HANDBOOK OF C...

... ...MENT

SECOND EDITION

We would like to thank Rachel Hills and Sophie Easterby-Smith for their tremendous help at editing, citation analysis, proofreading, formatting, and general management in drawing this new edition together.

HANDBOOK OF ORGANIZATIONAL LEARNING AND KNOWLEDGE MANAGEMENT

SECOND EDITION

Edited by

MARK EASTERBY-SMITH
AND
MARJORIE A. LYLES

A John Wiley and Sons, Ltd, Publication

This edition first published in 2011
Copyright © 2011 John Wiley & Sons

Registered office
John Wiley & Sons Ltd, The Atrium, Southern Gate, Chichester, West Sussex, PO19 8SQ,
United Kingdom

For details of our global editorial offices, for customer services and for information about how to
apply for permission to reuse the copyright material in this book please see our website at
www.wiley.com

Wiley also publishes its books in a variety of electronic formats and by print-on-demand. Some
content that appears in standard print versions of this book may not be available in other formats.
For more information about Wiley products, visit us at www.wiley.com.

Designations used by companies to distinguish their products are often claimed as trademarks. All
brand names and product names used in this book are trade names, service marks, trademarks or
registered trademarks of their respective owners. The publisher is not associated with any product
or vendor mentioned in this book. This publication is designed to provide accurate and authoritative
information in regard to the subject matter covered. It is sold on the understanding that the publisher
is not engaged in rendering professional services. If professional advice or other expert assistance is
required, the services of a competent professional should be sought.

Library of Congress Cataloging-in-Publication Data

Handbook of organizational learning and knowledge management edited by Mark Easterby-Smith,
    Marjorie A. Lyles. -- 2nd ed.
    p. cm.
Originally published: Blackwell handbook of organizational learning and knowledge
    management. 2003.
ISBN 978-0-470-97264-9 (pbk.)
1. Organizational learning--Handbooks, manuals, etc.   2. Knowledge management--
Handbooks, manuals, etc.   I. Easterby-Smith, Mark.   II. Lyles, Marjorie A.   III. Blackwell
handbook of organizational learning and knowledge management.
    HD58.82.B56 2011
    658.3'124--dc22

ISBN: 9780470972649 (pbk); ISBN: 9780470972809 (ebk)
ISBN: 9780470972816 (ebk); ISBN: 9781119977902 (ebk)

A catalogue record for this book is available from the British Library.

Typeset in 10/12 BaskervilleMT by MPS Limited, a Macmillan Company, Chennai, India
Printed in Great Britain by CPI Antony Rowe, Chippenham, Wiltshire

Contents

1

The Evolving Field of Organizational Learning and Knowledge Management

MARK EASTERBY-SMITH
AND MARJORIE A. LYLES

Organizational learning (OL) and knowledge management (KM) research has gone through dramatic changes in the last twenty years and, without doubt, the field will continue to change in the next ten years. Our research suggests that Cyert and March were the first authors to reference organizational learning in their publication of 1963. It was just twenty years ago that a conference was held at Carnegie Mellon University to honor March and his contribution to the field of organizational learning. Many of these presentations were published in a special issue of *Organization Science* in 1991.

Since that time we have seen a rapid expansion in the number of journal articles—both academic and practitioner—devoted to organizational learning. Fields such as information technology, marketing and human resources have also jumped on the bandwagon. Doctoral programs are including seminars on organizational learning, and MBA courses on organizational learning are appearing. All of this reflects acceptance of the concept that organizations have knowledge, do learn over time, and consider their knowledge base and social capital as valuable assets. It also reaffirms the legitimacy of research on organizational learning and its practical applications to organizations.

The first edition of this Handbook was published in 2003 but most chapters were completed in 2001 or 2002. Our first edition was widely used and it was clear—given the advancement of the field—that a second edition was necessary. Some people might claim that it is foolhardy to seek to cover the full range of the literature within one volume. Our intent is to provide a resource that is useful to academics, practitioners, and students who want an overview of the current field with full recognition that—to our delight—the field continues to have major impact on research and management practices. Our response is to highlight four features of the current literature, which provide a general rationale for compiling this Handbook.

First is the novelty and speed of development of the field. Overall, there was very little activity before 1990, and in some sub-areas almost everything dates after 1995. The speed of development, coupled with the lead times of publishing, means it is hard to develop a cumulative sense to the field where studies and publications are able to build systematically on previous work. Many of the chapter authors show how the present position has evolved from prior work, and then proceed to speculate on potential future directions (for example, see Argote, Denomme, and Fuchs, Chapter 29; and Van Wijk, van den Bosch, and Volberda, Chapter 22).

The second feature is the increasing diversity and specialization of the field. This has led to tighter definitions and the isolation of problems such as the political implications of organizational learning and knowledge management; it has also led to developments taking place in parallel which result in limited awareness of what is happening elsewhere at the same time. There is therefore a need to locate different sub-areas in relation to each other, so that overlaps and potential areas of synergy can be identified. In preparing the chapters of this book the authors have been aware of topics of other chapters and had access to the chapter drafts so that they could also identify potential commonalities and differences, whether there are overlaps of subject material, similar theoretical roots, or shared problem areas. This also implies a need for some mapping exercises, and several of the chapters (in addition to this one) aim to do just that (for example, see Shipton and DeFillippi, Chapter 4; and Vera, Crossan, and Apaydin, Chapter 8).

The third feature is that debates and arguments have started to flourish largely as a consequence of this diversity. Debates have focused around the definition of terms and the meaning of concepts, the appropriateness of methods of inquiry, ways of influencing learning processes within organizations, and the purposes to which we should put our knowledge of organizational learning and knowledge management. Because they lead to clarification of terms, sharpening of distinctions, and development of new ideas, these debates are invaluable. Consequently, we have encouraged authors to identify ongoing debates in their areas; and in a number of places we have juxtaposed chapters that represent different perspectives on particular contemporary debates.

Fourth, despite the growing diversity we have also been surprised at the number of citations that appear repeatedly across the chapters of the Handbook, which suggests that there still remains considerable commonality in the field. If we reach back to some of the earlier papers, there are several common points of departure, which may have become a form of 'tacit knowledge' that underlies the work of most scholars. Accordingly we devote much of this chapter to looking at the sources of key concepts, and to the works that have had a disproportionate influence on the evolution of the field. We see these as being similar to the watersheds of rivers which provide essential starting points for distinct streams, but which may subsequently be forgotten as the downstream rivers gather both strength and importance.

This opening chapter has three main sections. In the first section we offer a preliminary mapping of the field that is covered by the Handbook, which is elaborated in the chapters that follow. In the second section we present an analysis of the citations given by the chapters in this Handbook. In order to give an indication of changing priorities since the first edition was published we have divided this into two separate tables: Table 1.1 covers the references that predate 2000 and Table 1.2 covers references after 2000. There are 1160 citations to work predating 2000 out of a total of over 2229 references across the twenty-nine chapters of the book. In the third section we develop the theme of watersheds by focusing on the older publications, some of which score well in our analysis of citations, and all of which appear to have had a significant impact on the evolution of the fields of organizational learning and knowledge management.

The Field and Scope of the Handbook

For reasons of space, the title of the handbook refers to organizational learning and knowledge management; but two other important topics, 'the learning organization' and 'organizational knowledge', are also covered here. At first glance they may all seem very similar; but there are a number of important distinctions which we will explain below. The distinction between the first two terms was clearly articulated by Tsang (1997) to the extent that *organizational learning* refers to the study of the learning processes of and within organizations, largely from an academic point of view. The aims of such studies are therefore primarily to understand and critique what is taking place. On the other hand the *learning organization* is seen as an entity, an ideal type of organization, which has the capacity to learn effectively and therefore to prosper. Those who write about learning organizations generally aim to understand how to create and improve this learning capacity, and therefore they have a more practical impact and a performance agenda. We have gathered together papers in Part II of this volume, which reflect different aspects of the domain covered by these two terms.

A similar distinction can be made between the terms *organizational knowledge* and *knowledge management*. Those who write about the former often adopt a philosophical slant in trying to understand and conceptualize the nature of knowledge that is contained within organizations. Hence many of the discussions relate to distinctions between individual and organizational knowledge, whether the distinction between tacit and explicit knowledge is useful, or whether knowledge is a strategic advantage or asset. Also covered is how and what knowledge is shared and how knowledge is stored. Those who write about the latter generally adopt a technical approach aimed at creating ways of measuring, disseminating, storing, and leveraging knowledge in order to enhance organizational performance. The role and design of information technology is also important to such discussions. Part III of the Handbook considers issues in the domain of organizational knowledge and knowledge management (for example, see Almeida, Hohberger, and Parada, Chapter 18; Teece, Chapter 23; Zollo and Verona, Chapter 24; and Ahuja and Novelli, Chapter 25).

Part IV recognizes the importance of organizational learning and knowledge within the expanding international context of research in this area. The chapters in this section of the Handbook address areas of intercultural exchange, international context, and learning across borders.

In Figure 1.1 we offer an initial mapping of these four terms, based on the dichotomies of theory-practice and content-process. The first of these dichotomies follows the concerns of academics against those of practitioners, as described above. Even this is not necessarily straightforward. For example, a critical study of a learning organization would fit into the organizational learning box, and a study of the way knowledge is constructed

Figure 1.1 Mapping of Key Topics in the Handbook

within corporate knowledge management systems would belong to the organizational knowledge box.

The second dichotomy, the distinction between learning and knowledge, also seems fairly obvious: knowledge being the stuff (or content) that the organization possesses, and learning being the process whereby it acquires this stuff. Again, things are not quite so simple, as several of the chapters will demonstrate. For example, some chapters build on the paper by Cook and Brown (1999) which distinguishes between the epistemologies of possession and practice. In this case 'possession' fits well with the view of knowledge as content, but the epistemology of practice (or knowing) fits more closely with the process of learning from experience. We mention these potential limitations in passing because we still believe that it is valuable to start with some clear organizing principles, as an initial map for the reader. But we would also hope that those who get to the end of the book will become very clear about the inadequacies of such dichotomies!

There are also a number of themes and issues, which cut across the whole field, and therefore touch on all four quadrants of Figure 1.1. Some of these are fundamental issues about the nature of knowledge (Tsoukas, Chapter 21) and the processes of learning (Vera et al., Chapter 8); others relate to the role played by culture (Taylor and Osland, Chapter 26), emotion (Vince and Gabriel, Chapter 15), forgetting (de Holan and Phillips, Chapter 20), social identity (Child and Rodrigues, Chapter 14), and organizational identity (Corley et al., Chapter 16).

Many of the chapters review and update key concepts such as knowledge sharing (Salk and Simonon, Chapter 27), dominant logic (Bettis et al., Chapter 17), communities of practice (Plaskoff, Chapter 10; von Krogh, Chapter 19), teams (Roloff, Woolley, and Edmondson, Chapter 12), fluidity (Calhoun et al., Chapter 11), knowledge assets (Teece, Chapter 23), knowledge structures (Ahuja and Novelli, Chapter 25), absorptive capacity (Van Wijk, Van den Bosch, and Volberda, Chapter 13), and dynamic capabilities (Zollo and Verona, Chapter 24). Not only is it possible to locate these concepts on the general map of Figure 1.1, but it is also worth noting that they are often informed by different disciplinary and ontological assumptions (Easterby-Smith, 1997). That is why we have grouped a number of chapters into Part I, which considers the disciplinary perspectives underlying current developments in the field. We therefore hope that these chapters will enable readers to locate more clearly the different papers in subsequent parts of the book.

This brings us to the next section of the initial chapter. On the grounds that knowledge of the past is useful in making sense of the present, our aim here is to consider some of the formative influences in the field from a historical perspective. Thereby we hope to explain both similarities and differences between distinct parts of the field.

MAJOR SOURCES

If we start with the four terms in Figure 1.1, although all of them are relatively new, some are newer than others. Thus, the idea of knowledge management only emerged in the mid-1990s, whereas the first references to organizational learning appeared as far back as the early 1960s (Cyert and March, 1963; Cangelosi and Dill, 1965). But all four areas draw on literature and ideas that are older than their immediate concerns, and in a number of places there are overlaps between these initial sources.

Moreover, the field as a whole has been characterized by sudden surges of interest in particular topics, often followed soon after by rapid decline. (See Calhoun, Starbuck, and Abrahamson, Chapter 11, for further discussion of fads and fashions). These surges can often be explained by the changes in the business or technological environment. But literature also plays a significant part, and a number of books or papers have managed to capitalize on latent interest which then creates a major sub-industry in its own right. One obvious example is the book by Peter Senge (1990) which is one of the most cited texts in this volume. Although Senge was not the first person to coin the term 'learning organization,' it was the publication of his book which led to international awareness of the learning organization across both academic and practitioner communities. Thereafter, many large companies started claiming they were learning organizations, or that they were aspiring to this status; academics rushed to identify the characteristics of learning organizations, or to critique and deconstruct the very concept. As such, the publication of Senge's book represents a watershed, in the same way that Peters and Waterman (1982) represented a watershed for academics, consultants, and practitioners in the previous decade.

Our aim now is to examine systematically the chapters in this book to see if there are patterns and trends that can be discerned. We do this by first looking at the citations that predate 2000, where the content of the item has some relevance to the fields of organizational learning and management. Then we look at citations to papers that appeared from 2000 onwards. This gives an indication of the rises and falls in the influence of different authors over the last decade.

In Table 1.1 we list the authors of books or papers according to how many of the chapters in this Handbook have cited them. For each cited work we give the author names and date, but we do not provide full bibliographical details at the end of this chapter because all are cited in subsequent chapters.

There are a few points to note about this table. First, the list provides most of the names one would expect to see. If we take the total number of citations for authors, then the leading figures in the field are March, Nonaka, Argyris, Senge, Szulanski, and Huber, along with the pairs of Lave and Wenger, Brown and Duguid, Nelson and Winter, Cohen and Levinthal, Cook and Brown, and Kogut and Zander. Second, the dominance of the

Table 1.1   References prior to 2000 most cited in this Handbook

12 hits (1)
Nonaka and Takeuchi (1995)

10 hits (2)
Huber (1991)
Kogut and Zander (1992)

8 hits (5)
Argyris and Schön (1978)
Cohen and Levinthal (1990)
Cook and Brown (1999)
Nelson and Winter (1982)
Teece, Pisano, and Shuen (1997)

6 hits (4)
Grant (1996)
Lane and Lubatkin (1998)
Nonaka (1994)
Simon (1991)

4 hits (14)
Argote (1999)
Barney (1991)
Daft and Weick (1984)
Darr, Argote, and Epple (1995)
Davenport and Prusak (1998)
Garvin (1993)
Lyles and Schwenk (1992)
Mowery, Oxley, and Silverman (1996)
Nahapiet and Ghoshal (1998)
Polanyi (1962)
Powell, Koput, and Smith-Doerr (1996)
Simon (1947)
Walsh and Ungeson (1991)
Zander and Kogut (1995)

11 hits (1)
Brown and Duguid (1991)

9 hits (6)
Lave and Wenger (1991)
Levitt and March (1988)
March (1991)
Senge (1990)
Szulanski (1996)
Wenger (1998)

7 hits (2)
Cyert and March (1963)
Fiol and Lyles (1985)

5 hits (8)
Alavi and Leidner (1999)
Cook and Yanow (1993)
Dyer and Singh (1998)
Gherardi, Nicolini, and Odella, (1998)
Lyles and Salk (1996)
March and Simon (1958)
Penrose (1959)
Polanyi (1966)

3 hits (33)
Almeida and Kogut (1999)
Argote, Beckman, and Epple, (1990)
Barnard (1938)
Bettis and Prahalad (1995)
Brown and Duguid (1998)
Burt (1992)
Doz (1996)
Easterby-Smith (1997)
Easterby-Smith, Snell, and Gherardi(1998)
Galunic and Rodan (1998)
Hamel (1991)
Hansen, Nohria, and Tierney (1999)
Inkpen and Crossan (1995)
Inkpen and Dinur (1998)
Jaffe, Trajtenberg, and Henderson (1993)

Table 1.1 (*Continued*)

	Khanna, Gulati, and Nohria (1998)
	Kogut (1988)
	Lave (1988)
	Lyles (1988)
	Miner and Mezias (1996)
	Nicolini and Meznar (1995)
	Nonaka (1998)
	Orr (1996)
	Simonin (1999)
	Spender (1996)
	Teece (2007)
	Tsoukas (1996)
	Wegner (1986)
	Weick (1991)
	Weick and Roberts (1993)
	Williamson (1985)
2 hits	**1 hit**
102 further papers	982 further papers
Total number of references prior to 2000 cited in this Handbook: 1160	**Total number of references cited in the Handbook:** 2229

top publications is balanced by considerable diversity once one gets down to the level of detail. Thus, although the top ten were cited repeatedly, nearly half of the papers were only cited once or twice. This is because many of the authors are working in specialist areas, which have limited overlap with others.

A comparison between the present analysis and the same analysis conducted for the first edition shows that these classics of the learning literature are still important, but that their relative influence has diminished somewhat. Thus Nonaka and Takeuchi (1995), Brown and Duguid (1991), Huber (1991), Kogut and Zander (1992), and Nelson and Winter (1982) are still there, but a few other papers have grown in significance, notably Lave and Wenger (1991), Teece, Pisano, and Shuen (1997), and Wenger (1998).

Table 1.2, which covers the period from 2000–2010 provides an indication of trends in the field since the first edition was written. It shows the continuing dominance of some established scholars, notably Nonaka, and Brown and Duguid, but also the rise of some new stars including Argote and Ingram, Gherardi, von Krogh, Carlile, and Orlikowski. The topics covered by these authors demonstrate the growing interest in organizational knowledge creation and the social processes underlying organizational learning and knowledge.

Table 1.2   References for 2000-2010 cited in the Handbook

8 hits (1) Brown and Duguid (2001)	**7 hits** (0)
6 hits (1) Argote and Ingram (2000)	**5 hits** (2) Gherardi (2006) von Krogh, Ichijo, and Nonaka, (2000)
4 hits (4) Carlile (2002) Nonaka and von Krogh (2009) Orlikowski (2002) Zollo and Winter (2002)	**3 hits** (28) Ahuja (2000) Ahuja and Katila (2001) Almeida and Phene (2004) Argote, McEvily, and Reagans (2003) Baum, Calabrese, and Silverman (2000) Brown and Duguid (2000) Carlile (2004) Easterby-Smith, Crossan, and Nicolini (2000) Easterby-Smith, Lyles, and Tsang (2008) Eisenhardt and Martin (2000) Gavetti, Levinthal, and Rivkin (2005) Gourlay (2006) Gupta, and Govindarajan (2000) Lane, Salk and Lyles (2001) Menon and Pfeffer (2003) Nonaka, von Krogh, and Voelpel (2006) Obstfeld (2005) Oddou, Osland, and Blakeney (2009) Rashman, Withers, and Hartley (2009) Reagans and McEvily (2003) Rosenkopf and Almeida (2003) Rosenkopf and Nerkar (2001) Teece (2007) Tsai (2001) Volberda, Foss, and Lyles (2010) Wasko and Faraj (2005) Zollo and Singh (2004)
2 hits 93 further papers	**1 hit** 940 further papers

Total number of references
    included in analysis: 1069
	Total number of references cited in the
	    Handbook: 2229

WATERSHEDS

As suggested above, we are using the term 'watershed' to indicate a significant turning-point in the development of the subject area. In making sense of key watersheds we need to take account of (a) the absolute frequency of citation, (b) the timing of each publication, (c) the topic of the paper that does the citing, and (d) the text in which the citation is embedded. Given the natural tendency of academics to cite more recent work, there is a good case for giving extra weight to some of the older works which have been cited, especially where they are identified by authors working in different fields.

On this basis we may identify three main groups of literature as the timeline moves forward: (i) *classic* works that pre-date the identification of the ideas of organizational learning and knowledge management *per se*, (ii) *foundational* works which represent some of the first writings that set the agenda for subsequent work, and (iii) *popularizing* works which have acted as the most visible watersheds in the development of the field. It is important to note in passing that we do not regard the third term as being in any way pejorative; indeed, some of the 'popularizing' works were highly scholarly and all of them managed to generate streams of extremely valuable work. It is not possible to give single time-bands within which the three groups of literature appeared because different sub-areas have emerged at different times and at different rates; hence, the relevant watersheds come at slightly different times. We start with classic works which are presented for the whole field; we then consider separately the time lines within each of the four sub-areas defined at the outset of this chapter.

Classic works

Here we identify four main authors who have had a significant influence and who were active before the earliest mentions of terms such as organizational learning appeared: John Dewey, Michel Polanyi, Edith Penrose, and Frederick Hayek. They are not the most frequently cited in the present volume, partly because they have been overlaid by more recent authors (and as academics we are encouraged to focus more on recent publications than on classic works). Nevertheless, each of them has a substantial rating in the ISI Web of Science (running to several thousand for Dewey, Polanyi, and Hayek). We comment briefly here on their contributions primarily in the light of chapters within this Handbook, and in a few cases we will also refer to other key works in the field, including those listed in Table 1.1.

Dewey is the only one of these authors who explicitly focused his attention on learning. His ideas of learning from experience fit most easily into models of individuals' learning within organizations, and the notion of iterations between experience and reflection is frequently seen to underlie action learning, which is one of the key tools of the learning organization (Pedler, Boydell, and Burgoyne, 1989). Dewey's view that learning takes place through social interaction and yet cannot be passed from person to person as if it were a physical object is also seen to underlie the social learning perspective (Brandi and Elkjaer, Chapter 2). Other authors who take a social constructionist approach to organizational knowledge (Cook and Brown, 1999; Nicolini and Meznar, 1995; Shipton and DeFillippi, Chapter 4) follow Dewey's ideas, while Nonaka and Takeuchi (1995) acknowledge the impact of his philosophical contribution to 'pragmatism' in asserting that there cannot be a clear distinction between the observer and the observed.

Polanyi is best known for his distinction between tacit and explicit knowledge. The key idea of 'tacitness' has parallels to Dewey's experiential learning, because it is something that is held within the individual. Naturally, there are many different interpretations of what this all means. One version of tacit knowledge is that it is conscious, but not articulated; another version is that it is unconscious and hence inarticulable, as Tsoukas discusses (Chapter 21). Polanyi's ideas are based on philosophical analysis and argument, rather than on any empirical investigation, and of course, some would argue that the notion of tacit knowledge cannot be examined empirically because it is unconscious.

The influence of Polanyi is most evident in contemporary discussions about the nature of organizational knowledge. The idea of tacit knowledge is important for those trying to understand the roots of competitive advantage because it is the unexpressed knowledge and experiences of organizations which provide the unique competencies that cannot be easily replicated by competitors (Barney, 1991). While tacit knowledge may give unique advantages to a company, it also poses problems because it cannot easily be moved across cultural boundaries (Taylor and Osland, Chapter 26), nor is it easy to move between different parts of the same organization (Argote, Denomme, and Fuchs, Chapter 29).

Penrose is cited less frequently, but her ideas on the significance of the internal (human) resources of the firm are fundamental, and as she puts it: 'the dominant role that increasing knowledge plays in economic processes' (1959: 77). Penrose proposes the importance of 'excess resources' within an organization which can lead to innovation, paralleling the need for slack to allow experimentation. There are many other points made by Penrose which mirror those made both by her contemporaries and by recent authors. Thus, in discussing the role of top teams she comments: 'the administrative group is more than a collection of individuals; it is a collection of individuals who have had experience in working together, for only in this way can teamwork be developed' (1959: 46). And 'success depends upon a gradual building up of a group of officials' experiences in working together' (1959: 52). These views anticipate the ideas of social constructionists who emphasize that organizations know more than the sum of the knowledge of individuals within them; they also emphasize the role of experience and the fact that 'Knowledge comes from formal teaching and from personal experience' (1959: 53), which is very close to the distinction that Polanyi was developing at the same time between explicit and personal (tacit) knowledge.

It is not surprising that the work of Hayek is seen to underlie the thinking of those who adopt an economics perspective on organizational learning and knowledge. In particular, his view that one of the fundamental problems of economics is to use the knowledge initially dispersed around different individuals in a way that contributes to producing good decisions for the organization or society as a whole (see, Foss and Mahnke, Chapter 7). But he has also had a wider influence, possibly because his 1945 paper was extensively quoted by March and Simon (1958). Here, the emphasis that he places on the knowledge held by individuals naturally focuses attention on 'the knowledge of the particular circumstances of time and place' (Hayek, 1945: 80), which may be seen to anticipate the current attention given to 'situated' knowledge. Moreover, it starts to provide a methodological justification for the use of qualitative methods which are sensitive to contextual factors, such as narrative method, in trying to understand processes of organizational learning (see Bettis, Wong, and Blettner, Chapter 17, and Hayes, Chapter 5).

Not only are the contributions of these four authors still recognized by contemporary scholars, but we can also see that their ideas overlapped with each other in several respects. But all of their work contributed to early work in the management field as well as to the invention of the concept of organizational learning.

Organizational learning

The idea that an organization could *learn* and knowledge could be stored over time was the key breakthrough, which was first articulated in the book by Cyert and March (1963). Evidently the book was the product of much discussion and debate which had been going on among the team at Carnegie Tech during the 1950s (Augier, 2001) and it was foreshadowed, but not explicitly, by March and Simon (1958). Cyert and March propose a general theory of organizational learning as part of a model of decision making within the firm, and emphasize the role of rules, procedures, and routines in response to external shocks and which are more or less likely to be adopted according to whether or not they lead to positive consequences for the organization. A number of specific ideas were outlined in their book, which were subsequently developed further by other scholars. Noteworthy points in the book are: the idea that it is through 'organizational learning processes (that) . . . the firm adapts to its environment' (1963: 84); the view that 'the firm learns from its experience' (1963: 100); and an early version of the distinction between single and double-loop learning, to wit, 'An organization . . . changes its behavior in response to short-run feedback from the environment according to some fairly well-defined rules. It changes rules in response to longer-run feedback according to some more general rules, and so on' (1963: 101/2).

Cyert and March's book is often described as *the* foundational work of organizational learning, but others made fundamental contributions in the early days as well. Cangelosi and Dill (1965) produced the first publication in which the words 'organizational learning' appeared in the title, and although the paper is based on tendentious data, it already makes a distinct contribution to debates in the field because it starts to argue against the rationality of assumptions underlying the Cyert and March model. It is suggested that the model may be appropriate for established organizations in stable circumstances, but it has limited relevance to organizations developing within dynamic circumstances. Thus, Cangelosi and Dill propose a model based on tensions between individual and organizational levels of learning, which is similar to the notion of organizational learning being a discontinuous process (Argyris and Schön, 1978).

The book by Argyris and Schön (1978) was very important since it laid out the field as a whole very clearly, and their distinction between organizations with and without the capacity to engage in significant learning (Models II and I) received a great deal of attention. In it, the authors take a different critique of the assumptions of Cyert and March by pointing out that human behavior within organizations frequently does not follow the lines of economic rationality. Both individuals and organizations seek to protect themselves from the unpleasant experience of learning by establishing defensive routines. During the 1970s and 1980s there were a number of other *foundational* works, such as Hedberg (1981), Shrivastra (1983), Daft and Weick (1984), and Fiol and Lyles (1985), which made important contributions to the definitions of terminology, and to deeper perspectives on organizational learning, such as the distinction between learning and unlearning.

Perhaps the most significant *popularizing* force in the study of organizational learning was the publication of the Special Edition of *Organization Science* in 1991. This contains a number of highly cited articles including March (1991), Huber (1991), Epple, Argote and Devadas (1991), and Simon (1991). These have been very influential, and set the academic research agenda for much of the 1990s. They follow, in the main, the Carnegie tradition which suggests that it is desirable to maximize the efficient use of knowledge in organizations, while recognizing that there are substantial, largely human, antecedents. Many of the chapters in the current volume build explicitly upon their foundations (for example, van Wijk, van den Bosch, and Volberda, Chapter 13; and Teece, Chapter 23).

However, it is also interesting that the same issue of *Organization Science* included a paper by Brown and Duguid (1991) which has come to represent an alternative tradition that regards the social processes of organizational learning as pre-eminent. This tradition has also been developed through the work of Nicolini and Meznar (1995), Wenger (1998), Brown and Duguid (2000, 2001), and Gherardi (2006). In the current volume it is evident that it underpins the work of authors such as Hayes (Chapter 5), Gherardi (Chapter 4), Taylor and Osland (Chapter 26), von Krogh (Chapter 19), and Plaskoff (Chapter 10). From the early 1990s these two traditions, emphasizing either the efficiency or the social processes of organizational learning, have developed largely independently and have had increasing difficulty in communicating with each other. One of our aims in both editions of this Handbook has been to provide good coverage of both traditions in order to facilitate dialogue and better mutual understanding between the two.

The learning organization

The idea of the learning organization is of more recent provenance. It emerged towards the end of the 1980s largely on the basis of European work, with UK authors such as Garratt (1987) and Pedler, Boydell, and Burgoyne (1989) making early contributions, although the paper by de Geus (1988), which was published in the *Harvard Business Review*, brought the concept to wider attention. Nevertheless, the major watershed was the book by Senge (1990) which attracted enormous interest particularly because companies and consultants were searching for new ideas to replace the largely discredited concepts of corporate excellence (Peters and Waterman, 1982). Senge's book was both a *foundational* work and a *popularizer* because it rapidly became a key source for academics as well as an inspiration for practitioners. His ideas were highly attractive because they provided the potential for renewal and growth, with an underpinning of both technical and social ideas drawn respectively from the systems dynamics developed by Jay Forrester at MIT, the psycho-dynamic organizational theory developed by Chris Argyris, and process consultation of Ed Schein.

Despite the huge success of Senge's initial book, his perspective has not been widely adopted by the North American academic community (see Calhoun, Starbuck, and Abrahamson, Chapter 11),[1] and it has continued to be primarily a practitioner affair (for

---

[1] Even though James March uses the term 'learning organization' in March (1988), it is without the normative implications subsequently associated with the term following the work of Senge (1990).

example, Swieringa and Wierdsma, 1992; Burgoyne, Pedler, and Boydell, 1994; Örtenblad, 2004; Yeo, 2005). The few academics who write in the USA on this issue, for example, Dixon (1994) and Torbert (1994), are often influenced by European ideas, such as the work of Revans (1980) on Action Learning. In the present volume, diBella (Chapter 9) provides valuable updating and development of the concepts related to the learning organization by proposing a more flexible method than that originally laid down by Senge. Plaskoff (Chapter 10) describes strategies for implementing learning in organizations using ideas drawn from the communities of practice literature, and Roloff, Woolley, and Edmondson (Chapter 12) stress the importance of evaluating the contribution of teams.

Early critical work (Coopey, 1995; Coopey and Burgoyne, 2000; Snell and Chak, 1998) raised a number of concerns about the learning organization, including charges that it was politically naïve, contained an ideology that was exploitative of employees, and that it was not necessarily transferable to other cultural contexts. While not necessarily against the idea of the learning organization, later authors stressed that theories and practices needed to include ideas such as power, politics, and culture (Lawrence, et al., 2005; Simm, 2009), and the lack of clear links to business success (Thomas and Allen, 2006). Calhoun, Starbuck, and Abrahamson (Chapter 11) also point to the difficulty in demonstrating the benefits of the learning organization and discuss how it can be seen as part of the wider rise and fall of management ideas.

Organizational knowledge

Organizational knowledge as a subject of study has been around for a long time, but primarily within the economics community. Thus, as we have noted above, the 'classical' influence of economists such as Hayek and Penrose, and the philosopher Polanyi, has been significant. One of the major *foundational* works, also from an economics perspective, is Nelson and Winter (1982), which is particularly strong on the importance of 'tacit knowing' as a basis for individual and organizational competence. Other foundational works emerged in the early 1990s, especially from two Special Issues of the *Journal of Management Studies* on knowledge work (Alvesson, 1993; Starbuck, 1992, 1993); the elaboration of six different forms of organizational knowing by Blackler (1995) was also an important foundational work.

But the key *popularizing* influence was Ikujiro Nonaka who produced a series of papers and a highly respected book (Nonaka and Takeuchi, 1995) that set the standard for the emergent field with a rich mixture of concepts and field data. Key ideas expounded in the book include: the notion of knowledge creation through transformations of tacit and explicit knowledge; the importance of national culture and philosophy for understanding the construction and communication of knowledge; the interrelationship between the policy domain and the operational levels in the creation of knowledge; and the general principle that most dichotomies, such as tacit/explicit and mind/body, are false.

Given the importance of Nonaka's work, it is to be expected that he should attract his share of criticism. For example, there are suggestions that he misunderstands the nature of tacit knowledge, that his methodology is flawed and that his theory is not adequately supported by the evidence available (Gourlay, 2006). Nonaka has responded robustly to these criticisms through both restating the main principles of his theory and introducing new research results (Nonaka, von Krogh, and Voelpel, 2006; Nonaka and von Krogh, 2009).

In the background, the influence of Polanyi remains strongly evident in the works of dominant figures like Nelson and Winter (1982) and Nonaka; his ideas are also central to debates about the nature of organizational knowledge (Spender, 1996) in this Handbook by von Krogh (Chapter 19) and Tsoukas (Chapter 21). But it is also possible to see the influence of Hayek and other neo-classical economists in Nonaka's discussion about the problem of resolving the perspectives of the policy and operational domains, which can be solved, Nonaka argues, through the process of knowledge conversion.

Knowledge management

The idea of knowledge management arrived only in the mid 1990s, and is still developing (Alavi and Denford, Chapter 6). Its early evolution was rapid and chaotic, even though it has settled down with some distinctive themes over the last decade. To some extent, knowledge management gained academic legitimacy on the back of Nonaka's work; the driving force in the corporate world, however, has come from major consultancy companies seeking to capitalize on the enormous potential of information technology in a period following disenchantment with the methods and prescriptions of re-engineering (Hammer and Champy, 1993; Grint and Case, 1998). The idea is pretty simple, since it starts with the neo-economic view of the strategic value of organizational knowledge and then uses familiar IT software such as databases and electronic conferencing to facilitate the acquisition, sharing, storage, retrieval, and utilization of knowledge. As such, the conceptual logic follows the technical view of organizational learning as expounded by Huber (1991).

Early critiques of knowledge management initiatives were made on the grounds that they ignore the social architecture of knowledge exchange within organizations (Hansen, Nohria, and Tierney, 1999), and it is not surprising that some of these came from the 'social' school of organizational learning theorists (for example, Brown and Duguid, 2000). In a practical sense the social perspective has adapted technologies from elsewhere (such as Facebook) into the organizational context which enables flexible communication and sharing of supposedly tacit knowledge between members (McAfee, 2006). These technologies are also being applied to the absorption of external knowledge through, for example, the creation of online user communities who provide feedback on existing products and generate new ideas for innovation (Di Ganji et al., 2010). Alavi and Denford (Chapter 6) and Hayes (Chapter 5) review the development of social networking technology over the last decade and point to some of the limitations. Some of the other chapters also discuss the role of technology in knowledge sharing, storage, and databases (see Argote, Denomme, and Fuchs, Chapter 29; Ahuja and Novelli, Chapter 25).

FUTURE DIRECTIONS

In view of the size, complexity and diversity of the field it is hard enough to come up with an encapsulation of the current state of OLKM, and even more difficult to be definitive about future directions. However, undaunted by the task, we offer here some speculation about future directions. These are based on three main sources: an informal review of current citation patterns for recently-published papers; an overview of the predictions from authors who have contributed to this Handbook; and the results of our own discussions as we have developed the Handbook.

Our review of recent papers used ISI citation data for papers published since 2006. In this relatively short period of time, a few papers have already received over a hundred citations, and many have received over thirty. We can identify four main clusters of papers, around which recent energy has been focused, and hence which may be indicative of future trends. The strongest interest is around the drivers of corporate performance and competitive advantage. Two very influential papers (Teece, 2007; Simon, Hitt, and Ireland, 2007) examine the inner mechanisms whereby dynamic capabilities can sustain corporate performance, and Rai, Patnakayuni, and Seth (2006) and Hult et al. (2006) both look at the way knowledge can be managed in supply chains to drive competitive advantage. Other examples of well-cited papers in this area include Krishnan et al. (2006) on trust and alliance performance, and Zellmer-Bruhn and Gibson (2006) on the relation between team learning and performance in multinationals.

A second major theme is around the generation of enterprise and innovation. Zahra, Sapienza, and Davidsson (2006) provide a review and research agenda on the links between dynamic capabilities and enterprise, and Rothaermel and Hess (2007) examine how they link to innovation. Thorpe et al. (2005) look at the role of knowledge in small- and medium-sized firms. More recently both Alegre and Chiva (2008) and Liao et al. (2008) have looked at the links between organizational learning and innovation.

Our third theme is about learning and knowledge transfer between organizations. Several authors have written influential papers which both critique and develop the idea of absorptive capacity (Jansen et al., 2005; Lane et al., 2006; Todorova and Durisin, 2007). Others have conceptualized and examined the process of inter-organizational knowledge transfer (Paulraj et al., 2008; Easterby-Smith, Lyles, and Tsang, 2008; and van Wijk et al., 2008), and a third sub-group have focused on the way that learning takes place between clusters and networks of firms to produce competitive advantage (Dyer and Hatch, 2006; Lavie, 2006; Giuliani, 2007).

A fourth theme takes a more strategic perspective with examination of the interplay between exploration and exploitation especially within alliance relationships (Gupta et al., 2007; Lavie and Rosenkopf, 2006), and the way that capabilities can be built through alliances (Kale and Singh, 2007). The compromise position between exploration and exploitation is expressed in the idea of ambidexterity (Raisch and Birkinshaw, 2008; O'Reilly and Tushman, 2008).

In sum, there is strong evidence that organizational learning can impact the performance of a firm, but the problem is that this relationship may not hold at all times, and in all settings. Although we are aware of the existence of intervening variables, it is still not entirely clear which ones contribute the most, and under what circumstances, to organizational learning and performance. Consequently, this is likely to remain a research priority for a long time.

Related to this, we recognize that there is a relationship between learning and the exploitation or utilization of knowledge; yet we do not know the constructs that influence knowledge or learning utilization. Few studies address how knowledge is stored, when it is used and the timeliness of that usage. Examining real-time learning poses many difficulties beyond access to organizations and data. Exceptions exist such as those studies that evaluate how experience affects future organizational strategies. We want to understand organizational learning, but lack research on actual learning processes and knowledge. This, as several of the chapter authors imply, suggests that we should consider learning and knowledge as the dependent variables. Hence we might look at how social networks, communities of practice, and power structures influence knowledge and learning.

The quick and wide-spread development of emerging economies opens the door for future research addressing localized knowledge, knowledge trajectories, and outsourcing of knowledge, possibly through open innovation. Several recent papers have addressed the issues of globalization (Tsui et al., 2007; Sapienza et al., 2006), and it is due to the growing importance of cross-national learning and knowledge transfer that we have included a separate part of the Handbook on these issues. Future studies will need to consider how to build capacity for global learning, how knowledge is created, the uses of technology for knowledge transfer, the impact of social and organizational identity, and the processes of inter-organizational knowledge transfer.

CONCLUSIONS

In this opening chapter we have offered a general mapping of the field covered by the Handbook, and have also tried to demonstrate some of the inter-linkages over time and between parallel, but independent, areas of development. It has also been possible to identify some significant influences, which predate the invention of the concepts of organizational learning and knowledge management, and which might be seen as providing a common heritage, or similar watersheds.

It should be clear by now that the different sub-areas of the field are at different stages of maturity. Some of them are major rivers which have flowed gently for a long time; some are shorter streams which flow very quickly; and others are sudden torrents which emerge almost overnight—and which could disappear again equally quickly.

Several of the chapters from the first edition are now well on the way to becoming foundational works because they provide clear maps and overviews of their areas and have provided authoritative agendas for future research. As a whole, the first edition offers a major statement of the state of the field in the 'noughties'—at the start of the twenty-first century; this second edition builds on the foundational work and attempts to encapsulate the rapid development and the growing importance of the field as we enter the 'teens.'

REFERENCES

Alegre, J. and Chiva, R. (2008) Assessing the impact of organizational learning capability on product innovation performance: An empirical test. *Technovation*, 28(6): 315–326.

Alvesson, M. (1993) Organization as rhetoric: Knowledge-intensive firms and the struggle with ambiguity. *Journal of Management Studies*, 30: 997–1016.

Argyris, C. and Schön, D.A. (1978) *Organizational Learning: A Theory of Action Perspective*. Reading, MA: Addison-Wesley.

Augier, M. (2001) Simon Says: Bounded rationality matters. Introduction and interview. *Journal of Management Inquiry*, 10(3): 268–275.

Barney, J. (1991) Firm resources and sustained competitive advantage. *Journal of Management*, 17(1): 99–120.

Blackler, F. (1995) Knowledge, work and organizations. *Organization Studies*, 16(6): 1021–1045.

Brown, J.S. and Duguid, P. (1991) Organizational learning and communities-of-practice: Toward a unified view of working, learning and innovation. *Organization Science*, 2(1): 40–57.

Brown, J.S. and Duguid, P. (2000) *The Social Life of Information*. Boston, MA: Harvard Business School Press.

Brown, J.S. and Duguid, P. (2001) Knowledge and organization: A social-practice perspective. *Organization Science*, 12(2): 198–213.

Burgoyne, J., Pedler, M., and Boydell, T. (1994) *Towards the Learning Company: Concepts and Practices*. London: McGraw-Hill.

Cangelosi, V.E. and Dill, W.R. (1965) Organizational learning: Observations toward a theory. *Administrative Science Quarterly*, 10(2): 175–203.

Cook, S.D.N. and Brown, J.S. (1999) Bridging epistemologies: The generative dance between organizational knowledge and organizational knowing. *Organization Science*, 10(4): 381–400.

Coopey, J. (1995) The learning organization: Power, politics and ideology. *Management Learning*, 26(2): 193–213.

Coopey, J. and Burgoyne, J. (2000) Politics and organizational learning. *Journal of Management Studies*, 37(6): 869–885.

Cyert, R.M. and March, J.G. (1963) *A Behavioural Theory of the Firm*. Englewood Cliffs, NJ: Prentice-Hall.

Daft, R.L. and Weick, K.L. (1984) Toward a model of organizations as interpretation systems. *Academy of Management Review*, 9(2): 284–295.

de Geus, A.P. (1988) Planning as learning. *Harvard Business Review*, 66(2): 70–74.

Dewey, J. (1916) *Democracy and Education: An Introduction to the Philosophy of Education*. London: Collier-Macmillan.

Di Ganji, P.M., Wasko, M.M. and Hooker, R.E. (2010) Getting customers' ideas to work for you: Learning from Dell how to succeed with online user communities. *MIS Quarterly Executive*, 9(4): 213–218.

Dixon, N. (1994) *The Organizational Learning Cycle: How we can Learn Collectively*. London: McGraw-Hill.

Dyer, J.H. and Hatch, N.W. (2006). Relation-specific capabilities and barriers to knowledge transfers: Creating advantage through network relationships. *Strategic Management Journal*, 27(8): 701–719.

Easterby-Smith, M. (1997) Disciplines of organizational learning. *Human Relations*, 50(9): 1085–1116.

Easterby-Smith, M., Lyles, M.A., and Tsang, E.W.K. (2008) Inter-organizational knowledge transfer: Current issues and future prospects. *Journal of Management Studies*, 45(4): 661–674.

Epple, D., Argote, L., and Devadas, R. (1991) Organizational learning curves: A method for investigating inter-plant transfer of knowledge acquired through learning by doing. *Organization Science*, 2(1): 58–70.

Fiol, C.M. and Lyles, M.A. (1985) Organizational Learning. *Academy of Management Review*, 10(4): 803–813.

Garratt, B. (1987) *The Learning Organization*. London: Fontana.

Gherardi, S. (2006) *Organizational Knowledge. The Texture of Workplace Learning*. Oxford: Blackwell.

Giuliani, E. (2007) The selective nature of knowledge networks in clusters: Evidence from the wine industry. *Journal of Economic Geography*, 7(2): 139–168.

Gourlay, S. (2006) Conceptualizing knowledge creation: A critique of Nonaka's theory. *Journal of Management Studies*, 43(7): 1415–1436.

Grint, K. and Case, P. (1998) The violent rhetoric of re-engineering: Management consultancy on the offensive. *Journal of Management Studies*, 35(5): 557–577.

Gupta, A.K., Tesluk, P.E., and Taylor, M.S. (2007) Innovation at and across multiple levels of analysis. *Organization Science*, 18(6): 885–897.

Hammer, M. and Champy, J. (1993) *Reengineering the Corporation: A Manifesto for Business Revolution*. London: Nicholas Brealey.

Hansen, M.T., Nohria, N., and Tierney, T. (1999) What's your strategy for managing knowledge? *Harvard Business Review*, 77: 106–116.

Hayek, F.A. (1945) The use of knowledge in society. In F. A. Hayek (Ed), *Individualism and Economic Order*. London: Routledge and Kegan Paul: 1949.

Hedberg, B. (1981) How organizations learn and unlearn. In P.C. Nystrom and W.H. Starbuck (eds.), *Handbook of Organizational Design*. London: Cambridge University Press.

Huber, G.P. (1991) Organizational learning: The contributing processes and the literature. *Organization Science*, 2(1): 88–115.

Hult, G.T.M., Ketchen, D.J., Cavusgil, S.T., and Calantone, R.J. (2006) Knowledge as a strategic resource in supply chains. *Journal of Operations Management*, 24(5): 458–475.

Jansen, J., Van den Bosch, F.A.J., and Volberda, H.W. (2005) Managing potential and realised absorptive capacity: how do organizational antecedents matter? *Academy of Management Journal*, 43(6): 999–1015.

Kale, P. and Singh, H. (2007) Building firm capabilities through learning: The role of the alliance learning process in alliance capability and firm-level alliance success. *Strategic Management Journal*, 28(10): 981–1000.

Kogut, B. and Zander, U. (1992) Knowledge of the firm, combinative capabilities, and the replication of technology. *Organization Science*, 3(3): 383–397.

Krishnan, R., Martin, X., and Noorderhaven, N.G. (2006) When does trust matter to alliance performance? *Academy of Management Journal*, 49(5): 894–917.

Lane, P.J., Koka, B., and Pathak, S. (2006) The reification of absorptive capacity: A critical review and rejuvenation of the construct. *Academy of Management Review*, 31(4): 833–863.

Lave, J. and Wenger, E. (1991) *Situated Learning: Legitimate Peripheral Participation*. Cambridge: Cambridge University Press.

Lavie, D. (2006) The competitive advantage of interconnected firms: An extension of the resource-based view. *Academy of Management Review*, 31(3): 638–658.

Lavie, D. and Rosenkopf, L. (2006) Balancing exploration and exploitation in alliance formation. *Academy of Management Journal*, 49(4), 797–818.

Lawrence, T.B, Mauws, M.K., Dyck, B., and Kleysen, R.F. (2005) The politics of organizational learning: Integrating power into the 4I framework. *Academy of Management Review*, 30(1): 180–191.

Liao, S.H., Fei, W.C., and Liu, C.T. (2008) Relationships between knowledge inertia, organizational learning and organization innovation. *Technovation*, 28(4): 183–195.

March, J.G. (1988) *Decisions and Organizations*. Oxford: Blackwell.

March, J.G. (1991) Exploration and exploitation in organizational learning. *Organization Science*, 2(1): 71–87.

March, J.G. and Simon, H.A. (1958) *Organizations*. New York: John Wiley & Sons.

McAfee, A.P. (2006) Enterprise 2.0: The dawn of emergent collaboration. *Sloan Management Review*, 47(3): 21–28.

Nelson, R.R. and Winter, S.G. (1982) *An Evolutionary Theory of Economic Change*. Cambridge, Mass: Harvard University Press.

Nicolini, D. and Meznar, M.B. (1995) The social construction of organizational learning: Concepts and practical issues in the field. *Human Relations*, 48(7): 727–746.

Nonaka, I. and Takeuchi, H. (1995) *The Knowledge-Creating Company: How Japanese Companies Create the Dynamics of Innovation*. Oxford: Oxford University Press.

Nonaka, I. and von Krogh, G. (2009) Tacit knowledge and knowledge conversion: Controversy and advancement in organization knowledge creation theory. *Organization Science*, 20(3): 635–652.

Nonaka, I., von Krogh, G., and Voelpel, S. (2006) Organizational knowledge creation theory: Evolutionary paths and future advances. *Organization Studies*, 27(8): 1179–1208.

O'Reilly, C.A. and Tushman, M.L. (2008) Ambidexterity as a dynamic capability: Resolving the innovator's dilemma. *Research in Organizational Behavior*, 28: 185–206.

Örtenblad, A. (2004) The learning organization: towards an integrated model. *The Learning Organization*, 11(2): 129–144.

Paulraj, A., Lado, A.A. and Chen, I.J. (2008) Inter-organizational communication as a relational competency: Antecedents and performance outcomes in collaborative buyer-supplier relationships. *Journal of Operations Management*, 26(1): 45–64.

Pedler, M., Boydell, T., and Burgoyne, J.G. (1989) Towards the learning company. *Management Education and Development*, 20(1): 1–8.

Penrose, E.T. (1959) *The Theory of the Growth of the Firm*. Oxford: Blackwell.

Peters, T.J. and Waterman, R.H. (1982) *In Search of Excellence: Lessons from America's Best Run Companies*. New York: Harper and Row.

Polanyi, M. (1966) *The Tacit Dimension*. London: Routledge and Kegan Paul.

Rai, A., Patnayakuni, R., and Seth, N. (2006) Firm performance impacts of digitally enabled supply chain integration capabilities. *MIS Quarterly*, 30(2): 225–246.

Raisch, S. and Birkinshaw, J. (2008) Organizational ambidexterity: Antecedents, outcomes, and moderators. *Journal of Management*, 34(3): 375–409.

Revans, R.W. (1980) *Action Learning: New Techniques for Management*. London: Blond and Briggs.

Rothaermel, F.T. and Hess, A.M. (2007) Building dynamic capabilities: Innovation driven by individual-, firm-, and network-level effects. *Organization Science*, 18(6): 898–921.

Sapienza, H.J., Autio, E., George, G., and Zahra, S.A. (2006) A capabilities perspective on the effects of early internationalization on firm survival and growth. *Academy of Management Review*, 31(4): 914–933.

Senge, P.M. (1990) *The Fifth Discipline: The Art and Practice of the Learning Organization*. London: Century Business.

Shrivastva, P. (1983) A typology of organizational learning systems. *Journal of Management Studies*, 20(1): 7–28.

Simm, D. (2009) *The 'Celebritization' of a 'Learning Organization': The Case of Rover*. PhD Thesis, Lancaster University.

Simon, H. (1991) Bounded rationality and organizational learning. *Organization Science*, 2(1): 125–134.

Simon, D.G., Hitt, M.A., and Ireland, R.D. (2007) Managing firm resources in dynamic environments to create value: Looking inside the black box. *Academy of Management Review*, 32(1): 273–292.

Snell, R. and Chak, A. M-K. (1998) The learning organization: Learning and empowerment for whom? *Management Learning*, 29(3): 337–364.

Spender, J-C. (1996) Making knowledge the basis of a dynamic theory of the firm. *Strategic Management Journal*, 19: 45–62.

Starbuck, W.H. (1992) Learning by knowledge-intensive firms. *Journal of Management Studies*, 29: 713–740.

Starbuck, W.H. (1993) Keeping a butterfly and an elephant in a house of cards: The elements of exceptional success. *Journal of Management Studies*, 30: 885–922.

Swieringa, J. and Wierdsma, A. (1992) *Becoming a Learning Organization: Beyond the Learning Curve*. Wokingham, England: Addison-Wesley.

Teece, D.J. (2007) Explicating dynamic capabilities: The nature and microfoundations of (sustainable) enterprise performance. *Strategic Management Journal*, 28(13): 1319–1350.

Teece, D.J., Pisano, G., and Shuen, A. (1997) Dynamic capabilities and strategic management. *Strategic Management Journal*, 18(7): 509–533.

Thomas, K. and Allen, S. (2006) The learning organization: A meta-analysis of themes in literature. *The Learning Organization*, 13(2): 123–139.

Thorpe, R., Holt, R., Macpherson, A., and Pittaway, L. (2005) Using knowledge within small and medium-sized firms: A systematic review of the evidence. *International Journal of Management Reviews*, 7(4): 257–281.

Todorova, G. and Durisin, B. (2007) Absorptive capacity: Valuing a re-conceptualization. *Academy of Management Review*, 32(3): 774–786.

Torbert, W.R. (1994) Managerial learning, organizational learning: a potentially powerful redundancy. *Management Learning*, 25(1): 57–70.

Tsang, E.W.K. (1997) Organizational learning and the learning organization: A dichotomy between descriptive and prescriptive research. *Human Relations*, 50(1): 73–89.

Tsui, A.S., Nifadkar, S.S., and Ou, A.Y. (2007) Cross-national, cross-cultural organizational behavior research: Advances, gaps, and recommendations. *Journal of Management*, 33(3): 426–478.

Van Wijk, R., Jansen, J.P., and Lyles, M.A. (2008) Inter- and intra-organizational knowledge transfer: A meta-analytic review and assessment of its antecedents and consequences. *Journal of Management Studies*, 45: 815–838.

Wenger, E. (1998) *Communities of Practice: Learning, Meaning, and Identity*. Cambridge: Cambridge University Press.

Yeo, R.K. (2005) Revisiting the roots of learning organization: a synthesis of the learning organization literature. *The Learning Organization*, 12(4): 368–382.

Zahra, S.A., Sapienza, H.J., and Davidsson, P. (2006) Entrepreneurship and dynamic capabilities: A review, model and research agenda. *Journal of Management Studies*, 43(4): 917–955.

Zellmer-Bruhn, M. and Gibson, C. (2006) Multinational organization context: Implications for team learning and performance. *Academy of Management Journal*, 49(3): 501–518.

Part I

DISCIPLINARY PERSPECTIVES

2

Organizational Learning Viewed from a Social Learning Perspective

ULRIK BRANDI AND BENTE ELKJAER

ABSTRACT

This chapter reviews the literature on organizational learning through a social learning lens. We start with an individual learning perspective, before moving on to a social learning approach with a particular focus upon pragmatism. The literature review covers the following four issues: the content of learning, the process of learning, the relation between individual and organization, and the concept of organization. An important separator between individual and social learning perspectives is the different emphasis on learning as acquisition of skills and knowledge, versus learning as encompassing development of identities and socialization to organizational work and life. A pragmatist social learning perspective emphasizes both learning as acquisition through experience and inquiry, and learning as development of identities and socialization through individuals' capacities to both adapt and change. Further, a pragmatist social learning perspective also provides tools for the analysis of learning as process by the notions of learning initiated by tensions and ruptures.

INTRODUCTION

Many reviews have, over the years, been made to create an overview of literature on organizational learning (Babuji and Crossan, 2004; Dodgson, 1993; Easterby-Smith, 1997; Fenwick, 2008; Fiol and Lyles, 1985; Huber, 1991; Levitt and March, 1988; Miner and Mezias, 1996; Rashman, Withers, and Hartley, 2009; Shrivastava, 1983). The amount of reviews led to the following remark: 'there appear to be more reviews of organizational learning than there is substance to review' (Weick and Roberts, 1996 [1993]: 440). This statement should, however, be modified today because of an increase in published empirical papers on organizational learning, which indicates a certain maturation of the research field of organizational learning (Babuji and Crossan, 2004: 401). This chapter is, nevertheless, yet another review of literature on organizational learning. Further, it is a review that primarily is focused on literature on organizational learning in which the understanding of learning is based on social learning theory. Social learning theory in organizational learning literature has been coined under several names such as: 'situated learning' (Brown and Duguid, 1991; Richter, 1998); 'practice-based learning' (Gherardi, 2000); 'actor-network theory' (Fox, 2000); 'cultural-historical activity theory' (Engeström, 2001); and 'learning as cultural processes' (Cook and Yanow, 1993; Yanow, 2000).

We prefer the term 'social learning theory' to indicate that we are in the realm of social theory, and that the point of departure for learning is the lived and living experience of everyday life. All social learning theory departs from an understanding of learning as participation in social processes emphasizing both issues of knowing and issues of being and becoming. This means that social learning theory encompasses both the epistemology and the ontology of learning. Thus, social learning theory considers both the issue of human existence, development, and socialization (ontology) and the issue of people coming to know about themselves and what it means to be part of the world (epistemology). In social learning theory, socialization and learning are, in other words, inseparable processes; and they constitute each other in an understanding of learning as participation in social processes.

The overall governing question for this review is: How does social learning theory contribute to an understanding of organizational learning? And what does it add to an understanding of organizational learning that cannot be included in a deviation of individual learning theory? A lot of the literature on organizational learning and its counterpart, the Learning Organization, is founded in individual learning theory, and social learning theory in the organizational learning literature has grown out of a criticism of that (see e.g. Elkjaer, 2004 and the references mentioned in note 1). The criticism is elaborated later, but, in short, it is that individual learning theory focuses on learning as inner mental processes related to the acquisition and processing of information and knowledge. It leads to mind being the locus of learning and, as a consequence, a separation of body and mind; emotion and cognition as well as learner and context. This, in turn, means that the focus for learning is on how learners become knowledgeable in a purely cognitive sense, and not on how a context for learning (e.g. an enterprise) is key both to learning and to the development of identity and socialization. Individual learning theory is, in other words, criticized for neglecting the ontological dimension of learning, coming to be, and only focusing on the epistemological dimension, getting to know.

Having said that, it may be argued that social learning theory in organizational learning literature is not fully explicit about how to conceptually bind the two dimensions of learning (ontology and epistemology) together. This is the background for introducing John Dewey's concepts of experience and inquiry in this review (Dewey, 1933 [1986], 1938 [1986]). Dewey's concept of experience is not to be confused with the concept of experience found in humanistic and individual-oriented psychology in which experiencing is viewed as intrinsically psychical, mental, and private processes. Dewey's notion of experience is a non-dualist concept covering the individual and the world, and experience is always culturally mediated (Bernstein, 1960; Dewey, 1917 [1980]; Miettinen, 2000). Likewise, Dewey's concept of inquiry is not to be confused with plain communication skills (Senge et al., 1999), but to be related to the overall creation of individual and collective, cultural and historical knowledge. We return to Dewey's concepts of experience and inquiry as notions that hold potential for bridging conceptual gaps in coining a social learning theory for organizational learning.

A word about method for making this review is needed. The review consisted of four successive steps: First, we started out by searching for the term 'organizational learning' on the *Web of Science* database and the *SwetsWise* database with the search criteria set to 'topic' and 'title.' Secondly, we refined the results from the initial search by only including articles from the fifteen highest ranked journals measured by number of articles on the search term 'organizational learning.' Thirdly, from a surface reading of the abstract we selected the pool of potential articles that claimed to rest upon social learning theory, and which were critical of individual learning theory. Fourthly, we did an in-depth reading of the selected articles deciding which articles were of relevance and which were not.[1]

The way of reading the texts was inspired by a phenomenological approach (Giorgi, 1975). This means bracketing any theoretical knowledge the reader/interpreter may have in order to read the text as a text, that is as a phenomenon of words put together in order to give meaning. After this the interpreters apply their own theoretical framework or structure in order to give the texts new meaning according to the purpose of the phenomenological reading. In this case, the purpose was to explore the contribution of social learning theory to the field of organizational learning. Social learning theory, however, builds upon a critique of individual learning theory, which means that we find it helpful to introduce the two learning theories along the same structure.

Jean Lave's pioneering work on coining the essence of learning as the telos of learning, the learning mechanism, and the subject-world relation has served as an important source of inspiration for creating a structure for this review (Lave, 1997). In our adoption of Lave's notions of learning they have become the content of organizational learning, the process of organizational learning, and the relation between the individual and the organization. In other words, what do proponents of individual and social learning theory regard as the content of organizational learning; how is organizational learning to come about; and how is the relation between the individual and the organization understood and conceptualized? Lave's model for understanding learning does not explicitly include an organizational concept although it can be read into the subject–world relation. We have, nevertheless, chosen to add an organizational component in order to include the notion of organization that resides in the different organizational learning perspectives.

The flow in the chapter is that organizational learning based upon individual learning theory is introduced shortly followed by an introduction of social learning theory in organizational learning literature. Then follows a section, 'inspiration from pragmatism,' in which the above-mentioned Deweyan concepts of experience and inquiry are

---

[1] The main texts are in alphabetical order: Brown and Duguid, 1991; Cook and Brown, 1999; Cook and Yanow, 1993; Easterby-Smith, Snell, and Gherardi, 1998; Gherardi, 1999, 2000; Gherardi, Nicolini, and Odella, 1998; Hong and Fiona, 2009; Jacobs and Coghlan, 2005; Macpherson and Clark, 2009; Nicolini, Gherardi, and Yanow, 2003; Nicolini and Meznar, 1995; Patterson, 2009; Raz and Fadlon, 2006; Richter, 1998; Yanow, 2000. Others have been included and are mentioned in the text.

introduced as a way to conceptually bridge the gap between the ontological and the epistemological dimension of learning. Finally, in the 'conclusion and discussion,' implications for organizational learning of a social learning theory are suggested.

ORGANIZATIONAL LEARNING BASED UPON INDIVIDUAL LEARNING THEORY

Literature on organizational learning was first coined as theories of organizational behavior within the field of management science (Cyert and March, 1963; March and Simon, 1958). These early contributions to the emerging field of organizational learning dealt with information processing and decision making in organizations. The purpose was to help organizations learn to adapt to changes in the environment and to provide prescriptive managerial techniques. About thirty years later, with the publication of Senge's book, the counterpart of organizational learning, the Learning Organization, appeared as yet another way to create organizational learning (Senge, 1990). Judging from the many books and guidelines that have been published on how to develop a Learning Organization and pave the way for organizational learning, the Learning Organization and organizational learning have proved to be powerful models for organizational development (Argyris and Schön, 1996; Pedler and Aspinwall, 1998; Senge et al., 1999).

The learning theory in much of the literature on organizational learning and the Learning Organization is inspired by an individual-oriented psychological field. Enhancing information processing and decision making in organizations are seen as something that is done by individuals, and processes that can be enhanced by individuals' learning. Individuals' learning outcome can then, by way of individuals' acting on behalf of an organization, be crystallized in organizational routines and values and become organizational learning. The idea is that individuals hold a mental model in their mind, which is an abstract representation of their actions. It is that mental model, which can be enhanced in order for individuals, and subsequently organizations, to enhance information processing and lead to better decision making in organizations.

Thus, learning is, according to individual learning theory, identical to the enhancement of individuals' mental models, and happens when individuals acquire information and knowledge, which subsequently can guide their individual—and, thus, the organizational—behavior. The focus on mental modeling as the essence of learning in individual learning theory is the reason for naming individual learning theory 'cognitive learning theory.' Similarly, mental models may also be termed 'cognitive structures.' It is a focus on learning, which is directed towards what goes on in the minds of people.

A cognitive learning theory gives privilege to abstract, general, verbal, and conceptualized knowledge over and above the learning that derives from body and actions (Lave, 1988; Nicolini and Meznar, 1995). An example is when Senge talks about the importance of learning to think of organizations as systems, which is to learn 'systems thinking' in order to develop Learning Organizations (Senge, 1990). This is an understanding of organizational learning, which first coins the organization as an abstract entity, a 'system,' and then the organizational members should learn to relate to the system by thinking, in order to behave in adequate ways.

A system based understanding of organizations is composed of a predetermined set of elements that each has a different function in the rational constitution of the organization connecting to what we denote a functionalistic approach. For example, Leavitt (1965) presents five central elements in a system understanding of organizations that include social structure, participants or actors, goals, technologies, and the environment. In the understanding of organizations as systems, the focal point for organizational learning is to acquire explicit and abstract knowledge and integrate the acquired knowledge in organizational activities and routines. The knowledge acquiring process is done by the organizational members—who are viewed as given to the organization—on behalf of the organization and the goal is to optimize the organizational outputs. Thus, the basic maxim is to be knowledgeable about the system and for individual members of the system to be able to think of the organization as just that, a system (DiBella, Nevis, and Gould, 1996; Huber, 1991).

Organizational learning understood in light of individual learning theory is actually individual learning in organizations, which creates the problem of transferring individual learning outcome to that of the organization. The individual–organization split-up has been one of the major problems in the organizational learning literature that rests upon individual learning theory (Argyris and Schön, 1996; Mumford, 1991). One answer provided has been to view individuals as acting on behalf of the organization (Argyris and Schön, 1996; Senge, 1990). This view of the relation between individual and organization creates a conceptual separation between individuals and an organization. To use a metaphor, it is a relation resembling that between soup and bowl, the soup does not shape the bowl, and the bowl does not alter the substance of the soup. Thus, individual and organization, soup and bowl, 'can be analytically separated and studied on their own without doing violence to the complexity of the situation' (R. P. McDermott, 1993: 282).

In sum, in organizational learning literature viewed from the outpost of individual learning theory, learning is for individuals to become knowledgeable for the benefit of the enterprise. Learning comes about through individuals' work with their cognitive structures and it is possible to analytically separate individuals and enterprise in an organization understood as a system. The acknowledged problem in organizational learning based upon individual learning theory is the individual–organization dissociation, that is, how to make individual learning outcome organizational.

Organizational learning that rests upon individual learning theory separates epistemology, to come to know about the world, from ontology, to act in and become part of the world. It is a split between learning and socialization, which indicates a possibility for individuals' learning of particular content for the purpose of changing a system. The question is, however, on the one hand, is it possible to change systems through individual learning? And, on the other hand, is it possible to make this separation between learning something and being socialized into an enterprise? In the next section, social learning theories in organizational learning are explored. Neither of these comes without problems, because social learning theory has been formulated as a negation of individual learning theory in the organizational learning literature.

SOCIAL LEARNING THEORY IN ORGANIZATIONAL LEARNING LITERATURE

The appearance of social learning theory in organizational learning literature falls in time together with a social constructivist turn in social science and educational studies (Berger and Luckmann, 1966 [1991]; Bredo, 1997; Larochelle, Bednarz, and Garrison, 1998).

The individual mind as the locus of learning is, in other words, questioned within many fields of research. The main criticisms are that if learning begins with change in cognitive structures, how is it possible to learn from practice and practicing, i.e. from body, emotions, and from the taken for granted and unspoken history and culture (Cook and Yanow, 1993)? Further, if it is possible to coin the individual and the enterprise as separate entities, how is it possible to understand knowledge as situated, i.e. that an individual can be knowledgeable in one organizational context, and not in another comparable one (Lave, 1988)?

The argument from social learning theory is that a situation posits certain possibilities for some actions and knowledge being legitimate and other knowledge and actions not. Access to participation and power are, thus, important issues to take into account in organizational learning. Further, individuals both 'produce' and are 'products' of situations mirroring access and power. This 'situated' view of learning moves it away from individual mind to the social sphere of interaction, activity, and practice; and this has paved the road for another view on learning and knowledge (Cook and Brown, 1999; Gherardi, 2000; Nicolini et al., 2003). It is, however, a view that has ancient roots in American pragmatism, and early twentieth century Russian psychologist Vygotsky and the tradition of the cultural-historical activity theory (Bredo, 1997; Elkjaer, 2000; Popkewitz, 1998). We will return to that, but, first, social learning theory in organizational learning literature is introduced with regard to the content and process of learning and the relation between the individual and the organization as well as an understanding of organization.

Content and process in social learning theory

In organizational learning literature, viewed from a social learning theoretical perspective, learning is ubiquitous and part of everyday organizational life and work. Learning cannot be avoided; it is not a choice for or against learning. Further, learning is not restricted to taking place inside individuals' minds but as processes of participation and interaction. In other words, learning takes place among and through other people and artifacts as a relational activity, not an individual process of thought. This view changes the locus of the learning process from that of the mind of individuals to the participation patterns of individual members of organizations in which learning takes place (Gherardi et al., 1998; Lave and Wenger, 1991; Wenger, 1998).

In individual learning theory, learning is to come to know about actions and practices; in social learning theory, learning is a way of being and becoming part of the communities of practice that make up an organization, and in which the central issue of learning is to become a skilled practitioner (Brown and Duguid, 1991; Clegg, Kornberger, and Rhodes, 2005; Handley, Sturdy, Fincham, and Clark, 2006; Richter, 1998). Learning is a practical rather than an epistemic accomplishment, and it is a matter of identity development and socialization. Changing the content of learning from knowledge acquisition to socialization expands the concept of learning to include an ontological dimension. It also involves a change of the term 'knowledge' as knowledge becomes the embedded or situated knowledge of the organization, and not something stored in books, brains, and information systems (Cook and Brown, 1999; Gherardi, 2006, 2009; Gherardi et al., 1998). In social learning theory, knowledge is the active process of knowing, the processes and results of participation in organizational practices. Learners are to make sense of their participation in the social processes of organizing. It is not just the individuals who solely retain knowledge; rather knowledge is distributed within and among artifacts and organizational members (Brown and Duguid, 1991; Orlikowski, 2002, 2007; Richter, 1998).

The content being learned is context specific, and the learning itself is the discovery of what is to be done, when and how to do what according to the specific organizational routines, as well as which specific artifacts to use where and how. Learning also involves being able to give a reasonable account of why things are done and of what sort of person one must become in order to be a skilled member of a specific organization. In social learning theory, to know is to be capable of participating with the requisite competence in the complex web of relationships among people, artifacts, and activities. Learning is to acquire a 'situated curriculum,' which means to denote the pattern of learning opportunities available to newcomers in their encounter with a specific community inside a specific organization (Raz and Fadlon, 2006). Learning is what enables actors to modify their relations to others while contributing to the shared activity. Moving learning away from inside mind to social relations is also moving learning into an area of conflicts and power (Blackler and McDonald, 2000; Contu and Willmott, 2003; Coopey and Burgoyne, 2000). This makes the issue of empowerment essential, as learning requires access and opportunity to take part in the ongoing practice. The social structure of this practice, its power relations and its conditions for legitimacy, define the possibilities for learning (Gherardi et al., 1998; Hong and Fiona, 2009; Macpherson and Clark, 2009).

Language is, according to social learning theory, a central element of any process of learning as language is conceived to be the main way of acting in contemporary organizations. Language is, however, not merely a medium of knowledge transmission. Language is the medium of culture and as such it constitutes a crucial element in the process of learning, when the latter is perceived as the result of interaction among individuals in a specific occupational and organizational culture. The study of organizational learning is to explore the specific contexts of activities and social practices in which learning may occur. Only by understanding the circumstances and how the participants construct the situation can a valid interpretation of a learning activity be made (Gherardi et al., 1998).

In sum, regarding the content and process of social learning theory in organizational learning, a social learning theory emphasizes informality, improvisation, collective action, conversation, and sense making; and learning is of a distributed and provisional nature. Learning is not to acquire already known knowledge but is processes of moving into unknown territory to 'face mystery' (Gherardi, 1999). Learning is to make a journey into the land of discovery rather than to follow an already paved road. In the next section, the issue of the relation between the individual and the organization is taken up.

Relation between individual and organization

According to social learning theory, learners are social beings that construct their understanding and learn from participation in practice within the specific socio-cultural settings of an organization. The role of individual learners is to be engaged in sense making and to create knowledge within and among their trajectory of participation. The individual in social learning theory is to be understood as a participant in the social processes of everyday life of an organization. The organization provides occasion for interpretations of what goes on in an organization.

The understanding of the organizations within social learning theory of organizational learning can be understood as communities of practice (COP). COP is founded upon an idea that organizations are cultural, historical, and material collectives constituted by social interaction (Lave and Wenger, 1991; Wenger, 2000). Thus, there is no rational and technical organization of elements 'out there' to be fully described and explained as in a 'system' perspective. Organizations are, in a COP approach, constructed from social interaction and are dependent on the situated and contextualized aspects of the specific social practices. The main assumption for organizational learning in this perspective is that knowing—not knowledge—is something that emerges from social collective practices (Amin and Roberts, 2008; Beckhy, 2003; Brown and Duguid, 2001).

Continuing the metaphorical image from individual learning theory, the separation of soup and bowl may be replaced by the blending together of individuals and organizations like a rope. 'The fibres that make up the rope are discontinuous; when you twist them together, you don't make *them* continuous, you make the *thread* continuous. (...) The thread has no fibres in it, but, if you break up the thread, you can find the fibres again' (R. P. McDermott, 1993: 274). Thus, one cannot talk of the relation between individuals and organizations, or individual and context, as individuals in an organization, but individuals as part of a specific organizational practice as well as of patterns of participation and interaction.

There are, however, two views of context represented in social learning theory in organizational learning literature. The two understandings of context are whether context is a historical product of which persons are parts, or whether context is constructed as persons interact. To quote:

> One argues that the central theoretical relation is historically constituted between persons engaged in socio-culturally constructed activity and the world with which they are engaged. (...) The other focuses on the construction of the world in social interaction; this leads to the view that activity is its own context. Here the central theoretical relation is the intersubjective relation among co-participants in social interaction.
>
> (Lave, 1993 [1996]: 17)

The first view is represented in activity theory (Blackler, 1993; Engeström, 2001) and American pragmatism (see later). The second is inspired by social constructionism and phenomenological social theory. The latter is represented in the following much cited definition of learning in organizational learning literature based upon social learning theory, namely that learning is 'the acquiring, sustaining, or changing of intersubjective meanings through the artifactual vehicles of their expression and transmission and the collective actions of the group' (Cook and Yanow, 1993: 384). The group—or the collective actions of the group—and not the individual, is suggested here as the primary level of analysis. This is a social constructionist view on the relation between the individual and the organization. In the organizational learning literature, this view is also called a cultural approach to organizational learning (Yanow, 2000). The focus is on 'situated meaning (in this case, what is meaningful to those actors engaged in organizational learning activities)' (Yanow, 2000: 248). Context as a historical product in organizational learning literature can be expressed like this:

> The context must (...) be conceived as a historical and social product which is co-produced together with the activity it supports: agents, objects, activities, and material and symbolic artifacts all constitute a heterogeneous system that evolves over time.
>
> (Gherardi et al., 1998: 275)

Whether one views context as socially constructed in the situation or as a historical and social product is, we believe, a complicated matter consisting of many circumstances like political attitudes, academic traditions, taste, etc. For our part, we have a hard time not to view situations as consisting of people and contexts with a history mirroring social and cultural backgrounds. Our major problem is that a view of context as nothing other than a process of construction in social interaction and by the use of artifacts restricts the interventionist activities to ways of interacting with artifacts (in the broadest meaning of this term, which means that language is also an artifact, that is, a tool for action and interaction). With activity as its own context, it is difficult to see how change can be directed at changing contexts themselves, that is, of changing the conditions for learning and development. But, naturally, we also subscribe to a view of context as historically and culturally produced because we have our theoretical roots in American pragmatism. This connection is elaborated shortly.

To sum up, in social learning theory individuals' minds and actions are regarded as related to their participation in social practices formed by culture and history. This means that knowing, according to social learning theory, is always an integral part of broader changes of being, which can be traced to learners' participation in COP or activity systems. Knowing is, in other words, at the same time 'a way of participating and of relating' (Packer and Goicoechea, 2000: 234). Thus, in social learning theory it is not possible to separate knowing from being and becoming. To be and become or emerge as a knowledgeable person demands participation in social processes, which also involves relating to other beings and to (and with) the cultural and historically produced artifacts of the social worlds.

In the following, we introduce the work of John Dewey (Dewey, 1916 [1980], 1933 [1986], 1938 [1986]) because his concepts of experience and inquiry help bind the processes of epistemology and ontology in learning together. These are, as we have argued, at the heart of social learning theory in organizational learning literature but lack the conceptual elaboration here. Dewey's notions of experience and inquiry help to see that the ontological dimension of learning, how individuals come to be, and the epistemological dimension, how individuals come to know, cannot be separated. This means that socialization and learning are inseparable processes.

Inspiration from Pragmatism

Individuals gain experiences as a result of how they live their lives and how they associate with others. This, in turn, depends on who they are as people and how they enter into these relations. If individuals are to learn from their experiences, they have to use their ability to not only contemplate the relation between their actions and their consequences, but also to relate them to their past, present, and future experiences. The provocative element in the development of experience is when there is a sense of habitual actions being upset. This feeling cannot be forced upon anybody from the outside, but must come from experience or from within the parameters of expanding experience. Dewey is aware of the aesthetics of experience and the sensation that they perfect or complete; any delight and comfort in a situation is also an experience, and knowing is just one way of experiencing (J. J. McDermott, 1973 [1981]). There is only an analytical distinction between an intellect that knows and a body that acts.

This anti-dualistic approach in Dewey's works echoes one of the core principles in pragmatism, that is, that there are no dualisms such as, for example, psychological-physical, fact-value, culture-nature, and theory-action. Rather than understanding intellectual capacities and bodily actions as two different activities and phenomena, Dewey regards theories as tools or instruments in the human endeavor to cope with situations and events in life and to construct meaning by applying concepts in an experimental way. Some experiences may not be apprehended as knowledge, because they do not enter a sphere of communication with self and others, that is, they do not come with a verbal language. Along the continuum of experience, there is a vague transfer between non-cognitive and cognitive experience, but if learning is to occur from experience, experience must get out of the physical, non-discursive, and emotional and into the cognitive and communicative sphere. Only when individuals' experiences turn into communicative experiences and become learning experiences can they inform future practice:

> To 'learn from experience' is to make a backward and forward connection between what we do to things and what we enjoy or suffer from things in consequence. Under such conditions, doing becomes a trying; an experiment with the world to find out what it is like; the undergoing becomes instruction—discovery of the connection of things. Two conclusions important for education follow. (1) Experience is primarily an active-passive affair; it is not primarily cognitive. But (2) the *measure of the value* of an experience lies in the perception of relationships or continuities to which it leads up. It includes cognition in the degree in which it is cumulative or amounts to something, or has meaning.
>
> (Dewey, 1916 [1980]: 140, Dewey's emphasis)

In the Deweyan universe, there are no universal cognitive structures that shape human experience of reality. Dewey argued against Cartesian dualism and Kant's *a priori* and innate to mind categories (space, time, causality, and object) as structuring human thinking. For Dewey knowledge always refers directly to human experience and the origin of knowledge is living experience and not the other way around, as if logical theorems might govern thinking (J. J. McDermott, 1973 [1981]; Putnam, 1995; Sleeper, 1986). This does, however, not mean that pragmatism rejects cognition:

> thinking is a process of inquiry, of looking into things, of investigating. Acquiring is always secondary, and instrumental to the act of inquiry. It is seeking, a quest, for something that is not at hand
>
> (Dewey, 1916 [1980]: 148)

It is important to specify that it is a different kind of knowledge that Dewey talks about to that in the individual perspective. In the individual perspective, knowledge is something that attempts to represent the world while in the Deweyan perspective it is an answer to a problem. Thus, Dewey tries to discriminate between knowledge as propositional knowledge, which is a part of inquiry processes, and knowledge or warranted assertions, that is, the result of the inquiry process that is fallibilistic in nature (Dewey, 1941 [1988]).

In pragmatism, ideas, theories, and concepts, that is different forms of thinking and abstraction, function as instruments for actions. In one of his later works co-authored with Arthur Bentley, Dewey writes of the practice oriented function of thinking as a tool applied by 'men (sic!) themselves in action' (Dewey and Bentley, 1949 [1991]: 6). The nature of actions is always delimited or selective, because humans cannot act in general or in a vacuum. The essence of action is irremediably conditioned by the social (Dewey, 1938 [1986]). It follows that thinking and ideas or meanings developed through inquiry are social and cultural as well. Thus, a reflected action is created in relation to a specific situation or problem.

The concept of inquiry in pragmatism developed out of the criticism leveled at the concept of knowledge in formal logic with its references to *a priori* knowledge above and beyond the human world of experience (Dewey, 1929 [1984]). Dewey's development of logic as a theory of inquiry is based on everyday life experiences. Inquiry cannot be reduced to a response to purely abstract thoughts as it is anchored in situations as part of our everyday life. It is part of life to inquire, turn things around intellectually, come to conclusions, and make evaluations. This is how people learn and become cognizant human beings.

Inquiry is a process that starts with a sense that something is wrong. Intuitively, the inquirer suspects there is a problem. The suspicion does not necessarily arise from an intellectual wit. It is not until the inquirer begins to define and formulate the problem that inquiry moves into an intellectual field by using the human ability to reason and think verbally. In other words, the inquirer uses previous experiences from similar situations. According to Dewey, the inquirer tries to solve the problem by applying different working hypotheses and concludes by testing a solution model. The initial feeling of uncertainty, the uncertainty that started the inquiry process must disappear before a problem has been solved. If the inquiry is to lead to new experiences, to learning, it requires thinking and reflection over the relation between the problem's definition and formulation and the solution. It is not until deliberation has been applied to establish a relation between the action and the consequence(s) of the action that learning takes place in the sense that it is possible to act more informed in a new and similar situation.

In the understandings of the organization as a system and the organization as communities of practice, the individual is made sub-ordinate to the organization, either by 'choice,' that is, to adhere to the organization as a systemic entity, or by dissolving the individual in the communities of practice (see also Casey, 2002). We argue that a theory of the organization in organizational learning based on pragmatism is able to avoid this kind of sub-ordination. To conceptualize an organizational learning theory based on pragmatism, we draw upon the social arenas/worlds theory of Anselm Strauss (Strauss, 1993). Strauss's concept of organizations understood as arenas consisting of transactional social worlds has the same ontological basis as the COP and the cultural approach to organizations. The social world metaphor is, however, more strongly oriented towards processes of conflicts, negotiation, and tensions within and between social worlds, and the analysis of how these conflicting situations generate the possibility of changing arenas and social worlds (Brandi, 2010; Elkjaer and Hyusman, 2008).

The concept of social worlds originates from early social studies characteristic of the Chicago School of sociology. Firmly rooted in the classical pragmatism of Dewey and symbolic interactionism of Mead, one of its most prominent scholars, Anselm Strauss, developed social arenas/worlds theory as a conceptual frame for understanding the emergence and flow of activities in organizations. Social worlds are defined as:

> Groups with shared commitments to certain activities, sharing resources of many kinds to achieve their goals, and building shared ideologies about how to go about their business.
>
> (Clarke, 1991: 131)

In a social worlds perspective there are 'commitments,' 'goals,' and 'ideologies' that 'belong' to a group. There are not only patterns of access and participation, although they are also present. In a social worlds understanding, organizations are arenas of coordinated collective actions in which social worlds emerge as a result of commitment to organizational activities. It is the tensions and ruptures between these commitments within and between social worlds that may create avenues for questioning existing practices.

One especially relevant aspect of social worlds theory is that it explicitly focuses on the intersecting and segmentation processes between and within social worlds (Strauss, 1978: 123; 1993: 39). Intersecting looks at the bridging and interpenetrating processes of social worlds where social worlds and their actors engage in collaborative inquiry. Strauss (1982) underlines the significance of organizations characterized as a negotiated order. Negotiation denotes a fundamental trait that illustrates both the dynamic and political characteristics of social worlds. Every social world is characterized by intersections, caused by both internal and external (between social worlds) conflicts and contradictions, which convey negotiations and give rise to segmentation/intersecting processes. These processes create avenues for organizational learning by creating new relations between social worlds and practices within social worlds. Thus, segmentation/intersecting is a highly political process through its dependence on negotiations or processual ordering, as Strauss (1993: 254) later argued. This understanding of organization is a way of grasping the mutual relationship between individual and organization (social worlds) as both encompassing the organizational processes of ordering and the individuals as potential active participants who may or may not engage in the organizational activities.

In sum, pragmatism is a reminder of agency but agency grounded in and part of the shared and non-shared social worlds as well as individual capacities. Inquiry is useful because it can enact new practices by way of working hypotheses, and is necessary in order to produce learning and not only socialization. The organizational members and the organization are weaved together in social worlds in which inquiry and experiencing goes on as a continuous process. In pragmatism, the learning content may be coined as the development of human experience, which at the same time is to come to know about the world and be able to act in the world. Social learning theory for organizational learning inspired by pragmatism does not make a separation between coming to know about practice and coming to be a practitioner. It is not possible to develop experience as either processes of knowledge or processes of being and becoming. Experience and inquiry encompass both processes.

The learning method is inquiry, which includes thinking as a way to define problems, and reflection as a way to move learning outcome into the verbal and conscious arena, which paves the way for change and new practice. Inquiry begins in the senses, the bodily feelings and emotions, which may be turned into words in order to provide a way to learn from inquiry. Thus, inquiry is a way to enact knowledge that does not begin with language and conscious reflection. Inquiry cannot be restricted to mind or bodies, thinking or actions, but encompasses both. And their consequences are not to be restricted to knowledge acquisition but to include development of experience, creation of identity, and becoming a member of social worlds.

In pragmatism, it is not possible to separate the individual from the social, the context and/or the organization. The two are mutually constituted as human beings and human knowing, and as such they are products of history and culture, encompassed in social worlds theory of organizations. For a summary of the three positions, see Table 2.1.

Table 2.1   Summary of the three positions

	Individual Learning Theory	Social Learning Theory	Pragmatist Learning
Content	Individual information and knowledge about actions to guide organizational behavior	Context specific A 'situated curriculum'	Know about world and become part of world (knowing and socializing)
Process	Individuals' work with their cognitive structures mirroring actions	Participation in organizational practice to become skilled practitioners	Tensions and ruptures in situations Inquiry as a way to change experience
Relation between Individual– Organization	Can be analytically separated and worked upon seperately ('soup and bowl')	Weaved together 'a rope' Two understandings of context: 1) individual and context as historically produced 2) organizational activity as its own context	Mutual constituents Individual and context 'products' of human being and knowing
Organizational Concept	A system	Communities of Practice	Social arenas/worlds

CONCLUSION AND DISCUSSION

This review describes how the field of organizational learning can be understood from a social learning perspective and what social learning theories add to an understanding of organizational learning that cannot be included in an individual learning theoretical approach. In the review, we set out by characterizing the main elements of an individual approach followed by an in-depth review of organizational learning literature viewed from a social learning perspective. Finally, we refined the social learning perspective by including a pragmatist inspired understanding of organizational learning. The pragmatist approach to organizational learning echoes the philosophy from social learning theory without losing the individual capacity to inquire and enact new organizational experiences in the organizational learning processes. We have structured the answers to the governing questions of the review in four elements: the learning content; the learning process; the relation between the individual and the organization; and the organizational concepts.

Applying a social learning theory in organizational learning takes the focus of learning away from the individual mind and 'places' it in the organizational context as a setting for organizational learning. This means that the organizational actions directed to develop organizational learning cannot be solely focused on changing individuals' ways of thinking but should be focused on the organizational context, its patterns of participation and interaction. Social learning theory also moves the focus away from knowledge as the learning input to that of developing and socializing organizational members in order to turn them into skilled practitioners. Knowledge or knowing as the often preferred verb within social learning theory then becomes a way of enacting artifacts, routines, experiences, rules, etc. competently in the organization instead of something that resides inside the human mind ready to be used whenever needed.

A point of departure in social learning theory for organizational learning means that learning is viewed as an ongoing activity, which cannot be controlled, only the environments, the organization, can be made to facilitate organizational learning to a larger or lesser degree (Thompson, 2005). Some critique of social learning theory is that it focuses too much on the organizational context, and, thus, cannot for example encompass the mobile, knowledgeable, and potentially influential individuals. This may be the transformational leader or the ordinary professional who imports new ideas and who perhaps gets changed by outside encounters. The answer to this criticism is that the focus on context does not omit the individual as the two are viewed as mutually constituted and continuously changing with the participants 'moving' in and out of the specific context at hand. Thus, one cannot just change the organizational context without including the concrete and present participants in this context. The essence of applying a social learning theory is that it is not possible to work with ideal-typical individuals who learn by way of changing their ways of thinking. Organizations consist of real people each with their own experiences, history, and hopes for the future. This makes up the organizational context together with the specific work practice, the artifacts, the organizational rules and regulations. And it is from this starting point that learning and organizational learning begins to occur.

The contribution to social learning theory from pragmatism is to stress the coexistence between epistemology and ontology in learning. This is done by focusing on the development of human experience as both encompassing processes of knowledge acquisition and being and becoming part of the world. And it is to stress the interconnectedness of the development of individuals and organizations. The most beneficial contribution from pragmatism for organizational learning is, however, the notion of inquiry, which provides a method in which thinking is regarded as a tool, a way to define problems, and reflection is included as a way of sharing learning outcome.

Given the already mentioned wide-spread contemporary interest in viewing learning as participation in social processes, we have been interested in adding an organizational dimension by a social arenas/worlds understanding with its emphasis on tensions and ruptures as pathways for potential organizational learning experiences through inquiry.

Looking forward and into the future of the field of organizational learning in light of a social learning theoretical perspective, we believe that a pragmatist understanding will be beneficial in a globalized economy in which knowledge is no longer a scarce resource but the ability to find and select the right knowledge at the right time is. This means that learning not only demands cognitive skills or the power to access and participate in relevant practices, but both. The most important skill will, however, be an ability to make judgments, personal and collectively, and in that way be able to stand out as something separate and unique, as a person or an enterprise. The immense emphasis on branding products and enterprises that we currently witness especially in the economic sector of intangibles will afford more than ever anticipatory skills and knowledge to always be one step ahead and to be able to account for the initiatives taken. The emphasis will be on innovation and the ability to learn innovatively, for which pragmatism with its notions of inquiry and experience in the past, present, and future will be a good theoretical instrument in this pursuit. Also, the globalized economy is bringing enterprises together with an abundance of different cultures, races, ethnicities, etc. which will put an emphasis on learning as not only cognition or socialization skills but both, that is, an ability to learn to not only think or be but to be and think in a differentiation of workplaces where knowledge and judgmental power are distributed and demand continuous ability to learn and socialize.

REFERENCES

Amin, A. and Roberts, J. (2008) Knowing in action: Beyond communities of practice. *Research Policy*, 37(2): 353–369.

Argyris, C. and Schön, D. A. (1996) *Organizational Learning II. Theory, Method, and Practice.* Reading: Addison-Wesley.

Babuji, H. and Crossan, M. (2004) From questions to answers: Reviewing organizational learning research. *Management Learning*, 35(4): 397–417.

Beckhy, B. A. (2003) Sharing meaning across occupational communities: The transformation of understanding on a production floor. *Organization Science*, 14(3): 312–330.

Berger, P. L. and Luckmann, T. (1966 [1991]) *The Social Construction of Reality. A Treatise in the Sociology of Knowledge.* Harmondsworth: Penguin.

Bernstein, R. J. (1960) *John Dewey. On Experience, Nature and Freedom. Representative Selections.* New York: The Liberal Arts Press.

Blackler, F. (1993) Knowledge and the theory of organizations: Organizations as activity systems and the reframing of management. *Journal of Management Studies*, 30(6): 863–884.

Blackler, F. and McDonald, S. (2000) Power, mastery and organizational learning. *Journal of Management Studies*, 37(6): 833–851.

Brandi, U. (2010) Bringing back inquiry – Organizational learning the Deweyan way. In S. Jordan and H. Mitterhoffer (eds.) *Beyond Knowledge Management – Sociomaterial and Sociocultural Perspectives within Management Research.* Innsbruck: Innsbruck University Press: 95–121.

Bredo, E. (1997) The social construction of learning. In G. P. Phye (ed.) *Handbook of Academic Learning. Construction of Knowledge.* San Diego: Academic Press: 3–43.

Brown, J. S. and Duguid, P. (1991) Organizational learning and communities-of-practice: Toward a unified view of working, learning, and innovation. *Organization Science*, 2(1): 40–57.

Brown, J. S. and Duguid, P. (2001) Knowledge and organization: A social-practice perspective. *Organization Science*, 12(2): 198–213.

Casey, C. (2002) *Critical Analysis of Organizations. Theory, Practice, Revitalization.* London: Sage Publications.

Clarke, A. E. (1991) Social worlds/arenas theory as organizational theory. In D. R. Maines (ed.) *Social Organization and Social Process. Essays in the Honor of Anselm Strauss*. New York: Aldine de Gruyter: 119–158.

Clegg, S. R., Kornberger, M. and Rhodes, C. (2005) Learning/becoming/organizing. *Organization*, 12(2): 147–167.

Contu, A. and Willmott, H. (2003) Re-embedding situatedness: The importance of power relations in learning theory. *Organization Science*, 14(3): 283–296.

Cook, S. D. N. and Brown, J. S. (1999) Bridging epistemologies: The generative dance between organizational knowledge and organizational knowing. *Organization Science*, 10(4): 381–400.

Cook, S. D. N. and Yanow, D. (1993) Culture and organizational learning. *Journal of Management Inquiry*, 2(4): 373–390.

Coopey, J. and Burgoyne, J. (2000) Politics and organizational learning. *Journal of Management Studies*, 37(6): 869–885.

Cyert, R. M. and March, J. G. (1963) *A Behavioral Theory of the Firm*. Englewood Cliffs, NJ: Prentice-Hall.

Dewey, J. (1916 [1980]) Democracy and education: An introduction to the philosophy of education. In J. A. Boydston (ed.), *Middle Works 9*. Carbondale and Edwardsville: Southern Illinois University Press.

Dewey, J. (1917 [1980]) The need for a recovery of philosophy. In J. A. Boydston (ed.), *Middle Works* Vol. 10). Carbondale and Edwardsville: Southern Illinois University Press: 3–48.

Dewey, J. (1929 [1984]) The quest for certainty: A study of the relation of knowledge and action. Gifford Lectures. In J. A. Boydston (ed.), *Later Works 4*. Carbondale and Edwardsville: Southern Illinois University Press.

Dewey, J. (1933 [1986]) How we think: A restatement of the relation of reflective thinking to the educative process. In J. A. Boydston (ed.), *Later Works 8*. Carbondale and Edwardsville: Southern Illinois University Press: 105–352.

Dewey, J. (1938 [1986]) Logic: The theory of inquiry. In J. A. Boydston (ed.), *Later Works 12*. Carbondale and Edwardsville: Southern Illinois University Press.

Dewey, J. (1941 [1988]) Propositions, warranted assertibility, and truth. In J. A. Boydston (ed.), *Later Works 14*. Edwardsville and Carbondale: Southern Illinois University Press: 168–188.

Dewey, J. and Bentley, A. F. (1949 [1991]) Knowing and the known. In J. A. Boydston (ed.), *Later Works 16*. Carbondale and Edwardsville: Southern Illinois University Press: 1–294.

DiBella, A. J., Nevis, E. C., and Gould, J. M. (1996) Understanding organizational learning capability. *Journal of Management Studies*, 33(3): 361–379.

Dodgson, M. (1993) Organizational Learning: A review of some literatures. *Organization Studies*, 14(3): 375–394.

Easterby-Smith, M. (1997) Disciplines of organizational learning: Contributions and critiques. *Human Relations*, 50(9): 1085–1113.

Easterby-Smith, M., Snell, R., and Gherardi, S. (1998) Organizational learning: Diverging communities of practice? *Management Learning*, 29(3): 259–272.

Elkjaer, B. (2000) The continuity of action and thinking in learning: Re-visiting John Dewey. *Outlines. Critical Social Studies*, 2: 85–101.

Elkjaer, B. (2004) Organizational learning: The 'Third Way.' *Management Learning*, 35(4): 419–434.

Elkjaer, B. and Huysman, M. (2008). Social Worlds Theory and the Power of Tension. In D. Barry & H. Hansen (eds.), *The SAGE Handbook of New Approaches in Management and Organisation*. London: SAGE: 170–177.

Engeström, Y. (2001) Expansive learning at work: Toward an activity theoretical reconceptualization. *Journal of Education and Work*, 14(1): 133–156.

Fenwick, T. (2008) Understanding relations of individual-collective learning in work: A review of research. *Management Learning*, 39(3): 227–243.

Fiol, M. C. and Lyles, M. A. (1985) Organizational learning. *Academy of Management Review*, 10(4): 803–813.

Fox, S. (2000) Communities of practice, Foucault and actor-network theory. *Journal of Management Studies*, 37(6): 853–867.

Gherardi, S. (1999) Learning as problem-driven or learning in the face of mystery. *Organization Studies*, 20(1): 101–124.

Gherardi, S. (2000) Practice-based theorizing on learning and knowing in organizations. *Organization*, 7(2): 211–223.

Gherardi, S. (2006) *Organizational Knowledge: The Texture of Workplace Learning*. Malden, Oxford, Carlton: Blackwell Publishing.

Gherardi, S. (2009) Knowing and learning in practice-based studies: an introduction. *The Learning Organization*, 16(5): 352–359.

Gherardi, S., Nicolini, D., and Odella, F. (1998) Toward a social understanding of how people learn in organizations. The notion of situated curriculum. *Management Learning*, 29(3): 273–297.

Giorgi, A. (1975) An application of phenomenological method in psychology. In A. Giorgi, C. T. Fischer and E. L. Murray (eds.), *Duquesne Studies in Phenomenological Psychology*, II. Pittsburgh: Duquesne University: 82–103.

Handley, K., Sturdy, A., Fincham, R., and Clark, T. (2006) Within and beyond communities of practice: Making sense of learning through participation, identity and practice. *The Journal of Management Studies*, 43(3): 641–653.

Hong, J. F. L. and Fiona, K. H. O. (2009) Conflicting identities and power between communities of practice: The case of IT outsourcing. *Management Learning*, 40(3): 311–326.

Huber, G. P. (1991) Organizational learning: The contributing processes and the literatures. *Organization Science*, 2(1): 88–115.

Jacobs, C. and Coghlan, D. (2005) Sound from silence: On listening in organizational learning. *Human Relations*, 58(1): 115–138.

Larochelle, M., Bednarz, N., and Garrison, J. (eds.). (1998) *Constructivism and Education*. Cambridge: Cambridge University Press.

Lave, J. (1988) *Cognition in Practice. Mind, Mathematics and Culture in Everyday Life*. Cambridge: Cambridge University Press.

Lave, J. (1993 [1996]) The practice of learning. In S. Chaiklin and J. Lave (Eds.), *Understanding Practice. Perspectives on Activity and Context*. Cambridge: Cambridge University Press: 3–32.

Lave, J. (1997) Learning, apprenticeship, social practice. *Nordisk Pedagogik*, 17(3): 140–151.

Lave, J. and Wenger, E. (1991) *Situated Learning. Legitimate Peripheral Participation*. Cambridge: Cambridge University Press.

Leavitt, H. J. (1965) Applied organizational change in industry: Structural, technological and humanistic approaches. In J. G. March (ed.), *Handbook of Organizations*. Chicago: Rand McNally: 1144–1170.

Levitt, B. and March, J. G. (1988) Organizational learning. *Annual Review of Sociology*, 14: 319–340.

Macpherson, A. and Clark, B. (2009) Islands of practice: conflict and a lack of 'Community' in situated learning. *Management Learning*, 40(5): 551–568.

March, J. and Simon, H. A. (1958) *Organizations*. New York: John Wiley & Sons.

McDermott, J. J. (1973 [1981]) *The Philosophy of John Dewey. Two Volumes in One: 1. The Structure of Experience; 2. The Lived Experience*. Chicago and London: The University of Chicago Press.

McDermott, R. P. (1993) The acquisition of a child by a learning disability. In S. Chaiklin and J. Lave (eds.), *Understanding Practice. Perspectives on Activity and Context*. Cambridge: Cambridge University Press: 269–305.

Miettinen, R. (2000) The concept of experiential learning and John Dewey's theory of reflective thought and action. *International Journal of Lifelong Education*, 19(1): 54–72.

Miner, A. S. and Mezias, S. J. (1996) Ugly duckling no more: Pasts and futures of organizational learning research. *Organization Science*, 7(1): 88–99.

Mumford, A. (1991) Individual and organizational learning—the pursuit of change. *Industrial and Commercial Training*, 23(6): 24–31.

Nicolini, D., Gherardi, S., and Yanow, D. (2003) Introduction: toward a practice-based view of knowing and learning in organizations. In D. Nicolini, S. Gherardi and D. Yanow (Eds.), *Knowing in Organizations. A Practice-Based Approach*. Armonk, New York: M.E. Sharpe: 3–31.

Nicolini, D. and Meznar, M. B. (1995) The social construction of organizational learning: Conceptual and practical issues in the field. *Human Relations*, 48(7): 727–746.

Orlikowski, W. J. (2002) Knowing in practice: Enacting a collective capability in distributed organizing. *Organization Science*, 13(3): 249–273.

Orlikowski, W. J. (2007) Sociomaterial practices: Exploring technology at work. *Organization Studies*, 28(3): 1435–1449.

Packer, M. J. and Goicoechea, J. (2000) Sociocultural and constructivist theories of learning: Ontology, not just epistemology. *Educational Psychologist*, 35(4): 227–241.

Patterson, J. A. (2009) Organizational learning and leadership: On metaphor, meaning making, liminality and intercultural communication. *International Journal of Learning and Change*, 3(4): 382–393.

Pedler, M. and Aspinwall, K. (1998) *A Concise Guide to the Learning Organization*. London: Lemos and Crane.

Popkewitz, T. S. (1998) Dewey, Vygotsky, and the social administration of the individual: Constructivist pegagogy as systems of ideas in historical spaces. *American Educational Research Journal*, 35(4): 535–570.

Putnam, H. (1995) *Pragmatism: An Open Question*. Oxford: Blackwell.

Rashman, L., Withers, E., and Hartley, J. (2009) Organizational learning and knowledge in public service organizations: A systematic review of the literature. *International Journal of Management Reviews*, 11(4): 463–494.

Raz, A. E. and Fadlon, J. (2006) Managerial culture, workplace culture and situated curricula in organizational learning. *Organization Studies*, 27(2): 165–182.

Richter, I. (1998) Individual and organizational learning at the executive level. Towards a research agenda. *Management Learning*, 29(3): 299–316.

Senge, P. M. (1990) *The Fifth Discipline. The Art and Practice of the Learning Organization*. New York: Doubleday Currency.

Senge, P. M., Kleiner, A., Roberts, C., Ross, R., Roth, G., and Smith, B. (1999) *The Dance of Change. The Challenges of Sustaining Momentum in Learning Organizations. A Fifth Discipline Resource*. London: Nicholas Brealey Publishing.

Shrivastava, P. (1983) A typology of organizational learning systems. *Journal of Management Studies*, 20(1): 7–28.

Sleeper, R. W. (1986) *The Necessity of Pragmatism. John Dewey's Conception of Philosophy*. New Haven and London: Yale University Press.

Strauss, A. L. (1978) A social world perspective. *Studies in Symbolic Interaction*, 1: 119–128.

Strauss, A. L. (1982) Interorganizational negotiations. *Journal of Contemporary Ethnography*, 11(3): 350–367.

Strauss, A. L. (1993) *Continual Permutations of Action*. New York: Aldine de Gruyter.

Thompson, M. (2005) Structural and epistemic parameter in communities of practice. *Organization Science*, 16(2): 151–164.

Weick, K. E. and Roberts, K. H. (1996 [1993]) Collective mind in organizations. Heedful interrelating on flight decks. In M. D. Cohen and L. S. Sproull (Eds.), *Organizational Learning*. Thousand Oaks, London, New Delhi: SAGE Publications: 330–358.

Wenger, E. (1998) *Communities of Practice. Learning, Meaning, and Identity*. Cambridge: Cambridge University Press.

Wenger, E. (2000) Communities of Practice: The key to knowledge strategy. In E. Lesser (ed.), *Knowledge and Communities*. London: Butterworth Heinemann: 3–20.

Yanow, D. (2000) Seeing organizational learning: A cultural view. *Organization*, 7(2): 247–268.

3

Organizational Learning: The Sociology of Practice

SILVIA GHERARDI

ABSTRACT

A practice approach to organizational learning is based on the assumption that knowing and doing are inextricably entangled. Therefore, organizational learning takes places within working practices as a situated activity. The sociological roots of the concept of practice are traced and the expression 'practice-based studies' (PBS) is introduced as an umbrella-term. Within these studies two orientations are apparent: one which considers practices to be the object of empirical analysis (the site of learning and knowing), and one which assumes practice as epistemology.

If we consider the becoming of a practice and its function as a guide for knowledgeable collective doing, we can show that the epistemology of practice subtends a relational vision and an ecological model of inquiry within which practice is explored as sensible and tacit knowledge enacted in socio-material relations. It is then explored whether and how a practice theory of organization could come about and the theoretical and substantive contribution that it could make.

INTRODUCTION

Practice perspectives are inscribed mainly within a sociological approach to organizational learning and knowing that considers knowledge as something that people do together. Knowing and doing are therefore inextricably entangled.

While psychological approaches are better known and have founded, for better or worse, the interpretative model of organizational learning (see the critique of Weick, 1991; and Chapter 1 in this Handbook) sociological perspectives have been slower to establish themselves. The sociological contribution to the study of organizational learning (Gherardi and Nicolini, 2001) can be summarized in the terms of an invitation to view organizational learning from a cultural perspective as a metaphor (derived from the juxta-position of the two terms 'learning' and 'organization') that makes it possible to develop a system of representation (a theory) with which to interpret organizing as if it were a learn-ing process. Therefore, identifiable within studies on organizational learning are various narratives concerning what constitutes that relationship and how it can be understood. The sociological concepts that have contributed most to the understanding of organiza-tional learning have been first that of learning as participation, then of reflexivity as a dynamic of social reproduction, and, more recently, that of practice. And it is on this last concept that I shall concentrate in what follows.

Studies on organizational learning and knowing have re-appropriated the concept of practice since the late 1990s and the early 2000s. This has enabled a shift from knowledge to knowing—and therefore from an epistemology of possession (Cook and Brown, 1999) to one of practice—that is, to a conception of knowing as a practical activity. The 'practice turn' (Schatzki et al., 2001) began within studies on organizational learning and knowl-edge simultaneously with rediscovery of the concept of practice by other communities of scholars, such as those concerned with social studies on science and technology, feminist studies, researchers on strategy, workplace studies, and studies on activity systems. There are obviously different ways to use the term 'practice,' also because its polysemy allows its polymorphous exploration. Nevertheless, widely used in organization studies is the expres-sion 'practice-based studies' (PBS henceforth), which is a general label for a multiplicity of diverse studies whose shared feature is an interest in the study of social practices.

In the sections that follow I shall explore the potential of the sociology of practice by reviewing the intellectual tradition that can be considered the basis for PBS. I shall then return to the polysemy of the term to draw a distinction between considering practice as an empirical object and considering it as a relational epistemology with which knowledge can be produced on the basis of an ecological model of relations, primarily that between knowing and doing. I shall then use this model to show how a practice can be analyzed during its recursive unfolding, and how it develops within an equipped environment and interactions in a texture of practices. Finally, I will organize the discussion on the potential of the sociology of practice by analyzing its theoretical and substantive contribution to organizational learning.

THE GROUNDING OF THE 'PRACTICE-BASED STUDIES' LABEL

The concept of practice has manifold sociological roots. Implicit reference to one or another of them brings out a different phenomenon of practice, so that the same term is used to shed light on different aspects. At the cost of excessive simplification, and refer-ring the reader for more detailed treatment to Gherardi (2006, 2008), the main socio-logical theorizations of the concept of practice consist in phenomenological sociology (Schutz, 1962), symbolic interactionism (Mead, 1934; Strauss, 1991), ethnomethodology (Garfinkel, 1967), social praxeology (Bourdieu, 1972), and the theory of structuration (Giddens, 1984).

The phenomenological tradition in sociology concerns itself with the intersubjective production of sense and meaning through interaction and assembled knowledge. The world of everyday life is a province of meaning dominated and structured by what Schutz

(1962) calls the 'natural attitude', so that the world is from the outset not the world of the private individual but an intersubjective world, shared by us all, and in which we have not a theoretical but eminently practical interest. The bulk of what an individual knows does not originate from his or her experience alone, but is knowledge of social origin that has been transmitted to the individual by social relations of all types. Schutz (1946) distinguishes three components of the stock of knowledge: (i) the reserve of experience that arises from reflection on past experiences (as toolboxes, recipes and practical or theoretical routines); (ii) knowledge of social derivation (the testimony of others); (iii) socially approved knowledge (the knowledge approved by the group of membership, or by other trusted authorities). The complementarity of individual bodies of knowledge explains cooperation among individuals, so that collective knowledge derives from an assemblage of different kinds of knowledge. Knowledge is therefore social, and it is assembled knowledge. The social interaction of actors is a crucial element in understanding the acts of meaning production by knowledgeable subjects, and it is this aspect which inspired the 'practice turn' in social theory (Chia and Holt, 2008; Rasche and Chia, 2009; Reckwitz, 2002).

Put briefly, intersubjectivity gives rise not to a matching of meanings, but to the assumption that meanings are shared or, as Garfinkel (1967) puts it, to an agreement on methods of understanding. Therefore, within ethnomethodology shared understanding is a collective activity and the result of local procedures and devices. The researcher should therefore pay constant attention to the competent display of members' methods to accomplish 'sense' and 'order.' Members of any concrete setting acquire their sense or knowledge of it 'only in the doing' which is done 'skilfully, reliably, uniformly (. . .) as an unaccountable matter' (Garfinkel, 1967: 10). For members, 'the hows of these accomplishments are unproblematic' (Fox, 2006: 430), they are not the topic of competent remarks. Accordingly, the most significant innovation by ethnomethodology with respect to traditional sociology is its replacement of cognitive categories with the categories of action, and the consequent view of the creation and transmission of knowledge as a socially important practice.

This means that sociology, too, has taken up Austin's assertion that 'knowing is doing in everyday life, and it is doing society' (Giglioli, 1990: 85). In ethnomethodological studies, in fact, the transmission of knowledge as a social practice has been the focus of studies on work (Garfinkel, 1986; Garfinkel and Sacks, 1970), and ethnomethodology and conversation analysis provide one way to access how people recognize and reproduce the organizational location of their actions in and through each successive action (Llewellyn and Hindmarsh, 2010).

The phenomenological and ethnomethodological tradition is particularly attentive to the details of ordinary work practices in naturally occurring interactions (Alby and Zucchermaglio, 2006; Heath and Luff, 2007; Llewellyn and Spence, 2009; Rawls, 2008). It assumes that order is the ongoing achievement of members' methods for producing it. This tradition is therefore concerned to describe work practices in their becoming 'a practice' (Bjørkeng et al., 2009). The assumption, even if it is not always made explicit, is that knowing, learning, working, and innovating are not separate activities but are closely bound up with each other in their occurrence in time (Brown and Duguid, 1991; Orr, 1993; Cook and Yanow, 1993; Clegg et al., 2005). By contrast, the tradition of Bourdieu's social praxeology and that of structuration theory work on oppositions.

Bourdieu's methodological point of view can be defined as simultaneously 'anti-functionalist, anti-empiricist and anti-subjectivist' (Sulkunen, 1982: 103). He is profoundly convinced that it is impossible to grasp the deepest-lying logic of the social world without immersing oneself in the particularity of an empirical reality, historically situated and dated, even if only to construct it as a 'particular case of the possible.' On this view, the science of society is a two-dimensional system of power relations and meaning relations among groups. It therefore requires a twofold reading. The first treats society as a 'social physics': that is, as an objective structure grasped from outside, whose articulations can be observed, measured, and projected independently of the representations of those who live within it. This is the objectivist or structuralist point of view which analyzes society using statistical tools or formal models in order to bring out its regularities. Bourdieu believes that this is possible because people do not possess the totality of the meaning of their behavior, as if it were a given of consciousness, and because their actions always comprise more meanings than they realize.

However, a science of society must recognize that the awareness and interpretation of actors is also an essential component of analysis: individuals have practical knowledge about the world which they invest in their ordinary activities. It is by combining the two components of analysis that Bourdieu creates his 'social praxeology,' in which, however, the two components, although both necessary, are not of equal weight because epistemological priority is given to objectivist rather than subjectivist understanding.

It is here that the gap with ethnomethodology emerges, in that Bourdieu has the actor's point of view depend upon the place that he or she occupies in the objective social space. Whilst this is an idea rooted in the structuralist tradition, Bourdieu introduces two new concepts to explain the importance of relations: (i) the concept of 'field' as constituted by a set of objective and historical relations among positions anchored in specific forms of power or capital; (ii) the 'habitus', defined as a set of historical relations deposited in the bodies of individuals in the form of mental and corporeal schemes of perception, evaluation, and action. Both these concepts—field and habitus—are relational in the sense that they function completely only in relation to each other, so that a field exists only if the actors in it 'play with or against the other.' This signifies for Bourdieu that there is action, history, and the conservation or transformation of structures constituting a specific type of field only because there are agents 'in action'; and that these agents, in their turn, are efficacious only because they have not been reduced to the simple notion of 'individual' but are viewed as socialized organisms endowed with a set of dispositions which imply both the propensity and the ability to 'play the game' (Wacquant, 1992: 19–21).

Practices are collectively orchestrated without their being the outcome of the organizing action of an orchestra conductor (Bourdieu, 1972: 207). It means that we find certain games interesting because they have been imported into and imposed upon our minds and bodies in the form of what Bourdieu calls the 'sense of' or the 'feel for' the game. The practical sense—which is not weighed down by rules or principles, even less by calculations and deductions—is what makes it possible to grasp the meaning of a situation instantaneously, and to produce the appropriate responses at the same time. Only this type of acquired knowledge, in that it functions with the automatic reliability of an instinct, can furnish instantaneous responses to all the uncertain and ambiguous situations of practice.

Like Bourdieu, Giddens maintains that the prime concern of the social sciences should be neither the experience of the individual actor nor the existence of some or other form of 'social totality', but rather a set of social practices ordered in space and time. Like certain self-reproducing phenomena in nature, human social activities are *recursive*. They are not brought into being by social actors but are constantly recreated by the same means whereby they express themselves as actors (Giddens, 1990: 4). The concept of recursiveness is central to Giddens' thought. His theory of structuration views the production of social life as a 'skilled performance,' so that social practices are construed as procedures, methods, or practical techniques appropriately performed by social agents—a definition, for that matter, which derives from ethnomethodological theory.

In his attempt to reconcile and connect the concept of action with those of structure and institution, Giddens proposes the replacement of that dualism with the notion of 'duality of structure,' where the latter is viewed both as a medium and as a result of recursively organized human action: 'a medium because it is through its use that social conduct is produced, and an outcome because it is through the production of this conduct that rules and resources are reproduced in time and space'(Mouzelis, 1989: 615). The theory of structuration is therefore an attempt to analyze both structure and action within a single and coherent theoretical framework that yields an account of social life as a series of social activities and practices performed by individuals and by means of which, at the same time, those individuals reproduce social institutions and structures.

The influence of structuration theory is particularly evident in the study of technology and technological practices, and especially in the work of Wanda Orlikowski and the group at MIT which employs the concept of practice. Inspired by Giddens' practice theory, Orlikowski (2000; Orlikowski and Iacono, 2001) suggests an analytical distinction between the technological artifact (i.e. in IT its software and hardware components) and technology-in-use, (i.e. what agents do with the technological artifacts in their situated practices). A simple type of office software, for instance, acquires different meanings for different professions, because different professionals (secretaries, accountants, consultants) develop distinct uses of the same artifact. Through their practices of the technology, people reshape IT-in-use in a situated way. Orlikowski (2002) expressly uses the term 'knowing in practice' to suggest that knowing is not a static, embedded capability or stable disposition of actors, but rather an ongoing social accomplishment constituted and reconstituted as actors engage the world in practice. The competence of the individual in knowing how to get things done is both collective and distributed, grounded in the everyday practices of organizational members.

Social interactionism, ethnomethodology, social praxeology, and structuration theory have furnished the sociological background for the linkage between knowing and acting. In general, the term 'practice' has generated in organization studies a 'bandwagon' dynamic (Fujimura, 1988) whereby various denominations—none of which has prevailed—have been proposed in order to institutionalize PBS as a field of inquiry with many elements in common. The metaphor of the bandwagon calls to mind the idea of a collective 'journey.' The concept expresses an involving activity able to bring together a heterogeneous group of subjects in pursuit of the same goal. In chronological order, the following labels have been proposed (Corradi, Gherardi, and Verzelloni, 2010): practice-based standpoint (Brown and Duguid, 1991); science as practice (Pickering, 1992); strategy as practice (Whittington, 1996); practice-based learning (Raelin, 1997, 2007); practice lens and practice-oriented research (Orlikowski, 2000); knowing-in-practice (Gherardi, 2000); work-based learning (Billett, 2001); practice-based perspective (Sole and

Edmondson, 2002); practice-based approach (Carlile, 2002); practice-based approaches (Yanow, 2004).

The label 'practice-based studies' may serve as an umbrella-term to denote a shared problematic without forcing the numerous differences that it covers into a single category. In fact, as Miettinen et al. (2009: 1313) write in the introduction of a special issue devoted to the 're-turn to practice,' 'a new organizing buzzword must be imprecise and open enough to allow people from different traditions to join without renouncing their respective worldview.'

For that matter, this plurality of theoretical origins is not surprising if one considers that organization studies constitute a multidisciplinary—and at times also interdisciplinary—field of study which also comprises a variety of eclectic approaches.

How can one find one's bearings among such a diversified array of theories developed amid the ambiguity and the polysemy of the term 'practice' (Strati, 2007; Geiger, 2009)? Ambiguity is an asset and a resource with which to develop plural interpretations. Let us therefore explore it.

THE POLYSEMY OF PRACTICE

In everyday language the term 'practice' has different meanings. For example, it expresses something 'concrete' or 'real,' often in opposition to something 'abstract' or 'theoretical.' The theory/practice dichotomy expresses the tension or the gap between decontextualized and universal knowledge and knowledge that is situated, pragmatic, and used in a temporally defined context of action. I shall not enter into the debate on this matter here. Instead, I merely point out that use of the term 'practice' in this sense has recently spread within management studies, provoking the accusation that the interests of practitioners are neglected. The theory/practice gap has led to this charge being brought especially against Critical Management Studies, followers of which have responded by studying the practices of middle managers and redefining them in terms of the 'negotiation across interfaces of multiple rationalities' (Hotho and Pollard, 2007: 599). However, the view of practice as antithetical to theory is not one which contributes greatly to knowledge about practice, although it may subvert the symbolic relationship which sets value on theory rather than practice and conceals a gender subtext in the devaluing of situated, local, and non-theorized knowledge (Gherardi, 2010). At least three further significations are comprised in the commonplace meaning of the term 'practice.'

1. *Practice as a learning method.* People learn by 'doing' through constant repetition of their activities and discussions on the canons of their collective doing. To quote a proverb commonplace in numerous languages: 'Practice makes perfect'.
2. *Practice as an occupation or field of activity.* 'Practice' is a word able to express the field of activity in which an individual works and the body of knowledge that grounds its knowledge. Every work setting is in fact an arena of interconnected practices in continuous becoming: medical or legal practice, for example.
3. *Practice as the way something is done.* Practice is a processual concept able to represent the 'logic of the situation' of a context. The study of practice, or better 'practicing,' yields important insights into how practitioners recognize, produce, and formulate the scenes and regulations of everyday affairs.

It is not easy to reconcile the idea of practice as an empirical object (a working practice within legal practice, i.e. body of professional knowledge), particularly repeated and rehearsed action (as in practicing a distraint), with the fact that the practice in question is sustained by a specific mode of practicing that may vary from one legal firm to another. In other words, the usual act of distraint responds to criteria of good or bad practice within that community of practitioners. Practice may therefore be an object of doing, a time of doing, and a socially sustained way of doing. And in all three cases knowledge is present in the form of learning intrinsic to the doing—a knowledgeable doing—and knowledgeable doing sustained by social norms appreciative of the doing of things well, beautifully, usefully, etc. The complexity of these three senses can coexist without having to resort to a definition of practice which restricts it to the activities or operations internal to the practice, or to only the processual dimension of practice that develops through time and according to the specific modes of that doing, or only to the institutionalization of the social canons of good or bad practice. We may say with the words of Llewellyn and Spence (2009: 1420) that 'practice is reproduced through ordinary activity, but at the same time practice is a resource that enables people to recognize and assemble situated activities.'

The polysemy of the term 'practice' is apparent in everyday language (Antonacopoulou and Pesqueux, 2010). When the term is transferred to academic settings not only does it not disappear but it acquires a further element which, ironically, refers precisely to the everyday life and to that knowledge which is difficult to articulate. Generally, when the concept of practice enters academic settings, it is associated with the following elements: (i) intentional and goal-seeking actions that also have a habitual character and follow certain general principles of procedure (Turner, 1994: 8); (ii) the kind of practical and 'hidden' knowledge that supports them (see Tsoukas' chapter in this Handbook; and Tsoukas, 1998).

In this regard, a tension arises in the literature because—as Joseph Rouse (2001: 191) maintains—there are two fundamentally different conceptions of practices:

1. Practices identified with regularities or commonalities in the performances or presuppositions of some community of human agents.
2. Practices characterized in terms of normative accountability of various performances.

According to the first definition, practices are 'arrays of activities' that constitute models, or bundles of activities; while in the second definition, practices can instead be viewed as 'ways of doing things together.' Those who adopt the first definition are interested in knowing and describing 'the what question' (inside a practice), while those who choose the second are interested in 'the how question' (a practice is practiced).

Rouse criticizes the former conception and argues that the accountability which binds a practice together need not involve any underlying regularity, nor even presuppose an uncontested formulation of norms. Of interest is the footnote where he argues in favor of the second conception by citing Davidson (1984: 445) to draw an analogy with understanding and using a natural language, which 'involves no learnable common core of consistent behaviour, no shared grammar or rules, and no portable interpreting machine set to grind out the meaning of an arbitrary utterance.' This analogy with the use of a language and the concept of accountability highlights the crucial role played by language, which by means of discursive practices produces not only intelligibility but also moral order. The concept of accountability enables us to view reason not as an innate mental faculty but as a practical accomplishment. The social dimension is the key to understanding the reasons that induce a group of actors to practice continuously and repetitively, adjusting their activities to ongoing changes and molding their 'doing' to the situational rationality of the context in which they interact. Paradoxically, the term 'practice' has the connotation of being something transferable, teachable, transmittable, or reproducible (Turner, 1994), but at the same time practices are difficult to access, observe, measure, or represent because they are hidden, tacit, and often linguistically inexpressible in propositional terms.

To conclude this section on the polysemy of the term, and therefore on the difficulty of understanding what we are talking about when the term 'practice' is used, I shall now itemize the different linguistic uses made of it. I have already mentioned its *oppositional* theory-versus-practice use which subtends analysis of practice as concrete action in contrast with an abstract theory. A second use is *analogical*: a certain phenomenon is studied 'as practice.' In this case, there are two well-known strands of analysis that have developed on the basis of analogical use of the term: science as practice, and strategy as practice. The former arose in the 1990s with the laboratory studies that focused on the practices that produce science, and therefore described the manufacture of science (Knorr-Cetina, 1981). Their purpose was to criticize science as discovery and to dethrone rationalism and positivism. They were consequently interested in the working practices whose subject matter was knowledge and in interpretation of how epistemic objects and epistemic communities are formed. The second strand—strategy as practice—assumes the term 'practice' to study strategy as a doing and as a process (strategizing). It has little interest in practice, and its intention is not to contribute to a theory of practical knowledge, but rather to criticize prescriptive and top-down models of strategy.

A further use of 'practice' is *topological*. Practice is the place where knowledge and learning come about, are preserved, transmitted, and changed. The metaphor of practice as a container is the most accredited in the literature since its beginnings with the concept of community of practice and identification of specific working practices in which practical knowledge can be studied as knowledgeable collective competence and capacity for action. Hence, practice is the site of knowing and also the site of organizing (Brown and Duguid, 1991). With regard to this ontological meaning of practice as the site of knowing and organizing, it is interesting to note how it objectifies practices as empirical objects and the building blocks of an organization, while at the same time blurring the boundaries between working and organizing. The terms 'working practice' and 'organizational practice' are often interchangeable. Having identified a specific practice, the researcher is concerned to describe the activities that constitute it. Studies of this kind have been conducted on flute making (Yanow, 2003), the construction of safety (Gherardi and Nicolini, 2000; Styhre, 2009), bridge-building (Suchman, 2000), animal qualification practices (Labatut et. al, 2009), and making of nanoreactors (Olsen, 2009).

A final meaning of the term 'practice' is *transformative*, and it refers to the fact that knowledge transforms itself through its use: a process which can be studied and described in light of the circuits which reproduce practices and networks of practices (Brown and Duguid, 2001) or of the texture of practice (Gherardi, 2006). In this sense, practice constitutes an epistemology of the relationship between knowing and acting. The question of the true value of knowledge and of the manner in which it is acquired is replaced by questions concerning how knowledge circulates, how it is transformed by being transferred, and how it is produced in contexts of practices. Epistemology usually concerns itself with the conditions for the validity of knowledge (logic of verification) or, as in pragmatism, with the conditions for the production of knowledge (logic of discovery). What is still beyond its reach is study of the epistemological conditions for the circulation of knowledge, or, in other words, how knowledge transforms itself through its use; what I term a 'logic of transformation.'

A logic of transformation implies a relationship of equivalence or of non-difference between knowing and practicing. The expression designates a relational epistemology in that the two terms are ontologically inseparable from the outset (1987), but are instead performed in the course of specific material-discursive practices. Let us see in detail what adopting a relational epistemology entails, and how practice as epistemology can contribute both theoretically and substantively to looking at organizational learning as a situated activity.

The Epistemology of Practice

To gain better understanding of the epistemology of practice—and therefore move away from analysis that privileges action as the product of actors in a given context—it is useful to recall how Ira Cohen (1996) distinguishes between theories of action and theories of practice. We may say that whilst the former theories privilege the intentionality of actors, from which derives meaningful action (in the tradition of Weber and Parsons), the latter locate the source of significant patterns in how conduct is enacted, performed, or produced (in the tradition of Schutz, Dewey, Mead, Garfinkel, and Giddens). Hence, theories of practice assume an ecological model in which agency is distributed between humans and non-humans and in which the relationality between the social world and materiality can be subjected to inquiry. Whilst theories of action start from individuals and their intentionality in pursuing courses of action, theories of practice view actions as 'taking place' or 'happening,' as being performed through a network of connections-in-action, as life-world and dwelling (as the phenomenological legacy names them, see Sandberg and Dall'Alba, 2009).

The adoption of an ecological model that gives ontological priority to neither humans nor non-humans, or discursive practices, constitutes the fundamental difference between theories of action and of practice. It is in this interpretative framework that the difference can be grasped between the study of practice as an empirical object and the use of practice as epistemology. The difference is based on the attribution to practice of a realist ontology (that objectifies practices as primary units) and a social constructionist conception that does not distinguish between the production of knowledge and construction of the object of knowledge (between ontology and epistemology). From this derive different methodologies for the conduct of practice-based studies (Charreire-Petit and Huault, 2008).

One may answer the question as to what type of epistemology the epistemology of practice is by referring to Østerlund and Carlile (2005), who illustrate, through a re-reading of three classic studies on communities of practice (Lave and Wenger, 1991; Wenger, 1998; Brown and Duguid, 1991, 1998, 2001), how practice epistemology is based on a relational thinking in which the practice is the locus for the production and reproduction of social relations. The three studies not only select a specific practice to study (Lave and Wenger focus on the relation between newcomers and old-timers, Wenger on identity formation, and Brown and Duguid on community knowledge and canonical versus non canonical practices) but also choose to study this practice with regard to a limited set of relations characterized by specific differences, dependencies, changes, and power dynamics. But aside from the specific practice that can be studied and the relationships on which an author may choose to focus, the main feature of practice as relational epistemology is its focus on the emergence of relations through ongoing interaction and their normative stabilization.

Not only do subject and object define each other within a context of interaction, but the relationship between the material and the discursive comes about as a single phenomenon in which materiality is social—as social studies on technology have shown (Law, 1994)—and the process of meaning-making encompasses material semiosis. The term 'sociomateriality' has come into use after removal of the hyphen between the two terms (Orlikoswki, 2007; 2009). And the term 'intra-action,' coined by Barad (2003; 2007) to locate the relationship of mutual determination between subject and object, has also entered the lexicon of organization studies (Iedema, 2007; Nyberg, 2009) in relation to practice as epistemology. In other words, it is in the historically situated context of a practice that the knowing subject, the object of knowledge, and sociomateriality are involved in the processes of 'becoming' through which their identities are materially negotiated and (re)confirmed (Chia 2003: 106).

The epistemology of practice makes it possible to articulate the dynamic that occurs between the becoming of a practice as a socially sustained mode of action in a given context and the 'given' sociomaterial context in which it develops. Practice is situated between the given and the emergent as an element in the social order. If, therefore, practice is different from action, if it is not an ontologically distinct entity, we may ask how a practice becomes such, what relationship it assumes with other practices, and what effects it produces.

The Becoming of a Practice and its Stabilization

A metaphor which aptly illustrates the way in which a practice emerges and is socially and materially sustained is that of climbing, as described by Hennion:

> What climbing shows is not that the geological rock is a social construction, but that it is a reservoir of differences that can be brought into being. The climber makes the rock as the rock makes the climber. The differences are indeed in the rock, and not in the 'gaze' that is brought to it. But these are not brought to bear without the activity of the climb which makes them present. There is co-formation. Differences emerge, multiply and are projected. The 'object' is not an immobile mass against which our goals are thrown. It is in itself a deployment, a response, an infinite reservoir of differences that can be apprehended and brought into being.
>
> Hennion (2007:100–1)

Hennion thus illustrates the relationship of co-formation between sociomateriality and identity, but he only alludes to the fact that the same relationship exists between the doing—climbing—and the knowing: that is, knowing how to read the rock, seeing the handholds that become such only at the moment when the climber sees them and makes them handholds for his or her next move. This knowing how to read the context as a 'reservoir of differences,' knowing how to identify the handholds for the next action, knowing what the next action will be (Garfinkel's 'what next,' 1996), and possessing the vocabulary to talk competently about climbing, are things that are collectively learned, transmitted, and transformed during practice and as an effect of it.

We may imagine what can constitute a handhold for the development of practical knowledge by assembling an ideal toolbox that enables description of a practice while it is being practiced.

Professional vision

We may start with the image of the climber who looks at the rock with expert eyes and for a practical purpose. We may say that the climber possesses and develops by doing what Goodwin (1994: 606) has called 'professional vision.' He defines professional vision as 'socially organized ways of seeing and understanding events that are answerable to the distinctive interests of a particular social group.' All vision is perspectival and lodged within endogenous communities of practitioners. An archaeologist, a farmer, or a builder will see different things in the same patch of dirt because they look at it from different professional 'visions.' The skill of seeing (and looking) is gained through constant and situated use of directions and micro-explanations: the novice is *taught how to see* (Goodwin and Goodwin, 1996); the climber, while climbing, enacts his or her background knowledge of how to look in order to see. The ability to see a meaningful event is the effect of a socially situated activity accomplished through discursive practices which employ specific professional vocabularies. As we have seen, objects of knowledge emerge from the interplay between a domain of scrutiny and a set of discursive practices deployed within a specific activity.

Three activities shape a domain of occupational knowledge (Goodwin, 1994):

- coding, which transforms phenomena observed in a specific setting into the objects of knowledge that animate the discourse of an occupation;
- highlighting, which gives salience to specific phenomena in a complex perceptual field by marking them in some manner; and
- producing and articulating material representations, which embed and structure the knowledge produced and transfer it through space and time.

I shall interpret the term 'professional vision' in a broader sense in order to include both the physical act of seeing and its outcome, that is, a professional vision as a culture of practice. In fact, the same act of developing a professional vision comprises the two principles of stabilization of a practice, and its institutionalization. When material representations are codified and articulated, some ways of doing are inscribed in tools and artifacts (vocabularies as well); when 'phenomena' are highlighted, not only are they marked in order to distinguish them, but they are also marked according to an ethical and aesthetic code of practice. When Garfinkel says that members make settings accountable, that is 'observable and reportable', he means accountable rationally *and* morally. Moral order and social order are shown to be inseparably intertwined in-and-as the practical details of work interactions (Fox, 2008).

Aesthetic knowledge

Let us return briefly to the metaphor and the practice of climbing. Note that it has induced first Hennion and then us (via Goodwin) to use the metaphor of vision, but to neglect another form of knowledge embodied in the climber, namely touch. A handhold is one of the circumstances that aids the becoming of the action, but knowing how to see a handhold is not enough. For it to be a handhold, the fingers must have touched it and tested its firmness in relation to the climber's physique and agility. This further elaboration of the initial metaphor serves to highlight that the activity of knowing is not only situated in a context that furnishes resources for action but is also a bodily activity that relies on sensible knowledge and that mobilizes the perceptual faculties of the five senses. Aesthetic knowledge is always involved whenever flesh-and-blood human beings act. Put otherwise, the study of practices gives visibility to that form of practical knowledge which is anchored in the body, in the sensory faculties, and which is developed in corporeal patterns and cultivated as aesthetic judgment and as the aesthetic code of a practice.

On the other hand, all this makes practice difficult to express verbally both for practitioners and for researchers, who have difficult access to this knowledge resource and a paucity of vocabulary with which to describe it. I shall return to the methodological aspect later. Here I wish to emphasize that practitioners are in no better position than researchers regarding their capacity to know in terms of objectified knowledge and to express in words a *savoir faire*, an embodied knowledge, and an ability that resides in the fingers, the eyes, the nose, or the ears. These abilities, which are apparently an individual 'endowment,' and seemingly reveal a particular talent, are in reality the effect of a social practice and a collective process of learning and knowledge transmission.

Discursive practices

To provide an example of how language and discursive practices constitute 'handholds' for practice, I refer to an article by Geneviève Teil (1998) which describes how she learned to develop taste during a course to train the sense of smell. This sense and the professional skills associated with it constitute a field of expertise in demand by both the food and perfume industries. This ability can be learned in the surprisingly short period of five days, but its maintenance requires constant practice. In order to study the transmission of this knowledge, Teil attended the course and conducted self-ethnography as well as participant observation.

How, therefore, does one become a taster? Teil describes how learning produced changes in tastes and in olfactory practices during the training course, and how this brought about a change in the relationship between the novice and the object through:

- ◆ learning how to manage one's body and brain, so that the 'olfactory tool' is circumscribed within the body;
- ◆ learning how to use it in accordance with collective norms; and above all
- ◆ learning how to check its operation in a suitable way.

The trajectory of learning therefore proceeds through (a) feeling (perception of sensory impressions which delimit a context and an olfactory measure, and control over the brain's interpretations), (b) describing (development of a classificatory language with which to categorize sensations and to communicate, abandonment of the hedonism of feeling oneself naive, acquisition of an expert aesthetics to judge sensations), (c) using (to stabilize the link between the odor and its olfactory descriptor, gaining control over application of the metrological criteria that enable measurement of the relationship between describer and odor, and relying on the network of practitioners in order to heighten the performance of the olfactory tool).

From Teil's theoretical analysis we learn not only that the learning of sensory knowledge develops through stages extending from the mundane knowledge of the novice to the mastery of expert knowledge within a professional community, but also how participation in the community is contextual to the learning of an expert language with which to express aesthetic judgments.

Discursive practices, as in the community studied by Teil, also support the formation of aesthetic judgments and their negotiation within a particular occupational community. But all occupational communities comprise the collective process of taste-making (Gherardi, 2009) that lays down the aesthetic canons for judgment of what must be considered a beautiful practice or an ugly one, a correct but inelegant practice, and so on. This reference serves, on the one hand, to emphasize how a certain mode of practicing is sustained by aesthetic (and ethical) criteria intrinsic to the activity itself and formulated during its performance, and, on the other, how situated discursive practices are intrinsically reflexive, that is, provide their own accountability.

To be noted is that, contrary to a widespread tendency to overestimate the role of sharing (shared understanding, shared signification, shared values) in collective action, it is non-sharing—or better minimal and partial sharing—that is a circumstance for both the action of looking for signification, and a driver of constant change in practice which comes about through negotiation on meanings and the ethical (Clegg et al., 2007) and aesthetic criteria of that practice. In other words, to use a musical metaphor, it is dissonance and not the canon which produces new music (Gherardi and Nicolini, 2002).

The equipped environment

Returning once again to the metaphor of the climber and the co-production of handholds during a climb, we may ask what happens to the interpretation if the material environment, besides addressing the subject and being in a certain sense 'active' in the interaction, is somehow equipped to facilitate the climb if the climber regularly returns to the rock face or leaves pegs to help other climbers, or, again, sets up a rock climbing gym. What I want to show with this shift of perspective is that when a practice becomes such—that is, it has become recurrent and coalesced into habits—the context of the practice is very probably an equipped context in which the main handholds for regular performance of the practice are known; they have been made familiar by repetition of the practice; they have been equipped so as to elicit their habitual use. It is now that artifacts, tools, objects, and technologies come into play, and therefore the relationship with materiality (Svabo, 2009) which anchors relations and meanings and 'suggests actions.' Numerous concepts have been proposed to express this interpretative shift from the context as a 'container' more or less neutral and indifferent to the actions that develop within it to the context as a resource (Lave's 'arena' and 'setting'): the idea of in-strumentation (Rabardel, 1995) as an arrangement to have a relationship of instrumentality (i.e. that instruments are not such in themselves but become so in the relation with the action that they serve); the affordance (Gibson, 1979) of materiality that suggests its use to support a utilization; the intra-action of Barad (2003) which co-articulates meanings and materialities; the concept of 'jigging' (Kirsh, 1995: 37) as a way to prepare and structure the environment. The more completely prepared the environment is, the easier it becomes to accomplish one's task.

In other words, the recursiveness of practices establishes a relationship of co-production with the environment in which not only are the handholds for action discovered in the course of that action, but delegated to these handholds is the execution of certain operations of the same practice or certain functions, such as reminding (Grosjean and Bonneville, 2009), where helping not to forget is anchored in the materiality of signaling artifacts and technologies.

Finally, embedded in the theme of the equipped environment that anchors activities by suggesting to practitioners 'what next' in performance of the practice is a metaphor which conveys the sense of how humans and artifacts intertwine for the fluid performance of a practice. This concerns the idea of improvised choreography proposed by Whalen et al. (2002) when describing the arrangement of the objects and the gestures, as well as the body, of a call center operator. Just as choreography is a matter of space and time, so the operator conveys to the caller that the latter's request is being handled fluidly—without impeding the interaction and therefore with competence—by skilful management of an equipped environment and with a cadence that does not leave gaps in the interaction.

Recursiveness as stabilization and legitimation

In my use of climbing as a metaphor for seeing organizational learning as the becoming of a discursive and material practice, situated in the relationship between knowing and doing, I have tried to highlight both the dynamics of becoming—as a sequential discovery of handholds for doing—and the dynamic which stabilizes relations for a recursive and knowledgeable doing. I shall now dwell on this latter dynamic to synthesize how stabilization of a practice—that is, acting on the circumstances in the expectation that they will re-occur and therefore form a historical and cultural knowledge which supports the practice—is founded as much upon social elements as material ones. Stabilization in materiality takes place through anchorings in discursive and technological practices, in the artifacts of the practice, but these are not unconnected from the cultural process that a practice institutionalizes by attributing ethical and aesthetic values to the modes of doing and stabilizes them as a normative system (creating further artifacts of the practice such as codes, norms, auditing systems, laws). Finally the practice is further stabilized by being embedded in a texture of practice that the action connects and recalls.

THE THEORETICAL CONTRIBUTION
MADE BY THE STUDY OF PRACTICES

We have seen that importing the concept of practice into organizational learning studies has given rise to a large body of literature on practice, thus confirming the intuition of Easterby-Smith et al. (2000) that the emergence of practice as a unit of analysis would be one of the most promising developments within organizational learning. Let us now see whether we can intuit the components of a practice theory of organizations.

An organizational theory is nothing other than a system of representations, and in this case it is based on the idea that 'organizing' derives from the practical modes in which the entanglement between doing and knowing finds its direction and purpose by anchoring itself in materiality and discursiveness.

The base components of a practice theory of organizing are given by defining practice as a collective knowledgeable doing which is socially sustained. The feature which distinguishes practice from action is its recurrent nature. The recursiveness of practices is what enables the reproduction of the organization in its everyday routine. Working practices, in fact, are the elements of shared meaning that allow us to go to work day after day without having to invent every morning what we must do, and without having to negotiate it with our colleagues. Just as society and social relationships must be reproduced day after day and meeting after meeting, so organizations are reproduced every day through the repetition of their relational and normative elements. If a practice were to cease owing to the various reasons for which it is practiced, it would no longer be a practice.

The idea that for a practice to be a practice it must be seen as such by its practitioners, and must therefore be socially sustained, comprises two notions: first that sustaining a practice requires the concurrence of action, so that it is recurrent; second, that it is recurrent because it is institutionalized, that is, sustained by values, beliefs, norms, habits, and discourses. In this process, materiality concurs in the coalescence of the practice through artifacts, the 'equipped' environment, the limitation of interpretative possibilities. We can accordingly say that practice also functions as a guide to action. Not only, therefore, does practice contain a concatenation of operations that make sense to practitioners; it also provides for its accountability in terms of good, correct, wrong, beautiful, and so on, practice.

Just as the everyday reproduction of an organization is driven by the recursiveness of practices, so the idea of change has a particular meaning. It should of course be specified that the idea of reproduction is more similar in its social meaning to the reproduction of the species than to mechanical reproduction by a photocopier. Consequently, intrinsic to the reproduction of practices is the idea of change as a continuous process, a 'repetition without repetition' (Bernstein, 1996; Clot, 2002a), a dynamic that follows the logic of transformation. Just as an orchestra never repeats its performance of a symphony in exactly the same way, so organizational practices are recurrent but never identical. In a certain sense, inherent to the concept of practice is the operation of a contingent logic, not an *a priori* rationality, in that the bravura of practitioners (like orchestra members) resides in their capacity to reproduce the 'same' performance in spite of the varying conditions in which they do so. This is the criticism that the concept of situatedness has brought against the logic of formal and rational prescription. The distinctive dynamic of change in practice, moreover, does not consist solely in the use of the resources 'at hand' to deal with variability and shortages, and thereby reproduce 'the same' amid the changeable. It also involves the social process whereby practitioners are attached to their practices. Hence, refining the object of the practice is to celebrate the ability of the practitioners, their self, and the feelings of care and pleasure that practicing produces. Put otherwise, practices are meaningful to practitioners, they can be objects of love or hate, and they indubitably constitute emotionally involving relations.

Finally, another theoretical contribution that may be forthcoming from a practice theory of organization consists in resolution of the dichotomy between organization and environment. Practices are more directly and closely interconnected, but every practice links with another one. We may therefore say that it is connection-in-action which weaves practices into a texture, or into a 'seamless web,' to use Star's expression (1995). A practice does not stop at the boundaries of the organization; vice versa social practices extend into an organization, just as the knowledge involved in a practice does not stop at the boundaries among different professionals.

The way in which the concept of practice has been appropriated by organization studies has, I believe, the potential to develop a practice theory of organization of which we can see today only the first glimmerings. To buttress this opinion of mine, I shall now examine, even if briefly, the main substantive contributions made by PBS.

THE SUBSTANTIVE CONTRIBUTION MADE BY THE STUDY OF PRACTICES

In focusing on the contribution of organization studies concerned with practice, and to outline the problems studied from this perspective, one must start from the fact that—at least within studies on learning and knowledge in organizations—the practice perspective has emerged as the third way between mentalism, on the one hand, and the commodification of knowledge on the other (Gherardi, 2000). Hence, the inseparability of knowing and doing is assumed, yet practice-based learning is elusive (Contu and Willmott, 2000).

The interest in working practices arises from the fact that they are opaque: new technologies are embedded in already-stabilized practices; new technological systems have spatially dispersed communities working together. It is therefore necessary to know work practices to design technology to support them. Working practices are also opaque to their practitioners. The practice perspective has proved very productive when it has been linked with action research understood in the broad sense as practice development. That is to say, the main beneficiaries from the description and discussion of working practices are the practitioners themselves. In this regard, there are numerous initiatives that can be mentioned. The Helsinki Center for Activity Theory and Developmental Work Research has a 'Change Laboratory' designed to arrange a space comprising a rich set of instruments for analyzing disturbances and for constructing new models for work practice (Engeström, 2000). Opportunities given to homogeneous groups of practitioners, or to groups with members from several departments or organizations, to discuss their working practices not only foster reflexive learning but also lay the bases for bringing tools of daily work and the tools of analysis and design closer together—in a new dialectic of instrumentalities.

To be emphasized from the methodological point of view is the potential of video-recordings made of working situations and then shown to practitioners. Video-recordings have been widely used by workplace researchers interested in the fine-grained analysis of the real-time organization of work practice (for a review see Hindmarsh and Heath, 2007). This approach encourages close consideration of the discursive, embodied, embedded, radically contingent, deeply interactional, and tacit production and organization of work practice (Borzeix and Cochoy, 2008).

We may say that whilst the Change Laboratory is concerned with the intersection between working practices and organizational practices, workplace studies are more attentive to the performance and the spatial and temporal details of work activities and cooperation organized through interaction. A more clinical concern is shown by the French 'Clinique de l'Activitè' group (Clot et al., 2002b). Here researchers attempt to create a framework that favors the development of professional experience for the group engaged in the co-analytical process aimed at increasing individual subjects' power to act. The first stage is dedicated to the creation of a group for the co-analysis of work processes. The main idea is that of self-confrontations and crossed-self confrontations: subjects are confronted with their activity and then become involved in professional controversies. A cycle builds up around what the workers do, what they say about what they do, and ultimately what they do about what they say. A similar approach is adopted by a set of methods— which Shotter and Katz (1996; and Katz and Shotter, 1996) call 'social poetics'—for use by a group of practitioners in achieving a more composite grasp of their own practices, and thus to develop them.

What is important in this methodology is less how a group of people involved in the joint conduct and discussion of a practice respond to each other's different activities within it than how they are each 'struck by' certain fleeting moments within the ongoing conduct of the practice. The assumption is that these moments 'gesture towards,' 'express,' or 'manifest' something special in their shared lives together, and suggest connections and relations which were previously unnoticed.

My purpose in reporting these four initiatives in what we may call 'developmental practice' has been to underline how the representation of practice, by the researcher or with the researcher, is a stimulus for explicitation of that knowledge entangled in doing which may enable better verbal expression of what is known and is enacted in doing, and of which the individual may have scant awareness. At a collective level it is an opportunity for the explicitation and negotiation of the assumptions implicit in practice and which practitioners do not have opportunities to confront. Articulating practice discursively and collectively may become the situation where that part of practice which is obscure because it is not perceived or not recorded acquires an objectified existence and becomes a collective experience for the group (Blackler and Regan, 2009). This may engender a revision of the practices of organizing.

Finally, it must be pointed out that the methodological contribution to the study of practices has been an important factor in the development of PBS. But it should also be said that the representation of practices, although crucial, is not particularly advanced, with the exception of Nicolini's (2009) study on projective techniques and of those by Mondada (2003) and Hindmarsh and Heath (2007) on the use of video-recordings for the study of practices.

CONCLUSIONS

The highly symbolic transition from the term 'knowledge' to that of 'knowing' has opened the way for a view of knowledge as first a process and, subsequently, as a practical activity. In this way, the community of organizational learning and knowing scholars has appropriated the concept of practice to develop a practice theory of organization.

In the foregoing brief description of the developments brought and promises offered by the 'practice turn,' I have shown how 'practice' is a polysemous term with a long pedigree in sociology which ideally continues the sociological contribution to the study of organizational learning. The polysemy of the term may be an obstacle, but it is also a source of interpretative richness.

The richness of the term is evidenced by the proliferation of labels intended to unify and synthesize the approach, which by so doing have set the bandwagon of studies on practice in motion. We may therefore assume the expression 'practice-based studies' (PBS) as an umbrella-term which covers a host of practice-based studies. Within these studies two orientations are apparent: one which considers practices to be the object of empirical analysis (the site of learning and knowing) and one which assumes practice as epistemology.

In privileging the second of these meanings, I have highlighted that it subtends a relational vision and an ecological model of inquiry within which practice is regarded as a phenomenon emerging from the entanglement of knowing and doing. If we consider the becoming of a practice and its function as a guide for knowledgeable collective doing, we can show that the epistemology of practice enables appropriate exploration of sensible and tacit knowledge enacted in practice, together with the body as an active source of knowing, as well as materiality and sociomaterial relations.

I have then explored whether and how a practice theory of organizations could come about and the theoretical and substantive contribution that it could make. Further reflection should indicate directions for future analysis. But given the way in which this field is flourishing in such disorderly and haphazard manner, I would say that exploration in any direction is justified. When the one hundred flowers have given way to more mature theoretical inquiry, the problems and aspects that should be explored systematically will become clearer.

REFERENCES

Alby, F. and Zucchermaglio, C. (2006) Afterwards we can understand what went wrong, but now let's fix it: How situated work practices shape group decision making. *Organisation Studies*, 27(7): 943–966.

Antonacopoulou, E.P. and Pesqueux, Y. (2010) The practice of socialization and the socialization of practice. *Society and Business Review*, 5(1): 10–21.

Barad, K. (2003) Posthumanist performativity: Toward an understanding of how matter comes to matter. *Signs*, 28(3): 801–831.

Barad, K. (2007) *Meeting the University Halfway: Quantum Physics and the Entanglement of Matter and Meaning*. Durham: Duke University Press.

Bernstein, N.A. (1996) On dexterity and its development. In M.L. Latash and M.T. Turvey (eds.), *Dexterity and its Development*. Mahwah, N.J.: Lawrence, Erlbaum.

Billett, S. (2001) Knowing in practice: Re-conceptualising vocational expertise. *Learning and Instruction* 11 (6): 431–452.

Bjørkeng, K., Clegg, S., and Pitsis, T. (2009) Becoming (a) practice. *Management Learning*, 40(2): 145–160.

Blackler, F. and Regan, S. (2009) Intentionality, agency, change: Practice theory and management. *Management Learning*, 40(2): 161–176.

Borzeix, A. and Cochoy, F. (2008) Travail et theories de l'activité: Vers des workspace studies? *Sociologie du Travail*, 50(3): 273–286.

Bourdieu, P. (1972) *Esquisse d'une Théorie de la Pratique Précédé de Trois Etudes de Ethnologie Kabyle*, Switzerland: Librairie Droz S.A. (English trans. *Outline of a Theory of Practice* (1977). Cambridge: Cambridge University Press.

Brown, J. and Duguid, P. (1991) Organizational learning and communities of practice: Toward a unified view of working, learning and bureaucratization. *Organization Science*, 2: 40–57.

Brown J. S., and Duguid, P. (1998) Organizing knowledge. *California Management Review*, 40: 90–111.

Brown, J. and Duguid, P. (2001) Knowledge and organization: A social-practice perspective. *Organization Science*, 12(2):198–213.

Carlile, P.R. (2002). A pragmatic view of knowledge and boundaries: Boundary objects in new product development. *Organization Science*, 13: 442–455.

Charreire-Petit, S.C. and Huault, I. (2008) From practice-based knowledge to the practice of research: Revisiting constructivist research works on knowledge. *Management Learning*, 39(1): 73–91.

Chia, R. (2003) Ontology: organization as 'World Making'. In R. Westwood and S. Clegg (Eds.). *Debating organization: Point–Counter-Point in Organization Studies*. Oxford: Blackwell Publishing, 98–113.

Chia, R. and Holt, R. (2008) On managerial knowledge. *Management Learning*, 39(2): 141–158.

Clegg, S.R., Kornberger, M., and Rhodes, C. (2005) Learning/becoming/organizing. *Organization*, 12(2): 147–167.

Clegg, S. R., Kornberger, M., and Rhodes, C. (2007) Business ethics as practice. *British Journal of Management*, 18: 107–122.

Clot, Y. (2002a) Clinique de l'activité et répétition. *Cliniques Méditeranéennes*, 66: 31–53.

Clot, Y., Fernandez, G., and Carles, L. (2002b), Crossed self-confrontation in the 'Clinic of Activity'. In proceedings of the 11th European congress of cognitive ergonomics (cognition, culture and design), 7–10 September, Catania, Italy.

Cohen, I. J. (1996) Theories of action and praxis. In B.S Turner (ed.) *The Blackwell Companion to Social Theory*. Cambridge: Blackwell Publishers, 111–142.

Contu, A. and Willmott, H. (2000) Comment on Wenger and Yanow. Knowing in practice: a 'Delicate Flower' in the organizational learning field. *Organization*, 7(2): 269–276.

Cook, S. and Brown, J.S. (1999) Bridging epistemologies: The generative dance between organizational knowledge and organizational knowing. *Organization Science*, 10(4): 381–400.

Cook, S. and Yanow, D. (1993) Culture and organizational learning. *Journal of Management Inquiry*, 2(4): 373–390.

Corradi, G., Gherardi, S., and Verzelloni, L. (2010) Through the practice lens: How the bandwagon of practice-based studies was set in motion and where it is heading. *Management Learning*, forthcoming.

Davidson, D. (1984) *Inquiries into Truth and Interpretations*. Oxford: Oxford University Press.

Easterby-Smith, M., Crossan, M., and Nicolini, D. (2000) Organizational learning debates: Past, present and future. *Journal of Management Studies*, 37(6): 783–796.

Engeström, Y. (2000) From individual action to collective activity and back: developmental work research as an interventionist methodology. In P. Luff, J. Hindmarsh, and C. Heath, (eds.), *Workplace Studies*. Cambridge: Cambridge University Press.

Fox, S. (2006). Inquiries of every imaginable kind: Ethnomethodology, practical action and the new socially situated learning theory. *The Sociological Review*, 54(3), 426–445.

Fox, S. (2008) That miracle of familiar organizational things: Social and moral order in the MBA classroom. *Organization Studies*, 29(5): 733–761.

Fujimura, J. H. (1988) Molecular biological bandwagon in cancer research: Where social worlds meet. *Social Problems*, 35(3): 261–283.

Garfinkel, H. (1967) *Studies in Ethnomethodology*. Englewood Cliffs: Prentice-Hall.

Garfinkel, H. (ed.) (1986) *Ethnomethodological Studies of Work*. London: Routledge and Kegan Paul.

Garfinkel, H. (1996) Ethnomethodology's program. *Social Psychology Quarterly*, 59(1): 5–21.

Garfinkel, H. and Sacks, H. (1970) On formal structures of practical actions. In J. McKinney and E.A. Tiryakian (eds.) *Theoretical Sociology*, New York: Appleton-Century-Crofts, 337–366.

Geiger, D. (2009) Revisiting the concept of practice: Toward an argumentative understanding of practising. *Management Learning*, 40(2): 129–144.

Gherardi, S. (2000) Practice-based theorizing on learning and knowing in organizations: An introduction. *Organization*, 7(2): 211–223.

Gherardi, S. (2006) *Organizational Knowledge: The Texture of Workplace Learning*. Blackwell: Oxford.

Gherardi, S. (2008) Situated knowledge and situated action: What do practice-based studies promise? In D. Barry and H. Hansen (eds.), *Sage Handbook of the New and Emerging in Management and Organization*. London: Sage, 516–527.

Gherardi, S. (2009) Practice? It's a matter of taste! *Management Learning*, 40(5): 535–550.

Gherardi, S. (2011) Ways of knowing: Gender as a politics of knowing? In E. Jeanes, D. Knights, and P.Y. Martin (eds.), *Handbook of Gender, Work and Organizations*. Oxford: Blackwell.

Gherardi, S. and Nicolini, D. (2000) The organizational learning of safety in communities of practice. *Journal of Management Inquiry*, 9(1): 7–18.

Gherardi, S. and Nicolini, D. (2001) The sociological foundation of organizational learning. In M. Dierkes, A. Berthoin-Antal, J. Child, and I. Nonaka (eds.), *Handbook of Organizational Learning and Knowledge*. Oxford University Press: Oxford, 35–60.

Gherardi, S. and Nicolini, D. (2002) Learning in a constellation of interconnected practices: Canon or dissonance? *Journal of Management Studies*, 39(4): 419–436.

Gibson, J.G. (1979) *The Ecological Approach to Visual Perception*. Boston: Houghton-Mifflin.

Giddens, A. (1984) *The Constitution of Society*. Cambridge: Polity Press.

Giddens, A. (1990) *The Consequences of Modernity*. Cambridge: Polity Press.

Giglioli, P.P. (1990) *Rituale, Interazione, Vita Quotidiana*. Bologna: Il Mulino.

Goodwin, C. (1994) Professional vision. *American Anthropologist*, 96(3): 606–633.

Goodwin, C. and Goodwin, M. H. (1996) Seeing as a situated activity: Formulating planes. In Y. Engeström and D. Middleton (eds.), *Cognition and Communication at Work*, Cambridge: Cambridge University Press, 61–95.

Grosjean, S. and Bonneville, L. (2009) Saisir le processus de remémoration organisationnelles des actants humain et non humain au cœur du processus. *Revue d'Anthropologie des Connaissances*, 3(2): 317–347.

Heath, C. and Luff, P. (2007) Ordering competition: The interactional accomplishment of the sale of art and antiques at auction. *British Journal of Sociology*, 58: 63–85.

Hennion, A. (2007) Those things that hold us together: Taste and sociology. *Cultural Sociology*, 1(1): 97–114.

Hindmarsh, J. and Heath, C. (2007) Video-based studies of work practice. *Sociology Compass*, 1: 1–18.

Hotho, S. and Pollard, D. (2007) Management as negotiation at the interface: Moving beyond the critical-practice impasse. *Organization*, 14(4): 583–603.

Iedema, R. (2007) On the multi-modality, materiality and contingency of organizational discourse. *Organization Studies*, 28(6): 931–946.

Katz, A. and Shotter, J. (1996) Resonances from within the Practice: Social Poetics in a Mentorship Programme. *Concepts and Transformations*, 1(2/3): 239–247.

Kirsh, D. (1995) The intelligent use of space. *Artificial Intelligence*, 73(1–2), 31–68.

Knorr-Cetina, K. (1981) *The Manufacture of Knowledge*. Oxford: Pergamon Press.

Labatut, J., Aggeri, F., Astruc, J.M., Bibé, B., and Girard, N., (2009) The active role of instruments in articulating knowing and knowledge: The case of animal qualification practices in breeding organizations. *The Learning Organization*, 16(5): 371–385.

Lave, J. and Wenger, E. (1991) *Situated Learning. Legitimate Peripheral Participation*. Cambridge: Cambridge University Press.

Law, J. (1994) *Organizing Modernity*. Oxford: Blackwell.

Llewellyn, N. and Hindmarsh, J. (2010) Work and organisation in real time: An introduction. In N. Llewellyn, and J. Hindmarsh, (eds.) *Organization, Interaction and Practice: Studies in Ethnomethodology and Conversation Analysis*. Cambridge: Cambridge University Press.

Llewellyn, N. and Spence, L. (2009) Practice as a members' phenomenon. *Organization Studies*, 30(12): 1419–1439.

Mead, G. H. (1934) *Mind, Self, and Society*. Chicago: The University of Chicago Press.

Miettinen, R., Samra-Fredericks, D., and Yanow, D. (2009) Re-turn to practice: An introductory essay. *Organization Studies*, 30(12): 1309–1327.

Mondada, L. (2003) Working with video: How surgeons produce video records of their actions. *Visual Studies* 18: 58–73.

Mouzelis, N. (1989) Restructuring structuration theory. *The Sociological Review*, 37(4): 613–634.

Nicolini, D. (2009) Articulating and writing practice through the interview to the double. *Management Learning*, 40(2):195–212.

Nyberg, D. (2009) Computers, customer service operatives and cyborgs: Intra-actions in call centers. *Organization Studies*, 30(11): 1181–1199.

Olsen, D.S. (2009) Emerging interdisciplinary practice: Making nanoreactors. *The Learning Organization*, 16(5): 398–408.

Orlikowski, W. J. (2000) Using technology and constituting structures: A practice lens for studying technology in organizations. *Organization Science*, 11(4): 404–428.

Orlikowski, W. J. (2002) Knowing in practice: Enacting a collective capability in distributed organizing. *Organization Science*, 13: 249–273.

Orlikowski, W. J. (2007) Sociomaterial Practices: Exploring Technology at Work. *Organization Studies*, 28(9): 1435–1448.

Orlikowski,W. and Iacono, C. (2001). Research commentary: Desperately seeking the 'IT' in IT research – A call to theorizing the IT artifact. *Information Systems Research*, 12: 121–134.

Orr, J. (1993) Sharing knowledge, celebrating identity: War stories and community memory among service technicians. In D.S. Middleton and D. Edwards (eds.), *Collective Remembering: Memory in Society*. Beverly Hills, CA: Sage, 169–189.

Østerlund, C. and Carlile, P. (2005) Relations in practice: Sorting through practice theories on knowledge sharing in complex organizations. *The Information Society*, 21: 91–107.

Pickering, A. (1992) *Science as Practice and Culture*. Chicago: University of Chicago Press.

Rabardel, P. (1995) *Les Hommes et les Technologies, Approche Cognitive des Instruments Contemporains*. Paris: Armand Colin.

Raelin, J.A. (1997) A Model of Work-Based Learning. *Organization Science*, 8(6): 563–578.

Raelin, J.A. (2007). Toward an Epistemology of Practice. *Academy of Management Learning and Education*, 6(4): 495–519.

Rasche, A. and Chia, R. (2009) Researching strategy practices: A genealogical social theory perspective. *Organization Studies*, 30(7): 713–734.

Rawls, A. (2008) Harold Garfinkel, ethnomethodology and workplace studies. *Organisation Studies*, 29(5): 701–732.

Reckwitz, A. (2002) Toward a theory of social practices: A development in culturalist theorizing. *European Journal of Social Theory*, 5(2): 243–263.

Rouse, J. (2001) Two concepts of practices, in T.R. Schatzki, K. Knorr-Cetina and E. von Savigny (eds.) *The Practice Turn in Contemporary Theory*. London: Routledge, pp. 189–198.

Sandberg, J. and Dall'Alba, G. (2009) Returning to practice anew: A life-world perspective. *Organisation Studies*, 30(12): 1349–1368.

Schatzki, T.R., Knorr-Cetina, K., and von Savigny, E. (eds.), (2001) *The Practice Turn in Contemporary Theory*. London and New York: Routledge.

Schutz, A. (1946) The well-informed citizen: An essay on the social distribution of knowledge. *Social Research* 13(4): 463–478.

Schutz, A. (1962) *Collected Papers I. The Problem of Social Reality*. The Hague: Nijhoff.

Shotter, J. and Katz, A. (1996) Articulating A Practice From Within The Practice Itself: Establishing Formative Dialogues By The Use Of A 'Social Poetics'. *Concepts and Transformation*, 1(2/3): 213–237.

Sole, D. and Edmondson, A. (2002) Situated knowledge and learning in dispersed teams. *British Journal of Management*, 13 S2: 17–34.

Star, S. L. (1995) *Ecologies of Knowledge*. Albany: State University of New York Press.

Strati, A. (2007). Sensible knowledge and practice-based learning. *Management Learning*, 38(1): 61–77.

Strauss, A.L. (1991) *Creating Sociological Awareness. Collective Images and Symbolic Representations*. New Brunswick and London: Transaction Publishers.

Styhre, A. (2009) Tinkering with material resources: Operating under ambiguous conditions in rock construction work. *The Learning Organization*, 16(5): 386–397.

Suchman, L. (2000) Organizing alignment: A case of bridge-building. *Organization*, 7(2): 311–328.

Sulkunen, P. (1982) Society made visible. On the cultural sociology of Pierre Bourdieu. *Acta Sociologica*, 25(2): 103–115.

Svabo, C. (2009) Materiality in a practice-based approach. *The Learning Organization*, 16(5): 360–370.

Teil, G. (1998) Devenir expert aromaticien: Y a-t-il une place pour le goût dans le goûts alimentaires? *Sociologie du Travail*, 4: 503–522.

Tsoukas, H. (1998) Forms of knowledge and forms of life in organized contexts. In R. Chia (ed.), *In the Realm of Organization*. London: Routledge, 43–66.

Turner, S. (1994) *The Social Theory of Practices*. Chicago: The University of Chicago Press.

Wacquant, L. (1992) The structure and logic of Bourdieu's sociology. In P. Bourdieu and L. Wacquant (eds.) *An Invitation to Reflexive Sociology*. Chicago: University of Chicago.

Weick, K.E. (1991) The non-traditional quality of organizational learning. *Organization Science*, 2: 116–123.

Wenger, E. (1998) *Communities of Practice: Learning, Meaning, and Identity*. Cambridge: Cambridge University Press.

Whalen, J., Whalen, M., and Henderson, K. (2002) Improvisational choreography in tel-eservice work. *British Journal of Sociology*, 53: 239–258.

Whittington, R. (1996) Strategy as practice. *Long Range Planning*, 29(5): 731–735.

Yanow, D. (2003) Seeing organizational learning: a 'Cultural View.' In D. Nicolini, S. Gherardi, and D. Yanow (eds.) (2003) *Knowing in Organizations: A Practice-based Approach*. Armonk. NY: ME Sharpe.

Yanow, D. (2004) Translating local knowledge at organizational peripheries. *British Journal of Management*, 15(1): 9–25.

4

Psychological Perspectives in Organizational Learning: A Four-Quadrant Approach

HELEN SHIPTON AND ROBERT DeFILLIPPI

ABSTRACT

Psychological learning theories are assessed along two continua. We start by examining theories which hold that learning is susceptible to control and direction as opposed to unfolding naturally in the workplace. Here, we examine behavioral reinforcement theory as well as cognitive learning theory and extend the discussion by highlighting the organizational-level implications of this perspective. By reference to notions of distributed cognitions as well as social cognitive theory, we examine person/context reciprocity, again drawing out the implications for organizational learning. The polar opposite for this dimension—which suggests that learning evolves naturally—draws on situated learning theory and the logic for 'learning by doing' and communities of practice. A second continuum in our framework investigates distinctions where individuals as opposed to groups have been taken as the focal point of inquiry. We conclude by examining an area that has received relatively scant attention: the role of emotion in learning.

INTRODUCTION

Psychology has offered multiple insights into the vagaries of human learning. The literature has also enriched our understanding of organizational learning, while at the same time opening channels for scholarly debate. For example, questions have been raised about positivist as opposed to constructivist perspectives and the role of context versus personal determinism. To what extent are these considerations taken into account where the focus is the organization rather than the individual? Another point is whether there are missing strands that deserve closer scrutiny, given the emphasis on cognitive processes and what may be broadly termed 'relational' factors. We take an overarching approach as we address these questions, bringing together key themes, in line with the suggestion in the last edition of this Handbook that the paradigmatic shift in psychology is in this direction (DeFillippi and Ornstein, 2003).

The purpose of this chapter, then, is to explore how psychological learning theories have been used in the development of theories about organizational learning. We do so by means of a comparative framework (or typology) which allows us to compare and contrast significant themes along defined parameters. Utilizing a four-quadrant typology (Shipton, 2006) we first explore key aspects of individual learning theory and then turn to theories connected with organizational learning, in particular, those which are either drawn from, or have strong parallels with, psychological traditions. This way of assessing the various literatures offers a structure for comparing theoretical perspectives across levels of analysis (for example, individual, team, and organization), while also taking into account different paradigms. Some scholars, for example, view learning as amenable to control and direction, while others insist that learning rather unfolds naturally in the workplace. Our quest is to identify the main areas where various psychological paradigms have influenced organizational learning given these identified themes.

The advantages of using a typology have been described in detail elsewhere (Shipton, 2006). In short, a typology can subdivide the literature in order to 'transform the complexity of apparently eclectic congeries of diverse cases into well-ordered sets of a few rather homogenous types, clearly situated in a property space of a few important dimensions' (Bailey, 1994: 33). Each comparative type is relatively independent of the other, the important point being that there is a basis for comparison across types. Overall, the cataloging system offers the opportunity to draw conclusions linked with the profiling parameters that have been pre-defined (Bailey, 1994).

With these points in mind, a typology has been devised to categorize (as far as possible) individual learning research using a comparative matrix (see Figure 4.1). Along one continuum, we depict perspectives that focus on how learning may be managed, controlled or directed. The contrast is with (relatively) more explanatory or descriptive orientations, where learning is conceptualized as a process implicit in day-to-day tasks. Along the other continuum we examine the level of analysis; do authors focus on the individual or are they rather concerned about the wider context within which work activities take place? In considering these themes, we make reference to organizational learning literature. Here, there are again contrasting schools of thought not dissimilar from those highlighted above; on the one hand, there are studies where the orientation tends to be either prescriptive or normative. In a contrasting line of thought, scholars have been pre-occupied with how learning takes place *in situ*. Regarding levels of analysis, just as in the individual learning literature there is a distinction between an emphasis on the individual as opposed to the wider environment, where exploring organizational learning, perspectives tend to fall into one of two categories: those that adopt a micro perspective, where the focal point of interest is the individual and the surrounding work group or team, as opposed to those that are pre-occupied with organizational-level factors, tending towards a macro orientation.

We reviewed approximately eighty books and journal articles in developing our ideas, having been guided in our reading by a number of principles. Firstly, we looked for seminal studies that have been widely cited and were published in world-leading journals such as the *Academy of Management Review, Academy of Management Journal, Organization Science,*

Human Relations, Organization Studies, and the *Journal of Management Studies.* We next supplemented the preceding search by examining more practitioner-oriented books and journals which have also significantly influenced thinking in this area (e.g. Argyris, 1990; Pedler, Burgoyne, and Boydell, 1999; Senge, 1990). To complete the review, we looked at long-standing seminal texts, such as Kelly (1955), Dewey (1938), Mead (1938), and Bandura (1982) whose principles are enshrined in common knowledge and to whom frequent reference is made in standard academic texts on learning, training, and development (e.g. Blanchard and Thacker, 2010; Harrison, 2009; Mankin, 2009). In this way, we hope to illustrate general trends in line with the parameters defined above, without attempting to categorize each and every paper (a task that is clearly impossible within a short book chapter). What follows offers a rough classification of these literature sources, given that there may at times be ambivalence in terms of where within the framework a certain piece of work is positioned. We have attempted to highlight this ambiguity while simultaneously presenting a reasonably consistent depiction of the framework itself.

THE FOUR QUADRANT FRAMEWORK

In the next section, we work through the four-phase quadrant one step at a time, then compare and contrast theoretical perspectives for the top half of the quadrant (where the orientation is primarily based on cognitive processes) with the seemingly greater preoccupation with relationships exhibited by scholars whose work is located in the bottom two quadrants. This leads us into considering future directions. In doing so, we reflect (briefly) on

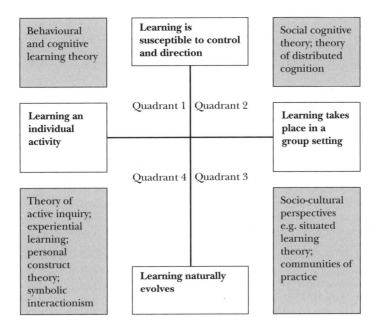

Figure 4.1 The Four Quadrant Framework

the scant attention that has been devoted to emotional factors in learning at both the level of the individual and the organization.

Quadrant one: learning is susceptible to control and direction: the individual perspective

Several learning theories can be seen to occupy this quadrant, which suggests that the learner is more or less passive and subject to stimuli from the outside environment. Implicit is the idea that acknowledged experts are responsible for learners' progress. Learning is achieved by creating an environment which reinforces desirable actions Skinner (1953). Here, we bring together both behaviorist traditions, which suggest that learning represents 'any change in behavior occurring as a result of practice or experience' (Bass and Vaughan, 1967) as well as traditional cognitive perspectives. For cognitive theorists, learning is not just a change in behavior, but rather a change in the way information is processed and the individual's mental schemata built or re-organized (Blanchard and Thacker, 2010). According to Piaget (1950), two cognitive processes are crucial for learning: accommodation and assimilation. The former term refers to the creation of new categories or schemata, while the latter is used to describe what happens when existing schemata are complemented with further information. Both approaches emphasize that some external driver is needed for learning to occur, behaviorists highlight the wider environment, while cognitivists instead emphasize the need to help learners to develop the necessary cognitive structures. The point is that learning can be enabled and controlled by a knowledgeable expert who has responsibility for supporting the learner to enable the necessary change.

The notions of double loop learning (Argyris and Schön, 1978) and generative learning (Senge, 1990) would also fall into this category. Here, the pre-occupation is again the individual, and the suggestion is that individuals can be helped to become more inclined to question the logic for performing work tasks, and to better understand their personal limitations. According to scholars in this area, people's so-called defensive thought patterns can be uncovered through creating an environment of openness and trust so that factors likely to inhibit learning are minimized (Argyris, 1990). One could argue that this approach is not dissimilar from suggestions by cognitive theorists that appropriate mental scaffolds need to be developed through the intervention of an expert third party.

Shifting the focus from the individual to the organization, one can see parallels with the wider literature. The learning organization model, for example, is seen as a context where learning improves as a result of proactive and empowering intervention by senior management (Sicilia and Lytras, 2005). Individuals are required to be increasingly proficient at articulating the issues they face whilst simultaneously listening actively to others before evaluating their input (e.g. Senge, 1990). There is also concern with creating the environment within which individuals can learn effectively. Thus, organizations should adopt flat, decentralized organizational structures that facilitate open communication and dialogue (Pedler, Burgoyne, and Boydell, 1999). Team working facilitates individual growth and empowerment, and therefore presents the ideal structural arrangement (Leonard-Barton, 1998). Other HR systems should be developed in line with this aspiration; for example, individuals should have opportunities to participate in organizational decision making and reward systems should be designed to recognize the achievement of learning goals

(Armstrong and Foley, 2003; Garvin, Edmondson, and Gino, 2008; Wang and Ahmed, 2004). Although outwardly there is a concern with organizational-level outcomes (competitive success, profitability, sustainability, etc), close reading suggests that the predominant orientation is the individual; furthermore, the underlying premise is that learning can be managed and controlled through external intervention.

Quadrant two: learning is susceptible to control and direction:
the group perspective

Unlike the first quadrant, this part of the typology encompasses work that is less straightforward to classify for several reasons. Scholars whose work is reviewed here generally posit a process of reciprocal determinism—whereby individuals and context have a mutually reinforcing effect (e.g. Bandura, 1997). This means that individual activities influence joint, distributed patterns of knowledge and cognitions, which in turn affect their own thinking and behavior (Pea, 1999). The precise boundary between the individual and the system to which he or she belongs, or between the person 'solo' and more widely distributed cognitions, is unclear, indeed there are likely to be some cognitions (such as higher-order knowledge) that are either not amenable to distribution at all or cannot be easily passed on to others (Salomon, 1999). Furthermore, mental representations—arising from individual thought processes—are seen as necessary in order to precipitate change in shared cognitions (denoting again a necessary emphasis on the individual).

Although there is acknowledgement in this quadrant about how the context and wider surroundings influence individuals, the precise role of individuals in specific settings will vary depending upon many factors, such as the need for higher-order knowledge and the meaning that is attributed by group participants to the joint activities involved (Salomon, 1999). To argue that scholars classified here emphasize context while those in the first quadrant highlight the individual would be simplistic; however, the emphasis seems to be in this second quadrant on unraveling the various strands that shape person/context dynamics, especially around learning and change.

The other point of contention concerns the susceptibility of learning to control and direction, as viewed from this quadrant. Here, there are parallels with the first quadrant. Although there is debate about the relative role of individuals within a social system, there is some notion of there being an external reality that can be aspired towards. Bandura (1982), for example, posited a model whereby social influence (e.g. observing peers) and social persuasion (e.g. having a supportive and positive mentor or line manager) would influence an individual's perception about his or her mastery at a given task, showing correlations between mastery perceptions and success in performing to be task high. According to this argument (again echoing quadrant one), the main impediment preventing an individual from gaining mastery may be the reinforcement detected by the individual in response to his or her actions. Other social psychologists argue that the environment is important for learning in a different way: through engaging in joint action (and thereby becoming part of a social system) individuals acquire a 'cognitive residue' or increased competency that can thereafter be applied to similar situations (Salomon, 1999). Managing and directing learning is necessarily complex according to this perspective, but nonetheless, where the reciprocal dynamics can be addressed, likely to yield fruitful returns.

Organizational learning scholars have embraced many of the insights derived from the psychological perspective outlined here. Their debate has been around individual versus organizational dynamics; for example, taking the individual perspective, Simon (1991: 125) stated that 'all learning takes place inside human heads and an organization learns in one of two ways: by the learning of its members or by ingesting new members who have knowledge that the organization didn't previously have.' Other scholars have rather emphasized the influence of organizational systems on individual attitudes, especially towards learning (e.g. Antonacopoulou, 2001). Reciprocity across levels is a re-occurring theme; novel insights from creative individuals may influence the wider work group, in turn, impacting on organizational functioning (e.g. Thomas, Sussman, and Henderson, 2001). According to the so-called '4-i' model, not only do individuals initiate organizational learning (through having a creative idea), they also, together with colleagues, implement the change in cognition and/or action required to effect organizational-level change, and in turn, through feedback processes, are themselves subject to change (Crossan, Lane, and White, 1999). This change could be described as a 'cognitive residue' which is retained by the individual, and necessary for building on-going capability across the system as a whole.

Much of the literature addressing the dynamics of reflection in action (e.g. Edmondson, 2002; Ron, Lipshitz, and Popper, 2006) is driven by a similar philosophical underpinning. Setting aside time for assessing how effectively work groups have dealt with their challenges builds individual competency (so that similar issues can be tackled elsewhere even when group members are engaged in different settings). Reflection may at the same time develop distributed cognitions, with group members increasingly cognizant of shared knowledge and able to take account of other members' expertise in their own endeavors. Arising from this, scholars (e.g. Huber, 1991) have suggested that insights are stored in a memory system that is drawn upon by organizational members as required (mirroring reference to the notion of cognitive residue).

One can also detect parallels with the sense-making literature insofar as it relates to organizational learning. For scholars whose work is explored above (in this quadrant), learning is characterized by a process of dynamic interaction between the learner and his or her wider environment, taking into account the perceptual framework that has evolved based on earlier experiences (cf. Bandura, 1982). The sense-making literature, taking an organizational-level perspective, holds similarly that learning involves a dynamic interplay between search, interpretation, and understanding (Thomas et al., 2001; Weick, 1995). Search routines alter patterns of understanding, which in turn produce new ways of making sense of complex and ambiguous experiences. Thus, sense making alters knowledge structures in organizations by heightening the need for change and influencing the processes whereby knowledge is interpreted. Shared understanding emerges as interpretative routines are internalized, so that learning and understanding become inextricably inter-connected. Studies have explored how sense making can be accelerated in line with strategic priorities, where, for example, a significant event provides the necessary 'jolt' in thinking (Christianson, Farkas, Sutcliffe, and Weick, 2009), or where the company effectively conveys the pressing need for change (Kim, 1998).

In some cases, in the above literature, there is a reality to be uncovered and behavior is influenced by a knowledgeable third party; in other cases, the position is more complex, in that interpretation and sense making may influence the 'reality' derived from complex and ambiguous settings. On the whole, there is a sense that learning can be managed either through effective exchange and dialogue, or through interpretation systems and (perhaps) appropriate reinforcement. To depict a contrasting perspective, we turn now to the third quadrant and review constructivist, rather than positivist, psychological perspectives.

Quadrant three: learning evolves naturally: the group perspective

Those of a social constructivist persuasion distance themselves from the idea that learning is an individual activity. Therefore, the separation between individual and organizational perspectives is dissolved. Person/environment interaction is important, but the individual is inevitably a product of his or her environment (Huysman, 2000). Context shapes what is learnt and how it is learnt and what is regarded as important. Thus, while learning involves self-reflection, it also involves working with others (Lave and Wenger, 1991). Gherardi et al. (1998: 274) have stated, for example, that 'people and groups create knowledge and negotiated meaning—in terms of words, actions, situations and artifacts.' Cognitive processes and conceptual structures are less important than the social engagements that provide a context for learning (Cook and Brown, 1999). 'Social groups provide the resources for their members to learn' (Brown and Duguid, 2001: 137). This happens as groups create knowledge and attribute meaning to certain words, actions, and artifacts, giving rise to a collective identity in terms of what activities are valued and how efforts should best be directed (Wenger, 2000).

What further distinguishes work located in this quadrant from the other perspectives concerns the way in which knowledge is depicted and the position of tacit versus explicit knowledge. This theme forms a central part of the 'situated learning' approach, which examines ideas surrounding 'knowing' rather than 'knowledge' (Cook and Brown, 1999). 'Knowing' involves gradually and almost subconsciously absorbing and understanding what is required to perform well, including the questions to ask, the language to use, how and where to best focus efforts. Through story-telling, for example, communities of practitioners share their experiences of work using their own unique language and terminology (Brown and Duguid, 1991). Accordingly, the way to promote organizational learning is to recognize its tacit dimension and to support communities as they develop the mechanisms required for sharing knowledge. By contrast, the various cycles of organizational learning portrayed in quadrant two deal with explicit knowledge and how such knowledge is embedded (e.g. Crossan et. al., 1999). Some theorists whose work logically fits into quadrant two assess tacit, implicit aspects of knowledge creation (e.g. Nonaka and Takeuchi, 1995; Zollo and Winter, 2002) but their concern is to make explicit and/ or codify this element. The 'practice-based' approach by contrast holds the 'tacit' aspects of knowledge creation and articulation to be central and not amenable to management and direction-setting.

Several strands of thought within the organizational learning literature arise from the social constructivist perspective described here. Firstly, because knowledge is socially constructed, rather than managed or directed by an external party, organizational boundaries are more fluid and less constricting than seems to be implicitly suggested by theorists whose work is portrayed in the first two quadrants. The logic seems to be in line with Nahapiet and Ghoshal (1998) in that social networks lead to the creation, transmission, and retention of intellectual capital, while going further by emphasizing that networks are not necessarily contained within any one specific context. By contrast, people are likely to gravitate towards those with similar professional interests, even where (or especially where) expertise is located outside. This development may be heightened in particular settings, for example, public sector bodies (given national policy strictures) (Rashman, Withers, and Hartley, 2009) or knowledge intensive service firms (where groups of firms work closely together to better meet client needs) (Miozzo, Lehrer, DeFillippi, Grimshaw, and Ordanini, 2010).

Secondly, work has alluded to the characteristics of source and recipient organizations where they are engaged in a process of mutual learning, stressing the role of openness to experience and the position of boundary scanners (Rashman et al., 2009). Work draws attention to the quality of the relationship between source and recipient organizations, implying that effectively managing such relationships may become increasingly pressing as boundaries across organizations are blurred. Thirdly, in a related development, scholars have examined network learning, whereby members of discrete but inter-connected organizations are represented in a collaborative setting where the intention is to learn and innovate (Knight and Pye, 2005). Insights from this line of research suggest that network learning can be understood by examining behavioral and cognitive change *within the network* over time, as shared meanings, structures, and commitment evolve in an iterative process. Finally, recent work has considered whether the learning organization model itself deserves further attention, taking into account not only internal attributes but also the extent of interaction with the external environment (Shipton, Zhou, and Mooi, under review).

Quadrant four: learning naturally evolves: the individual perspective

This quadrant considers theories that emphasize the practice-based nature of learning. Strictly speaking, the orientation is less to do with learning being emergent (as described above) and more connected with understanding the extent to which practice and experience may enrich learning. There are, of course, many different practice-based interventions (project learning, team-based learning, action learning, personal development plans, coaching and mentoring, job shadowing, and buddying to name but a few). This section explores underlying psychological perspectives (rather than comprehensively reviewing this literature). We first examine project learning, then consider the wider implications of this quadrant for organizational learning. The theme of emotion in learning—alluded to here in passing—is discussed in more detail in the final section of the chapter.

Project-based learning in all its forms emphasizes the importance of reflective practices, which refer to the means by which project participants make sense of their project experience and ponder the meaning of the experience for themselves and others (Raelin, 2001). However, project-based learning traditions differ in which focal audience they target for reflection. Action learning interventions often emphasize problem-based reflections on behavior and taken-for-granted assumptions that interfere with individual learning and effective work performance (Smith, 2001). Action research projects, by contrast, are more oriented toward reflecting on how the organizational and social-cultural context impacts project performance and, by implication, organization learning (Coghlan, 2001). Project-organized companies (e.g. construction, high technology) often employ project-learning interventions to capture 'lessons-learned' from completed projects onto company knowledge management databases for re-use by team members on subsequent projects (Keegan and Turner, 2001). In echoes of research examined in quadrant three, community-of-practice and network organization projects employ reflective practices oriented toward understanding how learning generated during projects is disseminated to external project sponsors and their relevant occupational and industry networks (Ayas and Zeniuk, 2001). Comparative assessments of problem and project-based learning approaches have detailed their implications for management education and management development interventions (DeFillippi and Milter, 2009).

Project learning research draws upon several theoretical traditions. Kolb (1984), for example, in line with Lewin (1946) has drawn attention to the stages involved in learning from experience, arguing that reflection, abstract thinking and experimentation are necessary for maximum benefit. Learning arises as a consequence of focusing on other (personal or career-related) goals, and learners can be helped to work through the various phases. Given the implication that meaning is unique to each learner, there are parallels with scholars whose work is reviewed in quadrant three (the social constructivist perspective). Project learning in a sense spans quadrants three and four: reality is based on the learners' experiences and perceptions, while at the same time a practical intervention that draws on opportunities provided by the work environment (DeFillippi and Milter, 2009).

Mead (1938) also posits that learning is part of everyday experience, the natural product of an inquiring mind. However, it is rather the mismatch between a person's anticipation of an experience and the experience itself that provides the momentum for learning and change. Perceptual changes arising from an experience are labeled 'validation' where there is correspondence with anticipation, as opposed to 'invalidation' where experience fails to meet with expectation. Mead's ideas are suggestive of emotion, a theme which is further developed below.

Psychological perspectives explored here have been applied to organizational learning by means of generalization. That is, as individuals learn more effective actions, this learning will aggregate or spill over to their employing organizations. Like work reviewed in quadrant one, the assumption is that organizations learn as a result of individual learning. For example, Kim's integrated model of organizational learning is premised on the assumption that 'the mental models in individuals' heads are where a vast majority of an organization's knowledge (both know-how and know-why) lies' (Kim, 1993: 44). His conceptual model links individuals' mental models (frameworks and routines) to individual single and double loop learning and suggests that single loop learning has more the character of conditioned behavioral response whereas double loop learning builds on the development of a higher level cognitive processing. At the organization level, it appears that organizational routines constitute the shared mental models that determine organizational action. However, these shared mental models slowly evolve in response to the mental models of the individuals comprising the organization. Hence, organizational learning is an additive function of the legacy of those individuals who collectively have contributed to the creation and maintenance of a shared mental model. This may suggest that the organization's culture is an additive, accumulative function of the legacy of individuals' shared cognitive perspectives.

EMOTION IN ORGANIZATIONAL LEARNING

Looking across the four-quadrant framework, it seems that emotional and motivational factors are either subsumed under broader headings such as 'learning culture' (e.g. Pedler, Burgoyne, and Boydell, 1996; Garvin et. al., 2008) or condensed to attributes like 'trust'

(Kang et. al., 2007; Nahapiet and Ghoshal, 1998). Similarly, although a wide literature has annotated the various factors that may facilitate both formal and informal learning—such as reward systems (Arthur and Aimant-Smith, 2001), personal commitment to self-actualization (Senge, 2006), and openness to new and different experiences (Pedler et. al., 1996) (touched on in quadrant one)—it is not clear how these mechanisms influence learning at a higher level than the individual. This lack of attention to emotion has, according to some scholars (e.g. Fineman, 2003), led to under-theorization in this area.

Close scrutiny indicates that there are suggestive links. Bandura (1982, 1997), discussed in quadrant two, has highlighted the role of self-efficacy in learning, suggesting that the momentum (and, by implication, the positive feelings) gained through achieving mastery may raise expectations and fuel an individual's willingness to take on new challenges. Defensive thought patterns (cf. Argyris and Schön, 1978), by contrast, are laden with fear and threat, and likely to undermine double loop learning. According to Kelly (1955), however, whose work follows on from Mead (1938), seeing emotions as either 'good' or 'bad' is simplistic; instead, emotions signal whether one's understanding of the world is evolving in the 'right' direction (according to expectations). Anxiety, for example, signals that the construct system is breaking down and requires revision.

Shifting the focus to the organization, Argyris and Schön (1978) have argued that only in an atmosphere of trust and openness are people likely to share their honest thoughts and fears. Vince and Saleem (2004) have shown that a culture indicative of caution and blame inhibits learning. Kang et al. (2007) concur that culture affects learning, but argue that exploratory learning may be suppressed in cultures emphasizing strong ties, indicating instead that exposure to new and different perspectives may be required. The suggestion is that feeling too 'comfortable' within a particular setting may not necessarily be conducive to deeper-level learning. The sense-making literature too hints at emotion (e.g. Christianson et al., 2009). According to this perspective, collective experiences with widespread implications prompt shared feelings, which, in turn, trigger new patterns of thinking across the organization. Again, emotions are suggested rather than made explicit, being associated with punctuations in the sense-making process, suggestive of the interplay between the negative and the positive. The question of how emotions and cognition interact to elicit the learning remains unaddressed.

In terms of future developments, a number of considerations are worth taking forward. Seeing emotion as somehow separate from cognition may be misleading. Emotion infuses both action and thinking, and arises from the socio-political context within which work activity takes place. We therefore concur with Fineman (2003) that social-constructivist approaches exploring how learning and change occur over time offer scope for assessing emotional dynamics in a particular setting. We also endorse theoretical perspectives that bring together cognitive and emotional elements (e.g. Kelly, 1955). According to Kelly, emotions signal when the existing construct system needs to be revised. Changes in construct systems arise from awareness of developments in the wider environment, and are likely to evolve in a shared way given a common setting. A construct is discarded once the person has evidence that it is no longer valid, that is, it no longer enables the environment to be effectively anticipated. At this stage, the person experiences anxiety (because a new construct has yet to evolve) but in time the construct is adjusted for optimal anticipation of events. Therefore, a sense of awakening or disturbance is necessary for the re-construal process. For example, if people can see that an existing operation in the company is no longer appropriate they are more likely to search for alternatives that fit better with their construal process (i.e. what needs to happen in order to better anticipate the challenges of the environment).

It would be informative to assess what this approach might mean for research located in the third quadrant, where social constructivist perspectives currently examine cognitive rather than emotional dynamics. This is also the case for the second quadrant, where analysis touches on issues around context and individual agency again without overtly addressing the question of emotion. A more processual perspective on organizational learning is suggestive of the re-construal of meaning rather than the transfer of knowledge across the organization in an exchange process (Shipton and Sillince, under review). We suggest that learning takes place as people frame meaning in a particular setting rather than through negotiating thought patterns (Argyris and Schön, 1978) or processing information (Huber, 1991).

Overall, this discussion leads us to suggest that there may be scope in bringing together organizational learning and emotional intelligence literatures (cf. Shipton and Sillince, under review). We wonder whether companies that are successful at learning treat emotion as a tool rather than as a barrier. We also ask whether leaders in companies with a strong propensity to learn are more aware of emotion and emotional transitions, making an explicit connection between emotion and organizational learning. Approaching some of the questions so might produce a more nuanced understanding of the way in which emotions in a collective setting seem most likely to influence learning and change.

CONCLUSION

Using a typology encompassing psychological learning theories across four quadrants, we have compared and contrasted various strands in the literature in an effort to detect synergies as well as points of difference. Doing so has enabled us to explore how psychological learning theories have been used in the development of (some) theories connected with organizational learning. To the left side of the model, theories which are essentially individualistic in orientation are reviewed. We have examined behavioral learning theory as well as simple cognitive models, in combination with theories that explore how the individual interacts with his or her environment to learn, change, and grow. To the right side of the model, we have explored theories such as distributed cognitions and learning-in-practice that highlight the shared sense of being that arises from working closely with others and the inseparability of learners from the social system to which they belong. Across the horizontal axis, we have reviewed (connected) themes asserting, firstly, the amenability of learning to control and direction, and, secondly, the natural evolution of learning, which occurs as people engage with their environments.

There are differences within each set of quadrants, taking into account the broad parameters described above. For example, looking to the left of the vertical axis, in the first quadrant, the individual is essentially passive, at the behest of his or her environment. Through appropriate reinforcement, desired behaviors are produced, which are, in turn, encouraged and rewarded by external parties in order to become a habitual state. In the fourth quadrant, by contrast, individuals are portrayed as active learners. Learning and progression may not necessarily be conscious, but rather a necessary part of the human condition.

Turning to perspectives outlined in the top and bottom parts of the typology, the point of contention is to do with control in learning, where we have asked questions about whether scholars perceive there to be an external reality against which learning can be held to account. For the first quadrant, the perspective seems to be that knowledge and expertise is concentrated in the hands of specific parties (for example, senior managers or learning and development specialists) who have responsibility for assisting and enabling the learning of those for whom they are responsible. In the second quadrant this line of reasoning is perhaps more subtly portrayed. Rather than people responding directly to their environments, it is suggested that there is a filtering process whereby a judgment is made about how effective or ineffective an action has been in the quest to achieve mastery (cf. Bandura, 1982). The social system influences mastery to the extent that there are role models portraying ideal behavior and providing guidance and support. The reciprocal nature of learning and the role of shared cognitions bring to mind several well known theories of organizational learning, such as the '4-i' framework (Crossan et al., 1999) and the SECI model posited by Nonaka and Takeuchi (1995).

Regarding constructivist perspectives, the typology suggests that there is a focus in the bottom two quadrants on how relationships influence learning within a work setting. Learning is social and is grounded in the concrete situations in which people participate with others. Social construction perspectives complement information processing and behavioral perspectives by focusing on organizational learning as involving socially mediated processes of interpretation and sense making. Weick (1995) conceives of the organization as a sense-making system that engages in recurring cycles of enactment, selection, and retention. These processes are the means by which the organization evolves as it makes sense of itself and its environment. The community of practice literature relies on the enactment of sense making, asserting that learning arises from communities sharing a common language, values, and practices. Newcomers to such communities learn through participation (Lave and Wenger, 1991).

Recent work has taken a knowledge co-creation and/or network learning perspective, which follows on from work reviewed in this quadrant. Because knowledge is socially constructed, rather than managed or directed by an external party, organizational boundaries are more fluid and less constricting than is implicitly suggested by theorists whose work is portrayed in the first two quadrants. The logic seems to be in line with Nahapiet and Ghoshal (1998) in that social networks lead to the creation, transmission, and retention of intellectual capital. Social constructivist perspectives suggest that such networks are not necessarily contained within any one specific context. By contrast, people are likely to gravitate towards those with similar professional interests, even where expertise is located outside. Turning to the applied learning school of thought (quadrant four), there are several theoretical perspectives largely drawn from individual learning literatures. Experiential learning theory, for example, draws attention to the stages involved in the learning experience; there is, however, a connection with social constructivist theory especially for interventions where learning tasks are anchored to naturally occurring work activity, such as projects (DeFillippi, 2001).

In conclusion, the emphasis across the four quadrants seems to have been on cognitive modeling based on theorizing at the individual level, developed for applicability at the level of the organization, or alternatively in exploring how learning arises informally, in a collective setting. The importance of building productive relationships and learning culture has been widely considered by organizational learning scholars, especially within work located in quadrants two, three, and four. We have suggested that there may be scope for developing these areas in future research by taking into account not just the cognitive aspects involved but also emotional dynamics.

References

Antonacopoulou, E. (2001) The paradoxical nature of the relationship between training and learning. *Journal of Management Studies*, (38)3: 327–350.

Argyris, C. (1990) *Overcoming Organisational Defenses: Facilitating Organisational Learning.* Boston, MA: Allyn and Bacon.

Argyris, C. and Schön, D. (1978) *Organisational Learning: a Theory of Action Perspective.* Reading: Addison-Wesley.

Armstrong, A. and Foley, P. (2003) Foundations for a learning organization: organization learning mechanisms. *The Learning Organization*, 10(2): 74–82.

Arthur, J. and Aimant-Smith, L. (2001) Gainsharing and organizational learning: An analysis of employee suggestions over time. *Academy of Management Journal*, 44: 737–754.

Ayas, K. and Zeniuk, N. (2001) Project-based Learning: Building Communities of Reflective Practitioners. *Management Learning*, 32(1): 61–76.

Bailey, K. (1994) Typologies and taxonomies: An introduction to classification techniques. *Sage University Paper No. 102*. London: Sage Publications.

Bandura, A. (1982) Self-efficacy mechanism in human agency. *American Psychologist*, 37: 122–147.

Bandura, A. (1997) *Self-efficacy: The exercise of control.* New York: W.H. Freeman and Company.

Bass, B. and Vaughan, J. (1967) *Training in industry: the management of learning.* London: Tavistock Publications.

Blanchard, P. and Thacker, J. (2010) *Effective training: Systems, strategies and practice*, 4th edition. New Jersey: Prentice-Hall.

Brown, J.S. and Duguid, P. (1991) Organisational learning and communities of practice: towards a unified view of working, learning and innovating. *Organisation Science*, 2(1): 40–57.

Brown, J.S. and Duguid, P. (2001) Knowledge and organization: a social-practice perspective. *Organization Science*, 12(2): 198–213.

Christianson, M., Farkas, M., Sutcliffe, K., and Weick, K. (2009) Learning through rare events: significant interruptions at the Baltimore and Ohio Railroad Museum. *Organization Science*, 20: 846–860.

Coghlan, D. (2001) Insider Action Research Projects: Implications for Practicing Managers. *Management Learning*, 32(1): 49–60.

Cook, S and Brown, J.S. (1999) Bridging epistemologies: the generative dance between organizational knowledge and organizational knowing. *Organization Science*, 10(4), 381–400.

Crossan, M., Lane, H., and White, R. (1999) An organizational learning framework: from intuition to institution. *Academy of Management Review*, 24(3): 522–537.

DeFillippi, R. (2001) Project-based learning, reflective practices and learning outcomes. *Management Learning*, 32(1): 5–10.

DeFillippi, R. and Milter, R. (2009) Problem-based and Project-based Learning Approaches: Applying Knowledge to Authentic Situations. In S. J. Armstrong and C. Fukami (eds.), *Handbook of Management Learning, Education and Development*. Oxford, UK: Oxford University Press: 344–363.

DeFillippi, R. and Ornstein, S. (2003) Psychological Perspectives Underlying Theories of Organizational Learning. In M. Easterby-Smith and M. Lyles (eds.), *Handbook of Organizational Learning and Knowledge*. Oxford: Blackwell Publishing: 19–37.

Dewey, J. (1938) *Experience and education*. New York: Simon & Schuster.

Edmondson, A. (2002) The Local and Variegated Nature of Learning in Organizations: A Group-Level Perspective. *Organization Science*, 13: 128–146.

Fineman, S. (2003) Emotions and learning. In M. Easterby-Smith and M. Lyles (eds.), *Handbook of Organizational Learning and Knowledge*. Blackwell Publishing, pp. 19–37.

Garvin, D., Edmondson, A., and Gino, F. (2008) Is yours a learning organization? *Harvard Business Review*, 86(3): 109–118.

Gherardi, S., Nicolini, D., and Odella, F. (1998) Toward a social understanding of how people learn in organizations. *Management Learning*, 29(3): 273–297.

Harrison, R. (2009) *Learning and development*. London: CIPD.

Huber, G. (1991) Organisational learning: the contributing processes and the literature. *Organisation Science*, 2(1): 88–115.

Huysman, M. (2000) An organizational learning approach to the learning organization. *European Journal of Work and Organizational Psychology*, 9(2): 133–145.

Kang, S., Morris, S., and Snell, S. (2007) Relational archetypes, organizational learning and value creation: Extending the human resource architecture. *Academy of Management Review*, 36: 236–256.

Keegan, A. and Turner J.R. (2001) Quantity versus Quality in Project-based Learning Practices. *Management Learning*, 32(1): 77–98.

Kelly, G. (1955) *The psychology of personal constructs*, Vols. 1 and 2. New York: Norton.

Kim, D.H. (1993) The link between individual and organisational learning. *Sloan Management Review*, 35(1): 37–50.

Kim, L. (1998) Crisis construction and organizational learning: Capability building in catching-up at Hyundai Motor. *Organization Science*, 9: 507–541.

Knight, L. and Pye, A. (2005) Network learning: An empirically derived model of learning by groups of organizations. *Human Relations*, 58: 369–392.

Kolb, D.A. (1984) *Experiential Learning; Experience as the Source of Learning and Development*. Englewood Cliffs, NJ: Prentice Hall.

Lave, J. and Wenger, E. (1991) *Situated legitimate peripheral participation*. Cambridge, UK: Cambridge University Press.

Leonard-Barton, D. (1998) *Wellsprings of Knowledge: Building and Sustaining the Sources of Innovation*. Boston: Harvard Business School Press.

Lewin, K. (1946) Action Research and Minority Problems. *Journal of Social Issues*, 2(4): 34–46.

Mankin, D. (2009) *Human Resource Development*. Oxford: Oxford University Press.

Mead, G. (1938) *The philosophy of the act*. Chicago: University of Chicago Press.

Miozzo, M., Lehrer, M., DeFillippi, R., Grimshaw, D. and Ordanini, A. (2010) Economies of scope through multi-unit skill systems: the organisation of large design firms. *British Journal of Management*: no. doi: 10.1111/j.1467–8551.2010.00699.x.

Nahapiet, J. and Ghoshal, S. (1998) Social Capital, Intellectual Capital, and the Organizational Advantage. *The Academy of Management Review*, 23(2): 242–266.

Nonaka, I. and Takeuchi, H. (1995) *The Knowledge Creating Company*. Oxford: Oxford University Press.

Pea, R. (1999) Practices of distributed intelligence and designs for education. In G. Salomon (ed.), *Distributed cognitions*. Cambridge: Cambridge University Press: 47–87.

Pedler, M., Burgoyne J. and Boydell P. (1996) *The Learning Company: a Strategy for Sustainable Development*. Maidenhead: McGraw-Hill.

Piaget, J. (1950) *The psychology of intelligence*. London: Routledge and Kegan Paul.

Raelin, J.A. (2001) Public Reflection as the Basis of Learning. *Management Learning*, 32(1): 11–30.

Rashman, L, Withers, E. and Hartley, J. (2009)Academic Journal Organizational learning and knowledge in public service organizations: A systematic review of the literature. *International Journal of Management Reviews*, 11(4): 463–494.

Ron, N., Lipshitz, R., and Popper, M. (2006) How organizations learn: post flight reviews in a F-16 fighter squadron. *Organization Studies*: 27(8): 1069–1089.

Salomon, G. (1999) *Distributed cognitions: Psychological and educational considerations*. Cambridge: Cambridge University Press.

Senge, P. (1990) *The fifth discipline: The art and practice of the learning organization*. New York: Double Day.

Senge, P. (2006) *The art and practice of the learning organization*. New York: DoubleDay.

Shipton, H. (2006) Cohesion or confusion? Towards a typology for organizational learning research. *International Journal of Management Reviews*, 8: 233–252.

Shipton, H. and Sillince, J. (under review). More than a cognitive experience: Emotion and meaning re-construal in organizational learning.

Shipton, H., Zhou, Q., and Mooi, E. (under review). The paradoxical nature of learning organizations.

Sicilia, M. and Lytras, M. (2005) The semantic learning organization. *The Learning Organization*, 12 (5): 402–410.

Simon, H. (1991) Bounded rationality and organizational learning. *Organization Science*, 2(1): 175–187.

Skinner, B.F. (1953) *Science and Human Behaviour*. London: Macmillan.

Smith, P.A.C. (2001) Action learning and reflective practice in project environments that are related to leadership development. *Management Learning*, 32(1): 31–48.

Thomas, J., Sussman, S., and Henderson, J. (2001) Understanding strategic learning: Linking organizational learning, knowledge management and sense-making. *Organization Science*, 12: 331–345.

Vince, R. and Saleem, T. (2004) The impact of caution and blame on organizational learning. *Management Learning*, 35(2): 133–154, 1350–5076.

Weick, K.E. (1995) *Sensemaking in organizations*. London: Sage.

Wenger, E. (2000) Communities of practice and social learning systems. *Organization*, 7: 225–246.

Zollo, M. and Winter, S.G. (2002) Deliberate learning and the evolution of dynamic capabilities. *Organization Science*, 13(3): 339–351.

5

Information Technology and the Possibilities for Knowledge Sharing

NIALL HAYES[1]

ABSTRACT

Information technology (IT) has been closely associated with the development of the great majority of knowledge management initiatives. However, most accounts have focused on technical aspects, while few have considered the use of it in relation to its social context. This chapter examines some of the challenges and opportunities that surround the use of IT in knowledge management initiatives from a relational perspective, which views knowledge as being processual, provisional, and highly context dependent. Specifically the chapter considers the lessons arising within the relational literature which has considered those technologies that have been used most extensively to support knowledge working (intranets, groupware, and databases), and compares and contrasts these insights with the issues that arose in a UK pharmaceuticals company which introduced a groupware application to support its knowledge management initiatives. Based on these lessons I briefly consider a new set of technologies (known as Enterprise 2.0), that some commentators are suggesting will transform knowledge management. Some practical implications are then provided.

INTRODUCTION

Knowledge work is still a relatively new and dynamic area of research that has emerged as a direct response to the changing organizing processes that pervade many organizations. Due to the emphasis on communication and information in knowledge work, information technology (IT) has been closely associated with the development of knowledge management initiatives (Zuboff, 1996; Hayes, 2001). Indeed, Easterby-Smith et al. (2000) estimate

---

[1] The author would like to acknowledge the contribution of Geoff Walsham to an earlier version of this chapter.

that seventy percent of publications on knowledge management have focused on the design of information technologies (ITs). In the commercial arena, most knowledge management initiatives have a strong IT focus, where knowledge is seen as being capable of being leveraged through the development of shared databases and knowledge warehouses (Sambamurthy and Subramani, 2005).

The objective of this chapter is to examine some of the challenges and opportunities that surround the use of IT in intra-organizational knowledge management initiatives. The chapter is structured as follows. Following this introduction, I will review some of the key issues that have been reported in the literature to date. Informed by the literature review, section three outlines a conceptual framework for understanding knowledge working through IT. I then draw on this framework to critically review some of the key challenges that arose in a knowledge management initiative undertaken by a UK pharmaceuticals company when making use of a leading groupware technology to support their knowledge management initiative. Based on the literature review, framework, and the case study, section five briefly discusses Enterprise 2.0 technologies (E2.0), a current category of technology that some claim offers new opportunities for knowledge working. Section six outlines some practical implications primarily with regard to long established knowledge management technologies such as groupware and intranets, but also provides some discussion of E2.0 technologies. The final section presents some brief conclusions.

LITERATURE REVIEW

This section reviews some key themes in the literature concerned with the role of IT in knowledge management initiatives.

Technologies and knowledge management

Over the last decade and more a plethora of technologies have emerged that have been associated with knowledge management; and specifically with the articulation, storage, transfer, creation, and retrieval of knowledge. Though not exhaustive, Table 5.1 highlights the most notable IT artifacts and platforms associated with knowledge management projects (Alavi and Leidner, 1999). Drawing on Zack (1999a) I distinguish between two types of ITs that have been associated with knowledge management projects: integrative and interactive applications. Much of the academic literature and practitioner accounts have focused on integrative applications which take the form of structured databases that allow employees to store and retrieve information on past projects. They also comprise expert finders, electronic bulletin boards through to best practice reports and working papers (Butler and Murphy, 2007; Zack, 1999b; Alavi and Leidner, 2001; Chua, 2004). Interactive applications take the form of email, desk-top conferencing, and discussion forums allowing for interactions with other staff and the garnering of their views and experiences regardless of physical location (Moffett et al., 2003; Leidner, 2000; Alavi and Leidner, 1999).

With regard to interactive applications, groupware and intranet platforms have dominated the academic and practitioner accounts to date (they are also the focus of much of this chapter). Most recently, interactive applications have come to include E2.0 platforms. E2.0 comprises a number of technologies that are typically associated with Web 2.0. The key

Table 5.1 Key technologies associated with knowledge management

Integrative IT Artefacts	*Interactive IT Artefacts*
Document management	Email
Knowledge databases	Collaborative authoring
Data mining	Discussion forums
Electronic bulletin boards	Social networking tools
Knowledge repositories	Blogs
Knowledge directories (Yellow Pages)	Wikis
	Information provision
Expert systems	Real time interactions
Workflow systems	Incremental categorization
IT Platforms	
Groupware	
Intranet	
Enterprise 2.0	

difference being E2.0 technologies are put in place to support collaboration and knowledge working within the organization. Key technologies include wikis, blogs, social networking and instant messaging, the ability to link out to other pages, and the categorization of data by users through tagging (McAfee, 2006). Tags are furthered through extensions, which is a form of automated tagging through pattern matching algorithms (e.g. Amazon). Such technologies are attracting considerable current attention amongst practitioners and are claimed to offer new ways to document, distribute, and retrieve knowledge within organizations (McAfee, 2006). This is a theme that I will return to towards the end of the chapter.

Understanding knowledge and technology

Within the academic literature, two contrasting epistemological approaches have underpinned accounts of knowledge management: the content and relational perspectives (Scarbrough and Burrell, 1997; Tsoukas, 1996). This chapter adopts the latter perspective. From a content perspective, knowledge is defined as being a predicative truth as it prescribes what to do (Nonaka and Takeuchi, 1994; Galliers and Newell, 2000). Knowledge is viewed as being able to be codified and stored in repositories, so that knowledge can be shared, built upon and retained regardless of employee turnover (Wasko and Faraj, 2000). This perspective is dominant in the information systems literature (see Sambamurthy and Subramani, 2005); and much of this literature has a practitioner orientation and has focused on collecting, distributing, reusing, and measuring existing codified knowledge (Lam and Chua, 2005; Bansler and Havn, 2004; Cohen, 1998; Knock and McQueen, 1998). Knowledge is considered to be an economic asset that can be codified, stored, and exchanged between individuals within a firm (Bohm, 1994; Shin et al., 2001; Pan and Scarbrough, 1999; Currie and Kerrin, 2004).

Relational writers are critical of this dominant view of knowledge (Lave, 1988; Blackler et al., 1997), and suggest that instead of treating knowledge as being a largely cerebral and tradable entity, knowledge should be viewed as being relative, provisional, and primarily context-bound (Scarbrough, 2008; Barley, 1996; Orr, 1990; Blackler et al., 1993). Critiques of much of the knowledge management literature suggest that knowledge is always embedded and as such can only be shared actively through social groups. Rather than knowledge, relational writers argue that the focus of enquiry should be on the process of knowing and the capability to act (Schultze, 2000; Blackler, 1995; Brown and Duguid, 1998). Furthermore, many are critical of the content approach for its weak empirical base and prescriptive standpoint (Pan and Scarbrough, 1999). They suggest that exchanging knowledge as if it were an economic asset via IT does not relate to the actual experience of the use of knowledge management applications within specific contexts (Schultze, 2000; Galliers and Newell, 2000). Within the literature, this focus on sharing explicit knowledge through IT systems has led to the terms 'information' and 'knowledge' often being used interchangeably and uncritically by many authors (Sambamurthy and Subramani, 2005).

Technology-centric

One pervasive theme in the literature has been the dominance of techno-centric accounts, as is exemplified by Sambamurthy and Subramani (2005: 2) who suggest that knowledge management involves 'developing searchable document repositories to support the digital capture, storage, retrieval, and distribution of an organization's explicitly documented knowledge.' Indeed, there has been a preoccupation with the problem of finding the location of knowledge (Sambamurthy and Subramani, 2005; Massey et al., 2002; Benbya, 2006; Gray and Durcikova, 2006). Such a position assumes knowledge can be codified and stored. Thompson and Walsham (2004) claim this has been at the expense of the more 'contextual elements of knowing.' Here they include a willingness to document and share information, an attention to detail, and the establishment of software tools and methodologies to support such changes. Similarly, based on his case studies of Technology Research Inc. and Buckman Laboratories, Zack (1999a) argues that the technology focus is a major obstacle to engendering an organizational climate that values and encourages co-operation, trust, and innovation (Butler and Murphy, 2007; Butler et al., 2007). Knox et al. (2008: 290) are also critical of such techno-centric accounts, arguing that managers know that 'their claims to expertise rest on their ability to perform the reconnections between the systems outputs and other more contingent "upstream" practices, situations and possibilities'. Thus, they argue that those that adopt a techno-centric perspective do not understand or appreciate the ways and the efforts to which the enactments of some people allow for such a perspective to 'work.'

Domain specific knowledge

From a relational perspective, knowledge is viewed as circulating easily when people work within a similar domain of practice, or have experience of working with other knowledge domains. This provides for a shared sense of what practice is and what the standards for judgment are (Brown and Duguid, 1998). Zack (1999a) argues that due to the shared understanding of practice, integrative applications that allow access to data stored centrally are sufficient to support work between employees from the same domain of work, though others still advocate more interactive applications (Boland and Tenkasi, 1995; McDermott, 1999). More recently Butler and Murphy (2007) argue that while technologies can assist knowledge creation and sharing within domains, they advocate the establishment of careful rules as to who can contribute posts to specific parts of the knowledge management system. This they claim ensures that only those who are expert are able to contribute, and reduces possibilities for misunderstandings between staff from different domains.

Orlikowski (2002) argued that the relative success that Kappa achieved with their knowledge management initiative was in part attributable to their ongoing reinforcement of a strong identity. This identity formation, Orlikowski (2002: 267) argued, allowed people from across the organization, regardless of their group or location 'to internalize and identify with a common way of thinking about and engaging in their product development work. This facilitates the communication and coordination of hundreds of product developers across time (19 time zones) and space (15 geographic locations).' Orlikowski (2002) goes on to explain that it also allowed people across the organization to share a common language. Importantly, such identity formation and the development of shared language were between staff from a similar knowledge domain, and consequently they shared aspects of their practice with each other.

Working between domains of knowledge

Sharing knowledge between employees with different professional backgrounds is viewed as more complex (Newell et al., 2000; Brown and Duguid, 1998; Ruhleder, 1995). Schultze and Boland's (2000a) study of US Company, a manufacturer of building materials, found that the introduction of KnowMor, a knowledge management application that bridged the different functions and locations, led to changing temporal and spatial work arrangements. They provide an example of the Notes administrators being required to perform not only technical activities, as previously, but also to write accounts of their actions into shared databases. Work practice changed in that they would now point users to these entries rather than deal with requests themselves. Schultze and Boland (2000a) explain that the new work practices required them to perform a dual role of acting (in terms of the technical change) and accounting self (in terms of making explicit their technical work).

A further challenge relates to the limited understandings that can be developed when reliance is placed on IT to share knowledge between communities. Brown's (1998) insightful study of the use of the Internet to support knowledge working found that a reliance on technology as a means of transferring knowledge is insufficient. Instead he contended that abstractions recorded and shared on the Internet need to be considered as being inseparable from their own historical and social locations of practice. McDermott (1999) provided a detailed analysis of why a reliance on abstractions is problematic. He cited the case of a diverse group of systems designers to illustrate what he termed the difficulties of thinking 'outside an expert's own territory.' He ascertained that, rather than needing each other's documentation stored on a common database, the system designers needed to understand the logic that other designers used in practice, such as the rationale behind the combination of specific software, hardware, and service plans. Similarly, Schultze's

(2000) case study of experts across US Company discovered that each group had their own conventions. She explained that the IT professionals emphasized the importance of documentation, while the competitive intelligence analysts emphasized secrecy and selective dissemination (Ruhleder, 1995; Hislop et al., 2000; Hayes, 2000). Currie and Kerrin's (2004:25) case study highlighted how the antagonistic relations between the sales and marketing teams were exacerbated following the introduction of the intranet as 'Sales and Marketing did not share the necessary language and context to effectively exchange knowledge.'

Thus, due to the difficulties of working between communities, many suggest that attention needs to be given to the nature of IT support. Butler and Murphy (2007) argue that knowledge management systems need to be designed so that they only allow people with relevant experience and insights to contribute to or review specific parts of them (Markus et al., 2002). When there is no shared history of working together, Zack (1999a) argues that integrative applications are unsuitable. Instead he recommends the use of interactive applications that support ad hoc collaboration (such as discussion databases and video conferencing).

Establishing social capital and social networks

Based on their study of an enterprise resource planning (ERP) implementation, Newell et al. (2004: 54) argue that a lack of social capital between organizational members from different knowledge domains made it impossible to 'expose and explore the different thought worlds.' Newell et al. (2004) thus argued that social capital was crucial for organizational knowledge to be accessed via an ERP system and integrated effectively (Huysman and Wulf, 2004). Similarly, Olivera's (2000) study of a consulting company found that users placed great effort on interacting with people rather than relying on computer based systems such as the intranet. Others have suggested working between communities requires the creation of new facilitating roles. Zack (1999b) emphasizes the importance of appointing facilitators charged with encouraging, interpreting and evaluating participation in cross-community electronic forums. Storck and Hill (2000) found that Xerox unit managers undertook facilitating roles so as to encourage knowledge sharing, such as presentations describing their initiatives, questioning participants about what they had learned, and electronically circulating what they considered to be key developments. Facilitators in Xerox looked for mutual interests, sought to mask differences in hierarchical status, encourage commitment, and reduce uncertainty (Schultze and Boland, 2000a; Storck and Hill, 2000).

Individualism versus collectivism

Orlikowski's (2002) case of Kappa found that staff staved off a lot of self interest by consciously making sure that they allowed all the different groups opportunities to engage in discussions, allocated work across functional and geographical boundaries, and reassigned staff to work across the world in different groups. This, Orlikowski (2002: 269) claims, provides for the 'crossing of temporal, geographic, technical, and political boundaries, because it provides for the distribution, and then the integration, of ideas and experiences.'

Storck and Hill's (2000) study of Xerox found that in addition to technology, the relaxing of centralized control had allowed participants to identify with, and be committed to, their community rather than to Xerox as a whole. They concluded that within communities, this engendered a climate that allowed for openness, trust, and commitment (Huysman, 2004; Pan and Scarbrough, 1999; Malhotra and Galletta, 2003). Newell et al.'s (2004) case study found that long established self interests meant the integration of dispersed organizational knowledge necessary for implementing the ERP system was never achieved. Overall, they argued that where people and teams have not worked together before considerable effort and resources need to be invested so as to encourage sociability and develop an understanding and familiarity with each other. They argue that such bonding is essential if people are to share knowledge for the public good as well as for their own self interests. Without doing this, Newell et al. (2004: 56) claim it will lead to 'a mechanistic pooling of knowledge that will not produce the knowledge integration leading to creativity and innovation that are needed in large-scale IT projects.' Orlikowski (2002) claims the emphasis that Kappa placed on the ongoing education of their employees with regard to their software development expertise, and career mentoring, encourages knowledge sharing (Wasko and Faraj, 2005; Zack, 1999a; Quinn et al., 1996).

In addition, several writers have suggested that reward structures can also encourage knowledge sharing. Orlikowski's (1993) study of a US consulting company argued that both the competitive promotion and financial reward structure led to Notes remaining largely unused by consultants. However, she found that the technologists and senior consultants who were not subject to the competitive culture did use Notes more formatively (McDermott and O'Dell, 2001; Hislop, 2003; Pan and Scarbrough, 1999; Zack, 1999b). Currie and Kerrin's (2004) case study of a global pharmaceutical firm who were in the process of downsizing also found that sales staff horded rather than shared knowledge with graduate trainees as they feared the trainees may become their replacements. Currie and Kerrin's (2004: 25) case also highlighted that when there is already animosity between different groups in an organization 'the intranet hardened existing cultural cleavages in the organization' rather than manufactured a sense of community.'

Visibility and control

A final important but often neglected theme to emerge in the literature relates to the inseparability of knowledge management initiatives from issues of power and politics (Easterby-Smith et al., 2007). Hislop et al. (2000) found that in a UK nuclear medicine company external expertise and information were utilized by groups as a political resource to reinforce and support their particular visions for change. They also described how groups supporting the interests of senior managers received the authoritative support and financial resources to bring about change. Similarly, Newell et al.'s (2000) study found that the introduction of communication forums reinforced the 'powerful centrifugal forces' in their firm.

Making work and views explicit on IT is also implicated in issues of power and control. Schultze and Boland's (2000b) study of US Company indicated how the IT consultants would visibly record their work in the databases as a means to protect themselves from any blame that may subsequently be leveled by their clients or other consultants. Schultze and Boland's case further indicated how the visibility that KnowMor provided could unintentionally have a negative effect on relationships within US Company. For example, one analyst felt that his role had inadvertently been threatened due to the way another employee had harnessed the visibility KnowMor provided. KnowMor had allowed this latter employee to be aware of and widely circulate some details about a merger that the analyst should have been aware of. The analyst resented the implication that he was not doing his job well and responded to the issue by revoking the employee's access to KnowMor. McDermott (1999) argued that, due to the pervasiveness of politics in knowledge working, one key challenge is not to homogenize views but to encourage diverse collaboration and an appreciation of the context specific insights of members from other communities. McKinley (2000) supports this view and warns against IT being used in knowledge management projects for surveillance and control activities. In a later study, McKinlay (2002: 81) argued that recording one's knowledge was sometimes viewed by staff in this case as 'being asked to give myself away.'

Thus, studies have pointed to the importance of attending to the link between power and making explicit a staff member's knowledge, hierarchical power relations, surveillance possibilities, and a competitive culture (Knights, 2008; Knights et al., 1993). Indeed, Currie and Kerrin (2004) argue that due to the overtly technological orientation, coupled with the broader issues of culture and power, the possibilities of IT to mediate knowledge sharing are limited.

CONCEPTUALIZING KNOWLEDGE SHARING AND IT

This section draws on the literature review and specifically Schultze and Boland's (2000b) work on narrative to develop a conceptual framework (Figure 5.1) pertaining to the ways in which knowledge is shared through ITs such as groupware and the intranet (Zack, 1999a). This comprises ongoing acting (practice) and accounting (textual narratives) processes.

Schultze and Boland's (2000b) study of US Company found that new work arrangements arose due to the reliance on the use of IT to work across spatial, temporal, and functional boundaries. They described how these new work practices required employees to perform dual 'acting' and 'accounting' processes. Acting involved employees undertaking their work (in their case IT consultancy activities which involved fixing machines and developing new applications) and accounting processes required them to record a narrative of their practice by making explicit their activities and views on the various shared discussion forums and lessons learned databases that cut across the organization's spatial, temporal, and functional boundaries. Based on this insight, acting and accounting can be conceived as comprising of three ongoing processes, sense making, sense giving, and sense reading.

Sense making is akin to what Schultze and Boland (2000b) refer to as an 'out of body' experience, where staff are required to consciously reflexively monitor and make sense of their own on-going activities (what they have done, how they achieved this in specific contexts, what their views are, etc.). They do this so they can account for their ongoing activity in a textual form and engage in sense giving.

Sense giving involves the provision of a textual account to others about their activity on a shared software application. This could be either an integrative application such as

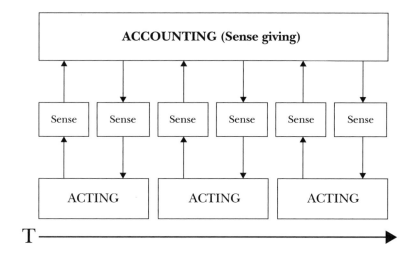

Figure 5.1 Acting and Accounting Processes

a 'repository' or an interactive application such as a shared discussion forum, a lessons learned database or a blog technology. Employees are required to account for their activities on such a technology in a way that is comprehensible to members of their own or other professional domains.

Sense reading refers to the process whereby a person makes sense of the accounts that other staff have made and then utilizes them in their ongoing activities. Sense reading depends on their familiarity with the knowledge domain, practice and political context of the sense giver, not to mention the sense giver's ability to account for their activity in a clear textual form. Importantly, we should not view this as being linear because when people make sense of accounts they are reading they do this by drawing on memories of other accounts they have read, discussions they have had, activities they have performed individually or while working with or observing others (Orr, 1996). Consequently, accounting processes are deeply rooted in practice and inherently collaborative and social as, even when posting accounts and reading accounts while working on their own, they do so by drawing on previous encounters. This is important as Figure 5.1 does not do sufficient justice to the social nature of acting and accounting processes. The following section draws on a case study; first, to illustrate the applicability of the acting and accounting framework and, second, to furnish the framework further by considering it in relation to knowledge domains and political dimensions.

INDICATIVE CASE EXAMPLE: KNOWLEDGE SHARING IN COMPOUND UK

Compound UK (a pseudonym) sells pharmaceutical products to hospitals and general practices, whilst also undertaking clinical trials of new drugs with participating doctors in Great Britain and Northern Ireland. It is part of a major multinational company and

Table 5.2 Key uses of Lotus Notes in Compound UK

Component	Intended Opportunity for Participation
E-mail	To enable one-to-one communication between individuals
Strategic selling	To enable employees in different functions to input their views and information in a structured way with the aim of bringing together the employees' shared knowledge so that they might contribute to a successful sale
Contact recording	To enable employees to record and review the views, interests, and requirements of particular doctors
Discussion databases	To enable employees to review the thread of discussions that had emerged on a particular issue

employs around 300 people, half of whom are involved in selling activities while the rest work in areas such as marketing, accounting, human resources, or as medical experts. Lotus Notes (Notes) was introduced as a means to encourage employees to draw on all areas of the organization to work and share information and knowledge across functional and geographic boundaries. Such knowledge sharing was seen as beneficial not least because of the complexity of sales situations which involved many different decision makers (such as different doctors, pharmacists, managers, and accountants), just as clinical trials involved many different physicians.

In addition to an electronic mail (e-mail) facility, there were three main uses of Notes, as summarized in Table 5.2. First, it was used to create a strategic selling database to support the co-operative activities of staff from different areas of expertise (such as sales, marketing, and medicine) involved in seeking to secure a sale to a particular hospital or general practice. The second and most prevalent use of Notes was the contact recording database. Any employees that visited a client were required to record specific details about doctors such as the outcome of the meeting, the doctor's personal and medical interests, and their involvement in clinical trials. Notes databases were also set up that focused on issues, products, or a particular role with the intention that employees would discuss relevant issues.

Sharing knowledge explicitly across boundaries

In relation to the framework represented in Figure 5.1, the introduction of Notes saw employees 'acting' in terms of selling products or undertaking clinical trials, and then 'accounted' for their practice by making explicit their activities and views on Notes' various databases which bridged the spatial, temporal, and functional boundaries. In trying to make explicit their sales and medical work, employees were required to make sense of their own activities in ways that were comprehensible to others (sense giving), and also make sense of (sense reading) and utilize the accounts of others. Sense making, giving, and reading are highly reflexive processes and are inextricably interlinked.

Acting and accounting on role or functional specific databases was relatively unproblematic. This was due to the intimate understandings and practice they shared with colleagues working in the same function. This local mastery was sustained not only through the use of Notes, but also through regular formal and informal face-to-face discussions and interactions.

However, when such practices spanned knowledge domains, acting and accounting practices were not as productive. Due to the limited number of company-wide meetings, staff had little experience of working directly with colleagues in different functions. This left the organization-wide Notes databases as the primary mode of collaboration. Such difficulties using Notes to work across functions were explained by one medical expert who said:

> You cannot put this level of detail into a Notes database, and much of what I do input must be meaningless to others.

Staff from across the different functions thus viewed much of what employees were able to provide on account of the shared databases as only being a simplistic representation of what they sought to convey (sense giving). Reps themselves were also sometimes unsure as to the meanings that others sought to convey in their posts, and they could not understand why some people would request further clarifications about posts they had recorded. This left them feeling ill disposed to record detailed information in the future and thus was further implicated in limiting sense making, giving, and reading processes.

This lack of familiarity with other domains of knowledge resulted in many employees experiencing considerable uncertainty about what they required from each other, and exactly how they could draw on each other's expertise. They feared not only that what they recorded may be misunderstood but that it might appear stupid or irrelevant to other employees, particularly by those in other professional domains. Further, as their use of Notes was in addition to their existing activities, many claimed that they did not have the time to review and/or contribute to the databases. Indeed, making their activities explicit in this way on an on-going basis was alien to most employees who were only typically required to account for what they had done when problems arose (Giddens, 1984: 6).

Understood from a practice perspective, overall the framework and the case indicate one key challenge pertaining to how knowledge management initiatives typically require people to make sense of the accounts recorded by members of other professions on shared forums and then utilize them in their own activities. The case has indicated that a reliance on accounts recorded on discussion forums, in order to collaborate across professional disciplines, are unlikely to provide a sufficient insight into the 'path of thinking' or different conventions that underpin the logic that other professions draw upon in their practice (Schultze, 2000; McDermott, 1999). Sense making, sense giving, and sense reading processes rest upon the shared practices of those posting to and reviewing shared databases. When practice is not shared then a reliance on reflexively monitoring and making sense of the accounts others have recorded on shared forums will always be limited as they are not fully representative of the histories, activities, and assumptions that underpin their formulation. As such, sense giving accounts are only likely to be partial rationalizations of the complexity that underpins their practice (Brown, 1998; Hayes, 2001). This again indicates the importance of recognizing that knowledge cannot be encoded on ITs, and instead is shared through social networks (Hislop et al., 2000). Consequently, for acting and accounting processes to be more productive they will require the ongoing development of social networks and reflexive engagement in joint practice, in addition to solely the use of shared forums (as was the case with the function specific databases). This ongoing sense making process provides a basis for people to develop a deeper understanding of the assumptions that underpin the work practices and formulation of accounts recorded by members of different professional groups (Brown, 1998).

Political and normative dimensions participation

This subsection focuses on the ways in which political and normative issues shape the extent and nature of acting and accounting processes. I draw on Hayes and Walsham's (2000a, 2000b, 2001) constructs of political and safe enclaves to do this. Political enclaves describe contexts for participation that resemble a public façade, while safe enclaves describe contexts for participation that allow for more genuine views and assumptions to be exposed.

Political enclaves. A first important theme pertaining to acting and accounting processes concerns the way senior managers may harness the surveillance capacity that political enclaves provide to reinforce their dominant positions (Newell et al., 2000; McKinley, 2000). Senior managers harnessed the surveillance capacity Notes provided to try to ensure that sales reps worked in the ways that they promoted. For example, not long after Notes was introduced, the Commercial Director instructed the Notes developer to devise a league facility which could indicate centrally how many contact records and strategic selling sheets had been completed by each rep. A senior manager would then send out electronic messages to field force managers commenting on their reps' position in the league tables. Further, some senior managers would regularly review detailed comments and observations that reps had recorded, and contact their area manager if they thought they could be approaching sales or recording contacts better. This confirmed many of the reps' suspicions about the intention behind the electronic contact recording and strategic selling databases, namely to increase central surveillance and control. This process of surveillance had the effect of simultaneously increasing the dominance of senior management while reducing the autonomy of middle managers dealing directly with the sales force, which strengthened hierarchical control and reduced trust and co-operation (Pan and Scarbrough, 1999; Zack, 1999a; Storck and Hill, 2000).

Such surveillance and control activities influenced the extent and nature of acting and accounting processes in Compound UK. When staff made sense of their own activities and then decided how they would convey (sense giving) this to others, they did this by identifying what would be politically and normatively acceptable to senior managers and others that may review their accounts. For example, in relation to the contact recording and strategic selling databases, even though non-careerist reps saw some of the use they made of them as being futile, they still felt normatively bound to record a sufficient amount and in enough detail so as to not be identified by senior managers. They felt frustration with their peers for having to undertake what they saw as being a futile and time-consuming task.

Similarly on the discussion databases careerist employees harnessed the visibility to indicate to senior managers that they were contributing to the development of new insights, while also concurring with their views. However, if non careerist reps disagreed with comments posted by senior managers, or those supporting the views of senior managers, rather than stating this on a database they considered it better not to post their own views. Indeed this led to a homogenizing of views that reflected those of senior management. Such examples highlight how sense making, giving, and reading processes are inextricably interlinked with the political and normative context (McDermott, 1999). Examining the latitude which employees have to distance themselves from received wisdom is a fundamental challenge for acting and accounting processes (Brown and Duguid, 1991).

In relation to sense making, giving, and reading, such career orientated politicking further reinforced the homogenizing of acting and accounting processes and had certain implications. For example, careerist reps formulated their activities and accounted for them in ways that they thought would meet senior management approval, and hence enhance their career prospects. Furthermore, when non-careerist reps made sense of the representations others recorded on the cross-functional discussion databases, many were aware of the dominating and careerist undertones that lay behind them. Further still, a result of this politicizing was that many non-careerist employees did not see any benefit to participating in discussions that were dominated by what one rep described as: 'ambitious people competing with each other about who could shout the loudest.' Though several studies have made a cursory reference to the importance of the reward structure in knowledge management initiatives, very few have explicitly considered how the career reward system can influence the shape and nature of participation. Of those that have, Orlikowski's (1993) study found that consultants did not make any use of Lotus Notes as it was not associated with either the career or the financial reward structure, while Quinn et al. (1996) discovered that modifying the reward structure to emphasize reciprocity was vital to the success of Merrill Lynch's and NovaCare's knowledge management initiatives. However, neither study highlighted how the visibility that political enclaves provide may exacerbate careerist motivations which arise from an individualistic reward structure, and how this may assist or hinder knowledge management initiatives. Such an understanding thus suggests that accounts of knowledge management need to be more sensitive to the hierarchical, coercive, and competitive nature of knowledge work (Knights et al., 1993).

Safe enclaves. In contrast, safe enclaves did provide opportunities for productive acting and accounting processes (Pan and Scarbrough, 1999; Zack, 1999a; Storck and Hill, 2000). Some discussion databases were considered to be safe(r) from heavy politicizing and careerism. Some non-careerist employees did include themselves in the functional or regional specific shared databases. On these databases, many non-ambitious reps would discuss the ways they had approached sales situations and other areas of interest that they shared. In addition, those employees that had experience of working with members of other functions would discuss and provide advice to less experienced members of their own community on how they could best interact with members of other functions. However, ambitious reps did not make much use of these local forums, as they viewed their time being better spent on career enhancing national discussion forums. In this sense, while safe enclaves did provide opportunities for staff to express their thoughts, and take into account the posts of others (sense reading) in their activities, there were still many other employees who did not participate, as they saw their time as being better spent using the community wide political enclaves to further their own career aspirations.

The concept of safe enclaves suggests that the relative success of acting and accounting processes rested upon several important features. First, they were all domain specific, which meant that employees felt confident that their representations would be understood by members of their own professional domain and that they could easily be made sense of as being genuine. Second, they were all optional, which meant they were not associated with the normative control structure. Third, senior managers were not privy to the discussions that occurred on safe enclaves.

IMPLICATIONS FOR ENTERPRISE 2.0 AND KNOWLEDGE MANAGEMENT

Even though E2.0 is still a relatively new technology, many anticipate that it will lead to a significant shift in the nature and form of knowledge sharing (McAfee, 2006). This enthusiasm was captured most emphatically by Thomas Davenport (2008) who stated:

> If E2.0 can give KM a mid-life kicker, so much the better. If a new set of technologies can bring about a knowledge-sharing culture, more power to them. Knowledge management was getting a little tired anyway.

Proponents claim that E2.0 technologies are easy to use due to everyone's familiarity with posting to and reviewing social networks, blogs, and wikis. McAfee (2006) also claims they benefit from relatively low set up costs as there is no need for sophisticated development tools or network infrastructures, nor is there a need for database administrators or designers (Whelen, 2007; Warr, 2008). Proponents such as McAfee (2006), based in part on the above, claim that this can allow for the potential for new knowledge sharing practices to emerge. These opportunities derive from its bottom-up orientation which McAfee (2006) claims allows for employees being better able to shape the nature and style of their contributions than was previously possible (Gilchrist, 2007). McAfee (2006) further claims that this allows employees to feel freer to express their thoughts, views, and knowledge on company-wide wikis and blogs than they did on company discussion databases, for example. Overall, advocates of E2.0 technologies claim that they more readily lend themselves to becoming a part of everyday work and, thus, are more representative of what people are doing, and who they are doing it with. Further, by tagging, users are more likely to categorize contributions that are related to what they are doing and, thus, result in more meaningful search requests and retrievals (McAfee, 2006; Whelen, 2007).

Viewed more critically, and in relation to the case specific literature already reviewed, such claims are technologically deterministic. Further, while the use of Web 2.0 technologies may provide some of the benefits claimed, the use of such technologies in the form of E2.0 within a specific organizational setting will vary greatly. What is lacking is the location of such claims within specific organizational contexts. If we take Orlikowski's (2002) relatively successful case study of the intranet in Kappa, then we may imagine that E2.0 technologies would offer similar and/or new possibilities for knowledge sharing as the current intranet system does. However, this possibility would derive primarily from the strong identity, the reward scheme, and the fact that knowledge sharing takes place within a specific domain of knowing (Orlikowski, 2002). In Compound UK, one would not anticipate E2.0 technologies necessarily bringing about much change due to the specific nature of their socio-political context (Hayes and Walsham, 2001). Why would knowledge sharing between professional domains in Compound UK be any more beneficial with E2.0 technology than groupware applications? Why would non careerist reps feel more included and thereby post their views on E2.0? Why wouldn't ambitious reps not write blogs and compose wikis to show to their senior managers they are working hard and in the ways advocated? Why would a wiki or a blog allow for views not to be homogenized? Clearly all of this is conjecture, but it seems hard to see how E2.0 technologies *per se* could result in significantly different use than the groupware and intranet applications already in place. To counter such technologically deterministic accounts what will be fascinating is the publication of a number of in-depth case studies that explore the possibilities of such technologies in different socio-political contexts. Only then will we better understand if, how, and to what extent E2.0 represents old wine in new bottles.

Practical Implications

This penultimate section draws upon the analysis presented in the previous sections to establish guidelines for developers to consider; first, when IT is used to support work between communities and, second, for work within communities. The term 'developers' is a deliberately broad category in order to refer to all those involved in the creation, introduction, and review of shared forums.

First and foremost, developers need to establish education programs to assist in countering the difficulties that have reportedly arisen in relation to acting, accounting, and sense-making processes. These programs should aim to provide staff with an insight into the conventions and rationales of members of other professional domains and, furthermore, a detailed understanding of their work practices. To achieve this, the program should first consist of experts from different professional backgrounds making presentations that outline the typical tasks they perform and the logic that they use to undertake their work. They should also present examples of the different types of information and expertise that they would like members of other functions to contribute.

Second, to solidify their sense making, giving, and reading processes, participants should undertake exercises on the knowledge management application with program participants from different professional domains, so as to provide them with feedback about how they could improve their accounting processes. Third, developers should rebuff access to organization-wide shared databases until they are satisfied that each employee's accounting and sense-making processes have reached an adequate level of competence. Further, developers need to develop one-off programs when there are any significant changes in the ways that specific professional domains undertake their work, and especially if any large-scale restructurings take place. Education programs of this sort will require levels of ongoing investment and senior management commitment that is typically not associated with groupware implementations (Grudin, 1990), which may be one of the most difficult issues to address.

A final guideline for developers to consider is the need for mentors to be assigned to less experienced staff. Mentors should be those staff experienced in working with employees in the varying professional domains. First, mentors should review the contributions made by less experienced colleagues and advise them how they could better meet the needs of members of other professions. Second, mentors should assist their charges in making sense of the representations recorded by members of other professions. Finally, mentors should highlight circumstances where in-depth face-to-face interactions may be more beneficial than relying on representations recorded on the IT.

With regard to E2.0 applications such as wikis and blogs, I would suggest the above guidelines would also be relevant. However, in addition I suggest one further normative guideline relating to education. Orlikowski and Gash (1994) developed the concept of technological frames to highlight how it is that people tend to interpret a new technology through their existing understandings and experiences of technology. For example, one of the challenges for groupware has been for users to shift from viewing groupware as an individual productivity tool to an application that was put in place to support collaboration (Orlikowski, 1993). With regard to E2.0, while proponents argue that as users are already familiar with wikis, blogs, and instant messaging, due to their prior personal and recreational use of the Internet, this may not necessarily be advantageous. Making sense of how to use E2.0 within a specific organizational context through a Web 2.0 technological frame may be problematical (Warr, 2008). For example, how will prior experiences of writing an Internet blog about a particular interest or hobby help in their understandings of posting to a work related audience? Would the same style of writing be relevant and if not what would be? What content should they post? How much practice will those reading their post share with them? Will the requirements and conditions for sense making, giving, and reading be substantially different to those relevant to a Web 2.0 technological frame? Secondly, the vast majority of people merely read and review the posts of others on wikis and blogs rather than contribute to them. Thus, an E2.0 technological frame will require a change in expectations if people are also to contribute. I suggest that understanding if and how technological frames shift following the introduction of E2.0 will be vital to shaping the extent and nature of sense making, sense giving, and sense reading activities. Understanding the changes to technological frames, I would suggest, is likely to be an important feature of an E2.0 specific education program.

In relation to countering the difficulties arising from political and normative issues, due to the complexity that surrounds how the political and normative context is continually produced and reproduced, generating guidelines in the relatively prescriptive form described so far in this subsection is more difficult. However, there are several issues relating to the symbolism that senior managers exhibit in their on-going use of shared discussion forums that organizations should bear in mind. Senior managers need to recognize that when people account for their activities on shared forums they endeavor to do so in a way that they deem to be politically and normatively acceptable to senior managers. They do this by continually monitoring the use that senior managers have made of the discussion forums. This will include the consistency of the tone and nature of views recorded, how the visibility that the technology provides has been harnessed to monitor and control their subordinates' practice, which discussion forums they have participated in or utilized, and their conduct and directives outside the discussion forums. It is important for senior managers to recognize that when the symbolism they exhibit leads to participation in discussion forums being of a highly political nature many staff will exclude themselves from participating in those forums that they consider to be normatively optional. Furthermore, it is also worth noting that sense-making processes are highly dependent on the history of previous organizational restructurings in specific contexts, which are often associated with increased workloads and new forms of control, rather than valuing professional autonomy. Finally, the above political issues need to be considered carefully when modifying the career or financial reward structure to emphasize reciprocity, as has been suggested in several previous studies (Zack, 1999a; Pan and Scarbrough, 1999), to analyze how this is likely to affect different forms of careerist and non-careerist activity.

Such implications are also relevant to E2.0 technologies. One could imagine in Compound UK, for example, that the tags chosen by staff will reflect those contributions that are provided by senior managers in an organization rather than necessarily tagging the most read or best contributions to a blog or a wiki. Further, one would expect communications via an instant messenger to be directed at those senior in the organization just as the introduction of email led to senior managers receiving large numbers of messages from ambitious staff who wanted to be 'seen' by their superiors. Further, in many organizations, the motivations for contributing to wikis and blogs would also be to politicize rather than merely to post on a blog contributions that were necessarily conceived of as being useful to others. In Kappa, such uses of E2.0 may not have arisen. Thus, I consider that the shape and nature of sense making, giving, and reading processes relating to E2.0 will be inextricably interlinked with the organization's political and normative context.

CONCLUSION

ITs such as groupware, the intranet, repositories, discussion forums, and E2.0 are likely to continue to have an ever-increasing role to play in knowledge management initiatives as they provide a way to record, store, and access textual accounts of people's activities. This allows for them to be made accessible regardless of time or location. This chapter has argued for a relational view of knowledge, and has highlighted some of the difficulties that arise from adopting a content view of knowledge management, and, specifically, adopting a technologically deterministic approach. From a relational perspective, knowledge cannot be conceived of as being an entity that can be possessed, codified, organized, and shared in the same way that data and information have been in the past. Instead, I have highlighted the importance for both academics and practitioners to view knowledge as being socially embedded and inseparable from practice.

Specifically I have offered the concepts of acting and accounting processes as a lens to think through the sense making, sense giving, and sense reading processes that take place as people are engaged in sharing knowledge through technology such as groupware. I have indicated that what is represented on the screen is merely a snapshot, reflecting an author's sense-making, giving, and reading abilities which are necessarily limited and inseparable from his or her own historical and social locations of practice. Furthermore, I have illustrated how the nature and extent of knowledge sharing is influenced by and influences each professional domain's socio-political context. I have also drawn on the lessons from the literature, the case, and the conceptual framework to consider how and if these issues may differ with regard to E2.0 technology.

Overall, I suggest that there are three important priorities for future research on the role of IT in knowledge management initiatives to consider. First, to examine sense-making, giving, and reading activities so as to better understand the activating and acting processes that take place as people make use of IT when working across diverse professional domains. Second, I suggest that future studies should also address how the use of ITs maintain or change the political and normative context, and what implications for knowledge working arise. Finally, I would suggest that future studies could contribute to considering how these lessons can be understood in the context of the development of new information technologies such as E2.0.

References

Alavi, M. and Leidner, D.E. (1999) Knowledge management systems: Issues, challenges and benefits. *Communications of the Associations for Information Systems*, 1(2): 1–36.

Alavi, M. and Leidner, D.E. (2001) Knowledge management and knowledge management systems: Conceptual foundations and research issues. *MIS Quarterly*, 25(1): 107–136.

Bansler, J.P. and Havn, E. (2004) Exploring the role of network effects in IT implementation: The case of knowledge repositories. *Information Technology and People*, 17(3): 268–285.

Barley, S. (1996) Technicians in the workplace: Ethnographic evidence for bringing work into organization studies. *Administrative Science Quarterly*, 41(1): 146–162.

Benbya, H. (2006) Mechanisms for knowledge management systems effectiveness: Empirical evidence from the silicon valley. *Academy of Management Conference*: 1–6.

Blackler, F. (1995) Knowledge, knowledge work and organisations: An overview and interpretation. *Organization Studies*, 16(6): 1021–1046.

Blackler, F., Crump, N., and McDonald, S. (1997) Knowledge, organisations and competition. In G. Krogh, J. Roos and D. Kleine (eds.), *Knowing in Firms: Understanding, Managing and Measuring Organisational Knowledge*. London: Sage: 67–86.

Blackler, F., Reed, M., and Whitaker, A. (1993) Editorial: Knowledge and the theory of organizations. *Journal of Management Studies*, 30(6): 851–861.

Bohm, R.E. (1994) Measuring and managing technological knowledge. *Sloan Management Review*, 26(1): 61–73.

Boland, R.J. and Tenkasi R.V. (1995) Perspective making and perspective taking in communities of knowing. *Organization Science*, 6(4): 350–372.

Brown, J.S. (1998) Internet technology in support of the concept of 'communities-of-practice:' the case of Xerox. *Accounting, Management and Information Technologies*, 8(4): 227–236.

Brown, J.S. and Duguid P. (1991) Organisational learning and communities of practice: towards a unified view of working, learning and innovation. *Organization Science*, 2(1): 40–57.

Brown, J.S. and Duguid, P. (1998) Organizing knowledge. *California Management Review*, 40(3): 90–111.

Butler, T., Heavin, C., and O'Donovan, F. (2007) A theoretical model and framework for understanding knowledge management system implementation. *Journal of Organizational and End User Computing*, 19(4): 1–21.

Butler, T. and Murphy, C. (2007) Understanding the design of information technologies for knowledge management in organizations: A pragmatic perspective. *Information Systems Journal*, 17(2): 143–163.

Chua, A. (2004) Knowledge management system architecture: a bridge between KM consultants and technologists. *International Journal of Information Management*, 24(1): 87–98.

Cohen, D. (1998) Towards a knowledge context: Report on the first annual U.C. Berkeley forum on knowledge and the firm. *California Management Review*, 40(3): 22–39.

Currie, G. and Kerrin, M. (2004) The limits of a technology fix to knowledge management epistemological, political and cultural issues in the case of intranet implementation. *Management Learning*, 35(1): 9–29.

Davenport, T. (2008) Enterprise 2.0: The new, new knowledge management? *Harvard Business Online*, Feb. 19.

Easterby-Smith, M., Antonacopoulou E., Graca, M., and Ferdinand J. (2007) Organizational learning and dynamic capabilities. In H. Scarbrough, (ed.) *The Evolution of Business Knowledge*, Oxford: Oxford University Press: 71–88.

Easterby-Smith, M., Crossan, M., and Nicolini, D. (2000) Organizational learning: Debates past, present and future. *Journal of Management Studies*, 37(6): 783–796.

Galliers, R.D. and Newell, S. (2000) Back to the future: From knowledge management to data management. London School of Economics, Information Systems Department, Working Paper Number 92.

Giddens, A. (1984) *The Constitution of Society*. Cambridge: Polity Press.

Gilchrist, A. (2007) Can Web 2.0 be used effectively inside organisations? *Information World*, 8(1): 123–139.

Gray, P. H. and Durcikova, A. (2006) The role of knowledge repositories in technical support environments: Speed versus learning in user performance. *Journal of Management Information Systems*, 22(3): 159–190.

Grudin, J. (1990) Groupware and co-operative work: Problems and prospects. In B. Laurel (ed.), *The Art of Human Computer Interface Design*. Cambridge: Addison Wesley, 97–105.

Hayes, N. (2000) Work-arounds and boundary crossing in a high tech optronics company: The role of co-operative work-flow technologies. *Computer Supported Co-operative Work: An International Journal*, 9(3/4): 435–455.

Hayes, N. (2001) Boundless and bounded interactions in the knowledge work process: The role of groupware technologies. *Information and Organization*, 11(2): 79–101.

Hayes, N. and Walsham, G. (2000a) Competing interpretations of computer supported co-operative work. *Organization*, 7(1): 49–67.

Hayes, N. and Walsham G. (2000b) Safe enclaves, political enclaves and knowledge working. In C. Prichard, R. Hull, M. Chumer and H. Willmott (Eds), *Managing Knowledge: Critical Investigations of Work and Learning*. London: Macmillan: 69–87.

Hayes, N. and Walsham, G. (2001) Participation in groupware-mediated communities of practice: A socio-political analysis of knowledge working. *Information and Organization*, 11(4): 263–288.

Hislop, D. (2003) Linking human resource management and knowledge management via commitment: A review and research agenda. *Employee Relations*, 25(2): 182–202.

Hislop, D., Newell, S. Scarbrough, H., and Swan, J. (2000) Networks, knowledge and power: Decision making, politics and the process of innovation. *Technology Analysis and Strategic Management*, 12(2): 399–411.

Huysman, M.H. (2004) Traps and challenges for knowledge sharing in practice. *Journal of Knowledge and Process Management*, 11(2): 81–92.

Huysman, M.H. and Wulf, V. (2004) Social capital and IT: Current debates and research. In M. Huysman and V. Wulf (ed.) *Social Capital and Information Technology*. Cambridge, MA: MIT Press: 1–16.

Knights, D. (2008) What knowledge or *knowledge* for what? Reforming/reinventing the business school. In Scarbrough H (ed.), *The Evolution of Business Knowledge*. Oxford: Oxford University Press: 89–114.

Knights, D., Murray, F., and Willmott, H. (1993) Networking as knowledge work: A study of strategic inter-organizational development in the financial services industry. *Journal of Management Studies*, 30(6): 975–995.

Knock, N. and McQueen, R. (1998) Knowledge and information communication within organizations: An analysis of core, support and improvement process. *Knowledge and Process Management*, 5(1): 29–40.

Knox H., O'Doherty D., Vurdubakis T. and Westrup C., (2008) Screenworlds: Information technology and the performance of business knowledge. In Scarbrough H (ed.), *The Evolution of Business Knowledge*. Oxford: Oxford University Press: 273–294.

Lam, W. and Chua, A. (2005) Knowledge management project abandonment: An explanatory examination of root causes. *Communications of the Association for Information Systems*, 16(1): 723–743.

Lave, J. (1988) *Cognition in Practice: Mind, Mathematics and Culture in Everyday Life*. Cambridge: Cambridge University Press.

Leidner, D. (2000) Editorial. *Journal of Strategic Information Systems*, 9(2–3): 101–105.

Malhotra, Y. and Galletta, D. F. (2003) The role of commitment and motivation in knowledge management systems: Theory, conceptualization and measurement of success. In *Proceedings of the 36th Hawaii Conference on Systems Sciences* (pp. 1–10).

Markus, L.M., Majchrzak, A., and Gasser, L. (2002) A design theory for systems that support emergent knowledge processes. *MIS Quarterly*, 26(3): 179–212.

Massey, A. P., Montoya-Weiss, M. M. and O'Driscoll, T. M. (2002) Knowledge management in pursuit of performance: Insights from Nortel Networks. *MIS Quarterly*, 26(3): 269–289.

McAfee, A.P. (2006) Enterprise 2.0: The dawn of emergent collaboration. *Sloan Management Review*, 47(3): 21–28.

McDermott, R. (1999) Why information technology inspired but cannot deliver knowledge management. *California Management Review*, 41(4): 103–117.

McDermott, R. and O'Dell, C. (2001) Overcoming cultural barriers to sharing knowledge. *Journal of Knowledge Management*, 5(1): 76–85.

McKinley, A. (2000) The bearable lightness of control: Organisational reflexivity and the politics of knowledge management. In C. Prichard, R. Hull, M. Chumer and H. Willmott (eds.), *Managing Knowledge; Critical Investigations of Work and Learning*. London: Macmillan: 107–121.

McKinlay, A. (2002) The limits of knowledge management. *New Technology, Work and Employment*, 17: 76–88.

Moffett, S., McAdam, R., and Parkinson, S. (2003) An empirical analysis of knowledge management applications. *Journal of Knowledge Management*, 7(3): 6–26.

Newell, S., Scarbrough, H., Swan, J., and Hislop, D. (2000) Intranets and knowledge management: de-centred technologies and the limits of technological discourse.

In Prichard C., Hull R., Chumer M. and Willmott H. (eds.), *Managing Knowledge: Critical Investigations of Work and Learning.* London: Macmillan: 88–106.

Newell, S., Tansley, C., and Huang, J. (2004) Social capital and knowledge integration in an ERP project team: The importance of bridging and bonding. *British Journal of Management,* 15(1): 43–57.

Nonaka, I. and Takeuchi, H. (1994) *The Knowledge Creating Company: How Japanese Companies Create the Dynamics of Innovation.* Oxford: Oxford University Press.

Olivera, F. (2000) Memory systems in organizations: An empirical investigation of mechanisms for knowledge collection, storage and access, *Journal of Management Studies,* 37(6): 811–832.

Orlikowski, W. (1993) Learning from notes: Organizational issues in groupware implementation. *The Information Society,* 9(3): 237–250.

Orlikowski, W.J. (2002) Knowing in practice: Enacting a collective capability in distributed organizing. *Organization Science,* 13(3): 249–273.

Orlikowski, W. and Gash, D. (1994) Technological frames: Making sense of information technology in organizations. *ACM Transactions on Information Systems,* 12(2): 174–207.

Orr, J. E. (1990) Sharing knowledge, celebrating identity: Community memory in a service culture. In Middleton, D. and Edwards, D. (eds.), *Collective Remembering.* Newbury Park CA: Sage: 169–189.

Orr, J. E. (1996) *Talking about machines: An ethnography of a modern job.* Ithaca NY: ILR Press.

Pan, S. L. and Scarbrough, H. (1999) Knowledge management in practice: An exploratory case study. *Technology Analysis and Strategic Management,* 11(3): 359–374.

Quinn, J. B., Anderson, P., and Finkelstein, S. (1996) Managing professional intellect: Making the most of the best. *Harvard Business Review,* 74(2): 71–82.

Ruhleder, K. (1995) Computerisation and changes to infrastructures for knowledge work. *The Information Society,* 11(2): 131–144.

Sambamurthy, V. and Subramani, M. (2005) Special issue on information technologies and knowledge management. *MIS Quarterly,* 29(1): 1–7.

Scarbrough, H. (2008) Introduction. In Scarbrough H, (ed.), *The Evolution of Business Knowledge.* Oxford: Oxford University Press: 1–23.

Scarbrough, H. and Burrell, G. (1997) The axeman commeth. In S. Clegg and G. Palmer (eds.), *The Politics of Management Knowledge.* London: Sage: 173–189.

Schultze, U. (2000) A confessional account of an ethnography about knowledge work. *MIS Quarterly,* 24(1): 3–41.

Schultze, U. and Boland, R. J. (2000a) Place, space and knowledge work: A study of outsourced computer systems administrators. *Accounting, Management and Information Technologies,* 10(3): 187–219.

Schultze, U. and Boland, R. J. (2000b) Knowledge management technology and the reproduction of knowledge work practices. *Journal of Strategic Information Systems,* 9(2–3): 193–212.

Shin, M., Holden, T., and Schmidt, R. (2001) From knowledge theory to management practice: Towards an integrated approach. *Information Processing and Management,* 37(2): 335–355.

Storck, J. and Hill, P.A. (2000) Knowledge diffusions through strategic communities. *Sloan Management Review,* 41(2): 63–74.

Thompson, M. and Walsham, G. (2004) Placing knowledge management in context. *Journal of Management Studies*, 41(5): 725–747.

Tsoukas, H. (1996) The firm as a distributed knowledge system: A constructionist approach. *Strategic Management Journal*, 17(Winter Special Issue): 11–25.

Warr, W. A. (2008) Social software: Fun and games, or business tools? *Journal of Information Science*, 34(4): 591–604.

Wasko, M. and Faraj, S. (2000) 'It's what one does': Why people participate and help others in electronic communities of practice. *Journal of Strategic Information Systems*, 9(2–3): 155–173.

Wasko, M. and Faraj, S. (2005) Why should I share? Examining social capital and knowledge contribution in electronic networks of practice. *MIS Quarterly*, 29(1): 35–58.

Whelen, E. (2007) Exploring knowledge exchange in electronic networks of practice. *Journal of Information Technology*, 22(1): 5–12.

Zack, M. H. (1999a) Managing codified knowledge. *Sloan Management Review*, 40(4): 45–58.

Zack, M. H. (1999b) Developing a knowledge strategy. *California Management Review*, 41(3): 125–145.

Zuboff, S. (1996) Foreword. In Ciborra, C. U. (ed.), *Groupware and Teamwork: Invisible Aid or Technical Hindrance?* Chichester: John Wiley & Sons.

6

Knowledge Management: Process, Practice, and Web 2.0

MARYAM ALAVI AND JAMES S. DENFORD[1]

ABSTRACT

In this chapter, we review the potential role of Web 2.0 in supporting knowledge creation and acquisition, storage and retrieval, transfer and sharing, and integration and application in the context of communities and networks of practice. We categorize applications based on their relative support to two key Web 2.0 principles. The first is that data is the new 'Intel Inside,' leading to the category of content publication platforms, where the content is supported by the social network. This category captures tools such as blogs, multimedia aggregators, and wikis. A second core concept is to leverage network effects, leading to the category of social media platforms, where the social network is supported by content. This category includes social tagging, synthetic worlds, and social networking software. We illustrate each category with cases and identify how different Web 2.0 platforms enable both knowledge management process and practice. Finally, we suggest a future evolutionary path of knowledge management-supporting technology through enterprise mash-ups and Web 3.0.

INTRODUCTION

Organizational knowledge management is a broad and multi-faceted topic involving socio-cultural, organizational, behavioral, and technical dimensions. Subsumed under the knowledge management rubric is a large set of behavioral strategies (e.g. learning organization and communities of practice), information-based approaches (e.g. best practices

---

[1] The authors would like to acknowledge the contribution of Amrit Tiwana to an earlier version of this chapter.

and competitive intelligence), and technologies (e.g. data mining and knowledge repositories). Knowledge and knowledge management are not new phenomena. Organizations
are continuously engaged in the creation or acquisition, accumulation, and application
of knowledge. According to Penrose (1959), the accumulation of knowledge is built into
the very nature of firms. In the 1990s emphasis on organizational knowledge and knowledge management increased among researchers and practitioners. This can be attributed
to several factors including globalization of the economy and markets, volatility of business and competitive environments, and a trend toward knowledge-intensive products and
services as well as rapid progress in information technologies (Alavi, 2000).

Effective knowledge management in organizations involves a combination of technological and social elements. Considering the pervasiveness and advances in information technologies, this chapter focuses on the technological components of knowledge
management and the potential relationships between technical and social dimensions.
This focus is based on the premise that large-scale knowledge management initiatives in
complex organizational settings can be enhanced and facilitated through the application
of advanced information technologies. In fact, it can be argued that the availability and
ubiquity of certain new technologies such as Web 2.0 tools and high-speed mobile communications can expand, facilitate, and expedite organizational knowledge management.

In this chapter, we first provide a perspective on organizations as knowledge systems
and describe the four underlying knowledge management processes: knowledge creation, knowledge storage and retrieval, knowledge transfer, and knowledge application.
We then present an overview of various categories of Web 2.0 technologies and present
case examples of their applications in support of knowledge management processes in
organizations.

Knowledge Management in Organizations

We adopt the knowledge management framework developed by Alavi and Leidner (2001),
which is based on the view of organizations as knowledge systems that include four knowledge processes: creation, storage and retrieval, transfer, and application. With over 600
academic citations at the time of this writing, this framework has received considerable
research support and remains valid in the current environment, though we incorporate
refinements to the processes based on evolution of the knowledge management literature.
In addition to the process view, we also adopt the view of practice, particularly in terms of
Brown and Duguid's communities of practice (1991) and networks of practice (2000).

Knowledge management processes

The knowledge-based view postulates that firms exist because it is difficult to generate, transfer, and apply all the required types of knowledge via markets. Thus, firms can be viewed as
systems created for creating, storing and retrieving, transferring and sharing, and applying
the knowledge required for development and delivery of products and/or services. Some
authors (Sambamurthy and Subramani, 2005; Takeishi, 2001; Teece, Pisano, and Shuen,
1997) have considered the processes of knowledge creation, storage and retrieval, transfer,
and application to be core and fundamental organizational capabilities. These processes,

briefly described below, provide a target of opportunity for the application of Web 2.0 technologies for facilitating and enhancing organizational knowledge management.

Knowledge creation process. Knowledge creation refers to the development of 'new' organizational know-how and capability (Nonaka, 1994; Nonaka and Nishiguchi, 2001). There are two approaches to organizational knowledge creation: (1) generating new knowledge inside the organization and (2) *acquiring* it from external sources. Knowledge originates within individuals or social systems (groups of individuals) (Alavi, 2000) and can take the form of a cycle of socialization, externalization, combination, and internalization (Nonaka, 1994). Some organizations allocate dedicated resources to the knowledge creation process. A useful example is employee training and development programs that aim to generate knowledge at the individual level. Another example is the establishment of units or groups (e.g. research and development departments) for the purpose of creating new knowledge. At the individual level, knowledge is created through cognitive processes such as reflection and learning. Social systems (i.e. groups) generate knowledge through collaborative interactions and joint problem solving. Information technology (IT) can thus play a role in the knowledge creation process through its support of the individual's access to existing knowledge sources as well as support of collaborative interactions among individuals.

Knowledge creation can be viewed as an activity that occurs inside the organization to generate new knowledge, whereas *knowledge acquisition* is focused on assimilating existing knowledge from outside the organization (Huber, 1991). The knowledge is 'new' to the organization and is appropriated to meet the firm's knowledge requirements (von Krogh, Nonaka, and Aben, 2001). This differentiation can be important, as some organizations may, in fact, prefer externally-acquired knowledge to that which is internally generated (Menon and Pfeffer, 2003). Tasks involved in knowledge acquisition include searching for, sourcing, and grafting of knowledge (King, 2007).

Knowledge storage and retrieval process. Knowledge storage and retrieval refers to development of organizational memory (i.e. stocks of organizational knowledge) and the means for accessing its content. We can identify two types of organizational memory: internal and external. Internal memory refers to the stocks of knowledge that reside within the individual or groups of individuals in an organization. Internal organizational memory as defined here consists of individuals' skills as well as the organizational culture (Walsh and Ungson, 1991). External memories contain codified and explicit organizational knowledge, and include formal policies and procedure, and manual and computer files. The development of external memory in organizations involves three key activities: (1) determining the knowledge content of the memory; (2) determining the sources of the content and specifying the means of collecting the targeted knowledge; and (3) developing the content of the external memory and specifying the means of accessing its content. Most IT initiatives for the creation of organizational memory have focused on the third activity, the development of the external and explicit knowledge stocks and mechanisms for retrieval of the contents.

Knowledge transfer and sharing process. While knowledge transfer and sharing have been used interchangeably, it is possible to differentiate the two concepts. *Knowledge transfer* takes a source-and-recipient view and can be defined as 'the communication of knowledge from a source so that it is learned and applied by a recipient' (Ko, Kirsch, and King, 2005: 62). The knowledge transfer process involves the transmission of knowledge from the initial location to where it is needed and is applied. Although the concept of knowledge transfer is simple, its execution in organizational settings is not. This is because organizations often do not know what they know, and often possess weak systems for locating and transmitting different forms of knowledge within their various locations (Huber, 1991). The lack of ability to transfer existing knowledge to the point of application is a key detriment to organizations' realization of the full value of their knowledge assets (Argote and Ingram, 2000).

In contrast to the source-and-recipient view of knowledge transfer, *knowledge sharing* is more concerned with 'the collective character of knowledge emerging from interaction and dialogue among individuals' (Renzl, 2008: 207). While knowledge transfer involves purposeful communication of knowledge in a known dyad, knowledge sharing is less-focused on dissemination, often involving repositories or unknown recipients (King, 2007). As opposed to knowledge transfer, knowledge sharing involves trust and community interest (Wasko and Faraj, 2000), as well as politics and self-interest (Hayes, 2011), and hence knowledge sharing is the more socially-oriented term.

We can identify three modes of knowledge exchange in organizations: (1) exchange of knowledge between individuals; (2) exchange between individuals and knowledge repositories (e.g. downloading a report from a document repository, or developing a report and storing it in a document repository); and (3) exchange among existing knowledge repositories (e.g. using RSS feeds to transfer pre-specified knowledge items among existing knowledge repositories). The use of the term exchange is intentional, as each of these modes can take the form of knowledge transfer or sharing. Considering the various modes of knowledge transfer and sharing, we can identify two models of IT applications in this area: the network model and the knowledge stock model. The network model focuses on facilitating person-to-person sharing of knowledge via establishing digital links between them. The stock model, on the other hand, focuses on the electronic transfer of codified knowledge to, from, and between computerized knowledge repositories.

Knowledge application process. Knowledge application refers to the use of knowledge for decision making, problem solving, and coordination by individuals and groups in organizations. Knowledge in and of itself does not produce organizational value. Its application for taking effective action does. On the other hand, absorption and application of 'new' knowledge by individuals is complex. For example, work in the area of individual cognition and knowledge structures has demonstrated that, in most cases, individuals in organizational settings enact cognitive processes (problem solving and decision making) with little attention and by invoking only pre-existing knowledge and cognitive 'routines' (Gioia and Pool, 1984). While this tendency leads to a reduction in cognitive load and is therefore an effective strategy for dealing with individual cognitive limitations, it creates a barrier to the search for and application of new knowledge in organizations. Thus, IT tools that facilitate knowledge application can potentially lead to significant organizational value.

We contend that Web 2.0 technologies provide a platform for enhancing organizational knowledge management by providing a 'field' for support of the timing, scope, depth, dynamics, and efficiency of the underlying knowledge management processes described here. In the next section, we provide a complement to the process view through the lens of practice.

Knowledge management practice

Brown and Duguid (1991) argue that work practice must be examined and understood in context, as abstractions of it distort and obscure its true form. Therefore, knowledge can be best understood by examining how it is used in practice (Brown and Duguid, 2001). The idea of knowledge management practice is not, however, antithetical to knowledge management process, as both are focused on linking sources of knowledge to deepen and widen knowledge flows within organizations (Alavi and Leidner, 1999).

Communities of practice. Communities of practice are individuals sharing common interests and the desire to learn from and contribute to a community with their knowledge and experiences (Lave and Wenger, 1991). They are characterized by their knowledge-sharing orientation, self-organizing nature, self-selective membership, and value proposition grounded in knowledge exchange (Smith and McKeen, 2002). In essence, they are an organizational expression of individuals' need to interact naturally with others who share their common understanding of practice (Plaskoff, 2003).

The process of internalizing explicit knowledge can be arduous for an individual, therefore mechanisms to assist this process should develop in organizations. Reflecting this need, some benefits of communities of practice include: decreasing the learning curve (as they allow new members to find experts and discover firm rules); reducing rework (as they encourage finding artifacts, their developers and their context); and increasing innovation (by leveraging weak ties, building safe environments to test new ideas, and generating common interests) (Lesser and Storck, 2001).

Reflecting their self-organizing and regulating nature, communities of practice tend to fail when mandated or forced (Wenger and Snyder, 2000). However, the benefits for encouraging them are substantial, as organizational learning is greatly enhanced by providing individuals with access to relevant communities of practice (Brown and Duguid, 1991). One of the primary methods to cultivate communities of practice is to provide the infrastructure required to support them (Wenger and Snyder, 2000). Within communities of practice, features of work practice include narration, which adds meaning to sparse corporate direction and accumulates knowledge; collaboration, which supports groups assembling to face difficult problems; and social construction, which develops a community identity and shared situational understanding (Brown and Duguid, 1991). Tools to support communities of practice should, therefore, provide support to these features.

As memberships in communities of practice are self-selected, they are based on interest and not solely expertise (Wasko and Faraj, 2000). This greatly widens the participation base in comparison to the development of expert systems (Lado and Zhang, 1998). Therefore, a significant challenge and opportunity for knowledge management is the use of peers in place of experts in the evaluation and refinement of knowledge (King, 2007). Cho, Chung, King, and Shunn (2008) demonstrated that multiple peers can, in fact, be more effective than experts in refining knowledge that will be used by their other peers. Again, tools supporting these communities should reflect the value of the knowledge of individual community members.

Networks of practice. Brown and Duguid (2000) identify communities of practice as being tightly-knit where face-to-face communication is the norm. In contrast, networks of practice can be conceived as geographically-dispersed but interest-linked individuals who share practice but do not necessarily meet face-to-face (Brown and Duguid, 2001). While both have shared practice at their core, communities of practice and networks of practice can be seen to exist at different points on a continuum of strength of ties, where the former are stronger than the latter (Wasko and Teigland, 2004). The weak ties in networks of practice are very important for exposure to new ideas which can lead to knowledge creation (Robertson, Swan, and Newell, 1996).

By definition, networks of practice rely on digital links to establish self-organizing, open activity systems focused on a shared practice (Wasko and Faraj, 2005: 37) and common interest. This definition leads to differentiation of networks of practice from other structural arrangements (e.g. project teams) in four key areas (Wasko and Teigland, 2004). First, self-organization and voluntary participation allow for a range of activities, in contrast to expected participation in work groups or teams. Second, open participation means any individual may use or contribute to the network, which is different from other social structures where membership is limited. Third, as an activity system focused on shared practice, the value of the network is in the exchange of knowledge through mutual interaction, which can be contrasted with static document repositories or databases. Fourth, the primary use of digital links means members of the network are unlikely to know one another well, which is differentiated from close knit communities of practice. Networks of practice are important to this discussion as they represent an environment in which Web 2.0 technologies are applied for support of knowledge management practice.

In the next section, we provide an overview of key Web 2.0 technologies, describe their role in support of organizational knowledge management processes and practice, and demonstrate their applications through case examples.

The Role of Web 2.0 Technologies in Support of Organizational Knowledge Management

Web 2.0 is the business revolution in the computer industry caused by the move to the internet as platform, and an attempt to understand the rules for success on that new platform. Chief among those rules is this: Build applications that harness network effects to get better the more people use them.

(O'Reilly, 2006)

Coined by Tim O'Reilly (2005), the term Web 2.0 refers to applications that facilitate interactive information sharing, interoperatibility, and collaboration on the World Wide Web (Wikipedia.org). Web 2.0 has also been defined as 'the philosophy of mutually maximizing collective intelligence and added value for each participant by formalized and dynamic information sharing and creation' (Hoegg, Martignoni, Meckel, and Stanoevska-Slabeva, 2006: 13). Each of these definitions focuses more on participation than technology. The linkage between knowledge management and Web 2.0 can be seen in the shift from process and stand-alone systems to network and collaboration.

A decade ago, we could identify specific types of systems that were designed to support individual knowledge processes. Knowledge management systems (KMS) can have core functionality that supports the coding and sharing of documents in repositories, the development of knowledge directories, and the creation of knowledge networks (Alavi and

Table 6.1   Knowledge management processes

	Creation	*Storage and Retrieval*	*Transfer*	*Application*
IT tools	E-learning Collaboration support systems	Data warehousing and data mining Repositories	Communication support systems Enterprise infor- mation portals	Expert systems Decision sup- port systems

Leidner, 2001). Reflecting the four knowledge processes, Alavi and Tiwana (2003) specified ITs supporting them in Table 6.1.

McAfee (2006) described knowledge management-supporting IT at the time as being comprised of channels and platforms. Channels encompassed technologies including e-mail and instant-messaging, where the audience was small or unique and the distribution of knowledge was limited. Platforms encompassed intranets or enterprise portals, and while the knowledge was highly visible and shared, it was generally created by a small group of gatekeepers. Channels were generally used more than platforms (Davenport, 2005). In addition, there has been an evolution away from static integrative IT artifacts, such as document management systems, expert systems, and workflow systems, to dynamic interactive IT artifacts, such as social networking tools, blogs, and wikis (Hayes, 2011). Today, elements of Web 2.0 technologies span the four knowledge processes and encompass the power of communities and networks.

In a Delphi study of KMS requirements, Nevo and Chan (2007) identified desirable capabilities, based upon the four knowledge management processes. First, incorporation of appropriate incentives for knowledge contribution is desirable for creation. Second, storage and retrieval should include multimedia capabilities, content management functionality, and a central repository, and enable easy and fast access to knowledge. Third, transfer and sharing should also include multimedia, report generation, and presentation functionality, and enable collaboration and knowledge sharing. Finally, a customizable interface and a 'push' strategy for knowledge were desirable for knowledge application. These ideal KMS capabilities mirror those available through many Web 2.0 technologies, which we will explore in the remainder of this chapter.

A common characteristic of all Web 2.0 platforms is their dynamic content, networked structure, and online edits, compared to static content, hierarchical structure, and controlled change of earlier Web content. A challenge in traditional KMS is the lack of social context surrounding both the content and individuals providing or seeking it (Parise, 2009). In contrast, Web 2.0 technologies support knowledge management by interlinking the conversations that sustain communities through user-friendly technological tools (Kosonen and Kianto, 2009). Levy (2009) compared Web 2.0 and KM principals, finding a high degree of correlation between the two. Platform orientation, value of networks, services development, individual participation, collective knowledge, and content as core are all principles that apply in both domains.

We have chosen to highlight two of the most prominent concepts of Web 2.0 as they relate to knowledge management in order to structure this chapter. One of the core concepts of Web 2.0 espoused by O'Reilly (2006) is that data is the new 'Intel Inside,' indicating that the value resides in content rather than structure or infrastructure. Reflecting the value of content over form, Web 2.0 tools are generally easy-to-use, lightweight, and primarily open-source, lowering barriers-to-entry to participation (Parameswaran and Whinston, 2007). A second core concept noted in the definition (O'Reilly, 2006), is to leverage network effects.

While all Web 2.0 tools support both concepts by definition, we have grouped several tools into categories, depending on whether they are platforms that support one concept more than the other. The first category we term *content publication platforms*, where the content is supported by the social network, capturing tools such as blogs, multimedia aggregators, and wikis. The second category we term *social media platforms*, where the social network is supported by content, including social tagging, synthetic worlds, and social networking software. The term 'platforms' is specifically used, reflecting the goal of Web 2.0 to view the Internet as a platform and differentiating them from point-to-point channels.

Content publication platforms

We define content publication platforms as Web 2.0 tools whose primary characteristic is adherence to the principle of data being the next 'Intel Inside.' Networks' effects are key components to their success; however, the content and the structuring of interaction around it place the network in an enabling role. In this section, we look briefly at two content publication platforms—blogs and multimedia content sites—before examining wikis in greater detail.

Weblogs, or blogs, are personally authored web pages in reverse chronological order, using specialized blogging software to simplify the publication task for end users (Wagner and Bolloju, 2005). As blogs are chronological, the content is rarely edited and simply accretes, often with critical content being referenced or brought-forward to be reinforced. A wide range of open-source software, primarily PHP or Perl-based, is available to support blogs, as are many blog websites, such as Blogger, Wordpress, or LiveJournal. Blogs tend to be authored by single users and hence often will present the personal view of the author (Wagner and Majchrzak, 2006). Specific types of blogs can include personal journals, commentaries on other websites, and knowledge logs (Herring, Scheidt, Bonus, and Wright, 2004). In its aggregate form, the proliferation of blogs is known as the blogosphere, which expanded rapidly in the early 2000s (Kumar, Novak, Raghavan, and Tomkins, 2004).

Blogs have been identified as supporting both knowledge processes and communities. Following Nonaka, Toyama, and Konno's (2000) work on the concept of *ba*, Martin-Niemi and Greatbanks (2010) suggest that the blogosphere acts as a knowledge creation space. As blogs are also storage mechanisms for individuals' knowledge, Wagner and Bolloju (2005) suggest that they can be 'harvested' for innovation communities, linking this Web 2.0 tool to the knowledge storage and retrieval process. Firms such as IBM have demonstrated how blogs can be used to encourage employees to share their knowledge (Razmerita, Kirchner, and Sudzina, 2009). Recognition as an expert and its consequent generation of social capital is a key component in developing these knowledge sharing communities (Huysman and Wulf, 2006). Blogs have been suggested as a component of decentralized, informal knowledge management that can, with appropriate metadata, be navigated and their knowledge retrieved (Cayzer, 2004). Finally, as the blogosphere can be navigated through interest-based linkages between blogs (Kumar et al., 2004), it can be seen as developing and supporting networks of practice.

While blogs and wikis can be viewed as conversational technologies supporting knowledge management through the written word (Wagner and Bolloju, 2005), there are other Web 2.0 tools supporting a range of other media types. A core application for these tools is podcasting, which enables the sharing of audio and video on a range of devices. The term 'podcasting' comes from a fusion of the ubiquitous Apple iPod with broadcasting (Crofts, Dilley, Fox, Retsema, and Williams, 2005). The technology allows the user to decouple the content from the producer's channel and gain more control over the media, allowing for a proliferation of content sources through multiple channels. Many specialized websites—multimedia aggregators—support this proliferation of media, including YouTube.com for video, Last.fm for music, and Flickr.com for pictures.

Multimedia aggregators have an important role to play in knowledge management of non-textual information. With many contributors throughout the world, YouTube has been effective in sharing knowledge without constraints of censorship, such as political speeches being posted, commented on, taken down, and reposted providing a forum for public discourse (Parameswaran and Whinston, 2007). Podcasts are an effective mechanism for transferring knowledge in the form of the spoken word, which previously had been confined to its point of origin or tightly controlled channels (Crofts, Dilley, Fox, Retsema, and Williams, 2005). As a repository for non-textual information, with proper metadata, these sites support oral and visual capture of content and support knowledge storage and retrieval processes. Finally, multimedia content sites are more than mere storage as they create communities through the tagging of media, the following of key contributors, and the generation of comments.

Content in blogs and multimedia aggregators is contributed individually and, in spite of comments by others, remains the unique contribution of the author. In contrast, wikis are content publication platforms that form a collaborative contribution of the community.

Wikis Wiki is the Hawaiian word for 'quick' or 'fast.' When Ward Cunningham invented the first wiki in 1995, his intent was to publish information rapidly and collaboratively on the Internet in a form that was the simplest online database that could possibly work. Leuf and Cunningham (2001) defined a wiki as 'a freely expandable collection of interlinked Web pages, a hypertext system for storing and modifying information—a database where each page is easily editable by any user with a forms-capable Web browser client' (2001: 14). Characteristics of wikis include their collective authorship, instant publication, extent of versioning, and simplicity of authorship (Prasarnphanich and Wagner, 2009). In contrast to the one-to-many monologue form of most blogs, wikis exhibit a many-to-many dialogue form, where participation is more equal (Wagner and Bolloju, 2005).

Stemming from these characteristics, the advantages of wikis include their ease of use, ability to act as a central repository of information, tracking and revision features, encouragement of collaboration between organizations, potential to solve the issue of information overload by e-mail, and development of a trusting culture (Grace, 2009). As they represent the collective knowledge of a community, wikis are suitable for maintaining best practices within the community (Wagner and Bolloju, 2005). Given wikis' open and dynamic nature, the key success factor in wiki adoption for firms appears to be a corporate culture that values collaboration, is less hierarchical, and recognizes innovation (Wagner and Majchrzak, 2006).

In comparison to the chronological nature of blogs, wikis are organized by topic. Therefore, unlike blogs which append material to older contributions or comment on those contributions, contributions to wikis are added directly to the existing body of knowledge. One of the concerns with wikis is their inherent openness, so trust is vital within a wiki community (Raman, 2006). Reflecting this openness and need for trust, wikis have been described both as a technology and the social norms that surround its use (Prasarnphanich and Wagner, 2009). Functionally, anyone can create a new wiki page, add or edit content in an existing wiki page, and delete content within a page, without any prior knowledge or skills in editing and publishing on the Web (Raman, 2006). This technical format requires a supporting social system, which can be described as wiki-etiquette or 'the Wiki way' (Prasarnphanich and Wagner, 2009). These social norms and supporting social system are key components to the network of practice enabled by the wiki.

An example of the 'wiki way' taking hold in a company can be found in IBM, where more than 2000 internal wikis are created and maintained by over 20,000 employees (Wagner and Majchrzak, 2006). The introduction of wikis was not planned, as they were often user initiated without the knowledge of IT management, but were embraced by the company. There appeared to be recognition that the communities and networks of practice that were supported by wikis were a valuable asset to the firm. The use of wikis is now well established at IBM, as individuals previously on wiki-enabled projects initiate wikis on their new projects. This degree of use has been made practical by the implementation of a wiki-appliance that creates a new wiki with a single click.

One of the key applications of wikis in IBM is in developer networks (Wagner and Majchrzak, 2006). Two critical problems with documentation reported by IBM include an inability to locate it and the fact that it quickly becomes inaccurate. One senior manager noted that documentation located in a team repository in Lotus Notes or on a shared drive often gets forgotten, whereas a wiki can be quickly located. Similarly, documentation is frequently inaccurate and difficult to update; however, with a wiki it is possible for a developer to modify the contents if an inaccuracy is found. Wikis in this context support storage and retrieval of knowledge for IBM.

Another application is client-facing wikis, with the goal of creating customer communities. IBM has been a leader in creating policies for this application, guiding employees' use of wikis with few unbreakable rules (such as non-disclosure of financials or unannounced product developments) and the aim to reflect IBM's knowledge and skills while adding value for the customer. Working within these guidelines, the IBM staff is able to engage with clients in creating a collaborative environment for the creation and acquisition of new knowledge.

Wikis have been found to be successful in supporting a range of knowledge management processes. In a study of the use of a wiki to structure the learning environment of a course in knowledge management, students found that wikis improved collaboration and the quality of work and were effective tools for knowledge creation (Chu, 2008). Openly shared collaborative writing, as supported by wikis, has been identified as a new form of collaborative knowledge creation (Wagner and Bolloju, 2005), which is primarily due to the instant publication of new knowledge (Wagner and Majchrzak, 2006). Additionally, considering Nonaka's (1994) SECI spiral, a wiki user can externalize his or her knowledge, see it instantly combined with other knowledge, and have it internalized by another wiki user, who can socialize it with his or her peers. Wagner and Bolloju (2005) identify that best practice communities can benefit from wikis, suggesting they are strongly related to the knowledge sharing process. This was supported in the knowledge management course study where students could read, amend, and comment on their peers' work (Chu, 2008). Storage and retrieval processes are enabled by capturing the current document and all previous versions, and by the use of built-in search tools. Wiki structure of forward and backward links assists in retrieval as the wiki can be navigated from any start point (Wagner and Majchrzak, 2006).

Wikis are ideal Web 2.0 tools as they exemplify the leveraging of network effects of communities. The basis of the success of wikis as a tool for knowledge management can be found in Surowieki's *The Wisdom of Crowds* (2004), where the consensus judgment of a large group of inexpert individuals (the crowd) can be superior to that of any individual member of the crowd or even an expert assessor. Supporting the network effects point of view, one study found that new articles tend to be written by different authors from the articles to which they are linked; hence the scalability of wikis is limited less by the capacity of individual contributors than by the size of the contributor pool (Spinellis and Louridas, 2008). Similarly, the age of a wiki is both an indicator and a contributing factor to its sustainability (Majchrzak, Wagner, and Yates, 2006). The longer a wiki exists, the more frequently it is accessed, both by lurkers and active participants, and hence the more likely it will be to continue.

Wikis are also exemplars of electronic networks of practice tools, as the underlying factors in the benefits generated from wikis are based primarily on the participants' belief in, capacity of, and reliance on collaboration (Majchrzak et al., 2006). Collaborative motivations for wiki contribution appear to outweigh individualistic ones (Prasarnphanich and Wagner, 2009; Wasko and Faraj, 2000). Even so, there are strong individual benefits to be achieved by participation in corporate wikis that include: enhancing reputation, making work easier, and helping improve organizational processes (Majchrzak et al., 2006).

The combination of collaborative motivation and individual benefits makes for a resilient form of organizational knowledge management, particularly from the point of view of use and misuse. While open wikis have been subject to misrepresentation as a form of attack, internal corporate wikis or closed community-based ones are likely to have minimal malfeasance due to their more focused use (Denning, Horning, Parnas, and Weinstein, 2005).

Nonetheless, organizational wikis, as they often include proprietary corporate knowledge, have to balance between openness and access control to ensure that critical knowledge is protected (Wagner and Majchrzak, 2006).

Of the content publication platforms—blogs, multimedia aggregators, and wikis—the last may be the most reliant on network effects to be effective, but content is still the core. In the next section, we examine social media platforms, where the exploitation of network effects is paramount.

Social media platforms

We define social media platforms as Web 2.0 tools whose primary characteristic is the exploitation of network effects. It is not that content is unimportant, but rather that in this grouping it is the social network that is being supported by content. In this section, we look briefly at two social media platforms—social tagging and virtual worlds—before examining social networking software in more detail.

Collaborative or social tagging and bookmarking are mechanisms for communities to share bookmarks of Internet resources. Tags and bookmarks are individual metadata linked to a particular web-page, and as such are not content themselves but paths between content. Tags can be public or private, supporting either the collective or personal navigation of content. Traditional tagging requires users to apply a predefined set of hierarchical terms that often takes the form of a centrally defined taxonomy. In comparison, collaborative tagging allows individual users to tag content and create connections between pages that share something in common (Levy, 2009). A folksonomy is the term coined by Thomas Vander Wal to refer to this aggregation of tags, combining the concepts of people (folk) and taxonomy (Smith, 2004).

Tags reflect individual users' schema of knowledge and the aggregation of this metadata is the main benefit of collaborative tagging to knowledge management. Similar to the convergence seen in wikis through the collective application of judgment, collaborative tagging systems also appear to converge on a stable distribution of tags (Halpin, Robu, and Shepherd, 2007), making them supportive of knowledge storage and retrieval processes. Also, social tagging is a mechanism that can support knowledge creation and acquisition, as it can identify knowledge that can either be combined with existing organizational knowledge to create something new or absorbed as knowledge that is 'new' to the organization. The navigation of the Web by tags supports networks of practice by combining and organizing the collective knowledge represented by individual community members.

While social tagging supports conceptual navigation of the Web, virtual worlds are conceived to support 'physical' navigation within worlds embedded in the Web. Synthetic or virtual worlds are three-dimensional graphically-intensive electronic environments where members assume a persona and engage in social and commercial interaction within a geographically dispersed community (Castronova, 2005). Interaction in virtual worlds is synchronous and three-dimensional, as users interact in real time and navigate the virtual world itself rather than web pages. While individuals can develop an image within the community based upon contributions to content publication and other social media platforms, image creation is direct in virtual worlds through the selection of self-presenting avatars and their directed interactions with others (Kaplan and Haenlein, 2009). Interest in virtual worlds by the business community has been primarily focused on marketing efforts within these synthetic environments (Hemp, 2006).

Virtual worlds can be used either to escape reality or to replicate it (Hemp, 2008), and it is in this latter use that their value to knowledge management can be seen. Synthetic worlds have the potential to assist in knowledge management through the development of collective knowledge and common understanding by addressing dispersion of participants (Burley, Savion, Peterson, Lotrecchiano, and Neshnavarz-Nia, 2010). Two of the key characteristics that help diminish the impact of distance are social presence and visualization (Ives and Junglas, 2008). Virtual worlds allow interaction including the social cues which are absent from other distance-spanning tools, providing context to knowledge sharing.

Through social tagging, networks of common interest can be discerned; through synthetic worlds, direct social interaction can take place and networks can be inferred. However, only through the use of social networking software can those social networks be made explicit and navigated.

Social networking software. Social networking sites (SNS) and their supporting software allow users to manage their contacts, share personal information, and socialize online. Boyd and Ellison (2008) define social networking sites as 'web-based services that allow individuals to (1) construct a public or semi-public profile within a bounded system, (2) articulate a list of other users with whom they share a connection, and (3) view and traverse their list of connections and those made by others within the system' (2008: 211). Sites can be oriented towards supporting friendships (Facebook.com), shared interests (MySpace.com), or professional relationships (LinkedIn.com), among other things. One of the key benefits of SNS is the generation and maintenance of social capital (Ellison, Steinfield, and Lampe, 2007). In keeping with the link to social capital, SNS are useful in the socialization of new organizational members, particularly if they already have a high degree of personal use (Leidner, Koch, and Gonzalez, 2010; Kane, Robinson-Combre, and Berge, 2010).

SNS first emerged in the late 1990s, with SixDegrees.com recognized as the first launched in 1997 to articulate and make visible social networks (Boyd and Ellison, 2008). The common core of SNS is their use of profiles and links between profiles, which map the social network. Users enter profiles that include personal and/or professional information and then identify other individuals registered with the site. Depending on the intent and culture of the site, these linkages can be termed 'friends,' 'fans,' 'followers,' 'contacts,' or other variations. The leveraging of network effects of SNS can be seen here in the value of the site being proportional to the number of users that can be connected. The utility of the networks is in a user's ability to navigate their contacts' links in order to discover new potential connections. To enable the development of social networks, SNS incorporate conversational mechanisms including commenting (public) and messaging (private) communications. Differentiation between SNS can be based upon network intent and audience, geographic or language specificity, or other methods of segmentation (Boyd and Ellison, 2008).

Military Bank (a pseudo name) is an organization in which social networking software plays an important role in the firm (Leidner et al., 2010). The 2500-employee IT department of the Military Bank was plagued with a sixty to seventy percent turnover rate in new hires during its second year of employment. As a mechanism of increasing retention of Generation Y hires faced with the tedious nature of their highly technical jobs, the organization deployed Nexus, a Web 2.0 platform to make the job more interesting. Nexus, based on SharePoint included features supporting both work and social interactions and was oriented towards the development of a community of practice of Generation Y IT personnel within the firm.

Nexus was seen by executive and middle managers as being responsible for decreased turnover, higher morale, and better engagement of employees (Leidner et al., 2010). In addition to the positive emotional responses of individuals, there were knowledge management-related benefits. Social networking tools facilitated establishing social and professional ties among new hires. These ties and emotional connections facilitated problem solving by providing an access to sources of knowledge and expertise, and encouraging knowledge sharing.

SNS can support knowledge processes by creating the paths through which they operate. For example, the groups that organizations use to create knowledge and the external contacts from which knowledge is acquired are both enabled by SNS. An example of retrieval of internal organizational knowledge in Military Bank was when a member was faced with a technical difficulty and was able to use Nexus to connect with a distant contact to provide direct assistance in resolving the issue outside of the normal bureaucratic request channels (Leidner et al., 2010). Similarly, the social capital generated by SNS set the conditions for knowledge sharing within organizations, where mutual friendship can create the required trust and motivation to affect the knowledge transfer (Huysman and Wulf, 2006). Finally, decision making in organizations is a complex process characterized both by information scarcity and overload. SNS can provide linkages to find the individuals in an organization with the scarce relevant information amongst the over-abundant irrelevant.

As SNS are focused on networks, their primary benefit is in the creation and maintenance of communities and networks of practice. Social networking software centers on the missing context in knowledge management through the navigation of social networks to find relevant content and sources of expertise (Parise, 2009). In addition to navigation of existing networks, Spertus, Sahami, and Buyukkokten (2005) suggested that SNS can use topographies of networks to recommend new communities to users based on membership characteristics. SNS have been demonstrated to support pre-existing social relationships more than the establishment of new ones, efficiently reinforcing weak ties (Ellison, Steinfield, and Lampe, 2007). This supports our view of networks of practice being primarily, but not exclusively, based on online activity.

SUMMARY AND CONCLUSION

In this chapter we have explored the information technology dimension of knowledge management, focusing on the emergence of an increased focus on practice and on the applicability of Web 2.0 tools to support it. We adopted Alavi and Leidner's (2001) framework that views firms as systems generated for creating, storing/retrieving, transferring/ sharing, and applying the knowledge required for development and delivery of products and/or services. We also adopt the concepts of communities and networks of practice, where both are composed of individuals sharing common interests and the desire to participate in a knowledge community (Lave and Wenger, 1991), while the latter is differentiated by its greater geographical dispersion, decreased face-to-face interaction, and reliance on electronic tools (Brown and Duguid, 2001). Our discussion complements and extends earlier work by Alavi and Tiwana (2003) that explored the enabling use of IT on knowledge management processes.

Traditional uses of ITs to support knowledge management have included the support of acquisition and retrieval of codified knowledge in formal systems (Huysman and Wulf, 2006). Organizations are expanding and complementing structured knowledge management systems with Web 2.0 applications. Wagner and Bolloju (2005) note that many Web 2.0 applications are conversational in nature, showing less formal structures than traditional knowledge management tools, and hence do not require structured databases of knowledge interpretation mechanisms. These lightweight tools do, however, require the ability to capture content and its social context within a community. In studying the impact of Web 2.0 tools in knowledge management, we have focused on differentiation along the lines of primacy of support for content or social networks, reflecting two key principles of Web 2.0 (O'Reilly, 2006).

We defined content publication platforms as Web 2.0 tools whose primary characteristic is the adherence to the principle of data being the next 'Intel Inside.' With their accretion of chronological authored content, blogs form a social space for knowledge creation and sharing, a repository of individual knowledge, and, taking the blogosphere as a whole, a collection of interest-sharing networks of practice. Using podcasting as a base technology to support the proliferation of audio and visual content, multimedia aggregators support the storage and retrieval of oral and visual histories and the communities and networks of practice that are generated and sustained by them. As a topically-organized knowledge repository using lightweight software, wikis support easy storage and retrieval of knowledge that can be applied quickly within an organization. With their collaborative nature and underlying social norms, wikis facilitate sharing within networks of practice and enable the social space for novel recombination of existing knowledge in the knowledge creation process.

We defined social media platforms as Web 2.0 tools whose primary characteristic is the exploitation of network effects. Through the aggregation of collaboratively-generated metadata on web pages and its convergence to stable distributions known as folksonomy, social tagging supports the sharing and absorption of new knowledge, the storage and retrieval of existing knowledge, and the navigation of networks of practice as represented by their shared interests. The combination of characteristics of virtual worlds that enable synchronous interaction of geographically dispersed individuals in replications of reality make them effective tools for knowledge sharing through the provision of social cues and visualization and the development of common understanding needed for knowledge application. Social networking software allows users to manage their contacts, share personal information, and socialize online, functions which are useful for developing a sense of community and linkages with it to apply the four knowledge processes.

Looking at the existing state-of-the-art in IT support to knowledge management, Alavi and Tiwana (2003) noted that ITs were starting to overlap the knowledge processes, an observation that we have supported in this chapter. While it is the network that is important, rather than content, the failure of SixDegrees.com, an early social networking site, was attributed to its lack of content—users complained that there was little to do once networks were created (Boyd and Ellison, 2008). Therefore, pure network with no content is unlikely to succeed and pure content with no network is a static, Web 1.0 presentation. Following this trend towards convergence of IT towards supporting processes and practice, content and networks, we extend our consideration of future research opportunities into two areas: mashups and Web 3.0.

Enterprise mashups are hybrid applications combining data and code from more than one existing source. They are 'situational' applications, in that they are created to address at-hand issues using available resources (Cherbakov, Bravery, Goodman, Pandya, and Baggett, 2007). The synergy of hobbyist programmers, available mashup-making tools, mashable data sources, and enterprise mashup hubs has provided a rich environment for the proliferation of these tools (Majchrzak and Maloney, 2008). The open-source origins of many individual Web 2.0 tools make them ideal for mashups which combine multiple applications into a single platform. Rapid interoperability is the key benefit of mashups, which makes the use of open data sources and application programming interfaces (APIs) essential to this technology (Kavanagh, 2010). Many SNS may already be considered mashups, for example the integration of Google Maps within Flickr or the proliferation of third-party applications in FaceBook. The reuse of existing enterprise applications and data to create new services is a key component of the value propositions of mashups (Majchrzak and Maloney, 2008) which is analogous to the firm's benefits of recombining existing knowledge to create new knowledge. In this manner, we would expect the parallel development of best practices in knowledge management and the IT supporting it to be beneficial to the organization and to warrant further empirical investigation.

The logical extension from Web 2.0 is to Web 3.0, which involves an evolution to the Semantic Web and artificial intelligence (AI) for platforms and increased personalization and mobility for users (Strickland, 2007). The Semantic Web is an initiative started by the World Wide Web Consortium to create a technological framework and medium for the exchange of data by automated tools as well as by people (Berners-Lee, Hendler, and Lassila, 2001). The AI sub-discipline concerned with constructing models of the world is related to knowledge representation (Lassila and Hendler, 2007). The marrying of AI with semantics was thus conceived to deal with the vast amount of data on the web and a growing interoperability problem (Hendler, 2008), both being significant issues for knowledge management. For the user, Web 3.0 will bring increased mobility and personalization, leading to a potential increase in personal knowledge management or PKM (Razmerita et al., 2009). This will allow for a differentiation between community- or organization-oriented Web 2.0-supported knowledge management tools and individual-oriented Web 3.0-supported PKM tools. The dual impacts of semantic-enabling and PKM are areas for further study.

In summary, Web 2.0 tools have the potential to provide significant support to organizational knowledge management initiatives. Technologies that support collectively-held knowledge should facilitate the exchange of ideas, the provision of expertise and the debating of issues in the community (Wasko and Faraj, 2000). Important success factors that relate to an ideal KMS itself include ease of use, value and quality of knowledge, system accessibility, and user involvement (Nevo and Chan, 2007). Web 2.0 tools can be seen to meet each of the success factors that previous developer- or expert-delivered tools may not have. We still hold that the information technology dimension of knowledge management, including the exploitation of Web 2.0 tools, remains understudied. Further empirical research on this facet of knowledge management offers unprecedented opportunities for connecting and unleashing the potential of what continues to be the most original source of new knowledge: the human mind.

References

Alavi, M. (2000) Managing organizational knowledge. In R.W. Zmud (ed.) *Framing the Domains of IT Management*. Cincinnati, OH: Pinnaflex Educational Resources.

Alavi, M. and Leidner D. (1999) Knowledge management systems: Issues, challenges, and benefits. *Communications of the Association for Information Systems*, 1(7): 1–35.

Alavi, M. and Leidner, D. (2001) Knowledge management and knowledge management systems: Conceptual foundations and research issues. *MIS Quarterly*, 25(1): 107–136.

Alavi, M. and Tiwana, A. (2003) Knowledge management: The information technology dimension. In M. Easterby-Smith and M.A. Lyles (eds.) *Blackwell Handbook of Organizational Learning and Knowledge Management*. Oxford: Blackwell Publishers: 104–121.

Argote, L. and Ingram, P. (2000) Knowledge transfer: A basis for competitive advantage in firms. *Organizational Behavior and Human Decision Processes*, 82(1): 150–169.

Berners-Lee, T., Hendler, J. and Lassila, O. (2001) The semantic web. *Scientific American*, 284(5): 34–43.

Boyd, D.M. and Ellison, N.B. (2008) Social network sites: Definition, history, and scholarship. *Journal of Computer-Mediated Communication*, 13(1): 210–230.

Brown, J.S. and Duguid, P. (1991) Organizational learning and communities-of-practice: Toward a unified view of working, learning, and innovation. *Organization Science*, 2(1): 40–57.

Brown, J.S. and Duguid, P. (2000) *The Social Life of Information*. Boston, MA: Harvard Business School Press.

Brown, J.S. and Duguid, P. (2001) Knowledge and organization: A social-practice perspective. *Organization Science*, 12(2): 198–213.

Burley, D., Savion, S., Peterson, M., Lotrecchiano, G., and Keshnavarz-Nia, N. (2010) Knowledge integration through synthetic worlds. *VINE*, 40(1): 71–82.

Castronova, E. (2005) *Synthetic Worlds: The Business and Culture of Online Games*. Chicago, IL: University of Chicago Press.

Cayzer, S. (2004) Semantic blogging and decentralized knowledge management. *Communications of the ACM*, 47(12): 47–52.

Cherbakov, L. Bravery, A, Goodman, B.D., Pandya, A., and Baggett, J. (2007) Changing the corporate IT development model: Tapping the power of grassroots computing. *IBM Systems Journal*, 46(4): 1–20.

Cho, K., Chung, T., King, W.R., and Shunn, C. (2008) Peer-based computer-supported knowledge refinement: An empirical investigation. *Communications of the ACM*, 51(3): 83–88.

Chu, S.K.-W. (2008) TWiki for knowledge building and management. *Online Information Review*, 32(6): 745–758.

Crofts, S., Dilley, J., Fox, M., Retsema, A., and Williams, B. (2005) Podcasting: A new technology in search of viable business models. *First Monday*, 10(9): 5 September 2005.

Davenport, T.H. (2005) *Thinking for a Living: How to Get Better Performance and Results from Knowledge Workers*. Boston, MA: Harvard Business Press.

Denning, P., Horning, J., Parnas, D., and Weinstein, L. (2005) Wikipedia risks. *Communications of the ACM*, 48(12): 152.

Ellison, N.B., Steinfield, C., and Lampe, C. (2007) The benefits of Facebook 'friends:' Social capital and college students' use of online social network sites. *Journal of Computer-Mediated Communication*, 12(4): 1143–1168.

Gioia, D.A. and Pool, P.P. (1984) Scripts in organizational behavior. *Academy of Management Review*, 9(3): 449–459.

Grace, T.P.L. (2009) Wikis as a knowledge management tool. *Journal of Knowledge Management*, 13(4): 63–74.

Halpin, H., Robu, V., and Shepherd, H. (2007) The complex dynamics of collaborative tagging. *Proceedings of the 16th International Conference on the World Wide Web (WWW'07)*. Banff, Canada: 211–220.

Hayes, N. (2011) Information technology and the possibilities for knowledge sharing, In M. Easterby-Smith and M.A. Lyles (eds.) *Handbook of Organizational Learning and Knowledge Management* (2nd edn). Chichester: John Wiley & Sons.

Hemp, P. (2006) Avatar-based marketing. *Harvard Business Review*, 84(6): 48–57.

Hemp, P. (2008) Getting real about virtual worlds. *Harvard Business Review*, 86(10): 27–28.

Hendler, J. (2008) Web 3.0: Chicken farms on the semantic web. *Computer*, 41(1): 106–108.

Herring, S. C., Scheidt, L. A., Bonus, S., and Wright, E. (2004) Bridging the gap: A genre analysis of weblogs. *Proceedings of the 37th Hawaii International Conference on System Sciences (HICSS-37)*. Los Alamitos, CA: IEEE.

Hoegg, R. Martignoni, R., Meckel, M. and Stanoevska-Slabeva, K. (2006) Overview of business models for Web 2.0 communities. *Proceedings of GeNeMe*, Dresden, GE.

Huber, G. (1991) Organizational learning: The contributing processes and the literatures. *Organizational Science*, 2(1): 88–115.

Huysman, M. and Wulf, V. (2006) IT to support knowledge sharing in communities: Towards a social capital analysis. *Journal of Information Technology*, 21(1): 40–51.

Ives, B. and Junglas, I. (2008) APC forum: Business implications of virtual worlds and serious gaming. *MIS Quarterly Executive*, 7(3): 151–156.

Kane, K., Robinson-Combre, J., and Berge, Z.L. (2010) Tapping into social networking: Collaborating enhances both knowledge management and e-learning. *VINE*, 40(1): 62–70.

Kaplan, A.M. and Haenlein, M. (2009) The fairyland of Second Life: Virtual social worlds and how to use them. *Business Horizons*, 52(6): 563–572.

Kavanagh, E. (2010) Transforming information management with enterprise mashups. *Information Management*, 20(1): 40.

King, W.R. (2007) IT strategy and innovation: Recent innovations in knowledge management. *Information Systems Management*, 24(1): 91–93.

King, W.R., Chung, T.R., and Haney, M.H. (2008) Knowledge management and organizational learning. *Omega*, 36(2): 167–172.

Ko, D.-G., Kirsch, L.J., and King, W.R. (2005) Antecedents of knowledge transfer from consultants to clients in enterprise system implementations. *MIS Quarterly*, 29(1): 59–85.

Kosonen, M. and Kianto, A. (2009) Applying wikis to managing knowledge—A sociotechnical approach. *Knowledge and Process Management*, 16(1): 23–29.

Kumar, R., Novak, J., Raghavan, P., and Tomkins, A. (2004) Structure and evolution of blogspace. *Communications of the ACM*, 47(12): 35–39.

Lado, A. and Zhang, M. (1998) Expert systems, knowledge development and utilization, and sustained competitive advantage: A resource-based model. *Journal of Management*, 24(4): 489–509.

Lassila, O. and Hendler, J. (2007) Embracing 'Web 3.0.' *IEEE Internet Computing*, 11(3): 90–93.

Lave, J. and Wenger, E. (1991) *Situated Learning: Legitimate Peripheral Participation*. New York, NY: Cambridge University Press.

Leidner, D. E., Koch, H., and Gonzalez, E. (2010) Assimilating generation Y IT new hires into USAA's workforce: The role of an enterprise 2.0 system. *MIS Quarterly Executive*, 9(4): 163–176.

Lesser, E. and Storck, J. (2001) Communities of practice and organisational performance. *IBM Systems Journal*, 40(4): 831–841.

Leuf, B. and Cunningham, W. (2001) *The Wiki Way: Quick Collaboration on the Web*, Boston, MA: Addison-Wesley.

Levy, M. (2009) Web 2.0 implications on knowledge management. *Journal of Knowledge Management*, 13(1): 120–134.

Majchrzak, A. and Maloney, J.T. (2008) *Enterprise Mashups: What Do They Mean for CIOs?* SIM APC Report.

Majchrzak, A., Wagner, C., and Yates, D. (2006) Corporate Wiki users: Results of a survey. *Proceedings of WikiSym '06*, August 21–23, 2006, Odense, Denmark: 99–104.

Martin-Niemi, F. and Greatbanks, R. (2010) The *Ba* of blogs: Enabling conditions for knowledge conversion in blog communities. *VINE*, 40(1): 7–23.

McAfee, A.P. (2006) Enterprise 2.0: The dawn of emergent collaboration. *MIT Sloan Management Review*, 47(3): 21–28.

Menon, T. and Pfeffer, J. (2003) Valuing internal vs. external knowledge: Explaining the preference for outsiders. *Management Science*, 49(4): 497–513.

Nevo, D. and Chan, Y.E. (2007) A Delphi study of knowledge management systems: Scope and requirements. *Information and Management*, 44(6): 583–597.

Nonaka, I. (1994) A dynamic theory of organizational knowledge creation. *Organization Science*, 5(1): 14–37.

Nonaka, I. and Nishiguchi, T. (2001) Social, technical, and evolutionary dimensions of knowledge creation. In I. Nonaka and T. Nishiguchi (eds.) *Knowledge Emergence: Social, Technical, and Evolutionary Dimensions of Knowledge Creation*. New York, NY: Oxford University Press: 286–289.

Nonaka, I., Toyama, R., and Konno, N. (2000) SECI, *Ba* and leadership: A unified model of dynamic knowledge creation. *Long Range Planning*, 33(1): 5–34.

O'Reilly, T. (2005) *What is Web 2.0*. http://oreilly.com/web2/archive/what-is-web-20.html, accessed 16 March 2010.

O'Reilly, T. (2006) *Web 2.0 Compact Definition: Trying Again*. http://radar.oreilly.com/2006/12/web-20-compact-definition-tryi.html, accessed 16 March 2010.

Parameswaran, M. and Whinston, A.B. (2007) Social computing: An overview. *Communications of the Association of Information Systems*, 19(37): 762–780.

Parise, S. (2009) Social media networks: What do they mean for knowledge management? *Journal of Information Technology Case and Application Research*, 11(2): 1–11.

Penrose, E. T. (1959) *The Theory of the Growth of the Firm*, New York, NY: John Wiley & Sons.

Plaskoff, J. (2003) Intersubjectivity and community building: Learning to learn organizationally. In M. Easterby-Smith and M.A. Lyles (eds.) *Blackwell Handbook of Organizational Learning and Knowledge Management* (1st edn). Oxford, UK: Blackwell Publishers: 161–184.

Prasarnphanich, P. and Wagner, C. (2009) The role of wiki technology and altruism in collaborative knowledge creation. *The Journal of Computer Information Systems*, 49(4): 33–41.

Raman, M. (2006) Wiki technology as a 'free' collaborative tool within an organizational setting. *Information Systems Management*, 23(4): 59–66.

Razmerita, L., Kirchner, K., and Sudzina, F. (2009) Personal knowledge management: The role of Web 2.0 tools for managing knowledge at individual and organizational levels. *Online Information Review*, 33(6): 1021–1039.

Renzl, B. (2008) Trust management and knowledge sharing: The mediating effects of fear and knowledge documentation. *Omega*, 36(2): 206–220.

Robertson, M., Swan, J., and Newell, S. (1996) The role of networks in the diffusion of technological innovation. *Journal of Management Studies*, 33(3): 333–359.

Sambamurthy, V. and Subramani, M. (2005) Special issue on information technologies and knowledge management. *MIS Quarterly*, 29(1): 1–7.

Smith, G. (2004) Folksonomy: Social classification, http://atomiq.org/archives/2004/08/folksonomy_social_classification.html, accessed 11 March 2010.

Smith, H.A. and McKeen, J.D. (2002) Creating and facilitating communities of practice. In C. Holsapple (ed.) *Handbook on Knowledge Management*, Vol 1. New York, NY: Springer-Verlag: 393–407.

Spertus, E., Sahami, M., and Buyukkokten, O. (2005) Evaluating similarity measures: A large-scale study in the Orkut social network. *Proceedings of the Eleventh International Conference on Knowledge Discovery in Data Mining (ACM SIGKDD)*, Chicago, IL: 678–684.

Spinellis, D. and Louridas, P. (2008) The collaborative organization of knowledge. *Communications of the ACM*, 51(8): 68–73.

Strickland, M. (2007) The evolution of Web 3.0. http://www.slideshare.net/mstrickland/the-evolution-of-web-30, accessed 16 March 2010.

Surowiecki, J. (2004) *The Wisdom of Crowds: Why the Many Are Smarter Than the Few and How Collective Wisdom Shapes Business, Economies, Societies and Nations*. New York, NY: Doubleday.

Takeishi, A. (2001) Bridging inter- and intra-firm boundaries: Management of supplier involvement in automobile product development. *Strategic Management Journal*, 22(5): 403–433.

Teece, D.J., Pisano, G., and Shuen, A. (1997) Dynamic capabilities and strategic management. *Strategic Management Journal*, 18(7): 509–533.

von Krogh, G., Nonaka, I., and Aben, M. (2001) Making the most of your company's knowledge: A strategic framework. *Long Range Planning*, 34(4): 421–439.

Wagner, C. and Bolloju, N. (2005) Supporting knowledge management in organizations with conversational technologies: Discussion forums, weblogs and wikis. *Journal of Database Management*, 16(2): 1–8

Wagner, C. and Majchrzak, A. (2006) *The Wiki in Your Company: Lessons for Collaborative Knowledge Management*, SIM APC Report.

Walsh, J.P. and Ungson, G.R. (1991) Organizational memory. *Academy of Management Review*, 16(1): 57–91.

Wasko, M. and Faraj, S. (2000) 'It is what one does:' Why people participate and help others in electronic communities of practice. *Journal of Strategic Information Systems*, 9(2/3): 155–173.

Wasko, M. and Faraj, S. (2005) Why should I share? Examining social capital and knowledge contribution in electronic networks of practice. *MIS Quarterly*, 29(1): 35–57.

Wasko, M. and Teigland, R. (2004) Public goods or virtual commons? Applying theories of public goods, social dilemmas, and collective action to electronic networks of practice. *Journal of Information Technology Theory and Applications*, 6(1): 25–41.

Wenger, E. and Snyder, W.H. (2000) Communities of practice: The organizational frontier. *Harvard Business Review*, 78(1): 139–145.

7

Knowledge Creation in Firms

An Organizational Economics Perspective

NICOLAI J. FOSS AND VOLKER MAHNKE

ABSTRACT

Knowledge creation has emerged as a very important organizational practice and has been extensively treated in a large body of academic work. Surprisingly, however, organizational economics (i.e. transaction cost economics, agency theory, team theory, and property rights theory) has played only a minor role in the development of the knowledge management literature. We argue that organizational economics insights can further the theory and practice of knowledge creation in several ways. Specifically, we apply notions of contracting, team production, complementarities, hold-up, and so on to knowledge management issues (i.e. creating and integration knowledge, rewarding knowledge workers, etc.), and derive from our discussion refutable propositions, to guide empirical research, that are novel to the knowledge management field.

KNOWLEDGE MANAGEMENT: PERILS AND PROMISES

During the last decade or so, knowledge management—a set of management activities, aimed at designing and influencing processes of knowledge creation and integration including processes of sharing knowledge—has emerged as one of the most influential new organizational practices. Numerous companies have experimented with knowledge management initiatives in order to improve their performance. At the same time, the literature on knowledge management has virtually exploded (e.g. Nonaka and Takeuchi 1995; Choo, 1998; von Krogh et al., 2000; Easterby-Smith et al., 2000; Nonaka and von Krogh, 2009).

Knowledge management would thus seem to be one of those areas where managerial practice and the academic literature develop simultaneously and perhaps even co-evolve.

Here knowledge management is not much different from many other management fads of the recent decades such as business process reengineering or total quality management that also promise to contribute to competitive advantage—although this is asserted rather than carefully demonstrated. The analogy goes further, for knowledge management is also akin to these fads in that there is no clear disciplinary foundation for it. Indeed, the underpinnings of knowledge management are a mixed bag, ranging from Eastern philosophical traditions over ideas from organizational behavior to notions from information science. Strikingly (to us, at least), organizational economics plays a limited role in the empirical literature on knowledge management (for recent exceptions see Mahnke and Venzin, 2003; Foss, 2007; Ambos and Mahnke, 2010). However, the knowledge management literature neglects organizational economics at its peril.

Organizational economics looks inside the firm by examining the tasks of motivating and coordinating human activity. It is taken up with explaining the nature of efficient organizational arrangements, and the determinants of such arrangements. Efficiency is understood in the sense of maximizing the joint surplus from productive activities, including processes of creating, sharing, and exploiting knowledge. A basic proposition is that the costs and the benefits of productive activities—and therefore joint surplus—are influenced by the incentives, property rights, and ways of disseminating and processing information that structure productive activities. Perhaps as a result of organizational economics playing at best a small role in the evolution of knowledge management, there is seldom any sustained attention to the *cost* of knowledge management activities. For example, when von Krogh, Ichijo, and Nonaka (2000) in a major survey of the knowledge management literature mention cost, they devote four pages (out of more than 250) to it, and then only treat costs of searching for knowledge, a category of cost that is only one among a multitude of relevant costs of knowledge management.[1] This neglect of organizational costs is quite representative of the whole knowledge management literature. Moreover, we would argue that even the potential *benefits* of alternative ways of organizing knowledge management are ill-understood in the literature. On the managerial level, something similar may be observed. This is, perhaps, best expressed in the words of a knowledge manager, who recently stated to us that:

> [t]he concept of KM for mutual benefit seems self-evident for the enthusiasts, which only increases their puzzlement when others in their organization show apathy or even negative interest in the concept. If there is no offsetting benefit for sharing knowledge in terms of money and recognition, or the process by which one does so is arcane or bureaucratic, or it is difficult to find the right fora, then organizational costs rise and participation drops proportionally.

Because neither the relevant costs of alternative ways of organizing knowledge in organizations, nor their benefits are addressed in any systematic manner in the knowledge

---

[1] von Krogh et al. (2000: 122) further observe that 'search costs are the total costs incurred by an organization's efforts to get individual members or a group to act effectively.' It is not so: search cost is a category that is entirely different from the incentive and coordination costs of getting 'members or a group to act effectively.' More on this later.

management literature, the attendant trade-offs, and how these may be influenced by managerial action also remain ill-understood. The result is that the literature does not allow propositions about *optimal* knowledge management strategies, and how these vary with changes in the relevant parameters, to be made. In other words, in its present manifestation, the knowledge management literature does not constitute a managerially relevant contingency framework; it may supply inspiration (and entertainment) for managers, but not much in the way of firm guidance.

Lest this be taken as a wholesale condemnation of knowledge management, let us state immediately that the knowledge management literature contains numerous salient observations on knowledge processes, that is, processes of creating, sharing, and exploiting knowledge (e.g. Lyles and Schwenk, 1992; Nonaka and Takeuchi, 1995; von Krogh et al., 2000). In addition, the literature does much to identify key characteristics of knowledge structures that surround knowledge processes in terms of knowledge type, knowledge distribution, complexity, and relatedness (e.g. Lyles and Schwenk, 1992; Weick and Roberts, 1993; Galunic and Rodan, 1998). In this chapter, we take some of these ideas as grist for a theoretical mill consisting of organizational economics. In particular, we focus on the *coordination* and *incentive* problems that processes of creating, sharing, and exploiting knowledge inside firms may give rise to, and how various aspects of governance may be understood as a response to such problems. We thus take steps towards meeting the challenge contained in the recent observation that 'the time is ripe to start addressing learning and knowing in the light of inherent conflicts between shareholders' goals, economic pressure, institutionalized professional interest and political agendas' (Easterby-Smith et al., 2000).

The remainder of the chapter is structured as follows. First, we highlight key insights from organizational economics, and briefly sketch general implications for the understanding of knowledge management practices. Second, we show that novel propositions about knowledge management may be derived from organizational economics. We also address from an organizational economics perspective a number of central phenomena (e.g. firm specific learning, teamwork, communities of practice, knowledge integration) that have been discussed in the knowledge management literature. Conclusions follow. A final reservation: our chosen subject in this chapter is a vast one. Considerable narrowing of the issues is necessary for space reasons. Thus, in the following we disregard knowledge management issues that relate to the matter of the boundaries of the firm (e.g. make-or-buy decisions, joint ventures, networks, etc.), and focus solely on knowledge management as it pertains to internal organization.[2]

ORGANIZATIONAL ECONOMICS: A NOVEL PERSPECTIVE ON KNOWLEDGE MANAGEMENT

Overall

Despite beginning as a theory of the existence and optimal scope of the firm (Coase, 1937; Williamson, 1985), during the last twenty years or so organizational economics has

---

[2]We have dealt with the issue of the boundaries of the firm in the context of knowledge management in Foss (2001, 2002) and Mahnke (2001).

increasingly been applied to internal organization issues. In particular, it has directed attention to the coordination and incentive problems that are caused by the pathologies that
unavoidably accompany an internal division of labor, such as asymmetric information,
diluted performance incentives, measurement difficulties, bargaining problems, moral hazard, duplicative (redundant) efforts, etc. In turn, organizational economists have explained
how a host of organizational arrangements, such as various kinds of authority, payment
schemes, delegation of decision rights, etc. serve to alleviate the severity of such problems.

Beginning our brief sampling of organizational economics perspectives, agency theory
perspectives have predominantly addressed issues related to payment schemes (Holmström,
1979, 1989) delegation of decision rights (Fama and Jensen, 1983; Jensen and Meckling,
1992; Aghion and Tirole, 1997), multitasking (Holmström and Milgrom, 1994), and managerial commitment (Baker et al., 1999) under assumptions of moral hazard and asymmetric information. Transaction cost economics (Williamson, 1985, 1996) and property
rights insights (Hart, 1995) have been brought to bear on issues related to allocation
of rights and design of contracts when investments in human capital are firm-specific,
agents may behave in an opportunistic manner, and contracts are incomplete. Team theory (Marschak and Radner, 1972; Casson, 1994; Carter, 1995) has addressed the optimal design of organizational structures, given the bounded rationality of individuals (but
absent conflicts of interest). Finally, work on complementarities between organizational
elements (e.g. payment schemes, delegation of rights, supervision methods, etc.) (Milgrom
and Roberts, 1990, 1995) lends strong formal support to the traditional notion that there
are stable, discrete governance structures that combine organizational elements in predictable ways (Thompson, 1967; Williamson, 1996). It is fair to say that the empirical base
of organizational economics, in terms of the number of corroborations of predictions of
these theories, is fairly strong (Shelanski and Klein, 1995; Prendergast, 2002).

Although organizational economics is constituted by a number of different theories,
nevertheless there are a number of common threads in the literature (cf. Foss, 2000).
On the method level, all of organizational economics is unabashedly 'individualistic'
in the sense that all organizational phenomena should be explained as the outcome of
the choice behavior of individual agents. At the theoretical base, the whole literature is
concerned with 'efficiency,' that is to say, how resources are allocated so that they yield
the maximum possible value. Two closely related implications follow immediately. First, the
organizational economics perspective is intimately taken up with value creation; as
noted, maximizing the value that can be created is the meaning of economic efficiency.
Second, since the allocation of resources is (also) a matter of how the relevant resources
are governed and organized, and since value-creation is dependent upon governance and
organization, it follows that an efficiency perspective allows one to discriminate between
alternative forms of economic organization in terms of efficiency. Rational actors will
choose those organizational forms, contracts, and governance structures that maximize
their joint surplus and will find ways to split this surplus among them.

In turn, the influence of alternative organizational arrangements on value creation
may be analyzed in terms of motivation, knowledge, information, and complementarity—
and how alternative arrangements embody different ways of influencing these variables
(cf. also Buckley and Carter, 1996). These are all in different ways related to those 'transaction costs' that (in various guises) are central in all organizational economics theories,
and the size of which influences the value that may be created from organizing and

governing scarce resources in particular ways. The value that can be created, in the presence of transaction costs, falls short of what may be created in a world with no problems of motivation, knowledge, information, and complementarity (a 'first-best'situation), and, hence, no transaction costs. While such a world may be imagined, it is not the world of managers and other inhabitants of organizations. However, the above may be manipulated so that the organization approaches it. We discuss motivation, knowledge and information, and the coordination of complementary actions *seriatim* in the following.

Motivation

The motivational assumptions of organizational economics have been subject to a good deal of scrutiny and critical discussion. Many scholars in, for example, organizational behavior, have been critical of the seemingly cynical assumptions with respect to human nature that drive much of organizational economics analysis. To these critics, opportunism ('self-interest seeking with guile,' Williamson, 1996) and moral hazard (i.e. using asymmetric information to one's advantage and the other party's disadvantage after a contract has been concluded) are not descriptively accurate. They may furthermore be 'bad for practice' to the extent that managerial action based on prescriptions from these theories may, by treating people as would-be opportunists, lead to self-fulfilling prophecies (Ghoshal and Moran, 1996). However, such motivational assumptions fundamentally serve to highlight the—presumably undisputed—fact that actors often have very different interests; opportunism and similar assumptions are stark ways of highlighting this. Moreover, the motivational assumptions serve to emphasize that economic organizations need to be designed with an eye to the possibility that some (by no means all) actors may act in a morally hazardous or opportunistic manner.

In the context of internal organization, the largest effort so far may well have been devoted to exploring how various aspects of internal organization—from accounting principles over payment methods to the nature and function of hierarchy itself—may be explained as efficient responses to various principal–agent problems. Thus, particular attention has been paid to differences between input and output-based payment, and how the choice between these is determined by the observability of effort and states of nature; the role of monitoring and of subjective and objective performance measurement (Prendergast, 2002); and of how a hierarchical structure may constrain 'rent-seeking,' that is, attempt to influence superiors to one's own advantage (Milgrom, 1988).

One perspective on all this is that various aspects of internal organization arise to curb the resource costs of agents pursuing their own interests in a way that is harmful to the organization. Under an organizational division of labor, management (and the owners of the firm) delegates some rights to employees, ranging from the trivial (the right to work with the company's vacuum cleaner) to the all-important (the right to make decisions on major investment projects). Management wishes these delegated rights to be exercised in an optimal manner. However, since the right holders cannot be constantly monitored, and since performance pay schemes trade-off incentives and risk, some losses (compared to a full-information situation) are usually unavoidable. Internal organization arises as a trade-off between these losses and the costs of designing monitoring schemes, incentive contracts, etc.

A particular set of incentive problems is caused by problems of managerial commitment. For example, often employees wish to specialize their human capital to the firm, thus becoming more productive and hoping to capture some of the marginal productivity created. In other words, they expect to be compensated for their investment. However, by specializing in this way, employees become subject to a potential hold-up problem (Williamson, 1985, 1996; Hart, 1995). To be sure, the possession of specialized knowledge may be a strong bargaining lever. However, there is another strong party to the bargain situation, namely the firm to which the employee specializes. The implication is that employees cannot expect to capture all or even most of the quasi-rent from their specialized human capital investments, which harms incentives to undertake the investments (Hart, 1995). Strong and credible managerial commitment to not using the hold-up option may solve the problem (Kreps, 1990). Another way of solving the problem is to allocate (more) decision rights to employees who undertake human capital investments (Rajan and Zingales, 1998). Thus, in professional service firms, often employees with a long tenure and good demonstrated performance become partners. A final managerial problem has to do with managerial interference in the business of agents to whom the same management have delegated rights (e.g. to run their own projects). This 'problem of selective intervention' (Williamson, 1985) arises because it is often hard for management to commit to not interfering. For example, it is not possible to make a court enforceable contract to prevent managerial interference once decision rights have been delegated. However, arbitrary intervention, the breaking of promises to not intervene, etc., all of which will often be very tempting for management, are very destructive for motivation (Baker et al., 1999; Foss, 2002).

These incentive problems are clearly relevant to the understanding of the costs of knowledge management practices. To the extent that agents' human capital investments consist in the gathering and building-up of specialized knowledge and skills, they are not likely to be willing to share the relevant knowledge and skills with other agents, unless they are properly compensated. They are not going to give up a strong bargaining lever without compensation. However, it is often difficult to contract over knowledge and skills. Moreover, there is a fundamental problem of managerial commitment: since it is difficult to write and enforce contracts on the sharing of the knowledge and the compensation to the employees between those employees who possess important specialized knowledge and the firm, it is tempting for management to renege on the promise after the sharing of knowledge has actually taken place. Two implications of direct relevance for knowledge management follow. First, forced knowledge management initiatives may well be experienced as hold-ups by those agents inside the firm who control specialized knowledge and skills. Their future investment incentives are harmed accordingly. Second, unless these agents can expect to be compensated they are unlikely to share their knowledge at all. It is likely that the best way to handle this (i.e. to invest in human capital *and* to share knowledge embodied in this capital) is by giving the relevant employees appropriate incentives, perhaps even making them partners through providing ownership rights.

Asymmetric knowledge and information

Even if agents can be motivated to take actions (i.e. exploit their decision rights) that are 'incentive-compatible' with those of other agents or principals, there is still no guarantee that they will also make optimal (i.e. value maximizing) choices. Willingness is not the same as ability. To some extent this is a problem of information transmission: under an organizational division of labor, no agent inside the firm is likely to have all the information needed for making an optimal choice, and transmitting all of this information to him or her is prohibitively costly. Delegation may arise as a cost economizing response to this. However, it is also a matter of the often fleeting, subjective, and tacit character of knowledge—a favorite theme of the knowledge management literature. As Hayek famously argued:

> The peculiar character of the problem of a rational economic order is determined precisely by the fact that the knowledge of the circumstances of which we must make use never exists in concentrated or integrated form but solely as the dispersed bits of incomplete and frequently contradictory knowledge which all the separate individuals possess. The economic problem of society is thus not merely a problem of how to allocate 'given' resources—if 'given' is taken to mean given to a single mind which deliberately solves the problem set by these 'data'. It is rather a problem of how to secure the best use of resources known to any of the members of society, for ends whose relative importance only these individuals know. Or, to put it briefly, it is a problem of the utilization of knowledge which is not given to anyone in its totality.
>
> (Hayek, 1945)

Arguably, firms face this problem of dispersed knowledge to a smaller extent than societies do; however, it is still relevant to them. Firms may cope with the problem in different ways. Again, they may delegate decision rights so that these rights are co-aligned with those who possess the relevant knowledge, balancing the attendant benefits with the agency costs that are caused by delegation (Jensen and Meckling, 1992). However, knowledge sharing is an alternative to this. Thus, rather than delegating decision rights in order to better utilize local knowledge, the existing rights structure (i.e. existing authority relations, payment schemes, organizational structures, etc.) remains unchanged and the relevant knowledge is gathered and shared among those who can make profitable use of this knowledge. Such knowledge sharing is, of course, a key focus of knowledge management.

However, in the knowledge management literature, knowledge sharing is often discussed and endorsed without any examination of the *alternative* of delegating rights so that knowledge is better utilized in this way. An organizational economics perspective not only identifies the relevant (organizational) alternatives, but also allows us to say something about the costs and benefits of these alternatives. Thus, one obvious advantage of the knowledge-sharing alternative is that it does not necessarily involve any delegation of decision rights. Knowledge sharing, as portrayed in the knowledge management literature, may therefore impose smaller agency costs on an organization than the alternative of delegating decision rights. However, there are *other* costs to consider when the choice has to be made between the two alternatives of knowledge sharing and delegating decision rights. For whereas knowledge sharing that takes place within an existing organizational structure may not impose the same agency costs as delegating decision rights does, knowledge sharing is likely to impose higher costs of, for example, communicating, storing, and retrieving knowledge than the delegation alternative. The point is not here that specialized IT systems have to be set up in order to reach the goal of knowledge sharing. Rather, the point is that knowledge sharing may introduce costs that are caused by the bounded rationality of individuals, that is, their limited ability to identify, absorb, process, remember, and so on, knowledge. And, of course, there are costs associated with trying to transform knowledge that only exists in a tacit form into an articulate form. As Hayek (1945) argued, decentralization economizes on these costs. In firms, delegation may be an attractive means of economizing on the costs associated with bounded rationality and tacit knowledge (Jensen and Meckling, 1992). The bottom line is that a full assessment of what alternative is superior in a specific situation—the improved utilization of knowledge by means of knowledge sharing or delegation of decision rights—generates a number of costs that have to be balanced against the relevant benefits. In its present manifestation, the knowledge management literature identifies neither the relevant alternatives nor the relevant net benefits.

The coordination of complementary actions

Even if agents can be motivated to take incentive-compatible actions and even if they possess the right information or knowledge (because they are specialists or because this information or knowledge is somehow transmitted to them), there is still a problem of coordinating actions inside the firm. In particular, the more complementary actions are, the more closely they need to be coordinated. Through the use of the price mechanism, markets cope well with the coordination problem (Hayek, 1945). However, the more complementary actions are, the more necessary is it to supplement the use of the price mechanism with other mechanisms, such as communication (Richardson, 1972). Firms have only limited access to the price mechanism, but they may have privileged access to the mechanism of communication (relative to markets). In this perspective, one advantage of knowledge management may actually be that it assists the coordination of complementary actions by spreading knowledge, effectively bringing about common knowledge conditions (see Foss, 2001 for such an argument). Knowledge management thus reduces what Koopmans referred to as 'secondary uncertainty:'

> In a rough and intuitive judgment the secondary uncertainty arising from a lack of communication, that is, from one decision maker having no way of finding out the concurrent decisions and plans made by others . . . is quantitatively at least as important as the primary uncertainty arising from random acts of nature and unpredictable changes in consumers' preferences.
>
> Koopmans (1957: 162–163)

When the acquisition (creation, sourcing) of knowledge in a firm is delegated to specialist knowledge workers, the firm faces this kind of secondary uncertainty (cf. Buckley and Carter, 1999). One possible function of knowledge management is thus to reduce secondary uncertainty, although this is not one that is identified in the knowledge management literature.

Summing up: Organizational economics aspects of knowledge management

In the frictionless world that dominated microeconomics textbooks before the revolution in information, property rights, and transaction costs economics about three decades ago, there are no problems of motivation, knowledge, information, and coordination. In this nirvana, resources, including knowledge resources, are allocated in the best possible way ('first-best'). Contracts can be written and enforced without cost and information is free. Therefore, there are no losses from lacking motivation, defective or missing knowledge, or coordination that goes wrong. There are no problems of exchanging knowledge either, so that markets are as efficient for this purpose as firms are. However, in a more realistic world, contracts are imperfect so that, for example, it is hard and perhaps impossible to write contracts that compensate those who 'give up' (i.e. share) valuable knowledge; commitment (including managerial commitment) may be broken; employees may be held-up by management so that their incentives to invest in and share knowledge are harmed, etc. Lest managers live in a paradise or nirvana, knowledge management practices are subject to these incentive costs.

The argument so far is therefore that organizational economics is able to illuminate the practice of knowledge management in important ways. In particular, by focusing on incentive compatibility problems, particularly as these relate to issues of investing in the production and sharing of knowledge, organizational economics identifies important, but hitherto neglected, incentive costs and benefits of knowledge management practices. This is the reason why organizational economics should be seen as an indispensable part of the disciplinary foundation of knowledge management. In the following section we deal further with processes of knowledge creation and integration in an organizational economics perspective.

KNOWLEDGE MANAGEMENT: ORGANIZATIONAL ECONOMIC INSIGHTS

In this section, we shall more concretely apply specific organizational economics insights to two clearly central aspects of knowledge management: knowledge creation and knowledge integration. The former category encompasses learning (by doing, using, being instructed, etc.) and innovation processes such as knowledge combination, while the latter refers to how to make best use of existing knowledge in the firm. We develop propositions based on organizational economics regarding how firms may stimulate investments by employees in firm specific knowledge, resolve incentive problems in knowledge-creating teams, and make choices between alternative means in the integration of knowledge, including knowledge sharing.

Knowledge creation

It is now almost an axiom that knowledge creation in firms lies at the heart of competitive advantage (Nonaka and Takeuchi, 1995; von Krogh et al., 2000; Nonaka and von Krogh, 2009). Expressions such as 'firms learn' and 'firms know' have become commonplace in much of the strategy and knowledge management literature.[3] However, it is not firms as such that learn, and firms themselves do not possess knowledge. So-called 'firm knowledge' is composed of knowledge sets controlled by individual agents. We stress this admittedly basic methodological individualist point in order to emphasize the point that

---

[3]Part of the motivation for the interest in, and growth of, various knowledge-oriented approaches to organizations appears to be the widespread belief that organizational economics approaches to organizations have very little to offer with respect to an understanding of learning processes in firms (Kogut and Zander, 1992; Madhok, 1996). This is, in our view, something of a misunderstanding. It is true that organizational economics approaches do not conceptualize firms as knowledge-based entities *per se*. However, that does not mean that it has little to offer of the processes whereby knowledge is created in firms.

by focusing on the level of the individual agent, rather than the firm, organizational economics highlights questions that are neglected in the knowledge management literature *because* much of this literature operates on the firm level and does not have an explicitly individualistic starting point.

In particular, an organizational economics perspective directs attention to the possible incentive conflicts that may arise in connection with issues such as, for example,

> *How can employees be induced to making firm-specific human capital investments?*
> *How can firms enable knowledge creation in teams?*

Perhaps somewhat contrary to intuition, such questions are central to successful knowledge management in practice and they are particularly prone to an organizational economics treatment. This is because processes of creating knowledge—for example, in the form of innovation projects—are typically risky, unpredictable (the knowledge-to-be-created can only be partly foreseen), often long term, labor intensive, idiosyncratic (that is, hard to compare to other processes), and often require substantial human capital investments (Holmström, 1989). A number of these characteristics are the basic stuff that contracting problems are made of.[4] In the following we discuss a number of ways in which firms may motivate employees to expend effort in the production of new knowledge. In this connection, we discuss how the return stream from such new knowledge is shared between the firm and the employee. Thus, the problems of motivating employees and capturing rents from new knowledge are two sides of the same coin.

We assume throughout that an asymmetric information setting prevails, and that incentive conflicts are present. To see why these assumptions are appropriate ones, consider a world where asymmetric information and incentive conflicts (agency problems, hold-up problems) are absent. Here, the interests of the various agents involved in the creation of new knowledge can be easily aligned. First, employees and employers would assess the value of new knowledge in the same way (because information about this is symmetric). Second, bargaining will take place immediately, because the symmetry of information means that there will be no strategic behavior. Third, the employee's reward for any learning investments will be guaranteed since the employer will not attempt to hold-up the employee. In a nirvana world where both employee and employer access the same information on the value of ideas and each other's outside options, inducing optimal human capital investment can be achieved by writing complete contracts. If more realistic assumptions are introduced, an incentive perspective on knowledge creation is particularly

---

[4]For example, incentives need to be provided so that agents are motivated to supply an efficient (i.e. second-best) level of effort, and undertake the required human capital investments; care must be exercised in connection with multi-stage projects where the firm may wish to stop projects at a certain stage and the project leader (who may be better informed) may not; risk-allocation is particularly pertinent here; etc. This is not to say that understanding knowledge creation is trivial in the context of organizational economics—far from it. In fact, because processes of knowledge creation are more uncertain in terms of the variance of the benefit distribution, and because the distribution of those benefits over time is harder to anticipate than in the case of more routine investment projects, analysis is comparatively more complicated.

appropriate, because it stresses not only that agents making learning investments must somehow share in the extra surplus from those investments to be properly motivated, but also that providing such motivation is no easy matter under asymmetric information, possibly incomplete contracts, and self-interested behavior.

Earning rents from knowledge creation. The knowledge management literature seldom makes clear exactly how the mechanism from knowledge creation to new rents works. However, the resource-based view in strategic management has gone some way towards clarifying this by identifying a set of criteria that resources must meet to be sources of (sustained) competitive advantages, such as being valuable, rare, and costly to imitate (Barney, 1991). Moreover, the relevant resources should not be fully mobile (Peteraf, 1993). Knowledge assets, particularly newly created ones, are particularly likely to meet these criteria (Winter, 1987). Given this, managers may wish to induce knowledge creation by means of providing incentives to employees to upgrade their own knowledge capital and by spending corporate resources on having employees do this (e.g. training, setting up incentives, etc.). From the perspective of the firm, earning rents from employee upgrading of knowledge is far from trivial. For example, accumulation of valuable knowledge capital in firms may require employees to make asset specific learning investments. In particular, whether or not firms are likely to earn rents from employees' knowledge depends on (1) the type of learning investment (e.g. firm specific or general knowledge); (2) the resolution of agency conflicts in firms (e.g. remuneration schemes and promotion rules); and (3) transaction costs in labor markets (e.g. signaling and screening). We consider these *seriatim.*

Types of learning investments. Firms' investments in augmenting the knowledge of their employees may be of two kinds, namely general and firm-specific ones. Both may increase an employee's productivity, but they have different implications with respect to who is likely to appropriate the returns and who will carry the costs of the investment. General learning investments may increase an employee's productivity in a range of employment opportunities. Such general investments include the learning of languages and generic skills, such as learning word processing programs, for example, that are equally useful for current and potential employers. Becker (1962) suggests that employees will pay for their general training, because in competitive markets they are the sole beneficiaries of the improvements of their productivity. A firm will not pay for an employee's learning of general knowledge, because of the weakness of its bargaining position after having made the investment. In contrast, the learning of firm-specific knowledge restricts an employee's possibility to capture returns on this knowledge outside of the firm that undertakes the investment. Becker (1962) argues that to the extent that an employee's productivity increase exceeds his or her wage increase after learning, the firm can earn rents even if it alone incurs the costs of firm specific learning investments. As far as such investments are concerned, the relative bargaining position of firms is strong because employees cannot credibly threaten to leave the firm to bargain for higher wages that reflect their productivity increase after specific learning investments. Thus, it is very likely that firms will appropriate a substantial part of the relevant rents. Of course, firms that undertake more specific learning investments will also create more rents, because the benefits (e.g. in terms of productivity or increased innovativeness) are larger to the firm in the case of specific than in general learning investments. Thus, the following refutable proposition may be put forward:

P1: Firms with a high ratio of specific to general learning investments will earn and appropriate relatively more rents than firms with a low ratio.

Inducing firm specific learning

Consider next the situation from the perspective of employees. From their point of view, learning is an investment of effort for which they wish to be compensated. Firms will have to provide inducements for such investments. However, as we have seen, making firm-specific learning investments restricts an employee's outside employment options (and therefore his or her bargaining power), which will tend to reduce firm-specific learning investments below the optimal level. Due to the incentive problem, undertaking these investments means becoming more vulnerable to managerial hold-ups. Resolving this problem turns on management's ability to credibly signal that it will not take advantage of employees who by making firm-specific learning investments have put themselves at risk. An organizational economics interpretation of (beneficial) corporate culture is that it is essentially an embodiment of such signals (Kreps, 1990). Thus, firms with corporate cultures that credibly signal that management is committed to a non-opportunistic approach in dealing with subordinates will induce higher learning investments on the part of employees. Such a corporate culture makes the provision of incentives credible, so that employees correctly believe that management will not renege on promises with respect to compensation. With respect to the issue of providing incentives for employees' investment in firm specific knowledge, organizational economics suggests at least four solutions:

◆ high-powered incentives (i.e. making employees more of residual claimants);
◆ promotion rules; and
◆ conferring access to critical resources.
◆ making credible commitments

Consider these in turn.

High-powered incentives   High-powered incentives—often represented as the contingent portion of pay—may be used to induce contributions through providing larger shares of quasi-rents to employees (Williamson, 1996). Firm specific learning investments may be induced by providing equity to employees (e.g. in the form of stock options or equity) or other high-powered incentives, such as performance pay (Demsetz and Lehn, 1989; Williamson, 1985). However, offering such high-powered incentives may also lead to a number of distortions. This is the case, for example, when the corresponding costs (e.g. of using the firms' assets) are not borne by those to whom high-powered incentives are offered (Holmström, 1989). Thus, as Williamson (1985) argues, this is exactly why incentives in firms are often comparatively low-powered. Another problem with high-powered incentives is that they expose employees to considerable risks. For example, performance (e.g. the value of stock options) may fluctuate for reasons beyond an employee's control. In addition, employees may be highly dependent on the fixed, risk free part of their income if they lack alternative sources of income. Risk-averse employees may therefore shy away from high-powered incentives. On the other hand, risk estimates may be in the eye of the beholder, and more highly skilled employees may judge risk differently from other employees.

Moreover, for incentive pay to be effective, either observability of output or behavior must prevail. If behaviors or output for tasks cannot be specified as cause-effect relationships are not well understood, then high performance ambiguity poses a problem because neither behaviors nor outputs can be related to specific skill acquisition with any precision. Thus, the less output and behavior can be pre-specified so as to reflect employees' specific skill development, then the less effective high-powered incentives become (Ouchi, 1980). Thus, the following refutable proposition may be put forward:

P2: The use of high-powered incentives to induce firm specific learning will be more common in firms with higher skilled, wealthier employees, and pre-specified output.

Promotion rules   The design of promotion rules is an alternative way of inducing firm specific learning investments. Consider inducing investments in firm-specific knowledge by means of 'up-or-stay' rules (e.g. the worker is either promoted or stays in the original job) relative to 'up-or-out' rules (e.g. the worker is promoted or fired) (Prendergast, 1993; Huberman and Kahn, 1988; Gibbons, 1998). Generally, when workers bear the costs of acquiring specific skills they will do so only if the wage (W^s) obtainable after skill acquisition minus their opportunity costs (C^s) exceeds current payment (W^{us}). The principal will pay the wage (W^s) only if the productivity difference ($P^s - P^{us}$) exceeds the difference of wages ($W^s - W^{us}$). With 'up-or-stay' rules principals distinguish jobs and attach different wages to them. This promotion rule creates a tension between needing a large enough wage gap to induce the worker to invest and keeping the gap small enough so that the principal is willing to promote the worker after the worker has invested (Prendergast, 1993). Gibbons (1998) illustrates this point, as follows.

For example, suppose that an untrained worker produces 10 in the easy job, that a trained worker produces 20 in the easy job and 30 in the difficult job, and that the opportunity cost of training is 15. Then training is efficient ($30 - 10 > 15$) but we cannot find wages that simultaneously induce the worker to invest (wage difference greater than opportunity cost, 15) and induce the firm to promote a trained worker (wage difference smaller than productivity difference, $30 - 20$). As a consequence, employees' investment in firm-specific skills may be low, *although* such investments would be efficient. Huberman and Kahn (1988) suggest that 'up-or-out rules' can solve this incentive problem. For example, with this rule the principal makes a commitment to promote the worker after a pre-specified time span or otherwise fire him (e.g. tenure in academic jobs, moving up career ladders in consultancies). The resulting rat-race creates incentives for investments in firm-specific knowledge. To illustrate, consider the example above. As before, specific learning investments only lead to firm rents when they are efficient ($P^s - P^{us} > 15$). If a worker expects promotion, he or she will invest at any wage (W^*) which exceeds his or her opportunity costs plus the best alternative (e.g. $W^* > W^{ALT} + 15$). The principal promotes the worker if his or her productivity (P^s) exceeds his or her high wage ($P^s > W^*$). Although with up-or-out rules there is always a wage (W^*) that is low enough to induce the principal to promote the worker who has made sufficient investments in firm-specific capital, up-or-out rules come at a cost. Because it is not possible to keep the worker in the firm when the productivity after investment does not exceed his or her high salary, this up-or-out rule may waste investments in firm-specific skills. This is especially obvious when there are different layers where such up-or out rules apply and workers survive the first rounds but drop out at a higher level (cf. Gibbons, 1998).[5] Thus, the following refutable proposition may be put forward:

> P3: Firms utilizing up-or-out rules will induce higher investments in firm specific human capital than firms using up-or-stay rules.

Additionally, once employees have invested in firm specific capital, a firm also needs to tie employees long enough to the firm, so that firm specific human capital investments can be recouped. Turnover of key knowledge carriers is a major problem in this respect. Typically, to prevent turnover from happening firms use deferred rewards and pensions, which benefit employees only in the distant future (Milgrom and Roberts, 1990).

Providing access to assets   Firms may positively influence learning investments by providing access to critical resources (Rajan and Zingales, 1998), such as critical knowledge resources. Access may be defined as the ability to use or work with a critical resource including other human resources. It generates an opportunity for employees to specialize relatively to these assets. We earlier analyzed this as giving rise to a potential hold-up problem, since the firm may hold-up the specialized employee. However, the other side of the coin is that specialization to a critical asset in combination with an employee's right to withdraw his or her (also critical) human capital gives him or her considerable bargaining power with respect to the sharing of the surplus from productive activities, that is, bargain for a higher salary. It can be shown that when investments are additive (i.e. the total surplus is dependent on the sum of the investments), granting access and, as it were, giving away bargaining power, may be a superior incentive mechanism to induce firm specific learning. In contrast, when investments are complementary (i.e. the marginal return of one investment rises in the level of the other investment), which is likely to take place in team-based firms, we are back to the familiar hold-up problem (Williamson, 1985; Hart, 1995). Not only will the employee directly influence the size of the surplus if he or she withdraws their human capital; he or she will also influence it indirectly, because his or her human capital investments are complementary to the human capital investments of other employees. In this situation, it will not be advantageous to grant the employee (too much) access (see Rajan and Zingales, 1998 for details).

The three mechanisms above (incentives, promotion rules, access to resources) may be substitutes or complements, depending on the circumstances. Thus, tournaments in the form of up-or-out rules may be a substitute for performance pay when employees are sufficiently risk-averse. Access may replace incentives in the same situation. Promotion rules and incentives may be swapped for access, when giving an employee access would be giving him or her too much bargaining power. On the other hand, all three mechanisms are

---

[5]This argument holds important lessons for remuneration practices and career paths in consultancies, which employ up-or-out rules. When senior consultants do not make enough investments to be qualified as a partner, they are fired, but their value to the firm may exceed their value in the best alternative due to previously acquired firm-specific skills. Firing thus means that firms waste firm specific investments in human capital. Thus, although up-or-out rules may be better than up-or-stay rules, they are still inefficient compared to the first-best.

often seen together; for example, in consultancies partners have obtained their position through a tournament that works according to certain promotion rules, they are granted access to assets contingent on learning investments, and they are usually residual claimants. We may now put forward the following proposition:

P4: Firms that resolve incentive conflicts in knowledge production by means of incentives (and/or promotion rules and/or deferred payment and/or access) will gain competitive advantage relative to firms that do not use these means.

Making credible commitments   The above analysis of firm-specific human capital has made the simplifying assumption that costs of concluding labor market transactions can be neglected. This, of course, is not the case as such costs aggravate complications of inducing firm specific investments. Asymmetric information between current and potential employers is one source of switching costs in labor markets (Akerlof, 1970). Employees must search for new job opportunities and firms must search for fitting employees. In this search process, there may be several complications. For example, a current employer usually knows more about employees' human capital and learning ability than potential employers do (Spence, 1973, 1974). In wage negotiations employees will have to credibly signal to new employers their ability to perform. However, because some employees will overstate their ability in order to drive up wages, employers will not only incur costs of screening employees, but may also reduce wages offered to account for the risk of picking a wrong employee (i.e. a lemon). If this is the case, employees willing to switch from their current employer would find the wage offered by new employers unattractive. The higher transaction costs in labor markets are, the more difficult it is for employees to switch between employers. By implication, high transaction costs in labor markets lower incentives for employees to invest in firm specific knowledge without appropriate safeguarding and compensation. Thus, firms that operate in labor markets with high transaction costs will incur greater costs to induce employee's firm specific learning compared to firms that do not.

One particularly interesting way to induce firm specific learning in such situations is to offer employees the possibility to engage in the acquisition of certified general knowledge such as management training or language and computer skills (Laing, 1994). Employees might face lower lock-in as a result, because the acquisition of certified general skills reduces labor market transaction costs such as screening and matching (Spence, 1974; Barzel, 1982). Nonetheless, a firm offering such general training possibilities to its employees can benefit in several ways. First, investments in general skills can increase the productivity effects of firm-specific skill investments because common knowledge between employees facilitates the combination and blending of specific skills (Kogut and Zander, 1992; Foss, 2001). Second, sponsoring general training as a form of pay also signals the commitment of employers to their employees (Kreps, 1990), and that their investments in firm-specific knowledge will not be opportunistically exploited. Thus, the following refutable proposition may be put forward:

P5: Firms sponsoring certified acquisition of general skills as a form of merit pay will induce higher employee investments in firm specific human capital.

Knowledge creation in teams

Many contributions to the knowledge management literature recommend the use of teams in the form of work groups, inter-disciplinary, and cross-functional teams to foster knowledge creation (e.g. Brown and Eisenhardt, 1995; Meyer and deTore, 1999; von Krogh et al., 2000). Teamwork may bring knowledge together that hitherto existed separately, resulting in 'new combinations' (Schumpeter, 1950); it may facilitate cross-functional communication, cross-fertilization of ideas, and enhance worker involvement. Through the integration of knowledge of individual members, teams may not only blend knowledge and insights beyond what individual members may achieve, but the development of new knowledge may also be stimulated by conversations and language-based learning in teams (Brown and Duguid, 1991; Nonaka and Takeuchi, 1995). However, while knowledge creation in teams has its virtues, there are special difficulties associated with aligning interests of team members (Scott and Einstein, 2001). Not only will teams be particularly prone to moral hazard, notably in the form of shirking, but the right form of incentive may also be contingent on the type of team at hand. Questions arise that remain neglected in the knowledge management literature such as: Who should be rewarded—teams or individuals? Who should evaluate contributions of team members—other team members, a specialized monitor, or an external manager? What measures of performance should be used and when? An organizational economics perspective suggests that the success of teams' knowledge-creating efforts depend, *inter alia*, on (1) the size of the team, (2) trade-offs between individual and team incentives, (3) exclusion rules, and (4) matching the varying degrees of uncertainty to incentive design.[6]

Free rider problems and team size   Alchian and Demsetz provide a classic treatment of incentive problems in team-production—a process 'wherein individual cooperating inputs do not yield identifiable, separate outputs' (1972: 779). Where measuring individual input productivity and rewarding accordingly become difficult, team members may free-ride on other team-members' contribution to knowledge creation. This is so because the benefits of withholding marginal effort accrue to each shirking member while the resulting losses accrue to the team as a whole. In principle, knowledge production in teams could be organized through a set of bilateral agreements between team members who promise best effort and ensure mutual control. However, such agreements are difficult to manage and will most likely incur large resource costs; for example, time spent on negotiation and haggling means that less time is available for knowledge creation. As teams grow in size, the larger these costs become, in fact, they increase exponentially with

---

[6]A further complication prevails when intrinsic motivation is an important consideration. In that case, high-powered (extrinsic) incentives may be counter-productive (Kreps, 1997). Moreover, social comparison processes may complicate the situation further. When such processes are strong, team members may be rewarded as a unit, rather than individually because differential individual rewards impede cooperation (Balkin and Gomez-Mejia, 1992; Jones, 1987; Ouchi, 1980). However, sometimes differentiated incentives may be used, particularly when it is up to the team itself to reward performance. Pfeffer and Langton (1993) add that distributive justice relates to individuals' perception of whether they are receiving a fair share of the available rewards, proportionately to their contribution to the group, personal risk, and responsibility assumed.

the number of team members (Rosen, 1991). In addition, free rider problems become more prevalent, the larger the knowledge-creating team becomes. Thus, one can derive the following refutable proposition:

P6: Knowledge creation in teams will be less effective the larger the team size because shirking and free-riding will increase.

Individual and/or team incentives   Team size problems are aggravated if incentives are exclusively allocated to a team as a whole rather than also considering incentives for individuals (Laursen and Mahnke, 2001). When capable and willing team members are forced to support free riders, they often withdraw effort or else leave the team. On the other hand, relying exclusively on individual incentives can inhibit cooperation in teams—especially when task performance crucially depends on the exchange of information and mutual adaptation (Thompson, 1967; Balkin and Gomez-Mejia, 1992). Nonetheless, many recommendations in the knowledge management literature are mistaken when they note that individual rewards may be the antithesis to teamwork. An organizational economics perspective urges managers not to neglect possibilities to induce individual contributions on which team performance ultimately rests.

One possibility for resolving incentive conflicts in the knowledge-creating team is that a team member specializes in monitoring other members' contributions to generate reliable information based on which rewards may be distributed (Alchian and Demsetz, 1972). A positive effect of monitoring is that knowledge about talents is discovered which can be used to reduce shirking but can also lead to better recombination or new uses of skills and talent. However, as specialized monitors become increasingly removed from actual teamwork, possible knowledge gaps between those creating new knowledge and those specializing in monitoring may increase over time, eventually compromising effective monitoring. As an alternative, management may provide incentives for achievements of the group as a whole and let the group members distribute team rewards among themselves based on subjective performance evaluation (e.g. 360 degree reviews).[7] This utilizes the fact that team members will often have information about each other's contributions, behavior, and ability that is superior to that of external management (Gibbons, 1998). Thus, specialized incentive procedures may cope with some of the incentive problems by combining incentives to teams with incentives to individual team members. This leads us to the following refutable proposition:

P7: Knowledge creation in teams will be more effective in firms that use combinations of team based and individual incentives.

Exclusion rules   We mentioned earlier that firms often use promotion rules in order to solve incentive conflicts by setting up competition between employees. Similar mechanisms may reduce incentive problems in teams. Lazear (1989) suggests that tournaments may involve self-selection and exclusion mechanisms. These drive up effort levels, because

---

[7]Such exercises can be associated with 360 degree feedback mechanisms. For a review of this vast and specialized literature, see Baron (1988).

only those who believe in their survival and exercise effort and skills in a team's knowledge creation effort are attracted (Dillard and Fisher, 1990). In particular, giving teams the right to exclude team members (Lazear, 1989; Malcomson, 1998) on the basis of subjective performance measures (e.g. peer evaluation, group leader assessment, or a combination) is clearly relevant in this context.

Setting up tournaments inside firms may be a viable control mechanism in team-based knowledge creation. But it can also be dangerous. If tournament rules cannot exclude sabotage among team members they may lead to outright breakdown of knowledge creation in teams (Lazear, 1989). An exaggerated emphasis on competition may also drive out exploration by team members who prefer to make quick wins through exploiting ideas of others rather than exploring new ideas on their own. This has two harmful effects on the knowledge-creating team (March, 1994). First, explorers benefit from developing absorptive capacity based on which they can pick up good ideas that others engaged in the same team process cannot exploit on their own. The less others involved in the knowledge-creating team are able to develop and exploit ideas themselves, the more important it becomes that others can relate to their ideas. Second, as team members increasingly engage in exploitation to the neglect of exploration, fewer ideas are available for exploitation. When competition provides disincentives for exploration and the revealing of ideas openly, the loss of relative absorptive capacity (Lane and Lubatkin, 1998) among team members diminishes the capacity for knowledge creation in the team as a whole.[8] Thus, we suggest the following refutable proposition:

P8: Knowledge creation in teams will be more effective the more team members are entitled to exclude non-exploring team members by self-selection.

Uncertainty and team types   Knowledge-creating teams may operate under varying degrees of means and end uncertainty. To illustrate, the knowledge management literature distinguishes two types of knowledge-creating teams: 'communities of practice' and learning in 'epistemic groups.' The former denotes a team of peers who learn during and about the execution of pre-specified tasks with defined outcomes (Lave and Wenger, 1990; Brown and Duguid, 1991; Brown and Duguid, 1998).[9] The key problem is how to create knowledge about means whose ends are well known. Examples include how to fix a working process that has broken down, how to deal with customer demands more quickly, etc. By contrast, 'epistemic communities' deal with knowledge creation for non-routine problems whose ends and means cannot be specified *ex ante* (Cohen, 1998). Here the key

---

[8]In the words of March (1994: 248): 'Since returns from exploration are preliminary returns from absorbing ideas generated by others, those returns are insignificant if no one else is engaging in exploration. As long as nobody else is engaging in exploration, there is inadequate incentive for any individual participant—or potential new entrant—to do so.'

[9]For example, Brown and Duguid (1991) in a study of informal networks among Xerox repair representatives illustrate how informal 'war stories' about painstaking customers and unusual repairs helped its members to deal with situations in their daily practices that were nowhere in the official manuals of the company. Learning in communities of practice is task-oriented, in the sense that there is less uncertainty about what should be achieved than about how to achieve it.

problem is how to discover means for ends that are unknown at the time the team starts developing knowledge. An example comes from a knowledge management team at a software security firm that described their situation as follows: 'In 2–3 years' time, our company will be designing security products we don't know, incorporating technologies which haven't been invented, made in processes yet to be defined, by people we have not yet recruited.'

One complication of means and ends uncertainty is that both complicate the provision of incentives in a team. This is because measurement bases for the provision of incentives become increasingly noisy the less means and end can be pre-specified *ex ante*. In other words: uncertainty leads to performance ambiguity, which complicates the provision of incentives (Ouchi, 1980). Only if performance ambiguity is low does performance pay seem effective in aligning conflicting interest. If this is not the case, variable rewards might be appropriate if pay and control can relate to specified behavior or to other forms of standardization (e.g. processes) which can serve as a basis for measuring performance. Unfortunately, to the extent that standardization of behavior or processes is prevented, such as in the case of many epistemic communities, neither behaviors nor outputs can be determined with precision. In this case, Ouchi (1980) suggests, clan control might be the solution to promote cooperation and mitigate conflict of interest: the basis of control becomes a set of internalized values and norms. It should be noted, however, that clan control can lead to normative fixation and group thinking that are both detrimental rather than conducive to knowledge creation in teams (e.g. Grandori, 2001). Comprehensive empirical research regarding managerial control dilemmas in knowledge-creating teams remains sparse and inconclusive. However, contrary to popular recommendations in the literature to abandon incentives in favor of normative control altogether,[10] recent evidence shows that incentives for knowledge-creating teams seem to prevail in practice across a number of industries (Laursen and Mahnke, 2001; Laursen and Foss, 2002). An organizational economics perspective on knowledge creation would not expect otherwise. Thus, we suggest the following refutable proposition:

P9: Teams employing combinations of individual incentives, team incentives, and exclusion rules will be more effective at knowledge creation than teams relying on clan control.

Nonetheless, as we move from inducing individual learning to knowledge creation in teams, complications of providing incentives have vastly increased. Given these complications of knowledge creation in teams, an organizational economics perspective suggests that team-based learning is a particularly expensive knowledge-creation mechanism that is riddled with many problems that include but are not limited to providing incentives.

---

[10]Recent contributions to the knowledge management literature have suggested creating a knowledge-creating atmosphere (Prusak and Davenport, 1998), generating corporate spirit, or enhancing a climate of mutual care based on reciprocity (von Krogh, 1998). Additionally, appeals are made to intrinsic motivation (McGregor, 1960; Deci, 1975), peer recognition, or symbolic rewards such as Texas Instruments' annual 'best practice celebration and sharing day' (O'Dell and Grayson, 1998). We agree. However, while these possibilities play their part in stimulating knowledge creation, explicit forms of incentives may also supplement them.

Seen this way, organizational economic insights might serve as reminders that knowledge creation in teams yields benefits at substantial costs. These may be compared to the benefits and costs of individual learning in firms as well as hiring of external expertise in the form of employment or contingent work, two alternative mechanisms of organizational learning (Simon, 1991).

Integrating knowledge: insights from organizational economics

Organizational economic insights (Coase, 1937; Demsetz, 1988; Jensen and Meckling, 1992; Williamson, 1985) have already substantially fertilized the literature on knowledge in organizations that characterizes the firm as a knowledge-integrating institution (Conner and Prahalad, 1996; Grant, 1996; Kogut and Zander, 1992, 1993).[11] Therefore, this section is restricted to briefly reviewing key insights on knowledge integration needs and mechanisms.[12]

Specialization of tasks leads to focused learning in narrowly defined domains (Smith, 1978). However, because the division of tasks also leads to the division of knowledge, knowledge integration may be required when several activities are interdependent and individuals need to adapt their action to each other (Thompson, 1967). If individuals are specialized in different knowledge domains this will limit the rate at which knowledge that lies outside a narrow specialization can be assimilated, accumulated, and applied (Simon, 1991; Lane and Lubatkin, 1998). Three coordination mechanisms may be conducive to address such knowledge-integration problems—direction, common knowledge, and autonomous adaptation—but their efficacy may vary with varying task dependencies at hand.

Autonomous adaptation is the marvel of market. As Hayek (1945) argues, markets (be they between or in companies) make individuals do desirable things without anyone having to tell them how to do them. While the price mechanism economizes on investments in common knowledge, it only facilitates thin communication among individuals that co-ordinate their tasks and action. Its applicability may also be limited to situations where task-coordination is signified by low uncertainty and low interdependence between tasks that make autonomous adaptation possible (Grandori, 2001). Moreover, pricing knowledge in exchange faces a fundamental paradox: the value of knowledge to a purchaser is not known until after the knowledge is revealed; however, once revealed, the purchaser has no need to pay for it (Arrow, 1984). Second, Arrow also argues that 'authority, the centralization of decision-making, serves to economize on the transmission and handling of knowledge' (Arrow, 1974: 69). Demsetz (1988) agrees when he suggests that '[d]irection substitutes for education (that is, for the transfer of the knowledge itself).' For example, employees transfer

---

[11]There are also several studies on product development that have argued that varying degrees of knowledge integration is conducive to explain firm performance (e.g. Clark and Fuijimoto, 1991; Iansiti, 1997; Henderson, 1994). Others suggest that patterns of common knowledge in the guise of combinative capabilities, routines, or core competencies are conducive in explaining differences in what firms can do well and how they perform (Hoopes and Postrel, 1999; Grant, 1996).

[12]For a more detailed review on the relation between organizational economic insights and claims associated with a 'new' knowledge-based theory of the firm see Foss (1996a, 1996b) and Foss and Foss (2000).

reports and memos rather than the knowledge on which they are crafted; superiors give advice on what to do and intervene at times rather than transfer the knowledge on which their judgment is based. Building on this argument, Conner and Prahalad (1996) stress that authority not only provides a low cost method of communicating, but also allows the flexible blending of expertise when contingencies emerge that were not foreseeable when, for example, an employment contract was concluded. This nicely corresponds to Coase (1937) who makes co-ordination by entrepreneurial direction based on employment contracts the distinguishing mark of the firm as an institution. Like price coordination, direction economizes on investments in common knowledge. In addition direction saves communication cost not because communication is restricted to thin communications as was the case with price coordination, but because communication (be it thin or thick) is restricted to top-down interaction on particular occasions. However, the application of top-down direction to coordinate knowledge finds its limits when superiors do not understand what and how results are achieved at a lower level—as is often the case with knowledge work (Foss, 1999, 2002). Finally, common knowledge (Grant, 1996) in the form of combinative capabilities, routines, shared context or codes, or social capital (Kogut and Zander, 1992, 1993; Nelson and Winter, 1982; Nahapiet and Ghoshal, 1998) may ease coordination, particularly when tasks are highly interdependent. However, as a discussion of knowledge-codification tools illustrates, investments in common knowledge and knowledge sharing—both in terms of managerial effort (see Zollo and Winter, 2002) and aligning diverging interest (Mahnke, 1998)—is particularly expensive. Thus, an organizational economics perspective suggests:

P10: Firms investing in common knowledge and engaging in substantial knowledge sharing only in the presence of high task interdependence will outperform firms that do so even under conditions of low task interdependence.

Conclusions

Since its take-off in the beginning of the 1970s (e.g. Alchian and Demsetz, 1972), organizational economics has been centrally concerned with what is a very recent recognition in the knowledge management literature, namely 'that social relations and learning processes do not happen in a political vacuum and, on the contrary, take place in a landscape of interests and differential power positions and relations' (Easterby-Smith et al., 2000: 793). Fundamentally, organizational economics represents a body of theory that allows the theorist to understand the nature of the obstacles to coordination within and between firms, as well as such issues as how the allocation of incentives and property rights influence the actions and investment decisions of individual agents (i.e. their human capital investments). It does so on the basis of precise assumptions about technologies (e.g. team production, complementarities), the distribution of information, the allocation of incentives and property rights, the degree of rationality and foresight possessed by agents, etc. In other words, organizational economics is taken up with the benefits as well as the costs of alternative contractual, organizational, and institutional structures. It puts forward comparative propositions on this basis.

Organizational economics advances research on knowledge management in organizations by allowing the derivation of novel refutable propositions that are of direct relevance for the empirical research on the practice of organizational knowledge creation. We have provided a number of examples. More fundamentally, it provides a micro-foundation (much needed, in our view) that allows focused research regarding the relation between knowledge management, value creation, and value appropriation by the involved stakeholders. We are confident that further research along these lines will continue to be fruitful.

REFERENCES

Aghion, P. and Tirole, J. (1997) Formal and real authority in organization, *Journal of Political Economy*, 105: 1–29.

Akerlof, G.A. (1970) The market for lemons: Quality and the market mechanism. *Quarterly Journal of Economics*, 84: 488–500.

Alchian, A.A. and Demsetz, H. (1972) Production, information costs, and economic organization. *The American Economic Review*, 62(5): 777–795.

Ambos, B. and Mahnke, V. (2010) When do MNC headquarters add value? *Management International Review*, 4: 403–412.

Arrow, K. (1974) *The Limits of Organization*. New York: W.W. Norton and Co.

Arrow, K.J. (1984) Information and economic behaviour. *Collected Papers of Kenneth J. Arrow – The Economics of Information*. Cambridge: The Belknap Press of Harvard University Press: 136–152.

Baker, G., Gibbons, R., and Murphy, K.J. (1999) Informal authority in organizations, *Journal of Law, Economics and Organization*, 15: 56–73.

Balkin, D. and Gomez-Mejia, L. (1992) Matching compensation and organizational strategies. *Strategic Management Journal*, 11: 153–169.

Barney, J. (1991) Firm resources and sustained competitive advantage. *Journal of Management*, 17: 99–120.

Baron, J.N. (1988) The employment relation as a social relation. *Journal of the Japanese and International Economies*, 2(4): 492–525.

Barzel, Y. (1982) Measurement costs and the organization of markets. *Journal of Law and Economics*, 25: 27–48.

Becker, G.S. (1962) Investment in human capital: A theoretical analysis. *Journal of Political Economy*, 70: 7–44.

Brown, J.S. and Duguid, P. (1998) Organizing knowledge. *California Management Review*, 40(3): 90–111.

Brown, J.S. and Duguid, P. (1991) Organizational Learning and Communities of Practice: Toward a Unified View of Working, Learning, and Innovation. *Organization Science*, 2(1): 40–57.

Brown, S. and Eisenhardt, K. (1995) Product development: Past research, recent findings, and future directions. *Academy of Management Review*, 20(3): 343–378.

Buckley, P.J. and Carter, M.J. (1996) The economics of business process design: Motivation, information and coordination within the firm. *International Journal of the Economics of Business*, 3: 5–24.

Casson, M. (1994) Why are firms hierarchical? *International Journal of the Economics of Business*, 1: 47–76.

Choo, C.W. (1998) *The Knowing Organization*. Oxford: Oxford University Press.

Clark, K. and Fujimoto, T. (1991) *Product Development Performance*. Boston: Harvard University Press.

Coase, R.H. (1937) The nature of the firm. In N. J. Foss (ed.), (2000) *The Theory of the Firm: Critical Perspectives in Business and Management, vol II*. London: Routledge.

Cohen, D. (1998) Toward a knowledge context. *California Management Review*, 40(3): 22–38.

Conner, K.R. and Prahalad, C.K. (1996) A resource based theory of the firm: Knowledge versus opportunism. *Organization Science*, 7(5): 477–501.

Deci, E. (1975) *Intrinsic Motivation*. New York: Plenum Press.

Demsetz, H. (1988) The theory of the firm revisited. *Journal of Law, Economics, and Organization*, 4: 141–161.

Demsetz, H. and Lehn, K. (1989) The structure of corporate ownership: Causes and consequences. *Journal of Political Economy*, 93 (6): 1155–1177.

Dillard, J. and Fisher, J. (1990) Compensation schemes, skill level and task performance: An experimental examination. *Decision Sciences*, 21: 121–137.

Easterby-Smith, M., Crossan, M., and Nicolini, D. (2000) Organizational learning: Debates past, present and future. *The Journal of Management Studies*, 38(6): 783–796.

Fama, E. and Jensen C. M. (1983) Separation of ownership and control. *Journal of Law and Economics*, 26: 301–325.

Foss, N.J. (1996a) Knowledge-Based Approaches to the Theory of the Firm: Some Critical Comments. *Organization Science*, 7: 470–476.

Foss, N.J. (1996b) More Critical Comments on Knowledge-Based Theories of the Firm. *Organization Science* 7: 519–523.

Foss, N.J. (1999) The use of knowledge in firms. *Journal of Institutional and Theoretical Economics*, 155: 458–486.

Foss, N.J. (2000) The theory of the firm. In N.J. Foss (ed.) *The Theory of the Firm: Critical Perspectives in Economic Organization* (4 vols.), London: Routledge.

Foss, N. J. (2001) Selective intervention and internal hybrids. *Manuscript*.

Foss, N. J. (2002) 'Hayek vs Coase': Economic organization and the knowledge economy. *International Journal of the Economics of Business*, 9(1): 9–35.

Foss, N.J. (2007) The Emerging Knowledge Governance Approach. *Organization*, 14: 29–52.

Foss, N.J. and Foss, K. (2000) Competence and Governance Perspectives: How Much Do They Differ? And How Does It Matter? In N.J. Foss and V. Mahnke (eds.), *Competence, Governance, and Entrepreneurship*. Oxford: Oxford University Press.

Galunic, D.C. and Rodan, S. (1998) Resource re-combinations in the firm: Knowledge structures and the potential for Schumpeterian innovation. *Strategic Management Journal*, 19:1193–1201.

Ghoshal, S. and Moran, P. (1996) Bad for practice: A critique of the transaction cost theory. *Academy of Management Review*, 21: 13–47.

Gibbons, R. (1998) Incentives in organizations. *Journal of Economic Perspectives*, 12: 115–132.

Grandori, A. (2001) *Organizations and economic behavior*. London: Routledge.

Grant, R. (1996) Toward a knowledge-based theory of the firm. *Strategic Management Journal*, 17: 109–122.

Hart, O. (1995) *Firms, Contracts, and Financial Structure*. Oxford: Oxford University Press.

Hayek, F.A. (1945) The use of knowledge in society. *American Economic Review*, 35(4): 519–530.

Henderson, R. M. (1994) The evolution of integrative capability: Innovation in cardiovascular drug discovery. *Industrial and Corporate Change*, 3: 607–630.

Holmström, B. (1979) Moral Hazard and Observability. *Bell Journal of Economics*, 10: 74–91.

Holmström, B. (1989) Agency Costs and Innovation. *Journal of Economic Behavior and Organization*, 12: 305–327.

Holmström, B. and Milgrom, P. (1994) The Firm as an Incentive System. *American Economic Review*, 84: 972–991.

Hoopes, D. and Postrel, S. (1999) Shared knowledge, glitches, and product development performance. *Strategic Management Journal*, 9: 837–865.

Huberman, G. and Kahn, C. (1988) Limited contract enforcement and strategic renegotiation. *American Economic Review*, 78(3): 471–484.

Iansiti, M. (1997) *Technology Integration: Making Critical Choices in a Dynamic World.* Boston: Harvard Business School Press.

Jensen, M.C. and Meckling, W. H. (1992) Specific and general knowledge and organizational structure. In L. Werin and H. Wijkander (eds.), *Contract Economics*. Oxford: Blackwell: 251–274.

Jones, G.R. (1987) Organization-client transactions and organizational governance structures. *Academy of Management Journal*, 30: 197–218.

Kogut, B. and Zander, U. (1992) Knowledge of the firm, combinative capabilities, and the replication of technology. *Organization Science*, 3: 383–397.

Kogut, B. and Zander, U. (1993) Knowledge of the firm and the evolutionary theory of the multinational corporation. *Journal of International Business Studies*, 24: 625–645.

Koopmans, T. (1957) *Three Essays on the State of Economic Science*. New York: McGraw-Hill.

Kreps, D. (1990) Corporate culture and economic theory. In J. Alt and K. Shepsle (eds.), *Perspectives on positive political economy*. New York: Cambridge University Press.

Laing, D. (1994) Firm Specific Human Capital as an Employer Discipline Device. *Economic Inquiry*, 32(1): 128–137.

Lane, P. J. and Lubatkin, M. (1998) Relative absorptive capacity and inter-organizational learning. *Strategic Management Journal*, 19(8): 461–477.

Laursen, K. and Foss, N.J. (2002) New HRM Practices, complementarities, and the impact on innovation performance. *Cambridge Journal of Economics*, 27(2): 243–263.

Laursen, K. and Mahnke, V. (2001) Knowledge strategies, firm types, and complementarity in human-resource practices. *Journal of Management and Governance*, 5(1): 1–27.

Lave, J. and Wenger, E. (1990) *Situated Learning: Legitimate Peripheral Participation*. Cambridge: Cambridge University Press.

Lazear E. (1989) Pay, equality and industrial politics. *Journal of Political Economy*, 97: 561–580.

Lyles, M.A. and Schwenk, C. R. (1992) Top management, strategy and organizational knowledge structures. *Journal of Management Studies*, 29: 155–174.

Madhok, A. (1996) The organization of economic activity: Transaction costs, firm capabilities, and the nature of governance. *Organization Science*, 7(5): 577–590.

Mahnke, V. (1998) The economies of knowledge sharing. *IVS/CBS working paper.*

Mahnke, V. and Venzin, M. (2003) Governing knowledge teams in the MNC. *Management International Review*: 43(3): 47–69.

Malcomson, J. (1998), Incentive Contracts in Labor Markets. In O. Ashenfelter and D. Card, (eds.), *Handbook of Labor Economics*, Volumes III and IV. New York: North Holland: 2291–2372.

Marschak, J. and Radner, R. (1972) *The Theory of Teams*. New Haven: Yale University Press.

McGregor, D. (1960) *The Human Side of the Enterprise*. New York: McGraw-Hill.

Meyer, M and deTore, A.D. (1999) Product development for services. *The Academy of Management Executive*, 13(3): 64–76.

Milgrom, P. (1988) Employment Contracts, Influence Activities and Efficient Organization Design. *Journal of Political Economy*, 96: 42–60.

Milgrom, P. and Roberts, J. (1990) 'The Economics of Modern Manufacturing: Technology, Strategy and Organization. *American Economic Review*, 80(3): 511–528.

Milgrom, P. and Roberts, J. (1995) Complementarities and fit strategy, structure, and organizational change in manufacturing. *Journal of Accounting and Economics*, 19: 179–208.

Nelson, R.R., and Winter, S. G. (1982) *An evolutionary theory of economic change*. Cambridge, MA: Belknap Press of Harvard University Press.

Nonaka, I. and Takeuchi, H. (1995) *The Knowledge-Creating Company*. Oxford: Oxford University Press.

Nonaka, I. and von Krogh, G. (2009) Tacit knowledge and knowledge conversion: Controversy and advancement in organizational knowledge creation theory. *Organization Science*, 20(3): 635–652.

O'Dell, C. and Grayson, J.C. (1998) If only we knew what we know: Identification and transfer of internal best practices. *California Management Review*, 40(3): 183–197.

Ouchi, W. (1980) Markets, bureaucracies and clans. *Administrative Science Quarterly* 25: 129–141.

Peteraf, M.A. (1993) The cornerstones of competitive advantage: A resource-based view. *Strategic Management Journal*, 14(3): 179–191.

Pfeffer, J. and Langton, N. (1993) The effect of wage dispersion on satisfaction, productivity, and working collaboratively: Evidence from college and university faculty. *Administrative Science Quarterly*, 38: 382–408.

Prendergast, C. (1993) The role of promotion in inducing specific human capital acquisition. *Quarterly Journal of Economics*, 108(2): 523–534.

Prendergast, C. (2002) The Tenuous Tradeoff of Risk and Incentives. *Journal of Political Economy* 110(5): 1071–1102.

Prusak, L. and Davenport, T. (1998) *Working Knowledge*. Boston: Harvard Business School Press.

Rajan, R.G. and Zingales, L. (1998) Power in a Theory of the Firm. *The Quarterly Journal of Economics*, 113(2): 387–343.

Richardson, J. B. (1972) The organization of industry. *Economic Journal*, 82: 883–896.

Rosen, S. (1991) Transaction costs and internal labor markets. In O.E. Williamson and S.G. Winter (eds.), *The Nature of the Firm*. Oxford: Basil Blackwell.

Schumpeter, J. A. (1950) *Essays on Entrepreneurs, Innovations, Business Cycles, and the Evolution of Capitalism*. New Brunswick: Transaction Publishers.

Scott, S.G., and Einstein, W.O. (2001) Strategic Performance Appraisal in Team-Based Organizations: One Size Does Not Fit All. *Academy of Management Executive*, 15: 107–117.

Shelanski, H. and Klein, P.G. (1995) Empirical research in transaction cost economics: A review and assessment. *Journal of Law, Economics, and Organization*: 335–361.

Simon, H. (1991) Bounded rationality and organizational learning. *Organization Science*, 2: 125–134.

Spence, A. M. (1973) Job market signalling. *Quarterly Journal of Economics*, 87: 355–377.

Spence, A. M. (1974) Market signalling informational transfer in hiring and related screening processes. *Harvard economic studies*. Cambridge: Harvard University Press.

Thompson, J.D. (1967) *Organizations in Action*. New York: Wiley.

Von Krogh, G. (1998) Care in knowledge creation. *California Management Review*, 40(3): 133–153.

Von Krogh, G., Ichijo, K, and Nonaka, I. (2000) *Enabling knowledge creation*. Oxford: Oxford University Press.

Weick, K. E. and Roberts, K.H. (1993) Collective mind in organizations: Heedful interrelating on flight decks. *Administrative Science Quarterly*, 38: 357–381.

Williamson, O.E. (1985) *The Economic Institutions of Capitalism*. New York: Free Press.

Williamson, O.E. (1996) *The Mechanisms of Governance*. Oxford: Oxford University Press.

Winter, S. (1987) Knowledge and competence as strategic assets. In D. Teece (ed.), *The competitive challenge*. Cambridge, MA: Ballinger: 159–184.

ADDITIONAL READING

Boisot, M. (1998) *Knowledge Assets: Securing Competitive Advantage in the Information Economy*. Oxford: Oxford University Press.

Bolton, P. and Farrell, J. (1990) Decentralization, duplication, and delay. *Journal of Political Economy*, 98: 803.

Brynjolfsson, E. (1994) Information assets, technology, and organization. *Management Science* 40: 1645–1662.

Burns, T. and Stalker, G.M. (1961) *The Management of Innovation*. London: Tavistock.

Cheung, S.N.S. (1983) The contractual nature of the firm. *Journal of Law and Economics*, 26:1–22.

Chow, C. (1983) The effects of job standard tightness and compensation scheme on performance: An exploration of linkages. *Accounting Review*, 58: 667–685.

Coff, R.W. (1999) When competitive advantage doesn't lead to performance: The resource-based view and shareholder bargaining power. *Organization Science*, 10: 119–134.

Grandori, A. (1997) Governance structures, coordination mechanisms and cognitive models. *Journal of Management and Governance*, 1: 29–42.

Harryson, S. J. (2000) *Managing know-who based companies*. Cheltenham: Edward Elgar.

Helper, S., MacDuffie, J.P., and Sabel, C. (2000) Pragmatic Collaborations: Advancing Knowledge While Controlling Opportunism. *Industrial and Corporate Change*, 9: 443–487.

Henderson, R.I. (2000) *Compensation Management in a Knowledge-Based World*. London: Prentice-Hall.

Holmström, B. (1999) The Firm as a Subeconomy. *Journal of Law, Economics, and Organization*, 15: 74–102.

Holmström, B. and Roberts, J. (1998) The Boundaries of the Firm Revisited. *Journal of Economic Perspectives*.

Mahnke, V., Pedersen, T., and Venzin, M. (2009) When does knowledge sharing pay? A MNC subsidiary perspective on knowledge outflows. *Advances in Marketing and Management*, 10: 234–272.

Matusik, S.F. and Hill, C.W.L. (1998) The Utilization of Contingent Work, Knowledge Creation, and Competitive Advantage. *Academy of Management Review*, 23: 680–697.

Meyer, C. (1994) How the Right Measures Help Teams Excel. *Harvard Business Review* 72(3): 95–103.

Miller, G. (1992) *Managerial Dilemmas*. Cambridge: Cambridge University Press.

Osterloh, M. and Frey, B. (2000) Motivation, Knowledge Transfer and Organizational Form. *Organization Science*, 11: 538–550.

Prusak, L. (1998) Introduction to Series – Why Knowledge, Why Now? In D. Neef (ed.), *The Knowledge Economy*. Boston: Butterworth-Heinemann.

Putterman, L. (1995) Markets, Hierarchies and Information: On a Paradox in the Economics of Organization. *Journal of Economic Behavior and Organization*, 26: 373–390.

Rabin, M. (1993) Information and the control of productive assets. *Journal of Law, Economics and Organization*, 9: 51–76.

Radner, R. (1993) The organization of decentralized information processing. *Econometrica*, 61: 1109–1146.

8

A Framework for Integrating Organizational Learning, Knowledge, Capabilities, and Absorptive Capacity

DUSYA VERA, MARY CROSSAN, AND
MARINA APAYDIN

ABSTRACT

The literature on organizational learning (OL), knowledge management (KM), dynamic capabilities (DC), and absorptive capacity (AC) is characterized by the use of very diverse terminology, where concepts often overlap, but it is unclear how all the pieces fit together.

Recognizing that no single overarching framework has been proposed to clear up this conceptual confusion, this chapter proposes a framework that integrates OL, KM, DC, and AC, and establishes a theoretical link between these constructs and performance. Our integrative model acknowledges the distinct roots of each field, identifies conceptual boundaries, and establishes relationships between the constructs and firm performance. We propose this framework as an instrument to facilitate communication between researchers in order to avoid the risk of continuously 'reinventing the wheel' in the learning field.

INTRODUCTION

We started our original chapter published in 2003 in the *Blackwell Handbook of Organizational Learning and Knowledge Management* by stating that 'organizational learning' and 'knowledge management' had become terms commonly used in the business environment that were usually associated with large-budget projects pursued by firms convinced that the only competitive advantage the company of the future will have is its ability to learn faster than its competitors (DeGeus, 1988). Although early academic discussions about these concepts date to the 1960s (Cangelosi and Dill, 1965; Polanyi, 1967), it was not until the 1990s that these topics dramatically captured the attention of managers, when Senge (1990) popularized the concept of the 'learning organization' and Nonaka and Takeuchi (1995) described how to become a 'knowledge-creating company.' It was also in the 1990s when the rapid evolution of information technology and the Internet allowed the development of sophisticated knowledge management tools.

Our concern in 2003 was that, while consultants were providing learning and knowledge management solutions to managers, academics (e.g. Huber, 1991; Simon, 1991; Weick, 1991) were expressing their concern about the lack of consistent terminology, cumulative work, and a widely accepted framework that connected the learning and knowledge fields. Miner and Mezias (1996) even called organizational learning theory 'an ugly duckling in the pond of organizational theory: interesting, but living on the fringes' (1996: 88). Furthermore, organizational learning (OL) and knowledge management (KM) were rarely discussed together. Since then, the field has evolved toward increasing integration of concepts and cross-fertilization of ideas between organizational learning and knowledge management scholars. Academic journals and conferences have been the forum in which dialogue and connections have been created. The new challenge in the twenty-first century has been the evolution of two concepts, dynamic capabilities (DC), and absorptive capacity (AC), which, again, emphasize the notion of learning and knowledge as critical for organizational success. How all the pieces fit together, however, is not clear and consensus has not been achieved.

The purpose of this chapter is to provide a conceptual framework that defines and integrates OL, KM, DC, and AC and establishes a theoretical link between these constructs and performance. We begin by defining the constructs and acknowledging their distinct roots. Then, we establish the fields' domains and their boundaries. It is important to note that since these fields are in flux, the term 'boundary' should be interpreted as the salient differences that distinguish the fields given the current dialogue. Next, propositions that integrate OL, DC, KM, and AC, and link them to performance are offered. Finally, we present conclusions and directions for future research.

DEFINITION OF CONSTRUCTS

Organizational learning

In defining 'organizational learning,' we agree with the growing group of theorists (e.g. Argyris and Schön, 1978; Duncan and Weiss, 1979; Miller, 1996) who emphasize the interrelationship between cognition and behavior and conclude that the learning process encompasses both cognitive and behavioral change. Individuals and groups learn by understanding and then acting or by acting and then interpreting (Crossan, Lane, White, and Djurfeldt, 1995). The definition of OL adopted for this chapter incorporates this thinking: organizational learning is the process of change in individual and shared thought and action, which is affected by and embedded in the institutions of the organization. When individual and group learning becomes institutionalized, organizational learning occurs and knowledge is embedded in non-human repositories such as routines, systems, structures, culture, and strategy (Crossan, Lane, and White, 1999; Nelson and Winter, 1982; Walsh and Rivera, 1991). The organizational learning system is comprised of the continually evolving knowledge stored in individuals, groups, and the organization and constitutes the fundamental infrastructure that supports a firm's strategy formulation and implementation processes.

Early work in organizational learning, spearheaded by James March (Cohen and Sproull, 1996) made use of learning concepts that were translated from the psychology literature on individual learning (e.g. choice, decision making, information processing). For example, Argyris and Schön (1978) proposed that organizations learn through individuals acting as agents for them. When defining single-loop and double-loop learning, they explained learning in terms of individual level error detection and error correction. Today, authors offer more comprehensive frameworks of OL that link the different levels of learning and that study learning from a systemic view. Furthermore, the study of the OL phenomenon has been enriched by the contributions from diverse disciplines (Easterby-Smith, 1997) and new perspectives such as interpretive systems (Daft and Weick, 1984), communities of practice (Brown and Duguid, 1991), dialogue (Isaacs, 1993), and memory (Casey, 1997; Walsh and Rivera, 1991). Finally, because of its intrinsic notion of change, organizational learning research has been associated with questions of how organizations evolve, transform (e.g. Barnett, Greve, and Park, 1994; MacIntosh, 1999), and renew themselves (e.g. Crossan et al., 1999; Lant and Mezias, 1992; Mezias and Glynn, 1993) in order to face the challenges of a continuously changing environment.

When defining organizational learning, it is important to note its relationship to the 'learning organization' (LO). Senge (1990:1) defines a learning organization as 'a place where people continually expand their capacity of creating results they really want, where patterns of thinking are broadened and nurtured, where collective aspiration is free and where people are continually learning to learn.' Organizational learning and the learning organization belong to different streams of theorizing in the field (Easterby-Smith, Snell, and Gherardi, 1998). OL is a descriptive stream, with academics who pursue the question 'how does an organization learn?' In contrast, LO is a prescriptive stream, targeted at practitioners who are interested in the question 'how should an organization learn?'

Knowledge management

In 2003, we noted that, in defining knowledge management, a major source of confusion arose from the failure to differentiate 'knowledge management' (KM) and 'organizational knowledge' (OK). In its origins, the term knowledge management was often used in conference programs and book titles, but seldom defined and incorporated in academic papers, where the concept of organizational knowledge was the one frequently used. Knowledge management has been defined as 'the explicit control and management of knowledge within an organization aimed at achieving the company's objectives' (Van der Spek and Spijkervet, 1997: 43), 'the formal management of knowledge for facilitating creation, access, and reuse of knowledge, typically using advanced technology' (O'Leary, 1998: 34), 'the process of creating, capturing, and using knowledge to enhance organizational performance' (Bassi, 1999: 424), and 'the ability of organizations to manage, store, value, and distribute knowledge' (Liebowitz and Wilcox, 1997: i).

As the field has evolved two main paradigms have emerged: a computational view of knowledge management which approaches knowledge management as a process of identifying empirically validated facts and managing them through technology, and an organic view of knowledge management which emphasizes the role of people, group dynamics, social and cultural factors, and networks (Argote, 2005). These two views have been combined in an integrated socio-technological approach to managing actual and potential flows of knowledge creation, transfer, and retention (Prieto and Easterby-Smith, 2006). Two chapters in this Handbook address the issues within the domain of KM. Hayes (Chapter 5) discusses the role of information technology within the organic or 'relational' view of KM. Alavi and Denford (Chapter 6) adopt a combined socio-technological approach and move the discussion forward by assessing the role of Web 2.0 in KM practice. They advocate the necessity of having both technological capability of information processing and relevant social content for a KM platform to be successful.

In contrast to the knowledge management concept, which was initially considered a prescriptive term, organizational knowledge is an established theoretical construct. Knowledge has been proposed as a key firm resource and a source of competitive advantage. This research is rooted in the resource-based view (RBV) of the firm (Barney, 1991; Penrose, 1959). Several authors argue for a 'knowledge-based' theory of the firm as a theory that explains the organizational advantage of firms over markets (Ghoshal and Moran, 1996; Grant, 1996; Kogut and Zander, 1992).

To develop a theory where the creation, transfer, and application of knowledge is the reason why firms exist, researchers have engaged in a passionate debate about what knowledge is and what forms or types of it are available (Collins, 1993). Whereas the term learning has not been bound up in questions of veridicality and accuracy, the term knowledge has witnessed many debates. Different philosophical views and conceptual paradigms offer different perspectives about what knowledge is and how it can be studied. For example, based on their distinct epistemological and ontological assumptions, positivists argue that reality is objective and can be comprehended accurately, while for post-modernists all meanings are context specific. While it is impossible to integrate these theories or resolve their disagreements, Gioia and Pitre (1990) propose that there is 'similarity despite disparity' across paradigms, and that a multi-paradigm approach to theory building would help researchers achieve a more comprehensive understanding of organizational phenomena. In the study of knowledge, the positivist view ('knowledge as justified true belief') is the predominant one in Western culture and a generally accepted assumption in organizational theory (Nonaka and Takeuchi, 1995). However, it has been increasingly challenged and complemented by more constructivist perspectives that argue that knowledge cannot be conceived independently from action, shifting the notion of *knowledge* as a commodity that individuals or organizations may acquire, to the study of *knowing* as something that they do (Blackler, 1995; Cook and Brown, 1999; Nicolini and Meznar, 1995; Polanyi, 1967). Polanyi's (1967) work, in particular, has been highly influential in defining knowledge as dynamic, when he argues that knowledge is an activity, which could be better described as a process of knowing.

Although the knowledge (explicit and tacit) and knowing constructs come from different paradigms, we believe that efforts towards integrating them are consistent with Gioia and Pitre's (1990) call for more multi-paradigm research. According to Polanyi (1967), explicit knowledge is articulated and specified either verbally or in writing, while tacit knowledge is unarticulated, intuitive, and non-verbalizable. Perception, the process of getting to know an external object by the impression made by it on our senses, underlies the paradigm of tacit knowledge (Polanyi, 1967). In perceiving a simple object, there are clues that are unspecifiable, thus, all empirical knowledge has an indeterminate content. Building on this work, Cook and Brown (1999) propose that explicit and tacit knowledge are not enough to understand the nature of knowledge and that to account for all somebody knows, it is necessary to add the notion of knowing. For them, while explicit and tacit knowledge are 'possessed' by people, knowing is not about possession, but about 'practice' and about interacting with the things of the social and physical world. For example, when riding a bike, people use their explicit knowledge about the parts of a bike and the tacit knowledge about how to keep balance on a bike. People possess this knowledge even when they are not riding a bike. The difference is that while biking, people practice their knowing, that is, they put knowledge into action.

In Figure 8.1, we summarize the relationships we observe between knowledge, knowing, and learning. First, knowledge can be obtained through the mind (learning by reflection, anticipatory learning) and through the body (learning by doing, experimental learning). Second, knowledge is accumulated in our minds (know what, declarative knowledge) and also in our bodies (know how, procedural knowledge). Third, knowing is practice, it is something we do. Knowing is not knowledge *used in* action, but knowledge that is *part of* action (Cook and Brown, 1999). Last, learning is the change in knowledge and the change in knowing, which involves, as mentioned before, changes in cognition and changes in behavior. Knowledge and knowing are the content of the learning process, in other words, what we learn or get to know. The main distinction between knowledge and knowing is that knowledge is mainly cognitive, including the facts and the skills we possess, while knowing is mainly behavioral, it is knowledge as action.

In this Handbook, Tsoukas (Chapter 21) continues the discussion about tacit knowledge by providing a review of the previous work on the subject by Polanyi, Nonaka, Takeuchi,

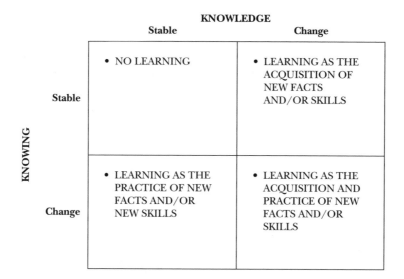

Figure 8.1 Knowledge-Knowing-Learning Matrix

Table 8.1 Dimensions of organizational knowledge

Authors	Dimensions
Polanyi (1962)	Tacitness
Barney (1991)	VRIN dimensions
Garyd and Kumaraswamy, (1995)	Modularity
Inkpen and Crossan (1995)	Channel/means (cognitive-behavioral)
Crossan et al. (1999)	Level of embeddedness (I/G/O/N)
Orlikowski (2002)	Actualization (possessed-practiced)
McEvily and Chakravarthy, (2002)	Complexity
Argote et al. (2003)	Access (internal-external, public-private)
	Concentration (degree to which the knowledge is shared by org members
Simonin (2004)	Ambiguity
Prieto and Easterby-Smith (2006)	Type (technological-social)
	Nature (additive-recombinative)

and others, and a clarification of the construct. Contrary to Nonaka and Takeuchi, he maintains that tacit knowledge is not hibernating explicit knowledge waiting to be articulated: 'tacit and explicit knowledge are not the two ends of a continuum but two sides of the same coin: even the most explicit kind of knowledge is underlain by tacit knowledge.'

In addition to the explicit/tacit dimension, recent developments in the field offered a plethora of other dimensions, which are summarized in Table 8.1. Furthermore, another important focus of the organizational knowledge literature is studying the processes through which knowledge is created, developed, retained, and transferred (e.g. Argote and Ingram, 2000; Nonaka and Takeuchi, 1995; Pisano, 1994; Szulanski, 1996). Thus, this second branch of research steps back from the questions about knowledge types and forms and emphasizes the need to understand the micro-processes by which knowledge is created or acquired, communicated, applied, and utilized in organizations.

Dynamic capabilities

The concept of 'dynamic capabilities' (DC) was introduced by Teece, Pisano, and Shuen (1997) to offer a more dynamic perspective of the resource-based view (Barney, 1991). They argue that because the value of a resource can change over time, competitive advantage comes not only from organizational resources, but also from the firm's capability to continually create, integrate, and reconfigure new resources. While building on the work of Teece et al., (1997), Eisenhardt and Martin (2000) provide a different perspective on dynamic capabilities. They define dynamic capabilities as the process by which firms use resources, i.e. the 'organizational and strategic routines by which firms achieve new resource configurations' (2000: 1007). In contrast to Teece et al. (1997), Eisenhardt and Martin argue that competitive advantage 'lies in the resource configurations that they create, not in the capabilities themselves' (2000: 1106), because dynamic capabilities exhibit commonalities among effective firms and become what managers call 'best practices.'

The last decade has witnessed great confusion in the DC field because of a lack of agreement about what dynamic capabilities actually are (Cepeda and Vera, 2007). Some definitions are prescriptive in nature in the sense that they assume that dynamic capabilities are always good and are a source of competitive advantage; these definitions have been criticized as tautological (Priem and Butler, 2001). Furthermore, if there is always a capability behind a capability, we face an infinite regress problem and it is impossible to identify the ultimate source of competitive advantage (Collis, 1994).

In an effort to understand the true nature of dynamic capabilities, several authors propose the need to differentiate among the types of processes and routines available in firms. Collis (1994) distinguishes between a first category of capabilities, which reflect an ability to perform the basic functional activities of the firm (e.g. plant layout, distribution logistics, and marketing campaigns), and a second category of capabilities, which deals with the dynamic improvement to the activities of the firm. In his detailed treatment of the subject, Winter (2003) defines capabilities as 'high level routine(s)' which in turn are 'learned and repetitious behaviors' (Winter, 2003: 991). He categorizes capabilities into a hierarchy using a mathematical metaphor of derivatives:

1. Zero-level operational capabilities (how a company earns a living now).
2. Dynamic capabilities, which are mathematically speaking 'first derivatives' of operational capabilities, i.e. their change.
3. Second-order capabilities are 'second derivatives' of operational capabilities and the 'first derivatives' of dynamic capabilities, i.e. their change.

Winter (2003) proposes learning as the ultimate second-order capability, and creates an explicit link between the concepts of organizational learning and dynamic capabilities. This hierarchical classification has increasingly been adopted in recent models of dynamic capabilities (e.g. Helfat and Peteraf, 2003; Zahra and George, 2002; Zahra, Sapienza, and Davidsson, 2006) and helps to eliminate the tautological flavor associated with dynamic capabilities. In addition, Teece (2007: 1319) establishes an explicit connection between dynamic capabilities and knowledge management, when he proposes that 'dynamic capabilities can be disaggregated into the capacity (1) to sense and shape opportunities and threats, (2) to seize opportunities, and (3) to maintain competitiveness through enhancing, combining, protecting, and, when necessary, reconfiguring the business enterprise's intangible and tangible assets,' and includes knowledge management as part of the third type of process.

In this Handbook, Teece (Chapter 23) extends this theorizing by connecting DC and 'knowledge assets' with the theory of the firm. Teece argues that the economic theory of the firm currently dominated by the contracting perspective should be augmented by the DC/KM perspective where learning is viewed as a way of development and maintenance of knowledge assets.

Absorptive capacity

The concept of 'absorptive capacity' (AC) was first[1] introduced by Cohen and Levinthal as 'the firm's ability to identify, assimilate and exploit knowledge from the environment' (Cohen and Levinthal, 1989: 569–570) and the 'ability of the firm to recognize the value of new external information, assimilate it, and apply it to commercial ends' (Cohen and Levinthal, 1990: 128). There have been three recent efforts to review the literature with the goal of reconceptualizing the construct from theoretical and definitional perspectives (Lane, Koka, and Pathak, 2006; Todorova and Durisin, 2007; Zahra and George, 2002). In fact, although the concept of absorptive capacity was introduced earlier than that of dynamic capabilities, the former has been greatly influenced by the latter, and absorptive capacity is increasingly being positioned as a firm's dynamic capability (Easterby-Smith, Graca, Antonacopoulou, and Ferdinand, 2008).

Zahra and George (2002) define absorptive capacity as a set of organizational routines and processes, by which firms acquire, assimilate, transform, and exploit knowledge to produce a dynamic organizational capability. They were the first to differentiate between potential and realized absorptive capacity. Potential absorptive capacity is a firm's capability to value and acquire external knowledge, but does not guarantee the exploitation of this knowledge. Realized absorptive capacity reflects the firm's capacity to leverage the knowledge that has been absorbed. Zahra and George (2002) also furthered the ideas about the role of the internal knowledge base as an antecedent of potential absorptive capacity, and added (1) activation triggers as moderators of the relationship between internal knowledge and potential absorptive capacity and (2) social interaction mechanisms as factors that reduce the gap between potential and realized absorptive capacity.

In a critical review, Lane et al. (2006) defined absorptive capacity as a firm's ability to utilize externally held knowledge through three sequential organizational learning processes: (1) recognizing and understanding potentially valuable new knowledge outside the firm through exploratory learning, (2) assimilating valuable new knowledge through transformative learning, and (3) using the assimilated knowledge to create new knowledge and commercial outputs through exploitative learning. They concluded that the construct has become reified; i.e. become a taken-for-granted, general-purpose concept and identified fundamental weaknesses in our understanding of AC calling for a 'rejuvenation of the construct' (Lane et al., 2006). They ask researchers to engage in empirical analysis and integrative theoretical work that: characterizes the construct as a capability rather than a knowledge asset, focuses at the micro level to broaden understanding of the role of team cognition, emphasizes the multiple dimensions of the concept, and considers the impact of team structural factors on the efficiency of applying assimilated knowledge.

In fact, an important debate in the AC field has been the dimensionality of AC (Nemanich, 2008). Lane et al. (2006) argued that the concepts of potential and realized AC bias the construct definition toward the short-term benefits of AC. They offered a

---

[1] The term 'Absorptive Capacity' was first used by Kedia and Bhagat (1988) to describe an organization which has 'cosmopolitan orientation, existing sophisticated technical core and strategic management process,' which would enable them to effectively manage technology transfers (1988: 568). However, it was Cohen and Levinthal (1989) who actually introduced AC as a defined concept.

model that returned to the three dimensions identified by Cohen and Levinthal (1990). Todorova and Durisin (2007) also made theoretical arguments for explicitly rejecting the idea of potential and realized AC constructs. Their model returned to the roots of Cohen and Levinthal's (1990) work and then expanded it by incorporating the following learning processes as dimensions: recognize the value, acquire, assimilate, transform, and exploit. Building on this work and addressing Lane et al.'s (2006) criticisms, Nemanich, Keller, Vera, and Chin (2010) recently added team shared cognition to the three traditional dimensions of AC—evaluate, assimilate, and apply capabilities—and argued that these capabilities manifest themselves in different levels of analysis, individual or team.

Finally, linking the AC and DC concepts, and emphasizing the micro-processes involved, not just the dimensions, Easterby-Smith et al. (2008) positioned absorptive capacity as a dynamic capability and pursued qualitative work that identified power and boundaries as central features of a process view of absorptive capacity.

Having discussed the roots and definitions of the four constructs of interest, the next section will delineate not only connections, but also the boundaries of each research area.

DEFINITION OF BOUNDARIES

Figure 8.2 summarizes our conclusions about the domains and boundaries of the OL, KM, DC, and AC fields. We see these boundaries as fluid. They will evolve as the dialogue between members of these fields continues.

In Figure 8.2, we show OL, KM, and DC as overlapping fields of research, but we recognize that there are topics that are dealt with primarily in one of the fields, and topics in which one field is more advanced in its development than the others. For example, we see OL as the most advanced in terms of providing a multilevel theory of learning in organizations. We also note that OL advances the view of an OL system or infrastructure where organizational level storehouses of knowledge—strategy, structure, systems, culture, and procedures—are aligned. In contrast, we see the KM field focused on creating a knowledge-based view of the firm, where the creation and integration of knowledge is the reason why firms exist. Similarly, the dynamic capabilities perspective is unique in providing a dynamic perspective of the resource-based view of the firm and in suggesting the ability to change routines and reconfigure resources (including knowledge routines and knowledge resources) as the ultimate source of competitive advantage.

The boundary between OL and KM

From a positivist perspective, one basic difference between OL and KM is that where one of KM's main focuses is understanding the nature of knowledge as an asset or a stock, OL primarily emphasizes the processes through which knowledge changes or flows. That is, there is a distinction between studying *what* is learned and studying the *process* of learning, or between studying *content* and *process*. Schendel (1996), for example, emphasizes the need to understand learning as a process, when he states that 'the capacity to develop organizational capability may be more important in creating competitive advantage than the specific knowledge gained' (1996: 6). KM views knowledge as a firm resource that can lead to sustainable competitive advantage. Thus, we position the knowledge-based view of

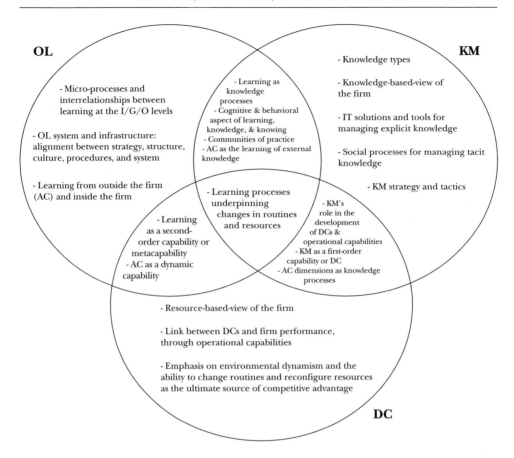

Figure 8.2   Boundaries of the Organizational Learning (OL), Knowledge Management (KM), Dynamic Capabilities (DC), and Absorptive Capacity (AC) Fields

the firm in Figure 8.2 within the boundaries of the OK domain. Discussion is focused on trying to understand what knowledge is, on defining knowledge typologies, and contrasting explicit and tacit knowledge and the technical and social mechanisms to support them. We conclude that OK has a more content view of knowledge, while OL is primarily interested in the underlying processes.

There is a growing agreement in the OL literature that for learning to occur, changes in cognition and/or behavior must take place. Whereas the KM literature has a strong cognitive side, it also addresses knowledge and knowing as grounded in action and as processes that require both cognitive and behavioral activity. Furthermore, constructivist approaches to knowledge emphasize that knowledge is constructed in interaction with the world, that knowledge is situated in practice, and that knowledge is relational, mediated by artifacts, contextualized, and dynamic (Blackler, 1995). We conclude that although the OL field has been the most explicit in explaining the cognitive and behavioral aspects of the learning phenomenon, KM has extended its focus on cognition, to incorporate the action orientation.

As suggested earlier in this chapter, OL and KM also overlap, because learning has been increasingly defined in terms of knowledge processes. For example, Argote (1999) defines learning as 'knowledge acquisition' and states that learning involves the processes through which members share, generate, evaluate, and combine knowledge. On the knowledge management side, process views take the form of 'life cycle' models. King, Chung, and Haney (2008) offer the most comprehensive of them consisting of several parallel paths, starting from creation (or acquisition), refinement, storage, then transfer (or sharing), and ending with utilization leading to organizational performance. In addition, as mentioned in the previous point, knowledge is not viewed as purely cognitive any more. Thus, when the notion of static knowledge is replaced by dynamic knowing and the agenda switches from managing knowledge assets to studying the knowledge-associated processes, such as creation, retention, and transfer, there is a powerful opportunity to unify the insights from both the organizational learning and organizational knowledge communities.

When studied from a social constructivist perspective, OL and KM share the recognition that learning and knowing are situated in practice. This research includes the study of communities of practice (Brown and Duguid, 1991) and activity systems (Blackler, 1995; Spender, 1996). The fundamental idea is that it is impossible to separate learning from working (Brown and Duguid, 1991) and that knowledge exists in socially-distributed activity systems, where participants employ their situated knowledge in a context which is itself constantly developing (Gherardi, Nicolini, and Odella, 1998).

In terms of the levels of analysis, several authors in the OL and KM fields (e.g. Crossan et al., 1999; Kogut and Zander, 1992; Nonaka and Takeuchi, 1995) have proposed that learning occurs and that knowledge exists at the individual, group, organizational, and inter-organizational or network levels. This fourth level of analysis has attracted a great deal of attention from researchers interested in the role of learning in alliances, joint ventures, strategic groups, and inter-firm relationships in general (e.g. Doz, 1996; Inkpen and Crossan, 1995; Lyles and Salk, 1996). An early debate, particularly in the OL field, questioned the existence of organizational-level learning. According to Argote (1999), a 'litmus test' for determining whether organizational learning has occurred is analyzing whether organizational knowledge persists in the face of individual turnover. Furthermore, work by Nelson and Winter (1982) describes knowledge at the organizational level and refers to organizational routines as the organization's genetic material, some explicit in bureaucratic rules, some implicit in the organization's culture. As the field has evolved, OL and KM researchers seem to agree that organizations are more than the sum of individuals and that by acknowledging the existence of non-human repositories of knowledge and organizational learning systems (Shrivastava and Grant, 1985), the capacity to learn, to know, and to have a memory (Walsh and Rivera, 1991) can be attributed to firms.

Once the different levels of analysis are recognized, the next step is to provide a theory that links the levels, explaining the micro-processes by which learning and knowledge at one level become learning and knowledge at another level. Schwandt's (1995) Dynamic Organizational Learning Model, for example, moves in this direction. In this model, organizational learning is a dynamic social system defined as 'a system of actions, actors, symbols, and processes that enables an organization to transform information into valued knowledge, which, in turn, increases its long-run adaptive capacity' (Schwandt, 1995: 370). Four learning subsystems (environmental interface, action-reflection, dissemination and diffusion, and meaning and memory) and their associated processes explain how individuals and groups in organizations collectively engage in social actions of learning. Work from Crossan et al. (1999), Nonaka and Takeuchi (1995), and Spender (1994, 1996) are other examples of ambitious efforts towards multilevel research. From our analysis of this work, we argue that OL is more advanced than KM in terms of providing this multilevel theory of how learning occurs at the individual, group, and organizational levels, how learning at one level impacts learning at other levels, and how knowledge flows from one level to the others. When discussing multiple levels of knowledge, the KM agenda has centered on tacit versus explicit knowledge and person to person transfer. For example, Spender (1994, 1996) has integrated the tacit and explicit taxonomy with the individual and social levels of analysis to present a matrix of four types of organizational knowledge: conscious, automatic or non-conscious, objectified or scientific, and collective. He discusses the 'action-domains' of each of the four types of knowledge and describes learning as the conversion from one type of knowledge to another. Still, the cognitive and behavioral processes involved in these learning flows need to be identified in order to provide useful prescriptions to firms.

To develop a multilevel theory of knowledge in organizations, KM also needs to establish relationships between the different knowledge-associated processes at different levels. For example what for one individual is knowledge sharing may be knowledge acquisition (learning) for a group or what for one individual is knowledge creation (learning) may be knowledge access for a group. In addition, when, for example, the knowledge transfer process is discussed at the group level, what is viewed as a transfer of current knowledge in the eyes of the sender may be seen as the acquisition of new knowledge by the receiver. These examples show that OL and OK involve many knowledge and learning processes and that there are significant opportunities for the two fields to work together to build a theory that relates the processes at different levels of analysis.

Finally, we propose in Figure 8.2 that the OL literature has most explicitly discussed the development of a learning system or infrastructure, which consists of embedded learning in the strategy, structure, culture, systems, and procedures of the firm. This learning infrastructure affects and is affected by learning processes and the different elements of the systems need to be aligned with each other for the firm to be successful.

The boundaries of OL and KM with DC

At its core, the dynamic capabilities perspective studies how change in routines and resources leads to competitive advantage. Because dynamic capabilities involve change, they involve learning—change in cognition and change in behavior, and because dynamic capabilities work on routines and resources, they involve knowledge—the most valuable, rare, and hard-to-imitate firm resource. Winter's (2003) hierarchy of capabilities was instrumental in making these connections explicit: operational capabilities represent how things are currently done (current knowledge), dynamic capabilities change operational capabilities, and learning is the ultimate capability that guides the development, evolution, and use of dynamic and operational capabilities (Eisenhardt and Martin, 2000).

In one of the most comprehensive efforts to link knowledge and dynamic capabilities explicitly, Zollo and Winter (2002) propose a 'knowledge evolution cycle' to describe the development of dynamic capabilities and operational routines; this cycle enables firms to change the way they do things in pursuit of greater rents. The knowledge evolution cycle includes four phases: generative variation, internal selection, replication, and retention. In the variation phase, individuals and groups generate ideas on how to approach old problems in novel ways or how to tackle new challenges. The selection phase implies the evaluation of ideas for their potential for enhancing the firm's effectiveness. Through knowledge articulation, analysis, and debate, ideas become explicit and the best are selected. The replication phase involves the codification of the selected change initiatives and their diffusion to relevant parties in the firm. The application of the changes in diverse contexts generates new information about the routines' performance and can initiate a new variation cycle. In the retention phase, changes turn into routines and knowledge becomes increasingly embedded in human behavior. There is stark similarity in these learning processes to those that have been well developed in the OL and KM literatures.

Building on this work, Cepeda and Vera (2007) delineated the connections between KM and DC when they stated that: (1) capabilities are organizational processes and routines rooted in knowledge; (2) the input of dynamic capabilities is an initial configuration of resources and operational routines; (3) dynamic capabilities involve a transformation process of the firm's knowledge resources and routines; and (4) the output of dynamic capabilities is a new configuration of resources and operational routines.

Finally, Easterby-Smith and Prieto (2008) have offered an integrative framework of the learning, knowledge, and capabilities concepts. They argue that because learning capabilities act as the source of dynamic capabilities (Zollo and Winter, 2002) and learning can be defined in terms of the processes of knowledge creation, transfer, and retention, the distinctions between knowledge management and dynamic capabilities are more of terminology than of essence. Easterby-Smith and Prieto (2008) proposed a complex link to performance that can be summarized by the following points: (1) dynamic capabilities and knowledge management are first-order capabilities that modify existing resources and operational routines over time; (2) learning is a second-order capability that contributes to the evolution of both dynamic capabilities and knowledge management; (3) dynamic capabilities themselves do not lead to competitive advantage, but competitive advantage depends on the new configurations of resources and operational routines resulting from them; and, finally, (4) dynamic capabilities enabled by knowledge management are antecedents of specific operational/functional competences, which in turn have a significant effect on firm performance.

These connections are presented in Figure 8.2 in the overlapping areas between OL and KM, KM and DC, and DC and OL, respectively. In addition, the center of the Venn diagram represents the core of the learning field, the belief that organizational learning processes underpin changes in routines and resources, that is, in the knowledge base of the firm. It should be noted that the sizes of the circles and geography of overlap are not intended to capture depth or breadth. When we consider the unique contributions of each field, we find that KM has contributed a great deal to the epistemological and ontological basis of knowledge and knowing. OL contributes depth in the multilevel processes that underpin changes in cognition and behavior and these processes are the same ones that underpin dynamic capabilities, knowledge management, and absorptive capacity. Dynamic capabilities contribute largely to the type of activities to which we can apply these learning processes in the drive for competitive advantage. The unfortunate short-coming in each of these literatures has been the predominant failure to draw on these associated strengths as each seems to try and 'reinvent the wheel.' We hope Figure 8.2 provides an opportunity for researchers to elevate organizational learning processes as the fundamental elements underpinning knowledge management, dynamic capabilities, and absorptive capacity constructs and theories.

Absorptive capacity and the OL, KM, and DC fields

The case of absorptive capacity is special in the sense that we see this concept as overlapping with different aspects of the OL, KM, and DC fields. AC is a subset of organizational learning because it focuses on the value and assimilation of one specific type of learning: learning from external sources. AC is also part of KM and OL because the different dimensions of AC are OL or KM processes (e.g. evaluating, assimilating, and applying external knowledge). Finally, AC has been positioned as a dynamic capability that is instrumental in changing and reconfiguring routines and resources.

We see absorptive capacity as a research area that builds on concepts from OL, KM, and DC fields, and that is specialized on the strategic value of learning and knowledge for technology innovation. An example of a study that makes AC's foundations in the OL and KM fields explicit is recent work by Nemanich et al. (2010), who incorporate research on the micro-level learning and knowledge processes into each of the AC dimensions and link AC dimensions to Nonaka and Takeuchi's (1995) knowledge spiral and to Crossan et al.'s (1999) 4I Framework of Organizational Learning (Crossan et al., 1999). We summarize these two models here briefly before making the connections to AC.

Nonaka and Takeuchi (1995) suggest four basic modes of knowledge creation: socialization, externalization, internalization, and combination; and four types of content: sympathized knowledge, conceptual knowledge, operational knowledge, and systemic knowledge. Mintzberg, Ahlstrand, and Lampel (1998) summarize these 'four modes of knowledge conversion:'

> *Socialization* describes the implicit sharing of tacit knowledge, often even without the use of language—for example, through experience . . . *Externalization* converts tacit to explicit knowledge, often through the use of metaphors and analysis—special uses of language. *Combination* combines and passes formally codified knowledge from one person to another . . . *Internalization* takes explicit knowledge back to the tacit form, as people internalize it, as in 'learning by doing'. Learning must therefore take place with the body as in the mind.
>
> Mintzberg et al. (1998:211)

In their 4I framework of Organizational Learning, Crossan et al. (1999) argue that learning takes place on the individual, group, and organizational levels, and that four sub-processes link the three levels, involving both behavioral and cognitive changes. According to this model, the process of OL can be conceived as a dynamic interplay among the organization belief system, the behaviors of its members, and stimuli from the environment, where beliefs and behaviors are both an input and a product of the process as they undergo change. Mintzberg et al. (1998) summarize the four sub-processes embedded in the 4I framework:

Intuiting is a subconscious process that occurs at the level of the individual. It is the start of learning and must happen in a single mind. *Interpreting* then picks up on the conscious elements of this individual learning and shares it at the group level. *Integrating* follows to change collective understanding at the group level and bridges to the level of the whole organization. Finally, *institutionalizing* incorporates that learning across the organization by imbedding it in its systems, structures, routines, and practices.

Mintzberg et al. (1998: 212)

Nemanich et al. (2010) argue that the first two dimensions of AC, the capabilities to *evaluate and assimilate external knowledge*, are highly cognitive in nature, and thus depend on the intuition and interpretation of individual team members (Crossan et al., 1999). Interpretation is also associated with Nonaka and Takeuchi's (1995) externalization process. For Nemanich et al. (2010), the *collective assimilation* capability requires that the unique external knowledge gathered externally by an individual be shared among others through social interpretation processes for integration at the team level. In the 4I framework of OL, Crossan et al. (1999) describe interpretation as the process of achieving a shared understanding of knowledge by reducing equivocality among cognitive maps held by team members. Shared cognition is also related to Nonaka and Takeuchi's (1995) socialization and combination processes. Finally, Nemanich et al. (2010) argue that the capability to *apply external knowledge* requires both cognitive skills and the collective behavioral skills that are essential to team task effectiveness, such as decision making and problem solving. Crossan et al. (1999) describe the process whereby teams make mutual adjustments and take coherent collective action as integration, which is a learning process of teams rather than individuals. Integration is closely associated with the notion of internalization proposed by Nonaka and Takeuchi (1995).

Building on the conclusions from this initial review, the following section presents propositions that relate OL, KM, DC, and AC to firm performance.

INTEGRATIVE FRAMEWORK

In this section, we integrate existing work to propose relationships between our constructs of interest and firm performance. We define performance as the organization's success or failure in achieving its financial and non-financial (e.g. quality, reputation, growth) goals. Our integrative model is shown in Figure 8.3.

Connecting learning types to the capability hierarchy

The study of organizational learning dates back to the 1930s, when the first work on organizational learning curves appeared (reviewed in Argote, 1999). Argyris and Schön might be considered the 'founding fathers' of the discussion about the learning types of which they identified three (Argyris and Schön, 1978). 'Single-loop learning' occurs when a mismatch between intended and obtained outcomes is detected and corrected without changing the underlying routines that govern the behaviors. 'Double-loop learning' occurs when a mismatch is detected and corrected by first changing the routines based on a new conception of the universe. 'Deutero-learning' is the second-order

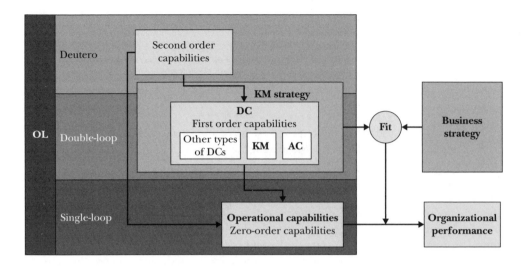

Figure 8.3 Integrative Framework

learning enacted on single- or double-loop, which can be described as learning to learn (Argyris, 2003). This typology has been clarified but not significantly challenged, modified, or connected to the new theories of knowledge and capabilities since its inception. Therefore, we based our theoretical development on the premise summarizing this conceptualization.

> Premise: OL is a comprehensive process consisting of single-loop, double-loop and deutero- learning.

Since OL is conceptualized as a process, the process theory is an appropriate theoretical framework to employ. A typical process theory holds that similar inputs transformed by similar processes will lead to similar outcomes; that there are specific necessary conditions for the outcome to be reached. Thus, a process level explanation identifies the generative mechanisms that cause observed events to happen in the real world, and the particular circumstances or contingencies when these causal mechanisms operate (Van de Ven and Poole, 1995). Therefore, OL provides what Bunge (1997) calls a 'mechanismic' explanation, i.e. an explanation of the mechanisms which underline a particular relationship between constructs.

In contrast to process theories, content theories such as RBV, DC, and others prioritize nouns over verbs and provide conceptual explanations of organizational outcomes (Garud and Van de Ven, 2002). In this sense, content theories are more static than process theories.

Based on our foregoing discussion, we propose the following connection between OL types and different levels of capabilities. This explanation is visualized in Figure 8.3 via a multilayer rectangle representing different types of OL.

Proposition 1: OL is the mechanism for development or change of capabilities of any order (zero, first, second) whereby single-loop learning is related to zero-order capabilities, double-loop learning is related to first-order capabilities, and deutero-learning is related to second-order capabilities.

Easterby-Smith and Prieto's (2008) model proposes that DC, as the first-order capability, modifies existing resources and routines over time, whereas OL, as the second-order capability, mediates between KM and DC and contributes to the evolution of both (see fig. 2 in Easterby-Smith and Prieto, 2008: 243). Our position is consistent with Easterby-Smith and Prieto's approach, but differs from theirs in that we propose that the organizational learning system of processes—including single-loop, double-loop, and deutero-learning processes—is behind all levels of the capability hierarchy, and underlies the creation and development of dynamic capabilities (including knowledge management and absorptive capacity) and operational capabilities. This position is consistent with our argument behind Figure 8.2, when we concluded that organizational learning processes were the core elements behind the concepts of KM, DC, and AC. We summarize these propositions below.

Proposition 2a: OL is positively related to the development and change of DC (including KM and AC), and of operational capabilities.
Proposition 2b: DC (including KM and AC) is positively related to the development and change of operational capabilities.

In Figure 8.3, our visual representation also differs from Easterby-Smith and Prieto's (2008) model in that it is presented as a series of cascading rectangles to highlight the idea of different levels ('orders') of capabilities that correspond to the different types of OL processes.

THE MODERATING ROLE OF A KNOWLEDGE STRATEGY

In Figure 8.3, we link operational capabilities to firm performance. Increasingly, dynamic capability researchers are agreeing that it is not dynamic capabilities, *per se*, that lead to competitive advantage, but it is the resulting configuration of operational capabilities and resources—including knowledge—that has an impact on performance (e.g. Eisenhardt and Martin, 2000; Winter, 2003). As described earlier, operational capabilities are rooted in knowledge and learning and, in particular, in single-loop learning. Thus, the link to examine is the relationship between learning/knowledge and performance.

Researchers have opposite views about the impact of learning and knowledge on firm performance. On one side of this discussion are those scholars who establish a positive link between these constructs. In their pioneering work, Cangelosi and Dill (1965) mention that improved performance is learning. Later, Fiol and Lyles (1985) propose that, irrespective of the underlying interpretations of organizational learning, 'in all instances the assumption that learning will improve future performance exists' (1985: 803). The perspective of the knowledge-based view further stresses a positive link between knowledge and performance. It is expected that a particular sub-category of knowledge, which is valuable, rare, inimitable, and non-substitutable (Barney, 1991), would lead to competitive advantage.

On the other side of the discussion are authors (Argyris and Schön, 1978; March and Olsen, 1975) who do not see a direct relationship between learning, knowledge, and performance. For example, Levitt and March (1988) state that 'learning does not always lead to intelligent behavior' (1988: 335) and Huber (1991) adds that 'learning does not always increase the learner's effectiveness or even potential effectiveness . . . Entities can incorrectly learn, and they can correctly learn that which is incorrect' (1991: 89). Complementary to this view is Leonard's (1992) description of how core rigidities are deeply embedded knowledge sets that hinder innovation. Arthur's (1989) law of increasing returns also supports the equivocal link between knowledge and performance. While having a good base of knowledge means that a company can leverage it and increase its advantage over competitors, having a poor base of knowledge means that the company that is losing advantage can only lose further advantage. Finally, from their review of the OL literature, Crossan et al. (1995) conclude that good performance is not a sign of learning and that learning may negatively impact performance in the short term.

In conclusion, OL and KM views of the impact of learning and knowledge on performance are diverse. While the OL literature presents an equivocal link between the learning process and performance, the knowledge literature suggests that knowledge—if recognized as a source of competitive advantage—explains differences in performance. Essentially, the attention is given only to the knowledge that is valuable, rare, inimitable, and organized in a manner that enables exploitation.

Empirical efforts have found support for the direct impact of learning, knowledge, and human and social capital on performance (e.g. Appleyard, 1996; Bontis, Crossan, and Hulland, 2002; Decarolis and Deeds, 1999; Hitt, Bierman, Shimizu, and Kochhar, 2001; Yeoh and Roth, 1999). It is important to note that the conclusion of these studies is not that 'the more learning the better' or 'the more knowledge the better,' but that learning that is effective and that knowledge that is relevant may have positive effects on performance. In our model, we emphasize that when studying learning and knowledge as antecedents of firm outcomes, it is critical that contextual variables, and in particular strategic variables, be included. The effectiveness of learning can only be assessed on the basis of its utility in guiding behavior relative to the organization's relevant domain (Crossan, 1991).

Capturing this thinking, we include in our integrative framework a fit construct, which represents the fit or mutual alignment between a firm's business strategy and a firm's knowledge management strategy. The notion of fit has been extensively used in contingency theories to study alignment among organizational factors such as the environment, structure, culture, leadership, and the strategy of firms (e.g. Thomas, Litschert, and Ramaswami, 1991; Venkatraman and Prescott, 1990). Argote, McEvily, and Reagans (2003) explicitly call for application of the fit or congruence concept in the field of OL/KM. In our third proposition, fit is a moderator of the impact of operational capabilities—rooted in learning and knowledge—on performance. Building on Teece (2007), we position a KM strategy as part of the development of the KM dynamic capability that allows firms to maintain competitiveness through enhancing, combining, protecting, and, when necessary, reconfiguring the business enterprise's intangible and tangible assets (Teece, 2007). We propose that if learning and knowledge are not relevant to, and consistent with, the firm's purpose, they do not guarantee positive results. For knowledge to become a source of competitive advantage, firms need to match their KM strategy with their business strategy. When a firm's KM strategy matches its business strategy, the impact of knowledge and learning is positive. If this match is not achieved, knowledge and learning may have no impact or even have a negative impact on performance.

In the late 1990s, authors in the OL and KM fields started to develop the 'learning strategy' and 'knowledge strategy' constructs. These learning/knowledge strategies can be explicit or implicit. Bierly and Chakrabarti (1996) define a knowledge strategy as the set of strategic choices that shape and direct the organization's learning process and determine the firm's knowledge base. In contrast to Bierly and Chakrabarti's definition, Zack's (1999) definition of knowledge strategy explicitly includes the notion of fit with the firm's business strategy. He suggests that a knowledge strategy describes the overall approach an organization intends to take to align its knowledge resources and capabilities with the intellectual requirements of its business strategy. Through a knowledge strategy, organizations identify the knowledge required to execute the firm's strategic intent, compare that to its actual knowledge, and recognize its strategic knowledge gaps (Zack, 1999).

There are also initial efforts in the late 1990s and 2000s in the OL and KM fields towards understanding the dimensions of an OL/KM strategy. As part of their knowledge strategy taxonomy, Bierly and Chakrabarti (1996) describe four tensions in the learning process: the tension between external and internal learning, radical and incremental learning, fast and slow learning, and a narrow and wide knowledge base. Building on this work, Zack (1999) adds that a knowledge strategy includes decisions regarding the creation, development, and maintenance of a firm's knowledge resources and capabilities. These decisions are the choices between internal and external knowledge, and between exploration and exploitation. These two pieces of research cut across the KM and the strategy fields. In addition, Argote (1999) lists several tensions or tradeoffs in the learning process, which define a learning strategy. These are the tensions between group and organizational learning, heterogeneity and standardization, learning by planning and learning by doing, and the tension between fast and slow learning. Argote's (1999) work cuts across the OL and KM fields. Vera and Crossan (2004) propose a connection between different styles of strategic leadership (transformational and transactional) and the different components of an OL system. Although this work is positioned in the OL/ strategy theoretical domain, it does not presuppose the deployment of a particular type of leadership as an intentional knowledge strategy but suggests mechanisms that leaders can use to support the elements of an OL system.

Given that these three lists of learning/knowledge choices barely overlap each other, it appears that neither list is comprehensive. However, for the purposes of this chapter, we are not interested in providing a comprehensive list of the dimensions of a KM strategy, but in emphasizing the importance of studying the impact of learning and knowledge on performance within the strategic context of the firm. In addition to the work of Bierly and Chakrabarti (1996), Argote (1999), and Zack (1999), other authors have introduced similar concepts such as 'learning styles' (Ribbens, 1997), 'learning modes' (Miller, 1996), 'learning orientations' (Nevis, DiBella, and Gould, 1995), and 'knowledge management styles' (Jordan and Jones, 1997). Table 8.2 summarizes the dimensions discussed in these conceptualizations. There is ample room for future research in the integration of these concepts and for new studies on this topic.

Table 8.2 Examples of dimensions incorporated into learning/knowledge strategies

Author	Typology / Taxonomy	Dimensions
Bierly and Chakrabarti (1996)	Four knowledge strategies	• External-Internal learning • Incremental-Radical learning • Fast-Slow learning • Breadth of knowledge base
Argote (1999)	Four tensions in the learning process	• Group-Organizational learning • Heterogeneity-Standardization • Learning by planning-Learning by doing • Fast-Slow learning
Zack (1999)	Six knowledge strategies	• External-Internal knowledge • Exploration-Exploitation
Nevis, DiBella and Gould (1995)	Seven learning orientations	• Knowledge source (internal-external) • Product-process focus • Documentation mode (personal-public) • Dissemination mode (formal-informal) • Incremental-radical learning • Value-chain focus (design-deliver) • Skill development focus (individual-group)
Hansen, Nohria, and Tierney (1999)	Knowledge management strategies	• 'people-to-documents' and 'person-to-person' KM approaches • Codification-personalization strategies
Birkinshaw and Sheehan (2002)	Knowledge life cycle and its strategies	• Four stages: creation, mobilization, diffusion, and commoditization • Codification-personalization strategies
Ribbens (1997)	Four organizational learning styles	• Random-Sequential knowledge • Abstract-Concrete knowledge

Author	Typology / Taxonomy	Dimensions
Jordan and Jones (1997)	Knowledge management styles	• Knowledge acquisition • Focus: internal-external • Search: opportunistic-focused • Problem-solving • Location: individual-team • Procedures: trial and error-heuristics • Activity: experimental-abstract • Scope: incremental-radical • Dissemination • Processes: informal-formal • Breadth: narrow-wide • Ownership • Identity: personal-collective • Resource: specialist-generalist • Storage/memory • Representation: tacit-explicit

The previous discussion leads to our third proposition:

Proposition 3: The fit between a firm's KM strategy and its business strategy moderates the positive relationship between operational capabilities (rooted in knowledge and learning) and firm performance, so that the greater the fit, the more positive the relationship between operational capabilities and firm performance.

In the next section, we provide conclusions and directions for future research based on the discussion in this chapter.

CONCLUSIONS AND DIRECTIONS FOR FUTURE RESEARCH

The objective of this chapter has been to reduce the conceptual confusion in the organizational learning, knowledge management, dynamic capabilities, and absorptive capacity fields by providing synthesis and integration of these closely related concepts. To achieve this purpose, we have critically reviewed previous research in an effort to understand how these literatures fit together and how they can be integrated into a more meaningful conceptual model for both academics and practitioners. We propose the present framework as an instrument to facilitate communication between researchers. It is not our intent to force fit the model, but to build on previous research to open up the possibility for provocative and creative dialogue that will further develop this integrative model.

A key contribution of this chapter has been to sketch the boundaries of each of the field's domains. The conclusion from Figure 8.2 was that the fields greatly overlap. Although there are topics that are mainly being studied by one field (e.g. the knowledge-based view of the firm in KM, or how processes can be a source of sustainable competitive advantage in DC) and topics in which one community is more advanced in its theoretical development (e.g. a multilevel theory of learning in OL, and the specific importance of acquiring external knowledge for innovation in AC), there are also multiple topics that are being studied by OL, KM, DC, and AC researchers at the same time. We believe there are significant opportunities for each of the communities to learn from the experience and developments of the others.

In our original 2003 chapter in this Handbook, we called for authors to acknowledge multiple literature bases in their work. Since then, learning research has definitely moved towards increasing integration. We have emphasized in our present discussion the strong link between learning processes and knowledge-associated processes and capabilities. For example, Argyris and Shön's (1978) organizational learning types and Winter's (2003) dynamic capability hierarchy have many elements in common, and we think an integration of these two models would help to move the still young perspective of dynamic capabilities forward in its theoretical development. Elevating organizational learning processes as the core element of these diverse theories will go a long way to reduce risks to continuously 'reinvent the wheel' in the learning fields.

A final conclusion from our model is that learning and the accumulation of knowledge only leads to better performance when they support and are aligned with the firm's strategy. We have argued in this chapter that researchers interested in studying the impact of OL, KM, DC, and AC on performance need to be more specific about the characteristics of the knowledge that enhances performance and the conditions under which learning leads to competitive advantage. We have proposed the fit between a firm's knowledge management strategy as a moderator of the impact of learning and knowledge on performance. We see potential in the further theoretical development of the 'learning/knowledge strategy' construct and invite researchers in the two fields to work together to define the critical decisions or tradeoffs that managers need to address regarding learning and knowledge resources in their firms.

One important direction of future theoretical work is to build on Gioia and Pitre's (1990) call for a multi-paradigm approach to theory building and to link, or at least juxtapose, the multiple views about knowledge, learning, and capabilities that have been created by different paradigms. Although researchers are likely to root their work in the assumptions of one paradigm, it is important to acknowledge and incorporate some of the insights coming from multiple perspectives. In our case, we come from a positivist perspective, but have tried to emphasize in our analysis the value of incorporating insights from social constructivist and interpretivist paradigms.

A final direction for future empirical work is to test our propositions. In testing them, future research needs to address the choice of appropriate measures and methodology. Several instruments are available in the academic and managerial OL, KM, DC, and AC literatures. Furthermore, future research can build on Bierly and Chakrabarti's (1996) operationalization of a knowledge strategy in the pharmaceutical industry. To operationalize the fit between a firm's business strategy and a firm's learning/knowledge strategy, researchers can build on empirical work in contingency and configurational theories (e.g. Thomas, Litschert, and Ramaswami, 1991; Venkatraman and Prescott, 1990) that study fit among constructs and how this fit impacts performance outcomes.

To conclude, we hope this study provides researchers in organizational learning, knowledge management, dynamic capabilities, and absorptive capability with a preliminary map of how these fields relate to one another. There is much to be learned from each domain and we are hopeful that researchers will seek to expand the literature bases from which they draw to advance the field as a whole.

REFERENCES

Appleyard, M. (1996) How does knowledge flow? Interfirm patterns in the semiconductor industry. *Strategic Management Journal*, 17: 137–154.

Argote, L. (1999) *Organizational Learning: Creating, Retaining, and Transferring Knowledge.* Norwell, MA: Kluwer.

Argote, L. (2005) Reflection on two views of managing learning and knowledge in organizations. *Journal of Management Inquiry*, 14(1): 43–48.

Argote, L. and Ingram, P. (2000) Knowledge transfer: A basis for competitive advantage in firms. *Organizational Behavior and Human Decision Processes*, 82: 150–169.

Argote, L., McEvily, B., and Reagans, R. (2003) Managing knowledge in organizations: An integrative framework and review of emerging themes. *Management Science*, 49(4): 571–582.

Argyris, C. (2003) A life full of learning. *Organization Studies*, 24: 1178–1192.

Argyris, C. and Schön, D. (1978) *Organizational learning: A theory of action perspective.* Reading, MA: Addison-Wesley.

Arthur, W. (1989) Competing technologies, increasing returns, and lock-in by historical events. *Economic Journal*, 99: 116–131.

Barnett, W., Greve, H., and Park, D. (1994) An evolutionary model of organizational performance. *Strategic Management Journal*, 15: 11–28.

Barney, J. (1991) Firm resources and sustained competitive advantage. *Journal of Management*, 17: 99–120.

Bassi, L. (1999) Harnessing the power of intellectual capital. In J. Cortada and J. Woods (eds.), *The Knowledge Management Yearbook 1999–2000.* Boston: Butterworth Heinemann: 422–431.

Bierly, P. and Chakrabarti, A. (1996) Generic knowledge strategies in the U.S. pharmaceutical industry. *Strategic Management Journal*, 17: 123–135.

Birkinshaw, J. and Sheehan, T. (2002) Managing the knowledge life cycle. *MIT Sloan Management Review*, 44(1): 75–83.

Blackler, F. (1995) Knowledge, knowledge work, and organizations: An overview and interpretation. *Organization Studies*, 16: 1021–1046.

Bontis, N., Crossan, M., and Hulland, J. (2002) Managing an organizational learning system by aligning stocks and flows. *Journal of Management Studies*, 39(4): 437–469.

Brown, J.S. and Duguid, P. (1991) Organizational learning and communities of practice: Toward a unified view of working, learning, and innovation. *Organizational Science*, 2: 40–57.

Bunge, M. (1997) Mechanism and explanation. *Philosophy of the Social Sciences*, 27(4): 410–465.

Cangelosi, V. and Dill, W. (1965) Organizational learning observations: Toward a theory. *Administrative Sciences Quarterly*, 10: 175–203.

Casey, A. (1997) Collective memory in organizations. In J.P. Walsh and A.S. Huff (Eds.), *Advances in Strategic Management: Organizational Learning and Strategic Management*, 14: 111–151.

Cepeda, G. and Vera, D. (2007) Dynamic capabilities and operational capabilities: A knowledge management perspective. *Journal of Business Research*, 60: 426–437.

Cohen, D. and Sproull, D. (1996) *Organizational Learning*. London, Sage.

Cohen, W.M. and Levinthal, D.A. (1989) Innovation and learning: The two faces of R and D. *The Economic Journal*, 99: 569–596.

Cohen, W.M. and Levinthal, D.A. (1990) Absorptive capacity: A new perspective on learning and innovation. *Administrative Science Quarterly*, 35(1): 128–152.

Collins, H. (1993) The structure of knowledge. *Social Research*, 60: 95–116.

Collis, D.J. (1994) How valuable are organizational capabilities? *Strategic Management Journal*, 15: 143–153.

Cook, S. and Brown, J.S. (1999) Bridging epistemologies: The generative dance between organizational knowledge and organizational knowing. *Organization Science*, 10: 381–400.

Crossan, M. (1991) Organization learning: A sociocognitive model of strategic management. *PhD Dissertation*, The University of Western Ontario.

Crossan, M., Lane, H., and White, R. (1999) An organizational learning framework: From intuition to institution. *Academy of Management Review*, 24: 522–538.

Crossan, M., Lane, H., White, R. and Djurfeldt, L. (1995) Organizational learning: Dimensions for a theory. *The International Journal of Organizational Analysis*, 3: 337–360.

Daft, R. and Weick, K. (1984) Towards a model of organizations as interpretation systems. *Academy of Management Review*, 9: 284–295.

Decarolis, D.M. and Deeds, D. (1999) The impact of stocks and flows of organizational knowledge on firm performance: An empirical investigation of the biotechnology industry. *Strategic Management Journal*, 20: 953–968.

DeGeus, A. (1988) Planning as learning. *Harvard Business Review*, 2: 70–74.

Doz, Y. (1996) The evolution of cooperation in strategic alliances: Initial conditions or learning processes? *Strategic Management Journal*, 17: 55–79.

Duncan, R. and Weiss, A. (1979) Organizational learning: Implications for organizational design. In B. Staw (ed.), *Research in Organizational Behavior*. Greenwich, CT: JAI Press: 75–124.

Easterby-Smith, M. (1997) Disciplines of organizational learning: Contributions and critiques. *Human Relations*, 50: 1058–1113.

Easterby-Smith, M. and Prieto, I. (2008) Dynamic capabilities and knowledge management: An integrative role for learning? *British Journal of Management*, 19: 235–249.

Easterby-Smith, M., Graça, M., Antonacopoulou, E., and Ferdinand, J. (2008) Absorptive capacity: A process perspective. *Management Learning*, 39: 483–501.

Easterby-Smith, M., Snell, R., and Gherardi, S. (1998) Organizational learning: Diverging communities of practices? *Management Learning*, 29: 259–272.

Eisenhardt, K.M. and Martin, J.A. (2000) Dynamic capabilities: What are they? *Strategic Management Journal*, 21: 1105–1121.

Fiol, C.M. and Lyles, M.A. (1985) Organisational learning. *Academy of Management Review*, 10: 803–813.

Garud, R. and Van de Ven, A. (2002) Strategic change processes. In A. Pettigrew, H. Thomas and R. Whittington (eds.), *Handbook of Strategy and Management*. London: Sage: 206–231.

Garyd, R. and Kumaraswamy, A. (1995) Technological and organizational designs for realizing economies of substitution. *Strategic Management Journal*, 16: 93–109.

Gherardi, S., Nicolini, D., and Odella, F. (1998) Toward a social understanding of how people learn in organizations. *Management Learning*, 29: 273–297.

Ghoshal, S. and Moran, P. (1996) Bad for practice: A critique of the transaction cost theory. *Academy of Management Review*, 21: 13–47.

Gioia, D. and Pitre, E. (1990) Multiparadigm perspectives on theory building. *Academy of Management Review*, 15: 584–603.

Grant, R. (1996) Toward a knowledge-based theory of the firm. *Strategic Management Journal*, 17: 109–122.

Hansen, M., Nohria, N., and Tierney, T. (1999) What is your strategy for managing knowledge? *Harvard Business Review*, 77(2): 106–116.

Helfat, C.E. and Peteraf, M.A. (2003) The dynamic resource-based view: Capability lifecycles. *Strategic Management Journal*, 24: 997–1010.

Hitt, M., Bierman, L. Shimizu, K., and Kochhar, R. (2001) Direct and moderating effects of human capital on strategy and performance in professional service firms: A resource-based perspective. *Academy of Management Journal*, 44: 13–28.

Huber, G. (1991) Organizational learning: The contributing processes and the literatures. *Organization Science*, 2: 88–115.

Inkpen, A. and Crossan, M. (1995) Believing is seeing: Joint ventures and organizational learning. *Journal of Management Studies*, 32: 595–619.

Isaacs, W. (1993) Taking flight: Dialogue, collective thinking, and organizational learning. *Organizational Dynamics*, 22: 24–39.

Jordan, J. and Jones, P. (1997) Assessing your company's knowledge management style. *Long Range Planning*, 30: 392–398.

Kedia, B.L. and Bhagat, R.S. (1988) Cultural constraints on transfer of technology across nations: Implications for research in international and comparative management. *The Academy of Management Review*, 13(4): 559–571.

King, W.R., Chung, T.R., and Haney, M.H. (2008) Knowledge management and organizational learning. *Omega-International Journal of Management Science*, 36: 167–172.

Kogut, B. and Zander, U. (1992) Knowledge of the firm, combinative capabilities, and the replication of technology. *Organization Science*, 3: 383–397.

Lane, P.J., Koka, B.R., and Pathak, S. (2006) The reification of absorptive capacity: A critical review and rejuvenation of the construct. *Academy of Management Review*, 31(4): 833–863.

Lant, T. and Mezias, S. (1992) An organizational learning model of convergence and reorientation. *Organization Science*, 3: 47–71.

Leonard, D. (1992) Core capabilities and core rigidities: A paradox in managing new product development. *Strategic Management Journal*, 13: 111–125.

Levitt, B. and March, J. (1988) Organizational learning. *Annual Review of Sociology*, 14: 319–340.

Liebowitz, J. and Wilcox, L. (1997) *Knowledge Management and its Integrative Elements*. Boca Raton: CRC Press.

Lyles, M. and Salk, J. (1996) Knowledge acquisition from foreign parents in international joint ventures: An empirical examination in the Hungarian context. *Journal of International Business Studies*, 27: 877–903.

MacIntosh, R. (1999) Conditioned emergence: A dissipative structures approach to transformation. *Strategic Management Journal*, 20: 297–316.

March, J. and Olsen, J. (1975) Organizational learning under ambiguity. *European Journal of Policy Review*, 3: 147–171.

McEvily, S.K. and Chakravarthy, B. (2002) The persistence of knowledge-based advantage: An empirical test for product performance and technological knowledge. *Strategic Management Journal*, 23: 285–305.

Mezias, S. and Glynn, M.A. (1993) The three faces of corporate renewal: Institution, revolution, and evolution. *Strategic Management Journal*, 14: 77–101.

Miller, D. (1996) A preliminary typology of organizational learning: Synthesizing the literature. *Journal of Management*, 22: 485–505.

Miner, A. and Mezias, S. (1996) Ugly duckling no more: Pasts and futures of organizational learning research. *Organization Science*, 7: 88–99.

Mintzberg, H., Ahlstrand, B., and Lampel, J. (1998) *Strategy Safari: A Guided Tour through the Wilds of Strategic Management.* New York: The Free Press.

Nelson, R. and Winter, S. (1982) *An Evolutionary Theory of Economic Change.* Cambridge, MA: Harvard University Press.

Nemanich, N. (2008) What are the impacts of absorptive capacity? A meta-analysis. *Working paper*, Arizona State University.

Nemanich, N., Keller, R., Vera, D., and Chin, W. (2010) Absorptive capacity in RandD project teams: A conceptualization and empirical test. *IEEE Engineering Management* (forthcoming).

Nevis, E., DiBella, A., and Gould, J. (1995) Understanding organizations as learning systems. *Sloan Management Review*, Winter: 73–85.

Nicolini, D. and Meznar, M. (1995) The social construction of organizational learning: Conceptual and practical issues in the field. *Human Relations*, 48: 727–740.

Nonaka, I. and Takeuchi, H. (1995) *The Knowledge-Creating Company: How Japanese Companies Create the Dynamics of Innovation.* Oxford: Oxford University Press.

O'Leary, D. (1998) Using AI in Knowledge management: Knowledge bases and ontologies. *IEEE Intelligent Systems*, 13: 34–39.

Orlikowski, W.J. (2002) Knowing in practice: Enacting a collective capability in distributed organizing. *Organization Science*, 13(3): 249–273.

Penrose, E. (1959) *The Theory of the Growth of the Firm.* Oxford: Blackwell.

Pisano, G. (1994) Knowledge, integration, and the locus of learning: An empirical analysis of process development. *Strategic Management Journal*, 15: 85–100.

Polanyi, M. (1962) *Personal Knowledge: Towards a Post-Critical Philosophy.* Chicago, IL: University of Chicago Press.

Polanyi, M. (1967) *The Tacit Dimension.* London: Routledge.

Priem, R.L. and Butler, J.E. (2001) Is the resource-based 'view' a useful perspective for strategic management research? *Academy of Management Review*, 26: 22–40.

Prieto, I.M. and Easterby-Smith, M. (2006) Dynamic capabilities and the role of organizational knowledge: An exploration. *European Journal of Information Systems*, 15: 500–510.

Ribbens, B. (1997) Organizational learning styles: Categorizing strategic predispositions from learning. *The International Journal of Organizational Analysis*, 5: 59–73.

Schendel, D. (1996) Knowledge and the firm. *Strategic Management Journal*, 17: 1–4.

Schwandt, D.R. (1995) Learning as an organization: A journey into chaos. In S. Chawla and J. Renesch (Eds.), *Learning Organizations: Developing Cultures for Tomorrow's Workplace*. Portland, OR: Productivity Press: 365–379.

Senge, P. (1990) *The Fifth Discipline: The Art and Practice of the Learning Organization*. New York: Doubleday/Currency.

Shrivastava, P. and Grant, J. (1985) Empirically derived models of strategic decision making processes. *Strategic Management Journal*, 6: 97–114.

Simon, H. (1991) Bounded rationality and organizational learning. *Organization Science*, 2: 125–134.

Simonin, B.L. (2004) An empirical investigation of the process of knowledge transfer in international strategic alliances. *Journal of International Business Studies*, 35: 407–427.

Spender, J. (1994) Knowing, managing, and learning. *Management Learning*, 25: 387–412.

Spender, J.C. (1996) Making knowledge the basis of a dynamic theory of the firm. *Strategic Management Journal*, 17: 45–62.

Szulanski, G. (1996) Exploring internal stickiness: Impediments to the transfer of best practice within the firm. *Strategic Management Journal*, 17: 27–43.

Teece, D. (2007) Explicating dynamic capabilities: The nature and microfoundations of (sustainable) enterprise performance. *Strategic Management Journal*, 28: 1319–1350.

Teece, D., Pisano, G., and Shuen, A. (1997) Dynamic capabilities and strategic management. *Strategic Management Journal*, 18: 509–534.

Thomas, A., Litschert, R., and Ramaswami, K. (1991) The performance impact of strategy-manager coalignment: An empirical examination. *Strategic Management Journal*, 12: 509–522.

Todorova, G. and Durisin, B. (2007) Absorptive capacity: Valuing a reconceptualization. *Academy of Management Review*, 32: 774–786.

Van de Ven, A.H. and Poole, M.S. (1995) Explaining development and change in organizations. *Academy of Management Review*, 20(3): 510–540.

Van der Spek, R. and Spijkervet, A. (1997) Knowledge management: Dealing intelligently with knowledge. In J. Liebowitz and L. Wilcox (Eds.), *Knowledge Management and its Integrative Elements*. Boca Raton: CRC Press: 31–59.

Venkatraman, N. and Prescott, J. (1990) Environment-strategy coalignment: An empirical test of its performance implications. *Strategic Management Journal*, 11: 1–23.

Vera, D. and Crossan, M.A. (2004) Leadership and organizational learning. *The Academy of Management Review*, 29(2): 222–240.

Walsh, J.P. and Rivera, G. (1991) Organizational memory. *Academy of Management Review*, 16: 57–91.

Weick, K.E. (1991) The nontraditional quality of organizational learning. *Organization Science*, 2: 116–124.

Winter, S. (2003) Understanding dynamic capabilities. *Strategic Management Journal*, 24: 991–995.

Yeoh, P. and Roth, K. (1999) An empirical analysis of sustained advantage in the U.S. pharmaceutical industry: Impact of firm resources and capabilities. *Strategic Management Journal*, 20: 637–653.

Zack, M. (1999) Developing a knowledge strategy. *California Management Review*, 41: 125–145.

Zahra, S.A. and George, G. (2002) Absorptive capacity: A review, reconcepualisation, and extension, *Academy of Management Review*, 27(2): 185–203.

Zahra, S., Sapienza, H.J., and Davidsson, P. (2006) Entrepreneurship and dynamic capabilities: A review, model and research agenda. *Journal of Management Studies*, 43: 917–955.

Zollo, M. and Winter, S.G. (2002) Deliberate learning and the evolution of dynamic capabilities. *Organization Science*, 13: 339–351.

Part II

ORGANIZATIONAL LEARNING AND LEARNING ORGANIZATIONS

9

Learning Portfolios: An Alternative to Learning Organizations

ANTHONY J. DIBELLA

ABSTRACT

The labels and names we give to constructs reflect our underlying assumptions and theories yet shape their practical implications and our research agendas. This chapter advocates a view of 'organizations as learning portfolios' and contrasts their characteristics with the image of 'the learning organization'. In the former, learning is considered an innate aspect of all organizations whose learning styles represent an acquired capability. A firm's investments in learning can be allocated and managed within the context of its portfolio. Learning portfolios can be managed to maximum effect when the impact and time value of learning are considered. The role of chief learning officers is to oversee a firm's learning portfolio or architecture. A set of research implications is presented.

INTRODUCTION

Metaphors and images are powerful tools that shape how we perceive and interact with the world (Morgan, 1986, 1993). The presumptions we carry about people, places, and things guide our expectations and actions; and the words we use to label, characterize, or describe our world embed or reflect what those presumptions are. It is no different in the domain of organization studies. The labels we give to our constructs carry with them meanings and assumptions that, although usually unstated, guide our hypothesis making and testing, and the actions of those who apply our theories.

In this chapter I examine images and characterizations that pertain to the nature of learning in and of organizations. In particular I offer and advocate a view of 'organizations as learning portfolios' by specifying presumptions necessary to substantiate this image and identifying critical dimensions and their implications, both theoretical and practical. Part of this elaboration is to differentiate the image from that of 'the learning organization' which has become a customary way to juxtapose the words 'learning' and 'organization.' To exemplify an organization as a learning portfolio, I include and draw from a case study of FIAT Auto.

An image of 'organizations as learning portfolios' affirms the multi-dimensionality of learning in and of organizations. This perspective has significant implications for the design of interventions to promote learning and change. Instead of viewing organizations as monoliths and then prescribing singular learning practices that are universally viewed as optimal (i.e. 'best practices'), advocates for organizational effectiveness respond to the particularities that exist within complex organizations by choosing to manage multiple learning activities. Specific activities are valued for their unique contributions and for the synergistic possibilities created through their complementarity with other activities. What is valued is not the best form or type of learning but a breadth of learning activities, relative effectiveness, and alignment with the organization's mission.

IMAGES OF ORGANIZATIONS AND LEARNING

Organizations as learning portfolios

Howard Gardner (1993) and Daniel Goleman (1995) have shown that understanding the learning capability of individuals requires more than just testing for IQ. Learning and intelligence are multi-dimensional concepts that cannot be determined with a single measure. Reliance on single measures simplifies reality but, more critically, devalues ways of learning and forms of intelligence that deviate from social norms.

Much as individuals learn in different ways (Kolb, 1979), so too is the case with organizations. To some extent these differences are a function of the diverse environments in which organizations must operate. For example, in stable environments with established products like ketchup or cement, what and how organizations learn will be very different from what occurs in industries that are volatile and involve new products or evolving technologies, such as computer hardware and software. Learning differences between organizations also occur as a result of differences in history, culture, size, and age. New, entrepreneurial firms are apt to learn differently from larger, established firms. This creates opportunities for firms, like Apple's chance in the 1970s and 1980s to take market share away from IBM. However, more critically the social complexity of organizations supports multiple cultural realities or segments (Van Maanen and Barley, 1985), and how learning occurs in one segment will differ from how it occurs in another (DiBella, 2001).

Organizational learning style is a function of how organizations learn as represented by the different learning activities that they undertake (DiBella and Nevis, 1998). An organization's pattern of learning activities reflects its learning style (Shrivastava, 1983). Such styles do not indicate how well an organization is learning nor judge the value of what is learned, but they do indicate a great deal about what is learned and how learning takes place. In aggregate, a complex organization is bound to support numerous learning practices that represent different learning styles. These practices and styles constitute the raw elements of an organization's learning portfolio. By recognizing a range of learning styles within an organization, we can focus on how certain styles are matched to work demands and provide complementary or strategic advantages.

Learning styles represent an organization's acquired capability. To use that capability for competitive advantage, organizational members must first recognize what that capability consists of. Identifying current capabilities provides a starting point for strategic action to change, augment, or enhance one's style or portfolio of styles. Rather than presume no existing competence and dictate its development top down, managers work with, and from what already exists.

Research has revealed that some organizations have a dominant learning style, while many more use a variety of styles, each of which provide some learning capability (DiBella et al., 1996). Companies with a large portfolio of styles are apt to have multiple competencies and a greater capacity to adapt to change than companies that rely on a single learning style. By focusing on a company's learning portfolio in its entirety, learning advocates re-orient themselves from wondering whether the company has the right learning style (or is, or is not, a learning organization) to considering the complementarity of its styles. Instead of evaluating the style of a particular part of a company, the learning advocate takes a systems view to consider synergistic possibilities. Recognizing the presence of multiple styles within a company can also explain inter-group conflicts and barriers to learning. If different parts of a company learn in different ways, then it is highly unlikely that knowledge will be transferred across functional or project boundaries. Once we recognize such differences, they can be managed as a potential source of competitive advantage.

One possible reason why managers often ignore existing capabilities is their attention to the plea that organizations must first unlearn before they can learn (Hedberg, 1981; McGill and Slocum, 1993). However, to develop learning capability organizations must distinguish between unlearning *what* they know and do and *how* they learn as represented by their learning portfolio. Managers can then make more informed assessments about how present capabilities realize or inhibit learning and whether barriers to improved performance exist because of what is being learned versus how learning takes place.

Table 9.1 contains a set of characteristics about learning and organizations. I start with the major presumption that learning is an essential process of all organizations. From this core, a set of related characteristics can be derived.

All organizations learn   Rather than face a bi-modal world consisting of organizations that learn and those that do not, I make the presumption that all organizations learn. Hence the notion of the learning organization is as redundant as the notion of hot steam or a breathing mammal. Organizations don't have to be developed so they can learn, they already do.

Source of learning   Learning occurs through the natural social interaction of people being and working together (Brown and Duguid, 2000). Organizations as contexts for social interaction naturally induce learning. Learning occurs through the very nature of organizational life.

Learning is rooted in culture   As cultures, all organizations have embedded learning processes. For example, acculturation, which every organization must have to integrate new employees (Van Maanen and Schein, 1979), is an embedded learning process. As organizational culture evolves so too does the nature and process of learning.

Table 9.1   Organizations as learning portfolios

Uni-modal world: All organizations have learning capability

Source of learning: Organizational existence

Culture: Culture is created and survives through embedded learning processes

Organizations are heterogeneous: Complex organizations house different structural units and sub-cultures

Learning style: Multiple and complementary, or in conflict

Managerial focal point: Understanding and appreciating current capability

---

Organizations are differentiated structures   Different organizational units promote different behaviors and forms of interaction. There is differentiation in behaviors and social interaction both vertically and horizontally in organizations (Trice and Beyer, 1993). Types and forms of learning vary between these different units. The cacophony of differences is consistent with a view of complex systems as organized anarchies (Cohen et al., 1972).

Learning styles   Organizations learn in divergent ways. There is no one way to learn or better ways for organizations to learn. Learning styles will vary across an organization that may house multiple styles in different organizational units.

Managerial focal point   Managers need to understand the nature of social interaction in their organizations and how existing behavior and routines engender learning. Once management understands how their organizations learn, they can direct those learning processes towards what is strategically desirable.

To understand the distinctiveness of the 'organization as learning portfolio' metaphor or framework, I now review the quite popular view of the learning organization. Those who advocate for the learning organization carry, like the rest of us, a set of presumptions about learning and organizations (Edmondson, 1996). These are infrequently stated and may be subconscious but can be deduced from the nature of their writing and its implications.

The 'Learning Organization'

In the 1990s, the learning organization became synonymous with long-term success. As elaborated by Arie deGeus (1988) and Peter Senge (1990), the learning organization is a template for an organization that continually creates its future by adapting to environmental change and pro-actively shaping its environment. The learning organization is a powerful vision and metaphor for change (Calhoun and Starbuck, 2003), but what does this juxtaposition of the words 'learning' and 'organization' represent?

Table 9.2 contains a set of characteristics derived from some of the writing on learning organizations. The key point is that presumptions may be derived from the connotations of the term itself.

Bi-modal world   By conceiving of 'learning organizations' and advocating for their creation or development, theorists effectively bifurcate the world of organizations. When learning is used as an adjective to describe a particular type of organization, one underlying assumption is that some organizations learn and others do not. Such a division suggests that learning is optional and not indigenous to the life of organizations.

Source of learning   Why do some organizations learn and others do not? Learning, as a mechanism to foster organizational improvement, does not occur through chance or random action but through the development and use of specific skills. Without disciplined action or intervention from their leaders, organizations fail to learn due to the impact of the many forces that constrain learning. For example, Senge (1990) states that it takes five component technologies or disciplines to establish a learning organization—personal mastery, mental models, shared vision, team learning, and systems thinking. What distinguishes learning organizations (from non-learning organizations) is their mastery or focus on these five disciplines. Another normative modeler (Garvin, 1993) claims that learning organizations are skilled at systematic problem solving, experimentation, learning from their own experiences and from others, and transferring knowledge.

Culture and learning   For organizations to learn, they must have the right culture, a learning culture. Mayo and Rick (1993) claim that a learning organization can be recognized by the interdependence of language and culture. In a similar manner, Beckhard and Pritchard (1992) discuss building a learning organization by creating a culture that values learning and rewards progress not just results.

Organizations as homogeneous, structured systems   Duncan and Weiss (1979) explain that learning occurs when organizations match their structures to their environments in order to maximize the understanding of members of action–outcome relationships. Purser and Pasmore (1992) claim that learning is dependent on the design of knowledge work. To maximize learning, the design of knowledge work must be formalized and aligned with the influence of decision makers. These theoreticians base their argument on the presumption that becoming a learning organization is predicated on having the right organization structure or design. Adler and Cole (1993) argue that this is so empirically as well. They claim that the work design at NUMMI Motors, the Toyota-GM

Table 9.2   The learning organization

Bi-modal world: There are organizations that learn and those that do not
Source of learning: Strategic action promotes the prerequisite conditions
The role of culture: Organizations must have the right culture for learning to occur
Organizations are homogeneous: Organizations learn systemically or they do not
Learning style: Learning processes are singular and specific
Managerial focal point: Innate organizational disabilities which prevent learning

joint car manufacturing venture, provided greater learning opportunities than did the design of Volvo's Uddevalla plant. Through standardization of work methods, NUMMI was able to identify problems and areas for improvement that led to learning.

Learning style   An oft-cited theoretical distinction in learning styles is Argyris and Schön's (1978) familiar contrast between single- and double-loop learning. More recently, 'triple-loop learning,' learning about learning, has been identified as yet another learning style (Bartunek and Moch, 1987; Torbert, 1994). Learning organizations promote double- and triple-loop learning since those styles are considered more advanced.

Managerial focal point   Learning disabilities occur due to the fundamental ways in which individuals have been trained to think and act (Argyris and Schön, 1974, 1978; Senge, 1990) and from organizational barriers to discover and utilize solutions to organizational problems (Tucker et al., 2002). Snyder and Cummings (1992) identify the problems of amnesia (lack of organizational memory), superstition (biased interpretation of experience), paralysis (inability to act), and schizophrenia (lack of coordination among organizational constituencies). Watkins and Marsick (1993) address three barriers to learning—learned helplessness, truncated learning, and tunnel vision—with the latter paralleling Senge's call for a systems perspective. To avoid or solve learning disabilities, organizational leadership must establish the normative conditions essential for learning to take place. The focus may be on enhancing competencies of individual members or teams, changing the organizational culture, or redesigning structure or systems (Edmondson, 1996).

Contrasting Images: Implications

To talk about developing 'learning organizations' means focusing on certain prescribed organizational and managerial characteristics. With its emphasis on managerial initiatives to establish the pre-conditions or skills for learning, a research agenda based on the need for 'learning organizations' would be oriented towards micro or individual-based factors. Another key issue pertains to establishing a vision and moving the firm towards that vision. By invoking the need for 'learning organizations,' theorists lay out a prescription for organizational improvement. While visions are powerful tools that motivate, one effect is to denigrate rather than appreciate the strengths of an organization. This implication may be one of the liabilities of the learning organization fad as suggested by Calhoun et al., 2003. Also, to regard learning as somehow antithetical to organizations is contrary to appreciative inquiry (Shrivastava, 1999).

To consider 'organizations as learning portfolios' produces a view of learning and organizations that is fundamentally different from the prescriptive vision of the 'learning organization'. Instead of focusing on some future state to be attained through managerial action and executive leadership, any desire to enhance an organization's learning must focus on understanding the organization as it now exists through its culture and differentiated structures. Organizations house diverse learning activities and styles that ideally are complementary but may, in fact, be in conflict.

Instead of perceiving organizations as some unified, homogeneous, or monolithic entity that does or does not learn, one can view learning as innate to all organizations but allow for its different manifestation in different parts of the organization. Instead of focusing on the dilemmas:—Why don't organizations learn, or how do we build learning organizations?—the focusing questions become: What do organizations learn and in how many different ways? More specific research questions can then be derived, such as: What's in the portfolio? How are the contents of the portfolio aligned with the mission/vision of the organization? What are the complementarities of learning styles across the organization? How are learning processes aligned across the organization? What are the ROIs of the different learning styles?

The notion of an 'organization as a learning portfolio' helps us recognize that firms may simultaneously support multiple and diverse learning activities (DiBella and Nevis, 1998; DiBella, 2001). Rather than view an organization that as a whole progresses through a series of learning stages, different components of a firm can function in different stages. Instead of learning stages being regarded or treated as sequential stages (Carroll, Rudolf, and Hatakenaka, 2003), they are seen as concurrent ones; and learners themselves function simultaneously in multiple learning environments (Plaskoff, 2011, this volume).

FIAT Auto: Case Example of a Company's Learning Portfolio

The following case was produced from field research I conducted over the course of two trips to Italy. Data were collected through structured and unstructured interviews, participant observation, and content analysis of internal documents. Additional background on this case was previously reported elsewhere (Nevis et al., 1995; DiBella et al., 1996; DiBella and Nevis, 1998.) The case shows how learning takes place through multiple activities supported at FIAT Auto.

FIAT Auto's learning portfolio

FIAT Auto designs, manufactures, and markets automobiles worldwide under a variety of trademarks including Fiat, Lancia, and Alfa Romeo. Staffed by approximately 3000 managers and professionals, *Direzione Technica* (DT) is FIAT Auto's engineering division responsible for the design of new automobiles. DT is organized into functional departments which each specialize in a particular aspect of car design, such as body style or engines.

FIAT Auto once produced vehicles under the Fiat trademark only. Subsequently, it acquired Lancia and then Alfa Romeo. Each trademark was produced in separate companies, which gave FIAT Auto a product focused organization structure. In 1991, the three car companies were reorganized as FIAT Auto into a functionally based structure with a heavy emphasis on project management. Trademark models are designed by new product development teams that reside in staff groups (*piattaforma*) responsible for the new models of a certain size or cost, e.g. subcompact, luxury. Staff from functional units are assigned to the *piattaformas* on a full-time basis to develop new models.

In 1989, FIAT Auto had one of its most successful years ever. In the same year, its CEO authorized benchmarking studies to compare FIAT Auto's performance to that of other world automobile manufacturers and a few consumer durable goods companies. Approximately fifty of FIAT Auto's top managers participated in this study by visiting other firms and their plants worldwide. The study group discovered that not only was the market-place changing due to different consumer tastes and expectations, but the processes whereby firms designed and manufactured products were also rapidly changing. The group became convinced that, although FIAT Auto was having a successful year, unless it changed how it worked and how it learned, it would lose its ability to compete with global companies.

One of the process changes DT made was to simultaneous engineering. New product development teams now work together in *co-location* in common, open work areas to facilitate communication and coordination. Staff from the *Direzione Technica* and other FIAT Auto divisions, such as manufacturing and marketing, who are also assigned to the *piatta-formas*, work in *co-location*. Where engineers and other functional staff once worked sequentially on related tasks, now they work concurrently in parallel rather than in series. In this form of simultaneous engineering, new models are completed without the time delays that occurred when components were designed sequentially or when newly designed components had to pass from function to function.

In describing the roots of FIAT Auto's organizational culture, staff often refer to Italy's tradition of paternalistic, religious, and militaristic organization forms. Particular reference is made to the heavy reliance on authority that stems from rigid, hierarchical structures and the acceptance of formal authority. There was significant concern at DT that FIAT Auto's traditional culture generated too much of a Taylorian division between those staff who did the thinking and those who acted. In the 1990s, DT learned about making the transition to a more open and flexible organization. This transition reflects the desire to shift the style of management from *capo* (head, commander) to *leader*. In the former, the framework is to command and obey; in the new framework of management the focus is cooperation and integration.

While discrete projects aimed at improvement and learning have been completed or are still underway, management's aim is to spawn institutionalized processes that facilitate continuous improvement. It is expected that changing the culture, structure, and management style at DT will accomplish this. Among the formal mechanisms to spawn learning is the use of Total Quality Planning (PQT) to identify areas needing improvement. PQT is required of all organizational units to identify both product and process issues that can be improved upon.

Staff also expects learning to occur through the very mechanisms whereby work is accomplished. DT's functional departments learn through the acquisition of know-how engineering and the establishment and improvement of shelf engineering. Each functional unit is also expected to build a *Memoria Technica*, a database containing knowledge about components and processes. Learning also occurs in the *piattaformas* through the application and utilization of know-how engineering in car design. In solving design problems for specific models, functional staff may generate solutions that, once communicated back to the function, may subsequently be applied in the design of other models.

Learning at FIAT Auto

The experiences at FIAT Auto indicate a concerted effort to build learning capability by enhancing and extending the firm's learning portfolio. FIAT Auto has learned through acquisition (of Lancia and Alfa Romeo), through adaptation (of best practices obtained through its benchmarking studies), and through correction via its PQT process. Now shifts in work process will create new learning capabilities. For example, the *Memoria Technica* represents a bureaucratic learning style; the shift to concurrent engineering will create communities of practice; and the change in leadership style represents a shift from a learning style of authorized expert to role modeling.

ANALYZING LEARNING PORTFOLIOS

When an organization's learning portfolio is examined in its entirety, several questions and concerns come to mind. First, what's in the portfolio now? Answering this question requires having an inventory of the learning practices and profiles that exist throughout the organization or firm. This inventory of data about learning provides the basic building block for analysis. At FIAT Auto, knowledge acquisition, adaptation, correction, and communities-of-practice are all supported and used.

A second concern pertains to the relatedness of the items in the inventory. To what extent are the learning practices and styles complementary, in conflict, or redundant? We should expect, for example, that what gets learned at FIAT Auto through its internal methods of self-correction and communities-of-practice would complement the more externally focused activities of acquisition and adaptation. In another work context, nuclear power plants, we would expect to see incremental learning taking place among operations plant staff which would complement the learning of a research and development unit engaged in transformative learning. A transformative or double-loop style, which may lead to unanticipated consequences, would be inappropriate in an environment like nuclear power operations where controls are needed to avoid disastrous outcomes.

A third concern about learning portfolios is the extent to which current practices or styles align with or match learning needs and work demands. Consider a team or organization that is in a new industry where innovation is critical to success. If it has an overemphasis on learning practices that support formal dissemination or incremental learning, then what's getting learned (and the speed whereby that learning is disseminated) is apt to be less than helpful to the firm's competitiveness practices that support transformative learning. In another scenario, if a firm wants to emphasize teamwork, then it should give more support to learning practices that promote group rather than individual learning. In the auto industry where product innovation is becoming increasingly more critical to success, FIAT Auto's relative emphasis on learning through communities-of-practice should outweigh its investments in learning through correction.

The idea that a firm's learning portfolio might be misaligned with its learning needs or competitive demands raises the possibility of portfolio management. How can a firm manage its portfolio for maximum advantage? What criteria should be followed in making portfolio management decisions? How would a managed learning portfolio differ from an unmanaged one? These questions suggest that instead of blindly supporting learning practices or not supporting them at all, companies allocate their learning resources within their portfolio in such a way as to maximize their effectiveness. Learning capability and effectiveness must go hand in hand.

LEARNING PORTFOLIO MANAGEMENT

Managing a learning portfolio requires a sensitivity and appreciation for outcomes; and traditionally in most business environments, outcomes or outputs are examined in the light of inputs. Return on investment, or ROI, has been a key measure that reflects the ratio of outputs to inputs. Since business people aim to maximize the returns on their investments, they make management decisions about their investments using ROI as a guiding indicator.

Using ROI as a singular criterion for making management or investment decisions is a limiting approach. To determine the value of outputs and expected returns assumptions must be made about the future; and these assumptions can turn out to be invalid. Assumptions are also made about linear associations, that an investment (usually financial resources) will be converted to some measurable amount of inputs (material, labor, process technology) that will be converted to an expected set of outputs (products, services, benefits). Over time unanticipated events or circumstances occur which thwart the realization of the presumed causal linkage, as when the cost of material or labor increases. Consequently, many management decisions end up being based on projections that turn out to be inaccurate.

This problem is especially prevalent with learning investments since the period during which the returns from learning are realized can be quite lengthy; and the lengthier the period of returns to be gained from an investment, the more tenuous our assumptions. Also the usefulness of learning pertains to its timeliness. When employees learn something in a formal training program, such as how to use new software for group collaboration, it's often because they expect to use those new skills right away. In that scenario, the benefits and outcomes from the learning have immediate value. On the other hand, employees sometimes learn behaviors (such as how to deal with angry customers or aggressive competitors) that they hope they never have to use. If we never use such behaviors, does that mean they have no value and were not worth the initial learning investment? Of course not, but what criteria should be used to make decisions among learning investments that lead to uncertain outcomes?

Another difficulty in using ROI as a criterion to manage learning investments is that it only takes into account tangible assets or returns. When an employee learns a new skill, a work team learns how to work better together, or a firm develops a new process technology, nothing tangible is created, but obviously the learning has produced something of value. When managers take the customary route of basing investment decisions and allocating learning resources among practices that generate tangible benefits and hence promise a higher ROI, they neglect to account for several characteristics of learning.

INVESTMENT DIMENSIONS TO LEARNING

There are two critical aspects or dimensions to learning that have direct bearing on learning portfolio management. The first of these, which I have come to name 'Learning use,' came to my direct attention while researching and working with clients in healthcare. The second, 'Learning impact,' came from my consulting work in the field of education.

Learning use

Some of the learning that takes place in healthcare involves practices or techniques that are used immediately to care for sick patients. Healthcare is a unique context in which the effect of not learning (possible death) is so devastating that medical practitioners and caregivers continually explore new procedures and protocols to help their patients. Consequently, they learn new techniques because they are needed immediately to address a patient's condition and thereby improve their well-being, if not their very survival. Yet as part of their formal training, medical practitioners also learn about illnesses and diseases they may encounter at some future date.

One can think of this comparison as reflecting a time dimension to the value of learning. For some practices the usefulness of what's been learned is realized immediately in the short term, while for other uses the benefit comes later on. In industry this contrast is reflected in a manager's choice between focusing on production activities that create valued outcomes and benefits in the short term and investment activities that lead to benefits in the long term. This contrast may be depicted in the following continuum:

Learning use: immediate   ←——————→   future

The relative timeliness of when we use or apply what we have learned is an important criterion to weigh up when choosing between alternative learning investments. Considering a practice in the light of its learning use (immediate versus future) is a helpful marker.

Learning impact

It is one thing to use or apply what we have learned, it is another to realize the benefits from that use. For example, while a healthcare practitioner may learn and then use a new protocol to assist someone with poor health, whether the use of that protocol actually adds value or creates benefit to the patient may not be known for some time. In effect, there are time lags between the use of learning and its resultant benefits. Consequently, we can't be certain, at the outset, of the value of what we're learning.

For some uses of learning, the benefits are unambiguous, as when emergency room staff uses new protocols to save a patient. In other cases, whether a new form of surgery or a new protocol of radiation therapy will extend the life of a cancer patient may not be known until some time has passed. Whenever learned attitudes or behaviors are used without controls or comparisons, there should always be uncertainty over their impacts. Without controls, one cannot be sure whether the outcomes should be attributed to what had been learned or some other factor, such as chance, a change in the environment, or merely the passage of time. For example, if a sick patient is treated in some new way recently learned by medical staff and then feels better, medical staff cannot be sure that the patient would not have felt better without the new treatment.

Thus, while learning may be used immediately, the payoff from that use may be uncertain or lag behind in time. Often we learn and use new behaviors because the impact is empirically known. At other times the impact is unknown, but we invest in learning just the same because we believe that the payoff or benefit will ultimately be positive. This contrast may be depicted in the following continuum:

Learning impact: certain   ←——————→   uncertain

The field of education is forever having to cope with the challenges of this dichotomy. In our large research universities, those scholars who teach focus on developing theory whose impact is uncertain, while many of their students prefer learning which they perceive to have certain impact. In primary and secondary education we invest in the schooling of our children with the hope and expectation that they will learn how to lead meaningful and productive lives as adults. Of course, support for education also comes from competitive pressures that our children be as successful as possible (even as other competitive pressures lead investors to expect that our corporations be as profitable as possible). The uncertain but expected payoffs from elementary and secondary education help fuel the coffers of many local school committees.

Yet when it comes to supporting education or learning in corporate environments, decision makers aren't quite so generous when they rely on ROI and other business measures to assess the returns and value of investments in learning. Learning portfolio management aims to maximize that value. Considering the learning use and learning impact of a given practice can guide that management process and ensure the effectiveness of learning efforts.

Assessing Learning Effectiveness

To be learning effectively means investing and allocating resources with an organization's learning portfolio to maximize value. Assessing learning effectiveness involves identifying the relative value of practices in one's learning portfolio. Learning use and Learning impact can be used as indicators for such an assessment. Any learning practice can be scored on the basis of these two dimensions to determine *relative* value. (Relative is highlighted for emphasis since absolute value cannot be determined; and the focus should be on weighing the value of learning investments compared to one another.) Once practices are scored, learning resources can be allocated on the basis of those scores.

Guiding Learning Portfolios: The Role of the Chief Learning Officer

After a company allocates its learning investments, patterns of learning activity are created which culminate in the establishment of the company's learning portfolio. As an organization's learning portfolio takes shape, a learning architecture is created with the hope that what gets learned adds value. Many firms have come to recognize the need to take a systems view of learning and to proactively shape their learning architecture. Many firms have created corporate universities to oversee all learning activities, while others have developed roles for learning strategists and chief learning officers (CLOs).

Companies that are oriented towards the use of computers or information technology to promote learning have created the role of the chief knowledge officer. In some cases the transition to this role merely involved re-labeling previous job titles such as chief information officer or director of management information systems. In general, their focus is on managing and utilizing existing, computerized databases through data mining rather than learning portfolio management.

The role of the CLO is, however, to oversee a company's learning architecture and ensure that what's in the portfolio actually matches the architecture. Doing so involves several activities to design, develop, and maintain learning. First is the task of designing the learning architecture in the light of the organization's culture and learning demands. A CLO should take a comprehensive view of the entire organization or firm to understand learning requirements and to profile current and desired learning. The second task is supporting those learning practices required to meet the firm's strategic needs; and the third is to evaluate practices for their quality and impact, and redesign the learning architecture as necessary.

Many firms have given their CLOs the role of running their corporate universities. Unfortunately, the activities of corporate universities emphasize practices that engender formal learning such as training and classroom teaching. The domain of a strategically focused CLO should be on all learning practices that exist within the firm's learning portfolio and on how best to allocate resources among them.

With a systems view, a CLO looks comprehensively at an organization's learning portfolio, sees how it aligns with the strategic demands on the firm, and allocates resources accordingly. Yet, perhaps more importantly, the role of the CLO is to be the organization's or firm's learning advocate. As economies transition more and more into the post-industrial age with an emphasis on services, companies are placing greater emphasis on knowledge management. When firms learn by creating or acquiring knowledge, they develop a growing capacity for effective action. It is difficult to place a value on that capacity since it is an intangible asset; a CLO must champion the allocation and use of resources that produce such intangible assets.

Learning use and learning impact are important markers to look at in allocating resources among alternative learning practices. Yet it is the value created from learning practices that many managers view as the ultimate criterion. The challenge for many CLOs is to promote learning, which in many cases creates intangible assets, in contexts that may only value what is tangible.

TAILORING THEORY AND APPLICATION

As the study of organizational learning has grown and matured during the past decade, it has become increasingly obvious that no single theory, model, or mode of learning applies equally to the diversity of organizations. If learning is fundamentally a process of adaptation, then what and how organizations need to learn will be a function of the environments in which they operate. While we increasingly share the same global economic environment on a macro level, micro operational environments remain distinct. For example, the competitive environment (and hence learning demands) of a city-wide franchise of hair salons is distinct from that of an inter-state shipping company. No one theory can offer applications that are equally effective across the wide array of operational environments in which organizations must function (Pettigrew, 2005).

If our goal is improved or more relevant learning, then our focus needs to be less on theory and more on practical learning tools or methods. The need for, and greater recognition of, tailored learning practices is reflected in the growth of research in particular contexts. Such research has allowed for the identification and evaluation of specific learning practices or techniques. In particular, the healthcare field has been a major area of interest. That is due in part to the publicity given to medical error and the interest among hospital administrators in how a learning environment can reduce preventable accidents

(DiBella, 2002). Among the key insights and focal points of research in healthcare is the link between learning and change (Berta and Baker, 2004; Leape and Berwick, 2005) and the particular challenges of retaining learning (Institute of Medicine, 2004; Tucker, Nembhard, and Edmondson, 2007).

Healthcare systems can engender data-, theory-, and practice-rich learning portfolios. From teaching hospitals to research labs, post-mortems, experimental drug therapies, and innovative surgical techniques, health services offer a range of learning events and practices. These different learning activities provide complementary contributions to the development of improved healthcare.

Another domain of growing interest is the public sector (Rashman, Withers, and Hartley, 2009) and in particular national security (Darling, Parry, and Moore 2005; DiBella, 2010). The military is an especially intriguing context in which to consider learning from a portfolio perspective. Each service branch of the military (Air Force, Army, and Navy) has a distinct history, performs a different function, and has different values. When it comes to learning about military strategy or operations, each service has a different sense of priorities associated with learning and hence invests in different learning activities. For example, the Army does far more to reward officers who attend formal programs of graduate study compared to the Navy which values learning-in action, aka on-the-job training (DiBella, 2010).

Yet challenges for the application and implementation of learning practices and better portfolio management remain. In particular, growing competitiveness and financial constraints lead to a greater focus on learning that ensures more immediate rather than long-term gain. Success in application is dependent on tailoring tools to the idiosyncratic nature of different organizational contexts and the pressures for organizational improvement.

CONCLUSION

The image of a firm, company, or organization as a learning portfolio is an alternative paradigm to the more popular notion of the learning organization. Its characteristics lead us to frame the issue and challenge of learning in and of organizations in different ways. It also provides a bridge from the processes of learning to the content of the knowledge that is generated and used in our organizations. For if knowledge is in the notes, learning makes the music.

The result is different research questions and different avenues and approaches for interventions. For example, what types of knowledge are valued across an organization's portfolio and how is that knowledge aligned with its strategic direction? What are the diverse ways in which knowledge is acquired, disseminated, and used? How do various forms or styles of learning across an organization conflict or complement one another? Finally, how are resources allocated within the portfolio and how might they be re-allocated to increase a firm's return on its learning investments?

As theorists and practitioners struggle to make their organizations more adaptable and more resilient (Deevy, 1995), the call to learning will endure. Until a proven formula for learning is found or generated, alternative paradigms will be needed to explore what does or does not help executives make their organizations learn. The 'organization as learning portfolio' broadens the view about how learning and organizations can best fit together. It also legitimizes the idiosyncrasy of portfolios tailored to maximize learning effectiveness in different operational environments.

REFERENCES

Adler, P.S. and Cole, R.E. (1993) Designed for learning: A tale of two auto plants. *Sloan Management Review*, 34: 85–94.

Argyris, C. and Schön, D.A. (1974) *Theory in Practice: Increasing Professional Effectiveness.* San Francisco: Jossey-Bass.

Argyris, C. and Schön, D.A. (1978) *Organizational Learning.* Reading, MA: Addison-Wesley.

Bartunek, J.M. and Moch, M.K. (1987) First-order, second-order, and third-order change and organization development interventions: A cognitive approach. *Journal of Applied Behavioral Science*, 23: 483–500.

Beckhard, R. and Pritchard, W. (1992) *Changing the Essence: The Art of Creating and Leading Fundamental Change in Organizations.* San Francisco: Jossey-Bass.

Berta, W.B and Baker, R. (2004) Factors that impact the transfer and retention of best practices for reducing errors in hospitals. *Health Care Management Review*, 29(2): 90–97.

Brown, J.S. and Duguid, P. (2000) *The Social Life of Information.* Boston: Harvard Business School Press.

Carroll, J., Rudolph, J.W., and Hatakenaka, S. (2003) Learning from organizational experience. In M. Easterby-Smith and M.A. Lyles (Eds.), *The Blackwell Handbook of Organizational Learning and Knowledge Management*, London: Blackwell: 575–600.

Cohen, M.D., March, J.D., and Olsen, J.P. (1972) A garbage can model of organizational choice. *Administrative Science Quarterly*, 17: 1–25.

Darling, M., Parry, C., and Moore, J. (2005) Learning in the thick of it. *Harvard Business Review*, July-August: 1–8.

Deevy, E. (1995) *Creating the Resilient Organization: A Rapid Response Management Program.* Englewood Cliffs, NJ: Prentice-Hall.

deGeus, A.P. (1988) Planning as Learning. *Harvard Business Review*, March-April: 70–74.

DiBella, A.J. (2001) *Learning Practices: Assessment and Action for Organizational Improvement.* Upper Saddle River, NJ: Prentice-Hall.

DiBella, A.J. (2002) Building the context for learning: An executive priority. In P.L. Spath (Ed.) *Guide to Effective Staff Development in Health Care Organizations: A Systems Approach to Successful Training.* San Francisco: Jossey-Bass: 3–21.

DiBella, A.J. (2010) Can the army become a learning organization?: A question re-examined. *Joint Forces Quarterly*, 56(1): 117–122.

DiBella, A.J., Nevis, E.C., and Gould, J.M. (1996) Understanding organizational learning capability. *Journal of Management Studies*, 33: 361–379.

DiBella, A.J. and Nevis, E.C. (1998) *How Organizations Learn: An Integrated Strategy for Building Learning Capability.* San Francisco: Jossey-Bass.

Duncan, R. and Weiss, A. (1979) Organizational learning: Implications for organizational design. *Research in Organizational Change and Development*, 1: 75–123.

Edmondson, A.C. (1996) Three faces of Eden: The persistence of competing theories and multiple diagnoses in organizational intervention research. *Human Relations,* 49: 571–575.

Gardner, H. (1993) *Multiple Intelligences: Theory in Practice.* New York: Basic Books.

Garvin, D.A. (1993) Building a learning organization. *Harvard Business Review*, July-August: 78–91.

Goleman, D. (1995) *Emotional Intelligence.* New York: Bantam Books.

Hedberg, R. (1981) How organizations learn and unlearn. In P. Nystrom and W. Starbuck (eds.), *Handbook of Organizational Design*, Oxford: Oxford University Press: 3–27.

Institute of Medicine. (2004) *Keeping Patients Safe: Transforming the Work Environment of Nurses.* Washington, DC: National Academy Press.

Kolb, D.A. (1979) On management and the learning process. In D. Kolb, I. Rubin, and J. McIntyre (Eds.), *Organizational Psychology: A Book of Readings* (2nd edn.). Englewood Cliffs, NJ: Prentice-Hall: 27–42.

Leape, L.L. and Berwick, D.M. (2005) Five years after to err is human: What have we learned? *Journal of the American Medical Association*, 293: 2384–2390.

Mayo, A. and Rick, S. (1993) Recognising a learning organization. *European Forum for Management Development*, 93/1: 14–17.

McGill, M.E. and Slocum, J.W. (1993) Unlearning the organization. *Organizational Dynamics*, 22: 67–78.

Morgan, G. (1986) *Images of Organization*. SAGE: Newbury Park, CA.

Morgan, G. (1993) *Imaginization*. SAGE: Beverly Hills, CA.

Nevis, E.C., DiBella, A.J., and Gould, J.M. (1995) Understanding organizations as learning systems. *Sloan Management Review*, 36: 73–85.

Pettigrew, A. (2005) The character and significance of management research on the public sector. *Academy of Management Journal*, 48: 973–977.

Purser, R.E. and Pasmore, W.A. (1992) Organizing for learning. *Research in Organizational Change and Development*, 6: 37–114.

Rashman, L., Withers, E., and Hartley, J. (2009) Organizational learning and knowledge in public sector organizations: A systematic review of the literature. *International Journal of Management Reviews*, 11: 463–494.

Senge, P.M. (1990) *The Fifth Discipline*. New York: Doubleday.

Shrivastava, P. (1999) A typology of organizational learning systems. *Journal of Management*, 20: 7–28.

Snyder, W.M. and Cummings, T.G. (1992) Organizational learning disabilities. Paper presented at the annual meeting of the Academy of Management, Las Vegas.

Srivastva, S., Cooperrider, D. L., and Associates. (1990) *Appreciative Management and Leadership: The Power of Positive Thought and Action in Organizations*. San Francisco: Jossey-Bass.

Torbert, W.R. (1994) Managerial learning, organizational learning: A potentially powerful redundancy. *Journal of Management Learning*, 1: 57–70.

Trice, M. and Beyer, J. (1993) *The Cultures of Work Organizations*. Englehard, NJ: Prentice-Hall.

Tucker, A.L., Edmondson, A.C. and Spear, S. (2002) When problem solving prevents organizational learning. *Journal of Organizational Change Management*, 15: 184–201.

Tucker, A.L., Nembhard, I.M., and Edmondson, A.C. (2007) Implementing new practices: An empirical study of organizational learning in hospital intensive care units. *Management Science*, 53: 894–907.

Van Maanen, J. and Barley, S. (1985) Cultural organization: Fragments of a theory. In P.J. Frost, L.F. Moore, M.R. Louis, C.C. Lundberg, and J. Martin (eds.) *Organization Culture*, Beverly Hills: Sage, 31–53.

Van Maanen J. and Schein, E.H. (1979) Toward a theory of organizational socialization. In B.M. Staw, and L.L. Cummings (eds.) *Research in Organizational Behavior*, Vol. 1. Greenwich, CT: Jai Press.

Watkins, K.E. and Marsick, V.J. (1993) *Sculpting the Learning Organization*. San Francisco: Jossey-Bass.

10

Intersubjectivity and Community-Building: Learning to Learn Organizationally

JOSH PLASKOFF

ABSTRACT

It has been twenty years since the paradigm-shifting introduction of the constructs of communities of practice and legitimate peripheral participation, which have become central to understanding learning in both an academic and organizational setting. The construct has not been without criticism—for insufficient treatment of power, for a lack of historical perspective, and for its theoretical slipperiness. What is required to meet this criticism is more examination of those elusive intersubjective elements of community relationships, identity, the negotiation of meaning. Building communities requires that individuals learn how to learn organizationally. A key to developing powerful communities is developing expanding circles of intersubjectivity about what it means to be a community and how to operate as one. A philosophy and a methodology have been developed and applied that foster three elements of intersubjectivity (believing, behaving, and belonging) called the **APPLE** process (assess, plan, prepare, launch, and establish). This work derives from the socio-cultural work of Vygotsky, Luria, and Leontiev, and develops a way to bridge the theoretical with the practical.

INTRODUCTION[1]

It has been twenty years since Lave and Wenger (1991) first introduced the constructs of communities of practice and legitimate peripheral participation, considered 'nothing short

[1]Many thanks to my community team, Tom Schwen, the CPSquare Consortium (especially Etienne Wenger, Richard McDermott, and Bill Snyder), Marjorie Lyles, Mark Easterby-Smith, and especially my wife Robyn.

of a paradigm shift in the study of learning' (Hughes et al., 2007). It has been almost fifteen years since Wenger (1998a, 1998b, 1999) more fully developed the community of practice lens. In that time, the construct has been voraciously applied by practitioners and academicians alike, in a wide variety of settings, both live and online (Gunawardena et al., 2009). They have served numerous disciplines especially in learning and education (Pane, 2010), but also law (Hara, 2009), medicine (Egan and Jaye, 2009) and corporate functions and organizational theory (Ha, 2008; Thompson, 2005), and have even influenced governmental and social theory in general. Arguably unlike any learning construct since behavioristic programmed learning, communities of practice have become central to understanding learning in both academic and organizational settings.

Despite its popularity and pervasiveness, or perhaps because of it, the community of practice perspective is not without its criticism and critique. Some point to an insufficient focus on a particular aspect of practice or community, such as the role of power in CoPs and the situatedness of learning (Contu and Willmott, 2003). Others point out a lack of historical perspective (Engeström, 2007). Still others bemoan Wenger's seeming abandonment of the neo-liberal political undertones of Lave and Wenger to an overtly conventional managerialism (Hughes et al., 2007). One criticism that takes center stage in most critiques, however, is a slipperiness and elusiveness unbefitting of a theory of strong learning (Barton and Tusting, 2005), which potentially could threaten its theoretical power. Interestingly, most of the criticisms seem to ignore the further comprehensive treatment of communities of practice (Wenger, 1998a). Indeed, much of the research focuses primarily on Lave and Wenger (e.g. Fuller, 2007) and pays little attention to the modes of belonging, economies of meaning, reification and participation, and other more phenomenological concepts introduced in later works.

Communities, the core of the human social system, have been studied for decades in anthropology, sociology, and psychology. Tönnies (2001), the nineteenth-century sociologist, distinguishes between *Gemeinschaft* (the personal community as a living organism) and *Gesellschaft* (society as a mechanical aggregate). Dewey (1916) treats the community's relationship to a public education system. Marx, Weber, and Durkheim embrace the collective as the foundation for their philosophical systems. Current focus, then, is a continuation of a tradition started some hundred years ago examining a human tendency to commune that is thousands of years old. In past and present works, the elusiveness and abstractness which serves as a critique of CoPs needs to be recognized as inherent in the subject matter itself. Modernity has liquidated many traditional forms of relating and seeking them out is a complex task. As Bauman so keenly points out:

> [C]ommunity stands for the kind of world which is not, regrettably, available to us—but which we would dearly hope to inhabit and which we hope to repossess. . . . [I]t is always in the future. 'Community' is nowadays another name for paradise lost—but one which we dearly hope to return, and so we feverishly seek the roads that may bring us there. Paradise lost or a paradise still hoped to be found; one way or another, this is definitely not a paradise that we inhabit and not the paradise that we know from our own experience.
>
> (Bauman, 2001: 3)

What is required, then, is to examine those elements that are most difficult to put our finger on: the intersubjective components of community relationships, identity, the negotiation of meaning through participation and reification that are outlined in Wenger

(1998a). This chapter provides one instantiation of how to theoretically and practically address some of these less tangible elements. It derives from my work as chief architect for a community infrastructure at a global pharmaceutical company. The purpose of this project was to seek ways to expedite the building shared history in communities through stable membership. What proved critical was fostering the intersubjective elements of community: identity, models of belonging, mutual trust, and reciprocity concerning the practice and communities in general. This chapter will examine this work and its outcomes.

KNOWLEDGE, COGNITION, AND ORGANIZATIONAL LEARNING

To understand why CoPs have attained such visibility in organizational learning, we must start with the core epistemological questions of what constitutes knowledge and how (and perhaps whether) it is transferred.

The individualist view

Until recently, behaviorist and cognitivist models have been the primary underlying forces influencing learning and organizational epistemologies (Von Krogh and Roos, 1995). According to these theories, knowledge is an object that can reside outside individuals and can be delivered to a learner as one would deliver food as nourishment (Gherardi, Nicolini, and Odella, 1998). The primary emphasis has been on individual minds and explicit knowledge (Baumard, 1999; Cook and Brown, 1999), knowledge that is easily represented through a formal symbol system (Nonaka and Takeuchi, 1995; Polanyi, 1966).

Employee development, therefore, has taken the form of event-driven training mechanisms for the individual (corporate universities, training, seminars, computer-based self-studies, etc.) which embody this epistemology. In addition, knowledge management and organizational learning champions have emphasized best practice capture, codification, and distribution (Fahey and Prusak, 1998; Hansen, Nohria, and Tierney, 1999; O'Dell and Grayson, 1998), even when the results are questionable, such as best practice databases that are merely 'information junkyards' (McDermott, 1998). Although these tools are worthwhile, they represent only a small fraction of the knowledge that exists and learning that can and does take place in an organization. To see this potential requires a paradigmatic shift in thinking.

A social view of knowledge and cognition

While the individualist view is still dominant, a more collective view of knowledge is strengthening. Building on Marx's and Hegel's historical materialism, the Russian psychologists Vygotsky and Leontiev formulated a socio-historical theory of activity and higher mental functions (see Leontiev, 1978; Vygotsky, 1978). This revolutionary approach to knowledge and cognition spawned current constructivist thinking, which posits the social and constructive nature of knowledge.

Knowledge, from this perspective, is not an object that is 'passed physically from one to another, like bricks; [it] cannot be shared as persons would share a pie by dividing it into physical pieces' (Dewey, 1916: 4). Rather, it is socially constructed through collabora-tive efforts with common objectives or by dialectically opposing different perspectives in dialogic interaction (Bakhtin, 1981; Pea, 1993). Knowledge is built into or, perhaps better stated, is equivalent to the patterns inherent in culture: in the reifications of artifacts, the behavioral patterns, and actions set in history. Thus, explicit knowledge only represents the 'tip of the iceberg' (Nonaka and Takeuchi, 1995), since most knowledge is tacit. Cook and Brown (1999) have even postulated that beyond tacit knowledge there is a knowledge inherent in practice itself which they call 'knowing.' In this sense, knowledge is a diffused and emergent property rather than a discrete entity unto itself.

If knowledge is distributed, then cognition and intelligence are distributed as well. Studies of airline pilots and ship navigation have shown that completion of actions and problem solving (or cognition) is based on distributed access to information and knowl-edge and a coordinated shared understanding amongst participants (Hutchins, 1995, 1996; Hutchins and Klausen, 1998). No person alone can complete an action—it must always be the 'person plus' (Perkins, 1993), a collective phenomenon. Cognitive resources are by no means restricted to people; they can also be embedded in tools, as a calcula-tor has the ability to compute a square root. The resources to complete any action are distributed amongst people, environments, and situations (Pea, 1993); in fact all cultural resources, and the coordination and configuration of those resources is the collective task of those completing the action.

Implications for organizational learning

The organizational learning implications of this alternative epistemology are profound. First, learning is situated (Brown, Collins, and Duguid, 1989; Gherardi, Nicolini, and Odella, 1998; Lave and Wenger, 1991) and contextual, historically tied to the situation in which knowledge is being created and used. It is situated in context of the activity or practice, part and parcel of the work itself. Learning does not only happen in the classroom; in fact, most learning results from interaction with co-workers during shared collaborative tasks. Learning and meaning are constructed from participation in social practice (Star, 1998). Lave and Wenger (1991) describe this learning phenomenon as legitimate peripheral participation (LPP). According to this model, learning is not a mat-ter of obtaining individual, objective knowledge or formal expertise. Rather, it is the attainment of the subjective perspective of a group of individuals engaged in a shared enterprise (a CoP) that is contained within artifacts, behaviors, and language. Individuals become encultured (Brown, Collins, and Duguid, 1989) to the group, acting like physi-cians, cabinetmakers, or insurance claims adjusters in the eyes of the other practitioners in the community. Thus, learning is more about developing an identity and becoming a practitioner through social interaction with others than about learning objectively about the practice (Brown and Duguid, 1991).

If learning is situated in practice, then practice precedes knowledge (Hedegaard, 1995). Higher mental functions as social processes within the practice manifest themselves exter-nally first and then are internalized through a transformational process. As Vygotsky states:

> It is necessary that everything internal in higher forms was external, that is, for others it was what it now is for oneself. Any higher mental function necessarily goes through an external stage in its development because it is initially a social function.
>
> (Vygotsky, 1981: 162)

For Vygotsky, learning appears in two planes, the social plane and the psychological plane, first interpsychological then intrapsychological. Internalization occurs as a result of a genetic relationship in which those possessing less mature cultural forms of behavior interrelate with those more culturally mature (Wertsch, 1985). Vygotsky calls the distance between the actual development level of individuals using their own means and the potential development level of individuals under the guidance of those more capable the *zone of proximal development*. The apprenticeship model from which Lave and Wenger derive the concept of CoPs demonstrates these Vygotskian principles in action. The longevity and evolution of the community is dependent on the perpetuation of the practice. This occurs through members negotiating meaning, a dialectical interplay of participation and reification, and through the concurrent negotiation of identity that membership entails (Wenger, 1998a). This process establishes the learning trajectories of both the novices and full member practitioners and indeed of the community as a whole.

Since knowledge is socially constructed, focus on knowledge creation, rather than knowledge transfer, becomes paramount for organizational learning. Knowledge creation has been described as a cyclical knowledge conversion process between tacit and explicit knowledge comprised of four conversion steps: socialization, externalization, combination, and internalization (Nonaka, 1991; Nonaka and Takeuchi, 1995). Socialization is key to knowledge creation. During socialization, individuals share experiences and develop common mental models. Often this happens through dialogue and observation. The concepts generated during this socialization process are then externalized through the use of metaphor and analogy, which helps to 'understand the unknown through the known and bridges the gap between the image and a logical model' (Nonaka and Takeuchi, 1995: 67). The model derived from externalization is then systematized through combination. Finally, the concept is re-embodied into tacit knowledge through 'learning-by-doing.' Note the similarity between Nonaka and Wenger's specification of how meaning negotiation occurs in CoPs. Wenger, however, unlike Nonaka, recognizes that the socialization process (participation) is a process affecting the person and the group through the forging of identity which then feeds not only the innovation, but also the practice itself.

INTERSUBJECTIVITY: THE KEY TO COMMUNITIES AND COMMUNITY BUILDING

From the discussion above, it should be clear that processes such as Nonaka's socialization, Wenger's participation, and Vygotsky's zone of proximal development entail an interhuman relationship, or intersubjectivity (Crossley, 1996; Rogoff, 1990; Rommetveit, 1974; Wertsch,1985).[2] Intersubjectivity is the act of transcending the private and becoming one with the other. As Rommetveit (cited in Wertsch, 1985) states:

> The basic problem of human intersubjectivity becomes . . . a question concerning in what sense and under what conditions two persons who engage in a dialogue can transcend their different private worlds. And the linguistic basis for this enterprise, I shall argue, is not a fixed repertory of shared 'literal' meanings, but very general and partially negotiated drafts of contracts concerning categorization and attribution inherent in ordinary language.
>
> (Rommetveit, in Wertsch, 1985: 160)

---

[2]Intersubjectivity derives from the phenomenology of Husserl (1965) and later appears in the writing of Buber (1974) and the existential system of Sartre (1966).

Individuals bring different perspectives and preliminary interpretations to a situation and, through semiotically mediated negotiation, attain a state of intersubjectivity (Wertsch, 1985). Language and other cultural tools that mediate shared activity serve as a means of creating this temporary shared social reality. Thus, one way to view intersubjectivity is the result of an alignment of cultural elements.

Identifying common reference points for an activity (experiences and frameworks) helps develop intersubjectivity (Rogoff, 1990). Metaphors and analogies, for example, serve as good tools for gaining a sense of intersubjectivity. They develop understanding of a new concept through comparison with one that is already well understood. The depth of intersubjectivity reached, however, can vary. According to Crossley (1996), intersubjectivity can take two forms: radical and egological. In the radical phase, relationships involve an unconditional communicative openness between parties and a lack of self-awareness of each individual. The self and other become one. In the egological phase, the individual empathizes with the other by transposing him or herself into the other's position. Both forms emerge in communities.

If intersubjectivity is responsible for the efficiency and effectiveness by which learning and activity are carried out, then the converse would also be true; breakdowns in intersubjectivity lead to inefficiencies in activity. This is only partially true. Activity theory argues that contradictions occur among various elements of an activity (or cultural) system. Rules, division of labor, and tools may be at odds with the overarching objectives or with each other. Though contradictions lead to breakdowns in intersubjectivity, they are also catalysts for change. If 'holes' in intersubjectivity are explored and new views of reality are constructed as a result, then the system progresses. If they remain obstacles to activity, then they negatively impact the system.

The impact on practice participation is obvious, but how does this impact building of communities? First, community building involves developing a stronger sense of intersubjectivity around practice. This may consist of merely surfacing what is latent, or it may require developing a completely new understanding of the practice itself. Addressing the intersubjectivity of the practice leads to the identity of the community.

What is more critical, however, is building intersubjectivity the concept of community. Most US organizations assume the primacy of the individual. Though they express in their vision espoused values of collective action, human resource systems promote radical individuals, their true basic assumptions. CoPs, which grew from a collective philosophy, challenge this culture. Thus, systematic processes for learning how to operate this way are necessary. Since learning and practice are inseparable, learning how to operate as a community of practice within a corporation and 'practicing' as a community of practice are integrated as well.

From Theory to Practice: Community Building

CoPs have been viewed as naturally forming, informal social phenomena. So, can we create CoPs? Creation implies developing something from nothing, and this is not a good approach to communities. Community building, however, differs from community creation. Where there is practice, there is community. The involvement of members or the depth of relationship in that community may be minimal, but the potential for community exists.

Community building is not creating something from nothing; it is molding what exists and catalyzing previously unknown opportunities.

These activities are critical for two reasons. First, communities that have a relatively high degree of relationship and involvement can benefit from reflecting on their current status and how they can better achieve their desired goals. More important, however, is introducing community 'novices' to how the community model can enhance their work and practice. Particularly in companies with strong individualistic cultures, collaborative working and a sense of community may involve very foreign behaviors that must be learned. Community building, thus, can be viewed as learning how to learn organizationally.

Approaching community building

Community building is culture-dependent. The approach to community building that follows is based on the particular challenges inherent in one company's culture. This approach could be called 'cautiously prescriptive.' Many of the frameworks and processes are modifications to or direct borrowings from the work of others, and the resulting frameworks have been shared with practitioners in a variety of industries to confirm their applicability. No framework, though, is 'plug and play.' All cultural interventions should be examined and interpreted in light of the particular cultural challenges and values of the target organization.

This approach considers community building learning community behaviors through expanding circles of intersubjectivity that narrow zones of proximal development in community participants. Intersubjectivity expands in four phases of meaning negotiation. First, the community development team, by defining philosophical underpinnings, development processes, and desired behaviors, creates a common understanding about what constitutes communities. While developing the framework, the team models community behaviors. Next, the development group works with a subset of the potential community to develop a sense of intersubjectivity concerning the specific practice and communities. This subset then expands the intersubjectivity circle to other potential members. Finally, community members, through their interactions with others outside the community, develop intersubjectivity with non-members. In addition, the foundation of intersubjectivity developed in the community serves to enculturate new members. Each step involves a Wengerian negotiation of meaning, blending participation and reification. At the same time, an 'expert' is able to scaffold the behaviors of other individuals in learning community activity, following the Vygotskian principles addressed earlier. Figure 10.1 depicts the expanding intersubjectivity circle and how groups interact during the development process.

The development process is systematic, yet evolving and flexible. It is built around an underlying philosophy of what constitutes community, how a community differs from other organizational structures (a community 'vocabulary'), and methods for handling existing cultural elements that impact community behaviors. By approaching things systematically, the development team is better able to create a common understanding amongst potential community members of common goals and activities necessary to evolve a community. In the next sections, I will describe these frameworks and processes.

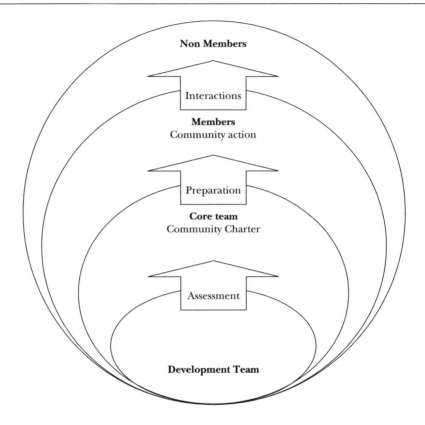

Figure 10.1 Expansive Intersubjectivity in Community Development

Defining communities

Language is critical to developing a sense of intersubjectivity (Rommetveit, 1974). Therefore, the first community development team task prior to facing any community is to define the term *community of practice* in order to more clearly communicate with potential members what constitutes this social structure and how it differs from others. In both the corporate and academic worlds, the word *community* has become confusing. Science students have been called a community of practice (Brown et al., 1993). Some groups in the work environment have been referred to as learning communities (Ryan, 1995). Online conversation groups have been referred to as virtual communities (Smith and Kollock, 1998). Even photography clubs or bridge groups have donned the title of CoPs. Use of the term community makes sense semantically since it characterizes well the groups' unity of purpose.

Overuse of the terms community and community of practice can cause significant problems for community building, however—a lapse in intersubjectivity caused by misaligned vocabulary. Consider two groups in a corporation: a group of scientists responsible for product development and a photography club. Wenger and Snyder define CoPs as 'groups of people informally bound together by shared experience and passion for a joint enterprise'

(2000: 139). According to this definition both groups are communities since members share a passion for their joint enterprises and have shared histories, experiences, and identities. Putting them on equal footing, however, creates potential discrepancies, because the socio-historical relationship between the scientists' community and the organization and the photography club and the organization are different. The scientists' community contributes significantly to the bottom-line profits of the company, and community goals may conflict with management desires and HR systems. Management designed as control systems that seek to direct all aspects of work may unknowingly interfere with community activities and growth. This is not the case with the photography club. The scientists' community offers a much more complex development challenge than does the photography club.

Consistency in terminology is also a problem. As CoPs proliferate around a company, multiple memberships become commonplace. If the concept community differs radically from group to group, intersubjectivity about community life within the corporation will break down, and participation could be threatened.

Arguing semantics in a company is difficult: people will continue to call any group a community. Two approaches can be taken to labeling communities: (1) distinguish among departments, teams, learning communities, and CoPs with those willing to discuss terminology, or (2) define community types for each social structure in the company. No matter how it is done, distinguishing structure types is critical. Figure 10.2 depicts the four

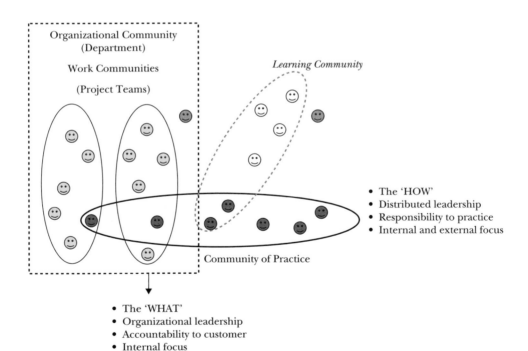

Figure 10.2 Types of Social Structures

organizational structures in this framework. Descriptions of these categories expand on work by Wenger and Snyder (2000).

Most departments (organizational communities) are hierarchical in nature, driven by a reporting structure from employee to management to executive leadership. In general, they provide employee accountability structures and focus for the project work to create company profits. Employees identify with departments through their reporting structure and are driven by compliance systems, such as performance management, succession planning, and reviews. The primary departmental knowledge activities are communication and coordination concerning events, projects, promotions, strategy, and vision.

The project team is unified by a very specific goal—the creation of deliverables. Members are associated with the team through their accountability for a portion of the project. Management systems are similar to departments—performance directly affects succession, reviews, and salary increases; management is often hierarchical, with the project manager the ultimate decision maker. Though some teams have elements of community (common beliefs for example), many, influenced by systems of individual accountability rather than team responsibility, still have departmental trappings. The primary team knowledge activities are coordination of tasks, timelines, and resources and communication about constraints, changes, and barriers.

A learning community in this framework is an informal group that shares knowledge about a topic. The topic can be a computer program, a hobby, or a job task. The topic, however, is not the members' dominant work activity. This community is not an organizational structure and is generally free from ties to management structures (performance management, salary increases, etc.), and leadership is distributed amongst the members. The primary learning community knowledge activities are learning and connection: sharing techniques or ideas, and networking expertise. The photography club treated earlier would be an example of a learning community.

The community of practice addresses critical work processes. Although some theorists see the fundamental purpose of a community of practice as learning (e.g. Wenger, 1998a) they are also engines for practice innovation and diffusion, since knowledge creation and learning are inseparable (Brown and Duguid, 1991; Nonaka and Takeuchi, 1995; Von Krogh et al., 2000). Project teams within departments produce the 'what,' the deliverable that ultimately provides profit, either directly or indirectly, for the company. The community of practice is orthogonal to the project team (see Figure 10.2), providing a venue in which practitioners from a variety of company settings commit to defining and refining their practice, or addressing the 'how.' This creates a double-knit organizational structure (McDermott, 1999).

CoPs are the identity containers and 'shared histories of meaning' (Wenger, 1998a: 89) for members of the corporation. While a learning community focuses on a supplementary skill, task, or interest, the community of practice focuses on the dominant work done by its members. Members identify themselves both inside and outside the corporation through their practice ('I am a cardiologist,' 'I am an engineer,' 'I am a chemist'), and take ownership for their practice, driven by feelings of responsibility and passion for its quality and integrity. Table 10.1 summarizes the attributes of these four types of organizational structures.

Table 10.1 Attributes of organizational structures

Attribute	Department (Organizational Community)	Project Team (Work Community)	Interest Group (Learning Community)	Community of Practice
Primary Activities	Communication, Coordination	Coordination, Communication	Learning, Connection	Innovation, Learning
Member Association	'I report into X'	'I am accountable for part of X'	'I am interested in X'	'I am an X'
Leadership	Organizational	Organizational	Distributed	Distributed
Purpose	Accountability for customer	Accountability for customer	Responsibility to self and community	Responsibility for practice and community
Motivation	Charge for career	Drive for deliverables	Interest in ideas	Passion for practice

Developing the community-building process

Once these discriminations have been made, the development team can then set its sights on developing a community-building process designed to foster intersubjectivity. The process presented here has three components: a stage model for community development, the APPLE development process, and the three dimensions of intersubjectivity. The stage model identifies how a community evolves over time, and is used to educate about community goals. The APPLE development process provides a step-by-step framework for moving a community along the development stages. The three intersubjectivity dimensions describe relationships within communities and serve as the guideposts for all the activities in both developing and maintaining a community. Each of the development components will be treated below.

Stages of community development

Wenger (1998b) defines five stages of development for a community: potential, coalescing, active, dispersed, and memorable. During the potential stage, individuals begin to find others with common interests but have no structure in which to share their experience. During the coalescing stage, the members begin to come together to define their practice, to define the function of their community, and to recognize the potential of their interconnections. During the active stage, the members develop the practice by defining artifacts, tools, creating relationships, and enhancing the practice. When members no longer engage in the practice, the community enters the dispersed stage. The members stay in contact and call each other for advice, but the community relationships dissipate. When the community is no longer viable, it enters the memorable stage, in which it completely dissipates, but the knowledge and experience still resides in its members who tell stories about the experience in the community and collect 'memorabilia' from it.

Wenger's stage model provides a useful tool for educating potential community members and leaders, creating in them a sense of common goals and a common understanding of the development direction. An expansion to Wenger's work is that the active stage can be divided into two parallel streams. Some communities are solely internally focused (Active I). The members create commitment and connection to each other and develop the practice, but the community scope is limited to its boundaries. They often remain anonymous or understated in the company. Some communities, on the other hand, see their role not only as innovating on their practice, connecting with others, and building competency, but also as influencing the company by publicly defining the role of their practice in the greater activities and business goals of the corporation (Active II). Their influencing may include changing work processes to better enable their effectiveness, lobbying for retaining or attracting staff, or even altering high-level decision making. They may also actively seek to partner with other communities to enhance their collaboration and the potential for radically changing their practice. Active II is not more evolved or advanced than Active I. These descriptors are merely used to help communities define their goals and needs. Figure 10.3 summarizes these stages of development.

APPLE *process*

Communities form naturally and will do so at the stage at which they are most comfortable (Wenger, 1999). A community-building process, however, can help catalyze the

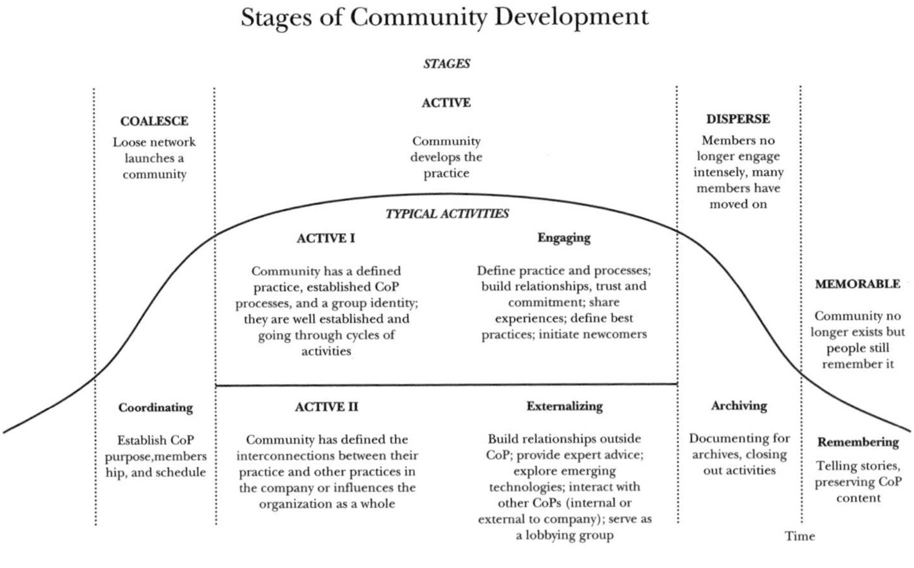

Stages of Community Development

Figure 10.3 Stages of Community Development

Adapted from Wenger (1998b)

evolutionary process and provide guidance for more quickly reaching levels of interaction and involvement (Active I or II). Loosely based on traditional system design models, the development model presented here leads the developer and the community from identification of the situation through establishment of the community. The process bears the acronym APPLE to represent the five steps of the process: assessment, planning, preparation, launch, and establishment and evolution. Before treating these phases in detail, it is important to review the dimensions of intersubjectivity, since they form the framework for community-building activities.

Dimensions of intersubjectivity: the three Bs

Communities are founded upon relationships built on common understandings, vision, values, and beliefs, or intersubjectivity. The three pathways to intersubjectivity are intellectual, social, and emotional (Rogoff, 1990). Based on these three dimensions, this model puts forward the three Bs of community: believing, behaving and belonging.[3] Each of these three dimensions informs activities from community start up to its continuing growth and evolution. These three components form a system; none can truly exist alone. The dimensions, however, can exist in varying degrees. The key is proper balance for the needs of the group. Segmenting community cohesion and intersubjectivity in this way enables members to identify existing imbalances and needed changes in community dynamics.

Believing. Believing encompasses the cognitive, thinking components of intersubjectivity. Key to believing is the establishment of the community identity and an understanding of the practice. The belief structure creates a common value system for the members, defines the community boundaries, and specifies how the practice holds strategic relevance for the enterprise in which it resides. Believing generally surfaces the specific problems that the community wishes to address and the mental models and body of knowledge needed to solve them. The focus areas should be both long term and short term, providing both a framework to strive for in the future and a specific set of problems to address in the present.

Believing questions

- What are the boundaries of the practice? What is 'in' and what is 'out'?
- How is this practice relevant to the success of the enterprise as a whole?
- What are our values?
- What is our practice responsible for?
- What types of problems does the community wish to address?

---

[3]My study of Reconstructionist Judaism uncovered the three Bs, but I have been unsuccessful identifying the specific source. They may be the work of Mordecai Kaplan, the philosopher behind Reconstructionism.

Behaving. As the community develops, members establish ways of working with each other, tools in the domain, and processes and procedures in their practice. These behaviors become accepted by the community and guide communication, actions, and problem formulation for members. Behaving focuses on two components: behavioral norms and artifacts. First, there is a socially accepted way of performing tasks that, though it can be challenged by innovation, is solidly entrenched in the community members. Second, in performing these behaviors, members generate and use artifacts—tools, documentation, knowledge bases, websites, and applications—that can facilitate or expedite processes. The knowledge of the community is passed on to existing and future members by becoming embedded in these artifacts.

Behaving questions

- What knowledge should be shared, created, and documented?
- How should members share their insights with each other and collaborate on community work?
- What tools do members of the community currently use in participating in the practice and what tools need to be created to enable it further?
- How does the community determine what practices should be standardized?
- How does the community operate outside the boundaries of the company and the community?

Belonging. What people believe and how they behave creates a sense of belonging—an emotional feeling that they are part of joint enterprise with others of the same mind. Belonging is nurtured through personal relationships that must be developed and supported. Relationships, in this model, thrive on three elements: trust, equal representation, and understanding.

At the heart of productive work relationships and extensive knowledge sharing stands trust (Bukowitz and Williams, 1999; Handy, 1995; Lesser and Prusak, 2000). Accountability models drive most organizations. This type of model is built on an individualistic reward and punishment system, which, by creating an environment of judgment, often stifles risk taking and discourages sharing behaviors. Communities need to foster a sense of trust to counter these external forces, providing a safe environment for innovation, testing ideas, and knowledge sharing. Trust is fostered through deep relationships and through personal interaction and a personal 'testing' and understanding process.

Most organizations are hierarchically structured, with certain positions imbued with a level of power to direct, evaluate, decide, hire, and fire. With this stratification of power comes the potential for dissolution of trust at multiple levels and barriers to creating personal relationships required to develop a sense of belonging. Communities, by adopting a distributed leadership model, eliminating corporate 'castes' within their walls, and allowing all members of the practice to participate equally, develop thriving relationships.

Because multiple voices characterize the community structure, conflict and disagreement is a norm rather than an exception. Good communities turn disagreements into learning experiences and chances to foster understanding. Through managed conversations (Von Krogh et al., 2000), members express different opinions, approaches, and philosophies and find ways to reconcile differences, combine approaches, and create new knowledge.

Belonging questions

- What kinds of activities generate a sense of unity?
- How can members help each other?
- How can members generate trust with each other?
- How can the community become a safe place for members to try out ideas?
- What conflicts exist in the community and how can they help in sparking conversations?
- Do all members have an equal say? Are some members excluded?
- How are new members brought into the community and given a sense of belonging?

Assessment

The purpose of the assessment phase is to gather information about the current state of the existing or potential community to determine whether community building is necessary, and if so, what direction to take. Generally, communities develop initiators—practitioners who have been exposed to the concept and have taken it upon themselves to either spark conversations among practitioners or to seek out help in developing a community. These initiators serve as good information sources about the potential community. The assessment phase serves as a good opportunity to educate the initiators about community development. Dialogue between the development team and the initiators is the first opportunity to develop intersubjectivity about communities with potential members, positioning them to do the same with new members.

Several criteria determine community readiness: the maturity level (according to the stages presented earlier), geographic dispersion, technological comfort (if technology is to be used), and value to the business (if sponsorship needs to be gained). In addition to these criteria, the assessment should focus on the current levels of the three Bs. The perceived identity should be examined. Excitement and passion for the practice and certain topics within it can serve as entry points for community conversations. Questions about behaving reveal the current tools and ways that potential members interact, share knowledge, collaborate, and learn. Belonging questions focus on the current levels of trust and relationship among practitioners and how the various members or sites view each other. In some cases these data are difficult to gather directly from practitioners, especially if the relationships are negative. In these cases, observation of work processes is helpful as well as interviews with individuals who interact with the practitioners who are more objective and able to help describe the relationships they have observed.

From this data, a determination must then be made as to whether a community of practice is the right solution, if there is enough desire for community and passion for practice to sustain a community effort and whether the current situation can be changed enough to allow the community to be successful.

Planning and preparation

Once the initiators have determined that building a community would benefit the practice, they enter the most important and most intensive community-building activity—planning. During this phase the foundations for the community are laid. Once this strategic phase is completed, the community prepares for launch, specifying the tactical steps necessary for this event. Because the preparation phase is comprised of relatively mundane tasks, it will not be covered in depth here.

The planning phase is critical to community success. Because this work lays the foundation for the future of the community, commitment and attention to this phase cannot be overemphasized. It involves three major tasks: building the core of the community, developing the community charter, and developing strong community relationships.

Building the core group. The first task during this phase is to build a core group. The core group serves as the generator of the community charter and as the engine for the community. The core group can be analogized to the founders of a company. As the founding leadership of a company determines its culture (Schein, 1992), so the core group of the community determines the culture of the community. Therefore, extreme care must be taken in bringing members into the core.

Core group members should have a number of characteristics. The core group should represent a mix of experienced (five years' tenure) and inexperienced members of the practice. Also, if the community spans multiple organizations, and most do, the core group should represent a mix of these organizations. This composition provides an innovative spirit that is informed and balanced by experience. Second, core group members should personally be willing to participate actively, share willingly, and influence others to participate. Both passion for the community enterprise as well as a willingness to network with others helps to build enthusiasm and recruit new members into the community. Finally, some core group members should be well-respected members of the practice to give legitimacy to the enterprise.

As with any organization, involving too many members too fast prevents efficient development of intersubjectivity and relationships. Between five and ten core group members is optimal. During their recruitment, they should be educated about the development process, what their role will be, and how they can help contribute to community success.

To both build relationships and to develop the common understanding about community work, the community development staff conducts an all-day session, the result of which is the community charter. During this all-day session, the key points and benefits of CoPs are reviewed. For learning about communities, analogies prove very helpful in developing an understanding about communities and the community values beginning to surface. Communities in the workplace have much in common with communities outside of it. Business people participate in communities on a regular basis outside of work.

Yet, they often do not make the connection between these communities and communities in the workplace. Analogies help to make this connection.

One analogy compares building a community to creating a city. Most large cities were formed near rivers that provide a lifeline of trade and a source of water and food. In the same way, communities in corporations congregate around a 'river'—a passion or need, either that enhances the social environment or ensures the 'survival' of workers by enabling them to do their jobs better. For community developers, the surveyors of the land, the task is to discover the 'rivers' where people congregate. Once discovered, the land must be surveyed, discovering the enabling peaks and distracting valleys, the dangerous mysteries of difficult relationships and the hidden treasures of passionate advocates and storehouses of knowledge. Once the terrain is determined, the boundaries are laid—the purpose and domain of the community. Finally, the social norms of the city are established—the behaviors and ground rules of the community. In the same way that a city's life evolves and is socio-historical in nature, so is the development of a community. The city continues to grow and change, and so does the community. This analogy helps the core group clearly understand the process of community development.

The second analogy provides a discussion activity during the all-day session. Core group members mentally leave the workplace and examine communities outside of work. First, they think of a community to which they currently belong. They then list what keeps them engaged in that community. Then, they think of a community that they consciously left, and they list why they left. In debriefing these 'attributes' of community, the core group becomes aware of some of the key enablers and barriers that create or prevent communal relationships. Not only does this align core group members about the definition of community, but it also serves as a basis for the values of their own particular community.

Developing the charter. The charter generated in the all-day session serves as the community's externalization of its conception of the three Bs. The charter is generated through active brainstorming activities and negotiation by the entire core group, and must have the fingerprints of all members. It is comprised of six components. The *Description of the Practice* provides a concise description of the practice on which the community is based. *Boundaries* contain a brief listing of who (or what) is part of the community (within its boundaries) and who or what is not (outside its boundaries). *Reason for Existence* describes an overarching statement about the purpose of the community. *Values* hold a concise statement or list of what the community believes is important and what value it brings to the company. *Objectives* enumerate a list of specific, measurable objectives that the community wishes to achieve. Generally these address specific issues in the practice. *Measures of Success* lists indicators that the community is achieving its objectives. Figure 10.4 is a sample charter from one of our communities.

Once the blueprint has been established, the group prepares to share its work with the rest of the community and to involve other members. The preparation phase educates the extended world of practitioners with the value of community. If the group decides to launch the community with a meeting, the meeting agenda is prepared, the activities are identified, and the logistics are addressed.

Quantitative Biology Community Charter

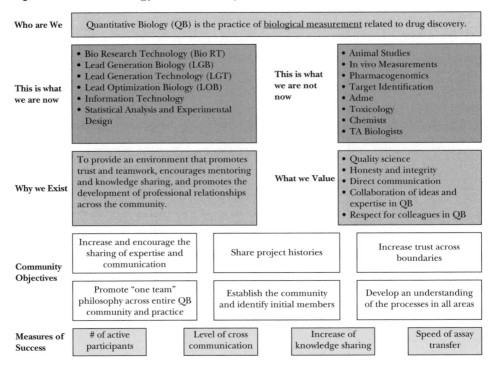

Figure 10.4 Quantitative Biology Charter

Building relationships in the core   The activities that generate the charter naturally develop relationships amongst members. Following the creation of the charter, a number of activities can continue this process. Beginning to work on specific projects to benefit the practice, conducting sharing meetings, continuing to strategize how to build the community, and working collaboratively on work projects can not only help build relationships, but can begin to demonstrate and embody the principles and desired behaviors of the community prior to launch. Launch should not occur until the core group members have established strong relationships and had time to behave as community members.

Launch

The launch of the community has four major purposes. First, it serves as a way of recruiting new members into the community—of bringing those from the periphery toward the core. Second, it tests whether the charter is compelling. If feedback from potential members shows confusion or resistance, the core group may need to revisit the community charter. Third, it educates the organization about communities and how they can benefit the organization. Finally, it represents an intersubjectivity transition point. The core group members begin to take responsibility for community education and developing intersubjectivity about communities and their specific community with potential members. The community developer transitions into a consultant and coach.

The launch can take a variety of forms. A 'metaphoric event' is very effective. The community charter can be communicated in the context of a meaningful metaphor, rather than in a formal business meeting. One of our communities created a small neighborhood. Participants followed a 'bus pass' that directed them to different venues, at which core group members explained a portion of the charter. The optometrist's office housed the vision. At the bank, participants learned about values. By the time participants completed the trip, they were well-acquainted with the purpose, activities, vision, and members of the community. Another group used the Olympics as its context, with each game serving as a discussion point. Others have used a presentation format. The preparation phase mentioned earlier is used to delegate tasks and design this event.

Certain messages should be delivered at launch. First and foremost, the community values and member commitment must be clearly communicated. Potential members need to understand that community is commitment to a set of values, a vision, and relationships. Second, management's expression of support can give the community legitimacy. Because communities are a different way of working, some individuals need to know that it is acceptable for them to participate. Communication from a member of management (however, not an insistence on participation) is helpful in sending this message. Third, core group members should make clear that active participation in the community is optional, yet desired. Finally, the core members should ensure that potential members of the community know that the charter and the community can and must evolve and change. The work done by the core group only serves as a base from which to grow. All members have a say in that evolution.

The launch meeting often results in attracting a few to the community concept. Immediate involvement of these individuals is critical. Growth, however, needs to be monitored carefully. Some may still not be attracted to the concept. This resistance naturally helps to control growth. Community growth and evolution is a complex topic worthy of its own treatment.

DISCUSSION—SOME KEY LEARNINGS FROM APPLYING THE MODEL

Communities provide an enabling context for knowledge creation. The organic and informal nature of the environment needed is often different from that which exists in American corporations today (Wenger and Snyder, 2000). The clashing of the new model with old and entrenched ways of working results in three major issues that should be specifically highlighted in the development and nurturing of CoPs:

♦ Creating communities is an emotional endeavor driven by passion in an environment that generally suppresses emotions.
♦ Communities thrive on responsibility; organizations drive through accountability.
♦ Communities hand control to the practitioners; management is often expected and seeks to control.

These are not independent issues, and to overcome them requires significant adjustment in the organization and in management's attitudes toward the structures within those organizations.

Communities and commitment

According to Von Krogh et al., the 'key quality of knowledge workers is their human-ness' (2000: 12); the goal of organizational learning, therefore, is to bring out this humanness by creating the proper *ba* (see Nonaka, 1998, for a treatment of this concept). Humanness arises in our relationships with others through communities. Dewey (1916) defines this relationship in this way:

> [People] live in a community in virtue of the things which they have in common. . . . What they must have in common in order to form a community or society are aims, beliefs, aspirations, knowledge—a common understanding. . . . The communication which insures participation in a common understanding is one which secures similar emotional and intellectual dispositions—like ways of responding to expectations and requirements.
>
> (Dewey, 1916: 4)

As mentioned earlier, the pathway to this sense of intersubjectivity is an emotional, social, and intellectual endeavor. Common understanding of aims and beliefs is achieved through emotional commitment, active empathy, personal responsibility for the self and others, honesty, and trust.

Unfortunately, though corporations are often good at reaching *cognitive* consensus, their recognition of the primacy of relationships and the importance of *emotional* connection is lacking. Humphrey and Ashford (1994) have shown that many organizations possess a set of 'feeling rules'—procedures for addressing emotional issues within company guidelines that suppress the individual's expression of personal emotions. Thus, public expression of frustration and enthusiastic celebrations are taboo and are often taken as signs of weakness or lack of control. At the same time, corporations invest significant funds in digital infrastructures assuming that relationships can be built and enhanced through computer networking. Yet, 'information systems are of limited usefulness in facilitating a group's commitment to a concept, sharing emotions tied to tacit experience, or embodying the knowledge related to a certain task' (Von Krogh et al., 2000: 27). So, to create this environment, a corporation must change some of its fundamental beliefs about the relationships between workers and what is acceptable and not acceptable in the workplace.

Responsibility *versus* accountability

What drives the current environment differs significantly from what drives communities. Companies operate under an individual accountability model. For the pay that each individual receives, he or she is expected to deliver a certain amount of production for the corporation. To foster this accountability, corporations have developed and implemented a system of rewards and punishments, of monitoring and feedback. This carries forward the same accountability model inherent in the school system in which children are educated as well as the Judeo-Christian religious frameworks that are infused in many cultures. Management's role is to monitor and enforce this accountability and to ensure delivery of the desired product (thus meeting their accountabilities) for the management above them.

Accountability is a control system that enforces with fear from without. Responsibility, on the other hand, is commitment established through caring and passion from within (for a description of the difference between accountability and responsibility, see Dunne and Legge, 2001). Unlike the accountability model, individuals driven by responsibility feel an emotional tie and commitment to other individuals or entities in their joint enterprise who, in turn, have the same emotional tie. They are driven by a common objective and intersubjectivity, which determines their coordinated actions.

What many companies do in their implementation of CoPs is turn to what they know best, and overlay an accountability model on the community, tying participation and performance in the community to organizational performance metrics, to end-of-year evaluations, and to salary increases. While this may build accountability to the organization, it creates a conflict for the community members and an inability to fully develop a sense of commitment and responsibility within the community. In imposing these systems, management often tries to make explicit the commitments and relationships with the hope of measuring their contribution to the company and use the results to evaluate the individual. As Baumard points out, however, 'commitment cannot be reduced to its explicitation' (1999: 204). In support of this thesis, he describes two examples of companies that created commitment of groups of employees from another corporate culture not by lecturing them about compliance, making their agreements explicit, or insisting on changing their behaviors, but by allowing them to work through their own choices, through discussion. While this approach is critical for the development and nurturing of communities, it often creates discomfort for corporate management.

Leadership and management

The implications for management of the two issues previously covered are profound. In this new community model, management must remove the control hat and put on a hat of facilitator and environment creator. The accountability for the deliverables associated with the department lies in the hands of the management, but the responsibility for the practice that determines how those projects are achieved lies in the hands of the practitioners. Management must trust the wisdom of practitioners and 'work for those practitioners' in creating a knowledge-enabling environment that nurtures communities, encourages and legitimizes, but does not require, participation, and values direction setting at all levels.

Some companies have tried establishing a new position called global practice leader— an individual, generally an executive, who is accountable for the performance of the practice at the company. This role can prove problematic for two reasons. First, a title attached to a role in the corporation immediately creates a different relationship between practitioners at the individual contributor level and the holder of the title. It creates an accountability relationship that has all the trappings of a reporting relationship. This relationship often stifles risk taking, challenges to establishment, and creative thought, since there is fear of being perceived as confrontational, incompetent, or emotional (see above). Second, it prevents commitment and responsibility from being established at the level of the practitioner, which would more likely produce effective results. What this position does is confuse organizational leadership (the vertical plane in Figure 10.2) with community leadership (the horizontal plane).

Leadership in a community of practice is distributed and takes two forms. The first form is administrative leadership. The tasks undertaken in this type of leadership ensure the continuity of the community from a tactical point of view—setting up meetings, distributing information, setting agendas, and facilitating gatherings. It does not carry with it the ability to reward or punish, and feedback is provided solely to enhance and enable community function. The second form is leadership by mentoring. In this role, those who step up to leadership in the community lead by encouraging participation in the community, connecting individuals who need knowledge from each other, transitioning new members and members on the periphery into the core of the community, and being a spokesperson or advocate of the community outside its boundaries. Leadership must be examined carefully in an organization seeking to develop a community culture.

Conclusion

As organizational learning takes hold in individualistic companies, employees must learn not only the content and techniques of their domain, but also new ways of interacting in the company—new cultural forms. CoPs are one such structure that promotes learning and at the same time requires its members to learn a new way of behaving.

Communities are houses of intersubjectivity. They are infused with common understanding of both the practice and communal activity. Though community creation, which seeks to create something from nothing, is unproductive, community development, which catalyzes intersubjectivity, the development of social norms, and the determination of the identity of a practitioner group, is crucial to achieving a strong organizational learning strategy.

Building communities, and organizational learning for that matter, is more about removing barriers instituted by the organization that prohibit employees' natural tendencies to socially construct knowledge, negotiate meaning, and internalize cultural enablers, rather than creating specialized learning programs or processes to codify and distribute all organizational knowledge. Communities are one step toward allowing people to interact naturally.

The work presented here introduces a number of topics for future work. First, as mentioned earlier, these frameworks only treat community startup. How communities evolve and change over a period of time, adopt new members, and adapt to outside organizational changes are rich areas for investigation. Intersubjectivity can provide a key to these activities as well, but research on this phenomenon is also sorely needed. Intersubjectivity literature is primarily philosophical, though many related ideas appear in the psychological and sociological literature. Synthesis of these concepts into a unified genetic conceptual framework and its application to community evolution could be very fruitful.

The continued work on this framework will focus on answering three questions. First, what type of leadership in the organization enables communities to thrive? Second, how can we further design technological solutions to enable intersubjective relationships in communities? Finally, how do the human systems (succession, promotions, and performance management systems) need to change in an organization with highly intersubjective communities? The foundation already created, however, can allow communities to continue to slowly reintroduce missing elements of humanness and belonging to meaning-seeking companies.

References

Bakhtin, M. (1981) *The Dialogic Imagination*. Austin: University of Texas Press.

Barton, D. and Tusting, K. (2005) *Beyond Communities of Practice*. New York: Cambridge University Press.

Bauman, Z. (2001) *Community: Seeking Safety in an Insecure World*. Cambridge: Polity.

Baumard, P. (1999) *Tacit Knowledge in Organizations*. London: Sage Publications.

Brown, A., Ash, D., Rutherford, M., Nakagawa, K., Gordon, A., and Campione, J. (1993) Distributed expertise in the classroom. In G. Salomon (ed.), *Distributed Cognitions: Psychological and Educational Considerations*. Cambridge: Cambridge University Press: 188–228.

Brown, J.S., Collins, A., and Duguid, P. (1989) Situated cognition and the culture of learning. *Educational Researcher*, 18(1): 32–42.

Brown, J.S. and Duguid, P. (1991) Organizational learning and communities of practice: Toward a unified view of working, learning, and innovating. *Organization Science*, 2(1): 40–56.

Buber, M. (1974) *I and Thou*. New York: Macmillan Publishing.

Bukowitz, W.R. and Williams, R.L. (1999) *The knowledge management fieldbook*. Upper Saddle River, N.J.: Financial Times, Prentice Hall.

Contu, A. and Willmott, H. (2003) Re-embedding situatedness: The importance of power relations in learning theory. *Organization Science*, 14(3): 283–296.

Cook, S. and Brown, J. S. (1999) Bridging epistemologies: The generative dance between organizational knowledge and organizational knowing. *Organization Science*, 10(4): 381–400.

Crossley, N. (1996) *Intersubjectivity: The Fabric of Social Becoming*. London: Sage Publications.

Dewey, J. (1916) *Democracy and Education*. New York: The Free Press.

Dunne, D. and Legge, J. (2001) US local government managers and the complexity of responsibility and accountability in democratic governance. *Journal of Public Administration Research and Theory*, 11(1): 73–88.

Egan, T. and Jaye, C. (2009) Communities of clinical practice: the social organization of clinical learning. *Health*, 13(1): 107–125.

Engeström, Y. (1995) Innovative organizational learning in medical and legal settings. In L. Martin, K. Nelson, and E. Tobach, (eds.), *Sociocultural Psychology: Theory and Practice of Doing and Knowing*. Cambridge: Cambridge University Press: 326–356.

Engeström, Y. (2007) From communities of practice to mycorrhizae. In J. Hughes, N. Jewson, and L. Unwin (eds.), *Communities of Practice: Critical Perspectives*. London: Routledge: 41–54.

Fahey, L. and Prusak, L. (1998) The eleven deadliest sins of knowledge management. *California Management Review*, 40(3): 265–276.

Fuller, A. (2007) Critiquing theories of learning and communities of practice. In J. Hughes, N. Jewson, and L. Unwin (eds.), *Communities of Practice: Critical Perspectives*. London: Routledge: 17–29.

Gherardi, S., Nicolini, D., and Odella, F. (1998) Toward a social understanding of how people learn in organizations. *Management Learning*, 29(3): 273–297.

Gunawardena, C. Hermans, M., Sanchez, D., Richmond, C., Bohley, M., and Tuttle, R. (2009) A theoretical framework for building online communities of practice with social networking tools. *Educational Media International*, 46(1): 3–16.

Ha, T.S. (2008) How IT workers learn in the workplace. *Studies in Continuing Education*, 30(2): 129–143.

Handy, C. (1995) Managing the dream. In S. Chawla and J. Renesch (eds.), *Learning Organizations: Developing Cultures for Tomorrow's Workplace*. Portland, Oregon: Productivity Press: 45–56.

Hansen, M., Nohria, N., and Tierney, T. (1999) What's your strategy for managing knowledge? *Harvard Business Review*, 77(2): 106–116.

Hara, N. (2009) *Communities of Practice: Fostering Peer-to-Peer Learning and Informal Knowledge Sharing in the Work Place*. Berlin: Springer.

Hedegaard, M. (1995) The qualitative analysis of the development of a child's theoretical knowledge and thinking. In L. Martin, K. Nelson, and E. Tobach (eds.), *Sociocultural Psychology: Theory and Practice of Doing and Knowing*. Cambridge: Cambridge University Press: 293–325.

Hughes, J., Jewson, N., and Unwin, L. (2007) Communities of practice: A contested concept in flux. In J. Hughes, N. Jewson, and L. Unwin (eds.), *Communities of Practice: Critical Perspectives*. London: Routledge: 1–16.

Humphrey, R. and Ashford, B. (1994) Cognitive scripts and prototypes in service encounters. In T. Swartz, D. Bowen, and S. Brown (eds.), *Advances in Service Marketing and Management: Research and Practice*. Greenwich, Connecticut: JAI Press.

Husserl, E. (1965) *Philosophy as Rigorous Science*. New York: Harper Torchbook.

Hutchins, E. (1995) *Cognition in the Wild*. Cambridge, MA: The MIT Press.

Hutchins, E. (1996) Learning to navigate. In S. Chaiklin and J. Lave (eds.), *Understanding Practice: Perspectives on Activity and Context*. Cambridge: Cambridge University Press: 35–63.

Hutchins, E. and Klausen, T. (1998) Distributed cognition in an airline cockpit. In Y. Engeström and D. Middleton (Eds.), *Cognition and Communication at Work*. Cambridge: Cambridge University Press: 15–34.

Lave, J. and Wenger, E. (1991) *Situation Learning: Legitimate Peripheral Participation*. Cambridge: Cambridge University Press.

Leontiev, A. (1978) *Activity, Consciousness, and Personality*. Englewood Cliffs: Prentice-Hall.

Lesser, E. and Prusak, L. (2000) Communities of practice, social capital and organizational knowledge. In E. Lesser, M. Fontaine, and J. Slusher (eds.), *Knowledge and Communities*. Boston: Butterworth Heinemann: 123–132.

McDermott, R. (1998) Why information technology inspired but cannot deliver knowledge management. *California Management Review*, 41(4): 103–117.

McDermott, R. (1999) Learning across teams: The role of communities of practice in team organizations. *Knowledge Management Review*, 8: 32–36.

Nonaka, I. (1998) The concept of 'ba': Building a foundation for knowledge creation. *California Management Review*, 40(3): 40–54.

Nonaka, I. and Takeuchi, H. (1995) *The Knowledge-Creating Company: How Japanese Companies Create the Dynamics of Innovation*. Oxford: Oxford University Press.

O'Dell, C. and Grayson, C. J. (1998) If only we knew what we know: Identification and transfer of internal best practices. *California Management Review*, 40(3): 154–174.

Pane, D.M. (2010) Viewing classroom discipline as negotiable social interaction: A communities of practice perspective. *Teaching and Teacher Education*, 26(1): 87–97.

Pea, R. (1993) Practices of distributed intelligence and designs of education. In G. Salomon (Ed.), *Distributed Cognitions: Psychological and Educational Considerations.* Cambridge: Cambridge University Press: 47–82.

Perkins, D. (1993) Person-plus: A distributed view of thinking and learning. In G. Salomon (ed.), *Distributed Cognitions: Psychological and Educational Considerations.* Cambridge: Cambridge University Press: 88–110.

Polanyi, M. (1966) *The Tacit Dimension.* Garden City, NY: Doubleday.

Rogoff, B. (1990) *Apprenticeship in Thinking: Cognitive Development in Social Contexts.* Oxford: Oxford University Press.

Rommetveit, R. (1974) *On Message Structure: A Framework for the Study of Language and Communication.* Chichester: John Wiley and Sons.

Ryan, S. (1995) Learning communities: An alternative to the 'expert model.' In S. Chawla and J. Renesch (eds.), *Learning Organizations: Developing Cultures of Tomorrow's Workplace,* Portland, OR: Productivity Press: 279–291.

Sartre, J. (1966) *Being and Nothingness.* New York: Washington Square Press.

Schein, E. (1992) *Organizational Culture and Leadership* (2nd edition). San Francisco: Jossey-Bass.

Smith, M. and Kollock, P. (1998) *Communities in Cyberspace.* London: Routledge.

Star, S. (1998) Working together: Symbolic interactionism, activity theory, and information systems. In Y. Engeström and D. Middleton (eds.), *Cognition and Communication at Work.* Cambridge: Cambridge University Press: 296–318.

Thompson, M. (2005) Structural and epistemic parameters in communities of practice. *Organization Science,* 16(2): 151–164.

Tönnies, F. (2001) *Community and Civil Society.* Cambridge: Cambridge University Press.

von Krogh, G. and Roos, J. (1995) *Organizational Epistemology.* New York: St. Martin's Press.

von Krogh, G., Ichijo, K., and Nonaka, I. (2000) *Enabling Knowledge Creation: How to Unlock the Mystery of Tacit Knowledge and Release the Power of Innovation.* Oxford: Oxford University Press.

Vygotsky, L. (1978) *Mind in Society: The Psychology of Higher Mental Functions.* Cambridge, MA: Harvard University Press.

Vygotsky, L. (1981) The genesis of higher mental functions. In J. Wertsch (ed.). *The Concept of Activity in Soviet Psychology.* Armonk, NY: M. E. Sharpe: 144–188.

Wenger, E. (1998a) *Communities of Practice: Learning, Meaning, and Identity.* Cambridge: Cambridge University Press.

Wenger, E. (1998b) Communities of practice: Learning as a social system. *Systems Thinker,* 9(5): 1–8.

Wenger, E. (1999) Communities of practice: The key to knowledge strategy. *Knowledge Directions: The Journal of the Institute for Knowledge Management,* 1: 48–63.

Wenger, E. and Snyder, W. (2000) Communities of practice: The organizational frontier. *Harvard Business Review,* 78(1): 139–145.

Wertsch, J. (1985) *Vygotsky and the Social Formation of Mind.* Cambridge, MA: Harvard University Press.

11

Fads, Fashions, and the Fluidity of Knowledge

Peter Senge's 'The Learning Organization'

MIKELLE A. CALHOUN, WILLIAM H. STARBUCK, AND ERIC ABRAHAMSON

ABSTRACT

This chapter uses the story of Peter Senge's The Learning Organization (TLO) and talks about 'learning organizations' to illustrate how management fads and fashions affect the spread of knowledge. Some commentators labeled Senge's successful TLO work a 'fad.' Implicit in such labeling is derision and suggestion that association with TLO lacks benefit. New management techniques often provoke skepticism and when miracles do not occur, receive the same derogatory 'fad' label. Is the negativism associated with management fads and fashions warranted? Analysis of the Senge TLO phenomena portrays fads and fashions as social processes, intrinsic to social change. They erupt from latency periods and may have brief or long lives. In retrospect, their consequences may be beneficial or harmful and may be short term or long term. Even brief fads may produce lasting benefits. TLO's story shows the complexity of social change and reveals the fluidity of knowledge, as ever-evolving fads and fashions weave older ideas into new beliefs and ways of problem solving.

INTRODUCTION

An organization's ability to learn, and translate that learning into action rapidly, is the ultimate competitive advantage.

Jack Welch

Peter Senge's 1990 book *The Fifth Discipline: The Art and Practice of the Learning Organization* presented a compelling frame for a collection of ideas and gave structure to a 'new' TLO concept. Senge explained that people need to conceive of the world as systems on which humans have imposed structures that both serve purposes and impose constraints. Senge explained TLO as a process of understanding and continually working to master five important disciplines. Each discipline has at its core a critical truth about a learning organization and adds to the total meaning of TLO. Senge's rich book was highly successful and attracted enthusiasts. Yet now, twenty years later, many commentators are dismissing TLO as a fad. This chapter evaluates Senge's TLO story and uses it to consider the contribution of fads and fashions to knowledge creation.

TLO is more than just a set of ideas promoted by a specific individual. Although TLO gained much impetus from its active champion, its emergence followed a latency period. Senge did not invent his concept of TLO out of nothing. He pulled together ideas that had originated separately in various places over several decades. Even the specific term 'the learning organization' had appeared in print earlier (Garratt, 1987; Korten, 1980). The success of Senge's book was partly a result of its timing. Senge spotted a developing societal trend, identified some relevant concepts, placed these concepts into a frame, and made the concepts accessible by retelling familiar stories and presenting interesting examples. Sales of Senge's books, public accolades, and formation of at least two societies testify that growing acceptance of TLO as valuable knowledge had widespread social support. Some consultants have promoted efforts to apply Senge's prescriptions, and some organizations may have benefited from trying to apply them.

This chapter describes the history of TLO and Senge's role in its emergence as a mainstream concept. This history suggests two questions. Why did Senge's book become popular and retain this popularity through two editions and two decades? Was the popularity of this book a consequence of its inherent properties or of its societal context? The chapter addresses these questions by drawing upon research into fads and fashions in business techniques. This research suggests that suppliers of management techniques—academics, consultants—promote them as efficient means to effective ends and also as novel and improved. By framing reactions to TLO in terms of prior research about fads and fashions, the chapter also raises questions about the nature of knowledge and what 'learning' means.

THE SUCCESS OF SENGE'S TLO

Peter Senge's *The Fifth Discipline* drew millions of readers and popularized the TLO concept. The book presented five techniques or 'disciplines' that Senge said 'must be studied and mastered to be put into practice' within a TLO (1990: 10). Senge defined TLOs as:

> organizations where people continually expand their capacity to create the results they truly desire, where new and expansive patterns of thinking are nurtured, where collective aspiration is set free, and where people are continually learning how to learn together.

The book sold over two and a half million copies, a result that encouraged Senge to say more about TLO. Over the following decade, he provided examples of the application of TLO principles in different contexts. In 1994, he and colleagues published *The Fifth Discipline Fieldbook: Strategies and Tools for Building a Learning Organization*. It has sold over

400,000 copies. A second fieldbook came out in 1999 under the title *The Dance of Change: The Challenges to Sustaining Momentum in Learning Organizations*. In 2000, Senge co-authored *Schools that Learn: A Fifth Discipline Fieldbook for Educators, Parents and Everyone Who Cares about Education*. A revised version of the original *Fifth Discipline* appeared in 2006.

Senge created a compelling vision. Jackson (2000: 207) claimed the TLO concept had dramatic qualities and inspired 'followers to see themselves actively engaged in building a learning organization.' As popularity of the TLO concept quickly grew, Senge founded a Center for Organizational Learning at MIT in 1991. Emerald Group Publishing launched a journal named *The Learning Organization* in 1994. Several prominent business magazines, including *Business Week* and *Fortune*, published articles about TLO. In 1997, *Harvard Business Review* named *The Fifth Discipline* as one of the most influential management books in the last seventy-five years. Also in 1997, Senge formed the Society for Organizational Learning, which subsequently spawned a journal entitled *Reflections: The SoL Journal* and which has developed consulting, coaching, conference, and publishing initiatives for its members. In 1999, the *Journal of Business Strategy* included Senge among the twenty-four people who had exerted the greatest influence on business strategy during the twentieth century. In 2000 and 2001, the *Financial Times* and *Business Week* called him one of the world's 'top management gurus.'

Figure 11.1 shows the numbers of documents that cited *The Fifth Discipline* from 1990 through 2005. The graph terminates in 2005 because the more recent data are less and less complete, so trends tend to appear to indicate that citations are leveling off or declining near the time of data gathering. Very likely, citations have continued to increase since 2005. Three fields account for ninety-eight percent of the documents that cited *The Fifth Discipline*. Documents classified by Google as 'social science,' which accounted for

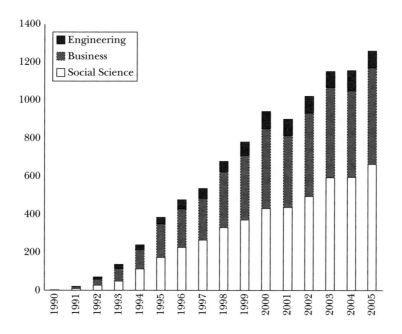

Figure 11.1 Citations of *The Fifth Discipline*

forty-nine percent of the citations, have mainly discussed educational organizations. Documents classified as 'business' have generated an additional forty-one percent of the citations. Documents classified as 'engineering,' which supplied an additional eight percent of the citations, have mainly discussed information systems.

Citations from the journal named *The Learning Organization* have also continued to increase. Indeed, articles published by this journal have had surprisingly long citation lives. A typical article from the early issues received less than half of its total citations during the first nine years following publication, and the articles published in the journal's first year were still receiving approximately one citation a piece per year, sixteen years later.

TLO's Latency Period

Research indicates that fads and fashions in business techniques typically have latency periods during which the techniques have little popularity (Abrahamson and Eisenman, 2008). Latency may give way to sudden upswings in techniques' popularity followed by equally sudden downswings, resulting in waves of diverse amplitudes and durations (Carson, Lanier, Carson, and Guidry, 2000). Some ideas may achieve wide acceptance and popularity; other ideas fail to gain much attention.

Both academic and nonacademic writers had been discussing components of Senge's TLO for several decades; an emergence and sudden surge in popularity could have occurred earlier. They did not. Senge's book could have been yet another incremental contribution to a continuing latency period. It was not. Instead, Senge brought TLO to prominence. Why Senge? Why his book? Why in 1990?

TLO and its five component disciplines build on a wide range of prior conceptual developments. Predecessor thinking concerns organizational learning, organizational rigidity, learning systems, systems thinking, and even prior discussions of similarly described 'learning organizations.' Senge devoted large portions of *The Fifth Discipline* to the ideas of other people. Table 11.1 shows the antecedents on whom Senge relied most strongly; they include both academics and practitioners.

Although Senge gave credit to the works listed in Table 11.1, he did not mention much of the research that had preceded his book. Even without attribution, current knowledge builds on prior knowledge. Sometimes similar ideas develop in different camps from a common pool of information, then proceed along different trajectories. Invention races and first-to-invent claims made by individuals in different parts of the world occur often. Senge's TLO draws from a wide range of prior knowledge concerning systems and organizational learning. Many other thinkers were on tangent paths. For instance, Senge did not report that, fifteen years earlier, Hedberg, Nystrom, and Starbuck (1976: 43) had written about how to keep organizations from rigidifying over time and how to foster continuing development. They argued, 'Designs can themselves be conceived as processes—as generators of dynamic sequences of solutions, in which attempted solutions induce new solutions and attempted designs trigger new designs.'

Academic studies of organizational learning. As early as 1936, engineers and economists noticed that the costs of producing aircraft grew less as workers produced more aircraft (Argote, 1999). By the early 1950s, academic economists and management scholars were debating the possible influence of evolutionary selection on decision making in populations of business

Table 11.1   Antecedents Senge acknowledged as important

	Definitional or Conceptual Works	Phenomenon Development and Analysis	Prescriptive Suggestions
Systems thinking	Bohm (1965): The universe is an indivisible whole. Forrester (1961, 1969, 1971): Simulation can demonstrate the dynamics of systems. Hardin (1968): What is good for individuals may be bad for the collectivity.	Bohm (1965): Fragmentation of problems and perceptions exacts a price. Kaufman (1980): Long cycles are hard to see. Sterman (1987): Systems' structures strongly influence behavior.	Roberts (1978, 1983): People have latent skills as systems thinkers; they can learn to do it quickly.
Mental models	Argyris and Schön (1978, 1985): Management teams do not behave as teams should; managers find collective inquiry threatening. Mitroff (1988): Mental models grow obsolete.	Argyris (1982): People create defensive routines and use other defensive routines to conceal these. Sterman (1987): People ignore the effects of their decisions on others. Tuchman (1984): People adhere to policies without watching the actual consequences.	Argyris (1982): People can become more aware of their mental models and the differences between their desired behaviors and their actual behaviors.
Personal mastery; shared vision, team learning	Bohm (1965): Thought can be more effective as the product of dialogue and discussion. Heisenberg (1971): Science can benefit from conversation among scientists.	Fritz (1989): People assume that they cannot fulfill their desires; they assume they are powerless or undeserving. Inamori (1985): For people to attain their fullest potential, they must have a 'sincere desire to serve the world'. O'Brien (1991): People need to feel part of an ennobling mission. Yankelovich (1981): Affluence has shifted work motivation from extrinsic goals toward intrinsic ones.	Bohm (1965): People should be willing to share their thinking and to have it influenced by others. de Geus (1988): Learning occurs in three ways – through teaching, through 'changing the rules' and through play. Schön (1983): Successful professionals reflect on their actions. Team learning is difficult so teams need to practice learning in 'virtual worlds.'

229

firms (Salgado, Starbuck, and Mezias, 2002). A decade later, Cyert and March (1963) wrote about adaptive learning by individual organizations. They characterized organizational learning as adapting decision rules to circumstances, changing goals and forecasts to reflect experience and updated perceptions, modifying goals to make them more realistic, and searching where previous searches have brought success. Such ideas have subsequently spawned many research studies and generated considerable debate. These studies indicate that organizational learning is deceptively treacherous and very likely to disappoint the learners.

Research studies indicate that the efforts of individual organizations to adapt to their environments are generally inadequate and frequently erroneous. Lessons that prove valuable in the short run tend to prove harmful in the long run (Hedberg et al., 1976). Unpredictable environmental changes may reward organizations that have acted incompetently or ineffectively (Starbuck and Pant, 1996). Intra-organizational politics and careerism may suppress evidence of poor performance and create false evidence of success (Baumard and Starbuck , 2005). Because organizations imitate each other, gains that organizations make *vis-à-vis* their competitors disappear rather rapidly (Simon and Bonini, 1958). Thus, some researchers have pursued the hypothesis that organizational learning is primarily a population-level phenomenon: evolutionary variation and selection might change the kinds of organizations that exist even if individual organizations change very little. However, over a decade of empirical studies showed that changes in organizational populations look very like random walks (Carroll, 1983; Levinthal, 1991). After more than fifty years of thought and study about organizational learning, March (2010: 114) surmised: 'Much of organizational and managerial life will produce vividly compelling experiences from which individuals and organizations will learn with considerable confidence, but the lessons they learn are likely to be incomplete, superstitious, self-confirming, or mythic.'

Nonacademic writing about organizational learning. Some of the people who have been working to facilitate organizational learning give credit to Revans, who wrote about 'The enterprise as a learning system' (1982). In parallel with Bohm, Argyris, and Schön, on whom Senge relies heavily, Revans argued that organizations should not rely on 'experts' for advice and that groups of organization members should discuss their own actions and experiences in a process he called Action Learning.

At least two authors used the exact term 'the learning organization' before Senge did, and David Korten (1980) used it a full decade earlier. Korten described five development projects in the Third World, and then argued that such projects should not adhere to plans that were designed top-down but should develop bottom-up through participation by people who understand events at first-hand. There will always be errors, and a learning organization should welcome evidence about errors as guidance about how to perform better. A learning organization also involves local people, takes advantage of what they know, and uses resources that are readily available. A learning organization integrates research, planning, and implementation. However, Korten was clearly talking about development projects that had specific goals and somewhat temporary lifespans, rather than learning that might go on indefinitely.

In a book titled *The Learning Organization*, Bob Garratt (1987) argued that business organizations typically have too little open discussion of issues, with one result being too little reflection about policies and strategies, and another result being too little information input from business environments. Garratt saw organizational learning as being the special responsibility of senior managers, and he proposed that senior executives ought to devote more effort to their personal learning and they should try to guide their organizations' continuing development.

In a third work, titled *The Learning Company*, Pedler, Burgoyne, and Boydell (1988) sought to identify properties of 'an organization that facilitates the learning of all its members and consciously transforms itself and its context.' They pointed to eleven properties that would enable such learning. These properties included strategizing as a learning process, wide participation by organization members and stakeholders, a culture that encourages continuous learning, and helpful accounting and information systems.

Clearly, both the term 'the learning organization' and the ideas echoed in *The Fifth Discipline* were well known in the 1980s, especially the late 1980s. Yet, it was Senge's interpretation of TLO that caught on and began to spread (Jackson, 2000).

SENGE'S FOCUS

Although Senge acknowledged that he was not the first person to write about organizational learning, his presentation seems to imply that his ideas have broader relevance than prior perspectives. Of course, he may have been unaware of the earlier research about organizational learning. He could have used the prior research he ignored to bolster his case for the need to approach organizational learning differently. The very fact that most organizational learning is ineffective or eventually causes problems gives reason for readers to pay attention to new ideas. At the same time, Senge's lessons do not focus on the kinds of organizational learning that typically do occur. He is not naïve and he recognizes that human behavior often impedes learning and that much organizational learning goes amiss. He is proposing that a more effective kind of learning could be occurring. He is a visionary who is trying to describe an idealized organizational form that does not exist today but, he says, could exist in the future.

What Senge said and how he said it

The Fifth Discipline has unusual properties. This fact should surprise no one, of course, because the book has had extreme success far beyond that of almost all other books. Even if the book's success is partly due to its timing and environment, it is unlikely to look exactly like less successful books. However, the book has properties that make it both attractive and unattractive to readers. Some evidence suggests that *The Fifth Discipline* is both easy to read and yet unread, that its popularity derives in part from its appeal for readers who see themselves as unusual, that its ideas have rarely been implemented and implementation has yielded unclear results. Does *The Fifth Discipline* afford a prototype for other books that aim at societal influence? Or has *The Fifth Discipline* succeeded because of its timing and despite its idiosyncrasies?

Much of *The Fifth Discipline* is very easy to understand, down-to-earth, and practical. Within the general themes, the text is fragmented and episodic. This fragmentation of text allows readers to read and digest segments. One need not read an entire chapter, sometimes not even an entire page, in order to extract a distinct point. Many of the segments tell great stories about human behavior, restate truisms, or contain quotable phrases. Although these segments fit into Senge's broader themes, they also stand alone as epigrams or illustrations of specific lessons (Ortenblad, 2007). For example, time delay in physiological reactions to ingesting food causes people to eat too much; trying to swim against a strong current may sap a swimmer's strength without producing progress toward shore. Such illustrations let readers draw useful lessons whether or not they buy into Senge's broader themes, and they make the lessons easy to remember. At the same time, the broader themes give the book some coherence and create an impression of communicating a message of grand significance.

However, the book also forwards ideas that are so abstract that many people do not see their value and the ideas are difficult and expensive to implement (Smith, 2008). The book offers rhapsodic discussion of interlinked systems, their importance and prevalence. It recognizes the complexity of organizational and behavioral challenges. It advocates holistic and dynamic appreciation of social systems (including organizations), and it criticizes much management practice as misguided efforts to apply simplistic mental frameworks to complex situations. Effective management, it says, requires 'systems thinking'—appreciation for interdependencies and change over time. The book (1990:14) asserts that effective organizational learning involves creativity as well as adaptation: 'it is not enough to survive. 'Survival learning' or what is more often termed 'adaptive learning' is important—indeed it is necessary. But for a learning organization, 'adaptive learning' must be joined by 'generative learning', learning that enhances our capacity to create'. Indeed, Senge concluded *The Fifth Discipline* with titillating predictions about a 'sixth discipline.' In an obscure manner, he suggested that an intellectual sequel awaits once the first five disciplines reach critical mass. Senge (1990: 363) predicted, 'there will be other innovations in the future' and 'perhaps one or two developments emerging from seemingly unlikely places, will lead to a wholly new discipline that we cannot even grasp today.'

Of course, his conceptual framework implies that Senge's prescriptions are themselves interdependent and idealistic. He urges people to practice five 'disciplines,' which Table 11.2 summarizes. The disciplines deal with individuals, groups, and whole organizations; and they overlap each other to some degree. Indeed, this overlap contributes to making the book very dense and difficult to synthesize. For example, in his discussion of systems thinking, Senge explains that the mental models are in many ways the results of the structures people impose on systems. In their efforts to understand and manage systems, people break systems down into more manageable pieces, organize them into structures, and then interpret them in these fragmented and organized forms. The structures may be literal but they are more often concepts about processes, procedures, or hierarchies. These imposed structures alter understandings of the entire system, often making the understandings less accurate. The structures also make systems more complex and hinder people's ability to learn. Thus, Senge prescribes awareness, reassessment of goals, and open exchange of ideas—individual and group actions—to improve system-wide learning.

Much of *The Fifth Discipline* is bizarrely abstract, nearly impossible to decipher, and impossible to translate into practical actions. People who have tried to use Senge's ideas have raised questions about *The Fifth Discipline*'s practical implications. Malone (1997: 72) pointed to three problems: (1) TLO has turned into training; (2) TLO had slipped into an MIS sinkhole; (3) 'No one has yet figured out quite how an organization "learns" the right things.' Smith (2001) suggested that Senge's work was 'simply too idealistic' and he observed that the self-reflection associated with the five disciplines daunts most people;

Table 11.2 Senge's five disciplines

Discipline	Discipline's Central Character	Discipline's Critical Truth	Discipline's Practical Meaning for TLO	What Senge Seems to be Trying to Say
Systems thinking	Foundation	Individuals and firms operate within systems and structures that influence behavior.	We need to think holistically and understand that how we organize our world adds to its complexity.	The world consists of interconnected phenomena. When we seek to impose order by fragmentation (breaking issues apart for easier management) and by imposing structures we add complexity, distort reality, and disconnect cause from effect.
Personal mastery	Prescription	Learning requires clear understanding of how current reality differs from desired reality.	We need to clearly understand where we are, where we want to go, and the distance between them.	We cannot develop a successful plan when our baseline information is wrong or our goal ill-designed.
Mental models	Constraints	'Facts' are collections of assumptions; the teachings of experience can perpetuate bias.	Question everything; we need to regard all facts as collections of assumptions ripe for reflection and inquiry.	Experience is not always a good teacher, and the changing world leads to changing truths. We need to challenge our beliefs about the world and best practices.
Shared vision	Motivation	Success requires commitment to goals and a belief in ability to achieve them.	We need an overriding belief that the collectivity can and *should* shape its future.	Achievement needs a strong motivating force that can exist only when everyone cares and believes in the possibility of shared goals.
Team learning	Structure	Open, non-judgmental communication leads to the best learning.	To find the best course of action, we need to test diverse ideas through non-judgmental brainstorming and dialogue.	Open exchange of ideas will best insure good decisions. We need to perfect our ability to put aside assumptions and personal motivations and to avoid defensive behaviors that waste energy and promote poor decisions.

many employees just want to earn a living and have no interest in the greater ideals of the organization. Ortenblad (2007) reported that managers do not read the book because it is so difficult to read and he complained that Senge provided no blueprint for implementation. Senge himself has expressed disappointment that companies 'either paid no more than lip service to [*The Fifth Discipline*] or turned their backs on it altogether' (Senge and Crainer, 2008: 71). In 2008, *The Learning Organization* journal published a fifteen-year retrospective issue on both TLO concept and on the journal itself. The editor concluded that 'although the learning organization concept is deemed narrow and out of date, it is judged to have significant positive influence on organizational thinking' (Smith, 2008: 441).

The foundation of TLO—systems analysis—may be its weakest component. *The Fifth Discipline* describes ten systems archetypes, which Senge characterized as tools to help managers learn systems thinking. The archetypes mix heterogeneous elements at different levels of abstraction—simplistic explanations involving phenomena such as delay and eroding goals alternate with complex theoretical descriptions such as the 'tragedy of the commons' and 'growth and underinvestment.' The conglomerate character of these archetypes underscores the substantial challenge of overcoming human nature and conditioning needed to achieve a broad, systemic mindset.

Senge clarified why people have trouble seeing the bigger picture and why systems thinking poses so many problems, but he nevertheless continued to insist that systems analysis should be the focal point of TLO. In doing so, Senge was attempting to override The Law of Requisite Variety, which says that for people to understand their environments, human comprehension abilities must be as complex and diverse as the environments (Ashby, 1958). However, human rationality is a rather crude and imperfect tool because humans need and demand simplicity. When Box and Draper (1969) attempted to use experiments to improve factory operations, they discovered that practical experiments have to alter no more than two or three variables at a time because the people who interpret experimental findings cannot make sense of interactions among four or more variables. Faust (1984) also observed that scientists have difficulties understanding interactions among more than three variables (Goldberg, 1970; Meehl, 1954). Faust remarked that the great theoretical contributions in the physical sciences have exhibited parsimony and simplicity rather than complexity, and he speculated that parsimonious theories have been very influential not because the physical universe is simple but because people find simple theories understandable.

A real-life example illustrates the constraints that human cognitive limitations place on systems analysis. In the summer of 2009, PA Consulting submitted a diagram to the officers who were in charge of US troops fighting in Afghanistan. The diagram presented the consulting company's analysis of the relationships officers ought to consider in planning military and political strategies—scores of relationships among scores of variables such as accomplishments, beliefs, capabilities, crime, expectations, fears, interest groups, manpower, needs, outcomes, perceptions, policies, political support, priorities, resources, setbacks, territory controlled, and time elapsed. According to Bumiller (2010), the officers reacted with laughter to this diagram's impenetrable complexity.

However, the complexity and abstraction of Senge's analysis may enable some readers to feel proud that they perceive issues and solutions that other people cannot see, and so these properties contribute to the development of a collectivity of superior insiders who appreciate Senge's message. The support organization Senge created, The Society for Organizational Learning, has already drifted away from the ideas in *The Fifth Discipline*. The

Society has recently been promoting 'Theory U' which promises to teach us 'to connect to our essential Self in the realm of presencing' and to use 'principles and practices that allow everyone to participate fully in co-creating and bringing forth the desired future that is working to emerge through us.' Similarly, much of Senge's own recent writing and speaking has centered on the more trendy topic of sustainability.

When Senge said it: Is TLO just a fad or more than that?

Perhaps *The Fifth Discipline* has succeeded mainly because it fits into its time and place, because it captures the spirit of its age. In his Foreword to the 2006 edition of *The Fifth Discipline*, Senge explained that he had realized in 1987 'that "the learning organization" would likely become a new management fad.' He assumed that the fad would rise and fall and he wanted to establish key ideas early on at the beginning of this fad and especially he wanted to influence the residual of ideas that remained after this fad abated.

Various commentators have declared TLO to be a short-term fad—indeed, a fad that is ending or has ended. Malone (1997) included TLO in a list of 'management fads which have come and gone.' Hodgetts, Luthans, and Lee (1998) claimed that TLO was an intermediate stage in a developmental evolution toward 'world-class organizations.' Scarbourgh and Swan (2001) evaluated ProQuest references to 'learning organization' and to 'knowledge management' from 1990 to 1998, and concluded that TLO had become unfashionable and had been replaced by knowledge management. Rebelo and Gomes (2008: 294) inferred that 'academic and managerial interest in these [organizational learning and TLO] started to wane slightly and the suspicion that organizational learning was merely a fashion has increased, as have the critical voices around it.'

Nevertheless, data do not yet demonstrate clearly that enthusiasm for TLO has waned. Figures 11.2a, 11.2b, and 11.2c compare the popularity of TLO with two management

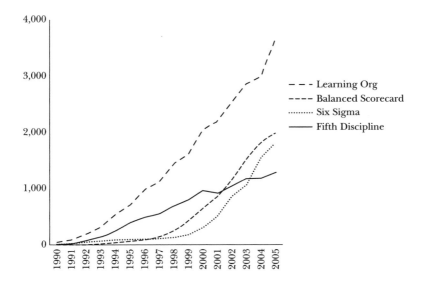

Figure 11.2a Citations About Three Management Ideas

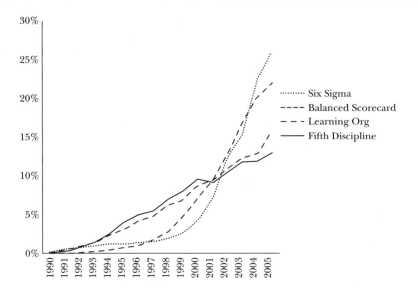

Figure 11.2b Normalized Citations About Three Management Ideas
(Normalized by Citations in First Sixteen Years)

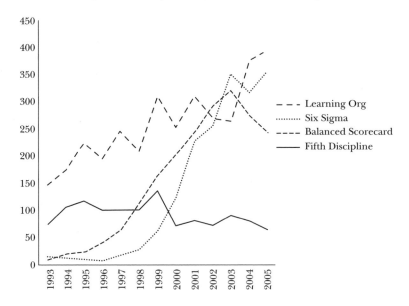

Figure 11.2c Changes in Citations About Three Management Ideas (Three-Year Averages)

ideas that were popular from 1990 to 2005—'six sigma' quality improvement and the
'balanced scorecard' assessment of business performance. The graphs show the numbers
of documents that cited *The Fifth Discipline* and the numbers of documents that used the
phrases 'learning organization,' 'six sigma,' or 'balanced scorecard.' Figure 11.2a presents

absolute numbers; many more documents used the phrase 'learning organization' than used the phrases 'six sigma' or 'balanced scorecard.' Only forty percent of the documents that used the phrase 'learning organization' also mentioned Senge; 'learning organization' is a broader concept than Senge's TLO.

To highlight the different shapes of the curves, Figure 11.2b shows data normalized so that all four lines appear to describe the same total number of documents over the sixteen years, and Figure 11.2c shows changes averaged over three years.

Citations to *The Fifth Discipline* and documents that mention 'learning organization' have increased more linearly than documents that mention the other two management ideas. Both six sigma and the balanced scorecard drew very few citations during the early 1990s; then both began rapid growth just before 2000. Rapid growth could be a sign that people are becoming more likely to do something as they see more people doing it, possibly because prevalence confers legitimacy. When people or organizations adopt an innovation partly because many other people or organizations have adopted this innovation, a bandwagon effect occurs. On the other hand, some studies have shown that rapid growth in the adoption of an innovation correlates with a parallel increase in marketing efforts, and Abrahamson and Rosenkopf (1993) ran simulations that showed very small differences could have massive impacts on the rise and collapse in the popularity of innovations. It is also worthwhile to beware of fallacious inferences about the processes that generate time series: a given process can generate quite different specific series; different processes can generate similar series (Starbuck, 2006: 25–26).

Citations to *The Fifth Discipline* rose very linearly: the annual increases in citations were nearly constant from 1993 to 2005. Uses of the phrase learning organization were somewhat less linear in that the annual *increases* in citations grew larger over time, approximately doubling over ten years. Mainly linear growth might reflect a gradual opening up of multiple new markets, and this interpretation is consistent with some of the shifting currents in the kinds of people who have cited *The Fifth Discipline*. All the earliest citations came from documents in the English language, and as time passed citations appeared in more and more languages. Loosely, one could say that the languages migrated from developed economies toward developing economies. There have also been adoption currents related to occupational groupings. For example, many citations have come from documents written by US Naval personnel and very few citations have come from documents written by other military personnel. Nurses have also shown special interest in *The Fifth Discipline*. Although each of these occupational groupings probably did engage in some bandwagon adoptions, each occupational grouping adopted TLO rather separately. With little contagion across groupings, exponential growth was restrained by boundaries between occupations, societies, and languages.

There is no clear reason why six sigma and balanced scorecard began spreading rapidly around 2000. Both ideas had been latent in the business culture for several decades, and although there were triggering events that brought them to the forefront, such triggering events could have happened much earlier or much later. The idea that businesses should consider factors other than financial ones originated in France in the early twentieth century, and General Electric developed a multidimensional assessment system for its profit centers during the 1950s. A 1992 article in *Harvard Business Review* gave balanced scorecard new visibility, but *Harvard Business Review* publicizes many ideas every year and 1992 was several years before the interest in balanced scorecard began to accelerate.

Very high quality became a popular theme in Japan during the 1960s, and this theme spread worldwide during the 1970s when it appeared that Japanese companies were having remarkable success. During the 1960s, statistical studies of the PIMS database (Profit Impact of Market Strategy) indicated that high-quality products are often very profitable. Then, in the 1980s, Motorola Corporation combined long-standing ideas about how to raise quality into a formal training program that the corporation marketed under the 'Six Sigma' trademark. For Motorola's corporate clients, six sigma offered easy implementation, quantitative measures of results, as well as some terminological pizzazz. However, Motorola's marketing of six sigma began almost two decades before interest in the idea began to accelerate.

Organizational learning is different. It seems quite unlikely that this idea could have started to become very popular before 1990. Although academics had written about organizational learning as early as the late 1950s, such ideas did not migrate into the literature of business practitioners. The phrase 'organizational learning' did not appear in *Harvard Business Review* until 1989 and it appeared in *Sloan Management Review* only once before 1991.

Senge's TLO is a poor candidate for exponential growth based on imitation. Imitation of managerial ideas is more likely if the ideas are easy to comprehend, quick to implement, and capable of producing visible results. Senge's ideas are sufficiently abstract that many people do not see their value and they are difficult and expensive to implement (Smith, 2008). Senge provides no simple prescriptions, and he advocates long-term, persistent commitment to unusual social processes. The benefits of TLO are elusive; there is no way to find out what would have happened in the absence of TLO. Thomas and Allen (2006) pointed to a lack of clear connection between learning and business success, and Smith said that some converts to TLO eventually shifted to other approaches after evidence of business success with TLO was not forthcoming.

The Fifth Discipline may continue to attract audiences less because it provides easy solutions than because it addresses challenging issues of current relevance. The book deals with management issues that have been becoming more and more relevant in affluent, developed economies during the late twentieth century. These issues seem likely to continue to gain relevance over the coming decades.

Senge wrote about a complex world, with many interdependencies—oligopolistic markets, corporations and governments that cooperate, externalities. The populace of this world does not have to scrabble around for existence and they aspire to do more than merely adapt to their environments; they reflect on their motives and actions and they seek to construct worlds with properties they desire. Workers are not lonely farmers at the mercy of weather or factory workers keeping pace with conveyor belts; they cooperate in teams, exchange ideas, analyze, and strategize.

Through the twentieth century, agriculture and manufacturing migrated toward developing economies, while the developed economies have shifted toward services. In the developed economies, the fastest-growing occupations have included professional and technical workers and managers. The US provides an extreme case. By 1990, the information sector accounted for three-fourths of US GNP, and over half of US workers were doing some type of information work.

Business in developed economies has been changing conceptually. New kinds of knowledge-intense and information-intense organizations have emerged that are devoted entirely to the production, processing, and distribution of information (Starbuck, 1992). These new kinds of organizations already employ many millions of people, with the Internet supporting new business and career opportunities. As well, facilitated by better telecommunications, business firms have been creating alliances and forming networks, and these larger entities have given business strategists license to think more about constructing environments that they desire instead of adapting to environments that already exist. Current thinking about strategic management emphasizes the usefulness of valuable resources that are rare and difficult to imitate (Barney, 1991), and many organizations seek to accumulate valuable and proprietary knowledge that they can exploit strategically. For instance, chemical and pharmaceutical companies employ skilled scientists and spend heavily on research aimed at developing proprietary products. Some manufacturing firms see experienced and highly trained managers as key assets, and many firms have appointed 'learning officers' who are charged with identifying useful knowledge and disseminating it to personnel who can use it. Managements have shifted focus from a more traditional input-and-output analysis to dealing with knowledge capital, information systems, logistics, and supply chains.

Senge saw these trends and responded to them, and it is unclear what forces might deflect changes from following the trends. It seems likely that information and knowledge will grow more and more important in developed economies. In particular, despite the fact that computers and electronic communications devices have existed for decades and they have become quite prevalent in Europe, Japan, and North America, only a fraction of the world population has use of computers, e-mail, or the Internet. At the same time, technological development has been accelerating. Organizations have been gaining access to more data more quickly. As this creates opportunities for surveillance from afar, competitive intelligence has been becoming easier and more productive, supervisors can more easily monitor distant subordinates, and organizations can more easily monitor their alliance partners. The technology also gives organizations more freedom to spread geographically, and they can collaborate effectively without actually merging.

WHAT RESEARCH INTO FADS AND FASHIONS SAYS ABOUT TLO's SUCCESS

TLO's history illustrates the rise in popularity and dissemination of a body of ideas, a particular way of thinking. Research about fads and fashions can make some interpretations of TLO's history more plausible and others less plausible. However, the history of TLO differs from most of the fads and fashions that researchers have studied. This means that much of the prior research is only indirectly relevant and it suggests some opportunities for future research.

The terms fad and fashion encompass a wide variety of social phenomena. They may spread across large populations of people or organizations, or they may occur within individual organizations or small subpopulations. Many business techniques have had very short life cycles (Brandes, 1976; Carson et al., 2000). By contrast, Aristotle's ideas dominated Western thinking about physics for over two millennia. As well, fads and fashions produce a wide variety of consequences, some beneficial and some harmful, some short term and others long term. Indeed, fads and fashions are kinds of social change, and change can be positive or negative, rapid or slow. Abrahamson and Rosenkopf (1993, 1997) characterized fads as forms of social change that incorporate contagion, and fashions as forms of social change in which followers imitate fashion setters.

It is helpful to consider fads and fashions as commodities bought and sold in markets. Some people and organizations act as buyers and others as sellers. A market perspective calls attention to some of the social structures that facilitate buying and selling and methods used to sell ideas. A market perspective aids in understanding the emergence of a fad and explains differences in popularity of some fads.

The market for business techniques

Senge's ideas about TLO and his more general ideas about the 'learning organization' are so ambiguous that they may not qualify as business techniques. They are less specific than many of the techniques that have been studied. However, research about fads and fashions in business techniques provides suggestions about the processes affecting the popularity and consequences of TLO.

Abrahamson (1996) analyzed changes in business techniques in a market framework. The techniques bought and sold in this market bear labels—such as 'The Learning Organization'—that provide concise characterizations for bundles of ideas, methods, requirements, and limitations that may be quite complicated. Both sellers and buyers of popular business techniques characterize them as 'rational' and 'progressive.' That is, the techniques supposedly help business firms and other organizations efficiently transform inputs into highly desirable outputs, and the techniques supposedly improve on previous techniques. The emphasis on progressive improvement guarantees that techniques will be constantly changing and that the sellers of techniques will claim that newer techniques are better.

Meyer and Rowan (1977) pointed out that criteria for judging rationality or improvement may have weak substantive support; there may be little or no clear evidence about efficiency, effectiveness, or benefits. However, the criteria have support from social norms. On the supply side, new techniques may allow consulting firms and gurus who market them to claim specialized expertise. On the demand side, stakeholders may withdraw support from organizations that do not use fashionable business techniques, and stakeholders may confer benefits on organizations that do adopt the latest techniques. Stakeholders may pursue fleeting opportunities or espouse new myths about organizational effectiveness (Abrahamson, 1996). Of course, societies differ in the degrees to which they value progressive change (Rogers, 1962). Competitive markets emphasize progressive change because competitors have to out-do each other (Campbell, 1985; Van Valen, 1973).

Several studies have found that claims about the effectiveness of new business techniques have very often been deceptive in that the buyers made little or no pragmatic use of the techniques (Staw and Epstein, 2000; Wang, 2010). For instance, Zbaracki (1998) found that the Total Quality Management (TQM) label was associated with very limited pragmatic use of TQM's prescriptions, and the superficial pragmatic use of prescriptions that did occur generally yielded poor results. However, users hid the poor results behind various organizational facades (Nystrom and Starbuck, 2006), and then told stories of TQM's successful implementation. Westphal, Gulati, and Shortell (1997) inferred that, among 2700 hospitals using TQM, early users showed a few performance increases, whereas later users tended to communicate TQM's use only for the rhetorical benefits they obtained. Chevalier's (1991) study of use of the Quality Circle (QC) label revealed two types of scenarios. In one scenario, each organization made very limited pragmatic use of QC's prescriptions but hid the lack of pragmatic use from stakeholders. In the second scenario, managers adopted behavioral approaches that fit their organizations' idiosyncrasies but that had little to do with QC's prescriptions. Delacroix and Swaminathan (1991) concluded that nearly all organizational changes in the Californian wine industry are cosmetic, pointless, or speculative.

For there to be significant changes in business techniques, there must be large numbers of buyers of these techniques, which in turn means that there must be even larger numbers of potential buyers (Abrahamson and Fairchild, 1999). One way for a pool of potential buyers to develop is for a new technique to produce noticeably better solutions to pervasive problems. Although the sellers of new techniques typically claim that their techniques do this, the evidence cited above suggests that the claims rarely have justification. Because people have been redesigning and adapting organizations for a very long time, the chances are remote of coming up with a genuinely original idea.

A second way for a pool of potential buyers to develop is for buyers of an existing technique to gradually lose confidence in it. In part because they face mutually inconsistent demands from different stakeholders, managers are endlessly trying to 'solve' some intrinsic organizational problems that have no solutions (Starbuck, 1994). As a result, techniques that supposedly solve these unsolvable problems inevitably disappoint those who have bought them. As the disappointed buyers accumulate, they become potential buyers of new solutions for the corresponding unsolvable problems. Abrahamson and Fairchild (1999) found that people talk about fads and fashions in more positive and emotional language while adopters are increasing, whereas the talk becomes more negative and logical while adopters are decreasing (Jönsson and Lundin, 1977).

A third way for a pool of potential buyers to develop is for social or technological evolution to create new organizational problems. The later part of the twentieth century brought many, many new organizational problems. Because agriculture and manufacturing industries competed with their counterparts in economies with lower wage levels, developed economies did less and less farming and manufacturing and shifted toward service industries that take advantage of education. In developed economies, and especially in the US, workers' educational levels rose dramatically. Because educated workers want autonomy and resent direct supervision, employers placed more emphasis on teamwork; team members supervise each other. Of course, the demand for organizations to 'learn' is partly one of those unsolvable organizational problems: to know what is worth learning requires coping with great complexity and predicting the future rather accurately. Therefore, Senge could not propose a lasting solution. He could, however, propose a solution that utilized computers and that would appeal to more highly educated workers who know how to collaborate in teams.

The marketing of business technique

Because social norms exert very strong influence in the market for fads and fashions, language and appearances are key properties in promoting success. Some fads and fashions also gain impetus from characteristics of their purveyors, including academics, consulting firms, and gurus.

A technique's name matters. 'The learning organization' sounds more proactive and progressive than 'the adaptive organization' or 'the reactive organization.' 'Six sigma' sounds quantitative and scientific, and quality-improvement personnel who bear the labels 'black belt' or 'green belt' certainly sound like they are capable of significant accomplishments. Buyers of business techniques use labels to communicate to their stakeholders that their organizations are using progressive, rational business techniques.

Jackson (1995: 38) commented, 'fads tend to recommend solutions which they believe hold in all circumstances.' Prescriptions that allow for many interpretations can be very successful. Organizations can clarify, particularize, and use such advice pragmatically in very different ways to fit various idiosyncrasies, from geographic locations (Giroux, 2006; Kieser, 1997) to distinctive swaths of time in different organizational sectors (Morris and Lancaster, 2006) or nations (Czarniawska-Joerges and Sevón, 2005). However, potential adopters also want or need easy-to-use tools that facilitate initial steps toward implementation. Many purveyors of business techniques supply tools for information gathering or self-training—questionnaires, forms, frameworks for discussing concepts—and many purveyors offer training.

The purveyors of business techniques come in at least three varieties. Academics come up with quite a few proposals about business techniques, but nearly all of these proposals lack easy means of implementation so they attract few adoptions. One exception to this pattern was a proposal by Richard Hackman, Ed Lawler, and Greg Oldham to 'enrich' jobs. Academic and mass-market publications by these academics included reports of field research that gave credibility to their ideas and questionnaires for assessing the characteristics of jobs (Hackman and Lawler, 1971; Hackman and Oldham, 1980). As a result, thousands of HR departments around the world used the questionnaires and attempted to redesign jobs.

Other purveyors are consultants. Consultants are continually searching for services that will entice clients to hire them (Kieser, 2001). Consultants perform activities such as information gathering and training that convert ideas into actions that appear practical. For example, in 1970, the Boston Consulting Group (BCG) began to advocate that a company should have a balanced portfolio of business activities that include (a) 'stars' with high market shares and high growth, (b) 'cash cows' that generate profits, and (c) 'question marks' that have potential to become stars. BCG's staff offered to put on strategic planning sessions to help client firms diagnose their existing strategic portfolios and to develop scenarios for future development. However, BCG gained limited advantage from its schema because it was so appealing, easily understood, and superficially logical that many other consultants imitated it and it appeared in all of the strategic management textbooks.

Many new business techniques, although not all, have support and stimulus from gurus (Abrahamson and Fairchild, 1999; Gill and Whittle, 1993). To be perceived as a guru, someone has to be a compelling spokesperson. Some gurus also serve as living symbols of the ideas they promote. However, all gurus have human defects and these defects sometimes undermine enthusiasm for their techniques. Peter Senge has been formally anointed a world-class guru by the *Financial Times* and *Business Week*, and he exhibits some characteristics that reinforce TLO and some that do not. His photo on the cover of *The Fifth Discipline* portrays him as boyish and idealistic, and, in person, he comes across as sincere and optimistic. However, his workbooks did not provide easily used implementation tools, and his efforts to create delivery systems for TLO have been less than successful. The Center for Organizational Learning at MIT, which Senge created in 1991, did not deliver solutions; rather it encouraged two score companies to attempt various experiments.

Next, in 1997, Senge founded the Society for Organizational Learning, but the members of this society seem to have drifted away from Senge's own ideas.

In general, research indicates that adoption of new business techniques involves strong reliance on rhetoric, weak results hidden behind facades, and strong claims of success (Hirsch, 1986; Strang and Macy, 2001; Strang and Meyer, 1994). Some business techniques involve easy-to-use implementation tools, other techniques offer very general prescriptions that adopters can interpret in many ways. Senge's affiliation with a prestigious academic institution, the complexity of his prescriptions, the jargon and scientific appearance of systems analysis, his emphasis on honesty, forthrightness, and collaboration, all give the TLO label a cachet. Yet, the idealism is so strong that very few people, if any, would try to implement TLO as Senge prescribes it. Indeed, Senge himself stated that he was talking about a kind of organization that could possibly exist someday in the future. Senge's audiences have expressed uncertainty about what TLO entails. Worrell (1995: 353) characterized the 'complete learning organization' of Senge's design as 'more of an ideal than a reality' and noted that firms had been adopting only one or two elements of TLO, not the entire package. Ortenblad (2007) collected some very diverse definitions of TLO, which led him to liken dissemination of the concept to children's 'whisper-down-the-lane' game. He remarked that people cite different passages from *The Fifth Discipline*, which, he said, leaves room for dynamic thinking and inspiration. Smith (2008) also commented that lack of clarity of the concept allows managers, researchers, students, and even editors to make TLO into what they wish.

FLUID KNOWLEDGE

All knowledge is imperfect and incomplete. Societies, human capabilities, social relations, resources, and technologies, all change. Even very ancient ideas have to be restated using modern language and metaphors to make them meaningful to the current age. Thus, how knowledge evolves is more important than what knowledge exists already.

Fads and fashions are media for knowledge development. They are a societal form of brainstorming where people try on new ideas, often quickly discarding those that do not work well; yet retaining others. Fads and fashions are processes by which knowledge accumulates and spreads. They draw upon aspirations, enthusiasm, fear, greed, mass media, social influence, and social pressure to inform people about new ideas and to induce them to investigate the value of these new ideas. Fads and fashions also make people aware that knowledge deteriorates, and they facilitate the discarding of obsolete ideas. People who discover the deficiencies of old ideas do so gradually and surrounded by other people who are making similar discoveries. The prevalence of so many fads and fashions provides constant reminders that knowledge is transitory, and there are usually several alternative ideas being offered as replacements for obsolete older ones (Abrahamson and Fairchild, 2009; Scarbrough and Swan, 2001).

At a microscopic level, the very process of change both produces knowledge and makes it obsolete. As people attempt change, they take fresh looks at what they have been doing, they develop new perceptions and make discoveries, and some of these have lasting value. The discoveries include deficiencies in older knowledge, and the process of discovery can be exhilarating. As a result, adoption of a new business technology can improve performance even if the new technology *per se* is not a meaningful improvement or if the 'technology' is a very ambiguous assortment of ideas with little practical content (Ogbonna and Harris, 2002). People who are struggling with very difficult, possibly unsolvable, problems need visions of possible improvement to keep them going.

Fads and fashions not only help to update knowledge; they help to formulate future knowledge by fostering mutation (Heusinkveld and Benders, 2001). Benders and Van Veen (2001: 37) argued that 'a certain degree of conceptual ambiguity' gives a business technique 'interpretive viability' that frees adopters to redefine what the technique means and entails. Senge's TLO possesses such conceptual ambiguity (Ortenblad, 2007). Jackson (2000: 207) inferred that *The Fifth Discipline* uses stories, parables, and well-established theoretical arguments to dramatize a 'socially rooted vision' that encourages readers to see themselves as 'actively engaged in building a learning organization.' TLO captures the fluidity of knowledge. Even if a fad, it is capable of dispersing and seeping into the very fabric of a firm. By choosing among the book's numerous stories and aphorisms, readers can adapt TLO to a multitude of complex contexts.

References

Abrahamson, E. (1996) Management fashion. *Academy of Management Review*, 21(1): 254–285.

Abrahamson, E. and Eisenman, M. (2008) Employee management techniques: Transient fads of trending fashions. *Administrative Science Quarterly*, 53(4): 719–744.

Abrahamson, E. and Fairchild, G. (1999) Management fashion: Lifecycles, triggers and collective learning processes. *Administrative Science Quarterly*, 44: 708–740.

Abrahamson, E. and Rosenkopf, L. (1993) Instititial and competitive bandwagons: Using mathematic modeling as a tool to explore innovation diffusion. *Academy of Management Review*, 18(3): 487–517.

Abrahamson, E. and Rosenkopf, L. (1997) Social network effects on the extent of innovation diffusion: A computer simulation. *Organization Science*, 8(3): 289–309.

Argote, L. (1999) *Organizational Learning: Creating, Retaining and Transferring Knowledge*. Boston: Kluwer.

Argyris, C. (1982) *Reasoning, Learning and Action: Individual and Organizational*. San Francisco: Jossey-Bass.

Argyris, C. and Schön, D.A. (1978) *Organizational Learning: A Theory of Action Perspective*. Reading, MA: Addison Wesley.

Ashby, W.R. (1958) Requisite variety and its implications for the control of complex systems. *Cybernetica*, 1(2): 83–99.

Barney, J. (1991) Firm resources and sustained competitive advantage. *Journal of Management*, 17 (1): 99–120.

Baumard, P. and Starbuck, W.H. (2005) Learning from failures: Why it may not happen. *Long Range Planning*, 18(3): 281–298.

Benders, J. and Van Veen, K. (2001) What's in a fashion? Interpretive viability and management fashions. *Organization*, 8(1): 33–53.

Bohm, D. (1965) *The Special Theory of Relativity*. New York: W.A. Benjamin.

Box, G.E.P. and Draper, N.R. (1969) *Evolutionary Operation*. New York: John Wiley & Sons.

Brandes, S. (1976) *American Welfare Capitalism, 1880–1940*. Chicago: University of Chicago Press.

Bumiller, E. (2010) We have met the enemy and he is PowerPoint. *The New York Times*, April 26: 1.

Campbell, J.H. (1985) An organizational interpretation of evolution. In D. J. Depew and B. H. Weber (eds.), *Evolution at a Crossroads: The New Biology and the New Philosophy of Science*. Cambridge, MA: MIT Press, 133–168.

Carroll, G.R. (1983) A stochastic model of organizational mortality: Review and reanalysis. *Social Science Research*, 12(4): 303–329.

Carson, P., Lanier, P. A., Carson, K. D., and Guidry, B. N. (2000) Clearing a path through the management fashion jungle: Some preliminary trailblazing. *Academy of Management Journal*, 43(6), 1143–1158.

Chevalier, F. (1991) From quality circles to total quality. *International Journal of Quality and Reliability Management*, 8(4): 9–24.

Cyert, R.M. and March, J.G. (1963) *Behavioral Theory of the Firm*. Englewood, NJ: Prentice Hall.

Czarniawska-Joerges, B. and Sevón, G. (2005) *Global Ideas: How Ideas, Objects and Practices Travel in a Global Economy*. Malmö, Sweden: Liber and Copenhagen Business School Press.

de Geus, A.P. (1988) Planning as learning. *Harvard Business Review*, 66(2): 70–74.

Delacroix, J. and Swaminathan, A. (1991) Cosmetic, speculative, and adaptive organizational change in the wine industry: A longitudinal study. *Administrative Science Quarterly*, 36: 631–661.

Faust, D. (1984) *The Limits of Scientific Reasoning*. Minneapolis: University of Minnesota Press.

Forrester, J. (1961) *Industrial Dynamics*. Cambridge, MA: MIT Press.

Forrester, J. (1969) *Urban Dynamics*. Cambridge, MA: MIT Press.

Forrester, J. (1971) The counterintuitive behavior of social systems. *Technology Review*, 73(3): 52–68.

Fritz, R. (1989) *The Path of Least Resistance*. New York: Fawcett-Columbine.

Garratt, B. (1987) *The Learning Organization*. London: Fontana Paperbacks.

Gill, J. and Whittle, S. (1993) Management by panacea: Accounting for transience. *Journal of Management Studies*, 30: 281–295.

Giroux, H. (2006) 'It was such a handy term': Management fashions and pragmatic ambiguity. *Journal of Management Studies*, 43(6): 1227–1260.

Goldberg, L.R. (1970) Man versus model of man: A rationale, plus some evidence, for a method of improving on clinical inference. *Psychological Bulletin*, 73: 422–432.

Hackman, J.R. and Lawler, E.E. (1971) Employee reactions to job characteristics. *Journal of Applied Psychology Monograph*, 55: 259–286.

Hackman, J.R. and Oldham, G.R. (1980) *Work Redesign*. Reading, MA: Addison-Wesley.

Hardin, G. (1968) The tragedy of the commons. *Science*, 162: 1243–1246.

Hedberg, B.L.T., Nystrom, P.C. and Starbuck, W.H. (1976) Camping on seesaws: Prescriptions for a self-designing organization. *Administrative Science Quarterly*, 21(1): 41–65.

Heisenberg, W. (1971) *Physics and Beyond: Encounters and Conversations*. New York: Harper and Row.

Heusinkveld, S. and Benders, J. (2001) Surges and sediments: Shaping the reception of engineering. *Information and Management*, 38(4): 239–251.

Hirsch, E.L. (1986) The creation of political solidarity in social movement organzations. *Sociological Quarterly*, 27(3): 373–387.

Hodgetts, R.M., Luthans, F., and Lee, S.M. (1998) New paradigm organizations: From total quality to learning to world-class. *Organizational Dynamics*, 22(3): 5–19.

Inamori, K. (1985) The perfect company: Goal for productivity. Speech given at Case Western Reserve University, June 5.

Jackson, B.G. (2000) A fantasy theme analysis of Peter Senge's learning organization. *The Journal of Applied Behavioral Science*, 36(2): 193–209.

Jackson, M.C. (1995) Beyond the fads: Systems thinking for managers. *Systems Research*, 12(1): 25–42.

Jönsson, S.A. and Lundin, R.A. (1977) Myths and wishful thinking as management tools. In P.C. Nystrom and W.H. Starbuck (eds.), *Prescriptive Models of Organizations*. Amsterdam: North-Holland: 157–170.

Kaufman, Jr., D. (1980) *Systems 1: An Introduction to Systems Thinking*. Minneapolis: Future Systems Inc.

Kieser, A. (2001) Applying theories of fashion to management consulting: How consultants turn concepts into fashions and sell them to managers. *Academy of Management Proceedings*. Cambridge, MA: MIT Press.

Korten, D.C. (1980) Community organization and rural development: A learning process approach. *Public Administration Review*, 40(5): 480–511.

Levinthal, D. (1991) Random walks and organizational mortality. *Administrative Science Quarterly*, 36: 397–420.

Malone, M.S. (1997) A way too short history of fads. *Forbes*, 159(7): April 7.

March, J.G. (2010) *The Ambiguities of Experience*. Ithaca, NY: Cornell University press.

Meehl, P.E. (1954) *Clinical versus Statistical Prediction: A Theoretical Analysis and a Review of the Evidence*. Minneapolis, MN: University of Minnesota Press.

Meyer, J.W. and Rowan, B. (1977) Institutionalized organizations: Formal structure as myth and ceremony. *American Journal of Sociology*, 83: 340–363.

Mitroff, I. (1988) *Break-away Thinking*. New York: John Wiley & Sons.

Morris, T. and Lancaster, Z. (2006) Translating management ideas. *Organization Studies*, 27(2): 207–233.

Nystrom, P.C. and Starbuck, W.H. (2006) Organizational facades. In W.H. Starbuck (Ed.), *Organizational Realities*. Oxford: Oxford University Press: 201–208.

O'Brien, B. (1991) *Advanced Maturity*. Available from Hanover Insurance, 100 North Parkway, Worcester, MA 01605.

Ogbonna, E. and Harris, L.C. (2002) The performance implications of management fads and fashions: An empirical study. *Journal of Strategic Marketing*, 10(1): 47–68.

Ortenblad, A. (2007) Senge's many faces: problem or opportunity? *The Learning Organization*, 14(2): 108–122.

Pedler M., Burgoyne J. and Boydell J. (1988) *Learning Company Project: A Report on Work Undertaken October 1987 to April 1988*. Sheffield: The Training Agency.

Rebelo, T.M. and Gomes, A.D. (2008) Organizational learning and the learning organization: Reviewing evolution for prospecting the future. *The Learning Organization*, 15(4): 294–308.

Revans, R.W. (1982) The enterprise as a learning system. In *The Origins and Growth of Action Learning*. London: Chartwell-Bratt.

Roberts, N. (1978) Teaching dynamic feedback systems thinking: An elementary view. *Management Science*, 24(8): 836–843.

Roberts, N. (1983) Teaching the world with simulations. *Classroom Computer News*, Jan/Feb: 28.

Rogers, E.M. (1962) *Diffusion of Innovation*. New York: Free Press of Glencoe.

Salgado, S.R., Starbuck, W.H., and Mezias, J.M. (2002) The accuracy of managers' perceptions: A dimension missing from theories about firms. In M. Augier and J. G. March (eds.), *The Economics of Choice, Change, and Organizations: Essays in Memory of Richard M. Cyert*. Cheltenham: Edward Elgar: 168–185.

Scarbrough, H. and Swan, J. (2001) Explaining the diffusion of knowledge management: The role of fashion. *British Journal of Management*, 12(1): 3–12.

Schön, D. (1983) *The Reflective Practitioner: How Professionals Think in Action*. New York: Basic Books.

Senge, P.M. (1990 and 2006) *The Fifth Discipline: The Art and Practice of the Learning Organization*. New York: Doubleday.

Senge, P. and Crainer, S. (2008) Senge and sensibility. *Business Strategy Review*, 19(4): 71–75.

Senge, P., Kleiner, A., Roberts, C., Ross, R., and Smith, B. (1994) *The Fifth Discipline Fieldbook: Strategies and Tools for Building a Learning Organization*. New York: Doubleday.

Senge, P., Kleiner, A., Roberts, C., Ross, R., Roth, G., and Smith, B. (1999) *The Dance of Change: The Challenges to Sustaining Momentum in Learning Organizations*. New York: Doubleday.

Senge, P., Cambron-McCabe, M., Lucas, T., Smith, B., Dutton, J., and Kleiner, A. (2000) *Schools that Learn: A Fifth Discipline Fieldbook for Educators, Parents and Everyone who Cares about Education*. New York: Doubleday.

Simon, H.A. and Bonini, C.P. (1958) The size distribution of business firms. *American Economic Review*, 48 (4): 607–617.

Smith, M.K. (2001) Peter Senge and the learning organization. *The Encyclopedia of Informal Education*. [www.infed.org/thinkers/senge.htm. Last update: September 3, 2009].

Smith, P.A.C. (2008) *The Learning Organization* turns 15: A retrospective. *The Learning Organization*, 15(6): 441–448.

Starbuck, W.H. (1992) Learning by knowledge-intensive firms. *Journal of Management Studies*, 29(6): 713–740.

Starbuck, W.H. (1994) On behalf of naïveté. In J.A.C. Baum and J.V. Singh (eds.), *Evolutionary Dynamics of Organizations*. London: Oxford University Press: 205–220.

Starbuck, W.H. (2006) *The Production of Knowledge: The Challenge of Social Science Research*. New York: Oxford University Press.

Starbuck, W.H. and Pant, P.N. (1996) Trying to help SandLs: How organizations with good intentions jointly enacted disaster. In Z. Shapira, *Organizational Decision Making*. Cambridge: Cambridge University Press.

Staw, B.M. and Epstein, L.D. (2000) What bandwagons bring: Effects of popular management techniques on corporate performance, reputation and CEO pay. *Administrative Science Quarterly*, 45(3): 523–556.

Sterman, J. (1987) Misperceptions of feedback in dynamic decision making. *MIT Sloan School of Management Working Paper* WP: 1933–87.

Strang, D. and Macy, M.W. (2001) In search of excellence: Fads, success stories and adaptive emulation. *American Journal of Sociology*, 107(1): 147–182.

Strang, D. and Meyer, J.W. (1994) Institutional conditions for diffusion. In W. R. Scott and J. W. Meyer (eds.), *Institutional Environments and Organizations: Structural Complexity and Individualism.* Newbury Park, CA: Sage: 100–112.

Sturdy, A. (1997) The consultancy process: An insecure business. *Journal of Management Studies,* 34 (3): 389–413.

Thomas, K. and Allen, S. (2006) The learning organization: A meta-analysis of themes in literature. *The Learning Organization,* 13(2): 123–139.

Tuchman, B. (1984) *The March of Folly: From Troy to Vietnam.* New York: Knopf.

Van Valen, L. (1973) A new evolutionary law. *Evolutionary Theory,* 1: 1–30.

Wang, P. (2010) Chasing the hottest IT: Effects of technology fashion on organizations. *Management Information Systems Quarterly,* 34(1): 63–85.

Westphal, J.D., Gulati, R., and Shortell, S.M. (1997) Customization and conformity: An institutional and network perspective on the content and consequences of TQM adoption. *Administrative Science Quarterly,* 42: 366–394.

Worrell, D. (1995) The learning organization: Management theory for the information age or a new age fad? *The Journal of Academic Librarianship,* 21(5): 351–357.

Yankelovich, D. (1981) *New Rules: Searching for Self-fulfillment in a World Turned Upside Down.* New York: Random House.

Zbaracki, M.J. (1998) The rhetoric and reality of total quality management. *Administrative Science Quarterly,* 43(3): 602–636.

12

The Contribution of Teams to Organizational Learning

KATHRYN S. ROLOFF, ANITA W. WOOLLEY,
AND AMY C. EDMONDSON

ABSTRACT

Organizational learning theorists have proposed that teams play a critical role in organizational learning (Senge, 1990; Edmondson, 2002). Indeed, as organizations become increasingly more global, teams are formed to leverage knowledge, to increase efficiency, and to streamline work processes. However, little empirical research clarifies the link between team and organizational learning. In this chapter, we explore three streams of literature on team learning as a way to understand how organizations learn. In particular, we suggest that in order to fully understand organizational learning, research on team learning should be expanded from understanding how learning occurs *within* teams to understanding how learning occurs *across* teams. One way learning occurs across teams is when individuals are simultaneously members of more than one team. Through multiple team membership, team learning can cross-fertilize across teams, building organizational learning. Therefore, we propose that studying multiple team membership can serve as a promising avenue for drawing connections between team and organizational learning.

INTRODUCTION

Many have argued that the main function of organizational design is to manage and direct the time, attention, and flow of information among individuals and organizational units (Cyert and March, 1963; March and Simon, 1958; Ocasio, 1997). This function has become increasingly challenging over time, as the dynamics of globalization have exerted simultaneous pressures on organizations to be more efficient and competitive, while at the same time increasing the need for learning so that organizations and the individuals within them can keep up with new technologies and demands. Though conceptually the time and energy put toward learning and skill development should foster improved performance, some analyses suggest that learning and productivity can work at odds with one another (Bunderson and Sutcliffe, 2003; Edmondson and Singer, 2008; Ren, Carley, and Argote 2006). To accommodate the demands for higher productivity and faster learning, organizations have increasingly turned to using smaller and more flexible work units, such as teams, to accomplish their most important tasks. Over time the use of teams has shifted from team-based work in hierarchical structures, to team-based work in matrix structures, and ultimately to team-based work in multi-team systems (Hatch and Cunliffe, 2006; Hobday, 2000; Malone, 2004; Marks, Dechurch, Mathieu, Panzer, and Alonso, 2005; Scott and Davis, 2006) in part to enable the knowledge and skills of individuals and smaller units to be leveraged across more projects in more parts of the organization.

One increasingly common design choice is to assign individuals to multiple teams simultaneously. Some surveys (for example, Lu, Wynn, Chudoba, and Watson-Manheim, 2003; Martin and Bal, 2006; O'Leary , Mortensen, and Woolley, 2011) estimate that simultaneous membership on more than one team appears to be the norm for at least sixty-five percent of knowledge workers across a wide range of industries and occupations in the US and Europe (Zika-Viktorsson, Sundstrom, and Engwall, 2006). Some surveys place the percentage of knowledge workers who are members of more than one team as high as 94.9 percent (Martin and Bal, 2006) and in at least one company (Intel) twenty-eight percent are on five or more (Lu et al., 2003). Multiple team membership seems especially common in many industries and settings in which learning and productivity are both especially critical, including information technology (Baschab and Piot, 2007), software development (Shore and Warden, 2007), new product development (Edmondson and Nembhard, 2009; Wheelwright and Clark, 1992), some consulting firms (Milgrom and Roberts, 1992), and education (Jones, 1990), but appears to be widespread in a variety of other contexts such as auto repair (Madono, 1998) and healthcare (Richter, Scully, and West, 2005).

As more teams share members, there is increased resource interdependence among different units of the organization. Researchers have begun to refer to this as a 'multi-coupled project organization' (Söderlund, 2002: 428) or as an instance of intra-organizational connectivity (Lazer and Friedman, 2007), or simply as multiple team membership (MTM) (Mortensen, Woolley, and O'Leary, 2007). Intra-organizational connectivity has positive effects on organizational learning. As noted by Kang, Morris, and Snell (2007), to understand organizational learning, it is important to consider the pattern of relationships among parties within a firm (Burt, 1992; Coleman, 1988; Uzzi, 1997). As intra-organizational connectivity increases, organizations have more paths along which information can flow, which increases the likelihood that any two potentially complementary pieces of information will be brought together and simultaneously decreases the likelihood that any potentially valuable piece of information is stuck in one part of the organization and 'lost.' The more often employees interact, the more opportunities they have to identify and utilize idiosyncratic knowledge (Hansen, 1999; Krackhardt, 1992; Nelson, 1989; Uzzi, 1997).

High interactivity across teams, such as that arising from shared membership, results in more integrated knowledge across those teams (Newell, Goussevskaia, Swan, Bresnen, and Obembe, 2007). Intra-organizational connectivity creates built-in boundary spanning capabilities across teams and improves information sharing in the organization (Ancona and Caldwell, 1992; Hansen, 1999; Lazer and Friedman, 2007). High levels of multiple team membership create embedded Simmelian ties, which are much stronger predictors of innovation than weak ties (Tortoriello and Krackhardt, 2010). People will carry lessons learned across units, managers at higher levels will have more sources of information about various projects and their staff (Meyer, 1994), and more opportunities will exist for the propagation of ideas across the organization (Subramaniam and Youndt, 2005). Noboeka, Cusumano, and others (Cusumano and Selby, 1995; Nobeoka, 1995) have shown how intra-organizational connectivity enhances organizational learning via enhanced cross-project learning. Such organizational learning by working across projects may break up 'collaborative dead-ends' more than simple interaction across team boundaries would (Dornisch, 2002) and improve organizational learning (Carlile, 2004; Hansen, 1999; Lazer and Friedman, 2007; Marrone, Tesluk, and Carson, 2007).

As teams within an organization become increasingly interconnected via shared members, organizations are more able to shift individuals fluidly and quickly from team to team to react to changing environmental conditions. In particular, this allows organizations to leverage their dispersed resources in multiple teams without incurring the costs typically brought about by restructuring or reassignment, allowing organizations to accomplish more with a given set of resources. This argument is consistent with Lojeski et al. (2007) who found that higher organization-wide multi-tasking is a key contributor to organizational productivity in the last decade.

Despite its advantages, it is possible that organizations can become too interconnected. Organizational slack refers to the supply of uncommitted resources in the organization (Bourgeois, 1981; Cyert and March, 1963). Slack resources allow organizations to respond to environmental events by allowing time to experiment and reflect on their responses (Meyer, 1982). Even in the absence of exogenous shocks, organizational slack can enable management to experiment with new postures in relation to the environment through innovations in new product development (Nohria and Gulati, 1996; Tushman and O'Reilly III, 1996) or in management style (Bourgeois, 1981). Such reflection and experimentation is critical for organizational learning. Thus, a reduction in organizational slack, which can occur by committing members to too many teams simultaneously, limits organizational learning.

In this chapter, we take a closer look at how team learning, both *within* and *across* organizational teams, serves as a fundamental building block of organizational learning. We start with a review of the literature on team learning, which has emphasized studies of learning within teams. We then draw connections between this research and a new research agenda to examine team learning across teams, with a particular focus on multiple team membership. Finally, we discuss the practical implications of how the tension between productivity and learning shapes organizational learning strategies in modern, global companies.

A REVIEW OF THE TEAM LEARNING LITERATURE

Research on team learning spans a vast range of organizational settings, research methods, and dependent variables. Although this diversity in scope is reflective of the rich array of learning performed by real teams in organizations, it can also lead to confusing inconsistency in terminology and difficulty in accumulating findings. Indeed, the field of organizational learning is similarly diverse, with a long history of well-studied, but varied theoretical perspectives (for example, Argyris and Schön, 1978; Huber, 1991; Leavitt and March, 1988). Given the strength of each divergent theoretical contribution, we argue that a highly specified definition of team learning would sacrifice breadth for depth. Therefore, similar to definitions of organizational learning, we broadly define team learning as the processes and outcomes that involve positive change as the result of investments in developing shared knowledge or skill (for a discussion of different definitions of team learning, see Edmondson, Dillon, and Roloff, 2007).

To date, the research on team learning falls into three general streams of work: learning curves in operational settings (outcome improvement), psychological experiments on team member coordination (task mastery), and field research on learning processes in teams (group process) (Edmondson, Dillon, and Roloff, 2007). Each of these research traditions provides a different contribution to the understanding of organizational learning. The outcome improvement stream is primarily concerned with issues related to learning measurement. The task mastery stream research is focused on knowledge management. The group process stream examines how to learn. In addition, each of these streams takes a different methodological approach, ranging from small psychological lab groups to large-scale organizational improvement efforts. See Table 12.1 for a summary of the three streams of team learning. By drawing on these three streams of research, we first review team learning from multiple perspectives, then consider how each perspective advances our understanding of organizational learning.

These three streams also vary with respect to how team learning is operationalized and to disciplinary foundations. Whereas the outcome improvement and the task mastery streams conceptualize team learning as improved task performance, usually related to clearly defined tasks with measurable success, the group process stream is more concerned with team learning as adaptive behaviors with the potential to promote success when tasks, success, and context are less certain. In addition, the task mastery and group process streams draw upon the theoretical foundations of the social psychology of group dynamics as both focus on interpersonal coordination in teams. On the other hand, the learning curve studies largely hail from a more objective conceptualization of efficiency improvement without a focus on the interpersonal behavior related to improvements.

Despite the differences across streams, team learning research has matured from an exploratory, qualitative orientation in the early theory-building phase to a more explanatory, quantitative orientation aimed at fine-tuning or moderating established models of team learning (Edmondson and McManus, 2007). As such, team learning research has begun to investigate the mediators that connect antecedents of team learning to outcomes and moderators that specify the contexts and conditions of team learning. Some moderators tested to date within team learning research include task type (Van der Vegt and Bunderson, 2005) and industry context (Zellmer-Bruhn and Gibson, 2006). In addition, researchers have shown that learning is different for different types of teams, such as the difference between routine production teams versus innovation teams (Wong, 2004).

These three streams of team learning research, with their similarities and important differences, yield a number of insights for future research on how team learning serves as the foundation of organizational learning (Senge, 1990). The learning curve stream shows that practice and experience are important sources of learning for improving

Table 12.1   The three streams of team learning

Concepts	Outcome Improvement	Task Mastery	Group Process
Motivating concern	At what rate do groups improve their efficiency?	How do team members coordinate knowledge and skill to accomplish tasks?	What drives learning-oriented behaviors and processes in organizational work groups?
Concept of team learning	Learning is performance improvement—usually efficiency improvement.	Learning is task mastery.	Learning is a process of sharing information and reflecting on experience
Dominant independent variables	Codified knowledge, collocation or shared ownership, team stability, knowledge sharing.	Group members trained together or separately; transactive memory system, communication.	Team leader behavior, psychological safety, team identification, team composition, organizational context.
Dominant dependent variable	Rate of cost or time reduction.	Performance on a novel task.	Team effectiveness or learning behavior.
Findings	Amount of experience working together improves team performance outcomes. In later work, how people work together and dimension of improvement affect rate of learning.	Having coordinated ways of codifying, storing and retrieving individual knowledge is necessary to access individual knowledge for coordinated task performance.	Team leadership and shared beliefs about team psychological safety, goals, or identity promote or inhibit team learning behaviors and, in turn, team performance.
Methods	Field research: Collection of quantitative data from teams producing a product or a service.	Lab experiments: Small teams of students as subjects; Random assignment to conditions to establish causality.	Largely field research: Qualitative and quantitative data that provide observations of real organizational work teams.

253

efficiency and productivity. Research on task mastery reveals that team learning involves knowledge coordination to effectively leverage team resources and skills in task execution. The group process work demonstrates that *how* teams learn is just as important as *what* teams learn, especially in the face of uncertainty.

Next, we review the related literature in each stream, and in the following section we build on this review by outlining how insights from these three streams form a foundation for a new research agenda aimed toward understanding the link between team learning and organizational learning. In particular, we suggest that considering learning across teams, such as through MTM, by leveraging what is known about learning within teams can provide an important link between the team and organizational levels of learning.

Measuring performance improvement: learning curves in teams

Learning curve research at the team level comes from a long and robust history of studying performance improvements with increased experience over time. In these studies, largely initiated in manufacturing settings, researchers documented the link between cumulative experience and improvements in operational performance such as increased productivity, reduced cost, or improved output. Since the early twentieth century, learning curve research has proliferated in the fields of technology management, economics, operations management, and competitive strategy. For the better part of its history, this stream of research has focused on the learning at the organizational level of analysis. However, the appeal of using objective, measurable performance data has attracted attention from team learning scholars, albeit later in the century. Whether the studies were focused on organizations or on teams, the core theme is that learning, in the form of experience over time, results in improved efficiency and performance.

Initial studies on learning curves in teams focused on improvement that is coincident with experience, or, 'practice makes perfect.' For example, in a study of thirty-six pizza franchises, Darr, Argote, and Epple (1995) found that unit cost decreased with experience. Similarly, two studies in the medical field found that procedure time decreased and number of procedures increased with experience (Edmondson, Winslow, Bohmer, and Pisano, 2003; Reagans, Argote, and Brooks, 2005). Studies in this stream consider the learning curve to be relevant at the start of a new project (product or process). As the project continues the learning curve reaches a peak level of performance and then plateaus as new learning slows down. Learning curve studies involve regression analysis models of longitudinal, quantitative outcome data from manufacturing or service organizations. The outcome variable of interest is usually related to a measure of efficiency such as cost reduction, increased productivity, or time. Recent research has studied the learning curve using data from multiple groups that implemented the same learning goal, and has stressed the importance of teamwork (such as communication and coordination) in generating improvements (Adler, 1990; Argote, Insko, Yovetich, and Romero, 1995). In general, learning curve research focused on finding and understanding differences in improvement rates across teams with the same task.

Studies of learning curves in teams have identified a number of factors associated with differences in improvement rates. One of the most widely noted factors is team stability (Argote, Beckman, and Epple, 1990; Argote, et al., 1995; Edmondson, et al., 2003). A recent study on self-managed production teams in a manufacturing setting showed that team turnover disrupts important interpersonal processes such as team learning behaviors and task flexibility, which are related to successful self management, in reducing the percentage of defects in production (Van der Vegt, Bunderson, and Kuipers, in press). In essence, teams with unstable membership improve less quickly than teams with stable membership, especially when task improvement involves the acquisition of tacit versus codified knowledge (Edmondson et al., 2003).

One reason team stability promotes learning from experience is simply the fact that team members who are familiar with each other have better coordination and teamwork (Reagans, Argote, and Brooks, 2005). In a study on surgical teams in hospitals, Reagans, Argote, and Brooks (2005) demonstrated that *learning by doing* increased team members' ability to coordinate knowledge at the team level and to improve familiarity with the organizational processes linked to the task, especially when teams had membership stability. Similarly, a study of software teams showed that team familiarity—members' prior experience working together—was a significant determinant of learning and performance in a setting where team membership was multiple and fluid (Huckman and Staats, 2009).

Task stability is another key factor associated with learning curves in teams. A recent field study of forty self-managed production teams in a high technology firm showed that when tasks are stable—are repetitive or continuous—team structure promotes learning (Bunderson and Boumgarden, 2011). The authors argue that when tasks are stable, team members that create clear roles and processes have an increased flow of information among members and reduced instances of conflict. Stability and structure create a safe and predictable environment where experience with tasks can lead to improvements. In an earlier and smaller sample study, Edmondson et al. (2003) showed that operating room teams that kept team members together over successive operations when learning a new cardiac surgery procedure reduced procedure time more quickly than teams with less stable membership.

In general, the results of learning curve studies show that rates of improvement are affected by the way learning is managed within teams. In using field-based research methods to build on the more traditional analytic approach, researchers have built on an established research paradigm on team learning from experience. In particular, the strength of learning curve research is its objective and measurable outcome variables with obvious practical implications. In addition, teams studied in this stream are often learning the same thing simultaneously, offering a view into comparisons across teams while holding the complexity of organizational contexts in which they work constant. Furthermore, this type of learning is likely the most easily translated across different teams and organizational units (Argote and Ingram, 2000; Wong, 2004), and thus more easily propagated in an MTM environment (O'Leary, Mortensen, and Woolley, 2011). On the other hand, the application of this research is limited to teams that perform repetitive, similar tasks and seek incremental improvements in efficiency and performance. Many organizational teams face challenges associated with innovation and radical improvement in highly uncertain contexts and, therefore, this work is limited with respect to insights for these types of teams.

Coordinating Team Knowledge: Task Mastery

A second area of research is focused on understanding how team members learn to master interdependent tasks through knowledge coordination. In this stream, team learning is the outcome of the communication and coordination that results from a shared knowledge base of team member skills, the task, team resources, and the task context. Success is measured in how well a team has learned, and mastered, their tasks.

Task mastery research emphasizes the importance of leveraging team member knowledge, skills, and abilities to increase the resources available to members during task execution. This work is primarily concerned with information processing in teams in the form of encoding, storing, retrieving, and communicating information (Wilson, Goodman, and Cronin, 2007). To say this another way, findings in this stream stress that teams are best able to perform interdependent tasks when members know what each other knows both collectively and individually. According to these researchers, team learning is not explicitly defined, *per se*, but rather learning is the outcome of improved performance of novel tasks.

Through tightly controlled laboratory studies of primarily student teams, researchers consider team learning from a cognitive perspective. Similar to how individuals develop knowledge, it is suggested that groups develop team-level cognitive systems that categorize and store collective knowledge. Teams of university students are assigned tasks such as simulating flight crews and assembling electronic devices. This type of research design allows for causal inferences about factors of team learning but is limited in terms of external validity. In addition, team members are often unfamiliar with each other before the task and disbanded afterward.

There are many terms for the team-level cognitive constructs studied in this stream including terms such as 'transactive memory systems' (Wegner, 1987), 'shared mental models' (Cannon-Bowers, Salas, Converse, and Castellan, 1993), and 'social cognition' (Larson and Christensen, 1993), among others. Despite different terms, these constructs share in common a characterization of team-level databases that encode, store, retrieve, and communicate knowledge in predicting task performance (for example, Hollingshead, 2001; Wegner, 1987).

These team level databases are thought to provide teams with a mechanism to create and organize a common understanding of team member knowledge, skills, and abilities in order to leverage team member strengths in task execution. The benefit of such a system is to enhance team coordination without the need for discussion. Creating a system of shared knowledge enhances team learning by enabling access to unique individual knowledge, promoting team member specialization, reducing redundancies in knowledge or skill, and creating informal rules about accountability. In general, this type of team learning is particularly important for teams that require diversity in expertise or knowledge to perform a task, such as in the case of product development teams. Developing these types of team-level databases requires effective communication among members, an area that merits further investigation given barriers to streamlined communication in modern, global organizations.

Studies on task mastery have focused on a number of factors associated with performance of novel tasks. First, researchers originally found that training team members on tasks together, rather than individually, was associated with improved task performance (Liang, Moreland, and Argote, 1995). Further research showed that it wasn't the training, *per se*, that led to improved performance but rather its effects were mediated by the development of a transactive memory system (Moreland and Myaskovsky, 2000).

The development of transactive memory systems was associated with increased team member complexity, accuracy, and agreement in perceptions of each other's expertise (Moreland et al., 1998), and a greater degree of tacit knowledge is shared during task execution (Gruenfeld, Mannix, Williams, and Neale, 1996). Quite notably, Stasser, Stewart, and Whittenbaum (1995) suggest that the formation of an effective transactive memory system is not due to simply mentioning differences in task expertise among members, but rather that explicitly recognizing these differences leads to informal schemas of accountability whereby 'experts' on the team are responsible for storing and retrieving specialized information.

Task mastery researchers have also suggested that teams develop different types of transactive memory systems related to, for example, task work and team processes (Mathieu, Heffner, Goodwin, Salas, and Cannon-Bowers, 2000). Of course, these various knowledge systems developed by teams are only useful in so far as they are accurate. Certain factors such as team size (Rentsch and Klimoski, 2001), previous task experience (Gino, Argote, Miron-Spektor, and Todorova, 2010), or organizational tenure (Smith-Jentsch, Campbell, Milanovich, and Reynolds, 2001) can inhibit or enhance transactive memory system development.

Furthermore, team processes such as communication are critical for achieving successful transactive memory system development (Lewis, Lange, and Gillis, 2005; Liang et al., 1995; Moreland and Myaskovsky, 2000; Rulke and Rau, 2000; Stasser et al., 1995). In particular, team climates that promote open and honest communication are more effective than climates that are interpersonally threatening. This is critical for diverse teams due to the tendency for team members to stereotype others in terms of the types of knowledge and experience they may bring to bear on the task (Hollingshead and Fraidin, 2003). Candid communication is also helpful for teams to surface unique individual knowledge because team members sometimes have a tendency to discuss shared knowledge as a method of creating social cohesion (Stasser, Stewart, and Whittenbaum, 1995; Whittenbaum, Hubbell, and Zuckerman, 1999). Finally, some have suggested that building team mental models is a highly political process in that team members are particularly concerned about how expertise labels affirm their identity or enhance their self-esteem (London, Polzer, and Omorgie, 2005; Walsh, Henderson, and Deighton, 1988).

In summary, the task mastery stream of research has contributed to an understanding of team learning by characterizing the cognitive dimensions of team level knowledge. That is, 'knowing who knows what' is an important feature of coordinating and leveraging team member strengths in learning together to perform novel tasks. Unlike the learning curve conceptualization of team learning, the task mastery form of learning is substantially more likely to be disrupted by MTM, as a larger number of team commitments tend to reduce the amount of time team members spend together which is critical for this type of learning to occur. Furthermore, the studies have predominantly employed laboratory methods, limiting an understanding about how organizational contexts and practices such as MTM affect team learning. Researchers have called for field studies to be performed to test these lab-based findings in real work contexts (Mohammed, Klimoski, and Rentsch, 2000). Such studies would help to expand our understanding about where and when developing coordinated ways of storing knowledge in teams is an essential aspect of the team learning process (for an example, see Lewis, 2004).

Learning How to Learn: Group Process

The third stream of research defines team learning as a group process instead of as a team outcome. Studies in this stream generally employ field research methods on work teams in real organizations. At its foundation, the group process stream originated from the input-process-output (I-P-O) model of team effectiveness, wherein team processes form the link between group inputs such as composition, structure, context, and group outputs such as innovation, quality, and performance (Hackman, 1987; see Ilgen, Hollenbeck, Johnson, and Jundt, 2005, for a review; McGrath, 1984). Whereas the prior two streams of team learning research have focused on inputs and outputs, the group process stream aims to understand the interpersonal processes in teams that constitute team learning. Typically, therefore, these researchers observe and measure the learning process in teams, rather than using performance outcomes as the measure of team learning.

Initially, group process researchers investigated the interpersonal processes in teams that fostered team learning behaviors. Evidence had begun to emerge that when team work is characterized by low quality interpersonal factors, teams are less likely to learn since members are not fully engaged and participating in the work due to fear of ridicule, embarrassment, or other forms of retribution for their actions (Brooks, 1994; Edmondson, 1996). In a study on fifty-three teams in a manufacturing firm, Edmondson (1999) identified psychological safety—a shared belief that it is safe to take interpersonal risks on the team— and demonstrated that it was a significant predictor of learning behavior in work teams. Group process work has shown that team leaders can play an important role in promoting team learning by fostering positive interpersonal climates in teams, involving members in decision making, clarifying team goals, and managing team boundaries with outsiders (Edmondson, 2003; Nembhard and Edmondson, 2006; Sarin and McDermott, 2003). When team leaders create a climate that is safe for risky interpersonal behavior, such as admitting mistakes, teams are more likely to learn. When teams learn, team performance improves as well. In addition to providing a safe climate for speaking up, team leaders can also neutralize power differences among team members (Edmondson, 2003; Nembhard and Edmondson, 2006; Van der Vegt, de Jong, Bunderson, and Molleman, in press).

Team learning scholars have also been interested in investigating the types of behaviors that promote learning first by broadly conceptualizing learning activities such as incremental learning, radical learning, vicarious learning, contextual learning behaviors, and local versus distal learning, among others (Bresman, 2006, 2010; Edmondson, 2002; Wong, 2004). A study of twenty-three process improvement teams in hospital intensive care units found that *learn-what* (learning behaviors related to acquiring knowledge or know-how) is conceptually distinct from *learn-how* (learning behaviors related to effective task strategies) in terms of the types of learning behaviors teams engage (Tucker, Nembhard, and Edmondson, 2007). Whereas learn-what behaviors were important for stocking a team's knowledge base, only learn-how activities were related to team effectiveness. Subsequently, the nature and type of team learning behaviors have been considered in greater detail. Recently, Savelsbergh, van der Heijden, and Poell (2009) developed a team learning behavior instrument containing eight distinct dimensions of team learning (such as reflection, feedback seeking, experimenting) and twenty-eight items.

Indeed new tools to measure team learning reflect the many varied operationalizations of team learning in the group process stream. Edmondson defined team learning as 'an ongoing process of reflection and action, characterized by asking questions, seeking feedback, experimenting, reflecting on results, and discussing errors or unexpected outcomes of action' (1999: 353). Wilson, Goodman, and Cronin define team learning as 'a change in the group's repertoire of potential behavior' (2007: 1043). Related constructs such as team reflexivity have also been used to define team learning. Team reflexivity is 'the extent to which group members overtly reflect upon and communicate about the group's objectives, strategies, and processes, and adapt them to current or anticipated circumstances' (West, 2000: 296). Across definitions, team learning involves a change in the way teams operate as a function of noticing and correcting problems. Most notably, team learning is considered to be a verb in this stream. Team learning is also similar to new conceptualizations of adaptation—adjustment to change—in teams (for example, Burke, Stagl, Salas, Pierce, and Kendall, 2006; Woolley, 2009) and also to notions of team reflexivity, or reflection and communication about objectives, strategies, and processes (De Dreu, 2007; Schippers, Den Hartog, Koopman, and Wienk, 2003; Schippers, Homan, van Knippenberg, 2009).

Recent work in this stream has employed a number of dependent variables related to team learning such as effectiveness, performance, creativity (Hirst, Van Knippenberg, and Zhou, 2009), and innovation, among others. Team performance variables have received the most attention, and, whereas the learning curve and task mastery streams operationalize changes in performance as a measure of team learning, the group process stream conceptualizes team performance as an outcome of team learning. Indeed terms such as 'performance' and 'effectiveness' are ubiquitous in group process research, but operationalizations of these variables lack consistency. However, these differences are necessary for connecting behaviors to outcomes, and, as the team learning literature grows, perhaps models of team learning could become more contingent and precise relative to the types of performance and effectiveness variables of interest.

In addition, models of team learning have begun to detail the antecedents, moderators, and contextual variables associated with team learning processes. As these models are refined, researchers have outlined where, when, and for whom. For example, team learning works best when teams have an interdependent learning goal whereby members must rely on each other to complete teamwork (Bunderson and Sutcliffe, 2003; Ely and Thomas, 2001; De Dreu, 2007; Tjosvold, Yu, and Hui, 2004). In addition, certain types of team tasks require different degrees of learning behavior—routine production teams require less learning than interdisciplinary action teams (Edmondson, 2003). However, most of the task characteristics explored in this stream of research are reflective of the research setting and participants rather than an investigation of task features (for example, Edmondson, 1999, included four types of team tasks and Wong, 2004, measured task routineness).

More recently, researchers have begun to investigate the effects of team composition on team learning and performance. Researchers suggest that moderate levels of team diversity, in terms of demographic identity and functional experience, among others, is optimal for team learning whereas too much or too little diversity can undermine or overburden team learning (Gibson and Vermeulen, 2003; Lau and Murnighan, 2005; Sarin and McDermott, 2003; Van der Vegt and Bunderson, 2005). And team diversity is most beneficial when differences among members are balanced rather than divided into strong subgroups (Lau and Murnighan, 2005). Indeed team composition is a critical area for further investigation as organizations increasingly form diverse teams to leverage unique knowledge and experience held by members in organizational learning efforts.

Furthermore, there are a number of proposed moderators in models of team learning. As discussed, psychological safety—a team climate factor—is an important interpersonal moderator of team learning (Edmondson, 1999). Team identification has been proposed as another influential moderator, especially as a common identity with others on the team can serve to unite diverse individuals and orient them toward a common goal. Van der Vegt and Bunderson (2005) found, in a study of fifty-seven multidisciplinary teams in the oil and gas industry, that collective team identification moderated the relationship between expertise diversity on learning behavior and team performance. When collective identification was high, teams experienced greater learning across expertise faultlines than teams with low collective identification. When teams are diverse in terms of power and hierarchical position, performance feedback moderates the relationship between power asymmetry and team learning (Van der Vegt, de Jong, Bunderson, and Mollerman, in press). In a study of forty-six teams in an industrial setting, Van der Vegt and colleagues (in press) found that when teams receive group performance feedback, as opposed to individual performance feedback, power asymmetry is associated with higher levels of team learning, and thus greater team performance.

Finally, group process researchers have begun to outline which organizational contexts are ideal for team learning. A study of ninety teams from the pharmaceutical industry showed that when teams were interrupted during the course of their work flow, teams had an opportunity to reflect on their current activities (Zellmer-Bruhn, 2003). Further, Zellmer-Bruhn and Gibson (2006) determined that organizations that grant teams greater decision-making autonomy experienced more team learning activities than teams in organizations with strong prescribed practices. Thus, various aspects of organizational contexts can enhance (or inhibit) a team's opportunities for learning.

This stream provides a detailed look into team learning through the diverse range of field research techniques ranging from rich qualitative data to meticulous quantitative measures. In addition, researchers in this stream acknowledge that individuals are nested within teams and teams are situated within larger organizational contexts through multi-level modeling techniques (for example, Edmondson, 1999; Zellmer-Bruhn and Gibson, 2006). However, the diversity of variables and methods is also limiting in that a comprehensive picture of team learning is difficult. It is difficult to compare results and to build knowledge across disparate terms and measures.

Some of the field-based findings in the team process tradition also suggest that multi-team membership (MTM) environments can be designed in such a way to optimize team learning and, ultimately, organizational learning. As teams come to recognize the potential benefits of the diverse experiences members bring from their work in other teams, they can develop routines for capturing and using that expertise. However, the time intensive nature of this form of learning may also lead it to be swept aside for the sake of efficiency. This underscores the importance of team leader behaviors and other moderating variables (such as team climate) to create the conditions that allow the sharing of new ideas that members may bring in from other teams to become a priority.

DISCUSSION

As work becomes more decentralized and more informally coordinated, members of organizations increasingly span the boundaries of multiple work teams and organizational units. Building a knowledge base about learning in these arrangements of teams and smaller work units is thus critical, as they constitute the basis for learning throughout the organization. Here, we have highlighted three different perspectives on conceptualizing and measuring team learning. Although these three streams of research involve different theoretical orientations, research methods, and samples, it would be shortsighted to say they represent the full taxonomy of learning teams.

Learning teams are concerned with improving outcomes, coordinating knowledge, and developing effective processes to one degree or another. Further, a team's focus may shift from one goal to another as the team's work evolves, integrating mechanisms that have traditionally been the focus of different lines of research. Similarly, team-learning researchers have begun to consider more than one stream in their research. For example, some research in the learning curve stream focused on improving efficiency by building effective group processes (Bunderson and Boumgarden, 2011). Another study combines the group process and task mastery streams by investigating the association between team learning behaviors (and its antecedents) and mutually shared cognition on team effectiveness (Van den Bossche, Gijselaers, Segers, and Kirshner, 2006). Therefore, we suggest that these streams are useful as organizing frameworks for considering the progression of team learning research, and are not meant to be prescriptive divisions for team learning research in the future. Rather, they highlight some of the differences in perspectives, assumptions, and terms that inhibit coherent progress in understanding these important phenomena.

The central argument in this chapter, as discussed at the outset, is that team learning increasingly takes place across teams rather than just within teams, because many organizations have become more complex and less hierarchical. Yet, to date, much of the research on team learning cited here has focused on the learning within focal teams as opposed to collective learning among teams. Scholars have begun to explore the theoretical implications of studying learning across teams (for example, Huckman and Staats, 2009; Woolley, 2009; Nembhard and Edmondson, 2006). Edmondson and Roberto (2003) refer to this type of learning as a team-based learning infrastructure.

Indeed, each stream of research has something to contribute to our understanding of learning across teams: the learning curve stream shows how learning is associated with experience, the task mastery stream outlines cognitive mechanisms for organizing team knowledge and skill, and the group process stream explores the numerous conditions associated with how to learn in teams. In addition, studies within each stream have indirectly examined some of the factors associated with learning across teams.

A few studies in the learning curve stream examined learning and knowledge transfer across teams. In a study of thirty-six stores in a service organization franchise, Darr, Argote, and Epple (1995) found that all the stores improved with experience, but only the stores with the same owner shared ideas and transferred knowledge across stores. In addition, Edmondson and colleagues (2003), in their study of cardiac surgery teams, showed that codified knowledge transferred across teams whereas tacit knowledge was difficult to transmit across teams. These studies reveal some important features of learning across teams such as: (1) it could be important to have an individual or individuals on both the original team and the team to which learning is to be transferred, and (2) teams should attempt to surface and codify tacit knowledge in order to transfer learning.

In the task mastery stream, researchers often performed experiments on teams by training them on tasks together—then reshuffling half the teams to explore what happened when members were required to work with new teammates. In one such study, Lewis, Lange, and Gillis (2005), found that teams performed equally well on the task irrespective of whether they were trained together and kept intact, or reshuffled. This study provided early evidence that team members can transmit certain types of knowledge and experience to new teams. More recently, researchers showed that direct experience yields higher team performance than indirect experience (such as learning by watching another team perform a similar task), further complicating methods of multi-team learning (Gino, Argote, Miron-Spektor, and Todorova, 2010). Another study in this stream investigated how teams leverage knowledge introduced by visitors from other 'foreign' teams. Gruenfeld, Martorana, and Fan (2000) found that although the 'indigenous' team was likely to use ideas from the foreign team member, they were less likely to surface unique ideas from the indigenous team members. This study suggests that knowledge transfer and learning across teams is difficult due to social processes that determine how team-level memory systems are formed.

Finally, the group process stream of research outlines team learning behaviors related to leveraging learning and knowledge across teams. Building on boundary-spanning research, Ancona and Caldwell (1992) identified three conceptually distinct forms of learning behaviors: experiential team learning, vicarious team learning, and contextual team learning. Both vicarious and contextual team learning refer to behaviors that leverage extra-team knowledge from other teams within the organization and outside of the organization, respectively. Similarly, Wong (2004) delineated the differences between *local* learning (learning from internal team activities) and *distal* learning, or learning from ideas, feedback, or help from external parties. When engaged in task mastery, distal learning actually hampered the team's performance whereas when engaged in innovation, distal learning enhanced team performance. Thus, the nature of the task can influence multi-team learning.

However, studies such as the ones mentioned have not examined learning across teams as the primary focus, but rather as a side-effect of the study design. Team scholars have called for more careful consideration of learning across teams (Mathieu, Maynard, Rapp, and Gilson, 2008). In particular, individual team members serve as conduits of learning through their simultaneous membership of more than one team (O'Leary, Mortensen, and Woolley, 2011). As mentioned above, researchers estimate that knowledge workers are members of more than one team anywhere between sixty-five and ninety-five percent of the time (Martin and Bal, 2006; Zika-Viktorsson et al., 2006). Given the considerable prevalence of multiple team membership, it is critical for organizational learning scholars to understand how MTM can foster the cross-fertilization of learning across teams.

Furthermore, as knowledge and specialization become commodities for employees—above and beyond job training and skills—team members are starting to consult extra-team members with task-relevant knowledge as a form of internal consulting for team learning (Ancona and Bresman, 2007; Bresman, 2010; Edmondson et al., 2001; Nembhard and Edmondson, 2006; Zellmer-Bruhn, 2003). Individual team members are valued more and more for depth of knowledge over breadth of knowledge, increasing the level of specialization of team member knowledge. As such, transactive memory systems are expanding beyond the single team unit to include strategies to leverage knowledge from local experts across teams.

However, as research from each of the three streams shows, there are significant differences between the types of tasks that benefit from the forms of learning studied (for example, learning curve research is focused on repetitive tasks whereas task mastery research examines novel, if well-structured, tasks). As such, the challenge of learning across teams (and of studying learning across teams) is further complicated by the variety of tasks and goals linked to these tasks. In particular, team tasks often reflect different types of learning goals, such as improving team productivity or fostering innovation. The nature of teamwork is correspondingly different for these goals as well. But, what is the relationship between productivity and learning across teams? How do individuals manage different goals as members of different teams? Thus, we will consider how these two linked, but distinct, team goals shape the experience of learning across multiple teams.

Tension Between Productivity and Learning

Learning and productivity are often related (and sometimes conflated), but conceptually distinct and often in tension (Sessa and London, 2006; Singer and Edmondson, 2008; Wilson, Goodman, and Cronin, 2007). For example, Bunderson and Sutcliffe (2003) provide evidence about how team learning can both hurt and help team effectiveness, and Edmondson, Dillon, and Roloff (2007) note how learning and execution are often at odds. The same is true at the individual and organizational levels of analysis. Thus, although there is the potential for a reciprocal relationship between productivity and learning, there are also features of the work environment that can foster one at the expense of the other.

Productivity is generally defined as the quantity of output produced with a given amount of resource (time, personnel, etc.). MTM evolved in some organizations initially in an effort to distribute employees' time across multiple smaller contracts (Mortensen, Woolley, and O'Leary, 2007) thus increasing organizational productivity. As the practice of MTM intensifies, particularly for knowledge work, individuals tend to deepen their knowledge base in a particular area and become deep subject matter experts whose knowledge is leveraged across an increasing number of teams. Initially this can provide a vehicle for sharing knowledge and skills across organizational units; however, when individuals belong to too many teams at once, this can severely limit the availability of slack resources (in particular, time) needed to schedule meetings and draw benefits from individuals' knowledge, resulting in the opposite effect. Moreover, the opportunity that teams provide to capitalize on unexpected opportunities for learning is also limited by multiple memberships. As the average number of team memberships increases, the ability of teams to meet or talk synchronously declines, often leading members (or project managers) to seek opportunities to carve projects into smaller parts so that progress can be made by members asynchronously. Consequently, while MTM can initially promote learning by exposing workers to a broader array of problems and encouraging expertise sharing, when left unchecked MTM can inadvertently encourage individuals to greater levels of specialization, and lead teams to create systems with lower levels of interdependence, undermining learning.

In summary, features of an MTM environment that lead to diversity of experience, people, and settings may foster learning at the expense of productivity, while conditions that encourage narrower and deeper individual task specialization, emphasizing efficient practices and reducing slack resources, foster productivity at the expense of learning. This tradeoff is not inevitable, however. For example, trends in medicine that have encouraged deeper specialization and a decline in the ability of collectives to learn have been addressed through interventions that enhance coordination, sometimes practices as simple as keeping surgical teams intact (Edmondson, Bohmer, and Pisano, 2001; Edmondson et al., 2003), conducting a weekly meeting (Gersick, 1989), or using a checklist that prompts conversations (Gawande, 2007; Pronovost et al., 2006). Thus, understanding the features that enhance team learning, coupled with understanding how MTM environments can inadvertently undermine it, can be helpful in developing interventions that can preserve and enhance team learning practices and, thus, the organizational level learning that can result.

Practical Implications and Future Research Directions

Given the fast pace of modern team learning environments, simply keeping up with the pace of change is challenging, and producing high performance necessarily requires continuous learning. Yet, the pace of business in contemporary global economies often demands results in the short term, creating pressures for organizations to sacrifice learning for productivity. Indeed, by their nature, MTM environments may involve a greater emphasis on productivity. Therefore, we suggest that managers should create work climates that foster learning and openness to increase the chance that quality feedback occurs. Studies on psychological safety and team learning have investigated teams in environments where productivity is paramount, such as operating rooms, manufacturing facilities, and research and development teams. In particular, as organizations are increasingly interested in leveraging the skills of highly specialized individual team members across groups, creating teams where team members feel safe to speak up is critical for success.

Team learning researchers must also perform studies in the same complex environment. To capture the dynamics of learning across teams through MTM, researchers should implement both quantitative and qualitative data collection strategies. Quantitative data collection will allow researchers to connect MTM to important outcomes such as performance, productivity, and efficacy—in the learning curve tradition—whereas qualitative data collection will allow researchers to begin to understand the complex inter-group processes and team member experiences, as in the group process tradition. Edmondson and MacManus (2007) suggested that both quantitative and qualitative methods of data collection are appropriate for 'intermediate theory,' or theories that draw new connections across potentially unconnected research paradigms by using established constructs in new ways. As such, research on MTM will marry the team and organizational learning literatures with established work in sociological fields such as social network theory.

In terms of data analysis, studying the link between team learning and organizational learning will require the use of multi-level analyses. It will be important to understand the individual's experience of learning across teams (MTM skills, knowledge, and ability), as they are nested in both team-level phenomena (for example, transactive memory systems) and in their connection to a greater notion of organizational learning (for example, adaptation to change). These models will help researchers to understand how team learning is embedded in the larger context of organizational learning.

CONCLUSION

Team learning has long been regarded as the fundamental building block of organizational learning; however, relatively few studies have established an empirical or methodological connection that clarifies this relationship. Here, we suggest that by building on team learning research about learning within teams by investigating learning across teams, through MTM, researchers can begin to draw connections between team and organizational learning. In support of this goal, we reviewed multiple studies that lay the foundation for future research, identifying essential constructs that have been in the literature for some years, such as transactive memory and psychological safety, as well as new concepts such as multiple team membership that reflect the changing nature of work. In so doing, we show the promise of research that examines teams and teamwork to highlight how today's complex organizations learn.

REFERENCES

Adler, P.S. (1990) Shared Learning. *Management Science*, 36(8): 938–957.

Ancona, D.G. and Bresman, H. (2007). X-*teams: How to build teams that lead, innovate, and succeed*. Cambridge, MA: Harvard Business School Press.

Ancona, D.G. and Caldwell, D. F. (1992) Bridging the boundary: External activity and performance in organizational teams. *Administrative Science Quarterly*, 37: 634–655.

Argote, L., Beckman, S.L., and Epple, D. (1990) The persistence and transfer of learning in industrial settings. *Management Science*, 36(2): 140–154.

Argote, L. and Ingram, P. (2000). Knowledge transfer: A basis for competitive advantage in firms. *Organizational Behavior and Human Decision Processes*, 82(1), 150–169.

Argote, L., Insko, C.A., Yovetich, N., and Romero, A.A. (1995) Group learning curves: The effects of turnover and task complexity on group performance. *Journal of Applied Social Psychology*, 25(6): 512–529.

Argyris, C. and Schön, D.A. (1978) *Organizational Learning: A Theory of Action Perspective*. Reading, MA: Addison-Wesley.

Baschab, J. and Piot, J. (2007) *Executives Guide to Information Technology*. New York: Wiley.

Bourgeois, L.J. (1981) On the measurement of organizational slack. *Academy of Management Journal*, 6(1): 29–39.

Bresman, H. (2006, August) Learning from the experiences of others: A process model of vicarious team learning. *Paper presented at the Annual Meeting of the Academy of Management*, Atlanta, GA.

Bresman, H. (2010) External learning activities and team performance: A multi-method field study. *Journal of Applied Psychology*, 21(1): 81–96.

Brooks, A.K. (1994) Power and the production of knowledge: Collective team learning in work organizations. *Human Resource Development Quarterly*, 5(3): 213–235.

Bunderson, J. S. and Sutcliffe, K. M. (2003) Management team learning orientation and business unit performance. *Journal of Applied Psychology*, 88(3): 552–560.

Bunderson, J.S. and Boumgarden, P. (2011) Structure and learning in self-managed teams: Why 'bureaucratic' teams can be better learners. *Organization Science*, 21: 609–624.

Burke, C.S., Stagl, K.C., Salas, E., Pierce, L., and Kendall, D. (2006) Understanding team adaptation: A conceptual analysis and model. *Journal of Applied Psychology*, 91(6): 1189–1207.

Burt, R.S. (1992) *Structural Holes*. Cambridge, MA: Harvard University Press.

Cannon-Bowers, J.A., Salas, E., Converse, S., and Castellan, N.J., Jr. (1993) Shared mental models in expert team decision making. *Individual and Group Decision Making: Current Issues*. Lawrence Erlbaum Associates, 221–246.

Carlile, P.R. (2004) Transferring, translating, and transforming: An integrative framework for managing knowledge across boundaries. *Organization Science*, 15(5): 555–568.

Coleman, J.S. (1988) Social capital in the creation of human capital. *American Journal of Sociology*, 94: S95–S120.

Cusumano, M.A. and Selby, R.W. (1995) *Microsoft Secrets: How the World's Most Powerful Software Company Creates Technology, Shapes Markets, and Manages People*. New York: Free Press.

Cyert, R.M. and March, J.G. (1963) *A Behavioral Theory of the Firm*. Englewood Cliffs, NJ: Prentice-Hall.

Darr, E.D., Argote, L., and Epple, D. (1995) The acquisition, transfer, and depreciation of knowledge in service organizations: Productivity in franchises. *Management Science*, 41(11): 1750–1762.

De Dreu, C.K.W. (2007) Cooperative outcome interdependence, task reflexivity, and team effectiveness: A motivated information processing perspective. *Journal of Applied Psychology*, 92(3): 628–638.

Dornisch, D. (2002) The evolution of post-socialist projects: Trajectory shift and transitional capacity in a Polish region. *Regional Studies*, 36(3): 307–321.

Edmondson, A.C. (1996) Learning from mistakes is easier said than done: Group and organizational influences on the detection and correction of human error. *Journal of Applied Behavioral Sciences*, 32(1): 5–32.

Edmondson, A.C. (1999) Psychological safety and learning behavior in work teams. *Administrative Science Quarterly*, 44(2): 350–383.

Edmondson, A.C. (2002) The local and variegated nature of learning in organizations. *Organization Science*, 13(2): 128–146.

Edmondson, A.C. (2003) Speaking up in the operating room: How team leaders promote learning in interdisciplinary action teams. *The Journal of Management Studies*, 40(6): 1419–1452.

Edmondson, A.C., Bohmer, R.M., and Pisano, G.P. (2001) Disrupted routines: Team learning and new technology implementation in hospitals. *Administrative Science Quarterly*, 46(4): 685–716.

Edmondson, A.C., Dillon, J.R., and Roloff, K.S. (2007) Three perspectives on team learning: Outcome improvement, task mastery, and group process. *Academy of Management Annals*, 1: 269–314.

Edmondson, A.C. and McManus, S.E. (2007) Methodological fit in management field research. *Academy of Management Review*, 32(4): 1155–1179.

Edmondson, A.C. and Nembhard, I.M. (2009) Product development and learning in project teams: The challenges are the benefits. *Journal of Product Innovation Management*, 26(2): 123–138.

Edmondson, A.C. and Roberto, M.R. (2003) Children's Hospital and Clinics Teaching Note 5–303–071. Boston: Harvard Business School Publishing.

Edmondson, A.C. and Singer, S.J. (2008) Confronting the tension between learning and performance. *The Systems Thinker*, 19(1).

Edmondson, A.C., Winslow, A.B., Bohmer, R.M., and Pisano, G.P. (2003) Learning how and learning what: Effects of tacit and codified knowledge on performance improvement following technology adoption. *Decision Sciences*, 34(2): 197–223.

Ely, R.J. and Thomas, D.A. (2001) Cultural diversity at work: The effects of diversity perspectives on work group processes and outcomes. *Administrative Science Quarterly*, 46(2): 229–273.

Gawande, A. (2007) The checklist. *The New Yorker*, December 10th.

Gersick, C.J. (1989) Marking time: Predictable transitions in task groups. *Academy of Management Journal*, 32: 274–309.

Gibson, C. and Vermeulen, F. (2003) A healthy divide: Subgroups as a stimulus for team learning behavior. *Administrative Science Quarterly*, 48(2): 202–239.

Gino, F., Argote, L., Miron-Spektor, E., and Todorova, G. (2010) First, get your feet wet: The effects of learning from direct and indirect experience on team creativity. *Organizational Behavior and Human Decision Processes*, 111: 102–115.

Gruenfeld, D.H., Mannix, E.A., Williams, K.Y., and Neale, M.A. (1996) Group composition and decision making: How member familiarity and information distribution affect process and performance. *Organizational Behavior and Human Decision Processes*, 67(1): 1–15.

Gruenfeld, D.H., Martorana, P.V., and Fan, E.T. (2000) What do groups learn from their worldliest members? Direct and indirect influence in dynamic teams. *Organizational Behavior and Human Decision Processes*, 82(1): 45–59.

Hackman, J.R. (1987) The design of work teams. In J. Lorsch (ed.), *Handbook of organizational behavior*. Englewood Cliffs, NJ: Prentice-Hall, 315–342.

Hansen, M.T. (1999) The search-transfer problem: The role of weak ties in sharing knowledge across organizational subunits. *Administrative Science Quarterly*, 44(1): 82–111.

Hatch, M.J. and Cunliffe, A.L. (2006) Organization theory: Modern, symbolic, and postmodern perspectives (2nd edn.). New York: Oxford University Press.

Hirst, G., Van Knippenberg, D., and Zhou, J. (2009) A cross-level perspective on employee creativity: goal orientation, team learning behavior, and individual creativity. *Academy of Management Journal*, 52(2): 280–293.

Hobday, M. (2000) The project-based organization: An ideal form for managing complex products and systems. *Research Policy*, 29: 871–893.

Hollingshead, A.B. (2001) Cognitive interdependence and convergent expectations in transactive memory. *Journal of Personality and Social Psychology*, 81(6): 1080–1089.

Hollingshead, A.B. and Fraidin, S. (2003) Gender stereotypes and assumptions about expertise in transactive memory. *Journal of Experimental Social Psychology*, 39(4): 355–363.

Huber, G.P. (1991) Organizational learning: The contributing processes and the literatures. *Organization Science*, 2(1): 88–115.

Huckman, R.S. and Staats, B.R. (2009) Fluid teams and fluid tasks: The impact of team familiarity and variation in experience. *Harvard Business School Working Paper* Series No. 09–145.

Ilgen, D.R., Hollenbeck, J.R., Johnson, M., and Jundt, D. (2005) Teams in Organizations: From Input-Process-Output Models to IMOI Models. *Annual Review of Psychology*, 56: 517–543.

Jones, N. (1990) *Refocusing Educational Psychology*. Bristol, PA: Falmer Press.

Kang, S.C., Morris, S.S., and Snell, S.A. (2007) Relational archetypes, organizational learning, and value creation: Extending the human resource architecture. *Academy of Management Review*, 32(1): 236–256.

Krackhardt, D. (1992) The strength of strong ties. In N. Nohria and R.G. Eccles (eds.), *Networks and Organizations: Structure, Form, and Action*. Cambridge, MA: Harvard Business School Press: 216–239.

Larson, J.R. and Christensen, C. (1993) Groups as problem-solving units: Toward a new meaning of social cognition. *British Journal of Social Psychology*, 32(1): 5–30.

Lau, D.C. and Murnighan, J.K. (2005) Interactions within groups and subgroups: The effects of demographic fault lines. *Academy of Management Journal*, 48(4): 645–659.

Lazer, D. and Friedman, A. (2007) The network structure of exploration and exploitation. *Administrative Science Quarterly*, 12: 1–30.

Lewis, K. (2004) Knowledge and performance in knowledge-worker teams: A longitudinal study of transactive memory systems. *Management Science*, 50(11): 1519–1533.

Lewis, K., Lange, D., and Gillis, L. (2005) Transactive memory systems, learning, and learning transfer. *Organization Science*, 16(6): 581–598.

Liang, D.W., Moreland, R.L., and Argote, L. (1995) Group versus individual training and group performance: The mediating factor of transactive memory. *Personality and Social Psychology Bulletin*, 21(4): 384–393.

Lojeski, K. S., Reilly, R., and Dominick, P. (2007). Multitasking and Innovation in Virtual Teams. *Proceedings of the 40th Annual Hawaii International Conference on System Sciences, 2007 (HICSS '07)*. Waikoloa, Hawaii. Vol. 40: 1–9: IEEE.

Lu, M., Wynn, E., Chudoba, K., and Watson-Manheim, M.B. (2003, December) Understanding virtuality in a global organization: Toward a virtuality index. International Conference on Information Systems, Seattle, WA.

Madono, K.E. (1998) Craft and regulatory learning in a neighborhood garage. In J.C. Singleton (ed.), *Learning in Likely Places: Varieties of Apprenticeship in Japan*. Cambridge, UK: Cambridge University Press: 134–152.

Malone, T.W. (2004) *The Future of Work: How the New Order of Business will Shape your Organization, your Management Style, and your Life*. Cambridge, MA: Harvard Business School Press.

March, J.G. and Simon, H.A. (1958) *Organizations*. New York: Wiley.

Marks, M.A., Dechurch, L.A., Mathieu, J.E., Panzer, F.J., and Alonso, A. (2005) Teamwork in multiteam systems. *Journal of Applied Psychology*, 90(5): 964–971.

Marrone, J.A., Tesluk, P.E., and Carson, J.B. (2007) A multilevel investigation of antecedents and consequences of team member boundary-spanning behavior. *Academy of Management Journal*, 50(6): 1423–1439.

Martin, A. and Bal, V. (2006) *The State of Teams*. Greensboro, NC: Center for Creative Leadership.

Mathieu, J.E., Heffner, T.S., Goodwin, G.F., Salas, E., and Cannon-Bowers, J.A. (2000) The influence of shared mental models on team process and performance. *Journal of Applied Psychology*, 85(2): 273–283.

Mathieu, J., Maynard, M. T., Rapp, T., and Gilson, L. (2008). Team effectiveness 1997–2007: A review of recent advancements and a glimpse into the future. *Journal of Management*, 34, 410–476.

McGrath, J.E. (1984) *Groups: Interaction and Performance*. Englewood Cliffs, NJ: Prentice-Hall.

Meyer, A.D. (1982) Adapting to organizational jolts. *Administrative Science Quarterly*, 27(4): 515–537.

Meyer, M.A. (1994) The dynamics of learning with team production: Implications for task assignment. *Quarterly Journal of Economics*, 109(4): 1157–1184.

Milgrom, P.R. and Roberts, J. (1992) *Economics, Organization, and Management*. Englewood Cliffs, NJ: Prentice-Hall.

Mohammed, S., Klimoski, R., and Rentsch, J.R. (2000) The measurement of team mental models: We have no shared schema. *Organizational Research Methods*, 3(2): 123–165.

Moreland, R.L., Argote, L., Krishnan, R., Tindale, R.S., Heath, L., and Edwards, J.(1998) Training people to work in groups. *Theory and research on small groups*. New York: Plenum Publishing, 37–60.

Moreland, R.L. and Myaskovsky, L. (2000) Exploring the performance benefits of group training: Transactive memory or improved communication? *Organizational Behavior and Human Decision Processes*, 82(1): 117.

Mortensen, M., Woolley, A.W., and O'Leary, M.B. (2007) Conditions enabling effective multiple team membership. In K. Crowston, S. Sieber, and E. Wynn (eds.), *Virtuality and Virtualization*, (vol. 236). Boston: Springer, 215–228.

Nelson, R.E. (1989) The strength of strong ties: Social networks and intergroup conflict in organizations. *Academy of Management Journal*, 32(2): 377–401.

Nembhard, I.M. and Edmondson, A.C. (2006) Making it safe: The effects of leader inclusiveness and professional status on psychological safety and improvement efforts in health care teams. *Journal of Organizational Behavior*, 27(7): 941–966.

Newell, S., Goussevskaia, A., Swan, J., Bresnen, M., and Obembe, A. (2007) Interdependencies in complex project ecologies: The case of biomedical innovation. *Long Range Planning*, 41: 33–54.

Nobeoka, K. (1995) Inter-project learning in new product development. *Academy of Management Journal*, 38: 432–436.

Nohria, N. and Gulati, R. (1996) Is slack good or bad for innovation. *Academy of Management Journal*, 39(5): 1245–1264.

Ocasio, W. (1997) Towards an attention-based view of the firm. *Strategic Management Journal*, 18: 187–206.

O'Leary, M.B., Mortensen, M., and Woolley, A.W. (2011) Multiple team membership: A theoretical model of its effects on productivity and learning for individuals and teams. *Academy of Management Review* 36 (3) July.

Pronovost, P., Needham, D., Berenholtz, S., Sinopoli, D., Chu, H., and Cosgrove, S. (2006) An intervention to decrease catheter-related bloodstream infections in the ICU. *New England Journal of Medicine*, 26(355): 2725–2732.

Reagans, R., Argote, L., and Brooks, D. (2005) Individual experience and experience working together: Predicting learning rates from knowing who knows what and knowing how to work together. *Management Science*, 51(6): 869–881.

Ren, Y., Carley, K.M., and Argote, L. (2006) The contingent effects of transactive memory: When is it more beneficial to know what others know? *Management Science*, 52(5): 671–682.

Rentsch, J.R. and Klimoski, R. (2001) Why do 'great minds' think alike?: Antecedents of team member schema agreement. *Journal of Organizational Behavior*, 22: 107–120.

Richter, A., Scully, J., and West, M. (2005) Intergroup conflict and intergroup effectiveness in organizations: Theory and scale development. *European Journal of Work and Organizational Psychology*, 14(2): 177–203.

Rulke, D. L. and Rau, D. (2000) Investigating the encoding process and transactive memory development in group training. *Group and Organization Management*, 25(4): 373–396.

Sarin, S. and McDermott, C. (2003) The effect of team leader characteristics on learning, knowledge application, and performance of cross-functional new product development teams. *Decision Sciences*, 34(4): 707–739.

Savelsbergh, C.M.J.H., van der Heijden, B.I.J.M. and Poell, R.F. (2009) The development and empirical validation of a multidimensional measurement instrument for team learning behaviors. *Small Group Research*, 40(5): 578–607.

Schippers, M.C., Den Hartog, D.N., Koopman, P.L., and Wienk, J.A. (2003). Diversity and team outcomes: The moderating effects of outcome interdependence and group longevity and the mediating effect of reflexivity. *Journal of Organizational Behavior*, 24(6): 779–802.

Schippers, M.C., Homan, A.C., and van Knippenberg, D. (2009, August). *Turning the team around: The importance of team reflexivity following poor performance.* Paper presented at the Annual Meeting of the Academy of Management, Chicago, IL.

Scott, W.R. and Davis, G.F. (2006) *Organizations and organizing: Rational natural, and open systems.* Upper Saddle River, NJ: Prentice Hall.

Senge, P.M. (1990) *The Fifth Discipline: the Art and Practice of the Learning Organization.* New York: Doubleday.

Sessa, V. I. and London, M. (2006). *Continuous learning: Individual, group, and organizational perspectives.* Mahwah, NJ: Lawrence Erlbaum Associates.

Shore, J. and Warden, S. (2007) *Art of agile development.* Sebastopol, CA: O'Reilly Media.

Singer S.J. and Edmondson A.C. (2008). When learning and performance are at odds: Confronting the tension. In P. Kumar and P. Ramsey (eds.) *Learning and performance matter* (pp. 33–61). Hackensack, NJ: World Scientific Books.

Smith-Jentsch, K.A., Campbell, G.E., Milanovich, D.M., and Reynolds, A.M. (2001) Measuring teamwork mental models to support training needs assessment, development, and evaluation: Two empirical studies. *Journal of Organizational Behavior*, 22: 179–194.

Söderlund, J. (2002) Managing complex development projects: Arenas, knowledge processes, and time. *R and D Management*, 32(5): 419–430.

Stasser, G., Stewart, D.D., and Wittenbaum, G.M. (1995) Expert roles and information exchange during discussion: The importance of knowing who knows what. *Journal of Experimental Social Psychology*, 31(3): 244–265.

Subramaniam, M. and Youndt, M.A. (2005) The influence of intellectual capital on the types of innovative capabilities. *Academy of Management Journal*, 48(3): 450–463.

Tjosvold, D., Yu, Z.-Y., and Hui, C. (2004) Team learning from mistakes: The contribution of cooperative goals and problem-solving. *The Journal of Management Studies*, 41(7): 1223–1245.

Tortoriello, M. and Krackhardt, D. (2010) Activating cross-boundary knowledge: The role of simmelian ties in the generation of innovations. *Academy of Management Journal*, 53(1): 167–181.

Tucker, A.L., Nembhard, I.M., and Edmondson, A.C. (2007) Implementing new practices: An empirical study of organizational learning in hospital intensive care units. *Management Science*, 53(6): 894–907.

Tushman, M. and O'Reilly, C. (1996) Ambidextrous organizations: Managing evolutionary and revolutionary change. *California Management Review*, 38(4): 8–30.

Uzzi, B. (1997) Social structure and competition in interfirm networks: The paradox of embeddedness. *Administrative Science Quarterly*, 42(1): 35–67.

Van den Bossche, P., Gijselaers, W.H., Segers, M., and Kirshner, P.A. (2006) Social and cognitive factors driving teamwork in collaborative learning environments: Team learning beliefs and behaviors. *Small Group Research*, 37: 490–521.

Van der Vegt, G. S. and Bunderson, J. S. (2005) Learning and performance in multidisciplinary teams: The importance of collective team identification. *Academy of Management Journal*, 48(3): 532–547.

Van der Vegt, G.S., Bunderson, J.S., and Kuipers, B. (in press) Why turnover matters in self-managing work teams: Learning, social integration, and task flexibility. *Journal of Management*.

Van der Vegt, G.S., de Jong, S.B., Bunderson, J.S., and Molleman, E. (in press) Power asymmetry and learning in teams: The moderating role of performance feedback. *Organization Science*.

Walsh, J.P., Henderson, C.M., and Deighton, J. (1988). Negotiated belief structures and decision performance: An empirical investigation. *Organizational Behavior and Human Decision Processes*, 42, 194–216.

Wegner, D. M. (1987) Transactive memory: A contemporary analysis of the group mind. In B. Mullen and G. R. Goethals (eds.), *Theories of Group Behavior*. New York: Springer-Verlag, 185–208.

West, M. (2000) Reflexivity, revolution and innovation in work teams. In M.M. Beyerlein, D.A. Johnson, and S.T. Beyerlein (eds.), *Product Development Teams* (vol. 5). Stamford, C.T.: JAI Press, 1–29.

Wheelright, S.C. and Clark, K.B. (1992) *Revolutionizing Product Development: Quantum Leaps in Speed, Efficacy, and Quality*. New York: The Free Press.

Wilson, J.M., Goodman, P.S., and Cronin, M.A. (2007) Group learning. *Academy of Management Review*, 32(4): 1041–1059.

Wong, S.S. (2004) Distal and local group learning: Performance trade-offs and tensions. *Organization Science*, 15(6): 645–656.

Woolley, A.W. (2009) Means vs. ends: Implications of process and outcome focus for team adaptation and performance. *Organization Science*, 20(3): 500–515.

Zellmer-Bruhn, M. (2003) Interruptive events and team knowledge acquisition. *Management Science*, 49(4): 514–528.

Zellmer-Bruhn, M. and Gibson, C. (2006) Multinational organizational context: Implications for team learning and performance. *Academy of Management Journal*, 49(3): 501–518.

Zika-Viktorsson, A., Sundstrom, P., and Engwall, M. (2006) Project overload: An exploratory study of work and management in multi-project settings. *International Journal of Project Management*, 24(5): 385–394.

13

Absorptive Capacity

Taking Stock of its Progress and Prospects

RAYMOND VAN WIJK,
FRANS A.J. VAN DEN BOSCH,
AND HENK W. VOLBERDA

ABSTRACT

As it influences the speed, frequency, and magnitude of innovation, the ability to recognize the value of new external knowledge, assimilate it, and apply it has rendered absorptive capacity arguably one of the most prominent constructs examined in organizational research. Even though a wealth of insights on absorptive capacity has been gained, the construct has suffered from inconsistent operationalizations, and has been refined and reconceptualized multiple times. Nevertheless, a large number of studies have examined the antecedents and outcomes of absorptive capacity. This chapter reviews the literature on absorptive capacity with the aim to set the coherent advancement of the construct. To that end, we provide an overview of how the definition of absorptive capacity has evolved, the levels of analysis involved and how studies have measured the construct, specifically by assessing refinements, extensions, and reconceptualizations of the construct. Given the inconsistent operationalizations, we review outcomes and antecedents heeded in prior research. Specifically, we distinguish between antecedents relating to the knowledge absorbed itself, the organization developing it, and the network organizations being operated in. Based on the review, we assess the progress made in the past two decades and seek to uncover central problems and prospects for future research.

INTRODUCTION

Knowledge and learning have become central to a firm's innovativeness and competitiveness (Argote and Ingram, 2000; Bogner and Bansal, 2007; Van Wijk et al., 2008).

Since valuable, relevant knowledge is often located outside firms' boundaries, the ability of firms and their units to acquire knowledge from external constituents has become a critical capability. The importance of the ability to acquire external knowledge has rendered absorptive capacity arguably one of the most prominent constructs examined in organizational research. Two papers by Cohen and Levinthal (1989, 1990) are generally heralded as the seminal contributions and have since been cited extensively in journals associated with a variety of disciplines, ranging from economics to sociology to psychology. According to the *Social Sciences Citation Index*, more than 4000 studies have cited the two seminal articles, and if the current popularity of the construct is a harbinger of the future, many more are to be expected.

Following Cohen and Levinthal (1989, 1990), absorptive capacity emerges as a byproduct of research and development, and the stock of knowledge developed confers on firms the ability to recognize the value of new external knowledge, assimilate it, and apply it to commercial ends. These three capabilities play a critical role in a firm's innovativeness and influence the speed, frequency, and magnitude of innovation (Lewin et al., 2010). Even though prior research has produced a wealth of insights on the functioning and value of absorptive capacity, only a limited number of studies have discussed its scope and sought to further develop it (Lane et al., 2006). Studies have relied on a wide variety of measures to gauge absorptive capacity, including patent-based measures, scales, and, consistent with Cohen and Levinthal (1990), notably research and development-based measures. Since many measures do not capture the richness of the construct and overlap with measures typically used for other prominent constructs, such as knowledge transfer and innovation, our understanding of the nomological network of absorptive capacity has been impeded. As a result, several studies have attempted to redefine the construct (e.g. Lane and Lubatkin, 1998; Lim, 2009). What is more, studies even sought to refine (Matusik and Heeley, 2005; Todorova and Durisin, 2007), reconceptualize (Zahra and George, 2002), reify (Lane et al., 2006), and rejuvenate (Volberda et al., 2010) the construct. Calls have also been made for a process perspective that uncovers the microfoundations of absorptive capacity (Easterby-Smith et al., 2008; Lewin et al., 2010).

The popularity of absorptive capacity has led scholars to empirically examine its relation to a variety of antecedents and outcomes in different contexts (Jansen et al., 2005; Lane et al., 2001; Lane and Lubatkin, 1998; Lichtenthaler, 2009; Mowery et al., 1996; Szulanski, 1996; Van den Bosch et al., 1999). In line with Cohen and Levinthal (1990), studies have particularly examined the role of absorptive capacity in innovation, but studies have also appeared considering knowledge transfer and performance as outcomes. Antecedents identified in prior research relate to the characteristics of the knowledge itself, to the organization in which it is developed, and to the dyad or network in which it is applied. In addition to a mediating role in explaining innovativeness and performance, studies have also assessed the extent to which absorptive capacity moderates relationships where innovation is the outcome (e.g. Rothaermel and Alexandre, 2009; Tsai, 2009). Because absorptive capacity has appeared an elusive construct and measuring it is fraught with difficulty, however, the insights gained on its antecedents and outcomes harbor suspicion.

In this chapter, we review the literature on absorptive capacity with the aim to advance the construct in a more coherent way. We assess the progress made in the past two decades and seek to uncover problems and prospects for future research. The chapter is structured as follows. First, based on the seminal contributions of Cohen and Levinthal (1989,

1990), we provide an overview of how the definition of absorptive capacity has evolved, the levels of analysis involved and how studies have measured the construct. Specifically, we assess the refinements, extensions, and reconceptualizations of the construct in the literature. Then, we review outcomes and antecedents heeded in prior research. Specifically, we distinguish between antecedents relating to the knowledge absorbed itself, the organization in which it is developed, and the network in which organizations operate. Next, we review more recent studies that have examined the moderating role of absorptive capacity in explaining innovation. Finally, based on this review, we address the progress made, identify central problems, and forward promising future research directions.

ORIGINS, DEFINITIONS, AND OPERATIONALIZATIONS

Even though Kedia and Bhagat (1988) were first to coin the term absorptive capacity, in the context of technology transfer across nations, Cohen and Levinthal (1989, 1990) are generally credited for forwarding the construct. The absorptive capacity construct evolved from research instigated in the 1970s and running through the 1980s on the role of internal research and development. Studies observed that internal research and development has a dual role. It not only shapes a firm's technological innovation, but also allows firms to keep abreast of technological developments and assimilate new technology (Tilton, 1971). Consistent with studies using an Industrial Organization-based perspective to explain firm strategy, Cohen and Levinthal (1989, 1990) sought to provide a set of explanations for the dual role of research and development from that perspective. While their 1989 paper focused on firms' incentives to learn and to invest in research and development as environmental opportunities vary from an economics perspective, their 1990 paper centered on the role of cognitive structures and took a more socio-economical approach. Borrowing from research on cognition and memory development (Ellis, 1965), in the latter paper they argue that individuals learn more efficiently when the knowledge to be learned is related to what is already known and emphasize the cumulative nature of learning.

Definitions

As our understanding of the construct has progressed over the years, the definition of absorptive capacity has evolved. An overview of most prominent definitions is given in Table 13.1. In their most widely cited paper, Cohen and Levinthal (1990: 128) define absorptive capacity as the 'ability to recognize the value of new information, assimilate it, and apply it to commercial ends.' This definition derives from their earlier definition, which emphasizes the 'ability to identify, assimilate and exploit knowledge from the environment' (1989: 569–570). They further argue that this ability is 'largely a function of the level of prior related knowledge' (1990: 128). Firms that have in place a body of knowledge in a certain domain will improve learning related knowledge. In other words, a firm's knowledge base renders three capabilities, which other studies have referred to as components (Lane et al., 2001) and dimensions of absorptive capacity (Lane and Lubatkin, 1998; Matusik and Heeley, 2005; Zahra and George, 2002). For a firm to have absorptive capacity it requires (1) the capability to identify, evaluate, and recognize the value of new external knowledge, (2) the capability to assimilate that knowledge into its existing knowledge base, and (3) the capability to exploit it to commercial ends.

Table 13.1   Definitions of absorptive capacity

Study	Definition
Cohen and Levinthal (1990)	'an ability to recognize the value of new information, assimilate it, and apply it to commercial ends' (p. 128).
Lane and Lubatkin (1998)	'the student's ability to value, assimilate, and commercialize its teacher's knowledge' (p. 473).
Zahra and George (2002)	'a set of organizational routines and processes by which firms acquire, assimilate, transform, and exploit knowledge' (p. 186).
Matusik and Heeley (2005)	'comprises . . . (a) the firm's relationship to its external environment (porosity of firm boundaries), (b) collective dimension (its structures, routines, and knowledge base), and (c) an individual dimension (individuals' absorptive capacities') (p. 550).
Lane et al. (2006)	'a firm's ability to utilize externally held knowledge through three sequential processes: (1) recognizing and understanding potentially valuable new knowledge outside the firm through exploratory learning, (2) assimilating valuable new knowledge through transformative learning, and (3) using the assimilated knowledge to create new knowledge and commercial outputs through exploitative learning' (p. 856).
Lewin et al. (2010)	'internal metaroutines [that] involve the regulation of activities related to managing internal variation-selection-retention processes . . . [and] external metaroutines . . ., which focus on the acquisition and utilization of knowledge from the external environment' (in press).
Todorova and Durisin (2007)	a firm's ability to recognize the value of new knowledge, to acquire it, to assimilate and/or transform it, and to exploit it.
Lim (2009)	Absorptive capacity consists in three forms, of which 'disciplinary absorptive capacity involves acquiring raw scientific knowledge in key scientific disciplines, and converting that knowledge into a form that is useful for solving practical problems, [while] domain-specific absorptive capacity refers to the ability to acquire knowledge directly related to solving those problems, so as to produce commercially useful innovations, [and] encoded absorptive capacity refers to a firm's ability to absorb knowledge that is already embedded in tools, artifacts, and processes' (p. 1252).

Firms are not necessarily equally endowed with these capabilities and may not have in place all three capabilities to the same degree. To that end, Zahra and George (2002) forward absorptive capacity as a dynamic capability. Based on the studies of Mowery and Oxley (1995) and Kim (1998), they introduce a fourth capability in addition to the three capabilities identified by Cohen and Levinthal (1990) and define absorptive capacity as 'a set of organizational routines and processes by which firms acquire, assimilate, transform, and exploit knowledge' (2002: 186). Their definition explicates that firms also need the ability to solve problems by transforming and modifying existing knowledge before they can exploit external knowledge. Based on the four capabilities, they make distinction between potential and realized absorptive capacity as two subsets of absorptive capacity that explain why firms vary in their ability to create value from their absorptive capacity. While potential absorptive capacity is a function of a firm's ability to acquire and assimilate new external knowledge, realized absorptive capacity reflects a firm's capacity to leverage that knowledge through transformation and exploitation. Minbaeva et al. (2003: 589) argue that 'potential absorptive capacity is expected to have a high content of employees' ability while realized absorptive capacity is expected to have a high content of employees' motivation.' Similar distinctions have been made between evaluation and utilization of knowledge (Arora and Gambardella, 1994) as well as between knowledge transfer and knowledge application (Bierly et al., 2009). Firms may have the ability to acquire and assimilate knowledge but lack the capacity to transform and exploit knowledge. Likewise, firms may have the capability to transform and exploit knowledge, but lack the capability to acquire knowledge from the environment. Such firms may be very efficient in realizing performance improvements, but the effect of their capability will be mitigated by the limited amount of external knowledge they acquire. Camisón and Forés (2010) found that potential and realized absorptive capacity are empirically distinct capabilities of absorptive capacity.

The empirical study of Jansen et al. (2005) indicates, however, that acquisition, assimilation, transformation, and exploitation should be viewed as four separate capabilities. Their four factor model was found to be superior to a two factor model revolving around potential and realized absorptive capacity. In their critique on the value of studying potential and realized absorptive capacity as two dimensions, Todorova and Durisin (2007) also make a case for considering the distinct capabilities as separate elements of absorptive capacity. Additionally, they suggest reintroducing the capability to recognize the value of external knowledge as originally put forth by Cohen and Levinthal (1990). Recognizing knowledge is implied by the acquisition capability identified by Zahra and George (2002). Todorova and Durisin (2007) make a case, however, that it is a separate process that elicits motivation to direct attention to the intensity, speed, and effort involved in acquiring knowledge. Moreover, based on research in cognitive science, they argue that transformation is not necessarily a process following but an alternative to assimilation. Even though Zahra and George (2002) also broadly imply this (see also Lane et al., 2006), Todorova and Durisin (2007) submit that firms may assimilate external knowledge without transforming it if it fits with the present knowledge base. In case new knowledge cannot be realistically altered to fit existing knowledge, firms may also need to transform knowledge before it is assimilated.

Showing how absorptive capacity aids firms in benefitting from knowledge spillovers, Lim (2009) delves into the processes revolving around the different capabilities constituting absorptive capacity. Specifically, he contends that absorptive capacity may be present in three forms: disciplinary, domain-specific, and encoded absorptive capacity. Disciplinary absorptive capacity refers to the acquisition of scientific knowledge and the transformation of that knowledge into useful forms for problem solving. Domain-specific absorptive capacity involves the ability to acquire additional knowledge to solve those specific problems, and to apply it to commercially useful innovations. Finally, encoded absorptive capacity denotes a firm's ability to absorb knowledge that is already embedded in tools, artifacts, and processes.

Since the variety in the use of absorptive capacity has led to inconsistent findings, Lane et al. (2006) have sought to reify the absorptive construct. To that end, they define absorptive capacity as the ability to recognize and understand potentially valuable knowledge through exploratory learning, to assimilate valuable knowledge through transformative learning, and to create new knowledge and commercial outputs through exploitative learning. Absorptive capacity revolves around three learning processes that reflect the innovative nature of absorptive capacity as emphasized by Cohen and Levinthal (1990). Exploration of new knowledge is necessary for innovation, but needs to be transformed before firms are able to exploit it.

In an empirical study among 175 German firms, Lichtenthaler (2009) argues that the exploratory learning process involves recognition and assimilation, the transformative learning process associates with maintaining and reactivating knowledge, and the exploitative process is characterized by the transmutation and application of knowledge. In line with Jansen et al. (2005), he found that a model reflective of the basic elements is superior to a model of higher order dimensions. Specifically, a six factor model around capabilities to recognize, assimilate, maintain, reactivate, transmute, and apply knowledge was superior to a three factor model around exploratory, transformative, and exploitative learning. However, a model in which the three learning processes were included as second order factors of the six first order factors, which subsequently loaded on absorptive capacity as a third order factor, proved to fit the data best. With that, current insights suggest that absorptive capacity involves different capabilities.

Levels of analysis

Prior research has shown that absorptive capacity is a construct operating at multiple levels. Cohen and Levinthal (1990) introduced absorptive capacity as a firm-level construct, but they emphasize that multiple levels are involved and focus on a firm's organizational units to explain how it develops. Since individual members are involved with absorbing knowledge within firms, they forward that 'an organization's absorptive capacity will depend on the absorptive capacities of its individual members' (1990: 131). Indeed, as Lane et al. (2006: 853–854) argue, 'individuals within the firm . . . scan the knowledge environment, bring the knowledge into the firm, and exploit the knowledge in products, processes, and services.' A firm is, however, a social community characterized by an architecture and organizing principles that make it more than a collection of individuals (cf. Kogut and Zander, 1992). Similarly, absorptive capacity 'is not . . . simply the sum of the absorptive capacities of its employees, and it is therefore useful to consider what aspects of absorptive capacity are distinctly organizational' (Cohen and Levinthal, 1990: 131). Similarly, Matusik and Heeley (2005) argue that a firm's absorptive capacity has an individual and a collective dimension. While absorptive capacity is partly dependent on the knowledge and abilities of its individual members, it is also dependent on a firm's knowledge that is collectively held in routines, procedures, documentation, systems, and shared experiences. Collective knowledge is defined by the discrete components of an organization's operations or parts, and an organization's architecture that enables how routines are developed to put a firm's components to productive use.

Taken that absorptive capacity is dependent on a relevant knowledge base, the link between absorptive capacity and learning is most evident at the individual level. Cohen and Levinthal (1990) derive from cognitive research on memory development (Ellis, 1965) that individuals learn more when the object of learning is related to what is already known. Research on memory development has shown that accumulated prior knowledge enables the ability to store new knowledge into one's memory and to recall and use it. The cumulative nature of learning and absorptive capacity entails that knowledge development is path-dependent and gives rise to specializations.

Since knowledge within firms is distributed among various individual members and subunits, firms have multiple entry points for external knowledge. Firms also coordinate interaction between individuals and subunits through communication structures, hence absorptive capacity 'also depends on transfers of knowledge across and within subunits that may be quite removed from the original point of entry' (Cohen and Levinthal, 1990: 131–132). Absorptive capacity rests, therefore, on individuals standing at the interface of both the environment and other subunits. In case external knowledge is dissimilar to what is known, an individual can consult other individuals within the organization that possess relevant related knowledge. In case the knowledge relates to what is known, individual members can translate knowledge in a meaningful way for others or relieve others from monitoring the environment. Cohen and Levinthal (1990) contend that organizations install group members that assume a gatekeeping or boundary-spanning role. Boundary spanners maintain ties that enable them to know where relevant knowledge resides in a firm and enhance individual performance in knowledge-intensive work (Cross and Cummings, 2004). Since a gatekeeper forms the point of entry and is dependent on the expertise of others within its group and the larger organization, designing a structure around gatekeepers cannot be disentangled from the distribution of expertise. The architecture that brings individuals together in groups and allows them to transfer knowledge and information renders a firm's absorptive capacity more than the sum of the absorptive capacities of its individual members and dependent on the ties between them.

A number of studies have also begun to examine the role of absorptive capacity in intrafirm knowledge transfer at the unit or subsidiary level (Tsai, 2001). While subunits need prior related knowledge to be able to evaluate, assimilate, and exploit knowledge originating in the external environment, studies found that absorptive capacity is also a critical determinant of knowledge transfer among peer subunits (Gupta and Govindarajan, 2000; Szulanski, 1996). Altogether, current insights illustrate that absorptive capacity is a phenomenon operating at multiple levels in an organization. As Figure 13.1 illustrates, absorptive capacity 'depends on the individuals who stand [either] at the interface of . . . the firm and the external environment or at the interface between subunits within the firm' (Cohen and Levinthal, 1990: 132).

Other relevant levels of analysis at which absorptive capacity has been studied include clusters of related industries, such as regions and nations (Wegloop, 1995), and even clusters of institutionally linked countries, such as the European Union (Meyer-Krahmer

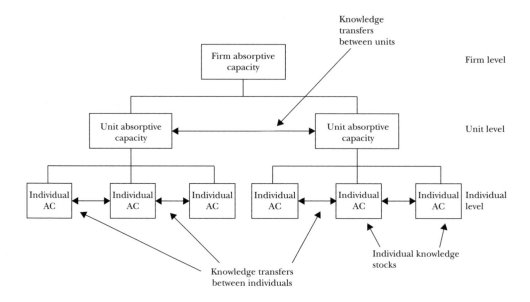

Figure 13.1 Levels of Absorptive Capacity

and Reger, 1999). Interaction among firms, universities, and governments in regions and nations shapes innovation infrastructures. To capitalize on such infrastructures, in different locations around the world clusters have emerged in which firms, universities, governments, and customers collaborate and drive innovation (Porter and Stern, 2001). Actors in a nation, region, or cluster have a stock of knowledge that creates absorptive capacity. Similar to collaboration among individuals shaping a firm's absorptive capacity beyond the sum of the knowledge held by individuals, two-way interactions between firms, nations, and clusters further enhance the ability of the region to attract talented individuals, companies, and institutes that bring new expertise and knowledge. As such, increasing the absorptive capacity of the economy becomes an important aspect of public policy (Mowery and Oxley, 1995; Keller, 1996).

The notion that absorptive capacity shapes knowledge transfer both between and within firms is supported by Lane and Lubatkin (1998), but they forward that absorptive capacity should be studied at the dyad level and introduce relative absorptive capacity. They argue that the level of absorptive capacity of a firm is not only dependent its own knowledge base but also on the knowledge bases of its interacting partners. If the knowledge bases of two firms do not overlap, they will experience difficulty learning from each other. Especially in the context of alliances where competitive advantage rests with the dyad, absorptive capacity is essentially relative (Lane and Lubatkin, 1998) and even partner-specific (Dyer and Singh, 1998).

Operationalizations

One of the root causes inhibiting progress in our understanding of the value of absorptive capacity is that empirical studies have estimated absorptive capacity in a wide variety of ways (see Table 13.2). Cohen and Levinthal's (1990) core argument centered on the

Table 13.2   Operationalizations of absorptive capacity

Level of analysis	Operationalization	Sample studies
Firm level construct	R&D measures:	
	R&D intensity	Cohen and Levinthal (1989; 1990); Mowery et al. (1996); Nichols-Nixon and Woo (2003); Puranam and Srikanth (2007); Singh (2008); Stock et al. (2001); Tsai (2001); Zhang et al. (2007a)
	R&D expenditures	Kamien and Zang (2000); Rothaermel and Alexandre (2009); Wiethaus (2005)
	R&D infrastructure	Cassiman and Veugelers (2006); Lichtenthaler and Ernst (2007)
	Patent stock	Almeida and Phene (2004); Bogner and Bansal (2007); Frost and Zhou (2005); Henderson and Cockburn (1996); Rosenkopf and Nerkar (2001); Somaya et al (2007); Zhang et al. (2007b)
	Prior experience	Kusunoki et al (1998); Lenox and King (2004); Macher and Boerner (2006)
	Proportion of foreigners/expats in management team	Gupta and Govindarajan (2000); White and Liu (1998)
	Scales	Björkman et al (2004); Camisón and Forés (2010); Haas (2006); Jansen et al. (2005); Lichtenthaler (2009); Lyles and Salk (1996); Szulanski (1996)
	Publications	Cockburn and Henderson (1998); Deeds (2001)
Dyad level construct	Patent overlap	Ahuja and Katila (2001)
	Technological relatedness/overlap	Mowery et al. (1996); Tallman and Phene (2007)
	Scales	Lane and Lubatkin (1998)
	Publications/citations	Lane and Lubatkin (1998)

role of in-house research and development in the acquisition of knowledge and in innovation. Therefore, they used business units' research and development intensities as a proxy for measuring absorptive capacity. A large number of studies have also adopted research and development intensity as the measure for absorptive capacity (e.g. Nicholls-Nixon and Woo, 2003; Puranam and Srikanth, 2007; Zhang et al., 2007a). However, 'R&D intensity measures inputs to the creation of capabilities and indicates little if anything about resultant changes in capabilities' (Mowery et al., 1996: 82; Helfat, 1997). Research and development intensity only coarsely gauges a firm's absorptive capacity and it is not fully reflective of the multidimensionality of absorptive capacity. Although research and development indeed develops a firm's knowledge base, it neither differentiates between different domains in which knowledge is developed nor makes a distinction between capabilities to recognize the value, to assimilate, to transform, and to commercially exploit knowledge. Moreover, since research and development intensity is measured by dividing its expenditures by sales, it does not indicate the absolute amount of absorptive capacity. Following this train of thought, a firm spending one million dollars on research and development with sales of twenty million dollars would have a higher level of absorptive capacity than a firm spending twenty million dollars on research and development with sales of one billion dollars. However, the latter firm would arguably have developed more knowledge enabling it to assimilate new external knowledge, even though its research and development intensity is lower. To address the problem of the denominator influencing the results, other studies have focused on the numerator and used research and development expenditures as a gauge for absorptive capacity (Kamien and Zang, 2000), while controlling for size (e.g. Rothaermel and Alexandre, 2009; Rothaermel and Hess, 2007).

Since patents are indicative of accumulated knowledge, another stream of research has used a firm's stock of prior patents as a measure for absorptive capacity (e.g. Ahuja and Katila, 2001; Almeida and Phene 2004; Bogner and Bansal, 2007; Frost and Zhou, 2005; Yayavaram and Ahuja, 2008; Zhang et al., 2007b). Measures based on patents to assess a firm's knowledge base create an opportunity to differentiate between different types of knowledge bases. For example, the number of patents is indicative of the depth and richness of a firm's knowledge stock, while different patent classes can be used to measure the breadth and diversity of a firm's knowledge stock (Almeida and Phene, 2004). Since data on patent stocks of all partners involved in a collaboration are generally available, studies have also used patent measures to assess overlap in patents (Ahuja and Katila, 2001), which is a proxy for relative or partner-specific absorptive capacity. Other measures used to assess the presence of relevant knowledge involve prior experience (Almeida and Phene, 2004), and the composition of management teams (Gupta and Govindarajan, 2000) and personnel (White and Liu, 1998).

Since the above measures appraise more than absorptive capacity and cannot differentiate between the various capabilities that firms need to be able to absorb knowledge, studies have resorted to using scales. While some studies have used scales to measure absorptive capacity directly as a singular construct (e.g. Lyles and Salk, 1996; Szulanski, 1996), more recently studies have begun to use scales to measure the various capabilities separately (e.g. Jansen et al., 2005; Lichtenthaler, 2009). Scales have also been used to assess a unit's or firm's knowledge stock (e.g. Björkman et al., 2004; Haas, 2006), as well as overlap in a firm's knowledge and technology (Lane and Lubatkin, 1998; Mowery et al., 1996).

The use of such a variety of measures for absorptive capacity has obfuscated current insights. The proxies used seem to gauge phenomena beyond absorptive capacity and do not necessarily correlate. For example, the evidence on the relation between research and development intensity, the proxy for absorptive capacity used in the original studies of Cohen and Levinthal (1989, 1990), and other variables that measure the various capabilities or dimensions of absorptive capacity is mixed. While Bierly et al. (2009) found positive correlations for research and development intensity with what may be considered potential and realized absorptive capacity, others found no relationship (e.g. Lane and Lubatkin, 1998; Matusik and Heeley, 2005; Mowery et al., 1996). Similarly, Björkman et al. (2004) found a non-significant correlation between subsidiary stock of knowledge and number of expatriate managers in the subsidiary, both previously used measures of absorptive capacity (e.g. Gupta and Govindarajan, 2000; Haas, 2006). Kotabe et al. (2007) found a non-significant correlation between the quality of the knowledge stock and research and development resources, also two measures of absorptive capacity that have been used in earlier studies.

Even in studies relying on a single type of source, consistency in measuring absorptive capacity has proven to be paramount. Using a patent database, Frost and Zhou (2005) assess the extent to which a subsidiary unit and headquarters engage in joint technical activity by measuring research and development co-practice, which is viewed as a flow variable that adds cumulatively to the stock variable measuring citations by a headquarters patent to a prior subsidiary patent. In that vein, their study illustrates that absorptive capacity is cumulative and a by-product of research and development investments. However, they also measure patent output weighed by patent quality of both headquarters and subsidiaries, which are indicators of existing knowledge-based resources. In line with the argument that absorptive capacity is dependent on prior knowledge, both headquarters' patent output stock in one period and headquarters' citations to subsidiary patents in the next are possible estimates of absorptive capacity. The question is whether the quality-corrected patent output measure or the citation measure is the preferred operationalization. Inter-firm patent citations are often used as proxies for knowledge transfer (e.g. Jaffe et al., 1993; Kotabe et al., 2007; Nerkar and Paruchuri, 2005; Rosenkopf and Almeida, 2003; Song et al., 2003), of which absorptive capacity is an antecedent and not its equivalent. The patent output measure, on the other hand, only seems to capture a firm's ability to exploit its knowledge, and not to evaluate and assimilate it. However, patent output determines the number of patents held by a firm, which have been used as measures of the knowledge held by a firm (Henderson and Cockburn, 1996; Rosenkopf and Nerkar, 2001) and innovative output (Ahuja, 2000; Rothaermel and Hess, 2007). Similarly, others have found a positive effect of research and development spending on co-citations (Deeds, 2001) and patenting performance as measured by counting patents (Somaya et al., 2007). While patenting performance is indicative of innovative performance, the count measure also gauges absorptive capacity as a higher patent count is reflective of a larger knowledge base. In contrast, using research and development expenditures and intensity respectively, Cattani (2005) and Singh (2008) did not find such a relation. While current insights support the argument that research and development spending has indeed a side effect in that it develops the knowledge base of a firm in addition to enhancing innovation, they are also indicative of the problems in operationalizing absorptive capacity. Altogether, different measures assess different dimensions of absorptive capacity as well as elements of which absorptive capacity is an antecedent or outcome.

Outcomes and Antecedents

A great number of studies have examined the antecedents and especially outcomes of absorptive capacity. A wide variety of insights have been gained in the past two decades, but such insights have also been obfuscated by the different ways in which absorptive capacity has been operationalized and by the different levels of analysis at which absorptive capacity's antecedents and outcomes have been examined.

Outcomes

Research on the various outcomes of absorptive capacity is extensive (see Table 13.3). One of the main reasons for Cohen and Levinthal (1990) to introduce absorptive capacity was to explain the side effects of research and development and their relation to innovation. In line with their argument, other research has adopted research and development-based measures as proxies for absorptive capacity to understand its effect on innovation. The evidence gained so far is mixed. Current insights lean towards a positive effect (e.g. Tsai, 2001), but studies have surfaced reporting negative (e.g. Ernst, 1998) and zero (e.g. Singh, 2008) effects of these measures on innovation. Also more complex relationships have been found. For example, Stock et al. (2001) found that absorptive capacity contributes to new product development up to a certain point but then its effect starts to decrease and becomes negative. Since research and development-based measures are antecedent to absorptive capacity and capture more than absorptive capacity alone, it

Table 13.3   Outcomes of absorptive capacity

Outcome	Key Studies
Innovation	Ahuja and Katila (2001); Cohen and Levinthal (1990); Frost and Zhou (2005); Haas (2006); Katila and Ahuja (2002); Kotabe et al. (2010); Kusunoki et al. (1998); Lichtenthaler (2009); Macher and Boerner (2006); Matusik and Heeley (2005); Nerkar (2003); Singh (2008); Smith et al. (2005); Tsai (2001); White and Liu (1998); Yayavaram and Ahuja (2008); Zhang et al. (2007b)
Exploration/exploitation	Bierly et al. (2009); Koza and Lewin (1998); Lane et al. (2006); Van den Bosch et al. (1999)
Firm performance	Bogner and Bansal (2007); Dushnitsky and Lenox (2005); Lane et al. (2001); Lichtenthaler (2009); Rothaermel and Hill (2005); Steensma and Corley (2000); Tsai (2001)
Knowledge flows	Gupta and Govindarajan (2000); Lane and Lubatkin (1998); Lyles and Salk (1996); Matusik and Heeley 2005); Minbaeva et al. (2003); Mowery et al. (1996); Rosenkopf and Almeida (2003); Song et al. (2003); Szulanski (1996; 2000)
Expectation formation	Cohen and Levinthal (1990; 1994)
Formation of alliances	Nicholls-Nixon and Woo (2003); Rothaermel and Hill (2005); Zhang et al. (2007b)

remains to be understood whether such curvilinear effect is due to research and development investments as such or to absorptive capacity.

The evidence of studies relying on experience-based measures as a gauge for absorptive capacity is also mixed at best with some studies finding positive relationships (e.g. Kusunoki et al., 1998; Macher and Boerner, 2006) and others finding negative and insignificant relationships (e.g. Haas, 2006). In contrast, with few exceptions (e.g. Singh, 2008), research relying on patent stocks to measure absorptive capacity tends to be evident of a positive relationship with innovation (e.g. Cattani, 2005; Yayavaram and Ahuja, 2008). Similarly, studies using scales (e.g. Lichtenthaler, 2009) and personnel measures (e.g. White and Liu, 1998) as proxies for absorptive capacity generally found positive effects on innovation.

The variety in earlier findings of the effect of absorptive capacity on innovation is due in part to the different ways in which studies have applied measures of absorptive capacity. Different measures allow researchers to emphasize distinct aspects of a firm's knowledge base. As mentioned, patent-based measures have been used not only to measure the volume and richness of a firm's knowledge base by counting patents but also to gauge its diversity by differentiating between patent classes that characterize a firm's patent stock (Almeida and Phene, 2004; Zhang et al., 2007b). This distinction is especially salient because richness and depth of knowledge enable a firm to master technological advances, while diversity and breadth of knowledge render a firm's capability to combine knowledge in new and novel ways (Katila and Ahuja, 2002; Subramaniam and Youndt, 2005). Absorptive capacity is a construct to explain why and how firms differ in their ability to acquire knowledge across organizational boundaries. Because it rests on the presence of a relevant knowledge base and its development is path dependent, firms tend to accumulate deep knowledge within a technological domain as this enables firms to exploit technological knowledge (Cohen and Levinthal, 1990, 1994). A firm seeking to innovate beyond its current technological trajectory needs to span technological boundaries in addition to spanning organizational boundaries, and use knowledge and technologies from domains beyond its current product offerings (Rosenkopf and Nerkar, 2001).

Both mastery of a single technology and the combination of different technologies may lead to innovation, albeit to different kinds of innovation. As innovation sheds light on the mixed evidence of the effect of absorptive capacity on innovation, studies have begun to make a distinction between its different dimensions and manifestations. A common distinction that is reflective of the difference between mastering and combining technologies is between exploitative and exploratory innovations. Exploitative innovations build on current knowledge and incrementally refine and extend existing products and competences, whereas exploratory innovations depart from existing knowledge and aim to develop new alternatives (March, 1991). Consistent with Cohen and Levinthal's (1990) argument, Bierly et al. (2009) found that technological relatedness, a measure of relative absorptive capacity, inhibits exploration. The more the technologies of partnering firms relate the more efficient knowledge acquisition will become and fewer opportunities exist for making new linkages. Similarly, Bergh and Lim (2008) differentiate absorptive capacity from improvisation and creativity. However, Van den Bosch et al. (1999) contend that knowledge absorption may vary in its efficiency, scope, and flexibility, and have found that efficiency facilitates exploitation whereas scope and flexibility contribute to exploration. Lane et al. (2006) take another perspective and argue that absorptive capacity caters for both exploration and exploitation. As part of their definition of absorptive capacity, they submit that the recognition and understanding of potentially valuable knowledge constitute the processes through which firms explore new knowledge, while using it is part of the exploitative learning process.

Seeking to further understand the effect of absorptive capacity on a firm's competitive position, studies have also examined its effect on performance. A variety of studies at the inter-firm (Lane et al., 2001), firm (Bogner and Bansal, 2007; Dushnitsky and Lenox, 2005; Rothaermel and Hill, 2005), and unit (Cohen and Levinthal, 1990; Tsai, 2001) level found a positive effect of absorptive capacity on performance. The effects found are, however, again dependent on the operationalization chosen by the investigators. A strong case in point is evident in the study of Steensma and Corley (2000) who used research and development intensity, size, and technological relatedness as proxies for absorptive capacity and only found relatedness to influence a firm's return on investment. In his study on 300 medium-sized and large German firms, Lichtenthaler (2009) differentiates between the three learning processes of absorptive capacity suggested by Lane et al. (2006) and found that especially the exploitative learning process influences firm performance. Likewise, Lane et al. (2001) found strong evidence that the application of external knowledge leads to performance increments.

In addition to providing evidence for the performance implications of absorptive capacity, the results of Lane et al. (2001) suggest that knowledge transfer mediates the relationship between absorptive capacity and performance. Differentiating between the three capabilities characterizing absorptive capacity, they found that the ability to understand and assimilate knowledge contributes strongly to the knowledge learned from foreign IJV parents. Using a variety of operationalizations of absorptive capacity, ranging from research and development-based measures to patents to psychometric scales, a growing number of studies indicate that absorptive capacity facilitates inter-organizational learning (Lyles and Salk, 1996; Mowery et al., 1996; Rosenkopf and Almeida, 2003). Similarly, the insights gained so far point out that absorptive capacity is a critical determinant of knowledge transfer across a firm's business units (e.g. Minbaeva et al., 2003; Szulanski, 1996). In their meta-analytic study, Van Wijk et al. (2008) corroborate the direct effect of absorptive capacity on knowledge transfer both across units and across firms.

Remarkably, Gupta and Govindarajan (2000) found no significant effect of absorptive capacity on knowledge transfers across peer subsidiaries. Their study on MNC knowledge flows shows partial support for the role of absorptive capacity in that it is limited to knowledge that originates in the parent organization and is transferred to subsidiaries. However, this finding is likely the result of their operationalization of absorptive capacity as mode of entry. Although their argument that acquired subsidiaries are less likely to have overlapping knowledge with other subsidiaries than greenfield subsidiaries makes sense, entry mode encompasses much more than the ability to absorb knowledge. Parent organizations are more likely to provide information and knowledge when they set up a greenfield subsidiary and will continue to do so because such subsidiaries will be perceived as more relevant and requiring more attention. In their study on manufacturing facilities in the information and communications industry, Lenox and King (2004) found that the provision of information by corporate managers enhanced both the adoption of pollution prevention practices by organizational subunits as well as the effect of subunits' absorptive capacity on such adoption.

Finally, studies have examined the effect of absorptive capacity on expectation formation (Cohen and Levinthal, 1990, 1994) and the formation of alliances (Rothaermel and

Hill, 2005; Veugelers and Kesteloot, 1996; Zhang et al., 2007b). Absorptive capacity enables firms not only to acquire knowledge but, since it involves knowledge of why certain technological trajectories are valuable and of who knows what, also to assess what may be potential future technological advances and the value of new partners it can collaborate with. Moreover, effective absorptive capacity rests on both the ability to communicate internally and the ability to acquire knowledge externally (Rothaermel and Alexandre, 2009), as well as on both internal and external research and development activities (Cassiman and Veugelers, 2006; Nicholls-Nixon and Woo, 2003). External knowledge may be supplied by potential alliance partners; hence, firms with high absorptive capacity are more likely to enter into an alliance because their expectations of its benefits are more certain.

Antecedents

In contrast to the outcomes of absorptive capacity, the antecedents and determinants of absorptive capacity have received limited attention. Most insights on the antecedents of absorptive capacity have been gained from research centering on the variables that have been used often to operationalize absorptive capacity. An overview of current research illustrates that characteristics of the knowledge involved are important to consider as they influence the learning process. Since firm or unit absorptive capacity is not simply the sum of the absorptive capacities of its constituent individual members, however, Cohen and Levinthal (1990: 131) make a case for considering the aspects of absorptive capacity that are 'distinctly organizational.' Moreover, since absorptive capacity is dependent on the knowledge bases of all actors involved, also dyad and network characteristics have been identified. An overview of the antecedents of absorptive capacity is provided in Table 13.4.

Table 13.4   Antecedents of absorptive capacity

Knowledge Characteristics	
Prior related knowledge	Bierly et al. (2009); Cockburn and Henderson (1998); Cohen and Levinthal (1989; 1990); Lane and Lubatkin (1998); Lane et al. (2001); Pennings and Harianto (1992); Shane (2000); Van den Bosch et al. (1999)
Technological overlap/similarity	Mowery et al. (1996); Lane et al (2001)
Knowledge richness vs. diversity	Almeida and Phene (2004); Argyres and Silverman (2004); Katila and Ahuja (2002); Leiponen and Helfat (2009); Zhang et al. (2007a)
Complexity of knowledge	Argote and Ingram (2000); Kotabe et al. (2007)
Tacitness of knowledge	Li et al. (2010)
Organizational characteristics	
Organizational structure	Cohen and Levinthal (1990); Van den Bosch et al. (1999); Yayavaram and Ahuja (2008)

(Continued)

Table 13.4   (*Continued*)

Organizational characteristics	
Centrality of R&D	Argyres and Silverman (2004); Zhang et al. (2007b)
Formalization	Jansen et al. (2005)
Communication	Cohen and Levinthal (1990); Minbaeva et al. (2003)
Corporate information provision	Lenox and King (2004)
Boundary-spanning	Cohen and Levinthal (1990); Cross and Cummings (2004); Easterby-Smith et al. (2008);
Combinative capabilities	Jansen et al. (2005); Van den Bosch et al. (1999)
Coordination mechanisms	Jansen et al. (2005)
Incentives	Cockburn and Henderson (1998); Minbaeva et al. (2003)
Strategic posture/entrepreneurial orientation	Bierly et al. (2009)
Financial leverage	Bierly et al. (2009)
Power	Easterby-Smith et al. (2008)
Socialization mechanisms	Björkman et al (2004); Jansen et al. (2005)
Flexibility	Lane et al. (2001)
Training	Lane et al. (2001); Lyles and Salk (1996); Matusik and Heeley (2005); Minbaeva et al. (2003)
Network characteristics	
Type of alliance	Arora and Gambardella (1990); Nicholls-Nixon and Woo (2003); Steensma and Corley (2000)
Similarity of compensation practices	Lane and Lubatkin (1998)
Similarity of dominant logics	Lane and Lubatkin (1998)
Similarity of organizational structure	Lane and Lubatkin (1998)
Bridging ties/brokerage	Cockburn and Henderson (1998); Li et al. (2010); McEvily and Zaheer (1999)
Bonding ties/connectedness	Cockburn and Henderson (1998); McEvily and Marcus (2005)
Trust	Dhanaraj et al (2004); Lane et al (2001); Li et al. (2010)
Shared vision/goals	Gupta and Govindarajan (2000); Li et al. (2010); Nahapiet and Ghoshal (1998)
Geographic proximity	Frost (2001); Zucker et al (1998)
Cultural compatibility	Gupta and Govindarajan (2000); Lane et al. (2001)

Knowledge characteristics. The basic tenet of Cohen and Levinthal's (1990) argument is that absorptive capacity is dependent on the level of prior related knowledge. Studies abound underscoring this notion at the unit and firm level (Bogner and Bansal, 2007; Helfat, 1997; Lane et al., 2001; Shane, 2000; Van den Bosch et al., 1999). Firms and units endowed with knowledge and expertise within a domain will more easily learn new knowledge in that domain and closely related domains. In that sense, 'accumulating absorptive capacity in one period will permit its more efficient accumulation in the next' (Cohen and Levinthal, 1990: 136). The efficiency and performance benefits derived from the cumulative quality of absorptive capacity lead firms and units to build on existing knowledge in domains relevant to current operations. The caveat of being driven by prior related knowledge is that firms and units may come to search locally and neglect domains that are less relevant and familiar (Stuart and Podolny, 1996; Van den Bosch et al., 1999).

The notion that absorptive capacity is dependent on a relevant knowledge base highlights the importance of considering the richness and diversity of knowledge (cf. Almeida and Phene, 2004; Zahra and George, 2002; Zhang et al., 2007b). Knowledge richness represents the depth and the extent of knowledge in domains. Knowledge diversity reflects the breadth and number of domains in which a firm or unit has knowledge. As Cohen and Levinthal argue (1990: 131; italics added), 'learning *performance* will be greatest when the object of learning is related to what is already known . . . [while] a diverse background . . . increases the *prospect* that incoming information will relate to what is already known.' Thus, both knowledge richness and knowledge diversity interact to determine in which domains a firm or unit can potentially learn and how well it can do so. Indeed, studies have empirically shown that technological relatedness increases a firm's ability to absorb new knowledge (e.g. Bierly et al., 2009; Mowery et al., 1996). Since efficiency and strategic considerations marshal firms and units to emphasize the most relevant related domains, relatedness deepens and enriches a firm's knowledge base and reduces its diversity.

Since units are main entry points for knowledge, firms wishing to absorb knowledge and develop absorptive capacity require interfaces between units and external constituents as well as across units. An important side effect of the path dependent nature of absorptive capacity is that units may come to experience difficulty to share knowledge with peer units as they diverge in developing their own knowledge bases. Cohen and Levinthal (1990) make, therefore, a distinction between outward-looking and inward-looking absorptive capacity. Outward-looking absorptive capacity facilitates externally-driven research and development and the potential to absorb knowledge, whereas inward-looking absorptive capacity fosters internal research and development and the realization of absorptive capacity into exploited knowledge (cf. Nagarajan and Mitchell, 1998; Nicholls-Nixon and Woo, 2003; Rothaermel and Alexandre, 2009; Zahra and George, 2002). Firms need to maintain a delicate balance between both as 'excessive dominance by one or the other will be dysfunctional' (Cohen and Levinthal, 1990: 133).

Cohen and Levinthal (1990: 134) argue that the 'ideal knowledge structure for an organizational subunit should reflect only partially overlapping knowledge complemented by nonoverlapping diverse knowledge.' Knowledge may be differentiated into different types. Prior related knowledge is not only characterized by substantive technological and product knowledge, but also by basic skills, learning skills, problem solving methods, prior learning experiences, and a shared language. In that sense, that two units in a diversified firm pursuing two seemingly unrelated technologies may be able to acquire knowledge from each other if they have a shared language and operate using similar problem-solving methods. Likewise, units may have unrelated technological knowledge but may have similar market and managerial knowledge and capabilities that provide an anchor for learning new, non-overlapping knowledge (cf. Sammara and Biggiero, 2008). Henderson and Cockburn (1996) found a positive effect of the knowledge held by a firm in one research domain on the knowledge developed in technologically related domains as well as on the number of research domains pursued by firms.

Intensity of effort is required if a firm or unit seeks to acquire non-overlapping knowledge and to develop absorptive capacity beyond domains it is familiar with and in which it has prior knowledge (Cohen and Levinthal, 1990; Kim, 1998). When knowledge is complex and comprised of multiple interconnected components, firms and units will experience difficulty acquiring and using such knowledge (Levitt and March, 1988). However, if some of these knowledge components are shared or can be understood through analogical reasoning they may be able to gradually understand knowledge that is completely new to them (Gavetti et al., 2005). Learning beyond familiar domains with the aim to create new knowledge is most effective at the individual level. Matusik and Heeley (2005) found that individual absorptive capacities are more likely to lead to the creation of new knowledge, whereas collective knowledge is more prone to the extension of existing knowledge. Similarly, Argote and Ingram (2000) argue that transferring knowledge from one site to another will be more effective if accompanied by moving people. People are more capable of adapting knowledge to the new context as their knowledge of how to use the transferred knowledge is interconnected. Consequently, characteristics of the knowledge to be transferred illustrate that firm absorptive capacity is dependent on the interplay between individuals and units as well as the links between them (see also Figure 13.1).

Organizational characteristics. Since the distribution of knowledge cannot be untied from the organization, Cohen and Levinthal (1990) argue that absorptive capacity is dependent on a set of organizational characteristics. Van den Bosch et al. (1999) found that organizational form influences absorptive capacity in that organizations with mechanistic properties are more likely to be efficient in absorbing knowledge, while organic organizations enjoy benefits in the scope and flexibility of knowledge absorption. In mechanistic organizations, organizational processes are formalized, which allows firms to exploit knowledge and realize absorptive capacity (Jansen et al., 2005), and research and development is more likely to be centralized, which leads to a broadening of knowledge and capabilities (Argyres and Silverman, 2004) and under stable environmental conditions enables firms to build on existing knowledge efficiently (Cohen and Levinthal, 1990; Van den Bosch et al., 1999). In organic organizations, local managers are closely located to action and are more likely to participate in decision making, which allows them to adapt to new circumstances and develop absorptive capacity (Gavetti, 2005; Jansen et al., 2005). In other words, firms that seek to develop absorptive capacity both to build on existing knowledge and to create new knowledge require both mechanistic and organic characteristics.

Consistent with Van den Bosch et al. (1999), Yayavaram and Ahuja (2008) found that a nearly decomposable knowledge base, which is characterized by clusters of knowledge which are connected and integrated by ties, is most advantageous when it comes to useful inventions, and they discuss how such knowledge bases can be created. Since knowledge bases should be viewed as networks of knowledge elements in which the ties are as important as the elements themselves, they argue that organization structures should permit differentiation across clusters and include integration mechanisms, such as personnel transfers across units, gatekeepers, and rewards for cross-unit innovations. Since 'firms are constrained to local search due to cognitive limitations and the lack of absorptive capacity required for long "jumps", . . . integration between clusters ensures that local moves at the level of a cluster can lead to adaptive walks that span cluster boundaries' (2008: 357).

Indeed, the evidence that mechanisms facilitating integration between individuals and units contribute to absorptive capacity is strongly growing. Creating a mosaic of links between individuals and units enables them (1) to realize that knowledge they assimilated is transformed and exploited (Rothaermel and Alexandre, 2009; Zahra and George, 2002), (2) to enlist others to absorb knowledge in case the knowledge is unrelated to their existing knowledge base, and (3) to relieve others from evaluating and assimilating knowledge (Cohen and Levinthal, 1990). An important way in which firms achieve integration is through their combinative capabilities (Kogut and Zander, 1992). To understand the impact of combinative capabilities on absorptive capacity, Jansen et al. (2005) and Van den Bosch et al. (1999) differentiate between system, coordination, and socialization capabilities. Based on two case studies, Van den Bosch et al. (1999) found that systems capabilities drive the efficiency at which firms absorb knowledge, whereas coordination and socialization capabilities foster the scope and flexibility in which firms absorb knowledge. Jansen et al. (2005) found that different types of combinative capabilities influence the different capabilities and dimensions constituting absorptive capacity. Specifically, they found that coordination capabilities, as manifested by cross-functional interfaces, participation in decision making, and job rotation, mostly influence the acquisition and assimilation of knowledge and a small portion of transformation of knowledge. Socialization capabilities, such as connectedness and socialization mechanisms, were found to be better predictors of the transformation and exploitation of knowledge. The effect of systems capabilities was more complex in that formalization contributed strongly to the exploitation of knowledge, but routinization had a negative impact on acquisition, assimilation, and transformation.

The study of Jansen et al. (2005) is one of the few exceptions having sought to understand the antecedents of the different capabilities or dimensions that make up absorptive capacity. Most studies empirically differentiating the capabilities constituting absorptive capacity have made a distinction between the transfer of knowledge from an outside source to the firm and the application of that knowledge, which are broadly understood as potential and realized absorptive capacity respectively (Bierly et al., 2009; Minbaeva et al., 2003; Mowery et al., 1996). Others have made a distinction between the three capabilities constituting absorptive capacity initially forwarded by Cohen and Levinthal (1990), and underscored that each capability requires discrete organizational processes and that using broad dimensions may be suboptimal (Lane et al., 2001). An important insight gained from these studies is that training fosters the ability to assimilate and acquire knowledge (Lyles and Salk, 1996; Minbaeva et al., 2003), and that competence in training facilitated the commercial application of that knowledge (Lane et al., 2001). Training extends and alters organizational members' knowledge bases, which enables them to assimilate knowledge they were previously not familiar with. Competence in training increases the efficacy in which firms and units are able to have organizational members understand, retain, and apply knowledge that is complex and causally ambiguous. The ability to acquire and assimilate knowledge is further enhanced by the degree of flexibility in adapting to changing circumstances and contexts (Lane et al., 2001). A firm's ability to transform and apply knowledge is dependent on internal communication between units and individuals (Cohen and Levinthal, 1990; Minbaeva et al., 2003), as well as on the strategy pursued by a firm (Lane et al., 2001) and the presence of performance-based compensation schemes and incentives (Minbaeva et al., 2003). Bierly et al. (2009) focused particularly on the antecedents of applying knowledge and made a distinction between exploitation and exploration. They found that financial leverage and the presence of technological capabilities expedites the application of knowledge to exploitative innovations, whereas entrepreneurial orientation fosters the application of knowledge to exploration.

Network characteristics. Lane and Lubatkin (1998) argue that absorptive capacity is not absolute but essentially relative, and should be considered at the dyad level since the capacity for learning is dependent on characteristics of the interacting parties involved. They found that absolute absorptive capacity as measured by research and development intensity has limited explanatory power as a predictor of knowledge absorption. Correspondingly, Dyer and Singh (1998) argued that absorptive capacity is inherently partner-specific. A firm or unit may have a substantial knowledge base, but its ability to learn from its partner depends on whether part of that knowledge base overlaps with the knowledge base of its partner (Lane et al., 2001; Mowery et al., 1996). In their study of research and development alliances between pharmaceutical and biotechnology firms, Lane and Lubatkin (1998) found that knowledge overlap determines a firm's ability to learn but that the effect of knowledge overlap is limited to overlap in basic knowledge of biochemistry since overlap in specialized knowledge had no effect. Overlap in basic knowledge facilitates the valuation of external knowledge extending or related to biochemistry. A specialized knowledge base is more likely to be rich and deep and overlap limits the opportunity set of firms to learn new knowledge. Corroborating this notion, Kotabe et al. (2007) found that the relative quality of knowledge has a positive impact on knowledge transfer, whereas a firm's absolute quality of knowledge diminishes knowledge transfer. Instead, the presence of a qualitatively extensive knowledge base leads to more innovation. Moreover, their evidence shows that prior experience with knowledge transfer contributes strongly to both knowledge transfer and innovation. Prior experience with knowledge transfer may serve as a template that shapes firms' ability to obtain and apply knowledge to innovation, even when such knowledge is unrelated to existing knowledge.

Along with prior knowledge, firms and units need in place similar knowledge processing systems to facilitate knowledge absorption, especially when such knowledge is new and dissimilar to existing knowledge. In keeping with Cohen and Levinthal's (1990) original argument that absorptive capacity has elements that are typically organizational, Lane et al. (2001) and Lane and Lubatkin (1998) also studied organizational characteristics at the dyad level. Lane et al. (2001) found a positive effect of trust and cultural compatibility, in addition to related knowledge bases, on the ability to understand knowledge. However, these effects disappeared when other antecedents were included in the model. Lane and Lubatkin (1998) found that similarities in lower management formalization, in centralization of research and development, and in compensation practices facilitate the assimilation of knowledge. The degree of upper management formalization and management centralization were, on the other hand, found to have a negative effect. These findings are in line with other studies that found that since local managers are more closely located to the action they should be able to participate in decision-making processes so that they can monitor the environment and broaden a firm's knowledge base (Gavetti, 2005; Jansen et al., 2005), while centralizing research and development enriches and deepens knowledge (Argyres and Silverman, 2004; Cohen and Levinthal, 1990). When firms or units are similar with regard to these organizational aspects, communication and understanding between them is facilitated. Altogether, current insights obtained from dyad level studies seem to substantiate that similarities in knowledge mainly influence the ability to evaluate knowledge, whereas organizational characteristics facilitate the assimilation and commercialization of knowledge.

In addition to examining the similarities and differences between pairs of firms, studies have assessed the effect of network-level characteristics (see Chapter 22 by Van Wijk et al. for an overview). A common approach in such studies is to distinguish between the structural, relational, and cognitive elements of the networks in which firms and units operate and from which they derive social capital (Adler and Kwon, 2002; Nahapiet and Ghoshal, 1998). Firms and units with a structurally central position in the network possess information benefits in that they have ties and access to redundant and non-redundant knowledge and are able to bridge these ties. For example, Cockburn and Henderson (1998) found that absorptive capacity is driven not only by internal basic research but also by the connectedness of researchers to a wide external community of other researchers. While redundant knowledge overlaps with existing knowledge, a non-redundant tie increases the range, novelty, and diversity of knowledge to which a firm or unit has access. By balancing redundant and non-redundant knowledge, firms and units receive valuable knowledge and know how to apply such knowledge to rewarding opportunities (McEvily and Zaheer, 1999).

While the ties reaped by a strong structural position in the network facilitate the transfer of non-complex, explicit knowledge, they are too weak for the transfer of complex, tacit knowledge (Hansen, 1999; Li et al., 2010). Firms and units also need strong relational and bonding ties characterized by trust. Trust facilitates knowledge absorption because it shapes the confidence of the recipient that the knowledge of the source is reliable and valuable, and increases its willingness to extend its efforts in absorbing the knowledge. Consequently, strong relational ties enable joint problem solving and the gradual learning of new and often tacitly held knowledge (McEvily and Marcus, 2005).

The ease with which new, unrelated knowledge can be understood, acquired, and applied is ameliorated by cognitive social capital, which manifests itself in the presence of a shared language, shared goals, and shared systems (Nahapiet and Ghoshal, 1998). While shared systems and a shared language facilitate understanding and acquiring new knowledge (cf. Cohen and Levinthal, 1990), shared goals allow firms and units to understand how knowledge consisting of multiple interconnected components can be applied. Marking the presence of shared values, cultural compatibility also has a positive effect on firms' abilities to absorb knowledge, although Lane et al. (2001) found that its effect is smaller than the effect of related knowledge bases. In the same vein, geographic proximity has been found to positively relate to the capacity to absorb knowledge (Frost, 2001; Gupta and Govindarajan, 2000). Geographic proximity enhances the strength of ties as opportunities to interact with partners are multifold. In that sense, Feinberg and Gupta (2004) found that the decision of MNCs to locate research and development in local subsidiaries is driven by potential knowledge spillovers in local markets.

Finally, prior research has examined the role of the type and governance structure of the collaboration. Li et al. (2010) found that formal contracts not only assist firms in the acquisition of explicit knowledge, but also govern the effect of shared goals and trust on knowledge acquisition. Arora and Gambardella (1990) suggest that firms seeking to access basic knowledge and to keep track of technological developments in domains in which they lack internal knowledge enjoy efficiency benefits if they enter into non-equity alliances with universities and minority equity investments in other firms. Non-equity agreements with other firms are effectively used to access products that are ready for commercialization.

Moderators and Absorptive Capacity as a Moderator

In recent years, studies have emerged examining moderators of how absorptive capacity relates to its outcomes, as well as the moderating effect of absorptive capacity on how organizational characteristics impact innovation and performance. In particular, studies have shown that the effect of absorptive capacity on innovation and performance is dependent on the environment in which firms operate (Lane et al., 2006; Lim, 2009). Van den Bosch et al. (1999) found that in a stable environment firms draw more exploitative innovations from their absorptive capacity since they are more likely to build on existing knowledge and increase the efficiency of knowledge absorption. In turbulent environments scope and flexibility of absorptive capacity are more important as they allow a firm to combine diverse knowledge and pursue exploratory innovations. Moreover, firms are more likely to decentralize their interface with the external environment to units, which increases the diversity of knowledge a firm can tap into and renders cross-functional relations more important (Cohen and Levinthal, 1990; Jones and Craven, 2001). Lichtenthaler (2009) distinguishes between technological and market turbulence has not found a moderating effect on the relation between the distinct dimensions of absorptive capacity and innovation. In contrast, his findings suggest that the effect of absorptive capacity on performance increases as market turbulence and, to a lesser degree, technological turbulence increase.

Following Cohen and Levinthal's (1990) argument, appropriability regimes faced by firms and other aspects influencing appropriability have been forwarded as moderating factors (Hurmelinna-Laukkanen and Blomqvist, 2007; Lane et al., 2006). Zahra and George (2002) argue that under a strong regime of appropriability realized absorptive capacity is likely to have a stronger effect on sustainable competitive advantage than in low appropriability regimes, because rivals will face higher costs imitating knowledge and internalizing knowledge spillovers. Unless they face no danger of exogenous spillovers or form a research joint venture, competing firms choose distinct research approaches to offset spillovers and to limit diffusion of knowledge to other firms (Kamien and Zang, 2000), especially when absorptive capacity effects are weak (Grünfeld, 2003). However, competing firms tend to adopt similar research and development approaches if the probability grows that their connectedness increases, which subsequently reduces appropriability concerns (Lim, 2009; Wiethaus, 2005). Another issue influencing the appropriability of knowledge is whether knowledge is tacit or not. Bierly et al. (2009) show that the more knowledge is tacit the more the effect of technological competence and prior experience on exploratory and exploitative innovation increases. Similarly, based on two case studies, Van den Bosch et al. (1999) illustrate that systems capabilities enable the combination of explicit knowledge across organizational units, while coordination and socialization capabilities enable the externalization of tacit knowledge.

Recently, studies have shown that absorptive capacity acts as a moderator itself. For example, Escribano et al. (2009) and Tsai (2009) have assessed absorptive capacity as a moderator of how knowledge flow between partners influences innovative performance. Similarly, Rothaermel and Alexandre (2009) found that absorptive capacity not only permits a firm to pursue ambidexterity in technology sourcing, but also enables it to capture more innovation and performance benefits resulting from that ambidexterity. Similarly, social network studies show and imply that the effect of social capital on innovativeness is moderated by absorptive capacity. Firms may have a substantial or strong social network from which they derive social capital, they also need a prior knowledge base if they seek to learn from the actors in their network (Reagans and McEvily, 2003; Tsai, 2009). Moreover, a social network not only provides firms with the opportunity to access outside knowledge, but also aids in acting on that knowledge (Obstfeld, 2005). Indeed, Kotabe et al. (2010) found that the ability to transform and exploit knowledge (realized absorptive capacity) increases the effect of knowledge acquisition through ties on new product performance. However, since research grows showing how positions in a social network are antecedent to absorptive capacity, it calls into question whether absorptive capacity is driven by social networks or whether it is a condition determining the efficacy with which firms deploy their social networks to innovate and become competitive.

PROGRESS, PROBLEMS, AND PROSPECTS

More than two decades after the publication of Cohen and Levinthal's (1989, 1990) seminal studies, an astounding number of studies has appeared taking absorptive capacity as one of the building blocks. Because of conceptual and methodological problems and challenges, studies have also sought to refine, reconceptualize, reify, and even rejuvenate the construct (Lane et al., 2006; Todorova and Durisin, 2007; Volberda et al., 2010; Zahra and George, 2002). Our review illustrates that, even though our understanding of the role and value of absorptive capacity has progressed strongly, problems and prospects for future research remain and merit discussion. An overview of the progress, problems, and prospects along the aspects covered in the current review is provided in Table 13.5.

The initial definition of absorptive capacity forwarded by Cohen and Levinthal (1990) has been refined multiple times and is reaching theoretical saturation. Our review of existing research shows that the distinction between potential and realized absorptive capacity has recently been most often applied as it is parsimonious and captures processes of external knowledge acquisition and the internal transformation of that knowledge to commercial ends, which underscores the importance of external and internal research and development (Bierly et al., 2009; Rothaermel and Alexandre, 2009; Zahra and George, 2002). Lane et al.'s (2006) definition revolving around exploratory, transformative, and exploitative learning processes has set the stage for enhancing our understanding of how absorptive capacity may lead to the acquisition and application of new and unrelated knowledge. However, it potentially harbors the predicament that absorptive

Table 13.5   Progress, problems, and future research

	Progress	*Future research*
Definition	High	Creating uniformity
		Definition should not broaden operationalizations
Dimensions	Medium	Consistency in dimensions
Measurement	Low	Consistency in operationalization
		More focus on the nature and type of knowledge stocks and existing knowledge bases for operationalizing absorptive capacity
		Less reliance on R&D-based and patent-based measures as measures of absorptive capacity
		Operationalize different capabilities constituting absorptive capacity separately
		Include measures that capture cumulativeness and learning dynamics of absorptive capacity
Levels of analysis	Low	More focus on individual level and individual absorptive capacity, how relationships between individuals create unit absorptive capacity, and subsequently how inter-unit relations create firm absorptive capacity
		Differentiate effects of absolute and relative absorptive capacity
Outcomes	High	Study the nomological network of absorptive capacity and its outcomes
		Study additional outcomes, such as transfer of different types of knowledge, exploitation vs. exploration, and ambidexterity.
Antecedents	Medium	Studying multiple antecedents to assess their strength
		Linking antecedents at multiple levels of analysis
Moderators	Low	Study the moderating effect of absorptive capacity on relationships of knowledge transfer variables and innovation/performance
		Introduce absorptive capacity as moderator in social network and capital studies

capacity is equated with its outcomes of exploratory and exploitative innovations. March (1991: 85) stated that the 'essence of exploration is experimentation with new alternatives,' whereas the 'essence of exploitation is the refinement and extension of existing competences.' Firms may acquire external knowledge they did not previously possess, but such knowledge may also refine existing knowledge and be more exploitative in nature. If

necessary at all, the exploratory learning process is limited to developing in-house expertise and problem solving that complements the activities of its partners prior to acquiring their knowledge (Mowery et al., 1996). Nevertheless, empirical studies have shown
that the capabilities underlying absorptive capacity are distinct organizational processes
and should be studied separately (e.g. Camisón and Forés, 2010; Jansen et al., 2005;
Lichtenthaler, 2009). Hence, future studies would benefit from differentiating the distinct
capabilities constituting absorptive capacity.

A side effect of the elusive nature of the construct is that it has not only hampered its
conceptualization, but also obfuscated its measurement in that studies have adopted absorptive capacity as a building block without questioning its scope and its relationship to other
constructs. Prior studies have pursued a wide variety of ways to measure absorptive capacity, but tend to use research and development-based measures. However, our review of the
insights gained so far indicates that using research and development intensity as a gauge for
absorptive capacity does not pay credit to the richness of the construct (Lane and Lubatkin,
1998; Lane et al., 2006; Mowery et al., 1996). As a remedy, studies have also relied on patent-based measures, experience-based measures, and scales. While these measures proxy a
firm's knowledge stock, they do not necessarily correlate with each other, with research and
development-based measures and with their antecedents and outcomes. For example, if firm
size is an antecedent of absorptive capacity and net earnings an outcome, the mediating
effect of absorptive capacity will be substantially stronger if it is measured using research and
development expenditures or patent stocks instead of using a measure assessing prior experience. There is no general agreement on how to measure absorptive capacity. More precise
measures are hence needed which more accurately capture the type and nature of a firm's
knowledge stock, and appraise the different capabilities underlying absorptive capacity.

A crucial way to deal with the operationalization issue and to advance research in general is to study the microfoundations of absorptive capacity (Gavetti, 2005; Lewin et al.,
2010). First, future research merits from including multiple levels of analysis in studying
absorptive capacity. Because individuals and people play a principal role in adapting and
absorbing knowledge (Argote and Ingram, 2000; Cohen and Levinthal, 1990; Lane et al.,
2006), further studies on the role of individuals and their subnetworks and on the interplay of absorptive capacity at the individual, unit, firm, and network level are needed.
Absorptive capacity of a unit is dependent on the knowledge stocks of individual members and on ties between them. In turn, firm absorptive capacity is dependent on unit
knowledge stocks and on the links between units. Considering the nature and type of
individual knowledge stocks as well as the tie and network correlates of individuals (cf.
Cross and Cummings, 2004) would more precisely uncover how the absorptive capacity
of units and firms is developed. Multilevel studies would also be able to uncover the antecedents and outcomes at various levels as well as interactions among them.

Second, future research would benefit from assessing the relative value of absolute and
relative absorptive capacity, preferably in conjunction with analyses for actors at multiple
levels of analysis. Absolute absorptive capacity centers on the presence of existing knowledge *per se* and explains the opportunity set of actors to acquire and assimilate knowledge.
In contrast, relative absorptive capacity revolves around knowledge similarities and technological overlap between interacting actors and explains whether they are able to absorb
knowledge in specific dyads and networks. However, in the context of alliances, Hoang
and Rothaermel (2005) examined the effect of general and partner-specific alliance experience, and found that general experience is a stronger predictor of alliance success.

Third, the nomological network surrounding absorptive capacity should be further disentangled. In addition to being a function of prior knowledge, absorptive capacity is dependent on organizational characteristics and cannot be detached from organizational structure (Cohen and Levinthal, 1990). However, if a firm's structure is part of its absorptive capacity, then, for example, so are the social networks creating that structure and it becomes inherently difficult to differentiate organization from absorptive capacity. It underscores the importance of considering absorptive capacity at multiple levels of analysis, as organizational structure does influence individual and unit knowledge stocks. Similarly, studies have assessed how combinative capabilities contribute to a firm's absorptive capacity (e.g. Jansen et al., 2005; Van den Bosch et al., 1999). However, as both emphasize firm's ability to synthesize and apply knowledge, both are dependent on internal and external interfaces, and both ultimately lead to new and refined capabilities, one may be equal, form a subset, or be antecedent to another. Uncovering the nomological network of absorptive capacity would also aid studies examining whether firms can acquire absorptive capacity through acquisitions, alliances, and hiring new employees from competing firms. Cohen and Levinthal (1990) argue that such means are suboptimal because knowledge is often routine-based, tacit, and firm specific, and cannot be easily integrated in the firm. In contrast, Rosenkopf and Almeida (2003) and Song et al. (2003) found that firms hiring employees from others are able to produce innovations that depend on new and unrelated knowledge. Such ability is, however, likely dependent on how new employees are integrated and how their knowledge gradually develops the knowledge of the hiring firm.

Finally, the development of dynamic models is needed. Absorptive capacity is cumulative and essentially a dynamic process. Learning in one period will increase the stock of knowledge and improve learning in the subsequent period (Cohen and Levinthal, 1989, 1990). Studies have shown complementary knowledge and capabilities may be instrumental in creating innovations (Helfat, 1997; Nagarajan and Mitchell, 1998). However, complementary knowledge does not necessarily have to be related to existing knowledge. Longitudinal studies may uncover how firms make local moves to acquire knowledge in domains in which they do not possess previous knowledge.

Based on a review of existing insights, our chapter sought to identify the central problems in absorptive capacity research and forward promising prospects for future research. Our review will hopefully motivate researchers into further developing the absorptive capacity construct and advance the field of absorptive capacity in a more coherent way. The problems identified will hopefully encourage future research in examining additional antecedents and outcomes of absorptive capacity at multiple levels of analysis to get a better grasp of how firms develop their knowledge base and how they apply it to innovation.

REFERENCES

Adler, P.S. and Kwon, S-W. (2002) Social capital: Prospects for a new concept. *Academy of Management Review*, 27 (1): 17–40.

Ahuja, G. (2000) The duality of collaboration: Inducements and opportunities in the formation of interfirm linkages. *Strategic Management Journal*, 21(3): 317–343.

Ahuja, G. and Katila, R. (2001) Technological acquisitions and the innovation performance of acquiring firms: A longitudinal study. *Strategic Management Journal*, 22(3): 197–220.

Almeida, P. and Phene, A. (2004) Subsidiaries and knowledge creation: The influence of the MNC and host country on innovation. *Strategic Management Journal*, 25(8/9): 847–864.

Argote, L. and Ingram, P. (2000) Knowledge transfer: A basis for competitive advantage in firms. *Organizational Behavior and Human Decision Processes*, 82(1): 150–169.

Argyres, N.S. and Silverman, B.S. (2004) R&D, organization structure, and the development of corporate technological knowledge. *Strategic Management Journal*, 25(8/9): 929–958.

Arora, A. and Gambardella, A. (1990) Complementarity and external linkages: The strategies of the large firms in biotechnology. *Journal of Industrial Economics*, 38(4): 361–379.

Arora, A. and Gambardella, A. (1994) Evaluating technological information and utilizing it. *Journal of Economic Behavior and Organization*, 24(1): 91–114.

Bergh, D.D. and Lim, E.N. (2008) Learning how to restructure: Absorptive capacity and improvisational views of restructuring actions and performance. *Strategic Management Journal*, 29(6): 593–616.

Bierly, P.E., Damanpour, F., and Santoro, M.D. (2009) The application of external knowledge: Organizational conditions for exploration and exploitation. *Journal of Management Studies*, 46(3): 481–509.

Björkman, I., Barner-Rasmussen, W., and Li, L. (2004) Managing knowledge transfer in MNCs: The impact of headquarters control mechanisms. *Journal of International Business Studies*, 35(5): 443–455.

Bogner, W.C. and Bansal, P. (2007) Knowledge management as the basis of sustained high performance. *Journal of Management Studies*, 44(1): 165–188.

Camisón, C. and Forés, B. (2010) Knowledge absorptive capacity: New insights for its conceptualization and measurement. *Journal of Business Research*, 63(7): 707–715.

Cassiman, B. and Veugelers, R. (2006) In search of complementarity in innovation strategy: Internal R&D and external knowledge acquisition. *Management Science*, 52(1): 68–82.

Cattani, G. (2005) Preadaptation, firm heterogeneity, and technological performance: A study on the evolution of fiber optics, 1970–1995. *Organization Science*, 16(6): 563–580.

Cockburn, I.M. and Henderson, R.M. (1998) Absorptive capacity, coauthoring behavior, and the organization of research in drug discovery. *Journal of Industrial Economics*, 46(2): 157–183.

Cohen, W.M. and Levinthal, D.A. (1989) Innovation and learning: The two faces of R&D. *The Economic Journal*, 99(397): 569–596.

Cohen, W.M., and Levinthal, D.A. (1990) Absorptive capacity: A new perspective on learning and innovation. *Administrative Science Quarterly*, 35(1): 128–152.

Cohen, W.M., and Levinthal, D.A. (1994) Fortune favors the prepared firm. *Management Science*, 40(2): 227–251.

Cross, R. and Cummings, J.N. (2004) Tie and network correlates of individual performance in knowledge-intensive work. *Academy of Management Journal*, 47(6): 928–937.

Deeds, D.L. (2001) The role of R&D intensity, technical development and absorptive capacity in creating entrepreneurial wealth in high technology start-ups. *Journal of Engineering and Technology Management*, 18(1): 29–47.

Dushnitsky, G. and Lenox, M.J. (2005) When do firms undertake R&D by investing in new ventures? *Strategic Management Journal*, 26(10): 947–965.

Dyer, J.H. and Singh, H. (1998) The relational view: Cooperative strategy and sources of interorganizational competitive advantage. *Academy of Management Review*, 23(4): 660–679.

Easterby-Smith, M.P.V., Graca, M., Antonacopoulou, E., and Ferdinand, J. (2008) Absorptive capacity: A process perspective. *Management Learning*, 39(5): 483–501.

Ellis, H.C. (1965) *The transfer of learning*. New York: MacMillan.

Ernst, H. (1998) Industrial research as a source of important patents. *Research Policy*, 27(1): 1–15.

Escribano, A., Fosfuri, A., and Tribo, J.A. (2009) Managing external knowledge flows: The moderating role of absorptive capacity. *Research Policy*, 38(1): 96–105.

Feinberg, S.E. and Gupta, A.K. (2004) Knowledge spillovers and the assignment of R&D responsibilities to foreign subsidiaries. *Strategic Management Journal*, 25(8/9): 823–845.

Frost, T.S. (2001) The geographic sources of foreign subsidiaries' innovations. *Strategic Management Journal*, 22(2): 101–123.

Frost, T.S. and Zhou, C. (2005) R&D co-practice and 'reverse' knowledge integration in multinational firms. *Journal of International Business Studies*, 36(6): 676–687.

Gavetti, G. (2005) Cognition and hierarchy: Rethinking the microfoundations of capabilities' development. *Organization Science*, 16(6): 599–617.

Gavetti, G., Levinthal , D.A., and Rivkin, J.W. (2005) Strategy making in novel and complex worlds: The power of analogy. *Strategic Management Journal*, 26(8): 691–712.

Grünfeld, L.A. (2003) Meet me halfway but don't rush: Absorptive capacity and R&D investment revisited. *International Journal of Industrial Organization*, 21(8): 1091–1109.

Gupta, A.K. and Govindarajan, V. (2000) Knowledge flows within multinational corporations. *Strategic Management Journal*, 21(4): 473–496.

Haas, M. (2006) Acquiring and applying knowledge in transnational teams: The roles of cosmopolitans and locals. *Organization Science*, 17(3): 367–384.

Hansen, M.T. (1999) The search-transfer problem: The role of weak ties in sharing knowledge across organization subunits. *Administrative Science Quarterly*, 44(1): 82–111.

Helfat, C. (1997) Know-how and asset complementarity and dynamic capability accumulation: The case of R&D. *Strategic Management Journal*, 18(5): 339–360.

Henderson, R. and Cockburn, I. (1996) Scale, scope and spillovers: The determinants of research productivity in ethical drug discovery. *Rand Journal of Economics*, 27(1): 32–59.

Hoang, H. and Rothaermel, F.T. (2005) The effect of general and partner-specific experience on joint R&D project performance. *Academy of Management Journal*, 48(2): 332–345.

Hurmelinna-Laukkanen, P. and Blomqvist, K. (2007) Fostering R&D collaboration: The interplay of trust, appropriability, and absorptive capacity. *Advances in Information and Communication Technology*, 243: 15–22.

Jaffe, A.B., Trajtenberg, M., and Henderson, R. (1993) Geographic localization of knowledge spillovers as evidenced by patent citations *Quarterly Journal of Economics*, 108(3): 577–598.

Jansen, J.J.P., Van den Bosch, F.A.J., and Volberda, H.W. (2005) Managing potential and realized absorptive capacity: How do organizational antecedents matter? *Academy of Management Journal*, 48(6): 999–1015.

Jones, O. and Craven, M. (2001) Expanding capabilities in a mature manufacturing firm: Absorptive capacity and the TCS. *International Small Business Journal*, 19(3): 39–55.

Kamien, M.I. and Zang, I. (2000) Meet me halfway: Research joint ventures and absorptive capacity. *International Journal of Industrial Organization*, 18(7): 995–1012.

Katila, R. and Ahuja, G. (2002) Something old, something new: A longitudinal study of search behavior and new product introduction. *Academy of Management Journal*, 45(6): 1183–1194.

Kedia, B.L. and Bhagat, R.S. (1988) Cultural constraints in transfer of technology across nations: Implications for research in international and comparative management. *Academy of Management Review*, 13(4): 559–571.

Keller, W. (1996) Absorptive capacity: On the creation and acquisition of technology in development. *Journal of Development Economics*, 49(1): 199–227.

Kim, L. (1998) Crisis construction and organizational learning: Capability building in catching-up at Hyundai Motor. *Organization Science*, 9(4): 506–521.

Kogut, B. and Zander, U. (1992) Knowledge of the firm, integration capabilities, and the replication of technology. *Organization Science*, 3(3): 383–397.

Kotabe, M., Dunlap-Hinkler, D., Parente, R., and Mishra, H.A. (2007) Determinants of cross-national knowledge transfer and its effect on firm innovation. *Journal of International Business Studies*, 38(2): 259–282.

Kotabe, M., Jiang, C.X., and Murray, J.Y. (2010). Managerial ties, knowledge acquisition, realized absorptive capacity and new product market performance of emerging multi-national companies: A case of China. *Journal of World Business*, 45: in press.

Koza, M.P. and Lewin, A.Y. (1998) The coevolution of strategic alliances. *Organization Science*, 9(3): 255–264.

Kusunoki, K., Nonaka, I., and Nagata, A. (1998) Organizational capabilities in product development of Japanese firms: A conceptual framework and empirical findings. *Organization Science*, 9(6): 699–718.

Lane, P.J., Koka, B.R., and Pathak, S. (2006) The reification of absorptive capacity: A critical review and rejuvenation of the construct. *Academy of Management Review*, 31(4): 833–863.

Lane, P.J. and Lubatkin, M. (1998) Relative absorptive capacity and inter-organizational learning. *Strategic Management Journal*, 19(5): 461–477.

Lane, P.J., Salk, J.E., and Lyles, M.A. (2001) Absorptive capacity, learning and performance in international joint ventures. *Strategic Management Journal*, 22(12): 1139–1161.

Leiponen, A. and Helfat, C.E. (2009) Innovation objectives, knowledge sources, and the benefits of breadth. *Strategic Management Journal*, 31(2): 224–236.

Lenox, M. and King, A. (2004) Prospects for developing absorptive capacity through internal information provision. *Strategic Management Journal*, 25(4): 331–345.

Levitt, B. and March, J.G. (1988) Organizational learning. *Annual Review of Sociology*, 14: 319–340.

Lewin, A.Y., Massini, S., and Peeters, C. (2010) Microfoundations of internal and external absorptive capacity routines. *Organization Science*, 21: in press.

Li, J.J., Poppo, L., and Zhou, K.Z. (2010) Relational mechanisms, formal contracts, and local knowledge acquisition by international subsidiaries. *Strategic Management Journal*, 31(4): 349–370.

Lichtenthaler, U. (2009) Absorptive capacity, environmental turbulence, and the complementarity of organizational learning processes. *Academy of Management Journal*, 52(4): 822–846.

Lim, K. (2009) The many faces of absorptive capacity: Spillovers of copper interconnect technology for semiconductor chips. *Industrial and Corporate Change*, 18(6): 1249–1284.

Lyles, M.A. and Salk, J.E. (1996) Knowledge acquisition from foreign parents in international joint ventures: An empirical examination in the Hungarian context. *Journal of International Business Studies*, 27(5): 877–904.

Macher, J.T. and Boerner, C.S. (2006) Experience and scale and scope economies: Trade-offs and performance in development. *Strategic Management Journal*, 27(9): 845–865.

March, J.G. (1991) Exploration and exploitation in organizational learning. *Organization Science*, 2(1): 71–78.

Matusik, S.F. and Heeley, M.B. (2005) Absorptive capacity in the software industry: Identifying dimensions that affect knowledge and knowledge creation activities. *Journal of Management*, 31(4): 549–572.

McEvily, B. and Marcus, A. (2005) Embedded ties and the acquisition of competitive capabilities. *Strategic Management Journal*, 26(11): 1033–1055.

McEvily, B. and Zaheer, A. (1999) Bridging ties: A source of firm heterogeneity in competitive capabilities. *Strategic Management Journal*, 20(12): 1133–1156.

Meyer-Krahmer, F. and Reger, G. (1999) New perspectives on the innovation strategies of multinational enterprises: Lessons for technology policy in Europe. *Research Policy*, 28(7): 751–776.

Minbaeva, D., Pedersen, T., Björkman, I., Fey, C.F., and Park, H.J. (2003) MNC knowledge transfer, subsidiary absorptive capacity, and HRM. *Journal of International Business Studies*, 34(6): 586–599.

Mowery, D.C. and Oxley, J.E. (1995) Inward technology transfer and competitiveness: The role of national innovation systems. *Cambridge Journal of Economics*, 19(1): 67–93.

Mowery, D.C., Oxley, J.E., and Silverman, B.S. (1996) Strategic alliances and interfirm knowledge transfer. *Strategic Management Journal*, 17 (Winter special issue): 77–91.

Nagarajan, A. and Mitchell, W. (1998) Evolutionary diffusion: Internal and external methods used to acquire encompassing, complementary, and incremental technological changes in the lithotripsy industry. *Strategic Management Journal*, 19(11): 1063–1077.

Nahapiet, J. and Ghoshal, S. (1998) Social capital, intellectual capital, and the organizational advantage. *Academy of Management Review*, 23(2): 242–266.

Nerkar, A. and Paruchuri, S. (2005) Evolution of R&D capabilities: The role of knowledge networks within a firm. *Management Science*, 51(5): 771–785.

Nicholls-Nixon, C.L. and Woo, C.Y. (2003) Technology sourcing and output of established firms in a regime of encompassing technological change. *Strategic Management Journal*, 24(7): 651–666.

Obstfeld, D. (2005) Social networks, the tertius iungens orientation, and involvement in innovation. *Administrative Science Quarterly*, 50(1): 100–130.

Pennings, J.M. and Harianto, F. (1992) Technological networking and innovation implementation. *Organization Science*, 3(3): 356–382.

Porter, M.E. and Stern, S. (2001) Innovation: Location matters. *Sloan Management Review*, 42 (4): 28–36.

Puranam, P. and Srikanth, K. (2007) What they know vs. what they do: How acquirers leverage technology acquisitions. *Strategic Management Journal*, 28(8): 805–825.

Reagans, R. and McEvily, B. (2003) Network structure and knowledge transfer: The effects of cohesion and range. *Administrative Science Quarterly*, 48(2): 240–267.

Rosenkopf, L. and Almeida, P. (2003) Overcoming local search through alliances and mobility. *Management Science* 49(6): 751–766.

Rosenkopf, L. and Nerkar, A. (2001) Beyond local search: Boundary-spanning, exploration, and impact in the optical disk industry. *Strategic Management Journal*, 22(4): 287–306.

Rothaermel, F.T. and Alexandre, M.T. (2009) Ambidexterity in technology sourcing: The moderating role of absorptive capacity. *Organization Science*, 20(4): 759–780.

Rothaermel, F.T. and Hess, A.M. (2007) Building dynamic capabilities: Innovation driven by individual-, firm-, and network-level effects. *Organization Science*, 18(6): 898–921.

Rothaermel, F.T. and Hill, C.W.L. (2005) Technological discontinuities and complementary assets: A longitudinal study of industry and firm performance. *Organization Science*, 16(1): 52–70.

Sammara, A. and Biggiero, L. (2008) Heterogeneity and specificity of inter-firm knowledge flows in innovation networks. *Journal of Management Studies*, 45(4): 800–829.

Shane, S. (2000) Prior knowledge and the discovery of entrepreneurial opportunities. *Organization Science*, 11(4): 448–469.

Singh, J. (2008) Distributed R&D, cross-regional knowledge integration and quality of innovative output. *Research Policy*, 37 (1): 77–96.

Somaya, D., Williamson, I.O., and Zhang, X. (2007) Combining patent law expertise with R&D for patenting performance. *Organization Science*, 18 6): 922–937.

Song, J., Almeida, P., and Wu, G. (2003) Learning-by-hiring: When is mobility likely to facilitate interfirm knowledge transfer? *Management Science*, 49 (4): 351–365.

Steensma, H.K. and Corley, K.G. (2000) On the performance of technology-sourcing partnerships: The interaction between partner interdependence and technology attributes. *Academy of Management Journal*, 43 (6): 1045–1067.

Stock, G.N., Greis, N.P., and Fischer, W.A. (2001) Absorptive capacity and new product development. *Journal of High Technology Management Research*, 12 (1): 77–91.

Stuart, T.E. and Podolny, J.M. (1996) Local search and the evolution of technological capabilities. *Strategic Management Journal*, 17 (Summer special issue): 21–38.

Subramaniam, M. and Youndt, M.A. (2005) The influence of intellectual capital on the types of innovative capabilities. *Academy of Management Journal*, 48 (3): 450–463.

Szulanski, G. (1996) Exploring internal stickiness: Impediments to the transfer of best practice within the firm. *Strategic Management Journal*, 17 (Winter special issue): 27–43.

Tilton, J.E. (1971) *International diffusion of technology: The case of semiconductors*. Washington DC: Brookings Institution Press.

Todorova, G. and Durisin, B. (2007) Absorptive capacity: Valuing a reconceptualization. *Academy of Management Review*, 32 (3): 774–786.

Tsai, K-H. (2009) Collaborative networks and product innovation performance: Toward a contingency perspective. *Research Policy*, 38 (5): 765–778.

Tsai, W. (2001) Knowledge transfers in intra-organizational networks. *Academy of Management Journal*, 44 (5): 996–1004.

Van Den Bosch, F.A.J., Volberda, H.W. and De Boer, M. (1999) Coevolution of firm absorptive capacity and knowledge environment: Organizational forms and combinative capabilities. *Organization Science*, 10 (5): 551–568.

Van Wijk, R., Jansen, J.J.P., and Lyles, M.A. (2008) Inter- and intra-organizational knowledge transfer: A meta-analytic review and assessment of its antecedents and consequences. *Journal of Management Studies*, 45 (4): 830–853.

Veugelers, R. and Kesteloot, K. (1996) Bargained shares in joint ventures among asymmetric partners: Is the Matthew effect catalyzing? *Journal of Economics*, 64 (1): 23–51.

Volberda, H.W., Foss, N.J., and Lyles, M.A. (2010) Absorbing the concept of absorptive capacity: How to realize its potential in the organization field. *Organization Science*, 21 (4): 931–951.

Wegloop, P. (1995) Linking firm strategy and government action: Towards a resource-based perspective on innovation and technology policy. *Technology in Society*, 17 (4): 413–428.

White, S. and Liu, X. (1998) Organizational processes to meet new performance criteria: Chinese pharmaceutical firms in transition. *Research Policy*, 27 (4): 369–383.

Wiethaus, L. (2005) Absorptive capacity and connectedness: Why competing firms also adopt identical R&D approaches. *International Journal of Industrial Organization*, 23 (5/6): 467–481.

Yayavaram, S. and Ahuja, G. (2008) Decomposability in knowledge structures and its impact on the usefulness of inventions and knowledge-base malleability. *Administrative Science Quarterly*, 53 (2): 333–362.

Zahra, S.A. and George, G. (2002) Absorptive capacity: A review, reconceptualization, and extension. *Academy of Management Review*, 27 (2): 185–203.

Zhang, Y., Li, H., Hitt, M.A., and Cui, G. (2007a) R&D intensity and international joint venture performance in an emerging market: Moderating effects of market focus and ownership structure. *Journal of International Business Studies*, 38: 944–960.

Zhang, J., Baden-Fuller, C., and Mangematin, V. (2007b) Technological knowledge base, R&D organization structure and alliance formation: Evidence from the biopharmaceutical industry. *Research Policy*, 36: 515–528.

14

Social Identity and Organizational Learning

JOHN CHILD AND SUZANA RODRIGUES

ABSTRACT

In this chapter we explore the relevance of social identity for organizational learning. Organizational learning is understood to be the acquisition, conversion, and creation of knowledge aimed at facilitating the attainment of organizational goals. We discuss how the identities that people internalize as members of social groups can impact on the organizational learning process, and how in turn that process can contribute to the evolution of an organization's identity. Nationality and occupation are important sources of social identity in organizations. The range of national and occupational identities found within organizations raises the question of how management can transcend social identity boundaries with the aim of generating collective learning. When this is achieved, its integrative effect can contribute to the development of an organizational identity and at the same time enhance the identification of sub-groups with the organization as an entity. We close by examining the significance for social identity and learning of new organizational forms and networks, which are presenting new challenges for aligning group social identities with the goal of organizational learning.

INTRODUCTION

Writers on organization have recognized the links between identity and learning (Brown and Starkey, 2000). However, with some exceptions such as Rothman and Friedman (2001), identity and learning are often treated as organizational-level phenomena in ways that are ontologically problematic and which oversimplify analysis of the subject. As Edmondson (1999a: 300) has noted, 'an implicit assumption in many accounts of organizational learning is that organizations are undifferentiated entities, such that within-organization variance is immaterial.' Given that organizational learning is a socially constructed process, surprisingly little attention has been paid to the relevance of how organizations are socially constituted in terms of different groups and their identities (Child and Heavens, 2001). Variations in the configuration of group identities, and in their compatibility with what the organization stands for (organizational identity), may well contribute to differences in organizational learning performance.

In order to clarify the links between social identity and organizational learning, we explore the constituent elements of both concepts. We begin by examining social identity and its sources, among which nationality and occupation are particularly relevant to organizations. This leads to a discussion of how social identity bears upon the process of organizational learning. Case examples of diverse occupational and national social identities raise the question of how managerial initiatives can transcend identity boundaries with the aim of generating a collective learning process. Successful initiatives of this kind can at the same time contribute to the development of organizational identity and reinforce identification with the organization. The closing section considers the significance for social identity and learning of the new organizational forms, including networks, which are becoming increasingly prevalent.

SOCIAL IDENTITY

The concept

Some economists view an organization, specifically the firm, as a nexus of contracts among individuals (e.g. Jensen and Meckling, 1976). This usefully draws attention to the economic interests of organizational members, and to the fact that these interests may conflict both among themselves and with those of the employer. Nevertheless, it is an inadequate perspective because it adopts an atomistic view of organizations, ignoring how they are socially constituted. Organizations are in fact complex systems of inter-group relations and networks. Some groups are employed within the organizational core; others contribute to value chains through outsourcing, sub-contracting, and various forms of partnership within a wider organizational network. The behavior and performance of these groups is not just defined in economic terms, but is also subject to logics of action that arise from what groups stand for in the eyes of the people who belong to them.

A sense of belonging to a group is reinforced when it possesses characteristics which are compatible with a person's own individual identity (Strauss, 1959). Indeed, such characteristics may contribute to the forming of that identity. They simultaneously make for uniformity within that group and for distinctiveness from other groups. Groups differ from one another in terms of values, experiences, and behaviors. The dynamics of social relations and the subtleties embedded in inter-personal interactions can encourage and reinforce the sense of belonging to a group.

Individual identity is related to the way that people conceive of themselves. Psychologists generally associate identity with those stable and enduring cognitive, emotional, and behavioral characteristics that are part of a person's biography and career (Weigert et al., 1986; Dubar, 1992). Identity is primarily informational and selective in the sense that it takes from the environment those sources of information considered useful or functional to the individual's self-concept (Tajfel, 1982; Turner et al., 1987). This self-concept is sustained importantly by what people value as their capabilities, including the competencies and knowledge they possess.

Various types of sources can inform the self: the activities individuals develop, the roles they perform in different contexts, and the groups they interact with. In order to inform their identity, people draw meaning from sources to which they attach an emotional and particular value—'the significant others', whether they be a person, a group, or an espoused value system (Foote, 1951). The notion of social identity builds upon this foundation by postulating that, while identity is an essentially subjective phenomenon, it normally has highly significant social referents. In other words, an individual's definition of the self is based (at least in part) on the group or other social categories to which he or she perceives they belong (Tajfel, 1982). Social identity is mostly relational and environmental in the sense that self-perception changes through the interaction of individuals with other people and with their environments. Goffman's (1959) concept of the 'performed self' suggests that an individual's identity can change in the course of social interaction. People interpret and enact their social identities in response to the situations in which they find themselves (Weick, 2001).

Students of organization have become increasingly aware of the relevance of identity for the expectations and behavior of organizational members (Hatch and Schultz, 2004). According to Ravasi and Schultz (2006: 435), 'identities reside in shared interpretive schemes that [organizational] members collectively construct in order to provide meaning to their experience.' Albert, Ashforth, and Dutton (2000: 13) comment that 'identity and identification . . . are root constructs in organizational phenomena and have been a subtext of many organizational behaviors.' The significance of social identity for organizational behavior in general, and for the process of organizational learning in particular, lies in the way that identification with a particular social group can be a referent for people to surface certain cognitive assumptions about themselves in relation to others. These assumptions, and the sense that people make of situations, influence the extent to which they are prepared to relate positively with those others including sharing their tacit or specialized knowledge. Social identity thus impinges on the 'semantic learning' that Corley and Gioia (2003) discuss in the previous edition of this Handbook. The enactment of social identity, and the potential barriers to collective learning that this introduces, is likely to take place primarily under certain conditions, especially those that are interpreted as posing a threat to the people concerned and/or when dependence on their membership group is perceived to be high (Weick, 1988; Salk and Shenkar, 2001). Moreover, as Corley and Gioia (2003) argue, the identity people attach to an organization can be quite fluid and subject to change as they reinterpret what it means to be 'us' as an organization.

The main challenge to organizational managements stems from the likelihood that individuals may be more inclined to identify with particular groups than with the organization itself (Martin, 1992). Identities can develop around a functional role, professional membership, gender, nationality, or a particular hierarchical status in an organization (Weigert et al., 1986; Ashforth and Mael, 1989). Occupational and national identities are of particular significance. Professionals, technical people, and other specialists may identify more with their occupational peer group or external reference groups than with their employing organizations. Functional specialists who work across the interface between the organization and the environment like sales personnel or purchasing officers tend to identify strongly with clients and partners (Alvesson, 2000). Similarly, it is quite possible that the members of ethnic or national groups working within a multinational corporation (MNC) or an international strategic alliance (ISA) will identify more closely with their fellow nationals, even those outside the organization, than with groups of different origin (Royce, 1982). Since people can belong to more than one group, it is possible for them to have multiple social identities, just as the pluralistic nature of organizations means that they will contain multiple social identities (Pratt and Foreman, 2000).

Occupationally-based identity. It is widely agreed that the strongest occupationally-based identity is to be found among members of the recognized professions. Many professionals work in units where they regulate or partially regulate their own work and careers—in private practice, professional firms, or public service organizations. This applies to most doctors, lawyers, and scientists, as well as to some accountants and engineers. However, many engineers and scientists are also employed within managerially-led organizations such as business firms, where they play a vital role in one of the most important fields of learning, namely product and process innovation. Other less professionally-recognized functional specialists such as HRM, IT, and marketing personnel are often heavily involved in organizational learning and change projects within firms.

Alvesson notes (2000: 1109) that people who see themselves primarily as professionals, albeit broadly defined, are likely to have weaker ties to an employing company and may as a result be more disloyal to that employer. Evidence suggests, however, that this does not necessarily mean that there will be a conflict between occupational and organizational commitments. Professionals who remain with non-professional organizations appear willing to accommodate their value orientations and professional self-perception to managerial expectations (Child, 1982). A significant factor here is whether non-professional organizations can satisfy the aspirations that professionals have for career advancement (Wallace, 1995).

Nationality-based identity. Nationality and ethnicity are two other bases for social identity that play an important role in contemporary organizations. Considerable attention has been paid to the cultural features that map onto different nationalities and their implications for behavior within organizations (Hofstede, 1991; Trompenaars, 1993). Nationality and ethnic group membership are strong life-long social points of reference for personal identity, and it is this identity that motivates adherence to the cultural values and behaviors associated with them (Weigert et al., 1986; Bloom, 1990; Sarup, 1996). As organizations increase their global reach, either through organic expansion or through mergers, acquisitions, and alliances, so their need to find a basis for people of different cultures to work together increases correspondingly. Given the intensity of global competition and the rapid rate of environmental change, much of this cross-cultural work will be directed towards the goals of innovation and learning.

A particular aspect of globalization concerns the international transfer of knowledge. When MNCs acquire local companies, they usually intend to transfer knowledge in the form of standard practices which are embedded in their domestic cultural contexts or that have been successful elsewhere. These practices extend beyond purely technical matters to involve particular ways of relating to people, authority, space, and time. These are sensitive issues because they impinge upon factors associated with social identity in the local context. What multinational managers understand as 'best practice' may be viewed by local staff as inappropriate or even illegitimate in their social and political context (Markóczy and Child, 1995). Differences associated with national cultures have been found to hinder knowledge transfer both between and within organizations (Lyles and Salk, 1996; Hong, Snell, and Easterby-Smith, 2006). Hence, the argument that a transfer of practices across national cultural boundaries requires their adaptation to local norms, or 'recontextualization' (Brannen et al., 1997). For this reason, corporate practices in areas like product promotion and personnel selection are not necessarily adopted by subsidiaries without modification. When imported practices are sensitive to local cultural norms, it may be necessary to de-construct and re-construct those practices in order to prevent social identity conflict.

Organizational identity

When corporate strategies affront meaningful values for identity, or go against already embedded values, role performance is subject to a struggle between a subjective and an objective identity (Berger et al., 1973). People can show how they reject these changes by cognitively distancing themselves and withdrawing commitment from these roles or from the organization (Burke, 1980; Weigert et al., 1986; Snow and Anderson, 1987). The multiple attachments that people have to roles, institutions, and situations inside and outside the place of work may vary in intensity and in the degree to which they overlap. This allows space for accommodation of identity; by negotiating their involvement, people may be committed to their work and/or to colleagues in different groups, without necessarily being committed to the organization.

Faced with a plurality of group identities, managements endeavor to develop organizational identities that offer a basis for enhancing identification with, and loyalty to, the organization and accord with their definition of its goals (Alvesson, 2000). A classic definition of organizational identity is what is central, distinctive, and enduring about an organization's character (Albert and Whetten, 1985). This definition, however, presents two problems in relation to the analysis of organizational learning. First, the assumption that organizational identity is enduring is inconsistent with the need for contemporary organizations to adapt to rapid and substantial external changes, some of which may require a fundamental redefinition of their strategic missions. In the extreme case, when adaptation is accomplished through merger and acquisition, an organization's previous identity may be destroyed. Adaptation places a premium on the capacity of organizations to learn, including learning to develop a new or modified organizational identity. Second, and most germane to the theme of this chapter, there is the danger that a unitary conception of organizational identity overlooks the other social memberships that provide identities for people within an organization and the implications these alternative identities have for the process of learning.

Corporate cultures are designed to enhance organizational identity, and identification with it, by creating a notion of a common enterprise, a sense of belonging, and a shared understanding (Brown, 1995). Most knowledge creation and organizational learning requires the members of different groups to collaborate and also to commit to the organizational goals that inform the investment in learning. The task of those who manage organizational learning is therefore to reconcile group social identities with a wider organizational identity. This can pose a significant challenge. The relations between groups in organizations often involve competition for power, status, and reward (Hogg and Abrams, 1988). Moreover, the collective identity and sense of common interest among group members are not necessarily aligned to a given employer or network partner. As we have noted, professional and national groups may identify more strongly with their peers outside the organization in which they are employed or to which they are contracted. Organizations can therefore become domains of contest between group identities and the meanings attached to them (Pratt and Foreman, 2000; Brown and Humphreys, 2006). Insofar as group identities are associated with perceived interests, they are far from neutral within the ambit of organizational politics (Rodrigues and Child, 2008). In turn, this can present a formidable challenge to securing the openness of communication and trust between different organizational groups that most commentators would see as essential conditions for effective organizational learning.

ORGANIZATIONAL LEARNING AND SOCIAL IDENTITY

A manufacturing or service value chain relies on the ability to combine and recombine the distinct competencies provided by different groups (Teece et al., 1997). These groups provide the knowledge and skills that enable organizations both to perform effectively in the present and to learn in preparation for the future. Thus, scientific professionals contribute knowledge essential to innovation, and foreign partners can provide invaluable knowledge for operating in new territories. However, while the source of their value resides in the differentiated competencies held separately by such groups, its realization for effective organizational learning requires a degree of reconciliation and integration between them. Here social identity can present obstacles.

The social identity of organizational groups is vested in the systems and bodies of knowledge that they perceive they own. Their members attribute symbolic value to that knowledge and regard themselves as having a right to arbitrate over this value. The implications for the management of organizational learning are very significant. First, the identity of the groups party to an organization will be attached to, and manifest in, their existing practices, thus legitimizing such practices as acceptable conventions. Changes to practice implicit in a policy of promoting organizational learning may therefore be perceived as a threat to social identity, with the result that the people concerned exhibit a reluctance to undertake the 'unlearning' that is a precondition for learning to proceed.

A second implication is that those involved in organizational learning will define its legitimate premises, such as learning goals, valid information, and appropriate schemes for classifying knowledge, in terms consistent with their social identities. While this diversity provides a richer palette of resources for learning, the distinct definitions and classifications are quite likely to be contested between the different groups involved. For example, Scarbrough's study of learning about the possibilities presented by IT for organizational redesign in six Scottish financial organizations led him to conclude that each of the interested specialist groups fought to promote 'classificatory world-views in which their own expertise is central' (1996: 200). If this conflict is not resolved, the willingness, indeed ability, of different groups to contribute to organizational learning will be compromised.

There is always a potential conflict between the values and interests signified by occupational, national, and organizational identities. The first two provide a basis for people to preserve some autonomy vis-à-vis the organization (even though this autonomy may in reality be primarily psychological). By contrast, the creation of an organizational identity forms part of a managerial armory not only to encourage knowledge generation but also to ensure conformity and control. The case of 'WorldDrug,' a US-owned pharmaceutical MNC studied by McKinlay (2001) illustrates how this conflict can impinge on the capacity to generate organizational learning. In the pharmaceutical sector, accelerating the process of drug development is critical for competitive advantage. Over a five-year period, WorldDrug had focused on leveraging employee knowledge of drug project processes, but with little success. Much of this failure was due to the resistance of knowledge workers to managerial monitoring and attempts to capture their tacit knowledge. This tacit knowledge about the high-level coordinative and improvisational skills essential to successful projects constituted the expertise that defined the knowledge workers' identities as experts. To surrender that essential tacit knowledge would turn a private asset into a corporate one and threaten the core of the workers' self-images and interests. McKinlay notes the knowledge workers' sense of rootlessness within the company as a factor that contributed to their reluctance to co-operate with management in transforming their knowledge into an organizational property.

Organizational learning, therefore, does not occur naturally. It requires the active management of different social identities and of the conflict these differences may entail. Managers cannot assume that an existing organizational identity provides an acceptable psychological contract for group members to willingly contribute their specialized knowledge and competencies to the learning process. People are likely to be comfortable in sharing their knowledge with others in the social group or category they identify with, and this sharing may be facilitated by the use of a common national or technical language. They are likely to be far less comfortable in sharing their knowledge with people outside that group. Groups can acquire an identity by developing a unique knowledge about ways of working successfully (Penrose, 1959), and be reluctant to give this away. Nevertheless, cross-group knowledge sharing is a requirement for an organization to convert fragmented knowledge into a useful generalized form. This means that the knowledge held by, or accessible to, individuals or groups has to be transformed into an organizational property, namely knowledge held in a form that makes it potentially accessible to the organization as a whole.

Overall, organizational learning includes three main processes. The first concerns the *acquisition* of knowledge from external sources. The acquisition of knowledge often involves the process of knowledge 'grafting' discussed by Huber (1991). Here the fact that some members of an organization share a social identity with such sources can facilitate the inward transfer of information and knowledge. For example, scientists employed by a firm will share a degree of professional identity with their specialist counterparts working in universities or research institutes, and this will often ease their access to information from these sources. Similarly, one of the reasons for joining with local joint venture partners in a different country is the expectation that they will enjoy favorable social ties to sources of local market and political information. The second process is the *conversion* of knowledge from a tacit to an explicit form. Rendering tacit knowledge explicit amounts to capturing it for wider organizational use and reducing management's dependence on a limited number of people who hold that knowledge. Even some explicit specialist knowledge is effectively tacit for the rest of the organization, and requires conversion to a form that is more generally accessible. In this way, knowledge already resident within an organization can be better exploited. The third process requires a collective contribution of different social groups towards the *creation* of new knowledge deriving from synergy between their distinct competencies. The distinction between knowledge conversion and knowledge creation is consistent with the one March (1991) has made between exploitation of existing knowledge and exploration of new knowledge.

Exploration depends heavily on the external acquisition of new knowledge, whereas exploitation can benefit both from access to external examples and internal experimentation. A common occupational identity and shared expertise between specialists located in different organizations should facilitate the identification and acquisition of relevant external knowledge. By contrast, the internal absorption of knowledge and its conversion into learning that can be applied may depend importantly on a shared intra-organizational identity that crosses specialist boundaries. Research on absorptive capacity indicates that a balance needs to be struck between external knowledge acquisition and internal knowledge processing for effective learning to take place (Raisch, Birkinshaw, Probst, and Tushman, 2009).

Knowledge acquired from external sources will need to be converted into a form that is intelligible and useful to the organization; in other words, it needs to be made more explicit to other organizational members, especially management. Moreover, imported knowledge may only contribute usefully to the organization's purposes if it can be brought together creatively and synergistically with knowledge held by other specialist groups. Here we arrive at the paradox that specialist group identity, when it spans the boundaries of an organization, is functional for the acquisition of knowledge but is potentially dysfunctional for the conversion and creation of knowledge. The identity boundaries between different groups within organizations or organized networks can render these last two processes problematic. For group members may be reluctant to release their tacit knowledge to management or to co-operate with people in other groups.

Learning within an organization therefore requires the bridging of identity boundaries on a basis that is acceptable to the parties concerned. For a learning process based on inter-group synergies to be accomplished, it is crucial that an integrating frame of reference be found. This higher order perspective will presumably reflect organizational goals and, if accepted by participants in the learning process, should serve to strengthen organizational identity and identification. If informed by learning, it will also adjust organizational strategies and practices to better suit the present and anticipated conditions for the organization's success and survival. Successful organizational learning thus strengthens organizational *identity* in the sense of providing a character (strategy and practices) for the organization that is compatible with its present and anticipated conditions. By providing a more convincing identity, the learning process should also make it easier for people to commit to what the organization stands for and so increase their organizational *identification*. Moreover, the experience of participating in goal-directed learning should enhance people's willingness to commit to the fruits of their knowledge creation, thus providing another means of enhancing organizational identification.

The alignment of group identities with organizational identity will be inhibited in circumstances where radical change is introduced in a purely top-down manner. Radical change requires new learning, but a forcing of the change is liable to inhibit identification with the new organizational mission except among the group(s) taking the lead in introducing the change. Such change implies a considerable adjustment of intersubjective meanings for many organizational members, and this may be strenuously resisted (Corley and Gioia, 2003). Thus, when the top management of Telemig, a major Brazilian telecommunications company, tried to introduce a completely new corporate culture and set of practices from the top, it merely succeeded in generating a counter-culture (Rodrigues, 1996, 2006). It was regarded as manipulative and failed to create an effective climate for organizational learning to support the desired change. In such circumstances, many employees shifted the basis of their attachment to the company to one of contract and economic necessity rather than identification.

The sensitivity of social identity for organizational learning is liable to vary depending on (1) the type of knowledge involved and (2) whether the organization in question is unitary in form as opposed to being an alliance or network. Three categories of knowledge can be distinguished, each of which is likely to be perceived differently by the parties concerned in terms of their social identities. The three categories are, respectively, technical knowledge, knowledge about the design of systems and procedures (systemic knowledge), and strategic understanding (Child and Rodrigues, 1996).

Technical knowledge can range from explicit and routine techniques such as statistical quality control and market forecasting to more complex and new technologies that evolve through a process of innovation. The process of acquiring and learning routine techniques may be confined to individuals or small specialist groups, whereas the development of new technologies will typically involve the contributions of several specialist groups. Systemic knowledge is embodied in systems for budgeting, compensation, and production control, in the definition of organizational responsibilities and reporting relationships, and in communication and information systems. This area of knowledge and its application impacts on relationships, across much if not the whole organization. Since new systems normally require a change in organizational behavior and relationships, they are liable to create considerable sensitivity for social identity. Strategic understanding concerns the mindsets of senior managers, especially their criteria of business success and their mental maps of factors that are significant for achieving such success. The prospect of acquiring new strategic understanding can threaten the self-perceived competencies of senior managers. Their social identity as organizational leaders is associated with the policies they have espoused and any substantial change in these promoted by strategic learning is liable to undermine the legitimacy of their position. It can be interpreted as a threat to the very basis of their social identity as senior managers, since this identity is nurtured by the claim to a special set of strategic competencies that identify them as a group of superior standing and privilege. The matter is made more sensitive insofar as the information speaking for strategic change typically comes from other parties, namely experts within and outside the organization.

For these reasons, within a unitary organization, social identity is likely to be more sensitive for systemic and strategic knowledge than it is for knowledge of a technical nature. Systemic and strategic knowledge, and its application, impinges on a range of groups within an organization. It is largely generated within the organization, though often with the help of consultants, and its development requires the willing co-operation of several different groups or units. Such knowledge, concerning as it does strategy and role definitions, comes closer to the core of an organization's identity than does knowledge of a more technical nature. Technical knowledge is often transferred into an organization and does not always have to be shared with other specialties. Several of its characteristics reduce the social sensitivity of acquiring technical knowledge. One is that it is often expressed in a widely accessible, explicit standardized form, some of it as international standards. Another is that technical knowledge is readily accepted as valid by trained specialists who avoid the 'not-invented-here' syndrome by virtue of their relatively cosmopolitan identity. Problems, however, tend to arise when the generation of new technology or new applications of technical knowledge requires the collaboration of people from different specialties, for then the presence of different externally validated technical standards and languages can increase the problem of integration.

The case of an alliance or international organizational network can be more complex. If the alliance or network partners are content to transfer technical knowledge between themselves, the fact that the gatekeepers for such transfer usually share a similar occupational identity can serve as a bridge between the organizations. As such, the transfer of technical knowledge is not likely to be perceived as carrying strong corporate values or involving a kind of imperialism by one national partner over the other. On the contrary, problems are more likely to arise when one partner is attempting to control access to its proprietary technology (cf. Hamel, 1991). This can place technical staff in a situation of dual loyalty and it may rapidly destroy trust between the partners and their staff.

The transfer of systemic knowledge from one partner to another, or pressure from one partner for an alliance to innovate in this area, may be perceived as more threatening to the recipient organization's identity. This is especially likely in international alliances or networks (Lyles and Salk, 1996). The more that systems introduced from abroad are concerned with ways of organizing and managing people, the stronger the implications for social identity. In these areas, systems and procedures brought in from another country impinge on issues that are deeply embedded in people's consciousness of the appropriate social order: on matters such as acceptance of responsibility, authority and power distance, relationships, personal dignity, and social equity. It can also be difficult to prove the superiority of foreign practices. One partner may take their superiority for granted and legitimize them as a reflection of 'global standards;' other partners may resent and resist this.

The case of strategic learning is different again. Alliances and networks are formed in order to benefit from asset complementarity, scale economies, or enhanced market power. To make economic sense they have to achieve a sufficient degree of strategic fit, which does not, however, mean that their objectives are identical (Child, Faulkner, and Tallman, 2005). If the underlying relationship between partner organizations remains a competitive one, or they regard links to the other partners as essentially short-term, it is unlikely that they will be willing to encourage any significant strategic learning by those partners. Defense of their own strategic identity will remain a paramount factor. Even with alliances between developed and developing or transition country partners, in which the latter explicitly state strategic learning to be one of their alliance objectives, the fact that they will be obliged to accept a learning role implies an inferior right to strategic control over the alliance. They may perceive this inferiority as threatening both their ability to protect their interests and their identity as a partner.

IDENTITY MANAGEMENT IN THE ORGANIZATIONAL LEARNING PROCESS

The implication of the above discussion is that the effective management of organizational knowledge acquisition, conversion, and creation speaks for policies that are sensitive to social identities and that can reconcile them with new organizational needs. There appear to be two key requirements for such policies to work. The first is to establish constructive relationships between the various participating groups based on trust and the preservation of what Edmondson (1999b) calls 'psychological safety' for the persons involved—in other words assuaging their fears of failure and personal harm. The second is a search for acceptable over-arching goals that integrate the participants' efforts and provide a sense of direction for the learning process. These points may be illustrated by examples from organizational learning processes, involving groups with respectively diverse occupational and national identities.

The use of teams as organizational learning vehicles that constructively reconcile identity differences is apparent in the examples below. Senge (1993) observes that 'teams, not individuals, are the fundamental learning unit in modern organizations' (1993: 10). Marshall (2001) sees project teams, comprising members from several contributing social groups, as exemplary of the tension between seeking a team identity (homogeneity) and preserving member differences (heterogeneity). Heterogeneity reflects the different yet complementary competencies and knowledge sets required to feed a constructive learning process. Homogeneity is required to unify diverse individuals and groups around a shared goal-directed activity. The managerial challenge is to resolve this tension in a manner that is conducive to organizational learning.

Learning and occupational identities

De Haen, Tsui-Auch, and Alexis (2001) offer the example of pharmaceutical companies that had to learn how to implement new regulations on Good Laboratory Practice (GLP). The first individuals in a pharmaceutical company to become familiar with GLP regulations were typically people with responsibility for preclinical drug safety assessment and regulatory compliance. However, compliance with GLP regulations required the cooperation of people from different specialties. Research protocols had to be endorsed by several investigators such as a pharmacotoxologist, veterinarian, statistician, manager, and a representative of a quality assurance unit. This degree of collective compliance threatened the identity of specialists who had previously conceived of themselves as individual researchers, especially as activities falling under GLP regulations became formalized into hierarchical systems of standard operating procedures (SOPs). The change was uncomfortable for researchers, for whom it sometimes lacked a scientific rationale and who had been trained to conduct experiments with a degree of operational flexibility that fosters chance discovery.

Companies learned to become creative in fostering their employees' compliance with GLP regulations in ways that were consistent with the social identities of such personnel. For example, they encouraged research staff to take an expert role in the writing of SOPs, and attached acceptable symbols and incentives to the change in ways that met the need for peer recognition. They also endeavored to motivate acceptance among researchers by encouraging peer pressure within teams. De Haen et al. comment that: 'The learning unit was always a group . . . This focus on groups signifies at least implicit acknowledgement of a social component in organizational learning needed for the implementation of GLP regulations' (De Haen et al., 2001: 915).

In ways such as these, managers in the pharmaceutical companies studied were able to effect a cultural change among scientific staff that built upon rather than violated their social identity. In fact, the application of GLP regulations eventually encouraged the emergence of new corporate-wide attitudes towards quality assurance based on the way they promote accountability and transparency in the acquisition and manipulation of laboratory data. The learning process led to staff eventually accepting the regulations as an embedded norm that became, at least in part, tacit in nature. In this respect it provided a bridge from group to organizational identity in a way that changed an important aspect of the latter.

Learning and national identities

Many international acquisitions, alliances, and collaborations are made with knowledge acquisition or synergistic learning as one of their objectives. In the case of international technology partnerships, knowledge creation is the primary objective. Yet many such arrangements fail and this is often attributed to difficulties in reconciling the partners' different national cultures and identities. The role that can be attributed to national identity is, however, often difficult to isolate because other sources of friction may be present which also stand in the way of creating the conditions for knowledge transfer, let alone mutual learning. For example, the learning intentions of international partners can be motivated by a desire to acquire the other's proprietary knowledge for competitive reasons, or in the case of an acquisition to subsequently close down the unit supplying the knowledge. Differences in the partners' abilities to learn from each other can rapidly undermine trust between them and engender a defensive attitude towards sharing knowledge (Hamel, 1991). Differences in the partners' organizational cultures and modes of working can also inhibit the evolution of effective learning relationships between them, due to factors other than nationality such as substantial differences in their size (Doz, 1996).

Heavens and Child (1999) examined the experience of six international project teams created to achieve specific knowledge-generating objectives. The cases pointed to problems caused by differences in national identity, and how the management of learning teams could reduce the gap created by these differences in the process of developing a new shared identity. The role of personal trust emerged as a vital facilitating factor for this process to take place, especially in terms of key relationships between individual team members. Trust informed the dynamics of team generated knowledge and its transformation into organizational learning. It also helped the team members to transcend the factors defining their separate social identities, and that otherwise threatened to jeopardize the collective learning process. As closer relationships developed between team members, they gradually became more comfortable in sharing their views and knowledge and they became more aware of a common learning goal.

These observations can be illustrated by one of the cases, a water company. The scenario for cross-national team learning in this case developed through a series of takeovers. These were prompted by a desire on the part of the British company to expand in a certain business area, with the initial acquisition of a Swedish firm in possession of the required technology. Subsequently, this latter firm bought out a smaller, Norwegian company, whose patents therefore went to the British water company as overall owner. It was the work with this smaller company on new waste water processes that was studied, one of a number of collaborative projects with the Scandinavians.

Issues of group identity impacted on the work of the project team, especially in the initial stages. The company's head of technology innovation, who had been with the British company for twenty years, noted that team work with the Swedes and Norwegians, based on technology developed by the latter, took a long time to evolve. His mission was to establish the ground rules and research program, but he was hindered by the fact that the Norwegian company was reluctant to tell him anything. There were two main reasons for this: first, the company, being small and therefore vulnerable, feared being 'emptied out,' with their patents being taken and sold on; second, and more generally, the Norwegians have a dislike of the English on account of contentious issues relating to their occupational identity as water engineers such as acid rain, and pollution from UK coastal outlets. It was only through withholding knowledge and distorting channels of information that the Norwegian subsidiary felt it could preserve its worth, and therefore its identity and security. A lack of trust held the Norwegians back from contributing to learning by the wider organization. It is significant that the initial formal framework of procedures and programs devised for mutual working, and intended also to promote mutual confidence, was insufficient to facilitate the learning process.

Barriers to knowledge sharing were becoming apparent about one year into the project. The initial barriers, created by fear and mistrust on the part of the Norwegian subsidiary, were overcome primarily through the personal relationship developed by the new project manager with his counterpart in Scandinavia. This relationship opened up communication between the British and Norwegian groups and enabled them to recognize mutual benefits and objectives. A joint research and development program also served importantly to assuage the Norwegians' fears and to provide a bridge across the national divide based on a sharing of their common scientific identities. This illustrates the importance of perceived goal congruence, a reconciliation of social identities, and a sense of psychological safety as conditions for team members to share knowledge and so generate organizational learning. The joint research and development program enabled findings from the project to be applied throughout the British and Scandinavian companies. Informants agreed that both operational processes, concerning the day to day running of waste water treatment works, and process knowledge—the actual technological processes of waste water treatment—were considerably enhanced through the teamwork that was developed. The program was also a symbolic indication of the new organizational identity that was being forged within the international corporate group.

National identities can clearly create sensitivities for learning within international partnerships, networks, and MNCs. National identity can manifest itself in ideas of national superiority both through categorizing other partners' attitudes as negative and through conceiving of learning as a one-way process. This is particularly common among the managers of MNCs, which are more likely to transfer practices within ISAs unilaterally than other firms. Child and Rodrigues report examples of this unilateralism and conclude that the definition of one partner as superior may, at worst, 'lead to a situation in which exchanges are unbalanced, information is concealed and people are excluded from opportunities to learn' (1996: 53). Even if there is a strong intention by the partners to learn from the strengths of each other's practices, their staff may consider the other's practices to be inappropriate or even illegitimate.

Salk conducted three detailed case studies of multi-management teams in IJVs that throw further light on the role of social identity as a referent for inter-personal attitudes and behavior (Salk, 1996; Salk and Brannen, 2000; Salk and Shenkar, 2001). While not focused explicitly on team learning, Salk's studies elucidate the problems that social identity can create for attaining the shared meanings and behaviors necessary for teams to succeed in achieving integrated knowledge conversion and creation. She found that although the three teams ultimately developed differently, in their first weeks and months they each passed through a similar phase of development which she terms the 'encounter phase.' During this phase, distinct social identities, primarily based on the members' nationalities, coexisted and sometimes competed with one another over how the team would work and the IJV would function. Cultural stereotyping and the creation of in-groups and outgroups characterized all three teams; this resulted from an enactment of social identity. In one of the IJVs, the dominant enactment of nationality-based identities within the teams persisted for several years. Salk argues that this persistence was partly explicable in terms of reinforcing factors such as a heavy resource dependence on its two parent companies, staffing the IJV's management through secondment from the parents, and the threat of market downturn. However, she also draws attention to the way that in this case the nationality-based social identities, once established, became 'a lens mediating the impact of contextual change on the enactments of the IJV setting and functioning by its members.' (Salk and Shenkar, 2001: 173).

The research we have reviewed points to the importance of attending carefully to the encounter phase in new teams composed of people who have different social identities. People coming together to work on a project create a discursive community which, on the one hand, enables them to compare their different perspectives and knowledge but, on the other hand, can give them a sense of being isolated, non-communicating, and even in conflict with others (Gherardi, 2005). Management's aim must be to encourage them to reach as quickly as possible an accommodation that constructively combines their different frames of meaning and behavioral assumptions. It is important for this reason to minimize personal concerns and threats that can induce team members to retreat into the psychological refuge of their separate social identities as an excuse for defensive stereotyping of other members and/or of management.

In the specific context of teams established to generate organizational learning, assurances may have to be offered that a sharing of tacit knowledge will not be to the detriment of personal careers and employment, efforts made to surface and then constructively overcome social stereotypes, and care taken to offer the team a clear objective for their work which they can understand and accept. Mixed identity teams can offer a rich combination of expertise, experience, and perspective to the learning process, but for this potential to be realized conditions of trust must prevail both within the team and in its relationship to management. If such teams are intended to have a continuing and evolving life, encouragement must be given to evolving trust to a point where the dominant social identity becomes one shared by the participants themselves (Child, 2001).

New Organizational Forms, Social Identity, and Learning

The globalization of markets and rapid advance of new technology is making competition increasingly knowledge-based in terms of the premium attached to innovation and to early awareness of changing market conditions. Non-business organizations are not immune either from pressures for new and improved services and responsiveness to public demands. These conditions clearly favor organizations that are fast learners and able to change quickly (March, 1995). Consequently, there has been a search for new forms of organization that reduce internal identity barriers, or transcend external identity differences, in the interest of improving learning capabilities and adaptability.

The new thinking on organization encompasses a move away from rigid bureaucratic structures toward the adoption of flexible unconventional forms. The contemporary design paradigm is shifting away from the hierarchy, in which it is assumed that the most valuable knowledge is held by top managers, and toward a 'distributed network of minds' (Gibson, 1997:8). Authority, power, responsibility, and resources are decentralized to semi-autonomous teams or work groups consisting of knowledgeable, professional, or multi-skilled, staff (Barley, 1996). They can also include relevant 'outsiders' such as suppliers and customers. These teams and work groups work with a high degree of local initiative, though it is recognized that their knowledge-creating activities need to be goal directed and contribute to the wider organization. (Hedlund, 1986; Wellins et al.,1994). Organizational teams are today formed around different axes of social identity such as professional and disciplinary groupings, as well as nationality, ethnicity, gender, and hierarchical position. Cheney's (1991) observation that in post-industrial societies organizational rhetoric is about the management of multiple identities is very pertinent to these developments.

One example of a relatively new organizational form that aims to transcend inter-organizational identity barriers with the intention of promoting learning and knowledge transfer is the strategic alliance. Globalization has encouraged the formation of international alliances between two or more partner organizations coming from different countries. This increasingly common kind of hybrid organization has to cope with differences in both organizational and national identities. Alliances with local partners are often seen as a means to accelerate learning about new markets that a firm seeks to enter (Luo, 2002). Technology partnerships are undertaken as a means of sharing knowledge or generating new knowledge, especially if the partner organizations possess complementary competencies and/or if the cost of innovation is high (Hagedoorn and Schakenraad, 1994).

The strategic alliance formed in 1999 between auto manufacturers Nissan and Renault faced considerable differences of organizational and national identity. This was one of the reasons why almost all commentators and industry experts predicted that the alliance would fail. As one said at the time, 'at their core they [Nissan and Renault] are both nationalistic and patriotic, and each believes its way is the right way to do things' (Morosini, 2006: 273). Moreover, Nissan was nearly bankrupt in 1999. However, within five years the Renault–Nissan alliance had become one of the world's most profitable car manufacturers accompanied by a substantial increase in market share. A willingness to transcend the different social identities of the two companies was initially founded on the trust built between their corporate presidents and then extended operationally through a number of organizational initiatives which promoted a great deal of shared knowledge exploitation. These initiatives included a mixed leadership team, a common language (English), the setting of a common mission in the form of a Nissan revival Plan, cross-country project teams to work on its implementation, and an open communications culture. As Morosini (2006: 285) notes, these developments created mutual social capabilities which became 'knowledge interactions.'

There can, however, be a negative side to the adoption of new organization forms. In some cases this can breach and destroy the very trust that was manifest in the Renault–Nissan alliance and had positive results for knowledge generation. For example, the downgrading of hierarchy involves de-layering and a hollowing out of middle manage-ment. The shift towards smaller units, combined with competitive pressures, has led to widespread downsizing and layoff (Cascio, 2002). The push towards greater flexibility has shifted the focus of the employment relationship from career to contract, undermined employment security, and thrown the onus of ensuring a long-term income stream onto the shoulders of the individual. The distinction between core and non-core activities has also increased the differentiation between primary and secondary status employment. These developments have often been associated with acquisitions which are intended to exploit the assets of the acquired company while failing to respect the social identity of its members (Rodrigues and Child, 2010).

Networks, Social Identity, and Learning

Many large organizations are also being deconstructed into systems of smaller compo-nents which then form a business or organizational network. Networks are regarded as a significant transformation from 'vertical bureaucracies' into 'horizontal corporations' (Castells, 1996). One incentive to form networks stems from the virtue of small units in order to avoid the rigidity, lack of focus and anonymity of large-scale organizations. It is argued that small units can more readily become 'self-organizing' than can larger units, and hence pursue their own learning initiatives when the need arises (Handy, 1992; Senge, 1997). Another incentive is that networks can provide a flexible means of quickly achiev-ing global reach in both supply chains and markets.

Studies in sociology have for some time addressed the question of how minorities and disadvantaged groups develop a social identity in forming relational networks (Proudford and Nkomo, 2006). However, the question of how social identity is developed across organizational networks so as to encourage learning within them requires more investiga-tion. Networks have been defined in several ways. A commonly accepted definition refers to social units that are loosely or tightly connected through shared activities, common val-ues or interests, whether these units are organizations, groups, or individuals (Brown and Duguid, 2001). While it is relatively easy to understand how a group develops a collective identity, this is less obvious in the case of networks. Groups are organized around a mis-sion or a sense of common purpose. They are contained within geographical boundaries and normally have the facility of visual contact. Organizational networks on the other hand are open ended and physically dispersed, with a membership and scope that may not be clearly demarcated.

A recent type of network which constitutes a form of social organization and has con-siderable potential for collective learning is the computer-based social network. These net-works such as Facebook, LinkedIn, and MySpace have attracted millions of users. They reveal not only how individuals learn from one another through sharing activities and interests, but also how this helps them construct self-identity. They also provide an exam-ple of how social identity is linked to social capital (Smith, Giraud-Carrier, and Purser, 2009) and how certain types of social capital provide opportunities for innovation and learning (Wineman, Kabo, and Davis, 2009). The link between social capital and social identity is clearly made in Bourdieu's (1984) work. He suggested that social capital is con-structed through unique relationships between individuals who recognize their group as possessing distinctive and rare characteristics which are not easily accessible to others. Such groups regulate membership through mechanisms of mutual recognition and acquaintance which provide the basis for inclusion and exclusion.

It is impossible to speak of learning in and through networks without reference to its relational dimensions and how people learn in the process of establishing social connections. Social identity is important to this equation insofar as when people build personal connections they not only outline the contours of the network but also what it stands for. In so doing, they build a common social identity which helps to dissolve barriers to communication and knowledge-sharing. There is evidence that connecting otherwise dispersed people within social networks and enhancing coordination between connected individuals are both predictors of innovation, especially when those people have differential contributions to offer (Obstfeld, 2005; Wineman et al., 2009).

Granovetter (1973) distinguished between networks that are based on strong ties and those that are characterized by weak ties. Strong ties are more intensive in nature; they are sustained through close kinship and friendship links. Weak ties are based on infrequent and impersonal relations. The implication of strong and weak network ties for learning and innovation has attracted interest. Burt (1992, 2004) argues that networks with structural holes, having low connectivity among those in a network, present opportunities for new ideas to be generated, especially if there are brokers who create links between heterogeneous items of information and fill the holes that characterize such networks. He suggests that, by contrast, close networks may create redundant information and encourage conformity, therefore jeopardizing learning (Burt, 2004). Similarly, Ferrary and Granovetter (2009) assume that forming weak ties is essential to learning. They argue that the learning basis of Silicon Valley rests on the development of multiple and heterogeneous connections across networks of different natures. They suggest that dynamic capability is developed as key agents—boundary spanning agents—engage with a multiplicity of ties that support the creation and development of high-tech start-ups. Thus, both the configuration of a network and the social capital it contains are seen as sources of learning. Connectivity appears to be a key factor in a network's success.

However, while the brokering of structural holes may promote invention, these weak networks may not be so effective in putting innovation into practice (Obstfeld, 2005). The development of strong ties is usually associated with locally embedded learning within a community of practice. 'Situated learning theory positions a "community of practice" as the context in which an individual develops the practices (including values, norms and relationships) and identities appropriate to that community' (Handley, Sturdy, Fincham, and Clark, 2006: 642). The notion of a community of practice implies that learning is interdependent with the process of forming a network identity. Forming an identity encourages stability among the central members of the network through the development of trust and commitment, and this is likely to encourage the open communication that enhances learning (Brown and Duguid, 2001). In turn, the satisfaction of achieving learning and new knowledge as a collective product may well enhance the sense of a common social identity (Corley and Gioia, 2003).

Experience to date suggests that achieving learning through organized networks presents a managerial challenge, but one that can be met. In some sectors such as biotechnology, the relevant knowledge for new product development is in any case scattered between research institutes, universities, and bio-tech firms, while the co-operation of venture capital firms is required for financing and that of hospitals or firms specializing in clinical trials is necessary for product development and testing. It is proving possible to co-ordinate networks of these separate organizations into effective learning systems (Powell et al., 1996). Much depends on developing the managerial skills to handle the process so that people do not feel obliged to enact their social identities defensively.

Do New Organizational Forms Threaten Social Identity and Learning?

Despite the growing technical possibilities for individuals and organizations to be connected through networks, the restructuring of many workplaces has detached people from a long-term stable association with employing organizations (Littler, 2000; Cascio, 2002). This creates insecurity and anxiety for many. It has often been accompanied by a breach of the trust which prevailed between employers and employees (Child and Rodrigues, 2004), and it therefore weakens the sources of work-related social identity. Albert, Ashforth, and Dutton (2000: 13–14) comment that 'given the massive corporate downsizings of recent years, the decrease in long-term relational contracts in favor of shorter-term transactional ones, and the growth in boundaryless careers . . . the notion of identification with and loyalty to one's employer, workgroup, or occupation may seem quite quaint, even naïve.' Insofar as identification with organizations is a condition for people to contribute to learning within them, this would be ironic because learning is one of the key processes that new organizational forms are intended to promote.

One feature in this trend is the disappearance of the former supports for occupational identity as new organizational forms are adopted. Previously, many specialists could rely on occupational credentialism (Collins, 1979) to provide an assured income stream and career progression within traditional functionally structured organizations. Today, many more people with specialized competencies have to rely on contract work secured on the basis of their standing in the labor market. The rise of a new educated managerial elite, and of new non-traditional specialties such as brand developers, software designers, and financial analysts, has added to the ranks of knowledge workers and further blurred the traditional lines of occupational identity. Some knowledge workers are typically located within the core of an organizational system, such as senior managers and key technical personnel. Others are today more usually hired in on contract in a consulting capacity, and this can even apply to groups who used to occupy core roles such as HRM specialists and maintenance engineers. These developments move the source of specialist identity away from the organized profession, skilled trade union, or other occupational association and towards the self-standing individual or specialized firms through which people offer their services in the market. The shift away from a credentialist occupational identity may assist organizational learning by increasing the willingness of specialists to work flexibly with others in learning-directed inter-disciplinary teams and work units. On the other hand, the forced removal of people from core to periphery, or the fear that they may be the next to go, is not likely to motivate them to contribute enthusiastically to the organizational learning process. Marketization is likely to limit their loyalty to a given organization and may qualify the extent to which they are willing to disclose their proprietary knowledge and skills.

By contrast, national identity appears to have been enhanced rather than weakened by the impact of globalization, and the modern information and communication technologies that facilitate it. Paradoxically, at the same time as national transactional boundaries weaken there is a increased awareness of cultural differences and a growing celebration of cultural diversity (Robertson, 1995). New technology dramatically improves communication between the members of cultural groups and provides opportunities for their self-expression. It also appears that people's awareness of their own culture and identity is promoted by the provision of more information about other societies or communities, which enables comparisons that clarify cultural distinctiveness. This enhanced awareness of national identity may add to the difficulties of achieving learning that relies upon integration between different national groups.

It thus appears that the nature and configuration of national and occupational identities are changing in the contemporary world. Much of this change is associated with the evolution of new organizational forms. They are presenting new challenges for aligning group social identities with the goal of organizational learning. Indeed, the greatest impact on organizational learning may actually come though the way that new forms reduce the identification people have with any one organization and the commitment they are willing to give to it. This puts people into a situation where they may have to devote considerable effort to re-establishing their identities through learning new inter-subjective meanings (Corley and Gioia, 2003). Many organizations are outsourcing activities and hollowing themselves out. This places a premium on the ability of the remaining core groups to achieve a requisite level and quality of learning though harnessing contributions from others that have become externalized. The issue becomes particularly acute with the 'virtual organization.'

According to Mowshowitz (1994: 270), 'the essence of the virtual organization is the management of goal-oriented activity in a way that is independent of the means for its realization. This implies a logical separation between the conception and planning of an activity, on the one hand, and its implementation on the other'. This concept could readily deny any sense of identification with the collective activity to people in the system other than those in the leading core group. It is partly for this reason that many corporations have been devoting considerable effort to enhancing their public identities, in the form of corporate images and brand names. For, in addition to the market appeal of strong images and brands, it is essential for the leaders of virtual organizations to create some basis of identification with, and understanding of, their goals if they are to generate the will and purpose to compete with more integrated companies. More specifically, there is a danger that the further an organization moves towards a virtual form, with arms length relationships based on contract rather than personal relationship, the less readily can it communicate the tacit knowledge that is essential for successful collective learning.

CONCLUSIONS

This chapter has explored one of the lacunae in the field of organizational learning, namely how the process of such learning is conditioned by the social identities that people internalize as members of groups within organizations. A monolithic focus on organizational identity at the cost of overlooking that of constituent groups is seen to be theoretically inadequate and practically misleading. Many organizations today contain a wide range of groups with their own social identities, often based on occupation and nationality. These social identities are sustained importantly by what people value as the special capabilities of the groups or communities to which they belong. The knowledge they possess is intrinsic to these capabilities. They are therefore concerned to protect this personal asset and may be cautious about sharing it either with the members of other organizational groups or with management.

Their constituent groups contain potentially valuable learning resources for organizations. The translation of that potential into reality, however, requires certain attributes of managers. They have to be sensitive to the social identities of the relevant groups, establish constructive relationships between the parties to the learning process, and reconcile their perspectives with the organizational needs to which learning is directed. Evidence from case studies indicates that these requirements can be satisfied, principally through two policies. The first is to create 'psychological safety' for the participating groups as the basis for their willingness to contribute to learning. The second is to search for acceptable over-arching goals that integrate the participants' efforts and provide a sense of direction for the learning process. Acceptance of organizational goals should also furnish an effective basis for promoting organizational identity, both in the sense of what an organization stands for and the willingness of its members to identify with that organization.

This chapter has also offered a number of analytical refinements that help to identify issues for further research. First, it has indicated that social identity may impinge on organizational learning differently according to whether the latter involves acquiring knowledge from external sources or processes primarily internal to the organization such as making tacit knowledge explicit and creating new knowledge. Second, it has argued that the significance of social identity for organizational learning depends on the type of knowledge involved. It postulated that the sensitivity of social identity for systemic and strategic knowledge is normally greater than it is for knowledge of a technical nature. Third, it has recognized the additional complications introduced by hybrid organizations such as alliances or networks, which encompass a myriad of identities and interests, especially when they are international. Fourth, and most far-reaching of all, the chapter has signaled the many unknowns brought into the picture by the emergence and evolution of new organizational forms.

The emergence of new organizational forms, which attenuate the attachment that many people have to their employer, presents both opportunities and challenges to organizational learning. One of the prime justifications for the new forms lies in their claim to promote the capacity to innovate and adapt on the basis of a superior learning capability. It is claimed that opportunities for learning are promoted by the decentralization of initiative, the deconstruction of lethargic bureaucracies into smaller units, and recourse to the market or external networks for accessing specialized knowledge. The challenges stem from the apparent consequences of these developments, particularly the ways in which the weakening of social ties to organizations and growing insecurity of employment jeopardize people's identification with their employer or even their occupation. The implications of new forms for organizational learning remain a particularly urgent and little understood issue for practitioners, and they present a very large agenda for further research.

It is clear that the ways in which social identity and organizational learning interact are complex. They have to be examined at different levels: individual, group, organization, and network. The relationship cannot be regarded as simply one whereby social identity impacts on organizational learning. The process of learning, and achievement, can itself be a source of identity for people and the groups to which they belong. When guided by clear goals, under non-threatening conditions, learning activities may serve to align the identities of groups with that of the organization as a whole. If, however, this alignment is not achieved, people are likely to adhere to their more immediate and longstanding social identities and may as a result choose to retain their knowledge rather than share it with the organization. We have suggested that this issue is becoming particularly acute in the changing circumstances of the contemporary organizational world.

REFERENCES

Albert, S. and Whetten, D. (1985) Organizational identity. In L.L. Cummings and B.M. Staw (eds.), *Research in Organizational Behavior*. Greenwich, CT: JAI Press, vol 7, 263–295.

Albert, S., Ashforth, B.E., and Dutton, J.E. (2000) Organizational identity and identification: Charting new waters and building new bridges. *Academy of Management Review*, 25: 13–17.

Alvesson, M. (2000) Social identity and the problem of loyalty in knowledge: Intensive companies. *Journal of Management Studies*, 32: 1101–1123.

Ashforth, B.E. and Mael, F. (1989) Social identity theory and the organization. *Academy of Management Review*, 14: 20–39.

Barley, S.R. (1996) Technicians in the workplace: Ethnographic evidence for bringing work into organization studies. *Administrative Science Quarterly*, 41: 404–441.

Berger, P.L., Berger, B., and Kellner, H. (1973) *The Homeless Mind: Modernization and Consciousness*. Harmondsworth: Penguin.

Bloom, W. (1990) *Personal Identity, National Identity and International Relations*. Cambridge: Cambridge University Press.

Bourdieu, P. (1984) *Distinction: A Social Critique of the Judgement of Taste*. London: Routledge.

Brannen, M.Y., Liker, J.K., and Fruin, M. (1997) Recontextualization and factory-to-factory transfer from Japan to the U.S.: The case of NSK. Paper presented to the 1997 Annual Meeting of the Academy of International Business, Monterrey, Mexico, 8–12, October.

Brown, A.D. (1995) *Organizational Culture*. London: Pitman.

Brown, A.D. and Humphreys, M. (2006) Organizational identity and place: A discursive exploration of hegemony and resistance. *Journal of Management Studies*, 43: 231–257.

Brown, A.D. and Starkey, K. (2000) Organizational identity and learning: a psychodynamic perspective. *Academy of Management Review*, 25: 102–120.

Brown, J.S and Duguid, P. (2001) Knowledge and organization: A social-practice perspective. *Organization Science*, 12: 198–213.

Burke, P. (1980) The self: measurement requirements for an interactionist perspective. *Social Psychological Quarterly*, 43: 18–29.

Burt, R.S. (1992) *Structural Holes: The Social Structure of Competition*. Cambridge, MA: Harvard University Press.

Burt, R. S. (2004) Structural holes and good ideas. *American Journal of Sociology*, 110: 349–399.

Cascio, W. F. (2002) *Responsible Restructuring: Creative and Profitable Alternatives to Layoffs*. San Francisco: Berrett-Koehler Publishers.

Castells, M. (1996) *The Rise of the Network Society*. Cambridge, MA: Blackwell.

Cheney, G. (1991) *Rhetoric in an Organizational Society: Managing Multiple Identities*. Columbia, SC: University of South Carolina Press.

Child, J. (1982) Professionals in the corporate world: values, interest and control. In D. Dunkerley and G. Salaman (eds.), *The International Yearbook of Organization Studies 1981*. London: Routledge and Kegan Paul: 212–241.

Child, J. (2001) Trust—the fundamental bond in global collaboration. *Organizational Dynamics*, 29: 274–288.

Child, J., Faulkner, D. and Tallman, S.B. (2005) *Cooperative Strategy: Managing Alliances, Networks and Joint Ventures*. Oxford: Oxford University Press.

Child, J. and Heavens, S. (2001) The social constitution of organizations and its implications for organizational learning. In M. Dierkes, A. B. Antal, J. Child, and I. Nonaka (eds.). *Handbook of Organizational Learning and Knowledge*. Oxford: Oxford University Press: 308–326.

Child, J. and Rodrigues, S.B. (1996) The role of social identity in the international transfer of knowledge through joint ventures. In S.R. Clegg and G. Palmer (eds.) *The Politics of Management Knowledge*. London: Sage: 46–68.

Child, J. and Rodrigues, S.B. (2004) Repairing the breach of trust in corporate governance. *Corporate Governance: An International Review*, 12: 143–151.

Collins, O. (1979) *The Credential Society: An Historical Sociology of Education and Stratification*. New York: Academic Press.

Corley, K.G. and Gioia, D.A. (2003) Semantic learning as change enabler: Relating organizational identity and organizational learning. In. M. Easterby-Smith and M.A. Lyles (eds.) *Handbook of Organizational Learning and Knowledge Management*. Oxford: John Wiley & Sons.

De Haen, C., Tsui-Auch, L.S., and Alexis, M. (2001) Multimodal organizational learning: from misbehavior to good laboratory practice in the pharmaceutical industry. In M. Dierkes, A. B. Antal, J. Child, and I. Nonaka (eds.). *Handbook of Organizational Learning and Knowledge*. Oxford: Oxford University Press: 902–918.

Doz, Y.L. (1996) The evolution of cooperation in strategic alliances: initial conditions or learning processes? *Strategic Management Journal*, 17: 55–83.

Dubar, C. (1992) Formes indentitaires et socialisation professionelle. *Revue Francaise de Sociologie*, 33: 505–529.

Edmondson, A.C. (1999a) The view through a different lens: investigating organizational learning at the group level of analysis. In M. Easterby-Smith, L. Araujo and J. Burgoyne (eds.) *Organizational Learning: 3rd International Conference*. Lancaster University, 6–8 June: 299–323.

Edmondson, A.C. (1999b) Psychological safety and learning behavior in work teams. *Administrative Science Quarterly*, 44: 350–383.

Ferrary, M. and Granovetter, M. (2009) The role of venture capital firms in Silicon Valley`s complex innovation network. *Economy and Society*, 38: 326–359.

Foote, N.N. (1951) Identification as a basis for a theory of motivation. *American Sociological Review*, 16: 14–21.

Gherardi, S. (2005) *Organizational Knowledge: The Texture of Workplace Learning*. Oxford: Blackwell.

Gibson, R. (ed.) (1997) *Rethinking the Future*. London: Nicholas Brealey.

Goffman, E. (1959) *The Presentation of Self in Everyday Life*. London: Allen Lane.

Granovetter, M. (1973) The strength of weak ties. *American Journal of Sociology*, 78: 1360–1380.

Hagedoorn, J. and Schakenraad, J. (1994) The effect of strategic technology alliances on company performance. *Strategic Management Journal*, 15: 291–309.

Hamel, G. (1991) Competition for competence and inter-partner learning within international strategic alliances. *Strategic Management Journal*, 12: 83–103.

Handley, K., Sturdy, A., Fincham, R., and Clark, T. (2006) Within and beyond communities of practice: Making sense of learning through participation, identity and practice. *Journal of Management Studies* 43: 641–653.

Handy, C. (1992) Balancing corporate power: A new federalist paper. *Harvard Business Review*, November-December: 59–72.

Hatch, M.J. and Schultz, M. (eds.) (2004) *Organizational Identity: A Reader*. Oxford: Oxford University Press.

Heavens, S. and Child, J. (1999) Mediating individual and organizational learning: The role of teams and trust. In M. Easterby-Smith, L. Araujo, and J. Burgoyne (eds.) *Organizational Learning: 3rd International Conference*. Lancaster University, 6–8 June: 496–532.

Hedlund, G. (1986) The hypermodern MNC—A heterarchy? *Human Resource Management*, 25: 9–35.

Hofstede, G. (1991) *Cultures and Organizations: Software of the Mind*. Maidenhead: McGraw-Hill.

Hogg, M.A. and Abrams, D. (1988) *Social Identifications: A Social Psychology of Intergroup Relations and Group Processes*. New York: Plenum.

Hong, J.F.L., Snell, R. and Easterby-Smith, M. (2006) Cross-cultural influences on organizational learning in MNCs: The case of Japanese companies in China. *Journal of International Management*, 12: 408–429.

Huber, G. P. (1991) Organizational learning: The contributory processes and the literatures. *Organization Science*, 2: 88–115.

Jensen, M.C. and Meckling, W.H. (1976) The theory of the firm: Managerial behavior, agency costs, and ownership structure. *Journal of Financial Economics*, 3: 305–360.

Littler, C.R. (2000) Comparing the downsizing experiences of three countries: A restructuring cycle? In R. J. Burke and C. L. Cooper (eds.), *The Organization in Crisis*. Oxford: Blackwell, 58–77.

Luo, Y. (2002) Contract, cooperation, and performance in international joint ventures. *Strategic Management Journal*, 23: 903–919.

Lyles, M.A. and Salk, J.E. (1996) Knowledge acquisition from foreign parents in international joint ventures: An empirical examination in the Hungarian context. *Journal of International Business Studies*, 27: 877–903.

March, J.G. (1991) Exploration and exploitation in organizational learning. *Organization Science*, 2: 71–87.

March, J.G. (1995) The future, disposable organizations and the rigidities of imagination. *Organization*, 2: 427–440.

Markóczy, L. and Child, J. (1995) International mixed management organizations and economic liberalization in Hungary: from state bureaucracy to new paternalism. In

Thomas, H., O'Neal, D., and Kelly J. (eds.), *Strategic Renaissance and Business Transformation*. Chichester: John Wiley & Sons: 57–79.

Marshall, N. (2001) Knowledge, identity and difference in project organizations. Paper presented to the 17th EGOS Colloquium, Lyon, July.

Martin, J. (1992) *Cultures in Organizations: Three Perspectives*. New York: Oxford University Press.

McKinlay, A. (2001) The limits of knowledge management. Paper presented to the 17th EGOS Colloquium, Lyon, July.

Morosini, P. (2006) Nuturing successful alliances across boundaries. In O. Shenkar and J.J. Reuer (eds.), *Handbook of Strategic Alliances*. Thousand Oaks, CA: Sage: 273–296.

Mowshowitz, A. (1994) Virtual organization: A vision of management in the information age. *The Information Society*, 10: 267–294.

Obstfeld, D. (2005) Social networks, the *Tertius Iungens* orientation, and involvement in innovation. *Administrative Science Quarterly*, 50: 100–130.

Penrose, E.T. (1959) *The Theory of the Growth of the Firm*. Oxford: Blackwell.

Powell, W.W., Koput, K.W., and Smith-Doerr, L. (1996) Interorganizational collaboration and the locus of innovation: Networks of learning in biotechnology. *Administrative Science Quarterly*, 41: 116–145.

Pratt, M. G. and Foreman, P. O. (2000) Classifying managerial responses to multiple organizational identities. *Academy of Management Review*, 25: 18–42.

Proudford, K. L. and Nkomo, S. (2006) Race and ethnicity in organizations. In A.M. Konrad, P. Prasad, and J.K. Pringle, (eds.), *Handbook of Workplace Diversity*. London: Sage: 323–345.

Raisch, S., Birkinshaw, J., Probst, G., and Tushman, M.L. (2009) Organizational ambidexterity: Balancing exploitation and exploration for sustained performance. *Organization Science*, 20: 685–695.

Ravasi, D. and Schultz, M. (2006) Responding to organizational identity threats: Exploring the role of organizational culture. *Academy of Management Journal*, 49: 433–458.

Robertson, R. (1995) Globalization: Time-space and homogeneity-heterogeneity. In M. Featherstone, S. Lash, and R. Robertson (eds.) *Global Modernities*. London: Sage: 25–44.

Rodrigues, S.B. (1996) Corporate culture and de-institutionalization: Implications for identity in a Brazilian telecommunications company. In G. Palmer and S.R. Clegg (eds.) *Constituting Management, Markets, Meanings and Identities*. Berlin: De Gruyter: 115–133.

Rodrigues, S.B. (2006) The political dynamics of organizational culture in an institutionalized environment. *Organization Studies*, 27: 537–557.

Rodrigues, S.B. and Child, J. (2008) The development of corporate identity: A political perspective. *Journal of Management Studies*, 45: 885–911.

Rodrigues, S.B. and Child, J. (2010) Private equity, the minimalist organization and the quality of employment relations. *Human Relations*, 63: 1321–1342.

Rothman, J. and Friedman, V.J. (2001) Identity, conflict and organizational learning. In M. Dierkes, A. B. Antal, J. Child, and I. Nonaka (eds.). *Handbook of Organizational Learning and Knowledge*. Oxford: Oxford University Press: 582–597.

Royce, A.P. (1982) *Ethnic Identity: Strategies of Diversity*. Bloomington, IN: Indiana University Press.

Salk, J.E. (1996) Partners and other strangers: Cultural boundaries and cross-cultural encounters in international joint venture teams. *International Studies of Management and Organization*, 26: 48–72.

Salk, J.E. and Brannen, M.Y. (2000) National culture, networks, and individual influence in a multinational management team. *Academy of Management Journal*, 43: 191–202.

Salk, J.E. and Shenkar, O. (2001) Social identities in an international joint venture: An exploratory case study. *Organization Science*, 12: 161–178.

Sarup, M. (1996) *Identity, Culture and the Postmodern World*. Edinburgh: Edinburgh University Press.

Scarbrough, H. (1996) Strategic change in financial services: The social construction of strategic IS. In W. J. Orlikowski, G. Walsham, M. R. Jones, and J. I. DeGross (eds.), *Information Technology and Changes in Organizational Work*. London: Chapman and Hall: 197–212.

Senge, P.M. (1993) *The Fifth Discipline*. London: Century.

Senge, P.M. (1997) Through the eye of the needle. In R. Gibson (ed.). *Rethinking the Future*. London: Nicholas Brealey: 123–145.

Smith, M., Giraud-Carrier, C., and Purser, N. (2009) Implicit affinity networks and social capital. *Information Technology and Management*, 10: 123–134.

Snow, A. and Anderson, L. (1987) Identity work among the homeless: The verbal construction and avowal of personal identities. *American Journal of Sociology*, 92: 1336–1371.

Strauss, A. (1959) *Mirrors and Masks: The Search for Identity*. Glencoe, Il: Free Press.

Tajfel, H. (1982) *Social Identity and Intergroup Relations*. Cambridge: Cambridge University Press.

Teece, D. J., Pisano, G., and Shuen, A. (1997) Dynamic capabilities and strategic management. *Strategic Management Journal*, 18: 509–533.

Trompenaars, F. (1993) *Riding the Waves of Culture: Understanding Cultural Diversity*. London: The Economist Books.

Turner, J.C., Hogg, M.A., Oakes, P.J., Reicher, S.D., and Wetherell, M.S. (1987) *Rediscovering the Social Group: A Self Categorization Theory*. Oxford: Blackwell.

Wallace, J. E. (1995) Organizational and professional commitment in professional and-nonprofessional organizations. *Administrative Science Quarterly*, 40: 228–255.

Weick, K.E. (1988) Enacted sensemaking in crisis situations. *Journal of Management Studies*, 25: 305–317.

Weick, K.E. (2001) *Making Sense of the Organization*. Oxford: Blackwell.

Weigert, A.J., Teitge, J.S. and Teitge, D.W. (1986) *Society and Identity*. Cambridge: Cambridge University Press.

Wellins, R. S., Byham, W.C., and Dixon, G.R. (1994) *Inside Teams: How 20 World-Class Organizations are Winning Through Teamwork*. San Francisco: Jossey-Bass.

Wineman J.D, Kabo F. W., and Davis, G.F. (2009) Spatial and social networks in organizational innovation. *Environment and Behavior*, 41: 427–442.

15

Organizations, Learning, and Emotion

RUSS VINCE AND YIANNIS GABRIEL

ABSTRACT

In this chapter, the authors identify some of the main organizational learning discourses in which emotion has established a foothold and indicate some of the core insights that it has provided, mainly linked to the theories of emotional labor and socially constructed emotions. They then explore in greater detail the emotional dimension of learning, both in classroom settings and in organizations more generally, developing some of Fineman's earlier arguments regarding the politics of learning. While acknowledging the significance of the socially constructed aspect of emotions, they emphasize that not all emotions can be easily accommodated, contained, or managed in organizations and not all learning can be safely guided towards enhancing organizational objectives. They suggest that learning evokes powerful emotional responses, positive and negative, ranging from excited curiosity to fear of failure and humiliation, and that many of these emotions may be traced to childhood experiences. In this connection, they examine transference as a powerful psychological process through which such experiences can resurface in later life, especially when people encounter intense authority relations individually or in groups. The chapter concludes with an analysis of the emotional dynamics present in two indispensable aspects of learning, criticism, and caring. They argue that criticism is a vital feature of feedback without which learning is impossible, but emphasize that criticism must be balanced by an ethic of care which supports learning and acts as a container for those emotions that may inhibit or incapacitate the learning process.

INTRODUCTION

When a new wave of immigrants arrives in a country, they often settle in particular parts of cities and towns, where they discover ways of starting their new lives and supporting each other. Such pockets or ghettoes provide relative security as well as ways of maintaining traditions and links with the old country. It is tempting to view the study of emotion in organizations as a wave of immigration that started some thirty years ago and initially settled in specific pockets of organizational discourses, such as leadership, service interactions, and learning. When Fineman (2003) wrote his contribution to the earlier edition of this Handbook, he rightly complained that learning literature had long disregarded emotion or viewed it as an obstacle to cognition and rationality. He also noted that much of the politics of organizations had been stripped of its emotional content and expressed ambivalence towards the concept of emotional intelligence. Here was a concept that promised to put emotion back into learning and organizational agendas, but at a considerable price—that of turning emotion into an organizational resource to be managed and exploited.

Since the publication of the first edition of *The Handbook of Organizational Learning and Knowledge Management*, emotion has started to diffuse across learning and organizational discourses. A count of article abstracts containing the word 'emotion' in business and management journals revealed twenty-five such articles in 2003, the year of the Handbook's first publication, and sixty-two and seventy such articles in 2008 and 2009 respectively. In the same period, the number of article abstracts with 'knowledge management' or 'knowledge transfer' in the same journals rose from eighty-three to 166 and 178 respectively. It would seem then that emotion continues to be a minority interest but it is becoming increasingly embedded in discourses of management and business—maybe, like the second generation of some immigrants, it is becoming increasingly accepted and assimilated in the wider picture.

In this chapter, we shall identify some of the main domains in which emotion has established a foothold and indicate some of the core insights that it has provided, mainly linked to the theories of emotional labor and socially constructed emotions. We will then explore in greater detail the emotional dimension of learning, both in classroom settings and in organizations more generally, developing some of Fineman's earlier arguments regarding the politics of learning. While acknowledging the significance of the socially constructed aspect of emotions, we will emphasize that not all emotions can be easily accommodated, contained, or managed in organizations and not all learning can be safely guided towards enhancing organizational objectives. We will suggest that learning evokes powerful emotional responses, positive and negative, from excited curiosity to fear of failure and humiliation, and that many of these emotions may be traced to childhood experiences. In this connection, we will examine transference as a powerful psychological process through which such experiences can resurface in later life, especially when we encounter intense authority relations individually or in groups. The chapter concludes with an analysis of the emotional dynamics we encounter in two indispensable aspects of learning, criticism, and caring. We argue that criticism is a vital feature of feedback without which learning is impossible, but emphasize that criticism must be balanced by an ethic of care which supports learning and acts as a container for those emotions that may inhibit or incapacitate the learning process.

LEARNING, KNOWLEDGE, AND EMOTION

'Why do people in organizations seek knowledge?' (Gherardi, 2004: 32) This may seem a question that leads to a certain dead end—people obviously look for knowledge in order to solve their problems and to gain advantage of some sort or other. So what happens if they fail to acquire knowledge or if the knowledge they acquire neither solves their problems nor gains them any advantage? What happens if the knowledge they crave turns out to redefine the nature of the problems they face or the nature of the competitive advantage they seek? And what if, as Gherardi (1999; 2004) reminds us, the pursuit of knowledge becomes an end in its own right, linked to desire, to curiosity, and to fascination with the unknown? Far from leading to a dead end, the 'why' question at the start of the paragraph inevitably leads to a view of learning and knowledge inextricably linked to emotion and passion—emotions, such as insecurity, fear, and anxiety may drive the quest for knowledge while passions of curiosity, exploration, and discovery may propel the quest for learning. Put this way, what seems surprising is that knowledge and learning are ever thought about without consideration to the emotions that drive them or the emotions they prompt along the way.

Why then are knowledge and learning so frequently considered independently of emotion and passion? As Fineman argued in 2003, learning and knowledge have long been approached in the rationalist tradition as cognitive domains, objective and pure, into which emotion can only introduce impurity and subjectivity. Yet, the parallel critical tradition has also existed, one that insists that knowledge and learning are inextricably linked to human interests (for classic statements, see Freire, 1970, 1996; Habermas, 1972) and, of course, to structures of domination and subordination (for the currently popular account of this view, see Foucault, 1978, 1980), not least those linked to masculine (Cooper, 1989) and colonial (Spivak, 1988) hegemony. But this critical tradition itself, in both its humanist and post-structuralist versions, has hesitated to engage with emotion as part of the discourses of knowledge and power.

More recently, emotions have started to attract the attention of different groups of scholars. This is related to wider social and cultural patterns that have brought emotion to the forefront of social life. Campbell (1989), for example, has argued that the suppression and denial of emotion were cardinal virtues of Puritanism, the Protestant ethic and even the Enlightenment project that saw everything as subordinate to the Commonwealth of Reason, Progress, and Science. Today, by contrast, argues Campbell, under the influence of consumerism, Puritanism has given way to a *Romantic ethic*. This castigates the choking of emotions, raising their free expression near the summit of values. All emotions, including fear, anger, and jealousy, argues Campbell can be vehicles for pleasure provided that we know how to express and contain them. 'Emoting' becomes a highly popular activity, whether it takes place in theatres and television shows, mass public festivals or intimate encounters. Thus, the 'stiff upper lip' ethic has given way to the mass demonstration of near-hysterical feeling, exemplified by the outpouring of emotion following the death of Princess Diana.

SOME PERSPECTIVES ON EMOTIONS

Currently many different perspectives on emotions are emerging. For example, biologists and evolutionary psychologists have been examining how human emotions were 'hard wired' into the evolution of our bodies over millions of years of adaptation to our natural and social environment. Neurologists have explored the relations between the functioning of the brain, emotions, and cognitive processes. By contrast, social constructionists have focused on the subtle ways that different national and organizational cultures shape the ways emotions are experienced and expressed. Psychoanalysts and psychodynamic scholars, for their parts, have examined how early life experiences influence our later emotional experiences. Many experimental and other psychologists have pursued the long tradition of seeking to measure emotions and economists have, more recently, sought to link emotions (like happiness and depression) to economic indicators like income per capita and unemployment rates.

Something on which all of these approaches agree is that most emotions are not fully willed; we do not choose freely whether and when to have them (although many actors become very skilled at experiencing emotions commensurable with their parts). Emotions often seem to overpower us and to influence our judgments in profound ways. Our decisions and our actions when we feel angry or frightened or enthusiastic appear not to agree with the dictates of reason and prudence. Emotion is often experienced as something standing in opposition to rationality—a theme that has been pursued by philosophers since Plato and Descartes. Yet, one of the most consistent and interesting findings of contemporary emotion research is that emotion and cognition cannot be separated. Research by Damasio (1994, 1999), Sacks (1995), and others suggests that both thought and emotion reside in the body rather than in an entity called 'the mind'; also, that emotion is an indispensable ingredient of rational action and rational decisions (though not a guarantee that a decision or an action will be rational). An emotional response to a situation always precedes a rational appreciation and almost invariably guides it. For example, being in a classroom may produce in us responses of anxiety and panic which inform how we experience what subsequently takes place in that space.

Theories of organizational learning draw on several of these approaches, most especially the social construction and psychodynamic traditions. The fundamental contributions of the former have been in highlighting the extent to which emotions are acquired, learnt, and socially constructed. Following Hochschild's (1979, 1983) pioneering early studies, emotional labor came to be seen as part of the work expected by many people, especially in service occupations; the emotions displayed by individuals in their workplace came to be accepted as much a part of the work they do as intellectual or manual work; and like intellectual and manual work, people can be trained to do emotional labor. This opened up the possibility that emotions are resources at the disposal of management, and that organizations that are able to deploy them effectively, in transactions with customers or among employees, can gain some advantage over their competitors. Social constructionist approaches to emotion, therefore, see emotions themselves as experiences, whose meanings emerge through culture, communicated through culture and even generated by culture. Specific cultural events call for appropriate emotional performances of those participating. Inspired by the work of Goffman (1959), different theorists have argued that emotions can be socially constructed just like other social phenomena. Far from being natural states that take possession of us, theorists like Heller (1979), Fineman (1993, 1996), Mangham (1998), and Flam (1990a, 1990b) argue that emotions are learned, just as theatrical roles are learned. And just as theatrical actors learn to experience anger, sorrow, joy, or fear when their roles call for them, so too social actors learn to experience feelings appropriate to specific social settings.

Psychodynamic approaches to emotion, on the other hand, tend to emphasize the involuntary character of emotions, their plasticity and mobility, not in response to external factors but as a consequence of psychological work. Thus, envy can easily be transformed into anger, which in turn may give way to guilt, which may manifest itself in attempts to console and repair. From a psychoanalytic perspective, emotions are not just 'movers' (from emovere) but also in motion; it is rare to capture an emotion in a steady state (as when we talk of 'consuming emotions'); frequently, the act of capturing the emotion instantly leads to its transformation (Antonacopoulou and Gabriel, 2001). In contrast to social constructionist approaches, psychoanalytic approaches insist that there is a primitive, pre-linguistic, pre-cognitive, and pre-social level of emotions, an inner world of passion, ambivalence, and contradiction which may be experienced or repressed, expressed or controlled, diffused or diluted, but never actually obliterated (Gabriel, 1998; Höpfl and Linstead, 1997). As Craib (1998: 110) has eloquently argued

> if we think of emotions as having a life of their own, which might be in contradiction to, or expressed fully or partially through our cognition to different degrees in different times, we can think through all sorts of situations with which most people must be familiar: experiencing feelings we cannot express to our satisfaction; having feelings that we can express but that others find difficult to understand; and most important perhaps, the regular experience of contradictions between our thoughts and our feelings.

The distinguishing feature of psychoanalysis and psychodynamic approaches is the assumption of an *unconscious* dimension to social and individual life, one in which both ideas and emotions may operate (Freud, 1923/1984, 1940/1986). The unconscious is not merely part of a psychic reality which happens to be concealed from consciousness, but functions both as a space in which dangerous and painful ideas are consigned through repression and other defensive mechanisms, and also as a source of resistance to specific ideas and emotions which present threats to mental functioning. Unconscious emotions, ideas, and desires often reach consciousness in highly distorted, camouflaged, or abstruse ways. The unconscious is not a marginal or pathological terrain into which we occasionally drift but a space that accounts for a substantial part of human emotion, motivation, and action; even where plausible conscious reasons and explanations are given for a particular emotional landscape, psychodynamic approaches will examine the possibility that unconscious factors are at play, factors that individuals, groups, or entire societies systematically repress or deny. Thus, at the cost of some simplification, while social constructionist approaches view emotion as derivative of social scripts, signs, and scenarios in which we become linguistically enmeshed, psychoanalytic and psychodynamic approaches view emotions and especially unconscious emotions as generating scripts, signs, and scenarios. Where, for instance, the former may identify anger as consequent of a scenario experienced as insult, the latter may view the experience of being insulted as derivative of a deeper anger and resentment (Gabriel, 1998).

ORGANIZATIONS, MANAGEMENT, AND EMOTION

Most perspectives agree that emotion contributes to 'seeing things differently' (Hochschild, 1983) and plays a significant part in rational thought and action (Williams, 2001). Asking questions about the ways in which emotions are connected to rational decisions raises opportunities for new knowledge and action and helps to redress the traditional imbalance whereby 'emotion is routinely subordinated to rationality' (Ten Bos and Willmott,

2001). It has thus been argued that the tendency of many managers to rationalize emotion creates additional *emotional* dynamics which provide opportunities for reflection, both in terms of understanding organizing processes and revealing the politics of managerial actions (Vince, 2006). Attempts to rationalize away emotions are themselves an exercise of political power which generates opportunities for further thought, critique, and development; they are themselves elements of the emotional dynamics of organizations. Emotion is a continuous and integral aspect of organizing, but this does not mean that emotions should be studied separately from the various rationalizations that relate to them. While studies of emotion challenge the dominance of rationalist assumptions, it is important to avoid, first, reversing this emphasis by privileging emotion at the expense of rationality (Ten Bos and Willmott, 2001) and, second, creating a fixed dichotomy or binary opposition which locks emotion and rationality into a relationship of permanent conflict (Carr, 2001). Instead, it is more useful to examine how particular organizational dynamics emerge, and the contribution that emotion and reason have made to creating and sustaining them. Emotion and reason may define each other, at times reinforcing each other and at times generating tensions and arguments.

One way of drawing emotion and reason closer has consisted of recent attempts to develop the idea of 'emotional intelligence.' Emotional intelligence emphasizes the impact that reason can make on emotion. The claim made for this perspective is that it represents 'an ability to perceive, to process, to understand, and to manage emotions in self and others' (Mayer and Salovey, 1997). Proponents of emotional intelligence maintain that there are distinct individual abilities and skills that relate to the explicit management of emotion; skills that can be developed over time and enhanced by training. Therefore, learning to perceive and manage the emotions of others and one's own is often viewed as 'an important tool in every manager's kit' (Ashkanasy and Daus, 2002: 82). Others have seen such approaches as being aimed to appropriate and commodify emotional displays and private feelings, turning them into 'yet another technology through which selves become enterprising and flexible . . . its objective (is) the rendering of subjectivity into a calculable force. By being made calculable, emotions are made amenable to management and control' (Landen, 2002: 517). The attempt to tame and control emotional displays and experiences in organizations represents in its own way a strong desire to avoid confronting complexities of the relationship between emotion and rationality in organizations. The discourse of emotional intelligence, under the guise of elevating and honoring the emotional dimensions of organizational life, ultimately subordinates emotions to managerial expediencies and organizational controls. Instead, we advocate a more complex *and* practical understanding to be had from appreciating the interplay between emotion and rationality. Our focus is not on individuals' competences in managing emotions and, ultimately, using them as an instrument of calculating and instilling compliance in others. Instead, we believe that understanding the interplay of emotion and rationality can provide a deeper knowledge to inform and guide our actions and relations.

Our discussion of organizations, learning and emotion can build on the idea that 'every organization . . . is an emotional place. It is an emotional place because it is a human invention, serving human purposes and dependent on human beings to function. And human beings are emotional animals: 'subject to anger, fear, surprise, disgust, happiness or joy, ease and unease' (Armstrong, 2000: 1). Here, we are concerned both with individuals' feelings in organizations and also with the collective production of emotional scripts that help people feel connected to organizational norms and guide their emotional responses to different situations. Fineman (2001) has offered a plausible explanation of the difference between feelings and emotions. He suggests that feelings are fundamentally private experiences and that emotion can be defined as *the public performance of feelings*. Emotional displays depend on an audience on which the performance of feelings is designed (consciously or unconsciously) to have a strategic effect. Thus, emotional displays are regulated by the actor's internal state as well as political webs of social rules and conventions.

While emotions are always located within webs of social rules or power relations, the view of feelings as private experiences may promote a misleading distinction. Psychodynamic theory offers the insight that feelings are not only private experiences, but are shaped by and linked to the internalization or denial of relations with other people (French and Vince, 1999). In this sense, therefore, both feelings and emotions are always social. In addition, one has to ask who is being represented in the public performance of feelings: is the performance of a feeling (such as outrage, shame or fear) the 'property' of an individual, or might it also include those persons and collectives whose influences, conflicts, and defenses encourage the acting out of specific emotional scripts? The experience of being a 'scapegoat,' for example, although private and isolating for the target, suggests that individuals can become conscious and unconscious victims and mouthpieces of group dynamics or organizational politics. The importance of this idea within this chapter is that such dynamics are not only linked to the labeling of an individual, but also to the unconscious labeling work of the collective (i.e. the ways in which definitions of 'how we do things here' emerge and become accepted). The definition of emotions as the public performance of feelings is important and useful because it reminds us that individuals' emotions are not detached from the context within which they are being expressed, managed, and/or organized.

From this perspective an interest in emotion in organizations is not about understanding personal emotions (whether this involves being reintroduced to early experiences, developing 'self-awareness,' or acquiring 'emotional intelligence'), so much as *discovering what emotions say about an organization as a system in context* (Armstrong, 2000). Emotions, both conscious and unconscious, which are individually felt and collectively produced and performed, are interwoven with politics and power in organizations. Emotion and politics inform and recreate each other within organizations.

ORGANIZATIONAL LEARNING, POLITICS, AND EMOTION

Despite the awareness that reason and emotion define each other, we often imagine that organizations are rational places, where we can use our intellectual abilities and our knowledge to implement decisions, to problem solve, and to take the organization forward. And this is true—we can do this through rational and intellectual endeavor. However, rationality is only one aspect of our experience and our knowledge in organizations. We also know that organizations overflow with stated and unstated emotions; with complex inter-personal relations; and with politics and power. Learning in organizations and the organization of learning processes are inevitably bound up with political dynamics, with power, and with resistance. So, how are we to understand politics in relation to learning? Politics is

> a term used to describe the activity of individuals, groups, organizations or institutions in mobilising resources and enrolling people to support a policy, plan or project . . . politics is a practice of securing compliance or consent . . . politics might be the practice of resistance to the established power relations . . . (or) it is just as likely to be a question of power struggles between different groups of managers

> (Odih and Knights, 2007: 336)

In our view, an interest in emotion in organizations should seek to address the ways in which emotions, as they interweave with political problems, are individually felt and collectively produced and performed. Thus, what seems like collaboration to managers may feel like control to their staff; what feels like a concession to managers may be experienced as an insult by their workers; or what is intended as reconciliation by one group may be experienced as a climb-down by another. Learning and knowledge, themselves, lie squarely at the heart of such emotional politics. Who gains and who is denied knowledge? What knowledge is on offer and on what terms? How is knowledge to be used and in whose interest? These are all deeply political issues and ones liable to arouse powerful emotions in individuals and groups. The complexity of relations that are mobilized by the interplay between emotions and politics create, for example, surprising, self-limiting, innovative, unexpected, uncomfortable, and unwanted structures for action.

The interplay between emotion and politics in organizations concerns *how* organizations function as emotional places (not how individuals within organizations can 'have' or 'manage' emotion); it concerns how decisions, strategies, and actions are shaped, subverted, and/or transformed by emotions; and it concerns how emotions become embedded in cultural and political practices that determine 'the way we do things here.' Engaging with the interplay between emotion and politics in organizations goes some way to unsettling the conventional view of organizations 'as rationally ordered, appropriately structured, and emotion free life spaces, where the right decisions are made for the right reasons by the right people, in a reliable and predictable manner' (Kersten, 2001: 452). Studies that have been concerned specifically with the relationship between emotion and politics have shown that emotion is essential to control processes, and that emotions need to be understood in terms of the social and political structures of which they are a part (Fineman and Sturdy, 1999). Emotions underpin and influence behavior in organizations in ways that create distinctive political dynamics and organizing processes (Vince, 2001, 2002). The generation of knowledge about the emotions and politics that underpin organizing adds to opportunities for behavior that can 'unsettle conventional practices' (Cunliffe and Easterby-Smith, 2004). Emotion guides individuals in appraising social situations and responding to them, therefore emotional display is part of an inter-personal, meaning creating process (Antonacopoulou and Gabriel, 2001).

An important distinction that illuminates the relation between emotion, politics, and learning is that between 'learning-in-action' and 'learning inaction' (Vince, 2008, 2010). The phrase 'learning-in-action' represents the productive relationship between learning and practice. For example, we know that learning can be 'generative' in the sense that it can underpin improvements in practice over time. Popular, action-based approaches to learning like 'action learning' are based on the premise that membership of action-learning groups can assist individuals in the development of strategic actions, which then can be tested and potentially transformed in practice (see Pedler, 2002). However, the politics surrounding learning in organizations also trigger a different and altogether less positive dynamic, one that leads to inertia and even paralysis. This is called 'learning inaction' because participants in learning groups also have (conscious and unconscious) knowledge, fantasies, and perceptions about when it is emotionally and politically expedient to refrain from action, when to avoid collective action, and the organizational dynamics that underpin a failure or refusal to act. We often know what the political limits of learning are in our organizations without having to be told; we collude with others in order to create limitations on learning; and we are often aware of what is and is not going to be seen as a legitimate result of our attempts to learn. We are (consciously or unconsciously) aware of the organizational dynamics that underpin a failure to act *at the same time* as we are positively engaged in learning activities to improve practice. The paradoxical tension of learning in organizations is that it is desired and resisted at the same time. Such tensions at the heart of both learning-in-action and learning inaction create anxiety for individuals, groups, and organizations.

ANXIETY

Anxiety is an emotion that has been widely discussed in relation to learning. Learning involves success and failure, trial and error, triumph and disappointment, presenting individuals and groups with formidable uncertainties and self-doubts liable to trigger anxiety. A common understanding of anxiety is that it is fear without an object—we can't easily say what makes us anxious. Here, we are using the word in the sense of an apprehensive expectation, or 'the expectation of a danger'—something to be avoided or controlled, because it 'incites the feeling of being uncomfortable' (Salecl, 2004). 'Being uncomfortable' is a common emotional state in organizations; indeed emotions have been described as 'uncomfortable knowledge' within organizations (Vince, 1999). Anxiety is a major aspect of human experience in organizations. We are not using the word anxiety here as a clinical term, but as 'a primary aspect of human experience' (Salecl, 2004). However, categories applied to the clinical diagnosis of anxiety also provide a general idea of the key components of everyday anxiety in organizations. These include: feelings of being 'on the edge,' keyed up, wound up, or nervous; the inability to relax; frequent preoccupation with painful thoughts; stress that is out of proportion to the subject matter of the thoughts; feeling apprehensive, a sense of being on the brink of some disaster; feeling restless, a need to be 'doing'/to be on the move; anticipating the worst; and difficulties in concentration.

Anxiety is an emotion that can emanate from the self, but equally may be co-created through interactions between people; it can be infectious both as a paralyzing and as a galvanizing force. Learning anxieties in organizations can afflict both individuals and groups and are capable of generating both paralyzing and productive effects. For example, anxiety about performing in public can be the very feeling that makes such action possible or impossible. Anxiety can provide the energy necessary to risk performing in public, as well as underpinning the fear and desire to avoid such performance. This dual potential of anxiety, to generate both insight and ignorance (Vince and Martin, 1993; Vince, 1998), has a profound impact on the organization of learning (as well as individuals' learning in organizations). Its management and containment is therefore an important aspect of the task of leaders and teachers alike.

An important starting point in understanding anxiety at work may be to recognize that 'what really produces anxiety is the attempt to get rid of it' (Salecl, 2004). This process can be seen within individuals, in groups, and in organizations. For example, consider the white manager who is reluctant to provide feedback on work performance with a black member of staff because she is anxious of being accused of racism. The manager's anxiety has already produced the discrimination she was seeking to avoid. Think of the MBA group that is anxious about the cultural and racial differences in the learning group. Their declaration that 'we are all equal in this group' makes difference almost impossible to talk about. Their anxiety reflects an unspoken awareness that differences are already making a difference in the group, and that it needs to protect itself from the imagined conflicts that might occur if this subject is spoken about.

Important as the management of anxiety is, in its very essence, it can generate additional anxieties, for example, by shifting the blame or making scapegoats of other people. If I do not want failures to be my fault then they must belong to someone else, to other people, or other parts of the organization where poor management, bad practices, or bad attitudes prevail. Anxieties about being seen to fail create blame of 'the other' and such blame undermines the ability of people within the organization to communicate across sub-system boundaries or to learn from honest mistakes (Vince and Saleem, 2004). In this example, anxiety about problems of communication is reinforcing communication problems in the organization. Individual and group attempts to address anxiety are referred to by psychodynamic thinkers as psychological defenses against anxiety. Some of these defenses, like shifting the blame or rationalizing away failure, may be conscious. Others, however, operate unconsciously as individuals and groups seek to fend themselves off from the unsettling effects of anxiety. These may include flights into fantasy, such as 'we are invulnerable, no-one can hurt us,' or denial 'this cannot possibly happen,' or 'this could never happen again.' Defense mechanisms then are a group of psychological processes aimed at reducing painful and troubling feelings, notably anxiety, or at eliminating forces that are experienced as threatening the integrity or mental survival of an individual or a group. These defenses, including projection, repression, denial, and splitting, seek to protect individuals, groups, and organizations from pain and anxiety, but the result can be precisely the opposite, since they may immerse them in individual or collective delusions or wish-fulfilling fantasies, whose result is to exacerbate organizational problems and failings. Under such circumstances, failure does not become the mother of success, as the old Chinese saying would have it, but the mother and grandmother of more failure.

TRANSFERENCE, ANXIETY, AND DEFENSES

If defense mechanisms generally inhibit learning, then learning (both individually and collectively) requires a certain type of psychological work in identifying, accepting, and tolerating the anxieties that it creates. Some of these anxieties may be triggered by earlier experiences of failure and disappointment or by threatening feelings of uncertainty, dependency, and vulnerability. Thus, learning is no spontaneous unleashing of potential but involves overcoming resistances to learning, many of which operate in unconscious and unacknowledged ways. One particular source of unconscious resistance to learning lies in each individual's narcissistic belief that he or she is already perfect and therefore needs no development or change (Freud, 1914/1984). Another source of resistance lies in the conviction that the individual knows what he/she needs to learn and nothing beyond it is necessary or desirable. Learning represents a challenge and a threat to all of us, endangering some valued ideas, habits, and beliefs about self and others and generating an unavoidable degree of discomfort or even pain.

For these reasons, psychodynamic writers pay great attention to early life learning experiences, its excitements and disappointments, which color subsequent learning in schools, universities, and, more generally, organizations. Learning is facilitated by an agent of learning, a parent, an older sibling, a teacher, who represents a figure of authority; this figure is in later life replaced by a leader, teacher, mentor, consultant, or clinician, who acts as the force facilitating and unleashing learning (Salzberger-Wittenberg et al., 1983; French 1997). This relationship between learner and the agent of learning is strongly influenced by the dynamics of transference and counter-transference, the complex and largely unconscious emotional forces which bind together student and teacher, practitioner and consultant, patient and analyst (Freud, 1940/1986). Transference is a process whereby feelings and images towards figures of authority or knowledge are repetitions of earlier experiences of relations with authority figures, notably parents. An important psychoanalytic insight derives from the work of Winnicott (1962, 1964, 1980), who argued that effective learning takes place within a 'holding environment,' an environment which allows enough space for experimentation and play, which is safe enough without being stifling or overbearing. The holding environment in organizations, including schools and universities, recreates the experience of the mother's embrace, an embrace which allows the child to realize that he or she has an independent existence in the world without, however, exposing him or her directly to the threats engendered by this world. The management of anxiety then becomes seminal in all learning situations, since too much or too little anxiety inhibits learning. Too much anxiety and learning is paralyzed; too little anxiety and learning never appears on the agenda.

GROUP EMOTIONS, COLLECTIVE DYNAMICS, AND LEARNING

Moving from individual to collective learning and its associated emotions, our theoretical knowledge originates in the work of Melanie Klein who identified two important mechanisms of defense against primitive anxiety—particularly the processes of 'projecting' bad feelings onto others and 'splitting' good and bad objects in order to focus on an ideal. The term primitive anxieties represents some of the overwhelming anxieties experienced by all children in early life, including fears of abandonment and betrayal, persecution, disintegration, and mutilation—which can resurface in later life in stressful situations. From these foundations, Elliott Jacques (1955) and Isobel Menzies (1960) developed a theory of the use of social systems as defenses against anxiety, arguing that, in addition to individual defenses, individuals and groups develop collective defenses against anxieties. This theory 'makes it possible to articulate the dilemma inherent in organizational life between adherence to professed definitions of purpose, and recognition of *unthought* purposes . . . concerned with providing the subject with an identity—purposes which, when threatened, arouse primitive anxiety' (Palmer, 2002: 161). When social defenses become dominant they also become dysfunctional for the organization as a whole, because defenses support organizational members' detachment from their experience. Social defenses do initially reduce anxiety, but they also eventually 'replace compassion, empathy, awareness and meaning with control and impersonality' (Kets de Vries, 2004: 198).

The inevitable intermingling of unthought purposes with deliberate intensions highlights further the importance of understanding the continuous connection between power, emotion, and learning in organizations (Vince, 2001). The emotions evoked through power relations promote a tendency towards defensive behavior; towards the evasion of feelings in context; towards the projection of bad feelings onto others as blame or criticism. One of the focal points for the intersection of power and emotion in organizations is the relation between a leader and his or her follower. Many approaches to learning about leadership emphasize the individual leader's role influence on followers, how in other words leaders may draw on specific traits, styles, and approaches in more or less effective ways. An individual leader may facilitate consensus or may initiate dispersed leadership in a group of followers, but both have to be recognized as political techniques to enhance performance through attempts to make hierarchical relations less overt. Looking at this emotionally as well as politically, 'leaders first and foremost spin dreams' (Gabriel, 1999) and they are subject to fantasies, which might stimulate defensive as much as desirable behavior. The leader's desire may be to share authority, to collaborate in a social context where 'none of us is as smart as all of us.' Thus, in organizational settings, individual accountability for outcomes in a political environment implies broader power relations, where regression to a dynamic of control often becomes an inevitable compromise.

Leaders stand at the boundary between rational and non-rational decision making, between realities and fantasies, helping to assess obstacles and to produce the necessary plans to overcome them. To understand leadership in organizations, it is important to understand how emotions are connected to fantasy; how fantasies provide hope or discourage action, as well as how they are communicated, for example, through projection onto others. The leader is never alone; he or she is also a product of the fantasies of followers (and vice versa). Such fantasies inevitably impact on the emotional and political dynamics and experiences surrounding attempts at leadership. The leader may be seen as someone who cares, can read my mind, is indifferent, accessible, aloof, omnipotent, unafraid, hopeless, brilliant, externally driven, or a fraud. In this way, emotional fantasies may reconfigure power relations in different ways, for instance by casting a leader into the role of benevolent mother figure or satanic schemer, and recasting the followers as heroic individualists, passive sheep, or recalcitrant children. All of these projections contribute to the complexity of leadership relations and reinforce the sense in which leadership is a product of the dynamics between self and other.

In organizations, it is impossible for leaders to remain dreamers; necessity requires that vision be turned into reality, something that inevitably calls for the assistance of others. Emotions, both conscious and unconscious, individually felt and collectively produced and performed, are intertwined with the political problems of leadership. For example, it is difficult to uncouple the desire to collaborate in organizations from the compulsion to dominate, or the desire to be protected from the impulse to scapegoat. We often know what good leadership feels like. However, leadership can also be an ambiguous process within a social and political context, one that mobilizes anxiety and self-doubt, encourages insecurity, gives rise to defensive behavior, fosters the development of avoidance strategies, and leads to detachment from reflection and from criticism. Our learning about leadership in organizations is individualistically orientated in part because this approach makes it easier to contain emotions and politics that might be capable of undermining organizational stability and create the potential for organizational learning and change. This individualism protects organizations by always providing the possibility of creating a scapegoat when things go wrong, replacing him or her, and resuming business as if nothing had happened, thus forfeiting all possibilities of learning along the way.

The ways in which leadership is exercised are the result not only of the person who leads or the people being led, but also of the organizational context that shapes leadership. For example, team building is seen as an individual skill that can be taught on management and leadership development courses. However, it may also be useful to recognize that the team builds the individual or individuals who represent and lead them. A team produces the behavior of the leader, as well as the leadership decisions and choices that are voiced, through their conscious and unconscious actions and inactions, through the various ways in which emotions and politics in a team impact on organizing. And team building itself may be a process that is systematically fostered or inhibited by organizational factors small and large, ranging from performance appraisals to the physical location of offices.

CRITICISM, LEARNING, AND CARE

Criticism and self-criticism lie at the heart of learning. We learn from our ability to reflect critically and assess the consequences of our actions, taking on board the criticisms of others and of ourselves. But criticism, as every child learns early in life, is painful and hurtful: and it is undoubtedly part of a technology of power. At its most extreme, criticism becomes bullying—incessant nit-picking and fault-finding which undermines a person's self-confidence and serves to perpetuate their subordinate dependent standing. In less extreme forms, criticism can still act to maintain hierarchical distinctions, to paralyze the willingness to experiment and innovate and to dread the prospect of failure, humiliation, and ridicule. Criticism can easily become internalized as self-criticism which is every bit as destabilizing as criticism by an external authority. As psychoanalysis teaches us, the voice of the super-ego can be harsher, more vigilant, more unreasonable, and harder to answer back than the voice of external authority. Yet, criticism is vital for learning. How can it be balanced and prevented from unleashing the kinds of dynamics that we identified earlier?

It is for this reason that we shall conclude this contribution by arguing that criticism and critical reflection are effective prompts for learning when balanced by an ethic of care which treats people in their different roles, as students, as subordinates and employees, as patients, and even as consumers, as ends in themselves rather than as means to specific ends. Since it was first articulated by Carol Gilligan (1982) in connection with the moral development of young girls, the discourse on the ethics of care has generated many insights in diverse fields ranging from international relations to psychology and moral philosophy (see, for example, Held, 2006). In the field of organizational studies and especially in management learning, however, it has been substantially ignored (for an exception, see Gabriel, 2009). The ethics of care sees caring as a vital dimension of most human interactions and as the foundation of a particular type of morality. In contrast to the 'ethics of justice,' the ethics of care does not rely on claims of universality, absolute judgments of right and wrong, and perfect virtues. Instead, it is a morality that grows out of the recognition that all people are embedded in different webs of social relations, being dependent on others for their survival and well-being and capable of supporting others in their moments of need and helplessness.

A large part of the debate on care concerns its gendered nature, whether in other words, women are more disposed by nature, culture, or other factors for caring than men and how this affects power relations between the genders (Held, 2006; Kittay, 1999; Kittay and Feder, 2002; Noddings, 1986; Tronto, 1993). What seems likely is that while both women and men can act in caring ways, at least in Western cultures, caring is associated with the feminine principle as against the ethic of impersonal objectivity, criticism, and judgment which represent a masculine or even patriarchal order. Being cared for is what every newborn child requires, and caring is attending to the needs of others with whom we feel close and for whom we are prepared to take personal responsibility. Caring is not a scripted emotional performance and cannot be reduced to emotional labor. Caring involves some of the qualities that are currently and fashionably grouped under the title of emotional intelligence, yet, unlike emotional intelligence, it entails no suggestion of emotional manipulation or deception. Instead, caring involves sensitivity to the emotional needs of the other person and an ability to guide and influence these emotions through a wide range of actions, utterances, and expressions. It requires an ability to 'notice what you are noticing' (James and Ladkin, 2008); and to anticipate the needs and vulnerabilities of the cared for. And, in spite of all this, it is a profound mistake to view an ethic of care as some kind of charitable principle of universal love or as a 'touchy-feely' ethic of intimacy. An ethic of care may sometimes dictate taking difficult, hard, and unpleasant actions in support of a person, an institution, or even a thing one cares for.

The ethic of care does not resolve the anxieties we signaled earlier, nor does it dissolve the political realities within which learning takes place; it can, however, contribute to learning in a number of different ways. First, it offers a counter-balance to the ethic of criticism, sustaining learning, especially in its early, tentative stages. Without compromising the commitment to rational discourse and rigorous knowledge, the ethic of care ensures that criticism is exercised in a responsible manner, a manner which tolerates disagreement and encourages learning. Within an ethic of care, criticism never degenerates to nit-picking, the compulsive pointing out of even trivial flaws with the aim of establishing hierarchies of authority and privilege. On the contrary, the caring critic acknowledges his or her own fallibility and the possibility that his or her judgment may be made in error.

An ethic of care offers a partial containment of anxieties unleashed by both the learning process and organizational politics. It allows for mistakes to be recognized and corrected, it supports experimentation and responsible improvisation, and it promotes respect for human fallibility and insecurity. Akio Morita, co-founder of Sony and a leader known both for his toughness and his caring qualities makes the point explicitly in his autobiography:

> Mistakes or miscalculations are human and normal, and viewed in the long run they have not damaged the company. I do not mind taking responsibility for every managerial decision I have made. But if a person who makes a mistake is branded and kicked off the seniority promotion escalator, he could lose his motivation for the rest of his business life and deprive the company of whatever good things he may have to offer later. . . . I tell our people, 'Go ahead and do what you think is right. If you make a mistake, you will learn from it. Just don't make the same mistake twice.'
>
> (Morita, 1987: 150)

The ethic of care does not function as a universal warm blanket of unconditional positive regard. Far from it—it can involve hard decisions, disappointing news and the management of disillusionment and pain without recourse to comforting untruths and false hopes. It can also dictate sharp political action in pursuit, defense, and support of individuals, groups, and organizations for which one cares. In this way, the ethic of care may extend to the process of learning itself and to the political realities with which it is intertwined. It may even extend to the organization itself as a valued entity, one that is cherished by those who work for it, support it, and nurture it. In a memorable piece inspired by the children's story of the velveteen rabbit, David Sims (2004) has argued that it is love that turns organizations into valued spaces in which people's actions 'come alive.' The velveteen rabbit is a children's toy that, in the story, comes to life or becomes 'real' only when the child who owns it develops a caring relation with it. The story's theme that love 'animates' what it touches is one that has been rehearsed endlessly by poets and storytellers, but Sims argues that it may also apply to organizations, some of which generate extraordinary amounts of loyalty and affection among their members whereas others remain objects of instrumental usefulness and emotional indifference. An ethic of care can in this way neutralize the widely commented cynicism that can so easily afflict our organizations and their attempt to foster a learning culture.

In this chapter, we indicated a number of different ways in which emotions in organizations enter into the learning processes of individuals and groups. We suggested that emotions neither enhance nor inhibit learning in a direct and straightforward manner; and emotions themselves are neither the direct products of learning nor its raw materials. Instead, we proposed that emotional configurations in organizations are themselves tied up with organizational politics and power and argued that to consider knowledge and learning outside organizational politics and power leads to blinkered accounts. Fear of failure or criticism, a key emotion in regard of organizational learning, is also the result of a political set-up focused on punishment and making scapegoats. We proposed, by contrast, an ethic of care that provides a secure environment in which people may learn, individually and collectively, from their mistakes and miscalculations, and engage in constructive criticism and self-criticism.

REFERENCES

Antonacopoulou, E. P. and Gabriel, Y. (2001) Emotion, learning and organizational change: Towards an integration of psychoanalytic and other perspectives. *Journal of Organizational Change Management*, 14(5): 435–451.

Armstrong, D. (2000) Emotions in organizations: Disturbance or intelligence? *International Society for the Psychoanalytic Study of Organizations Annual Symposium*, London, June.

Ashkanasy, N. M. and Daus, C. S. (2002) Emotions in the workplace: The new challenge for managers. *Academy of Management Executive*, 16(1): 76–86.

Campbell, C. (1989) The romantic ethic and the spirit of modern consumerism. Oxford: Macmillan.

Carr, A. (2001) Understanding emotion and emotionality in a process of change. *Journal of Organizational Change Management*, 14(5): 421–434.

Cooper, R. (1989) Modernism, postmodernism and organizational analysis 3: The contribution of Jacques Derrida. *Organization Studies*, 10(4): 479–502.

Craib, I. (1998) *Experiencing identity*. London: Sage.

Cunliffe, A. and Easterby-Smith, M. (2004) From Reflection to Practical Reflexivity: Experiential learning as lived experience. In M. Reynolds and R. Vince (eds.) *Organizing Reflection*. Aldershot, UK: Ashgate.

Damasio, A.R. (1994) *Descartes' error: Emotion, reason, and the human brain*. New York: Putnam.

Damasio, A.R. (1999) *The feeling of what happens: Body and emotion in the making of consciousness*. New York: Harcourt Brace.

Fineman, S. (1993) *Emotion in Organizations*. London: Sage.

Fineman, S. (1996) Emotion and organizing. In S. Clegg, C. Hardy, and W. R. Nord (eds.), *Handbook of Organization Studies*. London: Sage: 543–564.

Fineman, S. (2001) Managing emotions at work: some political reflections. Paper presented at the Academy of Management Conference, Washington, DC.

Fineman, S. (2003) Emotionalizing organizational learning. In M. Easterby-Smith and M. A. Lyles (eds.), *Handbook of Organizational Learning and Knowledge Management*. Oxford: Blackwell: 557–574.

Fineman, S. and Sturdy, A. (1999) The emotions of control: a qualitative exploration of environmental regulation. *Human Relations*, 52(5): 631–663.

Flam, H. (1990a) The emotional 'Man' and the problem of collective action. *International Sociology*, 5(1): 39–56.

Flam, H. (1990b) Emotional 'Man' II. Corporate actors as emotion-motivated emotion managers. *International Sociology*, 5(2): 225–234.

Foucault, M. (1978) *The History of Sexuality: An Introduction*, Harmondsworth: Penguin.

Foucault, M. (1980) *Power/knowledge: Selected interviews and other writings* 1972–1977. Brighton: Harvester Books.

Freire, P. (1970/1996) *Pedagogy of the Oppressed*. Harmondsworth: Penguin.

French, R (1997) The teacher as container of anxiety: Psychoanalysis and the role of the teacher. *Journal of Management Education*, 21(4): 483–495.

French, R. and Vince, R. (1999) *Group Relations, Management and Organisation*. Oxford: Oxford University Press.

Freud, S. (1914/1984) On narcissism: An introduction, *On Metapsychology: The Theory of Psychoanalysis*. Harmondsworth: Pelican Freud Library, 11: 59–97.

Freud, S. (1923/1984) The ego and the id, *On Metapsychology: The Theory of Psychoanalysis*. Harmondsworth: Pelican Freud Library, 11: 341–406.

Freud, S. (1940/1986) An outline of psychoanalysis. *Historical and Expository works on Psycho-Analysis*. Harmondsworth: Pelican Freud Library, 15: 371–443.

Gabriel, Y. (1998) Psychoanalytic contributions to the study of the emotional life of organizations. *Administration and Society*, 30(3): 291–314.

Gabriel, Y. (1999) *Organizations in Depth*. London: Sage.

Gabriel, Y. (2009) Reconciling an ethic of care with critical management pedagogy. *Management Learning*, 40(4): 379–385.

Gherardi, S. (1999) Learning as problem-driven or learning in the face of mystery? *Organizational Studies*, 20(1): 101–123.

Gherardi, S. (2004) Knowing as desire: Dante' Ulysses at the end of the known world. In
    Y. Gabriel (ed.), *Myths, Stories and Organizations: Premodern Narratives for Our Times*. Oxford:
    Oxford University Press: 32–48.

Gilligan, C. (1982) In a Different Voice: Psychological Theory and Women's Development.
    Cambridge, MA: Harvard University Press.

Goffman, E. (1959) *The Presentation of Self in Everyday Life*. Garden City, N.Y.: Anchor.

Habermas, J. (1972) *Knowledge and Human Interests*. London: Heinemann.

Held, V. (2006) *The Ethics of Care: Personal, Political, and Global*. Oxford: Oxford University
    Press.

Heller, A. (1979) *A Theory of Feelings*. Amsterdam: Van Gorkum Assen.

Hochschild, A.R. (1979) Emotion work, feeling rules, and social structure. *American Journal
    of Sociology*, 85(3): 551–575.

Hochschild, A.R. (1983) *The Managed Heart*. Berkeley: University of California Press.

Höpfl, H. and Linstead, S. (1997) Learning to feel and feeling to learn: Emotion and
    learning in organizations. *Management Learning*, 28(1): 5–12.

James, K.T. and Ladkin, D. (2008) Meeting the challenge of leading in the 21st century:
    Beyond the 'deficit model' of leadership development. In K.T. James and J. Collins
    (eds.), *Leadership Learning: Knowledge into Action*. London: Palgrave McMillian: 13–34.

Jaques, E. (1955) Social systems as a defense against persecutory and depressive anxiety.
    In M. Klein, P. Heimann, and R. E. Money-Kryle (eds.) *New Directions in Psychoanalysis*
    London: Tavistock Publications.

Kersten, A. (2001) Organizing for powerlessness: A critical perspective on psychodynam-
    ics and dysfunctionality. *Journal of Organizational Change Management*, 14(5): 452–467.

Kets de Vries, M. F. R. (2004) Organizations on the couch: A clinical perspective on
    organizational dynamics. *European Management Journal*, 22(2): 183–200.

Kittay, E. (1999) Love's labor: Essays on women, equality, and dependency. New York:
    Routledge.

Kittay, E. and Feder, E. (2002) *The Subject of Care: Feminist Perspectives on Dependency*. Lanham,
    MD: Rowman and Littlefield Publishers.

Landen, M. (2002) Emotion management: Dabbling in mystery—white witchcraft or
    black art? *Human Resource Development International*, 5(4): 507–524.

Mangham, I. (1998) Emotional discourse in organizations. In D. Grant, T. Keenoy, and
    C. Oswick (eds.), *Discourse and Organization*. London: Sage: 51–64.

Mayer, J. and Salovey, P. (1997) What is emotional intelligence? In P. Salovey and D.
    Sluyten (eds.) *Emotional Development and Emotional Intelligence: Implications for Educators*.
    New York: Basic Books.

Menzies, I. E. (1960) A case study of the functioning of social systems as a defense
    against anxiety: A report on a study of the nursing system in a general hospital. *Human
    Relations*, 13: 95–121.

Morita, A. (1987) *Made in Japan*. London: Fontana.

Noddings, N. (1986) *Caring: A Feminine Approach to Ethics and Moral Education*. Berkeley:
    University of California Press.

Odih, P. and Knights, D. (2007) Political organizations and decision making, In D. Knights
    and H. Willmott (eds.) *Introducing Organizational Behaviour and Management*. London:
    Thomson.

Palmer, B. (2002) The Tavistock Paradigm: Inside, Outside and Beyond. In R. D. Hinshelwood and M. Chiesa (eds.) *Organizations, Anxieties and Defenses: Towards a Psychoanalytic Social Psychology*. London: Whurr Publishers Ltd.

Pedler, M. (2002) Accessing local knowledge: Action learning and organizational learning in Walsall. *Human Resource Development International*, 5: 523–540.

Sacks, O. (1995) *An Anthropologist on Mars*. Oxford: Blackwell.

Salecl, R. (2004) *On Anxiety*. London: Routledge.

Salzberger-Wittenberg, I, Henry, G., and Osborne, E. (1983) *The Emotional Experience of Learning and Teaching*. London: Routledge.

Sims, D. (2004) The velveteen rabbit and passionate feelings for organizations. In Y. Gabriel (ed.), *Myths, Stories and Organizations: Premodern Narratives for Our Times*. Oxford: Oxford University Press: 209–222.

Spivak, G. (1988) Can the subaltern speak? In C. Nelson, and L. Grosberg (Eds.), *Marxism and the Interpretation of Culture*. Urbana: University of Illinois Press: 271–313.

Ten Bos, R. and Willmott, H. (2001) Towards a post-dualistic business ethics: Interweaving reason and emotion in working life. *Journal of Management Studies*, 38(6): 769–793.

Tronto, J. C. (1993) Moral boundaries: A political argument for an ethic of care. New York: Routledge.

Vince, R. (1998) Behind and beyond Kolb's learning cycle. *Journal of Management Education*, 22(3): 304–319.

Vince, R. (1999) 'Uncomfortable Knowledge' management: The impact of emotions on organizational learning. The 3rd International Conference on Organizational Learning and Knowledge Management, Lancaster University, UK, June 6–8.

Vince, R (2001) Power and emotion in organizational learning. *Human Relations*, 54(10): 1325–1351.

Vince, R. (2002) The politics of imagined stability: A psychodynamic understanding of change at Hyder plc. *Human Relations*, 55(10): 1189–1208.

Vince, R. (2006) Being taken over: Managers' emotions and rationalisations during a company takeover. *Journal of Management Studies*, 43(2): 343–365.

Vince, R. (2008) 'Learning-in-Action' and 'Learning Inaction': Advancing the theory and practice of critical action learning. *Action Learning: Research and Practice*, 5(2): 93–104.

Vince, R. (2010) Anxiety, politics and critical management education. *British Journal of Management*, 21(1): 26–29.

Vince, R. and Martin, L. (1993) Inside action learning: The psychology and the politics of the action learning model. *Management Learning*, 24(3): 205–215.

Vince, R. and Saleem, T. (2004) The impact of caution and blame on organizational learning. *Management Learning*, 35(2): 131–152.

Williams, S. (2001). *Emotion and Social Theory*. London: Sage.

Winnicott, D. (1962). The Maturational Processes and Facilitating Environment. London: Hogarth Press.

Winnicott, D. (1964) *The Child, the Family and the Outside World*. Harmondsworth: Penguin.

Winnicott, D. (1980) *Playing and Reality*. Harmondsworth: Penguin.

16

Subtle Learning and Organizational Identity as Enablers of Strategic Change

KEVIN G. CORLEY, DENNIS A. GIOIA, AND RAJIV NAG

ABSTRACT

Contrary to recent portrayals, we argue that the relationship between organizational identity and organizational learning is not only a strong one, but also one that facilitates organizational adaptability to a constantly shifting competitive environment. The implications of this relationship are perhaps most powerful in the context of change because both learning and identity are essential to both the strategic and personal aspects of organizational change. Most relevant to this volume, this adaptive interrelationship has implications for current conceptualizations of organizational learning that include: (1) the specification of a type of organizational learning heretofore downplayed in the literature—*subtle learning* and (2) the realization that organizational learning can be more subliminal and tacit than previously conceptualized and, therefore, can occur out of conscious awareness or without explicit articulation. These implications provide the foundation for inquiry into other organizational phenomena closely linked to the learning–identity relationship.

INTRODUCTION

The processes by which organizational members learn to change is intimately intertwined with their assumptions about who they are as an organization. Indeed recent research has found organizational identity to be a critical though relatively under-recognized factor that not only influences what is learned, but more importantly how members learn to respond to strategic change imperatives (Nag, Corley, and Gioia, 2003, 2007). In this chapter we consider the nature of the learning–identity interrelationship and attempt to draw out some of the consequent implications for both concepts, as well as implications for theorists and researchers who study both phenomena.

Although an overused catchphrase in today's society, the notion that 'change is everywhere; change is everything' still holds powerful sway over the modern organization. Because of fast-paced market changes confronting most industries, ever-accelerating technology cycles, insatiable desires for up-to-the-minute business news, and gyrating capital markets, as well as capricious terrorism, organizations are faced with tumultuous environmental relationships that require constant mindfulness and adaptability. Change *is*, in fact, everywhere in organizations and, to some extent, everything as well, in the sense that organizational well-being and even survival depend on organizational adaptability (Tsoukas and Chia, 2002).

Our research has discovered new ways in which organizational identity relates to transformational change. In our earlier conceptions we treated organizational identity as perceptions or implicit theories shared by organization members about 'who we are as an organization' (Albert and Whetten, 1985; Gioia, 1998; Stimpert, Gustafson, and Sarason, 1998). Recent research has urged us to enrich this conception of identity by appreciating a more situated, action-oriented, and pragmatic view of the concept (Carlsen, 2006, 2009; Nag, Corley, and Gioia, 2007). Issues of organizational identity arise not only as the members of an organization attempt to answer the question 'Who are we?' but also the questions 'How do we do things?', 'Why do we do those things?', and 'Who should we be in the future?' Attempting to answer these questions also prompts the question 'Who do others think we are?' which means that identity is closely interrelated with how insiders think outsiders perceive the organization (labeled as 'construed external image' by Dutton, Dukerich, and Harquail, 1994) and how outsiders actually perceive the organization (or reputation, see Fombrun, 1996).

Researchers have argued that because organizational identity involves answers to such fundamental questions, it is inherently stable and resistant to change (Albert and Whetten, 1985; Brown and Starkey, 2000). Our research has demonstrated that this is not necessarily the case, however, and that, quite to the contrary, organizational identity can change over relatively short periods of time (Corley and Gioia, 2004; Corley, Gioia, and Fabbri, 2000; Gioia, Schultz, and Corley, 2000; Gioia and Thomas, 1996). The underlying means by which identity change is possible while appearing to have endurance or continuity is that organization members maintain consistent labels for elements of their identity over time, but the meanings and practices associated with these labels change to accommodate emergent needs (Gioia, et al., 2000; Nag et al., 2007).

One major upshot of our theoretical and empirical efforts is the realization that processes of organizational learning are essential to the social construction and reconstruction of organizational identity in the now-common context of a fast-changing environment. In a general sense, identity construction and reconstruction are intertwined with a continuous process of organizational learning because an organization must continuously 'relearn' its identity as its enacted environment recursively influences further meaning making and action taking.

As our research has progressed, however, we have come to recognize that the type of learning involved in this dynamic process differs from the organizational learning typically described in management research. The predominant approach to studying learning in and by organizations is one of tracking *overt* change or tangible outcomes (Wilson, Goodman, and Cronin, 2007). Contrary to this approach, we find that learning associated with organizational identity change tends to be more discreet and based in changes to intersubjective meanings and underlying social practices as compared to the overt, knowledge- and behavior-based changes fundamental to the individual-level origins of the psychology and management perspectives on organizational learning (Easterby-Smith, 1997; Huber, 1991; Miller, 1996). This emerging distinction has forced us to explore more deeply the relationship between organizational identity and organizational learning and, as a result, to reconsider organizational learning as a theoretical concept.

The basic premise of this chapter is that processes of organizational learning are more closely interrelated with organizational identity than previously presumed, and that this relationship is adaptive for the organization. This interrelationship is most evident in the milieu of organizational change, where both identity and learning play key roles strategically and contextually. The intersection between the two phenomena not only provides a powerful set of implications for the continued study of organizational change, but also produces a number of significant insights for re-conceptualizing aspects of organizational learning that include:

- the formal recognition of a heretofore underspecified form of organizational learning based in intersubjective meanings and practices, which we term *subtle learning*;
- the appreciation that this form of learning provides the potential for organizational learning to be more inconspicuous, and its effects more covert, than previously presumed; and
- the pragmatically important insight that the influence an organization's identity has on learning processes can facilitate adaptability for the organization (as opposed to previous work depicting it as a constraint on adaptability).

We have two main purposes in writing this chapter that follow from these observations: (1) to act as interested outside observers who see value in bringing an identity perspective to the study of organizational learning (by highlighting and detailing the adaptive relationship between organizational identity and organizational learning); and (2) to explicate the argument that it is difficult to provide a definitive definition of organizational learning because learning takes so many different forms. Our contention here is parallel to Cook and Brown's (1999) argument that we should distinguish between different types of knowledge (and in our case, learning).

The remaining sections of this chapter explore more fully these expansions and reconsiderations of organizational learning, as well as exploring other implications of the interrelationship between organizational identity and learning. We begin with a discussion about the nature of organizational learning, followed by a more in-depth examination of how identity and learning are related at the organizational level. The chapter concludes with a discussion of both the theoretical and practical implications of this interrelationship, with particular attention paid to those implications involving organizational change.

THE NATURE OF ORGANIZATIONAL LEARNING

To explore the interrelationship between organizational identity and learning more deeply, it is first necessary to articulate our perspective on the nature of organizational learning. Similar to our arguments that organizational identity is more than just a collective version of individual identity (Corley et al., 2000), we believe that some types of organizational learning are more than just a collective version of individual learning.

Weick (1991) clearly articulates the strength of this position in his assertion that depicting organizational learning as following the same processes as individual learning limits our ability to gain insight into the phenomenon as a distinctive process in its own right. In its essence, Weick's argument contends that individual-level psychological theories of learning do not adequately describe the organizational learning process because the assumptions underlying those theories do not hold for organizations—organizations are a different type of entity than individuals and interact with environments differently than individuals. To depict organizations as learning the same way that individuals do results in an overly micro-centric view that does not do justice to the unique nature of organizational learning as a macro concept.

Weick and Westley (1999) further support this perspective in their citing of Normann's (1985) and Argote and McGrath's (1993) work. These researchers embed organizational learning in the practices and structures of groups rather than solely in the cognitions of individuals. Learning does not become a macro concept because groups (or in our case organizations) have cognitive structures like humans. Rather, it becomes a macro concept because learning is embedded in action and social interaction (see Ashforth, Rogers, and Corley, in press for a similar argument involving identity); in becoming a macro concept, these researchers argue that learning must transcend individual cognition.

Finally, our view of organizational learning is informed by Cook and Yanow's (1993) conceptualization of organizational learning as a cultural process. Attempting to circumvent the problems they see with viewing organizations mainly as cognitive entities, Cook and Yanow examined the Powell Flute Company's encounter with a technological change as an instance of organizational learning. The Powell Flute Company was world famous for making 'the best flutes in the world' using the Powell scale developed by the company's founder. When a new, highly-demanded scale (the Cooper scale) was introduced, the members of the Powell Flute Company had to face questions about who they were and how that might change given the advent of this new scale. Essentially, they were faced with a question of identity: 'Could the organization make a flute with a Cooper scale and still be the Powell organization?' (1993: 383). Cook and Yanow focus on the organizational learning that occurs around this identity issue, especially on how the organization learns to 'change without changing' and bring the new scale in to their operations without disrupting their sense of collective identity.

What emerges from their analysis is a depiction of organizational learning as 'the acquiring, sustaining, or changing of intersubjective meanings though the artifactual vehicles of their expression and transmission and the collective actions of the group' (1993: 384). The crucial insight here is that organizational learning can involve 'intersubjective meanings' created and sustained via cultural practices—an insight that has been magnified in recent works by Carlile (2002) and Bechky (2003). Similar to Weick and Robert's (1993) notion of collective mind embedded in group interaction, learning becomes collective when it is conceived at the level of social interaction, where 'boundary objects' such as language, symbols, and consensual practices (all supra-individual notions) facilitate the expression and transmission of *shared understanding* of actions and events throughout the organization.

SUBTLE LEARNING

As Weick (1991) points out, conceptualizing organizational learning at a bona fide collective level opens up the possibility of seeing previously hidden or neglected aspects of the phenomenon that differ from learning at the individual level. One such aspect, and an important part of understanding the adaptive nature of the identity–learning relationship, involves the subliminal nature of organizational learning that is based in meanings, or *subtle learning*. In choosing the label 'subtle' to describe this form of learning, we highlight changes in the meanings' underlying labels, symbols, and, importantly, practices that occur without explicit recognition or acknowledgement by those involved with those labels, symbols, or practices. Subtle learning, then, involves changes to the intersubjective meanings constituting the core of a collective's understanding of themselves. Instead of thinking of organizational learning as only involving changes in behavior and/or knowledge, this perspective emphasizes that changes in meaning around actions and symbols also form a viable conceptualization of organizational learning.

The 'deep processes'[1] of subtle learning

By moving the locus of the learning process away from an emphasis on individual cognition and placing its emphasis on the social interactions and intersubjective meanings embedded within a collective, it becomes possible to conceive of organizational learning as taking place without the explicit awareness of learning, without the recognition of learning, or even without the intention to learn by the members of the collective. It thus becomes possible to account for organizational learning that occurs without overt acknowledgement because changes in intersubjective meanings can exist and affect future cognition and action without members of the collective overtly recognizing them.

If a socially shared sense of meaning changes among the members of a collective, no one member of the collective need articulate that change to the other members for it to be implemented. It can be more subtle because learning and meaning can exist independently of the individual, in the interactions of the collective. Thus, simply by acting differently and picking up subtle cues based on others' behaviors, it is possible for meanings to change even without linguistic interaction. Taking this argument even further, we can say that, at the extreme, changes in intersubjective meanings might be so subtle that not only are they not articulated and made explicit in the collective's interactions, but that they also remain at a tacit level for the individuals within the collective.

A clear example of this process involves the shifting meaning of what it is to be a team for the members of, for example, a software development group. As the individuals come together and begin interacting with one another, a shared sense emerges that they are a team because their interactions are based in a consensus-seeking, decision-making process in which everyone participates equally to achieve the collective's goals. Over time, however, as resource and time constraints arise, the interaction patterns of these individuals

---

[1]We use the phrase 'deep processes' in pointed contrast to Chomsky's (1964) notion of 'deep structure.'

change such that each member takes on more autonomy, preferred task partnerships emerge, and important decisions are made individually, all the while accounting for the other members of the team and their shared goals. Even though the members of the collective might not be aware of the change or, if they are, do not articulate it in their verbal interactions, the meaning of what it is to be a team has changed for them. Not only have their individual and shared behaviors adapted to meet environmental constraints, but the meaning underlying their self-declaration as a 'team' has shifted, even though they continue to use the same label.

Learning has occurred within the collective, even though they might never label it as such, or, if they do, it will not be labeled until an occasion for retrospective sense making occurs or until external feedback raises their awareness of the change. Once it is brought to the collective's attention, it can officially be labeled 'learning' by those involved (Nicolini and Meznar, 1995) and become explicit in their actions and future meaning-making efforts. Nevertheless, the key point here is that conscious awareness and explicit articulation of the change in intersubjective meaning need not occur for organizational learning to take place.

It is even possible to argue that this form of subtle learning (and the subtle changes often accompanying it) is the norm at the organizational level. We are accustomed to thinking about learning as an explicit, conscious process that leads to some noticeable change in either knowledge or action. Taken in the context of meaning-based learning, however, this assumption seems heavily rooted in individual-level cognitive models of learning and, therefore, not as easily applied to the organizational level. Instead, we might posit that at the organizational level, subtle learning based in meaning changes is the normal state and that explicit, conscious learning is the exception. Subtle learning simultaneously preserves the past and generates the new. It enables finding new ways of doing the same things while still retaining existing meanings or tacitly changes meanings associated with the same ways of doing things. The key point here is that this form of learning brings about change that is less threatening because it is more continuous and connected to prior learnings.

Knowledge versus meaning making

It is also important to note that the distinction between knowledge and meaning is more than merely different labels for the same concept under the organizational learning scenario depicted in this chapter. An important theoretical difference exists between the two, in that any element of knowledge must have meaning ascribed to it before it becomes useful. That is, knowledge can be thought of generally as 'what we know,' whereas meaning involves understanding how that knowledge is applicable to the task at hand.

Thus, for instance, it is not that we know a particular competitor is about to release a new product that is important, but that such knowledge has meaning in how it will affect our strategic actions for the coming year. Meaning construction involves the contextual interpretation and reinterpretation of knowledge. Such interpretation involves discerning or constructing novel relationships between the situation and the actions that can be taken to address it. In a deep sense, then, we can only understand what a discrete bit of knowledge means if we can relate it to the context, and this relationship can only occur through the medium of meaningful actions (Brown and Duguid, 2001; Cook and Brown, 1999).

A fuller understanding of organizational learning requires the appreciation of 'knowing' as a dynamic process of interaction between meanings, narratives, actions, and context. Knowledge therefore is not merely a de-contextualized set of canons, but an evolving process of *knowing* that inheres in the practices by which actors create new meanings by engaging in generative dialogues with themselves, important others, and the emergent context (Tsoukas, 2009).

Building on this distinction then, it is possible to conceive of two different levels of subtle learning, with the common foundation being that both involve interpretations about knowledge (i.e. about what something that is important to the collective means for the collective). At one level, subtle learning is about the meanings underlying particular knowledge, whether that knowledge involves an object, event, or person, or even a label used to describe an object, event, or person. Subtle learning thus involves a collectively shared sense of what specific knowledge means. On a more fundamental level, however, subtle learning involves the meanings underlying what and how we do things as a collective; that is, coming to a collectively shared sense of how our practices shape who we are (Carlsen, 2006; Orlikowski, 2002). It is this deeper level that provides the strongest linkage between learning and identity, and where we next turn to provide a more in-depth discussion before exploring the implications of this interrelationship.

Organizational Identity ←→ Organizational Learning

Analogous to the expansion of the concept of knowledge, identity, too, ought to be seen as a more inclusive phenomenon that inheres in the recursive relationship between meanings and action patterns. Identity change therefore entails disruptions and revisions not only in perceptions, but also in social practices that provide 'justificational cues' to people about who they are as a collective and why they work in the ways they do. It is therefore possible to illustrate, both conceptually and empirically, how organizational identity and organizational learning are interrelated in an adaptive way. Based on a continuing line of research into the processes of organizational identity change, we suggest that instead of focusing on the potential for constraints to arise from identity and learning's mutual dependence (which inhibits adaptability), it is insightful to look at the enabling effects provided through their interrelationship (which facilitates adaptability).

Both Cook and Yanow (1993) and Nicolini and Meznar (1995) provide some insight into the relationship between learning and identity, albeit in a general sense. For example, in focusing on the cultural aspects of the learning undertaken by the Powell Flute Company, Cook and Yanow illustrate that learning can influence identity by strengthening or maintaining the current sense members have of who they are as a collective, or it can change that sense and lead to a redefinition of 'who we are.' Likewise, they also suggest that identity can either inhibit or facilitate learning, depending on how the organization's members deal with the potential for change in their collective sense of identity. In the end, Cook and Yanow posit that Powell Flute's learning about a new flute technology helped to strengthen their collective identity and that no change in identity occurred. We would argue, however, that through the meaning-based learning that occurred around Powell Flute's sense of collective self, their identity did in fact change in a subtle way that facilitated adaptation without loss of identity.

This is a key point, because treatments of the identity–learning relationship have explicitly reduced it to its inhibiting aspects by emphasizing the constraints placed on identity and learning because of their interdependence. For instance, Brown and Starkey (2000: 102) argue from a psychodynamic perspective that 'individuals and organizations are not primarily motivated to learn to the extent that learning entails anxiety-provoking identity change.' They explain that 'in practice, this means that individuals and organizations engage in learning activities and employ information and knowledge conservatively to preserve their existing identities.' Thus, they strongly imply that both identity change and learning are constrained because of their mutual dependence on each other.

Likewise, Lant (1999: 185) explains that because identity 'describes the boundaries of the collective [it] influences the interpretations of member firms and tends to constrain the range of strategic actions taken . . . both interpretation and actions will tend toward congruence with this identity' while Weick and Ashford (2001: 711) suggest that 'individuals learning about their own performance or that of their organization often make trade-offs between the desire for accurate information and the desire to defend the ego.'

These perspectives on the identity–learning relationship, however, hinge on the assumption that organizational identity is stable and, therefore, changes in organizational identity can be disconcerting for an organization and anxiety producing for its members. As our work on identity change has demonstrated, though, this conceptualization provides a rather incomplete picture of organizational identity and, in fact, prevents researchers from seeing complexities involved in its relationship with other key organizational phenomena. Nowhere is this more evident than in the relationship between organizational identity and organizational learning.

The fluidity of identity

Because organizational identity consists of collectively shared beliefs and perceptions of what it means to be 'us' as an organization, any change in that collective sense necessarily involves changes in intersubjective meanings. As noted above, changes in intersubjective meanings form the basis of subtle learning (see Figure 16.1). Yet, those changes are not always recognized by the members, nor explicitly labeled as learning, if recognized. Exploring why organizational identity changes and how this process comes about not only helps illustrate the adaptive nature of the identity–learning relationship, it also provides a clear example of subtle learning.

Our original conceptualization of a malleable identity grew out of past research on organizational identity, image, and reputation that demonstrated the potential for identity to change over relatively short periods of time, but did not explicitly explain it (cf. Corley and Gioia, 2004; Gioia and Thomas, 1996). In exploring these empirical examples, we posited that images of the organization communicated by outsiders are noticed by organization members and spur a social comparison process similar to James's (1918) 'looking glass self' (Gioia et al., 2000).

Specifically, members of an organization (especially top management members) implicitly and explicitly assess how they see the organization (i.e. provide answers to such questions as 'Who do we think we are?' and 'Who do we think we should be?') in relation to how they think outsiders see the organization (i.e. provide answers to questions such as 'Who do they think we are?' and 'Who do they think we should be?'). Arising from this

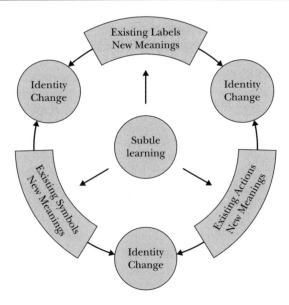

Figure 16.1 Illustration of Conceptual Links between Organizational Identity and Subtle Learning

comparison is either a sense of discrepancy ('How we see ourselves does not match with how we think others see us') or a sense of alignment ('We see ourselves in a similar way to how we think they see us') (Corley et al., 2000). A perception of alignment feeds back to reinforce organizational identity, whereas a perception of discrepancy can either result in a sense that something must be done in response to the disparity or in an acceptance of the discrepancy if it falls within some 'zone of indifference' (Barnard, 1938).

Regardless of whether a sense of alignment or discrepancy arises, identity is reconsidered and reconstructed (and, thus, destabilized to some degree) as organization members confront the implications of others' views of their organization. This instability of identity is actually adaptive, in that it allows an organization to cope better with the demands of an environment that itself is undergoing continuous change (Gioia et al., 2000). That is, an organizational identity that adapts to changing perceptions while maintaining a sense of continuity affords an organization the ability to cope with the changing expectations realized in interactions with a changing environment.

Perhaps the most useful aspect of our revised conceptualization of organizational identity, and the key to understanding its linkage with meaning-based organizational learning, was the recognition that changes in organizational identity can occur at the level of shared meanings that frame the social practices of organizational members, not just common language or labels. That is, an organization's identity consists of (1) the shared labels used to describe the 'who we are' and 'what we do,' and (2) the meanings associated with those labels by members. The seeming stability of an organization's identity resides in the stability of the consistent labels used to describe it, whereas the meanings and actions associated with those labels often change over time to match external expectations and internal goals. Thus, an organization can claim a stable identity, for instance, as a service organization focused on 'delivering the highest possible quality,' but the significance of such words as 'service,' 'quality,' and 'highest possible' can (and, in some circumstances, must) take on different meanings and practices at different times for members of the organization.

Changing the meanings underlying identity is as much a process of organizational learning as a pronounced change to the descriptive labels would be. The biggest difference, and the reason why the relationship between identity and learning can be adaptive, is that the learning can take place below the level of articulation, and possibly even awareness, for the individuals within the collective. Organizational learning occurs subtly as members focus on the labels used to describe 'who we are,' while the more tacit and unexplored meanings and practices underlying the labels change to match the shifting environment. This tacit process allows for a comforting sense of consensus, continuity, and stability among interested parties inside and outside the organization, while affording the organization the necessary adaptive learning to survive and grow in the face of changing environments. Thus, it is possible for learning to take place in the face of anxiety about changing identity because the identity change (and, thus, organizational learning) occurs at the level of intersubjective meanings embedded in social interaction.

In the context of Cook and Yanow's example of the Powell Flute Company, we suggest that, contrary to their original supposition, Powell Flute's identity did in fact change, albeit in a subtle manner that did not undermine the sense of continuity that was so important to its members. The concept of subtle learning as applied to organizational identity allows us the opportunity to see how an organization like Powell Flute can indeed 'change without changing.'

Changes in the external environment forced the organization to adapt and learn what it meant to be Powell Flute by reinterpreting the labels used to describe themselves. Yes, it was possible to continue making the best flutes in the world, regardless of whether the flutes have the Powell scale or the Cooper scale. The labels used to describe who they were remained the same, but their underlying meanings changed to reflect their new reality. The power of the change resides in its subtlety—the fact that it was subtle and precluded the kind of anxiety often attributed to changes in identity. One might even posit that because the change was successful and occurred without the anxiety that this event would normally be expected to generate, it helped inculcate change into the culture and break down many of the bases for resistance to change seen in other organizations.

IMPLICATIONS

The interrelationship between organizational identity and learning has a number of implications for organizations and for those of us studying them. Conceiving of organizational learning as occurring subtly, at a tacit level of collective awareness, affords researchers an opportunity to gain deeper insight into a diverse range of organizational phenomena. Some of the more relevant areas for this Handbook include conceptions of the 'learning organization,' leadership and organizational change, knowledge management, and the specification of the type of learning being examined in future conceptual and empirical work on the subject.

The learning organization

One of the clearest implications of this interrelationship is found in discussions of the 'learning organization.' As one might expect, the majority of definitions of the learning organization revolve around the management literature's individualistic approach to explicit organizational learning. Thus, some of the more traditional definitions include Pedler, Boydell, and Burgoyne's definition as 'an organization which facilitates the learning of all of its members and continually transforms itself' (1989: 2); Senge's original definition as 'organizations where people continually expand their capacity to create the results they truly desire, where new and expansive patterns of thinking are nurtured, where collective aspiration is set free, and where people are continually learning how to learn together' (1990: 3—see also Calhoun's chapter in this volume for more details); and a modified version of this definition used by Garvin as 'an organization skilled at creating, acquiring, and transferring knowledge, and at modifying its behavior to reflect new knowledge and insights' (1993: 80).

In reviewing this literature, our general expectation was that many of the insights researchers have produced about 'organizational learning' ought to translate into a better understanding of 'learning organizations,' especially given the apparent intent to create a more macro conceptualization of collective learning. Yet, this does not seem to be the case (exceptions can be found among the contributors to this Handbook—see especially diBella's chapter on organizations as learning portfolios). We feel, however, that the insights gained from examining the relationship between identity and learning, and the subtle learning that arises through their relationship, are directly applicable to our understanding of the learning organization. The following questions (and some answers) represent our attempt to do just that.

Perhaps the most obvious and enlightening place to start is with the observation that to become a learning organization, the organization must undergo some type of identity change. This is an implicit assumption of most treatments of the learning organization, but making it explicit provides some opportunities for discovery. For instance, must all identity changes involve formal, strategically planned efforts? No, as our discussions above have illustrated. What then happens to our notion of the learning organization if identity change, and thus organizational learning, occurs subtly and is more emergent than planned? One possibility is that the learning organization takes on a definition closer to 'an organization that is adaptive in its capacity for change' rather than the grand definitions most often found among practitioner writings on the subject.

One of the original intentions behind of the conceptualization of a 'learning organization' was to make learning explicit and to bring it to a level of awareness so that learning in organizations and by organizations could be better studied, understood, and translated into practice. Our reconceptualization of organizational learning carries with it an interesting twist: that is, to understand learning organizations properly we must account for their tacit, out-of-awareness dimensions, as well as their more explicit and evident dimensions. The upshot of this observation is that if we want to make manifest the subtlety of change and the critical role of meaning in the process, the best way to do so is to focus on the way that change occurs under the cover of stable labels.

A paradoxical question then arises: How can organizations maintain stability when stability itself is rooted in change? This paradox is evident in Barney's (1998) description of Koch Industries, an oil exploration company, whose ostensibly stable identity was that of a changing organization. The multiple-entendre meanings ascribable to Koch's own description of their organization ('We are a discovery company') vary on several enlightening levels (from the obvious 'we discover oil,' to the extensive 'we discover new ways of doing,' to the identity-reflective 'we discover who we are,' to the adaptive 'we discover how to learn and how to change'). Similarly, 3M bases their stable conception of themselves on the premise that they continuously change. They continuously invent new products and continuously reinvent themselves so they can continuously invent new products. Change as both process and outcome is so frequent and so pervasive and so undramatic that it becomes part of the unnoticed landscape. Subtle identity change and learning are everywhere all the time so that changes in identity and learning are almost unremarkable, but are always occurring in tandem.

Subtle leadership

Subtle learning also occurs in organizational processes other than organizational identity change, including the planning and implementing of strategic change initiatives, the development, growth, and intra-action of teams, and even the day-to-day practices that help define an organization's culture. All of these activities involve the sense making and sense giving efforts associated with leadership (Gioia and Chittipeddi, 1991). Using Smircich and Morgan's (1982) portrayal of leadership as the management of meaning, it is easy to see how the existence of a meaning-based form of organizational learning would affect leadership.

One particularly promising area for insight that emerges from considering subtle learning concerns the role of leadership in organizational change. If learning does occur at the level of intersubjective meanings, and thus is subtle enough that it often is not noticed or articulated within an organization, then one important aspect of leadership is the act of noticing, articulating, or even instigating changes in intersubjective meanings. These noticing and articulation processes can serve to heighten awareness among the organization's members that adaptive change is occurring and creates the opportunity to capture and codify valuable aspects of the change for future use. As this facet of leadership develops and progresses, subtle learning can become the basis for cultural change around learning processes, even helping the organization undergo the types of transformation necessary to become a learning organization.

There are important lessons to be learned on the other side of this coin, as well. Leaders too often presume that if change is to be successfully implemented, they must develop new labels and tout them explicitly to bring their followers' behavior and thinking into line with the proposed new paradigm. This approach often surprisingly produces not the hoped-for commitment, but rather an unexpected, increased resistance to change. Many organization members become weary and cynical about a 'flavor of the month club' mentality concerning yet another planned change effort that comes complete with its own set of clever new labels. Resistance does not need to be an automatic response to change, however, as is evident in our examples of identity changes involving subtle learning.

An alternative approach building on these insights involves the leader focusing on maintaining continuity through the use of familiar and long-held labels, but subtly beginning a process of changing the meanings underlying those labels. Change that is more adaptive and subtle, as opposed to more 'in-your-face,' can avoid some of the usual cynicism and resistance and increase the opportunity for collective learning. (Of course, we would be remiss if we did not acknowledge the possible dark side contained in this approach to the leadership of change efforts. The subtlety of meanings confers extraordinary power to those in a position to manipulate them, so Lord Acton's famous dictum—power corrupts, and absolute power . . . —applies even to this apparently inconspicuous realm. Most worrisome is that motivated meaning management is a stealth process with the capability to circumvent healthy debates and preferences about the character of change. It therefore plays directly to critical theorists' worst fears that organizational elites too often manipulate the construction of reality to favor their own interests at the expense of lower level members.)

Another area where leadership's role in the management of meaning is affected by the existence of subtle learning is the area of knowledge management. Knowledge management is often associated with organizational learning, although usually from the perspective of the information systems and procedures an organization relies on to exploit the knowledge gained through its learning. If knowledge only becomes valuable once meaning is attributed to it, however, then the management of meaning, and by extension the learning of that meaning, becomes a key aspect of knowledge management, so leaders have the responsibility to guide that process toward effectiveness. Although this dynamic is a direct outgrowth of recognizing a meaning-based form of organizational learning, it is not often discussed in current treatments of knowledge management.

On the need for specificity and clarity

Finally, our discussions of subtle learning raise important implications for future theoretical and empirical considerations of organizational learning. Perhaps one of the most important implications involves the use of the term 'organizational learning' itself. In many ways, this term has become so broad and now subsumes so many varied notions that its usefulness as a concept has become limited in both research and practice. Based on our own research experiences on the relationship between organizational identity and organizational learning, we feel that it is imperative for researchers and practitioners to recognize and define multiple types of organizational learning, each differing in its structure and process, each fulfilling different functions within an organization, and each resulting in different types of knowledge.

For instance, we have discussed the covert nature of subtle learning and the cultural processes involved in its occurrence. Subtle learning might also be more likely than other types of learning to lead to tacit, group-level knowledge, or what Cook and Brown (1999: 392) refer to as 'organizational genres.' Organizational genres represent 'the distinctive and useful meanings a given group attaches to its various literary artifacts [as well as] to its various physical and social artifacts.' Although 'these genres are not explicitly learned or known,' they represent knowledge 'possessed or "held in common" by that group' (ibid.) and confirmed or modified through continuing social interaction.

We believe that it is in our best interests as researchers, and in the best interests of the organizations we study and consult with, to be more specific and clear about the particular type(s) of organizational learning to which we are referring when we use this term. We hope our explication of semantic or meaning-based learning (cf. Corley and Gioia, 2003) provides the impetus for this kind of specification. Although past research has discussed issues that relate to meanings associated with learning, in this chapter we have attempted (1) to specify subtle learning in some detail; (2) to discuss its role in forming a type of learning different from more traditional notions of knowledge- or behaviorally-based learning; (3) to discuss its impact on the conceptualization of organizational learning; and (4) to label it in a fashion that allows researchers to see it as an interesting and useful domain for understanding and employing it in their work.

Although some might argue that specification of another form of organizational learning leads to further fragmentation of the concept, we feel that the inclusion of subtle learning within the spectrum of organizational learning types is a promising way for researchers to gain genuine insight into organizational phenomena related to organizational learning and to help the organizations they work with improve their learning processes. As researchers become more specific about the type of organizational learning they are describing and/or studying, our understanding of the role learning plays in organizational behavior and strategy will improve, thus enabling us as researchers to provide valuable knowledge for the organizations we study.

CONCLUSION

Our intent in this chapter has been to outline an argument for an adaptive relationship between organizational identity and learning. Contrary to (the few) current treatments of this relationship, we have attempted to articulate the case that changes in an organization's identity do not necessarily inhibit organizational learning, nor that organizational learning most often facilitates the maintenance of organizational identity. We believe, instead, that by focusing on changes to an organization's identity at the level of *meanings* (not language or labels), it is possible to see that organizational identity change and organizational learning are mutually facilitative and can help the organization in its adaptation to changing environments.

Focusing on this adaptive relationship has also led us to explicate a heretofore underspecified form of organizational learning, subtle learning. Subtle learning involves changes to the intersubjective meanings underlying a collective's labels and actions. Contrary to most treatments of organizational learning in the managerial literature, subtle learning is found only at a collective level, is more covert and tacit than previously conceived types of organizational learning, and provides insight into alternative relationships between organizational phenomena (such as our example of the adaptive nature of the organizational identity–learning relationship).

The implications arising from subtle learning and the interrelationships among organizational identity and learning pertain to a wide spectrum of organizational phenomena. Our hope is that by clarifying this relationship and specifying the characteristics of subtle learning, future research can develop a more comprehensive picture of the complexities inherent in organizational learning. Instead of shying away from these complexities, we feel it is better to confront them head on. We hope this chapter constitutes a start to that process.

REFERENCES

Albert, S. and Whetten, D. (1985) Organizational identity. In L.L. Cummings and B.M. Staw (eds.), *Research in Organizational Behavior*. JAI Press, vol. 7, 263–295.

Argote, L. and McGrath, J.E. (1993) Group processes in organization: Continuity and change. In C.L. Cooper and I.T. Robertson (eds.), *International Review of Industrial and Organizational Psychology*. New York: John Wiley & Sons.

Ashforth, B.E., Rogers, K.M. and Corley, K.G. (in press) Identity in organizations: Exploring cross-level dynamics. *Organization Science*.

Barnard, C.I. (1938) *The Functions of the Executive*. Cambridge: Harvard University Press.

Bechky. B.A. (2003) Sharing meaning across occupational communities: The transformation of knowledge on a production floor. *Organization Science*,14: 312–330.

Brown, A.D. and Starkey, K. (2000) Organizational identity and learning: A psychodynamic perspective. *Academy of Management Review*, 25: 102–120.

Brown, J. S. and Duguid, P. (2001) Knowledge and organization: A social-practice perspective. *Organization Science*, 12: 198–213.

Carlile, P. (2002) A pragmatic view of knowledge and boundaries: Boundary objects in new product development. *Organization Science*, 13: 442–455.

Carlsen, A. (2006) Organizational becoming as dialogic imagination of practice: The case of the indomitable gauls. *Organization Science*, 17: 132–149.

Carlsen, A. (2009) After James on identity. In P. S. Adler (Ed.), *The Oxford Handbook of Sociology and Organization Studies*, 421–443.

Cook, S.D.N. and Brown, J.S. (1999) Bridging epistemologies: The generative dance between organizational knowledge and organizational knowing. *Organization Science*, 10: 381–400.

Cook, S.D.N. and Yanow, D. (1993) Culture and organizational learning. *Journal of Management Inquiry*, 2: 373–390.

Corley, K.G. and Gioia, D.A. (2003) Semantic learning as change enabler: Relating organizational identity and organizational learning. In M. Easterby-Smith and M. Lyles (eds.) *The Blackwell Handbook of Organizational Learning and Knowledge Management*. Oxford: Blackwell: 621–636.

Corley, K.G. and Gioia, D.A. (2004) Identity ambiguity and change in the wake of a corporate spin-off. *Administrative Science Quarterly*, 49: 173–208.

Corley, K.G. Gioia, D.A., and Fabbri, T. (2000) Organizational identity in transition over time. In C.L. Cooper and D.M. Rousseau (eds.) *Trends in Organizational Behavior*. Chichester: John Wiley & Sons, 95–110.

Dutton, J.E., Dukerich, J.M. and Harquail, C.V. (1994) Organizational images and member identification. *Administrative Science Quarterly*, 39: 239–263.

Easterby-Smith, M. (1997) Disciplines of organizational learning: Contributions and critiques. *Human Relations*, 50: 1085–1113.

Fombrun, C.J. (1996) *Reputation: Realizing Value from the Corporate Image*. Boston: Harvard Business School Press.

Garvin, D.A. (1993) Building a learning organization. *Harvard Business Review*, 71: 78–91.

Gioia, D.A. (1998) From individual to organizational identity. In D. Whetton and P. Godfrey (eds.), *Identity in Organizations: Developing Theory Through Conversations*. Thousand Oaks, CA: Sage: 17–31.

Gioia, D. A. and Chittipeddi, K. (1991) Sensemaking and sensegiving in strategic change initiation. *Strategic Management Journal*, 12: 443–458.

Gioia, D.A., Schultz, M. and Corley, K.G. (2000) Organizational identity, image and adaptive instability. *Academy of Management Review*, 25: 63–81.

Gioia, D.A. and Thomas, J.B. (1996) Identity, image, and issue interpretation: Sense making during strategic change in academia. *Administrative Science Quarterly*, 41: 370–403.

Huber, G.P. (1991) Organizational learning: The contributing processes and the literatures. *Organization Science*, 2: 88–115.

James, W. (1918) *The Principles of Psychology*. New York: H. Holt and Company.

Lant, T.K. (1999) A situated learning perspective on the emergence of knowledge and identity in cognitive communities. In J. F. Porac and R. Garud (eds.), *Advances in Managerial and Organizational Information Processing*. JAI Press, 6:171–194.

Miller, D. (1996) A preliminary typology of organizational learning: Synthesizing the literature. *Journal of Management*, 22: 485–515.

Nag, R., Corley, K.G., and Gioia, D.A. (2003) Innovation tensions: Chaos, structure, and managed chaos. In L.V. Shavinina (Ed.) *International Handbook on Innovation*. Oxford: Elsevier Science: 607–618.

Nag, R., Corley, K.G., and Gioia, D.A. (2007) The intersection of organizational identity, knowledge, and practice: Attempting strategic change via knowledge grafting. *Academy of Management Journal*, 50: 821–847.

Nicolini, D., and Meznar, M.B. (1995) The social construction of organizational learning: Conceptual and practical issues in the field. *Human Relations*, 48: 727–746.

Normann, R. (1985) Developing capabilities for organizational learning. In J. M. Pennings (ed.), *Organizational Strategy and Change*. San Francisco: Jossey-Bass: 217–248.

Orlikowski, W.J. (2002) Knowing in practice: Enacting a collective capability in distributed organizing. *Organization Science*, 13: 249–273.

Pedler, M., Boydell, T., and Burgoyne, J. (1989) Towards the learning company. *Management Education and Development*, 20: 1–8.

Senge, P.M. (1990) *The Fifth Discipline: The Art and Practice of the Learning Organization*. New York: Doubleday.

Smircich, L. and Morgan, G. (1982) Leadership: The management of meaning. *The Journal of Applied Behavioral Sciences*, 18: 257–273.

Stimpert, J. L., Gustafson, L.T., and Sarason, Y. (1998) Organizational identity within the strategic management conversation: Contributions and assumptions. In D. Whetten and P. Godfrey (eds.), *Identity in Organizations: Developing theory through conversations*. Thousand Oaks, CA: Sage: 83–98.

Tsoukas. H. (2009) A dialogical approach to the creation of new knowledge in organizations. *Organization Science*, 20: 941–957.

Tsoukas H. and Chia, R. (2002) On organizational becoming: Rethinking organizational change. *Organization Science*, 13: 567–582.

Weick, K.E. (1991) The nontraditional quality of organizational learning. *Organization Science*, 2: 116–124.

Weick, K.E. and Ashford, S.J. (2001) Learning in organizations. In F. M. Jablin and L. L. Putnam (eds.), *The New Handbook of Organizational Communication: Advances in Theory, Research, and Methods*. Thousand Oaks, CA: Sage: 704–731.

Weick, K.E. and Roberts, K.H. (1993) Collective mind in organizations: Heedful interrelating on flight decks. *Administrative Science Quarterly*, 38: 357–381.

Weick, K.E. and Westley, F. (1999) Organizational learning: Affirming an oxymoron. In S. R. Clegg, C. Hardy, and W. R. Nord (eds.), *Managing organizations: Current issues*. Thousand Oaks: Sage: 190–208.

Wilson, J.M., Goodman, P.S., and Cronin, M.A. (2007) Group learning. *Academy of Management Review*, 32: 1041–1059.

Part III

KNOWLEDGE AND ITS MANAGEMENT IN ORGANIZATIONS

17

Dominant Logic, Knowledge Creation, and Managerial Choice

RICHARD A. BETTIS, SZE SZE WONG,
AND DANIELA BLETTNER

ABSTRACT

Dominant logic is a conceptual framework for thinking about the process and results of cognitive simplification in top management teams. It develops and evolves due to the characteristics of the firm's industry and strategy. With experience and success the dominant logic condenses into a variety of visible and invisible organizational features where it takes on a highly durable and self-reinforcing nature. Organizational learning becomes focused on current competencies because the dominant logic biases knowledge, know-how, and skill accumulation into path dependent pathways 'preferred' by the dominant logic. In this manner variance and exploration of alternatives are suppressed. This chapter also reviews current research related to dominant logic and potential areas of future research.

INTRODUCTION

The purpose of this chapter is to discuss the nature of the general management dominant logic concept (generally referred to below as simply 'dominant logic') and to connect it with key issues in learning, knowledge creation, and managerial choice. We also speculate on some potentially fruitful avenues for applying and extending the theory of dominant logic. This is not intended primarily as a review although many important aspects of a review are necessary to the fundamental purpose of the chapter. What is intended is to extend the usefulness of the dominant logic concept in understanding and exploring various organizational phenomena and connect it more firmly to various other concepts and literatures. Those interested in a basic review are referred to the original source (Prahalad and Bettis, 1986) and to a variety of other sources (e.g. Bettis and Prahalad, 1995; Bettis, 2000; Ginsberg, 1990; Grant, 1988; Ramanujam and Varadarajan, 1989; Von Krogh and Roos, 1996). Some relevant literature is also reviewed later in the chapter.

The concept of a general management dominant logic arose in response to the need to examine why firms find it so hard to manage (1) diversification (even 'related' diversification) and/or (2) rapid or discontinuous change in a core or base business (Prahalad and Bettis, 1986). Although superficially different, the issues of diversification and change in the core business both involve the necessity to change the mental models of managers. Such changes go far beyond the intellectual recognition of the need to change and have proven very difficult to accomplish in practice; and practitioner-oriented work by Sull (1999) and by Foster and Kaplan (2001) testifies to the difficulties involved.

Dominant logic provides a simple and potentially powerful way of thinking about various strategic issues. There are certainly other frameworks for thinking about these issues, and we claim no particular advantage for dominant logic. We do believe that it is one useful way for organizing reflection about and thoughtful inquiry into issues related to strategic change.

In what follows we first discuss the fundamental nature of the dominant logic concept. We then discuss two concepts important to understanding the impact of a dominant logic: (1) 'condensation' of dominant logic into visible and invisible organizational features and (2) 'variance suppression' at the dominant logic level, and how it interacts with variance suppression effects at other levels of analysis. We end with two sections reviewing some important literature and possible directions for future research.

The Nature of Dominant Logic

The theory of a general management dominant logic is one conceptual framework for thinking about the process and results of cognitive simplification in top management teams. As Schwenk (1984) suggests, strategic decision making in top management teams is subject to cognitive simplification. Top management, as with all humans, employ simplifying decision-making heuristics, such as prior hypothesis bias, adjustment and anchoring, illusion of control, and representativeness, that decrease their ability to appreciate the true complexity of problems and select the best solution.

The dominant logic represents the shared cognitive map (Prahalad and Bettis, 1986) and strategic mindset of the top management team or the dominant coalition, and is closely associated with the processes and tools used by top management. There may be minor variations in the details of the individual cognitive maps among top management team members, but the major features conform. From a managerial viewpoint, the congruence in cognition among top management team members offers advantages of efficiencies, but inevitably, it also introduces the disadvantages of rigidity. For example, the dominant logic may be inappropriately applied in diversification moves or when there are changes in the core industry. As Sull (1999) has observed, good companies go bad because they insist only on doing what worked in the past.

As shown in Figure 17.1, the dominant logic develops and evolves due to the characteristics of the industry and the strategy (or business model) the firm uses to compete in this industry. Essentially, experience and success in the presence of reasonable environmental stability breed shared patterns of thinking about key strategic and managerial issues.

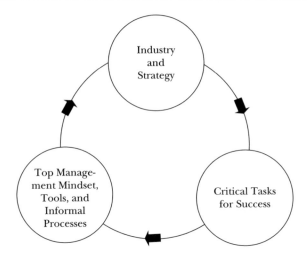

Figure 17.1 Evolution of General Management Dominant Logic

These shared cognitive patterns typically involve beliefs about issues such as causality in the industry, appropriate product cost structures, and desirable customer characteristics. As discussed below, this cognitive representation of the dominant logic eventually condenses or even ossifies into a variety of familiar organizational features where it takes on a highly durable and self-reinforcing nature. After condensation the dominant logic defines as much what the organization *cannot* do as what the organization *can* do (discussed below). The theoretical foundations of the shared mental encoding process lie in a variety of literatures including operant conditioning, decision heuristics, pattern recognition, cognitive simplification, and paradigms. The reader is referred to Prahalad and Bettis (1986) for an introductory discussion of some major foundation literatures.

The dominant logic concept also connects closely to the literature on complex adaptive systems (e.g. Axelrod and Cohen, 1999; Holland, 1995; Waldrop, 1992). Bettis and Prahalad (1995) point out that the dominant logic can be viewed as an emergent property of organizations. Such a view is entirely consistent with the cognitive mechanisms of individuals mentioned above. These cognitive mechanisms can be viewed as driving the micro-dynamics of agents in an organization. The outcome of these agents (senior managers) interacting with each other and with the common environment and common business model (or strategy) is seen at the aggregate level in the emergence of a dominant logic (and many other organizational properties). This emergence process is analogous to the way in which the particle mechanics of a large number of individual atoms within a gas interact with each other and the environment to produce emergent properties such as pressure and various thermodynamic relationships.

As an emergent property, it should be noted that the dominant logic is inherently an adaptive property as long as neither the domain of application nor the environment changes significantly. It allows the organization to 'anticipate' the environment by specifying the nature of cause and effect relationships. It economizes on managerial resources by simplifying and speeding decision making. However, this adaptive ability has obvious limitations and carries with it toxic side effects discussed below and in various references.

Condensation of dominant logic

This section examines how the dominant logic becomes embedded in the major features of the organization over time. The objective is to characterize the essential features of what we call the 'condensation process.' The objective is not to capture the complete complexity of this process and its relationship to a myriad of other issues.

The dominant logic develops over time. The process can be viewed as starting with the founding of a firm or with a major disruption of a firm (e.g. bankruptcy or near bankruptcy) that invalidates the dominant logic and management systems of a firm. As mentioned above and illustrated in Figure 17.1, there is an initial period during which the characteristics of the environment and firm strategy drive the formation of a shared mindset among the top management team. Obviously, in the presence of success (stability) this mindset becomes more uniform across managers and stronger over time. Up to this point the issue of significant change of the dominant logic is largely a matter of individual cognitive change across the top management team. This does not mean that change will be easy. However, it is likely to be much easier than when the dominant logic has condensed into a matrix of mutually reinforcing features within the organization.

As this mindset continues to develop, certain concepts and informal processes become associated with it within the top management team. For example, the authors have seen a firm in which 'cost plus' pricing became the only accepted way of thinking about pricing within the top management team. Also, the authors have observed firms in which the informal capital budgeting decision process among the top management team centered on rationing a percentage of sales proportionally across functions (e.g. manufacturing and sales). Increasingly the dominant logic places constraints on: (1) the search spaces associated with problems, (2) the conceptual frameworks used to help make decisions, and (3) the key features of acceptable solutions. The dominant logic at this point still remains largely invisible. It is cognitive with few or no obvious physical manifestations in the organization. It can only be examined through discussion with top managers and their direct reports.

As organizations grow and become more complex it becomes necessary and important to establish formal structure, procedures, systems, routines, and processes. These are usually designed in at least rough congruence with the dominant logic. In this sense the dominant logic begins to condense into 'visible' organization features. It also becomes 'invisibly' embodied as a significant part of the organization value system or culture. Formal structure, procedures, systems, processes, and controls are the hallmark of competent professional management. They standardize, simplify, and expedite decision making in line with the needs of the business. They focus attention on what are to be considered key issues. They establish priorities that conform to the strategic imperatives of the firm. In sum, they embody the dominant logic in the organizational features that direct attention and shape decisions for managers and employees throughout the organization.

By their very nature systems, procedures, controls, and processes are designed to be inflexible and difficult to change. Significant change in these features is undertaken only rarely, after considerable analysis, and at significant cost. Furthermore, they form a reinforcing web of relationships. For example, the job recruitment and selection routine, and organizational socialization process often result in the employment of individuals who share the organization's beliefs and values. Like a form of social control (O'Reilly and Chatman, 1996), employees' beliefs and interpretations of events, attitudes and behaviors become increasingly aligned with the dominant logic. This reinforces the existing systems, procedures, controls, and processes, which in turn fortifies the dominant logic.

Significant change in any one system, procedure, routine, control, or process is likely to require significant change in all or others to maintain alignment. All of these are interdependent (e.g. Siggelkow, 2001) to varying degrees, which makes the nature of relationships including causality difficult or impossible to discern. By contrast many techniques of change management, especially process reengineering have led many managers to conclude that major organizational changes are not all that difficult. However, as Christensen and Overdorf (2000) have observed, processes and systems are not nearly as flexible and adaptable as the proponents of these techniques suggest.

This process of condensation may take place over a considerable period of time with the dominant logic becoming more and more condensed. Once it has proceeded very far the problem of changing dominant logics becomes substantially more complex. As with physical solids, the process of moving back to a fluid state can require enormous amounts of energy if it can be accomplished at all. The condensation of a dominant logic is an irreversible process. One obviously cannot step backwards along the same path to the organization as it existed before condensation of the dominant logic. Change must involve creating a new path in the presence of a cognitive dominant logic and a mutually reinforcing web of 'visible' organizational features and a largely 'invisible' value system. Ultimately, this must involve unlearning of the inappropriate dominant logic. Success here is usually much more the exception than the rule. Dominant logics are extraordinarily resistant to unlearning.

As illustrated in Figure 17.2, as the process of condensation moves forward, a reinforcing feedback loop is established. The structure, systems, routines, and processes designed largely to conform to the dominant logic now provide information, controls, incentives, values, and decision rules that mirror the dominant logic to a substantial degree. Top management receives information and decision agendas framed in congruence with the dominant logic. Information systems ensure that attention is allocated to issues deemed important by the dominant logic. Decision rules are established to conform to the dominant logic. Metrics are those deemed important by the dominant logic. Controls assure compliance with the dominant logic. Hence a substantial portion of the organization becomes a reinforcing and interdependent system built largely around the dominant logic.

The focus narrows throughout the organization. Thoughtful action and creative analysis are increasingly displaced by 'unconscious' rules, processes, values, and systems (Ashforth and Fried, 1988). The capability for thoughtful independent action atrophies and decisions increasingly become automatic and habitual. Doing different things or even doing things differently becomes more and more difficult for the organization. This is suggestive of the common observation that the more successful organizations become the more difficult they find it to change. Of course as long as there is no necessity to make significant change, the condensed dominant logic can provide a highly effective and efficient means of managing the organization. The organization tends toward

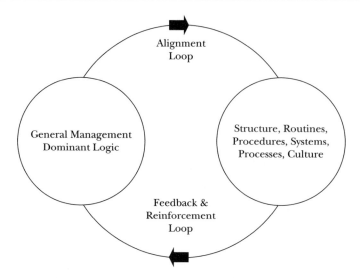

Figure 17.2 Condensation of General Management Dominant Logic

simplification, where it gradually weeds out 'unsuccessful' practices and builds 'architectures of simplicity' (Miller, 1993). In an earlier era, aligning organizational characteristics with strategy was considered the major mechanism of strategy implementation. In fact this paradigm of tight and long-term alignment of organizational activities with a 'semi-permanent' strategy is still followed pedagogically in some MBA programs. This is fine as long as the strategy is robust to the environment, but when significant change is necessary, it will be intensely difficult.

With continuous reinforcement in place, condensation may move to a stage best described as 'fossilization.' The organization becomes merely a rigid physical imprint of something that was once alive and able to move and to respond to some degree to the environment. In this state performance must decline catastrophically before an attempt is made to respond. The usual result is the dissolution or acquisition of the organization.

VARIANCE SUPPRESSION

The condensation process essentially suppresses variance within the organization. As discussed above, organizations increasingly emphasize *a* goal, structure, and/or set of routines, procedures, and processes, and preclude the consideration of others. This downward spiral toward simplification is likely to be the result of an interaction among several variance suppression processes existing at different levels of analysis, ranging from the cognitive top management level to the organizational field level.

Variance suppression occurs at several levels of analysis (Bettis, 2000). At the industrial and organizational field level, forces of competition and selection (Hannan and Freeman, 1977) and isomorphism (DiMaggio and Powell, 1983) result in increasing homogenization among firms. At the strategic group level (Reger and Huff, 1993), homogenization also occurs as firms in the same industry increasingly share similar beliefs and behaviors (Porac, Thomas, and Baden-Fuller, 1989). At the top management team level, the dominant logic also suppresses variance by directing top management decision making, among many things, into certain heuristics, models, concepts, beliefs, and types of analysis. Therefore, variance suppression is a general phenomenon that is prevalent in many different levels of analysis.

Variance suppression at each of these levels is likely to be interdependent. As discussed in the earlier section, dominant logic tends toward variance suppression as top management increasingly adopts a certain worldview (e.g. heuristic, beliefs, paradigm). How much variance it suppresses is likely a function of the variance the organization faced in the organizational field when the dominant logic was developing among the top management team. To the extent that more variance was faced during this period, the dominant logic is likely to be more robust, but even this has obvious limits. Furthermore, variance is not uniform and generic. It has a qualitative component. Different variables can be involved, such as technology, customer needs, or social values. Hence the dominant logic may be more robust to some variables than others. However, early in their lives, firms themselves may also be the source of environmental variance for others in an established industry. This is not the same as having to respond to variance caused by other factors. For instance Digital Equipment, as a new entrant, increased the variance in the computer environment by introducing the minicomputer. Incumbents (e.g. IBM, Burroughs, and NCR) found it hard to respond since their logics (and core competencies) were organized around mainframe computing. However, Digital Equipment subsequently developed a strong dominant logic based on the minicomputer. This logic prevented them from responding adequately when variance again was increased by the PC.

At the same time that environmental variance affects variance in the dominant logic it also affects the adaptability of the dominant logic. One way to think about this is the requisite variety principle from cybernetics, which suggests that the variety within a system (or the variety the system is capable of exhibiting or producing) must be matched to the environmental variety that the system faces (Ashby, 1956). The principle of requisite variety plainly suggests that organizations today must be capable of a greater variety of actions or variance, including learning, during a period of increased environmental variance. To illustrate metaphorically, consider the design of airplanes. Fighter planes must be designed for more rapid, frequent, severe, and unscripted maneuvers than passenger planes because they operate in a rapidly changing, unpredictable, and hostile environment. The tradeoff is that they are much less stable than passenger planes and, hence, rather unsafe, even in peacetime.

A second way to think about the implications of variance suppression for organizational change is in terms of ecological models of random variation and selective retention. In recent years these models, originating in biology, have shown considerable explanatory power in many fields. The models have been applied to a variety of organizational issues. For our purposes we will only mention two specific areas where they have been applied: learning (e.g. Campbell, 1960) and research and development (e.g. Nelson and Winter, 1982). (It should be noted that research and development is obviously a very specific kind of organizational learning.) In the former of these two cases suppression of variance reduces the rate of learning. In the latter it reduces the likelihood of a significant innovation. Obviously, if variation is suppressed there are profound implications for the random variation/selective retention model as it has been applied to various phenomena. Again, the implications for dominant logic should be obvious.

A third way to think of variance suppression that is closely related to the ecological approach is in terms of the exploration–exploitation tradeoff (March, 1991). Variance suppression by definition suppresses exploration, which means that the balance between exploration and exploitation is altered.

What this all suggests is that we need to give more attention to the non-recursive relationships between variance generation and variance suppression at different levels of analysis, and the issues of tradeoff between variance generation and suppression at these different levels. It is not a simple issue of more variance increases adaptive capability. Too little variance limits adaptation, but too much variance will simply swamp any organization. As such, we have to be cognizant of the tradeoffs, and explore ways in which they play out in different situations.

Review of some relevant literature

Dominant logic has been discussed in terms of the impact on resource allocation (Prahalad and Bettis, 1986) and in terms of filtering information (Bettis and Prahalad, 1995). While some papers deal with resource allocation (e.g. D'Aveni, Ravenscraft, and Anderson, 2004; Grant, 1988), others deal with information filtering (e.g. Porac, Mishina, and Pollock, 2002; Von Krogh, Erat, and Macus, 2000). Yet others understand dominant logic as a combination of behavioral and cognitive elements (e.g. Cote, Langley, and Pasquero, 1999; Jarzabkowski, 2001; Obloj and Pratt, 2005).

D'Aveni et al. (2004) associate dominant logic with resource allocation. Those authors associate resource congruence among lines of business with efficiency and profitability. In this case, dominant logic is a strictly behavioral concept and congruence of dominant logic is related to superior performance.

Porac et al. (2002) study growth logics of entrepreneurial teams using narrative analysis and cognitive mapping and show that there are inter-industry patterns in the clustering of growth logics. Von Krogh et al. (2000) suggest that the comprehensiveness of dominant logic is related to superior firm performance. The authors compared Nokia and Ericsson along six categories (internal conceptualization: people, culture, and product and brand; external conceptualization: competitors, consumer/customer, and technology). The method used by those authors is qualitative text analysis of annual reports.

Lampel and Shamsie (2000) also see dominant logic mainly as a cognitive concept, an information filter that then impacts strategic decisions and actions such as venture formation. Those authors claim that joint ventures that depart more from the corporate logic (General Electric in that case) are likely to be terminated earlier than ventures that are more consistent with the corporate logic. They argue that the consistency of the venture's logic with General Electric's logic creates cohesion (and harnesses entrepreneurial energies of the diverse businesses).

There are a number of empirical papers that base their measures of dominant logic on behavioral and cognitive elements. Cote et al. (1999), who investigate acquisitions, see the dominant logic of the mother firm (SNC was the firm studied) as rooted in its 'administrative heritage,' which they define as 'cultural values and historical practices that have been successful in the firm's core business' (Cote et al., 1999: 928). Hence, the authors operationalize the dominant logic in (1) conceptualization of the role of the firm and acquisitions, (2) criteria for choice and evaluation, and (3) organizing and management principles. On a more abstract level, the authors come to an interpretative and interrelated scheme of thinking, acting, and evaluating of the concrete strategic action by the management team. A difference in the timing of these components leads to inferior performance.

Similarly, Jarzabkowski (2001) proposes to understand dominant logic as the composite of three components: embedded administrative processes, top team thinking and acting, and the underlying strategic orientation of the firm. The potential of this operationalization relies on the fact that these processes are all encompassing and there is inevitably an interaction effect included. The interaction of these three components is self-reinforcing and brings about cohesion. Jarzabkowski associates the cohesion of the three elements of the organization (in this case the University of Warwick) with the responsiveness to the environment. Obloj and Pratt (2005) and Obloj, Obloj, and Pratt (2010) suggest an integrative view of dominant logic as containing cognitive elements (dominant logic as 'information filter') and behavioral components (learning and routines). The latter paper compares and contrasts logics of ventures in a transition economy (Poland).

The existing studies on dominant logic are insightful. Yet, there are still many unstudied or understudied issues. While the main focus of early empirical research on dominant logic has been diversification and performance, the emergence of (dominant) logic has recently received increased interest with studies focusing on the firm level (Obloj et al., 2010) and industry level (e.g. Santos and Eisenhardt, 2009). Obloj et al. (2010) examine the emergence of dominant logic in ventures in transition countries. Santos and Eisenhardt (2009) study the emergence of industry logic.

We think there is considerable potential for exploring the emergence of a dominant logic based on the competition of multiple competing logics. Beyond purely empirical considerations (e.g. choice of context, choice of method), it is essential to consider a theoretical foundation for the emergence of a coherent dominant logic. Coherence refers to how the elements of knowledge *cohere* (<lat. *cohaerere*) or hang together.[1] In the strategy literature, strategic coherence is associated with superior performance (e.g. Black, Hinrichs, and Fabian, 2005; Hamel and Prahalad, 1994). Yet, as indicated in earlier contributions, dominant logic can be seen not just as a 'filter' (Bettis and Prahalad, 1995) but also a 'blinder' (Prahalad, 2004). If a dominant logic is characterized by excessive coherence, it is resistant to change when strategic change becomes necessary. Only systematic studies of the coherence of the knowledge structure can reveal more about the positive or negative effects of certain coherence patterns. Several methods such as cognitive mapping (Eden, 1992; Eden and Spender, 1998; Fiol and Huff, 1992; Huff, 1990; Walsh, 1995) can be used. We believe studying the dynamics of coherence in a knowledge structure or mental map over time offers considerable promise. Changes in cognitive maps have

---

[1]'On an intuitive level, coherence is a matter of how the beliefs in a system of beliefs fit together or "dovetail" with each other, so as to constitute one unified and tightly structured whole. And it is clear that this fitting together depends on logical, inferential, and explanatory relations of many different sorts among the components of the system' (Bonjour, 1985: 107).

been examined in firm level studies (Barr, Stimpert, and Huff, 1992) and industry-level studies (Nadkarni and Narayanan, 2007), and specific reasoning processes (e.g. Gavetti, Levinthal, and Rivkin, 2005) greatly contribute to our understanding of managerial logics. Systematic analyses of such reasoning processes over time have the possibility of revealing features of potentially successful dominant logics.

Some Future Directions for the Study of Dominant Logic

Multiple dominant logics

By its very nature, dominant logic represents the *dominant* way in which managers think and act. It economizes on cognitive processing by offering a schema to classify environmental cues, and interpret their meanings. However, when the meaning of environmental cues change or the cues themselves change, it is inappropriate. Classification and interpretation of cues become inappropriate either because new cues are not recognized or categorized in inappropriate categories, or strategies to deal with these new cues are incompatible. A dominant logic that was once well adapted becomes non-adaptable.

Ashby (1956) argued that requisite variety in the internal environment is required to match variety in the external environment. Applied in the context of logics, this suggests that organizations in rapidly changing environments have to move beyond a dominant logic, and toward what is best characterized as multiple logics. As population ecologists have advocated (Hannan and Freeman, 1977), generalization is preferred over specialization in changing environments. Having a range of logics would not only allow organizations to scan and recognize a broader spectrum of environmental cues, but also select responses from a repertoire of logics. It is both easier and speedier to switch among multiple logics than to 'unfreeze' a deeply ingrained dominant logic and develop a new dominant logic. In the ideal (and perhaps unrealistic) case, the organization can flexibly change to another logic that is more appropriate as conditions change. Maintaining and executing a variety or continuum of logics might also mitigate against the condensation process that deeply and firmly embeds a dominant logic. By cultivating several logics and a meta-logic for choosing among them, organizations ostensibly could develop multiple ways of perceiving the environment.

Process Dominant Logics

Discussions of dominant logic thus far have focused at a general level. We use the term to refer to the mindset, casual map, or mental model of the top management team. However, the exact contents in the dominant logic are usually left unspecified. Most of the time, we assume dominant logic represents the strategic concepts and causal relations among these concepts because it is mostly applied to illustrate the strategies used by management teams. Of course, given strategic success, this logic condenses into many other visible and invisible features of the organization.

We want to focus briefly on the processes that top management teams develop to make decisions. Top management teams often develop stable ways of making strategic decisions. Like most other teams, top management team members over time develop a process logic that guides how they voice opinions, seek information, resolve differences, and make the final decision. Previous experiences, political dynamics, preference of the CEO, and interactions among members influence the process logic that emerges. Once created, the process logic as a component of the dominant logic endures and guides how strategic decisions are made. Unlike the issue-oriented aspects of a dominant logic that focuses on strategic concepts and their causal relationships, a process dominant logic focuses on the team processes involved in the top management team.

Considering the process aspects of dominant logic suggests a richer construct than is often envisioned. In addition to strategic issues logic, it also relates to the management team's model of how decision making should take place, and/or how information should be processed within the team. For instance, in Eisenhardt's (1989) study of decision making in high velocity environments, she found that top management teams in successful firms use more information, develop more alternatives, engage in a two-tiered advice process, and employ quick conflict resolution methods.

We believe that the study of the process aspects of dominant logic in top management teams represents a productive ground for future research. As shown in Eisenhardt's study, the decision-making process in top management teams is a key differentiator of successful and unsuccessful firms. So far, most of the discussion of dominant logic has been focused on how heuristics that capture rules of dealing with strategy develop and persist. We believe that it would be equally rewarding to turn research attention to the process aspects of logics that prevail in top management teams. By determining how information is sought and processed, process logics influence how information, knowledge, and opinions are combined to form the final strategic decision. Hence, the process logic of a top management team could help to explain why a particular decision is reached. More importantly, as we move toward more turbulent environments, it would be interesting to explore the types of process dominant logics that would allow members to more accurately sense new changes in the environment, and effectively integrate members' expertise to invent new responses.

REFERENCES

Ashby, W.R. (1956) *An introduction to cybernetics*. New York: John Wiley and Sons Inc.

Ashforth, B.E. and Fried, Y. (1988) The mindlessness of organizational behaviors. *Human Relations*, 41(4): 305–329.

Axelrod, R.M. and Cohen, M.D. (1999) *Harnessing Complexity: Organizational Implications of a Scientific Frontier*. New York: Free Press.

Barr, P.S., Stimpert, L.J., and Huff, A.S. (1992) Cognitive changes, strategic action, and organizational renewal. *Strategic Management Journal*, 13: 15–36.

Bettis, R. A. (2000) The iron cage is emptying, the dominant logic no longer dominates. In Baum, J.A.C. and Dobbins, F. (eds.) *Economics Meets Sociology in Strategic Management*. Stamford: JAI Press: 167–174.

Bettis, R.A. and Prahalad, C.K. (1995) The dominant logic: Retrospective and extension. *Strategic Management Journal*, 16(1): 5–14.

Black, J.A., Hinrichs, K.T., and Fabian, F.H. (2005) Fractals of strategic coherence in a successful nonprofit organization. *Nonprofit Management and Leadership*, 17(4): 421–441.

Bonjour, L. (1985) *The Structure of Empirical Knowledge*. Cambridge, MA: Harvard University Press.

Campbell, D.T. (1960) Blind variation and selective retention in creative thought as in other knowledge processes. *The Psychological Review*, 67: 380–400.

Christensen, C.M. and Overdorf, M. (2000) Meeting the challenge of disruptive change. *Harvard Business Review*, 78(2): 67–76.

Cote, L., Langley, A., and Pasquero, J. (1999) Acquisition strategy and dominant logic in an engineering firm. *Journal of Management Studies*, 36(7): 919–952.

D'Aveni, R.A., Ravenscraft, D.J., and Anderson, P. (2004) From corporate strategy to business-level advantages: Relatedness as resource congruence. *Managerial and Decision Economics*, 25: 365–381.

DiMaggio, P. and Powell, W. (1983) The iron cage revisited: Institutional isomorphism and collective rationality in organizational fields. *American Sociological Review*, 48: 147–160.

Eden, C. (1992) On the nature of cognitive maps. *Journal of Management Studies*, 29: 261–265.

Eden, C. and Spender, J.-C. (1998) Theory, Methods and Research. *Managerial and Organizational Cognition*. London: SAGE Publications, Ltd.

Eisenhardt, K.M. (1989) Making fast, strategic decisions in high-velocity environments. *Academy of Management Journal*, 32: 543–576.

Fiol, C.M. and Huff, A.S. (1992) Maps for managers. Where are we? Where do we go from here? *Journal of Management Studies*, 29(3): 267–285.

Foster, R. and Kaplan, S. (2001) *Creative Destruction*. New York: Currency.

Gavetti, G., Levinthal, D.A., and Rivkin, J.W. (2005) Strategy-making in novel and complex worlds: The power of analogy. *Strategic Management Journal*, 26(8): 691–712.

Ginsberg, A. (1990) Connecting diversification to performance: A sociocognitive approach. *Strategic Management Journal*, 15(5): 514–535.

Grant, R.M. (1988) On 'dominant logic', relatedness and the link between diversity and performance. *Strategic Management Journal*, 9(6): 639–642.

Hamel, G. and Prahalad, C.K. (1994) *Competing for the Future*. Boston: Harvard Business School Press.

Hannan, M.T. and Freeman, J. (1977) The population ecology of organizations. *American Journal of Sociology*, 82(5), 929–964.

Holland, J.H. (1995) *Hidden Order: How Adaptation Builds Complexity*. Reading, MA: Addison-Wesley.

Huff, A.S. (1990) *Mapping Strategic Thought*. Somerset, NJ: John Wiley & Sons.

Jarzabkowski, P. (2001) Dominant logic: An aid to strategic action or a predisposition to inertia? Working paper of Aston Business School Research Institute, RPO 110.

Lampel, J. and Shamsie, J. (2000) Probing the unobtrusive link: Dominant logic and the design of joint ventures at General Electric. *Strategic Management Journal*, 21: 593–602.

March, J.G. (1991) Exploration and exploitation in organizational learning. *Organization Science*, 2(1): 71–87.

Miller, D. (1993) The architecture of simplicity. *Academy of Management Review*, 18(1): 116–138.

Nadkarni, S. and Narayanan, V.K. (2007) The evolution of collective strategy frames in high and low velocity industries. *Organization Science*, 18(4): 688–711.

Nelson, S.G. and Winter, R.R. (1982) *An Evolutionary Theory of Economic Change*. Cambridge, MA: Harvard University Press.

Obloj, T., Obloj, K., and Pratt, M.G. (2010) Dominant logic and entrepreneurial firms' performance in a transition economy. *Entrepreneurship: Theory and Practice*, 34(1): 151–170.

Obloj, K. and Pratt, M.G. (2005) Happy kids and mature losers: Differentiating the dominant logics of successful and unsuccessful firms in emerging markets. In R.A. Bettis (Ed.) *Strategy in Transition*. Oxford: Blackwell: 81–104.

O'Reilly III, C.A. and Chatman, J.A. (1996) Culture as social control: Corporations, cults, and commitment. *Research in Organizational Behavior*, 18: 157–200.

Porac, J.F., Mishina, Y., and Pollock, T.G. (2002) Entrepreneurial narratives and the dominant logics of high-growth firms. In J. Huff and M. Jenkins (eds.) *Mapping Strategic Knowledge*. London: Cromwell Press: 112–136.

Porac, J.F., Thomas, H. and Baden-Fuller, C. (1989) Competitive groups as cognitive communities: The case of Scottish knitwear manufacturers. *Journal of Management Studies*, 26: 397–416.

Prahalad, C.K. (2004) The blinders of dominant logic. *Long Range Planning*, 37: 171–179.

Prahalad, C.K. and R.A. Bettis. (1986) The dominant logic: A new linkage between diversification and performance. *Strategic Management Journal*, 7: 485–501.

Ramanujam, V. and Varadarajan, P. (1989) Research on corporate diversification: A synthesis. *Strategic Management Journal*, 10(6), 523–551.

Reger, R.K. and Huff, A.S. (1993) Strategic groups: A cognitive perspective. *Strategic Management Journal*, 14: 103–124.

Santos F.M. and Eisenhardt, K.M. (2009) Constructing markets and shaping boundaries: Entrepreneurial power in nascent fields. *Academy of Management Journal*, 52(4): 643–671.

Schwenk, C.R. (1984) Cognitive simplification processes in strategic decision-making. *Strategic Management Journal*, 5: 111–128.

Siggelkow, N. (2001) Change in the presence of fit: the rise, the fall, and the renaissance of Liz Claiborne. *Academy of Management Journal*, 44(4), 838–857.

Sull, D.N. (1999) Why good companies go bad. *Harvard Business Review*, 77(4): 42–56.

Von Krogh, G. and Roos, J. (1996) A tale of unfinished research. *Strategic Management Journal*, 17: 729–737.

Von Krogh, G., Erat, P., and Macus, M. (2000) Exploring the link between dominant logic and company performance. *Journal of Creativity and Innovation Management*, 2(9): 83–93.

Waldrop, M.M. (1992) *Complexity: The Emerging Science at the Edge of Order and Chaos*. New York: Simon and Schuster.

Walsh, J.P. (1995) Managerial and organizational cognition: Notes from a trip down memory lane. *Organization Science*, 6(3): 280–321.

18

Informal Knowledge and Innovation

PAUL ALMEIDA, JAN HOHBERGER, AND PEDRO PARADA

ABSTRACT

This study provides a review of the literature, both conceptual and empirical, on informal knowledge flows and assesses the impact of this knowledge on organizational innovation. We examine various sources of informal knowledge such as the hiring of experts, communities of practice, board inter-locks, and geographic and ethnic communities. The chapter attempts to unbundle the process of knowledge absorption and utilization from informal and individual sources by analyzing its components to determine how firms can develop capabilities in search, transfer, and integration that enhance innovation and create competitive advantage.

KNOWLEDGE AND INNOVATION

The quest for identifying and assimilating knowledge that is useful to innovation poses a very real challenge for today's firms. Knowledge is now recognized as a key competitive asset that forms the basis of firm growth and sustainable competitive advantage (Grant, 1996). Since organizational innovation can be viewed as a result of the combination of existing and new knowledge (Kogut and Zander, 1992), firms that are adept at both sourcing and integrating knowledge are likely to be successful innovators in research and development, marketing, and operations.

Firms themselves are crucibles of knowledge—managerial, operational, and technical. However, they must exploit this internal knowledge in conjunction with external knowledge to compete successfully, gain profitability, and grow. Yet, which firm can claim to harness the potential of its knowledge fully and effectively? Which firm can find (within the organization or outside it) all the knowledge needed for innovation? Few, if any. Until the answers to these questions are in the affirmative, there will always be opportunities for firms to increase their operational efficiency, manage risk, and learn by further developing the capabilities to manage knowledge available within the organization or within their environment.

Previous research has extensively studied the various external sources of firm knowledge (including competitors, universities, and government bodies) and the formal mechanisms used to acquire knowledge (including strategic alliances and acquisitions) (Ahuja and Katila, 2001; Contractor and Lorange, 2004; Inkpen, 2002; Mowery, Oxley, and Silverman, 1996; Ranft and Lord, 2002; Schweizer, 2005). The literature on knowledge spillovers suggests that inter-organizational knowledge flows that are not captured by market contracts contribute to the competitive dynamics of regions and the success of organizations. Until the last decade, comparatively little attention had been paid to understanding informal knowledge flows across organizations especially those facilitated by the development of inter-organizational social communities. Individual actions such as mobility across firms, participation in consortia, and various geographically local, professional, or ethnic activities lead to the development of social communities. These communities provide individuals with potentially useful knowledge for innovation. Our chapter seeks to examine these informal, and often individual, sources of external knowledge. The study provides a review of the literature, both conceptual and empirical, on informal knowledge flows and assesses the impact of informal knowledge flows on organizational innovation. We examine how firms can scan for, absorb, and integrate knowledge obtained from informal sources. Thus, this chapter attempts to unbundle the process of knowledge absorption from informal and individual sources and analyzes its components to determine how firms can develop capabilities in search, transfer, and integration that enhance innovation and create competitive advantage.

WHY EXTERNAL KNOWLEDGE?

The resource-based view of the firm suggests that internal knowledge, embodied within a firm's resources is an important source of competitive advantage (Barney, 1991). The firm itself is often the source of much of the knowledge used in innovation. However, few firms possess all the inputs required for successful and continuous innovation. This is partly due to technological dynamism, reflected in an environment punctuated by competence destroying or altering technologies, that has forced firms to maintain a wide range of technological knowledge and skills (Tushman and Anderson, 1986). Very few firms can independently develop and master the wide range of knowledge and skills needed to compete in ever-changing innovative environments (D'Aveni, 1994; Lane and Lubatkin, 1998). Consequently, most organizations will develop a deficit within their boundaries as regards the critical knowledge needed to prosper and grow (Dussauge et al., 2000). Thus, although a firm's own research efforts play an important role in innovation, firms must turn to external sources of knowledge to maintain their innovative processes.

The notion that firms must often turn to external sources to fulfill their knowledge requirements is hardly new and dates back over fifty years (Jewkes et al., 1958). Early research identifies that major contributions to a firm's knowledge base often come from outside sources. In a classic study of seventeen research and development laboratories, Allen and Cohen (1969) found that vendors, 'unpaid outside consultants,' and informal contacts with government bodies and universities are important sources of research and development knowledge. Research of major product and process innovations at Du Pont between 1920 and 1950 by Mueller (1962) showed that the original knowledge sources of the most critical inventions were outside the firm. More recent research in strategy supports these arguments, suggesting that knowledge existing outside a firm's boundaries may be critical to success (Cassiman and Veugelers, 2006; Escribano et al., 2009; Menon and Pfeffer, 2003). Access to a broader knowledge base through external learning increases the flexibility of the firm, critical in a dynamic environment (Grant, 1996). The 'Yale' survey on appropriability, the results of which have been discussed in a series of papers by Klevorick et al. (1995), addresses the issue of external learning by examining inter-firm knowledge spillovers. In their survey of 650 research and development executives, the authors found that though own research and development was rated the most important channel of learning, external knowledge was also extremely important in most industries. Theoretical approaches are also being extended to incorporate the importance of external knowledge; the resource-based view of the firm, which originally focused on the role of internal capabilities, now encompasses resources that span firm boundaries—often embedded in inter-firm relationships (Dyer and Singh, 1998; Zollo and Winter, 2002).

Informal Modes of Knowledge Acquisition

Though existing research has emphasized the role of formal modes of external learning such as alliances (Contractor and Lorange, 2004; Inkpen, 2002; Mowery, et al., 1996) and acquisitions (Ahuja and Katila, 2001; Ranft and Lord, 2002; Schweizer, 2005), there is also significant evidence that knowledge is transferred across firms by informal means that may often not be easily identifiable and may not be linked to any formal organization level relationship or contract. From Porter's (1998) description of inter-firm knowledge flows in the Italian ceramic tile industry, to Saxenian's (1991) rich ethnography of semiconductor engineers sharing knowledge in Silicon Valley, and Liebeskind et al.'s (1996) description of communities of practice in biotechnology, informal mechanisms of knowledge transfer seem to play an important role in facilitating organizational learning. In her seminal work discussing the 'invisible college of scientists,' Diana Crane (1972) recognizes the fact that communities exist across organizations and these communities facilitate knowledge flows between their members. These communities have a strong social dimension (common language and norms) that governs the flow of knowledge between individuals often across firms, universities, and research institutions. These links act as informal bridges across firm and geographic boundaries (Allen and Cohen, 1969). Though the importance of these communities to inter-firm knowledge flows has been commonly acknowledged, there is need for further conceptual and empirical research that assesses the implications for organizational innovation and learning. In the next section we review the main modes of informal knowledge flows across firms facilitated by social communities (including those linked to individual mobility, ethnicity, geography, board inter-locks, and communities of practice) and subsequently evaluate the implications of these knowledge flows for innovation and learning. The informal social communities are not mutually exclusive—indeed they often overlap and build on each other—but each has a significant stream of research associated with them.

Mobility, hiring, and knowledge

An important mechanism for the transfer of knowledge across firm boundaries is through the mobility of people. Several primarily descriptive studies suggest that people are an important conduit of inter-firm knowledge transfer (Malecki, 1991). Most early research suggests only a connection between mobility and knowledge flows, offering, at best, indirect evidence. For instance, Markusen et al. (1986) find that regions with high concentrations of technical workers attract new high technology investment. In technology intensive industries as well, there are numerous descriptive studies of people carrying knowledge across firms (Hanson, 1982). In the semiconductor industry, interviews with engineers reveal many anecdotes of inter-firm knowledge flows associated with the mobility of engineers (Saxenian, 1991).

The most direct evidence linking mobility of engineers to inter-firm knowledge transfers may be accomplished through patent records. Almeida (1996) shows that after a semiconductor firm hired a new engineer, there was a significantly greater tendency for the hiring firm to cite the prior patents of the newly employed engineer than would be expected given its technology profile. In addition, Song et al. (2001) demonstrate that during the early stage of development of Korean semiconductor firms, the practice of bringing US-educated and US-employed nationals back home leads to similar patenting practices. An important mechanism for the transfer of knowledge across firm boundaries is through the mobility of people. Song et al. (2003) examine the conditions under which learning-by-hiring is more likely to be successful. Using patent applications from software engineers who moved from US firms to non-US firms, the authors demonstrate that mobility is more likely to result in inter-firm knowledge transfers if the hiring firm is less path dependent, if the hired engineers possess technological expertise distinct from that found in the hiring firm, and if the hired engineers work in non-core technological areas in their new firm. They also demonstrate that domestic mobility and international mobility are similarly beneficial to learning-by-hiring.

How does the knowledge obtained from mobility help firm innovation? Rosenkopf and Almeida (2003) demonstrate that the effectiveness of mobility increases with technological distance and is particularly helpful to overcome the challenge of learning from geographical distances. Tzabbar (2009) shows that the recruitment of experts from other organizations is positively associated with technological repositioning particularly in the case of hiring scientists who are experts in areas in which the firm does not have existing competence. Internal factors like breadth and the existence of star researchers moderate this relationship. In a recent study, Corredoira and Rosenkopf (2010) find that hiring can result in bi-directional knowledge flows and learning. Not only does the hiring firm gain knowledge but the firm that lost employees also appears to learn from the hiring firm. This suggests that mobility facilitates the formation of social relationships across firms that then permit the two-way flow of knowledge. Furthermore, the authors find that outbound mobility is a particularly relevant knowledge channel between geographically distant firms, but its importance decreases for geographically proximate firms since other knowledge channels exist within regions. Similarly, looking at the international dimension of inventor related knowledge flows, Oettl and Agrawal (2008) find that the inventor's new country and firm gains from the inflow of inventors and that there is also a reverse flow of knowledge. These studies suggest that hiring across organizations helps creates conduits for knowledge transfer across them, and perhaps even leads to the formation of inter-organizational and inter-country social communities that facilitate the flow of informal knowledge.

Geographically mediated communities and knowledge

Research points to the importance of geographic proximity in facilitating knowledge flows through the formation of spatially clustered social networks (Rogers and Larsen, 1984).

Localized knowledge sharing has been a well observed phenomenon through history. Allen (1983) points to the importance of knowledge sharing across organizations as a force in maintaining the supremacy of the nineteenth century steel industry in England. Case studies of regional clusters in Italy (Piore and Sabel, 1984) and Baden-Wuerttemberg in Germany (Herrigel, 1993) indicate extensive knowledge flows through networks in these regions. Why does co-location matter to the transfer of knowledge? Common to Alfred Marshall's (1920) 'industrial districts' and Porter's (1998) localized industry 'clusters' is the idea that industry-specific knowledge develops in geographically concentrated locations. This phenomenon is true not only of traditional, craft-based industries, but also of high-technology industries. This in turn leads to greater knowledge transfers between firms, due to the similarity in their knowledge bases and to the extensive linkages that develop within a region. In a recent article, Tappeiner et al. (2008) suggest that the geographical clustering of innovation may be best explained not so much by the direct flows of knowledge across neighboring organizations but by the underlying social networks and the commonality in the shared cultural and institutional setting that organizations and their employees share. Hence, some of the advantages of geography to knowledge acquisition and innovation may be indirect.

A question worth investigating is whether these geographically-mediated knowledge flows will grow less important in the face of globalization. For instance, Ponds et al. (2010) find that knowledge spillovers between universities and firms do take place locally but are not restricted to inter-regional flows. The authors do not separate formal and informal knowledge flow across organizations. In an extensive study of patents, Sonn and Storper (2008) find that the localization of inter-organizational knowledge flows has increased across time. Perhaps as more information becomes available to the individual and organization, local communities embedded in geography act as filters to highlight what knowledge is viewed as salient and therefore relevant to innovation and learning. In fact, Alcácer and Chung (2007) suggest that this phenomenon of geographically mediated informal knowledge flows is used strategically by multinational firms when deciding the location of activities to maximize knowledge inflows and minimize outflows.

So why do localized knowledge flows exist? Though linkages between firms could develop across geographic distances, proximity enhances the development of complex networks (Almeida and Kogut, 1999). Locational proximity reduces the cost and increases the frequency of personal contacts which serve to build social relations between players in a network (Saxenian, 1991; Zucker et al., 1998) that can be appropriated for learning purposes. Further, proximity builds common institutional and professional ties that help construct a context for knowledge transfers (Saxenian, 1991). In fact, Saxenian (1991) relates the dynamism and the vitality of Silicon Valley to the extensive networking both at the firm level (between firms and universities, buyers and suppliers, venture capitalists, etc.) and between individuals within the region. Porter's (1998) description of the localized Italian ceramic tile industry points to close and repeated interactions between the various small businesses in the region.

Ethnic communities and knowledge

Aldrich and Waldinger (1990) describe an ethnic community as having members of common culture and origin who are aware of their membership in a group. Ethnic social communities confer the benefits of social interaction, common value systems, and trust based relationships that facilitate social cohesion that can enhance the economic success of its members (Iyer and Shapiro, 1999; Tsai and Ghoshal, 1998). One well-researched area in economic sociology is the entrepreneurial role played by ethnic groups (Greene and Butler, 2004). In technology intensive industries, scholars point to the role of ethnic communities in facilitating not just entrepreneurship, but also innovation (Saxenian and Hsu, 2001). Saxenian (2002) believes that ethnic communities offer a flexible mechanism for transferring knowledge between participants even across distant regional regions. Similar to arguments made by Light (2002), she posits that immigrants often view themselves as outsiders to the mainstream community and consequently foreign-born engineers and scientists forge social relationships based on their national identity that enable the exchange of information and know-how. This would suggest that membership in ethnic communities should enhance an individual's and, therefore, his or her organization's innovativeness.

However, membership in an ethnic community could be a double-edged sword. After all, being embedded in any social community provides both opportunities and constraints (Uzzi and Lancaster, 2003). Porter (1998) suggests that the sense of altruism is especially strong in ethnic communities and helps bind community members together but this could lead to over-embeddedness. Karra et al. (2006), in their case study of Balkan immigrant communities, find that the strong sense of solidarity in the community does lead to over-embeddedness. Individuals are tied so strongly to the expectations of others in the community that their relationships with other non-ethnics are constrained (Bowles and Gintis, 2004) and they do not break away from these constraints due to the solidarity norms that bind the community. Porter (1998) cites the example of the narrow lines of business practiced by San Francisco's ethnic Chinese community to suggest that in many cases ethnic communities force solidarity on their members and the current practices and ways of thinking stifle the availability of new knowledge. This solidarity could take place to the extent to which an individual's ability to innovate or seek new ways of doing things is suppressed. Another way ethnic communities may stifle innovation is that, due to specialization and local learning, there could exist a lack of diversity of knowledge and expertise within the community, and therefore knowledge, resources, and competences obtained from the community could have limited usefulness.

Similar to the idea of path dependence in evolutionary economics, sociologists since Becker and Granovetter have referred to the idea of cumulative causation whereby historical decisions and actions determine future possibilities. Of course community norms and expectations can play a role in forming and directing the actions of individuals along particular paths. Waldinger (1994) attributes the dominance of Egyptian and Indian engineers in the New York City bureaucracy to cumulative causation where historical actions by early community members lead others to view possibilities and opportunities through a narrow historical lens. This leads to a continued reliance on community knowledge and ideas even when opportunities elsewhere may exist. The case study by Karra et al. (2006) suggests that this can lead to lock-in. They observed that individuals influenced by habit, social expectations, and limited world views continued to be a part of the ethnic community long after they played a constructive role or after it was useful. In a recent study, Almeida and Phene (2010) analyzing innovation influences of immigrant Indian inventors in the US find that this informal knowledge can have both positive and negative effects on innovativeness. While at low levels of interaction, ethnic communities can enhance innovation, as their influence increases innovation can actually be suppressed.

Communities of practice and knowledge

Lave and Wenger (1991) gave birth to the concept of communities of practice while examining apprenticeship as a learning model. The concept captured the idea of a community within an organization that collectively acts as a teacher to a new apprentice. Since community based learning is not limited to novices, and applies to numerous contexts and situations, the concept was quickly applied to more general learning and knowledge exchange situations. Brown and Duguid (2001), who worked mainly on the theoretical foundation of communities of practice, linked the concept to collective and social learning theories. They observed that learning and knowledge exchange is social and comes largely from experience with, and the relationship to, others. Communities of practice are institutions whose participants are informally bound by common activities and by what they have learned through their mutual involvement in these endeavors (Wenger, 1998). They can be seen as 'informal, spontaneous, self-organized groups of individuals who share knowledge, solve common problems and exchange insights and frustrations based on the similar work roles and a common context' (Lesser and Prusak, 2000). Since communities are not limited to organizations, they can be extremely important mechanisms for facilitating the flow of knowledge across organizations.

Scientific and technological communities can be seen as examples of communities of practice. Researchers have long studied how scientists interact with each other and under which socially constructed rules and norms they work. For example, Crane (1972) investigated the importance of individuals in creating knowledge bridges across organizations and the 'invisible college' of scientists that helps to diffuse knowledge within scientific communities. Her work is similar to related studies by Tushman (1977) and Allen and Cohen (1969) who argue about the positive effects of boundary spanning activities by certain individuals who are well-connected internally and externally. Boundary spanning scientists can use their social ties to develop links to experts in other firms, universities, and research institutions, and thereby act as informal bridges across organizational boundaries.

More recent research builds on this theme and tends to examine the effect of knowledge exchange by scientists on innovation. Looking directly at the benefits of firm–university collaboration, Cassiman et al. (2008) analyze the effect of science linkages to innovation performance at the patent level. The authors demonstrate that citations in scientific publications are not the main driver to explain forward citations, but they are positively related to their generality and geographical dispersion. Moreover, they illustrate that science linkages, at the firm level, matter more for forward citations with the exception of emerging technologies. Particularly, non-science related patents which have no scientific linkages are less frequently and less easily cited than comparable patents of firms with science linkages. When looking at the impact of high level scientific output on patents, Gittelman and Kogut (2003) find that publications, collaborations, and science intensity are associated to patented innovations; however, important scientific papers are negatively associated with high-impact innovations. The authors conclude that scientific and marketable innovations follow a different underlying logic and that the direct move from science to patent is more difficult and complex than previously assumed (Gittelman and Kogut, 2003). George et al. (2002) examine the effect of science linkages on patent variables and show that firms (in the Biotech sector) with university linkages have lower research and development expenses though they have higher levels of innovative output. However, they do not find support for the proposition that companies with university linkages show greater financial performance than similar firms without such linkages (George et al., 2002). An explanation for the, at best, mixed findings regarding the performance implication of firm–university collaborations is provided by Murray (2002). She argues that the underlying social structures are very different between 'science' and 'technology,' but that they co-evolve. Furthermore, she shows empirically that neither co-publishing nor citations as predicted from current literature drives performance, it is rather the co-mingling through founding, licensing, and consulting. Therefore, both theoretical and empirical studies suggest that knowledge exchange between scientists and engineers can have positive effects on firm innovation.

Board interlocks and knowledge

Board interlocks are another example of inter-organizational relationships that permit individual-level and informal knowledge exchange that potentially impacts corporate behavior and performance. The literature on board interlocks suggests that senior executives who sit on the boards of multiple firms form a unique social community and that the interaction within this community influences firm behavior. Even though board appointments are a formal and institutionalized function, they provide board members with a context in which to develop informal relationships resulting in knowledge exchange that extends beyond task specific information.

Since the 1980s research on board interlocks has produced numerous insights about their significance and usefulness and this stream of research has grown more prominent during the 1990s. Initial research conceptualized interlocks as a means of simultaneous cooperation and competition and as vehicles to reduce risk (Johnson et al.,1996; Murray, 2002). In further research, the learning and knowledge transfer aspects of board interlocks have also been highlighted. For instance, Useem's (1984) research explicitly discussed the learning effects of board interlocks as opposed to the control advantages these inter-firm linkages provided. He argued that interlocks provide managers with an additional source of knowledge regarding the latest business practices and developments in the broader business environment.

The social networks created by common board memberships have some specific characteristics that differentiate them from other informal exchange mechanisms. Board appointments enable executives to acquire and discuss knowledge related to new business and environmental trends at the highest organizational level (Haunschild and Beckman, 1998). These peer based interactions are otherwise less common for top-level executives. This high level interaction can be useful for benchmarking, identifying the adoption of new or different practices, and helping to clarify and evaluate these new practices (Davis, 1991; Gulati and Westphal, 1999). It is worth noting that the direct interaction between board members ensures the transfer of tacit components of knowledge. Hence, board membership provides executives with a context for social interaction that helps define the 'unwritten rules and traits of the game' (Westphal et al., 1997).

Not only do interlocks expose managers to new knowledge, but the direct contact between high level executives within an institutional setting is likely to make this knowledge appear more trustworthy. For example, in many countries (including the US), interlock partners are prohibited from being direct competitors and this reduces potential conflicts of interest (Zajac, 1988). A high level of trust created in part by the institutional setting probably motivates executives to share reliable knowledge (Haunschild and Beckman, 1998). Empirical research on board membership has documented several cases in which the exchange of knowledge—understood as knowledge of certain business practices—has directly influenced firm behavior. For example, Davis (1991) shows that firms are more likely to adopt a 'poison pill' as a takeover defense mechanism when their managers had board interlocks with firms that had already adopted poison pills. Haunschild (1993) investigated the type of knowledge transmitted by acquirers to other potential acquirers within board settings. She found that private information was not shared—rather it was broader knowledge related to 'how to' do things and other normative information. In another study of acquisitions and board interlocks, Haunschild and Beckman (1998) analyzed the interaction of alternative and often informal knowledge channels including business roundtables, business press, consultants, and private contacts with board interlocks on acquisition related knowledge. The paper finds that certain alternative knowledge channels (e.g. business roundtables) reduce the impact of interlocks while others (e.g. business press coverage) reinforce it. The authors argue that business roundtables provide rather similar knowledge as board interlocks whereas business press coverage of acquisitions is a complementary knowledge source. In a related study, Gulati and Westphal (1999) investigate the effect of interlocks on alliance formation. A CEO–board relationship characterized by independent board control reduces the likelihood of alliance formation by prompting distrust between corporate leaders, while CEO–board cooperation in strategic decision making appears to promote alliance formation by enhancing trust. In a recent study on alliance formation, Rosenkopf and Schleicher (2008) illustrate that interlocks and the participation in cooperative technical organizations facilitate alliance formation. However, interlocks only influence alliance formation positively when the common director serves as an officer in one of the firms. Hence, board interlocks can be seen to provide useful knowledge related to strategic decision making and organizational and managerial innovation.

THE STAGE OF ORGANIZATIONAL INNOVATION AND INFORMAL KNOWLEDGE

The previous section highlighted the fact that knowledge from informal external sources drawn from various social communities can play an important role in organizational innovation. However, effectively utilizing this knowledge is not without its challenges. We suggest here, that organizational learning from external and informal sources can be seen to have three distinct stages. The first stage involves the firm (or its employees) scanning the environment as it searches for informal knowledge useful to managerial, technological, or organizational innovation. Thus, the first stage is concerned solely with identifying potentially useful knowledge. Once the sources of potentially useful knowledge have been identified, the next challenge is to access and transfer this knowledge from the external constituent to the firm. It is in the second stage of transfer that knowledge actually crosses firm boundaries, and is brought in to the firm and becomes a part of the firm's internal knowledge stock. Finally, the organization must integrate the transferred knowledge with its internal knowledge to utilize it effectively and create value. In this last stage, we are concerned with the recombination of knowledge within firm boundaries that results in innovation. Given that informal sources of knowledge are important for organizations, yet varied and sometimes hard to identify, we examine the implications of this on each of the steps of innovation and learning.

The nature of search for external knowledge

How do firms search for external knowledge? An important idea emerging from the evolutionary perspective is that learning and search for external knowledge is typically 'path-dependent' (Nelson and Winter, 1982).This idea implies that a firm's past experience and expertise shapes its future decisions and hence the patterns of its knowledge search. The notion of path dependence is intertwined with that of local search. The concept of local search, embedded in evolutionary theory (Dosi and Nelson, 1994; Nelson and Winter, 2002) suggests that a firm, when seeking to innovate, will consider options in the neighborhood of its current activities, thus making radical change less likely. Research in organizational learning (Cyert and March, 1963; March and Simon, 1958) also makes a similar point regarding the search for new knowledge. This literature suggests that boundedly-rational decision makers rely on established organizational practices to drive the search for knowledge. Organizational theorists see learning as a process that involves trial, feedback, and evaluation. If too many parameters in the learning process are changed simultaneously, the ability of the firm to engage in meaningful learning is attenuated (Teece et al., 1997).

The evolutionary perspective of the firm suggests that routines, or 'socially constructed programs of action' drive organizational behavior. These routines are relatively stable and greatly influenced by the experience and history of the firm and the individuals therein (Baum and Ingram, 2002; Nelson and Winter, 1982). Firms thus recognize and absorb external knowledge close to their existing knowledge base and utilize them in established ways (Cohen and Levinthal, 1990). Hence, even as firms seek to expand their knowledge stocks by looking externally, the resultant search processes are restricted to familiar and proximate areas. Thus, the search for new knowledge is often restricted to a firm's current area of expertise and experience.

The local search argument assumes significant importance in the innovatory activities of the firm. Given the great size and uneven topography of all research projects that the firm is faced with, it turns to the 'neighborhood concept' to create an optimal strategy to allocate innovative effort across different technologies (Nelson and Winter, 1982). Technological learning tends to be local and opportunities for learning will be 'close in' to previous activities (Teece, 1988). The technological opportunity of a particular field of investigation will determine the strength of local search. Cantwell (1993) demonstrates that technological diversification has been greater for chemicals and pharmaceuticals than for electrical and electronic-related fields. He attributes this to the greater opportunities for innovation within the electrical and electronic fields than in chemicals and pharmaceuticals. Even for industries like semiconductors that are characterized by tremendous technological opportunities, technological search can be expected to remain fairly local.

It is not just technological search that is local but also geographic search. Studies of innovation and technology diffusion point to the geographic localization of knowledge.

Jaffe et al. (1993) analyzed patent citation data to demonstrate that firms and universities acquire knowledge from others in geographically proximate locations. A key reason for geographically localized knowledge flows, research suggests, is the establishment of inter-firm linkages between firms in the region (Saxenian, 1991). These relational linkages may be formalized, such as alliances and supply relationships (Von Hippel, 1988), or informal, such as regional social networks (Rogers and Larsen, 1984) and mobility of engineers (Almeida and Kogut, 1999). Firms exploit these regional relationships to access knowledge from other local firms. Thus, the underlying reason for geographically local search is both organizational and relational in nature.

There are some advantages to local, contextually-bounded search: it restricts the breadth and, therefore, the cost of the search process. Geographically and technologically proximate search also results in the acquisition of knowledge that can be more easily recognized and managed by the organization's existing routines and members. However, local search restricts the possibilities for innovation through recombination, since it blocks out the acquisition of novel and more distant knowledge. Indeed, Levitt and March (1988) warn of competence traps and Leonard-Barton (1992) suggests that core capabilities associated with existing routines can become core rigidities as circumstances change. Recent studies in the area of strategic management share the view that, given technological change and the dynamic nature of competition, firms must move beyond local search to compete successfully over time. Porter (1998) points to the emergence of geographically dispersed but specialized regions in various technologies and industries, emphasizing the need for geographically distant search. Kim and Kogut (1996) show that the dynamic of competition has encouraged semiconductor firms to diversify across technological sub-fields to maintain their competitive edge. Rosenkopf and Nerkar (2001) demonstrate that external exploration in distant technological domains yields innovations with more impact on a broader set of technological areas. No wonder March (1991) suggests that firms balance local search (exploitation) with more distant search (exploration).

One of the ways to achieve such a balance is by extending firms' scanning capabilities through the utilization of informal conduits of knowledge. A firm's scanning capability enables it to scan the environment and to recognize potentially useful knowledge in both local and distant contexts. So how can firms enhance their ability to stay abreast of new ideas and knowledge and, if necessary, innovate in emerging or new areas? Recent research gives us some hints about how firms may acquire and utilize the knowledge and capabilities to facilitate technological or organizational change. The evidence is that external, especially informal mechanisms can be used to absorb knowledge distant from a firm's current expertise. At the formal and organizational level, Karim and Mitchell (2000) show that acquisitions can reinforce previous business activities (resource deepening) or help them undertake new and 'path-breaking' activities (resource extending). Rosenkopf and Almeida (2003) show that firms can acquire knowledge informally from geographically or technologically distant domains through informal (mobility) means and this knowledge helps them reach beyond the localness of search processes. At the individual level, Song et al. (2003) both highlight the tendency towards local search and point to one way of overcoming it: by hiring experts from other countries and firms. Hiring was only useful when the new engineers and scientists were employed outside a firm's core areas. Hence, existing evidence suggests that in some instances external informal sources may be useful in helping organizations adjust their technological trajectories.

Why do informal sources help organizations scan more broadly? In technology, knowledge inputs and exchanges conducted at the individual level can provide them with an early and clearer picture of the emerging scientific and technological landscape and this expands the view of scientific and technological possibilities available to the firm. These external individual linkages across organizations can extend, not only the spectrum of possible scientific, technological, or managerial advances within the firm but, just as importantly, the perception of what is attractive (and unattractive) to them. Inputs, obtained and refined through external interaction and scientific collaboration, allow a firm to perceive global (rather than just local) optima and hence broaden the search process. Therefore, informal knowledge obtained through individual actions can play an important role in allowing firms to move beyond the constraints of local search but there is a need for firms to recognize the importance of this knowledge and specifically create routines that allow for the identification and subsequent absorption of this knowledge.

The sourcing and transfer of external knowledge

Recognizing the importance of outside knowledge does not necessarily permit a firm to access and transfer it. Nor does it explain which firms are best able to access knowledge or why firms are attentive to knowledge from certain sources and less attentive to others. To facilitate knowledge transfer firms must develop linkages to outside sources of knowledge that act as conduits for knowledge transfer (Cassiman and Veugelers, 2006; Dyer and Singh, 1998; Escribano, et al., 2009; Menon and Pfeffer, 2003). It is these conduits that channel the externally available knowledge, and determine which knowledge the firm actually uses in the innovative process. Of course, as outlined in the previous section, firms use a number of mechanisms that enable them to create conduits to external sources of useful knowledge. Besides traditional supply arrangements and the forming of strategic alliances (Mowery et al., 1996), the informal mechanisms include the hiring of scientists and engineers and the appropriation of informal networks in geographically proximate and other settings (Baum, Calabrese, and Silverman, 2000).

The utilization of mechanisms to access knowledge from external organizations (formal and informal) is facilitated by the possession of valuable internal knowledge, since a firm's or individual's knowledge base makes it more attractive to other organizations for the sharing of knowledge. For instance, Von Hippel (1988) describes how possession of knowledge serves as a prerequisite to arriving at inter-firm technology agreements that permit knowledge sharing and transfer. Thus, the ability of the firm to build and actively utilize mechanisms for external knowledge transfer is termed sourcing capability. Similar to scanning capability, it stems from the firm's internal knowledge base and the knowledge of the individuals employed by the firm.

Sourcing capability reflects the firm's ability to internalize knowledge existing in the environment and bring it within the scope of its own boundaries. For a firm to be successful at sourcing knowledge, it must understand the knowledge to be transferred, articulate it by coding it to facilitate transfer, and transfer it by using well-established reliable routines and then decode it once it has been transferred. This process is challenged when the firm draws upon knowledge obtained from numerous individual and often informal sources. The implication of obtaining knowledge from informal sources is that the sources of knowledge may be numerous and they are not restricted to identifiable levels of the hierarchy. Further, much of this knowledge may not coincide with the existing knowledge base of the firm or even match the established trajectories of innovation within the firm. It may, therefore, be more challenging to recognize the salience or the potential of newly acquired knowledge. Yet, absorbing this informal knowledge could be of critical importance, especially in dynamic industries. Hence, firms must develop new and wide-ranging routines that have been established to code and decode informal knowledge. This calls for a flexibility of organizational systems, processes, culture, and structures that recognize and validate knowledge that may emerge from unexpected and unconventional sources. Thus, while traditional thinking suggests the development of a few standardized routines that emphasize the reliability and durability of knowledge transfer routines, the extensive scope of knowledge from informal sources indicates the need for versatility of these routines and suggests that the underlying ability to articulate, code, and decode should be extended or applied to many types of knowledge. Firms with such flexible sourcing capabilities can transfer external knowledge from the environmental context to the firm. This leads to the last stage in the knowledge management process, integration.

Integrating knowledge

After knowledge has been absorbed from external sources and been transferred within firm boundaries, the challenge is to integrate it with knowledge existing in other parts of the firm. It was Schumpeter who first pointed out that innovation takes place by 'carrying out new combinations' (1939: 65). Henderson and Clark's (1990) concept of architectural knowledge reinforces this idea, suggesting that a critical feature of a firm's innovative ability may be the broader managerial capability to combine or link together knowledge within the firm. Thus, integration appears to be an important stage in innovation and value creation and may be specially challenging when external and informal knowledge sources are involved. The importance of the integration of knowledge within the firm becomes especially critical for firms with dispersed knowledge bases and for organization in dynamic technology environments.

The processes by which this geographically, technologically, and organizationally distributed knowledge is brought together by the companies may be different from the continual, intense knowledge sharing that has been advocated by some exponents of 'the learning company.' The key process is *integrating* specialized knowledge drawn from different locations—what Nonaka and Takeuchi (1995) refer to as 'knowledge combination' to create 'systemic knowledge.' The key to efficient integration from diverse external knowledge sources is the use of loosely-coupled modular designs that permits different individuals and groups to input their knowledge without overloading channels of communication and learning capacity of various units. For instance in interviews with engineers of semiconductor design firms, Fujitsu explained that its VLIW (Very Long Instruction Word) processor chip (used primarily for mobile phones, video compression, and other media-rich processing) was developed jointly by design teams in Tokyo, San Jose, and Frankfurt, but with each team working on specific modules and subsystems (these included a 16-bit instruction set, a 32-bit instruction set, a media instruction set, digital signal instruction set, and floating point instruction set). Segmented modular designs did not mean, however, that knowledge from different sources was reduced to codified knowledge capable of electronic transmission. Successful problem solving required linking with multiple knowledge bases often from a range of external sources: with university researchers on fundamental science, with customers on the functional and technical requirements of new products, with manufacturing engineers from a range of firms over fabrication issues, and with different design teams in order to access parallel experience and stimulate creative thinking. Most of these knowledge bases required accessing experience-based, intuitive knowledge of the tacit kind. A key characteristic of successful design teams was the ability to make full use of the form of computerized design tools and the company's library of designs, while exploring new opportunities through drawing upon the deeply-engrained know-how of seasoned engineers and the creativity and persistence of younger team members. Tacit knowledge is accumulated through experience and is inherently uncodifiable. The transfer of tacit knowledge depends not only upon trial-and-error imitation but also cultural and social context. This cultural and contextual knowledge is a function of socialization, often over a substantial period of time. So what capabilities should the firm emphasize to enable knowledge integration within its boundaries? Just as scanning capability and sourcing capability enhance search and transfer stages of the knowledge management process, we posit that combinative capability improves the stage of integration.

The firm's combinative capability is its ability to combine existing knowledge for innovation. This managerial ability of course, requires the transfer of knowledge from the points of access, with the boundary spanners and gatekeepers to other locations within the firm where this knowledge can be usefully exploited. How do organizations develop this combinative capability? The scale and scope of the firm's knowledge stock which is enhanced by external (often informal) knowledge increases the potential for re-combinations within the firm. However, to capitalize on this potential, firms need to develop internal mechanisms that enable re-combinations. The role of internal communication systems is crucial in this regard especially since the sources and users of potential knowledge are likely to be numerous. Zenger and Lawrence (1989) point out that the ability to communicate knowledge across organizational sub-units depends in part on the prevalence of a shared language and culture. But mere communication of knowledge may not be sufficient to ensure its exploitation. The nature of innovation and the tacit and complex nature of knowledge may require that several individuals and sub-units interact actively across extended periods of time to build new products or processes (Westney and Sakakibara, 1986). To facilitate this knowledge integration process, firms must establish intra-organizational mechanisms, processes and systems to link individuals with access to external knowledge and various sub-units across time.

INFORMAL KNOWLEDGE AND INNOVATION: NEXT STEPS

We have identified external knowledge drawn from informal sources (often linked by social communities) and the internal knowledge management process as the central process through which firms create innovation. Our inquiry into the sources of knowledge and the process by which it is utilized offers further insights into the literature on knowledge and innovation. We believe our study highlights the importance of knowledge from external informal sources. It also points to some of the challenges faced by firms in effectively utilizing this knowledge. By unbundling the components associated with utilization of this knowledge, we attempt to shed new light on the challenges faced by firms as they attempt to build and protect internal knowledge and yet fully utilize knowledge from external, and often informal, sources. The knowledge management process associated with innovation consists of three related yet distinct sub-processes: the search for external knowledge, its subsequent sourcing and transfer, and finally its integration.

We suggest that the fact that informal sources play an important role in enhancing organizational innovation has implications for how we design innovation processes in particular, but also organizational structures, systems, and processes in general. The challenge associated with designing and managing organizations has an added dimension and the processes get more complex as the process gets closer to culminating in value creation to innovation. The design and choice of different mechanisms of knowledge transfer must take careful account of the nature of the knowledge management process (e.g. the extent to which it seeks to replicate knowledge, to combine knowledge, or to create new knowledge through problem solving), the sources of knowledge (external versus internal, formal versus informal) and the types of knowledge being transferred (in particular, the less codifiable the knowledge, the richer the communication medium needs to be).

While firms have made huge strides in the use of information technology to transfer information and support communication worldwide, the next level of the innovation challenge lies in the design and operation of organizational structures, management systems, and shared values and behavioral norms that can facilitate the movement of complementary knowledge and link together different modes of communication and knowledge transfer.

REFERENCES

Ahuja, G. and Katila, R. (2001) Technological acquisitions and the innovation performance of acquiring firms: A longitudinal study. *Strategic Management Journal*, 22(3): 197–220.

Alcácer, J. and Chung, W. (2007) Location strategies and knowledge spillovers. *Management Science*, 53(5): 760–776.

Aldrich, H. and Waldinger, R. (1990) Ethnicity and entrepreneurship. *Annual Review of Sociology*, 16(1): 111–135.

Allen, R. (1983) Collective invention. *Journal of Economic Behavior & Organization*, 4(1): 1–24.

Allen, T. J. and Cohen, S. I. (1969) Information Flow in Research and Development Laboratories. *Administrative Science Quarterly*, 14(1): 12–19.

Almeida, P. (1996) Knowledge Sourcing By Foreign Multinationals: Patent Citations Analysis in the U.S. Semiconductor Industry. *Strategic Management Journal*, 17: 155–165.

Almeida, P. and Kogut, B. (1999) Localization of knowledge and the mobility of engineers in regional networks. *Management Science*, 45(7): 905–918.

Barney, J. B. (1991) Firms Resources and Competitive Advantage. *Journal of Management*, 17(1): 99–121.

Baum, J. and Ingram, P. (2002) Inter-organizational learning and network organization: toward a behavioral theory of the inter-firm. In M. Augier and J. G. March (eds.), *The Economics of Choice, Change, and Organization: Essays in Memory of Richard M. Cyert.* Cheltenham UK: Edward Elgar: 191–218.

Baum, J.A.C., Calabrese, T., and Silverman, B.S. (2000) Don't go it alone: alliance network composition and startups' performance in Canadian biotechnology. *Strategic Management Journal*, 21(3): 267–294.

Bowles, S. and Gintis, H. (2004) Persistent parochialism: trust and exclusion in ethnic networks. *Journal of Economic Behavior & Organization*, 55(1): 1–23.

Brown, J.S. and Duguid, P. (2001) Knowledge and Organization: A Social-Practice Perspective. *Organization Science*, 12(2): 198–212.

Cantwell, J. and Piscitello, L. (1993/2000) Accumulating technological competence: its changing impact on corporate diversification and internationalization. *Industrial and Corporate Change*, 9(1): 21–51.

Cassiman, B. and Veugelers, R. (2006) In search of complementarity in innovation strategy: internal RandD and external knowledge acquisition. *Management Science*, 52(1): 68–82.

Cassiman, B., Veugelers, R., and Zuniga, P. (2008) In Search of Performance Effects of (in)Direct Industry Science Links. *Industrial and Corporate Change*, 17(4): 611–646.

Cohen, W. M. and Levinthal, D. A. (1990) Absorptive Capacity: A new perspective on learning and innovation. *Administrative Science Quarterly*, 35: 128–152.

Contractor, F. and Lorange, P. (2004) Why should firms cooperate? The strategy and economic basis for cooperative ventures. In J. J. Reuer (ed.), *Strategic Alliances: Theory and Evidence*. Oxford, UK: Oxford University Press.

Corredoira, R. A. and Rosenkopf, L. (2010) Should Auld Acquaintance Be Forgot? The Reverse Transfer of Knowledge Through Mobility Ties. *Strategic Management Journal*, 31(2), 159–181.

Crane, D. (1972) *Invisible Colleges. Diffusion of Knowledge in Scientific Communities*. Chicago, IL: University of Chicago Press.

Cyert, R. M. and March, J. G. (1963) *A behavioral theory of the firm*. Englewood Cliff, NJ: Prentice-Hall.

D'Aveni, R. (1994) *Hypercompetition: Managing The Dynamics of Strategic Maneuvering*. New York: Free Press.

Davis, G. (1991) Agents without Principles? the Spread of the Poison Pill through the Intercorporate Network. *Administrative Science Quarterly*, 36(4): 583–613.

Dosi, G. and Nelson, R. (1994) An introduction to evolutionary theories in economics. *Journal of Evolutionary Economics*, 4(3): 153–172.

Dussauge, P., Garrette, B., and Mitchell, W. (2000) Learning from competing partners: Outcomes and durations of scale and link alliances in Europe, North America and Asia. *Strategic Management Journal*, 21(2): 99–126.

Dyer, J. H. and Singh, H. (1998) The relational view: Cooperative strategy and sources of interorganizational competitive advantage. *Academy of Management Review*, 23(4): 660–679.

Escribano, A., Fosfuri, A., and Tribó, J. (2009) Managing external knowledge flows: The moderating role of absorptive capacity. *Research Policy*, 38(1): 96–105.

George, G., Zahra, S. A., and Wood, D. R. (2002) The Effects of Business-University Alliances on Innovative Output and Financial Performance: a Study of Publicly Traded Biotechnology Companies. *Journal of Business Venturing*, 17(6): 577–609.

Gittelman, M. and Kogut, B. (2003) Does good science lead to valuable knowledge? Biotechnology firms and the evolutionary logic of citation patterns. *Management Science*, 49(4): 366–382.

Grant, R. M. (1996) Toward a knowledge based theory of the firm. *Strategic Management Journal*, 17: 109–125.

Greene, P. and Butler, J. (2004) The minority community as a natural business incubator. In J. S. Butler and G. Kozmetsky (eds.), *Immigrant and minority entrepreneurship: the continuous rebirth of American communities*. Westport, CT: Praeger Publishers: 107–122.

Gulati, R. and Westphal, J. (1999) Cooperative or controlling? The effects of CEO-board relations and the content of interlocks on the formation of joint ventures. *Administrative Science Quarterly*, 44(3): 473–506.

Hanson, D. (1982) *The new alchemists: Silicon Valley and the microelectronics revolution*. Boston: Little, Brown.

Haunschild, P. (1993) Interorganizational Imitation: The Impact of Interlocks on Corporate Acquisition Activity. *Administrative Science Quarterly*, 38(4): 564–592.

Haunschild, P. and Beckman, C. (1998) When Do Interlocks Matter?: Alternate Sources of Information and Interlock Influence. *Administrative Science Quarterly*, 43(4): 815–818.

Henderson, R. M. and Clark, K. B. (1990) Architectural Innovation – the Reconfiguration of Existing Product Technologies and the Failure of Established Firms. *Administrative Science Quarterly*, 35(1): 9–30.

Herrigel, G. (1993) Large Firms, Small Firms, and the Governance of Flexible Specialization: The Case of Baden Wuttemberg and Socialized Risk. In B. Kogut (ed.), *Country Competitiveness*. New York: Oxford University Press: 15–35.

Inkpen, A. C. (2002) Learning, knowledge acquisitions, and strategic alliances: So many studies, so many unanswered questions. In F. J. Contractor and P. Lorange (eds.), *Cooperative strategies and alliances*. Oxford: Pergamon: 267–289.

Iyer, G. and Shapiro, J. (1999) Ethnic entrepreneurial and marketing systems: implications for the global economy. *Journal of International Marketing*, 83–110.

Jaffe, A. B., Trajtenberg, M., and Henderson, R. (1993) Geographic Localization of Knowledge Spillovers as Evidenced by Patent Citations. *Quarterly Journal of Economics*, 108(3): 577–598.

Jewkes, J., Sawvers, D., and Stillerman, R. (1958) *The sources of invention*. London: Macmillan.

Johnson, J., Daily, C., and Ellstrand, A. (1996) Boards of directors: A review and research agenda. *Journal of Management*, 22(3): 409–438.

Karim, S. and Mitchell, W. (2000) Path-Dependent and Path-Breaking Change: Reconfiguring Business Resources Following Acquisitions in the US Medical Sector, 1978–1995. *Strategic Management Journal*, 21(10–11): 1061–1081.

Karra, N., Tracey, P., and Phillips, N. (2006) Altruism and agency in the family firm: Exploring the role of family, kinship, and ethnicity. *Entrepreneurship Theory and Practice*, 30(6): 861–877.

Kim, D. J., and Kogut, B. (1996) Technological Platforms and Diversification. *Organization Science*, 7(3): 283–301.

Klevorick, A. K., Levin, R. C., Nelson, R. R., and Winter, S. G. (1995) On the Sources and Significance of Interindustry Differences in Technological Opportunities. *Research Policy*, 24(2): 185–205.

Kogut, B. and Zander, U. (1992) Knowledge of the firm, combinative capabilities, and the replication of technology. *Organization Science*, 3(3): 383–397.

Lane, P. J. and Lubatkin, M. (1998) Relative absorptive capacity and interorganizational learning. *Strategic Management Journal*, 19(5): 461–477.

Lave, J. and Wenger, E. (1991) *Situated learning: Legitimate peripheral participation*: Cambridge University Press.

Leonard-Barton, D. (1992) Core Capabilities and Core Rigidities – a Paradox in Managing New Product Development. *Strategic Management Journal*, 13: 111–125.

Lesser, E. and Prusak, L. (2000) *Communities of practice, social capital and organizational knowledge*. Woburn, MA: Butterworth-Heinemann.

Levitt, B. and March, J. G. (1988) Organizational Learning. *Annual Review of Sociology*, 14: 319–338.

Liebeskind, J. P., Oliver, A. L., Zucker, L., and Brewer, M. (1996) Social Networks, Learning and Flexibility: Sourcing scientific knowledge in new biotechnology firms. *Organization Science*, 7(4): 428–443.

Light, I. (2002) Immigrant and ethnic enterprise in North America. *Entrepreneurship: Critical Perspectives On Business And Management*, 7(2): 179.

Malecki, E. (1991) *Technology and economic development: the dynamics of local, regional, and national change*. New York: Longman Pub Group.

March, J. G. (1991) Exploration and Exploitation in Organizational Learning. *Organization Science*, 2(1): 71–87.

March, J. G. and Simon, H. (1958) *Organizations*. New York: Wiley.

Markusen, A., Hall, P., and Glasmeier, A. (1986) *High Tech America: The what, how, where, and why of the sunrise industries*. Boston: Allen and Unwin.

Marshall, A. (1920) *Principles of economics* (8th edn.) London: Macmillian.

Menon, T. and Pfeffer, J. (2003) Valuing internal vs. external knowledge: Explaining the preference for outsiders. *Management Science*, 49(4): 497–513.

Mowery, D., Oxley, J., and Silverman, B. (1996) Strategic alliances and interfirm knowledge transfer. *Strategic Management Journal*, 17(2): 77–91.

Mueller, W. (1962) *The Origins of the Basic Inventions Underlying Du Pont's Major Product and Process Innovations 1920–1950*: Princeton University Press.

Murray, F. (2002) Innovation as Co-Evolution of Scientific and Technological Networks: Exploring Tissue Engineering. *Research Policy*, 31(8–9): 1389–1403.

Nelson, R. R. and Winter, S. (1982) *An Evolutionary Theory of Economic Change*. Cambridge: Belknap Press/Harvard University Press.

Nelson, R. R. and Winter, S. G. (2002) Evolutionary Theorizing in Economics. *Journal of Economic Perspectives*, 16(2): 23–46.

Nonaka, I. and Takeuchi, H. (eds.) (1995) *Knowledge-Creating Company: How Japanese Companies Create the Dynamics of Innovation*. Oxford: Oxford University Press.

Oettl, A. and Agrawal, A. (2008) International labor mobility and knowledge flow externalities. *Journal of International Business Studies*, 39(8): 1242–1260.

Piore, M. and Sabel, C. (eds.) (1984). *The Second Industrial Divide: Possibilities for Prosperity*. New York, NY: Basic Books.

Ponds, R., van Oort, F.G. and Frenken, K. (2010) Innovation, spillovers, and university-industry collaboration: an extended knowledge production function approach. *Journal of Economic Geography*: 10: 231–255.

Porter, M. (1998) Clusters and the new economics of competition. *Harvard Business Review*, 76(6): 77–90.

Ranft, A. L. and Lord, M. D. (2002) Acquiring new technologies and capabilites: A grounded model of acquisition. *Organization Science*, 13(4): 420–441.

Rogers, E. and Larsen, J. (1984) *Silicon Valley fever: Growth of high-technology culture*. New York: Basic Books.

Rosenkopf, L. and Almeida, P. (2003) Overcoming Local Search Through Alliances and Mobility. *Management Science*, 49(6): 751–766.

Rosenkopf, L. and Nerkar, A. (2001) Beyond Local Search: Boundary-spanning, Exploration and Impact in the Optical Disc Industry. *Strategic Management Journal*, 22(3): 287–306.

Rosenkopf, L. and Schleicher, T. (2008) Below the tip of the iceberg: the co-evolution of formal and informal interorganizational relations in the wireless telecommunications industry. *Managerial and Decision Economics*, 29(5): 425–441.

Saxenian, A. L. (1991) The Origins and Dynamics of Production Networks in Silicon Valley. *Research Policy*, 20(5): 423–437.

Saxenian, A. L. (2002) Silicon Valley's new immigrant high-growth entrepreneurs. *Economic Development Quarterly*, 16(1): 20–31.

Saxenian, A. L. and Hsu, J. Y. (2001) The Silicon Valley-Hsinchu connection: Technical communities and industrial upgrading. *Industrial and Corporate Change*, 10(4): 893–920.

Schumpeter, J. A. (1939) *Business Cycles. A Theoretical, Historical and Statistical Analysis of the Capitalist process*. London: McGraw-Hill.

Schweizer, L. (2005) Organizational integration of acquired biotechnology companies in pharmaceutical companies: The need for a hybrid approach. *Academy of Management Journal*, 48(6): 1051–1074.

Song, J., Almeida, P., and Wu, G. (2001) Mobility of engineers and cross-border knowledge building: The technological catching-up case of Korean and Taiwanese semiconductor firms. *Research on Technological Innovation, Management and Policy*, 7: 59–84.

Song, J., Almeida, P., and Wu, G. (2003) Learning-by-hiring: When is mobility more likely to facilitate interfirm knowledge transfer? *Management Science*, 49(4): 351–365.

Sonn, J. and Storper, M. (2008) The increasing importance of geographical proximity in knowledge production: an analysis of US patent citations, 1975–1997. *Environment and Planning A*, 40(5): 1020–1039.

Tappeiner, G., Hauser, C., and Walde, J. (2008) Regional knowledge spillovers: Fact or artifact? *Research Policy*, 37(5): 861–874.

Teece, D. (1988) Technological change and the nature of the firm. In G. Dosi, C. Freeman, R. Nelson, G. Silverberg and L. Soete (eds.), *Technical Change and Economic Theory*. New York: Pinter Publishers: 256–281.

Teece, D. J., Pisano, G., and Shuen, A. (1997) Dynamic Capabilities and Strategic Management. *Strategic Management Journal*, 18(7): 509–523.

Tsai, W. and Ghoshal, S. (1998) Social capital and value creation: The role of intrafirm networks. *Academy of Management Journal*, 41(4): 464–476.

Tushman, M. L. (1977) Special Boundary Roles in Innovation Process. *Administrative Science Quarterly*, 22(4): 587–605.

Tushman, M. L. and Anderson, P. (1986) Technological Discontinuities and Organizational Environments. *Administrative Science Quarterly*, 31(3): 439–465.

Tzabbar, D. (2009) When does Scientist Recruitment Affect Technological Repositioning? *Academy of Management Journal*, 52(5): 873–896.

Useem, M. (1984) *The Inner Circle: Large Corporations and the Rise of Business Political Activity in the US and UK*. New York: Oxford University Press.

Uzzi, B. and Lancaster, R. (2003) Relational Embeddedness and Learning: The Case of Bank Loan Managers and Their Clients. *Management Science*, 49(4): 383–399.

Von Hippel, E. (ed.) (1988) *The source of innovation*. New York: Oxford University Press.

Waldinger, R. (1994) The making of an immigrant niche. *International Migration Review*, 28(1): 3–30.

Wenger, E. (1998) Communities of practice: Learning as a social system. *Systems Thinker*, 9(5): 1–5.

Westney, E. and Sakakibara, K. (1986) Designing the designers: computer R&D in the United States and Japan. *Technology Review*, 89(3): 24–31.

Westphal, J., Gulati, R., and Shortell, S. (1997) Customization or conformity? An institutional and network perspective on the content and consequences of TQM adoption. *Administrative Science Quarterly*, 42(2): 366–394.

Zajac, E. (1988) Interlocking directorates as an interorganizational strategy: A test of critical assumptions. *Academy of Management Journal*, 31(2): 428–438.

Zenger, T. and Lawrence, B. (1989) Organizational demography: The differential effects of age and tenure distributions on technical communication. *Academy of Management Journal*, 32(2): 353–376.

Zollo, M. and Winter, S. G. (2002) Deliberate Learning and the Evolution of Dynamic Capabilities. *Organization Science*, 13(3): 339–351.

Zucker, L. G., Darby, M. R., and Armstrong, J. S. (1998) Geographically localized knowledge: Spillovers or markets? *Economic Inquiry*, 36(1): 65–86.

19

Knowledge Sharing in Organizations: The Role of Communities*

GEORG VON KROGH

ABSTRACT

Because it has become a central construct in theory and research, knowledge is utilized to explain and predict behavior at all levels. Knowledge not only links cognition and action, it also integrates individual and collective levels of analysis. This chapter addresses the need for research on how cognition and action could be tied to organizational performance. The key questions are: why, and under what circumstances, do people share knowledge in organizations? Inherent in this exploration are three important features of knowledge: knowledge is a function of our justified true beliefs; knowledge enables action; and knowledge is both explicit and tacit. In this chapter, the issue of knowledge sharing will be examined through a collective action framework, and two possible solutions to the sharing problem will be identified: the use of agency and the nurturing of a communal resource. The chapter also discusses how this nurturing can be achieved.

INTRODUCTION

There is an increasing body of work in organization behavior, organization theory, strategic management, information systems, technology and innovation management, marketing, and in the fundamental disciplines of economics, psychology, and sociology that makes knowledge a central construct in theory and research. Common to most of these contributions is the intent to demonstrate the power of knowledge for explaining and predicting behavior, at the level of societies and economies (Stehr, 1994); industries (Arthur,

*I am grateful for comments from Hilde Brune, Marla Kameny, Marjorie Lyles, Margit Osterloh, Petra Kugler, Mattaeus Urwyler, Sebastian Spaeth, and one anonymous reviewer. The paper is based on von Krogh (2002)

1997); firms and institutions (e.g. Nelson and Winter, 1982; Cohen and Levinthal, 1990; Grant, 1996; Spender, 1996; Kogut and Zander, 1992; Sabherwal and Sabherwal, 2005); networks (Dyer and Nobeoka, 2000); groups (Osterloh and Frey, 2000); and individuals (e.g. Cziksezentmihalyi, 1988). On the one hand, the knowledge construct has evolved since the cognitive revolution in the 1950s, and now bridges the chasm between cognition and action (von Krogh, Roos, and Slocum, 1994; Varela, Thompson, and Rosch, 1991). Knowledge gives rise to an array of behavioral patterns, decisions, and task solutions, observable in competent behavior. On the other hand, knowledge integrates individual and collective levels of analysis; what used to be a construct reserved for individual-level analysis, is now used by many scholars to explain and predict how individuals and groups mutually influence their thinking and acting (Nonaka and von Krogh, 2009).

For the purpose of this chapter, three important features of knowledge will be considered. The first is justified true beliefs. Individuals justify the truthfulness of their observations of the world, which depend on a unique viewpoint, personal sensibility, and individual experience (Nonaka and Takeuchi, 1995). When we have knowledge, we make sense of a situation by holding justified beliefs and committing to them.[1] Second, knowledge enables action. Our beliefs and our commitment to them enable our actions in a situation, for example formulating a problem or resolving a task (Stehr, 1992; 1994; Nonaka and von Krogh, 2009). Third, knowledge is both explicit and tacit (Nonaka, 1994). Some knowledge can be put on paper, formulated in sentences, or captured in drawings. Engineers, for example, convey knowledge of a product design through drawings and specifications, making what they know explicit. Yet, other kinds of knowledge are tied to the senses, movement skills, physical experiences, rules of thumb, and intuition (Merleau-Ponty, 1995). Such tacit knowledge can be costly to describe to others. Putting together the pieces of a high-precision luxury watch, for instance, or interpreting a complex seismic readout of an oil reservoir, demands knowledge that cannot be found in a procedure or easily conveyed to an apprentice. While the idea of tacit knowledge makes intuitive sense for most people, managers often have a hard time coming to grips with it on a practical level. Recognizing the value of tacit knowledge, that is, figuring out how to use it to enhance task performance, has become the key challenge for knowledge management practice in many organizations (Choo, 1998; Schulze and Hoegl, 2006).

Because of the merging of collective and individual cognition and action, and the power of explaining and predicting, scholars of organizational learning and knowledge management addressed the need for a more coherent body of research on how cognition and action could be tied to organizational performance. The central quest for knowledge management research became performance enhancement through various activities, enabling conditions, and information and communication technology tools that took into account the serendipitous and ambiguous nature of knowledge (Kluge, Stein, and Licht, 2001; Serenko et al., 2010). The research opportunities along these dimensions are still vast, but in order to progress fruitfully, we need to pay more attention to one of the core questions that bridges the chasm between individual and collective levels: *why*, and *under what circumstances*, do people share knowledge in organizations? While we understand *how* knowledge sharing occurs—for example, by organizational units transferring best practices

---

[1]For a discussion see von Krogh, Ichijo, and Nonaka (2000).

(Szulanski, 1996)—recent research suggests this problem has yet to be fully understood (Gaechter, von Krogh, and Haefliger, 2010).

In this chapter, light will be shed on the issue of knowledge sharing through a collective action framework, and two possible solutions to the sharing problem will be identified: the use of agency and the nurturing of a communal resource.[2] Whether or not a community is a resource for knowledge sharing depends on the interests of its affiliates. Generally, we do not assume that people in organizations have stable and shared interests (March, 1962). However, if there is some evolutionary stability of contributing to and benefiting from the community, over time, people may explore opportunities for joint learning in accordance with their interests. In this chapter some conditions enabling this stability will be discussed.

THE PROBLEM OF KNOWLEDGE SHARING

Knowledge sharing is found in most knowledge-management activities, from capturing and localizing knowledge, transferring knowledge and technology, to knowledge creation. The intent in capturing and localizing knowledge in the organization is to enhance the potential for linking and integrating knowledge dispersed throughout the organization, and to improve the efficiency of doing so (Davenport and Prusak, 1996; Choo, 1998). Knowledge and best-practice transfer within and between organizations is not a one-way activity; it is a sharing process, involving trial and error, feedback, and mutual adjustment (Szulanski, 1996; Powell, 1998; Kaeser, 2001). While the early literature on knowledge and technology transfer between and within organizations hinged on a simple model of

---

[2]A third solution refers to organization size, but space does not allow for further discussion here. For some collective action problems, the individual's benefit from participation depends on the success of a collective enterprise; and the success of the collective action hinges on the number of people who participate (Chong, 1991). This is a so-called 'critical mass' argument. If many people in the organization share their knowledge, more individuals might be interested to join and share as well, since sharing *ex ante* has provided a strong and valuable combination of individual experiences and benefits. Under conditions of diverse and distributed interests, the likelihood of more people being interested in collective action increases with the size of the organization (Oliver and Marwell, 1988). In a large organization it is likely that more people take an interest in sharing knowledge, even if structure and incentive mechanisms are not conducive to sustaining the sequence of these activities. There might be altruists interested in helping others to learn, but also self-interested individuals who find each other and discover opportunities to realize their immediate need satisfaction, or engage in sharing because they are deprived of other organizational resources (Darrah, 1990). There might also be 'pockets,' functions, departments, or areas in the organization, where extensive knowledge sharing has become an integral part of introducing newcomers into the firm (March, 1991), and where people feel 'obliged' to share by some professional code (Ferner, Edwards, and Sisson, 1995). An in-depth case study of organizational behavior in a consultancy showed that some professionals might even choose to leave a firm that lacks those pockets of sharing necessary to advance their careers (Ram, 1999). However, there is a cost involved in sharing knowledge that might rise with size of the group (Grant, 1996; see also Oliver and Marwell, 1988), in particular if the knowledge to be shared is tacit, and rates of learning and sharing slow down. Nahapiet and Ghoshal (1998) suggest that before knowledge can be shared, individuals must realize the potential for sharing and the benefits involved, and that the cost of identifying opportunities for sharing increases with the size of the organization.

information communication, new contributions in this area understand knowledge and technology transfer as a model of knowledge sharing and local knowledge (re)-creation (for a review, see von Krogh and Koehne, 1998). In theories of knowledge creation and innovation, the sharing of tacit knowledge among participants in an innovation process precedes the articulation of new concepts, the appraisal and justification of these concepts, and product prototyping (Leonard and Sensiper, 1998; von Krogh, Ichijo, and Nonaka, 2000; Nonaka, von Krogh, and Voelpel, 2006).

Often, apprentice training is used as an example of sharing, especially of tacit knowledge. Sharing tacit knowledge entails self-observation, reflection, and immersion in the routines of the master, as much as it does observation and imitative learning by the apprentice (Polanyi and Prosch, 1975). It also involves transformation of masters' cognition, as the training of apprentices confronts masters with new experiences that are tightly connected to, if not caused by, the performance of their own routines. Additionally, apprentices might bring a 'fresh' view to the tasks, which may help masters to perform them differently (Perkins, 1981). Masters' reflections on their own routines are indistinguishable from their observation of apprentices' attempts to re-create those routines at comparable standards of performance. Of course, it is this indistinctness of observation and reflection that could be said to be the very essence of being a 'master.' In this system of master and apprentice, masters' routines will change as a result of observation and reflection but to what extent, and in which direction, is dependent on individual masters' interest and willingness to adopt a shared identity with the apprentice (see Cohen, 1985). Some authors claim that good apprenticeship training can only be achieved when masters' routines include the observation and reflection that comes with training (Dreyfus and Dreyfus, 1986).

This example of tacit knowledge sharing reveals an important insight. If knowledge sharing is knowledge re-creation, as outlined, it could be construed as a *sequenced collective action problem* rather than the communication of information, representation of tasks, and procedural knowledge (see Gaechter, von Krogh, and Haefliger, 2010). Sharing, in its simplest form, needs a knowledge giver, e.g. master, and knowledge receiver or 're-creator,' e.g. apprentice, and a sequence of activities. The giver must be interested in transmitting knowledge, and the receiver must be interested in applying it; in both cases, cognition and action are altered. The receiver becomes a giver, who, by combining the new knowledge with gained experiences, rewards the giver with knowledge; and the giver in turn becomes the receiver.[3] As Merleau-Ponty (1995) remarked, individual learning often aims at producing a 'maximum grip' in a situation. Working in isolation, individuals direct their perception and positioning in relation to a task so that they can optimally control task execution and performance. This implies ignoring the presence of others during task performance. However, in a master–apprentice relationship, the 'other' becomes an integral part of task performance, cognition, and action simply because there is a master or apprentice observing, commenting, helping, or maybe even ignoring the person performing the tasks.[4]

---

[3] I am very grateful to a reviewer for pointing out that this process could alternatively be put in terms of Vygotsky's concept of 'zones of proximal development,' in which the process of knowledge sharing turns into a mediated social activity. For an analysis of this concept, see Wertsch (1985).

[4] When the master ignores the apprentice, this could be a sign of disinterest, dissatisfaction, or doubt. In any event, the task performance and learning of an apprentice who wants to look good in the eyes of the master will most certainly be affected.

Knowledge and interest are inter-dependent,[5] so interests should have an effect on knowledge sharing. For the purpose of this discussion, we use a broad understanding of interests based on Schutz (1970); a specific motivational focus determining an individual's definition of the situation as well as his particular rules of conduct, objective, or intent.[6]

As the literature on cognitive psychology shows, individual interest influences individuals' learning in a specific situation (Bruner, 1979), for example, how much of a particular subject matter they are willing to study and absorb. Stories people tell of their expertise and experience also reveal that their interests are varied and manifold and tightly connected to their own areas of tacit and explicit knowledge, history of action, and task performance (von Krogh, Ichijo, and Nonaka, 2000). Organizations create opportunities for people to realize their individual interests through learning; organizational task systems allow individuals to invest in learning and build expertise that is considered more or less costly, valuable, and even legitimate (see also discussion in Gourlay, 2006).

Were it not for the variation in individual interest throughout an organization, knowledge sharing would be a straightforward activity, without much shirking, guile, or resistance. In an organization populated only by altruists, who are interested beyond all else in helping others to learn, knowledge sharing would not represent a major issue to researchers concerned with organizational efficiency and innovation (Collard, 1978). However, empirical studies in many fields, for example Bruno Latour's work on how science proceeds as a collective enterprise, show that there are diverse and distributed interests behind knowledge production, barriers to knowledge sharing and people who find ways to teach less than they learn from others (e.g. Latour, 1987, 1993). Paul Carlile (2002) has shown that people's long-term investments in areas of expertise, for example in engineering disciplines, make them reluctant to share knowledge with representatives from other areas, and they tend to be very conscious of 'boundaries' and diverse interests, which separate their work practices from those of other disciplines. Darrah's (1990) ethnography of a high-tech manufacturing firm is also interesting in this respect. Fearing the loss of authority, manufacturing engineers who had full information about product design and specifications were reluctant to share this with front-line workers. As a (negative) result, the firm's attempts to lower quality costs by training led to more frustration than skill enhancement among the workers. Recent laboratory experiments have also confirmed that sharing explicit knowledge might easily break down with even the slightest change in the (economic) incentives affecting people's interests. We developed a game-theoretic model showing that explicit knowledge sharing is an activity with multiple equilibria (Gaechter, von Krogh, and Haefliger, 2010). Since there are many outcomes of knowledge sharing, we conducted an experiment involving 228 undergraduates. While we found more knowledge sharing than initially predicted, we also found that knowledge sharing depends on social

---

[5] The writing of Foucault (1980) gives a very good indication of how this interdependence has played out throughout human history. In contrast to Foucault, for example, Max Weber was concerned with 'legitimate power' arising from superior, sophisticated technical knowledge of operations (Weber, 1978).

[6] I deliberately define interests broadly because of the later need to capture their situational nature when elaborating on the evolutionary nature of communities.

preferences, for example, fairness. When people feel others benefit unfairly from what they share, they may be more reluctant to cooperate; this effect may be even more pronounced for tacit than for explicit knowledge. These studies, which pay explicit attention to people's diverse and distributed interests, conclude that knowledge sharing is a highly fragile and uncertain activity.[7]

A theory that explains why and under what conditions the collective act of knowledge sharing occurs, must take into account a variety of interests and personality traits, including self-interest and individuals who seek to maximize their own utility (see Ostrom, 2000).[8] Given the sequencing of activities and self-interest, free riding on others' knowledge is also of some concern (e.g. Olson, 1967). A free rider chooses to receive a higher payoff for defecting than for cooperating, even though contributors get a higher payoff if they all cooperate (Olson, 1967; Hardin, 1968; Mannix, 1991). Here, knowledge free-riding is taken to mean that an individual learns but hides the learning process from the knowledge giver (Gaechter, von Krogh, and Haefliger, 2010). Sometimes, the free rider will be able to obtain the same, or even more, benefits from the knowledge as a contributor (see also von Hippel and von Krogh, 2001). This raises the question, if people are prepared to give knowledge, why should others be interested in reciprocating?

It should be noted that diverse interests in the organization do not necessarily have a negative effect on organizational outcomes: think of innovation. Since knowledge and interest are connected, in the sense that individual interests influence an individual's learning, it stands to reason that diverse interests give rise to the miscellany and creativity organizations need to extract value from sharing knowledge. Moreover, when the 'mean level' of knowledge in a group is not sufficient for solving a particular problem, diverse interests may well facilitate knowledge sharing (e.g. Oliver, 1993). For example, a team of (self-interested) engineers might realize that the firm has not been efficient in adopting a new manufacturing technology, because they lack the basic knowledge needed for its implementation. Yet, engineering pride or a concern with building human capital makes each individual engineer interested in acquiring the new knowledge. This might be highly complex and demanding, requiring the dedicated effort of several people studying and acting together. Even if individually each thinks this new technology has potential for very different reasons, selfish or otherwise, the only way to realize individual interests is to learn jointly, especially under time pressure.

Given distributed and diverse interests, there are several ways to theorize why, and under what circumstances, people share knowledge in organizations. Two fruitful areas are concerned with agency and the community.

---

[7] Similar conclusions have been reached in other studies of collective action in an organization setting, such as Monge et al. (1998), McCaffrey, Faerman, and Hart (1995), Cabrera and Cabrera (2002).

[8] A similar discussion is continuing in economics, where the topic is how psychological research modifies conceptions of an individual's utility function. An important insight is that people occasionally depart from pure self-interest, to pursue 'other-regarding' goals, like altruism, fairness, and retaliation (Rabin, 1998).

Agency in Knowledge Sharing

In general, problems in collective action can be resolved by an agency[9] (management, for example) enforcing a regime of cooperation while outside the process itself. While an agency might enforce knowledge sharing in the organization, it might have limited concern for the details of the knowledge shared, and so its control might focus more on the structure for sharing, effectiveness of sharing, fairness and distributive justice, punishing free-riders, and so on. For example, a manager of a sales team might try to organize and motivate personnel to share information and experience in building customer relations, in order to improve the overall team sales performance.

The agency can make structural choices where changes are intended to increase points of contact or networks of organization members (Kransdorf, 1998). At the modest end of the scale, as Grant (1996) suggested, knowledge can be shared by forming a group that engages in problem solving and decision making. This alternative is particularly relevant if the task's complexity is very high and face-to-face interaction is needed to perform it. Moreover, management might create a unit to direct and oversee knowledge sharing. A comparison of manufacturing costs between a firm's activities in various countries might reveal strong differences. Case studies have shown that in order to exploit these differences, management typically creates a new knowledge management unit, or a knowledge and technology transfer unit whose task is to identify best practices among selected plants, and then foster the transfer and leverage of these practices throughout the firm on a worldwide basis (Dixon, 2000; von Krogh, Ichijo, and Nonaka, 2000; Kriwet, 1997). Typically, such units identify technologies and practices to be shared, document practice, structure knowledge, create manuals for training plant operators and other key people, revamp procedures, and encourage plants to participate in the practice-sharing program, and monitor progress (O'Dell and Grayson, 1998; Lu, Mao, and Wang, 2010).

At the larger end of the scale of organizational changes, Nonaka and Takeuchi's (1995) case studies show that management can choose a multi-layered organizational structure—what they term the 'hypertext organization:' a business system layer that covers the main tasks and business processes of the firm; a project layer where people collaborate to create new knowledge and innovation; and a knowledge-based layer that comprises organizational memory (e.g. positions, databases, organizational culture, etc.), and which organization members can access when needed for projects or operational activities. Employees of such organizations network on at least three different levels when solving operational tasks, working on projects, and storing and structuring knowledge. This networking is also instrumental in knowledge sharing between the various layers, and makes the organization increasingly adaptive to changes in the environment (Nonaka and Takeuchi, 1995; Nonaka, von Krogh, and Voelpel, 2006).

---

[9] An agent here means a person or group that exerts the power to produce an effect, and agency refers to the activities of this person or group. Agency is exogenous to the community. It is key to think of this solution as more encompassing than management in a company, since individuals in the organization may find various ways actually to enforce regimes of cooperation, like another colleague or an entity outside the organization.

Between these two extreme structural solutions to the sharing problem, we typically find the matrix organizational structures that combine business activities with a regional focus, or a functional focus with an industry or customer focus. The matrix structure is intended to increase the interconnectedness of functions, departments, groups, and regional centers. Decision making and resource allocation are federative rather than centralized (Doz and Prahalad, 1981). Resource allocation results from a bargaining process between the units, and thanks to the federative form, each unit in the matrix has an incentive to specialize, or in other words, create centers of excellence and knowledge that do not overlap, while seeking knowledge from other units as needed to conduct local tasks (Bartlett and Ghoshal, 1986).[10] However, as Bartlett and Ghoshal (1986) pointed out in their early writings on the topic, the matrix is more than a structure; it is a 'frame of mind.' This implies that performance expectations for both vertical and horizontal activities require extensive knowledge sharing, but that for such structures to work, local individual interests must be reflected in the overall corporate agenda, and effective human resource management must be put in place. In other words, organizational structure must be 'translated' into individual behavior (Gibbons, 1998).

The knowledge management literature comes to similar conclusions. Because human interest and tacit knowledge are often involved, there are strong limitations to structural solutions to the knowledge-sharing problem (see also Boisot, 1998; Grant, 1996; Tsai, 2002). Simply increasing people's exposure to functions, projects, and knowledge—and even to other people—fails to safeguard collective learning in the firm. Making a regional head talk to the supply chain expert at the corporate center will more often than not necessitate a real flow of technical expertise to other regions. Hence, within the agency solution, the knowledge management literature suggests that well-functioning HR management systems are imperative. Management can create management support systems, monetary or career incentives for individual organizational members, and conduct employee performance appraisals that take into account individuals' interests and attempts to share knowledge and information (e.g. Davenport and Prusak, 1998; Davenport and Probst, 2000; Grant, 1996; Pedler, Burgoyne, and Boydell, 1991). Management's investment in information and communication technology (ICT), including search capabilities, document management, messaging connectivity, expert systems, and pattern-recognizing technologies, all of which enable knowledge sharing, is strongly related to this emphasis on HR management systems (Allee, 1997; Alavi and Leidner, 2001). Yet, as case studies have shown, in modern organizations, although ICT enables people to connect more effectively, team performance and knowledge sharing are linked to individual and team-based incentives (Govindarajan and Gupta, 2001).

In those instances where tacit knowledge cannot be codified, sharing it between people is slow, costly, and uncertain, as was pointed out in the early work on knowledge in organizations (Kogut and Zander, 1992). Hence, the tacit nature of knowledge and the collective actions of knowledge sharing pose limitations to HR management systems.

---

[10] Grant (1996) argued that because of individuals' bounded rationality, efficiency in knowledge production requires specialization. Likewise, in a large organization, units have an incentive to specialize further and the agency's role must be to identify opportunities for sharing knowledge as necessary between units, facilitating a bargaining process between units to make knowledge flow.

In an important paper, Osterloh and Frey (2000) discussed whether self-interested individuals are motivated to share knowledge extrinsically, through material incentives such as money, or intrinsically, through the activity itself. Intrinsically motivated individuals act for their immediate need satisfaction, for example, for the inherent joy of performing a task. In the sharing of tacit knowledge in particular, intrinsic motivation outweighs extrinsic motivation. Material incentives cannot make people change their interest in codifying and sharing their tacit knowledge; neither can contracts assure effective and efficient knowledge sharing. The classic option through which organizations can achieve team production (Alchian and Demsetz, 1972) breaks down with tacit knowledge sharing, because there is no way for team members to monitor each other's sharing behavior.[11] If monitoring and sanctioning possible free-riding behavior is challenging for team members themselves, it is even more so for any outside agency that must base disciplinary action on retrieved information about individual team members' performance. Hence, intrinsic motivation, by which team members realize immediate need satisfaction by working together to solve complex tasks, is a prerequisite for (tacit) knowledge sharing.

However, it is important to know the conditions under which intrinsic motivation operates, one of which relates to cadence. Immediate need satisfaction might be a strong motivation for some organizational members, but the sequencing of activities involved in knowledge sharing[12] depends on the type of knowledge to be shared, as well as other individuals' rates of learning. Experiments have shown that if learning is slow, the rate at which people acquire tacit knowledge differs greatly (Shanks and Johnstone, 1998), and so immediate need satisfaction might fail to satisfy individual needs and provide sufficient stimulation for a change in individual interests. Moreover, the acquisition of tacit knowledge has uncertain outcomes. Since tacit knowledge is associated with both physiological and cognitive structures (Merleau-Ponty, 1995), people may differ greatly in their capacity to act, even after a long period of learning. In fact, it may be years before the apprentice's task performance comes within reach of the master's. Worse, some people may never reach the master's level.

THE COMMUNAL RESOURCE

The remainder of this chapter examines the role a community plays in explaining why people share knowledge in organizations. A brief review is provided of some of the key literature on communities within and outside the organizational context, followed by a discussion

---

[11] Of course, it is possible to observe certain knowledge-sharing behavior in a team. For example, a team member may take an active part in problem solving and decision making by offering valuable suggestions and contributions and by involving and integrating team members. This behavior can be observed by others. However, other team members will not know to what extent one individual has really shared everything she knows of value to the team. More importantly, if knowledge is tacit it can be costly to codify and beyond the reach of individual reflection and identification (Polanyi and Prosch, 1975). Hence, the interest in sharing knowledge, even beyond what people thought they knew, becomes a crucial factor for sustained sharing in the community.

[12] Recall that knowledge sharing is a sequential collective action problem.

on how diverse and distributed interests may influence knowledge sharing in communities. Assuming that organizations are populated by people with dynamic rather than static interests, the chapter ends with an examination of how opportunity structures and the social norms of care and authenticity could have a positive impact on knowledge sharing.

The term 'community' is derived from a classical sociological premise that people form social bonds through shared norms, traditions, identity, and solidarity. Historically, the concept of community stands in contrast to society, where competition, individualism, and self-interest rule (Toennies, 1887; Durkheim, 1893; Weber, 1978). Communities have their own languages, rituals, norms, and values that can only be developed and refined over a long period of time. Members of a community develop a shared and deep sense of identity through intense and sustained communication. Interestingly, this deep sense of identity, and the traditions, solidarity, and long-standing norms that come with it, can create a binding commitment among community members to mobilize large-scale societal changes. Sociologists have noted that when people experience grievances, or entrepreneurs see opportunities for action, feelings of solidarity can bind them together in collective action (Calhoun, 1986, 1994; Cohen, 1985; Fantasia, 1988).

Building on a long tradition in sociology, anthropology, and economics, a growing number of authors have focused on the role of communities in knowledge sharing. For example, the literature on rural and peasant communities emphasizes how farmers and village inhabitants acquire the skills of productive farming without depleting natural resources. Through processes of socialization, the very subtle rules and skills of farming are transferred from one generation to the next (see Foster, 1965). Related to this, a very important stream of work on occupational communities has shown how people who practice similar work develop a shared identity related to their occupations. Shared identity and work practice enable mutual learning, as well as solidarity (e.g. Van Maanen and Barley, 1984; Orr, 1996).

The Internet has become increasingly important for communication within and between organizations. Another literature stream reports on the characteristics of virtual communities, where protecting the anonymity of individuals often takes precedence over membership selection on the basis of social categories such as occupation. Anonymity is not a trivial issue. It enables a free flow of information between community members; for example, individual sharing is not inhibited by the fear of possible future retaliation due to the contents of messages (Myers, 1994). Virtual communities typically exist because people share an interest in exchanging information and explicit knowledge on particular topics at low cost (e.g. Rheingold, 1993; Castells, 1996; see also Wasko and Faraj, 2005). Research on communities of interest has focused on groups that are topic as well as relationship based. However, in these communities, anonymity might be less pronounced than for virtual communities. Learning and exchange of information are central activities in communities of interest, and interactions are mostly limited to the personal needs of members to obtain explicit knowledge and information at low cost and high speed. Common engagement in work, such as joint projects and tasks, is rare (e.g. Amstrong and Hagel, 1995). Virtual and interest communities do *not* necessarily bind people together by occupation or socialization into a village, rural district, or peasant group.

In contrast, there is an interesting stream of work relating to 'imagined communities.' Here, people 'imagine oneness' with others whom they have neither met nor seen. The foundation of this solidarity is a set of simple, effective socially transmitted constructs, such as an area of expertise or nationality. Imagined communities can be powerful forces for large-scale social change (Anderson, 1983; Calhoun, 1991). Case studies of communities for knowledge-sharing have observed that people tend to identify with similar groups of experts throughout the organization, even though they have never met face to face. This identification, in turn, seems to impact positively helping behavior across organizational boundaries (von Krogh, Nonaka, and Ichijo, 1997). Work on micro-communities of knowledge has argued that collective identity is formed as people jointly engage and commit to processes of knowledge creation.

The most systematic exploration of communities in organizations can be found in the practice-based perspective on organizational learning (Wenger, 1998; Brown and Duguid, 1991; Lave and Wenger, 1991; Lave, 1988; Orr, 1996). These studies provide insight into the social fabric of communities, how they work, and the conditions that enable or constrain them. A community of practice is characterized by members who share work activities and engagement, work together over a certain period of time, and develop a shared identity, language, artifacts, norms, and values. Learning through imitation, observation, narration, and storytelling gives rise to shared knowledge.

Returning to our initial problem, although communities are interesting for understanding how individuals behave apolitically and altruistically (Wolin, 1961) and how knowledge and learning happen in social practices (Tsoukas, 1996), systematic attention must also be paid to the collective action problem of knowledge sharing that results from the distributed and diverse interests of the individuals who comprise these communities (For a critique of the practice-based view of organizational learning, see Yakhlef, 2010.) A community acts collectively without outside intervention from an agency. In this sense, it exists outside the organization (see Bennis et al., 1958), and is not regulated by formal structure and incentive mechanisms, control, and sanctions (Wenger, 1998). A community attracts people around common tasks, work, knowledge, and experience, *as well as* emotions such as liking and empathy. Also, a community has a certain stability of affiliation over time;[13] it has multiple and direct relations between the actors (Taylor and Singleton, 1993), and there is some level of common information (cues) about other members' knowledge. The negative returns to size apply; not all needs can be satisfied immediately in knowledge sharing. However, the community could be a resource for knowledge sharing because the satisfaction of needs is suspended and the natural sequence of activities well preserved. This point will be scrutinized more closely later.

A community is different than the production team (Alchian and Demsetz, 1972). The community is established, developed, and maintained by its affiliates in a manner of self-production. The production team to some extent relies on the agency that allocates a complex production task and external inputs, performs external monitoring of production output, and sanctions the team. Empirical evidence has shown that communities produce less collective action when outside agencies monitor community activities and appropriate resources (Schmitt, Swope, and Walker, 2000). Yet, communities and production teams face the same challenge of self-monitoring. Within the production team, members can observe each other and sanction internal processes. If interests and effort diverge strongly in the production team and the community, members and affiliates can sanction others; but in the production team, members can appeal to an outside agency and rely on it to

---

[13] I think the word 'affiliation' is more appropriate than 'membership' here in order to highlight the informal nature of the communal resource.

take corrective and punishing action. However, as Osterloh and Frey argue, the problem is one of motivation and interests rather than agency function (2000). If knowledge to be shared is tacit, even self-monitoring can fail to produce the expected results. Also, tacit knowledge is shared if people are intrinsically motivated, but, as mentioned earlier, this in turn requires immediate need satisfaction related to tasks.

Because communities can be conducive to sharing knowledge, they can appropriately be termed resources (von Krogh, 2002; Spaeth et al., 2008).[14] Taylor and Singleton (1993), basing their argument on Coase (1960), suggest that where the community displays a high degree of collective interests, it can lower social (transaction) costs (Coase, 1960; Taylor and Singleton, 1993). First, affiliates of a community have access to information (cues) about others' knowledge. This is a resource because it reduces the affiliate's *costs of searching* for knowledgeable people in the organization. This is particularly relevant for communities where people share work practices or some set of common tasks and problems (Wenger, 1998). Second, *bargaining costs* are lower in a community because beliefs, preferences, and interests are shared. Stable affiliations in a community make it easier to conclude agreements between individuals, and relations on many fronts make it easier for individuals to make trade-offs that compensate for differences in cooperative gains between the parties in question. Third, the level of shared interests, expectations of continued interaction, and direct and manifold relations among individuals all reduce the *monitoring costs* involved in enforcing compliance in knowledge-sharing. Here it is important to note the multiplex character of relationships. In a community where interests are shared, relationships are enduring, and affiliates have options for seeking out who they will share knowledge with, affiliates are likely to attempt to share their best knowledge, even when tacit. In the types of communities described by Taylor and Singleton, recurring interactions give precedence to collective interests over self-interest (e.g. group utility). This has been described as a process where the community gains its own collective identity (Stoecker, 1995).[15]

For the organization in question, reduced monitoring costs and no need for an agency could potentially make the community a valuable resource. As an example, for a functioning community, management does not have to design a formal system for knowledge-sharing, monitoring members' behavior, and enforcing compliance with system procedures and rules. Knowledge-sharing happens due to the internal dynamics of the community and the gradual establishment of a collective identity (Kogut and Zander, 1996). The community also allows individuals to specialize and apply their knowledge to complex tasks within the firm (Grant, 1996). The community is also a resource because for many reasons—liking and emotion, deprivation, experience, etc.—it *attracts* individuals to identifiable social and virtual gatherings where people share interests, tasks, and knowledge.

Yet, the problem of knowledge-sharing is only partly resolved. As mentioned earlier, a common thread in the literature on communities within organizations seems to be that organizational members have a collective interest in sharing knowledge. In general,

---

[14] The term 'communal resource' was first introduced by Taylor and Singleton (1993), although I use it differently here.

[15] This situation is different than so called one-shot collective action. This is a class of problem that introduces very different reasoning, where the construct of 'communal resource' does not readily apply (see Franzen, 1995).

interests in organizations are very difficult to make meaningful, stable, and valid; and they are subject to constant bargaining and drift (March, 1962; Devine, 1999). Because communities comprise affiliates who are subject to changing work demands and conditions, an interesting dilemma arises. An organizational member may be accused of not being a responsible affiliate on the one hand, and of not being self-interested on the other (Hardin, 1968). In organizations that comprise communities, people are rewarded not only for sharing knowledge within the community, but also for being self-interested, rational, and free riding, in order to advance their career and improve their financial position (for related discussions, see Fife, 1977; McCay and Jentoft, 1998). In organizations where knowledge-sharing communities are explicitly fostered, supported by top management, and endowed with slack resources, this dilemma could potentially be powerful. A community consists of people with diverse and distributed interests, and it would be overly simplistic to assume that their individual interests would stabilize over time.

It follows from the discussion so far that the 'community' should not be defined by its level of shared interests, but rather by what we may call its *evolutionary stability*. In other words, the community is not a communal resource *per se*. Even if collective interests cannot be assumed, there is no reason to exclude the possibility of stable, multiplex, and direct relations between affiliates. Depending on the context of community interactions, an individual's interests, namely motivational focus, definition of a situation, personal objectives, and guidelines for conduct, evolve over time. As Massey (1994) points out in her criticism of Taylor and Singleton (1993), some communities are more inauspicious for collective action because of these possible changes in people's interests. Think of a community within the organization based on physical proximity, shared grievances, hobbies, or friendship, without much systematic knowledge sharing. For example, construction engineers might have strong friendships built around playing a game of cards at night, but might have very varied levels of interest in others' technical know-how beyond this hobby, as well as rules of conduct, such as 'no shop talk.' Moreover, in some communities it might be difficult to start knowledge sharing, because of a wish to conform and avoid later retaliation and punishment for breaking the rules. Conversely, think of a vibrant and creative community, where affiliates' diverse and distributed interests threaten the social fabric. The point of departure for defining a community should be to what extent it is able to maintain its community characteristics over time despite this diversity. For defining a communal resource, the start point is whether the community shares knowledge without the prerequisite of an agency to monitor and enforce cooperation.

So communities can be resources, or perhaps even liabilities, and there is a need to examine the conditions under which knowledge sharing can take place without the agency.[16] There are at least three factors associated with knowledge sharing in the community: opportunity structures, care, and authenticity.

---

[16] Interestingly, in their analysis of the community's ability to solve environmental problems, McCay and Jentoft (1998) come to very similar conclusions. Some environmental problems can be traced back to community failure rather than a failure of the market or environmental agencies. Although their analysis tackles a different complex of problems, their study shows that researchers need to show care in identifying both positive and negative factors associated with collective action in communities.

Opportunity structures

Opportunity structures refer to the benefits of sharing knowledge in the community and occasions for doing so. Since interest and knowledge are intimately connected, and since it takes more effort to identify sharing possibilities if affiliates have diverse interests (irrespective of community size), the opportunity structure of a community is a particularly important factor in the problem of knowledge sharing. The way opportunities present themselves to affiliates helps create structures for sharing relationships within the community. These structures hinge on factors such as individual and collective benefits of knowledge sharing; the cost of knowledge sharing; the sequence of knowledge-sharing activity; the history of sharing activities in the community; the search for sharing opportunities; affiliates' diverse and distributed interests, knowledge, and experience; bargaining; and helping behavior. The community is an arena or, as Nonaka and Konno (1998) understand it, a number of '*places*,' (Japanese: *Ba*) where affiliates can realize diverse interests over time as they see fit. Narrow opportunity structures imply that knowledge-sharing benefits can only be realized through a limited number of relationships with affiliates, sharing very specific knowledge at very specific times and places. In contrast, broad opportunity structures involve more relationships that share broader knowledge, in a continuous manner, and in several virtual and physical places (see Diemers, 2001). In other words, an opportunity structure can be within each affiliate's immediate reach, both cognitively and manipulatively. Cognitively, individuals within the community can *imagine* their interests being realized through cooperation with others, and how this realization could happen. Manipulatively, individuals can take concrete action to *meet* physically or virtually with other community affiliates in order to realize these opportunities.

The concept of opportunity structures does not rely on affiliates having full knowledge of others' knowledge; by our definition of knowledge this would be impossible. If this were the case, the social cost of monitoring compliance with knowledge sharing would not have been a problem. However, in his studies of the transfer of tacit knowledge involved in the design and manufacture of highly complex technologies, MacKenzie (1998) found that evoking an interest in sharing at a particular time and place needed only a *cue* about other affiliates' capabilities. The cue is both a stimulus to perception and a hint about how to behave in certain circumstances. Typically, in a work community, people will observe someone who performs tasks with originality, high precision, speed, and diligence. This individual's performance might be based on long-standing experience with the task. Other affiliates take cues from how the task is performed and how that performance differs from their own way of solving tasks (Dreyfus and Dreyfus, 1986).

Although cues about knowledge can elucidate opportunities for sharing, a lot of sharing is likely to be improvised in the community. It is this system of cues that Tilly (1999) referred to when he described a situation of collective action as 'deep improvisation,' where people do not necessarily follow predefined behavioral scripts (like in a wedding ceremony), but where strong social ties and a shared interpretation of cues allow people to improvise collectively (e.g. a jazz orchestra). A history of interaction among affiliates allows deeply improvised knowledge sharing within the community (see also Vendelo, 2009). People will send and interpret cues about when, where, and how knowledge sharing is appropriate. A wink, the wave of a hand, or a cough invites the apprentice into the master's workspace. A shake of the head and a sigh urge affiliates to approach the master and learn what has gone wrong. A system of cues allows sharing in a community to proceed without unnecessary interruption. Individuals can coordinate the realizations of their interests at a particular time and place, for example, avoiding everyone intruding on each other's activities all the time. In this sense there is a relationship between the system of cues in a community and social cost, both in terms of searching for knowledge and of bargaining about suitable times for sharing it. A system of cues is particularly useful for guiding the level, time, and type of interaction needed for sharing tacit knowledge, which must be shared on the fly. However, as Tilly (1999) underscores, collectively meaningful cues take a long time to evolve and learn, and easily mutate under conditions of discontinued interactions, for example, where turnover of group members is high.

In order to sustain collective knowledge sharing under adverse conditions, opportunity structures could rely less on a system of cues and deep improvisation, and more on behavioral rituals. In this case, the community will attempt to create a routine for its own knowledge sharing and expect everyone to engage in it. Such rituals could encompass the introduction of newcomers into the community, discussion platforms, weekly debriefs of tasks and activities, morning speeches and breakfast meetings, coffee breaks, trading posts, poster sessions, a 'speaker's corner' where people can state what's on their mind regarding the work of the community, and so on. However, rituals like these do not foster the spontaneous and impromptu realization of interests, and therefore might work better for sharing explicit rather than tacit knowledge.

Opportunity structures may be costly to identify and realize as the community grows in size. A large community will have an abundance of cues, more attempts at spontaneous sharing, and many rituals that serve the interests of powerful individuals. The community's efforts to monitor free-riding can also be important for its ability to sustain knowledge sharing. Several solutions to the free-rider problem have been suggested, such as convincing participants that they are engaging in long-term cooperative relationships (Axelrod, 1984); convincing participants to contribute using their particular resources, skills, and interests at various points in the unfolding collective action, where a match is found with a particular task (Granovetter, 1978; Oliver, et. al, 1985); convincing individual contributors that the importance of 'group fate' outweighs the cost of contributing (Schwartz and Paul, 1992); and convincing participants with diverse interests that they can trade control and participation over a range of ends (Coleman, 1973). However, most contributions to the concept of collective action note that the free-rider problem can be overcome in the creation and deployment of selective incentives (Friedman and McAdam, 1992; Oliver, 1980).

Selective incentives can be both monetary (for example, a non-participation fine) and non-monetary and, all else being equal, free riding is better dealt with when the community is small enough for selective incentives to be used effectively. Selective incentives are either positive (reinforcing behavior) or negative (changing behavior) and they are directed not at the group as a whole, but to each individual within it (Olson, 1967: 43–52; Fireman and Gamson, 1979; Taylor and Singleton, 1993). Selective monitoring of individual efforts is easier in a small group where people meet and communicate face to face (Ostrom, 1998). It is important to consider how this plays out in the realization of opportunity structures through cues and rituals. First, common knowledge of cues takes time and might involve considerable investment on the part of the individual newcomer to the community. The community determines affiliation on the basis of how well the newcomer has learned to interpret the cues necessary for knowledge sharing (Tilly, 1999). It is unlikely that a potential free rider would make this investment to engage in knowledge sharing with such uncertain outcomes.[17] Hence, there may be self-selection among extrinsically- and intrinsically-motivated people. Second, rituals give easier access to the community and formalize opportunity structures; the community could be expected to attempt to restrict its access to newcomers and deploy non-monetary selective incentives more strictly.

A typical immaterial selective incentive to mobilize people for collective action is membership of social categories (Friedman and McAdam, 1992; Tajfel, 1982). Empirical studies in sociology show that people tend to classify themselves and others in terms of cognitive categories (Turner, Brown, and Tajfel, 1979; Tajfel, 1982). Collective identity can be defined as

> people's sense of who they are in terms of some meaningful social category (e.g. occupational, gender, status, age, Community of Practice member, presence on the intranet, tech-clubs, etc.) that distinguishes how they interact with those inside from those outside the category
> (Roy and Parker-Gwin, 1999).[18]

Larger ritual-based communities benefit by bestowing credentials on affiliates, based on their observed efforts and/or skills. Individuals derive utility from these credentials if they give privileged access to resources, knowledge, social relations, status reputation, and so on. Hence, a value can be assigned to the social category that will be affected by past and current community affiliation. The higher the category's value in the mind of the affiliates, the more effective the non-monetary selective incentive.

In the larger community, opportunity structures tend to be less robust, since social relationships become increasingly scattered and ephemeral, and interests become more diverse. Therefore, the value of credentials might decrease with increasing community size (more people have access to scarce resources). Also, when the community increases in size, the impact of any individual's participation in knowledge sharing is negligible, and a self-interested, rational individual will choose to free ride under those conditions (Hardin, 1968). The cost of an individual's decision to free ride is spread over a greater number of people and the cost of organizing and using selective immaterial incentives to induce individual cooperation increases as well (Marwell and Oliver, 1988). It becomes even more costly for each group member to monitor and sanction others' free-riding behavior. Eventually, as the group grows, monitoring costs outgrow sharing costs, and could jointly outweigh the rewards from knowledge sharing itself. In addition, the value of the social category could become depleted, making it less attractive for newcomers to join the community. The expected outcome is that the opportunity structure will be underprovided and the value of the communal resource will decrease.

Affiliates' limited attention and cognition, and the cost of realizing knowledge sharing, make opportunity structures a constraint on the communal resource. As far as the practice of knowledge management is concerned, a popular way of facilitating knowledge sharing

---

[17] Free riders can only appraise the value of knowledge once they have learnt the system of cues.

[18] I used 'collective identity' here in a rather narrow sense. Some would include social norms, tradition, social relationships, and processes in identity (Stoecker, 1996).

in many organizations is through so-called 'technical share fairs' or 'knowledge fairs' (e.g. Davenport and Prusak, 1998). These are large exhibitions held over several days where research and engineering teams, technical groups, and so on, can exhibit information about their projects, areas of expertise, and technical pursuits. Some will already belong to a community of technical specialists at a research site. Others will not be affiliated with any particular community, but will discover new opportunities for establishing a community and sharing knowledge. Through these fairs, organizations enlarge the opportunity structure for knowledge sharing. The fair might also contribute to the evolutionary stability of the community, whereby social relations are reinforced and new ones are created. However, in spite of the abundant opportunities such fairs offer, it is not at all clear whether individuals will coordinate knowledge sharing. A fair might simply be a pleasant break in a somewhat dull and repetitive workday. For sharing to be enabled in an evolutionary stable manner, the right social norms have to be in place.

Care

A non-monetary selective incentive would result from members creating and enforcing social norms ('Thou shalt . . . Thou shalt not . . .') that compel affiliates to knowledge sharing in a customary fashion (e.g. Heckatorn, 1993). When the number of believers in the social norm increases, affiliates derive utility from the conformity of behavior to the norm, both due to reputation in the community as well as the individual's taste towards conformity (Hess, 1998). In effect, strong socialization and loyalty to the social norm could moderate free riding in the group (Ferre, 1982; Hirschman, 1970; Ostrom, 1999).

Care is a social norm in human relationships, and implies trust, active empathy, access to help, lenience in judgment, and the extent to which all of these are shared in the community (von Krogh, 1998).[19] Care can entail concrete action in helping others but does not necessarily do so. Depending on the needs of the recipient, care can mean merely presence and intimacy, without action. Moreover, care is sufficient to induce helping in others (Egan, 1986). In caring for another, a care provider may give information and support for task execution, integrate an individual socially, give guidance, and enhance social bonds, as well as help to choose what output of task performance is to be presented to a larger audience. However, assisting is not necessary for care to be relationship quality (Mayeroff, 1971). As stressed throughout this chapter, organizations are populated with individuals who have different interests and personalities. The only requirement for care to be a social norm is for more than one individual, even the self-interested, to derive utility from complying with it.

Let us look more carefully at these four dimensions of care and how they relate to knowledge sharing. First, the more affiliates trust each other to share knowledge, the lower

---

[19] An observer of open source software (OSS) development projects, such as the operating system Linux, Himanen (2001) suggests that care is one of the most important social norms of communities of OSS developers. Care involves experienced programmers helping newcomers to learn and improve the code others have made by debugging it. Although people are normally in widely dispersed locations, they work cooperatively over the Internet. Social norms make interactions and the expectations of individual programmers easier to express and comply with.

the social costs, as Taylor and Singleton (1994) mentioned (see also Nonaka and Takeuchi, 1995; Szulanski, 1996).[20] Second, the more leniently people judge others' knowledge, experience, and behavior, the more likely it is that diverse and distributed interests persist among affiliates in the community. Interaction can happen in spite of diverse interests; opportunities for knowledge sharing might emerge at a later point in time, when affiliates suspend their immediate realization of their own interests for the benefit of the community. Lenience also means that affiliates accept diverse rates of learning in the community. As we saw, learning rates may differ immensely among individuals, particularly for tacit knowledge, and a great deal of time can elapse before the giver realizes returns, if at all. In addition, newcomers into the community have to learn cues, especially where rituals are vague or absent. Lenience could be particularly important for integrating newcomers with different learning rates.

Active empathy, the third component of care, means that affiliates assess and understand others' interests and needs. Empathy is the attempt to put one's self in others' shoes, understanding their particular situation, interests, skills levels, successes, failures, opportunities, and problems (von Krogh, Ichijo, and Nonaka, 2000). Active empathy is the proactive attempt by community affiliates to understand the interests of others observed in ongoing conversations in the community. It allows many different interests to co-exist over time, and should impact positively the learning and the use of subtle cues needed for the sharing of tacit knowledge.

Fourth, while active empathy prepares the ground for helping behavior, care in the community also has to develop into real and tangible help when necessary. In the relationship between master and apprentice, for instance, the master teaches the design of a tool, how to use it, how to maintain it, where to acquire it, and so on. The master shows by example what to do to reach good task performance, listens to the apprentice's concerns and questions, and also extends a helping hand by being actively involved in the apprentice's task performance. But this interest in helping can be accompanied by various levels of access to the helper. Help might be offered based on an affiliate's own experience, by knowledge sharing, or simply by sharing the burden of the task, and learning together. As a social norm, care, through helping behavior, should moderate the free-rider problem in larger communities where knowledge sharing plays out as a deep improvisation rather than a ritual. Levels of trust and active empathy, as important as they are for knowledge sharing, may provide very vague information about people's compliance with the social norm, their inclusion or exclusion from the community. However, levels of access to help and levels of help given can be directly observed. Hence, where opportunity structures are narrow due to individual affiliates' lack of interest in helping, their future community status might be endangered; yet if helping matters to them, they are likely to change their behavior.

It was observed earlier that, in the communal resource, the natural sequence of the collective activities of (tacit) knowledge sharing must be preserved. When affiliates exhibit strong trust, active empathy toward each other, a strong inclination to help, as well as lenient judgment, this should have a positive impact on the suspended satisfaction of individual needs and the realization of interests. Imagine a community of engineers who have worked together for several years, all of whom know each other, and where there has been some

---

[20] Given the definition of interests in this chapter, shared interests are not a prerequisite for trust.

stability in relations. Enter a young engineering school graduate. Some affiliates exhibit a high level of help toward the newcomer, trying to integrate this person into the community. The newcomer will have to learn cues, rituals, and behavior according to social norms. Some experienced engineers might also recollect some long-gone feelings from their own inauguration process, where an experienced person took the time to introduce the 'subtle stuff' of the community. Because of the engineers' empathy with the newcomer, he or she is treated leniently. The newcomer gives no immediate learning feedback, so there is no immediate need satisfaction for the others from giving this help. Furthermore, without cues about the newcomer's capabilities, there is no guarantee that he or she will be a valuable affiliate of the community in the future. Learning the secrets of engineering in this way, where the opportunities of sharing are found, based on cues about what experienced engineers are capable of doing, the newcomer will eventually contribute new methods and theories from his or her education. It is care that allows for evolutionary stability—that is, for the community to persist as a resource for knowledge sharing.

Authenticity

When interests are shared in the community, we can assume that the 'best' knowledge will be spread among affiliates. In the absence of self-interested people or free riders, there is no reason why people should hide important details about task performance, pass on false information, sub-optimal procedures, unwarranted lessons, etc. However, where interests are diverse and distributed, it is possible that the social norm 'authenticity' could have an impact on the community as a resource for knowledge sharing. Authenticity means that legitimate knowledge in the community is shared directly with the source in a way that ensures its genuineness, accuracy, validity, and reliability. The master–apprentice dynamic illustrates what this means. An apprentice observes the genuine know-how of the master first-hand. The accuracy of their shared knowledge depends on the apprentice's ability to observe a certain level of detail in the master's work. Validity, in turn, refers to the master's and the apprentice's mutual ability to appraise observations, interpretations, and understanding of task performance. Validity also refers to the extent to which knowledge shared with the apprentice can also be extended to similar or different tasks the apprentice has to perform. Reliable knowledge enables the apprentice to resolve repeated tasks. Reliability, in turn, depends on affiliates' interests in applying shared knowledge in the collective action process. Hence, we have to revisit the system of social norms outlined thus far.

Care is a social norm from which people derive utility by giving. However, if care is the only norm in social relationships, the community might end up with more knowledge giving and limited collective knowledge sharing, or in other words, little learning and using. In the case of authenticity, people derive utility from searching out valid and genuine knowledge, but since sharing is a matter of collective action, people also derive utility from making this knowledge reliable by using it.

The best way to understand valuable authentic knowledge in the context of this chapter is to view it as cues about what others are capable of in terms of above-average performance in the community at large, in particular in a master–apprentice relationship. However, as mentioned, at one extreme communities can be self-preserving, conforming, retaliatory, and punitive, penalizing people who try to branch out and be inventive. Massey (1994) found that collective action is highly unlikely in groups with strong social norms and diverse interests, due to the social costs faced by individuals pursuing their own courses of action. Standing out in the crowd by proposing new ideas or criticizing the work of others could invite retaliation and exclusion from the social category (see also Hirschman, 1970).[21] Further, a community might have affiliates who detest any new knowledge, even if the benefits are immediate and collective. Rejection could be warranted by the costs of bargaining about what is really 'valuable' knowledge, or the unlearning of previous lessons learned. Individual interests in rejecting new knowledge could quickly transform into a collective protest against any new idea that someone tries to introduce into the community. The well-known not-invented-here (NIH) syndrome is a good example of such behavior; people who have worked hard and long to achieve a certain level of task performance might find it extremely difficult to change routines that have proved successful in the past (Kluge, Stein, and Licht, 2001). Even though new knowledge can have a potentially significant impact on people's task performance, those who would be in favor of trying the new way will withdraw their engagement in the process.

Perhaps NIH syndrome indeed results from a lack of authenticity. If authenticity is a social norm, the closeness of observation matters for the acceptance of new knowledge, and hence, new knowledge is best introduced by affiliates of the community. However, willingness to be taught by others is key to recognizing individual differences and accepting the new lessons as well. Furthermore, sharing depends on care among those with superior knowledge, and not necessarily collective interests associated with their knowledge, as in 'If I learn from you, you might not want to learn much from me, except for the way I apply that knowledge.'

For example, the newcomer to the engineering community might find that in some areas of practice, it is worthwhile learning lessons from experienced engineers. However, there are new methods that are more productive and will enhance the performance of the whole community, such as the use of a computer aided design (CAD) system. The experienced engineer might take cues about the newcomer's extraordinary and repeated ability to finish technical designs in a fraction of the time that it used to take. The newcomer may supply the other engineers with documents and manuals on the use of these systems. If care is strong, he might even personally teach the use of these systems to other engineers. In turn, some may take great interest in learning and using the newly shared knowledge. This sharing requires cues about capable behavior, and assumes that most community affiliates would be content to receive genuine, accurate, valid, and reliable solutions from those who have experience and insight. These experienced individuals in turn must be willing to share their experience with the new systems. This example underlines that interest in both teaching and learning is diffused widely in the community (among old timers as well as newcomers).

To summarize, communal resources are impacted by a community's characteristics, including the degree to which affiliates' interests are diverse and distributed. In particular, three factors taken together—opportunity structure, care, and authenticity—should impact knowledge sharing where interests are diverse and distributed. Opportunity structures here work as a constraint on knowledge sharing. As a social norm, care positively impacts affiliates' ability to suspend the immediate satisfaction of needs and to search for opportunities,

---

[21] In this sense, when social norms evolve, affiliates' social costs can be offset by anonymity (Massey, 1994) offered, for example, through electronic means of communication.

in spite of diverse interests. As a social norm, authenticity positively impacts affiliates' ability to realize 'better' knowledge within opportunity structures, to learn, and to improve. For example, in a community where there are ample opportunities for knowledge sharing, affiliates trying to determine with whom they want to interact will search out cues about others who demonstrate superior knowledge related to their interests and tasks at hand. Care in relationships makes affiliates patient with respect to returns on the knowledge they share, and allows them to realize varied interests, learning speeds, and behavior. It is important to note that even if interests are shared, the community can be characterized by opportunity structures, care, and authenticity. However, the argument does not assume *a priori* collective interests in sharing knowledge among affiliates, although the more collective the interests, the more powerful the communal resource for solving the problem of the social costs involved in the sequential collective action of knowledge sharing.

CONCLUSION AND RESEARCH IMPERATIVES

Knowledge sharing is a key process in many knowledge management activities, including the capture, transfer, and creation of knowledge. If we abandon the idea that knowledge can be shared as a simple process of communicating information, it might be more appropriate for future theory and research in knowledge management and organizational learning to consider knowledge sharing a problem of collective action among actors with diverse and distributed interests. The literature proposes different solutions to this problem that are worth examining. The first is to install an agency external to the knowledge-sharing process that structures, incentivizes, and monitors knowledge sharing, and punishes defiant behavior. Several problems are associated with this solution, such as choosing the right incentives for sharing and obtaining sufficient information for overseeing sharing activities with some degree of certainty.

Second, the communal resource reduces the social costs of sharing knowledge, eliminating the need to resort to an agency or to large numbers of organizational members. However, where interests are diverse and distributed, the effectiveness of the community as a communal resource depends on its opportunity structures and social norms. Opportunity structures for knowledge sharing work on cues observed among people in the community. These cues cover both task performance and ways to share knowledge. In terms of behavior, communities can deeply improvise or provide rituals. Care is a social norm that gives rise to trust, active empathy, helping behavior, and lenient judgment. Authenticity is a social norm that gives credence to knowledge directly observed in action, as well as the willingness to accept new knowledge. Hopefully, it has been demonstrated that the evolutionary stability of the community matters for a theory of knowledge sharing in organizations, assuming people in an organization hold diverse and distributed interests that change over time. Several poorly understood factors gain significance in determining whether or not the community will reduce the social costs of knowledge sharing. Hence, the role of the community as a resource has still to be determined.

A number of research questions arise out of this discussion that should interest any knowledge management and/or organizational learning scholar who cares about the communal resource. In the vein of the literature on communities within and outside organizations, the existence of community has been assumed *a priori*. However, as Wenger

(1998) argues, there are distinct phases in the formation of a community that should be taken into account. Future research might investigate the characteristics of community formation processes further: which support knowledge sharing? A related question concerns community composition. Both communities of practice and occupational communities consist of people who share work, tasks, problems, and some level of expertise. Nevertheless, during the process of community formation, a central question to pursue might be whether the new affiliate's background, diversity, and distribution of interests impact the effectiveness of knowledge sharing, as well as the duration of the community.

One consequence of basing the definition of a community on concepts of collective action (e.g. Olson, 1967; Taylor and Singleton, 1993) is that researchers should consider the activities going on within the community as well as its evolutionary stability. Therefore, a community that ceases to operate is just as interesting as communities that survive over long periods of time. A number of important questions about evolutionary stability emerge: How are opportunities for knowledge sharing found in the initial stages of community formation? What are the changes in opportunity structures as the community ages? To what extent do changes in opportunity structures explain the dissolution of communities? One could argue that the inflow of newcomers refreshes viewpoints and regenerates an urge and interest in new insights. How do opportunity structures change with fluctuations in affiliation? Does a constant inflow of newcomers really refresh viewpoints and regenerate new insights? What is the optimal turnover rate of affiliates and how does this relate to community size?

Furthermore, as Brown and Duguid (1991), Cook and Brown (1999), and Wenger (1998) argue, communities of practice need available resources and time to develop. A similar argument is found in studies of collective action. Meeting in so-called free spaces where resources and time are available, affiliates can act without being subject to agency monitoring; they can build social ties outside the existing social structures and develop particular shared norms (Polletta, 1999). Some of these free spaces might initially develop on the Internet or Intranet (Townsend, 2000). What is the relationship between ICT and the emergence of free spaces for community formation? What is the relationship between investments in ICT and emerging opportunity structures for knowledge sharing? What are the consequences of giving affiliates anonymity when sharing (explicit) knowledge? How is the norm of authenticity affected by the use of ICT?

Care is a social norm in the community from which individuals derive utility. It would be interesting to investigate further the emergent rewards related to caring. What factors impact on evolving care in community relationships? Do some caring people lead by example? What is the relationship between care and the integration of newcomers into the community? What is the role of care in the relationship between master and apprentice? Previous work has identified costs to this social norm as well (von Krogh, 1998). Care can be misused as a strategy of over-helping by ignoring what people really need. Care can be used as a strategy of taking others to their own party. What is the relationship between care and over-helping behavior, and what is the consequence of over-helping for knowledge sharing in the community? Researchers working on issues in HR management should observe that studies of caring occupations, such as nursing, have identified potential burnout among people who are expected to act both compassionately and effectively (Pines and Aronson, 1988; see also Sarason, 1985). In many service organizations, ranging from entertainment parks to consulting firms, 'customer care' is often the responsibility of communities. As Van Maanen (1991) observes, people who are expected to care for the well-being of customers while downplaying their own (often negative) emotions form strong bonds of solidarity and mutual compassion. Would a community among people who are expected to trade in emotions be related in any significant way to negative conditions, such as burnout or high personnel turnover? How does the pressure for externally-oriented care relate to the emergence of social norms in such communities? Moreover, an issue that deserves attention in the research on learning in service organizations is the effect of externally- and internally-oriented care on the individual worker—in other words, how much care can people take? Research on knowledge management and organizational learning in service organizations, particularly those trading in sentiments, which is blind to the role of social norms and individual emotions will be neither insightful nor practical.[22]

Schwart and Tomz (1997) show formally that over time, agency can have great advantages over the community in terms of securing superior expertise and knowledge. The reason is that social norms maintained by the community but not questioned by the outside agency could have an adverse impact on accepting and integrating new knowledge (as argued earlier). This finding also raises questions about the potentially negative impact of error-tolerance or lenient judgment. What is the interplay between lenient judgment and the cost of identifying valuable new knowledge? Also, there might be a noteworthy difference between tacit and explicit knowledge. If authenticity is at work, how can affiliates deal with the difference between ready-made explicit knowledge and tacit knowledge evolving through learning, in terms of quality and robustness? People might have a lot to learn from sharing an expert's trial-and-error with a task, flawed lessons, systematic reporting of experiences, etc. However, cues about valuable new knowledge are often recognized after the fact, that is, as ready-made knowledge. Furthermore, in terms of reducing learning time, preference might be given to explicit rather than tacit knowledge, even at the expense of authenticity.

And finally, as mentioned initially, many knowledge management researchers are interested in community and firm performance. Can we measure community performance, and if so, what are the best measures to use? How should we study community performance empirically? Researchers, in particular those interested in strategic management, should investigate what characteristics of a community impact firm performance. Moreover, in some industries, such as investment banking and management consulting, firms have hired whole teams rather than single individuals. If these teams display the community characteristics outlined in this chapter, it would be interesting to investigate and explain changes in the communal resource as it moves to a new organizational 'home.' Related to such investigations, what are the characteristics of capabilities that make firms outperform the industry average in terms of picking, developing, and deploying communal resources (Makadok, 2001)? Do some firms actually learn to distinguish communal resources from communal liabilities? And do they have some particular community nurturing capabilities that make these communities more effective than those in other firms at reducing the social costs of knowledge sharing?

---

[22] The work of Sandelands (1988), Foner (1995), Fisher, Nadler, and De Paolo (1983) provides a starting point for further exploration of this issue.

A starting point for answering these questions could be to investigate community perform-ance and the interaction effects of HR management systems. Empirical studies have shown that the quality of HR and HR systems matters for the implementation of strategy and impacts on firm performance (see Huselid, 1995; Slater and Olson, 2000; Lee and Miller, 1999). However, as reasoned in this chapter, communities and HR management systems can pull employees in two directions: individuals derive utility both from being self-interested and hoarding knowledge, and from sharing knowledge in accordance with social norms emerging in the community. Are there particular characteristics of HR management systems, beyond incentives that are conducive to knowledge sharing in communities? In those instances where communities change their organizational home, and individuals change their exposure to HR management systems, these interaction effects could be more pronounced.

Knowledge management and organizational learning as a field of inquiry has never been more exciting. As a construct, 'knowledge' offers a powerful bridge between cogni-tion and action at individual as well as social levels. This, in turn, improves our under-standing of how organizations work, and how individuals operate within, with, and without organizations. For those who take a serious interest in knowledge, learning and organization, the future is filled with opportunities, challenges, and questions.

REFERENCES

Alavi, M. and Leidner, D. (2001) Knowledge management and knowledge management systems: Conceptual foundations and research issues. *MIS Quarterly*, 15(1):107–136.

Alchian, A.A. and Demsetz, H. (1972) Production, information costs, and economic organization. *American Economic Review*, 62: 777–795.

Allee, V. (1997) *The Knowledge Evolution: Expanding organizational intelligence*. Boston: Butterworth-Heinemann.

Anderson, B.R. (1983) *Imagined communities: Reflections on the origin and spread of nationalism*. London: Verso.

Armstrong, A.G. and Hagel, J. (1995) Real profits from virtual communities. *McKinsey Quarterly*, 5: 128–141.

Arthur, W.B. (1997) *Increasing Returns and Path Dependence in the Economy*. Ann Arbor, MI: University of Michigan Press.

Axelrod, R. (1984) *The evolution of cooperation*. New York: Basic Books.

Bartlett, C.A. and Ghoshal, S. (1986) Tap your subsidiaries for global reach. *Harvard Business Review*, 64(6): 87–94.

Bennis, W.G., Berkowitz, N., Affinito, M., and Malone, M. (1958) Authority, power, and the ability to influence. *Human Relations*, 11: 143–156.

Boisot, M. (1998) *Knowledge assets: Securing competitive advantage in the information economy*. New York: Oxford.

Brown, J.S. and Duguid, P. (1991) Organizational learning and communities of practice: Toward a unified view of working, learning, and innovation. *Organization Science*, 2: 40–57.

Bruner, J. (1979) *On Knowing: Essays for the left hand*. Cambridge, MA: Belknap.

Cabrera, A. and Cabrera, E.F. (2002) Knowledge sharing dilemmas. *Organization Studies*, 23(5): 687–710.

Calhoun, C. (1986) The radicalism of tradition: Community strength or venerable dis-guise and borrowed language? *American Journal of Sociology*, 88(5): 886–924.

Calhoun, C. (1991) Indirect relationships and imagined communities: Large scale social integration and the transformation of everyday life. In P. Bordieu and J.S. Coleman (eds.) *Social Theory for a Changing Society*. Boulder, CO: Westview Press: 95–120.

Calhoun, C. (1994) Social theory and the politics of identity. In C. Calhoun (ed.), *Social Theory and the Politics of Identity*. Cambridge: Blackwell Publishers: 9–36.

Carlile, P. (2002) A Pragmatic View of Knowledge and Boundaries: Boundary Objects in New Product Development. *Organization Science*, 13(4): 442–455.

Castells, M. (1996) *The Rise of the Network Society*. Malden, MA: Blackwell Publishing.

Chong, D. (1991) *Collective action and the civil rights movement*. Chicago: University of Chicago Press.

Choo, C.W. (1998) *The Knowing Organization: How organizations use information to construct meaning, create knowledge, and make decisions*. New York: Oxford University Press.

Coase, R.H. (1960) The Problem of Social Cost. *Journal of Law and Economics*, 3: 1–44.

Cohen, A.P. (1985) *The symbolic construction of community*. London: Ellis Horwood/Tavistock.

Cohen, J.L. (1985) Strategy or identity: new theoretical paradigms and contemporary social movements. *Social Research*, 52(4): 663–717.

Cohen, W. and Levinthal, D. (1990) Absorptive capacity: A new perspective on learning and innovation. *Administrative Science Quarterly*, 35: 128–152.

Coleman, J. (1973) *The Mathematics of Collective Action*. Chicago: Aldine.

Collard, D. (1978) *Altruism and economy: A study in non-selfish economics*. New York: Oxford University Press.

Cook, S.D.N. and Brown, J.S. (1999) Bridging epistemologies: The generative dance between organizational knowledge and organizational knowing. *Organization Science*, 10(4): 381–400.

Czikszentmihalyi, M., (1988) The flow of experience and its significance for human psychology. In M. Czikszentmihalyi and I.S Czikszentmihalyi (eds.), *Optimal experience: Psychological studies of flow in consciousness*. Cambridge: Cambridge University Press: 15–35.

Darrah, C.N. (1990) Workplace training, workplace learning. *Human Organization*, 54: 31–41.

Davenport, T. and Probst, G. (eds.) (2000) *Knowledge Management Case Book*. Chichester: John Wiley & Sons.

Davenport, T. and Prusak, L. (1996) *Working Knowledge*. Cambridge, MA: Harvard Business School Press.

Devine, D.J. (1999) Effects of cognitive ability, task knowledge, information sharing, and conflict on group decision making. *Small Group Research*, 30(5): 608–634.

Diemers, D. (2001) *Virtual Knowledge Communities*, Unpublished Doctoral Dissertation. Seminar for Sociology, St.Gallen: University of St.Gallen.

Dixon, N. (2000) *Common Knowledge*. Cambridge, MA: Harvard Business School Press.

Doz, Y. and Prahalad, C.K. (1981) Headquarters influence and strategic control in MNCs. *Sloan Management Review*, 23(1): 15–30.

Dreyfus, H.L. and Dreyfus, S.E. (1986) *Mind over Machine: the power of human intuition and expertise in the era of the computer*. Oxford: Wiley-Blackwell.

Durkheim, E. (1893, translated 1933) *The Division of Labor in Society*. New York: Free Press.

Dyer, J. and Nobeoka, K. (2000) Creating and managing a high-performance knowledge sharing network: The Toyota Case. *Strategic Management Journal*, 21: 345–368.

Egan, G. (1986) *The skilled helper*. Monterey, CA: Brooks/Cole.

Fantasia, R. (1988) *Cultures of solidarity*. Berkeley, CA: University of California Press.

Ferner, A., Edwards, P., and Sisson, K. (1995) Coming unstuck—In search of the corporate glue in an international professional services firm. *Human Resources Management*, 34(3): 343–361.

Ferre, M.M. (1992) The political context of rationality: Rational choice theory and resource mobilization. In A.D. Morris, and C. McClurg (eds.), *Frontiers in Social Movement Theory*. New Haven: Yale University Press: 29–53.

Fife, D. (1977) Killing the goose. In G. Hardin and J. Baden (eds.), *Managing the Commons*. San Francisco: Freeman Press: 76–81.

Fireman, B. and Gamson, W.H. (1979) Utilitarian logic in the resource mobilization perspective. In M.M. Zald and J.D. McCarthy (eds.), *The Dynamics of Social Movements*. Cambridge, MA: Winthrop.

Fisher, J., Nadler, A., and De Paulo, B. (1983) *New Directions in Helping. Recipient Reactions to Aid (Vol. 1)*. New York: Academic Press.

Foner, N. (1995) The hidden injuries of bureaucracy. *Human Organization*, 54: 229–237.

Foster, G.M. (1965) Peasant society and the image of the limited good. *American Anthropologist*, 67: 289–315.

Foucault, M. (1980). *Power/Knowledge: Selected Interviews and Other Writings 1972–1977*. Brighton: Harvester Books.

Franzen, A. (1995) Group size and one-shot collective action. *Rationality and Society*, 7: 183–201.

Friedman, D. and McAdam, D. (1992) Collective identity and activism: Networks, choices, and the life of a social movement. In A.D. Morris, and C. McClurg (eds.), *Frontiers in Social Movement Theory*. New Haven: Yale University Press: 156–173.

Gaechter, S., von Krogh, G., and Haefliger, S. (2010) Initiating private-collective innovation: The fragility of knowledge sharing. *Research Policy*, 39(7): 893–906.

Gibbons, R. (1998) Incentives in organizations, *NBER Working paper 6695*, Cambridge, MA.

Gourlay, S. (2006) Conceptualizing knowledge creation: A critique of Nonaka's theory. *Journal of Management Studies*, 43(7): 1415–1436.

Govindarajan, V. and Gupta, A. (2001) Building an effective global business team. *Sloan Management Review*, 42(4): 63–71.

Granovetter, M. (1978) Threshold Models of Collective Behavior. *American Journal of Sociology*, 83(6): 1420–1443.

Grant, R.M. (1996) Towards a knowledge-based theory of the firm. *Strategic Management Journal*, 17: 109–122.

Hardin, G. (1968) Tragedy of the commons. *Science*, 162(3859): 1243–1248.

Heckatorn, D. (1993) Collective action and group heterogeneity–Voluntary provision versus selective incentives. *American Sociological Review*, 58(3): 329–350.

Hess, S. (1998) Individual behavior and collective action towards the environment: An economic framework based on the social customs approach. *Rationality and Society*, 10(2): 203–222.

Himanen, P. (2001) *The Hacker Ethic*. New York: Random House.

Hirschman, A.O. (1970) *Exit, Voice, and Loyalty*. Cambridge: Harvard University Press.

Huselid, M.A. (1995) The impact of human resource management practices on turnover, productivity, and corporate financial performance. *Academy of Management Journal*, 28: 635–673.

Kaeser, P. (2001) *Knowledge activists, knowledge transfer and creation*, Unpublished Ph.D. dissertation, University of St. Gallen.

Kluge, J., Stein, W., and Licht, T. (2001) *Knowledge Unplugged*. Basingstoke: Palgrave.

Kogut, B. and Zander, U. (1992) Knowledge of the firm, combinative capabilities, and the replication of technology. *Organization Science*, 3: 383–397.

Kogut, B. and Zander, U. (1996) What firms do: Coordination, identity, and learning. *Organization Science*, 7: 502–514.

Kransdorf, A. (1998) *Corporate Amnesia: Keeping know-how in the company*. Oxford: Butterworth-Heinemann.

Kriwet, C. K. (1997) Inter- and Intraorganizational Knowledge Transfer, dissertation, University of St. Gallen No. 2063.

Latour, B. (1987) *Science in Action*. Cambridge: Harvard University Press.

Latour, B. (1993) *The Pasteurization of France*. Cambridge: Harvard University Press.

Lave, J. (1988) *Cognition in practice*. Cambridge: Cambridge University Press.

Lave, J. and Wenger, E. (1991) *Situated learning: Legitimate peripheral participation*. Cambridge, MA: Cambridge University Press.

Lee, J. and Miller, D. (1999) People matter: Commitment to employees, strategy, and performance of Korean firms. *Strategic Management Journal*, 20: 579–591.

Leonard, D. and Sensiper, S. (1998) The role of tacit knowledge in group innovation. *California Management Review*, 40(3): 112–132.

Lu, I.Y., Mao, C.J., and Wang, C.H. (2010) Intrafirm technology and knowledge transfer: a best practice perspective. *International Journal of Technology Management*, 49(4): 338–356.

MacKenzie, D. (1998) *Knowing Machines: Essays on Technical Change*. Cambridge, MA: MIT Press.

Makadok, R. (2001) Towards a synthesis of the resource-based and dynamic capability view of rent creation. *Strategic Management Journal*, 22: 387–402.

Mannix, E.A. (1991) Resource dilemmas and discount rates in decision making groups. *Journal of Experimental Psychology*, 27: 379–391.

March, J.G. (1962) The Business Firm as a Political Coalition. *Journal of Politics*, 24: 662–678.

March, J.G. (1991) 'Exploration and Exploitation in Organizational Learning,' *Organization Science* 2: 71–87.

Marwell, G., and Oliver, P. (1993) *The Critical Mass in Collective Action*. Cambridge: Cambridge University Press.

Massey, R.I. (1994) Impediments to collective action in a small community. *Politics and Society*, 22(3): 421–435.

Mayeroff, M. (1971) *On Caring*. New York: Harper Row.

McCaffrey, D.P., Faerman, S.R., and Hart, D.W. (1995) The Appeal and Difficulties of Participative Systems. *Organization Science*, 6(6): 603–627.

McCay, B.J. and Jentoft, S. (1998) Market or community failure? Critical perspectives on common property research. *Human Organization*, 57: 21–29.

Merleau-Ponty, M. (1995) *Phenomenology of Perception* (Translated by Colin Smith). London: Routledge.

Monge, P.R., Fulk, J., Kalman, M.E., Flanagin, A.J., Parnassa, C., and Rumsey, S. (1998) Production of collective action in alliance-based interorganizational communication and information systems. *Organization Science*, 9(3): 411–433.

Myers, D.J. (1994) Communication Technology and Social Movements: Contributions of Computer Networks to Activism. *Social Science Computer Review*, 12(2): 250–260.

Nahapiet, J.S. and Ghoshal, S. (1998) Social capital, intellectual capital, and the organizational advantage. *Academy of Management Review*, 23: 242–266.

Nelson, R. and Winter, S.G. (1982) *An Evolutionary Theory of Economic Change*. Cambridge, MA: Belknap.

Nonaka, I. (1994) A dynamic theory of organizational knowledge creation. *Organization Science*, 5: 14–37.

Nonaka, I. and Konno, N. (1998) The concept of Ba: Building a foundation for knowledge creation. *California Management Review*, 40: 40–54.

Nonaka, I. and Takeuchi, H. (1995) *The Knowledge Creating Company*. New York: Oxford University Press.

Nonaka, I. and von Krogh, G. (2009) Tacit knowledge and knowledge conversion: Controversy and advancement in organizational knowledge creation theory. *Organization Science*, 20(3): 635–652.

Nonaka, I., von Krogh, G., and Voelpel, S. (2006) Organizational knowledge creation theory: Evolutionary paths and future advances. *Organization Studies*, 27(8): 1179–1208.

O'Dell, C. and Grayson, C.J. (1998) If only we knew what we know: Identification and transfer of internal best practices. *California Management Review*, 40(3): 154–174.

Oliver, P.E. (1980) Rewards and punishment as selective incentives for collective action: Theoretical investigations. *American Journal of Sociology*, 85: 1356–1375.

Oliver, P. (1993) Formal models of collective action. *Annual Review of Sociology*, 19: 271–300.

Oliver, P. and Marwell, G. (1988) The paradox of group size in collective action: A theory of critical mass II. *American Sociological Review*, 53: 1–8.

Oliver, P.E, Marwell, G., and Teixeira, R. (1985) Theory of the critical mass I: Interdependence, group heterogeneity, and the production of collective goods. *American Journal of Sociology*, 91: 522–556.

Olson, M. (1967) *The Logic of Collective Action*. Cambridge: Harvard University Press.

Orr, J. (1996) *Talking about machines: An ethnography of a modern job*. Itacha, NY: Cornell University Press.

Osterloh, M. and Frey, B.S. (2000) Motivation, knowledge transfer, and organizational forms. *Organization Science*, 11(5): 538–550.

Ostrom, E. (1998) A behavioral approach to the rational choice theory of collective action. *American Political Science Review*, 92(1): 1–22.

Ostrom, E. (1999) Coping with the tragedies of the commons. *Annual Review of Political Science*, 2: 493–535.

Ostrom, E. (2000) Crowding out citizenship. *Scandinavian Political Studies*, 23(11): 3–16.

Pedler, M., Burgoyne, J., and Boydell, T. (1991) *The Learning Company*. London: McGraw-Hill.

Perkins, D. (1981) *The mind's best work*. Cambridge: Harvard University Press.

Pines, A.M. and Aronson, E. (1988) *Career burnout*. New York: Free Press.

Polanyi, M. and Prosch, H. (1975) *Meaning*. Chicago: University of Chicago Press.

Polletta, F. (1999) Free-spaces in collective action. *Theory and Society*, 28: 1–38.

Powell, W. (1998) Learning from collaboration: Knowledge and networks in the biotechnology and pharmaceutical industries. *California Management Review*, 40(3): 228–240.

Rabin, M. (1998) Psychology and economics. *Journal of Economic Literature*, 36: 11–46.

Ram, M. (1999) Managing consultants in a small firm: A case study. *Journal of Management Studies*, 36(3): 875–879.

Rheingold, H. (1993) A slice of life in my virtual community. In L.M. Harasim (ed.), *Global Networks: Computers and international communication*. Cambridge, MA: MIT Press: 57–80.

Roy, W.G. and Parker-Gwin, R. (1999) Service learning as pedagogy and civic education: Comparing outcomes for three models. *Teaching Sociology*, 26(4): 276–291.

Sabherwal, R. and Sabherwal, S. (2005) Knowledge management using information technology: Determinants of short-term impact on firm value. *Decision Sciences*, 36(4): 531–567.

Sandelands, L.E. (1988) The concept of work feeling. *Journal for the Theory of Social Behavior*, 18: 437–457.

Sarason, S. (1985) *Caring and compassion in clinical practice*. San Francisco: Jossey-Bass.

Schmitt, P., Swope, K., and Walker, J. (2000) Collective action with incomplete commitment: Experimental evidence. *Southern Economic Journal*, 66: 829–855.

Schulze, A. and Hoegl, M. (2006) Knowledge creation in new product development projects. *Journal of Management*, 32(2): 210–236.

Schutz, A. (1970) *On Phenomenology and Social Relations*. Chicago: University of Chicago Press.

Schwart, E.P. and Tomz, M.R. (1997) The long-run advantages of centralization for collective action. *American Political Sciences Review*, 92(3): 685–693.

Schwartz, M. and Paul, S. (1992) Resource mobilization versus the mobilization of people. In A.D. Morris and C. McClurg (eds.), *Frontiers in Social Movement Theory*. New Haven: Yale University Press: 205–223.

Serenko, A., Bontis, N., Booker, L., et al. (2010) A scientometric analysis of knowledge management and intellectual capital academic literature (1994–2008). *Journal of Knowledge Management*, 14(1): 3–23.

Shanks, D.R. and Johnstone, T. (1998) Implicit knowledge in sequential learning tasks. In M.A. Stadler and P.A. Frensch (eds.), *Handbook of Implicit Learning*. Thousand Oaks: Sage: 533–572.

Slater, S.F. and Olson, E.M. (2000) Strategy type and performance: The influence of sales force management. *Strategic Management Journal*, 21: 813–829.

Spaeth, S., Haefliger, S., von Krogh, G., and Renzl, B. (2008) Communal resources in open source software development. *Information Research*, 13(1).

Spender, J-C. (1996) Making knowledge the basis for a dynamic theory of the firm. *Strategic Management Journal*, 17: 45–62.

Stehr, N. (1992) *Practical Knowledge*. London: Sage.

Stehr, N. (1994) *Knowledge Societies*. London: Sage.

Stoecker, R. (1995) Community, movement, organization: The problem of identity convergence in collective action. *Sociological Quarterly*, 36: 111–121.

Szulanski, G. (1996) Exploring internal stickiness: Impediments to transfer of best practice within the firm. *Strategic Management Journal*, 17: 27–44.

Tajfel, H. (1982) Social-Psychology of Inter-Group Relations. *Annual Review of Psychology*, 33: 1–39.

Taylor, M. and Singleton, S. (1993) The communal resource: Transaction cost and the solution to collective action problems. *Politics and Society*, 21(2): 195–214.

Tilly, C. (1999) *Durable Inequality*. Berkeley: University of California Press.

Toennies, F. (1887, translated 1963) *Community and society*. New York: Harper & Row.

Townsend, A.M. (2000) Solidarity.com? Class and collective action in the electronic village. *Journal of Labor Research*, 21(3): 393–405.

Tsai, W. (2002) Social structure of coopetition within a multiunit organization: Coordination, competition, and intraorganizational knowledge sharing. *Organization Science*, 13(2): 179–190.

Tsoukas, H. (1996) The firm as a distributed knowledge system: A constructionist approach. *Strategic Management Journal*, 17(SI): 11–25.

Turner, J.C., Brown, R.J., and Tajfel, H. (1979) Social-Comparison and Group Interest in Group Favoritism. *European Journal of Social Psychology*, 9(2): 187–204.

Van Maanen, J. (1991) The Smile-Factory: Work at Disneyland. In P. Frost, L.F. Moore, M.R. Louis, C.C. Lundberg, and J. Martin (eds.), *Rethinking Organizational Culture*. Newburry Park, CA: Sage: 58–76.

Van Maanen, J. and Barley, S.R. (1984) Occupational communities: Culture and control in organizations. In L. Cummings and B. Staw (eds.), *Research in organizational behavior*. Greenwich, CT: JAI Press: 287–365.

Varela, F.J., Thompson, E., and Rosch, E. (1991) *The Embodied Mind: Cognitive Science and Human Experience*. Cambridge, MA: MIT Press.

Vendelo, M.T. (2009) Improvisation and Learning in Organizations—An Opportunity for Future Empirical Research. *Management Learning*, 40(4): 449–456.

von Hippel, E. and von Krogh, G. (2001) Open source software development: Issues for organization research, Working paper.

von Krogh, G. (1998) Care in Knowledge Creation. *California Management Review*, 40: 133–154.

von Krogh, G. (2002) The Communal Resource and Information Systems. *Journal of Strategic Information Systems*, 11: 85–107.

von Krogh, G. and Koehne, M. (1998) Der Wissenstransfer in Unternehmen: Phasen des Wissenstransfer und Einflussfaktoren. *Die Unternehmung*, 52: 235–252.

von Krogh, G., Ichijo, K., and Nonaka, I. (2000) *Enabling Knowledge Creation*. New York: Oxford University Press.

von Krogh, G., Nonaka, I., and Ichijo, K. (1997) Develop knowledge activists! *European Management Journal*, 15(5): 475–483.

von Krogh, G., Roos, J. and Slocum, K. (1994) An essay on corporate epistemology. *Strategic Management Journal*, 15: 53–73.

Wasko, M. and Faraj, S. (2005) Why should I share? Examining social capital and knowledge contribution in electronic networks of practice. *MIS Quarterly*, 29(1): 35–57.

Weber, M. (1978) *Economy and Society: An outline of interpretive sociology*. Berkeley, CA: University of California Press.

Wenger, E. (1998) *Communities of Practice: Learning, Meaning, and Identity*. Cambridge: Cambridge University Press.

Wertsch, J. (1985) *Vygotsky and the social formation of mind*. Cambridge: Harvard University Press.

Wolin, S. (1961) *Politics and Vision*. London: Allen and Unwin.

Yakhlef, A. (2010) The three facts of knowledge: A critique of the practice-based learning theory. *Research Policy*, 39(1): 39–46.

20

Organizational Forgetting

PABLO MARTIN DE HOLAN
AND
NELSON PHILLIPS

ABSTRACT

While the creation and transfer of organizational knowledge have been the focus of intensive investigation by management researchers, another aspect of the dynamics of knowledge in organizations—'organizational forgetting'—has received much less attention. This aspect of organizational knowledge is, therefore, much less well understood than knowledge creation and transfer despite some recent encouraging efforts. In this chapter, we explore the notion of organizational forgetting and argue that it is an indispensable complement to theories of organizational learning. In addition, we argue that attempts to manage organizational learning and knowledge must also include efforts to understand and manage forgetting. We conclude with a discussion of an agenda for research on organizational forgetting.

INTRODUCTION

The imposing architecture of the Hotel Lutetia dominates the corner of Rue de Sevres and Rue de Babylone in Paris. The hotel has been renowned for more than a century for its beautifully decorated rooms, its impeccable service, and, not all that surprisingly for a Parisian luxury hotel, its gourmet restaurant. But this fine hotel has not always been simply a hotel. When the German Army entered the city during WWII, its commanders requisitioned the hotel to act as the Headquarters of the Abwehr Leitstelle, the French branch of the German Army's secret service.[*] And, in order to keep the hotel operating, the German army kept a significant part of the hotel staff on in their usual jobs.

This created a number of conflicts of interest for the retained staff. One of the most critical problems centered on the restaurant's impressive wine cellar that included some of the most prestigious and expensive French wines to be found in the city. The hotel staff took pride in the quality and variety of the cellar. So much pride, in fact, that when it became clear that the German Army would requisition the Lutetia, they decided they had to do something to protect the cellar. The decision was quickly made to eradicate all traces of the cellar, believing that if it were 'forgotten' it would survive the war. The staff proceeded to wall up the door that led to it and to hide or destroy all copies of the wine list. From an organizational point of view, the cellar was 'forgotten' by the hotel.

But it was not quite so simple. The new occupants of the building became suspicious when the staff claimed they could not serve wines selected by the German officers to accompany their meals, and their suspicions grew stronger when wine lists dating from the pre-occupation days were found. Upset by this evidence, the German officer in charge of logistics ordered a thorough search for the wine cellar, and then demanded to see the building's blueprints. To his great frustration, he could find neither and, faced with more pressing problems than a mysteriously absent wine cellar, dropped the matter.

After the war, and following a brief stint as a sorting center for returning French prisoners of war, the Lutetia once again became a luxury hotel. As the staff had hoped, the cellar had survived the war unscathed, and once the door was restored, the restaurant once again had one of the finest wine cellars in Paris. However, by that time all copies of the old wine list had disappeared, and the hotel had to embark on the time consuming task of making a new inventory of the cellar; a problematic task as old wines don't like to be disturbed and the task involved re-cataloguing the whole cellar bottle by bottle.

The story of the Hotel Lutetia raises a number of interesting questions for researchers interested in organizational knowledge. First, the decision to organizationally 'forget' the wine cellar highlights the fact that although the focus in the literature has been on organizational *learning*, in some situations organizations may need to get rid of existing knowledge rather than develop new knowledge; in other words, to forget rather than to learn (Bettis and Prahalad, 1995; Hedberg, 1981; Lyles and Schwenk, 1992; Nystrom and Starbuck, 1984; Starbuck, 1996). Forgetting is an intuitive concept, and it is a regular feature of everyday life; but how does the notion apply to organizations?

The difficulty experienced by the Lutetia when it tried to eliminate all traces of its cellar points to the fact that forgetting is often not an easy task. In some circumstances at least, it requires significant management effort and attention to succeed and, as the reappearing wine list attests, success is anything but guaranteed. This leads to our second question: how should managers manage forgetting?

Third, the accidental loss of all copies of the wine list is a good example of a less positive form of forgetting where an organization forgets something that it needs to remember. Organizations not only learn to do new things, but also forget to do things that they were able to do in the past. Research and practical experience show that organizational knowledge generally decays over time, and that valuable knowledge is often lost. But how this process works, how this kind of forgetting can be minimized, and how the organizational impact of forgetting can be reduced are not yet well understood.

---

*See Delarue, Jacques, *Histoire de la Gestapo*, Paris Arthème Fayard,1962. The authors are thankful to His Excellency Mr E. Calcagno y Maillmann, Ambassador of the Argentine Republic to France for referring the anecdote to us, and to Ms Virginie de La Fresnaye, Chargée de la Communication of the Hotel Lutetia for corroborating significant parts of the vignette.

In this chapter, we argue that the intense research focus on organizational learning has obscured the equally important process of organizational forgetting, and that the ongoing discussion of organizational learning needs to be complemented by a much clearer idea of how organizations 'forget' or 'unlearn.' In spite of significant and growing empirical evidence (Akgun, Byrne, Lynn, and Keskin, 2007; Argote and Epple, 1990; Fernandez and Sune, 2009) supporting the existence of 'knowledge decay,' 'unlearning' (Nystrom and Starbuck, 1984; Starbuck, 1996), or 'forgetting' (Carlson and Rowe, 1976; Smunt and Morton, 1985; Wickelgren, 1976), insufficient attention has been paid in the literature to the processes underlying the loss of organizational knowledge. Furthermore, while there has been some encouraging recent empirical (Martin de Holan and Phillips, 2004) and theoretical (Tsang and Zahra, 2008) work attempting to develop a comprehensive theory of organizational forgetting, there is still some distance to go to understand the types of organizational forgetting and how they relate to one another. Furthermore, we agree with Benkard's (2000) contention that 'the strategic implications of organizational forgetting have not been studied,' and believe this is detrimental to our full understanding of the dynamics of organizational learning, both for organizational theory and strategy (Besanko, Doraszelski, Kryukov, and Satterthwaite, 2010).

We present our argument in four steps. First, we provide an overview of the concepts of learning and forgetting and explain their common roots. Second, we distinguish between the two dominant schools of thought regarding organizational forgetting. Third, we present a comprehensive model of forgetting that integrates and extends existing views on the topic. We conclude by discussing some of the ramifications of a theory of forgetting for management research and practice and present some directions for future research.

LEARNING CURVES AND KNOWLEDGE DECAY

Organizational learning is commonly defined as modifications in the knowledge base of an organization induced primarily, but not exclusively, by the organization's experience (Huber, 1991). It is perceived as essential for sustained competitive advantage (Aldrich, 1999; Argote and Ingram, 2000; Eisenhardt and Martin, 2000; Kogut and Zander, 1992; Prahalad and Hamel, 1990; Rumelt, Schendel, and Teece, 1994; Teece, Pisano, and Shuen, 1997), as well as for strategic renewal (Crossan and Bedrow, 2003). Unsurprisingly, the concept of organizational learning has been of enduring interest to researchers and practitioners alike, and the chapters of this volume are a testament to the progress that has been made in understanding organizational learning.

At a practical level, organizational learning is the ability of an organization to create answers to problems that need to be solved, or to create a better answer to existing problems (Argote, 1999; Miner and Anderson, 1999; Miner and Mezias, 1996). It refers to the different processes by which organizations add to their stock of knowledge and to their repertoire of capabilities. Learning occurs most obviously when an organization encounters unusual events for which it has no solution in its collection of standard operating procedures (e.g. Cyert and March, 1963) and is therefore forced to do things in novel ways. More specifically, learning happens when the solution that has been found to that particular problem for which there was no solution is formalized in routines (Cyert and March, 1963; Nelson and Winter, 1982), rules (Levitt and March, 1988; Schulz, 1998; Schulz, 2001), operating procedures (Cyert and March, 1963), mental models, and dominant logics (Bettis and

Prahalad, 1995) that enable the organization to make further decisions and to take more actions in the future.

Early studies of learning in organizations were mostly based on learning curve models, which established a positive relationship between the experience gained by performing similar activities and gains in productivity. The theoretical details of gains-through-experience were first suggested by Wright, who showed a non-linear relationship between the average direct labor needed to produce a unit, and the cumulative number of units produced (Wright, 1936).

Thereafter, a large number of studies documented this 'learning-by-doing' and 'learning-through-experience' phenomenon such as Rapping (1965) who observed large gains in productivity in the production of war vessels, with average annual increases of 'about 40 per cent.' The same phenomenon was found in the production of rayon (Hollander, 1965), nuclear plants (Joskow and Rozanski, 1979), and ships (Searle and Goody, 1945), and also, later, in service organizations such as pizza parlors and hotels (Darr, Argote, and Epple, 1995; Martin de Holan and Phillips, 2004b).

At their core, learning curve models establish a positive relationship between experience and productivity: as organizations repeat a similar task, they learn, leading eventually to an accumulation of knowledge that translates into improved outcomes. Experience in these studies was usually assessed by cumulative production of similar units with relatively stable technology, and efficiency is seen to increase at some predictable rate with cumulative production. Several authors provide useful reviews of this literature (for a detailed review, see Adler and Clark, 1991; Argote and Epple, 1990).

Because of their apparent simplicity and intuitive appeal, learning curves quickly became popular among practitioners as useful instruments for cost estimation and control (Dutton, Thomas, and Butler, 1984). At the same time, they were a kind of 'black box' and suffered from several limitations. In particular, there was a lack of understanding of how learning from experience occurred in organizations and a lack of clear boundary conditions that would allow practitioners to understand under what circumstances learning through repetition would occur and when it would not (Abernathy and Wayne, 1974; Yelle, 1979, 1985).

Furthermore, one important conundrum rapidly became evident: because cumulative production can only increase over time, productivity should only rise over time also (Sterman, 2000). But this contradicts both intuition and what is observed in practice: often, performance in organizations deteriorates even in the presence of increasing cumulative volumes of production. Accordingly, the idea that knowledge accumulated by organizations can also deteriorate, decay, or otherwise disappear began to appear in the literature along with concerns with the ways it accumulates. These early learning curve studies led to both the blossoming of learning research and the beginnings of a concern with forgetting. This concern with forgetting was also encouraged by a small number of early theoretical discussions (Carlson and Rowe, 1976; Hedberg, 1981; Nystrom and Starbuck, 1984; Starbuck, 1996; Wickelgren, 1976).

However, in spite of this trickle of work and the general interest surrounding the concept (Besanko et al., 2010; Easterby-Smith, Antonacopoulou, Simm, and Lyles, 2004) organizational forgetting failed to gain traction among mainstream researchers. This is not, of course, to say that no research on forgetting has followed these early discussions. In early research, processes of forgetting or unlearning were mentioned explicitly by a few authors (Bettis and Prahalad, 1995; Day, 1994a, 1994b; Hedberg, 1981; Lyles and Schwenk, 1992; Nystrom and Starbuck, 1984; Starbuck, 1996), but seldom as the main object of the research, and often as a serendipitous finding that did not fit quite well with theory. Anand and associates, for example, present a clear example of forgetting as part of their argument, although the notion itself is not subsequently developed in their discussion.

> Managers at the propulsion systems division of a major aerospace company selected an engineer to become the in-house expert in a new technology. In a wave of management changes, the champions of the technology all moved out of the division. The expert engineer was reassigned to normal duties. After another wave of change management, it became apparent that the technology was critical, but no one remembered that there was an expert on staff, and the process was repeated.
>
> (Anand, Manz, and Glick, 1998: 798)

Similarly, but from a more practitioner-oriented perspective, Peters (1994: 128) argues that forgetting (or unlearning) is important for the performance of the organization, but doesn't take it much further than this vivid vignette:

> The issue for Ford Motor Co., home of the original whiz kids, and others in the 1980s was forgetting—that is, unlearning the habits attached to a once-viable way of life. . . . In 1938 the company tried to build a small car and failed miserably. 'Small car' was translated by Ford's engineers into 'shrunken big car'. A stubby, expensive, over-engineered product emerged. Not only was Ford snared by yesterday's routines (big-car design was the only variety the firm's engineers knew), but it then overlearned from its 1938 error—that is, 'We don't know how to build small cars.'

More recently, however, a number of researchers have begun to explore the nature and consequences of organizational forgetting, and some empirical evidence (Argote and Epple, 1990; Benkard, 2000; Darr et al., 1995; Epple, Argote, and Devadas, 1991; Martin de Holan and Phillips, 2004b) has begun to emerge, showing that the knowledge base of an organization can deteriorate, sometimes quite rapidly, which suggests that knowledge retention should be seen as a process requiring managerial effort and attention (Ocasio, 1997), and one that is prone to errors and mishaps.

From almost the beginning, then, both theoretical work and empirical findings gave rise to the concept of 'organizational forgetting,' highlighting that an organization not only acquires new knowledge, but also loses knowledge, either purposely or voluntarily. We will explore the literature on involuntary and purposeful forgetting in the next section.

Unlearning and Forgetting

As we discussed above, researchers have generally taken one of two approaches to knowledge loss. On the one hand, a number of writers have adopted Peters' approach and point to the importance of unlearning (Hedberg, 1981; Lyles, 1988) in breaking the inertia of past learning in the face of environmental change (Hannan and Freeman, 1984; Miller, 1993, 1994; Miller and Friesen, 1980; Romanelli and Tushman, 1986; Rumelt, 1995). Unlearning from this perspective is understood as a voluntary effort to rid the organization of knowledge that is no longer needed. This argument highlights the fact that organizations must somehow unlearn old routines and practices in order to learn new and more appropriate ways of doing things.

On the other hand, writers have also argued that organizations may forget accidentally; that is, knowledge may be lost without any explicit desire to eliminate the knowledge from the organization. Authors have documented how an organization's pool of knowledge may dissipate rapidly and unintentionally (Argote, Beckman, and Epple, 1990; Darr et al., 1995; Epple et al., 1991), and how this involuntary forgetting can have serious negative effects on productivity, profitability, and competitiveness (Argote, 1999: 60). We will consider these two views in the following subsections.

Unlearning

In discussions of unlearning, it is often argued that organizations must unlearn old practices in order to allow them to learn new ways of doing things. Learning from this perspective involves not just the creation of new knowledge, but also the active elimination of existing knowledge, especially when the new knowledge collides in some significant way with existing knowledge (Martin de Holan, 2006). From this perspective, unlearning is positive; when old knowledge prevents the organization from adjusting to the new requirements of the environment, unlearning is the solution.

This view of unlearning has largely been inspired by Hedberg (1981). In his seminal work, Hedberg claimed that unlearning was a necessary complement to the notion of organizational learning. He argued that unlearning is distinct from learning, but conceptually necessary to understand how organizations learn because 'knowledge grows and simultaneously becomes obsolete as reality changes' (Hedberg, 1981:3). As a result, organizations need to unlearn; that is, to engage in a 'process through which learners discard knowledge' (Hedberg, 1981: 18).

At the core of this thinking is the idea that organizational learning necessarily happens in a pre-existing organizational context with a pre-existing stock of knowledge. This 'canvas' over which learning happens has been conceptualized as a set (a 'collection of individual elements'), or as a network where 'knowledge elements are connected to other elements or not', creating a variety of connections and dependent relationships that vary in strength and direction (Ahuja and Novelli, 2010). Newstrom (1983) was one of the first to challenge the 'clean slate fallacy' (the idea that learning occurred in a void and did not interact in a significant way with existing knowledge). He proposed a typology of learning situations where the significance of unlearning depended on the motivations of the change. According to his typology, new knowledge that aimed to create a new behavior would require a limited amount of unlearning, whereas new knowledge whose objective would be to replace one behavior with another would require a considerable amount of unlearning. He defines unlearning as the 'process of reducing or eliminating preexisting knowledge or habits that would otherwise represent formidable barriers to learning' (Newstrom, 1983). From this definition, it is easy to see how managing unlearning could be beneficial for the organization.

Many other researchers have utilized this idea that unlearning is necessary for new learning to occur. For example, Anand and colleagues (1998: 806) noted that there are circumstances when 'the existing memory may be an obstruction rather than an aid.' The disruption and recreation of parts of the organization's memory may therefore be required. Similarly, Crossan and associates argue that 'the tension between assimilating new learning (feed forward) and using what has already been learned (feedback) arises because the institutionalized learning (what has already been learned) impedes the assimilation of new learning' (Crossan, Lane, and White, 1999: 533).

While these researchers have generally taken a behavioral learning approach focusing on routines and standard operating procedures, other researchers (e.g. Bettis and Prahalad, 1995; Miller 1990, 1994) have adopted a more cognitive view and argued convincingly that the failure to discard or 'unlearn' old dominant logics is one of the main reasons why organizations find it so difficult to adjust their behavior to new environmental conditions, even when they see clear evidence of changes in their environment. Noticing the difficulty that organizations have with diversifications, even related ones, and with rapid and or discontinuous change in a core business, these authors argue that it is not necessarily a problem of routines alone, but of collective representations of the world that make alternative views difficult or unlikely, and that prevent organizational members from either noticing the need for change (Freeman, 1999) or interpreting the changes to understand their consequences, making them blind to stimuli from their environment (Kiesler and Sproull, 1982).

Prahalad and Bettis (1995) are particularly notable in this line of thought as they claim that dominant logics, which are 'the mental maps developed through experience in the core business,' are often applied inappropriately in other circumstances. Because these dominant logics represent the shared cognitive map and the strategic mindset of the top management team in an organization, they are closely related to the processes and tools used in the organization and, consequently, with the types of behaviors that can be enacted and with those that cannot. (Bettis, Wong, and Blettner, 2010). Consequently, old dominant logics are one of the most important factors preventing organizations from discarding old knowledge, and a crucial part of organizational knowledge to unlearn when circumstances require, because they are 'inherently adaptive properties *as long as neither the domain of application nor the environment changes significantly*' (Bettis et al., 2010).

From this perspective, dominant logics represent the cognitive view of learning, where learning is seen as a lens that allows the organization and its members to understand in a collective way the environment in which it operates and the adequate responses to that environment. Unlearning is seen as the ability to discard an old logic in order to provide room for a new one: 'strategic learning and unlearning of the kind involved in the dominant logic are inextricably intertwined' (Bettis and Prahalad, 1995: 10), 'before strategic learning . . . can occur, the old logic must in a sense be unlearned by the organization' (Bettis and Prahalad, 1995). This is so because as organizations grow and become more complex 'it becomes necessary to establish formal structure, procedures, system, routines and processes (which) are designed in at least rough congruence with the dominant logic' (Bettis et al., 2010).

The crux of this approach, regardless of whether it is behavioral or cognitive, can be succinctly summarized as follows: 'firms that can unlearn and reframe their past success programs to fit with changing environmental and situational conditions will have a greater likelihood of survival and adaptation' (Lyles, 1988: 87). Ultimately, this approach sees unlearning as a fundamental dimension of change, because, as Tsang and Zahra (2008) argue in their exhaustive review, 'unlearning refers to the discarding of old routines to make way for new ones' (Tsang and Zahra, 2008). From this perspective, unlearning is best defined as the act of eliminating or discarding knowledge voluntarily, without necessarily the creation of new knowledge, although there is often a close association.

Forgetting

A parallel stream of research has focused on the negative consequences of forgetting. This perspective is concisely summarized by Day (1944: 44): 'Organizations without practical mechanisms to remember what has worked and why will have to repeat their failures and rediscover their success formulas over and over again,' wasting resources in the process.

In sharp contrast with the unlearning view, researchers here emphasize the importance of not losing knowledge, claiming that avoiding forgetting is critically important in order to maintain performance levels previously reached by the organization.

The notion of knowledge dissipating is particularly at odds with the standard learning curve theory and models, which establish a positive relationship between experience and productivity. Although learning curve studies are generally limited to production settings, the theory has been extrapolated to other dimensions of organizational learning, perhaps excessively (Abernathy and Wayne, 1974). In spite of the robust findings supporting learning curves in operations research (for a detailed review, see Adler and Clark, 1991; Argote and Epple, 1990), involuntary loss of knowledge (forgetting) has been well documented in intermittent production settings (Carlson and Rowe, 1976). Evidence that interruptions (either predictable interruptions, such as a national holiday, or random ones, such as a faulty machine) introduce considerable knowledge loss and consequently reduce learning rates has been documented for over half a century (Hirsch, 1952). This strongly suggests that in situations where changeovers and other interruptions make cumulative production non-continuous, learning arising from experience is followed by forgetting, which is followed by relearning (Carlson and Rowe, 1976). Bailey, for example, studies how interruptions in a process could impact the rate of forgetting and the rate of future relearning (that is, the amount of learning needed to achieve a state similar to the one reached in the past by the same organization) (Bailey, 1989).

These findings could, of course, simply be attributed to the interruption. However, similar results were found in continuous production settings where no interruption or resetting took place. Benkard (2000), for example, found that only sixty-one percent of the 'stock of experience' existing at the beginning of the year survived at its end. In other empirical studies available (Argote, 1990; Darr et al., 1995), knowledge retention (conceptually, the complement of knowledge deterioration) was even lower, in the range five to fifteen percent. The third, and most recent paper (Thompson, 2007) found lower, though 'still significant,' rates of forgetting, highlighting the difficulty of rigorously assessing forgetting.

Nevertheless, these studies show that the stock of knowledge of the organization diminishes as time passes, because organizational forgetting depletes it in a way that organizational learning cannot compensate. More importantly, they hint that knowledge retention is far from automatic as a naïve view of the learning curve would suggest. Furthermore, discovering how to perform an activity at a certain level of performance and being able to sustain the activity over time are far from the same thing.

In addition, researchers have begun to explore the important strategic ramifications of these observations. For example, Besanko et al. (2010) claim that 'if learning-by-doing can be "undone" by organizational forgetting, this raises the question whether organizational forgetting is an antidote to market dominance.' This important observation grows out of the fact that to the extent the market leader has more to forget than market followers, organizational forgetting should affect the market leader more than the followers and therefore work to equalize differences among firms. As a result, organizational forgetting suggests that improvements in competitive positions that grow out of organizational learning will be more transitory than those based in other aspects of the firm.

While work on the causes of involuntary forgetting does not provide a full account, some simulations and experiments have been run focusing on the role of turnover and structural design on rates of learning and forgetting (Carley, 1992; Devadas Rao and Argote,

2006). Carley (1992), for example, theorizes that personnel turnover has an effect on organizational performance because knowledge is lost as personnel leave. Bailey (1992) studies how interruptions in a process could impact the rate of forgetting and the rate of future relearning (that is, the amount of learning needed to achieve a state similar to the one reached in the past by the same organization); and in a similar vein, Argote hypothesizes that knowledge depreciation may happen because 'products or processes change and render old knowledge obsolete . . . , organizational records are lost or become difficult to access . . . [or] member[s] turnover' (Argote, 1999: 52–53).

Among the theoretical explanations for the cause of involuntary forgetting, we find the inability to codify knowledge in a way that can be captured by the organizational memory system, as is the case when there is significant individual or collective tacit knowledge involved that has not been made explicit by the organization (Nonaka, 1994). In these cases, organizational learning involves not simply the creation of new knowledge, but also the capacity to crystallize knowledge into routines (Nelson and Winter, 1982).

In that vein, Martin de Holan and associates (2004a), propose that 'knowledge entering an organization must be introduced in the organization's memory system, else the organization will rapidly forget the new knowledge.' They go on to argue that the degree of retention of new knowledge depends on the effort put into integration, hinting that knowledge acquisition and the integration of that knowledge into the organization are two distinct activities that require managerial attention, and probably different tools to manage effectively.

These studies suggest that in addition to unlearning as a positive event that helps the organization adapt to its environment, forgetting is an organizational phenomenon that can also have negative consequences: very much like learning, context matters in order to evaluate the outcomes of forgetting. In addition, available research shows that even in the most formalized of knowledge settings, knowledge retention and learning-by-doing is far from perfect and/or automatic.

A COMPREHENSIVE MODEL
OF LEARNING AND FORGETTING

The apparent contradiction of these two streams of work—knowledge loss as simultaneously necessary and competence enhancing and also unwelcome and competence destroying—requires some sort of theoretical explanation. It also raises the question of whether there are other types of knowledge loss. Beginning with these observations, we have developed a framework useful in understanding the types of knowledge loss that occur in organizations (see Figure 20.1). First, we begin by differentiating types of knowledge loss based on the intentionality associated with it. Focusing on the intention behind knowledge loss allows us to change the onus from the outcomes of the process of forgetting (e.g. whether it was good or bad for the organization) to the organizational activity that preceded it. At its most basic, all forms of knowledge loss are the same; it is the relationship between the knowledge loss and the intention behind it that makes it positive or negative. In refocusing on intentionality, we can capture the role of managers in the process and provide a more useful set of categories of knowledge loss: in the first case, the intention is that forgetting shouldn't occur; in the second, it is that unlearning should.

	New knowledge	**Established knowledge**
Unintentional	FAILED INNOVATION	FORGETTING
Purposeful	ABORTED LEARNING	UNLEARNING

Figure 20.1 Modes of Organizational Forgetting

In addition to intentionality, the degree of embeddedness of the knowledge that is lost needs to be taken into account. From our empirical work on knowledge loss, we believe it is important to differentiate between recent learning that has not yet been deeply incorporated into the routines of the organization, and pieces of knowledge that have been part of the organization's stock of knowledge for a long time and are therefore deeply embedded. We also found that the degree of embeddedness made a significant difference to how and why knowledge was lost, and we therefore argue for its use as a second dimension in our typology.

From these two dimensions, four types of organizational forgetting emerge: forgetting, unlearning, failed innovation, and aborted learning. These four types are presented and discussed below. We also provide a few illustrative vignettes for each of the categories drawn from a research project that we conducted and that served as the basis for a series of papers on the dynamics of forgetting (Martin de Holan and Phillips, 2004b), the management of organizational forgetting (Martin de Holan, Phillips, and Lawrence, 2004) and forgetting as a strategic activity for the organization (Martin de Holan and Phillips, 2004a).

Forgetting: the involuntary deterioration of embedded knowledge

We focus in this section on the degradation of knowledge after it has become embedded in the organizational memory system. As discussed above, we refer to this form of knowledge loss as forgetting. In our research, we observed several instances of forgetting where performance unexpectedly fell after having reached a level that was deemed satisfactory for some time. In these situations, instead of observing continued increasing gains in productivity and/or quality as cumulative output increased, we observed either higher costs or lower quality, or sometimes both. In these cases the learning curve predictions held, but only for a period: after reaching a plateau, the output then decreased. Furthermore, in some cases it was not just a matter of quality; the organization was, after a time, completely unable to invoke the routines that led to the satisfactory performance, regardless of the quality of the performance it had attained in the past.

We attributed that change in performance to an involuntary loss of established knowledge. A hotel manager in our study described the process as follows:

> We calculate the daily cost of food and beverages. As soon as a new manager (of Food and Beverages) starts, he starts well, and then there is a phase where you have to watch closely (or the cost of food will increase again). In a kitchen, the cost depends on how closely you watch everything. That is fundamental. You have to see what goes out, what comes in, and you have to monitor that very closely. As soon as (the manager) stops checking that, his performance (cost of food in relation to quality) goes down. We have seen that with our Cuban chefs. We hire one of them and in two weeks the cost of food is sky-high, and only then it stabilizes. We haven't been lucky with them.
>
> *(Resident Manager, Key Hotel)*

Based on our evidence, we can suggest that for traditional learning effects to occur, organizations need to initiate activities that ensure the learning is incorporated into the stock of knowledge, and then that it is maintained over time. Our findings give support to the view that learning and maintaining the acquired knowledge are two distinct activities that require significant managerial attention but are intrinsically different in nature. Furthermore, more and better maintenance activities will be needed to ensure lower rates of forgetting. It is not simply the level of attention given to the maintenance of the stock of knowledge, but also the quality of that attention that influences the levels of retention (or, as mentioned by Argote, 1999, the dissipation rates).

Unlearning: The purposeful destruction of established knowledge

The second dimension of knowledge loss identified is unlearning; that is, knowledge loss that is actively desired by the organization. As one of the hotel managers in our study observed:

> The Canadian (managers of the hotel) act as if this were some suburb of Montreal. They still have to understand that we are in Cuba and that certain things cannot be done their way. They want us to use their system (developed and tested in Canada), and that system does not work here, we need new ways of doing things that take into account the specificities of the country.
>
> *(Resident Manager, Montelimar Hotel)*

In these situations, unlearning was needed primarily as a way to make room for new knowledge; discarding knowledge that had once been functional for the organization but was now acting as a hindrance to required learning. Another insight we can draw from this statement is that unlearning is a separate process from the process of learning. It is distinct from it, but in at least some cases has an important influence on the outcome of the learning process.

From our findings, we argue that the rate of learning that an organization can exhibit is influenced by the rate of unlearning that the organization can deploy at a certain moment. Since unlearning involves the elimination of knowledge that is no longer needed, its existence influences the rate at which knowledge can be absorbed and, in extreme cases, whether future learning can happen at all.

The overall effectiveness of knowledge mobilization (including organizational learning, but also knowledge transfer from within the organization and vicarious learning) is likely to be influenced by the presence or absence of unlearning. When organizational learning requires that new routines and new standard operating procedures replace old ones, processes of forgetting can influence the success of these learning processes by facilitating or making more difficult the assimilation of what has been learned. These observations can be applied in parallel to the ones mentioned by Newstrom (1983): with the exception of the situation in which the objective of learning is simply to create a behavior that did not exist previously, all the other categories (sustaining previous behavior, increase or decrease behavior or skill level, add new behavior to repertoire and replace behavior with another one) will require less effort in the presence of unlearning and, conversely, will be more effortful when unlearning is not present or is poorly managed.

Also, the need for unlearning can be related to the quality of the memory systems of the organization. As Devadas Rao and Argote (2006) argue, '[u]nderstanding why organizational knowledge depreciates involves understanding where organizational knowledge is stored or retained in the organization's memory.' Building on these ideas, it is clear that the quality of the organizational memory system will have a strong influence on the rates of learning and forgetting: better, more developed memory systems will tend to retain knowledge longer, as the behaviors and the cognition will be deployed in a more comprehensive way in the organization, and will have more material supports than otherwise. In situations where memory systems are more developed, unlearning will be more important.

Failed innovation: the inability to integrate new knowledge

This sort of knowledge loss is related to the inability to integrate new knowledge into the organization once the original problem is solved. That is, a failed innovation occurs when knowledge is transferred from another organization, or created by the organization itself, but is not retained: the solution does not 'stick.' When this happened in our study, we observed that an organization was able to perform a task for the first time, but was unable to achieve the same level of performance the second time around, or in some cases even unable to perform it again at all.

In this case, what had been learned had dissipated rapidly; it involuntarily disappeared from the organization almost immediately after it was created. We found several instances of failed innovation in our research, and there was a clear common theme among the managers we interviewed. For example, 'if you do not follow-up, it is back to step 1' or 'you go on vacation, and when you are back, the standards are gone.' Although initially we hypothesized that these were examples of failure to transfer or to create knowledge, we later realized that the organization had been able to use that knowledge, but only for short periods of time.

For example, a gala dinner for the elite of the country and diplomatic representatives from abroad was organized at one hotel with great success: the general impression was that the quality of the premises, the food, and the service were impeccable. Yet, a few weeks later, a much more modest gathering failed, as the quality of the food and service was mediocre. Subsequent failures moved the organization to cancel its plans to add receptions to its service offering, depriving it of a profitable source of income. As one manager explained:

> I think it's easy to get to a high standard; it's not difficult. I can go to another hotel and we can have the best meal (banquet) tomorrow there, without a problem, the best service for one day. But to keep it, to keep the standard is very difficult.
>
> *(Food and Beverage Manager, Withwind Hotel.*

This quote suggests that the integration of knowledge into an organization's memory system is a difficult task with often imperfect results. We can hypothesize that the rates of knowledge dissipation are closely related to the quantity and quality of the efforts put in by the organization to store that knowledge, and to the quality of the memory system itself. More intense management effort and attention may lead to lower rates of dissipation, while less effort (or no effort at all) will likely produce a very high dissipation rate.

Our findings and the hypothesized relationships formalize Day's idea:

> [O]nce knowledge has been captured . . . it won't necessarily be retained or accessible. Retention requires that the insights, policies, procedures and on-going routines that demonstrate the lessons are regularly used and refreshed to keep up-to-date.
>
> (Day, 1994b: 23)

Without organizational members' effort to retain knowledge, forgetting is inevitable. Simple innovation or transfer is not enough. Rather, management attention must be spent as much on ensuring the new knowledge is embedded in the organization's memory as it is on its innovation in the first place.

Aborted learning: avoiding the integration of new knowledge

Innovation is often a central concern of organizations, but not everything that is new is useful or desirable. As one hotel manager pointed out:

> [At first] we imported the structure [sets of rules and procedures and formal descriptions of jobs] of Superb Hotel, and very quickly we realized that it did not work well here, perhaps it was because there were no foreigners among us, or maybe because our managers were not prepared for it. And we saw contradictions appearing at all levels, and our operating procedures were not implemented, and the same hierarchical level that decided on their implementation had to check to make sure they were actually applied. Then we decided to change the structure, to work differently so we would not drown in meetings that did not get the problems solved.
>
> *(General Manager, Caribbean Hotel)*

In this case, the organization developed new knowledge (a new structure was adopted, new operating procedures were introduced, and new patterns of communication established), but it became apparent that what the organization had learned was not appropriate, and the managers had to move quickly to break the new routines, change the new structure, and re-establish more workable routines and structures.

Although in the case cited above the knowledge had been transferred from another organization in the form of a structure, similar phenomena were observed in organizations that had developed their own knowledge in the form of successful innovations. We observed that organizations that were good at innovating also had to be good at forgetting, because they had no *a priori* guarantee that their innovation would be adequate for their organization in the particular context they found themselves. Organizations that created solutions for problems had to be prepared to acknowledge that the solution they had found may not be adequate for the overall organization and had to be dropped before it became embedded in the memory system.

In more general terms, organizations skilled at knowledge creation and learning in general often seemed to be in the situation where they needed to discard what they had developed. Many experiments meant a lot of forgetting, and inadequately managing this process led to a decrease in performance as organizations picked up undesirable innovations. Successful innovative organizations probably possess more and better mechanisms to prevent new knowledge from entering their memory systems.

CONCLUSIONS AND NEW AVENUES FOR RESEARCH

You can't live without an eraser.

Gregory Bateson

Organizational knowledge has proven to be a very fruitful concept. It has provided researchers with a useful frame for exploring a wide range of topics, as the diversity of the chapters in this volume attests. Yet, while researchers have gained a much better understanding of how knowledge is created and transferred, there are still important dynamics of knowledge that remain unexplored. In this chapter, we have begun to discuss one of these dynamics, knowledge loss, and its role in knowledge processes in organizations.

We hope it is clear from our discussion up to this point that knowledge loss plays an important role in the dynamics of knowledge, a much more important role than its current status in the literature would indicate. While there have been some initial empirical investigations, the study of knowledge loss has been largely neglected, and as a consequence we are still theorizing without much evidence.

Our own empirical work indicates that organizations spend considerable time either trying to unlearn something that is no longer (or never was) functional or trying not to forget things that are highly valued but in danger of being lost. In fact, the organizations we studied spent much more time on these activities than they devoted to knowledge creation or transfer. Managing knowledge loss was a major management concern and consumed a surprising amount of time and effort. Both anecdotal evidence and initial empirical work are telling us that knowledge loss is important and deserves a much more central role in theorizing about knowledge. Researchers need to respond to this and explore the causes of knowledge loss and the mechanisms that underlie it in much more detail.

More specifically, there are several areas that deserve further exploration. First, we have seen that some types of knowledge loss are involuntary, what we call forgetting in our framework. Further research should explore the causes of forgetting, and the types of errors and mishaps that increase forgetting rates. More specifically, we need to explain why knowledge that is stored in an organization's memory deteriorates over time, and what mechanisms prevent different parts of the organization from retrieving stored knowledge. Furthermore, we know that rates of forgetting vary across industries, but we don't know why. And it would be useful to know whether rates of knowledge dissipation differ between organizations in the same industry, or even within the same multi-unit organization, and why. In short, we need to pay more attention to the causes of forgetting, and try to understand under what circumstances forgetting happens.

Second, some knowledge loss is voluntary; what we have termed unlearning. We have argued that this type of knowledge loss can be understood as an organizational capability that can lead to increased rates of learning and change. Because of the theorized impact of unlearning (and even more a lack of unlearning) in the success of change efforts, of particular interest would be studies that shed light on exactly how and why unlearning has an impact on success. Furthermore, it is clear from the discussions above that organizations often need to unlearn and that managers are often involved in unlearning, but how does it actually work? How do managers do it and what are the strategies they use to create unlearning? These are critical questions for researchers interested in the theory and practice of knowledge management.

Third, we have little understanding of why some new knowledge is successfully integrated into the memory system while other new knowledge is not. A promising avenue for researchers would be to study where knowledge is embedded in the organization (i.e. routines, structures, understandings, assets) and to explore the factors that prevent or facilitate knowledge from being embedded in each one of these dimensions. Knowledge may well crystallize in some cases and in other cases may not, but why and how remain to be explored.

Our study highlights the contextual nature of forgetting: while forgetting was a common phenomenon in the organizations we studied, the effect of forgetting is context-dependent. If critical knowledge was forgotten, then competitiveness was lost and forgetting would have been better avoided. But, if the forgotten knowledge was extraneous or was actively interfering with the application of more appropriate knowledge, then forgetting was a positive occurrence. In some cases, managing to avoid organizational forgetting is critical; in others, managing to maximize the loss of organizational knowledge is equally adaptive. This renews the call for more studies of learning and forgetting, as the question is always there: learning and forgetting are important but what are they, why do they occur, and when can we expect them to happen?

In sum, how organizations can unlearn the things they want to unlearn, and avoid forgetting the things they do not want to forget, is an important question for management researchers. Furthermore, it is a question that has not been studied sufficiently to date and has the potential to make a much more significant contribution to our understanding of the dynamics of organizational knowledge. Our discussion in this chapter begins to draw together a number of threads from the literature, but much further research and writing is required to come to a deeper understanding of this fascinating phenomenon.

REFERENCES

Abernathy, W.J. and Wayne, K. (1974) Limits of the learning curve. *Harvard Business Review*, 52(5): 109.

Adler, P. and Clark, K.B. (1991) Behind the learning curve: A sketch of the learning process. *Management Science*, 37(3): 267–281.

Ahuja, G. and Novelli, E. (2011) Knowledge structures and innovation: Useful abstractions, lessons learnt and unanswered questions. In M. Easterby-Smith and M. Lyles (eds.), *Handbook of Organizational Learning and Knowledge Management* (2nd Edition). Chichester: John Wiley & Sons.

Akgun, A.E., Byrne, J.C., Lynn, G.S., and Keskin, H. (2007) Organizational unlearning as changes in beliefs and routines in organizations. *Journal of Organizational Change Management*, 20(6): 794–812.

Aldrich, H.E. (1999) *Organizations Evolving*. Thousand Oaks, CA: Sage.

Anand, V., Manz, C., and Glick, W. (1998) An organizational memory approach to information management. *Academy of Management Review*, 23(4): 796–809.

Argote, L. (1999) *Organizational Learning: Creating, Retaining, and Transferring Knowledge*. Boston: Kluwer Academic.

Argote, L., Beckman, S.L., and Epple, D. (1990) The persistence and transfer of learning in industrial settings. *Management Science*, 36(2): 140–155.

Argote, L. and Epple, D. (1990) Learning Curves in Manufacturing. *Science*, 247: 920–924.

Argote, L. and Ingram, P. (2000) Knowledge transfer: A basis for competitive advantage in firms. *Organizational Behavior and Human Decision Processes*, 82(1): 150–169.

Bailey, C. (1989) Forgetting and the learning curve: A laboratory study. *Management Science*, 35(3): 340–352.

Benkard, C. L. (2000) Learning and forgetting: The dynamics of aircraft production. *American Economic Review*, 90(4): 1034–1054.

Besanko, D., Doraszelski, U., Kryukov, Y.S., and Satterthwaite, M. (2010) Learning-by-doing, organizational forgetting, and industry dynamics. *Econometrica*, 78: 453–521.

Bettis, R. and Prahalad, C.K. (1995) The dominant logic: Retrospective and extension. *Strategic Management Journal*, 16: 5–14.

Bettis, R.A., Wong, S., and Blettner, D. (2011) Dominant logic, knowledge creation and managerial choice. In M. Easterby-Smith and M. Lyles (eds.), *Handbook of Organizational Learning and Knowledge* (2nd edition). Chichester: John Wiley & Sons.

Carley, K.M. (1992) Organizational learning and personnel turnover. *Organization Science*, 3(1): 20–46.

Carlson, J.G. and Rowe, A.J. (1976) How much does forgetting cost? *Industrial Engineering*, 8(9): 40.

Crossan, M.M. and Bedrow, I. (2003) Organizational learning and strategic renewal. *Strategic Management Journal*, 24(11): 1087.

Crossan, M., Lane, H., and White, R.E. (1999). An Organizational Learning Framework. Organizational Learning: From Intuition to Institution. *Academy of Management Review*, 24(3): 522–537.

Darr, E., Argote, L., and Epple, D. (1995) The acquisition, transfer and depreciation of knowledge in service organizations: Productivity in franchises. *Management Science*, 41(11): 1750–1762.

Day, G.S. (1994a) The capabilities of market-driven organizations. *Journal of Marketing*, 58: 37–52.

Day, G.S. (1994b) Continuous learning about markets. *California Management Review*, 36: 9–31.

Devadas Rao, R. and Argote, L. (2006) Organizational learning and forgetting: The effects of turnover and structure. *European Management Review*, 3(2): 77–85.

Dutton, J.M., Thomas, A., and Butler, J.E. (1984) The History of Progress Functions as a Managerial Technology. *Business History Review*, 58: 204–233.

Easterby-Smith, M., Antonacopoulou, E., Simm, D., and Lyles, M. (2004) Construction contributions to organizational learning: Argyris and the next generation. *Management Learning*, 35: 371–380.

Eisenhardt, K.M. and Martin, J.A. (2000) Dynamic capabilities: What are they? *Strategic Management Journal*, 21: 1105–1121.

Epple, D., Argote, L., and Devadas, R. (1991) Organization learning curves: A method for investigating intra-plant transfer of knowledge acquired through learning by doing. *Organization Science* 2: 58–70.

Fernandez, V. and Sune, A. (2009) Organizational forgetting and its causes: An empirical research. *Journal of Organizational Change Management*, 22(6): 620–634.

Freeman, S. (1999) Identity maintenance and adaptation: A multilevel analysis of response to loss. *Research in Organizational Behavior*, 21: 247–294.

Hannan, M.T. and Freeman, J. (1984) Structural inertia and organizational change. *American Sociological Review*, 49: 149–164.

Hedberg, B. (1981) How organizations learn and unlearn. In P. Nystrom and W. Starbuck (Eds.), *Handbook of Organizational Design*. Oxford: Oxford University Press: 3–27.

Hirsch, W. (1952) Manufacturing progress functions. *Review of Economics and Statistics*, 34: 143–155.

Hollander, S. (1965) *The Sources of Increased Efficiency: A Study of Du-Pont Rayon Plants*. Cambridge, MA: M.I.T. Press.

Huber, G. P. (1991). Organizational Learning: The contributing processes and the literature. *Organization Science*, 2(1): 88–115.

Joskow, P.L. and Rozanski, G.A. (1979) The effects of learning by doing on nuclear plant operating reliability. *Review of Economics and Statistics*, 61(2): 161–168.

Kiesler, S. and Sproull, L. (1982) Managerial response to changing environments: Perspectives on problem sensing from social cognition. *Administrative Science Quarterly*, 27(4): 548–570.

Kogut, B. and Zander, U. (1992) Knowledge of the firm, combinative capabilities and the replication of technology. *Organization Science*, 3(3): 383–397.

Lyles, M.A. (1988) Learning among joint venture-sophisticated firms. In F. Contractor and P. Lorange (eds.), *Cooperative Strategies in International Business*. Lexington, MA: D.C. Heath: 301–316.

Lyles, M.A. and Schwenk, C.R. (1992) Top management, strategy and organizational knowledge structures. *Journal of Management Studies*, 29(2): 155–174.

Martin de Holan, P. (2006) Out with the old, in with the new. *Financial Times, Mastering Uncertainty*.

Martin de Holan, P. and Phillips, N. (2004a) Organizational forgetting as strategy. *Strategic Organization*, 2: 412–430.

Martin de Holan, P., and Phillips, N. (2004b) Remembrance of things past?: The dynamics of organizational forgetting. *Management Science*, 50(11): 1603–1613.

Martin de Holan, P., Phillips, N., and Lawrence, T. (2004) Managing organizational forgetting. *Sloan Management Review*, 45(2): 45–51.

Miller, D. (1993) The architecture of simplicity. *Academy of Management Review*, 18(1): 116–138.

Miller, D. (1994) What happens after success: The perils of excellence. *Journal of Management Studies*, 31(3): 327–358.

Miller, D. and Friesen, P.H. (1980) Momentum and revolution in organizational adaptation. *Academy of Management Journal*, 23(4): 591–614.

Miner, A. and Anderson, P. (1999) Industry and population-level learning: Organizational, inter-organizational and collective learning processes, *Advances in Strategic Management*. Stamford, CT: JAI Press, 1–30.

Miner, A.S. and Mezias, S. J. (1996) Ugly duckling no more: Pasts and futures of organizational learning research. *Organization Science*, 7(1): 88–99.

Nelson, R. R. and Winter, S. (1982) *An Evolutionary Theory of Economic Change*. Cambridge, MA: Harvard University Press.

Newstrom, J.W. (1983) The management of unlearning: Exploding the 'clean slate' fallacy. *Training and Development Journal*, 37(8): 36–39.

Nonaka, I. (1994) A dynamic theory of organizational knowledge creation. *Organization Science*, 5(1): 14–37.

Nystrom, P.C. and Starbuck, W. (1984) To avoid organizational crises, unlearn. *Organizational Dynamics*, 12(4): 53–76.

Ocasio, W. (1997) Towards an attention-based view of the firm. *Strategic Management Journal*, 18: 187–206.

Peters, T. (1994) To forget is sublime. *Forbes*(April 11): 128–130.

Prahalad, C.K. and Hamel, G. (1990) The core competence of the corporation. *Harvard Business Review* (May-June), 79–90.

Rapping, L. (1965) Learning and World War II Production Functions. *Review of Economics and Statistics*, 47: 81–86.

Romanelli, E. and Tushman, M.L. (1986) Inertia, environments, and strategic choice: A quasi-experimental design for comparative-longitudinal research. *Management Science*, 32(5): 608–622.

Rumelt, R. P. (1995) Inertia and transformation. In C. A. Montgomery (ed.), *Resource-Based and Evolutionary Theories of the Firm: Towards a Synthesis*. Boston: Kluwer Academic Publishers, 101–132.

Rumelt, R.P., Schendel, D.E., and Teece, D.J. (1994) Fundamental issues in strategy: A research agenda. In R. P. Rumelt, D.E. Schendel and D.J. Teece (eds.), *Fundamental Issues in Strategy: A Research Agenda*. Boston, MA: Harvard Business School Press: 9–47.

Schulz, M. (1998). Limits to Bureaucratic Growth: The Density Dependence of Organizational Rules. *Administrative Science Quarterly*, 43 (December): 845–876.

Schulz, M. (2001). The Uncertain Relevance of Newness: Organizational Learning and Knowledge Flows. *Academy of Management Journal*, 44(4): 661–681.

Searle, A.D. and Goody, C.S. (1945) Productivity increases in selected wartime shipbuilding programs. *Monthly Labor Review*, 61: 1132–1147.

Smunt, T.L. and Morton, T.E. (1985) The effects of learning on optimal lot sizes—further developments on the single product case. *IIE Transactions*, 17: 33–37.

Starbuck, W. (1996) Unlearning ineffective or obsolete technologies. *International Journal of Technology Management*, 11: 725–737.

Sterman, J. (2000) *Business Dynamics*. Maidenhead: McGraw-Hill.

Teece, D.J., Pisano, G., and Shuen, A. (1997) Dynamic capabilities and strategic management. *Strategic Management Journal*, 18(7): 509–533.

Thompson, P. (2007) How much did the liberty shipbuilders forget? *Management Science*, 53(6): 908–918.

Tsang, E.W.K. and Zahra, S.A. (2008) Organizational unlearning. *Human Relations*, 61: 14–35.

Wickelgren, W.A. (ed.) (1976) *Memory storage dynamics*. Hillsdale, NJ: Lawrence Erlbaum Associates.

Wright, T.P. (1936) Factors affecting the cost of airplanes. *Journal of Aeronautical Science*, 3:122.

Yelle, L.E. (1979) The learning curve: Historical review and comprehensive survey. *Decision Sciences*, 10(2): 302.

Yelle, L.E. (1985) Common flaws in learning curve analysis. *Journal of Purchasing and Materials Management*, 21(3): 10.

21

How Should We Understand Tacit Knowledge? A Phenomenological View

HARIDIMOS TSOUKAS

ABSTRACT

In this chapter I argue that tacit knowledge has largely been misunderstood in organization and management studies, mainly because of the tacitly (!) accepted cognitivist framework and the associated conduit metaphor of communication. I present a phenomenological critique of the cognitivist view, especially as the latter has been manifested in the work of Nonaka and Takeuchi, by drawing on, primarily, Polanyi and, secondarily, more recent phenomenological philosophers such as Dreyfus and Taylor. I argue against the conversion model of tacit knowledge and present an alternative account, which acknowledges the possibility of the articulation (albeit perennially incomplete) of tacit knowledge when skilled activities are obstructed. In such a case, practitioners cease to be absorbed in their skilled performances by subsidiarily drawing on familiar patterns, thus becoming focally aware of how their tasks at hand are accomplished. Distinctions underlying skilled performances thus come to the fore, becoming available for inspection and re-punctuation. The latter occurs most effectively when individuals are engaged in productive dialogical interactions.

'*Nisi credideritis, non intelligitis.* (Unless ye believe, ye shall not understand.)
St Augustine (cited in Polanyi, 1962:266)

Something that we know when no one asks us, but no longer know when we are supposed to give an account of it, is something that we need to *remind* ourselves of.

Ludwig Wittgenstein (1953: No.89; italics in the original)

The act of knowing includes an appraisal; and this personal coefficient, which shapes all factual knowledge, bridges in doing so the disjunction between subjectivity and objectivity.

Michael Polanyi (1962:17)

[My interlocutor] draws from me thoughts which I had no idea I possessed.

Maurice Merleau-Ponty (1962: 354)

INTRODUCTION

Maybe Aristotle was right to optimistically assert that 'all men by nature desire to know' (Aristotle, 2006:3), but it is doubtful whether he could have anticipated the drastic changes the concept of 'knowledge' would undergo in the course of time. Philosophers such as Toulmin (1990), MacIntyre (1985), and Feyerabend (1999), among others, have helped us see how radical the change has been. Roughly, until the Middle Ages knowledge was conceived in essentially classical Greek (particularly Aristotelian) terms: knowledge was primarily self-knowledge and the search for the virtuous life; it did not so much imply the exercise of the individual cognitive faculty as the ability to participate effectively in a larger collective; it was context-dependent and infused with values. By contrast, with the mechanization and secularization of the world in the modern age, knowledge acquired a strongly utilitarian meaning. It gradually became identified with abstraction, general principles, and the ability to obtain results; it no longer incorporated ultimate values but acquired descriptive neutrality. *Phronesis* gave way to *episteme*, and *praxis* to *theoria*. Peter Drucker (1993) usefully pointed out that one of the key events that reflected the changing meaning of knowledge in the eighteenth century was the publication of *Encyclopedie* in France (edited by Diderot and d'Alembert between 1751 and 1772). For the first time knowledge ceased to reside in the heads of certain authoritative individuals. It was extracted from socio-material practices, taking instead the form of a manual, which contained generic statements, describing how the world works. In Drucker's words, the *Encyclopedie* 'converted experience into knowledge, apprenticeship into textbook, secrecy into methodology, doing into applied knowledge' (Drucker, 1993).

The increasing decontextualization of knowledge in the modern age has led to theoretical (or codified) knowledge acquiring a central place in the functioning of modern (especially, late modern) societies. Daniel Bell aptly captured this change as follows:

> Knowledge has of course been necessary in the functioning of any society. What is distinctive about the post-industrial society is the change in the character of knowledge itself. What has become decisive for the organization of decisions and the direction of change is the centrality of *theoretical knowledge*—the primacy of theory over empiricism and the codification of knowledge into abstract systems of symbols that, as in any axiomatic system, can be used to illustrate many different and varied areas of experience.
>
> (Bell, 1999: 20) (italics in the original)

Indeed, it is hard today to think of an industry that does not make systematic use of 'theoretical knowledge.' Products increasingly incorporate more and more specialized knowledge, supplied by research and development departments, universities, and research and consulting firms; and organizational processes, ranging from production to logistics and marketing, are increasingly based on systematic research that aims to optimize their functioning (Drucker, 1993; Mansell and When, 1998; Stehr, 1994). Late modernity is the age of *theoria par excellence*. Or is it not?

If one takes a closer look at how theoretical knowledge is actually *used* in practice, one will see the extent to which theoretical knowledge itself, far from being as self-sustaining and explicit as it is often taken to be, is actually grounded on tacit commitments. Even the most theoretical form of knowledge, such as pure mathematics, cannot be a completely formalized system, insofar as it is based for its application and development on the *skills* of mathematicians and how such skills are used in practice (Collins, 2001). To put it differently, theoretical knowledge necessarily contains a 'personal coefficient' (Polanyi, 1962: 17). Late modern knowledge-based economies certainly make great use of codified forms of knowledge, but that kind of knowledge is inescapably used in a *non-codifiable* (non-theoretical) manner. Ironically, it is the rapid proliferation of theoretical knowledge that has made us reflexively aware of its tacit presuppositions.

The significance of tacit knowledge and/or cognate concepts (i.e. intuition, know-how, procedural knowledge) for the functioning of organizations has not escaped the attention of organization and management theorists since the early days of the field. This has been especially so in the work of practitioners who systematically reflected on their practice (Barnard, 1968; Follett, 1924; Vickers, 1983) as well as in the research of some leading organizational scholars who took cognition seriously (Argyris, 1999; Schön, 1983; Simon, 1965). However, 'tacit knowledge' did not really take off before the mid 1990s with the publication of Nonaka and Takeuchi's (1995) influential *The Knowledge-Creating Company* (for more recent formulations, see Nonaka and von Krogh, 2009; Nonaka et al., 2006). Ever since then the concept has decisively entered the management theory and practice vernacular.

And quite rightly so: tacit knowledge underlies all skillful action, an important feature of organizational life. Organizational members know lots of things about what they do although, paradoxically, when they are asked to describe *how* they do what they do, they often find it hard to express it in words (Ambrosini and Bowman, 2001; Cook and Yanow, 1996: 442; Eraut, 2000; Nonaka and Takeuchi, 1995; Harper, 1987; Tsoukas and Vladimirou, 2001). Gregory (1999: 198), for example, an outstanding salesman, describes his frustration at being unable to teach other salesmen in the classroom. What is true of selling is also true of practicing law (Spaeth, 1999), medicine (Patel et al., 1999) and management (Hatsopoulos and Hatsopoulos, 1999). Effective performance depends on knowledge that cannot be explicitly formulated in full.

Although the importance of tacit knowledge is now widely recognized, and in spite of several studies that have sought to further explore the concept, there are still several misunderstandings surrounding it. The main one is that tacit knowledge is still mostly seen on the conversion model: as knowledge awaiting its conversion to explicit knowledge. The prevalent conceptualization has been a cognitivist one (Varela et al., 1991): tacit knowledge is thought to be a cognitive state awaiting its symbolic representation—its conversion to explicit knowledge. In that sense, tacit knowledge is merely a weak form of explicit knowledge; we simply need to retrieve it. Of course, in so far as tacit knowledge is a mental phenomenon, it should be accessible to consciousness (Searle, 1992). However, there are non-cognitivist ways in which tacit knowledge may be accessed, but these have not been widely explored in management studies (cf. Sandberg and Pinnington, 2009; Yanow and Tsoukas, 2009).

Nonaka and his associates certainly deserve credit for having done the most to bring tacit knowledge to our awareness, but their conceptualization has had its problems, as several researchers have pointed out (Cook and Brown, 1999; Gourlay, 2006; Styhre, 2004; Ribeiro and Collins, 2007; Tsoukas, 1996; Tsoukas and Vladimirou, 2001). Although it could be argued that conceptualizing something as elusive as tacit knowledge is bound to be problematic, this need not be the case. Tacit knowledge remains intractable only within a cognitivist framework that sees cognition as a computational program that operates on symbolic representations (Cleeremans, 1997: 226). In such a framework there is no space for tacit knowledge since the latter cannot be symbolically represented. By contrast, within a phenomenological framework (such as the one adopted here), tacit knowledge has a special place: it is a sine qua non condition for explicit knowledge to exist. We get access to tacit knowledge through action and in retrospect. Aspects of tacit knowledge may be articulated, which, however, is not the same as 'converted' or 'translated' to explicit knowledge. To paraphrase Weick (1995: 18), we do not know what we know until we see what we have done.

The purpose of this chapter is to suggest a phenomenological (mainly Heideggerian) perspective through which tacit knowledge may be viewed. Such a framework, I will argue, dispels the misunderstandings that have arisen and suggests a more fruitful way forward. I will first explore the nature of tacit knowledge by drawing primarily on Polanyi (the inventor of the term, whose philosophy largely follows a phenomenological, especially Heideggerian, line of thinking) and secondarily on more recent phenomenological philosophers, notably Dreyfus and Taylor. Then I will explore how tacit knowledge has been understood in management studies. More specifically, I will critically explore how Polanyi's phenomenological understanding of tacit knowledge has been interpreted by Nonaka and Takeuchi, the two scholars who, more than anyone else, have helped popularize tacit knowledge in management studies, and whose interpretation has been adopted by several management authors (see for example, Ambrosini and Bowman, 2001; Baumard, 1999; Boisot, 1995; Davenport and Prusak, 1998; Devlin, 1999; Dixon, 2000; Dyck et al., 2005; Leonard and Sensiper, 1998; Spender, 1996; von Krogh et al., 2000; for exceptions see Brown and Duguid, 2000; Cook and Brown, 1999: 385 and 394–395; D'Eredita and Baretto, 2006; Gherardi, 2006; Gourlay, 2006; Styhre, 2004; Kreiner, 1999; Ribeiro and Collins, 2007; Tsoukas, 1996: 14; 1997: 830–831; Wenger, 1998: 67). Following this I will flesh out a phenomenological understanding of tacit knowledge, focusing on how the latter may be articulated, and will conclude with a summary of the argument.

PERSONAL KNOWING, TACIT KNOWLEDGE, AND SKILLFUL PERFORMANCE: A PRIMER IN POLANYI

Personal knowing

One of the most distinguishing features of Michael Polanyi's work is his insistence on overcoming well established dichotomies, such as theoretical versus practical knowledge, sciences versus the humanities or, to put it differently, his determination to show the common structure underlying all kinds of knowledge. Polanyi, a chemist turned philosopher, was categorical that all knowing involves *skillful action* and that the knower necessarily participates in all acts of understanding. For him the idea that there is such a thing as 'objective' knowledge, self-contained, detached, and independent of human action, was wrong and pernicious. '*All* knowing,' he insists, 'is personal knowing—participation through indwelling' (Polanyi and Prosch, 1975: 44; italics in the original).

Take, for example, the use of geographical maps. A map is a symbolic representation of a particular territory. As an explicit representation, a map is, in logical terms, no different from a theoretical system or a system of behavioral rules: they all aim at enabling purposeful human action, that is, respectively, to get from A to B; to predict; and to guide behavior. We may be familiar with a map *per se* but to *use* it we need to be able to relate it to the world outside the map. More specifically, to use a map we need to be able to do three things. First, we must identify our current position on the map ('you are here'). Secondly, we must find our itinerary on the map ('we want to go to the National Museum, which is over there'). And thirdly, to actually reach our destination, we must identify the itinerary by various landmarks in the landscape around us ('you go past the train station, and then turn left'). In other words, a map, no matter how elaborate it is, cannot read itself; it requires the judgment of a skilled reader who will relate the map to the world through both cognitive and sensual means (Polanyi and Prosch, 1975: 30; Polanyi, 1962: 18–20).

The same personal judgment is involved whenever abstract representations encounter the world of experience. We are inclined to think, for example, that Newton's laws can predict the position of a planet circling round the sun, at some future point in time, provided its current position is known. Yet this is not quite the case: Newton's laws cannot do that, only *we* can. The difference is crucial. The numbers entering the relevant formulae, from which we compute the future position of a planet, are readings on our instruments—they are not given, but need to be worked out. Similarly, we check the veracity of our predictions by comparing the results of our computations with the readings of the instruments—the predicted computations will rarely coincide with the readings observed and the significance of such a discrepancy needs to be worked out, again, by us (Polanyi, 1962: 19; Polanyi and Prosch, 1975: 30). Notice that, like in the case of map reading, the formulae of celestial mechanics cannot apply themselves; the personal judgment of a human agent is necessarily involved in applying abstract representations to the world.

The general point to be derived from the above examples is this: insofar as a formal representation has a bearing on experience, that is to say the extent to which a representation encounters the world, personal judgment is called upon to make an assessment of the inescapable gap between the representation and the world encountered. Given that the map is a representation of the territory, I need to be able to match my location in the territory with its representation on the map if I am to be successful in reaching my destination. Personal judgment cannot be prescribed by rules but relies essentially on the use of our senses (Polanyi, 1962: 19; 1966: 20; Polanyi and Prosch, 1975: 30). To the extent this happens, the exercise of personal judgment is a skillful performance, involving both the mind and the body.

The crucial role of the body in the act of knowing has been persistently underscored by Polanyi (cf. Gill, 2000: 44–50). As said earlier, the cognitive tools we use do not apply themselves; *we* apply them and, thus, we need to assess the extent to which our tools match aspects of the world. Insofar as our contact with the world necessarily involves our somatic equipment—'the trained delicacy of eye, ear, and touch' (Polanyi and Prosch, 1975: 31)—we are engaged in the art of establishing a correspondence between the explicit formulations of our formal representations (be they maps, scientific laws, or organizational rules) and the actual experience of our senses. As Polanyi (1969: 147) remarks, 'the way the body participates in the act of perception can be generalized further to include the bodily roots of all knowledge and thought. . . . Parts of our body serve as tools for observing objects outside and for manipulating them'.

Rules, particulars, and tacit knowledge

If we accept that there is, indeed, a 'personal coefficient' (Polanyi, 1962: 17) in all acts of knowing, which is manifested in a skillful performance carried out by the knower, what is the structure of such a skill? What is it that enables a map-reader to make competent use of the map to find his or her way around, a scientist to use the formulae of celestial mechanics to predict the next eclipse of the moon, and a physician to read an X-ray picture of a chest? For Polanyi the starting point towards answering this question is to acknowledge that 'the aim of a skillful performance is achieved by the observance of a set of rules which are not known as such to the person following them' (Polanyi, 1962: 49). A cyclist, for example, does not normally know the rule that keeps his or her balance, nor does a swimmer know what keeps him or her afloat. Interestingly, such ignorance is hardly detrimental to their effective execution of their respective tasks.

The cyclist keeps his or her balance by winding through a series of curvatures. One can formulate the rule explaining why the cyclist does not fall off the bicycle—'for a given angle of unbalance the curvature of each winding is inversely proportional to the square of the speed at which the cyclist is proceeding' (Polanyi, 1962: 50)—but such a rule would hardly be helpful to the cyclist. Why? As we will see below, this is partly because no rule is helpful in guiding action unless it is assimilated and stored in the unconscious mind. It is also partly because there is a host of other particular elements to be taken into account, which are not included in this rule and, crucially, are not—cannot be—known by the cyclist. Skills retain an element of opacity and unspecificity; they cannot be fully accounted for in terms of their particulars, since their practitioners do not ordinarily know what those particulars are; even when they do know them, as for example in the case of topographic anatomy, they do not know how to integrate them (Polanyi, 1962: 88–90). It is one thing to learn a list of bones, arteries, nerves, and viscera and quite another to know how precisely they are intertwined inside the body (Polanyi, 1962: 89).

This is the reason why, contrary to what Collins (2007: 258) argues, 'somatic-limit knowledge' *cannot* 'be converted into explicit rules.' Ribeiro and Collins (2007: 1431) define 'somatic-limit knowledge' as 'knowledge that is tacit only because it is so complex that human beings can master it only though socialization—that is guided instruction in a social group' (Ribeiro and Collins, 2007: 1431). Collins (2007: 259) invites us to join a thought experiment to demonstrate the contingently tacit nature of somatic-limit knowledge. Imagine conditions, he says, in which you could cycle so slowly, as for example would be the case in the lower gravitational field of the Moon, that when you were in danger of falling over, this would happen so slowly as to enable you to read and follow a set of balancing instructions that would allow you to regain your balance.

If that were to be the case, the limits of somatic knowledge would be overcome. In certain conditions, somatic-limit knowledge can be turned to explicit knowledge, argues Collins (2007: 258).

However, this does not seem to be a particularly convincing claim. The rules of bike-riding cannot be used by humans when cycling not due to the size of our brains and the speed of our mental operations, as Collins (2007: 258) implies, but because of our *embodied* involvement in a skillful action. More is going on in bike-riding than is captured by formal rules, although we do not explicitly know what; personal knowledge is 'logically unspecificable' (Polanyi, 1962: 56). We cannot logically know the bodily particulars of skillful performance that lapse from our consciousness, since attempting to find out would stop the performance. The price we pay for skillfully carrying out a task is partial ignorance of how we do so. We come to know the particulars in terms of 'their contribution to a reasonable result' and, insofar as this is the case, 'they have never been known and were still less willed in themselves' (Polanyi, 1962: 63). We are, of course, capable of formulating rules, and as Collins points out, Polanyi himself formulated the rule for bike-riding, but he also pointed out that the reason we cannot ride by following his rule is that 'there are a number of other factors to be taken into account in practice which are left out in the formulation of this rule' (Polanyi, 1962: 50).

How, then, do individuals know how to exercise their skills? In a sense they don't— know how ignorance cannot be eliminated. 'A mental effort,' notes Polanyi (1962: 62), 'has a heuristic effect: it tends to incorporate any available elements of the situation which are helpful for its purpose.' Any particular elements of the situation which may help the purpose of a mental effort are selected insofar as they contribute to the performance at hand, without the performer knowing them as they would appear in themselves. The particulars are *subsidiarily* known insofar as they contribute to the action performed. As Polanyi remarks:

> this is the usual process of unconscious trial and error by which *we feel our way* to success and may continue to improve on our success without specifiably knowing how we do it—for we never meet the causes of our success as identifiable things which can be described in terms of classes of which such things are members. This is how you invent a method of swimming without knowing that it consists in regulating your breath in a particular manner, or discover the principle of cycling without realizing that it consists in the adjustment of your momentary direction and velocity, so as to counteract continuously your momentary accidental unbalance.
>
> (Polanyi, 1962: 62, italics in the original)

When engaged in action, we cannot identify the subsidiary particulars that render our action possible. This has nothing to do with the speed of our mental operations, but is an ontological feature of skilled action. Our tacit knowledge of subsidiaries is rather *manifested* in our patterns of action (Taylor, 1991b: 308; 1995: 68–69).

There are two different kinds of awareness in exercising a skill. When an individual uses a hammer to drive a nail (one of Polanyi's favorite examples—see Polanyi, 1962: 55; Polanyi and Prosch, 1975: 33), that individual is aware of both the nail and the hammer but in a different way. One watches the effects of his or her strokes on the nail, and tries to hit it as effectively as possible. Driving the nail down is the main object of the person's attention and they are *focally* aware of it. At the same time, that individual is also aware of the feeling in the palm of their hand of holding the hammer. But such awareness is *subsidiary*: the feelings of holding the hammer in the palm are not an object of the hammerer's attention but an instrument of it. The watching of the action of hitting the nail is caused by being aware of it. As Polanyi and Prosch (1975: 33) remark: 'I know the feelings in the palm of my hand *by relying on them for attending to the hammer hitting the nail.* I may say that I have a *subsidiary* awareness of the feelings in my hand which is merged into my *focal awareness* of my driving the nail' (italics in the original).

The structure of tacit knowledge

If the above is accepted, it means that we can be aware of certain things in a way that is quite different from focusing our attention on them. One has a subsidiary awareness of holding the hammer in the act of focusing on hitting the nail. In being subsidiarily aware of holding a hammer the individual sees it as having a meaning that is wiped out if that person focuses attention on how they are holding the hammer. Subsidiary awareness and focal awareness are mutually exclusive (Polanyi, 1962: 56). If we switch our focal attention to particulars of which we had only subsidiary awareness before, their meaning is lost and the corresponding action becomes clumsy. If a pianist shifts his or her attention from the piece being played to how his or her fingers are moving; if a speaker focuses his or her attention on the grammar being used instead of the act of speaking; or if a carpenter shifts his or her attention from hitting the nail to holding the hammer, they will all be confused. We must rely (to be precise, we must learn to rely) subsidiarily on particulars for attending to something else, hence our knowledge of them remains *tacit* (Polanyi, 1966: 10; Winograd and Flores, 1987: 32). In the context of carrying out a specific task, we come to know a set of particulars without being able to identify them. In Polanyi's (1966: 4) memorable phrase, 'we can know more than we can tell.'

From Figure 21.1 it follows that tacit knowledge forms a triangle, at the three corners of which are the *subsidiary particulars*, the *focal target*, and the *knower* who links the two. It should be clear from the above that the linking of the particulars to the focal target does not happen automatically but is a result of the *act* of the knower. It is in this sense that Polanyi talks about all knowledge being *personal* and all knowing being *action*. No knowledge is possible without the integration of the subsidiaries to the focal target by a person. However, unlike explicit inference, such integration is essentially tacit and irreversible. Its tacitness was earlier discussed; its irreversible character can be seen if juxtaposed to explicit (especially deductive) inference, whereby one can unproblematically traverse between the premises and the conclusions. Such traversing is not possible with tacit integration: once an individual has learned to play the piano they cannot go back to being

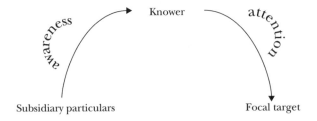

Figure 21.1 Personal Knowledge

ignorant of how to do it. While pianists can certainly focus their attention on how they move their fingers, thus making the performance clumsy to the point of paralyzing it, the musician can always recover their ability by casting their mind forward to the music itself.

With explicit inference, no such break-up and recovery are possible (Polanyi and Prosch, 1975: 39–42). When, for example, examining a legal syllogism or a mathematical proof an individual proceeds orderly from the premises, or a sequence of logical steps, to the conclusions. Nothing is lost and nothing is recovered—there is complete reversibility. The mathematician can go back to check the veracity of each constituent statement separately and how it logically links with its adjacent statements. Such reversibility is not, however, possible with tacit integration. Shifting attention to subsidiary particulars entails the loss of the skillful engagement with the activity at hand. By focusing on a subsidiary constituent of skilful action one changes the character of the activity one is involved with. There is no reversibility in this instance.

The structure of tacit knowing has three aspects: the functional, the phenomenal, and the semantic. The *functional* aspect consists in the *from–to* relation of particulars (or subsidiaries) to the focal target. Tacit knowing is from–to knowing: we humans know the particulars by relying on our awareness of them for attending to something else. Human awareness has a 'vectorial' character (Polanyi, 1969: 182): it moves from subsidiary particulars to the focal target (cf. Gill, 2000: 38–39). Or, in the words of Polanyi and Prosch (1975: 37–38), 'subsidiaries exist as such by bearing on the focus *to* which we are attending *from* them' (italics in the original). The *phenomenal* aspect involves the transformation of subsidiary experience into a new sensory experience. The latter appears through—it is created out of—the tacit integration of subsidiary sense perceptions. Finally, the *semantic* aspect is the meaning of subsidiaries, which is the focal target on which they bear (See Table 1).

Table 1   The three-dimensional structure of tacit knowing

◆ The *functional* dimension:
   From-to knowing: we know the particulars by relying on our awareness of them for attending to something else.
◆ The *phenomenal* dimension
   The transformation of subsidiary experience into a new sensory experience.
◆ The *semantic* dimension
   The meaning of subsidiaries (i.e. the focal target on which they bear).

The aspects of tacit knowing in Table 1 will become clearer with an example. Imagine a dentist exploring a tooth cavity with a probe. The exploration has a functional aspect: the dentist relies subsidiarily on his or her feeling of holding the probe in order to attend focally to the tip of the probe exploring the cavity. In doing so, the sensation of the probe pressing on the dentist's fingers is lost and, instead, he or she feels the point of the probe as it touches the cavity. This is the phenomenal aspect, whereby a new coherent sensory quality appears (i.e. the dentist's sense of the cavity) from the initial sense perceptions (i.e. the impact of the probe on the fingers). Finally, the probing has a semantic aspect: the dentist gets information by using the probe. That information is the meaning of his or her tactile experiences with the probe. As Polanyi (1966:13) notes, the dentist becomes aware of the feelings in his or her hand in terms of their meaning located at the tip of the probe, which is being attended to.

We engage in tacit knowing through virtually anything we do: we are normally una-ware of the movement of our eye muscles when we observe, of the rules of language when we speak, of our bodily functions as we move around. Indeed, to a large extent, our daily life consists of a huge number of small details of which we tend to be focally una-ware. When, however, we engage in more complex tasks, requiring even a modicum of specialized knowledge, then we face the challenge of how to assimilate the new knowledge—to interiorize it, dwell in it—in order to get things done efficiently and effectively. Polanyi gives the example of a medical student attending a course in X-ray diagnosis of pulmonary diseases. The student is initially puzzled: 'he can see in the X-ray picture of a chest only the shadows of the heart and the ribs, with a few spidery blotches between them. The experts seem to be romancing about figments of their imagination; he can see nothing that they are talking about' (Polanyi, 1962: 101).

At the early stage of training the student has not assimilated the relevant knowledge; unlike the dentist with the probe, the student cannot yet use it as a tool to carry out a diagnosis. The student, at this stage, is a remove from the diagnostic task as such: cannot think about it directly; the student rather needs to think about the relevant radiological knowledge first. If training is persevered with, however, 'he will gradually forget about the ribs and begin to see the lungs. And eventually, if he perseveres intelligently, a rich pano-rama of significant details will be revealed to him: of physiological variations and patho-logical changes, of scars, of chronic infections and signs of acute disease. He has entered a new world' (Polanyi, 1962: 101).

This is a useful illustration of the structure of tacit knowledge. The student has now interiorized the new radiological knowledge; the latter has become tacit knowledge, of which the student is subsidiarily aware while attending to the X-ray itself. Radiological knowledge exists now not as something unfamiliar, which needs to be learned and assimi-lated before a diagnosis can take place, but as a set of particulars—subsidiaries—which exist as such by bearing on the X-ray (the focus) *to* which the student is attending *from* them. Insofar as this happens, a phenomenal transformation has taken place: the heart, the ribs, and the spidery blotches gradually disappear and, instead, a new sensory expe-rience appears—the X-ray is no longer a collection of fragmented radiological images of bodily organs, but a representation of a chest full of meaningful connections. Thus, as well as having functional and phenomenal aspects, tacit knowledge has an important semantic aspect: the X-ray conveys information to an appropriately skilled observer. The meaning of the radiological knowledge, subsidiarily known and drawn upon by the stu-dent, is the diagnostic information received from the X-ray: it tells the student what it is that is being observed by using that knowledge.

It should be clear from the above that, for Polanyi, there is no difference between tan-gible (artifactual) things like probes, sticks, or hammers on the one hand, and intangible (symbolic) constructions such as radiological, linguistic, or cultural knowledge on the other—they are all *tools* enabling a skilled user to get things done. To use a tool properly we need to assimilate it and dwell in it. In Polanyi's (1969: 148) words, 'we may say that when we learn to use language, or a probe, or a tool, and thus make ourselves aware of these things as we are our body, we *interiorize* these things and *make ourselves dwell in them*' (italics in the original). The notion of *indwelling*, strongly reminiscent of a Heideggerian vocabulary (Dreyfus, 1991; Winograd and Flores, 1987; Spinosa et al., 1997), is crucial for Polanyi and turns up several times in his writings. It is only when we dwell on the tools we use, make them extensions of our own body, that we amplify the powers of our body and shift outwards the points at which we make contact with the world outside (Polanyi, 1962: 59, 1969: 148; Polanyi and Prosch, 1975: 37). Otherwise, our use of tools will be clumsy and will hinder getting things done.

We interiorize tools (artifactual and symbolic alike) when we are socialized into a socio-material practice (Benner, Hooper-Kyriakidis, and Stannard, 1999: 30–47; Polanyi, 1962: 101). For example, Gawande (2002), a surgical resident at a Boston hospital, gives a vivid account of his socialization in medical practice. Through dealing with particular incidents of patients, initially under the supervision of, and later in collaboration with, more experienced members of his practice, the trainee surgeon was learning to use the key categories implicated in a surgeon's job. Through his participation in this practice he was gradually learning to relate to his circumstances 'spontaneously' (Wittgenstein, 1980: 699), that is to say, 'uncritically' (Polanyi, 1962: 60): to use medical equipment, to recognize certain symptoms, to relate to colleagues and patients. The needles and how to use them in patients' chests, the X-rays and how to read them, and his relationships to others were not focal objects of thought for him, but subsidiary particulars—taken-for-granted aspects of the normal setting in all its recognizable stability and regularity.

The 'spontaneous' aspects of the activities practitioners undertake are primary and constitute what Wittgenstein (1979: 94) calls the 'inherited background,' against which practitioners make sense of their particular tasks (Shotter and Katz, 1996: 225; Taylor, 1993a: 325, 1995: 69). Practitioners are aware of the background but their awareness is largely 'inarticulate' (Taylor, 1991: 308) and implicit in their activity (Ryle, 1963: 40–41). The background provides the frame that renders their explicit representations comprehensible (Dreyfus, 1991: 102–4; Taylor, 1993a: 327–328; 1995: 69–70). As Wittgenstein (1979: 473–479) aptly noted, the basis of a socio-material practice is *activity*, not knowledge; *practice*, not thinking; *certainty*, not uncertainty. With the help of more experienced others we first learn to act, that is to accept the *certainties* of our particular socio-material practice (e.g. to use needles, to recognize the symptoms of pulmonary disease, to relate to patients) and, thus, relate spontaneously to our surroundings, and *later* we reflect on them. Experience comes first, reflection later.

Thus, in Gawande's case, the trainee surgeon was not training his mind alone, but also his hands and his whole body (how to interact with patients; the sort of footing he should be on with senior others). He may not have had descriptive terms for that embodied understanding—the manual dexterity he was developing with regard to feeling the human skin, for example. His embodied understanding was rather *manifested* in patterns of appropriate action, namely action that conformed to a sense of what was right. More generally, as Taylor (1991: 309) notes, agents' actions are responsive to this sense of rightness, although the 'norms' underlying their actions may be unformulated or in a fragmentary state.

The interiorization of a tool—its instrumentalization in the service of a purpose—is beneficial to users for it enables them to acquire new experiences and carry out more competently the task at hand (Dreyfus and Dreyfus, 2000). Compare, for example, one who learns driving a car to one who is an accomplished driver. The former may have learned how to change gear and to use the brake and the accelerator but cannot, yet, integrate those individual skills—the learner driver has not constructed a coherent perception of driving, the phenomenal transformation has not taken place yet. At the early stage, the driver is conscious of what needs to be done and feels the impact of the pedals on his or her foot and the gear stick on his or her palm; the driver has not learned to unconsciously correlate the performance of the car with the specific bodily actions he or she undertakes as a driver. The experienced driver, by contrast, is unconscious of the actions by which he or she drives—car instruments are tools whose use has been mastered, that is interiorized, and the experienced driver is therefore able to use them for the purpose of driving (Dreyfus and Dreyfus, 2000). By becoming unconscious of certain actions, the experienced driver expands the domain of experiences he or she can concentrate on as a driver (i.e. principally road conditions and other drivers' behavior).

The more general point to be derived from the preceding examples is formulated by Polanyi (1962: 61) as follows:

> we may say . . . that by the effort by which I concentrate on my chosen plane of operation I succeed in absorbing all the elements of the situation of which I might otherwise be aware in themselves, so that I become aware of them now in terms of the operational results achieved through their use.

This is important because we get things done, we achieve competence, by becoming unaware of how we do so. Of course one can take an interest in, and learn a great deal about, the gearbox and the acceleration mechanism but, to be able to drive, such knowledge needs to lapse into unconsciousness.

> This lapse into unconsciousness . . . is accompanied by a newly acquired consciousness of the experiences in question, on the operational plane. It is misleading, therefore, to describe this as the mere result of repetition; it is a structural change achieved by a repeated mental effort aiming at the instrumentalization of certain things and actions in the service of some purpose.
>
> Polanyi (1962: 62)

Notice that, for Polanyi, the shrinking of consciousness of certain things is, in the context of action, necessarily connected with the expansion of consciousness of other things. Particulars such as 'changing gear' and 'pressing the accelerator' are subsidiarily known, as the driver concentrates on the act of driving. Knowing something, then, is always a contextual issue and fundamentally connected to action (the 'operational plane'). My knowledge of gears is in the context of driving, and it is only in such a context that I am subsidiarily aware of that knowledge. If, however, I were a car mechanic, gears would constitute my focus of attention, rather than being an assimilated particular. Knowledge has a *recursive* form: given a certain context, we black-box—assimilate, interiorize, instrumentalize—certain things in order to concentrate—focus—on others. In another context, and at another level of analysis (cf. Bateson, 1979: 43), we can open up some of the previously black-boxed issues and focus our attention on them. In theory this is an endless process, although in practice there are institutional and practical limits to it.

In this way we can to some extent 'vertically integrate' our knowledge, although, as said earlier, what pieces of knowledge we *use* depends, at any point in time, on context. If the driver happens to be a car mechanic as well as an engineer he or she will have acquired three different bodies of knowledge, each having a different degree of abstraction, which, taken together, give his or her knowledge depth and make him or her a sophisticated driver (cf. Harper, 1987: 33). How, however, the driver draws on each one of them—that is, what is focally and what is subsidiarily known—depends on the context-in-use.

Moreover, each one of these bodies of knowledge stands on its own, and cannot be reduced to any of the others. The practical knowledge a driver has of their car cannot be replaced by the theoretical knowledge of an engineer; the practical knowledge an individual has of their own body cannot be replaced by the theoretical knowledge of a physician (cf. Polanyi, 1966: 20). In the social world, specialist, abstract, theoretical knowledge is necessarily refracted through the 'life world'—the taken-for-granted assumptions by means of which human beings organize their experience, knowledge, and transactions with the world (cf. Bruner, 1990: 35).

TACIT KNOWLEDGE IN MANAGEMENT STUDIES: THE GREAT MISUNDERSTANDING

Tacit knowledge in the SECI model

As mentioned earlier, 'tacit knowledge' has become very popular in management studies since the middle 1990s, thanks, to a large extent, to Nonaka and Takeuchi's (1995) influential *The Knowledge-Creating Company*. The cornerstone of Nonaka and Takeuchi's theory of organizational knowledge creation (the so-called SECI model) is the notion of 'knowledge conversion'—how tacit knowledge is 'converted' to explicit knowledge, and vice versa (Nonaka and Takeuchi, 1995: 61). The authors distinguish four modes of knowledge conversion: from tacit knowledge to tacit knowledge (socialization); from tacit knowledge to explicit knowledge (externalization); from explicit knowledge to explicit knowledge (combination); and from explicit knowledge to tacit knowledge (internalization). Tacit knowledge is converted to tacit knowledge through observation, imitation, and practice, in those cases where an apprentice learns from a master. Tacit knowledge is converted to explicit knowledge when it is articulated through concepts, models, hypotheses, metaphors, and analogies. Explicit knowledge is converted to explicit knowledge when different bodies of explicit knowledge are combined. And explicit knowledge is converted into tacit knowledge when it is first verbalized and then absorbed and internalized by the individuals involved.

The organizational knowledge creation process proceeds in cycles (in a spiral-like fashion), with each cycle consisting of five phases: the sharing of tacit knowledge among the members of a team; the creation of concepts whereby a team articulates its commonly shared mental model; the justification of concepts in terms of the overall organizational purposes and objectives; the building of an archetype which is a tangible manifestation of the justified concept; and the cross-leveling of knowledge, whereby a new cycle of knowledge creation may be created elsewhere (or even outside of the organization.)

To illustrate their theory, Nonaka and Takeuchi describe the product development process of Matsushita's Home Bakery, the first fully automated bread-making machine for home use, which was introduced to the Japanese market in 1987. There were three cycles in the relevant knowledge-creation process, with each cycle starting in order to either remove the weaknesses of the previous one or improve upon its outcome. The first cycle ended with the assemblage of a prototype, which, however, was not up to the design team's standards regarding the quality of bread it produced. This triggered the second cycle which started when Ikuko Tanaka, a software developer, took an apprenticeship with a master baker at the Osaka International Hotel. Her purpose was to learn how to knead bread dough properly in order to 'convert' later this know-how into particular design features of the bread-making machine under development. Following this, the third cycle came into operation whereby the commercialization team, consisting of people drawn from the manufacturing and marketing department, further improved the prototype that came out of the second cycle, and made it a commercially viable product.

To obtain a better insight into what Nonaka and Takeuchi mean by 'tacit knowledge' and how it is related to 'explicit knowledge' it is worth zooming into their description of the second cycle of the knowledge-creation process, since this is the cycle most relevant to the acquisition and 'conversion' of tacit knowledge. Below I quote in full the authors' description of this cycle (references and figures have been omitted).

> The second cycle began with a software developer, Ikuko Tanaka, sharing the tacit knowledge of a master baker in order to learn his kneading skill. A master baker learns the art of kneading, a critical step in bread making, following years of experience. However, such expertise is difficult to articulate in words. To capture this tacit knowledge, which usually takes a lot of imitation and practice to master, Tanaka proposed a creative solution. Why not train with the head baker at Osaka International Hotel, which had a reputation for making the best bread in Osaka, to study the kneading techniques? Tanaka learned her kneading skills through observation, imitation, and practice. She recalled:

> 'At first, everything was a surprise. After repeated failures, I began to ask where the master and I differed. I don't think one can understand or learn this skill without actually doing it. His bread and mine [came out] quite different even though we used the same materials. I asked why our products were so different and tried to reflect the difference in our skill of kneading.'

> Even at this stage, neither the head baker nor Tanaka was able to articulate knowledge in any systematic fashion. Because their tacit knowledge never became explicit, others within Matsushita were left puzzled. Consequently, engineers were also brought to the hotel and allowed to knead and bake bread to improve their understanding of the process. Sano, the division chief, noted, 'If the craftsmen cannot explain their skills, then the engineers should become craftsmen.'

> Not being an engineer, Tanaka could not devise mechanical specifications. However, she was able to transfer her knowledge to the engineers by using the phrase 'twisting stretch' to provide a rough image of kneading, and by suggesting the strength and speed of the propeller to be used in kneading. She would simply say, 'Make the propeller move stronger,' or 'Move it faster.' Then the engineers would adjust the machine specifications. Such a trial-and-error process continued for several months.

> Her request for a 'twisting stretch' movement was interpreted by the engineers and resulted in the addition inside the case of special ribs that held back the dough when the propeller turned so that the dough could be stretched. After a year of trial and error and working closely with other engineers, the team came up with product specifications that successfully reproduced the head baker's stretching technique and the quality of bread Tanaka had learned to make at the hotel. The team then materialized this concept, putting it together into a manual, and embodied it in the product.
>   (Nonaka and Takeuchi: 1995: 103–106; italics in the original)

How should we understand tacit knowledge?

Nonaka and Takeuchi's underlying assumption is that tacit knowledge is knowledge-on-its-way-to-symbolic-representation: a set of rules, as yet unformulated, that symbolically represent the activity an actor is involved in. The authors seem to think that what Tanaka learned through her apprenticeship with the master baker can be ultimately crystallized in a set of propositional 'if-then' statements (Tsoukas, 1998: 44–48), or what Oakeshott (1991: 12–15) called 'technical knowledge' and Ryle (1963: 28–32) 'knowing that.' In that sense, the tacit knowledge involved in kneading that Tanaka picked up through her apprenticeship—in Oakeshott's (1991: 12–15) terms, the 'practical knowledge' of kneading; and in Ryle's (1963: 28–32) terms, 'knowing how' to knead—the sort of knowledge that exists only *in use* and cannot be fully formulated in rules, is equivalent to the set of statements that represent it, namely it is equivalent to technical knowledge.

Tacit knowledge is thought to have the structure of a syllogism and, as such, can be reversed and, therefore, even mechanized (cf. Polanyi and Prosch, 1975: 40). What Tanaka was missing, the authors imply, were the premises of the syllogism, which she acquired through her sustained apprenticeship. Once they had been learned, it was a matter of time before she could put them together and arrive at the conclusion that 'twisting stretch' and 'the [right] movements required for the kneading propeller' (Nonaka and Takeuchi, 1995: 103–106) were what was required for designing the right bread-making machine.

However, although Nonaka and Takeuchi rightly acknowledge that Tanaka's apprenticeship was necessary because 'the art of kneading' could not be imparted in any other way, e.g. 'through reading memos and manuals' (Nonaka and Takeuchi, 1995: 103), they view her apprenticeship as merely an alternative mechanism for transferring knowledge. In terms of content, knowledge acquired through apprenticeship is not thought to be qualitatively different from knowledge acquired through reading manuals, since in both cases the content of knowledge can, ultimately, be formulated in rules—only the manner of its appropriation differs. The mechanism of knowledge acquisition may be different, but the result is the same.

The 'conduit metaphor of communication' (Lakoff, 1995: 116; Reddy, 1979; Tsoukas, 2005) that underlies Nonaka and Takeuchi's perspective—the view of ideas as objects which can be extracted from people and transmitted to others over a conduit—reduces practical knowledge to technical knowledge (cf. Costelloe, 1998: 325–326). However, while Tanaka, clearly, learned a technique during her apprenticeship, she acquired much more than technical knowledge, without even realizing it (Cleeremans, 1997; French and Cleeremans, 2002): she learned to make bread in a way that cannot be fully formulated in propositions but only *manifested* in her work. To treat practical knowledge as having a precisely definable content, which is initially located in the head of the practitioner and then 'translated' (Nonaka and Takeuchi, 1995: 105) into explicit knowledge, is to reduce what is known to what is representable, thus impoverishing the notion of practical knowledge. As Oakeshott remarks:

> a pianist acquires artistry as well as technique, a chess-player style and insight into the game as well as a knowledge of the moves, and a scientist acquires (among other things) the sort of judgment which tells him when his technique is leading him astray and the connoisseurship which enables him to distinguish the profitable from the unprofitable directions to explore.
>
> (Oakeshott, 1991: 15)

As should be clear from the preceding section, by viewing all knowing as essentially 'personal knowing' (Polanyi, 1962: 49), Polanyi highlights the skilled performance that all acts of knowing require: actors do not explicitly know all the rules they follow in the activity they are involved in. Like Oakeshott (1991), Polanyi (1962: 50) notes that 'rules of art can be useful, but they do not determine the practice of an art; they are maxims, which can serve as a guide to an art only if they can be integrated into the practical knowledge of the art. They cannot replace that knowledge.' It is precisely because what needs to be known cannot be specified in detail (Cleeremans, 1997) that the relevant knowledge must be passed from master to apprentice. It is not a question of mental speed, as Collins (2007: 258–259) implies, but of *radical ignorance*: even the master does not fully know what he or she knows; a lot of that knowledge is embodied and no descriptive terms to express it are possessed.

However, what cannot be expressed may well be manifested. And what may not be linguistically imparted may well be imitated.

> To learn by example is to submit to authority. You follow your master because you trust his manner of doing things even when you cannot analyse and account in detail for its effectiveness. By watching the master and emulating his efforts in the presence of his example, the apprentice unconsciously picks up the rules of the art, including those which are not explicitly known to the master himself. These hidden rules can be assimilated only by a person who surrenders himself to that extent uncritically to the imitation of another.
>
> (Polanyi, 1962: 53)

Like Polanyi's medical student discussed earlier, Tanaka was initially puzzled by what the master baker was doing—'at first, everything was a surprise' (Nonaka and Takeuchi, 1995: 104), as she put it. Her 'repeated failures' were due not to lack of knowledge as such, but due to not having interiorized the relevant knowledge yet. When, through practice, she began to assimilate the knowledge involved in kneading bread—namely, when she became subsidiarily aware of how she was kneading—she could, subsequently, turn her focal awareness to the task at hand: *kneading* bread, as opposed to imitating the master. Knowledge now became a tool to be tacitly known and uncritically used in the service of an objective. 'Kneading bread' ceased to be an object of focal awareness and became an instrument for actually kneading bread—a subsidiarily known tool for getting things done (Winograd and Flores, 1987: 27–37). For Tanaka to 'convert' her kneading skill into explicit knowledge, she would need to focus her attention on her subsidiary knowledge, thereby becoming focally aware of it. In that event, however, she would no longer be engaged in the same activity, namely *bread kneading*, but in the activity of thinking *about* bread kneading, which is a different matter. The particulars of her skill were 'logically unspecifiable' (Polanyi, 1962: 56): their specification would logically contradict and practically paralyze the performance at hand.

Of course, one might acknowledge this and still insist, along with Ambrosini and Bowman (2001) and Eraut (2000), that Tanaka could, *ex post facto*, reflect on her kneading skill, in the context of discussing bread kneading with her colleagues (the engineers), and turn it into explicit knowledge. But this would be a problematic claim to make for, in such an event, she would no longer be describing her kneading skill *in toto* but only its technical part: that which is possible to represent in rules, principles, and maxims—in short, in propositions. What she has to say about the 'ineffable' (Polanyi, 1962: 87–95) part of her skill, that which is tacitly known, she has already 'said' through her action—the kneading of bread (cf. Oakeshott, 1991: 14; Janik, 1992: 37). As Polanyi so perceptively argued, you cannot view subsidiary particulars as they allegedly are in themselves for they exist always in conjunction with the focus through which you attend to them, and that makes them unspecifiable. In his words:

> Subsidiary or instrumental knowledge, as I have defined it, is not known in itself but is known in terms of something focally known, to the quality of which it contributes; and to this extent it is unspecifiable. Analysis may bring subsidiary knowledge into focus and formulate it as a maxim or as a feature in a physiognomy, but such specification is in general not exhaustive. Although the expert diagnostician, taxonomist and cotton-classer can indicate their clues and formulate their maxims, they know many more things than they can tell, knowing them only in practice, as instrumental particulars, and not explicitly, as objects. The knowledge of such particulars is therefore ineffable, and the pondering of a judgment in terms of such particulars is an ineffable process of thought.
>
> (Polanyi, 1962: 88)

If the above is accepted, it follows that Tanaka neither 'transferred' her tacit knowledge to the engineers, nor did she 'convert' her kneading skill into explicit knowledge, as Nonaka and Takeuchi (1995: 104 and 105) suggest. She could do neither of these things simply because, following Polanyi's and Oakeshott's definitions of tacit and practical knowledge respectively, skillful knowing contains an ineffable element; it is based on an act of personal insight that is essentially inexpressible.

Articulating Tacit Knowledge

Even if the above is accepted, we still need to address a nagging question: how are we to understand Tanaka's concept of 'twisting stretch,' which turned out to be so crucial for the making of Matsushita's bread-making machine? If this concept did not help 'convert' tacit to explicit knowledge, what did it do? Or, to put it more generally, does the ineffability of skilled performance imply that we cannot talk about it? That the skills involved in, say, bread making, managing, teaching, selling, diagnosing patients, and so on will ultimately be mystical experiences outside the realm of reasoned inquiry? Are there ways to improve a practical activity if its core remains ineffable?

As argued earlier, a socio-material practice provides its members with an inarticulate background against which practitioners make focal sense of their particular tasks. When socialized in a practice, its members learn how to use the key distinctions that define it (for example, what constitutes competence, orientation to time, relations to others, etc.) (Tsoukas, 2009a: 943; 2010: 50; Yanow and Tsoukas, 2009: 1349–50). Through engagement in the world of their practice, its members acquire familiarity with it, which, later, they may seek to formulate explicitly in thought. Hatsopoulos and Hatsopoulos (1999: 144–5), for example, describe how, through trial and error, they discovered the usefulness of certain business principles, such as an empathic approach to employees, seeking diversity of backgrounds on the board, and understanding investors' non-financial motives.

Increased familiarity helps practitioners interiorize the tools they use in their practice and, thus, focus on the tasks at hand. Repeated experiences in the carrying out of tasks are unconsciously linked by practitioners to form a pattern (Klein, 1998: 31–33, 2003: 21). Patterns enable practitioners to recognize situations as typical or anomalous, and thus adopt relevant courses of action. Knowledge of patterns is tacit: repeated experiences, organized in patterns, are internalized and subsidiarily drawn upon by practitioners when faced with particular tasks. Patterns have a radial structure: the latter is formed around a relatively stable part made up of prototypical (central) members and an unstable part made up of non-prototypical (peripheral) members, radiating at various conceptual distances from the central members (Johnson, 1993; Lakoff, 1987). For example, Cimino describes this in the context of medical practice as follows:

> It is only by seeing patient after patient that the recognition patterns develop. From these experiences, the physician can build a set of case prototypes by which to compare future patients. These prototypes can help recognize patterns ... They can also help the physician recognize when something is out of place
> (Cimino, 1999: 116; for several similar examples, see Klein, 1998, 2003)

The radial structure of practical experience is important since it enables practitioners to judge prototypicality and to spontaneously undertake appropriate action (Klein, 1998: 149) without making tacit knowledge of patterns explicit. Rather, focal awareness of a particular issue subsidiarily draws on familiar patterns in the undertaking of action. In such cases, the practitioner is *absorbed* in the task at hand: he or she spontaneously *copes* with (responds to) the solicitations of the task at hand (Dreyfus, 1991: 69). When, however, the results of action undertaken do not meet the practitioner's tacit expectations, his or her absorbed coping with the situation calls for *deliberate* reflection. What was previously subsidiary now becomes focal (Patel et al., 1999: 95–96).

For example, Yanow and Tsoukas (2009) describe how Dr T., an experienced professor of psychology, deviated from his flow of teaching to respond to a feeling of puzzlement he had momentarily sensed in his students. 'What was previously transparent or subsidiary—namely, what he needed to do, as he had done many times before, to explain the subject of his lecture—becomes more explicitly focal,' note Yanow and Tsoukas (2009: 1356). Accordingly, Dr T. improvises and inserts a relevant example in his presentation. Notice, however, that the tacit background, the 'unexplicited horizon' (Taylor, 1995: 68) within which Dr T. was acting, is not something of which he was simply unaware as I am unaware of *Phobaeticus chani*, allegedly the longest insect in the world, recently discovered in Borneo. Rather, his unawareness was different: it was *focal* unawareness. The background was known, albeit subsidiarily, and could, thus, be in principle articulated. 'What I bring out to articulacy,' notes Taylor (1995: 69), 'is what I 'always knew,' as we might say, or what I had a 'sense' of, even if I didn't 'know' it.' The background has a paradoxical status. 'It can be made explicit, because we aren't completely unaware of it. But the expliciting itself supposes a background' (Taylor, 1995: 70).

Thus, when Dr T shifts his attention from being absorbed in the task at hand (i.e. lecturing) to the tool with which he was accomplishing it (e.g. what example to use to illustrate his point), that shift occurs against a new background—that of a *temporary breakdown*, namely a mild disruption of absorbed coping, which forces Dr T. to pay *deliberate* attention to how he is accomplishing the task at hand (Dreyfus, 1991: 72–3; Yanow and Tsoukas, 2009: 1352). The new background, created by disruption (temporary breakdown), makes it possible for aspects of the old background to be articulated. This is a process that can go on and on.

To put it differently, at any point in time, aspects of the background within which a particular task is carried out may be brought to awareness when probed in the context of a temporary breakdown. We are not aware of the full implications of what we do until we encounter an obstacle—a Platonic *aporia*—that forces us to look back at the patterns we tacitly know in order to resume our action afresh (Patel et al., 1999: 96; Cleeremans, 1997: 227). Thus, looked at patterns serve as 'displays' (Weick, 1977: 279) available for inspection: actors can articulate further what was already included in the background in an inchoate form. To paraphrase Weick (1995: 23), actors discover their tacit knowledge by undertaking action and observing the consequences. Since, as argued earlier, subsidiaries are *manifested* rather than specified, their patterns are accessed when they are given the opportunity to be *displayed*. Displays are brought forward (and thus a new background is created) by temporary breakdowns, thus forcing actors to reflect, even momentarily, on what they do.

What do we do when we reflect on our absorbed coping? We re-punctuate the distinctions underlying the practical activities we are involved in. We pay attention to certain hitherto unnoticed aspects of our activities and see connections among items previously thought unconnected (D'Eredita and Baretto, 2006: 1834; Weick, 1995: 87 and 126). Through attention-drawing forms of talk (e.g. 'look at this,' 'have you thought about this in that way?', 'try this,' 'imagine this,' 'compare this to that') we are moved to *re*-view the situation we are in, to relate to our circumstances in a different way. From a Wittgensteinian perspective, Shotter and Katz summarize succinctly this process as follows:

> to gain an explicit understanding of our everyday, practical activities, we can make use of the very same methods we used in gaining that practical kind of understanding in the first place— that is, we can use the self-same methods for drawing *our* attention to how people draw each other's attention to things, as they themselves (we all?) in fact use!
>
> (Shotter and Katz, 1996: 230)

Notice what Shotter and Katz are saying: we learn to engage in practical activities through our participation in socio-material practices, under the guidance of people who are more experienced than us (MacIntyre, 1985: 181–203; Taylor, 1993b); people who, by drawing our attention to certain things, make us 'see connections' (Wittgenstein, 1958: No.122; see also Shotter, 1993; 2005), similarly to the way in which the master baker was drawing Tanaka's attention to certain aspects of bread kneading. Through her subsequent conversations with the engineers, Tanaka was able to articulate her understanding of the kneading activity she had been involved in, by having her attention drawn to how the master baker was drawing her attention to kneading—hence the concept of 'twisting stretch' came up. It is in this sense that Wittgenstein talks of language as issuing reminders of things we *already* know: 'Something that we know when no one asks us, but no longer know when we are supposed to give an account of it, is something that we need to *remind* ourselves of' (Wittgenstein, 1958: No.89; italics in the original).

In other words, in her apprenticeship, Tanaka came eventually to practice 'twisting stretch' but she did not focally know it. She needed to be 'reminded' of it. How did it happen? Dialogically, through conversational interactions with the engineers (Tsoukas, 2009a, 2009b). 'Twisting stretch,' as I have explained elsewhere (Tsoukas, 2009a: 947), is a new distinction—a novel combination of two concepts, created through extensive dialogical exchanges between Tanaka and the engineers, whereby the property of the modifier ('twisting') applies to the head concept ('stretch'), thus providing an image of the kneading movement required. (For additional mechanisms whereby new distinctions come about, see Tsoukas, 2009a, 2009b).

More generally, when dialogue is productive we have opportunities to recursively punctuate our understanding and, thus, see new connections and '[give] prominence to distinctions which our ordinary forms of language easily makes us overlook' (Wittgenstein, 1958: No.132). As Merleau-Ponty (1962: 354) so perceptively remarked, when engaged in a productive dialogue, '[my interlocutor] draws from me thoughts which I had no idea

I possessed.' Through dialogical exchanges we are led to notice certain aspects of our circumstances that, due to their familiarity, remain hidden ('one is unable to notice something—because it is always before one's eyes' (Wittgenstein, 1958: No.129). This is, then, the sense in which, although skilled performance is ultimately ineffable, it nonetheless can be talked about: through dialogically reminding ourselves of it, we notice certain important features which had hitherto escaped our attention and can now be seen in a new context. Consequently, we are led to relate to our circumstances in new ways and, thus, see new ways forward.

CONCLUSIONS

Tacit knowledge has often been misunderstood in management studies, largely because of the tacitly (!) accepted cognitivist framework and the associated conduit metaphor of communication adopted by researchers. While Nonaka and Takeuchi were among the first to see the enormous importance of tacit knowledge in organizations and systematically explore it, their interpretation of tacit knowledge as knowledge-not-yet-symbolically-represented—namely, knowledge awaiting its 'translation' or 'conversion' into explicit knowledge—an interpretation that has been widely adopted in management studies, is erroneous: it ignores the essential ineffability of tacit knowledge, thus reducing it to what can be formulated in rules.

I have argued here that tacit and explicit knowledge are not the two ends of a continuum but two sides of the same coin: even the most explicit kind of knowledge is underlain by tacit knowledge. Tacit knowledge consists of a set of particulars of which we are subsidiarily aware as we focus on something else. Tacit knowing is vectorial: we know the particulars by relying on our awareness of them for attending to something else. Since subsidiaries exist as such by bearing on the focus *to* which we are attending *from* them, they cannot be separated from the focus and examined independently, for if this is done, their meaning will be lost. While we can certainly focus on particulars, we cannot do so in the same context of action (the inarticulate background) in which we are subsidiarily aware of them. Moreover, by focusing on particulars *after* a particular action has been performed, we are *not* focusing on them as they bear on the original focus of action, for their meaning is necessarily derived from their connection to that focus. When we focus on particulars we do so in a *new* context of action (a new inarticulate background), brought about by a temporary breakdown. Thus, the idea that somehow one can focus on a set of particulars and convert them into explicit knowledge is unsustainable.

The ineffability of tacit knowledge does not mean that we cannot discuss the skilled performances in which we are involved. We can—indeed, should—discuss them, provided we stop insisting on 'converting' tacit knowledge and, instead, start recursively drawing our attention to how we draw each other's attention to things. Dialogical interactions help us re-orientate ourselves to how we relate to others and the world around us, thus enabling us to talk and act differently. We can command a clearer view of our tasks at hand if we 're-mind' ourselves of how we do things so that distinctions which we had previously not noticed, and features which had previously escaped our attention, may be brought forward. Contrary to what some scholars suggest (Ambrosini and Bowman, 2001; Sternberg et al., 2000), we do not so much need to operationalize tacit knowledge (as explained earlier, we could not do this, even if we wanted to) as to find new ways of talking, fresh forms of interacting, and novel ways of distinguishing and connecting. Tacit knowledge cannot be 'captured,' 'translated,' or 'converted' but displayed—manifested— in what we do. New knowledge comes about not when the tacit is converted to explicit, but when tacit knowledge is re-punctuated (articulated) through dialogical interaction.

REFERENCES

Ambrosini, V. and Bowman, C. (2001) Tacit knowledge: Some suggestions for operation-alization. *Journal of Management Studies*, 38: 811–829.

Argyris, C. (1999) Tacit knowledge and management. In R.J. Sternberg and J.A. Horvath (Eds.), *Tacit Knowledge in Professional Practice*. Mahwah, NJ: Lawrence Erlbaum: 123–140.

Aristotle (2006) *Metaphysics*, Stilwell, KS: Digiereads.com, translated by: W.D. Ross.

Barnard, C. (1968) *The Functions of the Executive*. Cambridge, MA: Harvard University Press.

Bateson, G. (1979). *Mind and Nature*. Toronto: Bantam.

Bell, D. (1999) The axial age of technology foreword. In D. Bell (Ed.), *The Coming of the Post-Industrial Society*. New York: Basic Books, Special Anniversary Edition: 9–85.

Benner, P., Hooper-Kyriakidis, P., and Stannard, D. (1999) *Clinical Wisdom and Interventions in Critical Care*. Philadelphia, PA: Saunders.

Boisot, M.H. (1995). *Information Space: A Framework for Learning in Organizations, Institutions and Culture*. London, UK: Routledge.

Brown, J.S. and Duguid, P. (2000) *The Social Life of Information*. Boston: Harvard Business School Press.

Bruner, J. (1990) *Acts of Meaning*. Cambridge: Harvard University Press.

Cimino, J.J. (1999) Development of expertise in medical practice. In R.J. Sternberg and J.A. Horvath (eds.), *Tacit Knowledge in Professional Practice*. Mahwah, NJ: Lawrence Erlbaum: 101–120.

Cleeremans, A. (1997) Principles for implicit learning. In D.C. Berry (ed.), *How Implicit is Implicit Learning?* Oxford: Oxford University Press.

Collins, H. (2001) Tacit knowledge, trust and the Q of Sapphire, *Social Studies of Science*, 31: 71–85.

Collins, H. (2007) Bicycling on the moon: Collective tacit knowledge and somatic-limit tacit knowledge. *Organization Studies*, 28: 257–262.

Cook, S.D.N. and Brown, J.S. (1999) Bridging epistemologies: The generative dance between organizational knowledge and organizational knowing. *Organization Science*, 10: 381–400.

Cook, S.D.N. and Yanow, D. (1996) Culture and organizational learning. In M.D. Cohen and L.S. Sproull (eds.), *Organizational Learning*. Thousand Oaks, CA: Sage: 430–459.

Costelloe, T. (1998) Oakeshott, Wittgenstein, and the practice of social science. *Journal for the Theory of Social Behaviour*, 28: 323–347.

D'Eredita, M.A. and Baretto, C. (2006) How does tacit knowledge proliferate? An epi-sode-based perspective. *Organization Studies*, 27: 1821–1842.

Davenport, T.H. and Prusak L. (1998) *Working Knowledge*. Cambridge, MA: Harvard University Press.

Devlin, K. (1999) *Infosense*. New York: W.H. Freeman and Co.

Dixon, N.M. (2000) *Common Knowledge*. Boston: Harvard Business School Press.

Dreyfus, H.L. (1991) *Being-in-the-world: A Commentary on Heidegger's Being and Time, Division I*. Cambridge: MIT Press.

Dreyfus, H.L. and Dreyfus, S.E. (2000) *Mind over Machine*. New York: Free Press.

Drucker, P. (1993) *Post-Capitalist Society*. Oxford: Butterworth/Heinemann.

Dyck, B., Starke, F., Mischke, A., and Mauws, M. (2005) Learning to build a car: An empirical investigation of organizational learning. *Journal of Management Studies*, 42: 387–416.

Eraut, M. (2000) Non-formal learning and tacit knowledge in professional work. *British Journal of Educational Psychology*, 70: 113–136.

Feyerabend, P. (1999) *Conquest of Abundance*. Chicago: The University of Chicago Press.

Follett, M.P. (1924) *Creative Experience*. New York: Longmans.

French, R.M. and Cleeremans, A. (eds.) (2002) *Implicit Learning and Consciousness*. Hove, UK: Psychology Press.

Gawande, A. (2002) *Complications*. New York: Metropolitan Books.

Gherardi, S. (2006) *Organizational Knowledge: The Texture of Workplace Learning*. Oxford: Blackwell.

Gill, J.H. (2000) *The Tacit Mode*. Albany: State University of New York Press.

Gourlay, S. (2006) Conceptualizing knowledge creation: A critique of Nonaka's theory, *Journal of Management Studies*, 43: 1416–1436.

Gregory, S. (1999) Tacit knowledge in sales. In R.J. Sternberg and J.A. Horvath (Eds.), *Tacit Knowledge in Professional Practice*. Mahwah, NJ: Lawrence Erlbaum: 183–192.

Harper, D. (1987) *Working Knowledge*. Berkeley: University of California Press.

Hatsopoulos, N.G and Hatsopoulos, G.N. (1999) The role of tacit knowledge in management. In R.J. Sternberg and J.A. Horvath (eds.), *Tacit Knowledge in Professional Practice*. Mahwah, NJ: Lawrence Erlbaum: 141–152.

Janik, A. (1992) Why is Wittgenstein important? In B. Goranzon and M. Florin (eds.), *Skill and Education*. London: Springer-Verlag: 33–40.

Klein, G. (1998) *Sources of Power*. Cambridge, MA: MIT Press.

Klein, G. (2003) *The Power of Intuition*, New York: Currency Doubleday.

Kreiner, K. (1999) Knowledge and mind. *Advances in Management Cognition and Organizational Information Processing*, 6: 1–29.

Lakoff, G. (1995) Body, brain, and communication. In J. Brook and I.A. Boal (eds.), *Resisting the Virtual Life*. San Francisco: City Lights: 115–129.

Leonard, D. and Sensiper S. (1998) The role of tacit knowledge in group innovation. *California Management Review*, 40(3): 112–132.

MacIntyre, A. (1985) *After Virtue*. London: Duckworth, Second Edition.

Mansell, R. and When, U. (1998) *Knowledge Societies*. New York: Oxford University Press.

Merleau-Ponty, M. (1962). *Phenomenology of Perception*. London: Routledge [translated by C. Smith].

Nonaka, I. and Takeuchi, H. (1995) *The Knowledge-Creating Company*. New York: Oxford University Press.

Nonaka, I. and von Krogh, G. (2009) Tacit knowledge and knowledge conversion: Controversy and advancement in organizational knowledge creation theory. *Organization Science*, 20: 635–652.

Nonaka, I., von Krogh, G., and Voelpel, S. (2006) Organizational knowledge creation theory: Evolutionary paths and future advances. *Organization Studies*, 27: 1179–1208.

Oakeshott, M. (1991) *Rationalism in Politics and Other Essays*, New and Expanded Edition. Indianapolis: Liberty Press.

Patel, V.L., Arocha, J.F., and Kaufman, D.R. (1999) Expertise and tacit knowledge in medicine. In R.J. Sternberg and J.A. Horvath (eds.), *Tacit Knowledge in Professional Practice*. Mahwah, NJ: Lawrence Erlbaum: 75–100.

Polanyi, M. (1962) *Personal Knowledge*. Chicago: The University of Chicago Press.

Polanyi, M. (1966) *The Tacit Dimension*. London: Routledge and Kegan Paul.

Polanyi, M. (1969) In M. Grene (ed.) *Knowing and Being*. Chicago: The University of Chicago Press.

Polanyi, M. and Prosch, H. (1975) *Meaning*. Chicago: The University Of Chicago Press.

Ribeiro, R. and Collins, H. (2007) The bread-making machine: Tacit knowledge and two types of action. *Organization Studies*, 28: 1417–1433.

Ryle, G. (1963) *The Concept of Mind*. London: Penguin.

Sandberg, J. and Pinnington, P. (2009) Professional competence as ways of being: An existential ontological perspective. *Journal of Management Studies*, 46: 1138–1170.

Schön, D. (1983). *The Reflective Practitioner*. New York: Basic Books.

Searle, J.R. (1992) *The Rediscovery of Mind*. Cambridge, MA: MIT Press.

Shotter, J. (1993) *Conversational Realities*. London: Sage.

Shotter, J. (2005) 'Inside the moment of managing': Wittgenstein and the everyday dynamics of our expressive-responsive activities. *Organization Studies*, 26: 113–135.

Shotter, J. and Katz, A.M. (1996) Articulating a practice from within the practice itself: Establishing formative dialogues by the use of a 'social poetics.' *Concepts and Transformation*, 1: 213–237.

Simon, H. (1965) *Administrative Behavior*. New York: Free Press.

Spaeth, E.B. Jr (1999) What a lawyer needs to learn. In R.J. Sternberg and J.A. Horvath (eds.), *Tacit Knowledge in Professional Practice*. Mahwah, NJ: Lawrence Erlbaum: 21–36.

Spender, J. C. (1996) Making knowledge the basis of a dynamic theory of the firm. *Strategic Management Journal*, 17: 45–62.

Spinosa, C., Flores, F., and Dreyfus, H.L. (1997) *Disclosing New Worlds*. Cambridge, MA: The MIT Press.

Stehr, N. (1994) *Knowledge Societies*. London: Sage.

Sternberg, R.J., Forsythe, G.B., Hedlund, J., Horvath, J.A, Wagner, R.K., Williams, W.M., Snook, S.A., and Grigorenko, E. (2000) *Practical Intelligence in Everyday Life*. Cambridge: Cambridge University Press.

Styhre, A. (2004) Rethinking knowledge: A Bergsonian critique of the notion of tacit knowledge. *British Journal of Management*, 15: 177–188.

Taylor, C. (1991) The dialogical self. In D.R. Hiley, J.F. Bohman, and R. Shusterman (eds.), *The Interpretive Turn*. Ithaca, NY: Cornell University Press: 304–314.

Taylor, C. (1993a) Engaged agency and background in Heidegger. In C. Guignon (ed.), *The Cambridge Companion to Heidegger*. Cambridge, UK: Cambridge University Press: 317–336.

Taylor, C. (1993b) To follow a rule. In C. Calhoun, E. LiPuma and M. Postone (eds.), *Bourdieu: Critical Perspectives*. Cambridge, UK: Policy Press: 45–59.

Taylor, C. (1995) *Philosophical Arguments*. Cambridge, MA: Harvard University Press.

Thurow, L. (2000) *Creating Wealth*. London: Nicholas Brealey Publishing Ltd.

Toulmin, S. (1990) *Cosmopolis*. Chicago: University of Chicago Press.

Toulmin, S. (2001) *Return to Reason*. Cambridge, MA: Harvard University Press.

Tsoukas, H. (1996). The firm as a distributed knowledge system: A constructionist approach. *Strategic Management Journal*, 17: 11–25.

Tsoukas, H. (1997) The tyranny of light: The temptations and the paradoxes of the information society. *Futures*, 29: 827–843.

Tsoukas, H. (1998). Forms of knowledge and forms of life in organized contexts. In R.C. H. Chia (ed.), *In the Realm of Organization*. London: Routledge: 43–66.

Tsoukas, H. (2005) *Complex Knowledge*. Oxford: Oxford University Press.

Tsoukas, H. (2009a) A dialogical approach to the creation of new knowledge in organizations. *Organization Science*, 20: 941–957.

Tsoukas, H. (2009b) Creating organizational knowledge dialogically: An outline of a theory. In T. Rickards, M.A. Runco and S. Moger (eds.), *The Routledge Companion to Creativity*. London: Routledge: 160–176.

Tsoukas, H. and Vladimirou, E. (2001) What is organizational knowledge? *Journal of Management Studies*, 38: 973–993.

Varela, F.J., Thompson, E., and Rosch, E. (1991). *The Embodied Mind*. Cambridge, MA: MIT Press.

Vickers, G. (1983) *The Art of Judgment*. London: Harper and Row.

Von Krogh, G., Ichijo, K., and Nonaka, I. (2000) *Enabling Knowledge Creation*, New York: Oxford University Press.

Weick, K.E. (1977) Enactment processes in organizations. In B.M. Staw and G.R. Salancik (eds.), *New Directions in Organizational Behavior*. Chicago, IL: St Clair Press: 267–300.

Weick, K. (1995) *Sensemaking in Organizations*. Thousand Oaks, CA: Sage.

Wenger, E. (1998) *Communities of Practice*. Cambridge: Cambridge University Press.

Winograd, T. and Flores, F. (1987) *Understanding Computers and Cognition*. Reading, MA: Addison-Wesley.

Wittgenstein, L. (1958). *Philosophical Investigations*. Oxford: Blackwell.

Wittgenstein, L. (1979). *On Certainty*. Edited by G.E.M. Anscombe and G.H. von Wright. Translated by D. Paul and G.E.M. Anscombe. Oxford: Blackwell.

Wittgenstein, L. (1980) *Remarks on the Philosophy of Psychology*, vol.II. Edited by G.H. von Wright and H. Nyman, translated by C.G. Luckhardt and M.A.E. Aue. Chicago: University of Chicago Press.

Yanow, D. and Tsoukas, H. (2009) What is reflection-in-action?: A phenomenological account. *Journal of Management Studies*, 46: 1339–1364.

22

Organizing Knowledge in Social, Alliance, and Organizational Networks

RAYMOND VAN WIJK,
FRANS A.J. VAN DEN BOSCH, AND
HENK W. VOLBERDA

ABSTRACT

Reviewing the growing body of literature on how networks facilitate the management and organization of knowledge, in this chapter three types of networks are discerned: social networks, alliance networks, and organizational networks. Studies of social networks have mainly focused on how the structural and relational characteristics of ties influence knowledge seeking and transfer. Research on alliance networks has mainly concentrated on how firms access the multiple complementary knowledge bases of partners in an alliance portfolio, and on how knowledge is acquired among firms. Studies of organizational networks have centered on how different structures and management processes facilitate knowledge creation and transfer within firms. Since each research stream has contributed uniquely to the study of knowledge and networks, this chapter emphasizes how these three network types complement each other. Finally, studies examining the creation of relational and alliance capabilities are reviewed. The insights developed in this chapter are employed to identify promising future research directions.

INTRODUCTION

Both knowledge and networks are crucial to many organizations (Arikan, 2009; Cross and Cummings, 2004; Zaheer and Bell, 2005). The competitive landscape propels firms to innovate and explore new opportunities, so as to outmaneuver competitors and achieve a competitive edge. Since knowledge is a bedrock ingredient of innovation, it has become significant to success (Grant, 1996). However, the knowledge required to innovate is not always readily available within a firm. To meet such deficiencies, firms can create knowledge internally or they can acquire knowledge through external constituents (Van Wijk et al., 2008). Networks benefit firms in gaining access to knowledge, in facilitating learning processes, in transferring knowledge, and in fostering knowledge integration and creation. In this chapter, state-of-the-art and received insights of how networks facilitate the management and organization of knowledge and learning are reviewed and consolidated, while prospective research avenues are discussed.

The study of knowledge and networks in the management field traces its origins back to the 1950s and 1960s, with seminal contributions such as those of Cangelosi and Dill (1965), Penrose (1959), and Evan (1965). Over the years, research in knowledge and networks has developed into two strong individual research streams. Recently firms have started to establish networks to gain access to and facilitate the organization and management of knowledge. Research in which knowledge and networks are examined conjointly has therefore gained momentum predominantly during the past decades.

Networks are characterized by linkages between actors that are created in a temporal or semi-temporal fashion, commonly centering on a problem or issue (Baker, 1992). Actors in the network seek to access each other's resources, to learn from each other and to integrate each other's knowledge so as to solve the problem or to pass the issue, and a new series of linkages can be formed with the same or a different set of actors.

Firms progressively develop and nurture networks as a means to seek and transfer knowledge, yet their use has been surrounded by ambiguity. The term 'network' has become an evocative metaphor ascribed to many collaborative ventures or relationships (Baker, 1992; Jones et al., 1997; Nohria, 1992). The ambiguity surrounding networks has two main antecedents.[1] First, the study of networks involves multiple units and levels of analysis. Second, networks have advanced both as an analytical tool employed by researchers and as a governance mode applied by organizations (Nohria, 1992; see also, Koka and Prescott, 2002; Tsai and Ghoshal, 1998). The disparity in units and levels of analysis at which networks have been studied, and the different applications of networks have emerged and evolved along three streams of research: social networks, alliance networks, and organizational networks.[2] Mainly used as an analytical tool, a social network perspective considers every organization or set of organizations as a network regard

---

[1]Two alternative uses of the term 'network' exist that confound its meaning, but are beyond the scope of this chapter. First, by mentioning 'networks' in economics, scholars often refer to 'network economies' or 'network externalities,' which are present when goods interface with other goods, entailing conversion, consumption, and imitation effects. Especially imitation effects are impacted by knowledge-related considerations, since they occur when mimetic behavior brought about by inter-firm information flows drives firms to imitation (Majumdar and Venkataraman, 1998). Second, when considering the implementation of networks, often reference is made to information technology networks that link computers throughout an organization. While these networks certainly contribute to the sharing of knowledge within and across firms, and even contribute to the development of a 'network firm' (Antonelli, 1988), they do not typically emphasize and rely on richer face-to-face communications (Nohria and Eccles, 1992).

[2]This distinction is in line with other typologies commonly used in network studies such as intracorporate, strategic alliances and industrial districts (Inkpen and Tsang, 2005).

less of governance mode and structure. Alliance networks and organizational networks, on the other hand, have emerged as discrete modes of governance. Although the three perspectives are non-mistakenly concerned with network organization, each has contributed uniquely to the study of knowledge and networks. In this chapter, the facilitatory role of the three types of networks in seeking, transferring, integrating, and creating knowledge will be reviewed. Additionally, because some research streams have recently appeared instrumental to others, the areas are heeded in which the streams complement one another.

The chapter is organized as follows. In the next section, main conclusions drawn from research on the manifestation of knowledge in social, alliance, and organizational networks are presented. In the third section, the performance implications of networks and knowledge are heeded. Then, it is considered that networks by themselves may be a form of knowledge. In the final section, current understanding of knowledge and networks is discussed and future research directions are suggested.

KNOWLEDGE IN THREE NETWORK TYPES

The study of how various types of networks foster the management and organization of knowledge has been conducted under three banners: social networks, alliance networks, and organizational networks. The origins of the different research streams, as well as their applications, contributions to knowledge research, main parameters, and performance implications are listed in Table 22.1.

Social network perspective

Having its origins in sociology and anthropology, the study of social networks goes by the notion that 'the structure of any social organization can be thought of as a network' (Nohria and Eccles 1992: 288), and that the actions of network actors are shaped and constrained because of their position and embeddedness in the network (Nohria, 1992). Or, as Lincoln (1982: 26) argues, 'to assert that an organization is not a network is to strip of it that quality in terms of which it is best defined: the pattern of recurring linkages among its parts.' A social network perspective entails not only that all organizations are social networks, but also that the environment is a network of other organizations. With that, social network analysis provides management scholars with a tool to examine relations between actors, ranging from individuals and units (Brass and Burckhardt, 1993; Tsai and Ghoshal, 1998) to firms and groups of firms (Rowley et al., 2000; Wasserman and Faust, 1994), in which 'network' is essentially a construct created by the investigator. In that sense, it has also led to the economics critique that firms are far from atomistic agents but embedded in networks that influence competitive actions (Granovetter, 1985; Uzzi, 1997).

Social network research centers on the ties between actors and focuses on their content and benefits. Tie content may consist of assets, information, and status (Galaskiewicz, 1979). With the emergence of knowledge as a strategic asset (Grant, 1996), much research in social networks has come to center on how ties facilitate the seeking and subsequent transfer of knowledge. Tie benefits occur in the form of access, timing, and referrals (Burt, 1992). Access denotes the role of network ties in providing actors with access to parties and their knowledge. Timing allows actors to obtain information and knowledge sooner

Table 22.1   Research on networks: Three types

	Social Networks	Alliance Networks	Organizational Networks
Origin	Sociology and Anthropology	Economics, mainly socio-economics and institutional economics	Management, mainly International Business
Network conception	Network as an analytical tool to examine social relations and ties between individuals and organizations	Network as a governance mode intermediating markets and hierarchies	Network as a form of organizing
Manifestation of knowledge	- Provide timely access to knowledge and information, either directly or indirectly through referrals, about potential partners - Vehicle to transfer knowledge directly	- Combination of complementary knowledge bases - Accessing knowledge of partners - Acquiring knowledge from partners (internalization)	- Increase internal knowledge transfer to foster internal knowledge creation and integration processes
Main parameters	- Structural vs. relational embeddedness - Positional embeddedness - Brokerage vs. bonding - Structural, relational and cognitive social capital - Tie strength - Trust - Reputation	- Transparency, receptivity and intent - Absorptive capacity - Complexity/ambiguity of knowledge - Governance mode - Trust - Portfolio coordination	- Organization structure - Management/leadership style - Vertical vs. horizontal knowledge flows - Subsidiary roles - Power structure
Performance consequences	- Innovativeness - Financial performance	- Innovation - Ambidexterity - Financial performance	- Innovativeness - Financial performance

Table 22.1 *(Continued)*

| Typical studies | Adler and Kwon (2002); Ahuja (2000a; 2000b); Cross and Cummings (2004); Gulati (1998); Gulati and Gargiulo (1999); Hansen (1999; 2002); Inkpen and Tsang (2005); Koka and Prescott (2002); Nahapiet and Ghoshal (1998); Powell et al. (1996); Rowley and Baum (2008); Tsai (2000; 2001); Tsai and Ghoshal (1998) | Baum et al. (2000); Doz and Hamel (1998); Dyer (1996; 1997); Dyer and Singh (1998); Goerzen (2005; 2007); Grant and Baden-Fuller (2004); Hamel (1991); Mowery et al. (1996); Powell (1990); Sarkar et al. (2009); Tiwana (2008) | Argote et al. (2003); Cross and Cummings (2004); Ghoshal and Bartlett (1997); Gupta and Govindarajan (1991; 2000); Hedlund (1994); Hansen and Nohria (2004); Minbaeva et al. (2003); Monteiro et al. (2008); Nohria and Ghoshal (1997); Schulz (2001; 2003) |

than actors without contacts. Referrals involve the provision of information by actors in the network to the focal actor on available opportunities.

Since the benefits of ties are critical to understanding how social networks influence seeking and transferring knowledge, a body of research has begun to focus on social capital, which involves 'the actual or potential resources embedded within, available through, and derived from the network of relationships possessed by a social unit' (Nahapiet and Ghoshal, 1998: 243). Social capital involves the goodwill others have towards an actor, which is a valuable resource providing benefits in the realm of obtaining influence, facilitating solidarity, and getting superior access to information and knowledge (Adler and Kwon, 2002). Although organizations may benefit from having social ties, not all organizations possess comparable levels of network resources. Such heterogeneity depends on specific features of social networks that determine the value of social capital.

Main parameters. A common theme among social network studies is to describe the network position and ties of an actor in terms of its structural and relational embeddedness in the network (Gulati and Gargiulo, 1999; Uzzi, 1997). In studies of social capital an equivalent distinction is made to indicate the value actors derive from their position in the network. In addition to structural and relational social capital, Nahapiet and Ghoshal (1998) forward cognitive social capital as a third dimension. Structural capital refers to the structure and configuration of the network in terms of (mutual) contacts to one another. It involves the number of social ties maintained by an actor and the centrality of an actor in its network. Relational capital describes the kind of relationships actors have developed, and manifests itself in the strength of ties. Tie strength reflects the closeness of a relationship between partners, and increases with frequency of communication and interaction (Hansen, 1999). Cognitive capital indicates the resources that provide shared representations and systems of meaning, and is embodied in shared language and codes that facilitate learning, and common understanding of collective goals (Inkpen and Tsang, 2005; Nahapiet and Ghoshal, 1998).

In a study on the origins of networks, Gulati and Gargiulo (1999) suggested that, in addition to the structural and relational dimensions of embeddedness, an actor's positional embeddedness is an important characteristic. It indicates the extent to which actors derive information benefits from the ties and the network itself. Since network actors not only differ in number but also in characteristics, Koka and Prescott (2002) differentiated such benefits into volume, richness, and diversity of information and knowledge. Volume and richness refer to the quantity and quality of knowledge and information respectively. Diversity emphasizes the variety of knowledge and information available to network actors. These dimensions contribute to reconciling the different views as to how networks contribute to knowledge acquisition, innovation, and performance.

Two views have emerged as to which network typology creates most benefits when it comes to knowledge transfer (Burt, 1997; 2000; Coleman, 1988; Uzzi, 1997). The first view emphasizes the benefits of maintaining a strong structural position, and has been referred to as brokerage theory. It puts much emphasis on bridging social capital, which alternatively has been labeled linking or external social capital (Adler and Kwon, 2002). It stresses that the information benefits accruing to an actor are highest when that actor is central to the network and has a key role in bridging and linking multiple smaller actor networks between which no direct links exist. Every piece of information and knowledge must go through the central actor if it travels from one network to the other, making the central actor structurally autonomous and bridging structural holes. Brokerage theory views the network as an opportunity for entrepreneurs to exploit by seeking partners that are non-redundant and bring new and diverse information. Such diversity leads to firm heterogeneity in the development and acquisition of competitive capabilities (McEvily and Zaheer, 1999), as well as in the generation and appropriation of rents (Blyler and Coff, 2003).

The second view has been referred to as closure theory and takes that actors in a dense network enjoy most benefits from the network. Actors in a dense network share the same direct and indirect ties and are structurally equivalent. Because returns on investments in the resources needed to maintain the network are more certain, densely connected actors are likely to develop strong ties to redundant others. In that sense, this view focuses more on maintaining strong relational ties and it centers on bonding social capital, which has also been cited as communal or internal social capital (Adler and Kwon, 2002). A strong relational tie increases the opportunity to share richer information. The development of bonding positions also entails that the network is reproduced due to its value in preserving the social capital of an individual.

An ongoing debate has revolved around whether brokerage opportunities derived from a centralized position or closure accruing from relationally embedded ties foster knowledge transfer (Burt, 2007; Levin and Cross, 2004; Uzzi, 1997). Studies distinguishing between structural and relational properties of social networks show how these differences may manifest in specific contexts (Nahapiet and Ghoshal, 1998). Gargiulo and Benassi (2000) found that actors positioned in brokerage roles were better able to adapt to environmental changes, and that the network closure produced by cohesive ties fostered stability. Likewise, Lyles and Schwenk (1992) assert that a loosely coupled knowledge structure fosters adaptation. In contrast, the studies of Ahuja (2000a), Kraatz (1998), and Walker et al. (1997) found supporting evidence that cohesive and strong ties, which are information-rich, fostered adaptiveness by increasing innovation. Hite and Hesterly (2001) found that in the early growth stages of firms networks are likely to be dense, closed, and relationally embedded. In later growth stages, firms are likely to exploit structural holes in a balance of embedded, arm's-length relations. Likewise, Soda et al. (2004) found that the value of brokerage and closure is dependent on whether a structural position is current and a relational tie has proved its value in the past.

In an influential study of inter-unit knowledge transfer, Hansen (1999) found that one of the moderators influencing the value of a strong structural or relational position is the complexity of knowledge. He concluded that cohesive ties are less likely to allow firms to adapt to changes in coordination requirements, because strong ties are prone to network inertia and nodes in the network stay within their network. However, complex knowledge may contribute to joint problem solving (McEvily and Marcus, 2005) and to the novelty of innovation, and thus adaptation (cf. Galunic and Rodan, 1998). Social capital can therefore act as a resource, but also as a constraint in enforcing norms and values among network members and in developing political and cognitive lock-ins (Grabher, 1993). Hansen (1999) found that a trade-off exists in the use of ties when searching for relevant knowledge and transferring knowledge. This search-transfer problem indicates that weak ties are most effective for searching knowledge and transferring non-complex, easy-to-codify knowledge, and that strong ties characterized by close interaction and communication are necessary for transferring complex, difficult-to-codify knowledge. A similar result was found by Uzzi and Lancaster (2003) who argue that publicly available, hard knowledge is best transferred through an arm's length contract while the transfer of private knowledge benefits most from an embedded tie.

Since studies on networks and knowledge have been inconsistent in the measurement of network variables, recent studies have started to explore the extent to which the structural features of brokerage and closure act as opposites in explaining knowledge search and transfer, and the extent to which they associate with the relational feature of tie strength. Often prior studies have inferred structural properties from a relational variable (e.g. Hansen, 1999). Reagans and McEvily (2003) found that both brokerage and closure ease the transfer of knowledge independent of complexity. The evidence of a later study (Reagans and McEvily, 2008) indicates that structural and relational properties of networks are mutually reinforcing and promote both knowledge search and transfer but in different ways. Likewise, Tsai and Ghoshal (1998) found that both structural and cognitive social capital contribute to relational social capital, which subsequently increased knowledge combinations. In a study relating knowledge and power, Reagans and Zuckerman (2008) also show that non-redundancy generates greater potential returns, but that these returns are balanced by the more certain returns that result from having redundant partners. Both brokerage and closure serve as a locus of performance improvement and innovation because they provide access to different types of knowledge that may be unavailable otherwise. Cross and Cummings (2004) found that a strong structural position may account for both current and future performance in that centrality in the information networks facilitates access to current knowledge and centrality in the awareness network fosters the opportunity to act on future opportunities. Hence, both structural and relational capital have been suggested to provide an effective mechanism for seeking and transferring knowledge, as well as the creation of learning capabilities (Adler and Kwon, 2002).

Complexity of knowledge and the different dimensions of social networks and capital have been instrumental yet not sufficient to explain the ways in which networks contribute to knowledge transfer. An important moderating characteristic is the absorptive capacities of the actors involved in the exchange relation. Absorptive capacity is built on prior knowledge endowments: the more knowledge a firm possesses in a certain knowledge domain, the easier it is to learn new things in that domain (Cohen and Levinthal, 1990). Since studies of social network often take the dyad or network level of analysis, the role of absorptive capacity is especially salient. At the dyad level, absorptive capacity is relative (Lane and Lubatkin, 1998) and partner-specific (Dyer and Singh, 1998). Because the knowledge bases of the actors differ, the capacity to absorb knowledge from one partner is different from the capacity to absorb knowledge from another partner. When the knowledge stocks of actors in a network overlap, learning and knowledge transfer are fostered. An increasing number of studies found that relatedness in technologies, knowledge, and resources facilitates the creation of new linkages between actors, the transfer of knowledge and innovation (Ahuja, 2000a, 2000b; Stuart, 1998; Tsai, 2000).

Another characteristic examined in a variety of studies is the role of reputation and trust. Reputation primarily influences the search for knowledge, as it facilitates the creation of new linkages. As Granovetter (1985: 490) argues, individuals have 'widespread preference for transacting with individuals of known reputation'. Prestigious firms that have a track record of producing significant innovations and firms positioned in crowded network pockets where many innovations take place have more opportunities to create new ties (Stuart, 1998). Firms that have no information about the capabilities and intentions of actors in the network will first look for firms that have established a good reputation, because this creates a basis of trust. As such, trust is found important to network formation and maintenance: trust preserves the network through repeated ties and the creation of relational capital, which contribute to the development of trust (Gulati, 1995; Kale et al, 2000).

Alliance network perspective

Alliance network research focuses on network organization as a governance mode inter-jacent to market organization and firm organization and has its main roots in the economics discipline, mainly transaction-cost economics and socio-economics. Following transaction cost theorizing, firms choose an alliance when the costs they incur in negotiating, enforcing, and monitoring contracts are lower in cooperation than those associated with buying assets on the market and with making assets within their own firm (Powell, 1990; Williamson, 1975, 1985). A large part of alliance research has traditionally focused on joint ventures and strategic alliances that allow firms to reduce risk, to share costs, to enjoy economies of scale, and to block competitors. Additionally, firms use alliances as a means to access complementary resources and knowledge and to learn from their partners (Barringer and Harrison, 2000; Doz and Hamel, 1998; Kogut, 1988).

From a knowledge perspective, firms enter into alliances (1) to gain access to new knowledge and pool the knowledge bases of the partners involved or (2) to internalize the knowledge of the partner (Grant and Baden-Fuller, 2004; Inkpen and Dinur, 1998). Firms may have knowledge bases that are complementary or co-specialized so that innovation and competitive advantage only emerge when the knowledge of the alliance partners is brought together (Dhanaraj et al., 2004; Dyer, 1996, 1997; Larsson et al., 1998; Lavie, 2006). Especially in turbulent and converging industries, firms' product and knowledge domains may not be consistent. Organizations may not be able to develop products because they lack the necessary knowledge. Such inconsistencies trigger firms to look outside for knowledge. For example, Toyota cooperates with its suppliers as well as rival automotive companies in a diverse network to learn from each other and to be on the forefront of industry trends (Dyer and Nobeoka, 2000).

The emphasis in alliance research has moved from studying individual alliances at the firm or dyad level to multiple alliances in a complex network (Doz and Hamel, 1998; Goerzen, 2005). As Koka and Prescott (2002: 797) argue, 'firms have to go beyond traditional cost-benefit analyses of particular individual alliances ... [and] need to evaluate particular alliances not only in the context of the other alliances that they already possess but also in the context of the entire network of relationships.' A diverse set of cooperations provides a firm access to a larger and broader knowledge base that it can tap into (Baum et al., 2000; Mitchell and Singh, 1996; Powell et al., 1996). Since using multiple alliances as a means to improve performance requires more coordination, in addition to studying alliance networks *per se* alliance research has come to focus on how firms configure their alliances as part of an alliance portfolio (Baum et al., 2000; Sarkar et al., 2009; Tiwana, 2008).

Main parameters. Insights into main determinants of knowledge transfer in alliance networks have emerged from two types of studies. In addition to more recent research on alliances at the network level, studies that focus on individual alliances at the firm and dyad level have enriched our understanding of the antecedents and consequences of knowledge access and acquisition in alliances. For example, in his study of eleven US–Japanese alliances, Hamel (1991) found that learning outcomes were dependent on the intent of the partners, their transparency and their receptivity. Mowery et al. (1996) found that knowledge transfers between alliance partners increase as they share a common knowledge base, and that competition moderates this relationship since firms operating in industries with the same primary SIC tended to transfer less knowledge among each other. Learning in external networks is fraught with competitive motivations (Gnyawali and Madhavan, 2001), which may result in learning races. The ability to internalize knowledge and thus the outcome of such learning races is dependent on the relative market scope of the partnering firms and the alliance (Khanna, 1998; Khanna et al., 1998). The more the scope of the alliance overlaps with the scope of the firms involved, a relatively large share of common benefits would accrue to both firms, once they have internalized each other's knowledge and are able to co-develop new products within the scope of the alliance. Such learning within the alliance scope is likely facilitated because overlap in firm scope probably renders the knowledge bases of the involved firms partially overlapping as well, and this increases relative absorptive capacity (Lane and Lubatkin, 1998; Kumar and Nti, 1998). Partners may also appropriate permanent private benefits from the alliance, which accrue to firms when they are able to apply the knowledge they acquired to markets beyond the alliance.

In a study covering the alliances of 147 MNCs, Simonin (1999) found that ambiguity, which relates to knowledge tacitness and complexity, negatively impacts knowledge transfer. Cultural and organizational distance between partner firms is also found to negatively influence knowledge transfer, because such distance increases the ambiguity associated with inter-partner learning. Simonin's (1999) findings suggest, however, that as alliances become older firms are able to overcome problems associated with complexity, because firms develop alternate joint problem-solving styles and partner-specific collaborative know-how (cf. Dyer and Singh, 1998; Kumar and Nti, 1998) that enable them to adapt to each other and overcome problems associated with complexity.

Distinct interdependencies and complexities inherent in tasks lead to coordination costs (Gulati and Singh, 1998). Alliances are essentially incomplete contracts. Partners face the risk of opportunistic behavior emerging and knowledge leaking (Baum et al., 2000). Such risk is dependent on the motivations of the partners, the value creation logic driving the alliance and the resources involved in the alliance. Therefore, for alliances with different purposes and in which different types of resources are involved, firms use different governance structures (Das and Teng, 2000). The choice for governance structure and the extent to which firms enjoy competitive advantage is further influenced by whether firms create relation-specific assets and knowledge sharing routines. Such assets and routines not only create idiosyncratic inter-firm linkages to combine knowledge and other resources in unique ways (Dyer and Singh, 1998; Mesquita et al., 2008).

Governance structures are differentiated by the degree of formalization (Vlaar et al., 2007) and the amount of hierarchical controls (Gulati and Singh, 1998). When appropriation or opportunistic behavior is an issue, firms were found to use joint ventures and other equity-based arrangements as governance mode (Baum et al., 2000; Gulati and

Singh, 1998). Das and Teng (2000), however, suggest that firms may wish to use different governance modes depending on whether they bring property-based or knowledge-based resources into the equation. They argue that a joint venture is only worthwhile if the partner provides knowledge and the focal firm provides property-based resources, because a joint venture allows a firm to gain direct access to knowledge. A minority equity arrangement is more beneficial when the focal firm itself brings into the alliance knowledge-based resources, as a hostage without the creation of a separate entity will allow it to protect its knowledge from dissipating to its alliance partners.

Dyer and Singh (1998) argue that, in addition to the creation of formal hostages, effective self-enforced governance can occur informally through trust and reputation. Based on a study assessing whether firms in alliances finance the activities of their partners, Stuart (2003) found that the structural position of a firm in its alliance network influences the governance structure chosen in its alliances, as a structural position harbors a reputation effect and influences the knowledge potential partners have about the focal firm. As in social networks, trust is crucial in external networks and forms a substitute for price and authority as the coordination mechanism (Bradach and Eccles, 1989). Trust leads firms to make relation-specific investments and to create repeated ties with their partners and vice versa. Goerzen (2007) found evidence that forming repeated ties with the same alliance partners has a negative influence on the economic performance of firms at the corporate level, especially in uncertain environments. In that sense, he disconfirmed the transaction cost perspective that repeated ties lead to more efficient governance arrangements and mitigate challenges of acculturation and integration. While repeated ties create trust, they also lock out potential partners that possess new knowledge and may lead firms to exploit existing routines rather than exploring new ones (Zaheer and Bell, 2005). Firms need to configure their alliance network so that both diverse partners are bridged to increase innovation potential and strong relations are developed to develop integration capacity. Such a balanced network allows firms to use their alliances to both create innovation potential and realize that potential. In other words, it enables them to both explore and exploit, consequently becoming ambidextrous (Lavie and Rosenkopf, 2006; Tiwana, 2008).

Beyond dealing with partner coordination through relational governance, management of an alliance portfolio requires coordination among alliance partners. As firm boundaries blur and a firm's alliances become part of a wider ecosystem (Iansiti and Levien, 2004), different alliance partners in a firm's portfolio cater for the resources it does not possess. In case a firm seeks to acquire knowledge from multiple partners, it needs to develop absorptive capacity. Since absorptive capacity is dependent on a relevant knowledge base, it is inherently relative and partner-specific (Dyer and Singh, 1998; Lane and Lubatkin, 1998). In that vein, Kumar and Nti (1998) suggested that firms leverage absorptive capacity so that knowledge absorbed from one partner may increase the ability to absorb knowledge from another partner. Hence, the coordination of knowledge and strategies across a firm's alliance portfolio increases the success of a firm (Sarkar et al., 2009).

Organizational network perspective

Research on organizational networks is mainly rooted in the management field, notably in the field of international business. An organizational network's advantage is its 'ability to create new value through the accumulation, transfer, and integration of different kinds of knowledge, resources, and capabilities across its dispersed organizational units' (Nohria and Ghoshal, 1997: 208). Studies increasingly address the problems multinational firms face in transferring knowledge across their subsidiaries and in putting to effective use their distributed knowledge stocks in different locations. In that sense, they center on network organization as a feature of organizational design or as a form of organizing alternative to, for example, functional and multidivisional organization forms (Doz et al., 2001; Hedlund, 1994; Nohria and Ghoshal, 1997).

Organizational networks cater for the problem that 'knowledge is a resource that is difficult to accumulate at the corporate level . . . [and] those with the specialized knowledge and expertise most vital to the company's competitiveness are usually located far away from the corporate headquarters' (Bartlett and Ghoshal, 1993: 32). Subsidiaries and organizational units need to transfer knowledge among each other, because knowledge deemed valuable in one location may be valuable in other parts of an organization. When firms enter into alliance networks, little or no change takes place in internal organization. Organizational routines remain unimpaired and often prevent firms from deploying knowledge acquired externally as ambitiously internally (Ghoshal and Bartlett, 1997). These developments have triggered the emergence of an alternate corporate model that marks 'the selective infusion of market mechanisms into hierarchy and hierarchy into markets' (Zenger and Hesterly, 1997: 210). Alongside relying on alliances, this corporate model relies on intraorganizational networks to foster knowledge creation and integration inside a firm's boundaries.

Typically, organizational networks make use of organic systems of management, which are characterized by dispersed knowledge, horizontal knowledge transfer, and decentralized decision making (Burns and Stalker, 1961). They also depend on projects, less bureaucracy, open communication (Thomson, 1965), and are mainly self-designing (Hedberg et al., 1976). While the foundations of organizational networks were laid down in the 1960s, in international business, organizational networks have recently gained interest and have been further examined in studies on transnational corporations (Bartlett and Ghoshal, 1989), differentiated networks (Nohria and Ghoshal, 1997), integrated networks (Ghoshal and Bartlett, 1997), and metanational organizations (Doz et al., 2001). They also feature center stage in studies of organization forms such as cellular organizations (Miles et al., 1997), horizontal organizations (Ostroff, 1999), hypertext organizations (Nonaka and Takeuchi, 1995), and N-form corporations (Hedlund, 1994). Scholarly interest in these organizational forms has been progressing mainly because the proportion of firms with characteristics indigenous to network organization is increasing (Pettigrew et al., 2000).

Main parameters. A central theme in studies of how organizational networks influence knowledge transfer and integration is organization design. Ghoshal and Bartlett (1997) argue that the emphasis on strategy, structure, and systems so common in many organizations is changing towards purpose, processes, and people in organizational networks. Subsequent studies are indeed evident of this change as they emphasize that the most common barriers to collaboration and knowledge transfer revolve around the unwillingness and inability of people and units to share knowledge and help others (Hansen and Nohria, 2004; Szulanski, 1996; 2000). Ability and motivation are therefore central concerns of multinational corporations seeking to accumulate, integrate, and apply knowledge across different locations (Gupta and Govindarajan, 2000; Minbaeva et al., 2003), especially when faced with an opportunity (Argote et al., 2003), and are more effectively addressed by focusing on processes and people.

Structure in organizational networks remains important as it shapes ability and motivation by forming the context in which processes and people operate. Since co-locating knowledge and decision rights increases a unit's competitiveness (Doz et al., 2001; Jensen and Meckling, 1992), units in organizational networks are autonomous and granted operational and strategic responsibility. While this allows units to develop knowledge stocks attuned to local environments, units also become differentiated. Since stocks of knowledge developed by one unit may be effectively used by other units, in organizational networks integration mechanisms are in place connecting knowledge stocks through knowledge flows. Using an agent-based model, Siggelkow and Rivkin (2005) show that decentralization of decision-making power to local managers who can respond to idiosyncratic, local events and share knowledge laterally is a preferred structure when environmental turbulence increases in the face of high complexity. They also found, however, that the centralization of a hierarchical firm may be equally effective in such an environment as a select few can act speedily and decisively. Other studies suggest that the outcomes of adopting a (de)centralized design may be suboptimal and that combining hierarchy and network principles into one structure is most valuable. Networks are based on the principles of multiplication and combination rather than on the principle of division so characteristic of hierarchies (Hedlund, 1994), yet hierarchy remains indispensable to reach certain decisions quickly, to resolve disputes, and to obtain employees' allegiance to an organization's mission and objectives (Powell, 1990). A combination of these mechanistic and organic structures allows firms to pursue both exploration and exploitation and to become ambidextrous (cf. Raisch and Birkinshaw, 2008). Insights into how and the extent to which hierarchical and network structures need to be combined into one organization are, however, still inconclusive.

In addition to formal organization, changes in management and leadership style facilitate ability and in particular motivation to transfer knowledge (Hedlund, 1994; Hansen and Nohria, 2004; Pettigrew et al., 2003). Organizational networks require a management philosophy that is evident of an organic management system in which 'a network structure of control, authority, and communication' (Burns and Stalker, 1961: 121) is present. A commanding and monitoring role of the senior management team is ineffective to facilitate knowledge transfer. Organizational networks are better served by senior managers that act as architects and catalysts of network processes (Hedlund, 1994). Instead of *allocating* resources based on formal control mechanisms, executives of organizational networks facilitate the *leveraging* of knowledge and resources by institutionalizing common norms and values that breed a culture of trust, reciprocity and collaboration (Ghoshal and Bartlett, 1997; Powell, 1990). As a consequence, whereas in many organizations knowledge flows are primarily vertical from headquarters to units, in organizational networks knowledge flows are also configured horizontally among units (cf. Aoki, 1986). Senior managers in organizational networks are horizontal knowledge brokers 'linking and leveraging the company's widely distributed resources and capabilities,' rather than vertical information brokers (Bartlett and Ghoshal, 1993: 33).

The majority of studies have focused on how organizations influence the ability to transfer knowledge. While motivation to transfer knowledge is mainly influenced by characteristics of the organization, ability is additionally influenced by characteristics of the knowledge itself. For example, a variety of studies at the unit level found that the creation of vertical and horizontal knowledge flows in and out of a unit is dependent on whether old or new knowledge needs to be combined (Schulz, 2001), the volume of the unit knowledge base, the degree to which knowledge is codified, the extent to which knowledge is specialized (Schulz, 2003), the relatedness of knowledge (Hansen and Løvas, 2004), the absorptive capacity of the unit, the value of the unit knowledge stock (Gupta and Govindarajan, 2000), and the degree of ambidexterity (Mom et al., 2007). Similar findings have been reported in other studies with regard to the role of absorptive capacity (Szulanski, 1996; 2000), knowledge codification (Zander and Kogut, 1995), and knowledge specialization (Brusoni, 2005). Studies assessing organizational characteristics facilitating knowledge transfer have focused on the richness of transmission channels (Gupta and Govindarajan, 2000), integration mechanisms (Hansen and Nohria, 2004; Jansen et al., 2009), decentralization (Frost et al., 2002), incentives (Zenger and Hesterley, 1997), informal networks, and formal organization structure (Hansen and Løvas, 2004). Recently, studies have emerged examining how organizational and knowledge characteristics interrelate. For example, Szulanski et al. (2004) found that the positive effect of trustworthiness on knowledge transfer vanishes as causal ambiguity of the knowledge transferred becomes high. This negative effect may diminish when transmission channels become richer (cf. Daft and Lengel, 1986).

Cross and Cummings (2004) found that organizational structure renders some ties more important than others and may provide some actors with access to more knowledge and information. As a consequence, not every unit or subsidiary is equally embedded in an organizational network. Gupta and Govindarajan (1991) created a typology of subsidiary roles that centers on the strategic context of the subsidiary and the knowledge flow pattern involved. For example, subsidiaries that receive and distribute much knowledge are more integrated into the whole MNC network and play a central role in worldwide activities. On the other hand, subsidiaries who hardly share knowledge are likely to have the local expertise to innovate and implement knowledge and products tailored to local markets. Different subsidiaries will, therefore, differ as to their lateral interdependence, global responsibility and authority, and their need for autonomous initiative. In that sense, integrated subsidiaries will be more dependent on integrative mechanisms, corporate socialization, and communication than local players. Likewise, in integrated subsidiaries managers will be assessed on behavior more than on outcome, they need to be more tolerant of ambiguity, and their bonuses will be based more on the performance of multiple subsidiaries than the subsidiary that they are primarily responsible for.

Recently, a variety of studies have emerged examining how the power structure of an organization influences knowledge transfer. Monteiro et al. (2008) found that knowledge transfers between subsidiaries in MNCs typically occur between highly capable members. Units with expert status are likely to share more knowledge as it increases their power (Borgatti and Cross, 2003; Mudambi and Navarra, 2004). Wong et al. (2008) found that units that possess critical, non-substitutable, and central knowledge, and thus are deemed to have higher status and to be more powerful, are more likely to receive knowledge from others, but that this is dependent on the goal interdependence of the units involved. Andersson et al. (2007) found that subsidiary power is not only dependent on the importance of the subsidiary but also on the knowledge of corporate headquarters about the subsidiary's local network. Importance of the subsidiary has two conflicting roles in that it increases the power a subsidiary can exert, but also increases the likelihood that corporate headquarters has developed knowledge of that subsidiary's network and can lessen its power, which poses it a dilemma in that curtailing a subsidiary's power and influence may lead to a reduction in the subsidiary's interest in contributing to the overall performance of the MNC.

Networks: Integrative Perspectives

Given that every organization or set of organizations is essentially a social network (Lincoln, 1982), concepts of social network methods especially have been applied to understand how alliance and organizational networks emerge, function, and perform. Most notably, social network analysis has been deployed to increase our understanding of how firms obtain and use information about partner needs, knowledge, competencies, and reliabilities in their search for potential alliance partners (Gulati, 1995). Firms searching for partners are more likely to resort to their networks and choose their past partners or their partners' partners if they are faced with high levels of partnering uncertainty (Rowley and Baum, 2008). Information about partner reliability and competencies received increases trust, reduces the likelihood of opportunistic behavior, and influences the choice for governance structure. However, information about the capabilities and willingness of partners to cooperate may be more or less imperfect, which raises search costs. Reliable information may be difficult to obtain before an alliance is initiated, and thus firms face concerns of adverse selection and moral hazard. One way firms can overcome the possibility of opportunism occurring and obtain reliable information is to capitalize on the personal social ties between members of an alliance through which they obtain information about the reputation of a partner (Gulati, 1998; Ring and Van de Ven, 1994). In that sense, social network analysis has been instrumental to explain endogenous aspects of network formation (Gulati and Gargiulo, 1999). In the same vein, social network analysis has been instrumental in explaining intraorganizational linkage formation (Hansen, 2002; Tsai, 2000). In a meta-analytic review, Van Wijk et al. (2008) use concepts deployed in social network analysis to understand the antecedents and consequences of knowledge transfer in alliance and organizational networks.

In addition to explaining network formation, social network analysis has been applied in order to understand the performance benefits of alliance and organizational networks. For example, in a study of the Canadian biotechnology industry, Baum et al. (2000) found that startups can enhance their innovative performance by entering into alliances and by configuring them into a network through which access to diverse information and capabilities is provided. Similarly, using social network methods, a variety of studies (e.g. Dhanaraj et al., 2004; Hansen et al., 2001; Koka and Prescott, 2002) examined the role of structural and relational embeddedness on performance of alliances in different environments. Singh and Mitchell (1996: 112) argue that 'businesses that are able to work closely with current partners while at the same time identifying possible new partners are likely to succeed in an industry marked by ongoing technological change.' The studies of both Rowley et al. (2000) and Uzzi (1996) found that in exploitation-favoring environments, which are stable and predictable, strong ties between partners have a positive influence on performance. In exploration-favoring environments, which are turbulent and unpredictable, weak ties are more important for performance. Continuous formation of new relationships with diverse partners allows firms to maintain access to a broad knowledge base, which contributes to innovation and exploration. At the same time firms need to develop stable and strong relationships, which enable them to develop deep knowledge, which is essential in stable environments.

Since it has application in a variety of contexts and across a variety of levels, social network analysis is at the root of developing more general network theories (Jones et al., 1997) and of understanding how networks shape knowledge creation and transfer. Yet, even beyond social network methods, concepts used to understand the characteristics, functioning, and value of one type of network are increasingly used in the context of another network. For example, Lane and Lubatkin (1998) argue that relativity of absorptive capacity not only applies to partners within alliance networks, but could also explain learning processes between units in organizational networks. Indeed, absorptive capacity has been found important in social networks (Ahuja, 2000b; Tsai, 2001), alliance networks (Dyer and Singh, 1998; Lane et al., 2001), and organizational networks (Gupta and Govindarajan, 2000; Szulanski, 1996). Likewise, Dhanaraj and Parkhe (2006) argue that an alliance network needs a hub firm that occupies a central position in the network, spans structural holes, bridges positions, and orchestrates activities in the network. By the same token, Gupta and Govindarajan (2000) argue that corporate headquarters in MNCs continue to play a pivotal role in coordinating knowledge transfer between subsidiaries. Studies by Goerzen (2005) and Hoffmann (2005) show that successfully reaping benefits from an alliance portfolio requires coordination and the creation of synergies across internal units and subsidiaries.

MNC subsidiaries can tap into a variety of internal and external knowledge sources to produce innovations (Phene and Almeida, 2008). Andersson et al. (2002) found that the embeddedness of MNC subsidiaries in local networks has a positive impact on subsidiary performance and on the development of new products in the MNC. The extent to which subsidiaries become embedded in local business networks is, in turn, dependent on the extent to which the subsidiary provides technology within the MNC (Andersson et al., 2007). Similarly, Almeida and Phene (2004) found that subsidiaries maintaining close linkages to a local network of diverse partners contribute to innovation within the MNC as it enables them to tap into broad knowledge. While subsidiaries provide diverse, broad knowledge to an MNC's innovations, the necessary rich, deep knowledge is provided by the MNC itself. Tsai (2001) found that the degree to which such central network positions lead to increased innovative and financial performance is dependent on the capacity of units to absorb the diverse knowledge they have access to. To create synergies and to commercially use the knowledge that they share and receive, subsidiaries of an MNC need to balance demands from their alliance network and their position in the organizational network, while the MNC aligns the network of subsidiaries. In that sense, these findings may partially explain why MNCs provide different roles and power to the subsidiaries across the organizational MNC network (cf. Gupta and Govindarajan, 1991).

Network Capability

The study of knowledge and networks is not limited to how knowledge and knowledge transfers manifest in networks. As managing networks is fraught with difficulty, studies increasingly focus on the benefits of developing network capabilities. Research in social networks has focused on how relational capability increases the efficacy in which actors operate in their networks (Kale et al., 2000). Likewise, in the context of alliances, studies show that firms with alliance capabilities are more successful in their alliances (e.g. Anand and Khanna, 2000; Dyer et al., 2001; Kale and Singh, 2007; Lyles, 1988). As firms enter into alliances and alliance networks, they gain alliance experience. In their study of alliances in the manufacturing sector, Anand and Khanna (2000) found that firms learn to create more value as they accumulate experience, but only in the context of more extensive forms of collaboration, such as joint ventures. Since experience builds cumulatively, firms may become inert and may misattribute it across different contexts. Hence, firms need to learn from their experience and build know-how (Dyer et al., 2001; Kale and Singh, 2007), particularly of different alliance phases, such as partner search, negotiation, alliance management, and learning (Simonin, 1997). Gulati (1999) found that greater network alliance formation capabilities increase the chance that firms enter into alliances in the future (see also, Lyles, 1988). On the basis of a longitudinal case study, Lorenzoni and Lipparini (1999) proposed that the capability to interact with other firms improves learning and knowledge access and transfer. Simonin (1999) found that collaborative knowledge mitigated the negative effects of knowledge complexity, as well as the detrimental effects of cultural and organizational distance on learning.

The positive benefits gained through alliance capabilities have led many firms to develop a unit or multiple units dedicated to the alliance function (Hoffmann, 2005; Kale et al., 2002). In the context of alliance learning, 'knowledge consists . . . also of the know-how regarding cooperation . . . [and] of identifying who will cooperate and who has what capabilities' (Kogut et al., 1993: 77). A unit devoted to managing a firm's alliances facilitates the articulation, codification, sharing, and internalization of experiences learned in various alliances, provides a central point to develop alliance capability, and subsequently leads to greater alliance success (Kale and Singh, 2007). By creating and integrating alliance knowledge in a special unit, firms seek to increase external visibility, to enhance internal legitimacy, to provide internal coordination, to intervene in alliances (Dyer et al., 2001), and to facilitate alliance portfolio management (Hoffmann, 2005). These capabilities determine the efficacy in which firms act as hubs in an alliance network (Dhanaraj and Parkhe, 2006). However, a firm enters into alliances often at the business unit or subsidiary level. As a consequence, the degree to which a firm can learn from its various alliances is determined by a firm's internal knowledge sharing process. The sharing of knowledge that organizational networks facilitate at the same time facilitates the development of new alliance networks. In that sense, an alliance function serves as a *tertius iungens* in that it introduces disconnected units within the organization and facilitates new coordination among them as well as among a firm's alliance partners (cf. Obstfeld, 2005).

PROGRESS AND PROSPECTS

Research into how knowledge is created and integrated in networks has made substantial progress over the past decades. The topic has spawned so much interest that recently more quantitative reviews using meta-analytic techniques have emerged to further our understanding of the antecedents and consequences of knowledge transfer within and across companies (e.g. Van Wijk et al., 2008). Research into networks has developed under three banners. The thrust of social network analysis is that every organization is a social network, and that a social network can be used to disseminate knowledge and information. Alliance networks have been established as a governance mode to gain access to knowledge unavailable within a firm's boundaries. Organizational networks have emerged to facilitate the management of that knowledge internally.

Despite the insights and understanding gained, a substantial number of avenues for future research still remain. Most promising future research avenues essentially provide further cross-fertilization across the three network types, and apply concepts employed to examine one type to further understand the functioning of another. One such concept is the role of governance mode and organizational structure. For example, Stuart (2003) illustrated how a firm's structural and relational position may influence its choice for the governance structures used in its alliances. However, much remains to be discovered. For example, to co-develop products alliance partners may have to make relation-specific investments (Dyer and Singh, 1998). Such investments may lead partner firms to behave opportunistically and a governance structure that creates control. They also signal trust and may increase a firm's relational capital, requiring less control through governance. Likewise, received insights indicate that a strong structural position achieved through centrality provides knowledge access (Tsai and Ghoshal, 1998; Van Wijk et al., 2008). Actors may, however, be central in a strong administrative hierarchy, as a CEO or headquarters is, or may be central in an organizational network with only one layer, where an individual other than the CEO or a unit other than headquarters may be the most central actor. In that vein, the informational benefits accruing to a central actor may be moderated by organization structure. In that vein, the differentiation of units as to their structural and relational embeddedness and organization structure influence the ability of firms to develop alliance capability.

Studies may also incorporate other organizational characteristics. Typically, nodes in organizational networks are conceptualized as units, but they can also be products, activities, resources, and knowledge. Since each of the dispersed organizational units controls unique knowledge and resources giving rise to differentiated activities and abilities, these classes of variables are related to each other in the overall structure of the network. Units in an organizational network manufacturing a single product for a local market are more likely to perform specialist activities and to develop deep knowledge of those activities. In contrast, units producing multiple products for multiple markets are likely to develop broad knowledge covering the variety of activities they perform. Since absorptive capacity is dependent on the presence of a relevant knowledge base and the degree to which the knowledge bases of two units are overlapping, how do specialist and generalist units absorb knowledge from each other? Absorptive capacity was found to be an important determinant of knowledge transfer in social (Ahuja, 2000a), alliance (Lane and Lubatkin, 1998), and organizational networks (Jansen et al., 2006; Szulanski, 2000; Tsai, 2001). Since absorptive capacity is relative and partner-specific, firms face a trade-off in investing in deep, specialist, and broad, generalist knowledge with a variety of actors both within and outside organizational borders. Argote et al. (2003) argue that knowledge transfer within is easier than across organizational boundaries. If absorptive capacity is so central to knowledge transfer regardless of organizational boundary, which measures do firms with an organizational network take to foster the development of absorptive capacity, especially in cases where a firm has many specialist units with non-overlapping knowledge? Since it can trace individual actors, social network analysis may prove a valuable tool to advance our understanding of the interplay between alliance and organizational networks, provided concepts are incorporated that are typically employed outside the realm of social networks.

A related prospect for future research is further examination of barriers to knowledge transfer and learning in networks. While the most frequently cited studies of knowledge transfer address a variety of facilitators and barriers, much remains to be understood. Darr et al. (1995) found that knowledge was shared between stores of the same franchisee, but not of different franchisees. Since franchisees generally operate under the same brand and organization, boundaries that influence knowledge transfer here are likely legal. Another reason may be power issues, which potentially are a critical barrier to knowledge transfer (Andersson et al., 2007). In other frequently cited research, absorptive capacity (Mowery et al., 1996), causal ambiguity and arduous relationships among interacting parties have been found to be among the most important barriers to knowledge transfer (Szulanski, 1996; 2000). Geography may also play an important role. Intraplant transfers were found more common than interplant transfers, especially when the geographical dispersion of plants increased (Argote et al., 1990; see also, Schulz, 2001). Research in this area may be informed by studies on regional networks and clusters, in which firms have chosen to be co-located in order to allow knowledge to be transferred (Arikan, 2009).

We also still do not understand the extent to which firms with an extensive alliance network operate with organizational networks more often and more efficaciously than firms with less developed alliance networks, and *vice versa*. Firms endowed with a substantial amount of alliances increasingly develop alliance capabilities that allow them to create more value as experience in allying and in transferring knowledge increases (Anand and Khanna, 2000; Simonin, 1997). Coordinating alliance partners facilitates the creation of such capabilities (cf. Dhanaraj and Parkhe, 2006; Hoffmann, 2005; Sarkar et al., 2009), but also requires an organization equipped with systems and processes to share knowledge (Kale and Singh, 2007).

Likewise, knowing how to operate an organizational network may make firms more adept to network in alliance portfolios as well. This also raises the question as to whether the components that make up alliance capability are developed simultaneously or sequentially. Firms that have an organizational network in place may have developed a coordination capability that enables them to more efficiently and effectively create new alliance capabilities because that capability can be applied to coordinate alliance partners as well.

Another promising future research avenue involves exploring how the organization of knowledge in various networks contributes to organizational ambidexterity. Studies define ambidexterity as the ability to both exploit existing and explore new knowledge and have typically focused on its organizational antecedents (Raisch and Birkinshaw, 2008). For example, studies have examined how leadership (Jansen et al., 2008), formal and informal integration mechanisms (Jansen et al., 2009), cross-functional interfaces, and decision-making authority (Mom et al., 2009) influence organizational ambidexterity. Since many antecedents that have been studied differentiate organizational networks, such studies suggest that these networks foster ambidexterity. Recently, studies have examined how alliance networks contribute to organizational ambidexterity, and have done so borrowing concepts from social network studies such as the role of prior (Lavie and Rosenkopf, 2006), bridging, and strong ties (Tiwana, 2008). Research on how the organization of knowledge in networks leads to ambidexterity is, however, still in its infancy, which endorses studies seeking to understand how organizations use the three network types concurrently in becoming ambidextrous.

Space limitations prevent us listing the whole array of a seemingly endless number of promising future research avenues, but a final avenue for future research that would advance our understanding of knowledge in networks is differentiating knowledge into various types. Studies typically make a distinction between explicit information and tacitly-held know-how. Even tacitly-held knowledge comprises more than just know-how, and also includes know-what, know-when, know-where, know-who, and know-why components (Garud, 1997; Kogut et al., 1993). Studies of social networks have begun to make a distinction in type of knowledge, albeit coarse, by considering the role of transactive memory (cf. Soda et al., 2004), which relates to know-who, know-where, and know-when. Likewise, Tyler and Steensma (1995) found that executives with technical experience were more favorable of entering into a technology alliance than executives without that experience were. Such issues may be investigated by considering the different components of knowledge. The knowledge set of executive managers is different from that of functional managers. In that sense, differences in knowledge sets may place enormous demands on organizations, especially if they enter into alliances mostly at the business level for it likely requires more internal coordination. Firms may even choose to decentralize knowledge regarding who knows what and where knowledge resides, but may centralize know-how and know-what.

In sum, research into knowledge and networks has made substantial progress. The field of study is wide, however, and in its current state has left investigators with a variety of open terrains that deserve academic pursuit. Although first attempts at cross-fertilization have emerged, the three network types heeded in this chapter have been dealt with mostly separately. One of the main avenues for gaining further understanding of how networks facilitate learning, knowledge creation, and knowledge integration is consideration of the three networks in a complementary way. We hope the issues and questions raised in this review will set the stage for many future studies.

REFERENCES

Adler, P.S. and Kwon, S-W. (2002) Social capital: Prospects for a new concept. *Academy of Management Review*, 27(1): 17–40.

Ahuja, G. (2000a) The duality of collaboration: Inducements and opportunities in the formation of interfirm linkages. *Strategic Management Journal*, 21 (Special Issue): 317–343.

Ahuja, G. (2000b) Collaboration networks, structural holes, and innovation: A longitudinal study. *Administrative Science Quarterly*, 45(3): 425–455.

Almeida, P. and Phene, A. (2004) Subsidiaries and knowledge creation: The influence of the MNC and host country on innovation. *Strategic Management Journal*, 25(8/9): 847–864.

Anand, B.N. and Khanna, T. (2000) Do firms learn to create value? The case of alliances. *Strategic Management Journal*, 21 (Special Issue): 295–315.

Andersson, U., Forsgren, M., and Holm, U. (2002) The strategic impact of external networks: subsidiary performance and competence development in the multinational corporation. *Strategic Management Journal*, 23(11): 979–996.

Andersson, U., Forsgren, M., and Holm, U. (2007) Balancing subsidiary influence in the federative MNC: A business network view. *Journal of International Business Studies*, 38(5): 802–818.

Antonelli, C. 1988: The emergence of the network firm. In C. Antonelli (ed.), *New information technology and industrial change: The Italian case*, Dordrecht: Kluwer Academic, 13–32.

Aoki, M. (1986) Horizontal vs. vertical information structure of the firm. *American Economic Review*, 76 (5): 971–983.

Argote, L., Beckman, S., and Epple, D. (1990) The persistence and transfer of learning in industrial settings. *Management Science*, 36(2): 140–154.

Argote, L., McEvily, B., and Reagans, R. (2003) Managing knowledge in organizations: An integrative framework and review of emerging themes. *Management Science*, 49(4): 571–582.

Arikan, A.T. (2009) Interfirm knowledge exchanges and the knowledge creation capability of clusters. *Academy of Management Review*, 34(4): 658–676.

Baker, W.E. (1992) The network organization in theory and practice. In N. Nohria and R.G. Eccles (eds.), *Networks and organizations: Structure, form, and action*. Boston, MA: Harvard Business School Press: 397–429.

Barringer, B.R. and Harrison, J.S. (2000) Walking a tightrope: Creating value through interorganizational relationships. *Journal of Management*, 26(3): 367–403.

Bartlett, C.A. and Ghoshal, S. (1989) *Managing across borders*. Boston, MA: Harvard Business School Press.

Bartlett, C.A. and Ghoshal, S. (1993) Beyond the M-form: Toward a managerial theory of the firm. *Strategic Management Journal*, 14 (Winter Special Issue): 23–46.

Baum, J.A.C., Calabrese, T., and Silverman, B.S. (2000) Don't go it alone: Alliance network composition and startups' performance in Canadian biotechnology. *Strategic Management Journal*, 21 (Special Issue): 267–294.

Blyler, M. and Coff, R. (2003) Dynamic capabilities, social capital, and rent appropriation: Ties that split pies. *Strategic Management Journal*, 24(7): 677–686.

Borgatti, S.P. and Cross, R. (2003) A relational view of information seeking and learning in social networks. *Management Science*, 49(4): 432–445.

Bradach, J.L. and Eccles, R.G. (1989) Price, authority, and trust: From ideal types to plural forms. *Annual Review of Sociology*, 15: 97–118.

Brass, D.J. and Burkhardt, M.E. (1993) Potential power and power use: An investigation of structure and behavior. *Academy of Management Journal*, 36(3): 441–470.

Brusoni, S. (2005) The limits to specialization: Problem solving and coordination in 'modular networks'. *Organization Studies*, 26(12): 1885–1907.

Burns, T. and Stalker, G. (1961) *The management of innovation*. London: Tavistock.

Burt, R.S. (1992) *Structural holes: The social structure of competition*. Cambridge, MA: Harvard University Press.

Burt, R.S. (1997) The contingent value of social capital. *Administrative Science Quarterly*, 42(2): 339–365.

Burt, R.S. (2000) The network structure of social capital. *Research in Organizational Behavior*: 345–422.

Burt, R.S. (2007) *Brokerage and Closure.* New York: Oxford University Press.

Cangelosi, V.E. and Dill, W.R. (1965) Organizational learning: Observations toward a theory. *Administrative Science Quarterly,* 10 (2): 175–203.

Cohen, W.M. and Levinthal, D.A. (1990) Absorptive capacity: A new perspective on learning and innovation. *Administrative Science Quarterly,* 35(1): 128–152.

Coleman, J.S. (1988) Social capital in the creation of human capital. *American Journal of Sociology,* 94 (Supplement): S95–S120.

Cross, R. and Cummings, J.N. (2004) Tie and network correlates of individual performance in knowledge-intensive work. *Academy of Management Journal,* 47(6): 928–937.

Daft, R.L. and Lengel, R.H. (1986) Organizational information requirements, media richness and structural design. *Management Science,* 32(5): 554–571.

Darr, E.D., Argote, L., and Epple, D. (1995) The acquisition, transfer, and depreciation of knowledge in service organizations: Productivity in franchises. *Management Science,* 41(11): 1750–1762.

Das, T.K. and Teng, B-S. (2000) A resource-based theory of strategic alliances. *Journal of Management,* 26 (1) : 31–61.

Dhanaraj, C., Lyles, M.A., Steensma, H.K., and Tihanyi, L. (2004) Managing tacit and explicit knowledge transfer in IJVs: The role of relational embeddedness and the impact on performance. *Journal of International Business Studies,* 35(5): 428–442.

Dhanaraj, C. and Parkhe, A. (2006) Orchestrating innovation networks. *Academy of Management Review,* 31(3): 659–668.

Doz, Y.L. and Hamel, G. (1998) *Alliance advantage.* Boston, MA: Harvard Business School Press.

Doz, Y.L., Santos, J., and Williamson, P.J. (2001) *From global to metanational: How companies win in the knowledge economy.* Boston, MA: Harvard Business School Press.

Dyer, J.H. (1996) Specialized supplier networks as a source of competitive advantage: Evidence from the auto industry. *Strategic Management Journal,* 17 (4): 271–292.

Dyer, J.H. (1997) Does governance matter? *Keiretsu* alliances and asset specificity as sources of Japanese competitive advantage. *Organization Science,* 7(6): 649–666.

Dyer, J.H., Kale, P., and Singh, H. (2001) How to make strategic alliances work. *Sloan Management Review,* 42(4): 37–43.

Dyer, J.H. and Nobeoka, K. (2000) Creating and managing a high-performance knowledge-sharing network: The Toyota case. *Strategic Management Journal,* 21(3): 345–367.

Dyer, J.H. and Singh, H. (1998) The relational view: Cooperative strategy and sources of interorganizational competitive advantage. *Academy of Management Review,* 23(4): 660–679.

Evan, W.M. (1965) Toward a theory of inter-organizational relations. *Management Science,* 11(10): B217-B230.

Frost, T.S., Birkinshaw, J.M., and Ensign, P.C. (2002) Centers of excellence in multinational corporations. *Strategic Management Journal,* 23(11): 997–1018.

Galaskiewicz, J. (1979) *Exchange networks.* London: Sage.

Galunic, D.C. and Rodan, S. (1998) Resource recombination in the firm: Knowledge structures and the potential for Schumpeterian innovation. *Strategic Management Journal,* 19(12): 1193–1201.

Gargiulo, M. and Benassi, M. (2000) Trapped in your own net? Network cohesion, structural holes, and the adaptation of social capital. *Organization Science,* 11(2): 183–196.

Garud, R. (1997) On the distinction between know-how, know-why and know-what in technological systems. *Advances in Strategic Management*, 14: 81–101.

Ghoshal, S. and Bartlett, C.A. (1997) *The individualized corporation*. San Francisco, CA: Harper Business.

Gnyawali, D.R. and Madhavan R. (2001) Cooperative networks and competitive dynamics: A structural embeddedness perspective. *Academy of Management Review*, 26(2): 431–445.

Goerzen, A. (2005) Managing alliance networks: Emerging practices of multinational corporations. *Academy of Management Executive*, 19(2): 94–107.

Goerzen, A. (2007) Alliance networks and firm performance: The impact of repeated partnerships. *Strategic Management Journal*, 28(5): 487–509.

Grabher, G. (1993). The weakness of strong ties: the lock-in of regional development in the Ruhr Area. In G. Grabher (ed.), *The Embedded Firm: On the socio-economics of industrial networks*. London: Routledge: 255–277.

Granovetter, M.S. (1985) Economic action and social structure: The problem of embeddedness. *American Journal of Sociology*, 91(3): 481–510.

Grant, R.M. (1996) Prospering in dynamically-competitive environments: Organizational capability and knowledge integration. *Organization Science*, 7(4): 375–387.

Grant, R.M. and Baden-Fuller, C. (2004) A knowledge accessing theory of strategic alliances. *Journal of Management Studies*, 41(1): 61–84.

Gulati, R. (1995) Social structure and alliance formation pattern: A longitudinal analysis. *Administrative Science Quarterly*, 40(3): 610–652.

Gulati, R. (1998) Alliances and networks. *Strategic Management Journal*, 19(4): 293–318.

Gulati, R. (1999) Network location and learning: The influence of network resources and firm capabilities on alliance formation. *Strategic Management Journal*, 20(5): 397–420.

Gulati, R. and Gargiulo, M. (1999) Where do interorganizational networks come from? *American Journal of Sociology*, 104(5): 1439–1493.

Gulati, R. and Singh, H. (1998) The architecture of cooperation: Managing coordination costs and appropriation concerns in strategic alliances. *Administrative Science Quarterly*, 43(4): 781–814.

Gupta, A.K. and Govindarajan, V. (1991) Knowledge flows and the structure of control within multinational corporations. *Academy of Management Review*, 16(4): 768–792.

Gupta, A.K. and Govindarajan, V. (2000) Knowledge flows within multinational corporations. *Strategic Management Journal*, 21(4): 473–496.

Hamel, G. (1991) Competition for competence and inter-partner learning within international strategic alliances. *Strategic Management Journal*, 12(Summer Special Issue): 83–103.

Hansen, M.T. (1999) The search-transfer problem: The role of weak ties in sharing knowledge across organization subunits. *Administrative Science Quarterly*, 44(1): 82–111.

Hansen, M.T. (2002) Knowledge networks: Explaining effective knowledge sharing in multiunit companies. *Organization Science*, 13(3): 232–248.

Hansen, M.T. and Løvas, B. (2004) How do multinational companies leverage technological competencies? Moving from single to interdependent explanations. *Strategic Management Journal*, 25(8/9): 801–822.

Hansen, M.T. and Nohria, N. (2004) How to build collaborative advantage. *Sloan Management Review*, 46(1): 22–30.

Hansen, M.T., Podolny, J.M., and Pfeffer, J. (2001) So many ties, so little time: A task contingency perspective on the value of social capital in organizations. *Research in Organizational Behavior*, 18: 21–57.

Hedberg, B.L.T., Nystrom, P.C., and Starbuck, W.H. (1976) Camping on seesaws: Prescriptions for a self-designing organization. *Administrative Science Quarterly*, 21(1): 41–65.

Hedlund, G. (1994) A model of knowledge management and the N-form corporation. *Strategic Management Journal*, 15 (Summer Special Issue): 73–90.

Hite, J.M. and Hesterly, W.S. (2001) The evolution of firm networks: From emergence to early growth of the firm. *Strategic Management Journal*, 22(3): 275–286.

Hoffmann, W.H. (2005) How to manage a portfolio of alliances. *Long Range Planning*, 38(1): 123–143.

Iansiti, M. and Levien, R. (2004) Strategy as ecology. *Harvard Business Review*, 82(2): 68–78.

Inkpen, A.C. and Dinur, A. (1998) Knowledge management processes and international joint ventures. *Organization Science*, 9(4): 454–468.

Inkpen, A.C. and Tsang, E.W.K. (2005) Social capital, networks, and knowledge transfer. *Academy of Management Review*, 30(1): 146–165.

Jansen, J.J.P., George, G., Van den Bosch, F.A.J., and Volberda, H.W. (2008) Senior team attributes and organizational ambidexterity: The moderating role of transformational leadership. *Journal of Management Studies*, 45(5): 982–1007.

Jansen, J.J.P., Tempelaar, M.P., Van den Bosch, F.A.J., and Volberda, H.W. (2009) Structural differentiation and ambidexterity: The mediating role of integration mechanisms. *Organization Science*, 20(4): 797–811.

Jansen, J.J.P., Van den Bosch, F.A.J., and Volberda, H.W. (2006) Exploratory innovation, exploitative innovation, and performance: Effects of organizational antecedents and environmental moderators. *Management Science*, 52(11): 1661–1674.

Jensen, M. and Meckling, W. (1992) Specific and general knowledge and organizational structure. In L. Werin and H. Wikander (eds.), *Contract economics*. Oxford: Blackwell: 251–274.

Jones, C., Hesterly, W.S., and Borgatti, S.P. (1997) A general theory of network governance: Exchange conditions and social mechanisms. *Academy of Management Review*, 22(4): 911–945.

Kale, P., Dyer, J.H., and Singh, H. (2002) Alliance capability, stock market response, and long-term alliance success: The role of the alliance function. *Strategic Management Journal*, 23(8): 747–767.

Kale, P. and Singh, H. (2007) Building firm capabilities through learning: The role of the alliance learning process in alliance capability and firm-level alliance success. *Strategic Management Journal*, 28(10): 981–1000.

Kale, P., Singh, H., and Perlmutter, H. (2000) Learning and protection of proprietary assets in strategic alliances: Building relational capital. *Strategic Management Journal*, 21(3): 217–237.

Khanna, T. (1998) The scope of alliances. *Organization Science*, 9(3): 340–355.

Khanna, T., Gulati, R., and Nohria, N. (1998) The dynamics of learning alliances: Competition, cooperation and relative scope. *Strategic Management Journal*, 19(3): 193–210.

Kogut, B. (1988) Joint ventures: Theoretical and empirical perspectives. *Strategic Management Journal*, 9(4): 319–332.

Kogut, B., Shan, W., and Walker, G. (1993) Knowledge in the network and the network as knowledge: The structuring of new industries. In G. Grabher (ed.), *The embedded firm: On the socioeconomics of industrial networks*. London: Routledge: 67–94.

Koka, B.R. and Prescott, J.E. (2002) Strategic alliances as social capital: A multidimensional view. *Strategic Management Journal*, 23(9): 795–816.

Kraatz, M.S. (1998) Learning by association? Interorganizational networks and adaptation to environmental change. *Academy of Management Journal*, 41(6): 621–643.

Kumar, R. and Nti, K.O. (1998) Differential learning and interaction in alliance dynamics: A process and outcome discrepancy model. *Organization Science*, 9(3): 356–367.

Lane, P.J. and Lubatkin, M. (1998) Relative absorptive capacity and interorganizational learning. *Strategic Management Journal*, 19(5): 461–477.

Lane, P.J., Salk, J.E., and Lyles, M.A. (2001) Absorptive capacity, learning, and performance in international joint ventures. *Strategic Management Journal*, 22(12): 1139–1161.

Larsson, R., Bengtsson, L., Henriksson, K., and Sparks, J. (1998) The interorganizational learning dilemma: Collective knowledge development in strategic alliances. *Organization Science*, 9 (3): 285–305.

Lavie, D. (2006) The competitive advantage of interconnected firms: An extension of the resource-based view. *Academy of Management Review*, 31(3): 638–658.

Lavie, D. and Rosenkopf, L. (2006) Balancing exploration and exploitation in alliance formation. *Academy of Management Journal*, 49(4): 797–818.

Levin, D.S. and Cross, R. (2004) The strength of weak ties you can trust: The mediating role of trust in effective knowledge transfer. *Management Science*, 50(11): 1477–1490.

Lincoln, J.R. (1982) Intra- (and inter) organizational networks. In S.B. Bacharach (ed.), *Research in the Sociology of Organizations*, 1. Greenwich, CT: JAI Press: 1–38.

Lorenzoni, G. and Lipparini, A. (1999) The leveraging of interfirm relationships as a distinctive organizational capability: A longitudinal study. *Strategic Management Journal*, 20(4): 317–338.

Lyles, M.A. (1988) Learning among joint venture sophisticated firms. In F.J. Contractor and P. Lorange (eds.), *Cooperative Strategies in International Business*. Lexington: Lexington Books: 301–316.

Lyles, M.A. and Schwenk, C.R. (1992) Top management, strategy and organizational knowledge structures. *Journal of Management Studies*, 29(2): 155–174.

Majumdar, S.K. and Venkataraman, S. (1998) Network effects and the adoption of new technology: Evidence from the US telecommunications industry. *Strategic Management Journal*, 19(11): 1045–1062.

McEvily, B. and Marcus, A. (2005) Embedded ties and the acquisition of competitive capabilities. *Strategic Management Journal*, 26(11): 1033–1055.

McEvily, B. and Zaheer, A. (1999) Bridging ties: A source of firm heterogeneity in competitive capabilities. *Strategic Management Journal*, 20(12): 1133–1156.

Mesquita, L.F., Anand, J., and Brush, T.H. (2008) Comparing the resource-based and relational views: Knowledge transfer and spillover in vertical alliances. *Strategic Management Journal*, 29(9): 913–941.

Miles, R.E., Snow, C.C., Mathews, J.A., Miles, G., and Coleman, H.J. Jr. (1997) Organizing in the knowledge age: Anticipating the cellular form. *Academy of Management Executive*, 11(4): 7–20.

Minbaeva, D., Pedersen, T., Björkman, I., Fey, C.F., and Park, H.J. (2003) MNC knowledge transfer, subsidiary absorptive capacity, and HRM. *Journal of International Business Studies*, 34(6): 586–599.

Mitchell, W. and Singh, K. (1996) Survival of businesses using collaborative relationships to commercialize complex goods. *Strategic Management Journal*, 17(3): 169–195.

Mom, T.J.M., Van den Bosch, F.A.J., and Volberda, H.W. (2007) Investigating managers' exploration and exploitation activities: The influence of top-down, bottom-up, and horizontal knowledge inflows. *Journal of Management Studies*, 44(6): 910–931.

Mom, T.J.M., Van den Bosch, F.A.J., and Volberda, H.W. (2009) Understanding variation in managers' ambidexterity: Investigating direct and interaction effects of formal structural and personal coordination mechanisms. *Organization Science*, 20(4): 812–828.

Monteiro, L.F., Arvidsson, N., and Birkinshaw, J. (2008) Knowledge flows within multinational corporations: Explaining subsidiary isolation and its performance implications. *Organization Science*, 19(1): 90–107.

Mowery, D.C., Oxley, J.E., and Silverman, B.S. (1996) Strategic alliances and interfirm knowledge transfer. *Strategic Management Journal*, 17(Winter Special Issue): 77–91.

Mudambi, R. and Navarra, P. (2004) Is knowledge power? Knowledge flows, subsidiary power and rent-seeking in MNCs. *Journal of International Business Studies*, 35(5): 385–406.

Nahapiet, J. and Ghoshal, S. (1998) Social capital, intellectual capital, and the organizational advantage. *Academy of Management Review*, 23(2): 242–266.

Nohria, N. (1992) Is a network perspective a useful way of studying organizations? In N. Nohria and R.G. Eccles (eds.), *Networks and organizations: Structure, form, and action*. Boston, MA: Harvard Business School Press: 1–22.

Nohria, N. and Eccles, R.G. (1992) Face-to-face: Making network organizations work. In N. Nohria and R.G. Eccles (eds.), *Networks and organizations: Structure, form, and action*. Boston, MA: Harvard Business School Press: 288–308.

Nohria, N. and Ghoshal, S. (1997) *The differentiated network*. San Francisco, CA: Jossey-Bass.

Nonaka, I. and Takeuchi, H. (1995) *The knowledge-creating company*. New York: Oxford University Press.

Obstfeld, D. (2005) Social networks, the *tertius iungens* orientation, and involvement in innovation. *Administrative Science Quarterly*, 50(1): 100–130.

Ostroff, F. (1999) *The horizontal organization*. New York: Oxford University Press.

Penrose, E.T. (1959) *The theory of the growth of the firm*. New York: Oxford University Press.

Pettigrew, A.M., Massini, S., and Numagami, T. (2000) Innovative forms of organizing in Europe and Japan. *European Management Journal*, 18(3): 259–273.

Pettigrew, A.M., Whittington, R., Melin, L., Sanchez-Runde, C., Van Den Bosch, F.A.J., Ruigrok, W., and Numagami, T. (2003) *Innovative forms of organizing: International perspectives*. London: Sage.

Phene, A. and Almeida, P. (2008). Innovation in multinational subsidiaries : The role of knowledge assimilation and subsidiary capabilities. *Journal of International Business Studies*, 39(5): 901–919.

Powell, W.W. (1990) Neither market nor hierarchy: Network forms of organization. *Research in Organizational Behavior*, 12: 295–336.

Powell, W.W., Koput, K., and Smith-Doerr, L. (1996) Interorganizational collaboration and the locus of innovation: Networks of learning in biotechnology. *Administrative Science Quarterly*, 41(1): 116–145.

Raisch, S. and Birkinshaw, J. (2008) Organizational ambidexterity: Antecedents, outcomes, and moderators. *Journal of Management*, 34(3): 375–409.

Reagans, R. and McEvily, B. (2003) Network structure and knowledge transfer: The effects of cohesion and range. *Administrative Science Quarterly*, 48(2): 240–267.

Reagans, R. and McEvily, B. (2008) Contradictory or compatible? Reconsidering the 'trade-off' between brokerage and closure on knowledge sharing. *Advances in Strategic Management*, 25: 275–313.

Reagans, R. and Zuckerman, E.W. (2008) Why knowledge does not equal power: the network redundancy trade-off. *Industrial and Corporate Change*, 17(5): 903–944.

Ring, P.S. and Van de Ven, A.H. (1994) Developmental processes of interorganizational relationships. *Academy of Management Review*, 19(1): 90–118.

Rowley, T.J. and Baum, J.A.C. (2008) The dynamics of network strategies and positions. *Advances in Strategic Management*, 25: 641–671.

Rowley, T.J., Behrens, D., and Krackhardt, D. (2000) Redundant governance structures: An analysis of structural and relational embeddedness in the steel and semiconductor industries. *Strategic Management Journal*, 21 (Special Issue): 369–386.

Sarkar, M., Aulakh, P.S., and Madhok, A. (2009) Process capabilities and value creation in alliance portfolios. *Organization Science*, 20(3): 583–600.

Schulz, M. (2001) The uncertain relevance of newness: Organizational learning and knowledge flows. *Academy of Management Journal*, 44(4): 661–681.

Schulz, M. (2003) Pathways of relevance: Exploring inflows of knowledge into subunits of multinational corporations. *Organization Science*, 14(4): 440–459.

Siggelkow, N. and Rivkin, J. (2005) Speed and search: Designing organizations for turbulence and complexity. *Organization Science*, 16(2): 101–122.

Simonin, B.L. (1997) The importance of collaborative know-how: An empirical test of the learning organization. *Academy of Management Journal*, 40(5): 1150–1174.

Simonin, B.L. (1999) Ambiguity and the process of knowledge transfer in strategic alliances. *Strategic Management Journal*, 20(7): 595–623.

Singh, K. and Mitchell, W. (1996) Precarious collaboration: Business survival after partners shut down or form new partnerships. *Strategic Management Journal*, 17(Summer Special Issue): 99–115.

Soda, G., Usai, A., and Zaheer, A. (2004) Network memory: The influence of past and current networks on performance. *Academy of Management Journal*, 47(6): 893–906.

Stuart, T.E. (1998) Network positions and propensities to collaborate: An investigation of strategic alliance formation in a high-technology industry. *Administrative Science Quarterly*, 43(3): 668–698.

Stuart, T.E. (2003) Governing strategic alliances. *Research in the Sociology of Organizations*, 20: 189–208.

Szulanski, G. (1996) Exploring internal stickiness: Impediments to the transfer of best practice within the firm. *Strategic Management Journal*, 17(Winter Special Issue): 27–43.

Szulanski, G. (2000) The process of knowledge transfer: A diachronic analysis of stickiness. *Organizational Behavior and Human Decision Processes*, 82(1): 9–27.

Szulanski, G., Cappetta, R., and Jensen, R.J. (2004) When and how trustworthiness matters: Knowledge transfer and the moderating effect of causal ambiguity. *Organization Science*, 15(5): 600–613.

Tiwana, A. (2008) Do bridging ties complement strong ties? An empirical examination of alliance ambidexterity. *Strategic Management Journal*, 29(3): 251–272.

Tsai, W. (2000) Social capital, strategic relatedness and the formation of intraorganizational linkages. *Strategic Management Journal*, 21(8): 925–939.

Tsai, W. (2001) Knowledge transfer in intra-organizational networks: Effects of network position and absorptive capacity on business unit innovation and performance. *Academy of Management Journal*, 44(5): 996–1004.

Tsai, W. and Ghoshal, S. (1998) Social capital and value creation: The role of intrafirm networks. *Academy of Management Journal*, 41(4): 464–476.

Tyler, B.B. and Steensma, H.K. (1995) Evaluating technological collaborative opportunities: A cognitive modeling perspective. *Strategic Management Journal*, 16 (Summer Special Issue): 43–70.

Uzzi, B. (1996) The sources and consequences of embeddedness for the economic performance of organizations: The network effect. *American Sociological Review*, 61(4): 674–698.

Uzzi, B. (1997) Social structure and competition in interfirm networks: The paradox of embeddedness. *Administrative Science Quarterly*, 42(1): 35–67.

Uzzi, B. and Lancaster, R. (2003) Relational embeddedness and learning: The case of bank loan managers and their clients. *Management Science*, 49(4): 383–399.

Van Wijk, R., Jansen, J.J.P., and Lyles, M.A. (2008) Inter- and intra-organizational knowledge transfer: A meta-analytic review and assessment of its antecedents and consequences. *Journal of Management Studies*, 45(4): 830–853.

Vlaar, P.W.L., Van den Bosch, F.A.J., and Volberda, H.W. (2007) Towards a dialectic perspective on formalization in interorganizational relationships: How alliance managers capitalize on the duality inherent in rules and procedures. *Organization Studies*, 28(4): 437–466.

Walker, G., Kogut, B., and Shan, W. (1997) Social capital, structural holes and the formation of an industry network. *Organization Science*, 8(1): 109–125.

Wasserman, S. and Faust, K. (1994) *Social network analysis: Methods and applications*. Cambridge: Cambridge University Press.

Williamson, O.E. (1975) *Markets and hierarchies*. New York: Free Press.

Williamson, O.E. (1985) *The economic institutions of capitalism*. New York: Free Press.

Wong, S-S., Ho, V.T., and Lee, C.H. (2008) A power perspective to interunit knowledge transfer: Linking knowledge attributes to unit power and the transfer of knowledge. *Journal of Management*, 34(1): 127–150.

Zaheer, A. and Bell, G.G. (2005) Benefiting from network position: Firm capabilities, structural holes, and performance. *Strategic Management Journal*, 26(9): 809–825.

Zander, U. and Kogut, B. (1995) Knowledge and the speed of the transfer and imitation of organizational capabilities: An empirical test. *Organization Science*, 5(1): 76–92.

Zenger, T.R. and Hesterly, W.S. (1997) The disaggregation of corporations: Selective intervention, high-powered incentives, and molecular units. *Organization Science*, 8(3): 209–222.

23

Knowledge Assets, Capabilities, and the Theory of the Firm

DAVID J. TEECE* AND ABDULRAHMAN AL-AALI

ABSTRACT

Knowledge assets such as technical and organizational know-how undergird each firm's competitive position. Such assets are generally embedded in routines, the well-established and largely uncodified patterns that firms have developed for finding solutions to particular problems. Learning, the maintenance and development of these assets, is an inherently collective, organizational process that is grounded in, but surpasses, the experience and expertise of individuals.

Effective organizational learning—a continuous process in most industries—requires dynamic capabilities. These capabilities are activities that can usefully be thought of in three clusters: sensing opportunities (building new knowledge), seizing those opportunities to capture value, and transforming the organization as needed to adapt to the requirements of new business models and the competitive environment.

As sources of knowledge have become more organizationally and geographically diffuse, the coordination skills of managers are particularly important. Many of the resources to be coordinated can lie outside the boundaries of the firm as easily as inside; the extent of vertical integration must be carefully calibrated to reflect an array of strategic factors.

The economic 'theory of the firm,' currently dominated by the contracting perspective, needs to be augmented to account for these new factors, particularly the superiority of the firm over markets for the creation, transfer, and protection of intangible assets. Complementarities and co-specialization are advanced as two emerging concepts of particular relevance to a new theory of the learning firm.

* I'd like to thank the editors for many helpful comments. Greg Linden also provided substantial help with this chapter.

INTRODUCTION

In this chapter, knowledge and learning are seen as key factors impacting economic organization. In particular, the dynamic capabilities framework is used to explain how the distinctive experience-based and knowledge-based assets of firms drive their vertical (and lateral) integration, their heterogeneity, and indeed, their very existence. Mainstream economics has employed ideas from organizational learning in a piecemeal fashion (Boerner, et al., 2001). The resource-based view (RBV) of the firm, in which resources are built through experiential learning, can inform economic models (Conner, 1991) and business arrangements more generally.

In competitive market environments, firms must build assets and capabilities that enable positive differentiation. Knowledge assets such as technical and organizational know-how can provide this differentiation. Accordingly, they can undergird a firm's competitive position.

Knowledge is often embedded in routines, the well-established and largely uncodified patterns that firms have developed for finding solutions to particular problems (Nelson and Winter, 1982). More formal types of knowledge assets, such as patents, can also support competitive advantage.

Although the organizational knowledge that undergirds distinctive capabilities transcends the knowledge of individual firm employees, it must nonetheless be created and applied through the management of employees. With respect to knowledge assets, an important class of employees is that of experts (literati and numerati), whose management requires limited hierarchy, flexible teams, and performance-based incentives (Teece, 2011). Entrepreneurial managers with superior skills in asset orchestration are also vital to successful value capture.

Whereas firms may once have derived (and in some industries still do) advantage over rivals primarily from the efficient management of large scale manufacturing investment (Chandler, 1990), firms increasingly build competitive advantage and hence long-term profitability mainly through the creation, ownership, transfer, orchestration, and protection of non-tradable (intangible) assets. Knowledge itself is of course the prime example of an intangible asset.

An economic question of particular importance as more industries embrace outsourcing is why hierarchically-managed firms exist at all. Why not just organize the same activities using a nexus of contracts? Would a plethora of arm's-length contracts suffice to organize economic activity? If not, why not? These issues go to the heart of the 'theory of the firm' and are discussed later in this chapter.

KNOWLEDGE ASSETS AND LEARNING

Knowledge assets such as technical and organizational know-how undergird each firm's competitive position. Such assets are partially embedded in routines, the well-established and largely uncodified patterns that firms have developed for finding solutions to particular problems. Learning, which is necessary for the maintenance and development of these assets, is an inherently collective, organizational process that is grounded in, but surpasses, the experience and expertise of individuals (Fiol and Lyles, 1985; Simon, 1991) and individual competence. Ideally, this collective learning permits the organization to transcend individual-level bounded rationality (Teece et al., 1994). Value can also derive from the unique combination and alignment of intangible assets that entrepreneurs and managers assemble.

The pioneering description of organizational learning in Cyert and March (1963) saw learning as crisis driven and short term in focus, and inflexible to managerial intent. But for the field of strategic management, the key insight from Cyert and March was that the adaptive (and often path dependent) learning of firms, as embodied in their standard operating procedures, accounts for firm heterogeneity (Pierce et al., 2002). This notion, coupled with the insights of Penrose (1959) about the role of firm 'resources' in growth and innovation, eventually gave rise to the RBV of the firm. Over time, the dynamic capabilities framework (Teece et al., 1997) emerged as the dominant RBV-rooted approach to strategy.

In the dynamic capabilities framework, organizational learning (which is in part dependent on the orchestration talents of top management) is at the heart of a firm's capabilities. Effective organizational learning (and its associated value creation and capture) requires dynamic capabilities, and *vice versa* (Easterby-Smith and Prieto, 2008).

This section reviews the nature of firm resources and then outlines the dynamic capabilities framework. Dynamic capabilities can usefully be thought of in three clusters: sensing opportunities (building new knowledge), seizing these opportunities to capture value, and transforming the organization as needed to adapt to the requirements of new business models and the competitive environment.

Resources/competences

The core building blocks of stable and growing organizations are resources. Resources are firm-specific (generally intangible) assets that are difficult, or impossible, to imitate. Intangible assets are usually quite differentiated. They are stocks rather than flows.

Firm-specific assets are idiosyncratic in nature, and are difficult to trade because their property rights are likely to have fuzzy boundaries and their value is context dependent. As a result, there is unlikely to be a well-developed market for resources/competences; in fact, they are typically not traded at all. They are also generally difficult to transfer amongst firms. Examples include process know-how, customer relationships, and the knowledge possessed by groups of especially skilled employees.[1]

Competences are a particular kind of organizational resource. They result from activities that are performed repetitively, or quasi-repetitively. Organizational competences enable economic tasks to be performed that require collective effort. They are usually underpinned by organizational processes/routines. Indeed, they represent distinct bundles of organizational routines and problem-solving skills.[2]

---

[1]While the industrial workforce has always contained individuals with high education and/or exceptional talent, the economic significance of such literati and numerati has become more important as the traditional sources of firm profitability have been undermined (Albert and Bradley, 1997: 4). The nature and management of the firm's 'expert talent' are discussed later.

[2]Organizational competences have their roots in the work of Simon (1947), Nelson and Winter (1982), Winter (1988), Teece et al. (1994), and Dosi et al. (2000).

In short, ordinary competence defines sufficiency in performance of a delineated organizational task. It's about doing things well enough, or possibly very well, without attention to whether the economic activity is the right thing to do. Competences can be quantified because they can be measured against particular (unchanging) task requirements. The level of a competence can be benchmarked; the assessment of a competence does not require that the activity be aligned with the firm's environment and other assets/competences.

Some processes undergirding competence are formal, others informal. As employees address recurrent tasks, processes become defined. The nature of processes is that they are not meant to change (until they have to). Valuable differentiating processes may include those that define how decisions are made, how customer needs are assessed, and how quality is maintained. Organizational learning in these cases may evolve toward formal rules or remain as heuristics.[3]

As an organization grows, its capabilities are embedded in competences/resources and shaped by (organizational) values. Organizational values define the implicit norms and rules of the organization. They determine how it sets priorities with respect to how employees and affiliates work together.

While economics has often modeled firms as homogeneous, or asymmetric only in their access to information, the 'resource-based view' of the firm recognizes the unique attributes of individual firms. In the 1980s, a number of strategic management scholars, including Rumelt (1984), Teece (1980, 1982, 1984), and Wernerfelt (1984) began theorizing that a firm earns rents from leveraging its unique resources, which are difficult to monetize directly via transactions in intermediate markets.

As mentioned earlier, value can derive not only from routines but also from unique combinations of highly differentiated intangible assets. Such assets are traded only occasionally, if at all. Put differently, the markets on which they are bought and sold are very 'thin.' The ownership and orchestration of non-tradable (intangible) assets can therefore be a basis for long-term profitability in what we normally think of as competitive (final product) markets.

The Internet and the explosion of markets for everything have vastly expanded the number and type of goods and services that are readily accessed externally (Teece, 2000). As more and more activities become available from suppliers, the range of domains (thin markets) in which competitive advantage can be built narrows.

One class of very thin markets is the markets for intangibles. Intangible assets remain especially difficult—although not impossible—to trade. This is particularly true for knowledge assets and, more generally, 'relationship' (e.g. customer or supplier) assets. Knowledge assets are tacit to varying degrees and are both difficult to trade and costly to transfer (Teece, 1981a, 2000). So are relationship assets. Because the market for intangibles is thin and riddled with imperfections, this favors internalization (vertical or lateral integration) of the mechanics of capturing strategic value. Certain assets are more valuable to one firm than another, and because markets are thin, such assets, if procurable, can often be bought on the cheap.

---

[3]Evidence is mixed as to whether rules or heuristics are more desirable for firm performance. See Bingham et al. (2007) for an empirical study that supports heuristics and Zollo and Singh (2004) for an example of beneficial codification.

Dynamic capabilities

'Resources' such as intangible assets suggest stocks, not flows. However, for long-term competitive advantage, resources must be constantly renewed (Teece, 2009). The logic of renewal is amplified in fast-moving environments such as those characteristic of high-tech sectors (e.g. computers). However, a need to renew resources can also occur in 'low-tech' industries (e.g. home construction).

A framework is needed to help explain how business enterprises build and then renew their resource base, keeping it aligned with what's needed to serve customers and meet or beat the competition. The framework we offer is called dynamic capabilities.

Dynamic capabilities are the firm's ability to integrate, build, and reconfigure internal and external resources/competences to address and shape rapidly changing business environments (Teece et al., 1990, 1997; Teece, 2007a). They determine the speed at, and degree to which, the firm's idiosyncratic resources/competences can be aligned and realigned to match the opportunities and requirements of the business environment. The goal is to generate sustained abnormal (positive) returns.

Dynamic capabilities may sometimes be rooted in certain change routines (e.g. product development along a known trajectory) and analysis (e.g. of investment choices). However, they are more commonly rooted in creative managerial and entrepreneurial acts (e.g. pioneering new markets). Nevertheless, the learning that takes place in the dynamic capabilities framework is inherently collective, requiring coordinated search and communication in order to be effective (Pierce et al., 2002).

The essence of resources/competences as well as dynamic capabilities is that they cannot generally be bought; they must be built. As noted above, dynamic capabilities measure the capacity to build new intangibles when necessary and to align and realign, integrate and reintegrate such intangibles so that they are tuned to the business environment. Sensing, seizing, and transforming are meta-level categories of such attributes (opportunity seizing and adjustment mechanisms). Firms with these attributes can evolve and co-evolve with the business environment. Such capabilities create the potential for long-term profitability because markets do not price most resources/intangible assets at their real value to the buyer when the buyer possesses scarce complementary and, especially, co-specialized assets (Teece, 2007b). However, the required resources/intangible assets may not yet exist. They must first be built or created. In these situations, the business enterprise can create a distinctive competitive advantage by building the assets ahead of its competitors.

The sensing and seizing categories in the dynamic capabilities framework are similar to two activities discussed in the management literature as potentially incompatible within a single organization: exploration and exploitation (March, 1991). Exploration (e.g. research on a potentially disruptive technology) has a longer time horizon and greater uncertainty than exploitation (e.g. selling mature products). The two types of activities require different management styles; one solution is an 'ambidextrous organization' where two separate subunits with different cultures are linked by shared company-wide values and senior managers with a broad view—and appropriate incentives (O'Reilly and Tushman, 2004; O'Reilly et al., 2009).

As discussed above, a firm's basic competences, if well honed, enable it to perform its current activities efficiently. However, whether the enterprise is at present making the right products and addressing the right market segment, or whether its future plans are appropriately matched to consumer needs and technological and competitive opportunities, is determined by dynamic capabilities. Dynamic capabilities, in turn, require the organization (especially its top management) to develop conjectures, to validate them, and to realign assets and competences for new requirements. They enable the enterprise to profitably orchestrate its resources, competences, and other assets in order to take account of changing market and technological circumstances.

Dynamic capabilities are also used to assess when and how the enterprise is to ally with other enterprises. The expansion of trade has enabled and required greater global specialization. To make the global system of vertical specialization and co-specialization (bilateral dependence) work, there is a need (indeed an enhanced need) for firms to develop and align assets and to combine the various elements of the global value chain so as to develop and deliver a joint 'solution' that customers value.[4]

There is another realm in which dynamic capabilities are especially salient. Not infrequently, an innovating firm will be required to create a market, such as when an entirely new product is offered to customers, or when new intermediate products must be traded. Dynamic capabilities, particularly the more entrepreneurial competences, are a critical input to the market creating (and co-creating) processes.[5]

To summarize, dynamic capabilities reflect the capacity a firm has to orchestrate activities and resources/assets within the system of global specialization and co-specialization. They also reflect the firm's efforts to create/shape the market in ways that enable value to be created and captured. Dynamic capabilities require change routines and more. Fast-moving environments require modifying, or, if necessary, a complete revamping of what the enterprise is doing so as to maintain a good fit with (and sometimes to transform) the ecosystem and markets that the enterprise occupies. Some of this change management can be routinized. Some cannot.[6] Microfoundations and organizing principles have been laid out elsewhere (Teece, 2007a). The following is a brief overview of the major dynamic capability categories.

The continuous renewal enabled by dynamic capabilities requires an ongoing set of activities and adjustments that can be divided into three clusters: (1) identification and assessment of an opportunity (*sensing*), (2) mobilization of resources to address an opportunity and to capture value from doing so (*seizing*), and (3) regular realignment (*transforming*). These activities are required if the firm is to sustain itself as markets and technologies change, although some firms will be stronger than others at some or all of these.

One could imagine that a market economy would allow individuals and organizations to specialize in one of the three capability clusters. However, the markets for opportunities, inventions, and know-how are riddled with inefficiencies and high transaction costs, and most entrepreneurs are forced to bundle these activities together (i.e. do all three).[7]

---

[4]Co-specialization has strong implications for organization and strategy (Teece, 2007a).

[5]The entrepreneurial creation and co-creation of markets is often required to ensure the generation and appropriability of returns from innovation (Pitelis and Teece, 2009). The Internet keeps generating a myriad of such requirements every day.

[6]Entrepreneurial activity, inside or outside an enterprise, is by its nature non-routine.

[7]The market for opportunities is imperfect due both to problems of conveying the merits of ideas and also because of opportunism, which can lead to the 'lemons' problem identified by Akerlof (1970). In general, entrepreneurs will be reluctant to 'sell' or simply license ideas they believe are undervalued. The outcome thus tends towards internalization. For an early statement of some of these issues, see Teece (1981).

Table 23.1 Activities conducted to create and capture value
(organized by clusters of dynamic capabilities)

	Sensing	*Seizing*	*Transforming*
Creating value	• spotting opportunities	• investment discipline	• achieving recombinations
	• identifying opportunities for research and development	• commitment to research and development	
	• conceptualizing new customer needs and new business models	• building competencies	
		• achieving new combinations	
Capturing value	• positioning for first mover and other advantages	• intellectual property qualification and enforcement;	• managing threats
	• determining desirable entry timing	• implementing business models	• honing the business model
		• leveraging complementary assets	• developing new complements
		• investment or co-investment in 'production' facilities	

The relative importance of the competences and adjustment mechanisms that constitute sensing, seizing, and transforming varies according to circumstance. To simplify the analysis of dynamic capabilities even further, they can be grouped into two essential classes of activities: creating value and capturing value (see Table 23.1).

Dynamic capabilities are most relevant in a regime of rapid change, a condition that prevails in a growing number of industries. The global economy has undergone drastic changes that have accelerated the rhythm at which firms innovate. The decreased cost of communication and data flow, the reduced barriers to trade, and the liberalization of labor and financial markets in many parts of the world are forcing firms to confront agile and/or low-cost competitors early in life. This in turn has caused firms to undertake a major revision of their innovation strategies, such as a greater reliance on open innovation, which changes how firms must learn and 'store' new knowledge.[8]

---

[8]The enablement of open innovation by new technologies is in some ways the mirror image of the 'Second Industrial Revolution,' when earlier improvements to communications (telegraph) and transportation (railroad) induced a period of vertical integration on a continental scale with an emphasis on in-house research and development (Chandler, 1990).

KNOWLEDGE ASSETS AND COMPETITIVE ADVANTAGE

This section looks more closely at how the dynamic capabilities framework connects resources to performance through the creation and capture of value in markets.

Creating value with innovation

Despite its obvious importance, a theory of how firms create value is largely missing from the standard economics literature. To the extent it is addressed, the industrial organization literature dwells almost entirely on the funding of R&D, figuring (implicitly) that the R&D expenditure is the main driver of innovation. However, R&D activity is only one of several factors likely to determine the generation of new ideas.[9] The concept of dynamic capabilities—the sensing, seizing, and transformation that ongoing innovation requires—provides a broader framework to help one understand how firms create value.

Sensing is an entrepreneurial activity—whether conducted by a new or an existing firm—that involves the identification and conceptualization of opportunities both within and beyond prevailing technological paradigms (Teece, 2008). It involves cognition. As markets evolve, changes in consumer needs, product technologies, and the competitive positioning of other companies can threaten a firm's existing position or open the possibility of a new or better one. In some cases, as stressed by Kirzner (1973), the entrepreneur/manager may have differential access to existing information relative to rivals. More often, sensing opportunities involves scanning, interpretation, and learning across technologies and markets, both 'local' and 'distant', that are also visible to rival firms (March and Simon, 1958; Nelson and Winter, 1982). O'Reilly et al. (2009) describe well how IBM learned from its mistakes, having missed several emerging new market opportunities despite being involved in their early creation.[10]

In reality, management teams often find it difficult to look beyond a narrow search horizon tied to established competences (Levitt and March, 1988). Henderson (1994) cites General Motors, Digital Equipment, and IBM as companies that faced major problems from becoming trapped in their deeply ingrained assumptions, information filters, and

---

[9]The literature on cumulative innovation, with its emphasis on optimal patent policies (e.g. Scotchmer 1991), captures some of the larger context for innovation, as does that on learning from customers (e.g. von Hippel, 1998).

[10]'For example, IBM developed the first commercial router but Cisco dominated that market. As early as 1996, IBM had developed technologies to accelerate the performance of the web, but Akamai, a second-mover, had the product vision to capture this market. Early on, IBM developed speech recognition software but was eclipsed by Nuance. Technologies in RFID, Business Intelligence, e-Sourcing, and Pervasive Computing all represented disturbing examples of missed opportunities for the company. In each instance, the conclusion was that IBM had the potential to win in these markets but had failed to take advantage of the opportunity.' (O'Reilly et al., 2009: 85).

problem solving strategies. O'Reilly et al. (2009) put IBM's problems down to six factors, including the lack of discipline for evaluating new business opportunities.[11]

Seizing an opportunity requires investments in development via further creative and/ or combinatorial activity that addresses the opportunity with new products, processes, or services. It may involve building a necessary new competence or identifying an appropriate external alliance that can secure access to one. It can be aided by new organizational processes and structures, as IBM has discovered with its emerging business opportunities process. However, it took the leadership of Lou Gerstner to get this set up, indicating that it is not just routines and processes which undergird dynamic capabilities.

Transformation of the firm itself is the third capability required for creating (and capturing) value. Sensing and seizing marked out a path for the creation of value, but over time the firm still needs to periodically consider (and reconsider) its own 'fit' to the current opportunities it plans to exploit and the new possibilities it plans to explore (Siggelkow and Levinthal, 2005). Management must assess the coherence of the firm's business model, asset structure, and organizational routines with respect to its environment. Yet commitment to existing processes, assets, and problem definitions makes this extremely hard to do, especially in a firm that is currently performing satisfactorily.

Organizational innovation can allow the firm to escape unfavorable path dependencies. These dependencies themselves limit the speed and scope of the innovations that can be implemented (Teece et al., 1994). Reconfiguring the firm is costly in terms of both money and morale. When a planned innovation is incremental, routines and structures can probably be adapted gradually. Stinchcombe (1990), for example, describes how firms may make small adjustments to their structure as new information progressively reduces environmental uncertainty. Radical organizational innovation can potentially be accommodated by a 'break out' unit where new capabilities are established before being introduced to the firm as a whole (Teece, 2000).

Organizational innovation has a long history. As Chandler (1962; 1977) and Williamson (1975; 1981) have chronicled, the large, multidivisional (M-form) organization has its roots in the development of line-management hierarchies by the nineteenth-century railroads, which needed a system to manage a continent-spanning organization. In the twentieth century, large corporations such as DuPont and General Motors gradually shifted from a functionally organized (U-form) structure to an M-form structure that relieved top management of responsibility for operational details. Related innovations such as the conglomerate and the multinational forms allowed organizations to span a wider array of activities and locations than ever before.

---

[11]IBM's internal analysis of why the company had missed past emerging market opportunities yielded six major reasons: (1) 'The existing management system rewards execution directed at short-term results and does not value strategic business building;' (2) 'The company is preoccupied with current served markets and existing offerings;' (3) 'The business model emphasizes sustained profit and EPS improvement rather than actions oriented towards higher price/earnings;' (4) 'The firm's approach to gathering and using market insight is inadequate for embryonic markets;' (5) 'The company lacks established disciplines for selecting, experimenting, funding, and terminating new growth businesses;' and (6) 'Once selected, many new ventures fail in execution.' (O'Reilly et al., 2009: 85).

Organizational innovation has continued, with the benefits of greater decentralization being 'rediscovered' as the enterprise grows. John Chambers, the CEO of US network equipment company Cisco Systems, described how the management structure of Cisco changed some fifteen years after its founding: 'In 2001, we were like most high-tech companies—all decisions came to the top 10 people in the company, and we drove things back down from there' (McGirt, 2008).

Cisco developed a more decentralized and collaborative management system, with a network of councils and boards entrusted and empowered to launch new businesses, and incentives to encourage executives to work together flexibly. Chambers claimed that 'these boards and councils have been able to innovate with tremendous speed' (ibid.). Yet just a few years after saying this, Chambers dissolved the majority of the councils to overcome the bureaucratic sclerosis that had set in.

Organizational innovation is not only an important form of creating value but of capturing it as well. Armour and Teece (1978) showed that the petroleum industry firms that first adopted M-form structures retained a profit advantage until the innovation was eventually replicated generally throughout the industry by the early 1970s. Subsequent studies (Teece, 1981b) showed this same result across multiple industries.

Capturing value (profiting) from innovation

Companies that rely too heavily on creating value without an eye for the market will not perform well commercially. Many engineering-driven companies' brilliant ideas have never found (or created) a market. Invention without a commercialization strategy and access on competitive terms to complementary assets is unlikely to lead to commercial success. Although it is possible to disseminate some innovations (e.g. software over the Internet) without using complementary assets, most industrial innovations will not achieve marketplace success without deployment of considerable resources and complementary assets into production, distribution, and promotion.

For the value capture process, 'sensing' includes detecting the right timing for market entry. In some cases it's beneficial to be a first mover while in others it may be more advantageous to exploit a gap left by a pioneer.

'Seizing,' however, is the core competence cluster for capturing value and is encompassed by the profiting from innovation framework, which is discussed below. The capabilities involve choosing an appropriate mechanism for the protection of intellectual property (e.g. trade secrets versus patents), deciding which activities must be performed by the firm or procured in the market, and crafting a business model.

A business model (Chesbrough and Rosenbloom, 2002; Teece, 2010) defines a product's value proposition for customers and how the firm will convert that to profit.[12] A business model is an organizational and financial architecture which embraces and integrates in a consistent fashion (1) the feature set of the product or service; (2) the benefit (value proposition)

---

[12]Economics has for the most part not investigated business models. Some specific cases have been analyzed, especially the 'bundling' or 'tying' of goods for joint sale, typically discussed in an antitrust context (e.g. Adams and Yellen, 1976), and the provision of public goods (e.g. Demsetz, 1970). Even business studies have been slow to say what a business model is and why it matters.

to the user from consuming/using the product or service; (3) the market segments to be targeted; (4) the 'design' of revenue streams and cost structure; (5) the way products/services are to be combined and offered to the customer; and (6) the mechanisms by which value is to be captured.

Google, the leading Internet search engine, incorporated in 1998, provides clear examples of these business model elements in action. Initially, the company's investments in proprietary search algorithms and computing resources made it the most popular search engine on the Internet, but these innovations did not translate directly to profits. In late 2000, the company began auctioning ads linked to specific keywords (a system similar to that already employed by a competing search site, GoTo.com). Google recognized that part of its appeal was the minimalist design of its web site, and it has limited ads on the site to simple text. It was Google's combination of innovation, awareness of how it provided value both to search users and to advertisers, and a system for turning the advertising into revenue—and then into profit—that provided the foundation for the company's ongoing success.

To seize the opportunities created by innovation, innovators must excel at understanding not only customer needs, but also the possible future evolution of technology, costs, and customer willingness to pay. Even a successful business model, however, is insufficient to assure sustained profitability when imitation is easy. When hard to imitate—or when used to pioneer a winner-take-all market—a business model can be a source of sustained profitability.[13]

The business model also encompasses a firm's strategy toward its rivals. Positioning within fast-moving industries often takes the form of a standards competition, either in the market (e.g. Windows versus Mac) or through political maneuvering within a cooperative organization (e.g. the International Organization for Standardization).[14] Ownership of a successful standard has numerous potential benefits, including licensing revenue, privileged access to new technologies, and influence over the technology trajectory.

Seizing and transforming capabilities allow firms to refine and expand their business models in order to exploit new opportunities or defend against new competitive threats. They are the means by which organizations remake parts of themselves, possibly redrawing the firm's boundaries to respond to changes in the business environment. A reformulation of the business model may require radical shifts in the supply chain, asset ownership, or sales channels to ensure continued/improved value capture.

In fast-moving market and technology environments, firms must be ready to continuously reinvent themselves. Netflix is a good example of a firm that went through multiple business models in a short period of time. The initial Netflix business model was based on a pay-per-rental service, but this pricing model was unpopular and the company almost failed. It was clear to management Netflix had to rejig its business model and, between September and October 1999, it relaunched itself with a subscription model. For a fixed monthly fee, subscribers could rent any number of DVDs per month, limited only as to

---

[13]Features of markets that can produce winner-take-all outcomes include those in which network externalities (Katz and Shapiro, 1986), switching costs (Klemperer, 1987), or learning economies (Krugman, 1987) confer a substantial incumbent advantage.

[14]David and Greenstein (1990) provide a review of the extensive literature on the economics and competitive consequences of compatibility standards.

the number held at any one time. The model was supported by a system of regional distribution centers which ensured next day delivery to over 90% of subscribers. The Netflix business model was further refined as management figured out customer preferences and willingness to pay. The company had to adapt again as rental-via-download became a viable option. Since January 2008, Netflix has offered its subscribers unlimited use of the media it has available for streaming over the Internet.

Over the past two decades, our understanding of value capture from innovation and the link to firm strategy has expanded dramatically. A stream of research has stressed the importance of the architecture of the enterprise (especially the boundaries of its ownership and its control of complementary assets) for improving the chances of sustainable success when new technologies are commercialized. The role of supporting institutions and public policy—especially appropriability regimes—has also been highlighted.

This body of work has come to be known as the profiting from innovation (PFI) framework[15] and was the topic of a special issue of *Research Policy* in 2006 (v.35, n.8). PFI addressed a puzzle that had not been well explained in the previous literature, namely: why do highly creative, pioneering firms often fail to capture the economic returns from innovation? The original framework (Teece, 1986) cites several examples (e.g. EMI in CAT scanners, Bowmar in calculators), and the phenomenon does indeed endure. The first-generation PC manufacturers all but disappeared from the scene (and even IBM, which pioneered the Microsoft-Intel PC architecture, exited the business in 2005 by selling its PC business to a Chinese company, Lenovo). Xerox (PARC) and Apple invented the graphical user interface, but Microsoft Windows dominates the PC market with its follow-on graphical user interface. Netscape invented the browser, but Microsoft captured more of the market. Apple's iPod was not the first MP3 player, but it has a commanding position in the category today. Merck was a pioneer in cholesterol-lowering drugs (Zocor), but Pfizer, a late entrant, secured a superior market position with Lipitor.

At first glance, it is tempting to say that these examples reflect the result of Schumpeterian gales of creative destruction where winners are constantly challenged and overturned by entrants.[16] Indeed, entrants with potentially disruptive innovations are almost always waiting in the wings, but many of the cited cases involved mostly incremental/imitative entrants rather than the radical breakthroughs typically invoked in accounts of Schumpeterian competition.

More importantly, there is ample variance in the outcomes from entry, with many cases where first or early movers captured and sustained significant competitive advantage over time. Genentech was a pioneer in using biotechnology to discover and develop drugs, and thirty years later was the second largest biotechnology firm (and the most productive in

---

[15]The core paper in the profiting from innovation (PFI) framework is Teece (1986). The intellectual origins of the framework can be traced to Williamson (for his work on contracting), to Abernathy and Utterback (for their work on the innovation life cycle), to economic historians like Nathan Rosenberg and Alfred Chandler (for their work on complementary technologies), to Nelson and Winter (for their work on the nature of knowledge), and to Schumpeter (for his focus on the need for value capture). See Winter (2006) for a review of PFI's intellectual origins.

[16]There is a long literature on the role of new entrants in dislodging established firms. See for instance, Anderson and Tushman (1990), Clark (1985), Henderson and Clark (1990), and Christensen (1997).

its use of research and development dollars) right up to its acquisition by Hoffmann-La Roche in 2009. Intel invented the microprocessor and still has a leading market position more than thirty years later. Dell pioneered a new distribution system for PCs and, despite recent challenges and many would-be imitators, remained the leader until it was bypassed by Hewlett-Packard in 2007. Toyota's much studied 'Toyota Production System' has provided the auto maker a source of competitive advantage for decades despite numerous and sustained attempts at imitation, with the company finally becoming the world's biggest car manufacturer in 2008.

The profiting from innovation framework (Teece, 1986, 2006; Pisano and Teece, 2007) provides an explanation as to why some innovators profit from innovation while others lose out—often to rank imitators—and why it is not inevitable that the pioneers will lose.

The fundamental imperative for profiting from an innovation is that unless the inventor/innovator enjoys strong natural protection against imitation and/or strong intellectual property protection, then the potential future stream of income is at risk. The relevant appropriability regime is thus critical to shaping the possible outcomes.

Appropriability regimes can be 'weak' (innovations are difficult to protect because they can be easily codified and legal protection of intellectual property is ineffective) and 'strong' (innovations are easy to protect because knowledge about them is tacit and/or they are well protected legally). Regimes differ across fields of endeavor, not just across industries or countries.

The degree to which knowledge about an innovation is tacit or easily codified also affects the ease of imitation, and hence appropriability. The tacitness of knowledge varies to some extent over the product cycle. New products and processes are often highly nuanced. Thus, in the pre-paradigmatic phase of technological innovation (Abernathy and Utterback, 1978; Teece, 1986), the tacit component is likely to be high. Once a dominant design emerges, the rate of change of product design slows, and there is then the opportunity, if not the need, to codify technology. However, more rapid rates of innovation mean that there frequently isn't time to codify (make explicit) new knowledge even when it is technically feasible to do so.

Patents can in some cases be used to capture returns by slowing imitators and other rivals. However, patents rarely, if ever, confer strong appropriability, outside of special cases such as new drugs, chemical products, and rather simple mechanical inventions (Levin et al., 1987). Many patents can be 'invented around' at modest costs (Mansfield et al., 1981; Mansfield, 1985).[17] They are especially ineffective at protecting process innovation. Often patents provide little protection because the legal and financial requirements for upholding their validity or for proving their infringement are high, or because, in many countries, law enforcement for intellectual property is weak or non-existent.

The inventor of a core technology can also seek complementary patents on new features and/or manufacturing processes, and possibly on designs. The way the claims in the

---

[17]Mansfield, Schwartz, and Wagner (1981) found that about sixty percent of the patented innovations in their sample were imitated within four years. In a later study, Mansfield (1985) found that information concerning product and process development decisions was generally in the hands of at least several rivals within twelve to eighteen months, on average, after that decision was made. Process development decisions tend to leak out more than product development decisions in practically all industries, but the difference on average was found to be less than six months.

patent are written also matter. Of course, the more fundamental the invention then the better the chances of a broad patent being granted; and granted in multiple jurisdictions around the world.

While a patent is presumed to be valid in many jurisdictions, validity is never firmly established until a patent has been upheld in court. A patent is merely a passport to another journey down the road to enforcement and possible licensing fees. The best patents are those that are broad in scope, have already been upheld in court, and cover a technology essential to the manufacture and scale of products in high demand.

In some industries, particularly where the innovation is embedded in processes, trade secrets are a viable alternative to patents. Trade secret protection is possible, however, only if a firm can put its product before the public and still keep the underlying technology secret. Many industrial processes, including semiconductor fabrication, are of this kind.

The conundrum that managers confront beyond protecting the innovation itself is at least twofold. First, most innovations require complementary products, technologies, and services to yield value to users. Hardware requires software (and vice versa); operating systems require applications (and vice versa); digital music players require digital music and ways of distributing digital music (and vice versa); mobile phones need mobile phone networks (and vice versa); web browsers and web search engines require web content (and vice versa); airlines require airports (and vice versa). In short, technology must be embedded in a system to yield value to the user/consumer. Value capture becomes more difficult if other entities control required elements of the system.

Secondly, the delivery of product/process innovation requires the employment not just of complements but of many inputs/components up and down the vertical chain of production. Hence, when the inventor/innovator isn't already in control of the necessary inputs/components, the profitability of the inventor/innovator will be considerably compromised by whatever economic muscle is possessed by owners of required inputs/components. The firm must be prepared to change its assessment over time as the identity of the bottleneck asset may change due to innovation elsewhere in the system.

An obvious implication of this framework is that the firm's endowment of expert talent (literati and numerati), however brilliant, doesn't by itself guarantee that the organization will capture much of the value from innovation. Absent quality entrepreneurial managers, good intellectual property protection, and/or some control over complementary assets, superb performances by literati and numerati are likely to be in vain.

A THEORY OF THE LEARNING FIRM

The economic 'theory of the firm,' currently dominated by the contracting perspective pioneered by two Nobel laureates, Ronald Coase and Oliver Williamson, needs to be augmented to account for these new factors, particularly the superiority of the firm (i.e. internal organization) over 'markets' for the creation, transfer, protection, alignment, and realignment of intangible assets. Complementarities and co-specialization are advanced as two emerging concepts of particular relevance to a new theory of the learning firm, an organization 'which has the capacity to learn effectively and hence to prosper' (Easterby-Smith and Lyles, 2003: 2).

Context

As explained above, fundamental changes in the global economy are changing the way firms develop and deploy new knowledge. More open and competitive trading regimes have increased the importance of know-how and other intangible assets. There are significant implications for the theory of the firm, if such a theory is to connect meaningfully with the contemporary economy.

This section begins by introducing some of the theories of the firm that have emerged outside mainstream economics. Subsequent sections use the dynamic capabilities framework to reconsider the 'problems' for which firms are the solution, showing the complementarity of the contracting and capabilities perspectives. The final section argues that a more complete theory of the firm will recognize that firms exist in part to compensate for weak or non-existent markets for know-how. For the economic system to work, entrepreneurs and managers are required to orchestrate the resources/competences needed for creating and capturing the value of an innovation. Without managers and management, economic theory cannot explain the evolution and growth of the economy.

One would hope that the theory of the firm would provide some insight into firms as they exist today. Unfortunately, whether one uses the lens of transaction costs (e.g. Coase, 1937; Williamson, 1985), ownership perspectives (e.g. Hart and Moore, 1990), incentive perspectives (e.g. Holmstrom and Milgrom, 1994), or other 'modern' theories of the firm, nicely summarized and illustrated by Roberts (2004), the many theories available today still seem to caricature firms, at least those engaged in learning and innovation. Mainstream economics must reconceptualize how markets and market processes relate to learning and innovation and to the theory of the firm if economic theory is to have both relevance and rigorousness.

Furthermore, as Gibbons (2005) has noted, many theories of the firm today can more properly be characterized as theories of the boundaries of the firm. Gibbons further points out, following Cyert and March (1963), that the term 'theory of the firm' is more apt for descriptive and prescriptive models of firms' decision-making processes. Gibbons provides an excellent survey of four theories of the firm—what he calls (1) rent seeking, (2) property rights, (3) incentive systems, and (4) adaptations. He makes oblique reference to the resources/capabilities approach which he 'expects . . . to play key roles in future formal theories of the firm.' This section and those that follow are designed to turn some of Gibbons' perceived potential into actuality. The capabilities approach recognizes values in all four streams and incorporates some ideas from each.

First, however, a little history: to help overcome blatant deficiencies in standard production-function theory of the firm, transaction cost economics arose. Coase and Williamson were the pioneers. Both received Nobel Prizes in recognition of their significance. Williamson himself sees the 'relation between competence and governance as both rival and complementary—more the latter than the former' (1999a: 1106). Knowledge-based theories indirectly respond to challenges raised by Winter (1988), Demsetz (1988), and others. Emanating from the field of strategic management (e.g. Wernerfelt, 1984; Teece, 1982, 1986), they show considerable capacity to inform the theory of the modern firm.

Dynamic capabilities, co-specialization, and transaction costs

Ronald Coase in his classic (1937) article on the nature of the firm described firms and markets as alternative modes of governance, with a profit-seeking orientation causing the choice between them to be made so as to minimize transaction costs. The boundaries of the firm are set by bringing transactions into the firms so that at the margin the costs of internal organizing are equilibrated with the costs associated with transacting in the market. The Coasian firm has a simple decision-making calculus that supposedly explains the firm's boundaries. How resource allocation decisions inside the firm are made is not addressed in Coase's analysis of the nature of the firm.

A substantial literature has emerged since 1937 on the relative efficiencies of firms and markets. This literature, greatly expanded by Oliver Williamson (1975, 1985) and others, has come to be known as transaction cost economics. It analyzes the relative efficiencies of governance modes: markets and internal organization, as well as intermediate forms or organization such as strategic alliances.

Contractual difficulties associated with asset specificity are at the heart of the relative efficiency calculations in transaction cost economics. When irreversible investments in specific assets are needed to support efficient production, then the preferred organizational mode is internal organization. Internal organization minimizes exposure to the hazards of opportunistic recontracting and allows more flexible adaptation (Williamson, 1975, 1985).

In some ways, but not in others, the dynamic capabilities approach is consistent with a Coasian perspective. It conceptualizes the firm and markets as alternative modes of governance. However, the selection of what to organize (manage) internally versus through alliances or the market depends on a number of factors somewhat outside the realm of traditional transaction costs, including the availability and the non-tradability of intangible assets, capabilities, and to some extent on what Langlois (1992) has termed 'dynamic transaction costs.'[18]

The notion of 'non-tradability' advanced earlier and elsewhere (Teece, 1980) does not precisely match Coasian or Williamsonian concepts of 'transaction costs.' There is nevertheless a strong relationship between specific assets and non-traded or thinly traded assets. However, there are reasons why assets are not traded (or are thinly traded) that do not relate to asset specificity and transaction costs as such. For example, there may be no viable business model for licensing certain types of know-how in disembodied form.

Indeed, many companies will simply not license what they consider 'strategic' technological assets, especially not to direct competitors. The reason, at one level, is because a contract cannot be written that would compensate the licensor for the likely loss of customers if the licensee uses the licensor's technology to compete against the licensor.[19] Theoretically, a licensor ought to be indifferent between own sales and the sales of a licensee if the royalty rate is set to enable royalties to equalize with lost profits. However, such arrangements are rarely, if ever, seen, in part because there is likely to be ambiguity with respect to which customers and what sales are actually lost to the licensee (a standard

---

[18]Langlois defines dynamic transaction costs as 'the costs of persuading, negotiating, coordinating and teaching outside suppliers' (1992: 113).
[19]One could 'license' such technology by buying the entire enterprise, which would most likely involve paying a change-of-control premium.

transaction cost issue). Accordingly, it is uncommon in the actual world to see exclusive licenses (to direct competitors) when the licensor is able to sell in the same territory. At another level, it may simply be because there are differences in expectations with respect to the profit potential associated with the use of the technology. There are also likely concerns with respect to whether the licensor or the licensee will capture the 'learning by using' know-how associated with exploiting the technology. Negotiating and contractually specifying and monitoring sharing arrangements are also likely to be, as Williamson's framework suggests, very difficult.[20]

In short, the business model that firms use to capture value from innovation is usually one that involves selling products that contain new knowledge embedded in their design and manufacture. It is rare that firms will rely entirely on an unbundled business model in which patent/trade secret licensing is used as a mechanism to capture value from know-how. Rambus, Inc, and Dolby Labs are amongst the exceptions. Their success with this business model has not been unambiguously positive, especially for Rambus.[21]

In capabilities-based theories of the firm, the concept of co-specialization is particularly important (Teece, 1986, 2007a). Assets that are co-specialized to each other need to be employed in conjunction with each other, usually inside the firm (Teece, 1980). Co-specialization and the organizational challenges associated with achieving scope economies and seizing new opportunities isn't the emphasis in the path-breaking scholarship of Ronald Coase, Armen Alchian, Harold Demsetz, or Oliver Williamson. However, it is a phenomenon that requires (theoretical) attention. Some is provided below.

Cospecialized assets are the building blocks of firms. Building and assembling cospecialized assets inside the firm (rather than accessing them through a skein of contracts) is not done primarily to guard against opportunism and recontracting hazards, although in some cases that may be important. Instead, because effective coordination and alignment of assets/resources/competences is important, but difficult to achieve through the price system, special value can accrue to achieving good alignment. This is more easily done inside the firm. Achieving such alignment through internalization goes beyond what Barnard (1938) has suggested as the functions of the executive—which he sees in achieving cooperative adaptation.

The imperative for internalization is not just a matter of minimizing Williamsonian transaction costs. Rather, at least in the dynamic capabilities framework, the distinctive role of the (entrepreneurial) manager is to 'orchestrate' co-specialized assets. Performed astutely and proactively, such orchestration can: (1) keep co-specialized assets in value-creating alignment, (2) identify new co-specialized assets to be developed through the investment process, and (3) divest or run down co-specialized assets that no longer yield special

---

[20]Accordingly, Coca-Cola is unlikely to license its secret formula, and W.L.Gore is unlikely to license the technology behind Gore-Tex fabrics to anyone other than its wholly or partially owned subsidiaries. TSMC will likewise be reluctant to license its key semiconductor processes to competitors, except with severe restrictions and circumstances of high trust. Brands that signal particular values (e.g. Lexus, Tiffany) are likewise rarely licensed, partly for contractual reasons, partly for other reasons.

[21]Rambus, a supplier of specialty technology for memory chips, has had to finance years of litigation with memory chip manufacturers that have led to mixed results, including the invalidation of some patents in whole or in part (see, e.g. Cummings, 2010).

value. These goals cannot be readily achieved through contracting mechanisms in part because of dynamic transaction costs (the costs of negotiating, etc.) but also because there may not be a competent entity to build or 'supply' the assets that are needed. In short, capabilities must often be built, they cannot be bought, and there is limited utility in labeling this conundrum as a transactions cost problem.

Rather than stressing opportunism (although opportunism surely exists and must be guarded against), the emphasis in dynamic capabilities is on building specialized assets (that cannot be bought) and on change processes (to keep the enterprise aligned with its business environment). These processes include research and development, remolding the business architecture, asset selection, and asset orchestration. In dynamic capabilities, 'small numbers' bargaining is at the core, as in Williamson (1975). Importantly, the emphasis in dynamic capabilities is not just on protecting value from recontracting hazards; it's also on creating the assets that in transaction cost economics become the object of rent appropriation.

The basic unit of analysis for dynamic capabilities is not the transaction (as in transaction cost economies) but the firm and the (largely intangible) specific assets it creates and controls. To the extent that the emphasis in dynamic capabilities is on deals and contracts (explicit or implicit) it is less concerned with avoiding opportunism and more concerned with embracing opportunity. However, there is also considerable emphasis on 'production,' learning, and innovation. These considerations are largely absent from alternative theories of competitive advantage and from alternative theories of the firm.

The fundamental economic 'problems' to be solved by the (learning) firm

As earlier sections made clear, the fundamental problems solved by the learning firm are not just coordination to overcome high transaction costs (and other issues flowing from incomplete contracts) but also the design of opportunity and value capture mechanisms. These mechanisms can help solve the appropriability problems and help create the new organizational capabilities needed to address new opportunities as they arise. These theoretical challenges require the joining of transaction cost economics and capabilities theory. The problems associated with creating and capturing value are as important as coordination and incentive design in defining the nature of the (learning) firm.

Likewise, the economic problem being addressed here has little to do with incentive design and principal–agent problems. Managing expert talent (literati and numerati) has less to do with metering and monitoring to detect and punish *opportunism* than it has to do with detecting, monitoring, and metering *opportunity*.

Alchian, Demsetz, and Williamson have all emphasized opportunistic free riding as one organizing principle. This clearly is an important issue. Williamson assumes, correctly so, that human actors are boundedly rational, self-interest seeking, and opportunistic. The dynamic capabilities framework emphasizes other (arguably less ubiquitous and unevenly distributed but nevertheless more salient) traits of human nature: (1) entrepreneurship and pursuit of high-risk/high-reward opportunities, and (2) foresight and acumen. Williamson (1999a) appears to recognize that skills and foresight are not uniformly distributed. He quotes businessman Rudolf Spreckels—'Whenever I see something badly done, or not done at all, I see an opportunity to make a fortune.' Williamson comments: 'Those instincts, if widely operative, will influence the practice and ought to influence the theory of economic organization' (1999a: 1089). This statement invites a capabilities-based theory of the firm.

There are other differences between transaction cost and capabilities perspectives. Williamson makes the transaction the unit of analysis, with (the degree of) asset specificity a key explanatory variable in organizational design. In dynamic capabilities, complementary assets and the degree of their co-specialization are important explanatory variables. The firm is the focus if not the unit of analysis.

The utility of transaction cost economics and related frameworks for make-buy-ally and related governance decisions are not in dispute. But transaction cost economics leaves us without an understanding of the distinctive role of the manager. Executives must not only choose governance modes (between market arrangements, alliances, and internal organization), they must also understand how to design and implement different governance structures, to coordinate investment activities, and to design and implement business models, and choose appropriability strategies.

A dynamic knowledge-based theory of the firm is not at odds with Coase, Williamson, Hart, Moore, and others. In the dynamic capabilities framework, opportunism is not held in abeyance, nor are principal–agent and incentive issues ignored. But the essence of the learning firm lies in the generation, configuration, and leveraging of knowledge assets and organizational capabilities to allow the owners (shareholders) to create and capture value.

While the understanding of the existence and growth of the firm can be assisted by transaction cost theory, the advantages of organizing economic activity inside the firm go well beyond savings in transaction costs, however these are manifested. Advantages also flow from the ability of entrepreneurial managers to combine idiosyncratic co-specialized assets not just to achieve 'scope economies,' but to create and capture value by offering distinctive services (solutions) to customers while solving the firm's appropriability problems.

Each of these 'problems' has a transaction cost dimension; but, in some cases, over-reliance on the transaction cost economics apparatus will add unnecessary baggage. If, for instance, one wants to understand issues surrounding creating value, not simply protecting value created, transaction costs can only go part of the way. The firm's routines for sensing, seizing, and transforming can provide a basis for profitability well beyond the avoidance of contracting costs and hazards.

There is empirical evidence that outsourcing decisions do not depend on transaction cost (asset specificity) considerations alone. Studies show that 'system effects' such as interdependencies and complementarities (Monteverde and Teece, 1982)[22] and capability advantages (Argyres, 1996) impact economic organization in a statistically significant manner. These studies seem to indicate that boundary placement influences production learning and impacts research and development efficiency (Armour and Teece, 1980), resulting in lower costs and superior innovation potential.

What then is the role of managers in the theory of the firm? They are not primarily micromanaging creative people to stamp out opportunistic behavior. Nor are they merely engaged in adaptive sequential decision making. Rather, they are helping the organization to create and implement the systems and structures that enable the firm

---

[22]This article is often cited as reflecting empirical support for transaction cost economics, which indeed it does. But the variable for systems effects has more explanatory power and is consistent with the capabilities perspective advanced here.

to sense opportunities, act on them, and transform as the environment changes, which inevitably it will.

Opportunism is controlled not just through metrics and internal organization monitoring, but also through high commitment cultures/values. Innovative firms in which a great deal of learning must take place to commercialize new ideas typically need strong values because it's difficult in the loosely structured internal environments that innovation requires to define and measure performance and implement rigid controls. Incentive issues are powerful as well; creative and entrepreneurial activities need to be encouraged and rewarded.

The complementarity between capabilities-based views and contractual/transaction costs/property rights views is hopefully apparent. It has been remarked on by this author elsewhere, as well as by others (e.g. Foss, 1996).[23]

The transaction cost economics perspective clearly needs dynamic capabilities, and vice versa. Transaction cost economics assumes what might be referred to as capabilities neutrality. In transaction cost economics, so called 'production costs'—which might be thought of as a proxy for the firm's level of (operational) capability—are assumed to be the same across organizational types so that the choice between market and non-market arrangements swings entirely on transaction/governance costs. This assumption is a natural connection point to capabilities theory, which clearly indicates that the levels of capabilities are themselves a function of managerial activity/excellence (or lack thereof). Differences in capabilities can lead to wide disparities in 'production' costs within an industry. The very essence of the field of strategic management is built on the recognition that firms are different—not just in governance, but with respect to other features too (Rumelt, Schendel, and Teece, 1991)—and that this drives performance differences.

The (dynamic) capabilities framework, which posits that knowledge assets and their (dynamic) management have become central to profit maximization in an era of globalized commerce and information, suggests a new theory of the firm, one that is consistent with the observation of Alfred Marshall that:

> 'capital consists in a great part in knowledge and organization: and of this some part is private property and the other part is not. Knowledge is our most powerful engine of production—organization aids knowledge.'

> (Marshall, 1898: 213)

The proposed new capabilities-based theory opens up the black box of the firm and injects, into economic theory, new considerations which are generally not central to the theory of the firm as commonly presented.

Recapping complementarities, co-specialization, and the scope of the (learning) firm

The theory of the (learning) firm has benefited, and can benefit further, from a more rigorous exploration of the concepts of complementarities and co-specialization. The earliest

---

[23]The Profiting From Innovation framework (Teece, 1986) illustrates how a contracting framework is useful as a tool for building a (dynamic) capabilities-based theory of the firm (see also Winter, 2006).

use of the idea of complementarities in economics can be traced to Edgeworth (1881). Early applications to the economic development literature include Hirschman (1958) and to the innovation literature can be found in Rosenberg (1979; 1982) and Teece (1986). Work on complementarities in a strategic context includes Teece (1980), Milgrom and Roberts (1990a, 1990b), and Miller (1988).

Rosenberg notes: 'Time and again in the history of American technology it has happened that the productivity of a given invention has turned on the availability of complementary technologies . . . these linkages are both numerous and of varying degrees of importance' (1979: 26–27). Furthermore,

> the growing productivity of industrial economies is the complex outcome of large numbers of interlocking, mutually reinforcing technologies, the individual components of which are of very limited economic consequences by themselves. The smallest relevant unit of observation, therefore, is seldom a single innovation but, more typically, an interrelated clustering of innovations.
>
> (Rosenberg, 1979: 28–29)

Complementarities exist when various activities reinforce each other in such a manner that performing multiple activities together lowers/(raises) cost, increases economies/ (diseconomies) of scope, or otherwise improves/(depresses) payoffs.[24] More technically, complementarities exist when the mixed partial derivatives of a cost function or a payoff function provide positive returns at the margin associated with one variable increasing as the levels of other variables increase too. Doing more of one activity increases the returns from doing more of another. The aggregate economic value achieved by combining two or more complementary factors therefore exceeds the value that would be achieved by applying these factors in isolation.

Of course, as pointed out by Teece (1980), this in and of itself has no direct implication for the theory of the (boundaries of the) firm, although it has powerful implications for economic organization more generally. The existence of positive complementarities indicates the advantage of having separate activities occur together. However, without more structure to the concept, one cannot predict where the individual firm boundaries should lie, because contractual arrangements exist that, in theory, can enable joint activities to take place without common ownership of the parts.

While the importance of complementarities is now being recognized, the approach still needs additional specificity (with respect to causal relationships amongst key constructs) to allow it to morph fully into a falsifiable theory. Put differently, a robust theory of complementarities that provides economic insight is yet to emerge. While there is little doubt that complementary relationships exist among heterogeneous factors inside the firm (and that these can impact firm performance), the contexts in which such interactions occur is yet to be adequately specified. However, some evidence has been assembled. Monteverde and Teece (1982), while testing for the importance of asset specificity in predicting outsourcing decisions for General Motors and Ford, also found that a 'systems effect'—defined as 'the degree to which any given component's design affects the performance or [system-level

---

[24]The notion of complements has gained mathematical tractability through the concept of supermodularity (Topkis, 1978, 1987; Milgrom and Roberts, 1994). For an excellent review of the literature, see Ennen and Richter (2009).

integration] of other components' (1982: 210)—was statistically significant in explaining both firms' outsourcing decisions. The longstanding notion of strategic 'fit' is obviously consistent with notions of complementarity.

It should be noted that the notion of complementarity can be applied at a high level of aggregation, as with the Toyota System of production, or at a high level of specificity, such as the complementarity between the (integrated) design and manufacture of automobile components, e.g. an exterior grill and headlamp assemblies (Monteverde and Teece, 1982). Parmigiani and Mitchell (2009) use the example of automobile dashboards, which they note typically consist of multiple, interrelated, complementary components. Both levels of aggregation seem to provide insights, suggesting the power and generality of the complementarity insights.

Complementarities expressed through their mathematical corollary (supermodularity) break from classical economics. Most classical economics models of production recognize only traditional 'factors of production' like labor and capital and assume homogeneity with respect to the distribution of these factors amongst firms. The standard production function sees no benefit from the use of particular inputs—in the sense that, apart from diminishing returns related to fixed factors, there is no special significance to the identity of particular factors of production (Teece and Winter, 1984). Moreover, everything is infinitely divisible—indeed, twice differentiable—and firms maximize some objective function subject to constraints. Complementarity does not require divisibility; changes in one variable may require discrete (non-incremental) changes in another.

With production functions of the standard kind, decision makers need only equate marginal revenues to marginal cost and they will deliver global maxima in output. There are serious issues with this theory surrounding the search for, and the discovery of, a global maximum, if one exists. Complementarity modeled as supermodularity enables some departures from this extreme caricature by at least recognizing local maxima. It also accepts that payoff functions may be discontinuous. Design choices are recognized as being discrete and not necessarily continuous. These perspectives have received endorsement from organizational ecologists and strategic management scholars including Levinthal (1997), Porter and Siggelkow (2008), and Teece (2007a).

However, capabilities theory at present runs the risk of providing more *ex post* rationalization than *ex ante* guidance with respect to the particulars of the requirements—with Teece (1986, 2006) being the possible exception since these papers are quite explicit about the contexts in which complementary assets are important for capturing value from a specific innovation. These papers are also able to specify when complementary assets should be included inside the boundaries of the enterprise.

Toward a unified theory of the firm

Knowledge-based theories of the firm see business organizations as accumulating capabilities in path-dependent ways. Recognizing, creating, and exploiting complementarities is very much at the core of what firms do. Sustained 'abnormal' or 'supernormal' profitability occurs because factor markets for certain types of assets (particularly intangibles and idiosyncratic physical and human assets) are not fully efficient. To take full advantage and earn superior profits, firms need to sense, seize, and transform in ways that exploit inefficient factor markets. Indentifying and securing combinations and permutations of assets which enable the enterprise to address customer needs is key.

As firms build the microfoundations needed to sense, seize, and transform, all the while exploiting complementarities, they lay the foundations for sustained above-average profitability. There is nothing in Ronald Coase's or Oliver Williamson's work to explain how firms identify and exploit complementarities and develop competitive advantage. This raises the question of how the Coase/Williamson conceptualizations of the firm relate to dynamic capabilities.

As stated earlier, the knowledge and contracting perspectives are complementary theories/frameworks. No theory of the firm can ignore contractual issues. But neither Coase nor Williamson see a firm as a pure nexus of contracts. Nor do they see firms as merely 'social communities in which individual and social expertise is transformed into economically useful products and services by the application of a set of higher-order organizing principles' (Kogut and Zander, 1992).

There is clearly a way for knowledge-based theories and transaction cost perspectives to be brought together. Arrow (1974) provided a commanding and potentially unifying insight. He observed that the reason firms exist is not simply due to high transaction costs; rather, markets in some situations simply do not work and there is market 'failure.'[25] One can perform a thought experiment and conclude that if the transactions were forced into a market, transaction costs in such circumstances would be very high; but it's perhaps simpler to just recognize that there are many circumstances where internal organization is clearly a necessary and superior way to organize, and it is desirable for innovative activity to take place inside a firm orchestrated by entrepreneurial managers and surrounded by some kind of management structure.

For purposes of building an applied theory of the learning firm, it is important to specify the contexts in which these market failures are prevalent. The most important (and also the most under-researched) domain within which organization inside the firm is likely to be necessary is the creation, transfer, protection (appropriability), and orchestration (so as to exploit complementarities) of know-how and other intangibles.

As the author noted three decades ago:

> unassisted markets are seriously faulted as institutional devices for facilitating trading in many kinds of technological and managerial know-how. The imperfections in the market for know-how for the most part can be traced to the nature of the commodity in question.
>
> (Teece, 1981a: 84)

The market is also imperfect as a tool to create know-how. One can 'buy in' technology more easily than one can have it created through a contractual agreement and then transfer it in. 'Creation' must frequently be done internally, even though external sourcing

---

[25]Arrow acknowledged that in some cases markets might simply not exist. Williamson (1971), in his best-known statement on market failure, which he still endorsed 28 years later (Williamson, 1999b), restricted his attention to those that were 'failures only in the limited sense that they involve transaction costs that can be attenuated by substituting internal organization for market exchange' (1971: 114).

is usually a necessary complement to own development. 'Co-creation' is perhaps the more helpful concept.

It is only after industrially relevant know-how is first created that it can be traded (via licensing arrangements). Even once it is created, mutually beneficial trades frequently don't happen because the property rights covering know-how may be poorly defined (fuzzy),[26] the asset difficult to transfer, or its use difficult to meter. Internal resource allocation within the firm (a managerially directed activity) is the only viable alternative.

Moreover, because of complementarities and co-specialization, many intangible assets may be more valuable when they can co-evolve in a coordinated way with other assets. The ability to assemble unique configurations of co-specialized assets, as in the case of systemic innovation (Teece, 2000), can, therefore, enhance value. Rosenberg (1979) seems to go further and argues that such coordination and clustering is necessary for value to be created.

In short, managers often create great value by assembling particular constellations of complementary and co-specialized assets, especially knowledge assets, inside the enterprise to produce highly differentiated and innovative goods and services that customers want. This process of identifying, assembling, and orchestrating constellations of complementary and co-specialized assets is a fundamental function of management—and points to the fundamental nature of the modern firm. It's different from the Coasian firm.

In a globalized, knowledge-based economy, firms can secure short-term advantage from the coordination of bundles of difficult-to-trade assets and competencies, at least when such assets are scarce and difficult to imitate. Advantage that is sustainable over a longer term, however, can only flow from unique abilities possessed by business enterprises to continuously shape, reshape, and orchestrate those assets to create new technology, to respond to competition, achieve critical market mass, exploit complementarities, and serve changing customer needs. The particular (non-imitable) orchestration capacity of a business enterprise—its dynamic capabilities—is the irreducible core of the learning firm. It cannot be reproduced simply by assembling a constellation of contracts.

Fundamentally, business firms know how to do things. Most figure out how to adapt and possibly even shape their environment to some (small) degree. As noted earlier, even Harold Demsetz was willing to see the firm as a repository of knowledge.

However, it is not clear that many economists are willing as yet to recognize the implications of firms being repositories of knowledge and instruments for learning. One exception is Sidney Winter who correctly notes, 'it is the firms, not the people who work for the firms, that know how to make gasoline, automobiles, and computers' (1982: 76).

Organizational capabilities are what explain why an enterprise is more than the sum of its parts. They also help explain why the profits of the enterprise cannot be completely competed away in factor markets. Employees can come and go to a certain extent and the organization can continue without interruption.

Mainstream theory too often takes production functions and production sets as given, ignores complementarities and co-specialization, and fails to explain capabilities and heterogeneity amongst firms even in the same industry. Mainstream theory also completely

---

[26]See Teece (2000) for discussion of the fuzzy boundaries associated with intellectual property rights.

sidesteps the problem of how firms actually perform the tasks of storing the knowledge that underlies productive competence, transferring it internally (or externally), augmenting it in value-enhancing ways, and identifying and exploiting complementarities.

CONCLUSION

Learning and knowledge caution on the essential contributions of the firm to the post-industrial economy. In this chapter, a theory of the firm has advanced that goes beyond traditional industrial views of the enterprise. It is a perspective that views the generation, transfer, utilization, and protection of know-how as the essence of the enterprise. Learning in this perspective involves both learning inside the enterprise and learning about the changing needs of customers. Such learning, if accomplished continuously, undergirds dynamic capabilities, and these in turn undergird the competitive advantage of the business enterprise.

REFERENCES

Abernathy, W.J. and Utterback, J.M. (1978) Patterns of industrial innovation. *Technology Review*, 80(7): 40–47.

Adams, W.J. and Yellen, J.L. (1976) Commodity bundling and the burden of monopoly. *Quarterly Journal of Economics*, 90(3): 475–498.

Akerlof, G.A. (1970) The market for lemons. *Quarterly Journal of Economics*, 84(3): 488–500.

Albert, S. and Bradley, K. (1997) *Managing Knowledge Experts, Experts, Agencies and Organizations*. Cambridge: Cambridge University Press.

Anderson, P. and Tushman, M.L. (1990) Technological discontinuities and dominant design. *Administrative Science Quarterly*, 35(4): 604–633.

Argyres, N. (1996) Evidence on the role of firm capabilities in vertical integration decisions. *Strategic Management Journal*, 17(2): 129–150.

Armour, H.O. and Teece, D.J. (1978) Organizational structure and economic performance: A test of the multidivisional hypothesis. *Bell Journal of Economics*, 9(18): 106–122.

Armour, H.O. and Teece, D.J. (1980) Vertical integration and technological innovation. *Review of Economics and Statistics*, 62(3): 470–474.

Arrow, K.J. (1969) The organization of economic activity: Issues pertinent to the choice of market versus nonmarket allocation. In: *The Analysis and Evaluation of Public Expenditures: The PPB System*. Washington, DC: U.S. Government Printing Office, 47–64.

Arrow, K.J. (1974) *The Limits of Organization*. New York: Norton.

Barnard, C.I. (1938) *The Functions of the Executive*. Cambridge, MA: Harvard University Press.

Bingham, C.B., Eisenhardt, K.M., and Furr, N.R. (2007) What makes a process a capability? Heuristics, strategy, and effective capture of opportunities. *Strategic Entrepreneurship Journal*, 1(1/2): 27–47.

Boerner, C.S., Macher, J.T., and Teece, D.J. (2001) A review and assessment of organizational learning in economic theories. In M. Dierkes, A. Berthoin-Antal, J. Child and I. Nonaka (eds.), *Handbook of Organizational Learning and Knowledge*. Oxford University Press: New York, NY: 89–117.

Chandler, A.D. (1962) *Strategy and Structure*. Cambridge, MA: MIT Press.

Chandler, A.D. (1977) *The Visible Hand: The Managerial Revolution in American Business*. Cambridge, MA: Belknap Press.

Chandler, A.D. (1990) *Scale and Scope: The Dynamics of Industrial Capitalism*. Cambridge, MA: Belknap/Harvard University Press.

Chesbrough, H. and Rosenbloom, R.S. (2002) The role of the business model in capturing value from innovation: Evidence from Xerox corporation's technology spin-off companies. *Industrial and Corporate Change*, 11(3): 529–555.

Christensen, C.M. (1997) *The Innovator's Dilemma*. Boston, MA: Harvard Business School Press.

Clark, K.B. (1985) The interaction of design hierarchies and market concepts in technological evolution. *Research Policy*, 14(5): 235–251.

Coase, R.A. (1937) The nature of the firm. *Economica*, 16(4): 386–405.

Conner, K.R. (1991) A historical comparison of resource-based theory and five schools of thought within industrial organization economics: Do we have a new theory of the firm? *Journal of Management*, 17(1): 121–154.

Cummings, J. (2010) Rambus gets mixed patent ruling. *WSJ.com*, March 4. http://online.wsj.com/article/SB10001424052748704187204575102102378053906.html.

Cyert, R.M. and March, J.G. (1963) *A Behavioral Theory of the Firm*. Englewood Cliffs, NJ: Prentice-Hall.

David, P.A. and Greenstein, S. (1990) The economics of compatibility standards: An introduction to recent research. *Economics of Innovation and New Technology*, 1(1): 3–41.

Demsetz, H. (1970) The private production of public goods. *Journal of Law and Economics*, 13(2): 293–306.

Demsetz, H. (1988) The theory of the firm revisited. *Journal of Law, Economics, and Organization*, 4(1): 141–161.

Dosi, G., Nelson, R.R., and Winter, S.G. (eds.), (2000) *The Nature and Dynamics of Organizational Capabilities*. New York: Oxford University Press.

Easterby-Smith, M. and Lyles, M.A. (2003) Introduction: Watersheds of organizational learning and knowledge management. In Easterby-Smith, M., and Lyles, M. A. (Eds.) *The Blackwell Handbook of Organizational Learning and Knowledge Management*. Malden, MA: Blackwell Publishing, 1–15.

Easterby-Smith, M. and Prieto, I.M. (2008) Dynamic capabilities and knowledge management: An integrative role for learning? *British Journal of Management*, 19(3): 235–249.

Edgeworth, F.Y. (1881) *Mathematical Physics: An Essay on the Application of Mathematics to the Moral Sciences*. London: Kegan Paul.

Ennen, E. and Richter, A. (2009) The whole is more than the sum of its parts – or is it? A review of the empirical literature on complementarities in organizations. European Business School Research Paper. Wiesbaden, Germany: European Business School, 9–7.

Fiol, C.M. and Lyles, M.A. (1985) Organizational learning. *Academy of Management Review*, 10(4): 803–813.

Foss, N. (1996) Knowledge based approaches to the theory of the firm: Some critical comments. *Organizational Science*, 7(5): 470–476.

Gibbons, R. (2005) Four formal(izable) theories of the firm? *Journal of Economic Behavior and Organization*, 58(2): 200–245.

Hart, O. and Moore, J. (1990) Property rights and the nature of the firm. *Journal of Political Economy*, 98(6): 1119–1158.

Henderson, R.M. (1994) Managing innovation in the information age. *Harvard Business Review*, 72(1): 100–106.

Henderson, R.M. and Clark, K.B. (1990) Architectural innovation: The reconfiguration of existing product technologies and the failure of established firms. *Administrative Science Quarterly*, 35(1): 9–30.

Hirschman, A.O. (1958) *The Strategy of Economic Development*. New Haven, CT: Yale University Press.

Holmstrom, B. and Milgrom, P. (1994) The firm as an incentive system. *American Economic Review*, 84(4): 972–991.

Katz, M.L. and Shapiro, C. (1986) Technology adoption in the presence of network externalities. *Journal of Political Economy*, 94(4): 822–841.

Kirzner, I.M. (1973) *Competition and Entrepreneurship*. Chicago: University of Chicago Press.

Klemperer, P. (1987) Markets with consumer switching costs. *Quarterly Journal of Economics*, 102(2): 375–394.

Kogut, B. and Zander, U. (1992) Knowledge of the firm, combinative capabilities, and the replication of technology. *Organizational Science*, 3(3): 383–397.

Krugman, P. (1987) The narrow moving band, the Dutch disease, and the consequences of Mrs. Thatcher: Notes on trade in the presence of scale economies. *Journal of Development Economics*, 27(1–2): 41–55.

Langlois, R.N. (1992) Transaction-cost economics in real time. *Industrial and Corporate Change*, 1(1): 99–127.

Levin, R.C., Klevorick, A.K., Nelson, R.R., Winter, S. G., Gilbert, R. and Griliches, Z. (1987) Appropriating the returns from industrial research and development. *Brookings Papers on Economic Activity*, 1987(3): 783–831.

Levinthal, D.A. (1997) Adaptation on rugged landscapes. *Management Science*, 43(7): 934–950.

Levitt, B. and March, J.G. (1988) Organizational learning, *Annual Review of Sociology*, 14: 319–340.

Mansfield, E. (1985) How rapidly does new industrial technology leak out? *Journal of Industrial Economics*, 34(2): 217–223.

Mansfield, E., Schwartz, M., and Wagner, S. (1981) Imitation costs and patents: An empirical study. *Economic Journal*, 91(364): 907–918.

March, J.G. (1991) Exploration and exploitation in organizational learning. *Organization Science*, 2(1): 71–87.

March, J.G. and Simon, H.A. (1958) *Organizations*. New York: John Wiley & Sons.

Marshall, A. (1898) *Principles of Economics*. London: Macmillan and Co.

McGirt, E. (2008) Revolution in San Jose. *Fast Company*, 131: 90–93.

Milgrom, P. and Roberts, J. (1990a) The economics of modern manufacturing: technology, strategy, and organization. *American Economic Review*, 80(3): 511–528.

Milgrom, P. and Roberts, J. (1990b) Rationalizability, learning and equilibrium in games with strategic complementarities. *Econometrics*, 58(6): 1255–1277.

Milgrom, P. and Roberts, J. (1994) Complementarities and systems: Understanding Japanese economic organization. *Estudios Economicos*, 9(1): 3–42.

Miller, D. (1988) Relating Porter's business strategies to environment and structure: analysis and performance implications. *Academy of Management Journal*, 31(2): 280–308.

Monteverde, K. and Teece, D.J. (1982) Supplier switching costs and vertical integration in the automobile industry. *Bell Journal of Economics*, 13(1): 206–213.

Nelson, R.R. and Winter, S.G. (1982) *An Evolutionary Theory of Economic Change*. Cambridge, MA: Harvard University Press.

O'Reilly, C.A., Harreld, J.B., and Tushman, M.L. (2009) Organizational ambidexterity: IBM and emerging business opportunities. *California Management Review*, 51(4): 75–99.

O'Reilly, C.A. and Tushman, M.L. (2004) The ambidextrous organization. *Harvard Business Review*, 82(4): 74–81.

Parmigiani, A. and Mitchell, W. (2009) Complementarity, capabilities, and the boundaries of the firm: The impact of within-firm and interfirm expertise on concurrent sourcing of complementary components. *Strategic Management Journal*, 30(10): 1065–1091.

Penrose, E.G. (1959) *The Theory of the Growth of the Firm*. New York: Wiley.

Pierce, J.L., Boerner, C.S., and Teece, D.J. (2002) Dynamic capabilities, competence and the behavioral theory of the firm. In M. Augier and J. G. March (eds.) *The Economics of Choice, Change, and Organization: Essays in Memory of Richard M. Cyert*. Cheltenham, UK: Edward Elgar.

Pisano, G.P. and Teece, D.J. (2007) How to capture value from innovation: Shaping intellectual property and industry architecture. *California Management Review*, 50(1): 278–296.

Pitelis, C.N. and Teece, D.J. (2009) The (new) nature and essence of the firm. *European Management Review*, 6(1): 5–15.

Porter, M. and Siggelkow, N. (2008) Contextuality within activity systems and sustainability of competitive advantage. *Academy of Management Perspectives*, 22(2): 34–56.

Roberts, J. (2004) *The Modern Firm: Organizational Design for Performance and Growth*. New York: Oxford University Press.

Rosenberg, N. (1979) Technological interdependence in the American economy. *Technology and Culture*, 20(1): 25–50.

Rosenberg, N. (1982) *Inside the Black Box: Technology and Economics*. New York: Cambridge University Press.

Rumelt, R.P. (1984) Towards a strategic theory of the firm. In R. B. Lamb (ed.), *Competitive Strategic Management*. Englewood Cliffs, NJ: Prentice-Hall.

Rumelt, R.P, Schendel, D. and Teece, D.J. (1991) Strategic management and economics. *Strategic Management Journal*, 12: 5–29.

Scotchmer, S. (1991) Standing on the shoulders of giants: Cumulative research and the patent law. *Journal of Economic Perspectives*, 5(1): 29–41.

Siggelkow, N. and Levinthal, D.A. (2005) Escaping real (non-benign) competency traps: Linking the dynamics of organizational structure to the dynamics of search. *Strategic Organization*, 3(1): 85–115.

Simon, H.A. (1947) *Administrative Behavior*. New York: Macmillan.

Simon, H.A. (1991) Bounded rationality and organizational learning. *Organization Science*, 2(1): 125–134.

Stinchcombe, A.L. (1990) *Information and Organizations*. Berkeley: University of California Press.

Teece, D.J. (1980) Economies of scope and the scope of the enterprise. *Journal of Economic Behavior and Organization*, 1(3): 223–247.

Teece, D.J. (1981a) The market for know-how and the efficient international transfer of technology. *Annals of the Academy of Political and Social Science*, 458(1): 81–96.

Teece, D.J. (1981b) Internal organization and economic performance: An empirical analysis of the profitability of principal firms. *Journal of Industrial Economics*, 30(2): 173–199.

Teece, D.J. (1982) Towards an economic theory of the multiproduct firm. *Journal of Economic Behavior and Organization*, 3(1): 39–63.

Teece, D.J. (1984) Economic analysis and strategic management. *California Management Review*, 26(3): 87–110.

Teece, D.J. (1986) Profiting from technological innovation. *Research Policy*, 15(6): 285–305.

Teece, D.J. (2000) *Managing Intellectual Capital: Organizational, Strategic, and Policy Dimensions*, Oxford: Oxford University Press.

Teece, D.J. (2006) Reflections on profiting from innovation. *Research Policy*, 35(8): 1131–1146.

Teece, D.J. (2007a) Explicating dynamic capabilities: The nature and microfoundations of (sustainable) enterprise performance. *Strategic Management Journal*, 28(13): 1319–1350.

Teece, D.J. (2007b), Managers, markets, and dynamic capabilities. In C. Helfat, S. Finkelstein, W. Mitchell, M. Peteraf, H. Singh, D.J. Teece, and S. Winter (eds.), *Dynamic Capabilities: Understanding Strategic Change In Organizations*. Oxford, UK: Blackwell.

Teece, D.J. (2008) Dosi's technological paradigms and trajectories: Insights for economics and management. *Industrial and Corporate Change*, 17(3): 507–512.

Teece, D.J. (2009) *Dynamic Capabilities and Strategic Management: Organizing for Innovation and Growth*. New York : Oxford University Press.

Teece, D.J. (2010) Business models, business strategy and innovation. *Long Range Planning*, 43(2–3): 172–194.

Teece, D.J. (2011) Human capital, capabilities, and the firm: Literati, numerati, and entrepreneurs in the twenty-first century enterprise. In A. Burton-Jones and J. C. Spender (eds.) *The Oxford Handbook of Human Capital*. New York: Oxford University Press.

Teece, D.J., Pisano, G., Shuen, A. (1990) Firm capabilities, resources, and the concept of strategy. Center for research in management. University of California, Berkeley, CCC Working Paper 90–98.

Teece, D.J., Pisano, G., and Shuen, A. (1997) Dynamic capabilities and strategic management. *Strategic Management Journal*, 18(7): 509–533.

Teece, D.J., Rumelt, R., Dosi, G. and Winter, S. (1994) Understanding corporate coherence: Theory and evidence. *Journal of Economic Behavior and Organization*, 23(1): 1–30.

Teece, D.J. and Winter, S.G. (1984) The limits of neoclassical theory in management education. *American Economic Review*, 74(2): 116–121.

Topkis, D.L. (1978) Minimizing a submodular function on a lattice. *Operations Research*, 26(2): 305–321.

Topkis, D.L. (1987) Activity optimization games with complementarity. *European Journal of Operations Research*, 28(3): 358–368.

von Hippel, E. (1998) Economics of product development by users: The impact of 'Sticky' local information. *Management Science*, 44(5): 629–644.

Wernerfelt, B. (1984) A resource-based view of the firm. *Strategic Management Journal*, 5(2): 171–180.

Williamson, O.E. (1971) The vertical integration of production: Market failure considerations. *American Economic Review*, 61(2): 112–123.

Williamson, O.E. (1975) *Markets and Hierarchies*. New York: The Free Press.

Williamson, O.E. (1981) The modern corporation: Origins, evolution, attributes. *Journal of Economic Literature*, 19(4): 1537–1568.

Williamson, O.E. (1985) *The Economic Institutions of Capitalism*. New York: The Free Press.

Williamson, O.E. (1999a) Strategy research: Governance and competence perspectives. *Strategic Management Journal*, 20(12): 1087–1108.

Williamson, O.E. (1999b) Some reflections. In G. R. Carroll and D. J. Teece, (eds.), *Firms, Markets, and Hierarchies: The Transaction Cost Economics Perspective*. New York: Oxford University Press.

Winter, S.G. (1982) An essay on the theory of production in S. J. Hymans (Ed.) *Economics and the World Around It*. Ann Arbor: University of Michigan Press.

Winter, S.G. (1988) On Coase, competence, and the corporation. *Journal of Law, Economics, and Organization*, (4)1: 163–180.

Winter, S.G. (2006) The logic of appropriability: From Schumpeter to Arrow to Teece, *Research Policy*, 35(8): 1100–1106.

Zollo, M. and Singh, H. (2004) Deliberate learning in corporate acquisitions: Post acquisition strategies and integration capability in U.S. bank mergers. *Strategic Management Journal*, 25(13): 1233–1256.

24

The Human Side of Dynamic Capabilities: a Holistic Learning Model

GIANMARIO VERONA AND
MAURIZIO ZOLLO

ABSTRACT

In this chapter we review extant literature on dynamic capabilities with a view to move the debate towards the development of a positive theory on antecedents, consequences, and boundary conditions to the development and effectiveness of dynamic capabilities. To do so we propose to broaden the definition of the object of change beyond purely behavioral constructs such as processes and routines and to embrace the challenge of understanding how firms learn to influence the evolution of subtler aspects of human nature, and fundamental behavioral antecedents, such as emotions, motivation, and identity.

INTRODUCTION

The objective of this chapter is to extend the literature on dynamic capabilities (henceforth DC) to incorporate a more holistic model of human behavior, which includes micro-foundational elements, such as emotion, motivation, and identity, so far kept outside the debate around the evolution and consequences of DCs. The differential ability of firms to manipulate resources and routines to adapt to market and stakeholder expectations is in fact key to our understanding of competitive advantage (Teece, Pisano, and Shuen, 1997) and of strategic initiatives and processes such as mergers and acquisitions (M&A), product development, and knowledge management (Eisenhardt and Martin, 2000; Zollo and Winter, 2002). The construct itself has been capturing a growing attention from influential scholars of different fields coming from a wide variety of backgrounds and contributing to a more fine-grained understanding of change dynamics within organizations (Di Stefano, Peteraf, and Verona, 2010; see also Teece, Chapter 23 in this volume).

In a particularly influential statement for the development of the debate, Teece (2007) calls for a better understanding of the micro-foundational aspects of DC, echoing similar invitations from both critics (Felin and Foss, 2005) and contributors (Zollo and Winter, 2002) to the DC approach. In an attempt to provide a partial response to these calls, our intention is to move beyond definitional debates in the already rich landscape of DC literature (Bromiley, 2009) and to shift the focus towards the development of a more complete model of antecedents, consequences, and boundaries to the effectiveness of DCs. The inclusion of theoretical linkages of this sort appears to be important at this time not only because they are at least partially overlooked in our current understanding of capability dynamics. It is important also because empirical inquiry is still largely missing in this central domain for strategic management research, in part due to the missing articulation of these causal links.

In the effort to address this challenge, we propose a model that can accommodate the diverse nature of DCs with respect to the objects of change that they aim to act upon and can better serve the call for a better understanding of micro-foundations of strategy. In doing so, the model will include antecedents at both the organizational and the individual levels of analysis, as well as behavioral, cognitive, and emotional components of the change outcomes, which will then influence various aspects of performance. To illustrate the conceptual arguments, we will refer to cases and illustrative examples derived from the product development, the M&A, and the social/environmental sustainability contexts, since these are all processes that require, for their successful deployment, the reconfiguration of operating processes, structures, and resources, that is (by definition) the exercise of DCs as understood by some of the leading authors in the field (Helfat et al., 2007; Teece et al., 1997; Zollo and Winter, 2002; Winter, 2003).

In the remainder of this chapter we will first review the notion of DCs and then develop a theoretical model with the holistic traits described above. Finally, an agenda will be proposed for future work on both the theoretical and empirical fronts.

A REVIEW OF THE CONCEPT

The dynamic capability (henceforth DC) perspective has emerged in the last two decades as a promising attempt to untangle the complex problem of describing how firms learn to adapt their internal and external resource configurations and processes to shifting expectations and market conditions in pursuit of competitive advantage. In their original definition of the concept, Teece, Pisano, and Shuen posit:

> We refer to this ability to achieve new forms of competitive advantage as 'dynamic capabilities' to emphasize two key aspects . . . The term 'dynamic' refers to the capacity to renew competences so as to achieve congruence with the changing environment . . . The term 'capabilities' emphasizes the role of Strategic Management in appropriately adapting, integrating, and reconfiguring internal and external organizational skills, resources, and functional competences to match the requirements of a changing world.

> (Teece, Pisano, and Shuen, 1997: 510)

The fact that the achievement of 'new forms of competitive advantage' and of 'congruence with changing environment' is premised as a constitutive component of the concept rather than as a goal in pursuit of which the 'renewal' is made, has created significant debate in the literature. The difference is not trivial, for at least two reasons. First, it implicitly equates change with adaptation which is clearly false. The ability of a firm to change its configuration of resource and capabilities does not necessarily generate better fit with a rapidly changing environment, since the direction of change requirements might be wrongly perceived. Second, the inclusion in the definition of the *achievement* of the result (competitive advantage), rather than simply the pursuit of it, generates a well-known tautology (Zollo and Winter, 2002) which makes either the notion of DC or the notion of competitive advantage redundant. Even more worryingly, it makes it impossible for scholars to study the key question 'under what conditions does the presence of DC in firms generate competitive advantage?': arguably one of the most interesting questions in the field of strategic management today.

Alternative formulations that avoid this problem are those proposed by Zollo and Winter:

> A dynamic capability is a learned and stable pattern of collective activity through which the organization systematically generates and modifies its operating routines in pursuit of improved effectiveness.
>
> (Zollo and Winter, 2002: 340)

And by Helfat et al., in which the notion of performance outcomes has completely disappeared:

> A dynamic capability is the capacity of an organization to purposefully create, extend or modify its resource base. The resource base of an organization includes tangible, intangible and human assets (or resources) as well as capabilities which the organization owns, controls or has access to on a preferential basis.
>
> (Helfat et al., 2007: 4)

Moving beyond the definitional debate about the construct itself, there are several contributions about the characteristics and boundaries of the notion of DCs. In contrast to normal organizational capabilities, DCs are usually considered a higher-order phenomenon (Collis, 1994) because they build, integrate, and reconfigure existing resources and capabilities (Helfat and Peteraf, 2003). In this sense, DCs differ from ordinary capabilities since they are concerned with change, rather than with the contribution to the production or the delivery of a product or service to customers. Winter (2003) clarifies this point calling ordinary capabilities 'zero-level capabilities' in that they allow the firm to 'earn a living' by creating something valuable for a customer. Whenever the same firm triggers established patterns of actions (routines) dedicated to the identification and execution of change in the way it does so (for example, through innovation activities or reorganization processes), it would put into practice a 'first-order' capability, a change routine, a so-called DC. The fundamental condition for the existence of a DC, therefore, is the presence of a stable and repeatable pattern of action to address the change requirement, which (1) distinguishes the phenomenon from the execution of ad hoc problem-solving and implementation of a change process, and (2) makes DCs a relatively rare phenomenon compared to the ubiquitous *ad hoc* problem solving and change execution processes that any organization produces at any given time, across locations, and within all of its functional activities.

From a temporal standpoint, DCs are viewed as stable patterns of action that potentially build a string of temporary advantages by adding, integrating, and reconfiguring resources, which amount to sustained advantage once the entire pattern is taken into account (Blyler and Coff, 2003). DCs are therefore considered to be in the foreground of specific business processes, such as corporate acquisitions, resource allocations, reorganizations, and the management of product and (even more) process innovation (Eisenhardt and Martin, 2000: 1107, Zollo and Winter, 2002) whenever these business processes are carried out through the triggering and execution of change routines, rather than (solely) through *ad hoc* problem-driven search and solution implementation activities.

For the purpose of the present chapter, it is important to note that all these (and other) conceptualizations of DCs have in common the often implicit assumption that the object upon which DCs produce their effects is fundamentally of a behavioral nature: that is a pattern of action, a process, an operating routine, or any form of group activity characterized by some level of stability and predictability. This approach misses the fundamental aspect that organizational capabilities specific to managing change can hardly be reduced to the management of *behavioral* change.

Consider the example of the management of organizational change in the context of post-acquisition integration processes, which some organizations (a small minority in most industries and countries) have learned to handle through specialized change routines, therefore by exercising DCs. Can the ability to manage the integration of the acquired unit be reduced to the conversion of the information systems or the replication of reporting and control processes? Clearly not. The (dynamic) capability to manage post-acquisition integration change needs to include, for example, the capacity to understand and align emotional conditions felt by the personnel of the acquired unit with those of the acquirer (Huy, 1999). Even more profoundly, the capable acquirer will have developed processes to assess the cultural traits of the acquired unit, decide whether and what needs to be aligned with potentially conflicting traits present in the acquiring organization, and design appropriate types of interventions to achieve the desired type and level of alignment. A third, related aspect of fundamental importance for the success of most types of post-acquisition change processes relates to the use of motivational levers to create the necessary emotional and identity condition that can produce the degree and type of behavioral alignment that is aimed for. Again, some acquiring firms (not many) undergo these motivational change processes (Gottschalg and Zollo, 2007) by triggering specific patterns of action that aim to facilitate, for instance, the en masse socialization of the employees of the acquired firm to the 'way things are done' in the acquiring one.

These non-behavioral objects of change are not included in the original notion of dynamic capabilities, despite their obvious relevance in many (if not most) types of organizational change processes. They start, instead, being considered within the notions of 'intangible resources' and 'human assets' mentioned in the consensus definition proposed by Helfat et al. (2007: 4). This definition goes a long way towards the recognition of the type of 'objects' of change that we refer to in the post-acquisition integration example. It does not highlight, however, the differences between the received notion of dynamic capabilities aimed at behavioral adjustments and the notion of DCs required to adapt the more tacit and subtle aspect of human interactions (motivation, emotions, and identity, in particular) to environmental or contextual requirements. For example, one can easily consider the case of an acquiring company that has developed excellent competencies in the handling of change processes related to its procedures, systems, and operating routines in general. However, that same acquiring firm might be particularly bad at handling the change processes related to the more subtle human aspects, such as motivation, identification, and emotional status. Vice versa, a competitor might have much more developed procedures for the human interaction side of things in a post-acquisition context and be a lot less competent in handling change at the system and operating routine level. As noted by Vince and Gabriel:

> the interplay between emotions and politics in organizations concerns how organizations function as emotional places (not how individuals within organizations can 'have' or 'manage' emotion); it concerns how decisions or actions are shaped, subverted, and/or transformed by emotions; and it concerns how emotions become embedded in cultural and political practices that determine the 'way we do things here.'
>
> (Vince and Gabriel, Chapter 15 in this volume)

The distinction between these two aspects of the notion of dynamic capabilities is necessary, we argue, if we want to make progress on some of the key theoretical questions related to dynamic capabilities. In the quest to identify and assess the role played by potential antecedents to the development of DCs, for example, it seems sensible to expect that organizational characteristics conducive of the development of DCs aimed at changes in operating routines might be quite different from the factors explaining how firms learn to adapt motivations, emotions, and identity traits. Ditto for the consequences produced by the deployment of DCs. Depending on the type of task at hand and the type of performance objective aimed at, the impact of a firm's capabilities to adapt operating routines, as opposed to those specific to the adaptation of emotional/motivational states might be more or less relevant for both a model of organizational change and for models of organizational performance.

A 'Holistic' Framework of Dynamic Capabilities

The distinction made above between the (relatively) well-known characteristics of DC connected to the adaptation of behavioral patterns, and the hitherto under-explored notion of DC connected to the adaptation of antecedents to behavioral change is at the core of our proposed contribution. We use the word 'holistic' to indicate that the conceptual framework developed considers both notions of DC, those focused on the adaptation of firm behavior (operating capabilities in particular) and those focused on the adaptation of behavioral antecedents, such as cognition (e.g. cognitive frames) and motivation. The framework proposed is considered 'holistic' (complete) also because it aims to encompass, albeit in highly abstract and general terms, all the general categories of explanations for the formation and evolution of DC. As such, it will try to move beyond the role of learning processes highlighted by prior literature (Zollo and Winter, 2002) and consider the role of both organizational as well as individual traits in shaping the development of DC. Finally, the proposed framework aims to be holistic also in terms of identifying both the evolutionary and the technical aspects of performance highlighted by Helfat et al. (2007) to include notions of appropriateness in the direction of change (evolutionary fit), as well as of economic efficiency in the change process itself (technical fit, i.e. with value produced larger than the costs necessary to produce it). The overall logic of the framework is summarized in Figure 24.1.

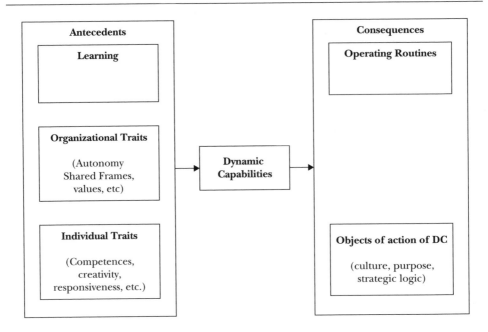

Figure 24.1 A Model of DC Antecedents and Consequences

The analysis is divided into three steps. We first focus on the mediations of behavioral and non-behavioral objects of change in shaping both the firm's evolutionary and technical fit. We then move on to consider the broad sets of factors that might distinguish one firm's ability to develop DC from another, over and above the notion of learning capabilities, which have already been discussed in the received literature. Finally, the dynamic nature of the framework is considered, including potentially important feedback loops that might shed new light on the advantages in order to expand the notion of DC to include the non-behavioral aspects of organizational change.

Mediating factors on the DC-performance link

The central point of departure from the received literature consists in the observation that, to fully capture the impact of DC on evolutionary and technical fitness, it is necessary to consider not only operating routines and organizational processes as objects of change, but also changes in cognitive and emotional/motivational traits of individual members of the organization, as well as shared cognitive and emotional/motivational traits among groups of individuals (eventually, albeit rarely, including all the members of the firm).

For instance, the absence of change in the case of Polaroid when faced by a technological discontinuity in the business of digital imaging was related to cognitive inertia (Tripsas and Gavetti, 2000) connected to the implicit framing of the competitive challenge facing Polaroid, and of its strategic response. It was Polaroid's inability to adapt its managers' mental models that led to the origins of the failure to adapt its competitive strategy and consequent operating routines to the rise of digital imaging. Similarly, Kodak and Anderson Co. have not been able to leverage the cognitive flexibility of their employees while coping with disruptive change respectively in the business of imaging and the business of consulting (Henderson and Kaplan, 2005). More recently, and along this line of reasoning, Danneels (2010) has described the inability of Smith Corona to face disruptive change in its typewriter business as an absence of dynamic capabilities specific to the adaptation of cognitive frames, first, and consequently of operating processes.

All the previous examples have in common a definition of cognition in terms of ways to frame the strategic challenge facing the firm (Schneider and Angelmar, 1993) and of the strategy connected to facing such challenge. Other cognitive traits that can be subject to systematic change processes through the deployment of DC might have to do with organizational identity traits connected with answers to questions like: what is the purpose of the company's existence and what defines or limits its role(s) within its social and economic environment (organizational identity)? What does it stand for (organizational values)? How are things done over here (organizational culture)?

In addition to all these cognitive dimensions, upon which the extended notion of DC that we have proposed displays its effects, there are several emotional and, in particular, motivational dimensions that also require specific attention. Gottschalg and Zollo (2007), for example, identify the mechanisms through which firms might learn to manipulate motivational levels of their managers and employees, encompassing explicit, normative implicit, and hedonic implicit motivations (Lindenberg, 2001). They also identify conditions under which these types of DCs generate sustainable competitive advantage, as well as conditions in which the advantage is not likely to be sustainable.

Besides motivational processes and connected organizational competencies for their static deployment as well as dynamic adaptation, the study of non-behavioral and non-cognitive objects of organizational change can be particularly vast, even though poorly appreciated. Consider all the dimensions of emotional traits that characterize in a stable, albeit not fixed, manner any organization. Positive effects (happiness, joy, excitement, etc.) are typically connected not only to stronger motivation to pursue the interests of the firm, but also to all sorts of intermediate goals such as creativity and innovation, capability development and transfer, and socially responsible decision making (Crilly et al., 2008). Negative effects, such as anger, frustration, and sadness (to name just a few), are typically connected to the opposite type of outcomes generated by positive effect. However, the causal linkages might be neither symmetric nor linear. For example, a moderate level of frustration is normally considered to be necessary in order to stimulate search for improved solutions, whereas anger with the status quo might be conducive to positive energy towards the initiation and/or acceptance of change. The key question, which has received very limited attention so far by scholars (Huy, 1999) concerns the development of processes dedicated to the change of these emotional traits within firms. DCs specialized in the manipulation of emotional traits are typically very difficult to observe in firms, but most of the processes connected with the internal communication function are geared towards the (more or less deliberate) adaptation of emotional traits.

Factors explaining the origins and the evolution of dynamic capabilities

The question related to the origins and development of DCs has received increasing attention from scholars, as the debate on the definition and content of DCs converged to some consensus (Zollo and Winter, 2002; Winter, 2003; Helfat et al., 2007). The most immediate explanations have to do with learning processes of a different nature that are expected to be at the basis of the development of any organizational capability, whether of dynamic nature or not. They have to do, for instance, with experience accumulation and learning-by-doing mechanisms, with deliberate investments in learning processes such as knowledge articulation and codification activities, as well as with vicarious learning and other imitative processes.

For the purpose of this chapter, however, we will focus on other factors that are not specifically related to learning processes but might nonetheless influence the ability of firms to undertake change processes through the development and deployment of DCs. Their discussion can be organized with respect to the level of analysis at work: organizational versus individual traits.

Organizational traits. To date, the conceptual and empirical effort directed towards the unbundling of the genesis and evolution of DC has been primarily devoted to studying the organizational base of the actions behind sustained product innovation. In an inter-industrial analysis of several product development projects, Leonard-Barton (1992) identified individual skills, technical systems, managerial systems, values, and norms as the key interrelated dimensions of the dynamics of sustained product innovation. Tushman and O'Reilly III (1997) also linked the nature of capabilities specific to the management of continuous product development to similar organizational variables and highlighted how an ambidextrous organization might prevent a firm falling into the trap of too much exploitation with no exploration. Verona and Ravasi (2003) found analogous results in the longitudinal analysis of a leading firm in the hearing-aid industry. According to their study, continuous product development was based on the ability to create, combine, and reconfigure knowledge. These three knowledge-based processes relied on the interconnection among organizational variables (namely, actors, physical resources, structure and systems, and organizational culture) and the ability of the firm to let them coexist within a loosely-coupled structure. Likewise, the work of Colanelli-O'Connor (2004) has recently investigated the organizational antecedents to the development of DCs specific to the management of radical product innovation. Findings show that these antecedents are deeply rooted in a system based on an identifiable organizational group, the practice of project management (a clear role system and a clear system of objectives), and a loosely-coupled organization, on an appropriate endowment of skills and talent, and on a (somewhat loosely defined) strong leadership. By comparing non-innovative and innovative organizations in mature industries, Dougherty, Barnard, and Dunne (2004) present an empirically-grounded theory that explains how the DC for sustained product innovation is closely linked to the organizational dynamics of power and control. Finally, Blyler and Coff (2003) point also to social capital as a key variable at the basis of a DC's formation and, consequently, at the basis of rent appropriation.

Beyond the sustained innovation context, there is comparably less work dedicated to the development of DCs in the management of organizational tasks of similar strategic importance, such as the selection, negotiation, and integration of corporate acquisitions, or the management of internal change geared towards the integration of principles of social and environmental (in addition to economic) sustainability. The reason why these other contexts might be very important for the development of the study of DC is that the management of M&A processes and the integration of social and environmental sustainability are organizational challenges that require particular attention to non-behavioral objects of the change process, such as the ones highlighted earlier: shared cognitive frames, beliefs and values, as well as collective emotional and motivational dynamics.

To illustrate, consider the recent evolution of the M&A literature specific to the problem of explaining performance variations studying the effects of experiential (Haleblian and Finkelstein, 1999; Hayward, 2002) and deliberate (Zollo and Singh, 2004) learning processes as antecedents to DCs specific to the management of organizational change related to the post-acquisition integration phase. What has been significantly under-explored, though, is the influence of other firm traits as antecedents of these specific types of DCs. What distinguishes some of the most successful acquirers from the others is still a matter of discussion in academic as well as practitioner debates, but it seems clear that it cannot be reduced to superior learning practices. By way of example, Charles O'Reilly's (1998) case on Cisco Systems focuses on specific organizational structures and HR management practices to explain Cisco's ability to integrate successfully high-tech start-ups and to retain the vast majority of their founders. In another example, GE Capital's competence in integrating acquired companies in the financial services sector is attributed to the development of innovative organizational arrangements, for example the novel role of 'integration manager' in a process leadership position, coupled with the business leader in the specific organizational unit of GE (see Ashkenas et al., 1998), and other process-specific innovations that are rooted in GE's organizational capacities to attract, motivate, and develop management talent, as well as in cultural traits that favor the emergence of managerial innovation.

The third context that we want to offer as illustrative example of DCs that could help identify the role of organizational traits in the evolution of these change capacities has to do with the significant efforts that an increasing amount of companies across industries and countries are making to understand and cope with the increasing demand by several types of stakeholders (employees, customers, suppliers, local communities, and, recently, even shareholders) to integrate principles of social and environmental sustainability within their operations, their strategic decision-making processes, and, eventually, even in their cultural fabric (Freeman, 1984; Donaldson and Preston, 1995; Blair and Stout, 1999; Freeman et al., 2010). Almost by definition, responding to these challenging expectations requires the development and deployment of DCs specific to the change of operating routines related, for instance, to the interactions with suppliers, customers, and local authorities in the communities where the firm operates. More challenging, and core to the argument in this chapter, is the change challenge connected to the more subtle aspects of the organization: the cognitive mindsets and shared beliefs that identify the purpose of work within the organization and the way it is supposed to compete and thrive, the cultural traits that could facilitate or hinder the openness to inclusion of stakeholders in the strategic decision-making processes of the firm, the motivational dynamics that affect (and are affected by) not only the system of incentives but also the type of social norms and of organizational identity traits that characterize the firm.

Individual traits. The development of this broader and more holistic notion of DC that encompasses the firm's ability to change not only its operating capabilities and resources, but also the other non-behavioral aspects of the organization that might influence sustainable performance, is also influenced by characteristics of individual traits. In fact, it is worth noting that some of the organizational traits highlighted by the literature on sustained innovation, such as skills, talent, and leadership, are really individual rather than collective constructs. In general, however, there is a broad recognition that human agency is fundamental to the explanation of the quality and the performance outcomes of the new product development process. Indeed the effectiveness and efficiency of the development of new products has been shown to be a direct consequence of the actions performed by project leaders and team members of new product development projects, senior management involved in new product development decisions, as well as customers and suppliers involved in the process (for reviews, see Brown and Eisenhardt, 1995; Verona, 1999). For instance, Krishnan and Ulrich (2001) reviewed research in product development with respect to the sequence of decisions made during the new product development process. This business process, which they consider a 'black box,' involves hundreds of decisions. Leveraging solely the literature in decision science or operations management, the authors identified in particular thirty major decisions made within organizational units dedicated to product development.

The decision-making activity behind new products and the role of human agency in the process give room to the importance of individual traits such as cognitive frames and beliefs, emotions, motivations, and identity. For instance, the recent work by von Hippel (2005) has shown how the alignment between the manufacturers' development process activities and customers' values favors the emergence of new products. Similarly, in the case of Ducati it has been shown how the alignment of values and norms and, more generally, of identity favors the exchange of knowledge between customers and members of the new product development team in the community of creation of new products called Tech Café (Sawhney et al., 2005).

With respect to the role of cognitive traits, recent work has shown their relevance in relation to opportunity recognition for entrepreneurial ventures (Shane and Ulrich, 2004). At the same time, though, Cardon et al. (2009: 517) show the importance and the positive role of entrepreneurial passion as a driver of opportunity recognition, pointing to the need to build a comprehensive ('holistic') model of opportunity recognition that encompasses both the cognitive and the emotional processes in human psyche. Beyond opportunity recognition, recent work focused on the role of motivation of entrepreneurs and team members in new ventures for the quality of new product development (Shane and Ulrich, 2004). With respect to psychological traits of individuals involved in new ventures, Hmieleski and Baron (2009), for instance, demonstrate how dispositional optimism (the tendency to expect positive outcomes even when they are not justifiable) is negatively related to the performance of their new ventures; they also show how this relationship is strengthened when moderated by industry dynamism and past experience.

These contributions exemplify, should it be necessary, the significant potential for the future development of our understanding of innovation processes provided by a serious investment in the exploration of the individual level antecedents to DC, sometimes referred to as the micro-foundations of innovation processes. For what concerns the M&A context, the discourse on the micro-foundations of M&A processes and performance is still in its embryonic stage. With very few exceptions, the literature has tackled the quest to understand M&A-related capabilities as a fundamentally collective phenomenon. This is understandable, since a corporate acquisition typically involves all the organizational functions of the acquired organization and, in all cases of operating, cultural or at least structural integration, the corresponding functions within the acquiring unit. However, the development of a firm's ability to handle the most complex phases of the M&A process, which are normally considered to center on the integration phase (Haspeslagh and Jemison, 1991), might be heavily influenced by individuals playing a particularly important role in these processes. In most cases of a sophisticated acquirer (Cisco Systems, Intel, GE Capital, Electrolux, Dow Chemical, to name but a few), the individuals heading the corporate development unit will shape the processes and the decisions characterizing their firm's approach to the integration phase in line with the objective requirements of the type of firms acquired and the rent generation logic of each acquisition. More subtly, they will also shape those processes and decisions in alignment with their own convictions (derived from their cognitive representations and frames) about how an acquisition should be handled, in alignment with their psychological dispositions vis-à-vis decision-making processes in general (e.g. consensus orientation), the emotional components of the integration process (e.g. resistance to change, uncertainty-driven anxiety, frustration and anger, hope and excitement, etc.), and the motivational dynamics that play such a significant role in the alignment and integration process (Jemison and Sitkin, 1986; Buono and Bowditch, 1990). However, what has not been tackled at all in the received literature is the role of the corporate leader in shaping, for better or worse, the way the firm learns how to cope with the complexities of the post-acquisition integration phase (Fubini et al., 2006). The authors identify several ways in which the corporate leader can influence the post-merger processes, including the way the firm learns to handle the key challenges during and after the completion of the integration phase. Despite these initial results, however, this line of work is still very much an open field since there is a lot more to understand on how individual traits of leaders and corporate development executives might influence the development of M&A-related DC.

In the third context considered, the one related to the embedding of social and environmental sustainability principles within the firm's operations, strategies and cultural traits, the study of firms' capabilities related to those internal change processes has yet to materialize in any empirical (or even theoretical) result. To the best of our knowledge, there are only a few case studies that attempt to unpack the learning challenge related to both sense making on the direction of change required and to enacting the internal changes against the resistance of internal and external stakeholders. Zadek (2004), for example, studied Nike's painful experience following the sweatshop scandal in the mid-1990s to conceptualize the challenge in terms of internal and external learning and change processes, but that can only be considered an initial exploration in largely uncharted territory. The field needs to begin a significant investment in the identification of the factors explaining superior performance in adapting internal processes to the evolution of multiple key stakeholders' needs and interests, and to refocus its attention to external stakeholder engagement practices towards the analysis of internal learning and change processes (Zollo et al., 2007). In that sense, the research agenda of scholars focusing on the study of social and environmental sustainability converges and overlaps with the one pursued by the larger field of scholars with a general interest in organizational learning and change, and, more specifically, in the origins and consequences of DC.

Dynamics and feedback loops

The focus of our argument above has been on the need to extend the received notion of DC to encompass a broader set of objects of learning and change (i.e. the non-behavioral aspects of the firm, beyond operating routines) as well as of antecedents to the learning and change process itself (organizational and individual traits, beyond learning processes). The call for extension of the theory of DC is not motivated solely by the need to build a more comprehensive model of organizational evolution, though. It is fundamentally driven by the observation that by extending the model to the dynamics of non-behavioral antecedents and consequences of DC, we might be able to observe and describe qualitatively different features of the dynamic interaction among the variables considered.

To illustrate, consider the version of the model exemplified by the sequential chain of causation from learning to change (i.e. DC) to operating routines proposed by Zollo and Winter (2002). In this received version of the story, the causation can only go in one direction, with learning processes influencing the development of capabilities (dynamic as well as 'static'), and with DCs influencing the development of operating capabilities and resources. If one, however, considers the extended version of the model proposed, the unidirectionality in the causation chain might not apply any more. More specifically, the 'holistic' notion of DC will influence the evolution of organizational traits that are in turn likely to influence at least some of the non-behavioral factors, at the organizational as well as individual level, that shape the ability of the organization to produce DC. It is the nature of these feedback loops that might allow future scholars to build a more complete picture not only of how business organizations evolve over time, but also (and most interestingly) about the interdependence between the evolutionary processes at the organizational and the individual levels (Figure 24.2).

To illustrate, consider the case of DCs specific to the integration of sustainability within the various dimensions of the firm, both behavioral (i.e. operating routines) and non-behavioral (e.g. cognitive framing of the strategic challenges, cultural traits, and emotional dispositions) in nature. Whereas it is difficult to imagine that changes in operating routines will influence 'backward' the development of the DC that might have created and eventually shaped them, that is quite possible when the influence of DC on cognitive and emotional components of the firm is taken into consideration. For instance, consider a firm that has developed a DC in adapting the cognitive frames of its managers related to the purpose of existence of their company to include the improvement of the well-being of the communities in which it operates. That firm will not only see its management change their decision-making patterns to include, for example, an explicit evaluation of the social and environmental consequences of their decisions, and perhaps to suggest process adjustments aimed at engaging the most relevant stakeholders in the decision itself. Most likely, that firm will also see its managers invest in learning to change internal processes, motivations, emotional traits, and social norms, thereby developing and upgrading the firm's collective DC specific to these sustainability domains. Ditto if the objects of change in the DC are the psychological dispositions of managers and entrepreneurs towards more caring for and openness with, for example, the key stakeholders of the enterprise (employees, customers, partners, and the local communities) in addition to the shareholders. Again, those dispositions might trigger learning processes which will further develop the same DC that initiated or developed them,

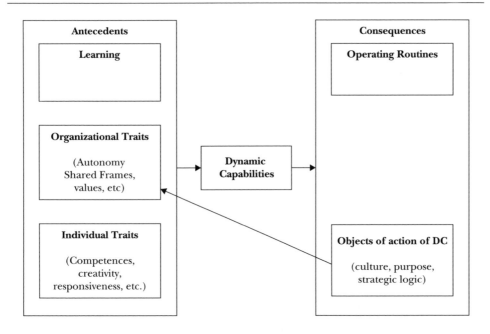

Figure 24.2 The Feedback Loops

creating, therefore, a positive feedback loop, a potential virtual cycle between holistic notions of DC and the non-behavioral objects of change. Note, by the way, that the presence of a positive loop does not necessarily mean that firms will spiral up (or down) to infinite levels of openness and caring for stakeholders (or lack thereof). The loops could simply follow each other with smaller and smaller magnitudes, therefore reaching a steady state in this dynamic system at high levels of DC, high levels of openness and inclusiveness in strategic decision making of stakeholders, and eventually high levels of evolutionary fit (assuming that openness and inclusiveness are part of the expectations and interests of stakeholders).

CONCLUSIONS

In this chapter we reviewed the extant literature on dynamic capabilities with a view to move the debate towards the development of a positive theory on antecedents and consequences of the development and effectiveness of dynamic capabilities. To do so we proposed a framework that broadens the object of change beyond purely behavioral constructs such as processes and routines, and embraces the challenge of understanding how firms learn to manipulate subtle aspects of human nature such as emotions, motivation, and identity. The core claim is that a broader notion of DC which includes non-behavioral aspects in both the objects and consequences of their deployment as well as in the factors explaining their origins and evolution will not only improve the descriptive power of the model of organizational evolution and long-term performance, compared to the received one based on solely behavioral mechanisms (learning, change, and operating routines). It will also produce a qualitatively different (and potentially powerful from a descriptive standpoint) set of dynamics among its main components. The non-behavioral objects of the change action of these holistic DCs could in fact influence the evolutionary patterns of the DCs themselves, potentially creating positive feedback loops which will enhance the self-generated emergence of change dynamics over and above the deliberate action of top management. The consequences could be particularly virtuous in terms of evolutionary and technical fit, if the management can appreciate the importance of these evolutionary processes, leverage the power of their change dynamics, and guide them appropriately towards the achievement of evolutionary and technical fit.

The argument has been developed and illustrated with the help of three managerial contexts, which provided some grounding into the change decisions that managers make and the change capabilities necessary to make them in the appropriate way. They are the new product development, the post-acquisition integration, and the social and environmental sustainability challenge. The managerial implications from the consideration of a broader concept of DCs, which includes the subtler aspects of human nature that antecede the overt behavioral outcomes, will be specific for each of the contexts analyzed. All those implications will have in common one important feature, however: they will potentially allow corporate managers and leaders to understand how to unleash the power of the human side of dynamic capabilities, leveraging the emergent nature of evolutionary change, and thus significantly amplifying, if properly guided, the firm's capacity to generate and sustain technical and evolutionary fit.

References

Ashkenas, R.N., DeMonaco, L.J., and Francis, S.C. (1998) Making the Deal Real: How GE Capital Integrates Acquisitions. *Harvard Business Review*, 76(1): 165–178.

Blair, M.M. and Stout, L.A. (1999) A Team Production Theory of Corporate Law, 85 *Virginia Law Review*,. No. 2, March 1999.

Blyler, M. and Coff, R.W. (2003) Dynamic Capabilities, Social Capital and Rent Appropriation: Ties that Split Pies. *Strategic Management Journal*, 24: 677–686.

Bromiley, P. (2009) A Prospect Theory Model of Resource Allocation. *Decision Analysis*, 6(3): 124–138.

Brown, S.L. and Eisenhardt, K.M. (1995) Product Development: Past Research, Present Findings and Future Directions. *Academy of Management Review*, 20: 334–378.

Buono, A.F. and Bowditch, J.L. (1990) *A Primer on Organizational Behavior*, 2nd edition. New York: John Wiley & Sons.

Cardon, M.S., Wincent, J., Singh, J., and Drnovsek, M. (2009) The nature and experience of entrepreneurial passion. *Academy of Management Journal*, 34: 511–532.

Colanelli-O'Connor, G. (2004) A Systems Approach to Building a Radical Innovation Dynamic Capability. *Working Paper AoM Conference*, New Orleans.

Collis, D.J. (1994) Research note: how valuable are organizational capabilities? *Strategic Management Journal*, 15: 143–152.

Crilly, D., Schneider, S.C., and Zollo, M. (2008) The psychological antecedents to socially responsible behavior. *European Management Review*, 5(3): 175–190.

Danneels, E. (2010) Trying to become a different company: Dynamic capabilities at Smith Corona. *Strategic Management Journal*, 32: 1–31.

Di Stefano, G., Peteraf, M.A., and Verona, G. (2010) Dynamic capabilities deconstructed: A bibliographic investigation into the origins, development, and future directions of the research domain. *Industrial and Corporate Change*, 19(4): 1187–1204.

Donaldson, T. and Preston, L.E. (1995) The Stakeholder Theory of the Corporation: Concepts, Evidence, and Implications. *Academy of Management Review*, 20 (1): 65–91.

Dougherty, D., Barnard, H., and Dunne, D. (2004) The Rules and Resources That Generate the Dynamic Capability for Sustained Product Innovation. *Working Paper*, AoM Conference New Orleans.

Eisenhardt, K.M. and Martin, J. (2000) Dynamic capabilities: what are they? *Strategic Management Journal*, 21(10–11): 1105–1121.

Felin, T. and Foss, N.J. (2005) Strategic organization: a field in search of micro-foundations. *Strategic Organization*, 3(4): 441–455.

Freeman, R.E. (1984) *Strategic Management: A Stakeholder Approach.* Boston: Pitman.

Freeman, R.E., Harrison, J.S., Wicks, A.C., Parmar, B.L., and de Colle, S. (2010) *Stakeholder Theory: The State of the Art.* Cambridge: Cambridge University Press.

Fubini, D., Price, C., and Zollo, M. (2006) *Mergers: Leadership, Performance and Corporate Health.* UK: Palgrave MacMillan.

Gottschalg, O. and Zollo, M. (2007) Interest alignment and competitive advantage. *Academy of Management Review*, 32(2): 418–437.

Haleblian, J. and Finkelstein, S. (1999) The Influence of Organizational Acquisition Experience on Acquisition Performance: A Behavioral Learning Perspective, *Administrative Science Quarterly*, 44 (1): 29–56.

Haspeslagh, P.C. and Jemison, D.B. (1991) *Managing acquisitions: Creating value through corporate renewal.* New York: Free Press.

Hayward, M.L.A. (2002) When do firms learn from their acquisition experience? Evidence from 1985–1995. *Strategic Management Journal*, 23: 21–39.

Helfat, C.E., Finkelstein, S., Mitchell, W., Peteraf, M.A., Singh, H., and Winter, S.G. (2007) *Dynamic capabilities: Understanding strategic change in organizations.* Malden, MA: Blackwell Publishing.

Helfat, C.E. and Peteraf, M.A. (2003) The dynamic resource-based view: Capability life-cycles. *Strategic Management Journal*, 24(10): 997–1010.

Henderson, R. and Kaplan, S. (2005) Inertia and Incentives: Bridging Organizational Economics and Organizational Theory. *Organization Science*, 16(5): 509–521.

Hmieleski, K.M. and Baron, R.L. (2009) Entrepreneurs' optimism and new venture performance: A social cognitive perspective. *Academy of Management Journal*, 52: 473–488.

Huy, Q.N. (1999) Emotional Capability, Emotional Intelligence, and Radical Change. *The Academy of Management Review*, 24(2): 325–345.

Jemison, D.B. and Sitkin, S.B. (1986) Corporate Acquisitions: A Process Perspective. *Academy of Management Review*, 11: 145–163.

Krishnan, V. and Ulrich, K. (2001) Product Development Decisions: A review of the literature. *Management Science*, 47: 1–21.

Leonard-Barton, D. (1992) Core capabilities and core rigidities: a paradox on managing new product development. *Strategic Management Journal*, 13: 111–126.

Lindenberg, S. (2001) Intrinsic Motivation in a New Light. *Kyklos*, 54(2/3): 317–342.

O'Reilly, C.A. (1998) *Cisco Systems: The Acquisition of Technology is the Acquisition of People.* Case Study.

Sawhney M., Verona G. and Prandelli, E. (2005) Collaborating to Create: The Internet as a Platform for Customer Engagement in Product Innovation. *Journal of Interactive Marketing*, 19(4): 4–17.

Schneider, S.C. and Angelmar, R. (1993) Cognition in organizational analysis: Who's minding the store? *Organizational Studies*, 14(3): 347–374.

Shane, S. and Ulrich, K. (2004) Technological innovation, product development and entrepreneurship in management science. *Management Science*, 50(4): 133–144.

Teece, D.J. (2007) Explicating dynamic capabilities: The nature and microfoundations of (sustainable) enterprise performance. *Strategic Management Journal*, 28: 1319–1350.

Teece, D.J, Pisano, G., and Shuen, A. (1997) Dynamic capabilities and strategic management. *Strategic Management Journal*, 18(7): 509–533.

Tripsas, M. and Gavetti, G. (2000) Capabilities, Cognition, and Inertia: Evidence from Digital Imaging. *Strategic Management Journal*, 21(10–11): 1147–1161.

Tushman, M. and O'Reilly, C. (1997). *Winning through Innovation: A practical guide to leading organizational change and renewal.* Boston, Mass.: Harvard Business School Press.

Verona, G. (1999) A Resource-Based View of Product Development. *Academy of Management Review*, 24 (1): 132–142.

Verona, G. and Ravasi, D. (2003) Unbundling dynamic capabilities: an exploratory study of continuous product innovation. *Industrial Corporate Change*, 12(3): 577–606.

Vince, R. and Gabriel, Y. (2011) Organizations, Learning and Emotion. In M. Easterby-Smith and M. Lyles (eds.), *Handbook of Organizational Learning and Knowledge Management* (2nd edition). Chichester: John Wiley & Sons.

Von Hippel, E. (2005) *Democratizing Innovation.* Cambridge, MA: The MIT Press.

Winter, S.G. (2000) The Satisficing Principle in Capability Learning. *Strategic Management Journal*, 21(10–11): 981–996.

Winter, S.G. (2003) Understanding Dynamic Capabilities. *Strategic Management Journal*, 24: 991–995.

Zadek, S. (2004) The Path to Corporate Responsibility. *Harvard Business Review*, 82(12): 125–132.

Zollo et al. (2007) Understanding and responding to societal demands on corporate responsibility (RESPONSE). Research report for the EU Commission. See http://portale.unibocconi.it/wps/allegatiCTP/RESPONSE_1.pdf

Zollo, M. and Singh, H. (2004) Deliberate learning in corporate acquisitions: post-acquisition strategies and integration capability in U.S. bank mergers. *Strategic Management Journal*, 25: 1233–1256.

Zollo, M. and Winter, S.G. (2002) Deliberate learning and the evolution of dynamic capabilities. *Organization Science* 13(3): 339–351.

25

Knowledge Structures and Innovation: Useful Abstractions and Unanswered Questions

GAUTAM AHUJA AND
ELENA NOVELLI*

Abstract

We examine the received research on organizational knowledge structures with a special focus on their link to innovation. We note that the literature has used the term knowledge structure to represent three quite distinct components of organizational knowledge: the cognitive templates used by management, the content knowledge of the organization, and the transactive systems used by an organization to organize its knowledge. We use the term organizational knowledge-base as an abstraction to capture the aggregative entity that includes these three components. We then examine the research to identify six primary dimensions along which organizational knowledge-bases differ: size, content, veridicality, degree of differentiation, degree of integration, and embeddedness. We identify the three common mechanisms by which organizations search for innovations, recombinant, cognitive, and experiential search and examine the implications of the knowledge-base dimensions in the context of these mechanisms. This discussion also helps to locate derived dimensions of organizational knowledge-bases such as relatedness, decomposability, and malleability. We then review the organizational antecedents that shape organizational knowledge-bases and conclude with some thoughts on key areas of future research in this literature.

*We gratefully acknowledge the financial support of the University of Michigan and Bocconi University—Kites Research Center. The authors are listed in alphabetical order.

> If only HP knew what HP knows—
>
> *Lew Platt, HP CEO (in Sieloff, 1999)*

A dramatic growth in organizational knowledge over the past few decades has made the problem of developing appropriate structures for capturing and storing knowledge in organizations especially salient. Concomitant with this growth in organizational knowledge and increased need for knowledge structuring, intensifying competition and high rates of technological obsolescence have created a need for greater and faster innovation in many industries. Addressing the challenges posed by these two problems, of structuring knowledge and managing it for innovation, are key tasks for organization theorists in the knowledge economy. Surveying and structuring the emergent literature in these domains, and thus cumulating our understanding of the relationship between knowledge structures and innovation, is the key objective of this chapter. Additionally, marking the current state of knowledge in this area is useful for identifying key problems and challenges that remain unaddressed and, therefore, for highlighting the gaps in our current understanding of these problems.

The organizational literature has defined and represented knowledge structures in several different ways, sometimes with slightly different meanings. Commonly, knowledge structures have been conceived of as cognitive templates. For instance, at the individual (rather than organizational) level Walsh (1995) suggests 'A knowledge structure is a mental template that individuals impose on an information environment to give it form and meaning.' Similarly, at the organizational level Lyles and Shwenk (1992) suggest that 'knowledge structure refers to shared beliefs at the organizational level. Further, these beliefs have a *structure*.' As they elaborate, 'the concept of knowledge structures deals with goals, cause-and-effect beliefs, and other *cognitive* elements.' Further, in their conceptualization, knowledge structures are characterized by some core features which remain invariant over long periods of time and some peripheral features which change (Lyles and Schwenk, 1992). Core features refer to the set of 'beliefs and goals on which there is widespread agreement,' while peripheral elements include knowledge about sub-goals and about the behavior or steps necessary to achieve the goals specified in the core set. Peripheral knowledge is open to much more debate and disagreement within the organization (Lyles and Schwenk, 1992). Similarly, in describing dominant logic, Prahalad and Bettis (1986) refer to knowledge systems, beliefs, theories, and propositions that have developed over time based on the manager's personal experiences. In other words, the term 'knowledge structures,' as emphasized by Galambos et al. (1986), has often referred to the cognitive structure underlying top-down or theory-driven information processing.

However, other authors (e.g. Walsh, 1995) have noted that organizational knowledge *per se*, includes not just process knowledge such as cognitive filters and beliefs, shared perspectives, and mental maps, but also content knowledge that includes information about (for instance) technological, production, and marketing concepts and relationships (e.g. see Yayavaram and Ahuja, 2008). Thus, knowledge about manufacturing of semiconductors, the properties of various types of integrated circuits, and the payment history of various customers are all parts of the content knowledge of a semiconductor manufacturer.

Finally, a third set of authors have drawn attention to another component of organizational knowledge—the set of procedures or transactive systems that are used by the organization for encoding, storing, retrieving, updating, and communicating organizational knowledge (Hollingshead, 2001; Wegner 1986; Lewis, Lange, and Gillis, 2005). Thus, who knows what, where specific pieces of knowledge are stored in the organization, and how they are to be retrieved are the kinds of knowledge stored in the transactive systems of an organization.

Clearly, any attempt to understand the implications of an organization's knowledge structures for innovation should encompass an analysis of not just organizational knowledge about beliefs, goals, and cognitive templates but also the organization of the substantive, task related content knowledge held by the organization as well as the transactive systems used by the organization to maintain, grow, and utilize its knowledge (see Figure 25.1). Accordingly, to facilitate our analysis of knowledge structures we synthesize the above notions of cognitive, content, and transactive knowledge in an organization to introduce the notion of an organizational knowledge base.[i]

We will use the concept of an organizational knowledge-base as a key organizing construct for this review. In its simplest sense an organizational knowledge-base refers to 'what an organization knows.' It is in essence a summation of the knowledge contained in the organization. Such knowledge may consist of 'content' knowledge about technologies, markets, products, customers, routines, or 'cognitive' knowledge such as beliefs, tem-

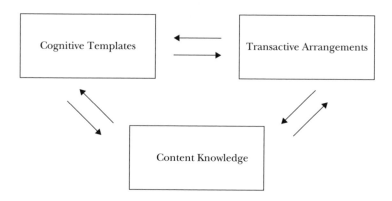

Figure 25.1 Organizational Knowledge-Base

---

[i] Making a distinction between different types of organizational knowledge has a long tradition in the literature. For instance, in a distinction similar to the distinction between procedural and declarative knowledge (Rogers, 1983; Winter, 1987; Kogut and Zander, 1992; Moorman and Miner, 1998; Tippins and Sohi, 2003), Kogut and Zander (1992) categorize organizational knowledge into information and know-how based knowledge. Information, as declarative knowledge, consists of a statement that provides a state description and know-how, like procedural knowledge, is a description of what defines current practice inside a firm. Cohen and Bacdayan (1994) emphasize the importance of organizational routines as a crucial component of organizations' knowledge in determining their performance and identify organizational routines as being part of what they define 'procedural memory,' i.e. memory for how things are done that encompasses cognitive as well as motor activities (Cohen and Bacdayan, 1994).

plates, cognitive frames, and heuristics or 'transactive' knowledge about how to access or update content knowledge. The organizational knowledge-base may reside in electronic or physical media, but also organization members, procedures, routines, and organizational structures. Knowledge-bases can be distinguished from ordinary databases in two ways. First, while databases are simply logical, structured classifications of data into logical categories and can be used to systematize, enhance, and expedite large scale intra- and inter-firm knowledge management (Alavi and Leidner, 2001), knowledge-bases also include conceptual maps that outline the interdependencies across contents, and include interpretations and beliefs about the data, as well as routines and rules for the storage, maintenance, and retrieval of the data themselves. Second, following from this, databases have usually an electronic or a physical manifestation. Knowledge-bases may however reside in people, relationships, organizational structures, and routines. Thus, all databases will be a part of a knowledge-base but a knowledge-base may not be captured entirely in databases.

The organizational knowledge-base construct is also related to, but distinct from, the construct of organizational memory (see Walsh and Ungson, 1991). As defined by Walsh and Ungson, the construct of organizational memory refers to 'stored information about a decision stimulus and response that when retrieved, comes to bear on present decisions.' Thus, organizational memory is derived from an organization's past experience and includes knowledge that is retained and recalled in the context of a specific decision stimulus. An organizational knowledge-base however has a broader scope of covered knowledge—it includes elements of knowledge that have not necessarily emerged from the organization's past experience or are not related to or recalled in the context of specific decision stimuli.

Note that the relationship between the three components of the organizational knowledge-base is likely to be bidirectional within each dyad. A management's cognitive template is likely to influence both the nature of content knowledge the organization accumulates and the kind of transactive systems it puts in place. In turn though, the content knowledge accumulated by an organization is likely to influence the cognitive templates of the management as well as the type of transactive systems it uses. Finally, the nature of transactive systems themselves may influence the content of a knowledge-base as well as the cognitive templates of the management.

Organizational Knowledge-Bases

Authors using this broader concept of organizational knowledge have sometimes invoked one of three broad abstractions to represent an organizational knowledge-base. First, they have used the concept of a set (Nelson and Winter, 1982; Kogut and Zander, 1992, 1996; Nonaka and Takeuchi, 1995; Ahuja and Katila, 2001; Nerkar and Roberts, 2004). A set representation assumes that an organization's knowledge can be represented as a collection of individual, discrete elements or quanta. A set representation enables the quantification of an organization's knowledge-base, is broad based and generic, and allows basic algebraic operations to be performed such as union and intersection. All these properties can be usefully exploited in organizational knowledge contexts.

For instance, the cardinal number of a set can be used to serve as an indicator of the size of an organization's knowledge-base, and can thus be used to describe both the absolute size of a knowledge-base as well as its relative size in a comparison between two knowledge-bases (Ahuja and Katila, 2001). The elements can reflect technical knowledge, knowledge about individual routines or procedures, or even organizational beliefs or heuristics (Nelson and Winter, 1982; Kogut and Zander, 1992; Grant, 1996; Nerkar and Roberts, 2004). Operations such as union and intersection can be meaningfully interpreted in the organizational context as the aggregation of knowledge-bases (for instance through mergers, alliances, acquisitions, franchising) and the degree of overlap or relatedness between two knowledge-bases, respectively (Kogut, 1988; Lyles and Salk, 1996; Simonin,1999; Khanna, Gulati, and Nohria, 1998; Inkpen, 2000; Gupta and Govindarajan, 2000; Ahuja and Katila, 2001; Sorenson and Sorensen, 2001). These properties can also be used to model the processes by which innovation occurs, such as recombination, or to explore the implications of knowledge depth and breadth. For instance, an organization's depth of knowledge can be conceived of as its frequency of reuse of its existing knowledge elements while breadth of knowledge can be conceived in terms of the number of knowledge elements in the knowledge-base (Katila and Ahuja, 2002).

However, representing a knowledge-base as a set also introduces limitations. First, the notion that all knowledge may be represented as discrete quanta or units may not be a useful simplification in specific contexts. Second, very importantly, the set abstraction assumes that the individual elements are all stand-alone pieces of knowledge, without connection to any other knowledge elements inside or outside the knowledge-base. Yet, most knowledge is usually related to and understood in the context of other knowledge. This limitation suggests that an alternate concept of organizational knowledge that allows the possibility of representing the knowledge elements with some recognition of the links between elements of knowledge may be a superior alternative in some cases. This suggests the possibility of at least two distinct representations incorporating this feature—the organizational knowledge-base represented as a matrix (Grant, 1996; Dyer and Singh, 1998; Helfat and Raubitschek, 2000; Eppinger, Sosa, and Rowles, 2004; Grant and Baden-Fuller, 2004; Siggelkow and Rivkin, 2005; Ethiraj, 2007), or as a network (Hansen, 2002; Reagans and McEvily, 2003; Yayavaram and Ahuja, 2008; Galunic and Rodan, 1998; Almeida and Phene, 2004; Owen-Smith and Powell, 2004; Nerkar and Paruchuri, 2005; Inkpen and Tsang, 2005).

The work on complexity theory and Simon's seminal work on the design of organizations (Simon, 1957; 1962; 1973) provides the precedent for the matrix representation of knowledge. In its simplest form this entails the listing of all knowledge elements as the two dimensions of a matrix with the actual cells of the matrix being denominated as ones or zeros (Steward, 1981; Smith and Eppinger, 1997) to indicate the presence or absence of a linkage between the knowledge elements. The relation specifying the presence of a one or zero can be defined in many different ways to reflect interdependencies of various types. This matrix can then be used to understand non-obvious relationships between knowledge elements, including potentially by using the power of matrix algebra.

An alternate, but similar, approach to addressing the issue of potential relationships between elements of knowledge is to conceive of the organizational knowledge-base as a network with the nodes representing individual bits of knowledge and the ties representing connections between specific pieces of knowledge. So considered, ties could represent many different forms of relationships. For instance Yayavaram and Ahuja (2008) define a tie between two knowledge elements as a coupling, the decision by an inventor or manager to consider two elements of knowledge jointly thus either using them together or not using them at all. According to them,

> couplings thus reflect an organization's revealed beliefs about which elements of knowledge are most likely to work well together and should be combined and, conversely, what kind of elements are unrelated to each other and do not need to be considered jointly. Couplings can vary in their intensity, going from strong (elements X and Y are always considered together) to weak (X and Y are considered together occasionally) to non-existent (X and Y are always considered independently).
>
> (Yayavaram and Ahuja, 2008)

They then demonstrate the use of coupling and knowledge elements to articulate the knowledge network of individual firms. The network representation of a knowledge-base is fairly general in that, as the above illustration shows, ties can be used to represent a wide variety of dependence relationships and can also be permitted to vary in strength (Ghoshal, Korine, and Szulanski, 1994; Hansen, 2002; Schulz, 2003; Levin and Cross, 2003).

To understand the implications of these various conceptualizations of organizational knowledge-bases it would be useful to have in mind the basic models through which we expect knowledge to create innovations. It is to this task that we turn our attention next. A survey of the literature suggests at least three broad (non-exclusive) processes through which innovations are commonly created—recombinant search, cognitive search, and experiential search (March and Simon, 1958; Cyert and March, 1963; Nelson and Winter, 1982; Huber, 1991; Kogut and Zander, 1992; Galunic and Rodan, 1998; Fleming, 2001; Gavetti and Levinthal, 2000; Winter, 2000; Fleming and Sorenson, 2004; Gavetti, Levinthal, and Rivkin, 2005).

THREE MECHANISMS OF INNOVATION SEARCH

Recombination as a mechanism for innovation can be traced back to at least Schumpeter (1934). More recently various organizational and strategy scholars have described the concept of recombination (Fleming, 2001; Kogut and Zander, 1992) with Fleming (2001) providing a seminal treatment of the recombinant process as it pertains to innovation search. As Fleming notes, inventions are fundamentally composed of combinations of prior existing components into new syntheses or the recombining of existing combinations (Fleming, 2001; Fleming and Sorenson, 2004; Fleming, Mingo, and Chen, 2007; Nasiriyar, Nesta, and Dibiaggio, 2010). Such recombinations may result in entirely new products and services or the application of existing products to new markets and uses (see Fleming and Sorenson, 2004, for famous examples). Pure recombination may however lead to the generation of far more combinations than can be meaningfully evaluated. To avoid a combinatorial explosion or 'complexity catastrophe' (Fleming and Sorenson, 2001) some decision rule needs to be invoked to reduce the set of combinations to a feasible number. Yayavaram and Ahuja (2008) suggest that 'coupling' may be one mechanism that organizations use to reduce the number of combinatorial choices to a meaningful number. Thus, recombination may work through the combining of 'coupled' groups of elements rather than individual elements.

Cognitive search processes work through the exercise of a causal reasoning logic (Fleming and Sorenson, 2004; Gavetti and Levinthal, 2000), the most common prototype of which is the scientific method. The inventor begins with an abstract model of the phenomenon of interest (Holland et al., 1986; Gavetti and Levinthal, 2000) and tries to understand the cause–effect mechanisms that underlie its behavior. To understand these cause–effect mechanisms the inventor may resort to one of two common processes, deduction or induction (Novelli, 2010). Deduction entails the identification of causes from systematic analysis using the tenets of established principles and general laws. These principles depict an architecture of relationships, a big picture of the terrain that the inventor can explore using causal reasoning and prior to or without observation of the phenomenon. In induction the researcher attempts to generalize backward from a set of observations to discover a common pattern that he or she uses as the basis of a general model of the phenomenon. Having understood the underlying causal effects the inventor can now design new products and processes that incorporate elements leading to desirable outcomes and eliminate elements that lead to undesirable effects.

When the process or product sought to be innovated upon is complex, embodying many simultaneous interactions, formulating a cognitive model of the process to engage in cognitive search may not be practical. In such situations experiential search processes may still provide a mechanism for innovation. Rather than rely upon a reasoned logic to explain the effects of a proposed change (impractical given the relative complexity of the change), in experiential search the inventor actually tries out the proposed change and then decides whether or not to accept the resultant product or process. Experiential search processes thus lead to innovation through a variation-selection-retention cycle. The decision maker varies an existing product or process and receives feedback from the environment on the performance of the entity after the mutation. If this feedback suggests that performance is improved following the mutation, the mutation is retained and the new version of the product or process is adopted. Subsequent variations continue the cycle of change leading potentially to further new products or processes.

Experiential search processes commonly differ from cognitive search processes on three key dimensions: the mode of evaluation, the range of alternatives considered, and the location of the search (Gavetti and Levinthal, 2000). Cognitive processes, since they can operate through the application of logic, may sometimes not require online evaluation. Logical analysis may suffice to provide an answer to whether some proposed change is a good idea or not. However, for experiential search processes putting the application into practice is necessary. Hence evaluation is, of necessity, on-line (Gavetti and Levinthal, 2000). Given the need to evaluate the effect of a proposed change experimentally, the number of alternatives that can be considered is also smaller than with cognitive search. Finally, experiential search is likely to be more incremental or local than cognitive search. Since the logic of experiential search involves assessing the effects of a change before accepting the change, it militates against simultaneous experimentation with multiple changes because the performance effects of the several changes would be confounded making it difficult to isolate what changes were beneficial and should be retained and what others were harmful (Sorenson, 2003).

Experiential search is also the basis of analogical reasoning (Gick and Holoyak, 1980; Gavetti, Levinthal, and Rivkin, 2005). Analogical reasoning deals with using experiential knowledge to cope with novel environments. It involves mapping from a source context of prior experience to a new target context (Gick and Holoyak, 1980). When the organization faces unfamiliar problems, analogizing managers choose a subset of the problem characteristics they believe distinguishes similar problems from different ones. Then, they transfer from the matching problem high-level policies or principles that guide search in the novel context (Gavetti, Levinthal, and Rivkin, 2005).

Dimensions of Organizational Knowledge-Bases

We now examine the relationship between the concept of an organizational knowledge-base and the three key innovation search processes. Understanding the implications of various knowledge-base dimensions becomes more meaningful, with the prior understanding of the innovation search processes in mind. We follow Walsh's suggestion that researchers focusing on the knowledge structure construct in relation to management need to address several distinct issues. First, in accordance with his suggestion, we survey the prior research to 'uncover the attributes' of knowledge structures that managers use. Second, following Walsh (1995), we need to understand the implications of these knowledge structures for consequences of relevance to managers; specifically we focus on the relationship between these various dimensions of knowledge structures and organizational innovation performance. Finally, in keeping with Walsh's third precept we try to 'uncover the origins' of organizational knowledge structures, i.e. understand the key determinants that shape knowledge structures in any organization. Going forward, unless it is contextually necessary, we use the term organizational knowledge-base everywhere as the term collectively captures all types of knowledge structures.

Research on organizational knowledge-bases has identified several key attributes or dimensions on which knowledge-bases differ. We focus on six such primary dimensions: size, content, veridicality, differentiation, integration, and embeddedness. However, in the course of the discussion we also mention some key 'derived' attributes of knowledge-bases such as decomposability, malleability, and relatedness. The distinction between the primary and derived attributes is that derived attributes emerge from the interaction or implications of primary attributes (see Figure 25.2).

Size

Knowledge-base size reflects 'how much' an organization knows. In the context of recombinant innovation, the size of a knowledge-base determines its recombination possibilities and, hence, its inventive potential (Fleming, 2001; Ahuja and Katila, 2001; Puranam, 2001). In the simplest conception the size of a knowledge-base should be a reflection of the resources committed by an organization to gain knowledge, for instance its research and development spending. However, the literature has identified several leveraging strategies by which firms increase the *de facto* size of their knowledge-bases by tapping into extra-organizational sources of knowledge. These include alliances with other firms (Kotabe and Swan, 1995; Lane and Lubatkin,1998; Mowery, Oxley, and Silverman,1996; Powell, Koput, and Smith-Doerr, 1996; Stuart, 2000; Rosenkopf and Almeida, 2003), investments through corporate venture capital units into start-ups (Dushnitsky and Lenox, 2005; Wadhwa and Kotha, 2006; Benson and Ziedonis, 2009), more effective organizational learning arrangements or location decisions that enable the firm to impound more of the knowledge created from prior searches (Zollo and Singh, 2004) or geographically

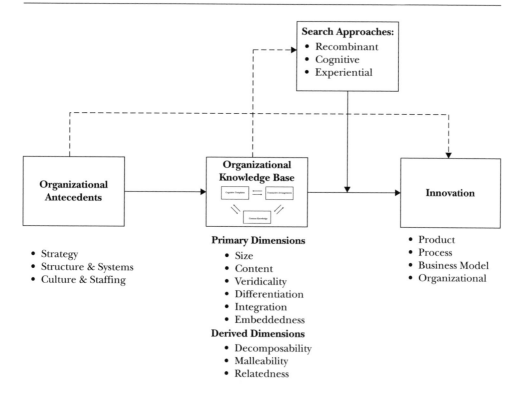

Figure 25.2 Antecedents and Consequences (Dotted line relationships are not within the scope of this study)

proximate organizations (Jaffe et al., 1993, Almeida and Phene, 2004; Lahiri, 2005; Singh, 2009), investments in absorptive capacity that enable a firm to internalize more of the spillovers from public science (Van den Bosch, Volberda and de Boer, 1999; Lenox and King, 2004), from competitors and complementors (Bowman and Hurry, 1993; Schilling, 2002; Lichtenthaler, 2009), or investments in network ties that enable them to occupy favorable positions in inter-organizational networks and, thus, foster the absorption of knowledge spillovers (Baum, Calabrese, and Silverman, 2000; Ahuja 2000; Owen-Smith and Powell, 2004).

Grafting new knowledge onto their knowledge bases through acquisitions is another mechanism by which firms expand knowledge-base size (Ahuja and Katila, 2001; Ranft and Lord, 2002; Puranam, 2001; Puranam, Singh, and Zollo, 2006; Puranam and Srikanth, 2007). In this context researchers have identified that a key issue is the integration paradox (Ahuja and Katila, 2001; Puranam, Singh, and Zollo 2006; Ranft and Lord, 2002). For grafted knowledge-bases to enhance the recombinant capacity of the firm, the acquired and acquiring firm's knowledge-bases have to be integrated. However, this integration may entail significant organizational disruption and may thus compromise innovative capability. Investigation of these ideas shows that whereas the absolute size of an acquired knowledge-base is positively associated with subsequent innovation (providing support for the recombination effect) large relative size of an acquired knowledge-base reduces innovation possibly by creating knowledge integration problems (Ahuja and Katila, 2001). Further, research suggests that as a given knowledge-base exploits its recombination potential, its need for recharging the knowledge-base with new elements that can be recombined grows (Fleming, 2001). Supporting this basic logic researchers find that firms facing recombinant exhaustion as indicated by their building on long chains of patents are more likely to invest in science, presumably as a means of adding new recombinant fodder (new elements) to their knowledge-base (Ahuja and Katila, 2004).

Merging knowledge-bases through acquisition integration may lead to fairly nuanced implications. For instance Puranam and Srikanth (2007) find that structural integration may enable firms to exploit the available existing knowledge (the empirical construct) but potentially at a cost to the development of the capabilities inherent in the acquired firm (knowledge in the latent sense). Puranam, Singh, and Zollo (2006) show that the effects of structural integration are contingent; firms that are early in the product development trajectory may be hurt by structural integration, but such effects may be attenuated for firms with more developed innovation trajectories. Puranam, Singh, and Chaudhuri (2009) indicate that under certain conditions coordination between the acquired and acquirer knowledge may be better achieved through mechanisms other than structural integration. Finally, it has been proposed that the nature of the knowledge (tacit or explicit) may also significantly affect successful integration of knowledge following an acquisition (Ranft and Lord, 2002).

The size of the knowledge-base is not only affected by the organization's capability to acquire new knowledge, but also by its capability to unlearn (deliberately) or its tendency to forget (unintentionally). Unlearning is necessary when established knowledge can constitute a barrier to further learning and has to be removed to make room for new knowledge (Bettis and Prahalad, 1995; Lyles and Schwenk, 1992; De Holan and Phillips, 2004, 2010). Forgetting, or the unintended loss of knowledge elements, can be productive (when obsolete knowledge is lost) or unproductive (when useful knowledge elements are lost).

Content

Content refers to the subject matter of the knowledge-base or the identity of the individual elements of knowledge. It is 'what' the organization knows. The most obvious use of the content of a knowledge-base is in terms of recognizing its overlap with other knowledge-bases. Such an approach can be used to operationalize the concept of relatedness between organizational knowledge-bases of different organizations (Mowery, Oxley, and Silverman, 1996; Ahuja and Katila, 2001). Research suggests that in the context of acquisitions moderate degrees of overlap between knowledge-bases lead to productive innovation performance after an acquisition (Ahuja and Katila, 2001). Similarly, the risk of knowledge appropriation is also likely to be higher in the context of knowledge relatedness (Mowery, Oxley, and Silverman, 1996).

In recognizing what an organization knows it is important to note the possibility that an organization's knowledge-base may extend beyond the organization's boundaries (Rosenkopf and Nerkar, 2001). Firms often use leveraging strategies or absorptive mechanisms to expand their knowledge-bases beyond their organizational boundaries. Such strategies could be informal, such as know-how exchange (Von Hippel, 1978; Rogers,

1983), or formal, such as licensing (Teece, 1986; Arora, Fosfuri, and Gambardella, 2001). Indeed, research suggests that some of the most important inventions may occur when firms use knowledge from beyond their own boundaries (Rosenkopf and Nerkar, 2001).

Noting this possibility we can make a distinction between an organization's knowledge from within its boundaries and that from beyond its boundaries. The latter may imply a broader search space available to the organization than the in-house experience would indicate; however, assessing the eventual value of such external elements of knowledge is more complicated. On the one hand, the mastery of knowledge situated outside the organization may be more limited and, further, the perceived value of internal versus external knowledge may differ with external knowledge subjected to a 'not invented here' bias that may limit its actual use by the organization (Katz and Allen, 1982). Conversely, knowledge obtained from outsiders could be valued more than internal knowledge because it appears more special and unique (Menon and Pfeffer, 2003). More broadly it appears that the relative utility of internal versus external knowledge is contingent on a variety of factors such as team composition, the proportion/number of local members versus cosmopolitans (Haas, 2006), characteristics of the knowledge-base such as size, specialization, and codification (Schulz, 2003), and even the perceptions of (or lack of) a shared or superordinate social identity (Kane, 2010).

Many different types of knowledge can be distinguished in talking about the content of a knowledge-base, but we will make a special note of just two kinds—technical knowledge versus scientific (Rosenberg, 1982; Brooks, 1994). Although it would appear that in science-driven sectors of the economy a knowledge-base that is significantly devoted to science may be an advantage, research suggests the need for caution in drawing such conclusions. Science can increase the recombinant potential of a knowledge-base by the identification of new elements, or provide a cognitive map of the landscape that can be used for search and recombination (Fleming, 2001; Fleming and Sorenson, 2004). It can also help to guide trial and error or experimental search (Gavetti and Levinthal, 2000); and it forms a very important basis for cognitive search (Ahuja and Katila, 2004; Gavetti and Levinthal, 2000). Yet, in spite of these advantages an excessive commitment to science may be detrimental to innovation because the institutional ethos of science is fundamentally different from technology (Stern, 2004). Science is about solving abstract problems, basic enquiry, and broad dissemination; technology is about creating pragmatic artifacts, commercial utility, and value appropriability. The conflicts between these modes of operation can undercut the science payoff to a technological knowledge-base (Gittelman and Kogut, 2003).

Veridicality

Veridicality refers to the fit between the external or 'true' information environment of an organization, and the reflection of that environment in the organization's knowledge-base (see Fiol and Lyles, 1985; Fiol, 1994; Walsh, 1995; Huber, 1991). A perfectly veridical organizational knowledge-base would imply that there is no difference between the reality of the true world and its image in the organization's cognition. This attribute is important because managerial and scientific decisions in an organization depend upon the information context perceived by the decision maker, not on what the true state of the world might be outside. Although at first glance higher veridicality might appear to be an unmitigated virtue (Hogarth, 1980), thoughtful analysis by scholars suggests that such a simplification or judgment may be premature for several reasons.

First, as Starbuck and Milliken (1988) and Walsh (1995) note, managers may not be well served by having the complexity of the real world replicated inside the organization's knowledge-base. *Au contraire*, functionally effective knowledge-bases may entail the suppression of some elements of knowledge and the highlighting of others. Perceptual filters that amplify some information and attenuate other information may be critical to managerial action (Starbuck and Milliken, 1988; Walsh, 1995). For instance, McNamara, Luce, and Thompson (2002) find that a cognitively parsimonious classification of the competitive environment is more predictive of firm performance than an in-depth representation of it.

Second, inaccurate knowledge-bases and templates can in themselves be the basis of learning (Weick, 1991; Yayavaram and Ahuja, 2008). Experiential or trial-and-error learning is often the way that complex realities are uncovered. Such realities often take the form of interdependence relationships between knowledge elements. In the absence of a veridical map of reality firms make assumptions about such interdependencies and act upon them. Their resultant experiments confirm or invalidate these assumptions. Under either circumstance this leads to an increase in the knowledge of the real world as either a true dependency is discovered or an assumed one is found to be falsified (Yayavaram and Ahuja, 2008).

Third, the existence itself of a true reality that is mirrored by firms' knowledge-bases is questioned by some research streams which suggest that there isn't such a thing as an objective reality, rather the world is subjectively defined (Berger and Luckmann, 1966) and different interpretations of reality coexist. Under these premises the utility of a knowledge-base does not depend on the accuracy with which it represents the external environment: rather it is situationally dependent and has to be evaluated on the basis of the actions that can be derived from it and the conditions of use (Weick, 1991; Walsh, 1995). If there is no such thing as a 'true reality' the idea of accuracy associated with the concept of veridicality can be used to identify the accuracy with which firms' knowledge-bases refer to the 'consensually defined environment,' i.e. the environment that constitutes the standard for organizations (Krackhardt, 1990). Under these circumstances less veridicality may be associated with greater system-level variety and innovation (e.g. Huber, 1991) for two reasons.

First, in the absence of definitive veridical mappings of the external informational environment firms need to make their own simplifying assumptions about such mappings. Such assumptions may increase the salience of different knowledge elements differentially *across organizations*, leading some to develop some elements of knowledge more than others (Yayavaram and Ahuja, 2008). Further, at the firm level a cognitive representation that moves away from the consensually defined environment may be the basis of new actions and strategies that have not already been implemented by other firms in the industry and may lead to more or breakthrough innovations.

Second, firms may generate more variety and potentially increase their innovative capabilities by increasing the salience of different knowledge elements differentially *within the organization*. Indeed organizations do not necessarily rely on a unique shared cognitive map. Rather, several representations may coexist within the same firm. For instance, Huber (1991) suggests that the wider the variety of interpretations held by the organization's various units, the wider the range of the organization's potential behaviors. Similarly, Fiol (1994) finds that learning involves the development of new and diverse interpretations of events and situations and it is fostered when managers actively encourage the development of different and conflicting views of what is thought to be true, while striving for a shared framing of the issues that is broad enough to encompass those differences.

The literature on interpretation and sense making (e.g. Daft and Weick, 1984; Milliken, 1990) suggests that firms scan the environment to collect information and then implement a process of information interpretation, which involves translating events to develop shared understandings and conceptual schemes. Two features of this sense-making process are important in the context of studying organizational knowledge-bases. First, organizational politics, organization structure, and managerial actions may all influence the final 'truth' that is recognized within the organization (Yayavaram and Ahuja, 2008; Lant et al., 1992, Walsh 1995, Mezias and Starbuck, 2003, Beck and Plowman, 2009). Second, the interpretive process itself may vary across organizations depending on the assumptions that the organization makes about the environment (Daft and Weick, 1984; Gavetti and Rivkin, 2007). A cognitive process involving linear thinking and logic is more likely to be used if the organization assumes that the external environment is concrete, that events and processes are hard, measurable, and determinant (Aguilar, 1967; Wilensky, 1967; Daft and Weick, 1984); an experiential process is more likely to be used instead when organizations assume that the external environment is unanalyzable, for instance as in the case of uncertain and quickly changing environments (Perrow, 1967; Duncan, 1972; Tung, 1979; Daft and Weick, 1984). In these cases the interpretation process is likely to be 'more personal, less linear, more ad hoc and improvisational' (Daft and Weick, 1984). The use of a cognitive as opposed to an experiential search for the development of the representation of the environment is also going to be a function of the extent to which an organization is active in intruding into the environment, a factor which may be determined by the characteristics of the firm, such as age and size, or of the environment itself (Daft and Weick, 1984; Gavetti and Rivkin, 2007).

Differentiation

Differentiation of knowledge-bases has been variously defined as the number of dimensions in a knowledge-base (Walsh, 1995) or as splitting a knowledge base into clusters Lawrence and Lorsch, 1967; Yayavaram and Ahuja, 2008). It refers to the partitioning of a knowledge-base into two or more components and has been argued to provide several innovation relevant benefits. First, differentiation permits the separation of knowledge into discrete categories and in turn this can facilitate specialization (Brusoni, Prencipe, and Pavitt, 2001). Relatedly, differentiation in an organizational knowledge-base may be necessary to optimally utilize external knowledge (Brusoni et al., 2001). The embodiment of knowledge into products requires the integration of different types of knowledge (often) from different sources. Having an internally differentiated knowledge-base can help the organization to coordinate the knowledge-flows from all these extra-corporate actors. In this sense large corporations may often maintain broader and more differentiated technological knowledge-bases than would appear necessary from their product range (Patel and Pavitt, 1997; Granstrand, Patel, and Pavitt, 1997; Brusoni et al., 2001).

In contrast to the coordination argument proposed above, researchers have also raised the possibility of a control motive for building a differentiated knowledge-base (Tiwana and Keil, 2006). Since firms often need to combine technology from different sources into their own technology or products, developing a differentiated knowledge-base that spans domains beyond their own core technologies may be useful in its own right. Investments in such 'peripheral' technologies can help the firm control and better govern the relationships through which external knowledge in such technologies is brought into the firm. In particular Zander and Kogut (1995) talk about system dependence of the knowledge to refer to the extent to which knowledge is dependent on many different groups of experienced people for its production.

Differentiation in knowledge-bases can also lead to the possibilities of cross-fertilization. From a recombinant perspective knowledge-base differentiation should provide the possibility of combining high search scope with search depth (Katila and Ahuja, 2002) with positive consequences for innovation (Quintana-Garcia and Benavides-Velasco, 2008). Searching across the differentiated sub-units of the knowledge-base provides the potential for search breadth while searching within the sub-units of the knowledge-base provides an opportunity for developing search depth. Miller, Fern, and Cardinal (2007) point out that, in the context of large multidivisional firms, knowledge from outside the division but inside the corporation has greater impact than knowledge from outside the corporation or within the sub-unit. Knowledge-base differentiation can also occur along functional lines (Nerkar and Roberts, 2004; Brown and Duguid, 2001) providing another basis for cross-fertilization. From an experiential perspective, differentiation can also provide the basis of search by analogy. Breadth and depth of experiential knowledge increase the likelihood that search will be more effective in new and complex contexts (Gavetti, Levinthal, and Rivkin, 2005) allowing managers to derive a favorable set of policies and principles from experienced settings and apply them in the new contexts.

Analogical reasoning can also enable organizations to translate differentiation in the knowledge-base into superior innovative performance (Novelli, 2010). By increasing the number and diversity of knowledge inputs to which an organization is exposed, differentiation increases the organization's ability to recognize more general patterns across variations, i.e. patterns of underlying constructs that minimize the distance across all the different variations observed (Novelli, 2010). These patterns constitute new knowledge that has the potential to be applied to contexts where such patterns have not been applied before. Thus, cross-fertilization via abstraction and superior generalization can become the basis of new product generation.

Additionally, differentiation can improve the performance of search for innovations through search simplification and narrowing (Yayavaram and Ahuja, 2008). In the context of recombinant search that we described above inventors create new products and processes by recombining elements or groups of elements into new syntheses. However, a key intermediate step is to recognize interdependencies between elements and group or cluster them on the basis of those interdependencies. This clustering helps to reduce the combinatorial complexity of the search process. However, identification of interdependencies between elements that can be used as the basis of grouping is itself difficult. Splitting up a knowledge-base into clusters, i.e. differentiating it, enables the recognition of interdependencies by limiting the number of elements that must be simultaneously studied (Yayavaram and Ahuja, 2008).

Integration

Integration refers to the building of connections across the differentiated components of a knowledge-base. Although integration of a differentiated knowledge-base may be desirable for a variety of reasons (see below), integration does not naturally or automatically or even beneficially *always* follow differentiation. The logic for integration following differentiation is fairly straightforward and broadly (though not universally) accepted (Postrel, 1998; 2002). The classical argument suggests that differentiation and integration are complements—to make the most of more differentiated knowledge integration mechanisms are needed (Grant, 1996; Nesta and Saviotti, 2004). While differentiation can enable an organization to collect information as a specialist in multiple areas, and possibly faster and deeper than a generalist would, integration of that knowledge is often required to produce successful applications (Lawrence and Lorsch, 1967). This basic intuition that differentiation should be accompanied by integration is, however, subject to several caveats. Integration may fail to follow differentiation because (1) it is needed but resources are not provided for it, (2) resources are provided for it but execution of integration is difficult, or (3) it is not needed or perceived to be not needed. Of these the first argument is relatively obvious, although no research appears to have examined it in detail. Several arguments suggest support for the second proposition. For instance, integration is hard because language differs across the differentiated components of a knowledge-base (Carlile, 2002). Similarly, integration can run into a legitimacy problem. Whereas the differentiated elements of knowledge are part of one hierarchy—the differentiated sub-unit that they belong to—and are regarded as legitimate within that hierarchy, integration by definition spans sub-unit hierarchies. Thus, it may be the case that integrative elements or arrangements simply do not get the organizational legitimacy, access, or attention that is required to make them effective.

The third argument against the occurrence of integration is probably the most controversial and the most interesting—integration may not necessarily be needed even in the presence of differentiation. The differentiation–integration duality draws attention to the fact that in any differentiated knowledge-base individual sub-units have to make resource choices in terms of investing in two different types of knowledge—investing in deepening their own specialist knowledge and investing in learning about the knowledge of others (Postrel, 1998; 2002). Postrel (2002) provides an interesting abstraction relating these two aspects of 'specialist capability' and 'trans-specialist understanding' with performance through the 'design production function.' Postrel's formal analysis then provides a counter-intuitive finding—that integration and differentiation may not necessarily be complements; indeed for certain ranges of parameters in his model they are actually substitutes. His explanation for this effect is that the high capability of very effective specialists buffers the other from needing to know too much about how the first does his or her job. Alternately, if the specialist is of low capability then high levels of trans-specialist knowledge are helpful because the others know the limitations of the focal actor's capabilities and adapt themselves accordingly.

Puranam and others highlight that strong integration may actually limit the potential and effectiveness of differentiated knowledge-bases (Puranam, Singh, and Chaudhuri, 2009). This suggests that the different mechanisms of integrating a knowledge-base may differ in their applicability to a given differentiation problem. It also draws attention to another important aspect of knowledge-base structuring, the balance between differentiation and integration. Following Simon's lead, researchers have examined knowledge-bases in terms of their decomposability—a derived attribute that emerges from the combination of differentiation and integration. When a knowledge-base is differentiated and thus has several distinct components, integration mechanisms span and connect these differentiated sub-units. These spanning linkages or couplings can be distributed in several different patterns. When the couplings are pervasive the knowledge-base can be described as non-decomposable, when there are no couplings, the knowledge-base can be thought of as modular or decomposable, with each sub-unit being essentially stand-alone. Between these two extremes stand nearly-decomposable knowledge-bases—knowledge-bases where the differentiated sub-segments are connected by a few linkages (Simon, 1962).

Yayavaram and Ahuja (2008) demonstrate that in the context of the semiconductor industry, nearly decomposable knowledge-bases out-perform fully decomposable and non-decomposable knowledge-bases in terms of the utility of the inventions generated from them as well as the knowledge-base's own malleability. Malleability, like decomposability, can be considered a derived property of a knowledge-base. It refers to the knowledge-base's capacity for change. Similarly, in the context of alliances, Schilling and Phelps (2007) show that alliance networks that secure both high clustering and high reach positively affect innovative output.

Embeddedness

The last major dimension of an organizational knowledge-base examined in this review is embeddedness. Embeddedness refers to the degree to which the knowledge in a given knowledge-base is formal, observable, codified, or articulated versus informal, tacit, or organizationally embedded (Nonaka, 1991, 1994; Zander and Kogut, 1995; Haas and Hansen, 2007; Nonaka and Von Krogh, 2009). Tacit knowledge refers to the knowledge that is 'unarticulated and tied to the senses, movement skills, physical experiences, intuition of implicit rules of thumb.' Conversely, explicit knowledge is 'uttered and captured in drawings and writing' and has 'a universal character, supporting the capacity to act across contexts' (Polanyi, 1966; Nonaka and Takeuchi, 1996; Nonaka and Von Krogh, 2009). Embeddedness is related to knowledge teachability and observability, i.e. the degree to which capable competitors can copy it (Zander and Kogut, 1995).

Research also finds that highly embedded knowledge-bases can be expected to be 'sticky' (Szulanski, 1996; Ahuja 2002). Diffusion of knowledge from such knowledge-bases may be difficult both from the perspective of competitors trying to extract knowledge as well as the organization itself trying to use the knowledge in a different location or application. Research also suggests that even for highly explicated forms of knowledge, there eventually remains an embedded component that limits its mobility. Subtle evidence to this effect is also provided by Rosenkopf and Almeida (2003), and their colleagues, who find that employee mobility is connected with higher rates of cross-citation between organizations.

The Antecedents of Organizational Knowledge-Bases

Why are there so many different types of knowledge-bases (Weick, 1991; Yayavaram and Ahuja, 2008)? Examining the literature that has developed along the six major dimensions of a knowledge-base it is natural to ask why organizations display so much variance between their knowledge bases. We next examine some of the leading organizational influences on organizational knowledge-bases.

Strategy

Organizational strategies are possibly the most salient influence in shaping several of the dimensional variations in knowledge-bases. Expansion into new geographic markets (Ahuja and Katila, 2004), seeking knowledge variety by tapping into different national contexts across the world (Luo, 1999; Tsang, 2002; Lahiri, 2005; Almeida and Phene, 2004; Alcácer and Chung, 2007; Chung and Yeaple, 2008; Meyer et al., 2009), and seeking research and development efficiencies and competitive advantage by knowledge-sourcing across low cost locations (Zhao, 2006) all contribute to knowledge-base differentiation as the organization distributes its research activities across geographic space. Knowledge-base differentiation may also emerge from foreign entry by acquisitions or joint ventures (Luo, 1999; Tsang, 2002; Almeida and Phene, 2004; Meyer et al., 2009).

Similarly, search for complementary skills and scale economies drive firms to seek collaborative alliances and these in turn affect several of the knowledge-base dimensions such as its *de facto* size (Ahuja, Lampert and Tandon, 2008); alliances with complementary partners may lead to increased specialization by organizations (Mowery, Oxley, and Silverman, 1996). The latter may thus alter knowledge-base content and may also potentially reduce the internal differentiation of their knowledge-bases (Nakamura, Shaver, and Yeung, 1996), though this last effect is yet to be conclusively established as evidence in the opposite direction has also been presented (Mowery, Oxley, and Silverman, 1996). Product market diversification and product portfolio expansion are also likely to be key drivers of knowledge-base differentiation (Helfat and Raubitschek, 2000). As firms expand the scope of their markets the research required to support the product–market activity may need to expand more than proportionately (Ethiraj, 2007; Brusoni et al., 2001). The need to obtain scope economies in research should then also serve to drive knowledge-base integration (Helfat and Raubitschek, 2000).

Organizational structure and systems

Organizational structure is likely to influence several knowledge-base dimensions (Van den Bosch, Volberda, and de Boer, 1999). Firms organized around product divisions are likely to develop differentiated knowledge-bases. However, the content dimension of knowledge-bases is also likely to be influenced by organization structure. As Argyres and Silverman (2004) show, research conducted by organizations with a centralized research and development structure is likely to differ in both the nature of search conducted as well as the impact of that search as measured by citations to the firm's inventions compared to firms where research is organized in a more decentralized fashion. Different communities of practice within an organization may lead to the development of a differentiated knowledge-base (Brown and Duguid, 2001). Conversely, the characteristics of the knowledge-base itself may affect the organizational structure. For instance Birkinshaw, Nobel, and Ridderstråle (2002) suggest that the observability and the system embeddedness of the knowledge-base impacts on the organizational structure.

Organizational systems, culture, and staffing practices

Organizational systems, culture, and staffing practices are additional sources of influence that are likely to shape organization knowledge-bases. For instance, Turner and Makhija (2006) establish that the type of control mechanism adopted (clan, outcome, process) may affect the usage of knowledge in an organization. An organizational climate of knowledge-sharing can provide a natural mechanism for integration as shared beliefs that constitute the core of the culture can perform the role of a coordination mechanism (Smith, Collins, and Clark, 2005; Collins and Smith, 2006) or formal interventions in micro level interactions can increase knowledge flexibility and enable integration within the organization (Okhuysen and Eisenhardt, 2002). By the same token, adoption of some organizational practices such as total quality management, while leading to a growth in one dimension of the knowledge-base and good performance outcomes by some metrics may lead to reduced experimentation, slower growth of the knowledge-base, and reduced innovation (Benner and Tushman, 2002; 2003). Similarly, a focus on reliable outputs may restrict innovative search and limit breakthrough inventions (Ahuja and Lampert, 2001). Decentralized interpersonal learning, however, can help in overcoming possible rigidities brought on by an organization-level emphasis on exploitation and aversion to experimentation (Miller, Zhao, and Calantone, 2006).

The mobility of knowledge workers can also serve to enhance differentiation in knowledge-bases as they carry with them imprints of their own informational environment which is distinctive from that of their new employers (Rosenkopf and Almeida, 2003; Corredoira and Rosenkopf, 2010). Culture and staffing practices can also serve as a complement to transactive interfaces, especially in the context of high embeddedness knowledge-bases. With key individuals serving as the repositories of indexing knowledge and as gate-keepers the effectiveness of the routines and artifacts that constitute the transactive system can be enhanced (Postrel, 2002).

Unanswered Questions

We begin with the relationship between organization strategy and knowledge-base differentiation. As organizations expand into new locations, do the differences in localized knowledge environments contribute to not just physical differentiation of the knowledge-base but also to distinctive development along localized trajectories? Further, following Brown and Duguid's (2001) development of the ideas of communities of practice it appears likely that the differences between functional perspectives should lead to greater differentiation of knowledge-bases in more complex functionally specialized corporations. If so, the current trends of outsourcing key functions may be leading to unintended consequences on their knowledge-bases. Not only are they losing expertise in the outsourced area (a 'budgeted for' effect), they may also be reducing the differentiation in their knowledge-bases which may lead to 'unbudgeted' and subtle deleterious effects in their innovation capability. More generally, how organizational boundaries affect the process of developing an integrated knowledge-base has not been investigated. For instance, what are the consequences of M&A among companies with different cognitive maps and how may the combination of elements from the different cognitive maps affect innovation?

Although some of the embeddedness of a knowledge-base is likely to be a function of its content—the nature of technologies and skills it includes—other factors such as organizational strategy are also likely to influence the degree of embeddedness of a knowledge-base. For instance the degree to which knowledge is eventually explicit or not is also partially a function of strategic context; the explication of knowledge may require substantial resources and is far more likely to be taken up when such efforts entail significant payoffs for the firm. Thus, it appears likely that organizations that seek to grow their business across distinct geographical settings may invest more in making knowledge explicit than single location firms in the same industry. However, direct evidence on this 'endogeneity of knowledge tacitness' is yet to emerge.

The concept of knowledge-base integration also draws attention to the possibilities of the opposite process—knowledge-base disintegration or fissibility. Research suggests that the size of a firm's knowledge-base influences the likelihood that the firm will generate spin-outs that will inherit the knowledge of the parent. For instance, Agarwal et al. (2004) show that an incumbent's capabilities at the time of a spin-out's founding positively affect the spin-out's knowledge capabilities and its probability of survival. However, study of the detailed effects of such fission processes remains limited, with a focus on the offspring knowledge-bases and far less work has outlined what effects such spin-outs have on the parent firm's knowledge-base and inventive fecundity. The public good characteristics of knowledge would suggest that fission processes should not hurt the parent knowledge-base. Yet, research has established that knowledge is not a true public good. The boundaries of these competing effects still need to be established in the context of knowledge-base fissibility. Relatedly, the implications of the diffusion of the content of a knowledge-base need to be studied. As the actual content of a knowledge-base becomes more widely diffused, does the value of the diffused knowledge, in terms of its inventive fecundity, decline? What trade-offs are there between using unique pieces of knowledge and pervasive elements of knowledge?

The vertical boundaries of firms are also likely to influence the contents of an organization's knowledge-base. Reduction in the vertical scope of a firm may lead to a broadening of its search scope as the stand-alone unit faces fewer coordination constraints now that it no longer has to restrict itself to the choices offered by its captive unit (Ahuja and Lahiri, 2010). However, direct evidence on the question is lacking. Future research may also look at how different interest groups associated with the firm (e.g. shareholders, managers, customers, etc.) may control the organization's working representation of the environment.

Examining the reverse set of relationships, i.e. how knowledge-bases might influence organization structure, is also important. For instance, researchers have shown that embeddedness has implications for organizational structure (Birkinshaw, Nobel, and Ridderstråle, 2002). Similarly, the pattern of knowledge-base differentiation may well lead to information reaching managers in certain ways that in turn influence strategy and scope decisions.

Finally, an intriguing area of potential investigation is to look at how organizations handle the trade-offs between the different dimensions of a knowledge-base. For instance, organizing a knowledge-base for innovation implies facilitating recombination. However, an organization that is structured in a way that maximizes recombination may face a challenge in producing reliably as the latter implies standardization of processes.

In summary, the field of knowledge structuring, having expanded significantly during the last decade, is nevertheless a fecund ground for many interesting and important questions. It combines the promise of theoretical advancement with practical relevance. The opportunity for organizational researchers now is to take up this challenge.

REFERENCES

Agarwal, R., Echambadi, R.. Franco, A. M. and Sarkar, M.B. (2004) Knowledge transfer through inheritance: Spinout generation, development, and survival. *Academy of Management Journal,* 47: 501–522.

Aguilar, F. (1967) *Scanning the business environment.* New York: Macmillan.

Ahuja, G. (2000) The duality of collaboration: Inducements and opportunities in the formation of interfirm linkages. *Strategic Management Journal,* 21(3): 317–343.

Ahuja, G. (2002) When Atlas shrugged: preemption, complexity and division of labor in a theory of appropriability. Paper presented at the *Academy of Management Conference,* Seattle, WA.

Ahuja, G.,and Katila, R. (2001) Technological acquisitions and the innovation performance of acquiring firms: a longitudinal study. *Strategic Management Journal,* 22(3): 197–220.

Ahuja, G. and Katila, R. (2004) Where Do Resources Come From? The Role of Idiosyncratic Situations. *Strategic Management Journal,* 25(8–9): 887–907.

Ahuja, G. and Lahiri, N. (2010) Explaining Exploration: Integration and Technological Search Behavior in the Semiconductor Industry. Working Paper, University of Michigan.

Ahuja, G. and Lampert, C.M. (2001) Entrepreneurship in large corporations: a longitudinal study of how established firms create breakthrough inventions. *Strategic Management Journal* 22: 521–543.

Ahuja, G., Lampert, C.M. and Tandon, V. (2008) Moving Beyond Schumpeter: Managerial Research on the Determinants of Technological Innovation. *Academy of Management Annals,* 2: 1–98.

Alavi, M. and Leidner, D. E. (2001) Review: Knowledge Management and Knowledge Management Systems: Conceptual Foundations and Research Issues. *MIS Quarterly,* 25: 107–136.

Alcácer, J. and Chung,W. (2007) Location strategies and knowledge spillovers. *Management Science,* 53(5): 760–776.

Almeida, P., and Phene, A. (2004) Subsidiaries and knowledge creation: The influence of the MNC and host country on innovation. *Strategic Management Journal,* 25(8/9): 847–864.

Argyres, N. S. and Silverman, B. S. (2004) R&D, Organization Structure, and the Development of Corporate Technological Knowledge. *Strategic Management Journal,* 25(8/9): 929–958.

Arora, A., Fosfuri, A. and Gambardella, A. (2001) *Markets for Technology: The Economics of Innovation and Corporate Strategy.* Cambridge, MA: MIT Press.

Baum, J.A.C, Calabrese, T., and Silverman, B.S. (2000) Don't go it alone: Alliance network composition and startups' performance in Canadian biotechnology. *Strategic Management Journal,* 21: 267–294.

Beck, T.E. and Plowman, D.A. (2009) Experiencing Rare and Unusual Events Richly: The Role of Middle Managers in Animating and Guiding Organizational Interpretation. *Organization Science*, 20(5): 909–924.

Benner, M. J. and Tushman, M. (2002) Process Management and Technological Innovation: A Longitudinal Study of the Photography and Paint Industries. *Administrative Science Quarterly*, 47(4): 676–706.

Benner, M. J. and Tushman, M. L. (2003) Exploitation, Exploration, and Process Management: The Productivity Dilemma Revisited. *Academy of Management Review*, 28(2): 238–256.

Benson, D. and Ziedonis, R.H. (2009) Corporate Venture Capital as a Window on New Technologies: Implications for the Performance of Corporate Investors When Acquiring Startups. *Organization Science*, 20(2): 329–351.

Berger, P.L. and Luckmann, T. (1966) *The social construction of reality: A treatise in the sociology of knowledge*. Garden City, NY: Doubleday.

Bettis, R. A. and Prahalad, C. K. (1995) The Dominant Logic: Retrospective and Extension. *Strategic Management Journal*, 16(1): 5–14.

Birkinshaw, J., Nobel, R. and Ridderstråle, J. (2002) Knowledge as a Contingency Variable: Do the Characteristics of Knowledge Predict Organization Structure? *Organization Science*, 13(3): 274–289.

Bowman, E. H., and Hurry, D. (1993) Strategy through the options lens: an integrated view of resource investments and the incremental-choice process. *Academy of Management Review*, 18 (4): 160–182.

Brooks, H. (1994) The Relationship Between Science and Technology. *Research Policy* Special issue from a seminar held in honor of Nathan Rosenberg at Stanford University, 9 (23): 477–486.

Brown, J.S., and Duguid, P. (2001) Knowledge and Organization: A Social-Practice Perspective. *Organization Science*, 12(2): 198–213.

Brusoni, S., Prencipe, A., and Pavitt, K. (2001) Knowledge specialization, organizational coupling, and the boundaries of the firm: why do firms know more than they make? *Administrative Science Quarterly*, 46(4): 597–621.

Carlile, P. (2002) A pragmatic view of knowledge and boundaries: Boundary objects in new product development. *Organization Science*, 13 (4): 442–455.

Chung, W. and Yeaple, S. (2008) International Knowledge Sourcing: Evidence from US Firms Expanding Abroad. *Strategic Management Journal*, 29(11): 1207–1224.

Cohen, M.D., and Bacdayan, P. (1994) Organizational routines are stored as procedural memory: Evidence from a laboratory study. *Organization Science*, 5: 554–568.

Collins, C.J. and Smith, K.G. (2006) Knowledge Exchange And Combination: The Role Of Human Resource Practices In The Performance Of High-Technology Firms. *Academy of Management Journal*, 49(3): 544–560.

Corredoira, R. A. and Rosenkopf, L. (2010) Should Auld Acquaintance Be Forgot? The Reverse Transfer of Knowledge through Mobility Ties. *Strategic Management Journal*, 31 (2):159–181.

Cyert, R.M. and March, J.G. (1963) *A Behavioral Theory of the Firm*. Englewood Cliffs, N.J.: Prentice-Hall.

Daft, R.L., and Weick, K.E. (1984) Toward a model of organizations as interpretation systems. *Academy of Management Review*, 9 (2): 284–295.

De Holan, P.M. and Phillips, N. (2003) Organizational Forgetting. In M. Easterby-Smith and M.A. Lyles (eds.), *The Handbook of Organizational Learning and Knowledge Management*, Blackwell.

De Holan, P.M. and Phillips, N. (2011) Organizational Forgetting. In M. Easterby-Smith and M. A. Lyles (eds.) *The Handbook of Organizational Learning and Knowledge Management*, Chichester: John Wiley & Sons Ltd.

Duncan, R.B. (1972) Characteristics of organizational environments and perceived environmental uncertainty. *Administrative Science Quarterly*, 17: 313–327.

Dushnitsky, G. and Lenox, M.J. (2005) When Do Firms Undertake R&D by Investing in New Ventures? *Strategic Management Journal*, 26(10): 947–965.

Dyer, J. and Singh, S. (1998) The relational view: cooperative strategy and sources of interorganizational competitive advantage. *Academy of Management Review*, 23: 660–679.

Eppinger, M.E., Sosa S.D. and Rowles, C.M. (2004) The Misalignment of Product Architecture and Organizational Structure in Complex Product Development. *Management Science*, 5(12): 1674–1689.

Ethiraj, S.K. (2007) Allocation of inventive effort in complex product systems. *Strategic Management Journal*, 28 (6): 563–584.

Fiol, C.M. (1994) Consensus, Diversity, and Learning in Organizations. *Organization Science*, 5(3): 403–420.

Fiol, C.M. and Lyles M.A. (1985) Organizational Learning. *Academy of Management Review*, 10: 803–813.

Fleming, L. (2001) Recombinant uncertainty in technological search. *Management Science*, 47: 117–132.

Fleming, L., Mingo, S., and Chen, D. (2007) Collaborative brokerage, generative creativity, and creative success. *Administrative Science Quarterly*, 52: 443–475.

Fleming, L, and Sorenson, O. (2001) Technology as a complex adaptive system: evidence from patent data. *Research Policy*, 30: 1019–1039.

Fleming, L. and Sorenson, O. (2004) Science as a map in technological search. *Strategic Management Journal*, 25: 909–928.

Galambos, J.A., Abelson, R.P., and Black, J.B. (1986) *Knowledge Structures*. Hillsdale, NJ: Lawrence Erlbaum Associates.

Galunic, D. and Rodan, S. (1998) Resource recombinations in the firm: knowledge structure and the potential for Schumpeterian innovation. *Strategic Management Journal*, 19(12): 1193–1201.

Gavetti, G. and Levinthal, D.A. (2000) Looking forward and looking backward: Cognitive and experiential search. *Administrative Science Quarterly*, 45: 113–137.

Gavetti, G., Levinthal, D.A. and Rivkin, J.W. (2005) Strategy making in novel and complex worlds: The power of analogy. *Strategic Management Journal*, 26: 691–713.

Gavetti, G. and Rivkin, J. W. (2007) On the origin of strategy: Action and cognition over time. *Organization Science*, 18: 420–439.

Ghoshal, S., Korine, H. and Szulanski, G. (1994) Interunit communication in multinational corporations. *Management Science*, 40: 96–110.

Gick, M. and Holoyak, K.J. (1980) Analogical Problem Solving. *Cognitive Psychology*, 12: 306–355.

Gittelman, M and Kogut, B. (2003). Does Good Science Lead to Valuable Knowledge? Biotechnology Firms and the Evolutionary Logic of Citation Patterns. *Management Science*, 49(4): 366–382.

Granstrand, O., Patel, P. and Pavitt, K. (1997) Multi-technology corporations: Why they have 'distributed' rather than 'distinctive' core competencies. *California Management Review* 39(4): 8–25.

Grant, R.M. (1996) Toward a knowledge-based theory of the firm. *Strategic Management Journal*, Winter Special Issue 17: 109–122.

Grant, R.M. and Baden-Fuller, C. (2004) A Knowledge Accessing Theory of Strategic Alliances. *Journal of Management Studies*, 41: 61–84.

Gupta, A.K. and Govindarajan, V. (2000) Knowledge flows within multinational corporations. *Strategic Management Journal*, 21: 473–496.

Haas, M.R. (2006) Acquiring and applying knowledge in transnational teams: The roles of cosmopolitans and locals. *Organization Science*, 17: 367–384.

Haas, M.R. and Hansen, M.T. (2007) Different Knowledge, Different Benefits: Toward A Productivity Perspective On Knowledge Sharing In Organizations. *Strategic Management Journal*, 28: 1133–1153.

Hansen, M.T. (2002) Knowledge networks: Explaining effective knowledge sharing in multiunit companies. *Organization Science*, 13: 232–248.

Helfat, E. and Raubitschek, R.S. (2000) Product Sequencing: Co-Evolution of Knowledge, Capabilities And Products. *Strategic Management Journal*, 21: 961–979.

Hogarth, R. (1980) *Judgment and Choice: The Psychology of Decision*. New York: Wiley and Sons.

Holland, J., Holyoak, K., Nisbett, R. and Thagard, P. (1986) *Induction: Processes of inference, learning, and discovery.* Cambridge, MA: MIT Press.

Hollingshead, A.B. (2001) Cognitive interdependence and convergent expectations in transactive memory. *Journal of Personality and Social Psychology*, 81: 1080–1089.

Huber, G.P. (1991) Organizational learning: the contributing processes and the literatures. *Organizational Science*, 2: 88–115.

Inkpen, A.C. (2000) A Note on the Dynamics of Learning Alliances: Competition, Cooperation, and Relative Scope. *Strategic Management Journal*, 21(7): 707–790.

Inkpen, A.C. and Tsang, E.W.K. (2005) Social capital, networks, and knowledge transfer. *Academy of Management Review*, 30(1): 146–165.

Jaffe, A. B., Trajtenberg, M. and Henderson R. (1993) Geographic Localization of Knowledge Spillovers as Evidenced by Patent Citations. *Quarterly Journal of Economics*, 108: 577–598.

Kane, A.A. (2010) Unlocking Knowledge Transfer Potential: Knowledge Demonstrability and Superordinate Social Identity. *Organization Science*, 21: 643–660.

Katila, R. and Ahuja, G. (2002) Something old, something new: A longitudinal study of search behavior and new product introduction. *Academy of Management Journal*, 45: 1183–1194.

Katz, R. and Allen, T. J. (1982) Investigating the Not Invented Here (NIH) Syndrome: A look at the performance, tenure, and communication patterns of 50 R&D Project Groups. *R&D Management*, 12(1): 7–19.

Khanna, T., Gulati, R. and Nohria, N. (1998) The dynamics of learning alliances: Competition, cooperation, and relative scope. *Strategic Management Journal*, 19: 193–210.

Kogut, B. (1988) Joint Ventures: Theoretical and Empirical Perspectives. *Strategic Management Journal*, 9: 319–332.

Kogut, B. and Zander, U. (1992) Knowledge of the firm, combinative capabilities, and the replication of technology. *Organization Science*, 3: 383–397.

Kogut, B. and Zander, U. (1996) What firms do: coordination, identity, and learning. *Organization Science,* 7: 502–518.

Kotabe, M. and Swan, S. (1995) The Role of Strategic Alliances In High-Technology New Product Development. *Strategic Management Journal,* 16: 621–636.

Krackhardt, D. (1990) Assessing the Political Landscape—Structure, Cognition, and Power in Organizations. *Administrative Science Quarterly,* 35: 342–369.

Lahiri, N. (2005) Geographic dispersion and innovation performance: It is utilization that matters! Working Paper, University of Michigan.

Lane, P.J. and Lubatkin, M. (1998) Relative absorptive capacity and interorganizational learning. *Strategic Management Journal,* 19: 461–477.

Lant, T. K., Milliken, F. J. and Batra, B. (1992) The role of managerial learning and interpretation in strategic persistence and reorientation: An empirical exploration. *Strategic Management Journal,* 13: 585–608.

Lawrence, P. and Lorsch, J. (1967) *Organization and Environment: Managing Differentiation and Integration.* Harvard University, Boston, MA.

Lenox, M. and King, A. (2004) Prospects For Developing Absorptive Capacity Through Internal Information Provision. *Strategic Management Journal,* 25: 331–345.

Levin, D.Z. and Cross, R. (2003) The strength of weak ties you can trust: the mediating role of trust in effective knowledge transfer. *Management Science,* 50(11): 1477–1490.

Lewis, K., Lange, D. and Gillis, L. (2005) Transactive Memory Systems, Learning, and Learning Transfer. *Organization Science,* 16(6): 581–598.

Lichtenthaler, U. (2009) Absorptive Capacity, Environmental Turbulence, and the Complementarity of Organizational Learning Processes. *Academy of Management Journal,* 52(4): 822–846.

Luo, Y. (1999) Dimensions of knowledge: comparing Asian and Western MNEs in China. *Asia Pacific Journal of Management,* 16: 75–93.

Lyles, M.A. and Salk, J.E. (1996) Knowledge acquisition from foreign parents in international joint ventures: An empirical examination in the Hungarian context. *Journal of International Business Studies,* 27(5): 877–903.

Lyles, M.A. and Schwenk, C.R. (1992) Top management, strategy, and organizational knowledge structures. *Journal of Management Studies,* 29: 155–174.

March, J.G. and Simon, H.A. (1958) *Organizations.* New York: Wiley.

McNamara, G.M., Luce, R.A. and Thompson, G.H. (2002) Examining the effect of complexity in strategic group knowledge structures on firm performance. *Strategic Management Journal,* 23: 153–170.

Menon, T. and Pfeffer, J. (2003) Valuing Internal vs External Knowledge: Explaining the Preference for Outsiders. *Management Science,* 49(4): 497–513.

Meyer, K., Wright M. and Pruthi, S. (2009) Managing Knowledge In Foreign Entry Strategies: A Resource-Based Analysis. *Strategic Management Journal,* 30: 557–574.

Mezias, J. M. and Starbuck, W. H. (2003) Studying the accuracy of managers' perceptions: A research odyssey. *British Journal of Management,* 14: 3–17.

Miller, D.J., Fern, M.J. and Cardinal, L.B. (2007) Distant search inside the diversified firm: The effect of interdivisional knowledge transfer on the impact of inventions. *Academy of Management Journal,* 50(2): 308–326.

Miller, K. D., Zhao, M. and Calantone, R. J. (2006) Adding Interpersonal Learning and Tacit Knowledge to March's Exploration-Exploitation Model. *Academy of Management Journal,* 49: 709–722.

Milliken, F.J. (1990) Perceiving and Interpreting Environmental-Change – an Examination of College Administrators' Interpretation of Changing Demographics. *Academy of Management Journal*, 33: 42–63.

Moorman, C. and Miner, A. S. (1998) Organizational Improvisation and Organizational Memory. *Academy of Management Review*, 23: 698–723.

Mowery, D., Oxley, J. and Silverman, B. (1996) Strategic alliances and interfirm knowledge transfer. *Strategic Management Journal*, Winter Special Issue 17: 77–91.

Nakamura, M., Shaver, J.M. and Yeung, B. (1996) An empirical investigation of joint venture dynamics: Evidence from US–Japan joint ventures. *International Journal of Industrial Organization*, 14: 521–541.

Nasiriyar, M., Nesta, L. and Dibiaggio, L. (2010) The organization of the knowledge base and innovative performance. Working Paper, SKEMA Business School.

Nelson, R. and Winter, S. (1982) *The Evolutionary Theory of the Firm*. Harvard University Press: Cambridge, MA.

Nerkar, A. and Paruchuri, S. (2005) Evolution of R&D capabilities: The role of knowledge networks within a firm. *Management Science*, 51: 771–786.

Nerkar, A. and Roberts, P.W. (2004) Technological and Product–Market Experience and The Success of New Product Introductions In The Pharmaceutical Industry. *Strategic Management Journal*, 25: 779–799.

Nesta, L. and Saviotti, P.P. (2004) Not-Sold-Here: How Attitudes Influence External Knowledge Exploitation, *SPRU Electronic Working Paper Series*.

Nonaka, I. (1991) The knowledge-creating company. *Harvard Business Review*, 69(6): 96–104.

Nonaka, I. (1994) A dynamic theory of organizational knowledge creation. *Organization Science*, 5(1): 14–37.

Nonaka, I. and Takeuchi, H. (1995) *The Knowledge-Creating Company: How Japanese Companies Create the Dynamics of Innovation*. Oxford University Press: New York.

Nonaka, I. and Takeuchi, H. (1996) A theory of organizational knowledge creation. *International Journal of Technology Management*. 11(7/8): 833–846.

Nonaka, I. and von Krogh, G. (2009) Tacit Knowledge and Knowledge Conversion: Controversy and Advancement in Organizational Knowledge Creation Theory. *Organization Science*, 20(3): 635–652.

Novelli, E. (2010) As You Sow, So Shall You Reap: General Technologies And Entry Into New Product Subfields In The Face Of Technological Uncertainty. *Working Paper*, University of Bath.

Okhuysen, G.A. and Eisenhardt, K.M. (2002) Integrating knowledge in groups: How formal interventions enable flexibility. *Organization Science*, 13: 370–386.

Owen-Smith, J. and Powell, W.W. (2004) Knowledge Networks as Channels and Conduits: The Effects of Spillovers in the Boston Biotechnology Community. *Organization Science*, 15(1): 5–2.

Patel, P. and Pavitt, K. (1997) The technological competencies of the world's largest firms: complex and path-dependent, but not much variety. *Research Policy*, 26: 141–156.

Perrow, C. (1967) A framework for the comparative analysis of organizations. *American Sociological Review*, 32: 194–208.

Polanyi, M. (1966) *The Tacit Dimension*. Doubleday, New York.

Postrel, S. (1998) *Combining knowledge in organizations*. Mimeo, Graduate School of Management, University of California at Irvine, Irvine, CA.

Postrel, S. (2002) Islands of Shared Knowledge: Specialization and Mutual Understanding in Problem-Solving Teams. *Organization Science*, 13(3): 223–353.

Powell, W.W., Koput, K.W. and Smith-Doerr, L. (1996) Interorganizational Collaboration and the Locus of Innovation: Networks of Learning in Biotechnology. *Administrative Science Quarterly*, 41(1): 116–145.

Prahalad, C.K. and Bettis, R.A. (1986) The dominant logic: A new linkage between diversity and performance. *Strategic Management Journal*, 7: 485–502.

Puranam, P. (2001) Grafting innovation: the acquisition of entrepreneurial firms by established firms. Doctoral dissertation, The Wharton School, University of Pennsylvania.

Puranam, P., Singh H. and Chaudhuri, S. (2009) Integrating Acquired Capabilities: When Structural Integration Is (Un)necessary. *Organization Science*, 20: 313–328.

Puranam, P., Singh, H. and Zollo, M. (2006) Organizing for innovation: managing the coordination–autonomy dilemma in technology acquisitions. *Academy of Management Journal*, 49(2): 263–281.

Puranam, P. and Srikanth, K. (2007) What they know vs. What they do: How acquirers leverage technology acquisitions. *Strategic Management Journal*, 28: 805–825.

Quintana-Garcia, C. and Benavides-Velasco, C.A. (2008) Innovative competence, exploration and exploitation: The influence of technological diversification. *Research Policy*, 37: 492–507.

Ranft, A.L. and Lord, M.D. (2002) Acquiring new technologies and capabilities: a grounded model of acquisition implementation. *Organization Science*, 13(4): 420–442.

Reagans, R. and McEvily, B. (2003) Network structure and knowledge transfer: The effects of cohesion and range. *Administrative Science Quarterly*, 48: 240–267.

Rogers, E. (1983) *Diffusion of Innovations*, 3rd ed. The Free Press, New York.

Rosenberg, N. (1982) *Inside the black box: technology and economics*. Cambridge, New York: Cambridge University Press.

Rosenkopf, L. and Almeida, P. (2003) Overcoming Local Search through Alliances and Mobility, *Management Science*, 49(6): 751–766.

Rosenkopf, L. and Nerkar, A. (2001) Beyond Local Search: Boundary-Spanning, Exploration, and Impact in the Optical Disk Industry. *Strategic Management Journal*, 22(4): 287–306.

Schilling, M.A. (2002) Technology Success And Failure In Winner-Take-All Markets: The Impact Of Learning Orientation, Timing, And Network Externalities. *Academy of Management Journal*, 45(2): 387–398.

Schilling, M. A. and Phelps, C.C. (2007) Interfirm collaboration networks: The impact of large-scale network structure on firm innovation. *Management Science*, 53, 1113–1126.

Schulz, M. (2003) Pathways of relevance: Exploring inflows of knowledge into subunits of multinational corporations. *Organization Science*, 14: 440–459.

Schumpeter, J. (1934) *The Theory of Economic Development*. Oxford: Oxford University Press.

Sieloff, C.G. (1999) 'If only HP knew what HP knows:' the roots of knowledge management at Hewlett-Packard. *Journal of Knowledge Management*, 3(1): 47–53.

Siggelkow, N. and Rivkin, J.W. (2005) Speed and search: Designing organizations for turbulence and complexity. *Organization Science*, 16(2):101–122.

Simon, H.A. (1957) *Administrative behavior* (4th ed.). New York: Macmillan.

Simon, H.A. (1962) *The sciences of the artificial*. Cambridge, MA: MIT Press.

Simon, H.A. (1973) Applying Information Technology to Organization Design. *Public Administration Review*, 106: 467–482.

Simonin, B. (1999) Ambiguity and the process of knowledge transfer in strategic alliances. *Strategic Management Journal*, 20(7): 595–623.

Singh, J. (2009) Collaborative Networks as Determinants of Knowledge Diffusion Patterns. *Management Science*, 51(5): 756–770.

Smith, K.G., Collins, C.J. and Clark, K.D. (2005) Existing knowledge, knowledge creation capability, and the rate of new product introduction in high-technology firms. *Academy of Management Journal*, 48: 346–357.

Smith, R.P. and Eppinger, S.D. (1997) Identifying controlling features of engineering design iteration. *Management Science*, 43: 276–293.

Sorenson, O. (2003) Interdependence and Adaptability: Organizational Learning and the Long-Term Effect of Integration. *Management Science*, 49(4): 446–463.

Sorenson, O. and Sorensen, J.B. (2001) Finding the right mix: Franchising, organizational learning, and chain performance. *Strategic Management Journal*, 22: 713–724.

Starbuck, W.H. and Milliken F.J. (1988) Executives' Perceptual Filters: What They Notice and How They Make Sense,' in D. Hambrick (Ed.), *The Executive Effect: Concepts and Methods for Studying Top Managers*. Greenwich, CT: JAI Press: 35–66.

Stern, S. (2004) Do Scientists Pay to Be Scientists? *Management Science*, 50(11): 1463–1476.

Steward, D.V. (1981) *Systems Analysis and Management: Structure, Strategy and Design*. New York: Petrocelli Books.

Stuart, T.E., (2000) Interorganizational Alliances and the Performance of Firms: A Study of Growth and Innovation Rates in a High-Technology Industry. *Strategic Management Journal*, 21(8): 791–811.

Szulanski, G. (1996) Exploring Internal Stickiness: Impediments to the Transfer of Best Practice within the Firm. *Strategic Management Journal*, 17: 27–43.

Teece, D.J., (1986) Profiting from technological innovation. *Research Policy*, 15(6): 285–305.

Tippins, M.J. and Sohi, R.S. (2003) IT Competency and Firm Performance: Is Organizational Learning a Missing Link? *Strategic Management Journal*, 24(8): 687–782.

Tiwana, A. and Keil, M. (2006) Does Peripheral Knowledge Complement Control? An Empirical Test In Technology Outsourcing Alliances. *Strategic Management Journal*, 28: 623–634.

Tsang E.W. K. (2002) Acquiring Knowledge By Foreign Partners From International Joint Ventures In A Transition Economy: Learning-By-Doing And Learning Myopia. *Strategic Management Journal*, 23: 835–854.

Tung, R.L. (1979) Dimensions or organizational environment: An exploratory study of their impact on organization structure. *Academy of Management Journal*, 22: 672–693.

Turner, K. L. and Makhija, M.V. (2006) The role of organizational controls in managing knowledge. *Academy of Management Review*, 31(1): 197–217.

Van den Bosch, F.A.J., Volberda, H. de Boer, M. (1999) Coevolution of Firm Absorptive Capacity and Knowledge Environment: Organizational Forms and Combinative Capabilities. *Organization Science*, 10(5): 551–568.

Von Hippel, E. (1978) Users as Innovators. *Technology Review* 80(3): 31–39.

Wadhwa, A. and Kotha, S. (2006) Knowledge creation through external venturing: Evidence from the telecommunications equipment manufacturing industry. *Academy of Management Journal*, 49: 819–835.

Walsh, J. (1995) Managerial and organizational cognition: Notes from a trip down memory lane. *Organization Science*, 6: 280–321.

Walsh, J. and Ungson, R. (1991) Organizational memory. *The Academy of Management Review*, 16(1): 57–91.

Wegner, D.M. (1986) Transactive memory: A contemporary analysis of the group mind. In B. Mullen and G. R. Goethals (Eds.), *Theories of group behavior*. New York: Springer-Verlag: 185–208.

Weick, K.E. (1991) The Nontraditional Quality of Organizational Learning. *Organization Science*, 2(1): 1–147.

Wilensky, H.L. (1967) *Organizational intelligence*. New York: Basic Books.

Winter, S. (1987) Knowledge and competence as strategic assets. In D. J. Teece (ed.), *The Competitive Challenge*. Cambridge, MA: Ballinger: 159–184.

Winter, S.G. (2000) The Satisfying Principle in Capability Learning. *Strategic Management Journal*, 21(10/11): 955–1173.

Yayavaram, S. and Ahuja, G. (2008) Decomposability in Knowledge Structures and Its Impact on the Usefulness of Inventions and Knowledge-base Malleability. *Administrative Science Quarterly*, 53: 333–362.

Zander, U. and Kogut, B. (1995) Knowledge and the speed of the transfer and imitation of organizational capabilities: an empirical test. *Organization Science*, 6: 76–92.

Zhao, M. (2006) Conducting R&D in countries with weak intellectual property rights protection. *Management Science*, 56 (7): 1185–1199.

Zollo, M. and Singh, H. (2004) Deliberate Learning in Corporate Acquisitions: Post-Acquisition Strategies and Integration Capability in U.S. Bank Mergers. *Strategic Management Journal*, 25: 1233–1256.

Part IV

LEARNING AND KNOWLEDGE IN
INTERNATIONAL CONTEXTS

26

The Impact of Intercultural Communication on Global Organizational Learning

SULLY TAYLOR AND JOYCE S. OSLAND

ABSTRACT

This chapter provides a look at organizational learning through the lens of intercultural communication. Since the organizational learning research seldom considers the impact of intercultural communication, we have written a conceptual piece based on reviews of both literatures and our own experience with global organizations. The chapter begins by first examining the role of communication in organizational learning. Next, we introduce the basic concepts of intercultural communication. We identify those aspects of intercultural communication that most directly affect knowledge transfer: marginality, stereotypes, style differences, linguistic ability, cosmopolitanism, satisficing, cultural intelligence, and intercultural sensitivity. We explore the relationship between stages of intercultural sensitivity and the readiness to learn, focusing on the trigger events that can move people and organizations to higher levels of sensitivity. Finally, we describe and discuss the practical implications that an understanding of intercultural communication has for organizational learning and the questions that need to be addressed by future research.

INTRODUCTION

In a global economy, success depends on accurately reading and responding to environmental complexity and competition (Bartlett and Ghoshal, 1989, 2000). Organizational learning would appear to be a prerequisite for surviving in the global context (de Geus, 1988: 7; Hamel and Prahalad, 1994). Moreover, the diversity of peoples and environments in which multinational corporations (MNCs) operate should increase the potential number and sources of innovations and learning. As Cohen and Levinthal note, 'interactions across individuals who each possess diverse and different knowledge structures will augment the organization's capacity for making novel linkages and associations—innovating—beyond what any one individual can achieve' (1990: 133). The MNC can thus be seen as a set of networked repositories of knowledge and capabilities (Leonard-Barton, 1995; Kogut and Zander, 1992; Gupta and Govindarajan, 1991; Zander and Zander, 2010). Makino and Inkpen's chapter in this Handbook focuses attention on the fact that potential for learning—what they term exploration—can in fact lead MNCs to invest in other countries. While there has been some research into how MNCs can tap the knowledge potential of their global networks of people and units (e.g. Nohria and Ghoshal, 1997), the exploration of the processes that enhance global knowledge transfer is still growing (e.g. Brannen and Peterson, 2009; Reiche et al., 2009).

The need to understand the processes of global knowledge transfer is especially important because there is some evidence to suggest that many MNCs fail to tap the knowledge or leverage the learning that occurs within them (Nohria and Ghoshal, 1997; Bartlett and Ghoshal, 1989). For example, expatriates and repatriates are potential conduits of organizational learning (e.g. Antal, 2001; Fink, Meirewert, and Rohr, 2005). Few firms, however, formally harvest their knowledge (Oddou, Osland, and Blakeney, 2009). Many expatriates find that the knowledge they have gained during their sojourns abroad concerning the foreign environment is ignored once they return to HQ, with little or no attempt to archive and distribute the learning that has occurred (Osland, 1995; Kamoche, 1996). One of the major challenges facing global firms is to develop processes and policies that will more effectively integrate the knowledge and experience of repatriates (Bernhut, 2001; Birkinshaw, 2001). Another challenge is knowing when and how to utilize expatriates in the knowledge transfer process. Fang et al. (2010) found that the type of knowledge and timing determined the impact of knowledge transfer by expatriates on the performance of foreign subsidiaries.

Given the limited success of MNCs in transferring knowledge, and the paucity of research on global organizational learning, this chapter will introduce one of the key barriers to global organizational learning: intercultural communication. Intercultural communication is defined as a 'symbolic process in which people from different cultures create shared meanings' (Lustig and Koester, 1999: 52). The basic research question posed in this chapter is: What factors in the intercultural communication process affect organizational learning and prevent global organizations from sharing and transferring the information and knowledge at both the individual and group level?

There are very few studies that deal with the link between intercultural communication and organizational learning (e.g. Heavens and Child, 1999). Therefore, this chapter is a conceptual piece based on a review of both literatures and our own experience with global organizations. The chapter begins by first examining the role of communication in global organizational learning. Next, we introduce the basic concepts of intercultural communication and identify the aspects that most directly affect knowledge transfer. We explore the relationship between stages of intercultural sensitivity, which we examine through the lens of cultural intelligence (Ang and Van Dyne, 2008; Early and Ang, 2003) and the readiness to learn. We focus on the trigger events (Osland, Bird, and Gundersen, 2008) or 'aha' moments (Napier, 2010; Napier and Taylor, 2010) that can move people and organizations to higher levels of sensitivity. Finally, we discuss the practical implications that an understanding of intercultural communication has for organizational learning in global organizations and examine how overcoming barriers to intercultural communication can imbue organization members with capabilities that enhance knowledge creation and transfer. Finally, we offer directions future research can follow in addressing this aspect of global organizational learning.

COMMUNICATION IN GLOBAL ORGANIZATIONAL LEARNING

At the base of all theories concerning organizational learning, whether from the information processing perspective (e.g. Huber, 1991) or the social construction perspective (Brown and Duguid, 1991; Cook and Yanow, 1993), lies the assumption that communication must occur in order for knowledge to be created or disseminated. When examining organizational learning in MNCs, it is particularly important to examine the impact of culture on communication because of the need to share knowledge across individuals and groups located in highly divergent cultural environments. Regardless of the type of knowledge to be transferred (tacit versus explicit; operational versus strategic) or the manner of transfer (archival versus verbal; experiential versus cognitive), the communication process will be affected by culture. If MNCs can fully leverage all the knowledge that they have within their global networks, they will greatly enhance their ability to respond to environmental changes and increase performance (Bartlett and Ghoshal, 2000). Therefore, the impact of intercultural communication on knowledge transfer merits attention.

Organizational learning theorists usually include within their definitions of the phenomenon the capability of organizations not only to create new knowledge, but also to transfer it (Senge, 1990; Garvin, 1993; Huber, 1991). Huber calls this 'information distribution,' and observes that it is 'a determinant of both the occurrence and breadth of organizational learning' (1991: 100). In other words, in order for organizations to learn, they must first have access to the knowledge that is available within the company. He goes on to observe the potential impediments to the effective distribution of knowledge in organizations, which include such factors as the perception of personal characteristics of the receiver (e.g. power and status), the workload of the sender, and the number of sequential links in the communication chain linking the sender and the receiver (Huber, 1991: 101). Thus, Huber (1991) makes salient the role of communication in information and knowledge transfer, but he does not address the potential barriers represented by differences in ethnic or national cultural patterns of communication.

National or ethnic cultural background of individuals has long been recognized as a major influence on communication, and hence it is reasonable to expect that knowledge transfer within MNCs will be affected by national culture. However, it should be noted that the effects of large cultural distance are complex (Chakrabarti, Gupta-Mukherjee, and Jayaraman, 2009; Reus and Lamont, 2009). There are many definitions of national culture—around 200 of them (Adler, 2002). We have chosen to use a representative definition:

> the shared beliefs, values, and practices of a group of people. A group's culture includes the language or languages used by group members as well as the norms and rules about how behavior can appropriately be displayed and how it should be understood.
>
> (O'Hair, Friedrich, Wiemann, and Wiemann, 1997: 9).

Communication of knowledge in MNCs can occur between different types of actors—between individuals, between individuals and groups, and among groups, internally or externally, nationally or internationally. In this chapter, we will focus on the internal transfer of knowledge among these various actors. While the sharing of knowledge with the external environment may be of some importance to business success, the major learning that the MNC can capture and turn into a distinctive competence (Barney, 1991) is most likely to be internal. Illustrations of such internal learning are knowledge about new markets, improvements in business processes, recent competitor behavior and relevant technological innovations.

Individuals are usually seen as the basis of learning within organizations (Inkpen and Dinur, 1998; Kim, 1993; Nonaka and Takeuchi, 1995). 'The prime movers in the process of organizational knowledge creation are the individual members of an organization' (Nonaka, 1994: 17). Individuals hold internal images of how the world works. These are called 'mental models.' The mental models arbitrate what new information we acquire, retain, use, and delete, but most important, 'they not only help us make sense of the world we see, they can also restrict our understanding to that which makes sense within the mental model' (Kim, 1993: 39). Through learning gathered by interaction with the environment, an individual's mental model changes, and these changes become embedded in the organization's mental model. 'The cycles of individual learning affect learning at the organizational level through their influence on the organization's shared mental models' (Kim, 1993: 43). Individual learning is combined, amplified, and changed into group mental models in the intermediate step of group learning, as emphasized by Nonaka (1994) and Inkpen and Crossan (1995). The process of embedding the individual's new mental model into the organization is never simple. Much knowledge, particularly tacit knowledge, can be lost in the process due to lack of connections between people or parts of the organizational structure.

Organizations as a whole, as well as their sub-units, are thus also important learners and communicators (Inkpen and Crossan, 1995; Kim, 1993). Organizations can be seen as interpretation systems (Daft and Weick, 1984; Inkpen and Crossan, 1995) that scan the environment, interpret events and develop concepts to guide future action. The mental models that the organization collectively holds help it in decision making through the schemas, scripts, and causal maps that result from the mental models. Very often this learning is embedded in the knowledge structure of the top management team and in the organizational structures and processes they create based on their shared mental models (Kim, 1993). The organization communicates its mental models internally through established standard operating procedures, organizational culture, assumptions, artifacts, and overt behavior rules that characterize the organization (Kim, 1993). Thus, communication becomes a key factor both in how the organization learns from the individuals within it and how it communicates its mental models to these same individuals.

Based on this framework of the interdependent and interactive nature of individual and organizational learning, we will examine the impact of intercultural communication on knowledge transfer. Before proceeding, however, the distinction between the mental models of individuals and organizations on the one hand, and national culture on the other, warrants clarification. While national culture can be seen as a type of mental model, it is a much broader and more deeply rooted 'way of seeing the world.' In this chapter, we will make the distinction that the term 'mental model' refers to a narrower, organizationally relevant perspective that focuses on an image or perception of what makes the organization successful. National culture refers to the broader, life-encompassing group influenced mental picture that people acquire early in life from membership in a particular ethnic group or culture.

INTERCULTURAL COMMUNICATION

When examining organizational learning in MNCs, it is clear that a strong intercultural component must be included in order to study and understand how organizations can be successful. MNCs by their very nature are engaged in business in a number of countries with often widely divergent cultures. This leads to increased ambiguity concerning meaning. 'It is the ambiguity of meaning that marks the boundaries of culture' (Cohen, 1985: 55)—'the boundary is where the ambiguity begins, where managers can no longer be sure of the correctness of their interpretation of what is going on' (Apfelthaler and Karmasin, 1998: 8). Ambiguity can lead to anxiety. Communicating with strangers (people from other cultures) is both a source of anxiety and a means for diminishing it. 'Reducing anxiety is one of the major functions of communication when we interact with strangers' (Gudykunst and Kim, 1997: 27), because it can lead to more accurate predictions and expectations about a stranger's meaning and behavior.

Ting-Toomey emphasizes the interactive nature of intercultural communication in this definition, 'the symbolic exchange process whereby individuals from two (or more) different cultural communities negotiate shared meanings in an interactive situation' (1999: 16–17). *Cultural communities* are 'groups of interacting individuals within a bounded unit who uphold a set of shared traditions and way of life' (Ting-Toomey, 1999: 18). The *symbols* they use are verbal and nonverbal. The *exchange process* is an interdependent one—two cultural strangers find themselves in a mutually interdependent, transactional relationship in which they are simultaneously encoding and decoding messages that influence the other person's communication. Furthermore, the intercultural process is irreversible (Barnlund, 1962) because receivers may not form the same impression of repeated messages, and they may not change their reaction to a communication the sender wants to 'take back' and edit. Shared meanings are *negotiated* in a creative, give-and-take process that involves adaptation and multiple levels of meaning (Ting-Toomey, 1999). The *interactive situation* refers to both concrete (physical setting, equipment, seating arrangements) and intangible or psychological features, (such as behavioral scripts, goals, motivations, norms, roles, social skills, etc.) (Burgoon, Buller, and Woodall, 1996).

The interaction of cross-cultural communication often faces barriers to success. 'Unfortunately, more often than not, intercultural encounters are filled with misunderstandings and second guesses because of language problems, communication style differences, and value orientation differences' (Ting-Toomey, 1999: 18). Accordingly, Gudykunst and Kim's (1997) well-accepted intercultural communication model highlights the filters present in intercultural communication. Their model depicts messages and feedback flowing between Person A and Person B that are transmitted and interpreted through the filters of cultural, sociocultural (e.g. social identity) and psychocultural (e.g. attitudes) influences. These filters are mechanisms that delimit the number of alternatives used to transmit and interpret messages, thereby limiting the predictions made about how people from another culture might respond to communication behavior. The filters also delimit what stimuli are attended to and how incoming messages are interpreted. In the next section of the chapter we elucidate how these filters affect the communication process in global organizational learning.

INTERCULTURAL COMMUNICATION BARRIERS TO ORGANIZATIONAL LEARNING

Based on our experiences with MNCs and an examination of the intercultural literature, we will address those factors or barriers in cross-cultural communication in the following sections that most directly influence organizational learning, generally by delimiting how messages are perceived and interpreted. The transactional nature of intercultural communication indicates that the parties involved are simultaneously senders and receivers, but for ease of categorization, we have divided the factors into sender- and receiver-related categories as shown in Figure 26.1. The sender-related factors consist of marginality, stereotypes, style differences that distinguish senders and receivers, and the linguistic ability of the sender. The receiver-related category includes the receivers' cosmopolitanism and their tendencies toward satisficing and plateauing of cultural knowledge. The aggregate of the factors that affect senders and receivers can be seen as their degree of intercultural sensitivity (Bennett, 1993) or cultural intelligence (Ang and Van Dyne, 2008; Early and Ang, 2003), which in turn relates to an MNC's 'level of readiness' and potential for organizational learning. We have chosen these factors carefully based on the cross-cultural communication literature, but, because this is a pioneering conceptual work, there is no way to gauge the relative weight and validity of these factors in global organizational learning without future empirical research.

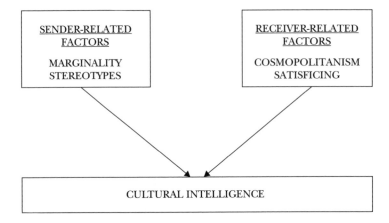

Figure 26.1 Intercultural Communication Factors that Affect Organizational Learning

Sender-related Intercultural Communication Barriers to Organizational Learning

Marginality of the sender

Marginality plays an important role in intercultural interactions. Cultural marginality refers to people who have internalized two or more cultural frames of reference (Stonequist, 1932). For example, Chinese-Americans can hold two distinct mental models concerning the importance of being independent of the group, and their self-descriptions will vary according to whether a Chinese or American cultural frame feels more appropriate (Hong, Morris, Chiu, and Benet-Martinez, 2000). This can lead to internal culture shock as two cultural voices vie for attention (J. Bennett, 1993). Marginal people are often ideally suited to boundary spanning or mediating roles between cultures (Bochner, 1982), since they understand both cultures objectively and subjectively. Some expatriates, for example, interpret the actions of the foreign subsidiaries for people at headquarters and vice versa, thereby contributing to organizational learning (Reiche et al., 2009). There may be, however, a less positive aspect to marginality. 'Marginal people [such as expatriates] feel that they live on the periphery rather than at the center of a group or community' (Osland, 1995: 113). This can translate into less opportunity to speak or be heard because they are not members of the dominant coalition. They may also consciously or unconsciously monitor their communication to reflect their marginal role.

With regard to organizational learning in MNCs, perceived marginality affects perception and, thus, the influence of the sender. This is reminiscent of Huber's (1991) reference to the status and power of the receiver as a potential barrier to information transfer. In many MNCs, employees who are not in the home country of the firm are seen as 'marginal.' Even well respected expatriates who have been sent from the home country can become marginalized by their physical absence from the corporate office. Ironically, people on the margins of organizations sometimes have a more accurate view of events and circumstances than central decision makers. Their position on the margin may bring them access to broader sources of information; in high power distance cultures (Hofstede, 1980), information is sometimes less censored in their presence. Yet, because the MNC views senders as marginal, the information or knowledge they transmit is considered of less value or relevance than similar information from a member within the home country. An organizational norm becomes established that discourages either seeking information from the marginal members, or from granting much attention when such people volunteer information. A classic example is the well known nineteenth-century incident of a low-level US Navy lieutenant on a posting in the China Seas who proposed a radical and extremely beneficial modification of sea fighting that was assiduously ignored by the War Department in Washington until Abraham Lincoln personally intervened to champion the innovation (Tushman and O'Reilly, 1997).

Perceived marginality can hamper both individuals and organizational units. The organization as a whole can marginalize all managers operating in foreign affiliates, including host-country, third-country, and expatriate managers, as well as certain affiliates (Inkpen and Dinur, 1998). In particular, affiliates in smaller foreign countries that neither command nor produce significant resources (Gupta and Govindarajran, 1991) are likely to be marginalized. Information and knowledge flowing from them is likely to have little influence on the knowledge base or decision making of either the home office or other units.

Generally speaking, marginality has to do with lack of membership in the dominant coalition of the organization, but it can also pertain to horizontal relations and individual communications. For example, a Japanese manager employed by an American MNC in Tokyo may be very receptive to information provided by the home office. He or she may, however, discount the same kind of information if it is received from a Korean manager in the company's affiliate in Seoul. This perceived marginality of the Korean is due to the historical animosity between Korea and Japan and the cultural superiority that many Japanese still feel they have over Koreans. This example points to the relationship between marginality and stereotypes.

Stereotypes concerning the stranger

Stereotyping is 'an exaggerated set of expectations and beliefs about the attributes of a group membership category ... an overgeneralization without any attempt to perceive individual variations' (Ting-Toomey, 1999: 161). According to research, stereotypes are based on relatively little information, are resistant to change even in light of new information, and are rarely accurately applied to specific individuals (Christensen and Rosenthal, 1982; McCauley, Stitt, and Segal, 1980). Stereotypes affect the senders' ability to communicate their messages because they interfere with their ability to be 'heard' and accurately judged. In a similar fashion, the senders' marginality interferes with their ability to be seen and heard. The senders' stereotype about receivers determines how much and what type of information they will share with them.

Stereotypes combine with attitudes (such as prejudice) to create expectations of how strangers will behave. These expectations, in turn, influence the way in which people interpret incoming stimuli and the predictions they make about strangers' behavior. 'Using our frame of reference invariably leads to misinterpretations of the strangers' messages, as well as inaccurate predictions about their future behavior' (Gudykunst and Kim, 1997: 48). While stereotyping is very normal behavior, it can inhibit organizational learning, particularly across organizational boundaries. If HQ staff does not expect to hear solid, innovative ideas from certain nationalities, they may not pay careful attention to all the information coming from the field. Subsidiaries can also discount input coming from headquarters if they do not perceive corporate staff as competent.

It should be noted that stereotyping is not always viewed as negative behavior in intercultural communication. Adler (2002) writes that stereotypes can be helpful if they are consciously held, descriptive rather than evaluative, accurate, and viewed as a 'first best guess' about a group or person, which means they are subject to modification once firsthand experience is obtained. When people are willing to continue learning about strangers, stereotypes are not necessarily harmful. In the absence of learning, however, stereotyping leads to a reduction in intercultural communication effectiveness.

Like individuals, organizations may hold stereotypes in the form of mental maps and shared assumptions. An organizational norm may exist, for example, in a Japanese MNC that Americans are so individualistic that no knowledge concerning effective team functioning could possibly exist in the company's US subsidiary. Even if the US subsidiary were to share codified or tacit knowledge about techniques for creating effective team functioning, the HQ in Japan is likely to ignore this knowledge because of stereotypes about Americans that are reflected in organizational values and norms.

Individual behavior can be affected by stereotypes as well, with negative consequences for organizational learning. A US HQ member of staff may receive a report from a French manager concerning dangerous moves by competitors in Europe and dismiss the news as an overreaction by 'those emotional French.' Thus, the stereotypes that individuals hold within the MNC can seriously, and negatively, affect the ability of senders to have their messages heard by key processors of information and knowledge.

Communication style differences

Another factor that has an effect on communication in global organizational learning is the area of communication style differences. The potential effect of communication style on organizational learning has received only passing attention in the research. Yet there is no doubt that it exists. In their study of organizational learning in a new intercultural team, Heavens and Child (1999) found that the Japanese members failed to communicate important information to British members. In this case, the Japanese communication reticence and formality with strangers led to a slowdown in reaching the team's goal.

Cultural and ethnic identities influence verbal and nonverbal communication styles (Ting-Toomey, 1999: 100). Mutual clarity is extremely hard to achieve without an understanding of these style differences, but few MNCs make the effort to educate their employees in intercultural communication. Table 26.1 presents the most common style differences that affect organizational learning: high versus low context, direct versus indirect, person-oriented versus status-oriented, self-enhancing versus self-effacing, and elaborate versus succinct styles.[1]

Table 26.1   Cultural Communication Styles

VERBAL STYLE	MAJOR CHARACTERISTIC
High- versus low-context	Meaning conveyed in context versus explicit verbal message
Direct versus indirect	Explicit versus implicit, camouflaged message
Person-oriented versus status-oriented	Emphasis on unique, personal identities versus honoring prescribed power-based membership identities
Self-enhancement versus self-effacement	Emphasis on boasting about accomplishments and abilities versus humility and self-deprecation
Succinct—Exacting—Elaborate	Low to moderate to high quantities of talk

---

[1]There are other communication differences related to culture, such as monochronic versus polychronic time schedules and instrumental versus affective styles, but they appear to have less potential direct impact on organizational learning.

High-context versus low-context. According to Hall (1976), low-context communication relies on explicit verbal messages to convey intention or meaning. In contrast, high-context communication tends to transmit intention or meaning via the context (such as social roles or positions) and the nonverbal channels (such as pausing, silence, tone of voice). High-context communication involves multilayered contexts (e.g. historical context, social norms, roles, situational and relational contexts), and the listener is expected to 'read between the lines' of indirect messages. In contrast, the onus lies on the sender in low-context communication to transmit a clear, direct message that listeners can easily decode (Ting-Toomey, 1999: 101). Knowledge transfer occurs differently and may be misinterpreted between high-context and low-context communicators.

Direct versus indirect verbal styles. These styles are differentiated by 'the extent to which intentions are revealed by tone of voice and the straightforwardness of the content message' (Ting-Toomey, 1999: 103). In the direct style, the speaker's intentions are specified in a forthright way and tone of voice; in the indirect style, in contrast, verbal statements hide the speaker's meaning, which is conveyed in nuances. Failure to understand these style differences allows for misinterpretation. Westerners, who prefer a direct style, often perceive the indirect style of the Chinese as 'insincere and untrustworthy' (Graf, 1994). The indirect style, characterized by an unwillingness to say 'no' directly or to force others into that position, allows for greater face-saving. People from cultures using indirect styles may perceive those with a direct style as both blunt and obtuse (Ting-Toomey, 1999). People and organizations with a direct style may be unaware that an indirect communicator is even trying to transfer knowledge to them.

Person-oriented versus status-oriented verbal styles. The person-oriented verbal style is individual-centered and emphasizes the importance of informality and role suspension. The status-oriented verbal style is role centered and emphasizes formality and large power distance (Ting-Toomey, 1999: 106). Power distance is the extent to which a society accepts the fact that power in institutions and organizations is distributed unequally (Hofstede, 1980). Koreans and Japanese are status-oriented whereas Americans are person-oriented. This style difference sometimes makes for uncomfortable interactions and misinterpretations; it may also determine who talks with whom in the hierarchy, who is allowed to come up with new knowledge and pass it along, and how much information and knowledge is shared.

Self-enhancement versus self-effacement verbal styles.

> The self-enhancement verbal style emphasizes the importance of boasting about one's accomplishments and abilities. The self-effacement verbal style, on the other hand, emphasizes the importance of humbling oneself via verbal restraints, hesitations, modest talk, and the use of self-deprecation concerning one's effort or performance.
>
> (Ting-Toomey, 1999: 107)

Collectivist Asian cultures are generally self-effacing while Arab and African-American cultures tend to be self-enhancing (Ting-Toomey, 1999). A person from a self-effacing culture may be so modest about knowledge they have acquired that people from self-enhancing cultures pay no attention. In contrast, the self-enhancers' boastful mode of transferring knowledge may be so distasteful to people from self-effacing cultures that they ignore or sabotage an effort at organizational learning.

Succinct versus elaborate verbal styles. This style refers to the amount of talk with which people feel comfortable. The continuum of speech quantity ranges from *succinct* (low quantity) to *exacting* (precision and 'just the right' amount of words) to *elaborate* (high quantity) (Gudykunst and Ting-Toomey, 1988). The elaborate style, found in Arab cultures, also includes detailed descriptions, repetition, verbal elaboration and exaggeration, and the use of metaphor, similes, and proverbs. The exacting style, typical of England, Germany, and Sweden, emphasizes clarity and precise meanings. These cultures perceive the use of too many words as exaggeration while the use of too few words is viewed as ambiguous. The succinct style, manifested in China, Japan, Korea, and Thailand, is characterized by understatements and meaningful pauses and silences (Gudykunst and Ting-Toomey, 1988). Rather than simply noting that another culture uses more or fewer words to communicate, these style differences are often the cause of cultural misattributions. People with a succinct style may discount elaborate speakers as illogical or inefficient and even stop listening to them. Elaborate speakers may assume succinct communicators have very little to say or contribute. Both these scenarios impact the effective transfer of knowledge. In multicultural meetings and teams, highly verbal Americans sometimes fill in the silences and do not allow enough room for people with a more succinct style (or for non-native speakers) to talk.

Ting-Toomey concludes,

> In individualistic cultures, people find themselves in numerous contexts that call for direct talk, person-oriented verbal interaction, verbal self-enhancement, and talkativeness. In contrast, in collectivistic cultures, people tend to encounter more situations that emphasize the preferential use of indirect talk, status-oriented verbal interaction, verbal self-effacement and silence.
>
> (Ting-Toomey, 1999:103)

Linguistic ability

The lack of language comprehension and fluency constitute other barriers to organizational learning. In addition to the obvious obstacles of mutual understanding and ease of transaction, people tend to restrict their communication to those who speak their own language. When large MNCs buy local companies in another country, they sometimes appoint as their liaison or local manager the host-country national who is most fluent in the language of the home country of the MNC. This person is not necessarily the most competent or best able to teach them about the local subsidiary and context; however, the transaction costs of communicating with them are the lowest.

RECEIVER-RELATED INTERCULTURAL COMMUNICATION BARRIERS TO ORGANIZATIONAL LEARNING

While the sender may encounter barriers to communicating information and knowledge to others for the reasons outlined above, the other part of the communication dyad is the receiver. Both the organization and individuals within the organization are potential receivers of information and knowledge critical to organizational learning.

There are two major factors that can affect the receptivity of both organizations and individuals: cosmopolitanism and satisficing behaviors.

Cosmopolitanism

Cosmopolitanism is an attitudinal stance or mindset that indicates an orientation toward the outside world (Merton, 1957). As originally conceived, it emphasized people who are oriented towards the outside world, and contrasted them with 'locals' who are more focused on local affairs (Merton, 1957). While later this was expanded to include a distinction between those in organizations who are oriented to a reference group outside the firm (Gouldner, 1957; 1958), it is this original external orientation to the world upon which we will draw. With increasing globalization, the concept of cosmopolitanism has received renewed attention, with an added emphasis on a willingness to engage with the external world. Some researchers (e.g. Levy, Beechler, Taylor, and Boyacigiller, 2007) identify cosmopolitanism as one of the two essential characteristics of global mindset. Hannerz (1996: 103) describes cosmopolitanism in this fashion:

> A more genuine cosmopolitanism is first of all an orientation, a willingness to engage with the other. It entails an intellectual and esthetic openness toward divergent cultural experiences, a search for contrasts rather than uniformity. To become acquainted with more cultures is to turn into an *aficionado*, to view them as artworks. At the same time, however, cosmopolitanism can be a matter of competence . . . a personal ability to make one's way into other cultures, through listening, looking, intuiting, and reflecting.

Cosmopolitanism can thus be seen as related to a key concept in intercultural communication called mindfulness. According to Thich (1991), this term means attending to one's internal assumptions, cognitions, and emotions, and simultaneously being attuned to the other's assumptions, cognitions, and emotions. It also involves being open to novelty and unfamiliar behavior (Ting-Toomey, 1999: 267–8). Langer wrote that mindfulness involves learning to (1) see behavior or information presented in the situation as novel or fresh; (2) view a situation from several vantage points or perspectives; (3) attend to the context and the person in which we are perceiving the behavior; and (4) create new categories through which this new behavior may be understood (1997: 111). In addition, cosmopolitanism at the organizational level can be seen as related to Kim's (1993) concept of organizational intrusiveness, or the willingness of the organization to look outside itself, as well as to Cohen and Levinthal's (1990) concept of absorptive capacity, which is the ability of an organization to recognize the value of new, external information and integrate it into existing knowledge.

In sum, the cosmopolitanism of the receiver is an important attitude that can influence the effectiveness of communication in global organizational learning. If a receiver at HQ (or HQ as a whole) is not interested in the external environment and not willing to engage with it, it is likely that he or she will ignore incoming communication as irrelevant to the local concerns. It is not that the receiver has a prejudice *per se* against externally generated knowledge, but simply a lack of interest in it. Similarly, entire work units or divisions may be so locally oriented that they are uninterested in knowledge generated elsewhere. In either case, the receiver misses potentially valuable input by failing to seek information relevant to organizational learning from external (i.e. external to their own site) sources due to a lack of interest and curiosity.

Satisficing

Satisficing is the second factor that influences receivers. In decision making this term refers to accepting a decision that is 'good enough' because the costs of maximizing are too great (Simon, 1976). In an intercultural context, we find satisficing in two areas—the plateauing that occurs in both language acquisition and cultural understanding (Osland, 1995: Osland and Bird, 2000). When these skills are good enough to get by, some people stop learning. There is no motivation to reach a higher level of fluency or understanding until a trigger event occurs, which initiates another round of cultural sense making (Osland and Bird, 2001) or a return to the dictionary or language teacher.

In terms of organizational learning, satisficing occurs when firms or individuals assume they understand enough to get by and be effective in a global context. MNCs that are not experiencing negative business results in foreign markets, or who are protected from the consequences of negative business results by subsidies at home, may feel satisfied with the level of cultural knowledge they possess. It can be argued that until the late 1980s many Japanese MNCs had high levels of satisficing behavior with regard to intercultural communication. The economic recession that began in the early 1990s and continues into the second decade of the new century, and the problems many Japanese MNCs have faced with overseas operations, such as Matsushita's troubles in Hollywood in the 1990s or Toyota's failure to listen to complaints about unexpected acceleration, have caused a re-examination of their level of intercultural understanding.

Individuals can also exhibit satisficing behaviors, particularly when their focus is restricted to short-term business goals. A US technical manager in a US MNC's subsidiary in China may have learned enough language and cultural knowledge to get by on a day-to-day basis when that country was still at an early stage of market opening, with few highly qualified engineers available. That manager may not realize fifteen years later that the skills and knowledge of the young Chinese engineers he or she is working with are considerably more sophisticated. Because the US technical manager is still using a set of behaviors that was good enough to get by in the short term, that manager is unlikely to recognize that the information environment around him or her has changed unless a trigger event, such as widespread resignations, occurs to jolt the manager out of complacency. Whether the manager responds to the trigger event depends in part on his or her level of readiness to continue learning about the particular work setting and the other culture.

Cultural Intelligence and Levels of Readiness

The third and final variable in the model represents an overall level of readiness to communicate in ways that are beneficial to global organizational learning. We use the concept of cultural intelligence (abbreviated as CQ) (Ang and Van Dyne, 2008; Early and Ang, 2003) to explore the characteristics of individuals who are more likely to have the capability to overcome the communication barriers to organizational learning in MNCs described above.

Cultural intelligence is conceptualized as having four main dimensions: meta-cognitive, cognitive, motivational, and behavioral (Ang and Van Dyne, 2008). Meta-cognitive CQ refers to the 'individual's level of conscious cultural awareness during cross-cultural interactions. People with strength in meta-cognitive CQ consciously question their own cultural assumptions, reflect during interactions, and adjust their cultural knowledge when interacting with those from other cultures' (Ang and Van Dyne, 2008: 5). It can thus be seen as a higher-order cognitive process. Cognitive CQ, on the other hand, is more concerned with understanding how cultures differ and includes knowledge of the norms and practices of other cultures that a person accumulates through study or personal experience. Motivational CQ refers to the 'capability to direct attention and energy toward learning about functioning in situations characterized by cultural differences,' that is, being willing to expend the energy to understand cultural differences, often due to intrinsic interest. Finally, behavioral CQ is the willingness to engage in actions, both verbal and non-verbal, that are different from those of one's own culture in order to facilitate interaction with people from different cultures.

While CQ is usually conceptualized and studied from the individual level of analysis, rather than societal or organizational (Elenkov and Pimentel, 2008), it has been argued that an organization such as a MNC can increase its 'cultural capital' by enhancing the CQ of its employees, often through 'enriching their multicultural experiences' (Klafehn, Banerjee, and Chiu, 2008: 327). Thus, we posit that both MNCs as a whole as well as the individuals within them have differing levels of CQ, and therefore 'readiness to transfer' information and knowledge across borders. The readiness to learn and transfer knowledge in a global organization rests on a threshold level of CQ possessed by a significant number of key employees within the organization.

How does a MNC know whether it has a high level of readiness to transfer information and knowledge across borders and that it has accumulated sufficient 'cultural capital' so that intraorganizational communication across cultures can occur without major misunderstandings? Drawing on Bennett's (1993) development model of intercultural sensitivity (DMIS), which is usually applied at the individual level, we can designate MNCs as being in either the ethnocentric or the ethnorelative stage of readiness. Within the ethnocentric level, companies and the individuals within them 'can be seen as . . . avoiding cultural differences, either by denying its existence, by raising defenses against it, or by minimizing its importance' (Bennett and Bennett, 2001: 14). In this stage, one's own culture is experienced as central to reality—hence the term 'ethnocentric.' In contrast, people experience their own culture in the context of other cultures in the ethnorelative stage. In this stage, companies and individuals seek cultural difference, 'either by accepting its importance, by adapting a perspective to take it into account, or by integrating the whole concept into a definition of identity' (Bennett and Bennett, 2001: 14). CQ is closely related to intercultural sensitivity; however, the CQ concept provides greater relevance to discussing the challenge of increasing organizational learning in MNCs (for a discussion of the differences between intercultural sensitivity and CQ, see Leung and Li, 2008, 352–353).

We believe that there is a relationship among CQ, intercultural sensitivity, and readiness to transfer knowledge for global organizational learning. Communicators' realization that they need to be aware of culture and open to knowledge regardless of its source (meta-cognitive CQ), and to question their assumptions through knowledge of their own culture and that of others (cognitive CQ), is more likely in the ethnorelative stages. At the organizational level, organizations in the ethnorelative stages are more likely to have a preponderance of key people who have both the motivation to learn about other cultural

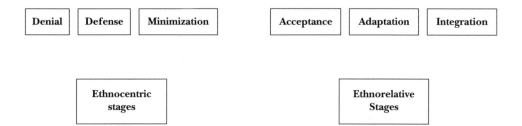

Figure 26.3 Bennett's Developmental Model of Intercultural Sensitivity

approaches to communication and to engage in the behaviors necessary to make their own ideas or others' clear during transfer of information or learning (motivational and behavioral CQ). In contrast, based on our examination of the barriers to communication in the first part of this chapter, we would expect ethnocentric organizations and individuals to show a greater tendency to marginalize other organizational members and units, to be more prone to stereotyping, and to be less conscious and tolerant of communication style differences and less flexible in adapting to other styles. We would also expect them to be less cosmopolitan and show a greater tendency toward satisficing.

Trigger events and increased readiness to learn

We argue that both organizations and individuals are unlikely to move from the ethnocentric to the ethnorelative level of readiness without a disruption of some sort. These disruptions can be viewed as trigger events (Griffith, 1998; Osland, Bird, and Gundersen, 2008) that cause the actors to become consciously engaged and question previous schemas of interpretation. Louis and Sutton (1991) identified three types of triggers. First, switching to a conscious mode is provoked when one experiences a situation as *unusual* or *novel*—when something 'stands out of the ordinary,' 'is unique,' or when the 'unfamiliar' or 'previously unknown' is experienced. Second, switching is also provoked by *discrepancy*—when 'acts are in some way frustrated,' when there is 'an unexpected failure,' a 'disruption,' 'a troublesome . . . situation,' when there is a significant difference between expectations and reality. The third trigger event refers to *deliberate initiatives*, usually in response to an internal or external request for an increased level of conscious attention— as when people are 'asked to think' or 'explicitly questioned' (Louis and Sutton, 1991: 60).

For an organization, the first kind of situation—an unusual or novel experience—can occur when a group or unit within the global network makes a positive and unexpected contribution of information or knowledge that has an impact on organizational performance. Hewlett-Packard, for example, had to re-examine its organizational view of the capabilities of its Singaporean affiliate when presented with a clear example of the ability of the Singaporean design team to move beyond adaptation to innovation. When such questioning leads to changes in attitude about the marginality of a particular unit, as well as a re-examination of the organization's view of its foreign operations, the trigger event moves the firm toward a more ethnorelative level of readiness.

For individuals, a similar trigger can occur when they are presented with valuable information or knowledge from an organizational member previously stereotyped as incapable of providing valuable input. A manager in the HQ of a Spanish telecommunications MNC might receive a report from its Chilean subsidiary on an innovative approach to billing customers for mobile services. Realizing that the innovation greatly enhances return on investment and is applicable world-wide could force the Spanish manager to re-examine his or her stereotypes about Chileans and other Latin American nationals, thus moving that manager toward greater ethnorelativism and openness to learning from international colleagues.

A trigger event can also be negative, a discrepancy between what is desired and what is obtained. For an organization, this could be the success of competitors' moves in its overseas markets and a consequent fall in its own performance. The experience of Procter and Gamble in Japan in the 1970s illustrates this kind of trigger. When Procter and Gamble first acquired a medium-sized Japanese firm to manufacture its disposable diapers, it held one hundred percent of the Japanese market due to its first mover status. However, it ignored the input from the managers in its Japanese subsidiary and failed to adjust the product to fit the smaller size of Japanese babies and other considerations of Japanese mothers. It soon found that Japanese competitors flooded the market with their own disposable diapers, which led to a drop of more than seventy percent in Procter and Gamble's market share in Japan. The company had been satisficing, basing its behavior on a superficial understanding of Japanese employees and the local context and failing to re-examine its assumptions. The reduced market share was a trigger event that led to a change in the way the company interacted with its Japanese subsidiary.

For individuals, such as the HQ-based leader of a global team, a discrepancy could include the inability to reach the goals set for the team. The leader could be facing possible negative impacts on his compensation or promotion. Examination of the hindrances to effective team performance could make the leader more aware of his tendency to discount important information or ideas because they were couched in elaborate descriptions rather than the succinct style he preferred. As a result, he might be motivated to learn more about communication style differences and attempt to reconcile his own language style with that of other team members.

Finally, an outside event such as a corporate initiative or training program can lead people to re-examine aspects of their intercultural communication. For organizations, this could include a change in corporate leadership, with a subsequent change in vision and norms. The CEO of a chemical company with a global strategy decided that international experience should be a prerequisite for promotion to senior management. The corporation's heroes became those people who worked abroad. Repatriates were promoted and given strategic responsibilities, which made it easier to transfer their knowledge back to headquarters. The firm acquired global expertise and transformed a formerly parochial mindset to a global mindset in a relatively short time frame.

For individuals, a deliberate initiative and important disruption often involves training. Hult, Nichols, Giunipero, and Hurley (2000), for example, found in their international study of organizational learning among supply chain managers that those who had received training in understanding and using organizational learning concepts had better supply chain relationships. One could argue that the training enhanced the cosmopolitanism of these individuals, leading to greater effectiveness in intercultural communication and learning with others in the supply chain.

Discussion

In this chapter, we argue that global organizational learning is affected by the process of intercultural communication at both the individual and organizational levels. Sender-related and receiver-related factors, such as marginality, stereotypes, and CQ, influence how messages are perceived and interpreted, and they filter the exchange of ideas in a global organization. This results in both individuals and organizations having varying levels of cultural intelligence and intercultural sensitivity, which can be characterized as either ethnocentric or ethnorelative (Bennett, 1993). Trigger events—novelty, discrepancy, and deliberate initiatives (Louis and Sutton, 1991)—can help move people and firms to higher stages of cultural intelligence, ethnorelativism, and global organizational learning. Our arguments are drawn from extant theory and research, as well as experience. The following discussion delineates the managerial implications and caveats of the framework presented in this chapter, along with their benefits and costs for MNCs. We also address the questions raised by the framework that require further research.

An understanding of the intercultural communication's impact on organizational learning yields many practical, managerial implications and caveats for global organizations. First of all, the most obvious way to diminish the effects of intercultural communication filters is through more training and emphasis on intercultural communication and the development of CQ for members of global organizations. Training and development needs to take into account the importance of intercultural sensitivity for global organizational learning. However, according to Bennett and Bennett (2001), such training should not be one-size-fits-all. To move individuals to higher levels of intercultural sensitivity, they recommend different types of training and experience for each stage.

Second, global managers should take into consideration the research findings on inter-group contact theory, which maintains that prejudice declines as a result of contact with other racial and ethnic groups (Williams, 1947; Allport, 1954). A meta-analysis of hundreds of studies concluded that contact does reduce prejudice when it is facilitated by (1) equal status; (2) group interdependent efforts toward common goals; (3) high potential for cross-group friendship; (4) positive experiences that counter negative stereotypes; and (5) authority sanction (Pettigrew and Tropp, 2000). MNCs could devote more attention and energy to these facilitating factors. Contact is needed not only between national groups, but also between different organizational cultures and different professions.

Third, while the greater heterogeneity and diversity of viewpoints and experiences inherent in MNCs can be a positive factor in organizational learning, there are also transaction costs for managers to recognize and handle. For example, stress is inherent in intercultural encounters, as evidenced in the literature on culture shock (Furnham and Bochner, 1986; Kim, 1988, 1989a) and intergroup anxiety (Barna, 1983; Gudykunst and Ting-Toomey, 1988; Stephan and Stephan, 1985). Pettigrew (2008) identified anxiety management as one of three core intercultural competencies. Learning to anticipate and deliberately manage this stress and anxiety could facilitate the transfer of knowledge.

Fourth, yet another transaction cost concerns intergroup relations. Relationships among different national or professional groups involve 'intergroup postures' that often cause 'in-group loyalties' and 'out-group discrimination' (Brewer and Miller, 1984; Brown and Turner, 1981). 'We–they' groups accentuate the perceived differences that divide them and are subject to attribution errors—inaccurate assumptions about the behavior of strangers, which are closely related to ethnocentrism and prejudice (Brewer and Miller, 1984). These tendencies are more pronounced when the groups involved have a history of dominance/subjugation or wide discrepancies in power and prestige (Kim, 1989b). More managerial attention, as well as research, could focus on the effects of marginality versus inclusion and on policies and practices that unwittingly reinforce unequal status. In MNCs, employees' expectations and interpretations of the behavior of people and groups from other cultures are frequently inaccurate, which can affect work performance as well as organizational learning. An awareness of these transaction costs and a deliberate effort to manage them could facilitate the transfer of knowledge.

Finally, if the intercultural communication process is both transactional and irreversible, that argues for greater mindfulness—paying more attention to the way employees of global firms, as well as the firms themselves, communicate and working to ensure that communications elicit more rather than less organizational learning. Mindfulness also involves increased awareness of the ethnocentric tendencies manifested in attitudes, policies, and procedures. Furthermore, mindfulness means identifying intercultural competence knowledge in the firm and transferring and institutionalizing that knowledge throughout the organization. By doing so, MNCs can eliminate some of the filters that impede organizational learning.

In sum, more managerial and organizational emphasis and attention to training, contact, transaction costs, intergroup relations, and mindfulness could increase global organizational learning in general. However, any investment that increases the competency of global talent represents a significant cost to MNCs, and one that should not be undertaken without evidence and research findings that prove its worth. Such research, however, should not overlook the potential collateral benefits of developing intercultural communication and CQ competence. By nurturing greater meta-cognitive CQ and communication competence in a MNC's employees, the firm is likely to increase its capacity, even in purely domestic settings, to become more aware of their own and other's assumptions when communicating important information and knowledge. This ability to stop and reflect during interactions, both about the context of the other as well as one's own, is a valuable skill that can lead to enhanced listening and understanding of others' ideas. It could also be argued that increased behavioral CQ, and the greater comfort of adapting one's behaviors to enhance communication across cultures, could also be useful when trying to interact across functional areas (say, engineers talking to marketers) or across organizational boundaries (for example, when supply chain managers in a large firm communicate with small-firm vendors). Moreover, increasing CQ generally has been found to be related to increased levels of creative performance (Leung and Chiu, 2010), which could have important implications for organizational knowledge creation in general. When MNCs have successfully managed to overcome the numerous barriers to successful intercultural communication discussed in this chapter and created greater ethnorelativism and CQ within the organization and its individual members, they may hold an advantage in organizational learning over purely domestic firms, as well as firms that lack intercultural expertise.

While the managerial implications of our framework suggest considerable benefits as well as costs, there is a clear need to substantiate the relationships we have discussed and to explore relationships the framework implies for other areas. First and foremost is to determine whether the set of intercultural communication factors chosen for discussion here is indeed the complete set of variables most relevant to global organizational learning. Second, we need to identify the relative weights each of these factors has in affecting successful transfer of knowledge in global firms. Again, without empirical research specific to this research question, it is difficult to predict which factors might be most important in explaining successful intercultural communication in global organizational learning.

A further question pertains to the relative importance of individual versus organizational actors in the intercultural communication process. Are highly ethnorelative firms in which most individual employees lag behind in CQ and ethnorelativism (which could occur through international acquisitions, for example) more or less successful than firms in which there are many ethnorelative individuals with high CQ within an overall fairly ethnocentric organization? The challenge of finding firms with these various configurations will make research into this area difficult, and require creative research methodologies. Yet the question could be an important task since the answer is likely to influence how scarce managerial resources are allocated in global firms wishing to increase their global organizational learning.

Several implications of the framework also need research to substantiate their effects. It is necessary to determine whether more intercultural training and intercultural sensitivity correlates with a higher level of both global organizational learning and firm performance, a relationship suggested by prior research (Williams, 1947; Allport, 1954). Further, while on the surface there appear to be linkages among intercultural communication competence, cultural intelligence, intercultural sensitivity, and the capacity for global organizational learning, more research is needed to test whether ethnorelative organizations are more successful at organizational learning and whether people with high levels of intercultural communication competence and cultural intelligence are more skilled at organizational learning.

In addition, the work of Bennett and Bennett (2001), upon which this framework draws, provokes several questions for organizational learning scholars. Is it possible to identify discrete stages of organizational readiness to learn globally and, if so, do we have the knowledge to move organizations to higher stages? We can readily borrow the ethnocentric and ethnorelative terms and apply them to an organization's openness to knowledge that is created within and outside corporate HQ, similar to Perlmutter's (1969) taxonomy. Would the identification of more narrow and discrete stages lead us to more systematic ideas for increasing organizational readiness to learn?

It is important to note that this chapter does not argue that effective intercultural communication is the most important determinant of global organizational learning. While we have argued that communication is extremely important, particularly for the transfer of tacit knowledge between individuals and groups, it may be that other mechanisms in MNCs are just as important to global organizational learning, such as information systems. Given the nature of global competition today, we believe that it is unlikely that a mechanistic system that rests on the transfer of largely archival or explicit knowledge can be a substitute for the individual and organizational communication as described in this chapter. However, we recognize that establishing the veracity of this belief is an empirical question requiring future research.

Finally, this chapter has focused on aspects of intercultural communication that filter or impede organizational learning. Scholars could take the positive perspective and examine how intercultural diversity and communication facilitates, rather than impedes organizational learning.

REFERENCES

Adler, N. (2002) *International Dimensions of Organizational Behavior,* 4th edition. Cincinnati: South-Western.

Allport, G.W. (1954). *The Nature of Prejudice.* Reading: Addison-Wesley.

Ang, S. and Van Dyne, L. (2008) Conceptualization of cultural intelligence: Definition, distinctiveness, and nomological network. In S. Ang and L. Van Dyne (eds.) *Handbook of Cultural Intelligence: Theory, Measurement, and Applications.* Armonk: M.E. Sharpe, pp. 3–15.

Antal, A. (2001) Expatriates' contributions to organizational learning. *Journal of General Management,* 26(4): 62–83.

Apfelthaler, G. and Karmasin, M. (1998) Do you manage globally or does culture matter at all? Paper presented at the Academy of Management Conference, San Diego, CA.

Barna, L. (1983) The stress factor in intercultural relations. In D. Landis and R. Brislin (eds.) *Handbook of Intercultural Training: Issues in Training Methodology.* New York: Pergamon, pp. 19–49.

Barney, J. (1991) Firm resources and sustained competitive advantage. *Journal of Management,* 17: 99–120.

Barnlund, D. (1962) Toward a meaning-centered philosophy of communication. *Journal of Communication,* 2: 197–211.

Bartlett, C. and Ghoshal, S. (1989) *Managing Across Borders.* Boston: Harvard Business School Press.

Bartlett, C. and Ghoshal, S. (2000) *Transitional Management.* Boston: Irwin McGraw-Hill.

Bennett, J. (1993) Cultural Marginality: Identity Issues in Intercultural Training. In R. M. Paige (ed.) *Education for the Intercultural Experience.* Yarmouth: Intercultural Press, pp. 109–135.

Bennett, J. and Bennett, M. (2001) *Developing intercultural sensitivity: An integrative approach to global and domestic diversity.* In D. Landis, J.M. Bennett and M.J. Bennett (eds.). *Handbook of intercultural training,* 3rd ed, pp 147–165. Thousand Oaks: Sage.

Bennett, M. (1993) Towards ethnorelativism: A developmental model of intercultural sensitivity. In R.M. Paige (ed.) *Education for the Intercultural Experience.* Yarmouth: Intercultural Press, pp. 21–71.

Bernhut, S (2001) Measuring the value of intellectual capital. *Ivey Business Journal,* 65(4): 16–20.

Birkinshaw, J. (2001) Making sense of knowledge management. *Ivey Business Journal,* 65(4): 32–36.

Bochner, S. (ed.) (1982) *The Mediating Person: Bridges Between Cultures.* Boston: Hall.

Brannen, M.Y. and Peterson, M. F. (2009) Merging without alienating: Interventions promoting cross-cultural organizational integration and their limitations. *Journal of International Business Studies,* 40(3): 468–489.

Brewer, M.B. and Miller, N. (1984) Beyond the contact hypothesis: Theoretical perspectives on desegregation. In N. Miller and M. Brewer (eds.) *Groups in Contact: The Psychology of Desegregation.* New York: Academic Press, pp. 281–302.

Brown, J.S. and Duguid, P. (1991) Organizational learning and communities-of-practice: Toward a unified view of working, learning, and innovation. *Organization Science,* 2(1): 40–57.

Brown, R. and Turner, J. (1981) Interpersonal and intergroup behavior. In J. Turner and Giles, H. (eds.) *Intergroup Behavior.* Chicago: University of Chicago Press, pp. 33–65.

Burgoon, J., Buller, D., and Woodall, W.G. (1996) *Nonverbal Communication: The Unspoken Dialogue*. New York: McGraw-Hill.

Chakrabarti, R., Gupta-Mukherjee, S. and Jayaraman, N. (2009) Mars–venus marriages: Culture and cross-border M&A. *Journal of International Business Studies*, 40(2): 216–236.

Christensen, D. and Rosenthal, R. (1982) Gender and nonverbal decoding skill as determinants of interpersonal expectancy effects. *Journal of Personality and Social Psychology*, 42: 75–87.

Cohen, A.P. (1985) *The Symbolic Construction of Community*. London/New York: Routledge.

Cohen, W. and Levinthal, D. (1990) Absorptive capacity: A new perspective on learning and innovation. *Administrative Science Quarterly*, 35(1): 128–152.

Cook, S. and Yanow, D. (1993) Culture and organizational learning. *Journal of Management Inquiry*, 2: 373–390.

Daft, R. and Weick, K. (1984) Toward a model of organizations as interpretation systems. *Academy of Management Review*, 3: 546–563.

De Geus, A. (1988) Planning as learning. *Harvard Business Review*, 66(2): 70–74.

Early, P. and Ang, S. (2003) *Cultural Intelligence: Individual Interactions Across Cultures*. Palo Alto: Stanford University Press.

Elenkov, D.S. and Pimental, J.R.C. (2008) Social intelligence, emotional intelligence and cultural intelligence: An integrative perspective. In S. Ang and L. Van Dyne, (eds.) *Handbook of Cultural Intelligence: Theory, measurement, and applications*. New York: ME Sharpe, pp. 289–305.

Fang, Y., Guo-Liang, F.J., Shige, M., and Beamish, P.W. (2010) Multinational firm knowledge, use of expatriates, and foreign subsidiary performance. *Journal of Management Studies*, 4(1): 27–54.

Fink, G., Meierewert S., and Rohr U. (2005) The use of repatriate knowledge in organizations. *Human Resource Planning*, 28(4): 30–36.

Furnham, A. and Bochner, S. (1986) *Culture Shock: Psychological Reactions to Unfamiliar Environments*. London: Methuen.

Garvin, D., (1993) Building a learning organization. *Harvard Business Review*, 71(4): 78–92.

Gouldner, A.W. (1957) Cosmopolitans and locals: Toward an analysis of latent social roles – I. *Administrative Science Quarterly*, 2: 281–306.

Gouldner, A.W. (1958) Cosmopolitans and locals: Toward an analysis of latent social roles – II. *Administrative Science Quarterly*, 2: 444–480.

Graf, J. (1994) Views on Chinese. In Y. Bao (Ed.) *Zhong Guo Ren, Ri Shou Le Shen Me Zhu Zhou? Chinese People, What Have You Been Cursed With?* Taipai: Xing Guang Ban She.

Griffith, T. (1999) Technology features as triggers for sensemaking. *Academy of Management Review*, 24(3): 472–488.

Gudykunst, W. and Kim, Y.Y. (1997) *Communicating With Strangers: An Approach to Intercultural Communication*. Boston: McGraw-Hill.

Gudykunst, W. and Ting-Toomey, S. with Chua, E. (1988) *Culture and Interpersonal Communication*. Newbury Park: Sage.

Gupta, A. and Govindarajan, V. (1991) Knowledge flows and the structure of control within multinational corporations. *Academy of Management Review*, 16(4): 768–792.

Hall, E.T. (1976) *Beyond Culture*. New York: Random House.

Hamel, G. and Prahalad, C.K. (1994) *Competing for the Future*. Boston: Harvard Business School Press.

Hannerz, U. (1996) Cosmopolitans and locals in world culture. In U. Hannerz (ed). *Transnational Connections: Culture, People, Places*. London: Routledge, 102–111.

Heavens, S. and Child, J. (1999) Mediating individual and organizational learning: The role of teams and trust. Paper Presented at the 1999 Organization Learning Conference, Lancaster University, Lancaster, England.

Hofstede, G. (1980) *Culture's Consequences*. Beverly Hills: Sage.

Hong, Y., Morris, M., Chiu, C-Y., and Benet-Martinez, V. (2000) Multicultural minds: A dynamic constructivist approach to culture and cognition. *American Psychologies*, 55: 709–720.

Huber, G. (1991) Organizational learning: The contributing processes and the literatures. *Organization Science*, 2(1): 88–115.

Hult, T., Nichols, E., Giunipero, L., and Hurley, R. (2000) Global organizational learning in the supply chain: A low versus high learning study. *Journal of International Marketing*, 8(3): 61–83.

Inkpen, A.C. and Crossan, M. (1995) Believing is seeing: Joint ventures and organizational learning. *Journal of Management Studies*, 32(5): 595–618.

Inkpen, A.C. and Dinur, A. (1998) Knowledge management processes and international joint ventures. *Organization Science*, 9(4): 454–468.

Kamoche, K. (1996) Strategic human resource management within a resource-capability view of the firm. *Journal of Management Studies*, 33(2): 213–234.

Kim, D. (1993) The link between individual and organizational learning. *Sloan Management Review*, 35(1): 37–50.

Kim, Y. (1988) *Communication and Cross-Cultural Adaptation: An Integrative Theory*. Clevedon: Multilingual Matters.

Kim, Y. (1989a) Intercultural adaptation. In M. Asante and W. Gudykunst (eds.) *Handbook of International and Intercultural Communication*. Newbury Park: Sage, pp. 275–299.

Kim, Y. (1989b) Explaining interethnic conflict. In J. Gittler (ed.) *The Annual Review of Conflict Knowledge and Conflict Resolution*, New York: Garland, pp. 101–125.

Klafehn, J., Banerjee, P.M., and Chiu, C. (2008) Navigating Cultures: The role of meta-cognitive cultural intelligence. In S. Ang and L. Van Dyne, (eds.) *Handbook of Cultural Intelligence: Theory, measurement, and applications*. New York: ME Sharpe, p. 327.

Kogut, B. and Zander, U. (1992) Knowledge of the firm, combinative capabilities, and the replication of technology. *Organization Science*, 3: 383–397.

Langer, E. (1997) *Mindfulness*. Reading: Addison-Wesley.

Leonard-Barton, D. (1995) *Wellsprings of Knowledge*. Boston: Harvard Business School Press.

Leung, A.K-Y. and Chiu, C-Y. (2010) Multicultural experiences, idea receptiveness, and creativity. *Journal of Cross-Cultural Psychology*. In press.

Leung, K. and Li, F. (2008) Social axioms and cultural intelligence: Working across cultural boundaries. *Annual Review of Psychology*, 58: 579–514.

Levy, O., Beechler, S., Taylor, S., and Boyacigiller, N. (2007) What we talk about when we talk about 'Global Mindset': Managerial cognition in multinational corporations. *Journal of International Business Studies*, 38(2): 231–258.

Louis, M.R. and Sutton, R. (1991) Switching cognitive gears: From habits of mind to active thinking. *Human Relations*, 44: 55–76.

Lustig, M. and Koester, J. (1999) *Intercultural Competence: Interpersonal Communication Across Cultures*. New York: Longman Addison-Wesley.

McCauley, C., Stitt, C.L., and Segal, M. (1980) Stereotyping: From prejudice to prediction. *Psychological Bulletin*, 29:195–208.

Merton, R.K. (1957). Patterns of influence: Local and cosmopolitan influentials. In R. K. Merton (ed.) *Social Theory and Social Structure*. Glencoe: Free Press, 368–380.

Napier, N.K. (2010). *Insight: Encouraging Aha Moments for Organizational Success*. Westport, CT: Praeger Publishers.

Napier, N.K. and Taylor, S. (2010) The aha experience in managing global organizations. In V. Kannan (ed.), *Going Global: Implementing International Business Operations*. Westport, CT: Praeger.

Nohria, N. and Ghoshal, S. (1997) The differentiated network. San Francisco: Jossey-Bass.

Nonaka, I. (1994). A dynamic theory of organizational knowledge creation. *Organizational Science*, 5(1): 14–37.

Nonaka, I. and Takeuchi, H. (1995) *The Knowledge-Creating Company*. New York: Oxford University Press.

Oddou, G., Osland, J., and Blakeney, R. (2009) Repatriating knowledge: Variables influencing the 'Transfer' process.' *Journal of International Business Studies*, 40: 181–199.

O'Hair, D., Friedrich, G., Wiemann, J., and Wiemann, M. (1997) *Competent Communication*. New York: St. Martin's Press.

Osland, J. (1995) *The Adventure of Working Abroad: Hero Tales From the Global Frontier*. San Francisco, CA: Jossey-Bass.

Osland, J. and Bird, A. (2000) Beyond sophisticated stereotyping: Cultural sensemaking. *Academy of Management Executive*, 14(1): 65–77.

Osland, J. and Bird, A. (2001) Trigger events in cultural sensemaking. Paper presented at the Institute for Research on Intercultural Cooperation Conference, the Netherlands.

Osland, J., Bird, A., and Gundersen, A. (2008) Trigger events in intercultural sensemaking. Paper presented at the Academy of International Business Meeting, Milan, Italy.

Perlmutter, H. (1969) The tortuous evolution of the multinational corporation. *Columbia Journal of World Business*, January–February: 9–18.

Pettigrew, T.F. (2008) Future directions for intergroups contact theory and research. *International Journal of Intercultural Relations*, 32(3): 182–199.

Pettigrew, T.F. and Tropp, L.R. (2000) Does intergroup contact reduce prejudice? Recent meta-analytic findings. In S. Oskamp (Ed.) *Reducing Prejudice and Discrimination*. Mahwah: Erlbaum: 93–113.

Reiche, B.S., Harzing, A., Kraimer, M.L., Reus, T.H., and Lamont, B.T. (2009) The Double-edged sword of cultural distance in international acquisitions. *Journal of International Business Studies*, 40(8): 1298–1314.

Reus, T.H. and Lamont, B.T. (2009) The double-edged sword of cultural distance in international acquisitions. *Journal of International Business Studies*, 40(8): 1298–1314.

Senge, P. (1990) *The Fifth Discipline*. London: Century.

Simon, H.A. (1976) *Administrative Behavior*. New York: Free Press.

Stephan, W. and Stephan, C. (1985) Intergroup anxiety. *Journal of Social Issues*, 41(3): 157–175.

Stonequist, E. (1932) *The Marginal Man: A Study in the Subjective Aspect of Cultural Conflict.* Chicago: Chicago University Press.

Thich, N.H. (1991) *Peace is Every Step: The Path of Mindfulness in Everyday Life.* New York: Bantam Books.

Ting-Toomey, S. (1999) *Communicating Across Cultures.* New York: Guilford.

Tushman, M. and O'Reilly III, C. (1997) *Winning Through Innovation.* Boston: Harvard Business School Press.

Williams, R.M., Jr. (1947) *The Reduction of Intergroup Tensions.* New York, NY: Social Science Research Council.

Zander, U. and Zander, L. (2010) Opening the grey box: Social communities, knowledge and culture in acquisitions. *Journal of International Business Studies,* 41: 27–37.

27

Collaborating, Learning and Leveraging Knowledge Across Borders: A Meta-Theory of Learning

JANE E. SALK AND BERNARD L. SIMONIN

ABSTRACT

Research on collaborative learning has not kept up with the proliferation of forms of organization and governance used in practice. Not only is research on collaborative learning weak in terms of breadth of forms, the structure of related research streams inhibits the degree to which the multilevel processes and mechanisms can be identified and linked. Joint ventures (JVs) and strategic alliances continue to garner much of the attention paid to learning across organizational boundaries, although many other types of inter-organizational collaboration occur where learning potential and needs also are strong. Many influential studies focus almost exclusively on organizational or inter-organizational level data and phenomena, usually with a structural orientation, despite the implicit or explicit importance accorded to group and individual level social processes and mechanisms in the learning theories drawn upon. Meanwhile, those most concerned with individual and group-level cross-boundary learning work in domains such as International HRM and within the rapidly developing area of Geographically Dispersed Teams. Hence, it is time to extend and revisit our earlier effort to create a broader conceptualization and more elaborated map of the domain. To that end, we offer a meta-framework to systematize and encapsulate learning and knowledge-driven issues rooted in a fast evolving and diverse set of literatures.

INTRODUCTION

Since the turn of the century, interest in diverse forms of inter-organizational relationships has proliferated in practice as well as in the most prestigious outlets for management studies. As the lowering of trade and investment barriers coincided with widespread access to ever cheaper and more sophisticated means of control, coordination, and communication (Friedman, 2006), many businesses and entrepreneurs have taken advantage of these changes to create more far-flung and complex supply chains, geographically dispersed teams, and network firms. Recent research has emphasized the importance of understanding the structural position of firms in inter-organizational networks (such as in the case with supply chains) and what sorts of structural arrangements encourage or impede knowledge transfer (Easterby-Smith, Lyles, and Tsang, 2008). Moreover, contemporary research that looks more closely at intraorganizational versus inter-organizational learning, frequently does so in order to link it explicitly to innovation and the creation and sustaining of firm capabilities (Hult, Ketchun, and Arrfelt, 2007; Easterby-Smith et. al., 2008).

This context creates a challenge for management scholars to redress the limits of theoretical and empirical understanding about structuring and the processes internal to an organization that foster taking both internally and externally generated knowledge and combining these to exploit current performance strengths or create new ones. The challenge is rendered more difficult by the tendency of research relevant to this larger question being dispersed across different scholarly communities. These boundaries have not been conducive to cross-fertilization and building more general theories of learning.

Our objective is to provide a new, more encompassing meta-framework to help map the inter-organizational collaborative learning and knowledge management field more rationally and systematically. Compared to Salk and Simonin's (2003) earlier overview of the field, the literatures that deal with one or more aspects of collaborative learning have become both more numerous and more diverse. Our contention is that learning and knowledge-driven issues rooted in diverse organizational settings can be encapsulated under this single, unifying paradigm. Hence, we shall review and attempt to distill commonalities and key issues across literatures that rarely address one another, even if they might invoke certain shared foundations as in March (1991) and Cohen and Levinthal (1989). Now that our intentions are clear, henceforth, when referring to collaborative learning alliances, we mean organizational collaborations of all types, from equity joint ventures, to outsourcing, to cross-functional/cross organizational development teams.

Collaborative learning refers to joint action and sense making in a purposive relationship for which the identification, transfer, and experimentation with knowledge originating with another entity has the potential to enhance existing competence or create new competence (Lane, Salk, and Lyles, 2001; Easterby-Smith et. al., 2008; Holmqvist, 2004). The notion of a purposive relationship is important because goals lead to theories or expectations about the experience and knowledge residing in the partner that might or might not manifest in actual collaboration. Hence, the key is 'purposive' and this need not (and usually will not) involve learning as the central objective. All three of the activities—identification, transfer, and experimentation—might entail active intent and involvement by more than one entity (e.g. one organization motivated to teach and the other motivated to learn). However, the experimentation with identified and transferred knowledge might often occur in multiple entities without interdependence (e.g. each partner takes knowledge from an IJV and brings it in house to experiment and recombine). The entities may be groups or individuals as well as organizations. In the case of new geographically dispersed teams, increasingly used for projects such as product development (Cramdon and Hinds, 2005; O'Leary and Mortensen, 2010), members' interdependencies translate into effective knowledge also leveraging learning via development of a transactive memory (Moreland

and Myaskovsky 2000). This memory becomes a property of the team when individuals can differentiate, identify, and integrate in action the different domains of expertise of individuals and across sites (O'Leary and Mortensen, 2010). We shall further expand upon this definition and its implications in mapping and synthesizing our framework from recent scholarly works.

Mapping the Collaborative Learning Field

Press accounts continue to be full of stories of underperforming or discontinued JVs and other inter-firm collaborations. JVs and strategic alliances more generally, thus, continue to have rates of failure estimated to be up to sixty percent. We are unaware of the precise figures for other cooperative arrangements, though we would assert that those outsourcing, geographically dispersed project teams and offshoring arrangements that involve knowledge application and exchange from more than one participant (unlike a typical sourcing arrangement by WalMart) do likely suffer from frequent failure to exploit learning potential to optimize the rents or other competitive advantages for the system of collaboration (i.e. the member organizations). The most modern organizations in one way or another extend their boundaries to gain strategic advantages (Cooper and Rousseau, 1999). Since the strongest and most enduring advantages accrue from unique configurations of structure, culture, and knowledge within the organization, this suggests that issues surrounding knowledge transfer and learning comprise a core issue for most modern organizations whether or not explicitly stated as a strategic priority.

In the following sections we organize our inquiry using questions that arose from our readings and discussions. Why should inter-organizational collaborations be viewed as platforms for learning? What is inter-organizational learning; who learns (the levels of analysis engaged)? Where does knowledge in inter-organizational collaborations accumulate, get transferred, and stored? What is the role of time (when)? How does learning occur? And how much learning does or should occur to reap benefits? We then synthesize from this exploration a framework of collaborative learning.

Why should inter-organizational collaborations be viewed as platforms for learning?

In the strategic alliance literature, many scholars, including Grant and Baden-Fuller (1995), Khanna, Gulati, and Nohria (1998), Kogut (1988), and Kogut and Zander (1992) have long viewed knowledge acquisition and learning as primary reasons for the formation of collaborative alliances. The 'learning race' perspective (Hamel, Doz, and Prahalad 1989; Khanna et al., 1998) assumes a strategic intent to learn from the partner, and advances the idea that competitive advantage accrues to the entity that learns faster and more effectively than the other. However, Hennart and Zeng, (2002), Hagedoorn and Sadowski (1999), and Inkpen (2000) all suggest that few partners have 'racing' intents and call into question the assumption that many or most alliances have clear learning objectives. Zeng and Hennart (2001) go a step further to suggest that 'many learning races are alliances "gone bad" rather than the normal and desirable way alliances should evolve' (2001: 1). In fact, Grant and Baden-Fuller (1995) argue that the main advantage of alliances over firms and markets is in accessing knowledge (rather than acquiring knowledge). They propose that the distinction between the acquisition and accessing of knowledge is similar to the difference between knowledge exploration and exploitation (Levitt and March, 1988). Thus, the main issue with alliances is the efficiency and effectiveness of knowledge utilization and the learning race, in itself, is immaterial.

These concepts of exploration and exploitation have received substantial attention in the strategy literature more generally (Birkinshaw and Gibson, 2004; Crossan and Bedrow, 2003; Lavie and Rosenkopf, 2006). Much recent literature assumes that exploration and exploitation each undermine the other due to contradictory requirements. However, Holmqvist (2004) suggests that this is incorrect. He identifies four interrelated organizational learning processes: opening-up/extension, opening-up/internalization, focusing/internalization, and focusing/extension. Opening-up/extension refers to a situation where intraorganizational exploitation (for example, a desire to extend products into new markets) motivates the search for external partners whose experience creates variety and hence can be seen as an opening up or exploration of the others' experiences. The ensuing inter-organization bargaining and learning, however, likely will lead to the organization choosing to focus and work upon translating particular knowledge for exploitation; hence it naturally becomes a process of focusing/exploitation (Holmqvist, 2004: 71).

It is also common that an organization looks for partners with related knowledge to generate learning that exploits or extends already existing internal capabilities (Lane and Lubatkin, 1998). Holmqvist (2004) refers to this as opening-up/internalization. As the partners interact, this again leads to variety, as the experiences are not identical. Eventually only some knowledge is focused upon by internal actors and this leads to focusing/extension; to completely internalize and use this knowledge it has to be experimented with—hence intra-organizational exploration will ensue in order to learn how to incorporate it in a reliable way to push experience curves or other factors that are part of the organizations' 'existing language' and experience base (Holmqvist, 2004:71).

By looking across levels at intraorganizational learning priorities and then at the inter-organizational dynamic, Holmqvist (2004) suggests that joint efforts or exploration can naturally lead to a phase of joint exploitation, since internal exploration ultimately is costly. Conversely, an example where joint exploitation is anticipated can quickly become one of internal exploration as one or both partner organizations get feedback from their interaction suggesting that the existing competencies cannot produce satisfactory results without translation and possible reinvention.

Hence, while many scholars would argue that firms choose 'learning' strategies emphasizing exploration as the path to innovation, we regard the implications of Holmqvist's research as an indication that at some point even the most self-confident and self-satisfied organizations are likely to experience an erosion of their competence relative to the competition and a diminished capacity to generate internal variety of experience. Hence collaborative learning, over the longer haul, is a key aspect to sustained value creation for all organizations and also for tightly linked inter-organizational networks. How collaborative learning plays itself out for different sorts of organizations and different forms of collaboration will be taken up in a later section.

A final issue highlighted by the literature is that the sense of dissatisfaction and urgency to look for knowledge and learn varies throughout an organization. In the case of alliances, for example, top management and members of a negotiating team often frame strategic intents, while groups and individuals actually responsible for the implementation and management of the collaboration are often different and might or might not fully understand and share these intents (Harrigan, 1986). It is also possible that individuals at lower levels of an organization have more dissatisfaction and better perceive learning opportunities than do their superiors. In the case of NUMMI, for example, General Motors' employees who actually went to Japan and trained in Toyota often were far more enthused by the different culture and systems they encountered than were their superiors back home. New knowledge brought back from NUMMI tended to be rejected by the General Motors organization where it more likely would be seen as a challenge to their competence or culturally inappropriate. Hence, understanding knowledge transfer and learning dynamics entails paying more attention to different actors' intents and their relationship to incentive systems, organizational structures, and other context factors.

What is learning and who/what is learned?

There is little convergence in defining and identifying proxies for 'learning.' Moreover, its definition may be virtually identical or quite different from knowledge acquisition. From a logical point of view, libraries, encyclopedias, and so on can be seen as vast repositories of 'knowledge.' Only when a book is dusted off and attentively read (or a web site discovered, opened, and studied by human eyes) does a potential for internalization and integration of that knowledge exist. Beyond internalization, the acquired knowledge can result in a change in the efficacy of current behaviors without fundamentally altering goals. Or it can result in changes of goals and routines not likely to have occurred without that particular knowledge.

A looser use of 'learning' is evidence of knowledge embedded in the experience of one entity moving across the boundary to become part of a knowledge base in another organization. A stricter definition requires that the entity acquiring the knowledge translates and at least experiments with using it. Hence evidence of learning comes from seeing changes in activities or new elements of practice somewhere in the organization (Lane, Salk, and Lyles, 2001). If the experience gains positive feedback and/or eludes various social or technical obstacles, it may result in an enduring change in routines. Other knowledge, as alluded to earlier in the example of NUMMI, might meet social and political opposition that greatly limits its potential to have an enduring and positive impact on the receiving organization (in our example General Motors). This is somewhat analogous to the strategic relevance or 'usefulness' of learning that emerged from the empirical analysis in Lane et al. (2001).

In terms of who learns, scholars increasingly concur that micro processes of perception and learning underpin macro-level routines and patterns of transfer and learning (Easterby-Smith et al. 2008; Lewin, Massini, and Peeters, 2010). This is an unfortunate lacunae in research. However, we suggest that macro-level scholars of alliances and other forms of inter-organizational learning should turn their attention to the theory development and empirical base of findings accumulated by the research stream devoted to geographically dispersed teams. There is a logical linkage between the motivations that lead to the creation of dispersed teams and creation of inter-organizational alliances. Experts recommend teams in situations that require diversity of information, complementary expertise, and resources. Similarly, alliances and JVs have been recommended for these same rationales, among others. What is interesting about the micro-level team research is that it concurrently has research and theory linking issues of structure, governance, and psychosocial dynamics such as identification and trust. (Articles providing a review of this literature include Polzer, Crisp, Jarvenpaa, and Kim, 2006.) Much like the Holmqvist (2004) research summarized earlier, among the relevant findings in this literature is preferred conditions to encourage identification and knowledge transfer. This includes minimizing the overlap of ethnic, organizational and other sources of faultlines (O'Leary and Mortensen, 2010) that gives a firmer theoretical grounding to similar suggestions stemming from a macro-level study of a fifty/fifty JV (Salk and Shenkar, 2001).

Turning to the 'What is learned?' question, four areas of interest have attracted attention: knowledge types, knowledge characteristics, cognitive versus behavioral manifestations of learning, and collaborative know-how as both a type of knowledge in itself and a possible moderator of the learning process in alliances.

Knowledge types. In alliances, whether or not organizations have a well-defined learning agenda and a clear strategic intent for seeking knowledge transfer, types of knowledge that may ultimately be developed or transferred in the context of an alliance remain constant. In the business world, knowledge related to markets, internationalization, marketing activities, research and development, design, procurement and logistics, production and manufacturing processes, human resource management practices, finance and accounting, and strategy have the potential to become sources of competitive advantage. As such, they may be both coveted and protected. In nonprofit organizations, fundraising and grant proposal development skills represent valuable knowledge-based counterparts. In the public sector, knowledge ranging from diplomatic savoir-faire to institutional and administrative expertise also represents critical assets. Alliances can be the stage for the deployment of, or exposure to, any of these knowledge types, some of which are more or less vital to a given organization. The same holds in intrafirm alliances. For instance, foreign subsidiaries of a multinational organization operating in various countries can benefit from the sharing of best practices, technologies, manufacturing processes, and new product development initiatives through collaborative programs.

Attempts to not only recognize, but also isolate and measure different types of knowledge are rare. In their study of learning by international joint ventures (IJVs), Lane, Salk, and Lyles (2001) look at the knowledge acquired from foreign parents, explicitly identifying the types of knowledge under consideration: managerial techniques, technological expertise, marketing expertise, manufacturing and production processes, and product development expertise. To date, a strong focus on technology dominates research related to organizational learning and alliances, be it a target for learning or a context for studying knowledge transfer. Among the numerous studies of technology-based alliances (e.g. Dodgson 1996, Eisenhardt and Schoohoven, 1996; Hagedoorn and Schakenraad 1994, Khanna, Gulati, and Nohria, 1998; Moensted, 2010) some have focused on research and development issues (e.g. Philbin, 2008; Olk 1997; Sampson 2001) while others have looked at specific industries ranging from biotechnology (e.g. Pisano 1988; Powell, Koput, and Smith-Doerr 1996; Mets, 2006) to semiconductors (e.g. Appleyard 1996 and 2001; Phene, Madhok, and Liu, 2005). The less plentiful studies focusing upon non-technology related knowledge include the study of marketing know-how (Simonin and Ozsomer, 2009; Simonin 1999b; Aulakh, Kotabe, and Sahay, 1996), franchising skills (Darr, Argote, and Epple,

1995), and collaborative know-how (Kale and Singh 2000; Simonin, 2000, 2004). Much remains unexplored in light of this imbalance between research focus and the diversity of knowledge types.

Knowledge characteristics. Understanding knowledge characteristics (and the organizational structures that support them) is key to understanding knowledge flows, transfers, storage, and lack thereof. In alliances, beyond the characteristics of knowledge seekers and knowledge providers, and the nature of their interrelationship, knowledge-specific variables shape the transferability of any given form of know-how (Simonin, 1999b; 2004). Alliance researchers overwhelmingly point to knowledge characteristics of tacitness and the work of Polanyi (1967), often ignoring all other facets or, at best, collapsing them into a single, uni-dimensional variable. Tacitness has been the proxy of choice for assessing the difficulty (or ease) of accumulating and transferring knowledge. However, since there are many types of knowledge, there are also many other distinct characteristics of knowledge to account for. Some characteristics are completely knowledge-intrinsic whereas others are also linked to the situation of both the knowledge seeker and provider.

Besides tacitness, complexity and specificity have been considered antecedents of causal and knowledge ambiguity (Reed and DeFillippi, 1990; Simonin, 1999a, 1999b, 2004). Complexity captures the number of interdependent routines, technologies, resources, and individuals linked to a specific asset or knowledge. More complex human or technological systems generate higher levels of ambiguity and, therefore, restrain imitation (Reed and DeFillippi, 1990). Research on these aspects yields mixed results. Zander and Kogut (1995) find no significant direct relationship between complexity and the speed of transfer of manufacturing related knowledge. Likewise, Simonin (1999b) observed no effect of complexity on the transferability of marketing know-how between alliance partners. On the other hand, he found significant effects in the case of the transfer of technology and manufacturing process know-how between partners (Simonin 1999a). Moreover, specificity was significant in the transfer of marketing know-how, particularly when collaborative experience of the knowledge seeker is limited and the alliance is not yet mature but not in the case of the transfer of technology and process knowledge. Here, specificity captures notions of durable investments and specialized knowledge undertaken or developed in the context of particular collaborative relationships.

Other knowledge characteristics likely to impact the pace, depth, and meaningfulness of learning in alliances include validity, novelty, relatedness, uniqueness, value, and actionability. *Validity* means that the knowledge is given accurately, reliably, and validly represents. *Novelty* captures the time dimension of knowledge; is it new, timely, or obsolete? *Relatedness* refers to the degree to which a knowledge seeker is familiar or has prior experience with a given knowledge platform, principles, or context—does it fit the existing knowledge base and portfolio? *Uniqueness* refers to the presence or absence of alternate, substitutable bodies of knowledge. Uniqueness differs from specificity in that the focus is not on the co-specialization of knowledge with the alliance, but rather on the presence of competing knowledge bases. *Value* can be construed as market value (absolute value) or as the value of knowledge to a partner given its specific capabilities, history, context, and ambitions (relative value). Finally, *actionability* relates to the readiness, receptivity (Hamel 1991), and ability of the organization to utilize and leverage particular knowledge. Obviously, we would expect new, valid, unique, related, and actionable knowledge to be more valuable.

Cognitive versus behavioral. The proper operationalization and measurement of learning and learning outcomes remains a challenge. At the heart of this challenge lies the dual manifestation of learning: both behavioral and cognitive (Fiol and Lyles, 1985). For instance, learning might be inferred from witnessing the adoption of a new product testing procedure inspired by an alliance partner (behavioral), or from observing the rise of a common and consistent conceptual understanding by JV managers about how to lobby in foreign markets (cognitive). Both manifestations of learning deserve research attention. Changes in routines, procedures, processes, actions, physical output, and structures (behavioral side) must be reconciled with changes in cognitive maps, conceptual representations, mental associations, shared beliefs, and understanding (cognitive side).

Collaborative know-how. In the context of alliances and organizational learning research, collaborative know-how plays an important role. By focusing on alliances and collaborative know-how, one draws and controls specific research boundaries under which to study organizational learning. Simonin (2002) argues that collaborative know-how can be considered a unique type of competence, one that may help explain why some alliances succeed brilliantly while others fail dramatically, and why some organizations are able to leverage their network of collaborative arrangements more effectively than others. Likewise, Kanter (1994), considering intercompany relationships as key business assets, maintains that the know-how to create and sustain fruitful collaboration, or collaborative advantage, 'gives companies a significant leg up.' In short, collaborative know-how is to collaborative advantage what a firm's core competency is to competitive advantage (Simonin, 2002). This alliance capability has increasingly captured the attention of researchers (e.g. Lyles, 1988; Simonin, 1997; Dyer and Singh, 1998; Gulati, 1999; Lorenzoni and Lipparini, 1999; Anand and Khanna, 2000; Appleyard, 2001; Kale, Dyer, and Singh, 2001; Heimeriks and Duysters, 2007; Mascarenhas and Koza, 2008; Weber and Khademian, 2008; Schreiner, Kale, and Corsten, 2009; Kale and Singh, 2009).

Thus, identifying, mapping, and measuring a firm's level of collaborative know-how constitute a critical first step in understanding organizational learning processes and performance in alliances. Most research to date has focused on prior experience as a proxy to actual knowledge and evidence of learning. Research results pertaining to the effects of experience remain mixed. Lei and Slocum (1992) trace the root causes of failures and alliance problems to ignorance and lack of experience. On the other hand, Barkema, Shenkar, Vermeulen, and Bell (1997) conclude that past JV experience does not favor alliance survival. Powell, Koput, and Smith-Doerr (1996) argue that collaborative experience is necessary not only to manage a diverse portfolio of alliances, but also to develop the capability to extract value from these alliances. Anand and Khanna (2000) report mixed results with a significant effect of experience in the case of JVs but not in the case of licensing agreements. More recently, using an event study methodology on US companies, Reuer, Park, and Zollo (2001) found that prior experience with international IJVs has no apparent effect on the performance of new IJVs (measured by the firm's valuation effects of the venture's announcement). Likewise, in her study of research and development alliances in the telecom equipment industry, Sampson (2001) found that prior experience increases collaborative benefits up to a point; whereas some degree of experience helps performance, extensive experience does not. More recently, Heimericks and Duysters (2007) showed that both experience and alliance capabilities shape alliance performance.

While collaborative experience is a construct of great theoretical importance in its own right, it nevertheless represents a concept distinct from collaborative know-how. In general, experience is considered a key antecedent of know-how. Research initiatives that have attempted to isolate the higher-order construct of collaborative know-how and its development include Appleyard (2001), Simonin (2000), and Schreiner, Kale and Corsten (2009). Simonin (2000) delineates empirically a multidimensional construct of collaborative know-how that singles out five distinct factors: partner search and selection, negotiating, managing and monitoring, knowledge and skill transfers, and exiting. Each one of these factors encompasses various specialized activities and types of skills. It is still unclear how collaborative know-how accumulates and decays, how it impacts performance, and why it varies across organizations. Of further interest, the comparison between inter-organizational and intraorganizational collaborative know-how as well as across units of analysis (in particular, what collaborative know-how means for individuals and network-like structures) represents a promising research area. At the individual level, for example, research on social intelligence (Goleman, 2006) or cultural intelligence (Thomas, 2006) could be explored as antecedents of alliance team performance and even in terms of whether and how these might be moderated by structural context. Finally, future research might shed additional light on the role of experiential versus non-experiential learning by isolating the respective effects of collaborative experience and collaborative know-how.

Who knows and who learns? Units of analysis, governance, and organization forms

Learning and knowledge acquisition occur at individual, team or group, organizational, and inter-organizational levels of analysis (Nonaka and Takeuchi 1995; Zander and Kogut, 2005). Learning also can occur via and in networks at any of these levels. Extended discussion of debates surrounding levels of analysis and their incorporation into models of learning exists (see Vera and Crossan, 2003). Alliance research has emphasized the inter-organizational level of analysis (cf. Inkpen and Crossan, 1995; Lyles and Salk, 1996; Lane, Salk, and Lyles 2001). That said, the mechanisms through which learning is realized and potentially converted into performance, often indirectly inferred rather than directly observed, imply structures and processes at the organizational and sub-organizational levels. These include social network interactions and proximity of groups and individuals and will be enumerated and described in the next section on how learning occurs.

It is important for researchers and research streams focusing narrowly on JVs, alliances, mergers and acquisitions, franchising, licensing, and so on, to track approaches and developments in research looking at other specialties. One reason is that an outsourcing arrangement might lead to a JV or acquisition, a JV might end with one partner buying out the other as the end game—hence over time these forms can be interrelated in a developmental sense. Second, though human resources are critical factors in many types of learning, it is outside the 'mainstream' of managerial alliance research that one finds exemplars focusing on the role of individuals (cf., Darr, Argote, and Epple, 1995a; Metiu, 2001; Kane, Argote, and Levine, 2002). Clearly individuals are conduits of, or sensors for, learning and knowledge in a collaborative setting (cf. Nonaka and Takeuchi, 1995) and the effect of context can interact with individual characteristics to affect learning (Dickson and Weaver, 1997). The practice of sending expatriates and secondees to alliances reflects the recognition by managers that individuals play a vital role in scanning, sense making and learning in alliances (Kogut, Walker, and Kim 1995; Almeida and Kogut, 1999; Salk and Shenkar, 2001). Almeida and Kogut traced movements of individuals across firms and within and across geographic areas, linking movements of personnel to knowledge acquisition. The classic literature on boundary-spanners further underscores the vital role individuals and groups play in channeling flows of knowledge and as learners themselves (cf. Allen, 1977; Tushman, 1977).

Groups can be particularly important influences in socialization of members (Van Maanen and Schein, 1979), and in providing social support and norms to push knowledge residing in individuals or subgroups toward institutionalization. Du Chatenier, Verstegen, Biemans, Mulder, and Omta (2009: 353) argue that 'At an organizational level, knowledge is often viewed as a commodity and at the group or individual level as something that is situated in a context, or a personal capability.' This likely underlies robust evidence that individuals can be willing to exchange expertise on-line with virtual strangers—as in open source development. Thus, if we want to understand the role of individuals and social groups in bearing, transferring, and transforming knowledge that ultimately becomes organizational, it is critical to examine the role of extrinsic and intrinsic motivation (Osterloh and Frey, 2000; Simonin and Ozsomer, 2009) and factors affecting psychological contracts (Rousseau, 1995). Salk and Shenkar (2001) and Salk (1996) describe highly effect-charged environments found in at least some multinational alliance teams, with rampant stereotyping and in-group out-group dynamics. A network perspective would suggest that these dynamics should affect communication and motivation and, hence, knowledge and learning transfer processes. Social identity theory predicts that perceptual group boundaries should affect which groups and individuals are chosen as referents for knowledge and as sources of learning. Kane, Argote, and Levine (2002) assigned groups to superordinate and sub-group identity conditions and found that when members were rotated between groups, learning of superior production techniques was significantly higher when the member rotated into the group shared a common superordinate identity. Hence, research on the role of social identity processes and emotional climate in organizational learning in alliances would contribute greatly to illuminating this heretofore dark corner. As developed in the next section, it is logical that the key to understanding alliances is not choosing one level of analysis, but seeking to develop and test cross-level models and constructs of learning and learning processes.

Governance forms likely hold a key to understanding how levels of analysis relate to one another, and the capacity and motivation of various participants to learn. Governance form as a mechanism shaping structures and flows of knowledge will be discussed in the section on 'How learning occurs'. Centralized organizations might learn less effectively than N-form or simply more decentralized organizations. Possibly both can learn and chose modally different forms of collaboration to do so. While the dominant conduits and repositories of knowledge might tend to pull toward the center in hierarchies, hence suggesting the importance of thoroughly accounting for learning occurring at the organizational level, in network organizations, inter-individual and inter-group networks might be the dominant loci of learning and knowledge repositories. Beyond simple structural typologies, the degree to which bureaucratic structures and rules or strong, shared cultures dominate as governance mechanisms matters. The roles of individuals, groups, and the organization might well differ in their roles *vis à vis* knowledge recognition, acquisition, driving change based on learning, and acting as repositories in bureaucratically, versus culturally driven organizations (Schein, 1998).

Haspeslaugh and Jemison (1991: 145) in their work on mergers and acquisitions, develop a framework for mapping strategic intents onto the mode of implementation. They distinguish between intents that have high needs for interdependence (high to low) and needs for organizational autonomy (high to low). High autonomy/low interdependence strategic rationales occur when what is being acquired are skills and knowledge embedded in a particular organizational context; in such a scenario, a governance approach that buffers the acquired organization to preserve its special capabilities is required. By contrast, a strategic intent to rationalize capacity would fall into a high integration, low autonomy needs category. Unlike the previous example, hierarchies and systems need to be either subsumed or merged. Harrigan (1986) made a similar qualitative observation that, depending on the goals, a JV culture and way of operating sometimes needs to diverge greatly from those of the parents. Such distinctions might help push discussions of sticky–bleeding, tacit–explicit toward a more nuanced way of viewing the role between governance structures and learning, though it has yet to be picked up and further developed.

Where does learning occur and where is it stored in collaborative alliances?

Learning can occur and knowledge can be stored at multiple levels of analysis. The concept of organizational memory (Walsh and Ungeson, 1991) focuses attention upon non-human repositories, such as systems, structures, rules, and routines. Other theorists focus upon individuals as bearers of, and repositories for, knowledge and organizational change more generally (Argyris and Schön, 1978; Schein, 1993; Simon, 1991). Learning takes place among entities throughout cooperative systems. Zeng and Hennart (1991: 7) correctly point out that much research focuses on one participant's learning rather than the behavior of partners simultaneously or a network as a whole. The majority of studies reviewed focused on learning by partners; learning by the joint organization formed by the collaboration (Inkpen, 1995; Lyles and Salk, 1996; Lane, Salk, and Lyles, 2001) has received more limited attention.

Variables such as power and influence, motivation, and individual skills of those involved in collaborations would likely moderate the relationship between alliance structure and learning. Szulanski (1996), studying intrafirm transfers of best practice, found that in addition to the nature of the knowledge to be transferred (especially causal ambiguity), the characteristics of the knowledge recipient and the nature of the relational context (arduous relationships; laborious and distant relationships) were major impediments to transferring knowledge. Despite some recent breakthroughs (e.g. Minbaeva, 2005; Minbaeva, Foss, and Snell, 2009; Simonin and Ozsomer, 2009), most research on internal knowledge transfer within MNCs fails to account fully for the critical role HRM practices and procedures play in creating and sharing knowledge. Both organizational design issues (Foss and Pedersen, 2004) and HRM questions such as the provision of incentives, mentoring and coaching, supervisory encouragement, training, and even expatriation, call for further research attention.

Focusing upon a particular cooperation or focal organization also leads to potentially missing secondary effects entailing changes located in institutional fields. Collaborative know-how entails accruals of knowledge about how to manage relations across time and different specific partnerships. Lawrence, Hardy, and Phillips (2002) studied NGO collaborations in Palestine. These collaborations varied in their degree of involvement and embeddedness and this accounted for differences in the degree to which a collaboration resulted in proto-institutions: 'new practices, rules and technologies that transcend the particular collaborative relationship and may become new institutions if they diffuse sufficiently.' Thus, there might be dynamics of innovation and change missed by researchers that might have very important ramifications for future behavior and other outcomes associated with performance over time. For example, in a highly embedded field of firms, it is possible that collaborative practices not only evolve from the direct partnering experiences of firms, but also via diffusion and mimesis across the field that might ultimately transform practices and create innovations.

When does learning occur and when can we observe its effects?

Time is most certainly a critical dimension to understand any change or learning process (Ancona, Goodman, Lawrence, and Tushman, 2001). Alliances evolve and change over time (Salk, 1996; Inkpen and Beamish, 1997; Das and Kumar, 2007; Duso, Pennings, and Seldeslachts, 2010; Greve, Baum, Mitsuhashi, and Rowley, 2010). Moreover, the degree to which such changes are anticipated in practice or predictable is highly variable. Looking at the same IJVs in 1993 and 1996, Lane, Salk, and Lyles (2001) found that the modal types of learning and variables most strongly associated with learning from the foreign parent changed over that period. The learning races and bargaining power perspectives (Yan and Gray, 1994; Inkpen and Beamish, 1997) suggest that alliances can be unstable over time and, when they do not end, the nature and content of the relationships can be expected to change. However, process remains a sorely understudied aspect of alliances (Salk, 2005) and of organizational knowledge management in MNCs (Foss and Pedersen, 2004).

Though emphasis on time and timing in the organization studies and strategy literatures has been increasing, there is a lack of definitional and methodological coherence (Ancona, Okhuysen, and Perlow, 2001). In terms of organizational learning, the question of time raises fundamental questions. One approach to studying organizational learning over time has entailed tracing learning curves (Darr, Argote, and Epple 1995a; Argote, 2000; Barkema and Schijven, 2008). While learning curves suit settings and questions, and potentially could be incorporated and applied in more studies of alliances, this so far leaves a number of other time-related issues unexplored. Among these issues are timing and sequences of interdependence and dependence of factors underpinning learning and the acquisition and transformation of that learning. Does one map learning and knowledge processes in alliances in terms of critical incidents and events, in terms of transitions in networks, group dynamics, in terms of looking at feedback loops into the system or systems, or measurable changes in routines, behaviors, and outputs? Do firm, functional, and culture-specific differences in approaches to time (Hall, 1983; Ancona, Okhuysen, and Perlow, 2001) entail different approaches to learning, embedding, using, and storing knowledge? To what extent, and on which dimensions and levels, might a life-cycle model of organizational learning be plausible and researchable and how might co-evolution of contexts and alliances relate to this? Salk (1996) found that developmental patterns of multicultural IJV top teams follow a sort of punctuated equilibrium (see Gersick, 1989); issues of social identity and role investment often impede coordination and communication flows until a critical incident creates shared performance pressures, giving team members an incentive for role investment and motivation to adapt.

In short, while the dimension of time and timing is implicit in most theories and frameworks of organizational learning in alliances, this aspect has so far received inadequate attention in empirical research. The degree to which this is possibly the most fundamental gap in studies of alliances and organizational learning (and perhaps much of the organizational learning literature more generally) is further highlighted by looking in the next section at approaches to the question of how organizational learning is thought to occur in alliances.

Collaborative Learning

Mapping the field

From our prior discussion, it is evident that a great deal of interesting research is taking place. However, it is also clear that most empirical studies in this area focus on a few specific explanatory variables, sometimes on an *ad hoc* basis, providing only a partial explanation to the overall phenomenon. Moreover, different streams of research have their own norms about levels of analysis data and variables. While each study has the potential to add to our comprehension of a given facet of alliance learning, it also contributes to the fragmentation of our understanding. The big picture is lost.

To address this problem, we propose a generic taxonomy of variables related to the 'how?' question in Figure 27.1. Four distinct blocks of explanatory variables compose this conceptual framework and help organize logically variables of interest: (1) alliance-specific variables, (2) partner-specific variables, (3) knowledge-specific variables, and (4) context-specific variables.

For each block, we provide a list of pertinent variables. Lists are illustrative rather than exhaustive. The first block, alliance-specific variables, refers to many of the variables we have already introduced and discussed that may facilitate or impede the learning process. For instance, the importance of the form of the alliance (e.g. equity versus non-equity based) on learning constitutes a significant research question for many researchers.

Partner-specific variables, the model's second block, subsume many critical research variables such as absorptive capacity, prior experience, strategic intent, trust, protectiveness, and collaborative know-how. Much attention has been paid to issues surrounding trust and protectiveness, a major concern being proprietary know-how bleeding to partners (Hamel, Doz, and Prahalad 1989; Hamel, 1991; Khanna, Gulati, and Nohria 1998; Kale, Singh and Perlmutter, 2000; Kale and Singh, 2009).

Effective management of networks at the inter-organizational level also serves as a vital mechanism for knowledge acquisition. There are different kinds of networks and different schools of thought about the types of networks most conducive to learning. Some theorists emphasize exploiting structural holes in inter-firm networks to limit redundancy and to have a unique combination of access to information and knowledge by virtue of a distinctive position. Social network theory stressing cohesion and strength of ties suggests that the trust and social capital built up through dense repeated relations increases knowledge flows within these networks. These approaches have divergent views concerning the mechanisms and operationalizations of their transmission. Both are promising avenues, though we believe they probably will prove to explain effectiveness of different types of learning and knowledge exploration.

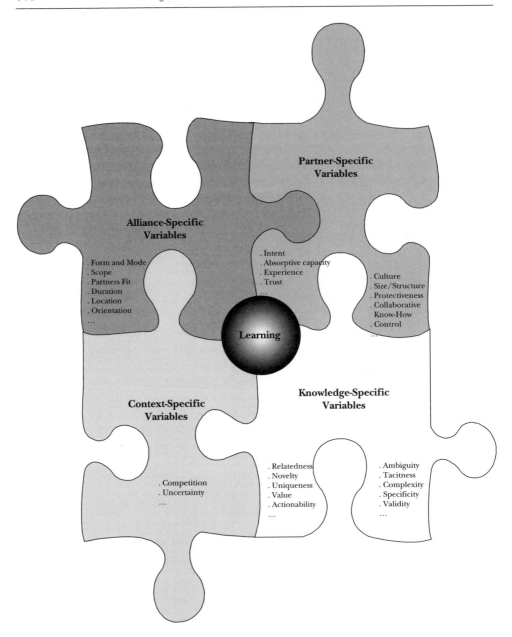

Figure 27.1 Learning and Alliances: Theoretical Building Blocks

A key concept underpinning both approaches so far and the concept underlying the 'how' in organizational learning more generally is that of absorptive capacity: the ability to identify, assimilate, and exploit knowledge (Cohen and Levinthal, 1989). To study knowledge transfers, it is helpful to distinguish between knowledge-seekers and knowledge-providers

(Simonin, 1999a; 2004) or learning versus teaching partners (Inkpen, 2001). In the IJV literature, Lyles and Salk (1996) identified structures and processes contributing to an IJV's capacity to absorb knowledge from the foreign parent. These included a flexible organization, written business plans and goals, a clear division of labor, and training by the foreign parent. These variables suggest (albeit indirectly) a mode of HRM and organizing that shapes cognitive orientations and informational networks within the alliance organization itself. Since then, Lane and Lubatkin (1998) have introduced the notion of relative absorptive capacity: the relatedness of the partnering firms' knowledge bases, organizational structure and compensation as proxies for similarity in the norms and learning processes in the organizations, and dominant logics as a proxy for the motivation and ability to use the knowledge acquired. Lane, Salk, and Lyles (2001) found support for the relative absorptive capacity construct in their study of IJVs. In their study, the relatedness of knowledge and organizational characteristics of flexibility and training by the foreign parent predicted knowledge acquisition by the foreign parent, while the dominant logic (differentiation) and training in the IJV (a diffusion mechanism) predicted performance.

Both experiential (through training, learning-by-doing) and non-experiential learning (via proximity, observation) are implied by these studies. In other research that looks at learning by firms in geographic clusters, flows of personnel are viewed as mechanisms for the grafting of new knowledge and skills from one firm to another (Almeida and Kogut, 1999). Moreover, proximity provides opportunities for mimetic learning. As such, expatriates are viewed as key agents and facilitators of knowledge transfer in MNCs (Minbaeva, 2005; Simonin and Ozsomer, 2009).

The third block, knowledge-specific variables, was discussed earlier under the 'What?' section. The central point here is the determination of knowledge characteristics that create ambiguity and value. Ambiguity affects comprehension and transferability. Value stimulates learning intent for the knowledge seeker and encourages protective behaviors by the knowledge holder. Finally, context-specific variables, the fourth building block of our model, subsume non-controllable variables that may be sources of noise, but also motivation enactment of strategic intent to become an active, focused, or better learner or teacher.

TOWARDS A META-FRAMEWORK OF COLLABORATIVE LEARNING

Figure 27.2 presents our mapping of the field. We discuss its dimensions in the following section.

Alliances: specifying the boundaries

A range of inter-firm relationships can be categorized as strategic alliances (Kale and Singh, 2009). Definitional ambiguities render assessing cooperation, particularly, inter-firm cooperation, difficult. Early on, O'Brien and Tullis (1989), Root (1988) and Shenkar and Zeira (1987) recognized that the term 'strategic alliances' already was becoming little more than a buzzword. These definitional ambiguities are a major source of difficulty when comparing the results of different studies (Terpstra and Simonin, 1993). In light of confusion created by this proliferation of terms, we favor the use of the more universal and inclusive term

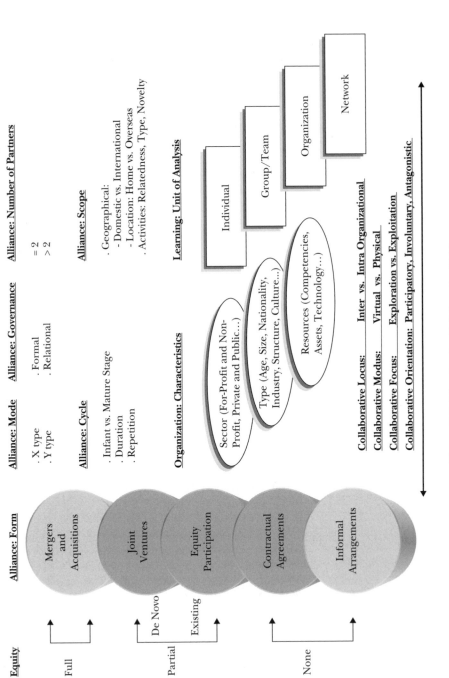

Figure 27.2 Mapping the Collaborative Field

'inter-organizational collaboration,' or simply 'alliances.' Although many definitional propositions exist, their practical value may be quite limited. Rather, researchers should focus on the key variables that help frame the boundaries of collaboration. In Figure 27.2, these key variables are: alliance form, mode, governance, scope, number of partners, and cycle. Alliance form (Terpstra and Simonin, 1993) refers to the structural organization of the alliance along an equity continuum from no equity involved to full equity participation in the case of an acquisition or a merger. Past research has focused essentially on three forms: contractual agreements (e.g. licensing, franchising; no equity is involved), equity participation (e.g. equity swaps and partial acquisition; here, no new legal entity is created), and JVs (formation of a new and separate legal entity).

At the extremes of the equity continuum, two other forms of collaboration deserve attention. First, informal arrangements correspond to the case when no equity, but also no contract, is involved (e.g. exchange of personnel, benchmarking). Often unnoticed in the literature, this form of cooperation appears to be widely used. For instance, Berardo (2009) looks at cooperative funding programs where partnering governmental and non-governmental organizations relate to each other essentially through informal links. In the corporate context, Hakanson and Johanson (1988) report in a study of cooperation between firms involved in technical development that more than two-thirds of the arrangements were informal. Second, the case of full equity (as opposed to no and partial equity) represents another, often ignored, case of cooperation. Mergers and acquisitions thus represent an ultimate form of collaboration where partners fully fuse their structures, legal existence, processes, cultures, and knowledge platforms. Research on knowledge acquisition and transfer in this area remains very promising and complementary (Zou and Ghauri, 2008; Westphal and Shaw, 2005; Henrik Bresman, Birkinshaw, and Nobel, 1999).

Similar to mergers and acquisitions, the multinational organization's network of subsidiaries and affiliates fits our expanded definition. Lately, this area has seen a tremendous surge of research interest aimed at understanding knowledge management and flows, the epitome of the learning organization (Foss and Pedersen, 2004; Minbaeva, 2005, 2007; Monteiro, Arvidsson, and Birkinshaw, 2008; Oddou, Osland, and Blakeney, 2009; Simonin and Ozsomer, 2009). Over two decades ago, Hamel, Doz, and Prahalad (1989) warned that ownership structure seems to capture managers' attention when, in fact, the learning place between partners is more important. Today, due to the growing interest in the learning organization and knowledge management, this impetus may have shifted. When looking at the alliance form, more is in play beyond the desire for control. The different structural forms of cooperation just identified may vary in their conduciveness to learning and types of prominent learning issues.

As form refers to the structural component of an alliance, mode focuses on the function of the collaboration (Terpstra and Simonin, 1993). These modes fall into two general categories Type X and Type Y (Porter and Fuller, 1986). Type X corresponds to joint activities (partners perform activities at the same level of the value chain; e.g. joint research and development) while Type Y relates to complementary activities (partners perform activities at different levels of the value chain; e.g. one partner provides the manufacturing capability whereas the other provides marketing). From a learning point of view, Type X is more propitious to maintenance and single-loop learning due to the likely presence of a common knowledge base. Type Y alliances may be sources of greater knowledge gaps between partners resulting in possible shifts of expertise (accumulation of radically different knowledge, double-loop learning), but, conversely, it is less likely that learning occurs due to the specialization and partitioning of knowledge across partners.

Next, governance refers to governance mechanisms (i.e. concrete management and control activities). We distinguish between two situations based on two common types (e.g. Hoetker and Mellewigt, 2009): (1) formal governance mechanisms that rely on the use of explicit agreements, indicators, reporting, and contracts to specify parties' roles, expected performance, and dispute resolution means; and (2) relational governance mechanisms that foster open communication, sharing of information, trust, and cooperation. Much research interest exists in this domain (Faems, Janssens, Bouwen, and Van Looy, 2006; Kok and Creemers, 2008; Hoetker and Mellewigt, 2009) that is paralleled by extensive work in the area of 'knowledge governance.' Influential in this area is the collective work emanating from the Copenhagen Business School (e.g. Foss, 2007; Foss and Pedersen, 2004; Pedersen and Mahnke, 2004) that has put some emphasis, in particular, on the question of micro-foundations and processes (Abell, Felin, and Foss, 2008; Felin and Foss, 2009) and has drawn attention to the role of HRM (Minbaeva, 2005; Minbaeva, Foss, and Snell, 2009; Simonin and Ozsomer, 2009). Ultimately, these domains of investigation intersect and specialized research on knowledge governance in strategic alliances starts to emerge (Knudsen and Nielsen, 2009).

Finally, geography and activities define the scope of an alliance. In terms of geographical scope, one should differentiate domestic from international alliances on the basis of the national and linguistic origin of the partners (Meschi, 1997) and the location of the alliance itself or its interface (home or overseas) particularly when the focus is on knowledge transfer. The role of 'cultural' is intrinsically linked to the issue of location. Much has been written about the effects of national and organizational culture in alliances (Barger, 2007; Meirovich, 2010). The process of knowledge transfer, itself, has been shown to be influenced not just by the nature of competitive regime (partners as competitors or not), the form of the alliance (equity versus non-equity), but also by the degree of organizational distance across partners (Simonin, 2004). Recently, this line of inquiry has also drawn a lot more research interest when applied to related cases of knowledge transfer in MNEs, between headquarters and subsidiaries (e.g. Welch and Welch, 2008; Lucas, 2006).

Turning to the scope of alliance activities, one can distinguish the type of activities contributed (e.g. marketing, product development), their relatedness to the partners' expertise and core competencies (central or peripheral), and the valence of their overall novelty (e.g. breakthrough or routine). The number of partners can influence learning processes and utilization. The case of two partners differs from cases with three or more partners because, in general, the degree of complexity in interactions grows in a non-linear way. At times, in specific collaborative context, the reverse may be true as well. For instance, when studying funding initiatives with government actors, Berardo (2009) found that collaborative efforts are more likely to succeed when the leading organization can secure the assistance of a larger number of partners. While most alliance research deals with dyadic relationships, studying consortia-like arrangements, particularly when assessing learning outcomes, processes, and performance levels, would contribute to the field.

Finally, when specifying alliance boundaries, one must isolate the components of an alliance cycle. Different challenges and problems exist at different stages of an alliance life (e.g. infant versus mature stage). Cooperation evolves and co-evolves over time and requires re-examination at various stages (Iyer, 2002; Duso, Pennings, and Seldeslachts, 2010).

Duration is also an important aspect. Over time familiarity can increase, trust may intensify, and the opportunities for accessing knowledge might increase while the system diversity might decrease (Meschi, 1997; Gulati, 1995). Lastly, repetition provides another facet of a collaborative cycle. It encapsulates the degree and frequency at which partners collaborated in the past: is the alliance a first encounter between specific partners or, rather, another episode of a long collaborative history between them.

Learning: specifying the unit of analysis

Our model of collaborative learning identifies four distinct units of analysis: individuals, teams, organizations, and networks. These different levels of analysis also correspond to different learning foci and outcomes that are interrelated. This approach is consistent with Tiemessen, Lane, Crossan, and Inkpen's (1997) organizational learning framework that recognizes three levels of learning (individual, group, organization). The alliance literature needs investigation into how to reconcile individual and organizational learning. Likewise, more research pertaining to knowledge structures and processes, with networks taken as a unit analysis, is needed. Overall, paying attention to units of analysis equates to more precision in the coverage and understanding of collaborative learning.

Organization: specifying the key characteristics

Beyond drawing alliance boundaries and the units of analysis, specifying key organizational characteristics that help further classify alliances and identify boundary conditions for learning outcomes and processes is necessary. Our model focuses on three categories: sector, type, and resources. Sector is a reminder that alliances go beyond business-to-business collaborations. Of particular interest, alliances between nonprofit organizations, public agencies, and hybrids with business organizations deserve greater attention (Austin, 2000). Under type, we regroup variables that characterize an organization and are likely to impact learning (e.g. age, size, nationality, industry, structure, culture, etc.). Finally, resources capture aspects of an organization pertaining to knowledge (competencies, technology, intangible assets).

Collaboration: specifying the locus, modus, focus, and orientation

Finally, we turn to four other key collaborative dimensions: collaborative locus, modus, focus, and collaborative orientation. *Collaborative locus* draws a distinction between inter- and intraorganizational collaborations. The bulk of alliance research deals with inter-firm collaborations. Our contention is that they are only a subset of the overall collaborative phenomenon. In a multinational enterprise, for instance, foreign subsidiaries or research teams from different SBUs collaborate with one another on specific projects. Best practices and global campaigns need to be shared within a network of affiliates. In a sense, we argue that the study of organizational learning and knowledge transfer in the context of multinationals and FDI is not so different from that in the context of traditional alliances: both fit under our model of collaborative learning. In one case the knowledge seeker may be a subsidiary in Spain and the knowledge holder/provider another subsidiary in Germany or HQ; in the other case (traditional alliance) two unrelated companies play these roles.

Collaborative modus corresponds to the degree of physical proximity and interaction between partners ranging from virtual collaboration to close physical proximity. As examined earlier, virtual collaboration has become a more prevalent phenomenon and area of research interest. *Collaborative focus* captures the degree to which an alliance falls under an 'exploitation' versus 'exploration' categorization or agenda for a given partner. As per our earlier discussion of Holmqvist's (2004) categorization of organizational learning processes, this dimension also underlines a rich and promising area of inquiry.

Collaborative orientation depicts the nature and climate of a given collaboration: participatory, involuntary, and antagonistic. This is particularly important when looking at knowledge flows across partners. Under a participatory setting, one would expect the most favorable conditions for learning. The roles of the teaching partner and learning partner (Inkpen, 2001) are well specified, harmonized, and accepted. At the opposite, under an antagonistic setting, partners fight or co-habit at best. Learning is difficult. Partners adopt explicit protective measures, deploy shielding mechanisms, and engage in defensive actions to protect the transparency of their competencies, particularly when the embodied knowledge is explicit and held by only a few experts (Hamel, 1991; Inkpen and Beamish, 1997, Simonin, 1999a, 1999b). The last category, involuntary collaboration, depicts a situation where one organization may not even be aware of its role as a contributing partner. Then, learning is likely to be moderate and truncated through partial access only. As an extreme form of involuntary collaboration, reverse engineering and hiring of competitors' talents open a window on learning. Assessing collaborative orientation will provide a reliable gauge on the boundaries of learning opportunities and challenges ahead.

CONCLUDING REMARKS

Though many of the observations and trends highlighted in our prior snapshot of the literatures in 2003 hold true today, there has been a proliferation of interest in different forms of knowledge transfer and learning. Moreover, the geopolitical and technological context has pushed the dissemination and practice of using IT mediated teams and supply chains. This has occurred faster than could have been anticipated in 2003, given that Web 2.0 was still in its infancy. Scholars seeking an integrative understanding of knowledge transfer and learning have a lot of diverse developments to catch up with out there 'in the real world' as well as within a larger set of conceptually complementary lines of research. Throughout we have repeatedly highlighted a number of aspects and avenues of inquiry that to our mind remain obscure and ripe for inquiry. Our recommendation in 2003 that scholars need to study a broader range of collaborative settings has occurred, though in piecemeal fashion. Our analysis confirms once again the reflection that the alliance literature in general pays insufficient attention to social processes (Doz, 1996). Research on learning in inter-organizational alliances remains overwhelmingly structural and macro in focus. One of the biggest gaps revealed time and again above is a relative lack of studies that look at inter-organizational collaborative learning at the intraorganizational, group, and individual levels of analysis; this gap recently has been acknowledged for research on outsourcing and offshoring (Lewin et. al., 2010). The work by Lyles and Salk (1996) and Lane, Salk, and Lyles (2001) attempts to find rough and ready proxies for inter-group and interpersonal contact and things that might affect it. If we look further afield, the micro work on teams that we have highlighted in this review might be a good place from which to pick up and push toward better understanding of meso and micro collaborative processes.

The flip side of the large gaps in research and islands of specialized scholarship is that these conditions contain exceptional opportunities for innovative and high impact research. Throughout the chapter, we have suggested topics that are un- or underdeveloped. We want to lend our support to the contention that using network approaches and theory to study processes of knowledge transfer and learning in such settings, especially across levels of analysis, should reap rich dividends for the field. Collecting network and other original multilevel survey data admittedly is time consuming since they cannot be generated from secondary sources. Hence, there is a need for rigorously conducted and comparative case studies. It would be highly informative for theory building to seek out and conduct studies of 'best practice' and 'worst practice' in developing collaborative know-how. Comparing outliers offers different benefits for expanding our knowledge of collaborative learning than focusing, as does virtually all of the current research, on averages. Finally, some interesting preliminary insights on geographically dispersed teams have come out of experimental research traditions (for example, Kane, 2009, whose research connects super-ordinate identity formation to knowledge transfer and learning in teams and O'Leary and Mortensen, 2010, who look at social isolates' team identity and performance). It is an important literature that finds insights and stimulation to begin filling in theory and an empirical agenda that crosses and connects levels of analysis.

In conclusion, while learning in alliances has deservedly captured the attention of management scholars, the boundaries of the phenomenon and the variables that need to be assessed to understand it holistically have not been encapsulated in one place. This is where we hope our inquiry will be of use. We have laid a foundation for new avenues of research and for more cross-fertilization and dialog across research paradigms and communities who, without explicitly acknowledging it, want to understand the same things.

References

Abell, P., Felin, T., and Foss, N. (2008) Building microfoundations for the routines, capabilities, and performance links. *Managerial and Decision Economics*, 29: 489–502.

Allen, T.A. (1977) Managing the Flow of Technology: Technology Transfer and The Dissemination of Technological Information Within the R&D Organization. Cambridge, MA: MIT Press.

Almeida, P. and Kogut, B. (1999) Localization of knowledge and the mobility of engineers in regional networks. *Management Science*, 45 (7): 905–917.

Anand, B.N. and Khanna, T. (2000) Do firms learn to create value? The case of alliances. *Strategic Management Journal*, 21: 295–315.

Ancona, D., Goodman, P., Lawrence, B., and Tushman, M. (2001) Time: A new research lens. *Academy of Management Review*, 26(4): 645–663.

Ancona, D., Okhysen, G., and Perlow. L. (2001) Taking time to integrate temporal research. *Academy of Management Review*, 26(4): 512–529.

Appleyard, M. (1996) How does knowledge flow? Interfirm patterns in the semiconductor industry. *Strategic Management Journal*, 17: 137–154.

Appleyard, M. (2001) Cooperative knowledge creation: The case of buyer–supplier co-development in the semiconductor industry. Paper presented at IMD's conference on Cooperative Strategies and Alliances: What We Know 15 Years Later.

Argote, L. (1999) *Organizational Learning: Creating, Retaining and Transferring Knowledge*. Norwell, MA: Kluwer.

Argyris, C. and Schön, D. (1978) *Organizational Learning: A Theory of Action Perspective*. Reading, MA: Addison-Wesley.

Aulakh, P.S., Kotabe, M., and Sahay, A. (1996) Trust and performance in cross-border marketing partnerships. *Journal of International Business Studies*, 27(5): 1005–1032.

Austin, J. (2000) Strategic collaboration between nonprofits and businesses. *Nonprofit and Voluntary Sector Quarterly*, 29: 69–97.

Barger, B. (2007) Culture and overused term and international joint ventures: A review of the literature and a case study. *Journal of Organizational Culture, Communication and Conflict*, 11(2): 1–14.

Barkema, H. and Schijven, M. (2008) How do firms learn to make acquisitions? A review of past research and an agenda for the future. *Journal of Management*, 34(3): 594–634.

Barkema, H., Shenkar, O., Vermeulen, F. and Bell, J.H.J. (1997) Working abroad, working with others: How firms learn to operate international joint ventures. *The Academy of Management Journal*, 40(2), Special Research Forum on Alliances and Networks: 426–442.

Berardo, R. (2009) Processing complexity in networks: A study of informal collaboration and its effect on organizational success. *Policy Studies Journal*, 37(3): 521–539.

Birkinshaw, J. and Gibson, C.B. (2004) Building ambidexterity into an organization. *Sloan Management Review*, 47–55.

Du Chatenier, E., Verstegen, J., Biemans, H., Mulder, M., and Omta, O. (2009). The challenges of collaborative knowledge creation in open innovation teams. *Human Resource Development Review*, 8(3): 350.

Cohen, W.M. and Levinthal, D.A. (1989) Innovation and learning: The two faces of R&D. *The Economic Journal*, 99: 569–596.

Cohen, W.M. and Levinthal, D.A., (1990) Absorptive capacity: A new perspective on learning and innovation. *Administrative Science Quarterly*, 35(1): 128–152.

Cooper, C. and Rousseau, D.M. (eds.) (1999) *The Virtual Organization. Trends in Organizational Behavior Series*, Volume 6. New York: John Wiley & Sons, Ltd.

Cramdon, C.D. and Hinds, P.J. (2005) Subgroup dynamics in internationally distributed teams: Ethnocentrism or cross-national learning? *Research in Organizational Behavior*, 26: 231–263.

Crossan, M. and Bedrow, I., (2003) Organizational learning and strategic renewal. *Strategic Management Journal*, 24: 1087–1105.

Darr, E., Argote, L., and Epple, D. (1995) The acquisition, transfer and depreciation of knowledge in service organizations: Productivity in franchises. *Management Science*, 41: 1750–1762.

Das, T.K. and Kumar, R. (2007) Learning dynamics in the alliance development process. *Management Decision*, 45(4): 684–707.

Dickson, P.H. and Weaver, K.M. (1997) Environmental determinants and individual-level moderators of alliance use. *Academy of Management Journal*, 40(2): 404–425.

Dodgson, M. (1996) Learning, trust and inter-firm technological linkages: Some theoretical associations. In R. Coombs, A. Richards, P. Saviotti, and V. Walsh (eds.) *Technological Collaboration*. Cheltenham, UK: Edward Elgar.

Doz, Y. (1996) The evolution of cooperation in strategic alliances: Initial conditions or learning processes? *Strategic Management Journal*, 17: 55–83.

Du Chatenier, E., Verstegen, J., Biemans, H., Mulder, M., and Omta, O. (2009) The challenges of collaborative knowledge creation in open innovation teams. *Human Resource Development Review*, 8(3): 350.

Duso, T., Pennings, E. and Seldeslachts, J. (2010) Learning dynamics in research alliances: A panel data analysis. *Research Policy*, 39(6): 776.

Dyer, J.H. and Singh, H. (1998) The relational view: Cooperative strategy and sources of interorganizational competitive advantage. *Academy of Management Review*, 23(4): 660–679.

Easterby-Smith, M., Lyles, M.A., and Tsang, E. (2008) Interorganizational knowledge transfer: Current themes and future prospects. *Journal of Management Studies*, 45(4): 661–674.

Eisenhardt, K.M. and Schoonhoven, C.B. (1996) Resource-based view of strategic alliance formation: Strategic and social effects in entrepreneurial firms. *Organization Science*, 7(2): 136–150.

Faems, D., Janssens, M., Bouwen, R., and Van Looy, B. (2006) Governing explorative R&D alliances: Searching for effective strategies. *Management Revue*, 17(1): 9–29.

Felin, T. and Foss, N. (2009). Organizational routines and capabilities: Historical drift and a course-correction toward microfoundations. *Scandinavian Journal of Management*, 25: 157–167.

Fiol, C.M. and Lyles, M.A. (1985). Organizational learning. *Academy of Management Review*, 10(4), 803–813.

Foss, N. (2007). Knowledge governance in a dynamic global context: the center for strategic management and globalization at the Copenhagen business school. *European Management Review*, 4(3): 183–191.

Foss, N. and Pedersen, T. (2004) Special issue on 'Governing Knowledge Processes in the MNC.' *Journal of International Business Studies*, 25.

Friedman, T. (2006) *The world is flat: A Brief History of the Twenty-First Century*. New York: Farrar, Straus and Giroux.

Gersick, C. (1989) Marking time: Predictable transitions in task groups. *Academy of Management Journal*, 32(2): 274–309.

Gibson, C.B. and Birkinshaw, J. (2004) The antecedents, consequences, and mediating role of organizational ambidexterity. *Academy of Management Journal*, 47(2): 209–226.

Goleman, D. (2006) *Social Intelligence: The New Science of Social Relationships*. New York: Bantam Books.

Grant, R. and Baden-Fuller, C. (1995) A knowledge accessing theory of interfirm alliances. Paper presented at IMD's Conference on Cooperative Strategies and Alliances: What We Know 15 Years Later.

Gravier, M., Strutton, D., and Randall, W. (2008) Investigating the role of knowledge in alliance performance. *Journal of Knowledge Management*, 12(4): 117–130.

Greve, H., Baum, J., Mitsuhashi, H., and Rowley, T. (2010). Built to last but falling apart: Cohesion, friction, and withdrawal from interfirm alliances. *Academy of Management Journal*, 53(2): 302.

Gulati, R. (1995) Does familiarity breed trust? The implications of repeated ties for contractual choice in alliances. *Academy of Management Journal*, 38(1): 85–112.

Gulati, R. (1999) Network location and learning: The influence of network resources and firm capabilities on alliance formation. *Strategic Management Journal*, 20: 397–420.

Hagedoorn, J. and Sadowski, B. (1999) The transition from strategic technology alliance to mergers and acquisitions: An exploratory study. *Journal of Management Studies*, 36 (1): 87–107.

Hagedoorn, J. and Schakenraad, J. (1994) The effect of strategic technology alliances on company performance. *Strategic Management Journal*, 15: 291–309.

Hakanson, H. and Johanson, J. (1988) Formal and informal cooperation strategies in international industrial networks. In F. Contractor and P. Lorange (eds.), *Cooperative Strategies in International Business*. Lanham, MD: Lexington Books.

Hall, E. (1983) *The Dance of Life*. New York: Anchor Books/ Doubleday.

Hamel, G. (1991) Competition for competence and inter-partner learning within international strategic alliances. *Strategic Management Journal*, 12: 83–103.

Hamel, G., Doz, Y., and Prahalad, C.K. (1989) Collaborate with your competitors and win. *Harvard Business Review*, 67 (1): 133–139.

Harrigan, K.R. (1986) *Managing for Joint Venture Success*. Lanham MD: Lexington Books.

Haspeslaugh, P.C. and Jemison, D.B. (1991) *Managing Acquisitions: Creating Value Through Corporate Renewal*. New York: Free Press.

Heimeriks, K. and Duysters, G. (2007). Alliance capability as a mediator between experience and alliance performance: An empirical investigation into the alliance capability development process. *The Journal of Management Studies*, 44(1), 25–49.

Hennart, J-F. and Zeng, M. (2002) Cross-cultural differences and joint venture longevity. *Journal of International Business Studies*, 33(4): 699–716.

Holmqvist, M. (2004) Experiential learning processes of exploitation and exploration within and between organizations: An empirical study of product development. *Organization Science*, 15(1): 70–81.

Hult, T., Ketchun, D., and Arrfelt, M. (2007) Strategic supply chain management: Improving performance through a culture of competitiveness and knowledge development. *Strategic Management Journal*, 28: 1035–1052.

Inkpen, A. (1995) Organizational learning and international joint ventures. *Journal of International Management*, 1: 165–198.

Inkpen, A. (1995) *The Management of Joint Ventures: An Organization Learning Perspective*. New York: Routledge Press.

Inkpen, A. (2000) A note on the dynamics of learning alliances: Competition, cooperation, and relative scope. *Strategic Management Journal*, 21: 775–779.

Inkpen, A. (2001) Learning, knowledge management and strategic alliances: So many studies, so many unanswered questions. Paper presented at IMD's conference on Cooperative Strategies and Alliances: What We Know 15 Years Later.

Inkpen, A. and Beamish, P. (1997) Knowledge, bargaining power and international joint venture stability. *Academy of Management Review*, 22: 177–202.

Inkpen, A. and Crossan, M. (1995) Believing is seeing: Joint Ventures and organization learning. *Journal of Management Studies*, 32: 595–618.

Iyer, K. (2002) Learning in strategic alliances: An evolutionary perspective. *Academy of Marketing Science Review*, 1:10.

Kale, P. and Singh, H. (2009) Managing strategic alliances: What do we know now, and where do we go from here? *Academy of Management Perspectives*, 45–62.

Kale, P., Dyer, J., and Singh, H. (2001) Alliance capability, stock market response, and long term alliance success. Paper presented at IMD's conference on Cooperative Strategies and Alliances: What We Know 15 Years Later.

Kale, P., Singh, H., and Perlmutter, H. (2000) Learning and the protection of proprietary assets in strategic alliances: Building relational capital. *Strategic Management Journal*, 21: 217–237.

Kane, A.A. (2009) Unlocking knowledge transfer potential: Knowledge demonstrability and superordinate social identity. *Organization Science*, 1–18.

Kane, A., Argote, L., and Levine, J. (2002) Knowledge transfer between groups via personnel rotation: Effects of social identity and knowledge quality. GSIA Working Paper, Carnegie Mellon University.

Kanter R.M. (1994) Collaborative Advantage. *Harvard Business Review*, 96–108.

Khamseh, H. and Jolly, D. (2008) Knowledge transfer in alliances: Determinant factors. *Journal of Knowledge Management*, 12(1): 37–50.

Khanna, T., Gulati, R. and Nohria, N. (1998) The dynamics of learning alliances: Competition, cooperation and relative scope. *Strategic Management Journal*, 19(3): 193–210.

Knudsen, L. G., and Nielsen, B. (2009) Antecedents of procedural governance in knowledge sharing alliances. In King, W. (ed.), *Knowledge Management and Organizational Learning*. London: Springer, 145–162.

Kogut, B. (1988) Joint ventures: Theoretical and empirical perspectives. *Strategic Management Journal*, 9: 319–332.

Kogut, B., Walker, W., and Kim, D.J. (1995) Platform technologies and national industrial networks. In J. Hagedoorn (Ed.), *Technical Change and the World Economy*. Brookfield, VT: Elgar, 58–82.

Kogut, B. and Zander, U.(1992) Knowledge of the firm, combinative capabilities, and the replication of technology. *Organization Science*, 3: 383–397.

Lane, P. and Lubatkin, M. (1998) Relative absorptive capacity and interorganizational learning. *Strategic Management Journal*, 19: 461–477.

Lane, P.J, Koka, B.R., and Pathak, S. (2006) The reification of absorptive capacity: A critical review and rejuvenation of the construct. *Academy of Management Review*, 31(4): 833–863.

Lane, P., Salk, J.E., and Lyles, M. (2001) Absorptive capacity, learning and performance in international joint ventures. *Strategic Management Journal*, 22(12): 1139–1162.

Lavie, D. and Rosenkopf, L. (2006) Balancing Exploration and Exploitation in Alliance Formation. *Academy of Management Journal*, 49: 797–818.

Lawrence, B., Hardy, C., and Phillips, N. (2002). Institutional effects of interorganizational collaboration: The emergence of proto-institutions. *Academy of Management Journal*, 45(1): 281–290.

Lei, D. and Slocum, J. (1992) Global strategy, competence-building and strategic alliances. *California Management Review*, 35(1): 81–87.

Levitt, B. and March, J.G. (1988). Organizational learning. *Annual Review of Sociology*, 14: 319–340.

Lewin, A.Y., Massini, S., and Peeters, C. (2010) Microfoundations of internal and external absorptive capacity routines. *Organization Science*, 1–18.

Lorenzoni, G. and Lipparini, A. (1999) The leveraging of interfirm relationships as a distinctive organizational capability: A longitudinal study. *Strategic Management Journal*, 20(4), 317–338.

Lucas, L.M. (2006) The role of culture on knowledge transfer: The case of the multinational corporation. *The Learning Organization*, 13(2/3): 257–275.

Lunnan, R. and Haugland, S. (2008) Predicting and measuring alliance performance: A multidimensional analysis. *Strategic Management Journal*, 29(5): 545–556.

Lyles, M. (1988) Learning among joint venture sophisticated firms. *Management International Review*, 28: 85–98.

Lyles, M. and Salk, J. E. (1996) Knowledge acquisition from foreign parents in international joint ventures: An empirical examination in the Hungarian context. *Journal of International Business Studies*, 29(2): 154–174.

March, J.G (1991) Exploration and exploitation in organizational learning. *Organization Science*, 2: 71–87.

Mascarenhas, B. and Koza, M. (2008). Develop and nurture an international alliance capability. *Thunderbird International Business Review*, 50(2): 121–128.

Meirovich, G. (2010) The impact of cultural similarities and differences on performance in strategic partnerships: An integrative perspective. *Journal of Management and Organization*, 16(1), 127–139.

Meschi, P.X. (1997) Longevity and cultural differences of international joint ventures: Toward time-based cultural management. *Human Relations*, 50(2): 211–227.

Metiu, A.M. (2001) Faraway, so close: Code ownership over innovative work in the global software industry. Unpublished PhD Dissertation, Wharton School, University of Pennsylvania.

Mets, T. (2006) Creating a knowledge transfer environment: The case of Estonian biotechnology. *Management Research News*, 29(12): 754–768.

Minbaeva, D. (2005) HRM practices and MNC knowledge transfer. *Personnel Review*, 34(1): 125–144.

Minbaeva, D. (2007) Knowledge transfer in multinational corporations. *Management International Review*, 47(4): 567–593.

Minbaeva, D., Foss N. and Snell, S. (2009) Bringing the knowledge perspective into HRM. *Human Resource Management*, 48(4): 477–483.

Moensted, M. (2010) Networking and entrepreneurship in small high-tech European firms: An empirical study. *International Journal of Management*, 27(1): 16–30.

Moreland, R.L. and Myaskovsky, L. (2000) Exploring the performance benefits of group training: Transactive memory or improved communication? *Organization Behavior and Human Decision Processes*, 82: 117–133.

Muthusamy, S. and White, M. (2005) Learning and knowledge transfer in strategic alliances: A social exchange view. *Organization Studies*, 26(3): 415–441.

Nonaka, I. and Takeuchi, H. (1995) *The Knowledge-Creating Company*. New York: Oxford University Press.

O'Brien, P. and Tullis, M. (1989) Strategic alliances: The shifting boundaries between collaboration and competition. *Multinational Business*, 4: 10–17.

Oddou, G., Osland, J., and Blakeney, R. (2009) Repatriating knowledge: Variables influencing the 'Transfer' process. *Journal of International Business Studies*, 40(2): 181–199.

O'Leary and Mortensen (2010) Go (con)figure: subgroups, imbalance, and isolates in geographically dispersed teams. *Organizational Science*, 21(1): 115–131.

Olk, P. (1997) The effect of partner differences on the performance of R&D consortia. In P. Beamish and J. Killing, (eds.), *Cooperative strategies, American perspectives*, San Francisco: The New Lexington Press.

Osterloh, M. and Frey, B. (2000) Motivation, knowledge transfer and organizational forms. *Organization Science*, 11(5): 538–550.

Pedersen, T. and Mahnke, V. (eds.) (2004) *Knowledge flows, governance, and the multinational enterprise*. London: Palgrave Macmillan.

Phene, A., Madhok, A., and Liu, K. (2005) Knowledge transfer within the multinational firm: What drives the speed of transfer? *Management International Review*, 45(2): 53–74.

Philbin, S. (2008) Process model for university–industry research collaboration. *European Journal of Innovation Management*, 11(4): 488–521.

Pisano, G. (1988) Innovation Through Markets, Hierarchies, and Joint Ventures: Technology Strategy and Collaborative Arrangements in the Biotechnology Industry. Dissertation, Berkeley: University of California.

Polanyi, M. (1967) *The Tacit Dimension*. Garden City, NY: Anchor.

Polzer, J.T., Crisp, B., Jarvenpaa, S L., and Kim, J.W. (2006) Extending the faultline concept to geographically dispersed teams: How collocated subgroups can impair group functioning. *Academy of Management Journal*, 49(4): 679–692.

Porter, M. and Fuller, M. (1986) Coalitions and global strategy. In M. Porter (ed.), *Competition in Global Industries*. Boston, MA: Harvard Business School Press.

Powell, W., Koput, K., and Smith-Doerr, L. (1996) Interorganizational collaboration and the locus of innovation: Networks of learning in biotechnology. *Administrative Science Quarterly*, 41: 116–145.

Reed, R. and DeFillippi, R. (1990) Causal ambiguity, barriers to imitation, and sustainable competitive advantage. *Academy of Management Review*, 15: 88–102.

Reuer, J., Park, K.M., and Zollo, M. (2001) Experiential learning in international joint ventures: Obstacles and opportunities. Paper presented at IMD's conference on Cooperative Strategies and Alliances: What We Know 15 Years Later.

Root, F. (1988) Some taxonomies of international cooperative arrangements. In F. Contractor and P. Lorange (eds.), *Cooperative Strategies in International Business*. Lanham, MD: Lexington Books.

Rousseau, D.M. (1995) *Psychological Contracts in Organizations: Written and Unwritten Agreements*. Thousand Oaks, CA: Sage.

Salk, J.E. (1996) Partners and other strangers: Cultural boundaries and cross-cultural encounters in international joint venture teams. *International Studies of Management and Organization*, 26(4): 48–72.

Salk, J.E. (2005) Often called for but rarely chosen: alliance research that directly studies process. *European Management Review*, 2(2): 117–122.

Salk, J.E. and Brannen, M.Y. (2000) National culture, networks and individual influence in a multi-national management team. *Academy of Management Journal*, 43(12): 191–202.

Salk, J.E. and Shenkar, O. (2001) Social identities and cooperation in an international joint venture: An exploratory case study. *Organization Science*, 12(2): 161–178.

Salk, J.E. and Simonin, B. (2003) Towards a meta-theory of organizational learning. In M. Easterby-Smith and M.A. Lyles (eds.), *The Blackwell Handbook of Organizational Learning and Knowledge Management*, Malden: Blackwell.

Sampson, R. (2001) Experience, learning, and collaborative returns in R&D alliances. Paper presented at IMD's conference on Cooperative Strategies and Alliances: What We Know 15 Years Later.

Schein, E.H. (1993) *Organizational Culture and Leadership*. San Francisco: Jossey-Bass.

Schein, E.H. (1998) *Process Consultation*. Reading, MA: Addison-Wesley.

Schreiner, M., Kale, P., and Corsten, D. (2009) What really is alliance management capability and how does it impact alliance outcomes and success? *Strategic Management Journal*, 30(13): 1395–1419.

Shenkar, O. and Zeira, Y. (1987) Human resources management in international joint ventures: Direction for research. *Academy of Management Review*, 12(3): 546–557.

Simon, H. (1991) Bounded rationality and organizational learning. *Organization Science*, 2: 125–134.

Simonin, B. (1997) The importance of developing collaborative know-how: An empirical test of the learning organization. *Academy of Management Journal*, 40(5): 1150–1174.

Simonin, B. (1999a) Ambiguity and the process of knowledge transfer in strategic alliances. *Strategic Management Journal*, 20: 595–623.

Simonin, B. (1999b) Transfer of marketing know-how in international strategic alliances: An empirical investigation of the role and antecedents of knowledge ambiguity. *Journal of International Business Studies*, 30(3): 463–490.

Simonin, B. (2000) Collaborative know-how and collaborative advantage. *Global Focus*, 12 (4): 19–34.

Simonin, B. (2002) The nature of collaborative know-how. In P. Lorange and F. Contractor (eds.), *Cooperative Strategies and Alliances: What We Know 15 Years Later*.

Simonin, B. (2004) An empirical investigation of the process of knowledge transfer in international strategic alliances. *Journal of International Business Studies*, 35(5): 407–427.

Simonin, B. and Ozsomer, A. (2009) Knowledge processes and learning outcomes in MNCs: An empirical investigation of the role of HRM practices in foreign subsidiaries. *Human Resource Management*, 48(4): 505–530.

Skerlavai, M. and Dimovski, V. (2007) Towards a network perspective of intraorganizational learning: Bridging the gap between acquisition and participation perspective[s]. *Interdisciplinary Journal of Information, Knowledge, and Management*, 2: 1–16.

Szulanski, G. (1996) Exploring internal stickiness: Impediments to the transfer of best practice within the firm. *Strategic Management Journal*, 17: 27–43.

Terpstra, V. and Simonin, B. (1993) Strategic alliances in the triad: An exploratory study. *Journal of International Marketing*, 1(1): 4–25.

Thomas, D. (2006) Domain and development of cultural intelligence: The importance of mindfulness. *Group & Organization Management*, 31(1): 78–99.

Tiemessen, I., Lane, H., Crossan, M., and Inkpen, A. (1997) Knowledge management in international joint ventures. In P. Beamish and J. Killing (eds.), *Cooperative strategies, North American perspectives*. San Francisco: New Lexington Press, 370–399.

Tushman, M.L. (1977) Special boundary roles in the innovation process. *Administrative Science Quarterly*, 22 (4): 587–605.

Van Maanen, J. and Schein, E.H. (1979) Toward a theory of organizational socialization. In M. B. Staw and L. L. Cummings (eds.) *Research in Organizational Behavior*. Greenwich.: JAI Press.

Vera, D., and Crossan, M. (2003). Organizational learning and knowledge management: Toward an integrative framework. In M. Easterby-Smith and M. A. Lyles (Eds.), *The Blackwell Handbook of Organizational Learning and Knowledge Management*. Malden, MA: Blackwell: 122–141.

Walsh, J. P. and Ungeson, G. (1991) Organizational memory. *Academy of Management Review*, 16(1): 57–92.

Weber, E., and Khademian, A. (2008) Wicked problems, knowledge challenges, and collaborative capacity builders in network settings. *Public Administration Review*, 68(2): 334–349.

Welch, D.E. and Welch, L.S. (2008) The importance of language in international knowledge transfer. *Management International Review*, 48(3): 339–360.

Westphal, T. and Shaw, V. (2005). Knowledge transfers in acquisitions – An exploratory study and model. *Management International Review*: 45(2), 75–100.

Yan, A. and Gray, B. (1994) Bargaining power, management control, and performance in United States–China joint ventures: A comparative case study. *Academy of Management Journal*, 37(6): 1478–1517.

Zander, U., and Kogut, B. (1995). Knowledge and the speed of the transfer and imitation of organizational capabilities: An empirical test. *Organization Science*, 6: 76–92.

Zeng, M. and Hennart, J.F. (2001) Learning races and cooperative specialization: Reconciling two views of alliances. Paper presented at IMD's conference on Cooperative Strategies and Alliances: What We Know 15 Years Later.

28

Organizational Learning in Asia

ROBIN SNELL AND JACKY HONG

Abstract

In this chapter, we review prior studies on organizational learning in Asia, including the distinguished work of Ikujiro Nonaka, whose theory of knowledge creation has been crafted to represent essentially Japanese characteristics. Therein lies a problem, in that emic learning practices across other Asian countries are not even considered in Nonaka's model. While many studies have been undertaken in Asia outside Japan, these have tended to focus on the importation of learning systems to such countries, without identifying and harnessing indigenous cultural and institutional resources. We shall begin this chapter with an overview of prior research into organizational learning in Asia ex-Japan. In the second part, we shall switch focus to Japanese owned organizations operating on Japanese soil. Thirdly,, we shall consider cultural and institutional features that apply more generally across Asia, and their implications for a pan-Asian theory of organizational learning.

Taking Stock of Past Research

Given the multitude of Asian countries and the diversity of Asian cultures and institutional contexts, it is not possible to distinguish substantive themes that cover each of these locations. Prior research into organizational learning in Asia (excluding Japanese organizations on home soil) has explored four broad issues, which we shall review below. The first two of these are theory-oriented while the latter two focus more on practice (Easterby-Smith and Lyles, 2003). The issues are:

- knowledge management involving joint ventures in Asia;
- knowledge management involving wholly-owned subsidiaries in Asia;
- transfer of organizational learning practices to Asia; and
- measuring organizational learning in Asia.

Knowledge management involving joint ventures in Asia

Among studies of Asia-based joint ventures, we can distinguish those undertaken in the People's Republic of China (PRC) from those undertaken in non-Chinese countries. Studies of PRC-based cross-national joint ventures involving partners from Hong Kong or Singapore indicate that the flow of managerial and technical expertise has been over-whelmingly one-way to the mainland partner (Wang and Nicholas, 2005). Learning for the overseas Chinese partners has derived from the joint venturing experience itself, including how to work amicably with PRC-based partners while signaling to them, without causing loss of face, that proprietary knowledge is not open to disclosure (Wang and Nicholas, 2005). Reflecting ethnocentricity, the more 'developed' partners have typically suffered 'learning myopia,' in two respects. First, they seem not to have been open to knowledge flow in the 'reverse' direction, whether through instruction or vicarious learning, and second, while they have engaged in serendipitous experiential learning both from overseeing operations from a distance and from hands-on, *in situ*, managerial effort, they have not sought systematically and proactively to acquire and capture such learning (Tsang, 1999; 2002). Evidence that operating PRC-based joint venture firms requires the development of dynamic capability, and hence the *in situ* creation of new knowledge (Zhan and Luo, 2008), and that prior joint venturing elsewhere in Asia provides useful preparation for managing PRC-based subsidiaries, suggests that failure to adopt systematic means to capture learning arising from joint venturing is an important omission by foreign parent companies (Tsang, 1999).

In a study of knowledge sharing between Korean firms in alliances with one another outside the *chaebol* structure, Bstieler and Hemmert (2008) found that interaction intimacy between partners at operational level contributed to effective knowledge exchange, indicating the importance for Koreans of *jeong*, the building of strong social bonds that cover personal as well as business matters. Berrell, Gloet, and Wright (2002) identified strong tensions between Australian and Malaysian partners involved in an educational alliance in Malaysia. The Australians, preferring critical enquiry, explicitness, and proactivity as approaches to addressing problems, became frustrated with the Malaysians' apparent preference to avoid overt conflict and to defer to instructions passed down from respected seniors. The authors attribute the break-up of the alliance to inadequate expatriate selection and training. In the context of international partnerships in Vietnam, Napier (2006) points out that the Vietnamese possess valuable knowledge resources and discusses the potential for reverse knowledge flow from Vietnamese to foreign partners. She argues that the foreigners should demonstrate willingness and openness to learning from the Vietnamese as mentors.

Knowledge management involving wholly-owned subsidiaries in Asia

Regarding inter-subsidiary knowledge flows in Asia, mainly within Western-owned multinational corporations (MNCs), Wang-Cowham (2008) discovered that there has been considerable networking and knowledge sharing between human resource management units based at different PRC-based sister subsidiaries, through forums and joint projects organized by PRC-based regional HQ offices. By contrast, Jonsson (2008) found that within a Western-headquartered MNC, cross-national, inter-subsidiary, lateral knowledge flows involving units in Japan and the PRC were driven by *personal* networks, characterized as 'your insurance policy for not making mistakes.' Jonsson (2008) found also that the value of undertaking inter-subsidiary projects was perceived to be higher if the respective markets were seen to pose similar challenges, unlike the markets of Japan *vis-à-vis* the PRC.

Other studies have examined transfer of knowledge from overseas headquarters to Asia-based subsidiaries. Jonsson (2007) found that employees in a Japan-based subsidiary faced considerable difficulties in interpreting and digesting knowledge in the form of lists, metaphors, and manuals from the headquarters of a Western MNC. They preferred instead to learn through face to face consultation with superiors, facilitators, and local experts or through brainstorming meetings. Staff canteens appeared to provide an open atmosphere for informal lateral knowledge sharing across business units.

Research into the transfer of knowledge from headquarters of Japanese MNCs to their subsidiaries in other Asian countries provides a mixed picture in terms of the transfer of organizational learning practices and systems. Takeuchi, Wakabayashi, and Chen (2003) found that the transfer of team-based problem solving approaches to overseas Asian subsidiaries was positively related to their financial performance, and that the likelihood of such transfer was increased by adopting Japanese-style policies of in-company welfare, long-term commitment, and employee skill development. Hong, Easterby-Smith, and Snell (2006a) found that some companies were able to implement a Japanization strategy, through various socialization vehicles and human resource policies, and by adopting open plan architecture, but that in some companies these methods were not applicable, limiting the extent to which Japanese learning systems could be transferred. With specific reference to a graduate trainee program in one Japan-headquartered MNC, Wong (1996) found that little attempt was made to transfer organizational learning systems to the Hong Kong subsidiary, where lifetime employment of graduate trainees was not assumed, and where the latter were not expected to play a significant role in organizational learning.

Regarding the attenuation of 'reverse' knowledge flow, and the neglect of the need to capture experiential learning arising from managing subsidiaries, Wong (2001; 2005) found evidence of institutionalized learning myopia, driven by ethnocentrism and xenophobia, at the Japanese HQ of a Hong Kong-based subsidiary. Japanese expatriates regarded their own international exposure as a form of exile and sought to remain aloof from local adaptation in order to avoid being seen by HQ as being contaminated by alien values and mindsets.

Transfer of organizational learning practices to Asia

Chwee (1999) found that among senior native Chinese executives in the PRC, those with prior employment experience within foreign-invested firms were more proactive, open-minded, outward-looking, and adventurous than those with prior experience only in state-owned enterprises, who were more passive, conservative, and inward-looking.

A number of studies have documented how organizational learning practices have, with some success, been introduced to the more 'traditional' cultures of Asia. Among them are three studies by Barry Elsey and his colleagues. Elsey and Leung (2004) describe a process improvement program based on action research in a foreign invested enterprise in the PRC. While employees' concern to maintain face between hierarchical levels appeared to rule out highly participative approaches, front-line staff participated in two cycles of action research, with facilitation by consultants and by selected supervisors and middle managers, and these activities led to improvements in service quality, as perceived by customers. Elsey and Tse (2007) describe action learning and action research oriented intervention, involving frontline workers at a Hong Kong-based bakery. The consultants found it possible to establish an open and democratic culture of workplace learning, with evidence of ongoing sharing of new knowledge and skills, and of the adoption of team-based problem solving approaches. Elsey and Sirichoti (2003) report on a program to establish integrated pest management (IPM) among durian growers in rural parts of Thailand, through adult education interventions by indigenous agricultural extension workers (AEWs). The growers became committed to the adoption of IPM, once they had seen the results of putting it into practice over time, and had experienced its value for their own practical survival. The AEWs lacked resources but were strongly motivated to serve as change agents and instructors, using a blend of transmission, learning facilitation, and learner-centered collaboration.

Among studies by other authors, Selamat and Choudrie (2007) investigated the impact, in a large manufacturing organization in Malaysia, of a training program, designed to motivate and equip professionals to participate in the externalization of implicit knowledge. The program appeared to improve trainees' ability to reflect on problems, and to engage in rational discourse. After the training, employees played an active part in bringing about constructive changes to information systems, by actively documenting their ideas and reflections in the course of their day to day work. Yeo (2006) reports the impact of introducing 'reflective-action learning groups' (RALGs) to teachers in a further education institution in Singapore. The group meetings appeared to be characterized by social bonding, and open and frank expression of views, with members psychologically engaging with the issues under discussion. Although there was some skepticism, especially among junior employees, about organizational impact, the RALGs appeared to help members to adopt more effective teaching approaches. Yeo (2007) also reports a two-year intervention into organizational learning within a Singaporean firm. Senior managers, as unifying leaders, sought to reassure and support less senior employees, who initially felt considerable stress and fear in the face of the unknown. They facilitated team learning and joint decision making, provided space for continuing dialog, and treated employees' ideas with respect.

Relatively unsuccessful attempts to introduce organizational learning practices have also been documented. Retna and Tee (2006) report an attempt by the head teacher of a Singaporean school to develop it into a learning organization, and suggest that progress was constrained by the wider societal culture and by pressures for quick results. Staff tended to accept the use of dialog as a means to solve problems, but preferred not to share knowledge and skills with one another. Some staff found the leader's adoption of egalitarian leadership unacceptable. Greater trust had developed, but this was tempered by a lingering, culturally-framed fear of authority. Kim (2003) reports an unsuccessful attempt by senior managers, all with Western-based education and working experience, to embed the structures and processes of a team-based organization into a medium sized IT company in South Korea. The prospect of nominal job titles, use of first names, and collaborative team learning appeared to break social taboos, and were strongly resisted. A middle layer of members preferred hierarchy and leadership based on command and control and denied developmental opportunities to younger members, who sought instead to acquire knowledge through private sharing with friends, and through external networks and courses.

Measuring organizational learning in Asia

A number of quantitative studies using Western-originated instruments have been conducted in Asia. Zhang, Zhang, and Yang (2004) established that the Dimensions of the Learning Organization Questionnaire (DLOQ) (Watkins and Marsick, 1993; 1997) had acceptable psychometric properties when used in six large companies in the PRC. Kumar (2005) used the DLOQ to discover that individual and organizational-level learning, but not team-level learning, were positively associated with the financial performance of private colleges in Malaysia.

Some studies have examined the impact of leadership styles and organizational culture on organizational learning. Based on data from various government departments in Brunei, concerning individual learning orientation (Ames and Archer, 1988), team learning (Edmondson, 1996), and organizational learning orientation (Baker and Sinkula, 1999), Chan, Lim, and Keasberry (2003) concluded that high power distance and emphasis on harmony maintenance may deter individual employees from challenging the assumptions of their leaders and may prevent individual learning from being shared at organizational level. In a study in the life insurance sector in Taiwan, Hsu, Lee, Chih, and Chiu (2009) found that organizational learning capacity (Hult and Ferrell, 1997) was a function of the innovativeness and supportiveness of the organizational culture (Wallach, 1983) and of leadership styles oriented toward contingent reward and individualized consideration (Bass and Avolio, 1996). Based on data from the Indian banking sector, Singh (2008) argued that vision articulation, intellectual stimulation, and high performance expectations, as dimensions of transformational leadership (Podsakoff et al., 1990) positively predicted scores on Marquardt's (1996) learning organization scale.

Limpibunterng and Johri (2009) developed their own measurement scales in a study of public and private sector telecommunication companies in Thailand. Their sub-scales of organizational learning capacity included shared understanding about company direction, the fostering of aspiration, team working, flexibility, envisioning, planning for handling impact, testing of new services, and testing of feedback channels. They found that various leadership tasks, such as doing alignment, cohesive teaming with commitment to common goals, empowering people, encouraging learning though mistakes, and resourcefulness, had positive impact on organizational learning capacity. They noted that the public sector companies had relatively poorly developed organizational learning capabilities and attributed this to their characteristics as 'power centric bureaucracies.'

Summary

Thus far, we have reviewed research on Asia-based organizational learning that has been undertaken outside Japan. Recurring emphases in such research appear to be attempts to transfer *etic* learning practices and concepts into Asian countries, which have either been met by resistance, or have been adapted and absorbed. Aside from a small number of studies highlighting the importance of interpersonal relationships and networks, and of particular styles of and approaches to leadership, very little has been done to identify *emic* characteristics of effective organizational learning in Asia, with the exception of Nonaka's theory of knowledge creation, which we review next.

NONAKA'S THEORY OF KNOWLEDGE CREATION

In the previous section, we reviewed the current state of research into organizational learning in Asia outside Japan, and concluded that indigenous Asian perspectives on the field are generally rare or under-developed. The tendency has been for Asia-based researchers to follow research traditions that have been imported from either North America or Europe, rather than developing *emic* approaches (Meyer, 2006).

There is, however, one notable exception, in the form of the work of Professor Ikujiro Nonaka of Hitotsubashi University, who, over two decades, through decoding the principles that underpin the innovative capability of Japanese organizations (Nonaka, 1988; Takeuchi and Nonaka, 1986) has developed a dynamic theory of knowledge creation in Japanese firms (Ichijo and Nonaka, 2007; Nonaka, 1991, 1994; Nonaka and Konno, 1998; Nonaka and Nishiguchi, 2001; Nonaka and Takeuchi, 1995; Nonaka and Toyama, 2002, 2003, 2005, 2007; Nonaka et al., 2000a, 2000b, 2006; von Krogh, Ichijo and Nonaka, 2000). Nonaka's research, which draws on data from inside Japan, provides highly credible insights into the dynamics of knowledge creation within a dozen or more large and successful Japanese multinationals across various industries (Nonaka and Takeuchi, 1995). However, doubts remain concerning the universality of the theory (Glisby and Holden, 2003; Gourlay, 2006; Gueldenberg and Helting, 2007; Weir and Hutchings, 2005), and hence about the transferability of Japanese organizational learning and knowledge management practices to other locations (Hong et al., 2006a; Hong et al., 2006b; Collinson and Wilson, 2006), with some critics arguing that the theory is applicable only in the specific context of Japanese culture and institutions (Easterby-Smith, 1998; Glisby and Holden, 2003; Lam, 2003).

It is against this background that we shall review Nonaka's theory of knowledge creation. First, we shall acknowledge the considerable impact of the theory. Second, we will summarize its core conceptual components, with particular emphasis on the SECI (socialization, externalization, combination, and internationalization) model, and the enabling factors that are embedded at the individual and organizational levels. Third, we will identify the taken-for-granted social and institutional factors underpinning the model. Fourth, with reference to existing critiques, we will assess whether these built-in assumptions imply limitations when attempting to transfer and localize the model to other settings, including other Asian countries.

Impact

The theory, and the extensive body of research upon which it has been based, has inspired a plethora of studies exploring how Japanese organizations might adapt and transfer their home-grown organizational learning and knowledge processing systems to overseas operations, and the impact thereof on organizational performance (Beechler and Bird, 1999; Cutcher-Gershenfeld et al., 1994; Giroud, 2000; Kidd, 1998; Lam, 2003; Whitley et al., 2003). The theory's influence has also had a broader beneficial impact on the fields of knowledge management and organizational learning, which owe much to Nonaka for the rapid increase in their popularity, research output, and academic legitimacy (Easterby-Smith and Lyles, 2003). Teece sums up Nonaka's contribution thus, 'there is no one who in recent years has done more to shape the field of (knowledge) management than Ikujiro Nonaka' (2008: 6).

Core conceptual components

The theory draws on the ontological ideas of Polanyi (1962), regarding the nature of tacit knowledge and its relation to explicit knowledge. Tacit knowledge is characterized by personal intuitions that arise from close and deep exposure to phenomena that are of compelling interest to the practitioner-cum-inquirer. Knowledge that is discovered in this way is difficult to articulate, and creates an urge for further sense making. Explicit knowledge, by contrast, is readily codified into precise formulae or verbal prescriptions. According to Nonaka and Takeuchi (1995), knowledge creation involves dynamic interplay between the creation of tacit and explicit knowledge, in what they label a 'knowledge creation spiral' in the SECI model. The model encompasses four distinct modes of knowledge conversion (see Figure 28.1), each of which entails distinctive knowledge sharing practices, and the interplay between them across individual, group, and organizational levels constitutes the foundation for the dynamic process of knowledge creation (Nonaka, 1991; 1994).

The theory contends that knowledge creation begins with tacit individually-held intuitions, and that the first mode of knowledge conversion is from the tacit knowledge of one individual to the tacit knowledge of one or more others, through socialization. In this mode, an individual employee shares his or her experientially-grounded insights about appropriate actions or conduct with colleagues, by means of demonstration to them or through soliciting their co-participation. For example, within a typical Japanese organization, it is taken for granted that those employees who have previously faced a particular problem and have improvised a workable *ad hoc* solution to it will offer hands-on help to their peers whenever the latter encounter a similar problem. Also, if a new member needs to learn the ropes, experienced colleagues will comprehensively role model the expected behaviors and norms throughout the day, both inside and outside the formal workplace.

	... to tacit knowledge	... to explicit knowledge
From tacit knowledge ...	**Socialization**	**Externalization**
From explicit knowledge ...	**Internalization**	**Combination**

Figure 28.1 The SECI Model

Source: Nonaka and Takeuchi (1995: 62)

However, tacit knowledge that is held among a few individuals is of limited value to the organization unless it is more widely shared through being made explicit. Thus, the second mode of knowledge conversion is from tacit knowledge to explicit knowledge, through the externalization of ideas or lessons derived from concrete experience, into stories, images, or other narrative forms of expression. For example, Japanese managements tend to use metaphors and analogies to convey otherwise hard-to-communicate ideas to subordinates (Nonaka, 1991). The third, and potentially most important, mode of knowledge conversion is explicit to explicit, or combination, where formally articulated knowledge is shared, merged, modified, and integrated among group members or across a set of groups (Hedlund and Nonaka, 1993). The combination mode serves to synthesize explicit knowledge from diverse sources (Nonaka and Johansson, 1985), and to organize, encapsulate, and codify them into knowledge repositories, maps of processes, and other boundary objects (Carlile, 2002; 2004). The fourth mode entails internalization, where shared understandings and prescriptions, such as newly-agreed routines, which have been developed through earlier modes of knowledge creation, provide a context for individuals to convert the explicit knowledge into embodied, tacit knowledge. Then, as fresh intuitions are triggered through engagement in newly-embodied practices, individual members interact with each other, first in order to work out common, tacit solutions to any further problems that may arise, and then to articulate these explicitly as potential procedural solutions, thus initiating a new spiral of knowledge conversion.

It has been argued that the effective functioning of the SECI knowledge conversion processes depends on the existence of two key enabling factors, one at the level of the individual behavior and the other at the level of organizational culture-cum-systems (von Krogh et al., 2000). At the individual level, enactment of the knowledge creation model may depend on each organizational member assuming a distinctly proactive role in knowledge conversion. For example, the promotion of 'middle-up-down' management practice (Nonaka, 1988) and cultivation of 'knowledge activists' (von Krogh et al., 1997), who are responsible for coordinating and energizing the knowledge creation efforts throughout the organization, indicate the importance of active contributions by middle-level managers. According to Nonaka, such individuals play a key role in combining the strategic, macro-level, context-free, 'abstract concepts' that originate from top-level management with the hands-on, micro-level, context-specific, 'experientially-grounded' concepts originating from the shop floor (1988: 9). Active participation by middle managers in open dialog with those both above them and below them in the organizational hierarchy is therefore essential for the development of practical wisdom, or phronesis (Nonaka and Toyama, 2007), through which unique problems arising in particular situations or contexts are solved.

The second key enabling factor is the existence, at the organizational level, of a shared context or *ba* (Nonaka and Konno, 1998), which is conducive for knowledge to be created, shared, and acted upon. This shared space for action is conceived as 'the dynamic, generative source of possibilities, providing the "room" or "space" for innovations to emerge' (Gueldenberg and Helting, 2007: 113). Translated literally as 'space' or 'place' in English, *ba* signifies 'an existential place where participants share context and create new meanings through interactions' (Nonaka and Toyama, 2003: 7). This place for engagement in knowledge creation and knowledge conversion may be psychological, physical, social, or virtual in nature. For example, Nonaka et al. (2000a) distinguish four types of *ba* based on the types of interaction and media used in such interactions. Originating *ba* refers to the occasion, during which individuals share experiences and feelings with each other on a face-to-face basis, whereas exercising *ba* supports individual knowledge contributions within a virtual space. For group-based and face-to-face interactions, it is necessary to establish a dialogically-based *ba* to promote open interchanges among participants, while systemizing *ba* offers a systemic infrastructure for various groups to combine knowledge within a virtual space. It is through participation in and engagement within the various types of *ba* that the members: (1) develop a shared sense of purpose, (2) transcend their own limited and subjective perspectives, (3) interact with each other, and (4) create new knowledge (Nonaka et al., 2008). In sum, *ba* provides a nexus of forums and platforms that supports and records a plethora of simultaneous, ongoing, and informal episodes, during which knowledge is shared and dialogs take place openly between people at various levels, and in various functional positions, both inside and outside the organization, thereby facilitating the operation of the SECI knowledge conversion modes.

Taken-for-granted social and institutional factors

Nonaka has drawn substantially and explicitly on the ontological insights of great Western philosophers, such as Aristotle and Polanyi (Gueldenberg and Helting, 2007), but there is also an explicitly Japanese influence, in that the concept of *ba* derives from the ideas of a Japanese philosopher, Kitaro Nishida.

Perhaps more important are the implicit theoretical assumptions. The two enabling factors explained above, i.e. proactive involvement in knowledge creation and *ba*, share, as a common foundation, the cultural expectation that everyone employed by the organization, or with an interest in it, will engage in dynamic, open-minded dialog with one another, regardless of differences in their functional backgrounds or position in the organizational hierarchy (Cole, 1992). This spirit of openness can be attributed to the Japanese tradition of designing organizations according to the principles of within-team and between-team cooperation (Abegglen, 1957; Kumazawa, 1996). Production operations are normally conducted in teams, within which each member co-operates with others, whether from the same or from different departments, to solve daily problems, and where recognition of individual contributions and narrow job demarcations are de-emphasized. The assumption that work is conducted in a collaborative manner is evident in the many types of work group, such as quality control (QC) circles, self-managing teams, and *kaizen* meetings (Cole, 1989). These ubiquitous organizational group settings, whether formal or informal, not only provide the primary context for contributing work, but also constitute powerful socializing vehicles that build and reinforce members' relationships with other members and with the organization itself. Engagement in group dialogs enables each member to acquire a shared nexus of tacit meanings and assumptions about knowledge creation that support the associated modes of knowledge conversion. We may note here the contrast with the example, cited earlier, of strong resistance to team-based learning in South Korea (Kim, 2003).

Glisby and Holden (2003) have also suggested that a number of other distinctly Japanese cultural and institutional assumptions are embedded in the SECI model. These include: close relationships between partner organizations within the business network, intense employee identification with and commitment to corporate goals and ideals, seniority-based promotion systems, and company-wide employee participation. The following section will identify the major critiques and limitations of the theory.

Critiques and limitations

We shall consider two main critiques of the theory, both of which relate to the distinctly Japanese cultural and institutional assumptions upon which the theory is based. The most commonly mentioned critique of the theory among knowledge management scholars concerns the lack of evidence to support its applicability *outside Japan*. The second critique, which by implication relates to the first, reflects various degrees of skepticism regarding the possibility of converting tacit knowledge to explicit knowledge.

The first critique focuses on the fact that the exemplary knowledge creation practices reported by Nonaka and colleagues (Nonaka et al., 2008) are all based on studies of the operations of major Japanese multinational corporations on home territory. Findings such as those by Wong (1996), cited earlier, along with the exclusive use of Japan-based studies in the generation of the theory, have raised questions of 'whether the SECI process is fully transferable to US and European contexts.'(Teece, 2008: xv), and of how Japanese multinational firms and their managers might overcome barriers to the implementation of the SECI process, which could arise when particular socio-cultural factors in the host country are substantially different from those in Japan (Glisby and Holden, 2003; Hong and Snell, 2008; Keys et al., 1998). In the face of this criticism, advocates of the theory, and of the knowledge management practices associated with it, can argue that the theory may still be adaptable to foreign soil, if managements adjust for differences between those features of Japanese culture and society that are factored into the theory, and local cultural assumptions and institutional circumstances. For example, a foreign subsidiary of a Japanese MNC might seek to create its own supportive enterprise context (Hong et al., 2006a), in order to bridge the cultural and institutional gaps between the host and home country environments (Hong and Snell, 2008; Kostova, 1999; Takeuchi, Wakabayashi, and Chen, 2003).

The second critique relates to Nonaka's emphasis on the role of externalization of tacit knowledge in knowledge creation (Tsoukas, 2003; Tsoukas and Vladimirou, 2001), represented in the proposition that 'subjective, tacit knowledge held by an individual is externalized into objective, explicit knowledge to be shared and synthesized within the organization, and even beyond' (Nonaka and Toyama, 2007: 17). This proposition may, at least in part, be attributed to Nonaka's Asian background (Gueldenberg and Helting, 2007), and even to the social embeddedness of Japanese cultural traditions and organizational forms for handling tacit knowledge (Lam, 1997). Nonaka's emphasis on the importance of contextualized experience to the knowledge creating firm can best be illustrated by the portrayal of the 'indwelling' activities conducted by Japanese employees when handling problems and issues at the workplace (Nonaka et al., 2008: 40).

The assumption that tacit knowledge is converted into explicit knowledge has been criticized on the grounds that people's knowing in action (Orlikowski, 2002) inevitably entails some tacitly known components, which are present regardless of conscious awareness (Polanyi, 1962). This tacit element of knowledge comprises 'non-reflectional experiences' and is 'the characteristic of our everyday living' (Gourlay, 2006: 1427), rather like water surrounding fish, thus making it extremely difficult to recognize, articulate, and externalize. Instead of being externalized, tacit knowledge may remain a nexus of meaning that remains a shared but tacit set of assumptions among employees. Although Gueldenberg and Helting note that, 'tacit knowing refers to the context, field or source from which more explicit forms of knowing evolve' (2007: 118), they argue that it does not follow from this that the explication of tacit knowledge is a typical consequence; instead it is merely a possibility. Whether explication takes place depends on whether the bearers are both able and willing to engage in the necessary amount of mindful reflection, which may be a rare occurrence. While Jonsson (2007) notes some difficulties of tacit to explicit knowledge conversion but attributes these to linguistic and semantic barriers, Tsoukas (2003) expresses even stronger skepticism, holding that while tacit knowledge can be shared through manifestation or display, it cannot, as such, be converted to explicit knowledge.

Towards a Pan-Asian Perspective on Organizational Learning

The previous section has reviewed the conceptual foundations of Nonaka's knowledge creation theory, along with critiques thereof. It appears that his original SECI model and enabling factors are imbued with assumptions that are derived from the unique socio-cultural characteristics in Japan, thereby constituting a barrier to its applicability across the rest of Asia.

Although Asia is populated by diverse institutional environments, the societies therein tend to have in common the two cultural characteristics of high collectivism and high power distance (Hofstede, 1980). We shall argue that the strong cultural propensity to form extensive social networks in Asia is driven by collectivistic values, and that this, combined with the high power distance evident in most Asian countries, generates a strong tendency for organization members to regard proprietary knowledge as a means for increasing one's personal power base and an extreme reliance on leaders to resolve problems. Thus it is that three sets of cultural practices or assumptions are especially salient in shaping and channeling organizational learning processes in Asian societies outside Japan (Bhagat et al., 2002). These are: (1) *guanxi* networks, i.e. personal connections, serving both as pervasive resources and as pervasive barriers; (2) possession of privileged knowledge as a powerful status symbol; and (3) paternalistic leadership.

In this section, we shall characterize the contribution of these factors to organizational learning as being interdependent, such that while pervasive *guanxi* networks can broaden the sources of external knowledge available to an organization, the effectiveness of learning inside an organization is likely to depend on the personal motivations of organization members to share their knowledge with other co-workers, and on the leadership quality to navigate asymmetric power relations within the organizational hierarchy (Easterby-Smith et al., 2008). Based on our final analysis, we will also suggest some possible adjustments to Nonaka's SECI model which may facilitate its wider generalizabilty and applicability across Asia.

Guanxi networks as pervasive resources and barriers

Collectivistic cultures entail strong predilection to act as members of groups. For example, the traditions of Confucianism assume that social order is governed by the specific roles and responsibilities of individuals, who are situated within relatively stable networks of relationships (Redding and Whitley, 1990; Whitley, 1991). Thus, the Chinese typically construct their social identity and derive experiential meaning with reference to close relationships with significant others.

The importance of cultivating and maintaining interpersonal relationships for achieving business success in Asia has been extensively documented (Yeung and Tung, 1996; Chen and Chen, 2004; Tsang, 1998). Across much of Asia, because legal systems and institutional rationality are relatively less developed than in the West, intricacies of social relationships permeate all aspects of life, such that even in formal working contexts the quality and effectiveness of interpersonal cooperation depends on the strength of the social and kinship ties that bind the parties, along with the associated particularistic obligations (Tsui et al., 2000). Such ties are inescapable considerations when managing and working within and between business organizations (Chen and Chen, 2004) and when interfacing with government bureaucracies (Xin and Pearce, 1996).

Among traditional Chinese, the relative closeness of any particular social relationship may be categorized into a small set of concentric circles (Luo, 1997; Redding and Wong, 1986), such as: family members, familiar persons, strangers with common identity, and strangers without common identity (Tsui and Farh, 1997). It is assumed that family members should be given unconditional support and assistance without obliging other parties to reciprocate, whereas there is an expectation of mutual commitment and reciprocity among familiar persons with whom the focal person shares some close connections. Transacting with strangers with common bonds, such as same origin, neighborhood, or school ties, is treated with depersonalized affection, but social exchanges with pure strangers are regarded as purely utilitarianistic and instrumental (Tsui et al., 2000).

In traditional Confucian societies, individuals interpret and apply the principles of reciprocity, mutual obligation, and loyalty in building and maintaining particularistic personal connections or *guanxi* (Xin and Pearce, 1996), which link into networks of informal and personal ties and which serve as bases for (1) securing useful resources and (2) developing a sense of social connectedness in the business context (Luo, 1997). Individuals, who are connected by *guanxi*, relate to one another on the basis of the particular social psychological meanings, expectations, and obligations that match the strength of their relationship ties (Tsui and Farh, 1997). Strong *guanxi* ties are characterized by mutual feelings of warmth and shared fate (Hwang, 1987). Social hierarchy is structured and supported by *guanxi* ties (Chen and Chen, 2004; Luo, 1997), which confer status and behavioral norms upon individuals and groups, depending on their location within the *guanxi* network. As argued by Chen (1995: 144), 'a Chinese should first and foremost know his place in society and how to interact with others in a proper manner.' Given the importance of the relational circles (Redding and Wong, 1986) people tend to invest considerable effort in maintaining and extending their *guanxi* networks and thereby improve their relative social standing. In the context of organizational learning, building *guanxi* with appropriate parties, including key employees, business partners, and members of central and local government agencies, may help a firm to gain access to necessary information about government policies (Tsang, 1998) and to overcome problems and barriers related to knowledge transfer (Buckley et al., 2006).

The cultural preference for collectivism extends from managing social relationships to the development of inter-firm relationships, as manifested by the prevalence of business groups in Asia, such as Japanese *keiretsus*, Korean *chaebols*, and Chinese family businesses (Chang, 2006). Although their structures and management practices have some distinctive national characteristics, a common feature of such business groups is that they operate as networks of affiliated companies that are connected by cross-shareholdings and interpersonal ties (Tipton, 2007; 2008). Members derive value from such arrangements through reduced transaction costs, availability of valuable resources, and increased flexibility (Carney, 2008). The recent emergence of Asian conglomerates can, to a certain extent, be considered a reflection of the effective utilization of *guanxi* networks at the firm level for mutual advantage. Such 'Dragon Multinationals' appear to thrive on a new linkage-learning-leverage (LLL) paradigm by developing strategic alliances with partner firms, sharing the partners' critical resources, and augmenting their own organizational capabilities (Mathews, 2002). For example, in a study tracking the past development of high-tech industries in Asia, Mathews and Cho (2000) described how new start-ups in Asia established extensive links with foreign advanced companies in order to achieve technological development.

The application and manifestation of *guanxi* practices also extends to relationships between private and public organizations (Chen, 2005). For example, a so-called 'main bank' system has been set up in Japan, with the purpose of ensuring that there is a supportive, relational basis to the financial resourcing of firms by banks, thereby reducing the threat of hostile takeovers and enabling managers to take a long-term view in their investment decisions (Chang, 2006). There is also a prevalent assumption among Asian governments that neither 'perfect' nor maximum competition constitutes optimal market conditions, and that the level of competition needs to be 'fine-tuned' to promote investment and technical change (Enderwick, 2005). Government regulation of business is enacted through 'administrative guidance,' and through visible and active co-participation, rather than through formal legislation (Tipton, 2007; 2008).

It is evident, however, that pervasive *guanxi* networks have substantial downsides at the societal level. Asia's economic crisis in 1997 has been attributed to 'crony capitalism,' a typical phenomenon in Asian societies (Singh and Zammit, 2006), describing an economic system in which successful businesspeople derive their success from close relationships with politicians and government officials. Thus, for Johnson (1998), crony capitalism means 'corruption, nepotism, excessive bureaucratic rigidity, and other forms of trust violation that can occur whenever a state tries to manipulate incentives or, in other words, alter the market,' while Thompson (1998) characterizes crony capitalism as 'a kind of subcontracting of corruption that relied on state power to provide monopolies for private accumulation.' Crony capitalism thus describes a capitalist economy in which contracts, loans, appointments, concessions, subsidies, tax incentives, and so on are awarded to friends, relatives, and other privileged clienteles rather than on the basis of due process and open contracting. Generally speaking, crony capitalism arises when political cronyism spills over into the business world, and when self-serving friendships and family ties between business people and government officials influence economic and social policies to the extent of corrupting public service and political ideals (Enderwick, 2005), such that business success is not determined by the disciplines of the free market and the rule of law, but depends instead on relationships with the ruling government.

We have thus highlighted the pervasiveness of *guanxi* networks in Asian societies as a manifestation of Asian collectivistic social values, and their salience at all levels of social and organizational behavior, extending to corporate strategy making and economic development. The following section will discuss how high power distance is manifest in the treatment of privileged knowledge as a powerful status symbol, and in paternalistic leadership.

Privileged knowledge as a powerful status symbol

Although knowledge is considered to be the most critical resource for the firm (Grant, 1996), perceptions and assumptions about its role and value differ across cultures (Bhagat et al., 2002; Buckley et al., 2006). While in some cultures, knowledge is treated pragmatically, as a means to achieving other ends, other cultures attach a high symbolic premium to the possession of valuable and rare knowledge, which mediates power relations and social interactions between providers and recipients of knowledge resources. Thus, across much of Asia, foreign partners with substantial knowledge resources have been revered as leaders in the upgrading of local business operations (Clark and Geppert, 2006). We have noted earlier the other side of the coin, in that the potential for 'reverse flow' knowledge appears to be neglected, and is even considered undesirable, not only by Japanese companies (Wong, 2001; 2005), but also by partners from Singapore and Hong Kong (Tsang, 1999, 2002; Wang and Nicholas, 2005).

Due to the influence of Confucianism, Asian societies have traditionally emphasized the value of education and learning opportunities. Those assumed to be in possession of knowledge, and with the associated academic or titular credentials, tend to be accorded greater trust and higher social status (Redding, 2002). This nexus of cultural assumptions is manifest in day-to-day organizational behavior activities and knowledge management practices (Glisby and Holden, 2003). Superiors are expected, by virtue of their position, to be knowledgeable and resourceful, and therefore it is rare for Chinese subordinates to query a superior's ideas, since this is likely to cause loss of 'face' and to be perceived as a sign of incompetence on the part of the subordinate. Superiors are also reluctant to be seen to receive advice from subordinates (Weir and Hutchings, 2005).

As a means of preserving their leadership legitimacy and the governmentality of subordinates, Chinese managers tend not to make their knowledge widely accessible across the firm, preferring instead to confine any sharing to a trusted few within their inner network circle (Weir and Hutchings, 2005). Through selective disclosure and sharing of information (Silin, 1976) they generate greater dependency (Mintzberg, 1983) and secure stronger commitment from some subordinates, while restricting others' access to intraorganizational knowledge. Subordinates may thus engage in *guanxi* building (Fu et al., 2006) and face giving (*mianzi*), in relation to their leaders (Buckley et al., 2006), as means of removing knowledge sharing barriers (Husted and Michailova, 2002).

Leader-centric relationships

Large power distance among Asian people, especially the Chinese, stems primarily from Confucian values and ethics, which emphasize respect for hierarchy (Hofstede, 1980). Leaders have considerably more power, privileges, and status than their subordinates, who expect and are expected to be submissive and compliant. Accordingly, relationships between leaders and subordinates are unequal, often authoritarian. Inside Chinese firms, decision making is typically concentrated in the hands of a small group of leaders (sometimes a single leader) who have absolute control and prefer not to delegate power

(Redding and Wong, 1986). Leaders typically use secrecy, cliquishness, and nepotism as means to secure the obedience and compliance of subordinates. They are likely also to seek to appear intelligent and resourceful, and to cast themselves as experts and role models (Silin, 1976). In reciprocation, subordinates are socialized to be loyal and submissive, and not to speak out (Kirkbride and Tang, 1992).

Chinese leaders appear also to assume the behavioral attributes of 'paternalistic leadership' (Farh and Cheng, 2000) and 'headship' (Westwood and Chan, 1992). Leader behavior toward subordinates is underpinned by benevolence and care as major guiding principles, whereas subordinate behavior toward superiors is characterized by compliance, obedience, gratitude, and respect. According to Chong (1987: 137), 'most owner-managers are paternalistic toward their employees and do feel responsible for their well-being, which is very much like the responsibility felt by most heads of families toward members of their own households.' They feel a sense of moral obligation to take care of the well-being of their subordinates, while in return the latter are expected to demonstrate their loyalty and support, thus maintaining harmonious and stable employment relations (Westwood et al., 2004).

The combination of authoritarian and paternalistic management (Westwood, 1997) fosters strong deference by subordinates to their leaders (Bond, 1991). This is reflected in studies of organizational learning in Sino-foreign joint ventures, which report that Chinese subordinates tend to avoid exposing ideas to public scrutiny, thus dampening the lateral flow and quality of knowledge available to other team members (Buckley et al., 2006), and are unwilling to participate in group decision making (Child and Markoczy, 1993; Hong et al., 2006b).

Implications for Organizational Learning and Knowledge Creation

Thus far, we have discussed some salient institutional and cultural features of Asian business environments and organizational practices, namely the pervasiveness of *guanxi* networks, knowledge as power symbol, and leader-centric relationships. We have argued that these characteristics reflect an underlying collectivistic orientation and widespread acceptance of the need for unequal power and authority in leader–subordinate relationships. We shall now identify one positive and three negative implications for organizational learning and knowledge creation in Asia.

On the positive side, Asian organizations are more likely than Western ones to have sufficient patience and long-term orientation to nurture and build networks of organizational *guanxi*, as cooperative resources. Network-based models of knowledge development differ from mainstream knowledge-based theory, which features individual firms as basic units of analysis (Grant, 1996: 114) relying on internal 'mechanisms for integrating specialized knowledge.' Pervasive *guanxi* networks, and the intimate and intense inter-firm linkages that are associated with them, potentially support unique processes of inter-organizational knowledge transfer, combination, and co-creation (Easterby-Smith et al., 2008; Hong and Snell, 2009). Networks of an informal and particularistic nature provide unique opportunities for knowledge sharing, mutual help and knowledge combination between trusted others at interpersonal and inter-organizational level (Helfat and Raubitschek, 2000;

Jonsson, 2008). Since knowledge creation requires a shared context, or *ba* (Nonaka and Konno, 1998), good *guanxi* can pave the way for a 'shared space of emerging relationships' (Nonaka et al., 2006: 1185), as a supportive social environment that is necessary for the emergence of shared meanings and knowledge repositories (Hong et al., 2006a). Furthermore, to the extent that networked relationships cut across conventional functional and proprietary boundaries, knowledge networking may facilitate cross-fertilization and thereby generate innovative ideas which may not otherwise be conceivable. Thus, for Asian multinationals, intimate linkages with selected partners may serve to diversify available knowledge and facilitate distinctive combinations of resources and capabilities (Mathews, 2006).

The first of three inhibitory social and/or cultural forces is the strong orientation to maintaining power differentials and hierarchical structures across Asia, which is likely to confine proprietary knowledge within elite cliques and thereby inhibit organizational learning. Since a key governance tool is information secrecy and manipulation (Westwood, 1997), there is a strong tendency to keep knowledge non-codified and undiffused (Boisot and Child, 1988; 1996). Without felt pressure to codify and diffuse knowledge that may be accessible outside immediate social networks, knowledge is likely to remain sticky (Szulanski, 1996), thus hindering implementation of the externalization and combination processes in the SECI model.

A second inhibitory factor for organizational learning is that deference to leaders may, for fear of reprisal, reduce subordinates' courage to challenge 'dominant logic' by offering ideas for change or improvement (Prahalad and Bettis, 1986), thereby inhibiting double-loop learning (Argyris and Schön, 1978). The role of 'knowledge activists,' regarded as important for kick-starting the knowledge creation spiral, thus appears to have no niche in Asian societies outside Japan (Von Krogh et al., 1997).

A third inhibitory factor is that leader-centricity confines knowledge sharing to vertical channels, serving to reduce the likelihood of knowledge creation through community-based learning, as practiced in exemplary Japanese knowledge-creating companies (Nonaka and Takeuchi, 1995). 'Didactic leaders' (Silin, 1976) choose only to socialize and communicate with their inner circle of trusted subordinates, instead of participating in open dialog to facilitate knowledge combination and knowledge internalization involving all members of workplace learning communities. This particularistic and individual-based knowledge sharing approach tends to marginalize the voices of those people located at the periphery, and generates substantive intercultural communication barriers (Taylor and Osland, 2003). It also inhibits the incorporation and synthesis of diverse ideas from various sources within the firm, which in the Japanese model is a cornerstone of knowledge creation dialogs (Nonaka et al., 2006).

The three barriers identified above constitute substantial organizational-level boundary-crossing challenges to learning and knowledge creation practices in Asia (Easterby-Smith et al., 2008: 685). It is possible to overcome such barriers through structured interventions, facilitation and guidance, and through the harnessing of managerial benevolence, as indicated in some studies quoted earlier (Elsey and Leung, 2004; Elsey and Tse, 2007; Selamat and Choudrie, 2007; Yeo, 2006, 2007). However, doing so requires special attention to the need to motivate, support, and mobilize the use of appropriate boundary objects and knowledge repositories. For example, simple conceptual models, common jargon, and selected middle managers, who are willing to serve as exemplars and role models, may serve as common interfaces for enabling and encouraging the externalization, sharing, and internalization of tacit knowledge (Carlile, 2002; Hong et al., 2009; Star and Griesemer, 1989).

REFERENCES

Abegglen, J.C. (1957) *The Japanese factory: Aspects of its social organization.* Glencoe, ILL: The Free Press.

Ames, C. and Archer, J. (1988) Achievement gals in the classroom: Students' learning behaviours and motivation processes. *Journal of Educational Psychology*, 18(3): 260–267.

Argyris, C. and Schön, D. (1978) *Organizational learning: A theory of action perspective.* London: Addison Wesley.

Baker, W.E. and Sinkula, J.M. (1999) The synergistic effect of market orientation and learning orientation on organizational performance. *Journal of the Academy of Marketing Science*, 27(4): 411–427.

Bass, B.M. and Avolio, B.J. (1996) *Manual for the multifactor leadership questionnaire.* Palo Alto, CA: Mind Garden.

Beechler, S. and Bird, A. (eds.) (1999) *Japanese multinationals abroad: Individual and organizational learning.* New York: Oxford University Press.

Berrell, M., Gloet, M., and Wright, P. (2002) Organisational learning in international joint ventures: Implications for management development. *Journal of Management Development*, 21(2): 83–100.

Bhagat, R., Kedia, B., Harveston, P., and Triandis, H. (2002) Cultural variations in the cross-border transfer of organizational knowledge: An integrative framework. *Academy of Management Review*, 27(2): 204–221.

Boisot, M. and Child, J. (1988) The iron law of fiefs: Bureaucratic failure and the problem of governance in the Chinese economic reform. *Administrative Science Quarterly*, 33(4): 507–527.

Boisot, M. and Child, J. (1996) From fiefs to clans and network capitalism: Explaining China's emerging economic order. *Administrative Science Quarterly*, 41(4): 600–628.

Bond, M. (1991) *Beyond the Chinese face.* Hong Kong: Oxford University Press.

Bstieler, L. and Hemmert, M. (2008) Influence of tie strength and behavioural factors on effective knowledge acquisition: A study of Korean new product alliances. *Asian Business and Management*, 7(1): 75–94.

Buckley, P., Clegg, J., and Tan, H. (2006) Cultural awareness in knowledge transfer to China: The role of guanxi and mianzi. *Journal of World Business*, 41(3): 275–288.

Carlile, P. (2002) A pragmatic view of knowledge and boundaries: Boundary objects in new product development. *Organization Science*, 13(4): 442–455.

Carlile, P. (2004) Transferring, translating, and transforming: An integrative framework for managing knowledge across boundaries. *Organization Science*, 15(5): 555–568.

Carney, M. (2008) The many futures of Asian business groups. *Asia Pacific Journal of Management*, 25(4): 595–613.

Chan, C.C.A., Lim, L., and Keasberry, S.K. (2003) Examining the linkages between team learning behaviours and team performance. *Learning Organization*, 10(4/5): 228–236.

Chang, S. J. (2006) Business groups in East Asia: Post-crisis restructuring and new growth. *Asia Pacific Journal of Management*, 23(4): 407–417.

Chen, M. (1995) *Asian Management Systems*. London: Routledge.

Chen, M. (2005) *Asian management systems* (2nd edn). London: Routledge.

Chen, X. and Chen, C. (2004) On the intricacies of Chinese guanxi: A process model of guanxi development. *Asia Pacific Journal of Management*, 21(3): 305–324.

Child, J. and Markoczy, L. (1993) Host-country managerial behavior and learning in Chinese and Hungarian joint ventures. *Journal of Management Studies*, 30(4): 611–631.

Chong, L.C. (1987) History and managerial culture in Singapore: Pragmatism, openness, and paternalism. *Asia Pacific Journal of Management*, 4(3): 133–143.

Chwee, W.W. (1999) Individual and organizational learning of Chinese executives at Compaq-China. *Advances in Developing Human Resources*, 1(4): 69–82.

Clark, E. and Geppert, M. (2006) Socio-political processes in international management in post-socialist contexts: Knowledge, learning and transnational institution building. *Journal of International Management*, 12(3): 340–357.

Cole, R.E. (1989) *Strategies for learning*. Berkeley: University of California Press.

Cole, R.E. (1992) Some cultural and social bases of Japanese innovation: Small group activities in comparative perspective. In S. Kumon and H. Rosovsky (eds.), *The Political Economy of Japan*, vol. 2. Stanford: Stanford University Press: 292–318.

Collinson, S. and Wilson, D. (2006) Inertia in Japanese Organizations: Knowledge Management Routines and Failure to Innovate. *Organization Studies*, 27(9): 1359–1387.

Cutcher-Gershenfeld, J., Nitta, M., Barrett, B.J., Belhedi, N., Chow, S.S., Inaba, T., Ishino, I., Lin, W., Moore, M.L., Mothersell, W.M., Palthe, J., Ramanand, S., Strolle, M.E., and Wheaton, A.C. (1994) Japanese team-based work systems in North America. *California Management Review*, 37(1): 42–64.

Easterby-Smith, M. (1998) Organizational learning and national culture: Do models of organizational learning apply outside the USA? *Bolletin de Estudios Economicos*, 53(164): 281–295.

Easterby-Smith, M. and Lyles, M. (2003) Introduction: Watersheds of organizational learning and knowledge management. In M. Easterby-Smith and M. Lyles (eds.), *The Blackwell Handbook of Organizational Learning and Knowledge Management*. Oxford: Blackwell Publishing: 1–15.

Easterby-Smith, M., Lyles, M., and Tsang, E. (2008) Inter-organizational knowledge transfer: Current themes and future prospects. *Journal of Management Studies*, 45(4): 677–690.

Edmondson, A.C. (1996) Group and organizational influences on team learning. Unpublished doctoral dissertation. Harvard University, Boston, MA.

Elsey, B. and Leung, J.S-K. (2004) Changing the work behavior of Chinese employees using organizational learning. *Journal of Workplace Learning*, 16(3): 167–178.

Elsey, B. and Sirichoti, K. (2003) The theory and practice of workplace learning in the adoption of integrated pest management by tropical fruit growers in Thailand. *Journal of Workplace Learning*, 15(2): 53–62.

Elsey, B. and Tse, R.C-H. (2007) Changing the behaviour of traditional bakers in a Chinese multi-family owned food company through workplace action learning in Hong Kong. *Journal of Workplace Learning*, 19(8): 511–525.

Enderwick, P. (2005) What's bad about crony capitalism? *Asian Business and Management*, 4(2): 117–132.

Farh, J. and Cheng, B. (2000) A cultural analysis of paternalistic leadership in Chinese organizations. In J. Li, A. Tsui, and E. Weldon (eds.), *Management and Organizations in the Chinese Context*. London: Macmillan Press: 84–127.

Fu, P., Tsui, A., and Dess, G. (2006) The dynamics of guanxi in Chinese high tech firms: Implications for knowledge management and decision making. *Management International Review*, 46(3): 277–305.

Giroud, A. (2000) Japanese transnational corporations' knowledge transfer to southeast Asia: The case of the electrical and electronics sector in Malaysia. *International Business Review*, 9(5): 571–586.

Glisby, M. and Holden, N. (2003) Contextual constraints in knowledge management theory: The cultural embeddedness of Nonaka's knowledge creating company. *Knowledge and Process Management*, 10(1): 29–36.

Gourlay, S. (2006) Conceptualizing knowledge creation: A critique of Nonaka's theory. *Journal of Management Studies*, 43(7): 1415–1436.

Grant, R. (1996) Toward a knowledge-based theory of the firm. *Strategic Management Journal*, 17(winter special issue): 109–122.

Gueldenberg, S. and Helting, H. (2007) Bridging 'The great divide': Nonaka's synthesis of 'Western' and 'Eastern' knowledge concepts reassessed. *Organization*, 14(1): 101–122.

Hedlund, G. and Nonaka, I. (1993) Models of knowledge management in the West and Japan. In P. Lorange, B. Chakravarthy, J. Roos, and A, Van de Ven (eds.), *Implementing Strategic Process: Change Learning and Co-operation*. Oxford: Blackwell: 117–144.

Helfat, C. and Raubitschek, R. (2000) Product sequencing: Co-evolution of knowledge, capabilities and products. *Strategic Management Journal*, 21(10/11): 961–979.

Hofstede, G. (1980) *Culture's consequences: International differences in work-related values*. Beverly-Hills, CA: Sage.

Hong, J. and Snell, R. (2008) Power inequality in cross-cultural learning: The case of Japanese transplants in China. *Asia Pacific Business Review*, 14(2): 253–273.

Hong, J. and Snell, R. (2009) Knowledge co-creation involving a foreign subsidiary in China and its local suppliers: A case study. Academy of Management (AOM) Meeting, Chicago, US.

Hong, J., Easterby-Smith, M., and Snell, R. (2006a) Transferring organizational learning systems to Japanese subsidiaries in China. *Journal of Management Studies*, 43(5): 1027–1058.

Hong, J., Snell, R., and Easterby-Smith, M. (2006b) Cross cultural influences of organizational learning in MNCs: The case of Japanese companies in China. *Journal of International Management*, 12(4): 408–429.

Hong, J., Snell, R., and Easterby-Smith, M. (2009) Knowledge flow and boundary crossing at the periphery of a MNC. *International Business Review*, 18(6): 539–554.

Hsu, Y-L., Lee, C-H., Chih, W-H., and Chiu, T-Y. (2009) Organizational learning as an intervening variable in the life insurance industry. *Business Review*, 12(1): 174–186.

Hult, T.G.M. and Ferrell, O.C. (1997) Global organizational learning capacity in purchasing: Construct and measurement. *Journal of Business Research*, 40(2): 97–111.

Husted, K. and Michailova, S. (2002) Diagnosing and fighting knowledge sharing hostility. *Organizational Dynamics*, 31(1): 60–73.

Hwang, K.K. (1987) Face and favor: The Chinese power game. *American Journal of Sociology*, 92(4): 944–974.

Ichijo, K. and Nonaka, I. (eds.) (2007) *Knowledge creation and management: New challenges for managers*. New York: Oxford University Press.

Johnson, C. (1998) Economic crisis in East Asia: The clash of capitalisms. *Cambridge Journal of Economics*, 22(6): 653–661.

Jonsson, A. (2007) Knowledge sharing at micro level: An observation at IKEA Japan. Paper presented at the 19th Business Administration Conference (NFF) Bergen, Norway, 9–11 August 2007.

Jonsson, A. (2008) A transnational perspective on knowledge sharing: Lessons learned from IKEA's entry into Russia, China and Japan. *International Review of Retail, Distribution and Consumer Research*, 18(1): 17–44.

Keys, J.B., Wells, R.A., and Denton, L.T. (1998) Japanese managerial and organizational learning. *Thunderbird International Business Review*, 40(2): 119–139.

Kidd, J.B. (1998) Knowledge creation in Japanese manufacturing companies in Italy: Reflections upon organizational learning. *Management Learning*, 29(2): 131–146.

Kim, Y-S. (2003) Learning one's way to implementing learning teams in Korea: The relationship between team learning and power in organizations. *Advances in Developing Human Resources*, 5(1): 64–83.

Kirkbride, P.S. and Tang, S.F.Y. (1992) Management development in the Nanyang Chinese societies of south-east Asia. *Journal of Management Development*, 11(2): 54–66.

Kostova, T. (1999) Transnational transfer of strategic organizational practices: A contextual perspective. *Academy of Management Review*, 24(2): 308–325.

Kumar, N. (2005) Assessing the learning culture and performance of educational institutions. *Performance Improvement*, 44(9): 27–32.

Kumazawa, M. (1996) *Portraits of the Japanese workplace*. Boulder, CL: Westview Press.

Lam, A. (1997) Embedded firms, embedded knowledge: Problems of collaboration and knowledge transfer in global cooperative ventures. *Organization Studies*, 18(6): 973–996.

Lam, A. (2003) Organizational learning in multinationals: RandD networks of Japanese and US MNEs in the UK. *Journal of Management Studies*, 40(3): 673–703.

Limpibunterng, T. and Johri, L.M. (2009) Complementary role of organizational learning capability in New Service Development (NSD) process. *Learning Organization*, 16(4): 326–348.

Luo, Y. (1997) Guanxi: Principles, philosophies and implications. *Human Systems Management*, 16(1): 43–51.

Marquardt, M.J. (1996) *Building the learning organization: A systems approach to quantum improvement and global success*. New York: McGraw-Hill.

Mathews, J. (2002) Competitive advantage of the late-comer firm: A resource-based account of industrial catch-up strategies. *Asia Pacific Journal of Management*, 19(4): 467–488.

Mathews, J.A. (2006) Dragon multinationals: New players in 21st century globalization. *Asia Pacific Journal of Management*, 23(1): 5–27.

Mathews, J.A. and Cho, D.S. (2000) *Tiger technology: The creation of a semiconductor industry in East Asia*. Cambridge: Cambridge University Press.

Meyer, K.E. (2006) Asian management research needs more self-confidence. *Asia Pacific Journal of Management*, 23(2): 119–137.

Mintzberg, H. (1983) *Power in and around organizations*. New York: Prentice-Hall.

Napier, N.K. (2006) Cross cultural learning and the role of reverse knowledge flows in Vietnam. *International Journal of Cross Cultural Management*, 6(1): 57–74.

Nonaka, I. (1988) Toward middle-up-down management: Accelerating information creation. *Sloan Management Review*, 29(3): 9–18.

Nonaka, I. (1991) The knowledge-creating company. *Harvard Business Review*, 69(6): 96–104.

Nonaka, I. (1994) A dynamic theory of organizational knowledge creation. *Organizational Science*, 5(1): 14–37.

Nonaka, I. and Johansson, J.K. (1985) Japanese management: What about the hard skills? *Academy of Management Review*, 10(2): 181–191.

Nonaka, I. and Konno, N. (1998) The concept of 'Ba': Building a foundation for knowledge creation. *California Management Review*, 40(3): 1–15.

Nonaka, I. and Nishiguchi, T. (2001) *Knowledge emergence: Social, technical, and evolutionary dimensions of knowledge creation.* New York: Oxford University Press.

Nonaka, I. and Takeuchi, K. (1995) *The knowledge creating company.* New York: Oxford University Press.

Nonaka, I. and Toyama, R. (2002) A firm as a dialectical being: Towards a dynamic theory of a firm. *Industrial and Corporate Change*, 11(5): 995–1009.

Nonaka, I. and Toyama, R. (2003) The knowledge creating theory revisited: Knowledge creation as a synthesis process. *Knowledge Management Research and Practice*, 1(1): 2–10.

Nonaka, I. and Toyama, R. (2005) The theory of the knowledge-creating firm: Subjectivity, objectivity and synthesis. *Industrial and Corporate Change*, 14(3): 419–436.

Nonaka, I. and Toyama, R. (2007) Strategic management as distributed practical wisdom (Phronesis). *Industrial and Corporate Change*, 16(3): 371–394.

Nonaka, I., Toyama, R., and Konno, N. (2000a) SECI, Ba and leadership: A unified model of dynamic knowledge creation. *Long Range Planning*, 33(1): 5–34.

Nonaka, I., Toyama, R., and Nataga, I. (2000b) A firm as a knowledge-creating entity: A new perspective on the theory of the firm. *Industrial and Corporate Change*, 9(1): 1–12.

Nonaka, I., Toyama, R., and Hirata, T. (2008) *Managing flow: A process theory of the knowledge-based firm.* New York: Palgrave MacMillan.

Nonaka, I., Toyama, R., and Voelpel, S. (2006) Organizational knowledge creation theory: Evolutionary paths and future advances. *Organization Studies*, 27(8): 1179–1208.

Orlikowski, W. J. (2002) Knowing in practice: Enacting a collective capability in distributed organizing. *Organization Science*, 13(3): 249–273.

Podsakoff, P. M., MacKenzie, S. B., Moorman, R. H., and Fetter, R. (1990) Transformational leader behaviors and their effects on followers' trust in leader, satisfaction, and organizational citizenship behaviors. *Leadership Quarterly*, 1(2): 107–142.

Polanyi, M. (1962) *Personal knowledge.* Chicago: The University of Chicago Press.

Prahalad, C.K. and Bettis, R.A. (1986) The dominant logic: A new linkage between diversity and performance. *Strategic Management Journal*, 7(6): 485–501.

Redding, S.G. (2002) The capitalist business systems of China and its rationale. *Asia Pacific Journal of Management*, 19(2/3): 221–249.

Redding, S.G. and Whitley, R. (1990) Beyond bureaucracy: Towards a comparative analysis of forms of economic resource co-ordination and control. In S. Clegg and S.G. Redding (eds.), *Capitalism in Contrasting Cultures*. Berlin: De Gruyter: 79–104.

Redding, S.G. and Wong, G.Y.Y. (1986) The psychology of Chinese organizational behavior. In M.H. Bond (ed.), *The Psychology of the Chinese People*. New York: Oxford University Press: 213–266.

Retna, K.L. and Tee, N.P. (2006) The challenges of adopting the learning organization philosophy in a Singaporean school. *International Journal of Educational Management*, 20(2): 140–152.

Selamat, M.H., and Choudrie, J. (2007) Using meta-abilities and tacit knowledge for developing learning based systems: A case study approach. *Learning Organization*, 14(4): 321–344.

Silin, R. (1976) *Leadership and values*. Cambridge, MA: Harvard University Press.

Singh, A. and Zammit, A. (2006) Corporate governance, crony capitalism and economic crises: Should the US business model replace the Asian way of doing business? *Corporate Governance: An International Review*, 14(4): 220–233.

Singh, K. (2008) Relationship between learning organization a transformational leadership: Banking organizations in India. *International Journal of Business and Management Science*, 1(1): 97–111.

Star, S. and Griesemer, J. (1989) Translations and boundary objects: Amateurs and professionals in Berkeley's museum of vertebrate zoology. *Social Studies of Science*, 19(3): 387–420.

Szulanski, G. (1996) Exploring internal stickiness: Impediments to the transfer of best practice within the firm. *Strategic Management Journal*, 17(Winter): 27–43.

Takeuchi, N., Wakabayashi, M., and Chen, Z. (2003) The strategic HRM configuration for competitive advantage: Evidence from Japanese firms in China and Taiwan. *Asia Pacific Journal of Management*, 20(4): 447–480.

Taylor, S. and Osland, J. (2003) The impact of intercultural communication on global organizational learning. In M. Easterby-Smith and M. Lyles (eds.), *The Blackwell Handbook of Organizational Learning and Knowledge Management*. Oxford: Blackwell Publishing: 212–232.

Teece, D. (2008) Foreword: From the management of RandD to knowledge. In I. Nonaka, R. Toyama, and T. Hirata (eds.), *Managing Flow: A Process Theory of the Knowledge-based Firm*. New York: Palgrave MacMillan: 9–17.

Thompson, M. R. (1998) The Marcos regime in the Philippines. In H.E. Chehabi, and J. J. Linz, (eds.) *Sultanistic Regimes*. Johns Hopkins University Press, Baltimore, pp. 206–229.

Tipton, F.B. (2007) *Asian Firms: History, Institutions and Management*. Cheltenham, UK: Edward Elgar.

Tipton, F.B. (2008) Southeast Asian capitalism: History, institutions, states and firms. *Asia Pacific Journal of Management*, 26(3): 401–434.

Tsang, E.W.K. (1998) Can guanxi be a source of sustained competitive advantage for doing business in China? *Academy of Management Executive*, 12(2): 64–73.

Tsang, E.W.K. (1999) Internationalization as a learning process: Singapore MNCs in China. *Academy of Management Executive*, 13(1): 91–101.

Tsang, E.W.K. (2002) Acquiring knowledge by foreign partners from international joint ventures in a transition economy: learning-by-doing and learning myopia. *Strategic Management Journal*, 23(9): 835–854.

Tsoukas, H. (2003) Do we really understand tacit knowledge?. In M. Easterby-Smith and M. Lyles (eds.), *The Blackwell Handbook of Organizational Learning and Knowledge Management*. Oxford: Blackwell Publishing: 410–427.

Tsoukas, H. and Vladimirou, E. (2001) What is Organizational Knowledge? *Journal of Management Studies*, 38(7): 973–993.

Tsui, A. and Farh, J. L. (1997) Where guanxi matters: Relational demography and guanxi in the Chinese context. *Work and Occupation*, 24(1): 56–79.

Tsui, A., Farh, J.L., and Xin, K. (2000) Guanxi in the Chinese context. In J. Li, A. Tsui, and E. Weldon (eds.), *Management and Organization in the Chinese Context*. New York: St. Martin's Press: 225–244.

Von Krogh, G., Ichijo, K., and Nonaka, I. (2000) *Enabling Knowledge Creation: How to Unlock the Mystery of Tacit Knowledge and Release the Power of Innovation*. New York: Oxford University Press.

Von Krogh, G., Nonaka, I., and Ichijo, K. (1997) Develop knowledge activists! *European Management Journal*, 15(5): 475–483.

Wallach, E. J. (1983) Individuals and organizations: The cultural match. *Training and Development Journal*, 37(2): 28–35.

Wang, Y. and Nicholas, S. (2005) Knowledge transfer, knowledge replication, and learning in non-equity alliances: Operating contractual joint ventures in China. *Management International Review*, 45(1): 99–118.

Wang-Cowham, C. (2008) HR structure and HR knowledge transfer between subsidiaries in China. *The Learning Organization*, 15(1): 26–44.

Watkins, K.E. and Marsick, V.J. (1993) *Sculpting the learning organization: The art and science of systematic change*. San Francisco, CA: Jossey-Bass.

Watkins, K.E. and Marsick, V.J. (1997) Dimensions of learning organization (DLOQ) [Survey]. Warwick, RI: Partners for the Learning Organization.

Weir, D. and Hutchings, K. (2005) Cultural embeddedness and contextual constraints: Knowledge sharing in Chinese and Arab cultures. *Knowledge and Process Management*, 12(2): 89–98.

Westwood, R. (1997) Harmony and patriarchy: The cultural basis of 'Paternalistic Headship' among the overseas Chinese. *Organization Studies*, 18(3): 445–480.

Westwood, R. and Chan, A. (1992) Headship and leadership. In R. Westwood (ed.), *Organizational Behavior: A Southeast Asian Perspective*. Hong Kong: Longman Group: 123–139.

Westwood, R., Chan, A., and Linstead, S. (2004) Theorizing Chinese employment relations comparatively. *Asia Pacific Journal of Management*, 21(3): 365–389.

Whitley, R. (1991) The social construction of business systems in East Asia. *Organization Studies*, 12(1): 1–28.

Whitley, R., Morgan, G., Kelly, W., and Sharpe, D. (2003) The changing Japanese multinational: Application, adaptation and learning in car manufacturing and financial services. *Journal of Management Studies*, 40(3): 643–672.

Wong, M.M-L. (1996) Organizational learning through graduate training programmes: A comparison between Japan and Hong Kong in a Japanese organization. *Journal of European Industrial Training*, 20(5): 13–19.

Wong, M.M-L. (2001) Internationalizing Japanese expatriate managers. organizational learning through international assignment. *Management Learning*, 32(2): 237–251.

Wong, M.M-L. (2005) Organizational learning via expatriate managers: Collective myopia as blocking mechanism. *Organization Studies*, 26(3): 325–350.

Xin, K. and Pearce, J. (1996) Guanxi: Connections as substitutes for formal institutional support. *Academy of Management Journal*, 39(6): 1641–1658.

Yeo, R. (2006) Learning institution to learning organization: Kudos to reflective practitioners. *Journal of European Industrial Training*, 30(5): 396–419.

Yeo, R. (2007) Change in(ter)ventions to organizational learning: Bravo to leaders as unifying agents. *Learning Organization*, 14(6): 524–552.

Yeung, I.Y.M. and Tung, R. (1996) Achieving business success in Confucian societies: The importance of guanxi. *Organizational Dynamics*, 25(2): 54–65.

Zhan, W. and Luo, Y. (2008) Performance implications of capability exploitation and upgrading in international joint ventures. *Management International Review*, 48(2): 227–253.

Zhang, D., Zhang, Z., and Yang, B. (2004) Learning organization in Mainland China: Empirical research on its application to Chinese state-owned enterprises. *International Journal of Training and Development*, 8(4): 258–273.

29

Learning Across Boundaries: The Effect of Geographic Distribution

LINDA ARGOTE, CAROLYN DENOMME, AND ERICA FUCHS*

ABSTRACT

This chapter analyzes the effects of the geographic distribution of organizational units on organizational learning and knowledge transfer. We argue that developments over the last several decades have led to the fragmentation and internationalization of organizational activities. The resultant distribution of employees and organizational units across spatial, temporal, and national boundaries both poses challenges to and provides opportunities for organizational learning. We analyze how characteristics of national, technological, and social contexts moderate the effect of geographic dispersion on organizational learning and knowledge transfer. We discuss how characteristics of the context can facilitate or impair organizational learning and knowledge transfer in geographically distributed organizations. The chapter concludes with a discussion of future research directions that are likely to be productive.

INTRODUCTION

Organizational learning and knowledge transfer are central to the performance and prosperity of organizations. Organizational learning is a process through which organizations interpret their experience, which can enable them to improve their performance and adapt to their environments. Organizations that are able to learn and transfer the resultant

*We wish to acknowledge the National Science Foundation (Grant SBE-0965442) for its support of our research.

knowledge throughout their establishments are more successful than organizations that are less adept at organizational learning and knowledge transfer (Argote and Ingram, 2000; Teece, Pisano, and Shuen, 1997).

New organizational forms that involve geographic distribution of organizational units pose challenges to organizational learning and knowledge transfer. Over the past few decades there has been a growing fragmentation and internationalization of firms' productive activities (Feenstra, 1998; Gereffi, Humphrey, and Sturgeon, 2005). We discuss the fragmentation and internationalization trends separately.

A number of changes over the past three decades have led to the increased fragmentation and, thereby, distribution of productive activity. Continued improvements in an ever-growing variety of electronic-based communication (such as email and video conferencing) and coordination media (including online collaborative tools such as Google documents) are increasing the viability of distributing teams across geographic distance and firm boundaries. In addition, advances in information technology (IT), such as enterprise resource planning and computer-aided design systems, are reducing traditional reliance on face-to-face communications.

At the same time, the last three decades have seen a dramatic change in the structure of many US industries. In the 1950s, 1960s, and early 1970s, much research and development was housed within corporate laboratories such as Bell Laboratories, GE Research, and Xerox Parc. By the 1980s and 1990s, key advantages to networked small and medium-sized enterprises appeared. Such enterprises were quicker, more flexible, and more innovative than their larger, slower-moving counterparts (Piore and Sabel, 1984; Pavitt and Townsend, 1987; Powell, 1990). Today, many firms outsource their innovation to universities and small firms through technology alliances and acquisitions (Cohen and Levinthal, 1990; Lamb and Spekman, 1997; Chesbrough, 2003). As a consequence, complex networks of firms, universities, and government laboratories are critical features of many industries, especially in fields with rapid technological progress, such as computers, semiconductors, pharmaceuticals, and biotechnology (Powell and Grodal, 2005).

Along with increased opportunities to fragment and distribute firm activities has come increased globalization of those activities. While globalization is as old as international trade (Hirst and Thompson, 1996), in recent years the extent and nature of globalized activities have changed dramatically. Empirical research through the 1980s broadly supported the theory that firms would initially innovate and locate production in their home country, and only move activities overseas as products commoditized and matured (Vernon, 1966; Mullor-Sebastian, 1983; Antras, 2004). Today, however, more and more firms are 'born global' (Oviatt and McDougal, 1994). These international new ventures are business organizations that from their very inception seek to derive competitive advantage from the use of resources and the sale of outputs in multiple countries (Oviatt and McDougal, 1994). At the same time as young, small firms are becoming increasingly international, pre-existing multinational firms have also expanded their global activities (Feenstra, 1998; Gereffi, Humphrey, and Sturgeon, 2005; Lewin and Couto, 2007). This distribution of employees across spatial, temporal, and national boundaries brings new challenges as well as opportunities for organizational learning and knowledge transfer.

From the fragmentation and internationalization of productive activity arise a variety of possible organizational forms. As shown in Figure 29.1, these organizational forms

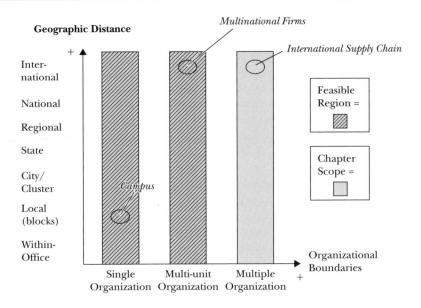

Figure 29.1 Organizational Forms Spanning Geographic Distance and Organizational Boundaries

can be distinguished along two axes. The horizontal axis is the organizational boundary; the vertical axis is geographic distance. On the organizational boundary axis, productive activities can occur within a single organization, within multi-unit organizations such as franchises and chains (Baum and Greve, 2001), and within multiple organizations including different firms (e.g. supply chain) and mixed organizational types such as firms, universities, and government laboratories. On the vertical axis, distances can range from those within an office space (Allen, 1977) to within a few city blocks (Allen, 1977) to within a city (Marshall, 1890; Porter, 1990) to spanning state, national, or international boundaries.

This chapter analyzes how organizational learning and knowledge transfer are affected by the geographic distribution of organizational units. We focus on studies that examine the effect of geographic distribution on learning and knowledge transfer processes and outcomes. In focusing on geographic distribution, our analysis encompasses both single- and multi-unit organizational forms. We leave the discussion of learning and knowledge transfer across different organizations to other studies.

In the subsequent sections, we first define organizational learning and knowledge transfer and then discuss a framework for analyzing them. We then describe geographic distribution, its underlying dimensions, and the challenges and opportunities it poses for organizational learning and knowledge transfer. We next turn to a discussion of the context and how it facilitates or impedes learning and knowledge transfer in geographically distributed organizations. We conclude the chapter with a discussion of future research directions that are likely to be fruitful.

THEORETICAL FRAMEWORK

Organizational learning is a change in the organization's knowledge that occurs as it acquires experience (Fiol and Lyles, 1985). Researchers have taken different approaches to assessing organizational learning and the knowledge that results from it. Taking a cognitive approach, researchers have measured organizational learning by assessing changes in the cognitions of organizational members (Huff and Jenkins, 2001). Taking a behavioral approach, researchers have studied how organizational routines or practices change as a function of experience (Gherardi, 2006; Levitt and March, 1988) or how characteristics of performance, such as speed or accuracy, change as a function of experience (Argote and Epple, 1990; Dutton and Thomas, 1984). Researchers have also measured knowledge by measuring characteristics of an organization's patent stock (Alcacer and Gittleman, 2006) or products (Mansfield, 1985).

Learning occurs at different levels of analysis in organizations: individual, group, organizational, and inter-organizational. We focus on learning at the organizational level of analysis but include research on group learning that sheds light on organizational learning (for reviews on group learning , see Argote, Gruenfeld, and Naquin, 2001; Edmondson, Dillon, and Roloff, 2007). Research on group learning is relevant for understanding organizational learning because groups are basic building blocks of organizations (Leavitt, 1996). Understanding learning within and between groups advances our understanding of organizational learning.

Although organizational learning generally occurs through individuals, individual learning does not necessarily imply that organizational learning has occurred. In order for organizational learning to occur, the individual would have to share knowledge with other organizational members or embed it in a repository that other members could use. That is, an individual's knowledge would have to be embedded in a supra-individual repository such as a routine or a transactive memory system that other members could access.

Because our focus is on learning within organizations, research on inter-organizational learning is beyond the scope of this chapter (see Miner and Haunschild, 1995; Ingram, 2002; and Easterby-Smith, Lyles, and Tsang, 2008, for reviews). A major component of the literature in inter-organizational learning focuses on the concept of absorptive capacity (Cohen and Levinthal, 1990) or the ability of an organization to recognize and assimilate information from external sources. Volberda, Foss, and Lyles (2010) provided a review and theoretical integration of research on absorptive capacity. Organizational learning and knowledge transfer in the context of alliances or joint ventures is also beyond the scope of this chapter (see Lavie and Miller, 2008; Zollo and Reuer, in press; Rosenkopf, 2000; Powell and Grodal 2005; Rosenkopf and Schilling, 2007).

A framework for analyzing organizational learning is shown in Figure 29.2. It builds on a theoretical framework developed by Argote and Miron-Spektor (in press). As can be seen from the framework, organizational learning begins with experience and depends on the context. That is, the context moderates the relationship between organizational experience and knowledge. We focus on the moderating effect of the context on the relationship between experience and knowledge in this chapter. Other relationships in the overall framework, such as how knowledge affects the context which in turn shapes future experience, are discussed in Argote and Miron-Spektor (in press). Major components of Figure 29.2 are now discussed.

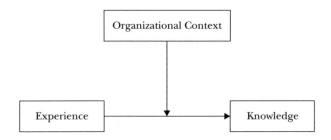

Figure 29.2 A Framework for Analyzing Organizational Learning

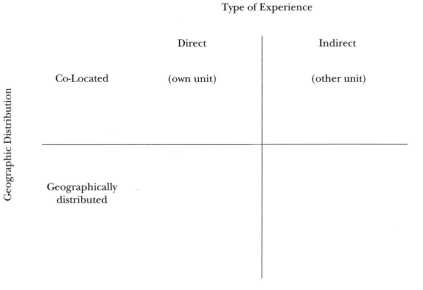

Figure 29.3 Experience domain

Experience

Experience is what occurs in the organization as it performs its tasks. Experience can be measured by the total or cumulative number of task performances. Several types and dimensions of experience have been proposed (Argote and Ophir, 2002; Argote and Todorova, 2007; Ingram, 2002; Schulz, 2002). In the current chapter, we focus on the extent to which experience is geographically distributed. The other important dimension of experience that we analyze in this chapter is whether experience is acquired directly by the focal organizational unit or indirectly from the experience of other organizational units. The latter form of learning is referred to as vicarious learning (Bandura, 1977) or knowledge transfer (Argote and Ingram, 2000).

These two dimensions can be crossed as is shown in Figure 29.3. In the upper left quadrant of the table, members of organizational units are co-located and learn from their own experience. For example, co-located members of a product development team learn from its own direct experience developing products. In the lower left corner, members of organizational units are geographically distributed but work together on the same units of experience or task performance. For example, a geographically dispersed product development team that learns from its own experience designing a product would fit in this quadrant. In the upper right quadrant, a product development team would learn from the experience of other co-located product development teams in the same establishment. By contrast, in the lower right quadrant, a product development team would learn from the experience of other product development teams in geographically different locations.

Thus, the difference between the left and right columns of Figure 29.3 is whether one is learning from one's own experience or from experience acquired by other organizational units. Organizations are made up of different groups and departments who can learn from their own experience as they perform a task or learn from the experience of other organizational units. The difference between the upper and lower rows of Figure 29.3 is geographic distribution: whether the organizational units are co-located or geographically dispersed. For purposes of this chapter, we define co-location as being part of the same establishment (i.e. an office building or campus).

Although the effect of experience on learning outcomes is generally beneficial (Argote and Epple, 1990; Dutton and Thomas, 1984), organizations vary dramatically in their ability to learn. In some organizations experience is associated with significant increases in knowledge, while in other organizations experience has little effect on knowledge or organizations learn the wrong knowledge. Experience can be challenging to interpret (March, Sproull, and Tamuz, 1991; Starbuck, 2009). Organizations sometimes derive inappropriate inferences from experience (Zollo, 2009; Tripsas and Gavetti, 2000). Levitt and March (1988) described the inappropriate lessons organizations can draw from experience as 'superstitious learning.' This sort of learning can occur when units are geographically distributed, which poses challenges to interpreting experience.

Organizational learning processes translate experience into knowledge. Organizational learning processes have been characterized in terms of their 'mindfulness.' Mindful processes are deliberative processes (Weick and Sutcliffe, 2006) while less mindful processes are automatic or routine ones (Levinthal and Rerup, 2006). Learning from both direct and indirect experience can occur in a mindful or less mindful way. Reflecting on experience, such as through after-action reviews, would be an example of mindful learning from direct experience. Stimulus-response learning would be an example of a less mindful process. Concerning learning from indirect experience, knowledge transfer attempts that adapt the knowledge to the new context would be mindful while 'copy exactly' approaches would be less mindful.

Context

The context includes the external and internal environments in which the organization is embedded. Competitors, clients, suppliers, trade associations, regulators, and nation states are part of the organization's external environment. The context also includes aspects of the organization's internal environment such as its culture, structure, strategy, technology, identity, and memory system. We organize our analysis of the context in three areas: national context, technical context, and social context. We examine how the context interacts with experience to affect organizational learning. Thus, we identify contextual conditions that facilitate learning from geographically distributed experience and contextual conditions that impair such learning.

Knowledge

Knowledge acquired through learning can be embedded in different repositories such as individuals, routines, tools, and transactive memory systems (Argote and Ingram, 2000; Walsh and Ungson, 1991). Further, knowledge can be characterized along several dimensions (see Alavi and Leidner, 2001). For example, knowledge can range from explicit knowledge that can be codified (Zander and Kogut, 1995) to tacit knowledge that is difficult to articulate (Nonaka and von Krogh, 2009; Polanyi, 1962). Similarly, researchers distinguish between 'know-what' or 'know-how' (Edmondson, Pisano, Bohmer, and Winslow, 2003; Lapré, Mukherjee, and Van Wassenhove, 2000). Knowledge can also vary in its complexity (Novak and Eppinger, 2001), its uncertainty and causal ambiguity (Szulanski, 1996), and its decomposability.

Geographic distribution

Geographic distribution poses challenges and opportunities for organizational learning and knowledge transfer. For example, Hong, Snell, and Easterby-Smith (2009) analyzed knowledge transfer between the headquarters of a Japanese multinational and its subsidiary in China and described the crossing of syntactic (communication), semantic (interpretation), and pragmatic (interests) boundaries (Carlisle, 2004). Firms are increasingly organized in a geographically distributed fashion that requires crossing such boundaries.

Geographic distribution has several underlying dimensions. Gibson and Gibbs (2006) investigated the separate dimensions of geographic dispersion, electronic dependence, and national context and found that each dimension had a negative effect on innovation. When members are dispersed across different locations, they may not share common knowledge and taken-for-granted understandings that facilitate information exchange and learning from experience (Cramton, 2001; Sole and Edmondson, 2002). Members of distributed organizations may depend on electronic communication to accomplish tasks, which reduces social cues (Sproull and Kiesler, 1991) and communication richness, and thereby impairs coordination (Boh, Ren, Kiesler, and Bussjaeger, 2007). Trust may be challenging to maintain in geographically distributed teams where members do not interact face-to-face (Jarvenpaa and Leidner, 1999).

National diversity also can impede learning because members may have different norms for communication (Gibson and Gibbs, 2006) and identify with their nation rather than with the organization. For example, Louis Gallois, the CEO of Airbus, which has French, German, British, and Spanish locations, banned national symbols in the organization because he attributed coordination problems with the A380 aircraft to national identities. He eliminated national flags because they reinforced identity at the national level and aimed instead to create a superordinate identity at the organizational level (Clarke, 2007).

Temporal dispersion is another dimension that is often associated with the geographic distribution of organizations. Geographically distributed teams that span time zones encounter more difficulties communicating and coordinating than those in the same time zone. Working across different time zones can provide opportunities for cultural faux pas if holidays and 'normal' work hours are not thoughtfully considered. For example, a US team scheduled an early Friday morning meeting that would correspond to the afternoon in France. The French work week, however, is thirty-five hours and Friday afternoon was out of normal work hours for the French collaborators who were too respectful to point out the oversight (Olson and Olson, 2000). The effect of temporal dispersion may be more difficult to overcome than the effect of spatial dispersion (Espinosa and Pickering, 2006; Cummings, 2009).

Geographic distribution poses challenges to organizational learning and knowledge transfer, which depend on members' abilities, motivations, and opportunities (Argote, McEvily, and Reagans, 2003). Geographic dispersion can reduce members' abilities to interpret experience by reducing common knowledge and social cues. In geographically distributed organizations, members may be more committed to their local units than to the superordinate organization, which reduces their motivation to learn and transfer knowledge. Because of temporal and spatial differences, members may not have many opportunities to interact and share knowledge in geographically distributed organizations. Thus, members' abilities, motivations, and opportunities to learn and transfer knowledge are likely to be lower in geographically distributed than in co-located organizations.

Although knowledge transfer across geographic boundaries is challenging, firms that are able to successfully transfer knowledge across geographic boundaries realize enormous advantages. For example, Cummings (2004) found that external knowledge transfer across units was more strongly related to performance when units were geographically distributed than when they were geographically concentrated. The different geographic locations exposed the groups to unique sources of knowledge that were very valuable in improving their performance.

EFFECT OF CONTEXTUAL FACTORS ON ORGANIZATIONAL LEARNING AND KNOWLEDGE TRANSFER

As is shown in Figure 29.2, the context interacts with experience to create knowledge. That is, the context moderates the relationship between experience and knowledge creation and transfer. In the sections that follow, we discuss how characteristics of the context can facilitate or impede organizational learning and knowledge transfer in geographically distributed organizations. Thus, we identify contextual conditions that enable organizations to overcome the barriers posed by geographic dispersion. We organize our analyses according to whether the contextual dimension pertains to national, technical, or social factors.

National context

While globalization may in some situations lead to greater commonality across nations (Hirst and Thompson, 1996), national diversity persists on a wide number of dimensions. Some of these dimensions are immediately obvious to the casual observer: different languages, different physical resources, and different legal rules and policy regulations. Other dimensions of national context can be subtle. Nations have different institutions—the formal and informal rules of the game that constrain human interaction (North, 1990).

As a consequence of these different institutions, nations also have different national organizations. These organizations can be of many forms including national firms, universities, government laboratories, or other organizations that are part of the government. In addition, in different nations, individuals and organizations also have different local knowledge (Patel and Pavitt, 1994). Combined, the different physical resources, organizational resources, knowledge resources, and rules of the game in each nation lead to very different contexts within which learning and knowledge transfer occur.

There are many examples of the different organizational structures, production environments, and team environments that emerge as a consequence of national contexts. In the US, industries tend to be vertically disintegrated with large firms often outsourcing technology development to small and medium-sized firms (Cohen and Levinthal, 1990; Lamb and Spekman, 1997; Chesbrough, 2003). In contrast, in Japan, firms tend to be vertically integrated, keeping many different functions in-house (Fransman, 1995; 1999). Thus, while knowledge and learning must often be coordinated across many different organizations in the US, this learning is more often centralized in a single firm in Japan.

The most efficient or economically viable production processes and products can also vary widely with national context. In the case of production environments, the Ford system of mass production emerged in the US (Hounshell, 1985), the Toyota production system and lean manufacturing emerged in Japan (Womack, Jones, and Roos, 1990), and the Mexican Maquiliadora system emerged in Mexico (Morris and Pavett, 1992; Vargas and Johnson, 1993; Prasad, Tat, and Thorn, 1995). In many ways, each of these production systems emerged by learning from and adapting the Ford mass production system to better fit a particular national context (Zeitlin and Herrigel, 2000).

In the case of products, research has shown in both the automotive and the photonic semiconductor industries, the most competitive design switches with the choice of manufacturing location, due to national differences in the organization of production (Fuchs, Field, Roth, and Kirchain, 2011; Fuchs and Kirchain, 2010). Significant work remains to understand the extent to which these differences are understood by managers, and the speed at which organizations may be able to learn and integrate these differences into their production decisions. Along these lines, Leonard-Barton (1988) described the implementation of new production technologies as mutual adaptation of technology and organization (Leonard-Barton, 1988). Also, Zeitlin and Herrigel (2000) found that countries that adapted mass production techniques to match the communication and work norms in their national contexts were most successful (Zeitlin and Herrigel, 2000).

Finally, accepted and successful methods of communication and working within and across teams can vary widely across national contexts (Cramton and Hinds, 2005). Working across different national contexts can lead to unexpected costs due to context mismatch (Zeitlin and Herrigel, 2000) and slowed cross-context learning or knowledge transfer (Gibson and Gibbs, 2006), but also can lead to many opportunities for increased learning through the adaptation of existing knowledge and the creation of new knowledge (Leonard-Barton, 1988; Zeitlin and Herrigel, 2000; Cramton and Hinds, 2005). Cramton and Hinds (2005) found that teams with mutual positive distinctiveness were likely to learn from sub-group differences, and developed sophistication in their understandings of cross-national relationships and competence in managing them. We return to the issue of managing differences across geographically distributed groups in our discussion of the social context.

Technical context

Learning and knowledge transfer often occur in a technical context. In the case of this chapter, we use technical context to encompass the extent of uncertainty around a problem, the amount and complexity of information, the architecture (or modularity) of a technology or design, the equipment and tools used in production, and the type of technology used to store or transfer the requisite knowledge. These dimensions of technical context have been shown to be important moderators of the relationship between experience and knowledge when geographic distance is involved.

Several technical contexts are particularly challenging for learning and the transfer of knowledge across geographic distance. Research has shown that technical contexts involving unfamiliar, unstructured problems often require experts to be physically present to recognize embedded clues, exploit specialized tools, use tacit knowledge, and interpret relevant information (Leonard-Barton, 1988; Tyre and von Hippel, 1997; Nadler, Thompson, and van Boven, 2003). The opportunity for in-person problem solving can be critical in production environments (Leonard-Barton, 1988), in particular in the early stages of technology development in chemical and process-based industries such as semiconductors, pharmaceuticals, and standard chemical production (Fuchs and Kirchain, 2010).

Another context involving unfamiliar, unstructured problems is new product development. Managing product development can involve a greater degree of process, marketing, and technical uncertainty than found in many other settings (Anderson, Davis-Blake, Erzurumlu , Joglekar, and Parker, 2008). In this context, ensuring information flows, cooperation, and collaboration can be critical (Anderson, Davis-Blake, Erzurumlu, Joglekar, and Parker, 2008). Thus, new product development can be particularly challenging across geographic distance. At the same time, new product development is a particularly interesting setting for understanding what systems, tools, and frameworks alleviate challenges in learning and knowledge flows created by distance. Previous research has suggested that distributed product development faces greater challenges than non-distributed product development (Sosa, Eppinger, Pich, and McKendrick, 2002; Anderson, Davis-Blake, Erzurumlu, Joglekar, and Parker, 2008). However, contrary to conventional wisdom, recent research has also suggested that project organization types that span country boundaries can outperform co-located insourcing projects, particularly in projects with higher uncertainty (Mishra, 2009). Mishra suggested that this finding may be a result of client firms increasingly leveraging offshore locations for strategic reasons that go beyond cost considerations—a discovery that echoes recent findings that companies are increasingly locating activities offshore to leverage local talent (Lewin and Couto, 2007; Mishra, 2009). Further research will be necessary to disentangle in what contexts distributed teams outperform local ones by leveraging location-specific capabilities versus in what contexts challenges in learning and knowledge transfer across geographic distance mean that co-location is most advantageous.

In addition to affecting the nature of problems, the technical context can also affect the quantity and complexity of the information to be transferred. For example, Von Hippel (1994) argued that successful anticipation and avoidance of all field problems that might affect, for example, a new airplane or a new process machine, require a very large amount of information transfer and, thus, are extremely costly, if not impossible. Likewise, a number of authors have argued that technical contexts with high complexity can lead to knowledge being difficult to communicate or transfer across distance (Patel and Pavitt, 1991; Pavitt, 1999; Novak and Eppinger, 2001). In their study of the automotive industry, Novak and Eppinger suggested that product complexity has three main elements: (1) the number of product components to specify and produce, (2) the extent of interactions to manage between these components (parts coupling), and (3) the degree of product novelty. Variations in product complexity are, in turn, driven by choices in performance, technology, and product architecture. Novak and Eppinger found a significant positive relationship between product complexity and vertical integration (Novak and Eppinger, 2001). Relatedly, Pavitt and Patel (1999) defined complexity as the levels of multi-field knowledge and differentiation required for a given technological competency, and found that multinational firms tend to concentrate activities with high complexity in their home country (Pavitt and Patel, 1999). Notably, however, these relationships may be changing. In particular, recent research suggests that more and more firms are choosing to source their research and development activities overseas, and that with firm experience access to local skills becomes an important driver of overseas location (Lewin and Couto, 2007).

While certain technical contexts can prove particularly challenging or even impossible to manage across geographic distance, other technical contexts can help enable or even support the separation of productive activities across geographic distance. One such technical context is design modularity. A module is a unit whose elements are powerfully connected to one another but weakly connected to elements in other units. Modules have thin crossing points, or points with low transaction costs, at their boundaries; and thick crossing points, or points with high transaction costs, in their interiors (Baldwin and Clark, 2000). Traditionally, product and process modularity have been considered critical to distributed production and product development (Sturgeon, 2002; Sosa, Eppinger, and Rowles, 2004; Gereffi, Humphrey, and Sturgeon, 2005; Eppinger and Chitkara, 2006; MacCormack, Rusnak, and Baldwin, 2008). More recent literature, however, suggests that this relationship may be more nuanced than originally thought (Hoetker, 2006). Colfer and Baldwin (2010) found that almost one third of the cases in their study did not support the hypothesis that organizational patterns, including employment ties, hierarchical groupings, and geographic location and communication links would correspond to the technical patterns of dependency in the system under development (Baldwin and Clark, 2000; MacCormack et al., 2008; Colfer and Baldwin, 2010). In all of the cases where independent and dispersed contributors made highly interdependent contributions to the design of a single technical system, 'actionable transparency' was used as a means of achieving coordination (Colfer and Baldwin, 2010). Colfer and Baldwin (2010) defined actionable transparency as the extent to which everyone with an interest in improving a given design has the right and the means to act on it.

In addition, Tripathy and Eppinger (2008) found that most components or processes can neither be termed completely modular or integral at the task level, and suggested an alternative structuring framework for distributed product development. Further, work transfer across distance did not behave monotonically with respect to modularity. Others, however, continue to find that design–interface misalignment has a significant negative impact on project performance, and that this impact is particularly severe when projects are distributed across nations and across firm boundaries (Mishra, 2009). Future work will need to explore the sources of these different findings.

The use of IT to coordinate and collaborate around problems and projects can also ease the difficulties of working across spatial and temporal distances. IT can include synchronous communication methods (i.e. instant messaging, group note-taking or document-editing systems, tele- and video-conferencing), asynchronous communication methods (i.e. email, electronic bulletin boards, web-based software, and data sharing software), information holding databases, and collaborative tools or tools that are designed to automate a manual task. IT tools can provide effective means for communicating and collaborating across distances. This 'virtual co-location' can allow collaborators to share information (Hameri and Nihtilä, 1997), provide a 'technical grammar' which can create social conventions around collaborating and coordinating (Argyres, 1999), and improve coordination (Sproull and Kiesler, 1991; Yates and Orlikowski, 1992; Sosa, Eppinger, Pich, and McKendrick, 2002).

The extent of integration of technology into processes and routines also matters. Boone and Ganeshan (2001) found productivity benefits from technology that was integrated into the production process but no benefits from technology that just held documents or served as a repository. Ashworth, Mukhopadhyay, and Argote (2004) found that the introduction of IT facilitated organizational learning and knowledge transfer across six geographically distributed units of a financial services firm.

Kane and Alavi (2007) noted that information systems support organizational learning. Hansen, Nohria, and Tierney (1999) argued that the effectiveness of knowledge management systems was contingent on the extent to which work was standardized. In particular, developing detailed databases or knowledge repositories was effective when work was standardized while providing directories that identified member expertise was effective when work was not standardized. These directories facilitated communication, which enabled the solution of non-standard problems.

A couple of studies examined empirically the effectiveness of knowledge management systems. Kim (2008) found that using a knowledge management system contributed positively to the performance of stores in a retail grocery chain. Further, the magnitude of the effect was greater for managers who were remotely located, for those with fewer alternative sources of knowledge and for managers dealing with products that did not become obsolete quickly.

By contrast, Haas and Hansen (2005) found that the number of documents used from a knowledge management system in a consulting firm was negatively associated with consulting team performance. Further, the researchers found interactions between the number of documents used and two contextual variables, team experience and the number of competitors. Using documents from a knowledge management system was particularly harmful for experienced teams and for teams with many competitors. It seems likely that experienced teams already possessed relevant knowledge. Because standard knowledge rather than knowledge that is a source of competitive advantage is likely to populate knowledge management systems, those systems are not very useful in competitive environments. Thus, although knowledge management systems can facilitate organizational learning and have positive effects on organizational performance (Kim, 2008), the positive effect is not guaranteed and depends on important contextual conditions, such as the experience of team members, their alternative sources of information, and their task environment. These factors will be discussed in our section on the social context.

Knowledge management systems are evolving and therefore their capability to contribute to organizational learning and knowledge transfer is also evolving. While early generations of knowledge management systems provided document repositories and directories of declared expertise of organization members, recent systems include communication capabilities and the identification of expertise based on who is consulted and who answers questions. Research is needed on the effects of knowledge management systems with these new capabilities on organizational learning and knowledge transfer.

Social context

By the social context we mean characteristics of the organization's members and relationships among members. Dimensions of the social context that have been shown to be important moderators of the relationship between experience and knowledge include: the similarity of the contexts; characteristics of members such as their social identity and experience working together; characteristics of relationships among members such as transactive memory systems; leadership; and the organization's structure, culture, and practices.

The extent to which a context is shared moderates the effect of geographic distance on knowledge transfer. Hinds and Mortensen (2005) found that geographically distributed teams had more conflict than co-located teams. Further, a shared context in which members possessed the same tools, information, and priorities weakened the effect of geographic distance on increased conflict. Thus, providing a shared context to members can be helpful in overcoming the negative effects of geographic distribution on member relations and knowledge transfer.

The similarity of social contexts affects knowledge transfer across them (Bhagat, Kedia, Harveston, and Triandis, 2002). Based on an analysis of three cases of multinational firms, Makela, Kalla, and Piekkari (2007) concluded that similarity in national-cultural backgrounds, language, and organizational status led to more interaction among the members of multinational firms, which increased knowledge transfer. Similarly, Tsai (2002) found that strategic relatedness facilitated knowledge transfer. Darr and Kurtzberg (2000) also found that strategic similarity increased knowledge transfer while they did not find evidence that geographic distance affected knowledge transfer. The units in the Darr and Kurtzberg study were located throughout the UK. Thus, geographic dispersion and language differences may not have been large enough to pose challenges to knowledge transfer. Alternatively, all of the units in the Darr and Kurtzberg (2000) study were affiliated with the same parent corporation, a superordinate structure that may have facilitated knowledge transfer.

When members identify with a superordinate group or organization, they are more likely to transfer knowledge across its units (Kane, Argote, and Levine, 2005). Members who feel that they belong to the same superordinate group are more likely to share information and thoughtfully consider the ideas of others than members who do not feel that they share an identity. Similarly, Sosa, Eppinger, Pich, and McKendrick (2002) found that team interdependence and strong organizational bonds helped overcome the negative effect of distance.

Investigating how a shared identity interacts with geographic distribution, Hinds and Mortensen (2005) found that a shared identity weakened the effect of geographic dispersion on interpersonal conflict. Although geographically distributed teams experienced more task and interpersonal conflict than co-located teams, the effect of geographic dispersion on interpersonal conflict was weaker for teams that shared an identity. In addition, communication weakened the effect of geographic distribution on conflict. Thus, a shared identity and communication hold promise for overcoming the negative effects of geographic distribution.

A transactive memory system can also be useful in mitigating the negative effects of geographic dispersion. A transactive memory system is a collective system for storing, encoding, and distributing information (Brandon and Hollingshead, 2004; Wegner, 1986). In organizations with well-developed transactive memory systems members know 'who knows what.' Transactive memory systems have been found to improve the performance of virtual (Kanawattanachai and Yoo, 2007) as well as co-located groups (Austin, 2003; Lewis, 2004; Hollingshead, 1998; Liang, Moreland, and Argote, 1995) and organizations. Further, Borgatti and Cross (2003) found that the effect of geographic distance on knowledge transfer was mediated by knowing what others know and being able to access that knowledge. Thus, a well-developed transactive memory system can overcome the effect of geographic dispersion on knowledge transfer.

Leadership affects the success of most organizational units, including geographically distributed ones. Joshi, Lazarova and Liao (2009) found that inspirational leaders fostered attitudes and relationships critical to the success of geographically distributed teams. Inspirational leadership enhanced members' trust in each other and commitment to the team, which in turn increased team performance. Further, the beneficial effects of inspirational leadership were stronger in geographically distributed teams than co-located teams.

Experience working together can also help groups overcome the challenges of geographic dispersion. Based on study of geographically distributed software teams, Espinosa, Slaughter, Kraut, and Herbsleb (2007) found that: (1) geographic dispersion had a negative effect on team performance; (2) team familiarity, or experience working together, had a positive effect on team performance; and (3) the positive effect of team familiarity or team performance was stronger for geographically distributed than co-located teams. Thus, team familiarity helped the teams overcome the negative effect of geographic dispersion on team performance.

Moving personnel across 'donor' and 'recipient' sites can facilitate knowledge transfer (Galbraith, 1990; Davenport and Prusak, 1998; Sole and Edmondson, 2002). Moving personnel is an especially effective mechanism for knowledge transfer because both tacit and explicit knowledge move with people when they move to a new task (Berry and Broadbent, 1984; 1987). Almeida and Kogut (1999) demonstrated that knowledge flowed across organizations through personnel movement. Similarly, Kane, Argote, and Levine (2005) showed that personnel rotation was an effective mechanism for transferring knowledge across groups, especially when members shared an identity.

How members are configured across geographically dispersed groups has important implications for knowledge transfer. Polzer, Crisp, Jarvenpaa, and Kim (2006) studied teams of graduate students from universities in different countries. Teams were assigned to three conditions: fully dispersed (six members in different, unique locations), three sub-groups (two members in each of three unique locations), and two sub-groups (three members in each of two unique locations). Results indicated that trust was higher in the fully dispersed than in the other two conditions, which did not differ significantly from each other. Team conflict was significantly higher in the two sub-group condition than in either the three sub-group condition or the fully dispersed condition, which did not differ significantly from each other.

O'Leary and Mortensen (2010) also analyzed the effect of the geographic configuration, or the number of team members at each location, on group processes and performance.

Similar to the Polzer et al. results, O'Leary and Mortensen (2010) found that totally dispersed teams, where members had no teammates at their sites, scored the best on outcomes such as identification with the team, effective transactive memory, coordination, and low conflict. Teams with two or more members per site score weaker on these outcomes than totally dispersed teams. Further, an imbalance in the size of sub-groups (i.e. the uneven distribution of members across sites) invoked a coalitional approach that led to even more negative effects than those observed in the balanced sub-groups.

The organizational structure also affects knowledge transfer. Tsai (2002) found that centralization impaired knowledge transfer in a large multi-unit firm. By contrast, social interactions facilitated knowledge transfer. In a study of multinational firms, Gupta and Govindarajan (2000) found that both formal integrative mechanisms and lateral socialization mechanisms facilitated knowledge transfer.

Organizational practices also affect the success of geographically distributed work. Leonardi and Bailey (2008) analyzed two cases of offshoring, including one case of offshoring from Mexico to India and another of offshoring from the US to India. The Mexican site interacted more directly with India than the US site, which interacted via third-party on-site coordinators or gatekeepers. Two work practices appeared to contribute to successful offshoring at both sites: defining task requirements by monitoring progress of task, and fixing work that was returned because the offshored site did not understand task requirements. From the perspective of the home site, satisfaction with the offshored arrangement was higher under the US gatekeeping model than under the Mexican direct contact model. By contrast, the recipients in India were more satisfied with the Mexican model of direct contact and felt they learned more from it than from the US model. This learning resulted in larger and more complex tasks being offshored from Mexico to India than from the US.

Interactions between national, technical, and social contexts

A given geographically distributed project will invariably have a particular instantiation of national, technical, and social contexts. Due to interaction effects between the different contexts, the specific combination of instantiations of each of these three contexts in a single project has significant implications for how the context moderates the relationship between experience and organizational learning and knowledge transfer. We discuss the possible interaction effects between different national, technical, and social contexts below.

The national and technical contexts found in a project can interact with one another. As discussed earlier, the national context can change the economic viability of particular production processes or products (Zeitlin and Herrigel, 2000; Fuchs, Field, Roth, and Kirchain, 2010; Fuchs and Kirchain, 2010). National context, in the form of culture, can also interact with the technical context, in the form of IT, and affect the extent to which IT can ease the negative impact of geographic distance on organizational learning. Particularly relevant to our discussion is the interaction of IT and national culture. The technology itself and cultural norms around its use can contribute to the challenges and successes of distance collaboration. Although some work has found no difference in use of technology by users from different national cultures (Setlock, Quinines, and Fussell, 2007), more recent work from Setlock and Fussell (2010) found that Asian users valued the support of social processes in addition to task processes in their online work more than American users. Other related work has found varying degrees of difference in technology usage as a function of cultural differences such as the extent of use of video and audio chat features in instant messaging (Kayan, Fussell, and Setlock, 2006), and the extent of participation in video chat based brainstorming sessions (Wang, Fussell, and Setlock, 2009). These differences are commonly related to contextual richness of communication expected in different cultures.

There are other national cultural aspects that affect collaboration when using IT to coordinate across distance. Echoing the findings detailed above, the more task-oriented Americans who are used to short-term teams can find it challenging to work with Europeans or Asians who may value long-term personal relationships (Hall and Hall, 1990). This difference can seem particularly pronounced when video or audio chats are used and norms about the extent of social conversation before and after business discussions are unclear (Olson and Olson, 2000). Speech norms that vary across cultures can create difficult environments for productive conversations over audio and video chats (Olson and Olson, 2000). These challenges in interacting and communicating over new technologies can extend to differences in management style and cultural norms around relationships with management (Hofstede, 1991). The subtleties around these issues can easily be lost over distance, but in some cases overcome with adaptation of the user. For example, if American team members are more conscious to build in pauses after their sentences, particularly in video conferences where timing delays are longer, it allows foreign collaborators more opportunities to comment (Olson and Olson, 2000). Finally, even inconsequential issues, such as different conventions about attire, are apparent on video conferences and can cause misunderstandings and misconceptions (Olson and Olson, 2000).

The social context also interacts with the technical context to affect organizational learning and knowledge transfer. For example, the frequency and timing of meetings and interaction can moderate the effectiveness of technology usage. In a study of three virtual teams within one organization, Maznevski and Chudoba (2000) found that effective global teams had a regular rhythm of face-to-face meetings with virtual communication in the interim. These face-to-face meetings helped build relationships and provided long-term stability and continuity to the teams. In a concurrent engineering context, Loch and Terwiesch (1998) concluded, based on an analytic model, that project characteristics (such as the speed of the evolution of a product design and extent of concurrency between design activities), precommunication, and uncertainty all contribute to determining communication frequency.

Olson and Olson (2000) provides a rich overview of research on IT and argued that its impact depends on social factors, including common ground, coupling (dependencies) of group work, collaboration readiness, and collaboration technology readiness. They conclude that geographically distributed collaborative work will be challenging for a long time, but as technology improves and work systems are adapted to utilize these evolving technologies, some of the hurdles that existed then (and still do now, a decade later) can be overcome. Common ground, context, trust, different time zones, culture, and interactions of these factors with technology are elements that make distance collaboration qualitatively different than physical collocation.

Social networks are another arena in which the social context interacts with the technical context. Social networks interact with characteristics of the task to affect organizational learning and knowledge transfer. Hansen et al. (1999) found that tacit knowledge was best transferred through strong ties while explicit knowledge was best transferred through weak ties.

The national context can also interact with the social context to affect organizational learning and knowledge transfer. For example, in their study of geographically distributed teams, Polzer, Crisp, Jarvenpaa, and Kim (2006) found that geographic distance between sub-groups led to more conflict and less trust when sub-group members were homogenous with respect to nationality. Thus, their results supported extending Lau and Murnighan's (1998) concept of 'fault lines' to geographically distributed teams. The overlapping of geographic dispersion and national differences strengthened fault lines and exacerbated conflict between groups. Despite such potential challenges, as discussed earlier, teams can also be constructed so as to be more likely to learn from sub-group differences, becoming more sophisticated in their understanding of cross-national relationships and competent in managing them (Cramton and Hinds, 2005).

FUTURE WORK AND CONCLUSION

Organizational learning and knowledge transfer are central to the performance of organizations. The growing fragmentation and internationalization of productive activities, however, has led to new organizational forms whose geographic distribution poses challenges to organizational learning and knowledge transfer. While a wealth of literature has begun to blossom in this area over the past decade, understanding the impact of geographic dispersion on organizational learning and knowledge transfer poses unique challenges.

One particularly challenging aspect of this area of study is teasing apart the relative effects of different variables associated with geographic distribution and the organizational context. At the beginning of this chapter we presented a framework in which organizational learning begins with experience and ends with knowledge. National, technical, and social contexts moderate the relationship between organizational experience and knowledge. As we noted in the last section, however, there are interactions between the national, technical, and social contexts and a given geographically distributed project will have a particular combination of the three.

Beyond the interaction between contexts, however, studying organizational learning in a geographically distributed context also poses other challenges for teasing apart the relative effects of different dimensions of geographic distribution. In particular, geographic dispersion has several underlying dimensions including geographic distance, electronic dependence, and whether temporal and national boundaries are crossed. Each of these dimensions poses different challenges for organizational learning and knowledge transfer. In this day and age it will be difficult to find geographic dispersion without some amount of electronic dependence, although the type of electronic dependence may vary. It is challenging to imagine a case of a multi-unit organization that does not involve geographic dispersion. Such challenges may make it difficult to distinguish between the challenges for communication and coordination posed by multiple units versus by geographic dispersion. On the other hand, a geographically distributed organization can, but must not necessarily, cross temporal and national boundaries. Conveniently, each of these variables can be found without examples of the other. For example, a geographically distributed organization can be imagined that crosses temporal but not national boundaries, that crosses national but not temporal boundaries, and that crosses both national and temporal boundaries. It is difficult, however, to imagine an organization that crosses national or temporal boundaries that is not geographically distributed.

In addition to challenges of teasing apart the effects of different variables, another challenging but also exciting aspect of geographically distributed organizations is the constant change in the environment being studied. Due to the growing fragmentation and internationalization of firm activities, today geographically distributed firms vary in the size, age, and the very reasons for which they are distributed. In addition, the technical, and in particular IT, options to support communication and collaboration in geographically distributed organizations also continue to change. Such changes provide exciting opportunities to continually reinvent and reinvigorate our understanding of geographically distributed learning and knowledge transfer.

Another particularly interesting area for future research is the rapidly changing relationship between technology—in particular the type of knowledge and the structure of the design—and geographic dispersion. Newly emerging research suggests that many cases do not support the hypothesis that organizational patterns will correspond to the technical patterns of dependency in a system under development (Colfer and Baldwin, 2010). Other work has questioned the extent to which any task can be labeled fully modular or integral (Tripathy and Eppinger, 2008). These results suggest a prime opportunity to reframe the existing discussion on the aspects of technology that may influence the geographic distribution of work. Particularly interesting will also be to understand the extent to which new developments in electronic media and team composition and management may be leading to these observed changes.

Both the challenges in teasing out the effects of different variables and the rapid change in the nature and opportunities for geographically distributed organizations provide exciting opportunities for future work in the study of organizational learning and knowledge transfer in geographically distributed organizations. One particularly interesting area for future work is teasing out the tension between the costs of geographic dispersion and the benefits that may come from being able to successfully leverage location-specific knowledge or capabilities. In the interaction between national and technical context, significant work remains to understand the extent to which local production differences and their significance for the economic viability of new technologies are understood by managers and the speed with which organizations may be able to learn and integrate these differences into their production and product development decisions. Likewise, it will be important to understand the extent to which new forms of electronic media and team composition and management may change outcomes in the above contexts. Finally, further research is needed to understand in which contexts distributed teams may be able to outperform local ones by leveraging location-specific capabilities versus in which contexts costs for organizational learning and knowledge transfer across geographic distance outweigh these benefits. Understanding these questions will enable us to advance the practice as well as theory of learning and knowledge transfer in geographically distributed organizations.

REFERENCES

Alavi, M. and Leidner, D.E. (2001) Review: Knowledge management and knowledge management systems: Conceptual foundations and research issues. *MIS Quarterly*, 25(1): 107–136.

Alcacer, J. and Gittleman, M. (2006) Patent citations as a measure of knowledge flows: the influence of examiner citations. *The Review of Economic Statistics*, 88(4): 774–779.

Allen, T.J. (1977) *Managing the flow of technology: Technology transfer and dissemination of technological information within the R&D organization.* Cambridge, MA: MIT Press.

Almeida, P., and Kogut, B. (1999). Localization of knowledge and the mobility of engineers in regional networks. *Management Science*, 45(7): 905–917.

Anderson, E.G., Davis-Blake, A., Erzurumlu, S.S., Joglekar, N., and Parker, G.G. (2008) The effects of outsourcing, offshoring, and distributed product development organizations on coordinating the NPD process. In C.H. Loch and S. Kavadias (eds.) *Handbook of New Product Development Management.* Oxford: Elsevier Press.

Antras, P. (2004) Incomplete contracts and the product cycle. Working Paper, Harvard University, NBER, CEPR.

Argote, L. and Epple, D. (1990, February 23) Learning curves in manufacturing. *Science*, 247: 920–924.

Argote, L., Gruenfeld, D., and Naquin, C. (2001) Group learning in organizations. In M. E. Turner (ed.), *Groups at work: Advances in theory and research.* Mahwah, NJ: Lawrence Erlbaum Associates: 369–411.

Argote, L. and Ingram, P. (2000) Knowledge transfer in organizations: A basis for competitive advantage in firms. *Organizational Behavior and Human Decision Processes*, 82: 150–169.

Argote, L., McEvily, B., and Reagans, R. (2003) Managing knowledge in organizations: An integrative framework and review of emerging themes. *Management Science*, 49: 571–582.

Argote, L. and Miron-Spektor, E. (in press) Organizational learning: From experience to knowledge. *Organization Science.*

Argote, L. and Ophir, R. (2002) Intraorganizational learning. In J.A.C. Baum (ed.), *Companion to organizations.* Oxford: Blackwell: 181–207.

Argote, L. and Todorova, G. (2007) Organizational learning: Review and future directions. In G.P Hodgkinson and J.K. Ford (eds.) *International Review of Industrial and Organizational Psychology.* New York: John Wiley & Sons: 193–234.

Argyres, N. (1999) The Impact of information technology on coordination: Evidence from the B-2 'Stealth' bomber. *Organization Science*, 10(2): 162–180.

Ashworth, M., Mukhopadhyay, T., and Argote, L. (2004) Information technology and organizational learning: An empirical analysis. *Proceedings of the 25th Annual International Conference on Information Systems (ICIS)*: 11–21.

Austin, J.R. (2003) Transactive memory in organizational groups: The effects of content, consensus, specialization, and accuracy on group performance. *Journal of Applied Psychology*, 88(5): 866–878.

Baldwin, C. and Clark, K. (2000) *Design Rules: The power of modularity.* Cambridge, MA: M.I.T. Press.

Bandura, A. (1977) *Social learning theory.*Englewood Cliffs, N.J.: Prentice-Hall.

Baum, J.A.C. and Greve, H.R. (eds.) (2001) *Multiunit organizations and multiunit strategy: Advances in strategic management*, Volume 18. Oxford: Elsevier.

Berry, D. and Broadbent, D.E. (1984) On the relationship between task performance and associated verbalizable knowledge. *Quarterly Journal of Experimental Psychology*, 36: 209–231.

Berry, D. and Broadbent, D.E. (1987) The combination of implicit and explicit knowledge in task control. *Psychological Research*, 49: 7–15.

Bhagat, R.S., Kedia, B.L., Harveston, P.D., and Triandis, H.C. (2002) Cultural variations in the cross border transfer of organizational knowledge: An integrative framework. *Academy of Management Review*, 27(2): 204–221.

Boh, W-F., Ren, Y., Kiesler, S., and Bussjaeger, R. (2007) Expertise and collaboration in the geographically dispersed organization. *Organization Science*, 18: 595–612.

Boone, T. and Ganeshan. R. (2001) The effect of information technology on learning in professional service organizations. *Journal of Operations Management*. 19(4): 485–495.

Borgatti, S.P. and Cross, R. (2003) A relational view of information seeking and learning in social networks. *Management Science*, 49(4): 432–445.

Brandon, D.P. and Hollingshead, A.B. (2004) Transactive memory systems in organizations: Matching tasks, expertise and people. *Organization Science*, 15: 633–644.

Carlisle, P. (2004) Transferring, translating, and transforming: an integrative framework for managing knowledge across boundaries. *Organization Science*, 15: 555–568.

Chesbrough, H. (2003) *Open Innovation: The new imperative for creating and profiting from technology*. Boston: Harvard Business School Press.

Clarke, N. (2007) Turnaround effort is challenging at Airbus, a stew of European cultures. *The New York Times*. New York: May 18, 2007: 3.

Cohen, W. and Levinthal, D. (1990) Absorptive capacity: A new perspective on learning and innovation. *Administrative Science Quarterly*, 35: 128–152.

Colfer, L. and Baldwin, C.Y. (2010) *The mirroring hypothesis: Theory, evidence and exceptions*. Harvard Business School Working Paper, No. 10–058, January 2010.

Cramton, C.D. (2001) The mutual knowledge problem and its consequences in geographically dispersed teams. *Organization Science*, 12(3): 346–371.

Cramton, C.D. and Hinds, P.J. (2005) Subgroup dynamics in internationally distributed teams: Ethnocentrism or cross-national learning? *Journal of Organizational Behavior*, 26: 62.

Cummings, J.N. (2004) Work groups, structural diversity, and knowledge sharing in a global organization. *Management Science*, 50(3): 352–364.

Cummings, J. (2009) Crossing spatial and temporal boundaries in globally distributed projects: A relational model of coordination delay. *Information Systems Research*, 30(3): 420–439.

Darr, E.D. and Kurtzberg, T.R. (2000) An investigation of partner similarity dimensions on knowledge transfer. *Organizational Behavior Human Decision Processes*, 82(1): 28–44.

Davenport, T. and Prusak, L. (1998) *Working Knowledge: How organizations manage what they know*. Boston, MA: Harvard Business School Press.

Dutton, J.M. and Thomas, A. (1984) Treating progress functions as a managerial opportunity. *Academy of Management Review*, 9: 235–247.

Easterby-Smith, M., Lyles, M.A., and Tsang, E.W.K. (2008) Inter-organizational knowledge transfer: Current themes and future prospects. *Journal of Management Studies*, 45(4): 677–690.

Edmondson, A.C., Dillon, J.R., and Roloff, K. (2007) Three perspectives on team learning: outcome improvement, task mastery, and group process. In J.P. Walsh and A.P. Brief (eds.), *The Academy of Management Annals*. London: Psychology Press, pp. 269–314.

Edmondson, A., Pisano, G.P., Bohmer, R., and Winslow, A. (2003) Learning how and learning what: Effects of tacit and codified knowledge on performance improvement following technology adoption. *Decision Sciences*, 34(2): 197–223.

Eppinger, S.D. and Chitkara, A.R. (2006) The new practice of global product development. *MIT Sloan Management Review*, 47(4): 22–30.

Espinosa, J.A. and Pickering, C. (2006) The effect of time separation on coordination processes and outcomes: A case study. *Proceedings of the 39th Hawaii International Conference on System Sciences*, Hawaii, IEEE.

Espinosa, A., Slaughter, S., Kraut, R., and Herbsleb, J. (2007) Familiarity, complexity and team performance in geographically distributed software development. *Organization Science*, 18: 613–630.

Feenstra, R. (1998) Integration of trade and disintegration of production in the global economy. *Journal of Economic Perspectives*, 12(4): 31–50.

Fiol, C.M. and Lyles, M. A. (1985) Organizational learning. *Academy of Management Review*, 10: 803–813.

Fransman, M. (1995*). Japan's Computer and Communications Industry: The Evolution of Industrial Giants and Global Competitiveness*. Oxford: Oxford University Press.

Fransman, M. (1999*) Visions of Innovation: The firm and Japan*. Oxford: Oxford University Press.

Fuchs, E.R.H., Field, F.R., Roth, R., and Kirchain, R. (2010) Plastic cars in China? The significance of production location over markets for technology competitiveness. *International Journal of Production Economics*, In press.

Fuchs, E.R.H. and Kirchain, R.E. (2010) Design for location: The impact of manufacturing offshore on technology competitiveness. *Management Science*, 56(12): 2323–2349.

Galbraith, C.S. (1990) Transferring core manufacturing technologies in high-technology firms. *California Management Review*, 32: 56–70.

Gereffi, G., Humphrey, J., and Sturgeon, T.J. (2005) The governance of global value chains. *Review of International Political Economy*, 12(1): 78–104.

Gherardi, S. (2006) *Organizational Knowledge. The Texture of Workplace Learning*. Oxford: Blackwell Publishers.

Gibson, C. B. and Gibbs, J. L. (2006) Unpacking the concept of virtuality: The effects of geographic dispersion, electronic dependence, dynamic structure, and national diversity on team innovation. *Administrative Science Quarterly*, 51: 451–495.

Gupta, A.K. and Govindarajan, V. (2000) Analysis of the emerging global arena. *European Management Journal*, 18(3): 274–284.

Haas, M.R. and Hansen, M.T. (2005) When using knowledge can hurt performance: An empirical test of competitive bidding in a management consulting company. *Strategic Management Journal*, 26: 1–24.

Hall, E.T. and Hall, M.R. (1990) *Understanding cultural differences: Germans, French, and Americans*. Yarmouth, ME: Intercultural Press.

Hameri, A.P. and Nihtilä, J. (1997) Distributed new product development project based on internet and world-wide web: a case study. *Journal of Product Innovation Management*, 14: 77–87.

Hansen, M.T., Nohria, N., and Tierney, T. (1999) What's your strategy for managing knowledge? *Harvard Business Review*, 77(2): 106–116.

Hinds, P. and Mortensen, M. (2005) Understanding conflict in geographically distributed teams: An empirical investigation. *Organization Science*, 16: 290–307.

Hirst, P. and Thompson, G. (1996) *Globalization in Question*. Oxford: Blackwell Publishers.

Hoetker, G. (2006) Do modular products lead to modular organizations? *Strategic Management Journal*, 27(6): 501–518.

Hofstede, G. (1991) *Cultures and Organizations: Software of the mind*. London: McGraw-Hill.

Hollingshead, A.B. (1998) Retrieval processes in transactive memory systems. *Journal of Personality and Social Psychology*, 74: 659–671.

Hong, J., Snell, R., and Easterby-Smith, M. (2009) Knowledge flow and boundary crossing at the periphery of a MNC. *International Business Review*, 18(6): 539–554.

Hounshell, D. (1985) *From the American system to mass production, 1800–1932: The development of manufacturing technology in the United States*. Baltimore: Johns Hopkins University Press.

Huff, A.S. and Jenkins, M. (2001) Mapping managerial knowledge. In A.S. Huff and M. Jenkins (eds.), *Mapping Managerial Knowledge*. Chichester: John Wiley & Sons.

Ingram, P. (2002) Interorganizational learning. In J.A.C. Baum (ed.), *The Blackwell Companion to Organizations*. Oxford: Blackwell Business, pp. 642–663.

Jarvenpaa, S. L. and Leidner, D.E. (1999) Communication and trust in global virtual teams. *Organization Science*, 10(6): 791–815.

Joshi, A., Lazarova, M.B., and Liao, H. (2009). Getting everyone on board: The role of inspirational leadership in geographically dispersed teams. *Organization Science*, 20: 240–252.

Kanawattanachai, P. and Yoo, Y. (2007) The impact of knowledge coordination on virtual performance over time. *MIS Quarterly*, 31(4): 783–808.

Kane, G.C. and Alavi, M. (2007) Information technology and organizational learning: an investigation of exploration and exploitation processes, *Organization Science*, 18(5): 796–812.

Kane, A.A., Argote, L., and Levine, J.M. (2005) Knowledge transfer between groups via personnel rotation: Effects of social identity and knowledge quality. *Organizational Behavior and Human Decision Processes*, 96: 56–71.

Kayan, S., Fussell, S.R., and Setlock, L.D. (2006) Cultural differences in the use of instant messaging in Asia and North America. *Proceedings of CSCW 2006*. NY: ACM Press, pp. 525–528.

Kim, S.H. (2008) *An empirical assessment of knowledge management systems*. Doctoral dissertation. Carnegie Mellon University.

Lamb, C. and Spekman, R. (1997) Alliances, external technology acquisition, and discontinuous technological change. *Journal of Product Innovation Management*, 14: 102–116.

Lapré, M.A., Mukherjee, A.S., and Van Wassenhove, L.N. (2000) Behind the learning curve: Linking learning activities to waste reduction. *Management Science*, 46(5), 597–611.

Lau, D. and Murnighan, J. K. (1998) Demographic diversity and faultlines: The compositional dynamics of organizational groups. *Academy of Management Review*, 23: 325–340.

Lavie, D. and Miller, S. R. (2008) Alliance portfolio internationalization and firm performance, *Organization Science*, 19(4), 623–646.

Leavitt, H.J. (1996), The old days, hot groups, and managers' lib. *Administrative Science Quarterly*, 41: 288–300.

Leonard-Barton, D. (1988) Implementation as Mutual Adaptation of Technology and Organization. *Research Policy*, 17: 251–267.

Leonardi, P.M. and Bailey, D.E. (2008) Transformational technologies and the ration of new work practices: Making implicit knowledge explicit in task-based offshoring. *MIS Quarterly*, 32 (2):159–176.

Levinthal, D. and Rerup, C. (2006) Crossing an apparent chasm: Bridging mindful and less-mindful perspectives on organizational learning. *Organizational Science*, 17: 502–513.

Levitt, B. and March, J.G. (1988) Organizational learning. *Annual Review of Sociology*, 14: 319–340.

Lewin, A. and Couto, V. (2007) *Next generation offshoring: The globalization of innovation*. Offshoring Research Network, Duke Fuqua School of Business and Booz Allen Hamilton.

Lewis, K. (2004) Knowledge and performance in knowledge-worker teams: A longitudinal study of transactive memory systems. *Management Science*, 50(11): 1519–1533.

Liang, D.W., Moreland, R., and Argote, L. (1995) Group versus individual training and group performance: The mediating role of transactive memory. *Personality and Social Psychology Bulletin*, 21: 384–393.

Loch, C.H. and Terwiesch, C. (1998) Communication and uncertainty in concurrent engineering. *Management Science*, 44(8): 1032–1048.

MacCormack, A., Rusnak, J., and Baldwin, C.Y. (2008) *Exploring the Duality between Product and Organizational Architectures: A Test of the Mirroring Hypothesis*. Cambridge, MA: Harvard Business School Press.

Makela, M., Kalla, H.K., and Piekkari, R. (2007) Interpersonal similarity as a driver of knowledge sharing within multinational corporations. *International Business Review*, 16: 1–22.

Mansfield, E. (1985) How rapidly does industrial technology leak out? *The Journal of Industrial Economics*, 34: 217–224.

March, J. G., Sproull, L.S., and Tamuz, M. (1991) Learning from samples of one or fewer. *Organization Science*, 2(1): 1–14.

Marshall, A. (1890) *Principles of Economics*. London: Macmillan.

Maznevski, M.L. and Chudoba, K.M. (2000) Bridging Space over Time: Global Virtual Team Dynamics and Effectiveness. *Organization Science*. 11(5): 473–492.

Miner, A.S. and Haunschild, P.R. (1995) Population level learning. In L.L. Cummings and B. M. Staw (eds.) *Research in Organizational Behavior*. Greenwich, CN: JAI Press, pp. 115–166.

Mishra, A. (2009) *Essays on global sourcing of technology projects* Minneapolis: University of Minnesota. Doctor of Philosophy: 219.

Morris, T. and Pavett, C. (1992) Management style and productivity in two cultures. *Journal of International Business Studies*, 23: 169–179.

Mullor-Sebastian, A. (1983) The product life cycle theory: Empirical evidence. *Journal of International Business Studies*, 14(3): 95–105.

Nadler, J., Thompson, L., and Van Boven, L. (2003) Learning negotiation skills: Four models of knowledge creation and transfer. *Management Science*, 49(4): 529–540.

Nonaka, I. and von Krogh. G. (2009) Perspective—tacit knowledge and knowledge conversion: Controversy and advancement in organizational knowledge creation theory. *Organization Science*, 20: 635–652.

North, D. (1990) *Institutions, Institutional Change, and Economic Performance*. Cambridge: Cambridge University Press.

Novak, S. and Eppinger, S. D. (2001) Sourcing by design: Product complexity and the supply chain. *Management Science*, 47(1): 15.

O'Leary, M.B and Mortensen, M. (2010) Go (con)figure: Subgroups, imbalance, and isolates in geographically dispersed teams. *Organization Science*, 21(1): 115–131.

Olson, G.M. and Olson, J.S. (2000) Distance matters, *Human–Computer Interaction*. 15(2): 139–178.

Oviatt, B. and McDougal, P. (1994) Toward a theory of international new ventures. *Journal of International Business Studies*, 25(1): 45–64.

Patel, P. and Pavitt, K. (1991) Large firms in the production of the world's technology: An important case of non-globalization. *Journal of International Business Studies*, 22(1): 1–21.

Patel, P. and Pavitt, K. (1994) Uneven (and divergent) technological accumulation among advanced countries: evidence and a framework of explanation. *Industrial and Corporate Change*, 3(3): 759–787.

Pavitt, K. (1999) *Technology, Management, and Systems of Innovation*. Cheltenham: Edward Elgar.

Pavitt, K. and Patel, P. (1999) Global corporations and national systems of innovation: who dominates whom? *Innovation Policy in a Global Economy*. Cambridge: Cambridge University Press.

Pavitt, K. and Townsend, J. (1987) The size distribution of innovating firms in the U.S. 1945–1983. *Journal of Industrial Economics*, 35: 291–316.

Piore, M. and Sabel, C. (1984) *The Second Industrial Divide: Possibilities for prosperity*. New York: Basic Books.

Polanyi, M. (1962) *Personal Knowledge: Towards a post-critical philosophy*. New York: Harper and Row.

Polzer, J.T., Crisp, B., Jarvenpaa, S.L., and Kim, J.W. (2006) Extending the faultline concept to geographically dispersed teams: How colocated subgroups can impair group functioning. *Academy of Management Journal*, 49(4): 679–692.

Porter, M.E. (1990) *The Competitive Advantage of Nations*. New York: The Free Press.

Powell, W. (1990) Neither markets nor hierarchies: Network forms of organization. *Research in Organizational Behavior*, 12: 295–336.

Powell, W. and Grodal, S. (2005) Networks of innovators. In J. Fagerberg, D.C. Mowery, and R.R. Nelson (eds.), *The Oxford Handbook of Innovation*. New York: Oxford University Press, pp. 56–85.

Prasad, S., Tat, J., and Thorn, R. (1995) Benchmarking Maquiladora operations relative to those in the USA. *International Journal of Quality & Reliability Management*, 13(9): 8–18.

Rosenkopf, L. (2000). Managing dynamic knowledge networks. In G. Day and P. Schoemaker (eds.), *Wharton on Managing Emerging Technologies*. New York: John Wiley and Sons: 337–357.

Rosenkopf, L. and Schilling, M. (2007) Competing alliance network structure across industries: Observations and explanations. *Strategic Entrepreneurship Journal*, 1: 18.

Schulz, M. (2002) Organizational learning. In J.A.C. Baum (ed.), *The Blackwell Companion to Organizations*. Oxford: Blackwell Business, pp. 416–441.

Setlock, L.D. and Fussell, S.R. (2010) What's it worth to you? The costs and affordances of CMC tools for Asian and American users. *Proceedings of CSCW 2010*. New York: ACM Press, pp. 341–349.

Setlock, L.D., Quinines, P.A., and Fussell, S.R. (2007) Does culture interact with media richness? The effects of audio vs. video conferencing on Chinese and American dyads. *Proceedings of HICSS 2007*.

Sole, D. and Edmondson, A. (2002). Situated knowledge and learning in dispersed teams. *British Journal of Management*, 13: 17–34.

Sosa, M.E., Eppinger, S.D., Pich, M., and McKendrick, D.G. (2002) Factors that influence technical communication in distributed product development: An empirical study in the telecommunications industry. *IEEE Transactions on Engineering Management*, 49(1): 45–58.

Sosa, M.E., Eppinger, S.D., and Rowles, C.M. (2004) The misalignment of product architecture and organizational structure in complex product development. *Management Science*. 50(12): 15.

Sproull, L. and Kiesler, S. (1991) *Connections: new ways of working in the networked organization.* Boston: MIT Press.

Starbuck, W.H. (2009) Cognitive reactions to rare events: Perceptions, uncertainty, and learning. *Organization Science*, 20: 925–937.

Sturgeon, T.J., (2002) Modular production networks: a new American model of industrial organization. *Industrial and Corporate Change*, 11(3): 451–496.

Szulanski, G. (1996) Exploring internal stickiness: Impediments to the transfer of best practice within the firm. *Strategic Management Journal*, 17: 27–43.

Teece, D., Pisano, G., and Shuen, A. (1997) Dynamic capabilities and strategic management. *Strategic Management Journal*, 18 (7): 509.

Tripathy, A. and Eppinger, S.D. (2008) Work distribution in global product development organizations. Paper presented at the 10th International Design Structure Matrix Conference, DSM'08. Stockholm, Sweden.

Tripsas, M. and Gavetti, G. (2000) Capabilities, cognition, and inertia: Evidence from digital imaging. *Strategic Management Journal*, 21: 1147–1161.

Tsai, W. (2002) Social structure of 'coopetition' within a multiunit organization: Coordination, competition, and intraorganizational knowledge sharing. *Organization Science*, 13: 179–190.

Tyre, M. and von Hippel, E. (1997) The situated nature of adaptive learning in organizations. *Organization Science*, 8(1): 71–83.

Vargas, G.A. and Johnson, T.W. (1993) An analysis of operational experience in the US/Mexico production-sharing (maquiladora) program. *Journal of Operations Management*, 11(1): 17–34.

Vernon, R. (1966) International investment and international trade in the product cycle. *Quarterly Journal of Economics*, 80: 190–207.

Volberda, H.W., Foss, N.J., and Lyles, M.A. (2010) Perspective—absorbing the concept of absorptive capacity: How to realize its potential in the organization. *Organization Science*, 21(4): 931–951.

Von Hippel, E.A. (1994) 'Sticky information' and the locus of problem solving: Implications for innovation. *Management Science*, 40(4): 429–439.

Walsh, J.P. and Ungson, G.R. (1991) Organizational memory. *Academy of Management Review*, 16: 57–91.

Wang, H-C., Fussell, S.R., and Setlock, L.D. (2009) Cultural difference and adaptation of communication styles in computer-mediated group brainstorming. *Proceedings of CHI 2009*. NY: ACM, pp. 669–678.

Wegner, D. M. (1986) Transactive memory: A contemporary analysis of the group mind. In B. Millen and G.R. Goethals (eds.), *Theories of Group Behavior*. New York: Springer-Verlag, pp. 185–205.

Weick, K.E. and Sutcliffe, K.M. (2006) Mindfulness and the quality of organizational attention. *Organization Science*, 17(4): 514–524.

Womack, J., Jones, D., and Roos, D. (1990) *The Machine that Changed the World*. New York: Rawson Associates.

Yates, J. and Orlikowski, W.J. (1992) Genres of organizational communication: A structurational approach to studying communication and media. *The Academy of Management Review*, 17(2): 27.

Zander, U. and Kogut, B. (1995) Knowledge and the speed of the transfer and imitation of organizational capabilities: an empirical test. *Organization Science*, 6: 76–92.

Zeitlin, J. and Herrigel, G. (2000) *Americanization and its Limits: Reworking US technology and management in post-war Europe and Japan*. Oxford: Oxford University Press.

Zollo, M. (2009) Superstitious learning with rare strategic decisions: theory and evidence from corporate acquisitions. *Organization Science*, 20: 894–908.

Zollo. M. and. Reuer, J.J. (in press) Experience spillovers across corporate development activities. *Organization Science*, published online before print Dec 4, 2009, DOI: doi:10.1287/orsc.1090.0474.

Index